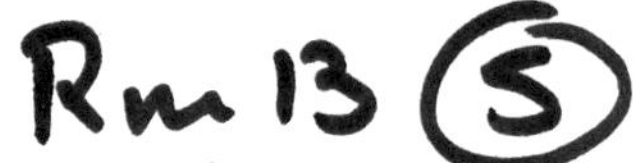

Complete Mathematics

for GCSE and Standard Grade

David Rayner

Oxford University Press

Oxford University Press, Walton Street, Oxford OX2 6DP

Oxford New York
Athens Auckland Bangkok Bombay
Calcutta Cape Town Dar es Salaam Delhi
Florence Hong Kong Istanbul Karachi
Kuala Lumpur Madras Madrid Melbourne
Mexico City Nairobi Paris Singapore
Taipei Tokyo Toronto

and associated companied in
Berlin Ibadan

Oxford is a trade mark of Oxford University Press

First published as *Mathematics for GCSE Books 1* and *2* and *Answer Book* 1987
This complete edition first published 1990
Reprinted 1991, 1992 (twice), 1993, 1994, 1995

Cartoons by David Simonds

British Library Cataloguing in Publication Data
Rayner, D. (David) 1949–
Complete mathematics for GCSE and standard grade
1. Finite mathematics
I. Title

ISBN 0 19 914350 1

Printed and bound in Great Britain by
Butler & Tanner Ltd, Frome and London

PREFACE

This book has been written for the majority of students approaching GCSE or Standard Grade Mathematics examinations. It is divided into two sections: Section A covers the groundwork; Section B offers opportunities for revising the groundwork before approaching harder topics.

Throughout the book there are a large number of practice questions which have been carefully graded. It is not expected that every student will want to answer every question and a selection can be made to suit a particular student's needs.

The 'Think about it' sections (identified by the stippling at the bottom corner of each page) provide opportunities for problem-solving and investigations, and hence for project work. Each section of the book includes a batch of mental arithmetic tests. When these are used in class the teacher or lecturer can read the questions out to the class with their books closed. Students working on their own can enlist the help of a friend or use these texts as written exercises but without writing down any detailed working.

The author wishes to record his thanks to Micheline Dubois, Philip Cutts and all his colleagues at Richard Hale School, Hertford. Thanks are also due to the following examination boards for kindly allowing the use of questions from their past papers:

London and East Anglian Group [L]
Midland Examining Group [M]
Northern Examining Association [N]
Southern Examining Group [S]
Welsh Joint Education Committee [W]

David Rayner
Hertford 1989

CONTENTS

Section A

Section B

Section A

Unit 1

1.1 WHOLE NUMBERS

Exercise 1

Work out

1. 27 + 31
2. 45 + 22
3. 234 + 17
4. 316 + 204
5. 50 + 911
6. 291 + 46
7. 299 + 197
8. 306 + 205
9. 45 + 275
10. 903 + 89
11. 415 + 207 + 25
12. 41 + 607 + 423
13. 206 + 114 + 8
14. 9 + 19 + 912
15. 157 + 16 + 24
16. 16 + 2341 + 27
17. 3047 + 265
18. 274 + 5061
19. 2941 + 4067
20. 8046 + 147
21. 401 + 609 + 21
22. 506 + 2615
23. 2947 + 4 + 590
24. 209 + 607 + 11
25. 6672 + 11 + 207
26. 994 + 27
27. 604 + 12 407
28. 9150 + 12 694
29. 53246 + 62141
30. 19 274 + 27 + 584

Exercise 2

Work out

1. 97 − 63
2. 69 − 41
3. 83 − 60
4. 87 − 5
5. 192 − 81
6. 214 − 10
7. 86 − 29
8. 52 − 37
9. 74 − 18
10. 91 − 68
11. 265 − 128
12. 642 − 181
13. 562 − 181
14. 816 − 274
15. 509 − 208
16. 604 − 491
17. 808 − 275
18. 250 − 127
19. 640 − 118
20. 265 − 184
21. 484 − 219
22. 6064 − 418
23. 5126 − 307
24. 6417 − 29
25. 8050 − 218
26. 406 − 22
27. 649 − 250
28. 6009 − 205
29. 1717 − 356
30. 843 − 295
31. 641 − 286
32. 2719 − 394
33. 7416 − 286
34. 5417 − 346

35. 2098 – 364
36. 2006 – 507
37. 4017 – 2138
38. 2094 – 1846
39. 4075 – 999
40. 732 – 159

41. Two hundred and six take away forty-eight.
42. Five hundred and seventeen take away one hundred and twenty.
43. Two thousand, four hundred and eight take away six hundred and eleven.
44. Ten thousand and twenty take away eight thousand six hundred and four.
45. Six hundred and nineteen take away two hundred and thirty-seven.
46. Nineteen thousand and twelve take away ten thousand.
47. Six hundred and seven take away five hundred and sixty.
48. Ten thousand take away six hundred and forty.
49. Six hundred and fifty take away two hundred and ninety-one.
50. Seventeen thousand and seventeen take away six hundred and eighty-four.

Exercise 3

In a 'magic square' you get the same number when you add across each row (↔), add down each column (↕) and add diagonally (↙, ↘). Copy and complete the following magic squares.

1.

3		
2		
7	0	

2.

9	7	5
		10

3.

8	1	6
4		

4.

7		
	6	4
		5

5.

12		14
	11	
8		

6.

17		
12		16
13		

7.

		7	14
	13	2	
	3	16	5
15			4

8.

	6		4
10		16	
		2	
1	12	7	14

9.

	10		
14	15		8
	4	18	
16	13		6

10.

18		12	7
	6		
11	16	5	14
4			

11.

11		7	20	3
	12	25		16
	5	13		9
	18		14	
		19	2	15

12.

16		10	17	4
3	15		9	21
20		14		8
	19			
24			5	12

13. This one is slightly different because there are not enough numbers given. Try different numbers for * until you find one which makes the square magic.

10		
5		
6		*

Tables test

Exercise 4

Copy and complete the multiplication squares.

1.

	4	7	3	5	9	11	8	6	2	12
4										
7										
3					27					
5										
9										
11									22	
8			24							
6										
2										
12										

2.

	7	5	9	6	8	11	4	2	12	3
7										
5										
9										
6										
8										
11										
4										
2										
12										
3										

Multiplication

Exercise 5

Work out

1. 21 × 3 **2.** 32 × 3
3. 42 × 6 **4.** 35 × 4
5. 213 × 3 **6.** 46 × 5
7. 205 × 6 **8.** 28 × 6
9. 211 × 7 **10.** 302 × 7

11. 213 × 5 **12.** 641 × 3
13. 21 × 8 **14.** 314 × 6
15. 131 × 9 **16.** 214 × 8
17. 820 × 6 **18.** 921 × 4
19. 2141 × 6 **20.** 3025 × 5

21. 324 × 8 **22.** 643 × 7
23. 295 × 9 **24.** 641 × 10
25. 846 × 10 **26.** 275 × 8
27. 631 × 7 **28.** 885 × 9
29. 497 × 8 **30.** 2153 × 6

Exercise 6

Work out

1. 23 × 15 **2.** 27 × 17
3. 41 × 23 **4.** 36 × 23
5. 61 × 25 **6.** 25 × 47
7. 73 × 61 **8.** 80 × 43
9. 29 × 16 **10.** 211 × 23

11. 406 × 24 **12.** 291 × 31
13. 382 × 42 **14.** 611 × 52
15. 952 × 73 **16.** 211 × 312
17. 314 × 215 **18.** 234 × 614
19. 812 × 316 **20.** 911 × 806

Division

Exercise 7

Work out

1. 69 ÷ 3 **2.** 286 ÷ 2
3. 844 ÷ 4 **4.** 345 ÷ 3
5. 712 ÷ 4 **6.** 1160 ÷ 5
7. 1581 ÷ 3 **8.** 2112 ÷ 4
9. 415 ÷ 5 **10.** 994 ÷ 2

11. 1092 ÷ 4 **12.** 18 072 ÷ 3
13. 3020 ÷ 5 **14.** 1626 ÷ 6
15. 1660 ÷ 4 **16.** 1915 ÷ 5
17. 4944 ÷ 6 **18.** 5616 ÷ 6
19. 2247 ÷ 7 **20.** 10 710 ÷ 5

21. 18 972 ÷ 2 **22.** 9256 ÷ 4
23. 1928 ÷ 8 **24.** 14 010 ÷ 2
25. 5859 ÷ 7 **26.** 55 305 ÷ 9
27. 21 104 ÷ 8 **28.** 3735 ÷ 9
29. 12 360 ÷ 6 **30.** 24 832 ÷ 8

Exercise 8

Work out

1. 1300 ÷ 4 **2.** 1863 ÷ 9
3. 2508 ÷ 6 **4.** 1664 ÷ 4

5. 31 805 ÷ 5
6. 3175 ÷ 5
7. 24 267 ÷ 3
8. 19 976 ÷ 8
9. 39 389 ÷ 7
10. 69 984 ÷ 4

There are 'remainders' in the next 10 questions.

11. 2143 ÷ 4
12. 6418 ÷ 5
13. 6027 ÷ 4
14. 24 081 × 7
15. 4135 ÷ 6
16. 1173 ÷ 9
17. 6798 ÷ 7
18. 7048 ÷ 3
19. 2035 ÷ 8
20. 26 525 ÷ 6

Sequences

Write down the next two numbers in each sequence.

(a) 2, 6, 10, 14,
(b) 60, 59, 57, 54,
(c) 240, 120, 60, 30,

(a) 2, 6, 10, 14, **18**, **22**.
(b) 60, 59, 57, 54, **50**, **45**.
(c) 240, 120, 60, 30, **15**, $\mathbf{7\frac{1}{2}}$

Exercise 9

Write down each sequence and find the next two numbers.

1. 2, 5, 8, 11,
2. 1, 6, 11, 16,
3. 20, 18, 16, 14,
4. 2, 9, 16, 23,
5. 74, 62, 50, 38,
6. 1, 2, 4, 7, 11,
7. 5, 7, 10, 14,
8. 50, 49, 47, 44,
9. 50, 43, 36, 29,
10. 44, 53, 62, 71,
11. 90, 82, 75, 69,
12. −4, −2, 0, 2,
13. −5, −2, 1, 4,
14. 6, 2, −2, −6,
15. 5, 8, 12, 17,
16. 10, 8, 5, 1,
17. −20, −14, −8, −2,
18. 93, 81, 70, 60,
19. 31, 40, 51, 64, 79,
20. 55, 49, 42, 34,

Exercise 10

Write down each sequence and find the next two numbers or letters.

1. 1, 2, 4, 8,
2. 1, 3, 9, 27,
3. 400, 200, 100, 50
4. 22, 31, 40, 49,
5. 3, 30, 300, 3000,
6. 128, 64, 32, 16,
7. 85, 92, 99, 106,
8. 40, 38, 35, 31,
9. A, C, E, G,
10. B, E, H, K,
11. A, B, D, G, K,
12. W, U, S, Q,
13. 2480, 1240, 620, 310,
14. 1, 4, 9, 16,
15. 1, 1, 2, 6, 24,
16. −5, −4, −2, 1,
17. A, D, G, J,
18. 7, 4, 0, −5,
19. 8, 11, 15, 20,
20. 3, 10, 19, 30,

The next ten are more difficult.

21. −21, −18, −13, −6,
22. 162, 54, 18, 6,
23. 63, 51, 65, 49,
24. 27, 9, 3, 1,
25. 1, 1, 2, 3, 5, 8,
26. C, C, D, F, I,
27. 1, 4, 20, 120,
28. 100, 79, 59, 40,
29. 2, 5, 11, 20,
30. 2, 3, 5, 7, 11, 13,

1.2 DECIMALS

Place value

Exercise 11

In questions **1** to **12** write down the line which is correct.

1. (a) 0.06 is equal to 0.6
   (b) 0.06 is greater than 0.6
   (c) 0.06 is less than 0.6
2. (a) 0.14 is equal to 0.41
   (b) 0.14 is greater than 0.41
   (c) 0.14 is less than 0.41
3. (a) 0.61 is equal to 0.6
   (b) 0.61 is greater than 0.6
   (c) 0.61 is less than 0.6
4. (a) 0.04 is equal to 0.040
   (b) 0.04 is greater than 0.040
   (c) 0.04 is less than 0.040
5. (a) 0.12 is equal to 0.1
   (b) 0.12 is greater than 0.1
   (c) 0.12 is less than 0.1

[In the following questions:
$>$ means 'is greater than' (e.g. $9 > 5$)
$<$ means 'is less than' (e.g. $7 < 10$)]

6. (a) $0.03 = 0.3$
   (b) $0.03 > 0.3$
   (c) $0.03 < 0.3$
7. (a) $0.214 = 0.241$
   (b) $0.214 > 0.241$
   (c) $0.214 < 0.241$

8. (a) $0.06 = 0.60$
(b) $0.06 > 0.60$
(c) $0.06 < 0.60$

9. (a) $2.01 = 2.010$
(b) $2.01 > 2.010$
(c) $2.01 < 2.010$

10. (a) $0.15 = 0.153$
(b) $0.15 > 0.153$
(c) $0.15 < 0.153$

11. (a) $0.313 = 0.331$
(b) $0.313 > 0.331$
(c) $0.313 < 0.331$

12. (a) $0.071 = 0.08$
(b) $0.071 > 0.08$
(c) $0.071 < 0.08$

In the remaining questions answer 'true' or 'false'

13. $0.8 = 0.08$
14. $0.7 < 0.71$
15. $0.61 > 0.16$
16. $0.08 > 0.008$
17. $0.5 = 0.500$
18. $0.4 < 0.35$
19. $0.613 < 0.631$
20. $0.06 > 0.055$
21. $8 = 8.00$
22. $7 = 0.7$
23. $0.63 > 0.36$
24. $8.2 < 8.022$
25. $6.04 < 6.40$
26. $0.75 = 0.075$
27. $5 = 0.5$
28. $0.001 > 0.0001$
29. $0.078 < 0.08$
30. $9 = 9.0$
31. $0.9 > 0.085$
32. $6.2 < 6.02$
33. $0.05 < 0.005$
34. $0.718 < 0.871$
35. $0.09 > 0.1$
36. $11 = 0.11$
37. $0.88 > 0.088$
38. $0.65 > 0.605$
39. $2.42 = 2.420$
40. $0.31 = 0.3100$

Exercise 12

Arrange the numbers in order of size, smallest first.

1. 0.21, 0.31, 0.12
2. 0.04, 0.4, 0.35
3. 0.67, 0.672, 0.7
4. 0.05, 0.045, 0.07
5. 0.1, 0.09, 0.089
6. 0.75, 0.57, 0.705
7. 0.41, 0.041, 0.14
8. 0.809, 0.81, 0.8
9. 0.006, 0.6, 0.059
10. 0.15, 0.143, 0.2

11. 0.04, 0.14, 0.2, 0.53
12. 1.2, 0.12, 0.21, 1.12
13. 2.3, 2.03, 0.75, 0.08
14. 0.62, 0.26, 0.602, 0.3
15. 0.5, 1.3, 1.03, 1.003
16. 0.79, 0.792, 0.709, 0.97
17. 1.23, 0.321, 0.312, 1.04
18. 0.008, 0.09, 0.091, 0.0075
19. 2.05, 2.5, 2, 2.046
20. 1.95, 9.51, 5.19, 5.1
21. 0.76, 0.674, 0.706, 0.71
22. 1, 0.99, 0.989, 0.09
23. 0.42, 0.24, 1, 0.204
24. 0.3, 0.33, 0.303, 0.222
25. 1.2, 1.02, 1.21, 0.95
26. 3.62, 0.632, 0.362, 0.662
27. 0.08, 0.096, 1, 0.4
28. 0.72, 0.732, 0.722, 0.7
29. 4.03, 3.99, 4, 4.025
30. 0.66, 0.658, 0.685, 0.08

Addition and subtraction

Exercise 13

Work out the following, without a calculator.

1. $2.84 + 7.3$
2. $18.6 + 2.34$
3. $25.96 + 0.75$
4. $212.7 + 4.256$
5. $3.6 + 6$
6. $7 + 16.1$
7. $8 + 3.4 + 0.85$
8. $12 + 5.32 + 0.08$
9. $0.004 + 0.0583$
10. $7.77 + 77.7$

11. $4.81 - 3.7$
12. $6.92 - 2.56$
13. $8.27 - 5.86$
14. $19.7 - 8.9$
15. $3.6 - 2.24$
16. $8.4 - 2.17$
17. $8.24 - 5.78$
18. $19.6 - 7.36$
19. $15.4 - 7$
20. $23.96 - 8$

21. $8 - 5.2$
22. $9 - 6.8$
23. $13 - 2.7$
24. $25 - 3.2$
25. $0.325 - 0.188$
26. $0.484 - 0.4352$
27. $7 - 0.35$
28. $6 - 1.28$
29. $2.38 - 1.814$
30. $11 - 7.4$

Multiplication

Work out (a) 5.2×0.6, (b) 12.4×1.3

(a)
$$\begin{array}{r} 52 \\ \times\ 6 \\ \hline 312 \\ \hline \end{array}$$

(b)
$$\begin{array}{r} 124 \\ \times\ 13 \\ \hline 1240 \\ 372 \\ \hline 1612 \\ \hline \end{array}$$

So $5.2 \times 0.6 = 3.12$ So $12.4 \times 1.3 = 16.12$

Exercise 14

Work out the following, without a calculator

1. 2.3×0.4
2. 3.6×0.3
3. 4.7×0.5
4. 21.3×0.4
5. 62.5×0.8
6. 4.26×0.7

7. 4.2×0.03
8. 6.04×0.05
9. 17.3×0.004
10. 25.2×0.002

11. 0.51×0.9
12. 0.063×0.04
13. 212×0.6
14. 543×0.02
15. 7104×0.04
16. 0.085×0.5
17. 1.33×0.04
18. 4.004×0.9
19. 1.09×0.0002
20. 584×0.001

21. 2.3×1.3
22. 3.4×1.4
23. 5.21×1.5
24. 6.22×0.21
25. 7.34×0.32
26. 0.831×1.5
27. 8.42×0.022
28. 81.4×0.26
29. 76.4×0.043
30. 0.708×0.034

Division

Work out $7.63 \div 0.4$

$7.63 \div 0.4 = 76.3 \div 4$

$$4\overline{)76.300} = 19.075$$

Exercise 15

Work out the following, without a calculator.

1. $8.76 \div 4$
2. $19.74 \div 2$
3. $7.02 \div 3$
4. $9.24 \div 4$
5. $8.34 \div 5$
6. $20.7 \div 6$
7. $0.318 \div 2$
8. $2.51 \div 8$
9. $40.88 \div 7$
10. $13.26 \div 5$

11. $17.2 \div 8$
12. $3.15 \div 9$
13. $25.96 \div 11$
14. $60.13 \div 7$
15. $525 \div 6$
16. $0.92 \div 5$
17. $0.638 \div 0.2$
18. $0.852 \div 0.4$
19. $5.73 \div 0.5$
20. $2.912 \div 0.8$

21. $0.3504 \div 0.06$
22. $2.527 \div 0.07$
23. $5.616 \div 0.9$
24. $0.004\,384 \div 0.008$
25. $0.446\,74 \div 0.07$
26. $0.028\,49 \div 0.11$
27. $0.039\,282 \div 0.006$
28. $5.2 \div 0.05$
29. $14.3 \div 0.004$
30. $2.63 \div 0.0008$

31. $51.093 \div 9$
32. $68.618 \div 11$
33. $0.347\,41 \div 0.7$
34. $7 \div 0.005$
35. $0.7612 \div 0.011$
36. $8 \div 0.002$
37. $0.643\,06 \div 1.1$
38. $0.015\,54 \div 6$
39. $5 \div 0.08$
40. $27.34 \div 0.000\,01$

Multiplication and division by 10's, 100's, 1000's

Exercise 16

Write down the answer to each of the following.

1. 0.634×10
2. 0.838×10
3. 0.815×100
4. 0.074×100
5. 7.245×1000
6. 0.6105×100
7. 0.064×100
8. 0.0075×1000
9. 27×10
10. 351×100

11. $6.24 \div 10$
12. $8.97 \div 10$
13. $17.5 \div 100$
14. $23.6 \div 1000$
15. $4.8 \div 100$
16. $0.73 \div 10$
17. $127 \div 1000$
18. $16.3 \div 100$
19. $580 \div 10$
20. $6300 \div 1000$

21. 0.751×100
22. $0.084 \div 10$
23. $0.111 \div 10$
24. 0.0084×1000
25. 16×1000
26. $7 \div 100$
27. $0.8 \div 100$
28. 317×10
29. $254 \div 1000$
30. 99×1000

The next two exercises are more difficult because they contain a mixture of questions on addition, subtraction, multiplication and division.

Exercise 17

1. $3.7 + 0.62$
2. $8.45 - 2.7$
3. $11.3 - 2.14$
4. 2.52×0.4
5. $3.74 \div 5$
6. $17 + 3.24$
7. $12 - 1.8$
8. $23.6 \div 8$
9. 82.1×0.06
10. 0.034×1000

11. $62.1 \div 100$
12. $11.4 - 3.16$
13. 0.153×0.8
14. $2.16 + 9.99$
15. $18.606 \div 7$
16. 6.042×11
17. 34.1×1000
18. $0.41 \div 100$
19. 52.6×0.04
20. $0.365 - 0.08$

21. $2.329\,56 \div 9$
22. 654×0.005
23. $0.7 + 0.77 + 0.777$
24. $54 \div 100$
25. 27×0.001
26. 6.007×1.1
27. $8.2 - 1.64$
28. $47.04 \div 6$
29. $58.4 \div 10\,000$
30. 0.742×1 million

Exercise 18

1. 2.06 × 0.05
2. 43.75 ÷ 7
3. 19.1 − 7
4. 7 − 3.6
5. 0.62 × 1000
6. 82.6 ÷ 10
7. 43.6 − 2.18
8. 0.5 + 0.55 + 0.555
9. 0.072 ÷ 8
10. 850 × 0.0004
11. 0.026 × 1 million
12. 962.4 ÷ 100 000
13. 54 − 6.2
14. 28.3 × 0.011
15. 586.26 ÷ 9
16. 2.84 ÷ 0.5
17. 48.6 × 0.07
18. 0.392 ÷ 0.04
19. 7 + 0.7 + 0.77
20. 180 − 2.5
21. 0.0714 ÷ 0.08
22. 0.004 × 10 million
23. 333 × 0.007
24. 17 + 8.8
25. 82 ÷ 10 000
26. 0.458 36 ÷ 0.07
27. 206 − 74.2
28. 18 + 1.8 + 0.18
29. 0.190 47 ÷ 0.003
30. 2.6 ÷ 0.005

1.3 PERCENTAGES

Change 15 out of 25 into a percentage.

As a fraction 15 out of 25 $= \frac{15}{25}$

$$\frac{15}{25} = \frac{15}{25} \times \frac{100}{1}\%$$
$$= 60\%$$

Exercise 19

Change to percentages

1. $\frac{3}{4}$
2. $\frac{2}{5}$
3. $\frac{1}{2}$
4. $\frac{4}{5}$
5. $\frac{1}{4}$
6. $\frac{5}{8}$
7. $\frac{9}{10}$
8. $\frac{17}{20}$
9. $\frac{5}{20}$
10. $\frac{7}{8}$
11. $\frac{17}{25}$
12. $\frac{7}{20}$
13. $\frac{7}{100}$
14. $\frac{1}{3}$
15. $\frac{2}{3}$
16. $\frac{1}{8}$
17. $\frac{49}{50}$
18. $\frac{15}{60}$
19. $\frac{61}{100}$
20. $\frac{250}{1000}$
21. $\frac{16}{50}$
22. $\frac{27}{40}$
23. $\frac{4}{12}$
24. $\frac{235}{1000}$
25. 17 marks out of 25
26. 18 marks out of 20
27. 52 marks out of 80
28. 12 marks out of 30
29. £45 out of £200
30. £17 out of £50
31. £98 out of £100
32. £65 out of £260
33. 19 kg out of 40 kg
34. 300 kg out of 900 kg
35. $67 out of $1000

Exercise 20

1. (a) In a test Ann obtained 11 marks out of 25. What is her percentage mark?
   (b) In a second test she obtained 13 marks out of 20. What is her percentage mark?
2. A motorist has to drive a distance of 400 km. After an hour he has driven 84 km. What percentage of his journey has he completed?
3. In a survey 1600 people were asked which television channel they preferred.
   800 chose ITV
   640 chose BBC
   160 had no television set.
   (a) What percentage chose ITV?
   (b) What percentage chose BBC?
   (c) What percentage had no television?
4. Of the people in a room 11 are men and 14 are women.
   (a) How many people are in the room?
   (b) What percentage of the people are men?
   (c) What percentage of the people are women?
5. Three girls in different classes all had maths tests on the same day.
   Jane scored 27 out of 50.
   Susan scored 28 out of 40.
   Jackie scored 39 out of 75.
   Work out their marks as percentages and put them in order with the highest first.
6. In a car park 23 cars are British made and 27 cars are imported. What percentage of the cars in the car park are imported?

7. The children in a class were asked to state which was their least favourite subject.

7 chose Maths
12 chose Music
6 chose R.E.

(a) What percentage of the class chose Music?
(b) What percentage of the class chose Maths or Music?

8. In an opinion poll 37% of the people preferred the Conservatives, 35% preferred Labour, 24% preferred Liberal/S.D.P. and the rest were 'Don't knows'. What percentage were 'Don't knows'?

9. John throws a die several times and obtains the following results

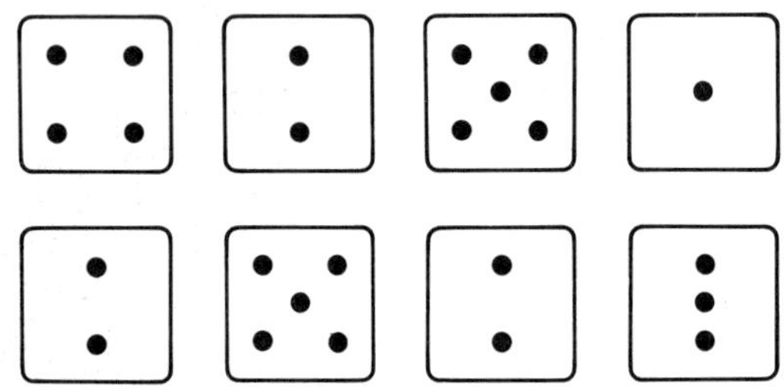

(a) What percentage of his throws gave a 'two'?
(b) What percentage of his throws gave a 'four'?
(c) What percentage of his throws gave a 'six'?
(d) What percentage of his throws gave more than three?

10. In a group of people 17 came from France, 22 came from Spain, 32 came from Germany and 9 came from Italy. What percentage of the group came from Germany?

Percentage of a number

> Work out 22% of £40.
>
> $$\frac{22}{100} \times \frac{40}{1} = \frac{880}{100}$$
>
> Answer: £8.80

Exercise 21

Work out

1. 20% of £60
2. 10% of £80
3. 5% of £200
4. 6% of £50
5. 4% of £60
6. 30% of £80
7. 9% of £500
8. 18% of £400
9. 61% of £400
10. 12% of £80

11. 6% of $700
12. 11% of $800
13. 5% of 160 kg
14. 20% of 60 kg
15. 68% of 400 g
16. 15% of 300 m
17. 2% of 2000 km
18. 71% of $1000
19. 26% of 19 kg
20. 1% of 6000 g

21. 67% of £2000
22. 35% of 700 kg
23. 22% of £440
24. 17% of £560
25. 26% of £85
26. 73% of £96
27. 110% of £60
28. 125% of £90
29. 140% of £80
30. 117% of £145

> Work out 6.5% of £17.50 correct to the nearest penny.
>
> $$\frac{6.5}{100} \times \frac{17.5}{1} = \frac{113.75}{100}$$
>
> $$= £1.1375$$
>
> Answer: £1.14 to the nearest penny.

Exercise 22

Give the answers to the nearest penny where necessary.

1. 4.5% of £6.22
2. 17% of £6.84
3. 15% of £8.11
4. 17% of £17.07
5. 37% of £9.64
6. 3.5% of £12.90
7. 8% of £11.64
8. 68% of £54.45
9. 73% of £23.24
10. 2.5% of £15.20

11. 6.3% of £12.50
12. 8.2% of £19.50
13. 87% of £15.40
14. 80% of £62.50
15. 12% of £24.50
16. $12\frac{1}{2}$% of £88.50
17. $7\frac{1}{2}$% of £16.40
18. $5\frac{1}{2}$% of £80
19. $12\frac{1}{2}$% of £90
20. 19% of £119.50

21. 1% of £11.79
22. 1% of £2.73
23. $6\frac{1}{2}$% of £17
24. 110% of £85
25. 117% of £82
26. 153% of £279
27. 1% of £3.51
28. 2% of £6.38
29. 19.1% of £35.60
30. 8.7% of £10.10

A coat originally cost £24. Calculate the new price after a 5% reduction.

Price reduction $= 5\%$ of £24

$$= \frac{5}{100} \times \frac{24}{1} = £1.20$$

New price of coat $= £24 - £1.20$

$= £22.80$

Exercise 23

1. Increase a price of £12 by 10%
2. Increase a price of £40 by 5%
3. Increase a price of £60 by 15%
4. Increase a price of £84 by 4%
5. Increase a price of £70 by 20%
6. Reduce a price of £50 by 8%
7. Reduce a price of £75 by 40%
8. Reduce a price of £64 by 5%
9. Reduce a price of £8.40 by 10%
10. Reduce a price of £9.90 by 10%

11. Increase a price of £60 by 5%
12. Reduce a price of £800 by 8%
13. Reduce a price of £82.50 by 6%
14. Increase a price of £65 by 60%
15. Reduce a price of £2000 by 2%
16. Increase a price of £440 by 80%
17. Increase a price of £66 by 100%
18. Reduce a price of £91.50 by 50%
19. Increase a price of £88.24 by 25%
20. Reduce a price of £63 by $33\frac{1}{3}$%

In the remaining questions give the answers to the nearest penny.

21. Increase a price of £8.24 by 46%
22. Increase a price of £7.65 by 24%
23. Increase a price of £5.61 by 31%
24. Reduce a price of £8.99 by 22%
25. Increase a price of £11.12 by 11%
26. Reduce a price of £17.62 by 4%
27. Increase a price of £28.20 by 13%
28. Increase a price of £8.55 by $5\frac{1}{2}$%
29. Reduce a price of £9.60 by $7\frac{1}{2}$%
30. Increase a price of £12.80 by $10\frac{1}{2}$%

Exercise 24

1. In a closing-down sale a shop reduces all its prices by 20%. Find the sale price of a coat which previously cost £44.
2. The price of a car was £5400 but it is increased by 6%. What is the new price?
3. The price of a sideboard was £245 but, because the sideboard is scratched, the price is reduced by 30%. What is the new price?
4. A hi-fi shop offers a 7% discount for cash. How much does a cash-paying customer pay for an amplifier advertised at £95?
5. A rabbit weighs 2.8 kg. After being shot its weight is increased by 1%. How much does it weigh now?

6. The insurance premium for a car is normally £90. With a 'no-claim bonus' the premium is reduced by 35%. What is the reduced premium?
7. Myxomatosis kills 92% of a colony of 300 rabbits. How many rabbits survive?
8. The population of a town increased by 32% between 1945 and 1985. If there were 45 000 people in 1945, what was the 1985 population?
9. A restaurant adds a 12% 'service charge' onto the basic price of meals. How much do I pay for a meal with a basic price of £8.50?
10. A new-born baby weighs 3.1 kg. Her weight increases by 8% over the next fortnight. What does she weigh then?
11. A large snake normally weighs 12.2 kg. After swallowing a rat, the weight of the snake is increased by 7%. How much does it weigh after dinner?
12. At the beginning of the year a car is valued at £3250. During the year its value falls by 15%. How much is it worth at the end of the year?

13. Copy and complete the table.

Basic price	VAT at 15%	Final price
(a) £24	£3.60	£27.60
(b) £38		
(c) £42		
(d) £212		
(e) £8.20		

14. During a sale a shopkeeper reduces prices by various amounts. Copy and complete the table.

Normal price	% reduction	Sale price
(a) £28	10%	
(b) £35	5%	
(c) £55	15%	
(d) £240	35%	
(e) £8.40	5%	

Exercise 25

(This exercise contains some harder questions.)
In questions **1** to **4** find the total bill.

1. 2 hammers at £5.30 each
   50 screws at 25p for 10
   5 bulbs at 38p each
   1 tape measure at £1.15
   VAT at 15% is added to the total cost.
2. 5 litres of oil at 85p per litre
   3 spanners at £1.25 each
   2 manuals at £4.30 each
   200 bolts at 90p for 10
   VAT at 15% is added to the total cost.
3. 12 rolls of wallpaper at £3.70 per roll
   3 packets of paste at £0.55 per packet
   2 brushes at £2.40 each
   1 stepladder at £15.50
   VAT at 15% is added to the total cost.
4. 5 golf clubs at £12.45 each
   48 golf balls at £15 per dozen
   100 tees at 1p each
   1 bag at £21.50
   1 umbrella at £12.99
   VAT at 15% is added to the total cost.
5. In a sale a dress priced at £35 is reduced by 20%. At the end of the week the *sale price* is reduced by a further 25%. Calculate
   (a) the price in the original sale
   (b) the final price.
6. In a sale a coat priced at £85 is reduced by 40%. At the end of the week the *sale price* is reduced by a further 20%. Calculate
   (a) the price in the original sale
   (b) the final price.
7. A dishonest shopkeeper increases all his prices by 10% and keeps the new prices for a week. At the end of the week he has a sale of 'all goods at 10% off!' What is the sale price of an article which cost £400 before the increase?
8. (a) In 1985 a club has 40 members who each pay £12 annual subscription. What is the total income from subscriptions?
   (b) In 1986 the subscription is increased by 35% and the membership increases to 65.
   (i) What is the 1986 subscription?
   (ii) What is the total income from subscriptions in 1986?

Exercise 26

1. A jacket costs £32 to make and the shopkeeper adds 25% to give the 'marked price'. During a sale all goods, are labelled 'Sale Price – 10% off Marked Price'.
   (a) What was the 'marked price' for the jacket?
   (b) What was the 'Sale Price' for the jacket?
   (c) How much profit did the shopkeeper make, if he sold 20 of these jackets in the sale?
2. The table shows the normal price of some television sets and how much they are reduced in a sale.

Make	Normal price	% reduction	Actual reduction
Sony	£280	10%	
ITT	£315	5%	
Phillips	£440		£44
Ferguson	£310	12%	
Sanyo	£250		£50

Copy and complete the table.

3. A car bought for £5950 loses £950 of its value during the first year, and then an annual depreciation of 20% of its value at the beginning of each following year.
   (a) What is the value of the car after one year?
   (b) By how much does the value decrease over the second year?
   (c) Work out the value of the car after
      (i) 2 years (ii) 3 years (iii) 4 years
4. A cooker is purchased by taking out a bank loan for £450, to which the bank adds interest equivalent to 10% of the loan.

   (a) How much interest is charged?
   (b) What is the total cost?
   (c) The bank loan plus interest has to be repaid by 12 equal monthly payments. How much is repaid each month?
5. In a survey 10 000 people were asked which television channel they liked best.
   4000 chose ITV
   3500 chose BBC1
   1000 chose BBC2
   500 chose Channel 4
   1000 did not have TV.

   What percentage chose
   (a) ITV (b) BBC1 (c) BBC2
   (d) Channel 4?
6. A shopkeeper bought 50 articles for £20 and sold them all at 50p each.
   Find the missing numbers below.
   (a) The cost price of each article was * p
   (b) The total selling price of all the articles was £*
   (c) The total profit was £*.
7. At blast-off a rocket consists of a structure of mass 800 kg together with 4000 kg of fuel. Calculate the total mass of the rocket when 15% of the fuel has been burned away.

   Picture
8. A man bought a house in 1982, for £30 000. He sold it, in 1985, for £35 000.
   (a) What was his profit, in £'s?
   (b) Express this profit as a percentage of the 1982 cost price.

1.4 RATIO

> Share £60 in the ratio 2:3
>
> Total number of shares = 2 + 3 = 5
> ∴ One share = £60 ÷ 5 = £12
> ∴ The two amounts are £24 and £36

Exercise 27

1. Share £30 in the ratio 1:2.
2. Share £60 in the ratio 3:1.
3. Share £20 in the ratio 3:2.
4. Share £42 in the ratio 1:5.
5. Divide 880 g of food between the cat and the dog in the ratio 3:5.
6. Divide $1080 between Sam and Chris in the ratio 4:5.
7. Share 126 gallons of petrol between Steve and Dave in the ratio 2:5.
8. Share £60 in the ratio 1:2:3.
9. Share £400 in the ratio 2:3:3.
10. Share £96 in the ratio 1:3:4.
11. Divide $5400 in the ratio 2:3:4.
12. Share out 260 marbles between three children in the ratio 2:3:5.
13. Divide 880 g of wedding cake between three guests in the ratio 2:4:5.
14. Alan, Brian and Dawn divided £560 between them in the ratio 2:1:5. How much did Brian receive?

15. A sum of £120 is divided in the ratio 3:4:5. What is the largest share?
16. Find the largest share when £192.50 is divided in the ratio 2:5.
17. Find the smallest share when 260 g is divided in the ratio 4:2:7.
18. At an election 7800 people voted Labour, Conservative or Alliance in the ratio 4:3:5. How many people voted Alliance?
19. Find the largest share when £1 is divided in the ratio 5:6:9.
20. £109.80 is divided between James and his twin sisters in the ratio 5:2:2. How much does each twin receive?

Exercise 28

(This exercise is more difficult.)

1. Divide $45 in the ratio 2:4:3:1.
2. Divide £330 in the ratio 3:2:5:5.
3. Share 4200 kg in the ratio 2:5:1:6.
4. Find the largest share when 480 g is divided in the ratio 1:3:4:7.
5. Find the smallest share when £91 is divided in the ratio 5:2:6:7.
6. £80 is divided between Sally and Jane in the ratio 2:3. How much more does Jane get than Sally?
7. $388.50 is divided between Charles and Jack in the ratio 2:5. How much more does Jack get than Charles?
8. Share £96 so that A has twice as much as B.
9. Share £120 so that A has one third as much as B.
10. Share £84 so that A has twice as much as B, who has twice as much as C.
11. Share £600 so that A has twice as much as B, who has three times as much as C.
12. Share £252 so that A has half as much as B, who has four times as much as C.
13. Share £350 so that A has half as much as C, who has half as much as B. (Make it clear how much each person receives).
14. Share £168 so that A has twice as much as C, who has twice as much as B.
15. Share £54 so that B has three times as much as C, who has twice as much as A.

In a class, the ratio of boys to girls is 3:4. If there are 9 boys, how many girls are there?

Boys:Girls = 3:4
Multiply both parts by 3.
Boys:Girls = 9:12
So there are 9 boys and 12 girls.

Exercise 29

1. In a room, the ratio of boys to girls is 3:2. If there are 12 boys, how many girls are there?
2. In a room, the ratio of men to women is 4:1. If there are 20 men, how many women are there?

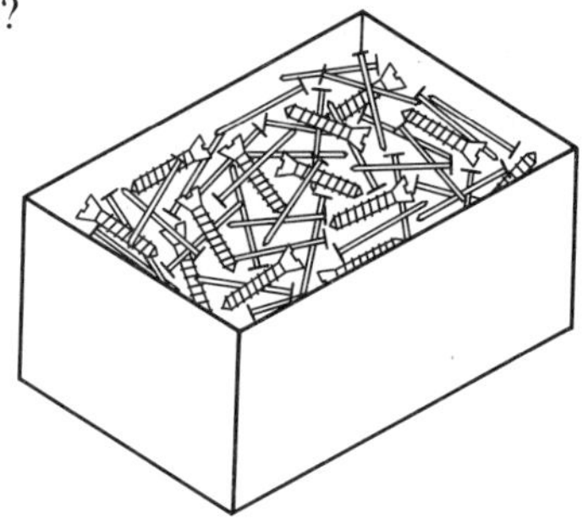

3. In a box, the ratio of nails to screws is 5:3. If there are 15 nails, how many screws are there?
4. A sum of money is divided in the ratio 4:5. If the smaller amount is £80, find the larger amount.
5. A sum of money is divided in the ratio 7:3. If the smaller amount is £18, find the larger amount.
6. An alloy consists of copper, zinc and tin in the ratios 1:3:4. If there is 10 g of copper in the alloy, find the weights of zinc and tin.
7. In a shop the ratio of oranges to apples is 2:5. If there are 60 apples, how many oranges are there?
8. In a train the ratio of adults to children is 7:2. If there are 126 adults, how many children are there?
9. In a bag, the ratio of red beads to white beads to green beads is 7:2:1. If there are 56 red beads, how many white beads are there and how many green beads?
10. On a farm, the ratio of cows to horses to sheep is 8:1:3. If there are 48 sheep, how many horses are there and how many cows?

1.5 PROPORTION

Direct proportion

If 12 calculators cost £54, find the cost of 17 calculators.

12 calculators cost £54
$\therefore$ 1 calculator costs £54 ÷ 12 = £4.50
$\therefore$ 17 calculators cost £4.50 × 17
= £76.50

Exercise 30

1. If 5 books cost £15, find the cost of 8.

2. If 7 apples cost 63p, find the cost of 12.

3. If 4 batteries cost 180p, find the cost of 7.

4. If 5 bottles of beer cost £2.45, find the cost of 12.

5. Toy cars cost £3.36 for 8. Find the cost of
(a) 3 toy cars
(b) 10 toy cars.

6. Crisps cost £1.32 for 12 packets. Find the cost of
(a) 20 packets
(b) 200 packets.

7. Stair carpet costs £78 for 12 m. Find the cost of 15 m.

8. The total weight of 7 ceramic tiles is 1750 g. How much do 11 tiles weigh?

9. A machine fills 2000 bottles in 10 minutes. How many bottles will it fill in 7 minutes?

10. The total contents of 8 cartons of fruit drink is 12 litres. How much fruit drink is there in 3 cartons?

11. Find the cost of 15 cakes if 9 cakes cost £2.07.

12. Find the cost of 7 screws if 20 screws cost £4.60.

13. How much would 7 cauliflowers cost, if 10 cauliflowers cost £5.70?

14. A machine takes 20 seconds to make 8 coins. How long does it take to make 50 coins?

15. A plane flies 50 km in 15 minutes. How long will it take to fly 300 km?

Exercise 31

1. If 8 pencils cost 56p, how many can be bought for 70p?

2. If 6 pineapples can be bought for £3.12, how many can be bought for £5.20?

3. If 20 m^2 of carpet costs £150, what area of carpet can be bought for £90?

4. Oranges cost £1.68 for 12. How many can be bought for (a) £2.80 (b) £4.90?

5. Twenty men produce 500 articles in 6 days. How many articles would 4 men produce in 6 days?

6. Forty women take 8 days to produce 400 articles. How many articles would 16 women produce in 8 days?

7. 12 men produce 600 components in 12 hours. How many components would 9 men produce in 12 hours?

8. 7 cycles cost £623.
(a) What is the cost of 3 cycles?
(b) How many cycles can be bought for £979?

9. 11 cassettes cost £9.35.
(a) What is the cost of 15 cassettes?
(b) How many cassettes can be bought for £17?

10. $2\frac{1}{2}$ m of metal tube cost £1.40. Find the cost of (a) 4 m (b) $7\frac{1}{2}$ m.

11. $3\frac{1}{4}$ kg of sweets costs £2.60. Find the cost of (a) 2 kg (b) $4\frac{1}{2}$ kg.

12. A car travels 210 km on 30 litres of petrol. How much petrol is needed for a journey of 245 km?

13. A light aircraft flies 375 km on 150 litres of fuel. How much fuel is needed for a journey of 500 km?

14. A tank travels 140 miles on 40 gallons of fuel. How much fuel is needed for a journey of 245 miles?

Inverse proportion

> If 12 men can build a wall in 8 hours, how long will it take 4 men?
>
> The less men there are, the more time it takes.
>
> 12 men take 8 hours
> 1 man takes 96 hours
> 4 men take 24 hours

Exercise 32

1. If 15 men can build a wall in 6 hours, how long will it take 5 men?
2. If 6 men can dig a trench in 12 hours, how long will it take 24 men?
3. A ship has enough food to supply 600 passengers for 3 days. How long would the food last for 300 passengers?
4. Four men can build a shed in 9 hours. How long would it take six men?
5. A farmer has enough hay to feed 8 horses for 2 days. How long would the hay last for
   (a) 2 horses (b) 32 horses?
6. Eight dockers can unload a ship in 15 hours. How long will it take 3 men?
7. A farmer employs 12 men to do a job in 10 days. How long would it have taken 5 men?
8. A bridge was painted by 8 men in 6 days. How long would it have taken 12 men?

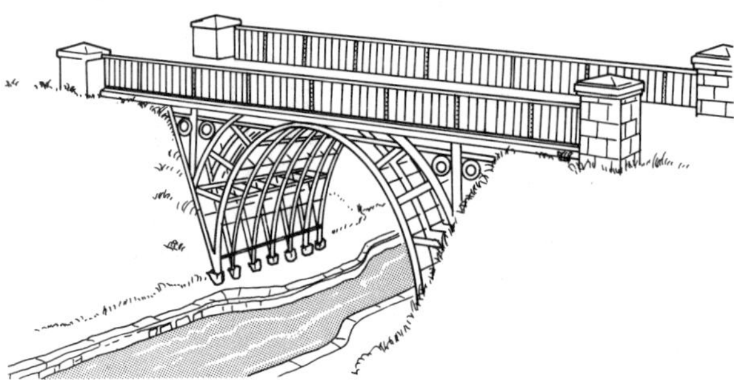

9. Four men can do a job in 12 hours. How many men would it take to do the job in 2 hours?
10. Six women can do a job in 8 hours. How many women would it take to do the job in 6 hours?
11. 8 sacks of corn will feed 30 hens for 6 days. Copy and complete the following:
    (a) 16 sacks of corn will feed 30 hens for * days.
    (b) 4 sacks of corn will feed 30 hens for * days.
    (c) 8 sacks of corn will feed 45 hens for * days.
    (d) 4 sacks of corn will feed 60 hens for * days (use part (b)).
12. 200 kg of food will feed 40 prisoners for 6 days. Copy and complete the following:
    (a) 200 kg of food will feed * prisoners for 3 days.
    (b) 200 kg of food will feed 10 prisoners for * days.
    (c) * kg of food will feed 40 prisoners for 30 days.
    (d) 50 kg of food will feed 40 prisoners for * days.
13. 6 swallows eat 300 flies in 5 hours. Copy and complete the following:
    (a) 30 swallows eat * flies in 5 hours.
    (b) 30 swallows eat * flies in 10 hours.
    (c) 6 swallows eat 60 flies in * hours.
    (d) * swallows eat 6000 flies in 5 hours.
14. Usually it takes 5 hours for 12 men to do a job. How many men are needed to do the job in 2 hours?
15. A car travelling at 80 km/h completes a certain journey in 60 minutes. How long would it take for a car travelling at
    (a) 40 km/h (b) 120 km/h?
16. A car travelling at 60 km/h completes a journey in 90 minutes. How long would it take for a car travelling at
    (a) 180 km/h (b) 15 km/h?

Unit 2

2.1 THE METRIC SYSTEM

(a) 0.314×100 $= 31.4$	(b) $17.4 \div 1000$ $= 0.0174$
(c) 1.2×1000 $= 1200$	(d) $8 \div 100$ $= 0.08$

Exercise 1

This exercise provides revision of multiplying and dividing by 10's, 100's and 1000's. Do not use a calculator.

Work out

1. 0.724×10
2. 0.41×10
3. 1.625×100
4. 0.231×100
5. 8×100
6. 17×10
7. 6×1000
8. 0.6×100
9. 0.2×1000
10. 1.3×1000
11. 1.1×100
12. 0.04×100
13. 3.2×1000
14. 15.6×100
15. 7×1000
16. 0.7×1000
17. 0.007×100
18. 0.002×100
19. 0.74×100
20. 6.23×1000

21. $82.4 \div 10$
22. $79.6 \div 10$
23. $97.3 \div 100$
24. $111.2 \div 100$
25. $27 \div 10$
26. $373 \div 100$
27. $24.2 \div 100$
28. $8.2 \div 100$
29. $6 \div 100$
30. $11 \div 100$
31. $4 \div 1000$
32. $2 \div 1000$
33. $2.3 \div 1000$
34. $1 \div 100$
35. $182 \div 1000$
36. $79 \div 1000$
37. $0.2 \div 10$
38. $0.71 \div 100$
39. $1.3 \div 100$
40. $84 \div 1000$

41. 2.3×100
42. $8.2 \div 10$
43. 0.41×1000
44. 17×100
45. $17 \div 10$
46. $0.6 \div 10$
47. 89.7×100
48. 1.1×1000
49. $8 \div 100$
50. $600 \div 100$
51. 20×100
52. 18×1000

Length	Weight	Volume
10 mm = 1 cm	1000 g = 1 kg	1000 ml = 1 l
100 cm = 1 m	1000 kg = 1 t	1000 l = 1 m^3
1000 m = 1 km	(t for tonne)	(l for litre)

Exercise 2

Copy and complete.

1. 1.27 m = cm
2. 0.65 m = cm
3. 3 m = cm
4. 0.07 m = cm
5. 11 m = cm
6. 8.1 m = cm
7. 2.34 m = cm
8. 0.002 m = cm
9. 17 cm = m
10. 24 cm = m
11. 240 cm = m
12. 11 cm = m
13. 2 cm = m
14. 18.2 cm = m
15. 3.1 cm = m
16. 5000 cm = m
17. 6.3 m = cm
18. 0.24 m = cm
19. 67 cm = m
20. 9 cm = m
21. 17 mm = cm
22. 25 mm = cm
23. 250 mm = cm
24. 12 mm = cm
25. 2 cm = mm
26. 15 cm = mm
27. 2.8 cm = mm
28. 9.6 cm = mm
29. 2 km = m
30. 1.5 km = m
31. 1.24 km = m
32. 0.324 km = m
33. 0.076 km = m
34. 18 km = m
35. 7.1 km = m
36. 0.07 km = m
37. 400 m = km
38. 875 m = km
39. 25 mm = cm
40. 65 m = km
41. 450 g = kg
42. 200 g = kg
43. 1400 g = kg
44. 2650 g = kg
45. 40 g = kg
46. 55 g = kg
47. 7 g = kg
48. 7000 g = kg
49. 2.2 kg = g
50. 0.65 kg = g
51. 2 t = kg
52. 3.2 t = kg
53. 500 ml = l
54. 4000 l = m^3
55. 6000 l = m^3
56. 8000 ml = l
57. 455 ml = l
58. 2.45 l = ml
59. 2.8 t = kg
60. 67 g = kg

Exercise 3

Copy and complete.

1. 32 cm = m
2. 15 mm = cm
3. 234 g = kg
4. 72 m = km
5. 7.5 m = cm
6. 0.041 kg = g
7. 260 ml = l
8. 0.71 cm = mm
9. 9 cm = m
10. 100 km = m
11. 27 g = kg
12. 7 mm = cm
13. 18 kg = g
14. 800 ml = l
15. 0.2 km = m
16. 11.1 m = cm
17. 400 kg = t
18. 1000 kg = g
19. 85 m = km
20. 0.3 mm = cm
21. 8 cm = m
22. 6 g = kg
23. 100 mm = cm
24. 950 ml = l
25. 7.8 t = kg
26. 0.07 kg = g
27. 20 cm = m
28. 60 m = cm
29. 18 g = kg
30. 880 m = km
31. 7000 cm = km
32. 600 mm = m
33. 0.03 m = mm
34. 0.71 km = m
35. 20 000 g = t
36. 50 000 ml = m^3
37. 600 cm = km
38. 17 g = kg
39. 250 m = cm
40. 0.1 mm = m

2.2 PROBLEMS

Exercise 4

1. John makes a tower using nine identical bricks, each of thickness 2.7 cm. How high is the tower?
2. Mrs Johnson bought 8 kg of potatoes at 31p a kilogram. She paid for her purchase with a £5 note. How much change did she receive?
3. A car dealer bought twelve cars. He bought a number of tyres so that each car had five new tyres and he had 13 left over. How many tyres did he buy?
4. A theatre has 460 seats arranged in 20 rows of equal length. How many seats are in each row?
5. The population of a town near a nuclear power station decreased from 8854 to 6278. How many people left the town?
6. A man bought five articles at £2.40 each and six articles at 95p each. How much did he spend altogether?
7. A chef cooks a Christmas pudding which weighs 24 kg. The pudding is shared equally between 40 people. How much does each person receive?

8. Find the next two numbers in each sequence
   (a) 61, 52, 43, . . .
   (b) 120, 60, 30, . . .
   (c) 2, 3, 5, 8, . . .
   (d) 80, 68, 56, . . .
9. John and Steven each have the same amount of money. How much must John give to Steve if Steve is then to have £10 more than John?
10. In a simple code A = 1, B = 2, C = 3, . . . Z = 26.
   Decode the following messages.
   (a) 23, 8, 1, 20
   20, 9, 13, 5
   4, 15
   23, 5
   6, 9, 14, 9, 19, 8.
   (b) 19, 4^2, (3×7), 18, $(90 - 71)$
   1^3, (9×2), $(2^2 + 1^2)$
   18, $(\frac{1}{5}$ of 105), 2, $(1 \div \frac{1}{2})$, 3^2, 19, 2^3.
   (c) 23, $(100 \div 20)$
   1, $(2 \times 3 \times 3)$, $(2^2 + 1^2)$
   21, $(100 - 86)$, $(100 \div 25)$, 5, $(2^4 + 2)$
   1, (5×4), $(10 \div \frac{1}{2})$, 1, $(27 \div 9)$, $(99 \div 9)$.

Exercise 5

1. There are 1128 pupils in a school and there are 36 more girls than boys. How many girls attend the school?
2. A generous, but not very bright, teacher decides to award 1p to the person coming 10th in a test, 2p to the person coming 9th, 4p to the person coming 8th and so on, doubling the amount each time. How much does the teacher award to the person who came top?
3. A tree was planted when James Wilkinson was born. He died in 1920, aged 75. How old was the tree in 1975?
4. Washing-up liquid is sold in 200 ml containers. Each container costs 57p. How much will it cost to buy 10 litres of the liquid?
5. A train is supposed to leave London at 11 24 and arrive in Brighton at 12 40. The train was delayed and arrived $2\frac{1}{4}$ hours late. At what time did the train arrive?
6. Big Ben stopped for repairs at 17 15 on Tuesday and restarted at 08 20 on Wednesday. For how long had it been stopped?

7 How much would I pay for nine litres of paint if two litres cost £2.30?
8. A television set was advertised at £282.50 for cash, or by 12 equal instalments of £25.30. How much would be saved by paying cash?
9. Eggs are packed twelve to a box. A farmer has enough eggs to fill 316 boxes with unbroken eggs and he has 62 cracked eggs left over. How many eggs had he to start with?
10. A car travels 30 miles on a gallon of petrol and petrol costs £2.20 per gallon. Over a period of one year the car travels a distance of 9600 miles. How much does the petrol cost for the whole year?

Exercise 6

1. In a rugby match the total number of points scored was 58. The home team won by 16 points. How many points did the away team score?
2. Every day at school a teacher uses 10 g of chalk. He teaches 200 days a year. How much chalk will he use if he teaches for 25 years? Give the answer in kg.
3. Mrs James saw flour on sale at 200 g for 28p. How much does she pay if she buys 650 g of flour?
4. A half is a third of it. What is it?
5. A third is a half of it. What is it?
6. A hotel manager was able to buy loaves of bread at £4.44 per dozen, whereas the shop price was 43p per loaf. How much did he save on each loaf?

7. David bought seven apples and received 88p change from £2.00. What was the average price of the apples?
8. In a cycle time-trial, John took 6 min 11 s for the course and Bill took only 5 min 47 s. By how many seconds was Bill quicker than John?

9. One day a third of the class is absent and 16 children are present. How many children are in the class when no one is away?
10. A train leaves Manchester at 09 00 and travels towards London at 100 mph. Another train leaves London for Manchester, also at 09 00, and travels at 80 mph. Which train is nearer to London when they meet?

Exercise 7

1. A special new cheese is on offer at £3.48 per kilogram. Mrs Mann buys half a kilogram. How much change does she receive if she pays with a £5 note?
2. A cup and a saucer together cost £2.80. The cup costs 60p more than the saucer. How much does the cup cost?
3. What number must be subtracted from both 25 and 42 so that one number is twice the other?
4. A generous school teacher gave each of her 30 pupils five sweets. There were 65 sweets left in the box. How many sweets were in the box to start with?
5. Six lamp posts lie at equal distances from each other along a straight road. If the distance between each pair of lamp posts is 20 m, how far is it from the first lamp post to the sixth?
6. A man worked 7 hours per day from Monday to Friday and 4 hours overtime on Saturday. The rate of pay from Monday to Friday is £4.50 per hour and the overtime rate is time and a half. How much did he earn during the week?
7. A man smokes 40 cigarettes a day and each packet of 20 cigarettes costs £1.15. How much does he spend on cigarettes in a whole year of 365 days?
8. A dealer bought a shirt for £4, sold it for £5, bought it back for £6 and finally sold it for £7. How much profit did he make?
9. Five 2's can make 25: $25 = 22 + 2 + \frac{2}{2}$
   (a) Use four 9's to make 100
   (b) Use three 6's to make 7
   (c) Use three 5's to make 60
   (d) Use five 5's to make 61
   (e) Use four 7's to make 1
   (f) Use three 8's to make 11
10. Find the missing digits.

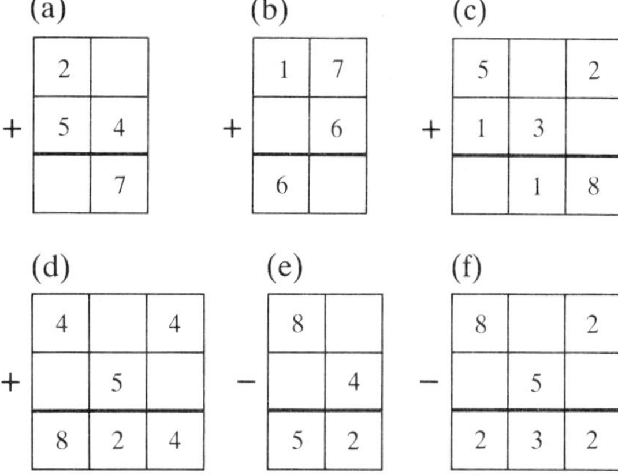

Exercise 8

1. If gas costs 31p for every therm used, what will be the cost in £'s of 200 therms?
2. The rent for a flat is £19 per week. How much rent is paid over a period of 30 weeks?
3. A man works from 07 30 until 16 45. How many hours and minutes has he worked?
4. A rectangular room measures 3.8 m by 2.7 m. A carpet measuring 4 m by 3 m is cut to fit the room.
   (a) Calculate the area of the room.
   (b) Calculate the area of carpet wasted.

5. Calculate the number of seconds in a day.
6. Write down the next two numbers in each of the following sequences
   (a) 2, 5, 8, 11, . . .
   (b) 7, 7, 8, 10, 13, . . .
   (c) 12, 11, 9, 6, . . .
   (d) 1, 3, 7, 15, 31, . . .
7. A roll of wallpaper is cut into five strips. A wall requires 35 strips of paper. How much will it cost if one roll of wallpaper costs £5.40?
8. A television set which costs £300 in England was on sale in France at 3630 francs. Assuming that the television set has the same value as in England, calculate the rate of exchange (i.e. how many francs to the pound?).
9. (a) Last season in the Football League 3 points were awarded for a win, 1 point for a draw and 0 points for a defeat. Copy and complete the table below.

Team	P	W	D	L	Points
Liverpool	18	12	3	3	
Notts. Forest	19	11	5	3	
Man. Utd	18	12	2	4	
West Ham	19	10	6	3	
Spurs	18	11	2	5	
QPR	19	9	4	5	
Everton	17	10	0	7	
Ipswich	17	8	4	5	

   (b) Calculate also how many points each team would have using the old system of
   2 points for a win
   1 point for a draw
   0 points for a defeat.
10. A shopkeeper buys coffee at £3.65 per kg and sells it at 95p per 100 g. How much profit does he make per kg?

Exercise 9

1. Mrs Jackson buys nine 15p stamps and twenty 18p stamps. How much change will she receive from a £5 note?
2. Place the following numbers in order of size, smallest first: 0.12, 0.012, 0.21, 0.021, 0.03.
3. The outline of a 50p coin is shown below.

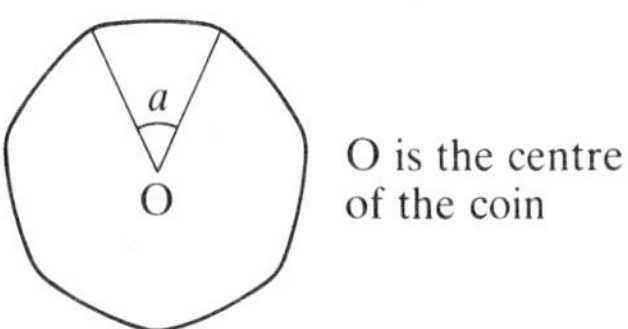

   Calculate the size of the angle a, to the nearest $\frac{1}{10}$ of a degree.
4. Which would cost less and by how much: 35 tins at 25p each or 23 jars at 37p each?
5. A car travels 12 km on 1 litre of petrol. How much petrol will it need on a journey of 54 km?
6. A wooden rod of length 4 m is cut into two pieces so that one piece is 10 cm longer than the other. How long is each piece?
7. (a) Increase £60 by 10%.
   (b) Decrease £900 by 20%.
   (c) Increase £2000 by 2%.
8. A 12-day holiday in Spain costs £285. Find the average cost per day, correct to the nearest pound.
9. Write as a single number:
   (a) 3^2 (b) 2^3 (c) 5^2
   (d) 10^3 (e) 2×4^2 (f) 3×2^4
10. In order to make the service more popular, bus fares are reduced by 40%. Find the new price of a ticket which used to cost
   (a) 10p, (b) 50p, (c) 35p.

Exercise 10

1. Twelve calculators cost £102. How many calculators could be bought for £76.50?
2. A car travels 35 m in 0.7 seconds. How far does it travel in
   (a) 0.1 s? (b) 1 s? (c) 2 minutes?

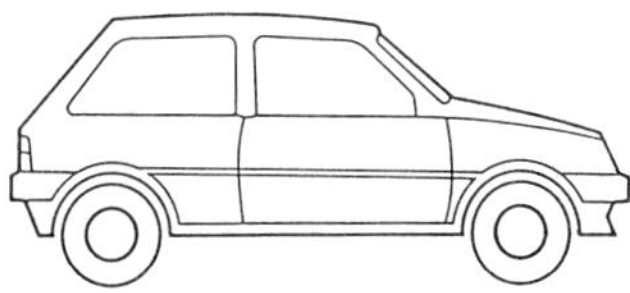

3. Class 4P has 22 pupils and class 4N has 20 pupils. Pupils in 4P give an average of 5p each to charity and pupils in 4N give an average of 7p each. How much was given to charity altogether?

4. Find two numbers which:
   (a) multiply to give 12 and add up to 7.
   (b) multiply to give 42 and add up to 13.
   (c) multiply to give 32 and add up to 12.
   (d) multiply to give 48 and add up to 26.
5. Copy and complete

	Fraction	Decimal
(a)	$\frac{4}{5}$	0.8
(b)	$\frac{1}{4}$	
(c)		0.3
(d)	$\frac{1}{8}$	
(e)		0.05

6. An engineering firm offers all of its workers a choice of two pay rises. Workers can choose either an 8% increase on their salaries or they can accept a rise of £800.
   (a) A fitter earns £5200 a year. Which pay rise should he choose?
   (b) The personnel manager earns £11 500 a year. Which pay rise should he choose?
7. A ship's voyage started at 20 30 on Tuesday and finished at 07 00 on the next day. How long was the journey in hours and minutes?
8. Work out, without using a calculator.
   (a) 0.6 − 0.06 (b) 0.04 × 1000
   (c) 0.4 ÷ 100 (d) 7.2 − 5
   (e) 10% of £90 (f) 25% of £160.
9. In 1984 the population of the United States was 232 million. The population was expected to grow by 12% by the end of the century. Find the expected population at the end of the century, correct to the nearest million.
10. Amongst other ingredients, 350 g of flour and 2 tablespoons of milk are needed to make 4 cakes.
    (a) What weight of flour is need to make 12 cakes?
    (b) How many tablespoons of milk are needed to make 6 cakes?

Exercise 11

1. How many oranges costing 9p each can be bought with £2?
2. A film lasting 1 hour 40 minutes finishes at 21 15. At what time does the film start?
3. Find the angle between the hands of a clock showing 4.00 p.m.

4. A roll of wallpaper costs £5.60 and each roll is sufficient for 6 strips. How much will it cost to paper a room which requires 24 strips of wallpaper?
5. Arrange the following numbers in order, smallest first:
   3210, 3120, 2333, 3211, 3301, 3102.
6. Work out, without a calculator:
   (a) 2.7 × 100,
   (b) 0.41 × 10 000,
   (c) 0.84 ÷ 100,
   (d) 0.005 23 × 1000.
7. How many seconds are there in 5 hours?
8. In a rugby match the total number of points scored was 50. The home team won by 14 points. How many points did the away team score?
9. A milkman delivers 2 bottles of milk to every house on his round.
   (a) If there are 648 houses on his round, how many bottles does he deliver?
   (b) After he has delivered to 487 houses, how many more bottles has he still to deliver?
10. Which of the shapes below can be drawn without going over any line twice and without taking the pencil from the paper? Write 'yes' or 'no' for each shape.

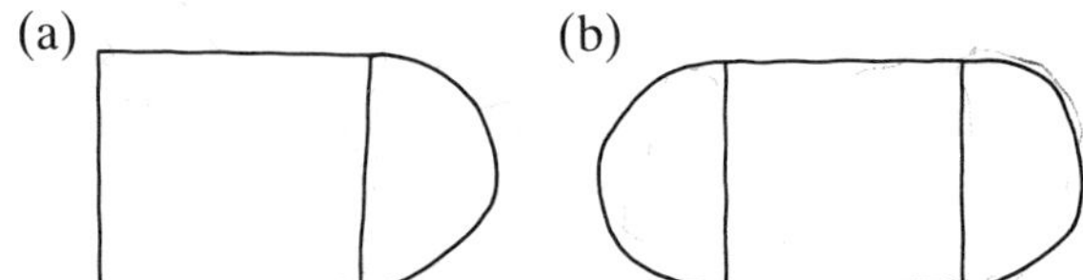

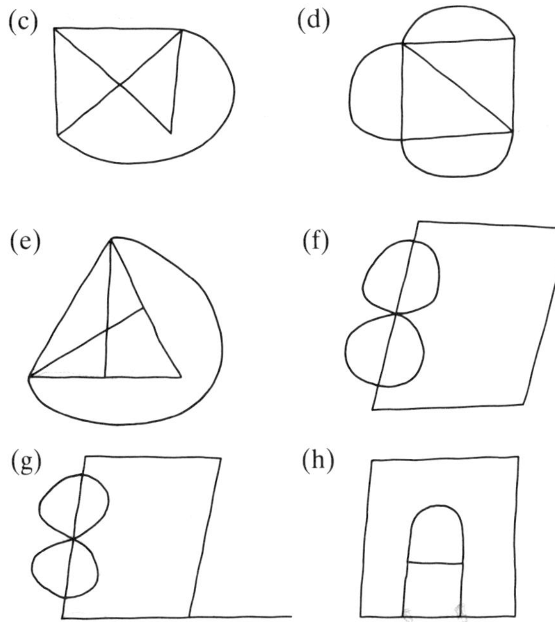

Exercise 12

1. A worker is paid £3.40 per hour for a 40 hour week. In addition to his basic pay he works 6 hours overtime at time and a half. Calculate
   (a) his basic pay for 40 hours
   (b) his overtime pay
   (c) his take-home pay, if he pays £8.75 National Insurance and £15.80 income tax.

2. Calculate the area of a square which has a perimeter of 20 cm.

3. The table below gives the cost of sending parcels by post. (Parts of a kilogram are charged as a whole kilogram).

Parcel not over	Cost
1 kg	£1.80
2 kg	£2.15
3 kg	£2.45
4 kg	£2.72
5 kg	£2.93

State the cost of posting a parcel of weight:
(a) 2 kg
(b) 2.8 kg
(c) 4.2 kg.

4. Calculate the perimeter of the shape below.

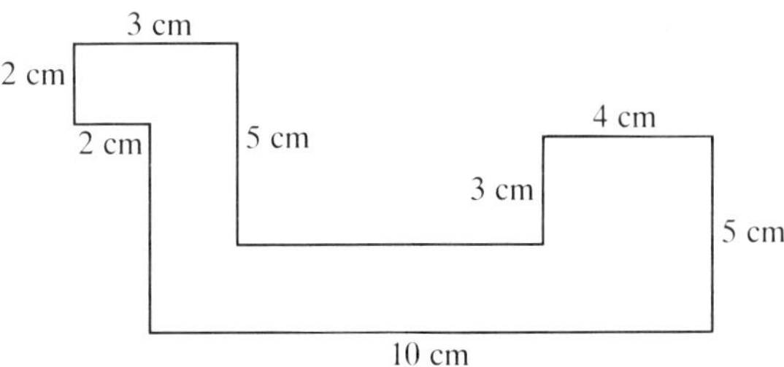

5. A hi-fi system is priced as follows:

Stereo amplifier	£119.50
Cassette deck	£92.50
Record deck	£46.00
Tuner	£75.50
Speakers	£124.00
Cabinet	£65.50

   (a) Find the total cash price of this system.
   (b) This system can also be bought using hire purchase with a deposit of £120 and 18 monthly payments of £28. Find the total hire purchase price.
   (c) In a sale the prices of all items are reduced by 30%. Find the cash price of the whole system in the sale.

6. The houses in a street are numbered from 1 to 60. How many times does the number '2' appear?

7. Draw a large copy of the square below.

1	2	3	4

Your task is to fill up all 16 squares using four 1's, four 2's, four 3's and four 4's. Each number may appear only once in any row (↔) or column (↕). The first row has been drawn already.

8. Between the times 11 57 and 12 27 the mileometer of a car changes from 23793 miles to 23825 miles. At what average speed is the car travelling?

9. In a simple code A = 1, B = 2, C = 3 and so on. When the word 'BAT' is written in code its total score is (2 + 1 + 20) = 23.
   (a) Find the score for the word 'ZOOM'
   (b) Find the score for the word 'ALPHABET'
   (c) Find a word with a score of 40.

10. Alan has 28p and John has 20p. How much must John give to Alan so that Alan has twice as much money as John?

Exercise 13

1. A woman hires a car from a car hire firm which charges £12 per day plus 8p per km travelled.
   (a) How much does it cost to hire a car for four days and drive 200 km?
   (b) How much does it cost to hire a car for six days and drive 650 km?
   (c) A woman hired a car for two days and had to pay £32. How far did she drive?

2. The table shows how much £100 amounts to when invested at the given rates for periods of 1, 3 or 5 years.

Period in years	Amount		
	6% per annum	8% per annum	10% per annum
1	£106	£108	£110
3	£119	£126	£133
5	£134	£147	£161

   (a) What does £100 amount to when invested
      (i) at 6% for 1 year
      (ii) at 10% for 5 years
      (iii) at 8% for 3 years
      (iv) at 6% for 3 years?
   (b) How much interest is earned when £100 is invested at 8% per annum for 5 years?
   (c) What does £500 amount to when invested at 10% for 3 years?
   (d) What is the interest on £2000 at 6% per annum for 3 years?

3. Find the missing numbers

   (a)
```
   3 * 4
 + * 2 *
 -------
   5 8 9
```
   (b)
```
     * 4 7
 +   8 * *
 ---------
   * 1 5 9
```

4. A restaurant adds a service charge of 10% to the basic price of meals.
   (a) Find the total cost of a meal with a basic price of £15.
   (b) Find the basic price of a meal which costs £22 after the service charge has been added.

5. Due to overproduction, the E.E.C. destroyed 41 cauliflowers for each minute of the year in 1984.
   (a) How many cauliflowers were destroyed per day?
   (b) How many cauliflowers were destroyed in the whole year?
   (c) If each cauliflower had been sold for 20p, how much money would have been raised by actually selling the cauliflowers?

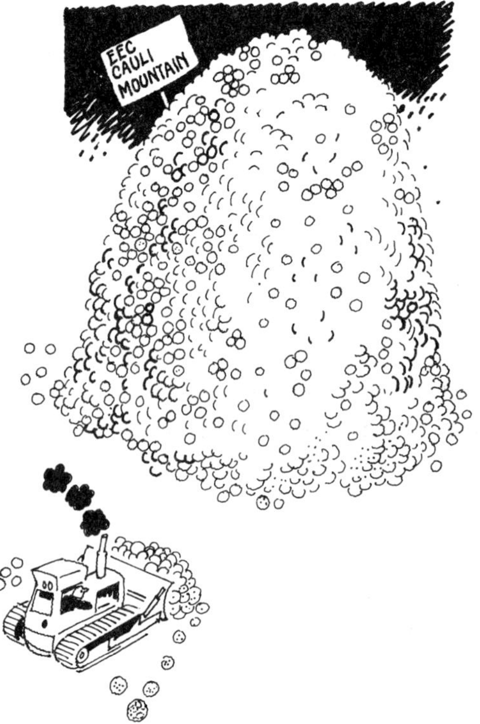

2.3 IMPERIAL UNITS

(a) 12 inches = 1 foot
3 feet = 1 yard
1760 yards = 1 mile

(b) 16 ounces = 1 pound
14 pounds = 1 stone
2240 pounds = 1 ton

(c) 8 pints = 1 gallon

Exercise 14

1. How many inches are there in two feet?
2. How many feet are there in three yards?
3. How many ounces are there in two pounds?
4. How many pints are there in two gallons?
5. How many pounds are there in three stones?
6. How many inches are there in five feet?
7. How many yards are there in ten miles?
8. How many ounces are there in five pounds?
9. How many pounds are there in two tons?
10. How many inches are there in a yard?
11. How many pounds are there in ten stones?
12. How many ounces are there in a stone?
13. How many inches are there in half a yard?
14. How many ounces are there in half a pound?
15. How many yards are there in a quarter of a mile?
16. How many inches are there in ten yards?

In questions **17** to **38** copy each statement and fill in the missing numbers.

17. 12 feet = yards.
18. 32 ounces = pounds
19. 4 stones = pounds
20. 2 gallons = pints
21. 6 feet = inches
22. 2 miles = yards
23. 40 pints = gallons
24. 4480 pounds = tons
25. 28 pounds = stones
26. 6 gallons = pints
27. 3 yards = inches
28. $1\frac{1}{2}$ feet = inches
29. $\frac{1}{2}$ mile = yards
30. $\frac{1}{2}$ gallon = pints
31. 4 feet 6 inches = inches
32. 3 pounds 6 ounces = ounces
33. 5 stones 2 pounds = pounds
34. 7 stones 4 pounds = pounds
35. 10 stones 12 pounds = pounds
36. 5 feet 3 inches = inches
37. 6 feet 1 inch = inches
38. 4 feet 10 inches = inches

Changing units

Exercise 15

You may use the following approximate conversions.

1 inch = 2.54 cm	1 gallon = 4.55 litres
1 mile = 1.61 km	1 km = 0.621 mile
1 pound = 0.454 kg	1 litre = 0.22 gallon
1 pint = 0.568 litre	1 kg = 2.2 pounds

Copy each statement and fill in the missing numbers.

1. 10 inches = cm
2. 10 gallons = litres
3. 100 pounds = kg
4. 100 pints = litres
5. 2 miles = km
6. 2 pounds = kg
7. 10 miles = km
8. 4 inches = cm
9. 5 pounds = kg
10. $\frac{1}{2}$ pint = litre
11. 10 km = miles
12. 100 litres = gallons
13. 3 kg = pounds
14. 100 km = miles
15. 400 litres = gallons
16. 2 kg = pounds
17. 2 km = miles
18. 5 litres = gallons
19. 20 kg = pounds
20. 20 km = miles
21. 1 foot = cm
22. 5 pints = litres
23. 3 litres = gallons
24. 3 inches = cm
25. 4 pounds = kg

2.4 FOREIGN CURRENCY

In this section we will use the following rates of exchange:

Country	Unit of money	Rate of exchange
France	franc	F12 = £1
Germany	mark	DM4 = £1
Greece	drachma	DR150 = £1
Spain	peseta	Ptas200 = £1
U.S.A.	dollar	\$1.40 = £1

Exercise 16

Change the British money into the foreign currency stated.

1. £10 = F
2. £20 = DM
3. £3 = DR
4. £100 = Ptas
5. £1000 = \$
6. £8 = DR
7. £7 = F
8. £100 = \$
9. £16 = DM
10. £500 = DM
11. £0.50 = F
12. £0.50 = Ptas
13. £0.50 = \$
14. £1000 = DR
15. £1000 = Ptas
16. £0.25 = DM
17. £0.25 = F
18. £50 = \$
19. £200 = DR
20. £0.10 = Ptas
21. £500 = \$
22. £600 = F
23. £65 = DM
24. £30 = DR
25. £1.50 = F
26. £1 = \$
27. £1.50 = DR
28. £2.50 = Ptas
29. £11 = Ptas
30. £12.50 = \$

Convert \$50 into British money to the nearest penny.

\$1.40 = £1 (from above)

$\therefore \$1 = £\frac{1}{1.40}$

$\therefore \$50 = £\frac{1}{1.40} \times 50 = £35.7142$

$= £35.71$ (to the nearest penny)

Exercise 17

Change the foreign currency into British money, correct to the nearest penny where necessary.

1. F36
2. DM40
3. \$2.80
4. Ptas1000
5. DR600
6. F120
7. \$140
8. DM80
9. Ptas5000
10. DR1500
11. F96
12. \$70
13. DM6
14. Ptas900
15. DR80
16. F65
17. \$60
18. DM82
19. F105
20. Ptas6500
21. DM62
22. \$900
23. DR70
24. F240
25. Ptas10 000
26. DR95
27. \$22.50
28. Ptas965
29. DM88.40
30. F72.65
31. Ptas8500
32. \$71
33. DR640
34. DR191
35. \$760
36. DM317
37. DM19 000
38. Ptas600 000
39. F22 500
40. \$255

Exercise 18

Give answers correct to the nearest penny where necessary. In questions **1** to **10** fill in the spaces.

1. £20 = F
2. £15 = DM
3. \$14 = £
4. DR450 = £
5. £5 = Ptas
6. F108 = £
7. DM60 = £
8. £600 = \$
9. F27 = £
10. DM84 = £

11. A record costs \$5.50 in the United States. What is the price in British money?

12. A car costs F40 000 in France. What is the price in British money?

13. A television costs £320 in Britain. What is the price in Greek money?

14. A bottle of wine costs Ptas185 in Spain. What is the price in British money?

15. A video recorder costs £500 in Britain and DM1900 in Germany. In which country is it cheaper and by how much (in £)?

16. A car costs F37 920 in France and Ptas680 000 in Spain. In which country is it cheaper and by how much (to the nearest £)?

17. A book costs DM26 in Germany and \$8.40 in the United States. In which country is it cheaper and by how much (in £)?

18. Copy and complete
(a) \$140 = £
(b) £100 = F
(c) \$140 = F

2.5 MAP SCALES

The map below is drawn to a scale of 1:50 000. In other words 1 cm on the map represents 50 000 cm on the land.

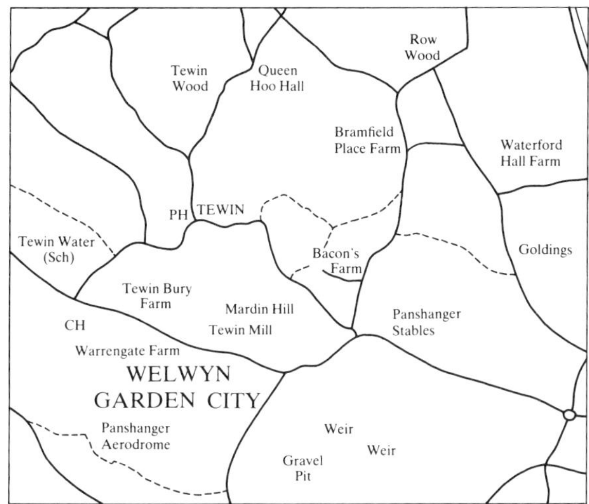

On a map of scale 1:25 000 two towns appear 10 cm apart. What is the actual distance between the towns in km?

1 cm on map = 25 000 cm on land
10 cm on map = 250 000 cm on land
250 000 cm = 2500 m
= 2.5 km

The towns are 2.5 km apart.

Exercise 19

1. The scale of a map is 1:1000. Find the actual length in metres represented on the map by 20 cm.
2. The scale of a map is 1:10 000. Find the actual length in metres represented on the map by 5 cm.
3. The scale of a map is 1:20 000. Find the actual length in kilometres represented on the map by
   (a) 10 cm (b) 15 cm (c) 4 cm
4. The scale of a map is 1:50 000. Find the actual length in kilometres represented on the map by
   (a) 10 cm (b) 6 cm (c) 12 cm
5. Copy and complete the table

Map scale	Length on map	Actual length on land
(a) 1:10 000	10 cm	1 km
(b) 1:2000	10 cm	m
(c) 1:25 000	4 cm	km
(d) 1:10 000	6 cm	km
(e) 1:50 000	3 cm	km
(f) 1:25 000	10 cm	km
(g) 1:100 000	2.2 cm	km
(h) 1:25 000	8 cm	km
(i) 1:50 000	3.1 cm	km
(j) 1:10 000	2.7 cm	m

6. How far apart are two places if they are 5.4 cm apart on a map whose scale is 1:20 000?
7. Find the actual distance in metres between two points which are 6.3 cm apart on a map whose scale is 1:1000.
8. On a map of scale 1:300 000 the distance between York and Harrogate is 8 cm. What is the actual distance in km?
9. On a map of scale 1:320 000 the distance between Adwick le Street and Knottingley is 6.1 cm. What is the actual distance in km?
10. On a map of scale 1:64 000 the distance between Pudsey Town Hall and Beeston cemetery is 9.2 cm. What is the actual distance in km?
11. A builder's plan is drawn to a scale of 1 cm to 10 m. How long is a road which is 12 cm on the plan.
12. A plan is drawn to a scale of 1 cm to 1 m. How long is a wall which is 5.6 cm on the plan?
13. The plan of a house is drawn to a scale of 1 cm to 5 m. How wide is the kitchen if its width is 1 cm on the plan?
14. The scale of a drawing is 1 cm to 10 m. How long is a road which is 9 cm on the drawing?
15. The scale of a drawing is 1 cm to 5 m. How long is a path which is 2.1 cm on the drawing?

> The distance between two towns is 18 km. How far apart will they be on a map of scale 1:50 000?
>
> 18 km = 1 800 000 cm
> 1 800 000 cm on land = $\frac{1}{50\ 000} \times 1\ 800\ 000$ cm on map
>
> Distance between towns on map = 36 cm

Exercise 20

1. The distance between two towns is 15 km. How far apart will they be on a map of scale 1:10 000?
2. The distance between two points is 25 km. How far apart will they be on a map of scale 1:20 000?
3. The length of a road is 2.8 km. How long will the road be on a map of scale 1:10 000?
4. The length of a reservoir is 5.9 km. How long will it be on a map of scale 1:100 000?
5. Copy and complete the table.

Map scale	Actual length on land	Length on map
(a) 1:20 000	12 km	cm
(b) 1:10 000	8.4 km	cm
(c) 1:50 000	28 km	cm
(d) 1:40 000	56 km	cm
(e) 1:5000	5 km	cm
(f) 1:1000	60 m	cm
(g) 1:60 000	30 km	cm
(h) 1:250 000	550 km	cm
(i) 1:2000	12 m	cm

6. The plan of a house is drawn to a scale of 1 cm to 1 m. The length of the house is 13 m. What length will the house be on the plan?
7. The scale of a drawing is 1 cm to 10 m. The length of a wall is 25 m. What length will the wall be on the drawing?
8. A builder's plan is drawn to a scale of 1 cm to 10 m. The length of a garden is 15 m. What length will the garden be on the plan?

Exercise 21

1. On a map of scale 1:55 000 the distance between two places is 8 cm. What is the actual distance in km?
2. The length of a canal is 50 km. How long will it be on a map of scale 1:20 000?
3. Copy and complete the table.

Map scale	Length on map	Actual length on land
(a) 1:10 000	5 cm	* km
(b) 1:10 000	* cm	12 km
(c) 1:20 000	8.4 cm	* km
(d) 1:50 000	* cm	8 km
(e) 1:200 000	3.2 cm	* km
(f) 1:1000	* cm	2 m
(g) 1:250	1.2 cm	* m
(h) 1:20 000	7.7 cm	* km
(i) *	20 cm	2 km
(j) *	8 cm	1.6 km
(k) *	3 cm	3 km
(l) *	9 cm	1.8 km
(m) *	2.7 cm	1.35 km

4. A farmer's field is 5 cm long on a map. If the field is actually 500 m long, find the scale of the map.
5. A road is 12 cm on a map. If the road is actually 2.4 km long, find the scale of the map.
6. Two towns are 14 km apart, but the distance between them on a map is 28 cm. Find the scale of the map.
7. The plan of the room below is drawn to a scale of 1 cm to 1.2 m.

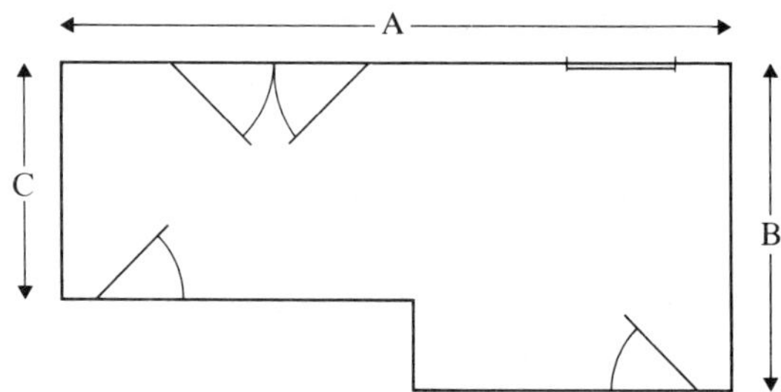

Use a ruler to find the actual dimensions marked A, B and C.

Unit 3

3.1 APPROXIMATIONS

Significant figures

Write the following numbers correct to three significant figures (3 S.F.).

(a) 2.6582 = 2.66 (to 3 S.F.)
↑

(b) 0.5142 = 0.514 (to 3 S.F.)
↑

(c) 84 660 = 84 700 (to 3 S.F.)
↑

(d) 0.04031 = 0.0403 (to 3 S.F.)
↑

In each case we look at the number marked with an arrow to see if it is 'five or more'.

Exercise 1

In questions **1** to **20** write the numbers correct to three significant figures.

1. 3.1782 **2.** 14.762
3. 8.0491 **4.** 2.6324
5. 51.252 **6.** 0.5567
7. 0.832 41 **8.** 7.3668
9. 0.076 14 **10.** 18.294
11. 426.72 **12.** 315.23
13. 6.0074 **14.** 11.355
15. 2.0943 **16.** 0.007 422
17. 318.24 **18.** 2418
19. 3561 **20.** 38 684

In questions **21** to **40** write the numbers correct to two significant figures.

21. 5.674 **22.** 18.34
23. 0.7666 **24.** 0.5151

25. 8.333 **26.** 7.2461
27. 11.624 **28.** 25.09
29. 18.555 **30.** 0.008 26
31. 0.071 38 **32.** 17.802
33. 30.542 **34.** 60.91
35. 18 740 **36.** 34 265
37. 889 **38.** 71 623
39. 40 027 **40.** 163.4

In questions **41** to **60** write the numbers correct to four significant figures.

41. 28.666 **42.** 3.0407
43. 2.994 81 **44.** 316.252
45. 8.0455 **46.** 0.007 1652
47. 0.031 111 **48.** 84 207
49. 65 525 **50.** 124 860
51. 5.6777 **52.** 193.24
53. 568.83 **54.** 2001.76
55. 0.038 1111 **56.** 76.0583
57. 80.0455 **58.** 6.0666
59. 77 777 **60.** 400 289

Decimal places

> Write the following numbers correct to two decimal places (2 D.P.)
>
> (a) 8.358 = 8.36 (to 2 D.P.)
> ↑
>
> (b) 0.0328 = 0.03 (to 2 D.P.)
> ↑
>
> (c) 74.355 = 74.36 (to 2 D.P.)
> ↑
>
> In each case we look at the number marked with an arrow to see if it is 'five or more'.

Exercise 2

In questions **1** to **20** write the numbers correct to two decimal places.

1. 8.486 **2.** 6.041
3. 1.042 **4.** 12.135
5. 11.618 **6.** 6.049
7. 0.555 **8.** 18.076
9. 2.0492 **10.** 8.946
11. 13.6241 **12.** 216.841
13. 0.0743 **14.** 0.0714
15. 7.823 **16.** 3.126
17. 4.114 **18.** 24.521
19. 206.125 **20.** 8.0895

In questions **21** to **40** write the numbers correct to one decimal place.

21. 8.621 **22.** 12.55
23. 9.047 **24.** 2.608
25. 8.614 **26.** 5.672
27. 0.714 **28.** 0.0961
29. 8.826 **30.** 0.666
31. 207.15 **32.** 10.72
33. 0.0923 **34.** 8.041
35. 4.261 **36.** 88.74
37. 217.14 **38.** 3.961
39. 0.85 **40.** 4.972

In questions **41** to **60** write the numbers to the degree of accuracy indicated.

41. 8.052 (2 D.P.) **42.** 17.62 (1 D.P.)
43. 6.777 (1 D.P.) **44.** 9.094 (2 D.P.)
45. 0.0714 (3 D.P.) **46.** 0.03328 (4 D.P.)
47. 19.62 (1 D.P.) **48.** 8.0755 (3 D.P.)
49. 8.092 (2 D.P.) **50.** 4.076 (2 D.P.)
51. 3.3355 (3 D.P.) **52.** 8.921 (1 D.P.)
53. 8.0496 (2 D.P.) **54** .0.078 (2 D.P.)
55. 0.07145 (4 D.P.) **56.** 2.342 (1 D.P.)
57. 8.0715 (3 D.P.) **58.** 1.3498 (3 D.P.)
59. 9.942 (1 D.P.) **60.** 15.981 (1 D.P.)

61. Use a ruler to measure the dimensions of the rectangles below.
(a) Write down the length and width in cm correct to one decimal place.
(b) Work out the area of each rectangle and give the answer in cm^2 correct to one decimal place.

(i)

(ii)

3.2 ESTIMATING

Estimate the answers to the following questions:

(a) $9.7 \times 3.1 \approx 10 \times 3$. About 30.
(b) $81.4 \times 98.2 \approx 80 \times 100$. About 8000.
(c) $19.2 \times 49.1 \approx 20 \times 50$. About 1000.
(d) $102.7 \div 19.6 \approx 100 \div 20$. About 5.

Exercise 3

In the table below there are 30 questions, each followed by three possible answers. In each case only one answer is correct.
Write down each question and decide (by estimating) which answer is correct. No calculating is required.

Question	Answer A	Answer B	Answer C
1. 5.1×9.9	4.69	94.69	50.49
2. 9×7.2	64.8	23.4	201.8
3. 1.01×80.6	19.302	81.406	304.206
4. 58.4×102	600.4	5956.8	2450.4
5. 6.8×11.4	19.32	280.14	77.52
6. 97×1.08	104.76	55.66	1062.3
7. 972×20.2	2112.4	19 634.4	8862.4
8. 7.1×103	74.3	731.3	7210.3
9. 18.9×21	396.9	58.7	201.9
10. 2.1×96	19.6	507.6	201.6
11. 3.85×1010	394.6	3002.5	3888.5
12. 11.6×40.3	467.48	811.48	48.48
13. 1.95×21	212.65	40.95	19.85
14. 6.9×103	710.7	2350.7	70.9
15. 207×3.9	317.3	8140.3	807.3
16. 21.1×19.2	708.12	405.12	41.12
17. 97.1×98	963.8	4810.8	9515.8
18. 4.01×960	3849.6	417.4	894.2
19. 33×2.7	35.1	89.1	342.1
20. 43×0.95	4.95	40.85	407.65
21. 7.8×9	20.4	711.2	70.2
22. 11.1×8.9	98.79	58.69	504.6
23. 88×4.9	195.4	431.2	904.2
24. 201×1.87	38.63	916.87	375.87
25. 0.9×115	103.5	62.5	309.5
26. 1200×0.89	121.4	1068	364.4
27. 10.9×61	61.8	2444.9	664.9
28. 0.1×98.2	29.42	9.82	98.2
29. 0.104×980	9.82	984.2	101.92
30. 0.21×1050	22.5	220.5	485.5

Exercise 4

In the table below there are 30 questions, each followed by three possible answers. In each case only one answer is correct.
Write down each question and decide (by estimating) which answer is correct. Do not do the calculations exactly.

Question	Answer A	Answer B	Answer C
1. 7.79 ÷ 1.9	8.2	4.1	1.9
2. 27.03 ÷ 5.1	5.3	0.5	8.7
3. 59.78 ÷ 9.8	12.2	2.8	6.1
4. 13.32 ÷ 1.8	7.4	4.7	12.1
5. 18.05 ÷ 0.95	1.9	19	7.6
6. 29.82 ÷ 7.1	1.8	8.6	4.2
7. 34.68 ÷ 10.2	3.4	7.1	11.4
8. 93.84 ÷ 9.2	7.6	10.2	19.4
9. 711 ÷ 7.9	90	51	175
10. 1.078 ÷ 0.98	6.4	10.4	1.1
11. 1250.5 ÷ 6.1	21.4	205	66.2
12. 20.48 ÷ 3.2	6.4	12.2	2.8
13. 25.25 ÷ 10.1	5.6	25	2.5
14. 881.1 ÷ 99	8.9	4.9	19.9
15. 1155 ÷ 105	3.5	11	23
16. 32 × 98	3136	1754	24 806
17. 2.1 × 5.01	7.641	10.521	17.21
18. 103 × 0.96	9.78	65.78	98.88
19. 7.2 × 6.9	112.68	49.68	73.48
20. 19.11 ÷ 9.1	5.2	2.1	0.23
21. 25.11 ÷ 3.1	8.1	15.1	19.3
22. 216 ÷ 0.9	56.3	24.3	240
23. 19.2 + 0.41	23.3	8.41	19.61
24. 207 + 18.34	25.34	225.34	1248
25. 68.2 − 1.38	97.82	48.82	66.82
26. 7 − 0.64	6.36	1.48	0.48
27. 974 × 0.11	9.14	107.14	563.14
28. 551.1 ÷ 11	6.92	50.1	5623
29. 207.1 + 11.65	310.75	23.75	218.75
30. 664 × 0.51	256.2	338.64	828.62

3.3 ORDER OF OPERATIONS

Work out × and ÷ before + and −

(a) 5 + 6 × 2 = 5 + 12 = 17
(b) 12 ÷ 3 − 2 = 4 − 2 = 2
(c) 8 − 15 ÷ 3 = 8 − 5 = 3
(d) 2 × 4 + 3 × 6 = 8 + 18 = 26

Exercise 5

Work out

1. 6 × 3 + 2
2. 5 + 2 × 4
3. 6 + 5 × 2
4. 8 + 7 × 2
5. 8 − 1 × 4
6. 7 + 18 ÷ 3
7. 9 + 6 ÷ 2
8. 26 − 2 × 8

9. $20 - 3 \times 5$
10. $11 + 8 \div 2$
11. $5 \times 5 - 5$
12. $16 - 30 \div 3$
13. $10 - 20 \div 4$
14. $7 \times 7 - 2$
15. $9 + 7 \times 3$
16. $20 \div 10 + 20$
17. $50 - 8 \times 4$
18. $55 - 8 \times 5$
19. $22 - 3 \times 7$
20. $19 + 24 \div 6$
21. $11 + 8 \div 1$
22. $60 - 7 \times 8$
23. $15 - 2 \times 6$
24. $15 \div 5 - 3$
25. $30 + 15 \div 3$
26. $9 \times 5 + 15$
27. $40 - 3 \times 8$
28. $12 - 36 \div 6$
29. $3 + 20 \div 2$
30. $13 + 8 \div 8$

31. $2 \times 4 + 3 \times 5$
32. $6 \times 6 + 7 \times 5$
33. $1 \times 6 + 7 \times 2$
34. $2 \times 8 + 2 \times 10$
35. $3 \times 5 - 12 \div 2$
36. $3 \times 5 - 28 \div 4$
37. $7 \times 4 + 2 \times 2$
38. $30 \div 3 + 5 \times 4$
39. $20 \div 2 - 3 \times 2$
40. $8 \div 8 - 1 \times 1$
41. $7 \times 3 + 32 \div 2$
42. $7 \times 5 + 33 \div 3$
43. $40 \div 8 - 60 \div 12$
44. $40 \div 8 + 6 \times 5$
45. $4 \times 12 + 13 \times 2$
46. $7 \times 3 - 100 \div 5$
47. $5 + 3 \times 2 - 6$
48. $28 - 7 \times 4 + 7$
49. $10 - 4 \times 2 + 4$
50. $15 + 60 \div 3 - 15$
51. $10 + 12 \div 3 - 7$
52. $2 + 9 \times 10 + 3$
53. $15 - 36 \div 12 + 2$
54. $40 - 216 \div 6 + 3$
55. $6 + 3 \times 8 - 10$
56. $9 + 9 \times 9 - 1$
57. $7 \times 7 + 10 \div 10$
58. $3 \times 8 - 2 \times 8$
59. $50 \div 2 - 5 \times 4$
60. $20 \times 20 - 306 \div 9$

When a calculation involves brackets, do things in the following order:

(i) brackets
(ii) $\times$ and $\div$
(iii) $+$ and $-$

(a) $15 - (7 - 2) = 15 - 5 = 10$
(b) $3 \times (8 \div 2) = 3 \times 4 = 12$
(c) $(12 + 8) \div (6 \div 3) = 20 \div 2 = 10$
(d) $24 - (3 + 2 \times 4) = 24 - 11 = 13$

Exercise 6

Work out

1. $6 + (3 \times 2) + 1$
2. $4 \times (4 - 2) + 7$
3. $8 + (8 - 3) \times 3$
4. $6 \times 6 - (3 \times 3)$
5. $(10 - 1) \times 2 - 3$
6. $8 \times (10 \div 2) - 12$
7. $7 + 3 \times (6 \times 5)$
8. $(3 \times 3) + 2 \times 4$
9. $8 - (3 \times 2) \div 6$
10. $5 \times (8 - 3) - 20$
11. $20 + 16 \div (4 \times 2)$
12. $12 + 8 \div (8 \div 4)$
13. $(5 - 2) \times 3 + 11$
14. $3 \times (12 - 7) - 10$
15. $15 \div (9 - 6) + 8$
16. $5 \times (9 + 1) + 8$
17. $8 + 3 \times (3 + 4)$
18. $85 - (15 + 45) \div 12$
19. $8 + (7 + 2) \div 9$
20. $6 + 16 \div (5 - 1)$
21. $(1 + 4) \times 7 - 15$
22. $10 + 8 \times (8 - 5)$
23. $24 - (9 + 21) \div 5$
24. $42 \div (11 - 5) - 2$
25. $(7 \times 2) \times 2 + 16$
26. $(11 - 7) \times 3 + 16$
27. $60 - (3 \times 20) + 13$
28. $17 + 5 \times (3 \times 1)$
29. $16 - 22 \div (23 - 21)$
30. $13 + (19 + 5) \div 3$

31. $(18 + 6) \div 6 + 13$
32. $(8 + 5) \times 2 + 10$
33. $15 + 8 \times (21 - 18)$
34. $129 - 7 \times (15 - 8)$
35. $(13 - 6) \times 8 - 5$
36. $35 \div (24 - 19) - 6$
37. $7 - (8 + 2) \div 5$
38. $12 + (5 + 2) \times 6$
39. $9 + (36 + 9) \div 9$
40. $(19 - 8) \times 6 + 12$
41. $(33 - 22) \times 4 + 7$
42. $7 + (21 + 7) \div 4$
43. $9 \times (9 + 2) - 2$
44. $6 \div (12 \div 2) + 3$
45. $96 - 8 \times (60 - 51)$
46. $8 \times 4 + (17 - 8)$
47. $7 \times (12 - 10) + 9$
48. $9 \times 3 - (20 \div 2)$
49. $37 - (26 - 19) \times 2$
50. $24 \div (12 \div 2) + 7$

51. $\dfrac{15}{(8 - 5)}$
52. $\dfrac{9 \times 2}{(9 - 6)}$
53. $\dfrac{18 + 2}{(3 + 2)}$
54. $\dfrac{15 + 15 - 2}{(8 - 1)}$
55. $\dfrac{27 + 3 \times 3}{(3 \times 2)}$
56. $\dfrac{6 + 8 \times 3}{(8 \times 2 - 10)}$
57. $\dfrac{13 - 12 \div 4}{4 + 3 \times 2}$
58. $\dfrac{11 + 6 \times 6}{5 - 8 \div 2}$
59. $\dfrac{12 + 3 \times 6}{4 + 3 \div 3}$
60. $\dfrac{24 - 18 \div 3}{1.5 + 4.5}$

The last ten questions are more difficult.

61. $(42 - 5 \times 6) \times (8 - 4 \times 2) + (7 + 3 \times 3)$
62. $(10 - 24 \div 3) + (8 + 3 \times 4) \div (8 - 6 \times 1)$
63. $7 + 9 \times (8 - 6 \div 2)$
64. $[(7 - 2) \times 5] - (6 \times 3 - 2 \times 4)$
65. $[(60 - 7 \times 5) \div 5] + (12 + 7 \times 10)$
66. $(15 - 3 \times 4) \times 4 + [60 \div (24 \div 2)]$
67. $[(9 - 7) \times 12] - (7 \times 3 - 5 \times 4)$
68. $(50 - 8 \times 6) \times 2 + [40 \div (5 \times 2)]$
69. $[(12 - 8) \times 4] \div (11 - 3 \times 1)$
70. $(7 \times 2 - 6) + (7 + 16 \div 8) \times (10 - 4 \times 2)$

3.4 USING A CALCULATOR

Exercise 7

Work out, correct to four significant figures.

1. 85.3×21.7
2. $18.6 \div 2.7$
3. $10.074 \div 8.3$
4. 0.112×3.74
5. $8 - 0.11111$
6. $19 + 0.3456$
7. $0.841 \div 17$
8. 11.02×20.1
9. $18.3 \div 0.751$
10. 0.982×6.74
11. $\dfrac{8.3 + 2.94}{3.4}$
12. $\dfrac{6.1 - 4.35}{0.76}$
13. $\dfrac{19.7 + 21.4}{0.985}$
14. $7.3 + \left(\dfrac{8.2}{9.5}\right)$
15. $\left(\dfrac{6.04}{18.7}\right) - 0.214$
16. $\dfrac{2.4 \times 0.871}{4.18}$
17. $19.3 + \left(\dfrac{2.6}{1.95}\right)$
18. $6.41 + \dfrac{9.58}{2.6}$
19. $\dfrac{19.3 \times 0.221}{0.689}$
20. $8.3 + \dfrac{0.64}{0.325}$
21. $2.4 + (9.7 \times 0.642)$
22. $11.2 + (9.75 \times 1.11)$
23. $0.325 + \dfrac{8.6}{11.2}$
24. $8.35^2 - 25$
25. $6.71^2 + 0.64$
26. $3.45^3 + 11.8$
27. $2.93^3 - 2.641$
28. $\dfrac{7.2^2 - 4.5}{8.64}$
29. $\dfrac{13.9 + 2.97^2}{4.31}$
30. $(3.3 - 2.84)^2$
31. $\dfrac{(12.9 - 8.45)^2}{4.3}$
32. $\left(\dfrac{4.4 + 6.23}{9.9}\right)^2$

Using the memory

> Work out $\dfrac{4.2 + 1.75}{3.63 - 2.14}$, correct to 4 S.F., using the memory buttons.
>
> Find the bottom line first:
>
> [3.63] [−] [2.14] [=] [M+] [C]
>
> [4.2] [+] [1.75] [=] [÷] [MR] [=]
>
> The calculator reads 3.9932886
>
> ∴ Answer= 3.993 (to 4 S.F.)

Exercise 8

Work out the following, correct to four significant figures. Use the memory buttons where necessary.

1. $\dfrac{7.3 + 2.14}{3.6 - 2.95}$
2. $\dfrac{2.3 + 0.924}{1.3 + 0.635}$
3. $\dfrac{5.89}{7 - 3.83}$
4. $\dfrac{102}{58.1 + 65.32}$
5. $\dfrac{18.8}{3.72 \times 1.86}$
6. $\dfrac{904}{65.3 \times 2.86}$
7. $12.2 - \left(\dfrac{2.6}{1.95}\right)$
8. $8.047 - \left(\dfrac{6.34}{10.2}\right)$
9. $14.2 - \left(\dfrac{1.7}{2.4}\right)$
10. $\dfrac{9.75 - 8.792}{4.31 - 3.014}$
11. $\dfrac{19.6 \times 3.01}{2.01 - 1.958}$
12. $3.7^2 - \left(\dfrac{8.59}{24}\right)$
13. $8.27 - 1.56^2$
14. $111.79 - 5.04^2$
15. $18.3 - 2.841^2$
16. $(2.93 + 71.5)^2$
17. $(8.3 - 6.34)^4$
18. $54.2 - 2.6^4$
19. $(8.7 - 5.95)^4$
20. $\sqrt{68.4} + 11.63$
21. $9.45 - \sqrt{8.248}$
22. $3.24^2 - \sqrt{1.962}$
23. $\dfrac{3.54 + 2.4}{8.47^2}$
24. $2065 - \sqrt{44\,000}$
25. $\sqrt{(5.69 - 0.0852)}$
26. $\sqrt{(0.976 + 1.03)}$
27. $\sqrt{\left(\dfrac{17.4}{2.16 - 1.83}\right)}$
28. $\sqrt{\left(\dfrac{28.9}{\sqrt{8.47}}\right)}$
29. $257 - \dfrac{6.32}{0.059}$
30. $75\,000 - 5.6^4$
31. $\dfrac{11.29 \times 2.09}{2.7 + 0.082}$
32. $85.5 - \sqrt{105.8}$
33. $\dfrac{4.45^2}{8.2^2 - 51.09}$
34. $\left(\dfrac{8.53 + 7.07}{6.04 - 4.32}\right)^4$
35. $2.75 + \dfrac{5}{8.2} + \dfrac{11.2}{4.3}$
36. $8.2 + \dfrac{6.3}{0.91} + \dfrac{2.74}{8.4}$
37. $\dfrac{18.5}{1.6} + \dfrac{7.1}{0.53} + \dfrac{11.9}{25.6}$
38. $\dfrac{83.6}{105} + \dfrac{2.95}{2.7} + \dfrac{81}{97}$
39. $\left(\dfrac{98.76}{103} + \dfrac{4.07}{3.6}\right)^2$
40. $\dfrac{(5.843 - \sqrt{2.07})^2}{88.4}$

3.5 STANDARD FORM

Very large numbers and very small numbers are more conveniently written using *standard form*.

$260\ 000\ 000 = 2.6 \times 10^8$
$4\ 187\ 000\ 000 = 4.187 \times 10^9$
$0.000\ 000\ 072 = 7.2 \times 10^{-8}$
$0.000\ 05 = 5 \times 10^{-5}$

Most calculators represent large and small numbers using standard form.

e.g. [1.541 ²⁴] means 1.541×10^{24}

Exercise 9

Write the following numbers in standard form.

1. 560 000
2. 244 000 000
3. 72 000
4. 131 000
5. 85 000 000
6. 900 000 000
7. 73 400 000 000
8. 8 420 000 000
9. 66 000
10. 2 000 000 000 000
11. 100 million
12. 2000 million
13. 440
14. 60 000
15. 160 000
16. 4 850 000 000
17. 18 472
18. 635 811
19. 3 333 333
20. 8 211 111
21. 0.000 004
22. 0.000 0052
23. 0.000 007 411
24. 0.004 32
25. 0.0075
26. 0.008 239
27. 0.000 000 007
28. 0.000 000 015
29. 0.000 000 000 2
30. 0.0046
31. 0.0074
32. 0.006 31
33. 84 000
34. 12 000 000
35. 0.000 002
36. 0.000 000 045 3
37. 16 000 000 000
38. 0.724
39. 284 444
40. 0.000 002 22
41. 320×10^4
42. 600×10^7
43. 18.2×10^5
44. 0.4×10^{-6}
45. 0.07×10^{-5}
46. 700×10^{-10}
47. 666×10^8
48. 7100×10^8
49. 320×10^{-10}
50. 16.2×10^{-7}

Exercise 10

Write the following numbers in the usual form.

1. 3.6×10^5
2. 7.22×10^7
3. 8.2×10^4
4. 6×10^6
5. 1.1×10^9
6. 3.24×10^5
7. 1×10^{11}
8. 6.36×10^6
9. 8.02×10^9
10. 3.2×10^4
11. 6.7×10^2
12. 3.03×10^4
13. 8.99×10^7
14. 1.02×10^{10}
15. 6.2×10^6
16. 2.6×10^{-4}
17. 8.1×10^{-2}
18. 1×10^{-5}
19. 3×10^{-6}
20. 4.4×10^{-7}
21. 8×10^{-3}
22. 1.2×10^{-7}
23. 9.5×10^{-8}
24. 4.6×10^{-11}
25. 8.8×10^4
26. 2.75×10^3
27. 1.01×10^{-3}
28. 9.6×10^{-6}
29. 7×10^{-5}
30. 3.2×10^2

Exercise 11

Work out

1. $10^2 \times 10^5$
2. $10^2 \times 10^7$
3. $10^4 \times 10^6$
4. $10^7 \times 10^{-2}$
5. $10^9 \times 10^{-3}$
6. $10^{-2} \times 10^4$
7. $10^{-5} \times 10^{-2}$
8. $10^8 \times 10^{-10}$
9. $10^4 \times 10^{-12}$
10. $10^{-2} \times 10^{-3}$
11. $10^{-1} \times 10^{-7}$
12. $10^8 \times 10^{-6}$
13. $10^6 \div 10^2$
14. $10^8 \div 10^3$
15. $10^{10} \div 10^2$
16. $10^5 \div 10^9$
17. $10^3 \div 10^{16}$
18. $10^4 \div 10^{-2}$
19. $10^7 \div 10^{-1}$
20. $10^8 \div 10^{-3}$
21. $10^{-3} \div 10^5$
22. $10^9 \times 10^{-2}$
23. $10^7 \times 10^{-10}$
24. $10^5 \div 10^{-3}$

Exercise 12

Work out the following and give the answer in standard form.

1. $(2 \times 10^4) \times (3 \times 10^5)$
2. $(1.5 \times 10^5) \times (2 \times 10^8)$
3. $(2.2 \times 10^7) \times (3 \times 10^{10})$
4. $(1 \times 10^{11}) \times (8.8 \times 10^2)$
5. $(4 \times 10^6) \times (2 \times 10^{-2})$
6. $(8.5 \times 10^{12}) \times (1 \times 10^{-3})$
7. $(2.3 \times 10^{-8}) \times (3 \times 10^2)$
8. $(3.5 \times 10^{-5}) \times (2 \times 10^{10})$
9. $(6.28 \times 10^8) \times (1 \times 10^8)$
10. $(7.2 \times 10^7) \times (1 \times 10^{-11})$
11. $(8.8 \times 10^8) \div (2 \times 10^2)$
12. $(9 \times 10^6) \div (2 \times 10^3)$
13. $(6 \times 10^8) \div (4 \times 10^2)$
14. $(8 \times 10^{11}) \div (1 \times 10^8)$
15. $(9 \times 10^5) \div (3 \times 10^{10})$
16. $(5 \times 10^3) \div (2.5 \times 10^9)$
17. $(7.2 \times 10^2) \div (2 \times 10^8)$
18. $(3.4 \times 10^4) \div (2 \times 10^{-2})$
19. $(7.5 \times 10^6) \div (2.5 \times 10^{-3})$
20. $(9.3 \times 10^5) \div (3 \times 10^{-2})$

Think about it 1

Project 1 THE CHESS BOARD PROBLEM

Look at the miniature chess board below. It is only a 4 × 4 square instead of 8 × 8. Your problem is to place four objects on the board so that nowhere are there two objects on the same row (↔), column (↕) or diagonal (↗) (↘).

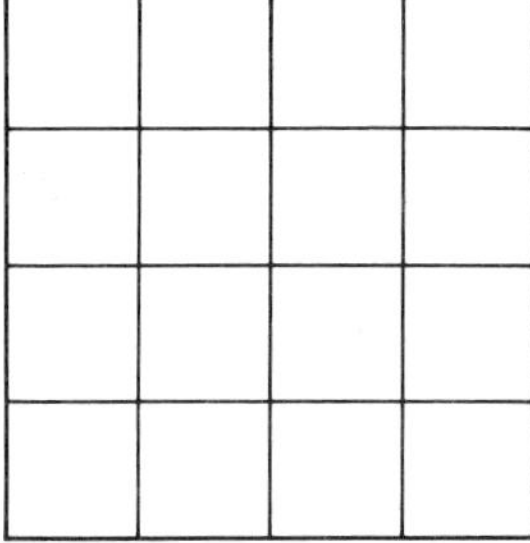

In the example below we have gone wrong because ① and ④ are on the same diagonal, and ② and ③ are on the other diagonal.

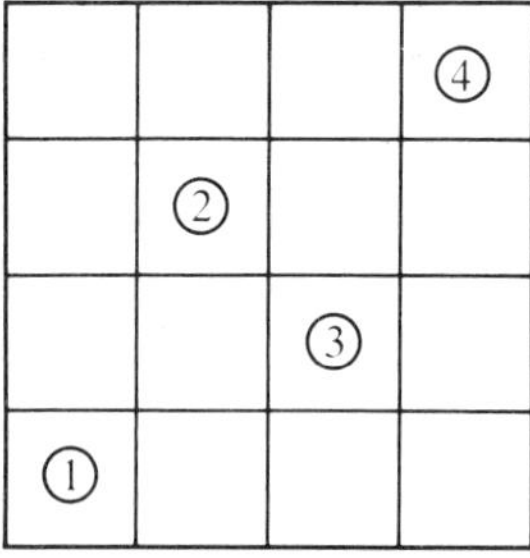

1. Find a correct solution for the 4 × 4 square.

2. Find a solution for a 5 × 5 square, using five objects.

3. Find a solution for a 6 × 6 square, using six objects.

4. Find a solution for a 7 × 7 square, using seven objects.

5. Finally, if you have been successful with the previous squares, try to find a solution for a full-size 8 × 8 square, using eight objects. It is called the chess board problem because one of the objects could be a 'Queen' which can move any number of squares in any direction.

Most people start off by trying to guess the solutions. After a little practice it is better to adopt a more systematic approach. Good luck!

Exercise A

1. Screws are sold in packets of eight and I need 182 screws for a job. How many packets must I buy and how many screws will be left over?
2. What number, when divided by 7 and then multiplied by 3, gives an answer of 18?
3. In an election 5090 votes were cast for the two candidates. Mr Wislon won by 260 votes. How many people voted for Wislon?
4. A 10p coin is 2 mm thick. Nicola has a pile of 10p coins which is 18.4 cm tall. What is the value of the money in Nicola's pile of coins?
5. The school morning lasts 3 hours 30 minutes. How many 35-minute lessons are there?
6. Find two numbers which multiply together to give 24 and which add up to 10.
7. A man runs around a rectangular field which is 160 m long and 90 m wide. How far does he run in km if he completes 12 laps of the field?
8. When a certain number is divided by 20 the answer is 37. What is the number?
9. An aircraft takes $2\frac{3}{4}$ hours to complete a journey. How long will the journey take if it travels at half the speed?
10. A garden 36 m long and 10 m wide is to be covered with peat, which is supplied in 60 kg sacks. 10 kg of peat covers an area of 20 m^2. How many sacks of peat are needed for the whole garden?

Project 2 PENTOMINOES

A pentomino is a set of five squares joined along their edges. You probably know of the game of dominoes. A domino is just two squares joined together; there is only one possible shape because the two shapes here count as the same.

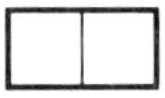

counts the same as

1. See how many different pentominoes you can design on squared paper. Here are a few.

(a) 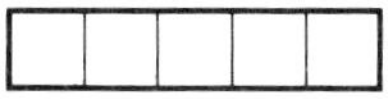 (b) 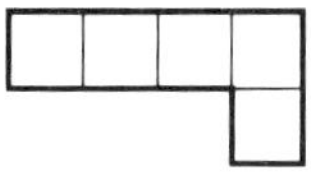 (c)

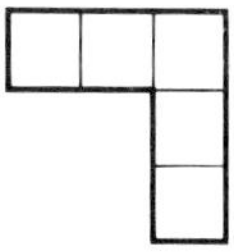

You may find that some of your designs are really the same, for example

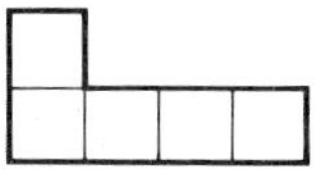

and

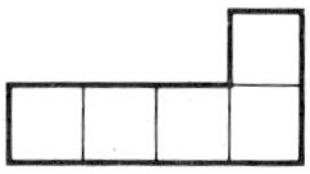

You can use a piece of tracing paper to check if some of your designs are really the same or different.

After about fifteen minutes, compare your designs with those of other people in your class. There are in fact twelve different pentomino shapes. Make a neat copy of these.

2. On squared paper, draw a square having eight units on each side. Somewhere inside the square draw a small square having two units on each side and shade it.

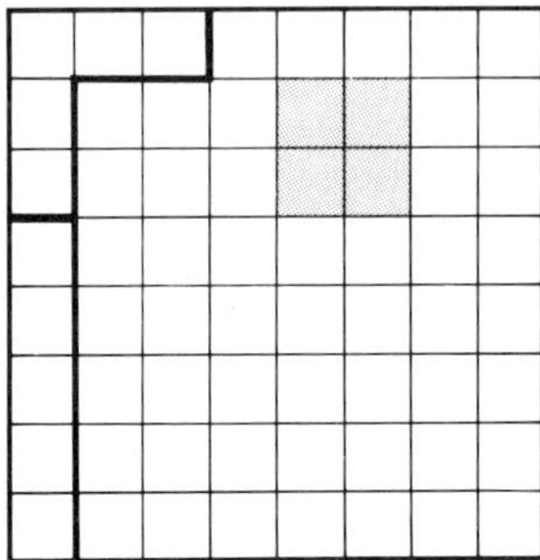

Now fill up the rest of the square with as many different pentominoes as you can. There should be no 'holes' left by the time you have finished.

A start has been made in the diagram above.

3. Take some more squared paper and draw a rectangle measuring 10 by 6. Fill up the rectangle with as many different pentominoes as you can.

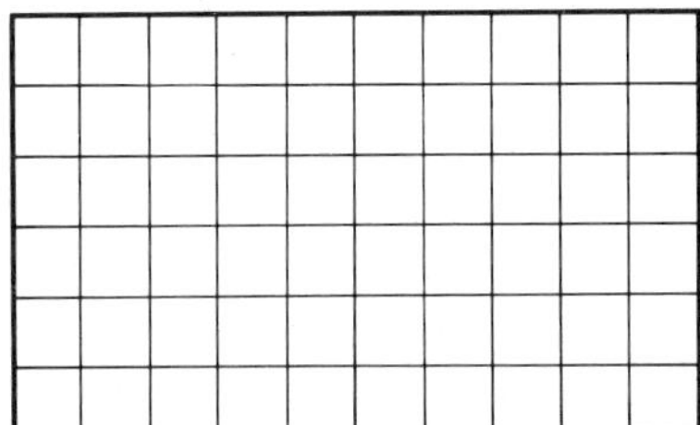

This problem is more difficult than the 8 by 8 square.

Exercise B

1. Find the result when two hundred and twelve thousand, five hundred and seven is added to sixty thousand, eight hundred and seventy.
2. Find the angle between the hands of a clock showing
   (a) 8.00 pm
   (b) 11.00 am
3. A badly typed three-digit number appears as 84*. It is known to be odd and divisible by 5. Find the number.

4. A car uses 9 litres of petrol for every 50 km travelled. Calculate the cost in £'s of travelling 750 km if petrol costs 43p per litre.

5. Add together the 19th odd number and the 12th even number. (The first odd number is 1 and the first even number is 2).

6. (a) Work out 8 × 125, without a calculator.
   (b) Use the result above to work out 12 000 ÷ 125.

7. A play was attended by 240 adults, each paying 80p, and 164 children, each paying 50p. How much in £'s was paid altogether by the people attending the play?

8. The exchange rate in Spain is 220 pesetas to the £.
   (a) How many pesetas will I receive for £20?
   (b) A bottle of wine is priced at 550 pesetas. What is the equivalent cost in £'s?

9. An extract from Mrs Brown's bank statement is shown below.

Date	Customer details	Debit	Credit	Balance
April 1	Balance forward			334.13
April 4	495466	46.00		288.13
April 8	495468	85.00		x
April 15	Salary		574.08	y
April 20	495467	24.00		
April 21	495470	110.00		
April 25	495469	57.50		z

Calculate the values of the missing balances x, y and z.

10. A man smokes 60 cigarettes a day and a packet of 20 costs £1.25. How much does he spend on cigarettes in a seven day week?

Project 3 STAMPS

I have lots of 4p and 9p stamps but I have no stamps of other values.

I could post a package costing 30p by using 9p + 9p + 4p + 4p + 4p. It is, however, impossible to put on an amount of 14p exactly.

Copy and complete the list below and show how to make up the amounts given. If it is impossible, write 'impossible'.

1p Impossible	14p	27p	40p
2p Impossible	15p	28p	41p
3p Impossible	16p	29p	42p
4p = 4p	17p	30p	43p
5p Impossible	18p	31p	44p
6p Impossible	19p	32p	45p
7p Impossible	20p	33p	46p
8p 4p + 4p	21p	34p	47p
9p = 9p	22p	35p	48p
10p	23p	36p	49p
11p	24p	37p	50p
12p	25p	38p	
13p	26p	39p	

Exercise C — 'SUPER LEAGUE' SOCCER

To avoid the football league programme becoming too crowded, an experimental 'super league' was formed with just six clubs: Liverpool, Manchester United, Nottingham Forest, West Ham, Arsenal and Everton.

Each team played each of the others at home and away and the results are shown below.

Home		**Away**		**Attendance**
Liverpool	2	Manchester United	1	46 250
Nottingham Forest	1	Liverpool	1	28 700
Liverpool	4	West Ham	1	33 610
Arsenal	0	Liverpool	2	47 420
Liverpool	1	Everton	1	49 840
Manchester United	2	Liverpool	0	56 815
Liverpool	2	Nottingham Forest	2	29 610
West Ham	1	Liverpool	2	28 250
Liverpool	2	Arsenal	1	36 460
Everton	1	Liverpool	1	48 890
Manchester United	3	Nottingham Forest	1	46 610
West Ham	0	Manchester United	1	31 295
Manchester United	2	Arsenal	0	51 605
Manchester United	1	Everton	1	46 240
Nottingham Forest	1	Manchester United	2	27 270
Manchester United	2	West Ham	0	38 615
Arsenal	1	Manchester United	0	43 720
Everton	2	Manchester United	1	45 610
Nottingham Forest	1	West Ham	2	19 265
Arsenal	1	Nottingham Forest	0	36 780
Nottingham Forest	1	Everton	1	24 815
West Ham	0	Nottingham Forest	1	23 370
Nottingham Forest	2	Arsenal	0	22 610
Everton	3	Nottingham Forest	1	35 470
West Ham	2	Arsenal	1	31 865
West Ham	1	Everton	1	25 700
Arsenal	1	West Ham	0	38 215
Everton	3	West Ham	1	28 320
Arsenal	2	Everton	2	32 610
Everton	2	Arsenal	1	35 815

1. Copy and complete the table of results for Liverpool.

Win	Draw	Lose
2-1		
	1-1	
4-1		
2-0		
	1-1	
		0-2

Games:	
Won:	5
Drawn:	
Lost:	
Goals	
For:	17
Against	

2. Work out similar tables of results for Manchester United, Nottingham Forest, West Ham, Arsenal and Everton.

3. Use the information you have obtained to work out the final league table. A team obtains 3 points for a win, 1 point for a draw and 0 points for a loss. If two teams have the same number of points, the team with the better goal difference is placed higher.

Team	Games played	Won	Drawn	Lost	Goals For	Goals Against	Points
Liverpool	10	5	4	1	17	11	19

Here is a list of prices charged by the six clubs.

Team	Average admission price	Price of programme
Liverpool	£2.50	50p
Man. Utd.	£2.00	40p
Notts Forest	£2.60	60p
West Ham	£2.60	50p
Arsenal	£2.40	60p
Everton	£2.70	65p

4. When Liverpool were at home to Manchester United the attendance was 46 250. Calculate the total sum of money paid for admission.
5. What was the total sum paid for admission to the Arsenal–Liverpool game? (i.e. Arsenal at home.)
6. Calculate the total sum paid for admission to Manchester United's five home games.
7. Exactly half of the people at the Arsenal–Notts Forest game bought a programme. Calculate the total money received from programme sales.

Project 4 MATCHSTICK SHAPES

1. Triangles

Diagram 1

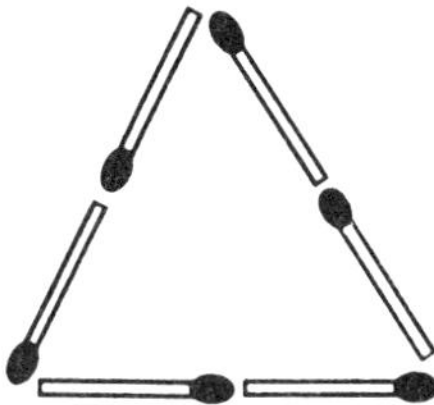
Diagram 2

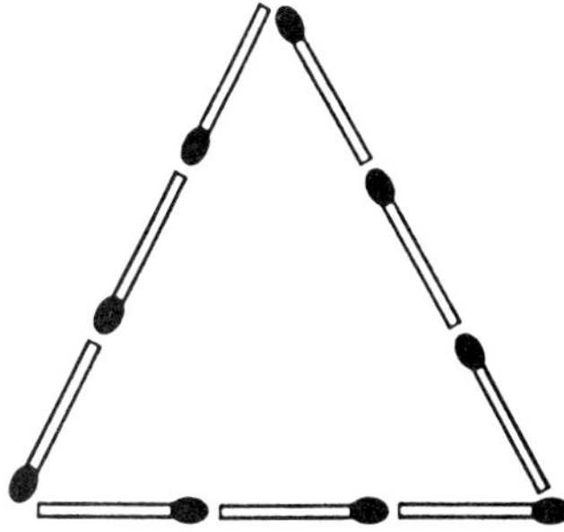
Diagram 3

Draw the next three triangles in the sequence.
Copy and complete this table.

Diagram number	1	2	3	4	5	6	10	30	45
Number of matches	3	6							150

2. Squares

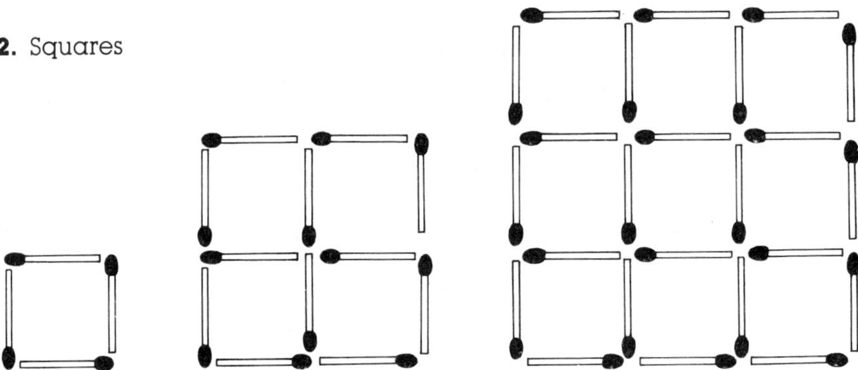

Diagram 1 Diagram 2 Diagram 3

Draw the next three diagrams in the sequence.
Copy and complete this table.

Diagram number	1	2	3	4	5	6	10	20	50
Number of matches									

3. Steps

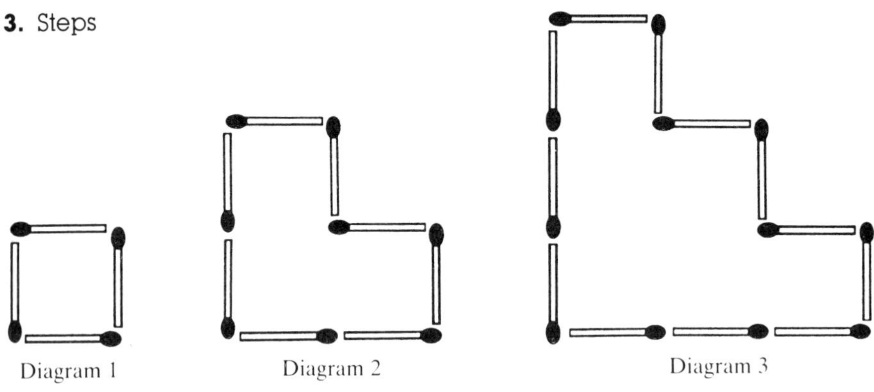

Diagram 1 Diagram 2 Diagram 3

Draw the next three diagrams in the sequence.
Copy and complete this table.

Diagram number	1	2	3	4	5	6	10	15	30		
Number of matches										150	168

4. Triangle nets

Diagram 1

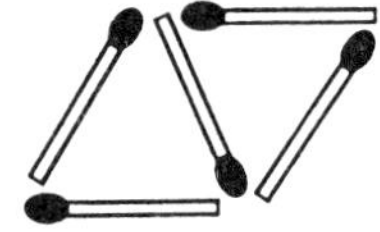

Diagram 2

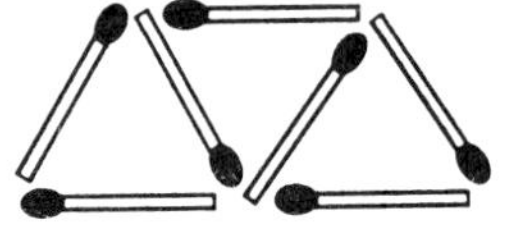

Diagram 3

Draw the next three diagrams in the sequence.
Copy and complete this table.

Diagram number	1	2	3	4	5	6	15	30	50		
Number of matches										111	125

5. Finding a formula

(a) For each of the four sequences of diagrams above, find a formula which connects the diagram number x with the number of matches n in the diagram, i.e. find an equation involving x and n.

(b) Make two tables, one for the sequence of squares (part 2) and one for the sequence of triangle nets (part 4), to show the number of matches p on the perimeter of each shape. The table for the sequence of squares starts like this.

Diagram number x	1	2	3	4	5	6
Number of matches p on the perimeter	4	8	12			

If p is the number of matches on the perimeter, find a formula (relationship) between p and x for each of the two sequences.

Exercise D

1. A suitcase is packed with 35 books, each weighing 420 g. The total weight of the suitcase and books is 17 kg. Find the weight of the suitcase.

2. Copy and complete the following:

(a) 200 cm = m, (b) 2.3 m = cm,
(c) 7.2 km = m, (d) 0.8 m = cm,
(e) 28 m = km, (f) 25 mm = cm.

3. A lady bought a car for £1200 and sold it six months later at a price 10% higher. At what price did she sell the car?

4. Copy and complete the pattern below.

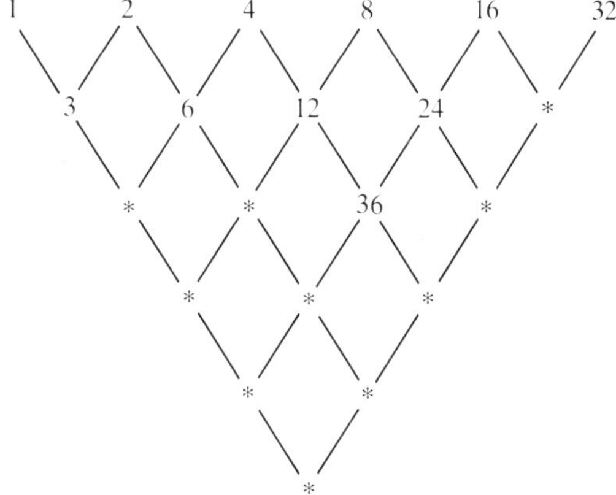

5. A box contains 200 assorted nails and screws and there are three times as many nails as screws.

(a) How many screws are there?

(b) What is the probability that an item chosen at random from the box will be a nail?

6. A 9-day holiday in Italy costs £170. Find the average cost per day, correct to the nearest pound.

7. In 1984 British Euro-MPs were paid a basic salary of £18 000 per year. The allowance for accommodation and subsistence was £75 a day. Travel allowances were 30p per mile travelled. Work out how much money was paid in one year to an MP who drew the accommodation allowance for 150 days and travelled a total of 80 000 miles during the year.

8. Mr Black's salary is £7800 per year. He pays no tax on the first £1600 of his salary but pays 30% on each remaining £. How much tax does he pay?

9. A man bought 20 plants at 85p each and a number of plants costing 45p each. In all he spent £22.40. How many of the less expensive plants did he buy?

10. ABCD is a square of side 10 cm. Side AB is increased by 30% to form rectangle AXYD.

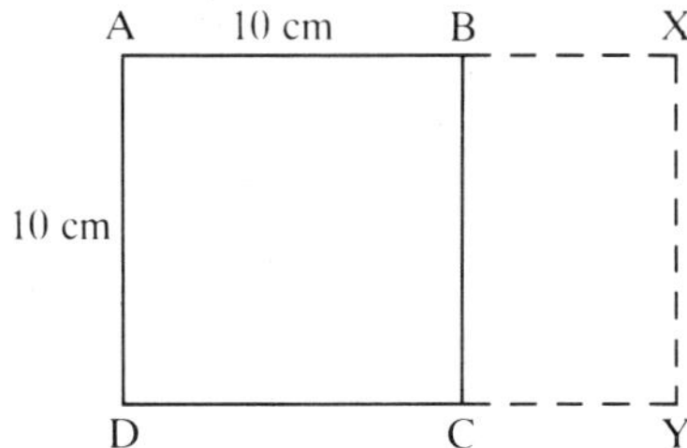

Calculate
(a) the area of ABCD (b) the length BX (c) the area BXYC

Project 5 MATHEMATICAL WORDSEARCH

Copy the square below. Find as many mathematical words as possible and make a list. The words appear written forwards or backwards in any row, column or diagonal.

A	M	P	T	R	I	A	N	G	L	E	O
R	N	C	Z	J	S	X	I	R	N	M	F
P	E	D	B	O	N	E	D	A	H	U	P
E	T	D	E	G	R	E	E	M	E	L	S
N	L	F	K	C	A	U	B	T	O	O	F
C	H	R	C	S	I	Q	L	D	G	V	T
I	C	A	J	E	R	M	O	E	S	D	U
L	N	C	D	V	Q	Z	A	N	R	D	L
E	I	T	H	E	E	U	R	L	T	A	V
Z	M	I	S	N	N	F	E	V	T	B	W
K	Y	O	W	T	X	O	A	O	R	U	N
C	E	N	T	I	M	E	T	R	E	C	O

Your rating:
10 Average
15 Good
18 Very good
20 Excellent

Exercise E

1. What is the weight of 15 biscuits if 9 biscuits weigh 288 g?
2. The area of an ordinary postage stamp is approximately (a) 5 mm^2 (b) 50 mm^2 (c) 5 cm^2 (d) 0.5 m^2. Select the correct answer.
3. An aircraft flies 210 m in 0.3 seconds.

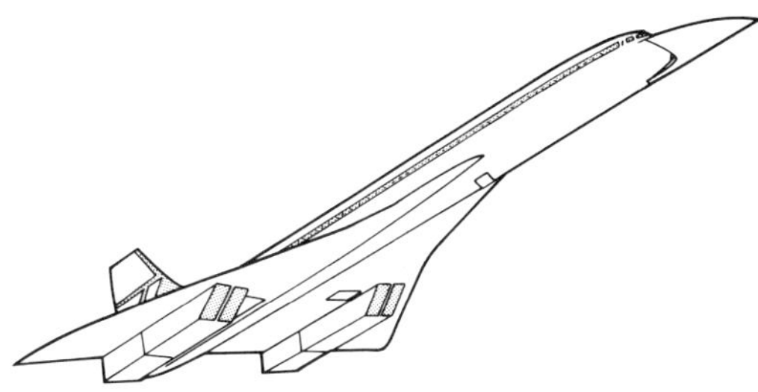

   (a) How far does it fly in 0.1 seconds?
   (b) How far does it fly in 1 second?
   (c) How far does it fly in 1 minute?
4. Nine mugs cost £7.65 and weigh 3.78 kg.
   Find (a) the cost and (b) the weight of 20 of these mugs.
5. The charges for parking a car at a car park are as follows:

0–1 hour	10p
1–3 hours	20p
3–8 hours	50p
Over 8 hours	80p

   Find the charge for a car parked from 08 40 to 12 20.
6. Which is more: (5% of £80) or (8% of £40)?
7. Write down the square root of the following (without a calculator)
   (a) 25 (b) 900 (c) 144
   (d) 10 000 (e) 81 (f) 0.01
8. Copy and complete

Percentage	Fraction
(a) 20%	
(b) 75%	
(c)	$\frac{1}{2}$
(d) 90%	
(e)	$\frac{1}{4}$
(f) 10%	

9. A box contains 45 assorted sweets and there are twice as many toffees as chocolates.
   (a) How many are toffees?
   (b) What is the probability that a sweet chosen at random from the box will be a chocolate?
10. A special offer for engine oil says: 'Buy 2 cans at £3.50 each and get a third can at half price'. Calculate the total cost of the 3 cans of oil.

Project 6 MATHSMAGIC

Here is a trick which you can perform to demonstrate your amazing powers of mental arithmetic. You will incidentally be learning some mathematics as you do it.

(a) Ask someone to give you a three-digit number. He may say '327'

(b) Write the number down twice

327   327

(c) Ask for another three-digit number. He may say '652'. Write this number underneath one of the 327's.

327   327
652

(d) Work out in your head the number which when added to 652 gives 999, in this case 347. Pretend you are just thinking of another number at random and write the 347 underneath the other 327.

327   327
652   347

(e) Pretend to concentrate very hard and 'in your head' you multiply 327 by 652 and add the result to 327 × 347

$$\begin{array}{r}327\\ \times\,652\\ \hline \\ \hline\end{array} \; + \; \begin{array}{r}327\\ \times\,347\\ \hline \\ \hline\end{array}$$

$$= 326673$$

How is it done?

The first 3 digits of the answer are (327 − 1) i.e. 326.

The next 3 digits are the figures which added to 326 make 999, i.e. 673. Here is another example.

$$\begin{array}{r}821\\ \times\,146\\ \hline \\ \hline\end{array} \; + \; \begin{array}{r}821\\ \times\,853\\ \hline \\ \hline\end{array} \; = 820179$$

Try this trick on your friends and relatives and see if they can work out how you do it.

Note It is best if they give you three-digit numbers which are 'all jumbled up'. Try to discourage numbers like '444' or '777' because they are 'too easy for you'.

Exercise F

1. Place the following numbers in order of size, smallest first: 0.085, 0.058, 0.11, 0.03, 0.07.
2. Reduce the cost of each of the following items by one tenth of its price: (a) T.V.: £300 (b) Car: £4500 (c) Book: £4.50
3. The average of three numbers is 11. If two of the numbers are 8 and 12, what is the third number?
4. Write down the next two numbers in each sequence:
   (a) 1, 5, 9, 13, . . .
   (b) 11, 16, 22, 29, . . .
   (c) 48, 24, 12, 6, . . .
   (d) 1, 4, 9, 16, . . .
5. How many pieces of wire of length 7.2 cm can be cut from a reel of wire of length 5 m?

6. A shopkeeper sells an average of 6 radios per day from Monday to Friday inclusive. On Saturday he sells 15 radios. What is the average number of radios sold per day over the six days, from Monday to Saturday?
7. Write in their simplest form:
   (a) $\frac{12}{16}$ (b) $\frac{30}{45}$ (c) $\frac{20}{32}$ (d) $\frac{24}{60}$.
8. Copy and complete the table.

Fraction	Decimal	Percentage
$\frac{1}{2}$		
	0.2	
		10%
$\frac{3}{8}$		
		90%

9. A manufacturer purchases materials to the value of £30 000 of which £5000 worth are zero-rated for V.A.T. and the rest carry V.A.T. at 15%.
   (a) Calculate the V.A.T. paid on these materials.
   (b) Write down the total cost of all materials and V.A.T.
10. A man drives a car at an average speed of 65 km/h and does an average of 10 km per litre of petrol.
    (a) How far does he drive in 4 hours?
    (b) How much petrol does he use?
    (c) How much does it cost, if the price of petrol is 42.5p/litre?

Project 7 ESTIMATING GAME

This is a game for two players. On squared paper draw out an answer grid with the numbers shown below.

Answer grid

1215	429	2475	1485	8415	275
315	975	1089	4050	750	2125
891	1050	165	2025	819	1701
585	3315	525	1950	231	3861
2079	6885	550	4950	375	1785
1275	1250	3159	8019	4250	935

The players now take turns to choose two numbers from the question grid below and multiply them on a calculator.

Question grid

11	25	81
15	39	85
21	50	99

The number obtained is crossed out on the answer grid using the player's own colour. The winner is the first player with four answers in a line (horizontal, vertical or diagonal).

Exercise G

Find the missing numbers.

1.

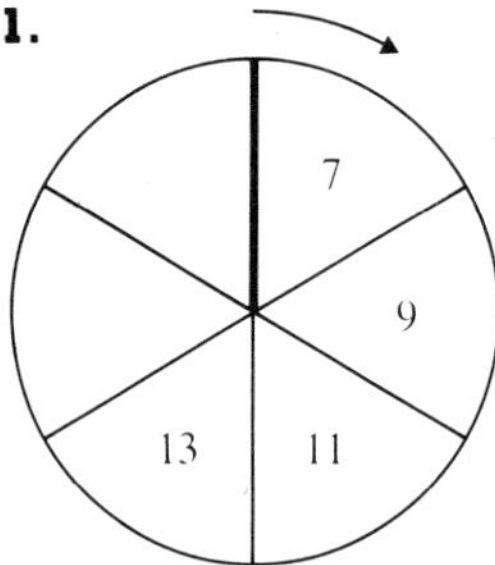

2.

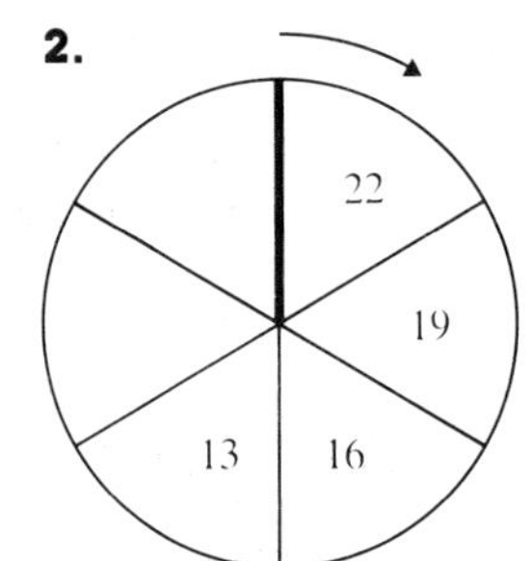

3.

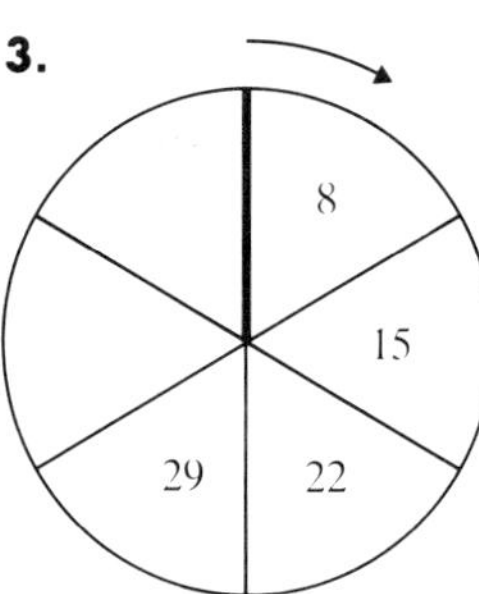

4.

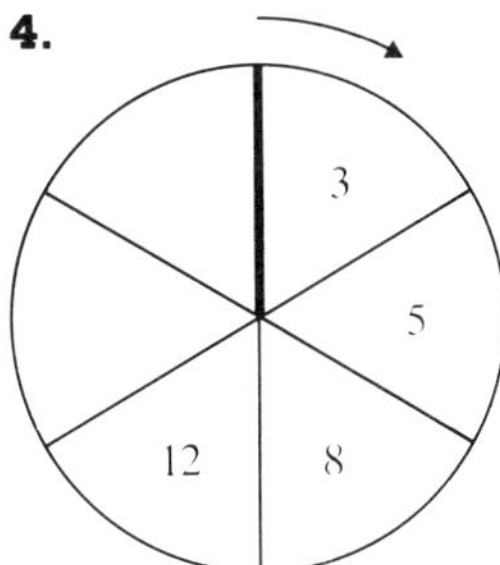

5.

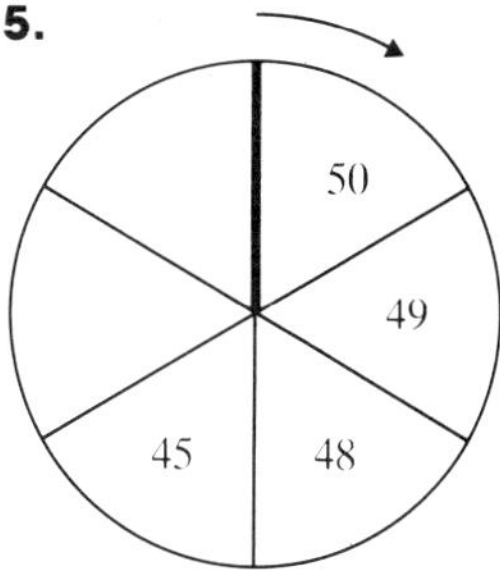

6.

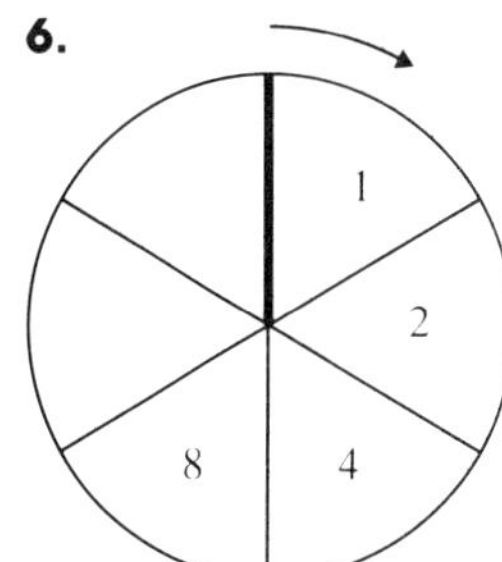

7.

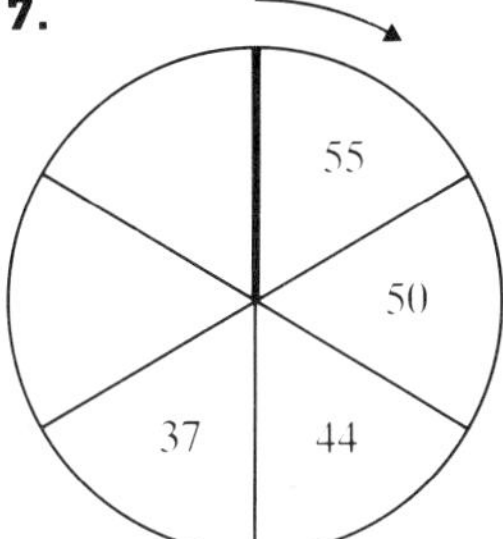

8.

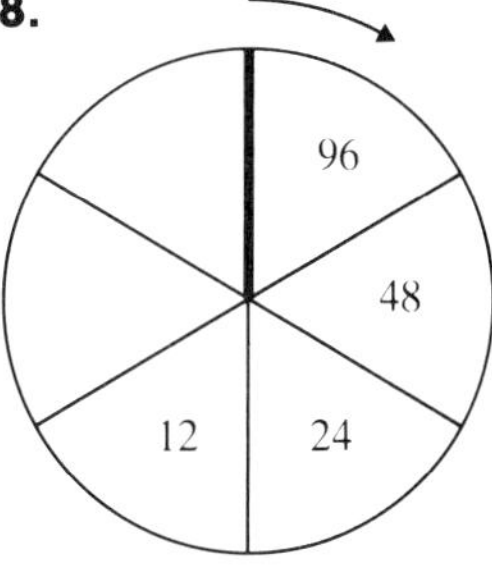

9.

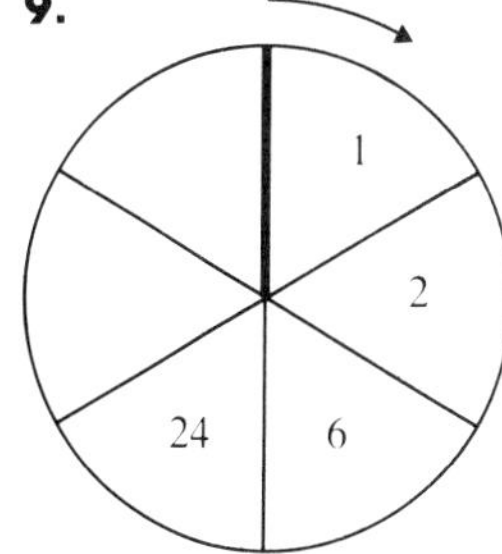

Write down the following sequences and work out the numbers indicated by $*$.

10. 1, 4, 7, $*$, $*$, 16.

11. 7, 6, 8, 7, 10, 9, $*$, $*$.

12. 11, 15, 21, 29, $*$, 51, $*$.

13. 1, 4, 9, 16, $*$, $*$, 49.

14. 144, 72, 36, $*$, 9, $*$.

15. 2, 1, $\frac{1}{2}$, $*$, $\frac{1}{8}$, $*$.

16. 1, 3, 5, $*$, $*$, 11.

17. 2, 4, 12, 48, $*$, $*$.

18. 60, 57, 51, 42, $*$, $*$.

19. 1, $*$, 27, 64, 125, $*$.

20. 20, 34, 49, 65, $*$, $*$.

21. (a) Write down the next two lines of the sequence:

$3 \times 4 = 3 + 3^2$
$4 \times 5 = 4 + 4^2$
$5 \times 6 = 5 + 5^2$
$=$
$=$

(b) Complete the lines below

$10 \times 11 =$
$30 \times 31 =$

22. (a) Write down the next two lines of the sequence:

$3^2 = 1^2 + 4 \times 1 + 4$
$4^2 = 2^2 + 4 \times 2 + 4$
$5^2 = 3^2 + 4 \times 3 + 4$
$6^2 = 4^2 + 4 \times 4 + 4$
$=$
$=$

(b) Complete the lines below

$12^2 =$
$22^2 =$

23. (a) Write down the next two lines of the sequence:

$1^2 = 1$
$2^2 = 1 + 3$
$3^2 = 1 + 3 + 5$
$4^2 = 1 + 3 + 5 + 7$
$=$
$=$

(b) Complete the lines below.

$10^2 =$
$15^2 =$

Project 8 HAPPY NUMBERS

(a)

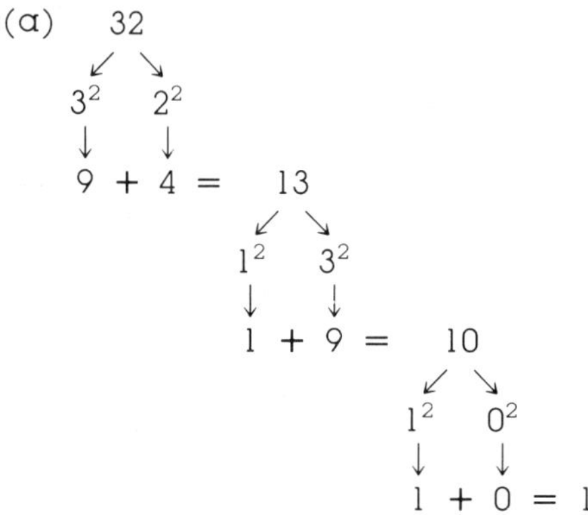

32 is a so-called 'happy' number because it ends with 1.

(b) Try a different number: 70. This time we will simplify the working by doing the squaring without writing it down.

70
↙ ↘
49 + 0 = 49
↙ ↘
16 + 81 = 97
↙ ↘
81 + 49 = 130
↙ ↓ ↘
1 + 9 + 0 = 10
↙ ↘
1 + 0 = 1

So 70 is also a 'happy' number.

(c) Find out whether the following numbers are 'happy' or 'unhappy': 23, 85, 49, 40, 44, 14, 15, 94

Hint: Write single digit numbers with a nought in front: 4 → 04
6 → 06

This helps to maintain the pattern.

Look out for patterns of numbers which repeat themselves. This will save a lot of working.

(d) If 23 is happy, is 32 happy?
If 24 is unhappy, is 42 happy?
If 25 is unhappy, is 52 happy?

Project 9 LARGEST PRODUCT

(a) Take any whole number (say 25) and split it into three smaller whole numbers. The three numbers must add up to 25. (We might choose 5, 8 and 12). Now multiply the three numbers together.

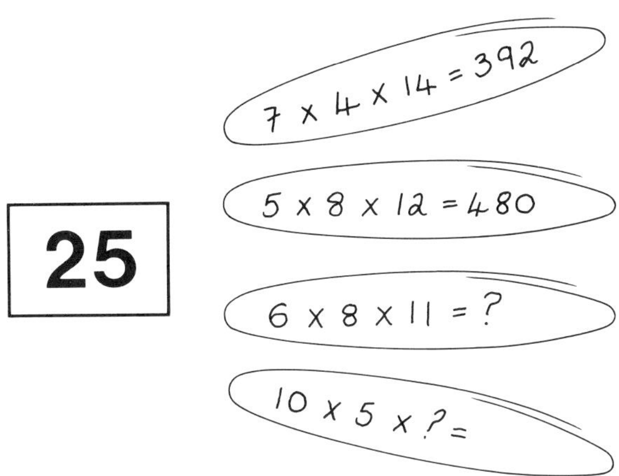

Try a different combination of three numbers and again find their product. Which three numbers give the largest possible product?

(b) Now try different starting numbers and for each one find the combination of three numbers which gives the largest product.

Is there a general rule for finding the numbers which give the largest product?

(c) Now split the starting number into four (or five or even six) smaller numbers and find the combination which gives the greatest product.

Is there a rule for finding the numbers which give the largest product?

Unit 4

4.1 AREA

Rectangle and triangle

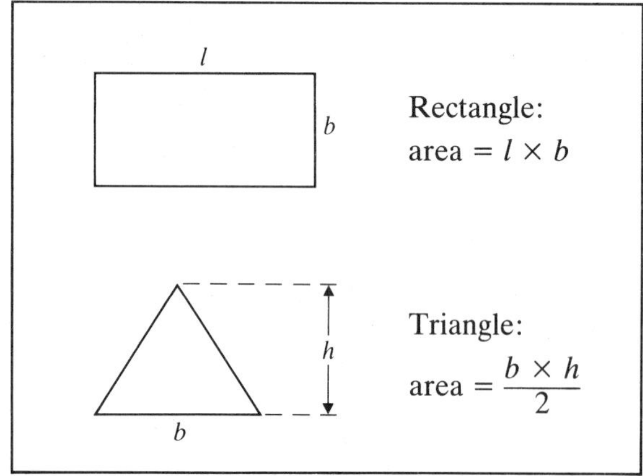

Exercise 1

Draw each diagram and work out the area.

1. 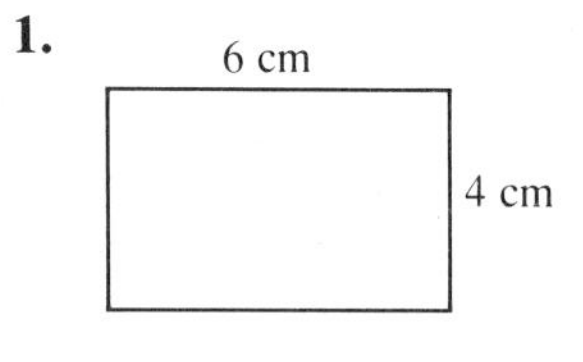

2. 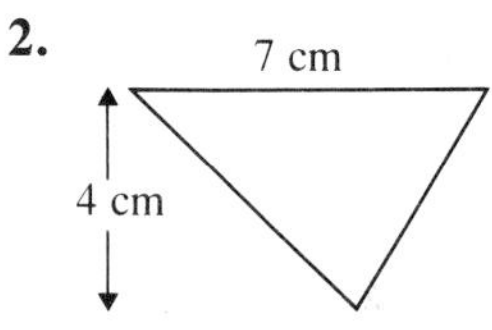

3. 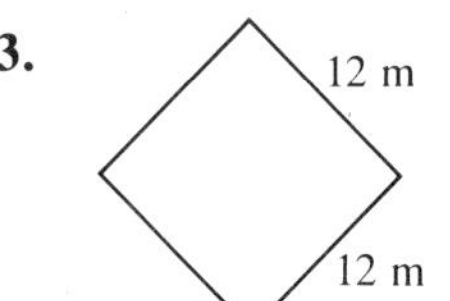

4. 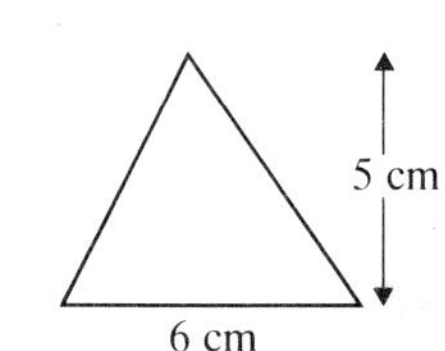

5. 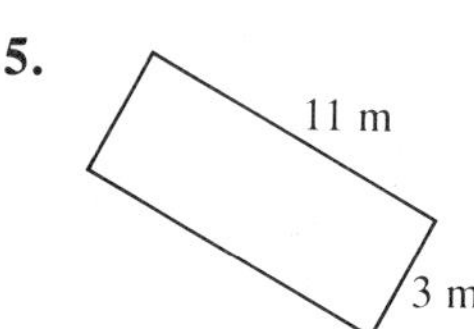

6. 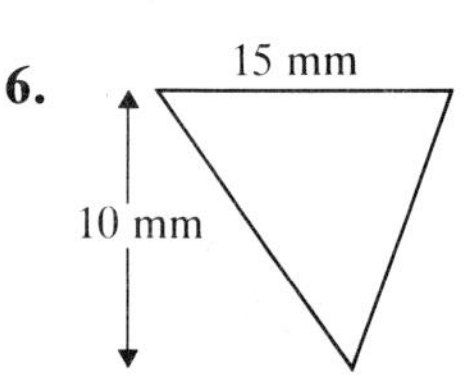

7.

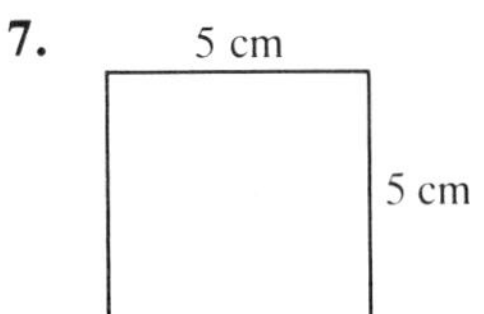

8.

8 cm
3 cm

9.

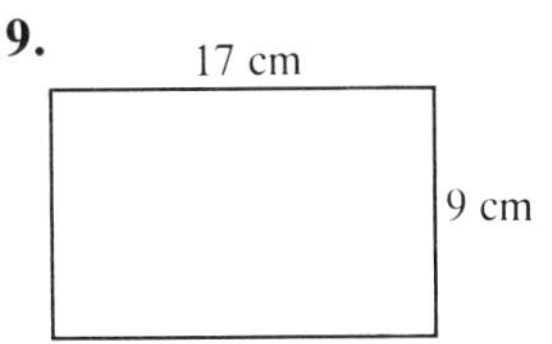

10.

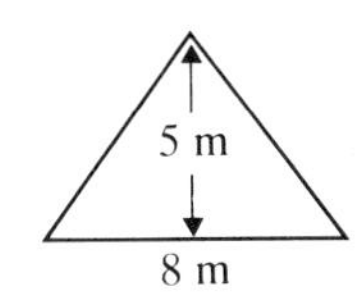

11.

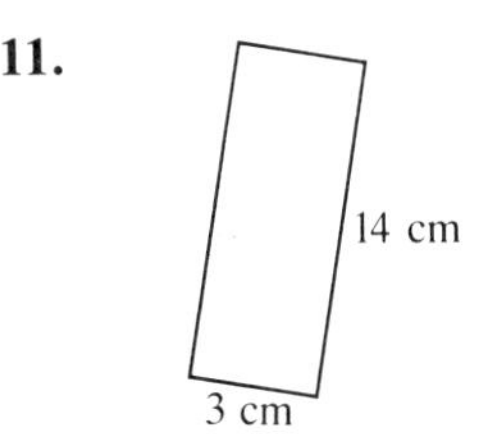

12.

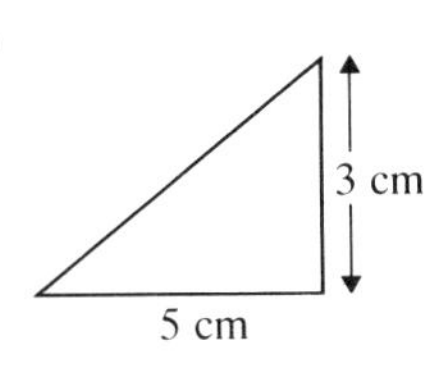

13.

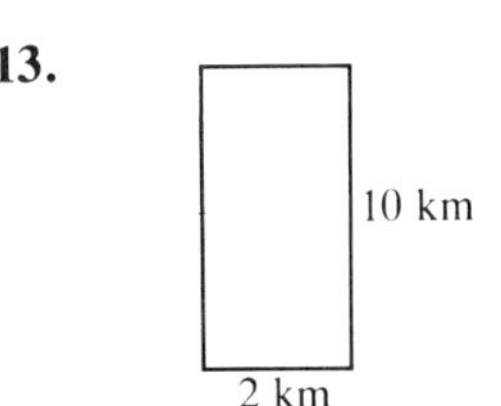

14.

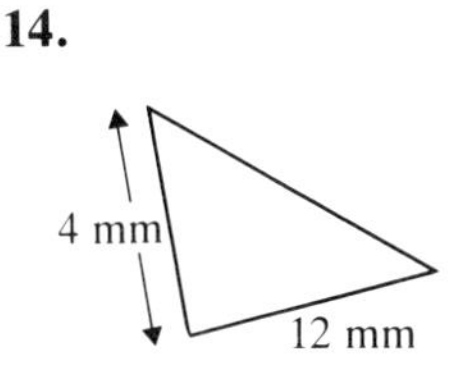

Exercise 2

Draw each diagram and then find the area.

1.

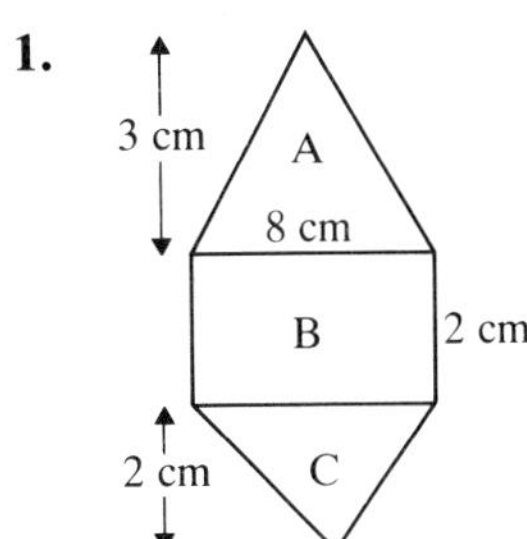

2.

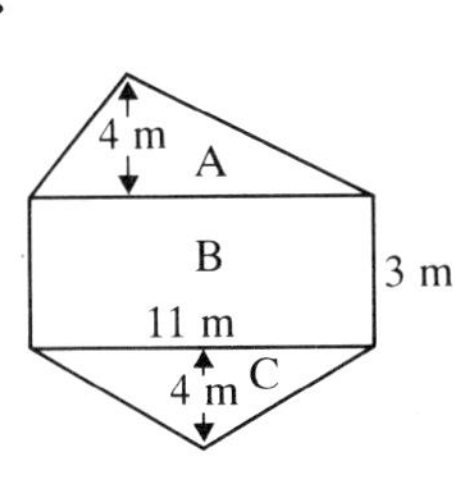

3.

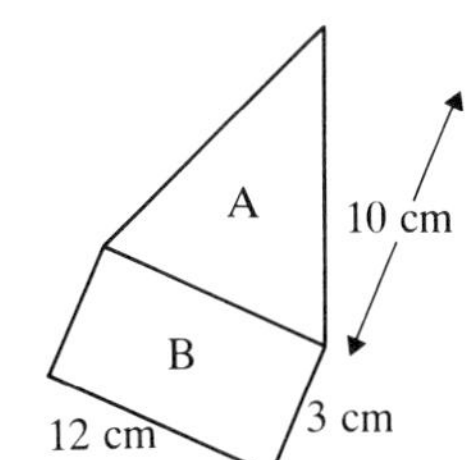

4.

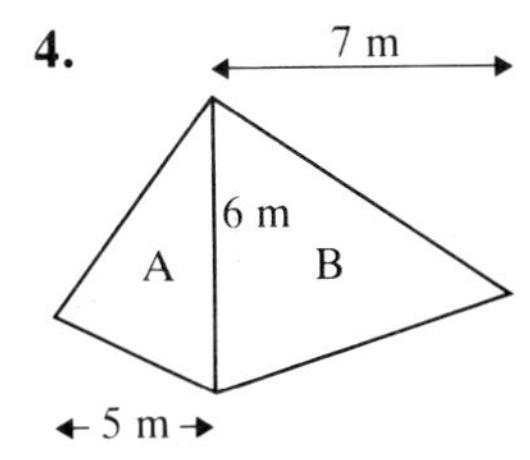

5.

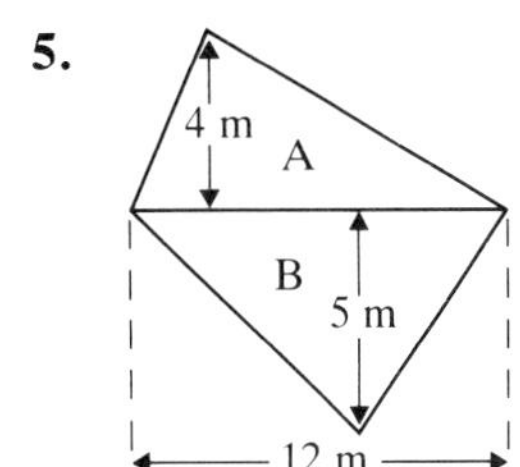

6.

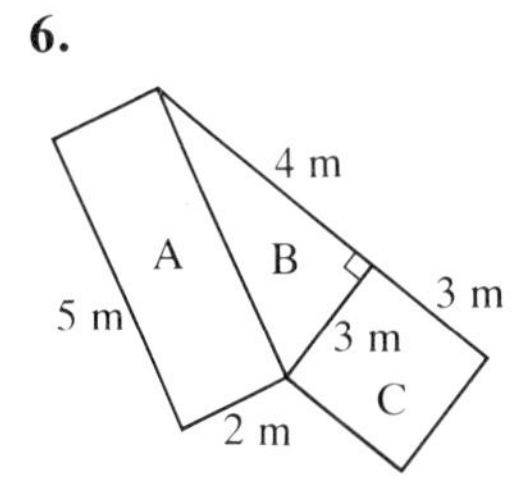

7.

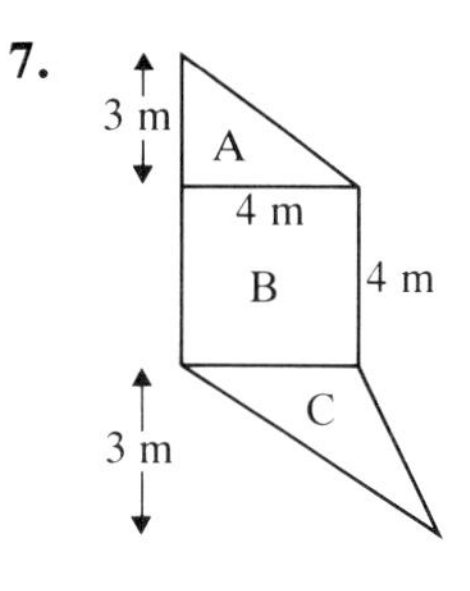

8.

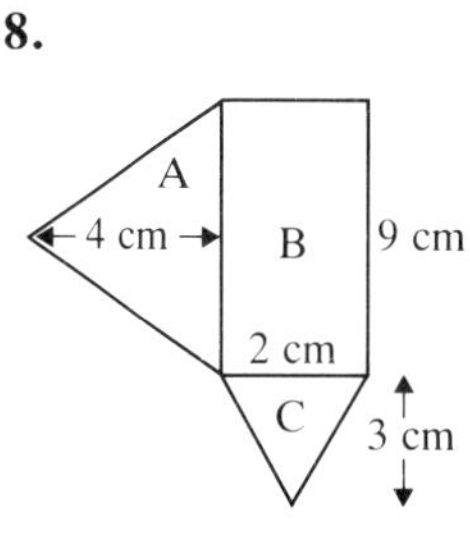

9.

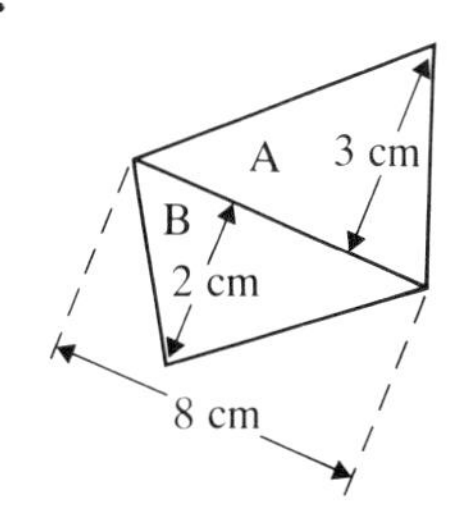

10.

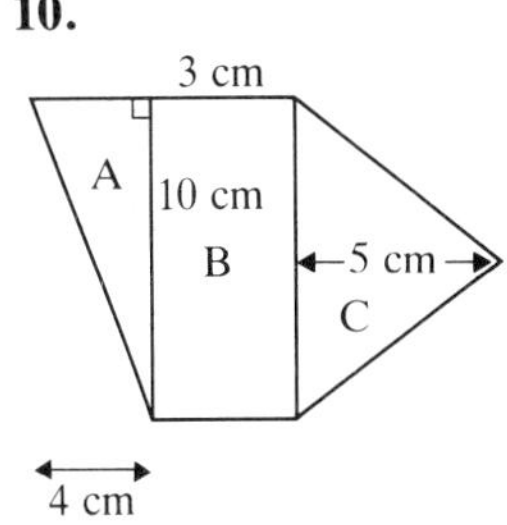

11.

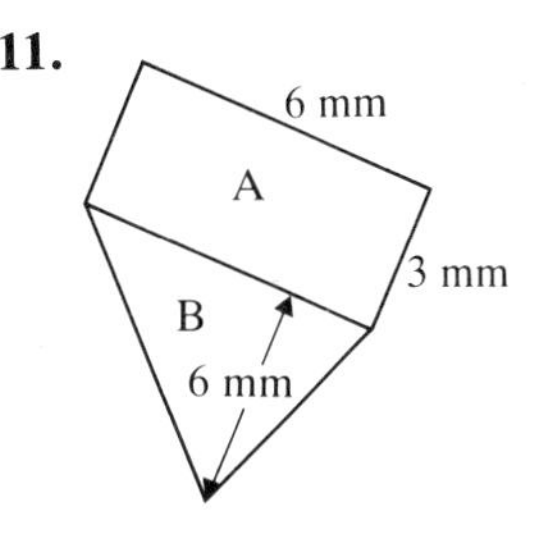

12.

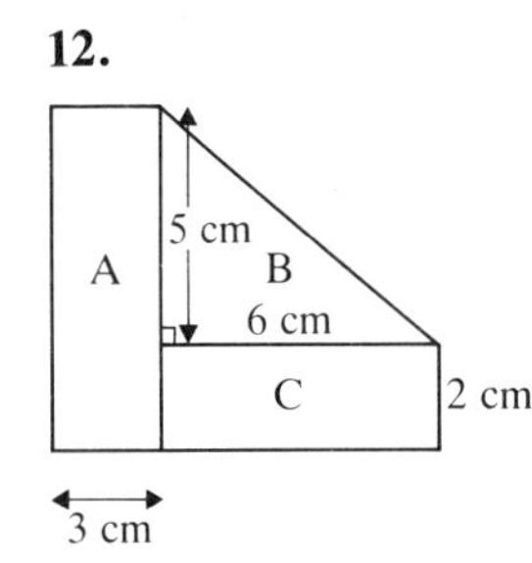

Exercise 3

Find the area of each shape.
All lengths are in cm.

1.

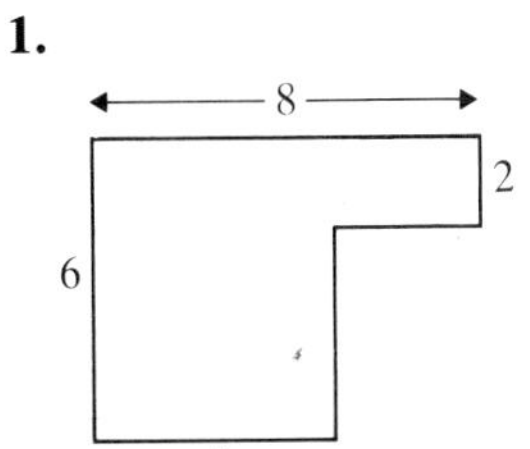

2.

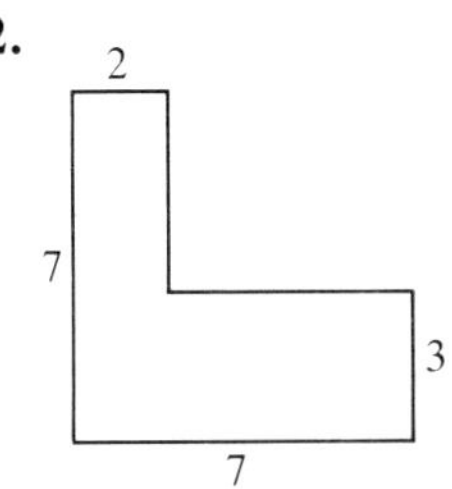

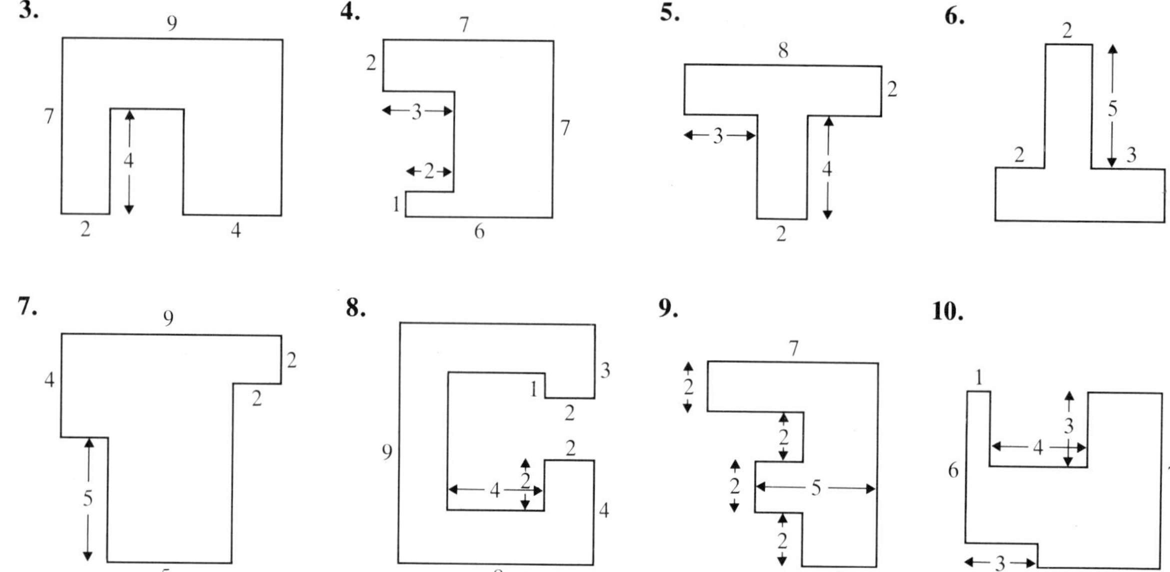

Exercise 4

A decorator works out how many rolls of wallpaper he needs for a room from the table below.

Height from skirting	Measurement round walls (including doors and windows) in metres									
	8.6	9.8	11.0	12.2	13.4	14.6	15.8	17.0	18.2	19.4
2.20 m	4	4	5	5	6	6	7	7	8	8
2.35 m	4	4	5	5	6	6	7	8	8	9
2.50 m	4	5	5	6	6	7	7	8	8	9
2.65 m	4	5	5	6	6	7	8	8	9	9
2.80 m	4	5	6	6	7	7	8	9	9	10
2.95 m	5	5	6	7	7	8	9	9	10	10
3.10 m	5	5	6	7	8	8	9	10	10	11

1. A plan of one room is shown below

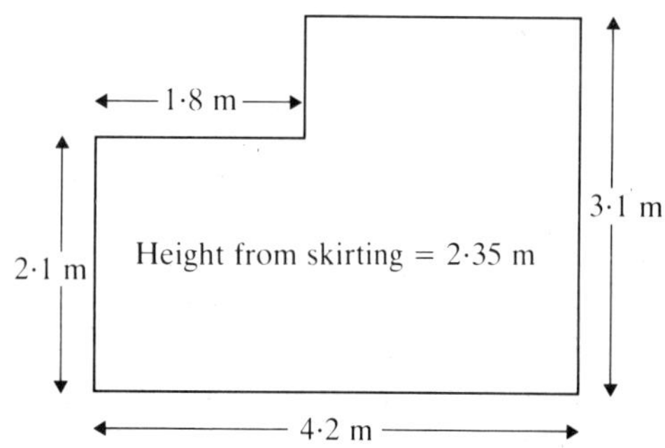

Work out
(a) the total length round the walls (the perimeter).
(b) the number of rolls of wallpaper he needs.
(c) the total cost of the wallpaper if one roll costs £3.20.
(d) the area of the ceiling of the room.

2. Work out the answers to parts (a), (b), (c) and (d) for each of the rooms shown below.

A.

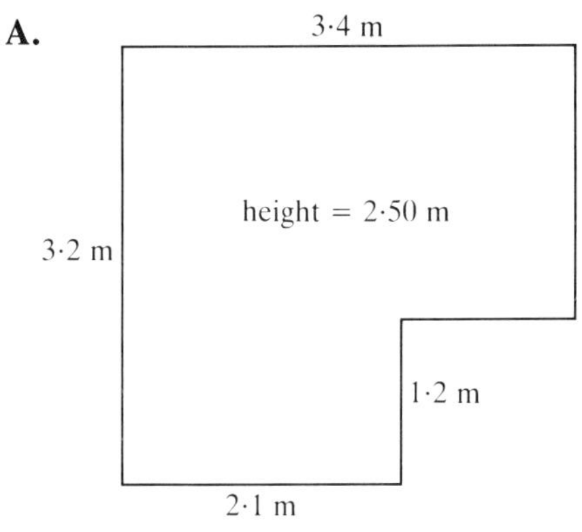

B.

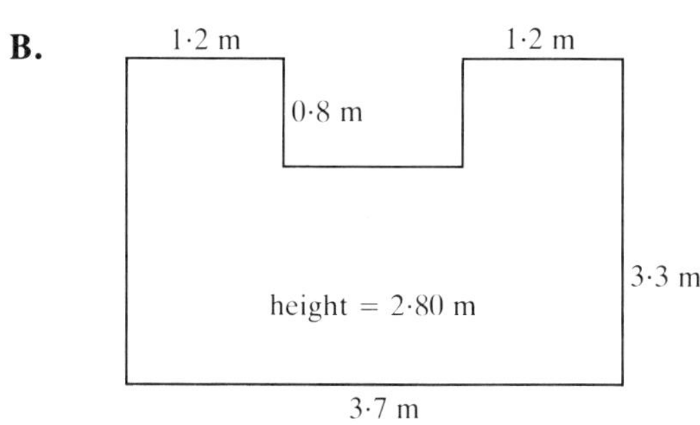

C.

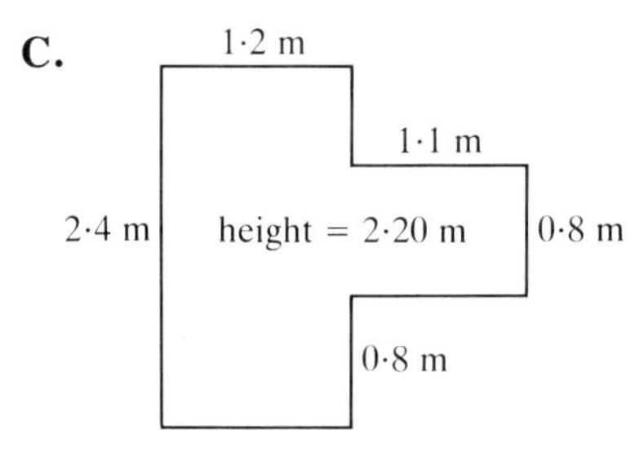

D.

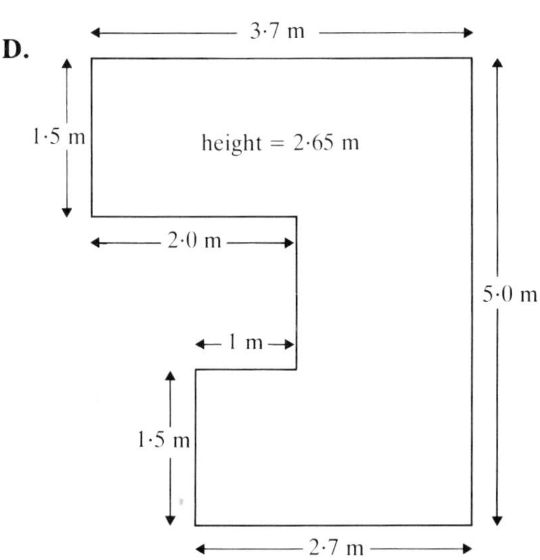

Exercise 5

1. (a) Copy the diagram below.

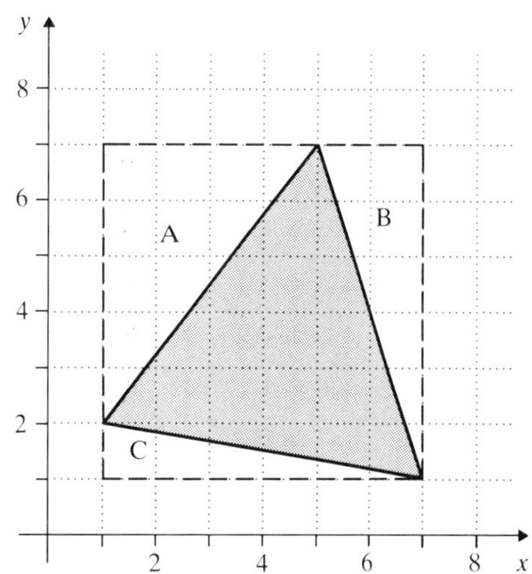

(b) Work out the areas of triangles A, B and C.

(c) Work out the area of the square enclosed by the broken lines.

(d) Hence work out the area of the shaded triangle. Give the answer in square units.

2. (a) Copy the diagram below.

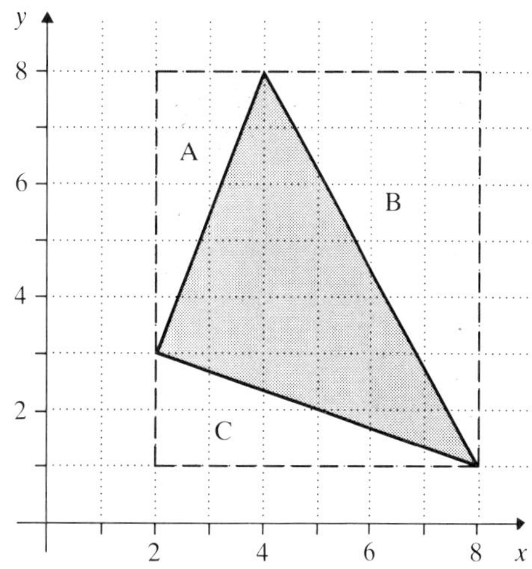

(b) Work out the areas of triangles A, B and C.

(c) Work out the area of the rectangle enclosed by the broken lines.

(d) Hence work out the area of the shaded triangle. Give the answer in square units.

For the remaining questions in this exercise draw a pair of axes similar to those in questions **1** and **2**. Plot the points in the order given and find the area of the shape enclosed.

3. (1,4), (6,8), (4,1)
4. (1,7), (8,5), (4,2)
5. (1,8), (8,6), (4,1)
6. (2,5), (6,2), (8,8)
7. (1,2), (7,3), (2,8)
8. (2,4), (6,1), (8,7), (4,8), (2,4)
9. (1,4), (5,1), (7,6), (4,8), (1,4)
10. (1,6), (2,2), (8,6), (6,8), (1,6)
11. (2,8), (4,5), (8,8), (4,1), (2,8)
12. (1,8), (8,5), (2,1), (4,5), (1,8)

13.

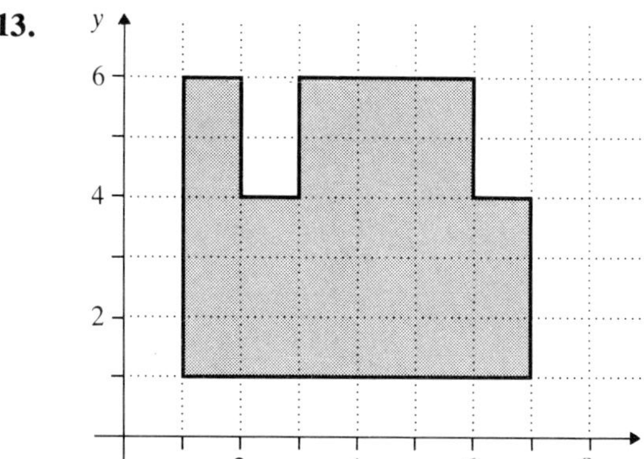

14. (1,8), (8,8), (8,6), (3,6), (3,5), (6,5), (6,4), (4,4), (4,2), (3,2), (3,1), (1,1), (1,8).

4.2 CIRCLES

Circumference of a circle

The circumference of the circle below is given by $C = \pi d$

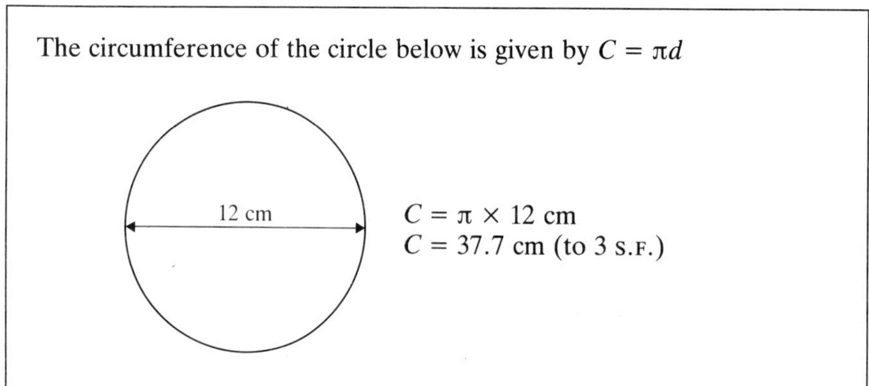

$C = \pi \times 12$ cm
$C = 37.7$ cm (to 3 S.F.)

Exercise 6

Find the circumference. Use the 'π' button on a calculator or take $\pi = 3.14$. Give the answers correct to 3 significant figures.

1.

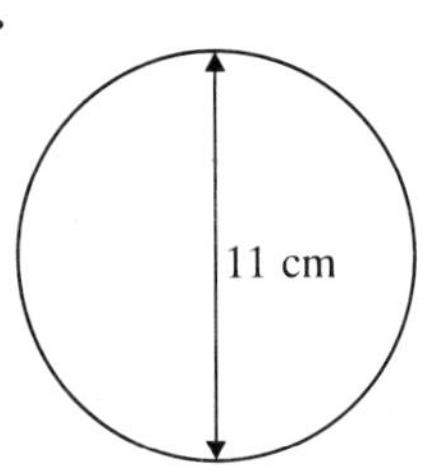

2.

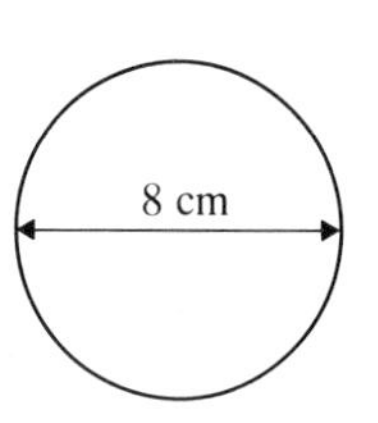

3.

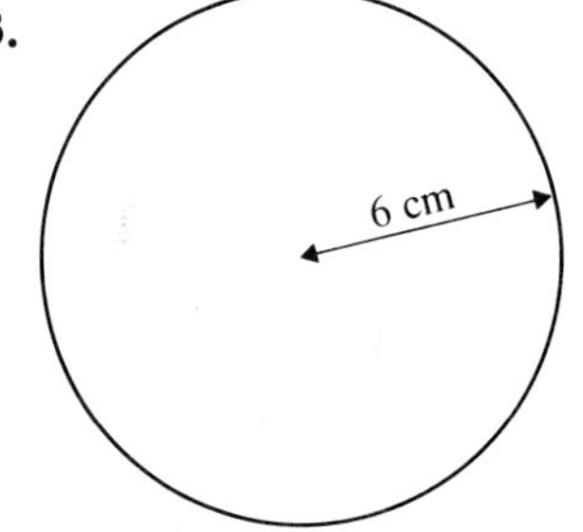

4.

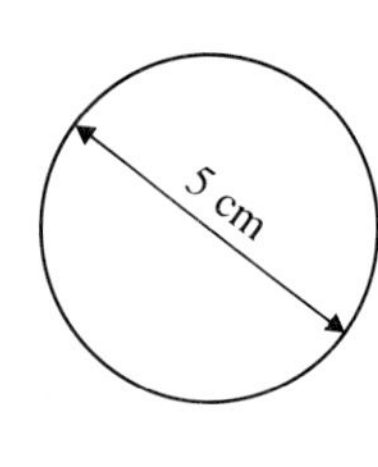

5.

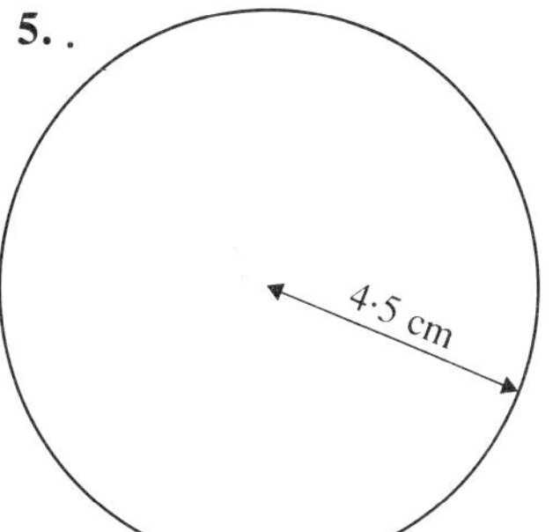

6.

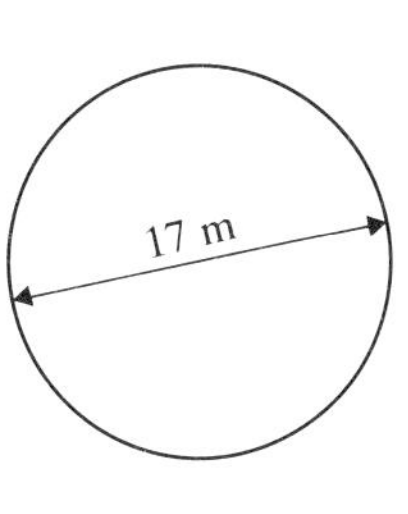

7.

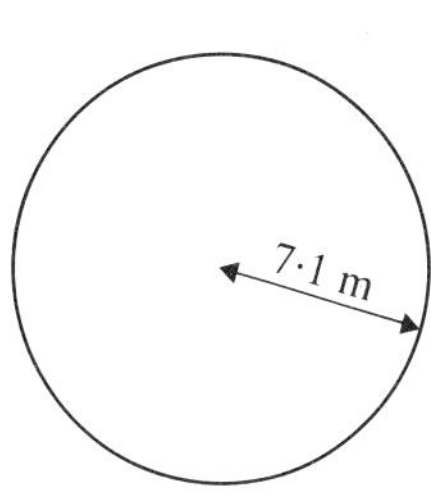

8.

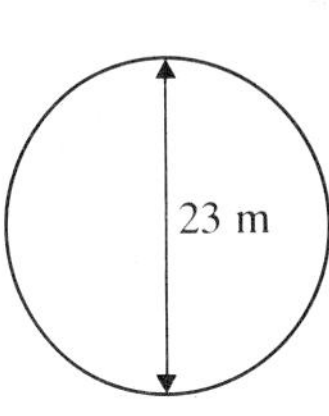

9.

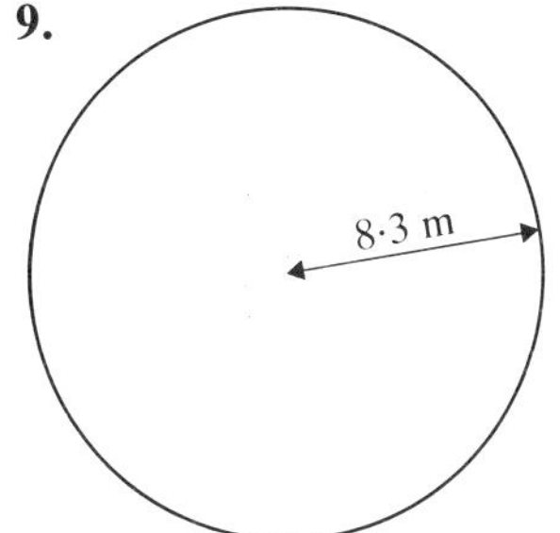

10.

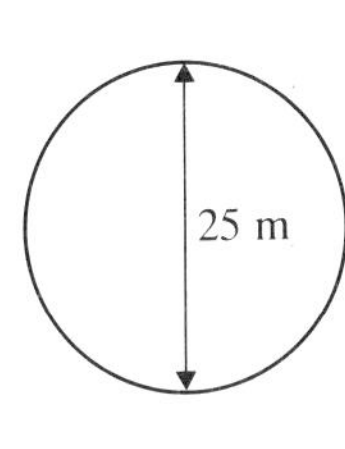

11.

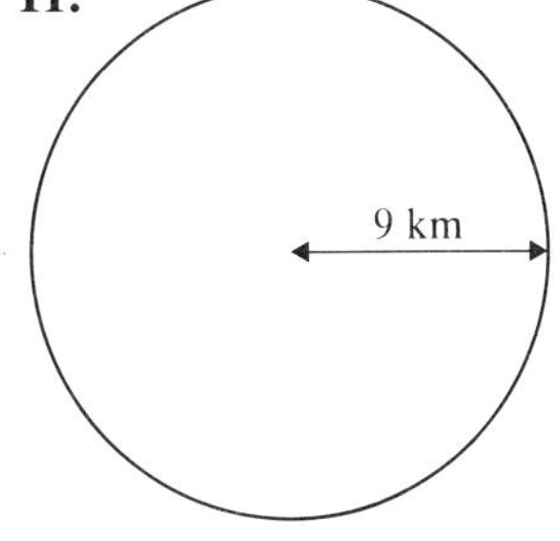

12.

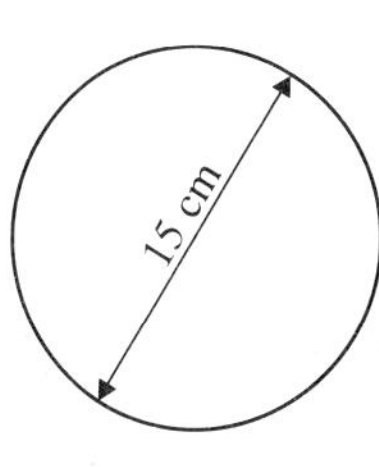

13.

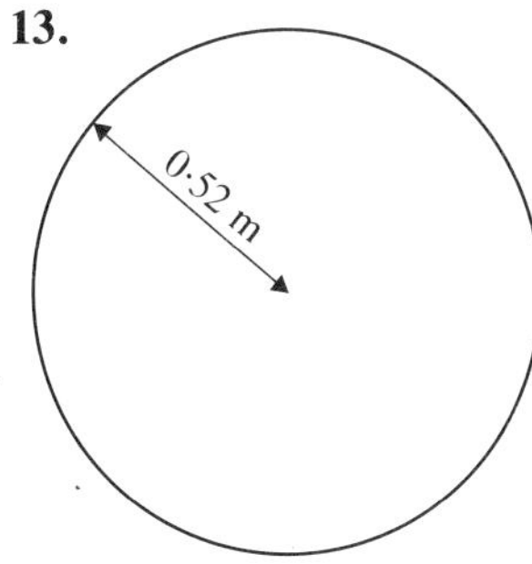

14.

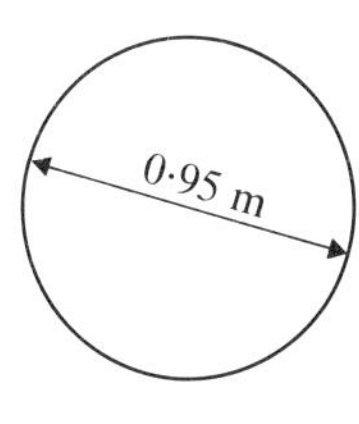

15.

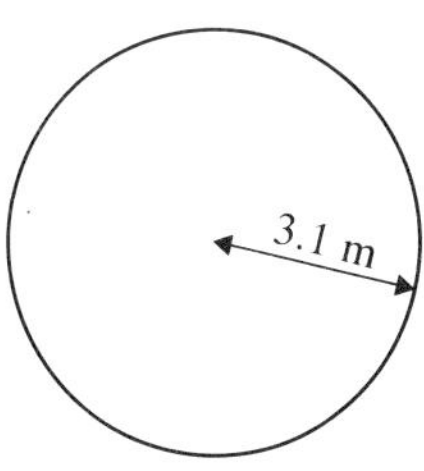

16. Diameter = 8.2 km
17. Radius = 0.84 mm
18. Diameter = 3.74 cm
19. Diameter = 18.2 m
20. Radius = 3.1 mm
21. Radius = 2.4 miles
22. Diameter = 8.3 feet
23. Radius = 3.9 km
24. Diameter = 0.092 m
25. Radius = 1.43 cm

Exercise 7

Find the perimeter of the shapes. Use the 'π' button on a calculator or take π = 3.14. Give the answers correct to 3 significant figures.

1.

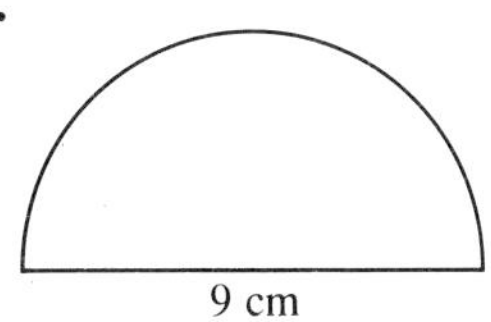

2.

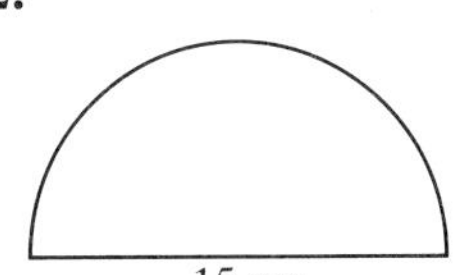

3.

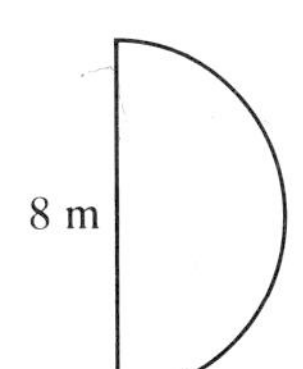

4.

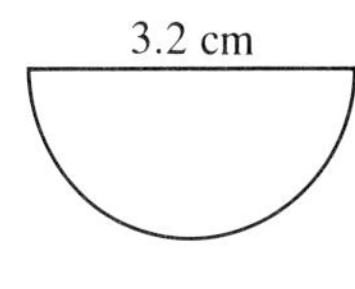

5.

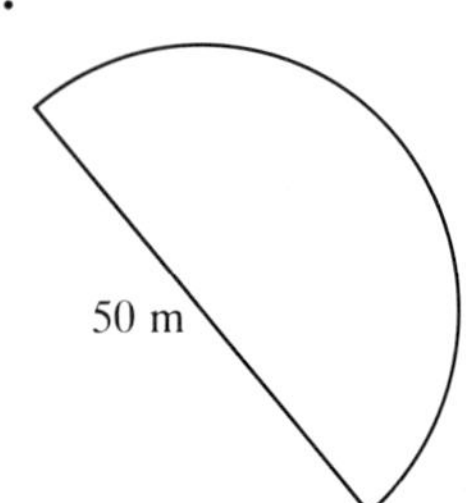

6.

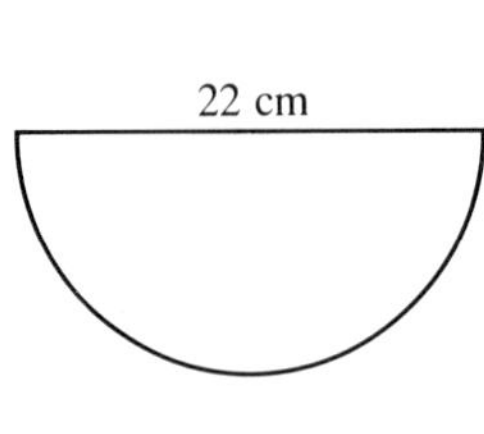

7.

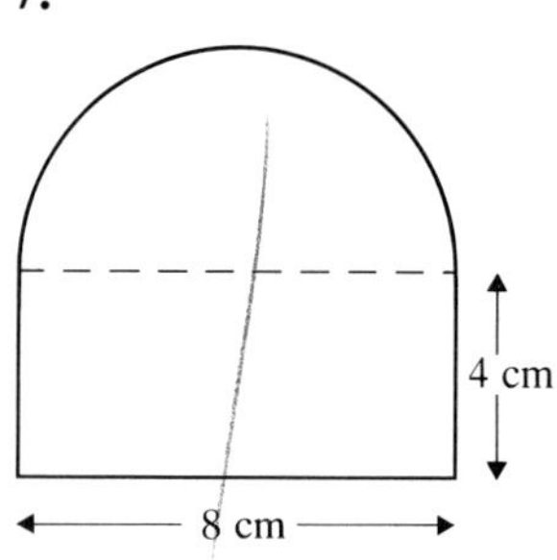

8.

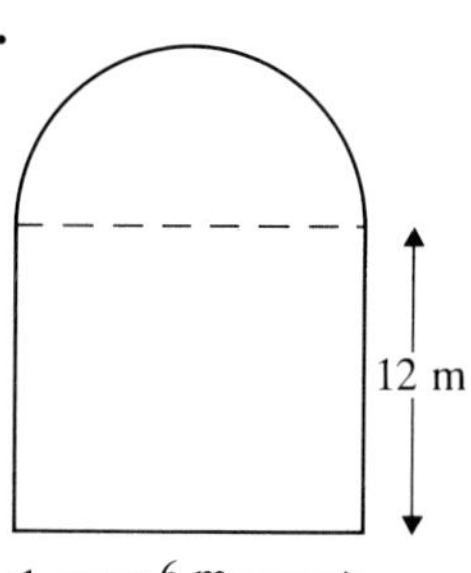

9.

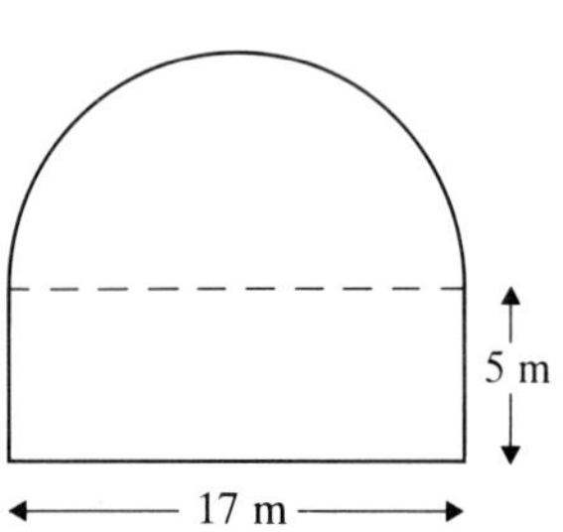

10.

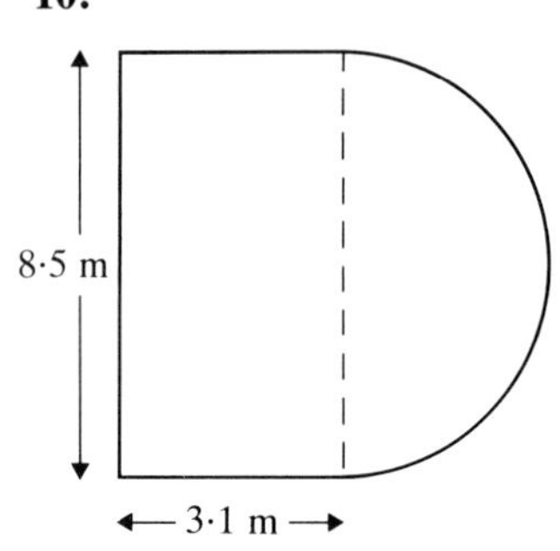

11.

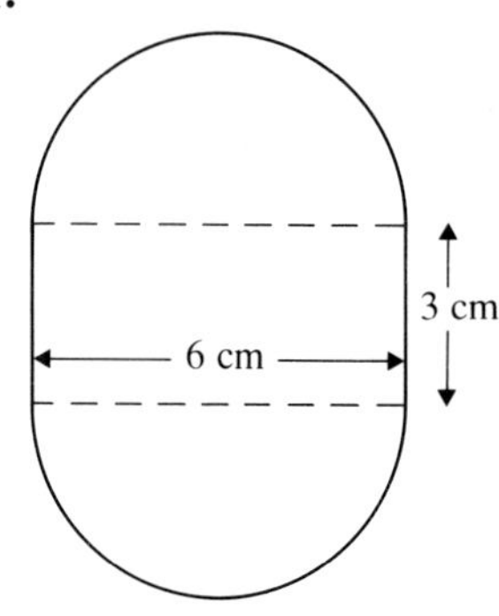

12.

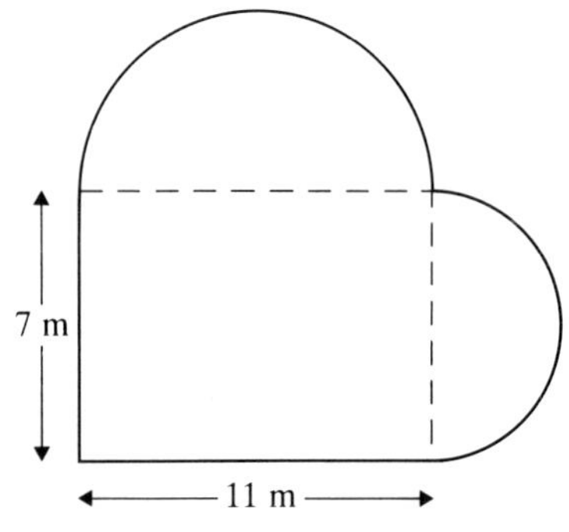

13.

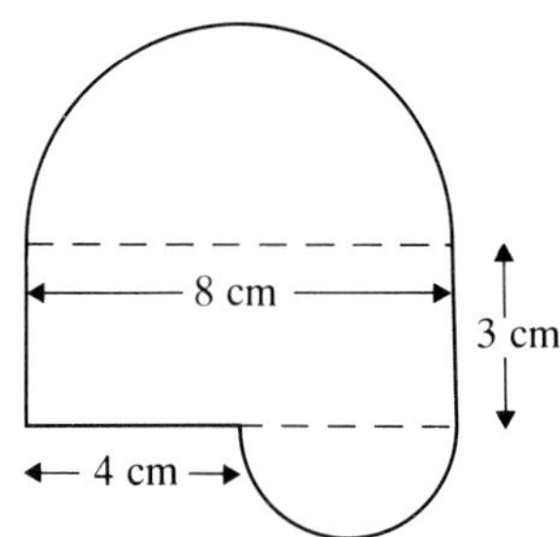

14.

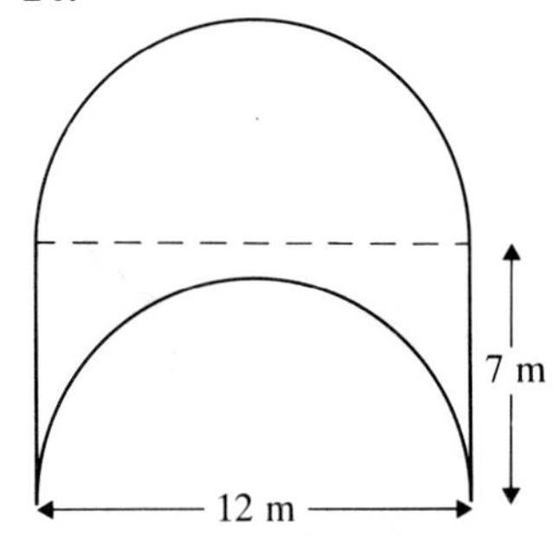

Area of a circle

Find the area of the circle shown.

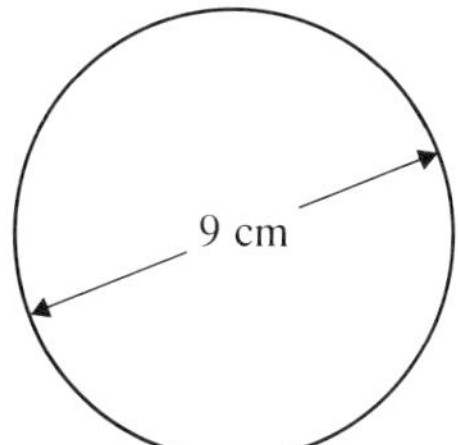

The area of a circle of radius r is given by
$A = \pi r^2$
In this circle $r = 4.5$ cm
$\therefore$ Area of circle $= \pi \times 4.5^2$
$= 63.6 \text{ cm}^2$ (to 3 S.F.)
[Here we have used the 'π' button on a calculator.]

Exercise 8

In questions **1** to **20** find the area of the circle. Use the 'π' button on a calculator or use $\pi = 3.14$. Give the answers correct to three significant figures.

1.
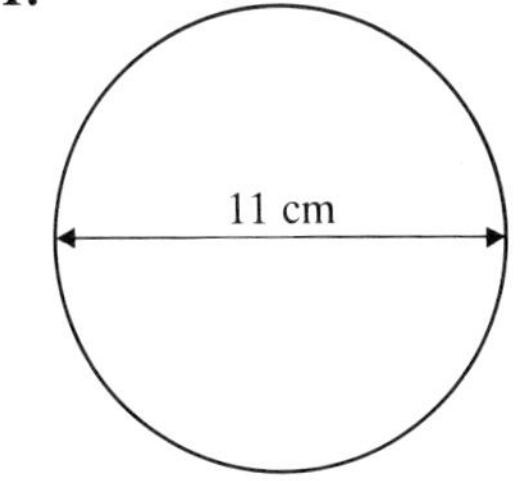

2.
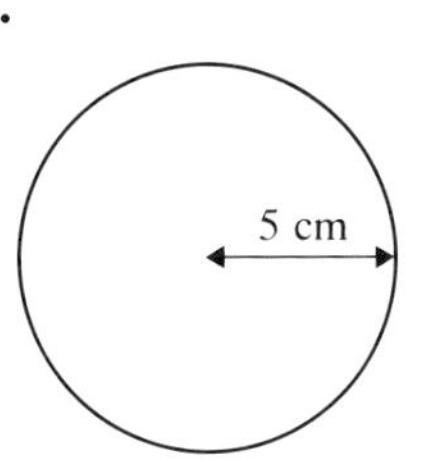

3.
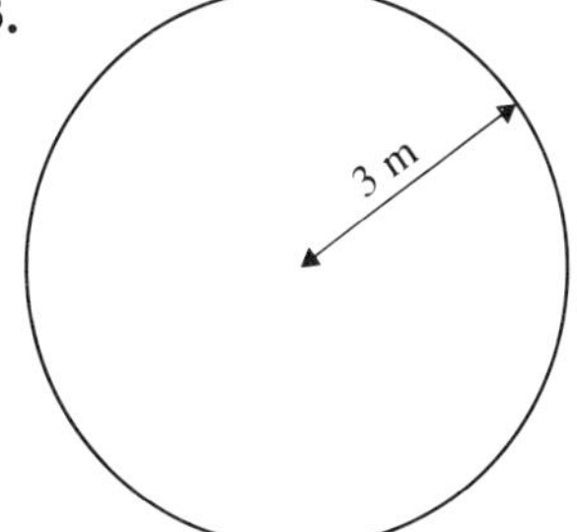

4.
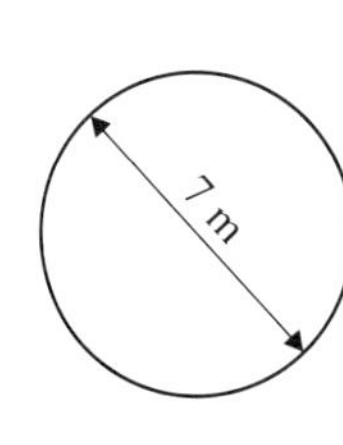

5.
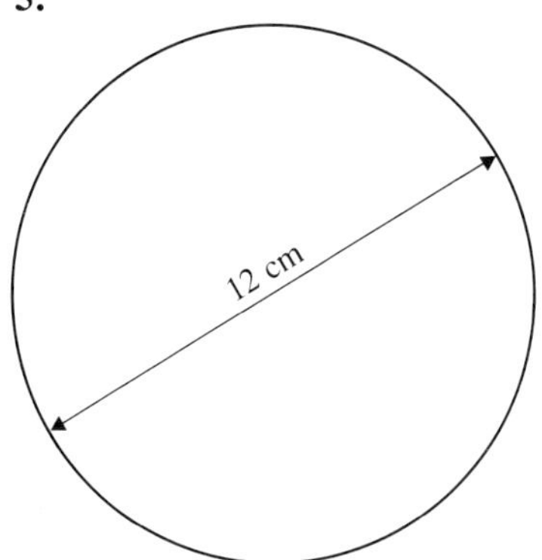

6.
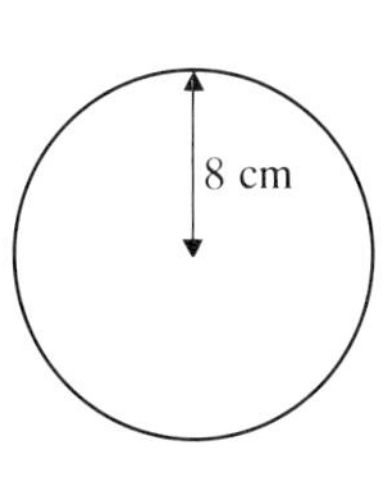

7.
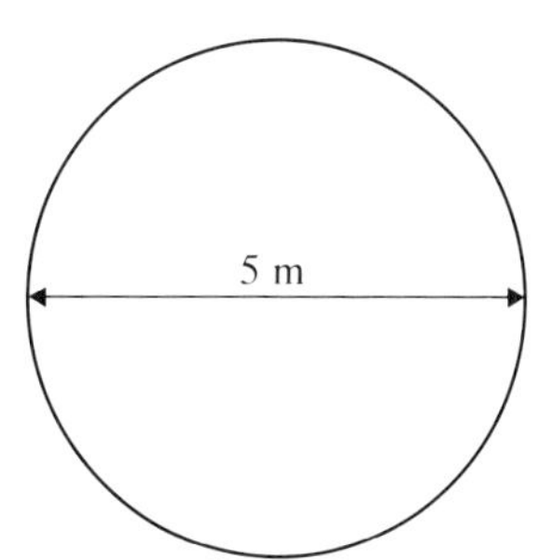

8.
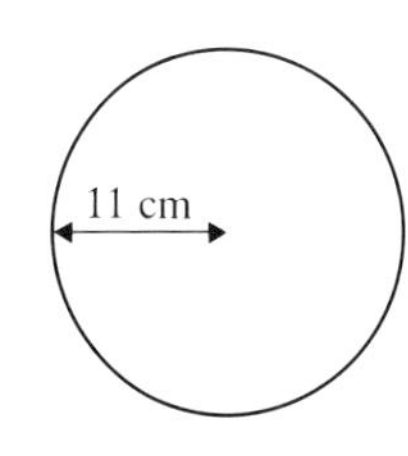

9.

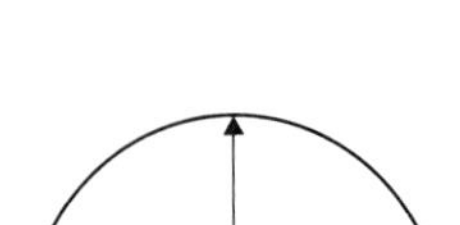

10.

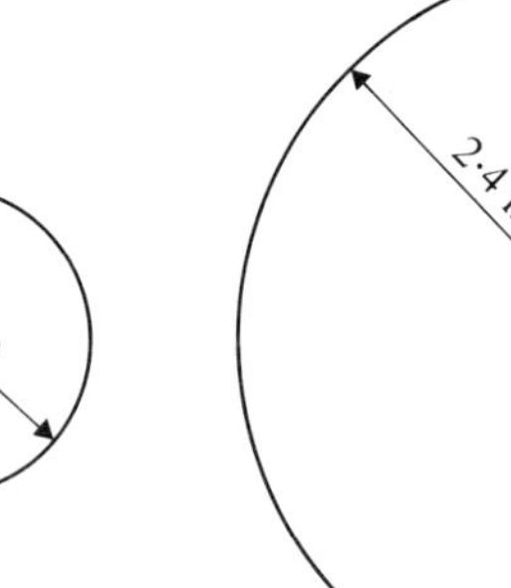

11.

12.

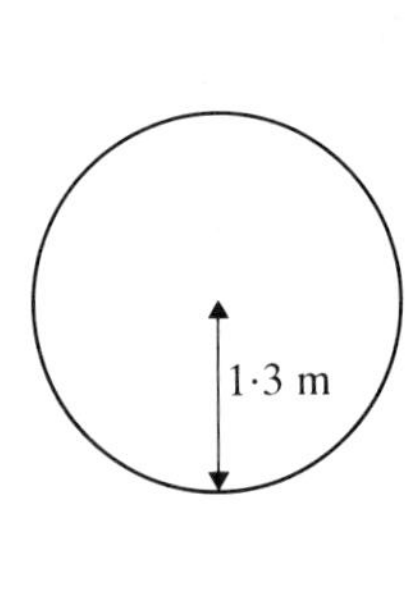

13. Radius = 9.7 cm
14. Diameter = 19 km
15. Diameter = 8.2 cm
16. Radius = 0.2 m
17. Diameter = 11.6 m
18. Radius = 1.8 cm
19. Radius = 0.85 m
20. Diameter = 3.9 km

Exercise 9

Find the area of each shape. Use the 'π' button on a calculator or use $\pi = 3.14$. Give the answers correct to three significant figures.

1.

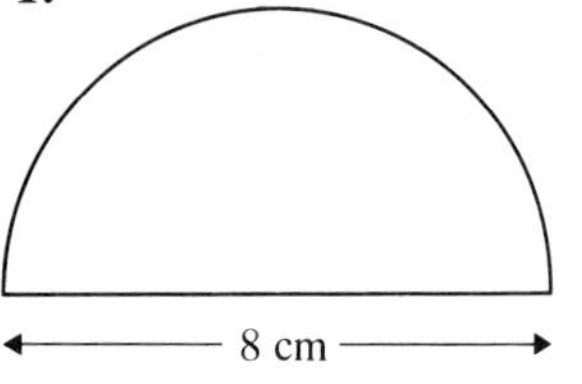

2.

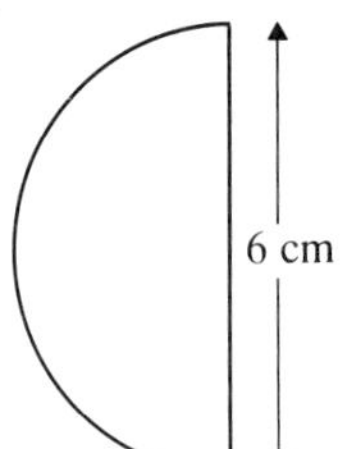

3.

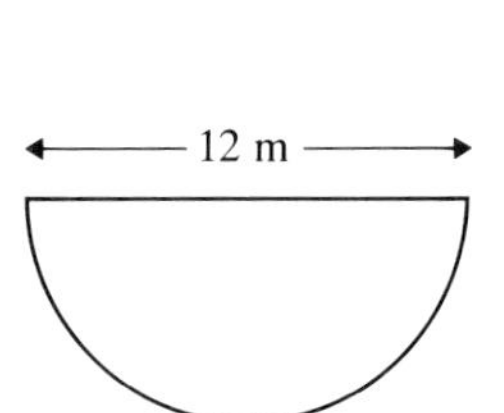

4.

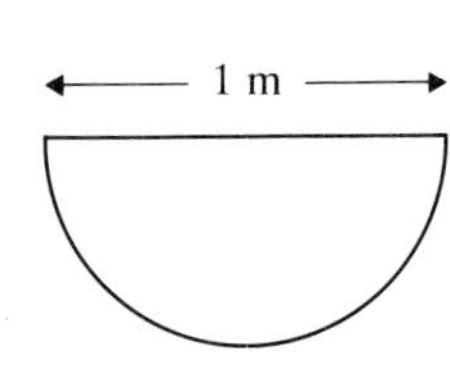

5.

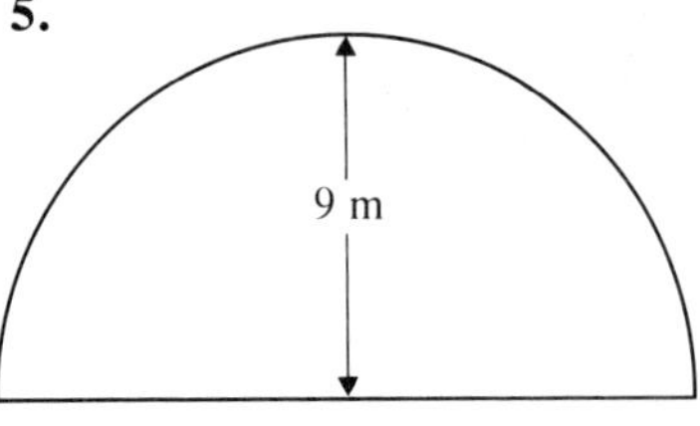

6.

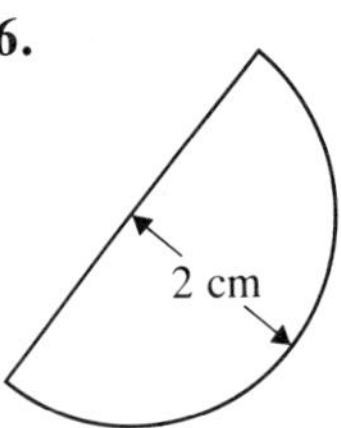

7.

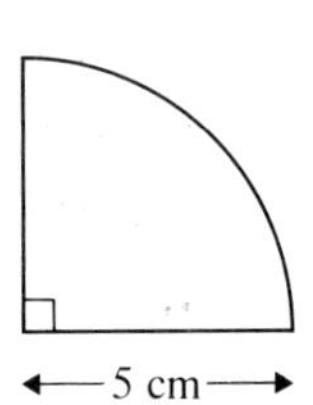

8.

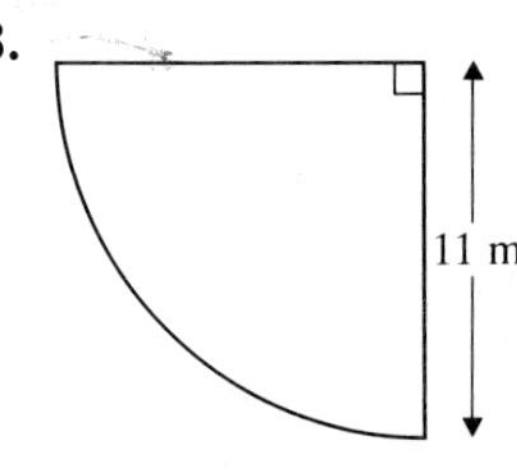

9.

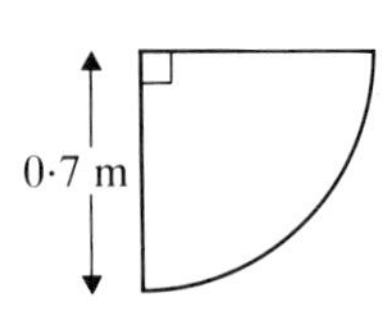

10.

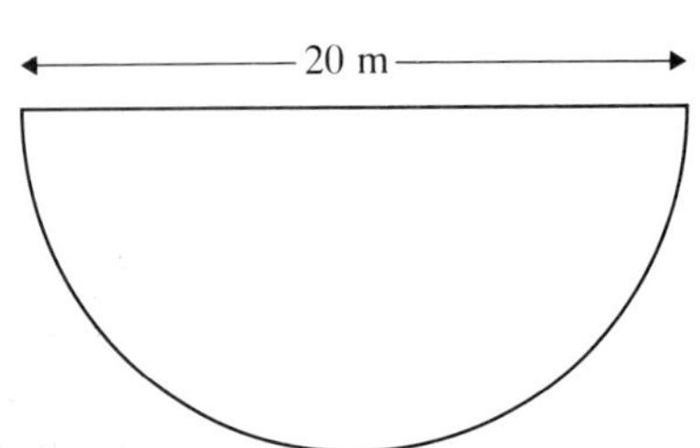

11.

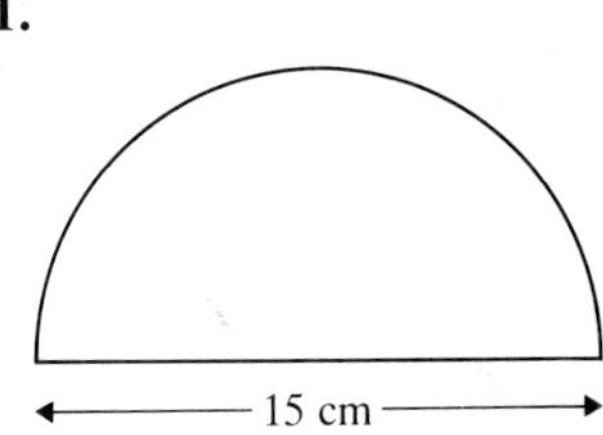

Exercise 10

Find the area of each shape. Use the 'π' button on a calculator or take $\pi = 3.14$. Give the answers correct to three significant figures. All lengths are in cm.

1.

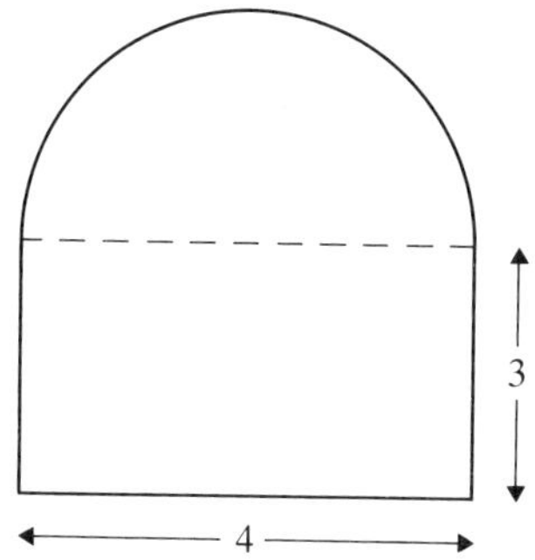

2.

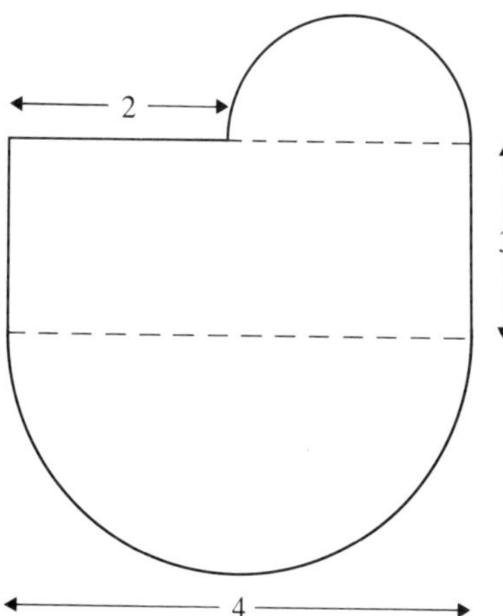

3.

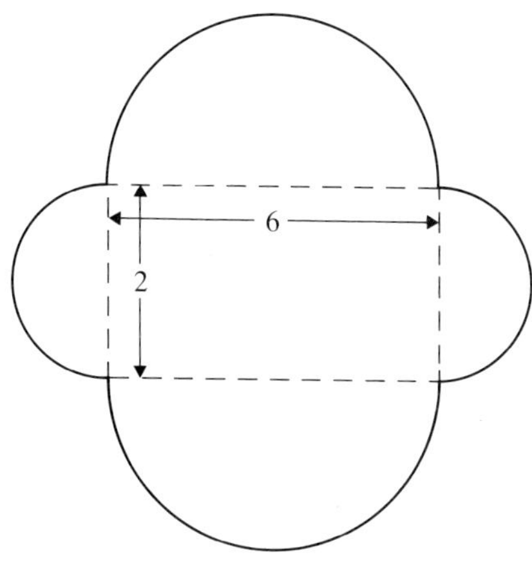

4.

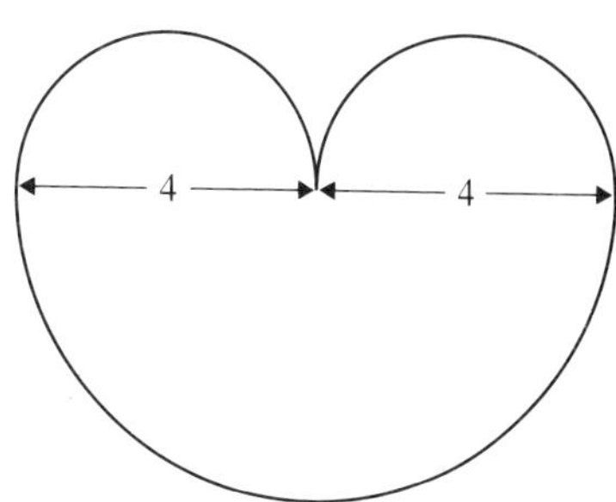

In questions **5** to **8** find the shaded area.

5.

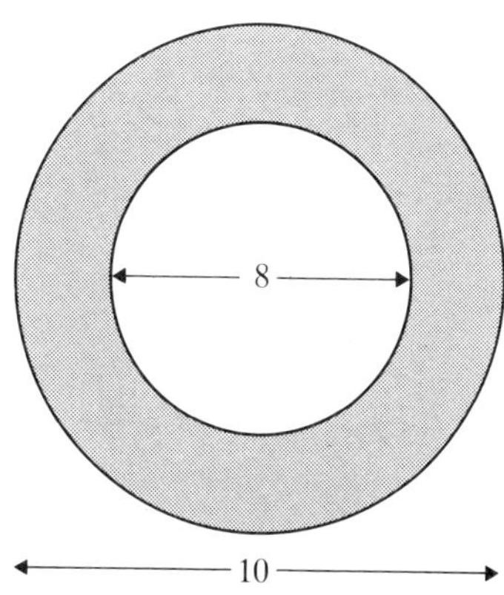

6.

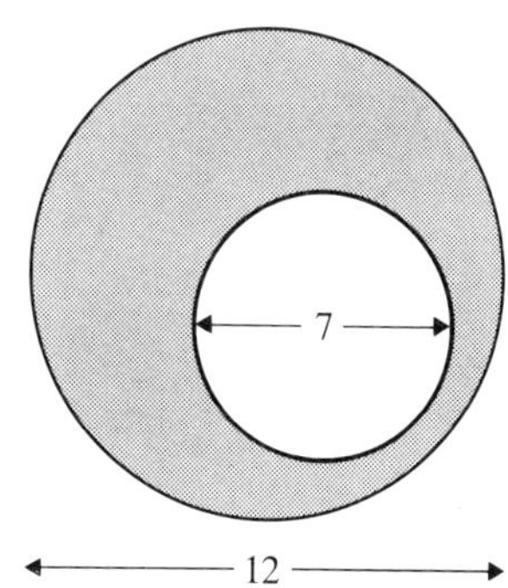

7.

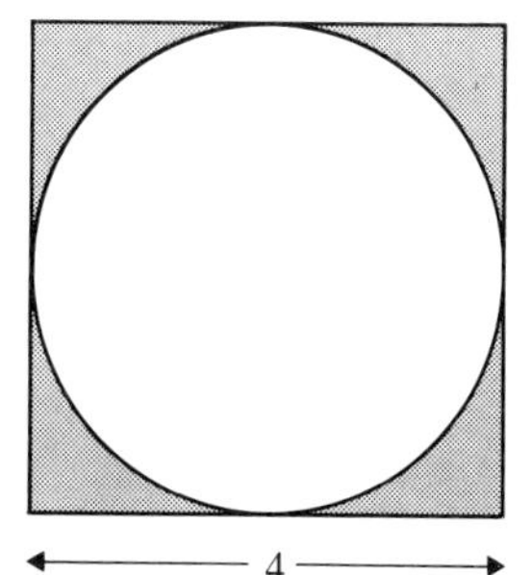

8.

9.

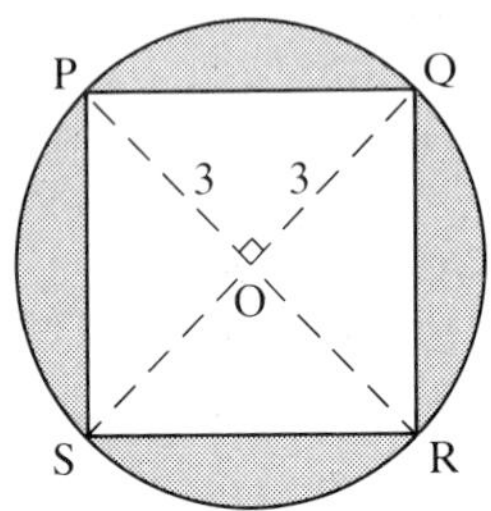

(a) Find the area of triangle OPQ.
(b) Hence find the area of the square PQRS.
(c) Find the area of the circle.
(d) Hence find the shaded area.

10.

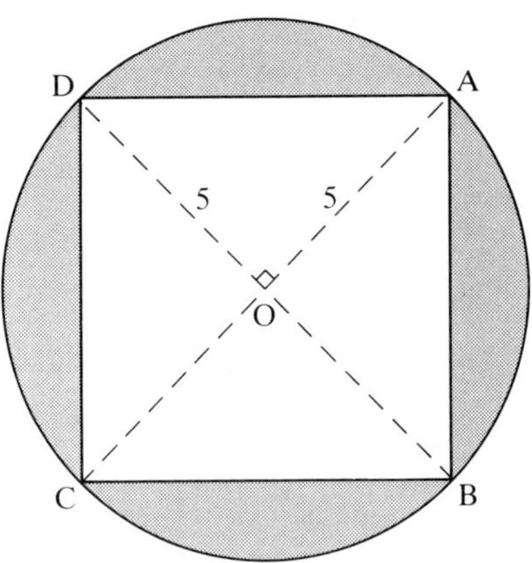

(a) Find the area of triangle OAD.
(b) Hence find the area of the square ABCD.
(c) Find the area of the circle.
(d) Hence find the shaded area.

4.3 VOLUME

The volume of a cuboid is given by the formula $V = l \times b \times h$.

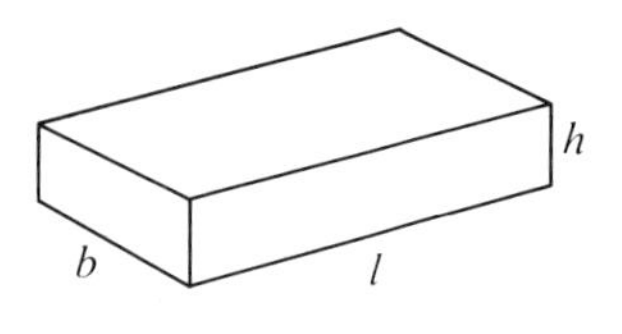

Exercise 11

In questions **1** to **8** find the volume of each cuboid.

1.

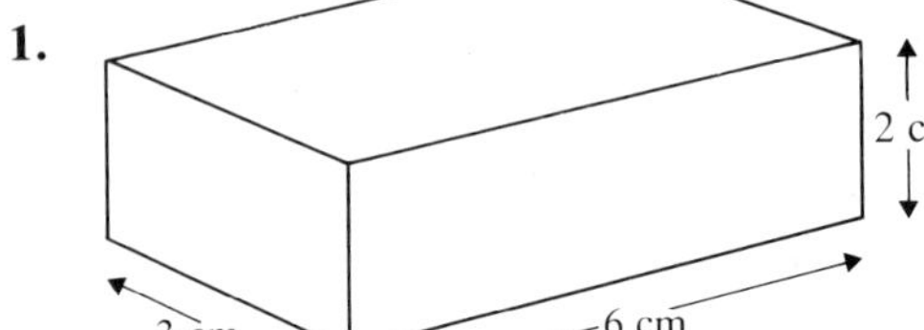

2.

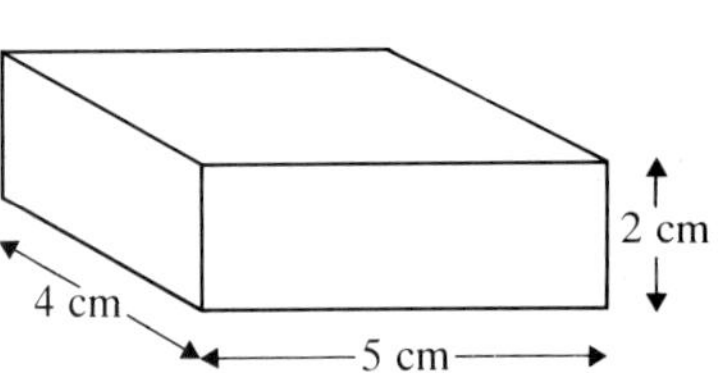

3.

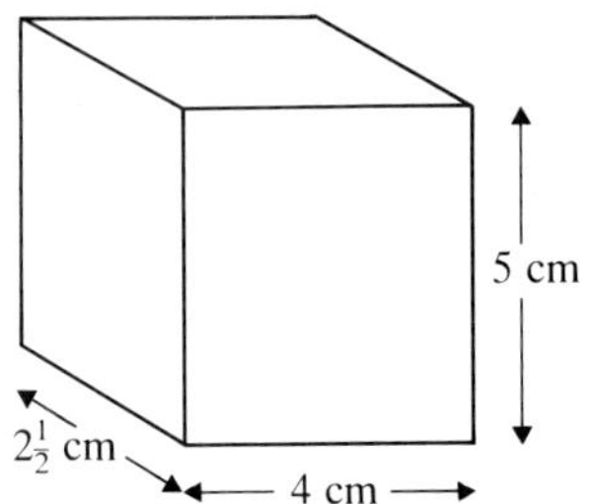

4. length = 7 m, breadth = 4 m, height = 3 m.
5. length = 10 cm, breadth = 5 cm, height = 100 cm.
6. length = 2 cm, breadth = 0.1 cm, height = 0.5 cm.
7. length = 3.1 cm, breadth = 3 cm, height = 10 cm.
8. length = 8.4 cm, breadth = 10 cm, height = 0.01 cm.

In questions **9** to **12** find the length of the side marked with a letter.

9.

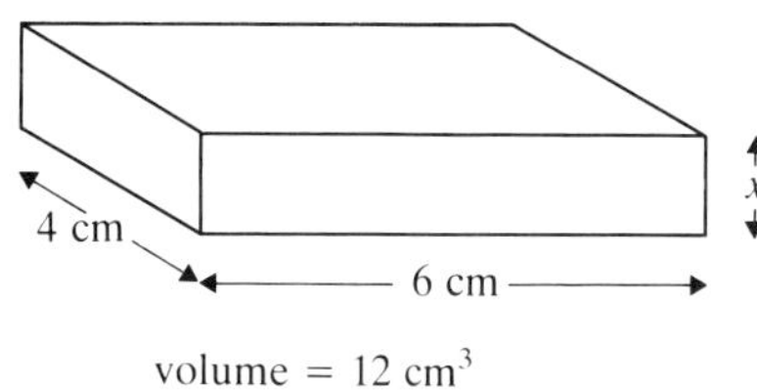

volume = 12 cm^3

10.

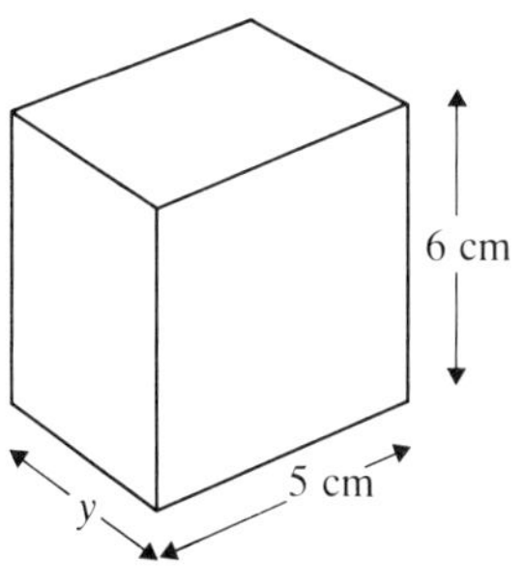

volume = 105 cm^3

11.

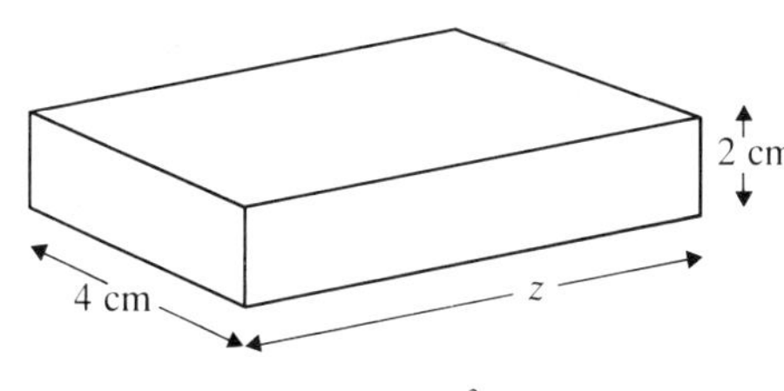

volume = 42 cm^3

12.

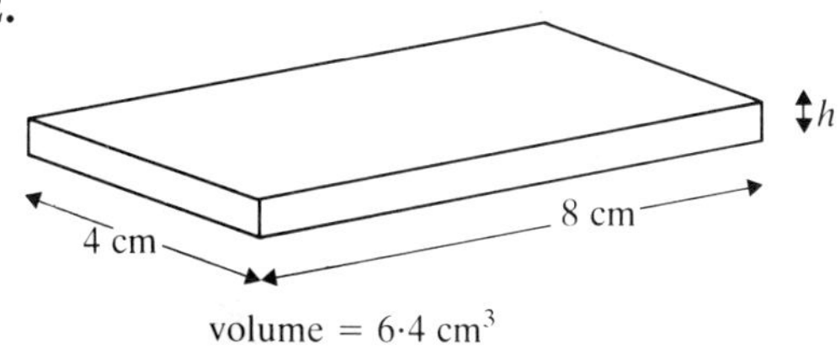

volume = 6·4 cm^3

For questions **13** to **19** find the volume of each solid. Each cube has a volume of 1 cm^3. Start each question by drawing a careful diagram.

13.

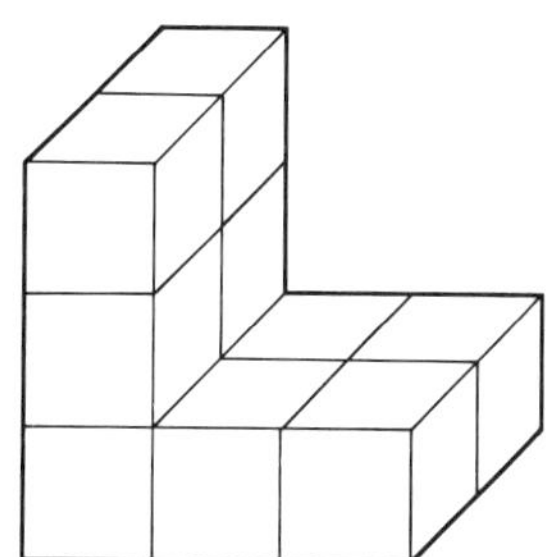

14.

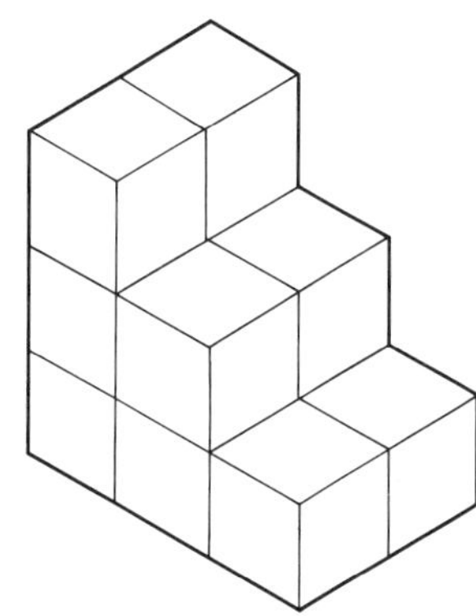

15.

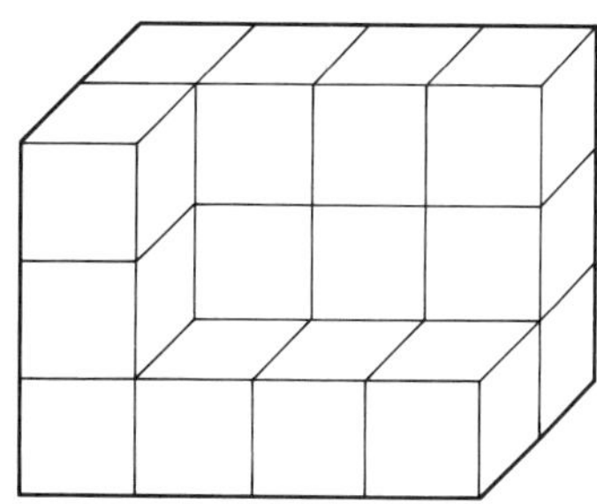

16.

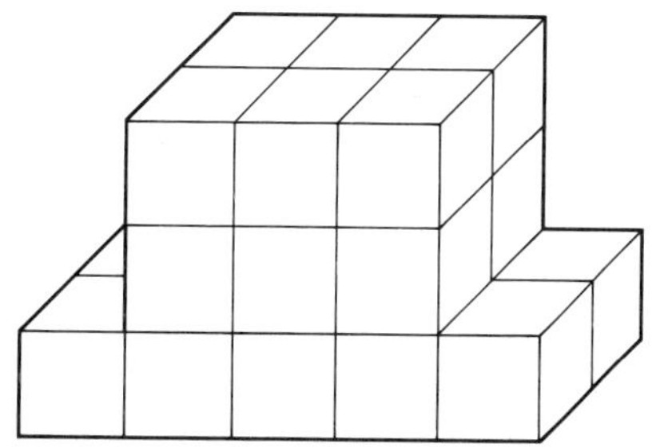

17.

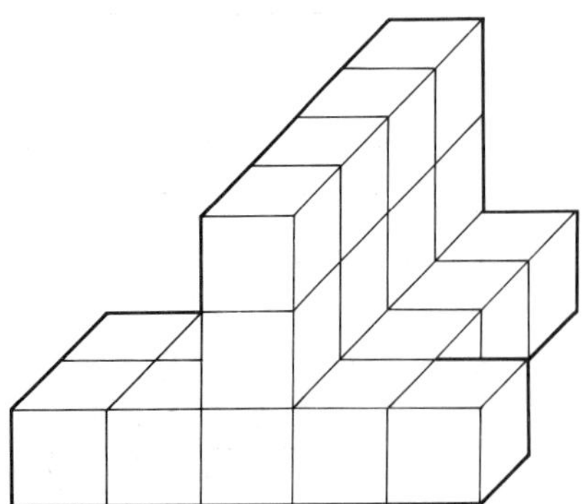

18.

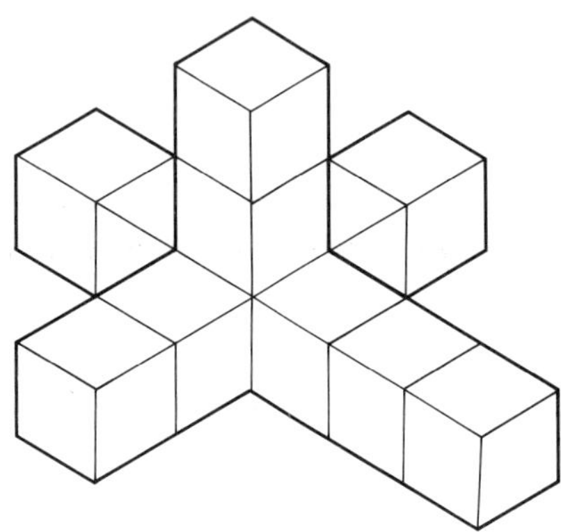

19.

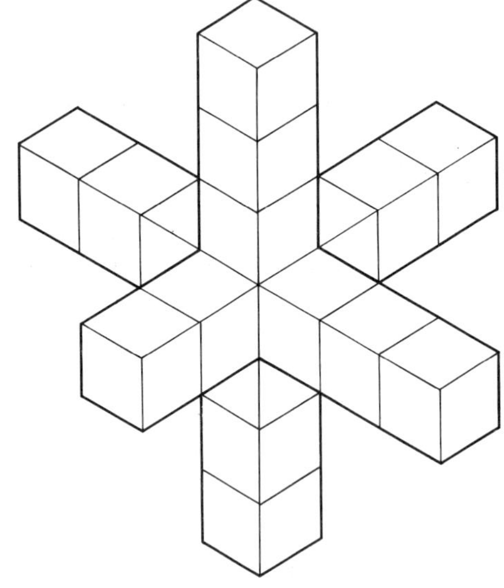

Prisms

A prism is an object with a uniform cross section

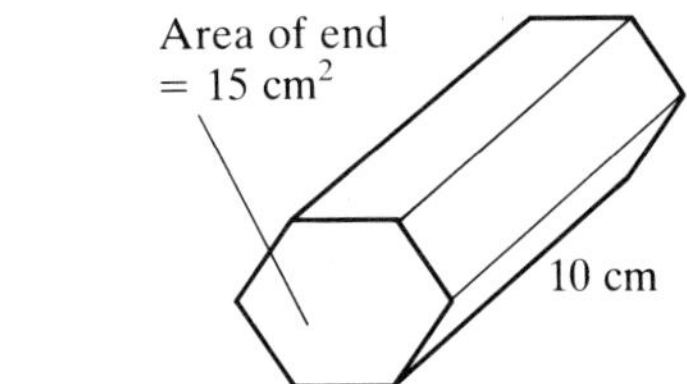

Volume = $A \times l$.

Exercise 12

Find the volume of each prism.

1. Area of end = 15 cm^2

10 cm

2. Area of end = 5 m^2

12 m

3. 12 cm

10 cm

8 cm

4. 20 m

2 m

3 m

5.

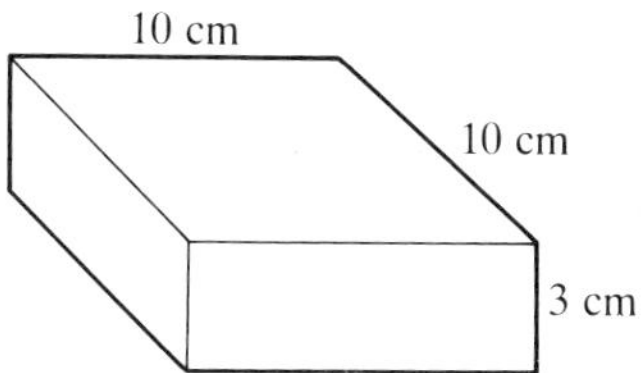

6.

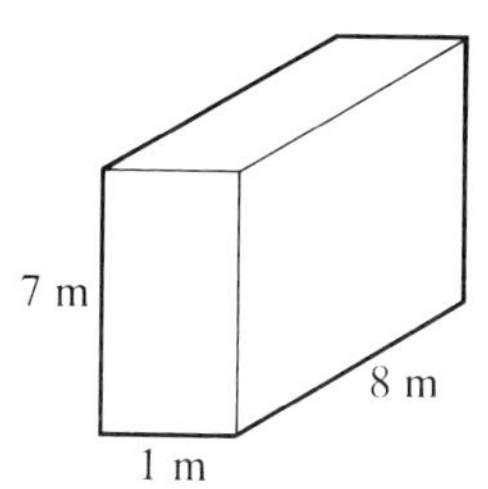

7.

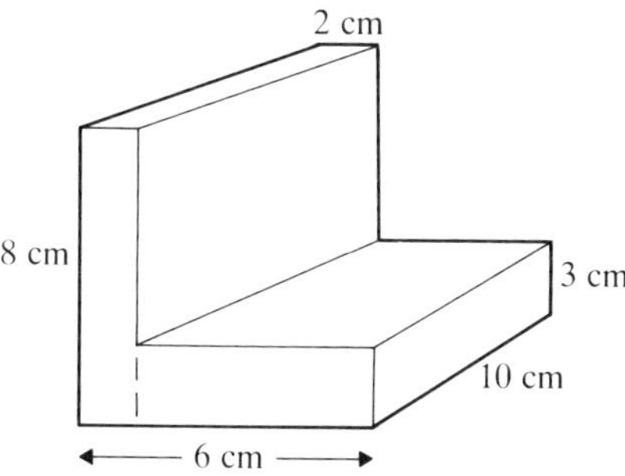

8.

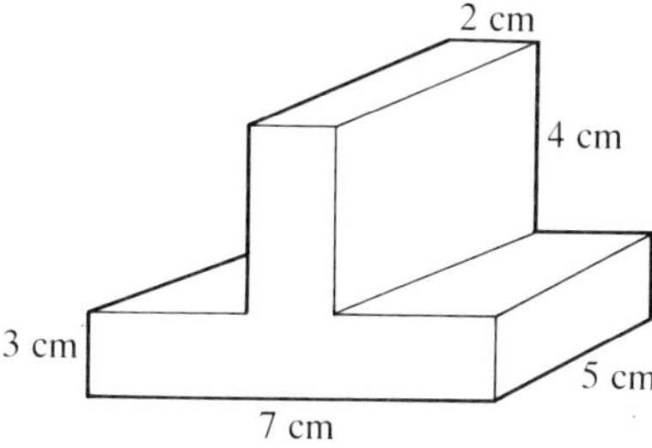

9.

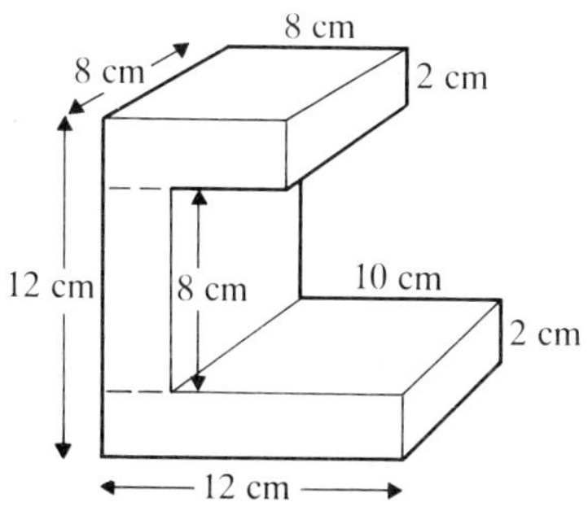

10.

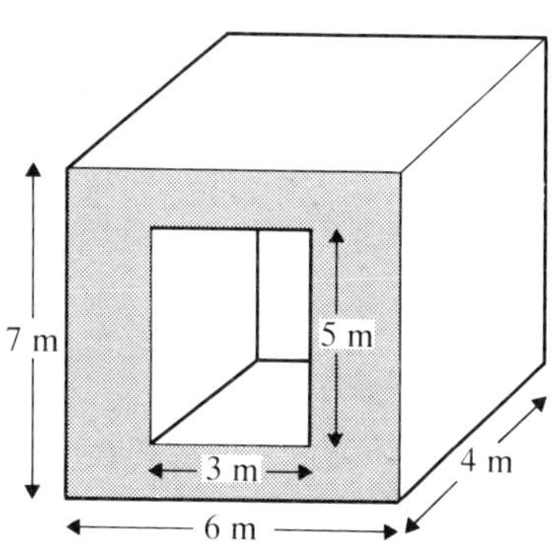

Cylinders

A cylinder is a prism with a circular cross section.

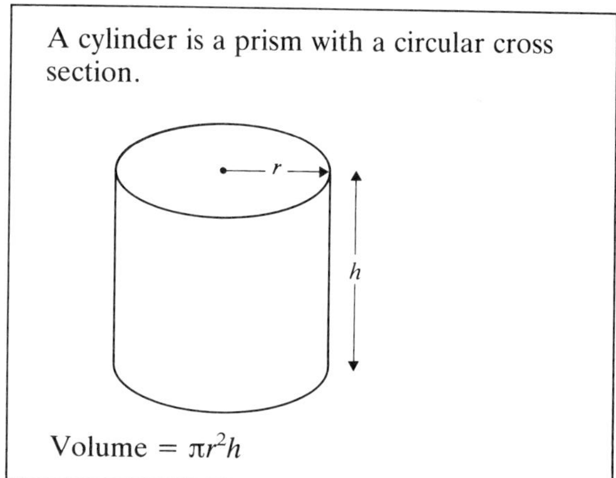

Volume $= \pi r^2 h$

Exercise 13

Find the volume of each cylinder. Use the 'π' button on a calculator or use $\pi = 3.14$. Give the answers correct to 3 S.F.

1. 2.

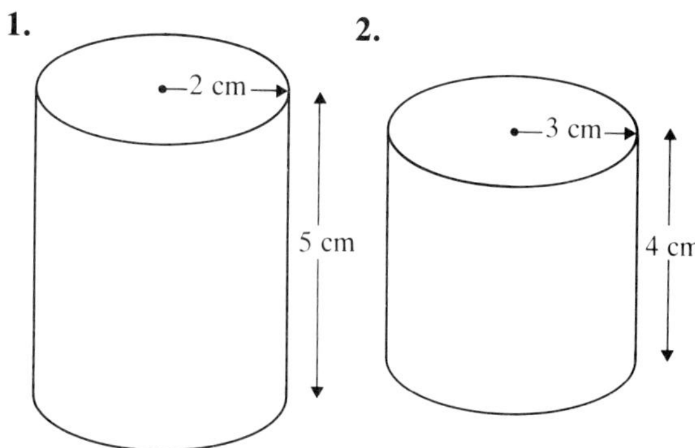

3.

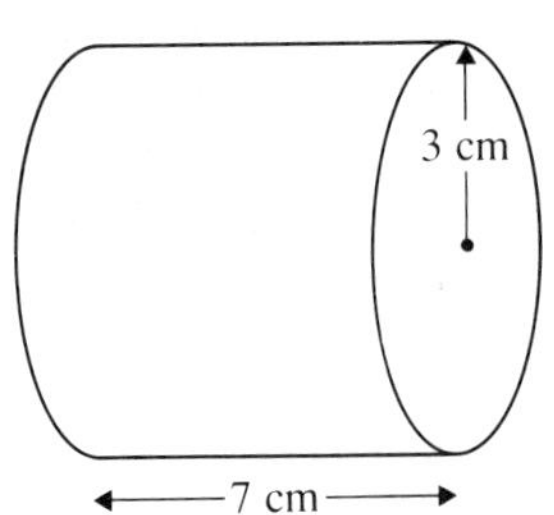

4.

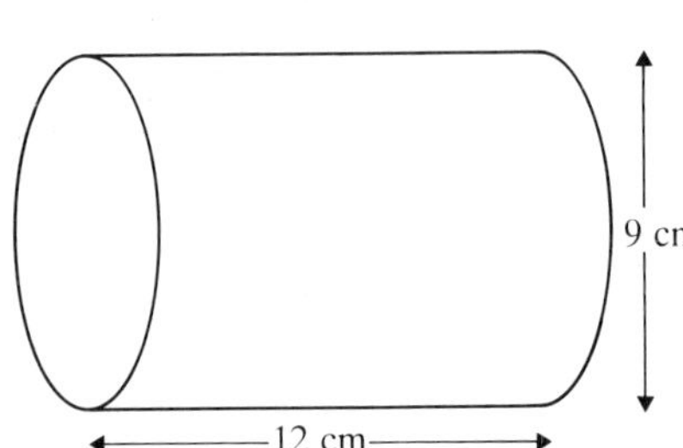

5.

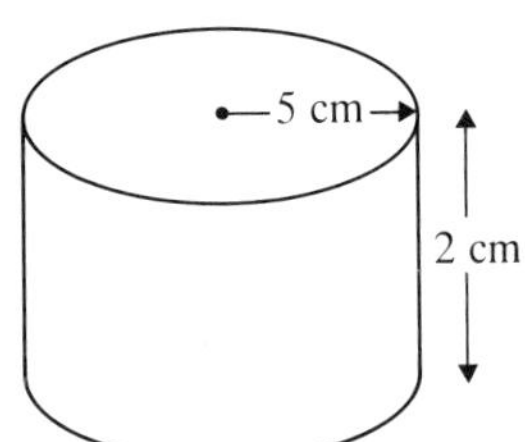

6.

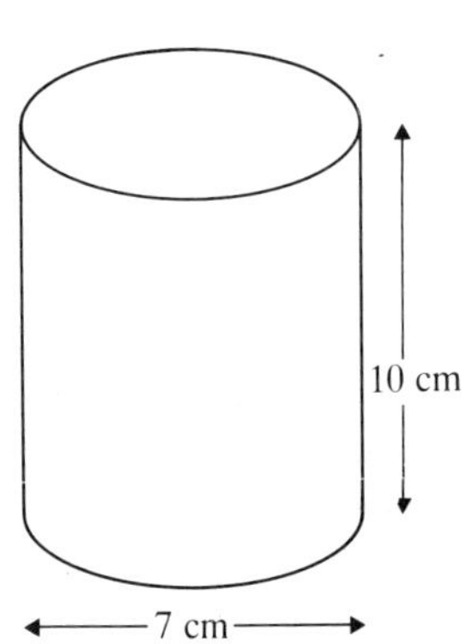

7. radius = 7 cm, height = 5 cm
8. diameter = 8 m, height = 3.5 m
9. diameter = 11 m, height = 2.4 m
10. radius = 3.2 cm, height = 15.1 cm
11. diameter = 0.84 m, height = 1.2 m
12. radius = 0.95 cm, height = 6.2 cm
13. diameter = 3.3 m, height = 0.7 m
14. radius = 4.01 m, height = 0.59 m
15. diameter = 5 feet, height = 6 feet
16. radius = 2.4 feet, height = 5.5 feet
17. diameter = 13 inches, height = 6.6 inches
18. radius = 0.658 cm, height = 24 cm

Exercise 14

This exercise contains a mixture of questions involving the volumes of a wide variety of different objects. Where necessary give answers correct to 3 S.F.

1. A cylindrical bar has a cross-sectional area of 12 cm^2 and a length of two metres. Calculate the volume of the bar
   (a) in cm^3,
   (b) in m^3.
2. The diagram represents a building.

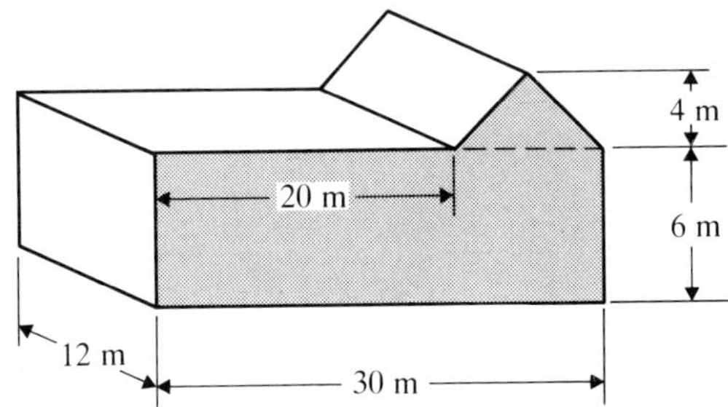

   (a) Calculate the area of the shaded end.
   (b) Calculate the volume of the building.

3. A rectangular block has dimensions 20 cm × 7 cm × 7 cm. Find the volume of the largest solid cylinder which can be cut from this block.

4. Brass washers are to be made 2 mm thick with a circular cross section as shown below.

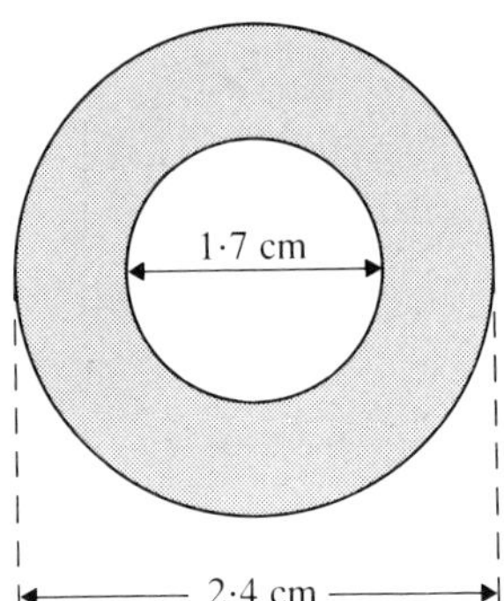

   (a) Find the area of the flat surface of the washer.
   (b) Calculate the volume of the washer.
   (c) Find in cm^3 the volume of brass needed to make 10 000 of these washers.

5. A cylindrical water tank has internal diameter 40 cm and height 50 cm and a cylindrical mug has internal diameter 8 cm and height 10 cm. If the tank is initially full, how many mugs can be filled from the tank?

6. The diagram shows the cross section of a steel girder which is 4 m long.

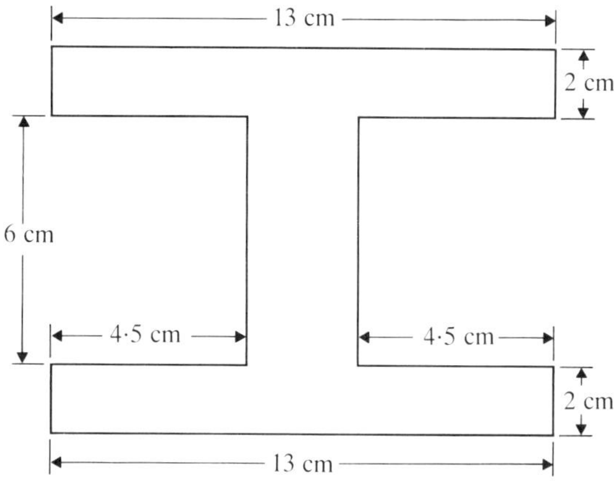

(a) Calculate the cross-sectional area in cm^2.
(b) Calculate the volume of the girder in cm^3.
(c) If 1 cm^3 of steel weighs 7.8 g find the weight of the girder in kg.
(d) How many girders can be carried on a lorry if its total load must not be more than 8 tonnes? (1 tonne = 1000 kg).

7. In the diagram all the angles are right angles and the lengths are in cm. Find the volume.

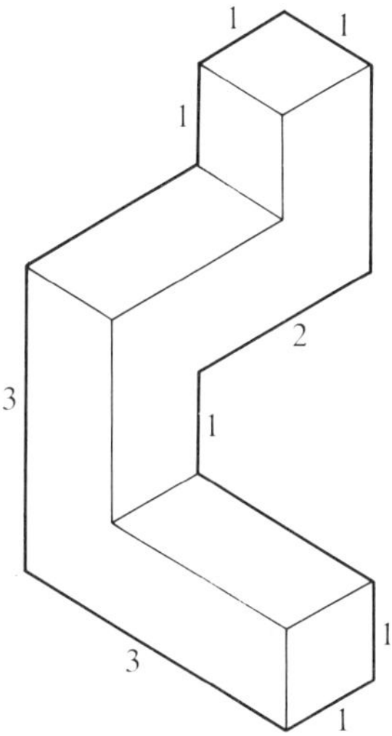

8. Mr Morton builds a fence at the end of his garden. The planks for the fence measure 1 m by 12 cm by 1 cm. The posts to which the planks are nailed are 10 cm square in cross section and 1.40 m long.

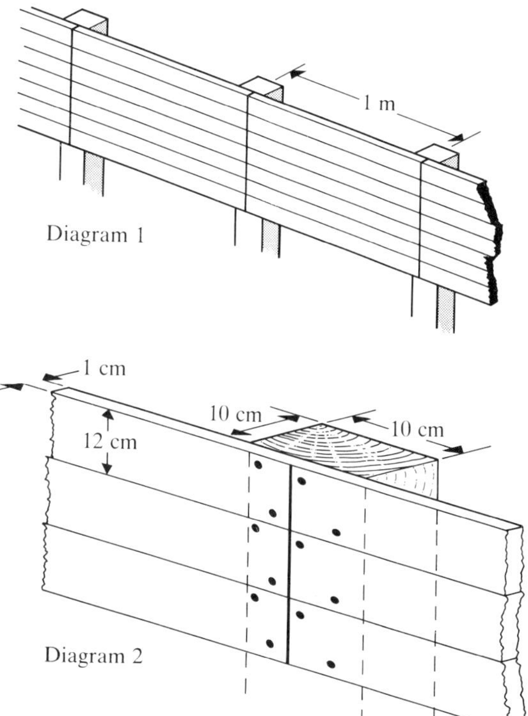

Diagram 1 shows a part of the fence and diagram 2 shows details of its construction.

(a) How many planks are there between each pair of posts?
(b) If the fence is 5 m long,
  (i) how many planks are needed?
  (ii) how many posts are needed? (There is a post at each end of the fence).
(c) Calculate the volume in cm^3 of
  (i) each plank
  (ii) each post
(d) Wood of the required quality costs 4p per 100 cm^3, irrespective of the thickness. Calculate the cost of
  (i) each plank
  (ii) each post
  (iii) all the wood for the whole fence.
(e) Each end of a plank is nailed to a post with two nails. How many nails are needed for the whole fence?

Unit 5

5.1 NEGATIVE NUMBERS

You are used to working with negative numbers when recording low temperatures. On a very cold day the temperature might be −4 °C. This means 4 °C *below freezing*. If the temperature falls by a further 3° the new temperature will be −7 °C.

Exercise 1

1. The temperature in a room is 6 °C. What is the new temperature after a fall of 10°?
2. The temperature in a store is −2 °C. What is the new temperature after a fall of 4°?
3. The temperature in a barn is −3 °C. What is the new temperature after a rise of 8°?
4. Copy and complete the table below.

original temperature	change in temperature	final temperature
(a) 10 °C	fall of 6°	4 °C
(b) 7 °C	fall of 10°	*
(c) −3 °C	rise of 8°	*
(d) −14 °C	rise of 6°	*
(e) 5 °C	−3°	*
(f) 8 °C	−11°	*
(g) 16 °C	−20°	*
(h) −7 °C	+8°	*
(i) −3 °C	+5°	*
(j) −15 °C	+10°	*
(k) −9 °C	+21°	*

original temperature	change in temperature	final temperature
(l) 4 °C	−7°	*
(m) 6 °C	*	10 °C
(n) −3 °C	*	2 °C
(o) 4 °C	*	−2 °C
(p) −2 °C	*	4 °C
(q) −8 °C	*	−5 °C
(r) −7 °C	*	1 °C
(s) *	−3°	7 °C
(t) *	−2°	1 °C
(u) *	−5°	−2 °C
(v) *	−8°	3 °C
(w) *	+4°	7 °C
(x) *	+6°	1 °C
(y) *	+5°	−1 °C
(z) *	+7°	−3 °C

Exercise 2

In questions **1** to **20** state whether true or false.

1. $3<4$ **2.** $10>7$ **3.** $-2<4$
4. $-2>1$ **5.** $4<-3$ **6.** $-3>-6$
7. $3<-5$ **8.** $6>-2$ **9.** $-4<-7$
10. $-6>-10$ **11.** $8<-7$ **12.** $-3>-1$
13. $-4<6$ **14.** $-7>-8$ **15.** $2>-2$
16. $16>-3$ **17.** $-3>0$ **18.** $2<0$
19. $-7<-1$ **20.** $10<-12$

In questions **21** to **40** insert $>$ or $<$ to make a true statement.

21. −2 4 **22.** 3 −5 **23.** −2 −6
24. 3 −1 **25.** 0 4 **26.** −3 0
27. −3 −8 **28.** 9 −7 **29.** −2 1
30. 0 −4 **31.** 8 −8 **32.** 7 −6
33. −3 0 **34.** 1 −1 **35.** −5 $-\frac{1}{2}$
36. $-\frac{1}{2}$ 1 **37.** 0 −8 **38.** −10 −11
39. −3 −7 **40.** 5 −2

In questions **41** to **60** put the numbers in order of size with the smallest first.

41. 2, −3, −4 **42.** −3, 7, −5
43. 0, 5, −5 **44.** 1, −3, −8
45. −4, −1, −2 **46.** 6, −3, 2, −4
47. −1, 3, −2, 1 **48.** −3, 0, −2, 4
49. −3, 1, −5, 4 **50.** −3, 7, −7, 2
51. −1, 0, 4, −4 **52.** −6, 2, −1, −2
53. −4, 5, −1, 6 **54.** −8, −1, 10, −4
55. −8, 7, −3, 1, 0 **56.** −6, 0, −5, −9, 1
57. −1, −3, 5, 4, −2 **58.** 8, −9, −1, 6, −2
59. −3, 5, −4, 1, 4 **60.** −6, −60, 17, 2, −20

In questions **61** to **80** find the next two numbers in each sequence.

61. 10, 8, 6, 4 **62.** 12, 9, 6
63. 3, 2, 1, 0, −1 **64.** 4, 2, 0, −2
65. 12, 6, 0 **66.** −3, −2, −1
67. −8, −6, −4 **68.** 10, 6, 2
69. 15, 5, −5 **70.** −10, −6, −2

71. −7, −4, −1 **72.** 6, 2, −2
73. 2, 3, 5, 8 **74.** 12, 11, 9, 6
75. 0, 1, 3, 6 **76.** 4, 3, 1, −2
77. −10, −9, −7, −4 **78.** 5, 2, −1, −4
79. 24, 10, −4 **80.** −11, −7, −3

Adding and subtracting with negative numbers

−6 + 4 = −2	−3 − 6 = −9
10 − 16 = −6	−8 + 14 = 6
−2 − 10 = −12	3 − 8 = −5

Exercise 3

1. −2 + 6 **2.** 7 − 10 **3.** −2 + 8
4. 8 − 12 **5.** −3 + 10 **6.** −3 + 8
7. 6 − 12 **8.** 8 − 14 **9.** −3 + 1
10. −5 + 6 **11.** −5 + 5 **12.** 7 − 20
13. 4 − 20 **14.** 7 − 6 **15.** −8 + 8
16. −8 + 11 **17.** 17 − 27 **18.** −6 + 1
19. −3 + 2 **20.** 10 − 12 **21.** −6 − 4

22. −7 + 3 **23.** −8 − 5 **24.** −6 − 14
25. −7 − 3 **26.** −8 − 1 **27.** −8 + 1
28. −7 + 2 **29.** 8 − 6 **30.** 4 − 3
31. −6 − 5 **32.** 10 − 24 **33.** −7 − 6
34. 10 − 15 **35.** −8 + 6 **36.** 12 − 24
37. −8 − 15 **38.** −7 − 16 **39.** 8 − 30
40. −7 + 10 **41.** −4 − 14 **42.** 20 − 31

43. 7 − 100 **44.** −8 − 82 **45.** −6 + 30
46. 4 − 50 **47.** −7 − 13 **48.** −9 − 9
49. 8 − 18 **50.** −11 + 11 **51.** −5 − 6
52. 21 − 32 **53.** 7 − 60 **54.** −100 + 1
55. −8 + 38 **56.** −17 − 3 **57.** 10 − 51
58. 17 − 18 **59.** −4 − 17 **60.** 6 − 4

$5 - -6$	$-8 - +4$
$= 5 + 6$	$= -8 - 4$
$= \mathbf{11}$	$= \mathbf{-12}$

Exercise 4

1. $5 + (-4)$
2. $7 + (-3)$
3. $8 + (-4)$
4. $9 - (-5)$
5. $7 - (-3)$
6. $6 - (+4)$
7. $-4 - (-5)$
8. $-10 + (-4)$
9. $-4 - (+4)$
10. $-7 - (-2)$
11. $6 + (-10)$
12. $8 + (-9)$
13. $3 - (-4)$
14. $10 + (-5)$
15. $-3 - (-5)$
16. $6 - (+11)$
17. $-8 + (-12)$
18. $-8 - (+7)$
19. $9 - (+11)$
20. $7 - (-9)$

21. $-5 + (-6)$
22 $-7 - (-13)$
23 $-6 + (-2)$
24. $-8 - (-2)$
25. $7 - (+9)$
26. $3 - (+20)$
27. $-6 + (+6)$
28. $-8 + (-8)$
29. $-2 + (+8)$
30. $7 - (-8)$
31. $19 - (+3)$
32. $6 - (+9)$
33. $-11 - (-3)$
34. $7 + (-14)$
35. $-6 + (-4)$
36. $8 + (+9)$
37. $-7 + (-5)$
38. $-11 - (-11)$
39. $17 - (+15)$
40. $80 - (-15)$

Multiplying and dividing with negative numbers

(a) When the signs are the same, the answer is positive.
(b) When the signs are different, the answer is negative.

$-3 \times (+4) = -12$	$-6 \times (-3) = 18$
$-12 \div (2) = -6$	$-4 \div (-1) = 4$

Exercise 5

1. $-3 \times (+2)$
2. $-4 \times (+1)$
3. $+5 \times (-3)$
4. $-3 \times (-3)$
5. $-4 \times (2)$
6. $-5 \times (3)$
7. $6 \times (-4)$
8. $3 \times (2)$
9. $-3 \times (-4)$
10. $6 \times (-3)$
11. $-7 \times (3)$
12. $-5 \times (-5)$
13. $6 \times (-10)$
14. $-3 \times (-7)$
15. $8 \times (6)$
16. $-8 \times (2)$
17. $-7 \times (6)$
18. $-5 \times (-4)$
19. $-6 \times (7)$
20. $11 \times (-6)$
21. $8 \div (-2)$
22. $-9 \div (3)$
23. $-6 \div (-2)$
24. $10 \div (-2)$
25. $-12 \div (-3)$
26. $-16 \div (4)$
27. $4 \div (-1)$
28. $8 \div (-8)$
29. $16 \div (-8)$
30. $-20 \div (-5)$

31. $-16 \div (1)$
32. $18 \div (-9)$
33. $36 \div (-9)$
34. $-45 \div (-9)$
35. $-70 \div (7)$
36. $-11 \div (-1)$
37. $-16 \div (-1)$
38. $1 \div (-\frac{1}{2})$
39. $-2 \div (\frac{1}{2})$
40. $50 \div (-10)$
41. $-8 \times (-8)$
42. $-9 \times (3)$
43. $10 \times (-60)$
44. $-8 \times (-5)$
45. $-12 \div (-6)$
46. $-18 \times (-2)$
47. $-8 \div (4)$
48. $-80 \div (10)$
49. $-16 \times (-10)$
50. $32 \div (-16)$

Exercise 6

1. $-7 + 3$
2. -3×4
3. $-3 - (-4)$
4. $8 \div (-2)$
5. $-4 \times (-4)$
6. $-8 - 5$
7. $4 + (-2)$
8. -3×1
9. $6 - 12$
10. $0 \times (-7)$
11. $-8 - 4$
12. $-1 \times (-8)$
13. $12 \div (-3)$
14. $10 \times (-10)$
15. $18 - 30$
16. $3 - (+8)$
17. $-16 \div 8$
18. $-7 - 4$
19. -4×5
20. $-8 + 13$

21 $-8 + 2$
22. $3 \times (-3)$
23. $8 \div (-8)$
24. $6 - (-3)$
25. $-6 \times (-1)$
26. -3×0
27. $-6 + 1$
28. $-8 - 7$
29. $-30 + 42$
30. $-2 + (-2)$

Exercise 7

1. -3×9
2. $10 - 23$
3. $-6 - 4$
4. $-7 - (-8)$
5. $12 \div (-6)$
6. -3×0
7. $-3 - (-3)$
8. $4 \times (-100)$
9. $-4 + 20$
10. $-6 \times (-7)$
11. $8 + (-9)$
12. $-3 \times (-11)$
13. $-30 \div (-2)$
14. $10 \times (-6)$
15. $-7 - 6$
16. $20 - 31$
17. 10×20
18. $-8 + 60$
19. $-4 - 40$
20. $0 \div (-8)$

21. $0 + (-9)$
22. $7 \times (-7)$
23. $14 - 24$
24. $-14 - 24$
25. $100 \div (-5)$
26. $-1 \times (-501)$

Exercise 8

1. Copy and complete the addition square below. The numbers inside the square are found by adding together the numbers across the top and down the side.

add	−2	1	4	0	−3	6	−1	5
−3		−2						
2								
4								
−2								
−1						5		
5								
−4								
1								

2. Copy and complete the multiplication square below. The numbers inside the square are found by multiplying together the numbers across the top and down the side.

multiply	−2	5	2	6	−4	0	−3	3
3	−6							
−1								
−2					8			
4								
5								
−4								
1								
−3								

5.2 USING LETTERS FOR NUMBERS

A large number of everyday problems can be solved using ordinary arithmetic with ordinary numbers. For example: 'work out 25% of £75'; 'take £8.85 away from £12.60'; 'divide 12.6 kg into ten equal parts'.

There are, however, an even larger number of mathematical problems which are much easier to solve when letters are used instead of numbers. Computer programs make use of algebra in statements like 'LET X = 2' or 'IF Y > 10 GO TO 70'.

Find what number I am left with.
(a) I start with x, multiply it by 7 and then add 10.
(b) I start with t, subtract 3 and then multiply the result by 5.

(a) $x \rightarrow 7x \rightarrow 7x + 10$
(b) $t \rightarrow t - 3 \rightarrow 5(t - 3)$

Exercise 9

In each question, find what number I am left with.

1. I start with x, multiply it by 3 and then add 6
2. I start with x, multiply it by 5 and then add 7
3. I start with x, double it and then subtract 4
4. I start with x, treble it and then add 10
5. I start with y, multiply it by 6 and then add 3
6. I start with y, double it and then subtract 7
7. I start with m, multiply it by 5 and then subtract 8
8. I start with x, multiply it by 6 and then subtract y
9. I start with y, treble it and then add t
10. I start with p, multiply it by 6 and then subtract a
11. I start with x, add 4 and then multiply the result by 3 [Hint: use brackets].
12. I start with x, add 3 and then multiply the result by 5

13. I start with y, add 11 and then multiply the result by 6
14. I start with m, subtract 5 and then multiply the result by 9
15. I start with t, multiply by 5 and then subtract 7
16. I start with x, subtract 6 and then multiply the result by 4
17. I start with x, add 3 and then divide the result by 4. [Hint: If you divide m by 5, write $\frac{m}{5}$ rather than $m \div 5$].
18. I start with x, subtract 7 and then divide the result by 3
19. I start with y, subtract 8 and then divide the result by 5
20. I start with x, add m and then divide the result by 7
21. I start with $2x$, add 7 and then multiply the result by 3
22. I start with $3x$, subtract y and then divide the result by 5
23. I start with $4a$, add 3, multiply the result by 2 and then divide the final result by 5
24. I start with m, subtract 6, multiply the result by 3 and then divide the final result by 4
25. I start with t, add x, multiply the result by 4 and then divide the final result by 5
26. I start with x, square it and then add 4
27. I start with x, square it and then subtract 6
28. I start with x, square it, add 3 and then divide the result by 4.
29. I start with n, add 2 and then square the result. [Use brackets]
30. I start with w, subtract x and then square the result
31. I start with y, add t and then square the result
32. I start with x, square it, subtract 7 and then divide the result by 3
33. I start with x, square it, multiply by 3 and then add 4.
34. I start with y, square it, add 4 and then multiply the result by 2
35. I start with a, cube it, subtract 3 and then divide the result by 7.
36. I start with z, cube it, add 6 and then divide the result by 8
37. I start with p, square it, subtract x and then multiply the result by 4
38. I start with x, subtract 9, square the result and then add 10
39. I start with y, add 7, square the result and then divide by x
40. I start with a, subtract x, cube the result and then divide by y.

Exercise 10

1. A plant is x cm tall at the beginning of the summer. During the summer it grows a further y cm and then the gardener prunes off 7 cm. How tall is it now?
2. When a man buys a small tree it is l cm tall. During the year it grows a further t cm and then he prunes off 10 cm. How tall is it now?
3. A piece of wood is l cm long. If I cut off a piece 3 cm long, how much wood remains?
4. A piece of string is 15 cm long. How much remains after I cut off a piece of length x cm?
5. A car in a showroom costs £c. The price goes up by £200 but is then reduced in a sale by £5. What is the cost in the sale?
6. The price of a book is x pence. The price goes up by 25p but is then reduced in a sale by y pence. What is the cost of the book?
7. On Thursday there are n people in a cinema. On Friday there are three times as many plus another 55. How many people are there in the cinema on Friday?
8. A soldier on an exercise crawls a distance of c metres, then walks a distance of w metres and finally runs a distance of 2000 metres. How far does he go?
9. A slug walks a distance of y cm, crawls a further d cm and finally runs x cm. How far does it go?

10. An athlete runs t km on Monday. On Tuesday she runs twice as far plus another 3 km. How far does she run (a) on Tuesday, (b) altogether on Monday and Tuesday?

11. A car dealer buys a car at an auction for £x. He puts it on sale at twice the price plus another £100. What is the price of the car?

12. A delivery van weighs l kg. At a depot it picks up goods weighing 200 kg and later delivers goods weighing m kg. How much does it weigh after making the delivery?

13. A box usually contains n chocolates. The shopkeeper puts an extra 2 chocolates into each box. A girl buys 4 boxes. How many chocolates does she have?

14. A brick weighs w kg. How much do six bricks weigh?

15. A sack weighs l kg. How much do x sacks weigh?

16. A man shares a sum of n pence equally between six children. How much does each child receive?

17. A sum of £p is shared equally between you and four others. How much does each person receive?

18. A cake weighing 12 kg is cut into n equal pieces. How much does each piece weigh?

19. A pie weighing m kg is shared equally between you and three others. How much does each person receive?

20. A small bag of sweets contains x sweets. A large bag contains three times as many sweets. John buys a large bag and then eats 11 sweets. How many sweets are left?

5.3 SUBSTITUTING FOR LETTERS

Exercise 11

1. $a = 3, b = 4, c = -1, d = -2, e = 5,$
$v = -2, w = -3, x = 6, y = 0, z = 2$

Copy and complete the table below. The number in each square is found by adding the numbers represented by the two letters in each square, for example $a + v = 1$.

a v 1	b v	d z	c x	d w
b y	c z	a z	e z	e x
e v	a w	b w	d y	c y
c w	d x	e w	a x	b x
d v	e y	c v	b z	a y

2. $f = 4, g = -2, h = 5, i = -1, j = 3,$
$p = -1, q = 3, r = -2, s = 4, t = -3$

Copy and complete the table below. The number in each square is found by subtracting the second letter from the first letter in each square, for example $f - p = 5$.

f p 5	h s	g r	i r	j s
g q	j q	i p	f s	h t
i q	f q	h q	g t	i t
h r	i s	j t	j r	f t
j f	g p	f r	h p	g s

3. Use the values for $a, b, c, d, e, v, w, x, y, z$ given in question **1**. Complete the table given in question **1**, but this time multiply together the two letters in each square, for example $av = -6$.

If $m = 3$, $n = -2$ and $t = 4$ find the value of (a) $m + n$, (b) $n - t$

(a) $m + n$
$= 3 + -2$
$= 3 - 2$
$= \mathbf{1}$

(b) $n - t$
$= -2 - 4$
$= \mathbf{-6}$

Work down the page. It is easier to follow.

Exercise 12

If $a = 3$, $b = 5$, $c = 1$, $d = 7$, work out

1. $a + c$	**2.** $a - d$
3. $b - c$	**4.** $b + d$
5. $c + d$	**6.** $a - 8$
7. $b + 2$	**8.** $d - 4$
9. $c + 5$	**10.** $5 + d$
11. $a - b$	**12.** $a + 11$
13. $d - a$	**14.** $8 + d$
15. $c - 3$	**16.** $d - 10$
17. $c + 6$	**18.** $c - b$
19. $7 - b$	**20.** $d + a$

If $n = 5$, $t = 2$, $x = 0$, $y = 4$, work out

21. $x + n$	**22.** $y - t$
23. $x - y$	**24.** $5 + n$
25. $y + n$	**26.** $x - t$
27. $t - 10$	**28.** $t + x$
29. $4 - y$	**30.** $n + 10$
31. $x + y - t$	**32.** $t - n - 5$
33. $y - t + 2$	**34.** $y + t + n$
35. $x - 10 - y$	**36.** $x - t - 13$
37. $7 + t - n$	**38.** $n - 9 + y$
39. $3 + t - x$	**40.** $2 - y - t$

Exercise 13

Work out the answers to questions **1** to **20** of Exercise 12 with $a = 2$, $b = -3$, $c = 0$, $d = 5$.

Work out the answers to questions **21** to **40** of Exercise 12 with $n = -1$, $t = 3$, $x = 2$, $y = -2$.

If $l = 5$, $m = -2$, $x = 3$, work out (a) $4x$, (b) lm

(a) $4x = 4 \times 3$
$= \mathbf{12}$

(b) $lm = 5 \times -2$
$= \mathbf{-10}$

Exercise 14

If $a = 4$, $b = -2$, $c = -3$, $d = 2$, $x = 3$, $y = -1$ work out

1. $3c$	**2.** ab	**3.** $2a$	**4.** $4d$
5. $6a$	**6.** $3d$	**7.** xc	**8.** $9c$
9. ya	**10.** $6c$	**11.** $8b$	**12.** $4y$
13. $6y$	**14.** bc	**15.** $5c$	**16.** $10d$
17. cd	**18.** $7a$	**19.** da	**20.** $2x$
21. $4c$	**22.** $9a$	**23.** $10b$	**24.** $4b$
25. $3a$	**26.** $2c$	**27.** bx	**28.** ax
29. $5b$	**30.** xd	**31.** $3y$	**32.** $11b$
33. ac	**34.** $5a$	**35.** $9b$	**36.** $7c$
37. $2b$	**38.** $10a$	**39.** $5x$	**40.** $9x$
41. $8d$	**42.** db	**43.** $4a$	**44.** $3b$
45. $11y$	**46.** $8y$	**47.** $2d$	**48.** yb
49. $3x$	**50.** $11x$	**51.** yc	**52.** $10c$
53. $10x$	**54.** $7x$	**55.** $10y$	**56.** $11a$
57. xy	**58.** $2y$	**59.** $4x$	**60.** dy

Exercise 15

Work out the answers to questions **1** to **60** of Exercise 14 with $a = 2$, $b = -4$, $c = 5$, $d = -3$, $x = -7$, $y = -6$.

If $x = 3$, $y = -4$, work out
(a) $2x + y$ (b) $xy - y$

(a) $2x + y$
$= 6 + -4$
$= 6 - 4$
$= \mathbf{2}$

(b) $xy - y$
$= -12 - -4$
$= -12 + 4$
$= \mathbf{-8}$

Do some of the working in your head

Exercise 16

If $a = -4$, $b = 5$, $c = -2$, work out

1. $2a + 3$	**2.** $3b - 7$
3. $4a - 1$	**4.** $2b + c$
5. $5c - 2a$	**6.** $6a - 3$
7. $2c + b$	**8.** $3a - 2b$
9. $6c - 2b$	**10.** $3c + 4a$
11. $3c - 4$	**12.** $2a - 3c$

13. $7b + 3a$ **14.** $8a + 6c$
15. $2b - 4a$ **16.** $4b + 5$
17. $3a + 8$ **18.** $2c - a$
19. $5a - 2c$ **20.** $3b + 7$

If $n = 3$, $x = -1$, $y = 6$, work out
21. $2x - 3$ **22.** $3y + 4n$
23. $5n + 2x$ **24.** $4y - x$
25. $7y - 2$ **26.** $3x + 2n$
27. $10x + 5$ **28.** $6x - y$
29. $4x - 5y$ **30.** $2y - 10$
31. $8n - 2y$ **32.** $7n + 3y$
33. $6y + 4$ **34.** $4n + 5x$
35. $2n + 3x$ **36.** $5y - 20$
37. $9y - n$ **38.** $8x + 2n$
39. $5x + 6$ **40.** $3n - 2x$

If $m = 3$, $h = -2$, $k = 4$, $t = -3$, work out
41. $2m + h - 2t$ **42.** $3k + 7 + 6t$
43. $hk - m + 3t$ **44.** $mt + 2h - 8$
45. $5k + 2 + 3h$ **46.** $2t - 3k - 2h$
47. $th - 2k - m$ **48.** $tk - m + 5h$
49. $3h + 10t - 9$ **50.** $6 - 8k - t$

Exercise 17

Work out the answers to questions **1** to **20** of Exercise 16 with $a = 3$, $b = -2$, $c = 4$.

Work out the answers to questions **21** to **40** of Exercise 16 with $n = -3$, $x = 2$, $y = -1$.

Work out the answers to questions **41** to **50** of Exercise 16 with $m = -2$, $h = 7$, $k = -1$, $t = -5$.

$a^2 = a \times a$

$a^3 = a \times a \times a$

$2a^2 = 2(a^2)$

$(2a)^2 = 2a \times 2a$

$a(b - c)$: Work out the term in brackets first

$\frac{a+b}{c}$: The division line works like a bracket, so workout $a + b$ first.

If $x = 2$, $y = -3$, work out

(a) y^2, (b) $3x^2$

(a) $y^2 = -3 \times -3$
$= \mathbf{9}$

(b) $3x^2 = 3 \times 4$
$= \mathbf{12}$

Exercise 18

If $m = 2$, $t = -2$, $x = -3$, $y = 4$, work out
1. m^2 **2.** t^2
3. x^2 **4.** y^2
5. m^3 **6.** t^3
7. x^3 **8.** y^3
9. $2m^2$ **10.** $(2m)^2$
11. $2t^2$ **12.** $(2t)^2$
13. $2x^2$ **14.** $(2x)^2$
15. $3y^2$ **16.** $4m^2$
17. $5t^2$ **18.** $6x^2$
19. $(3y)^2$ **20.** $3m^3$

21. $x^2 + 4$ **22.** $y^2 - 6$
23. $t^2 - 3$ **24.** $m^3 + 10$
25. $x^2 + t^2$ **26.** $2x^2 + 1$
27. $m^2 + xt$ **28.** my^2
29. $(mt)^2$ **30.** $(xy)^2$
31. $(xt)^2$ **32.** yx^2
33. $m - t$ **34.** $t - x$
35. $y - m$ **36.** $m - y^2$
37. $t + x$ **38.** $2m + 3x$
39. $3t - y$ **40.** $xt + y$

41. $3(m + t)$ **42.** $4(x + y)$
43. $5(m + 2y)$ **44.** $2(y - m)$
45. $m(t + x)$ **46.** $y(m + x)$
47. $x(y - m)$ **48.** $t(2m + y)$
49. $m^2(y - x)$ **50.** $t^2(x^2 + m)$

51. $\frac{2y+t}{3}$ **52.** $\frac{2t+m}{2}$

53. $\frac{x+t}{5}$ **54.** $\frac{y-t}{m}$

55. $\frac{y-m}{t^2}$ **56.** $\frac{x^2+m}{11}$

Exercise 19

Work out the answers to questions **1** to **56** of Exercise 18 with $m = -1$, $t = -4$, $x = 3$, $y = -5$.

5.4 COLLECTING LIKE TERMS

$7x + 3 + 3x + 5 + x = 11x + 8$
$3a + 2b - 2 + 4a + 7 = 7a + 2b + 5$
$x^2 + 3x + 9 + 4x + 3x^2 = 4x^2 + 7x + 9$
$2x - 3y + 2xy + 5x + 3xy = 7x - 3y + 5xy$

Exercise 20

Collect like terms together.

1. $2x + 3 + 3x + 5$
2. $4x + 8 + 5x - 3$
3. $5x - 3 + 2x + 7$
4. $6x + 1 + x + 3$
5. $4x - 3 + 2x + 10 + x$
6. $5x + 8 + x + 4 + 2x$
7. $7x - 9 + 2x + 3 + 3x$
8. $5x + 7 - 3x - 2$
9. $4x - 6 - 2x + 1$
10. $10x + 5 - 9x - 10 + x$

11. $6x - 3 + 2x - 5 + x - 1$
12. $3x + 2 - x - 7 + x$
13. $10x - 7 - 4x + 8 + 3x + 5$
14. $11x + 4 - x - 4 + 3x$
15. $6x - 5 - 5x + 10 - x + 1$
16. $5y - 6 + 2y + 4$
17. $3y + 4 + 6y - 6 + y$
18. $2y + 10 - y - 10 + 3y$
19. $5y - 6 - 4y - 2 - y$
20. $11y + 3 - 8y + 5 + y$

21. $4a + 6b + 3 + 9a - 3b - 4$
22. $8m - 3n + 1 + 6n + 2m + 7$
23. $6p - 4 + 5q - 3p - 4 - 7q$
24. $12s - 3t + 2 - 10s - 4t + 12$
25. $a - 2b - 7 + a + 2b + 8$
26. $3x + 2y + 5z - 2x - y + 2z$
27. $6x - 5y + 3z - x + y + z$
28. $2k - 3m + n + 3k - m - n$
29. $12a - 3 + 2b - 6 - 8a + 3b$
30. $3a + x + e - 2a - 5x - 6e$

Remember: You cannot add x^2 to $3x$
You cannot add y^2 to $5y$
You cannot add xy to $4x$

Exercise 21

Collect like terms together.

1. $x^2 + 3x + 2 + 4x + 1$
2. $x^2 + 4x + 3 + 3x + 5$
3. $x^2 + 5x + 2 - 2x + 1$
4. $x^2 + 2x + 2x^2 + 4x + 5$
5. $x^2 + 5x + x^2 + x - 7$
6. $2x^2 - 3x + 8 + x^2 + 4x + 4$
7. $3x^2 + 4x + 6 - x^2 - 3x - 3$
8. $5x^2 - 3x + 2 - 3x^2 + 2x - 2$
9. $2x^2 - 2x + 3 - x^2 - 2x - 5$
10. $6x^2 - 7x + 8 - 3x^2 + 5x - 10$

11. $3a^2 + 2a + 4 - 3a^2 + 6a + 5$
12. $m^2 + 6m - 7 + m^2 + 2m - 3$
13. $8 - 3x - x^2 + 2 + 4x - 2x^2$
14. $10 + 2x + x^2 - 8 - 6x - 4x^2$
15. $17 - 2t + 2t^2 + 4t + 5 + 2t$
16. $18 + t^2 - 3t + 5 + t^2 + 3t - 2t^2$
17. $n^2 - 2n + 3 + 2n^2 + 1 + 2n - 3n^2$
18. $3x^2 + 10 - 6x + 19 - x + x^2$
19. $5 - 2x - 3x^2 - 1 + x + x^2$
20. $2x^2 + 10x - 5 - 5 + x - 2x^2 + 10$

21. $x^2 + 2xy + 3x + 2x + 3xy$
22. $3x^2 + 4xy - 2x + x^2 + 2xy$
23. $5x^2 - 3x + 2xy + 2x^2 + 4x + 6xy$
24. $4x^2 + 6x + 4xy + x^2 - 5x - 2xy$
25. $x^2 - 5x - 2xy + 6x + 3x^2 + 5xy$
26. $m^2 + 4m + 2mn + 3m^2 - 2m + mn$
27. $a^2 - 3a + 2ab + 7a^2 - 2a + 2ab$
28. $c^2 + 3c + 4cd - c^2 - 3c + 2cd$
29. $z^2 - 3z + 2xz + 2z^2 + 8z + 8xz$
30. $5p^2 - 7p + 2pq - p^2 - 3p - 2pq$

31. $3y^2 - 6x + y^2 + x^2 + 7x + 4x^2$
32. $8 - 5x - 2x^2 + 4 + 6x + 2x^2$
33. $5 + 2y + 3y^2 - 8y - 6 + 2y^2 + 3$
34. $ab + a^2 - 3b + 2ab - a^2$
35. $3c^2 - d^2 + 2cd - 3c^2 - d^2$
36. $ab + 2a^2 + 3ab - 4a^2 + 2a$
37. $x^3 + 2x^2 - x + 3x^2 + x^3 + x$
38. $5 - x^2 - 2x^3 + 6 + 2x^2 + 3x^3$
39. $xy + ab - cd + 2xy - ab + dc$
40. $pq - 3qp + p^2 + 2qp - q^2$

Exercise 22

Find the perimeter of each of the following shapes. All the lengths are given in cm. Give the answers in the simplest form.

1.

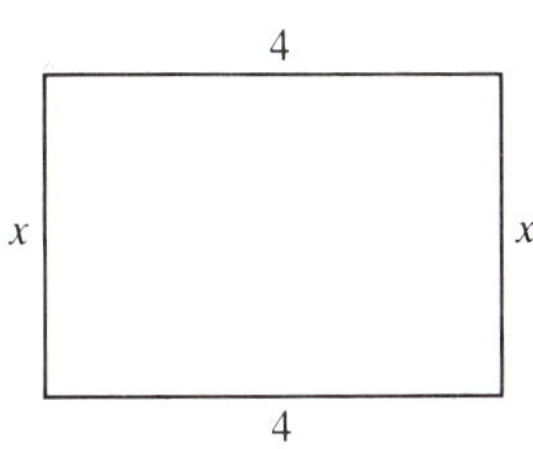

2.

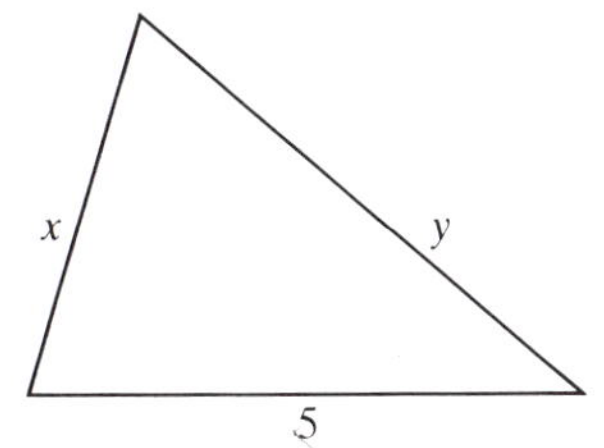

3.

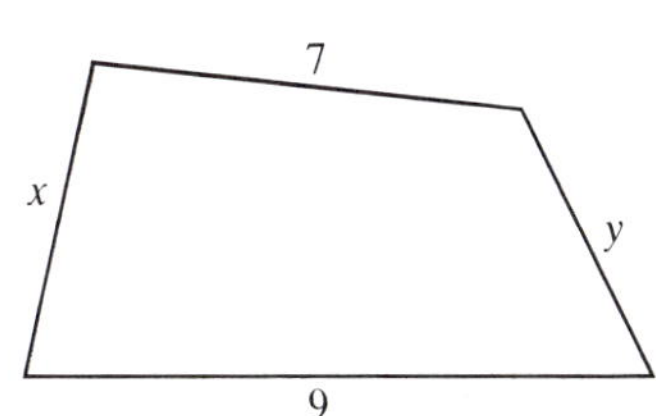

4.

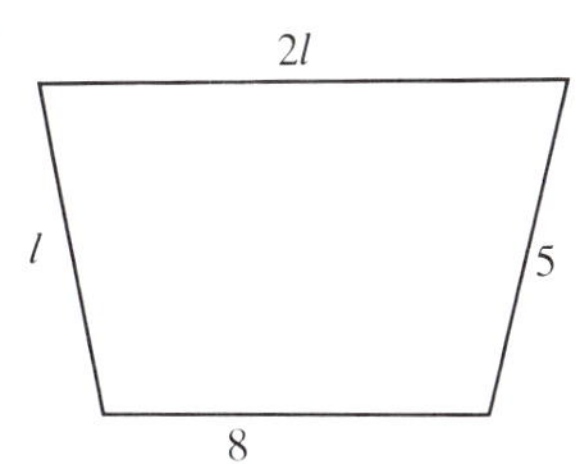

5.

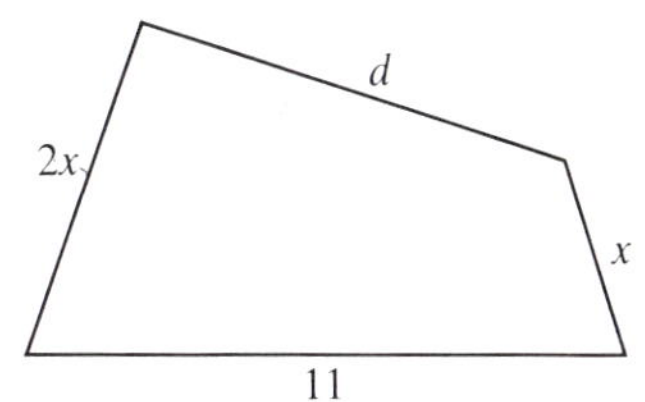

6.

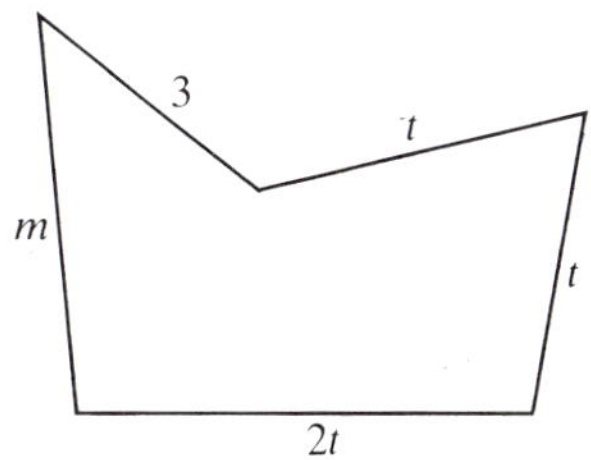

7.

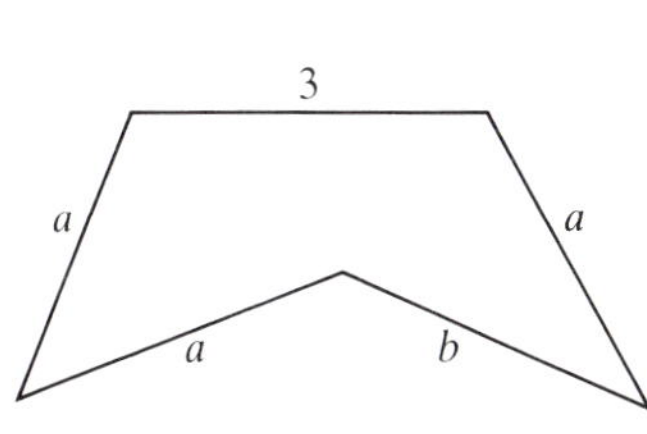

8.

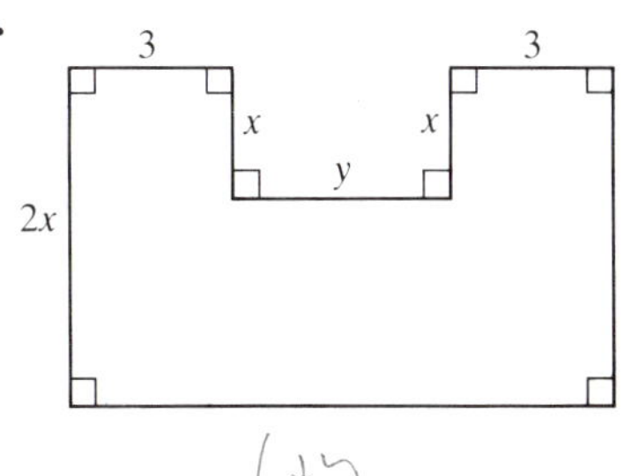

9.

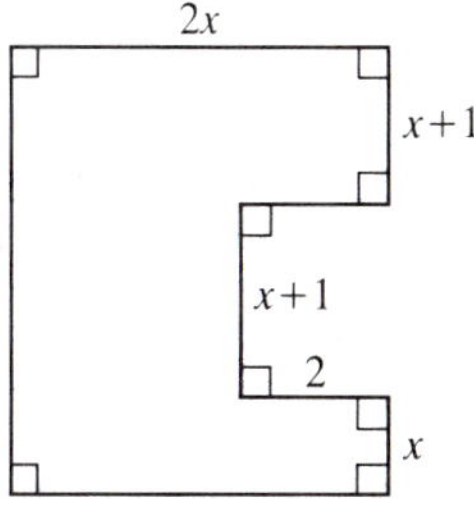

5.5 SIMPLIFYING TERMS AND BRACKETS

$3 \times 4x = 12x$	$x \times 3x = 3x^2$
$8 \times 6y = 48y$	$2z \times 4z = 8z^2$
$-3 \times 2x = -6x$	$4(2x \times 3x) = 24x^2$

Exercise 23

Write in a more simple form.

1. $2 \times 3x$ **2.** $4 \times 2x$ **3.** $3 \times 2x$
4. $5 \times 3x$ **5.** $3 \times 2y$ **6.** $4 \times 5y$
7. $7 \times 3x$ **8.** $-2 \times 3x$ **9.** $-5 \times 4x$
10. $-2 \times 5x$ **11.** $7 \times 4a$ **12.** $5 \times 3a$
13. $2x \times 3$ **14.** $3y \times 4$ **15.** $5y \times 5$
16. $x \times 2x$ **17.** $x \times 4x$ **18.** $x \times 6x$
19. $y \times 3y$ **20.** $y \times 10y$ **21.** $x \times 7x$
22. $a \times 5a$ **23.** $2x \times 3x$ **24.** $3x \times 4x$
25. $2x \times 5x$ **26.** $4x \times 2x$ **27.** $7x \times 2x$
28. $6x \times 3x$ **29.** $5y \times 2y$ **30.** $4t \times 6t$

31. $x \times 2x^2$ **32.** $2x \times 3x^2$ **33.** $4y \times y^2$
34. $3a \times 2a^2$ **35.** $3y \times 3y^2$ **36.** $5x^2 \times x$
37. $7p \times 3p$ **38.** $2(3x \times 2x)$ **39.** $4(3x \times 5x)$
40. $5(2x \times 3x)$ **41.** $3(2x \times 5x^2)$ **42.** $2(x \times 6x^2)$
43. $4(x \times x^2)$ **44.** $3(2y \times 2y)$ **45.** $6(a \times 2a^2)$

46. $x \times 3x^3$ **47.** $y \times 2x$ **48.** $2a \times 3a^2$
49. $2a \times 3b$ **50.** $2p \times 5q$ **51.** $3x \times 5y$
52. $6x \times 3x^2$ **53.** $3a \times 8a^3$ **54.** $3(3x \times 4x^2)$
55. $ab \times 2a$ **56.** $xy \times 3y$ **57.** $cd \times 5c$
58. $ab \times ab$ **59.** $2xy \times xy$ **60.** $3d \times 2c$

Exercise 24

Write down the area of each shape in its simplest form. All lengths are in cm.

1.

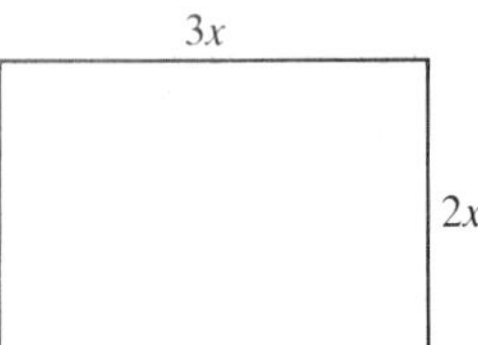

2.

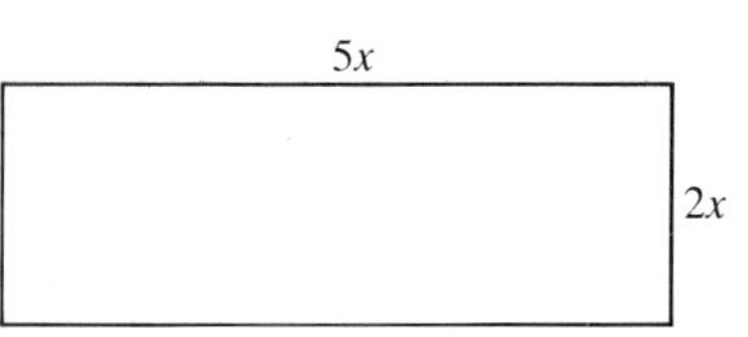

3.

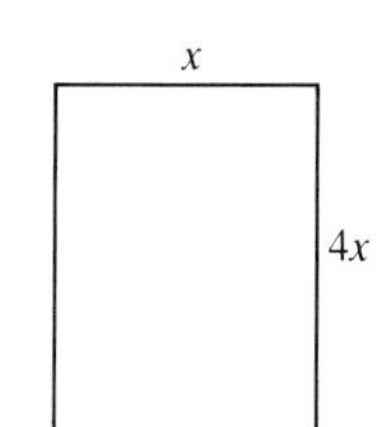

4.

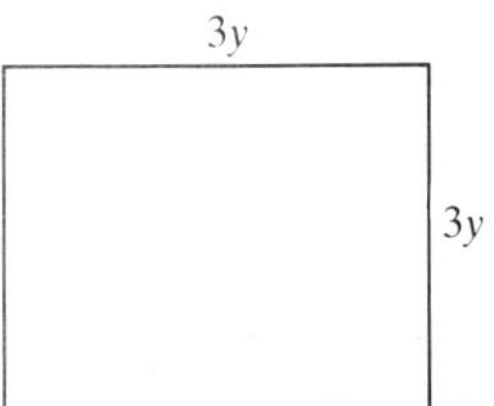

5.

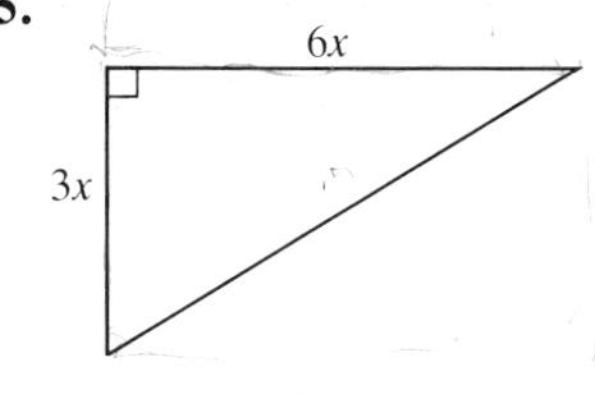

6.

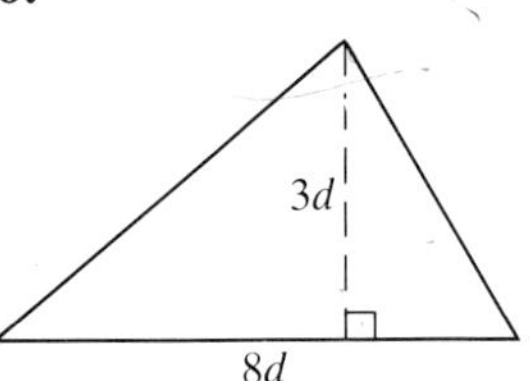

7.

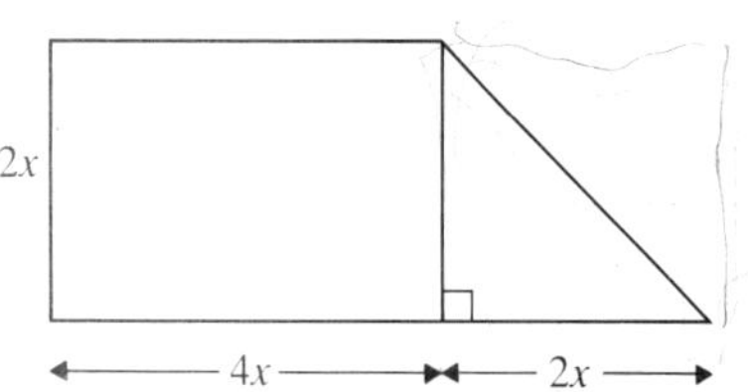

8.

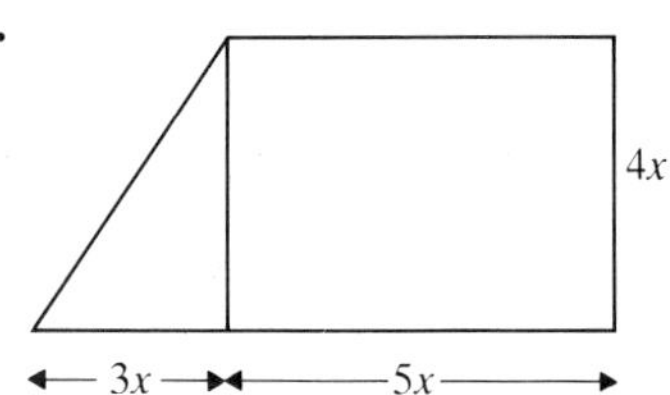

9.

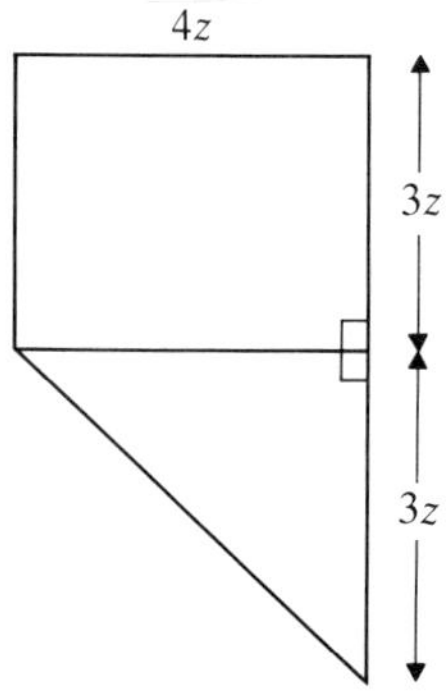

> Remove the brackets
> $3(x-2) = 3x - 6$
> $4(2x+3) = 8x + 12$
> $x(2x-3) = 2x^2 - 3x$
> $-2x(x-4) = -2x^2 + 8x$

Exercise 25

Remove the brackets

1. $2(x+3)$	**2.** $3(x+5)$	**21.** $-2(2x+3)$	**22.** $-4(2x+1)$
3. $4(x+6)$	**4.** $2(2x+1)$	**23.** $-3(x+2)$	**24.** $-2(3x+4)$
5. $5(2x+3)$	**6.** $4(3x-1)$	**25.** $-2(4x-1)$	**26.** $-5(2x-2)$
7. $6(2x-2)$	**8.** $3(5x-2)$	**27.** $-3(2x+1)$	**28.** $-(2x+1)$
9. $5(3x-4)$	**10.** $7(2x-3)$	**29.** $-(3x+2)$	**30.** $-(4x-5)$
11. $2(2x+3)$	**12.** $3(2x+1)$	**31.** $x(x+3)$	**32.** $x(x+5)$
13. $5(x+4)$	**14.** $6(2x+2)$	**33.** $x(x-2)$	**34.** $x(x-3)$
15. $4(x+3)$	**16.** $12(x+7)$	**35.** $x(2x+1)$	**36.** $x(3x-2)$
17. $3(2x-3)$	**18.** $10(x+4)$	**37.** $x(3x+5)$	**38.** $2x(x-1)$
19. $9(2x+5)$	**20.** $8(3x-6)$	**39.** $2x(x+2)$	**40.** $3x(2x+3)$

Exercise 26

1. Three rods A, B and C have lengths of x, $(x + 1)$ and $(x - 2)$ cm respectively, as shown

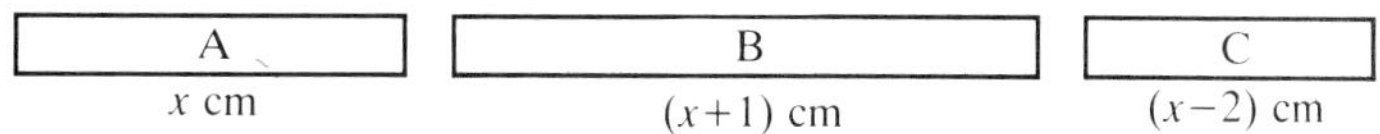

In the diagrams below express the length l in terms of x. Give your answers in their simplest form.

(a)
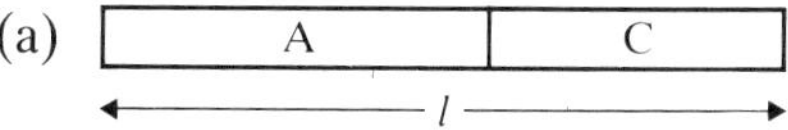

(b)
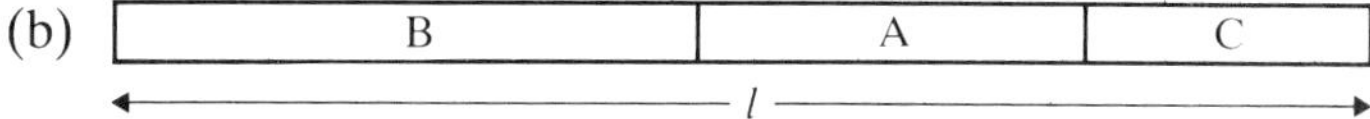

(c)
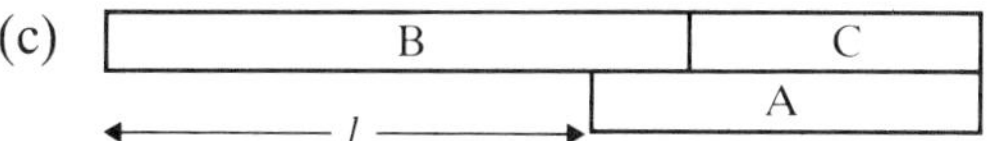

(d)
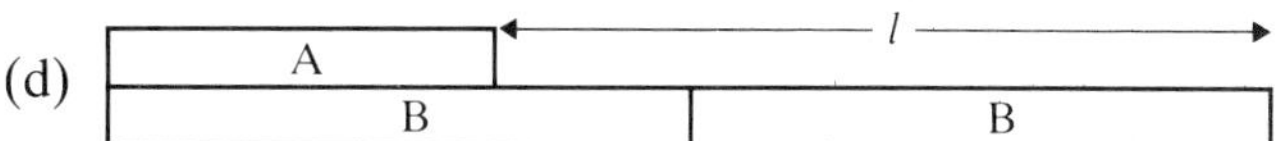

(e)
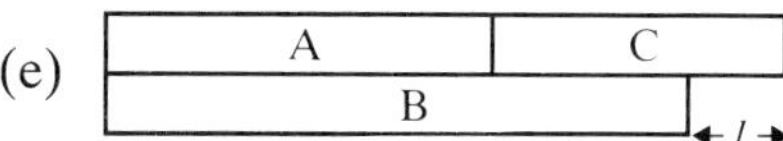

(f)
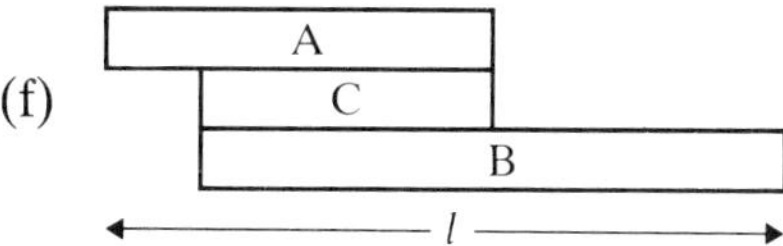

(g)
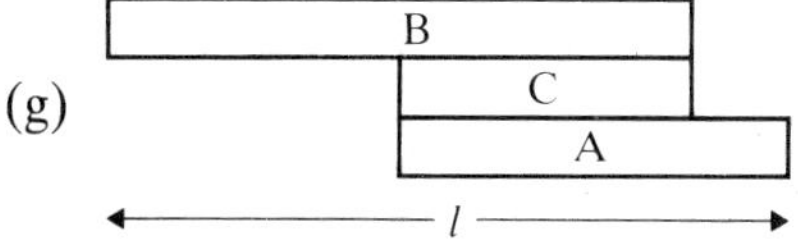

2. Four rods A, B, C and D have lengths as shown below.

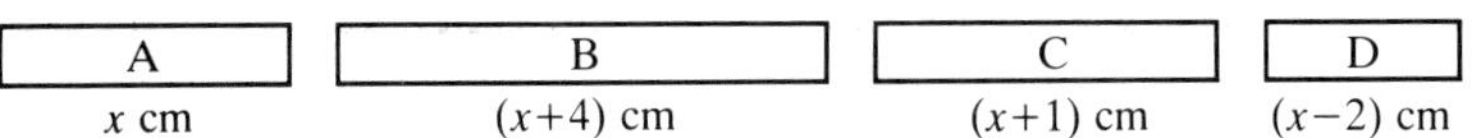

In the diagrams below express the length l in terms of x.
Give your answers in their simplest form.

(a)
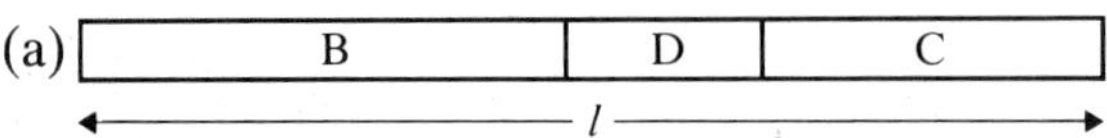

(b)
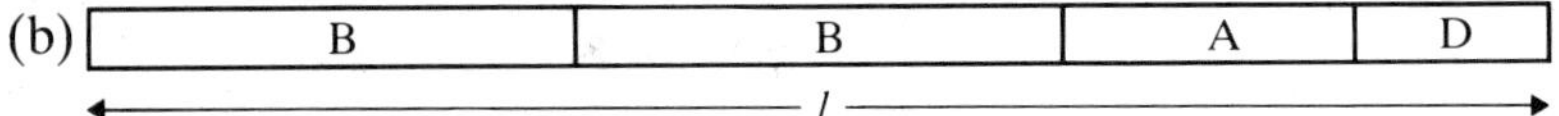

(c)

(d)
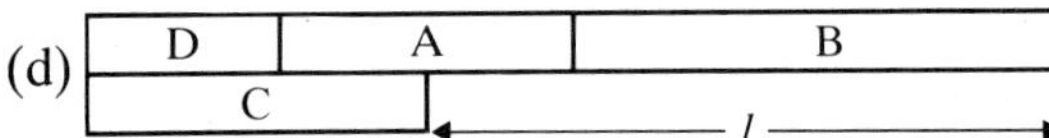

(e)
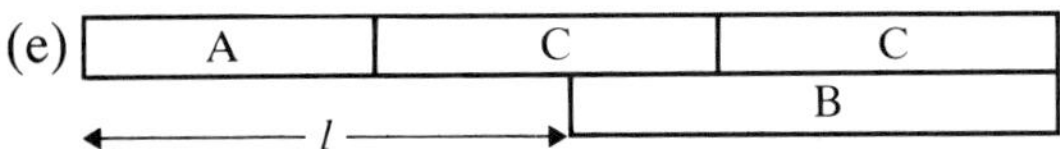

(f)
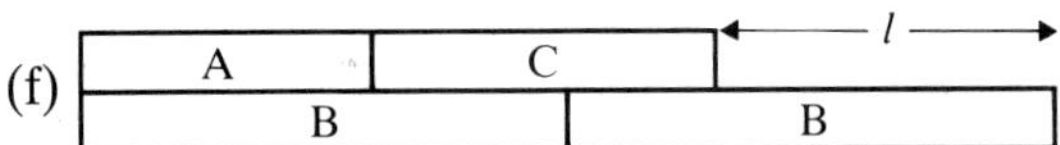

(g)
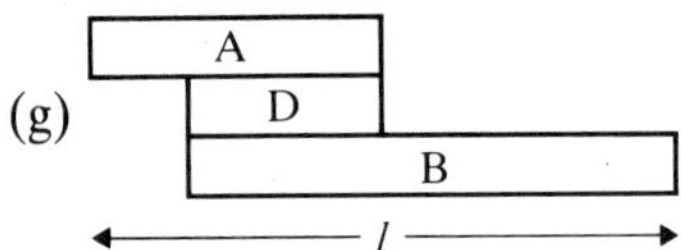

(h)
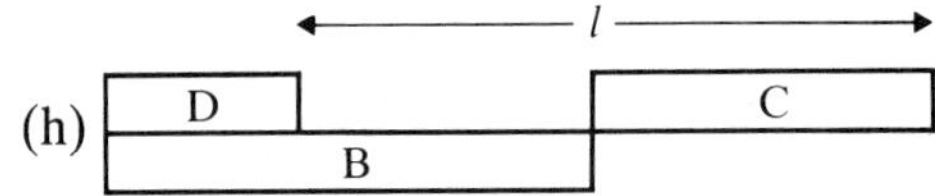

(i)
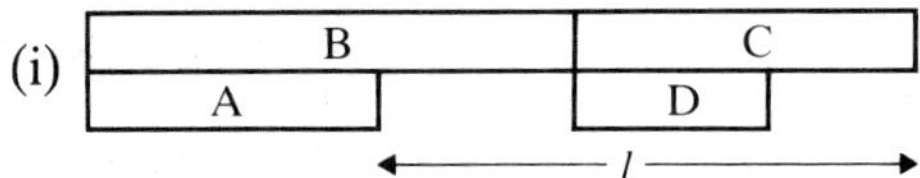

Unit 6

6.1 SOLVING EQUATIONS

(a) $x - 3 = 8$	(b) $7 + y = 2$
$x = 8 + 3$	$y = 2 - 7$
$x = \mathbf{11}$	$y = \mathbf{-5}$

Exercise 1

Solve the equations.

1. $x - 3 = 5$ **2.** $x - 4 = 6$
3. $x - 2 = 11$ **4.** $x + 5 = 8$
5. $x + 7 = 12$ **6.** $x + 15 = 21$
7. $x - 3 = 1$ **8.** $x + 4 = 5$
9. $x - 8 = 0$ **10.** $x + 4 = 2$
11. $x + 6 = 3$ **12.** $x + 8 = 3$

13. $y - 7 = -5$ **14.** $y - 8 = -10$
15. $y + 10 = 20$ **16.** $y + 9 = 4$
17. $y - 7 = -6$ **18.** $y + 25 = 15$
19. $4 + x = 9$ **20.** $5 + x = 7$
21. $8 + x = 24$ **22.** $a + 6 = -2$
23. $a - 7 = -3$ **24.** $a + 6 = 0$
25. $7 = x + 2$ **26.** $9 = x - 3$
27. $15 = x + 4$ **28.** $12 = x - 7$
29. $5 = x + 11$ **30.** $16 = x - 7$
31. $18 = 9 + x$ **32.** $23 = 11 + x$
33. $-10 = x + 6$ **34.** $7 = 6 + x$
35. $18 = 13 + x$ **36.** $-5 = 7 + x$

(a) $3x = 15$	(b) $4x = 3$
$x = \frac{15}{3}$	$x = \frac{3}{4}$
$x = 5$	

Exercise 2

Solve the equations.

1. $3x = 9$ **2.** $2x = 12$
3. $4x = 28$ **4.** $5x = 30$

5. $7x = 56$
6. $4x = 36$
7. $9x = 81$
8. $9x = 90$
9. $6x = 180$
10. $12x = 60$
11. $10x = 1000$
12. $8x = 96$

13. $5x = 2$
14. $7x = 5$
15. $8x = 3$
16. $4x = 1$
17. $2x = 1$
18. $9x = 5$
19. $3x = 5$
20. $4x = 7$
21. $3x = 7$
22. $2x = 9$
23. $3x = 10$
24. $5x = 11$

25. $5x = -4$
26. $6x = -24$
27. $5x = -10$
28. $4x = -36$
29. $3x = -2$
30. $12x = -1$
31. $7x = -10$
32. $5x = 1$
33. $4x = -9$
34. $10x = -10$
35. $18x = -18$
36. $17x = -68$

37. $8 = 4x$
38. $10 = 2x$
39. $12 = 3y$
40. $72 = 9a$
41. $6 = 5a$
42. $15 = 2z$
43. $-8 = 2y$
44. $-7 = 2x$
45. $9 = -3m$
46. $15 = -5n$
47. $-20 = -2x$
48. $-40 = -4y$

(a) $\frac{x}{2} = 4$
$x = 4 \times 2$
$x = 8$

(b) $\frac{x}{5} = -3$
$x = -3 \times 5$
$x = -15$

Exercise 3

Solve the equations.

1. $\frac{x}{3} = 4$
2. $\frac{x}{4} = 5$
3. $\frac{x}{5} = 4$
4. $\frac{x}{4} = 7$
5. $\frac{x}{8} = 9$
6. $\frac{x}{6} = -2$
7. $\frac{x}{2} = -2$
8. $\frac{x}{5} = 0$
9. $\frac{x}{10} = 0.1$
10. $\frac{x}{6} = 60$
11. $\frac{x}{2} = \frac{1}{2}$
12. $\frac{x}{6} = \frac{1}{3}$
13. $\frac{a}{7} = \frac{1}{2}$
14. $\frac{a}{8} = \frac{1}{4}$
15. $\frac{a}{7} = 10$
16. $7 = \frac{x}{5}$
17. $9 = \frac{x}{4}$
18. $7 = \frac{x}{11}$
19. $-3 = \frac{x}{3}$
20. $-1 = \frac{x}{8}$
21. $\frac{x}{10} = -\frac{1}{2}$
22. $\frac{x}{8} = -10$
23. $-2 = \frac{a}{80}$
24. $\frac{x}{2} = \frac{1}{4}$
25. $3x = 60$
26. $4x = 28$
27. $\frac{x}{2} = 8$
28. $\frac{x}{3} = 15$

(a) $2x - 1 = 7$
$2x = 7 + 1$
$2x = 8$
$x = \frac{8}{2}$
$x = 4$

(b) $3x + 4 = 6$
$3x = 6 - 4$
$3x = 2$
$x = \frac{2}{3}$

Exercise 4

1. $2x - 3 = 3$
2. $3x - 1 = 5$
3. $4x - 3 = 5$
4. $3x - 5 = 13$
5. $5x - 7 = 3$
6. $7x - 1 = 27$
7. $2x - 1 = 4$
8. $3x + 1 = 13$
9. $4x + 2 = 5$
10. $5x + 1 = 7$
11. $5x - 3 = 10$
12. $3x + 1 = 2$

13. $2y + 10 = 11$
14. $3y - 6 = -3$
15. $2y + 10 = 9$
16. $3y + 10 = 7$
17. $4y + 10 = 10$
18. $3y - 6 = -4$
19. $5a + 6 = 10$
20. $7a + 4 = 0$
21. $9a - 7 = 0$
22. $10a - 3 = 0$
23. $5n - 3 = 11$
24. $6n + 3 = -2$

25. $3x + 4 = -3$
26. $8x - 2 = 10$
27. $4t + 10 = 0$
28. $6 + 3x = 12$
29. $5 + 2x = 13$
30. $7 + 4x = 20$
31. $5 + 8x = 10$
32. $8 + 5x = 2$
33. $3 + 7x = 2$
34. $8 + 5x = 0$
35. $9 + 3x = 0$
36. $5 + 3x = -1$

37. $10 = 2x + 3$
38. $2 = 3x - 4$
39. $7 = 4x - 5$
40. $4 = 5x - 1$
41. $7 = 3x + 6$
42. $-11 = 3x - 5$
43. $6 = 3x - 4$
44. $-2 = 2x + 1$
45. $0 = 10x - 1$
46. $0 = 11x + 2$
47. $19 = 6x - 5$
48. $7 = 3x + 7$

Solve the equations

(a) $5x + 1 = 3x + 8$
$5x - 3x = 8 - 1$
$2x = 7$
$x = \frac{7}{2}$
$x = 3\frac{1}{2}$

(b) $4x - 2 = x - 6$
$4x - x = -6 + 2$
$3x = -4$
$x = -\frac{4}{3}$
$x = -1\frac{1}{3}$

Exercise 5

Solve the equations.

1. $3x + 1 = 2x + 3$
2. $5x + 3 = 2x + 12$
3. $4x - 1 = x + 2$
4. $6x - 2 = 2x + 6$
5. $5x + 7 = 4x + 11$
6. $3x - 3 = x + 3$
7. $10x + 1 = 4x + 4$
8. $7x - 8 = x - 2$
9. $5x - 7 = 3x - 3$
10. $11x - 20 = 6x + 5$

11. $4x + 2 = 17 - x$
12. $5x - 3 = 11 - 2x$
13. $6x + 1 = 33 - 2x$
14. $3x - 7 = 1 - 5x$
15. $4x - 1 = 5 - 2x$
16. $8x + 2 = 7 - 2x$
17. $6x - 7 = 2 - 4x$
18. $3x + 9 = 17 + 2x$
19. $10x - 8 = 20 + 6x$
20. $3x - 12 = 4 - 3x$

21. $5x - 2 = 6 + 4x$
22. $10x + 7 = 12 - 2x$
23. $3x + 5 = 8 - x$
24. $7x = 8 - 2x$
25. $3x = 10 + x$
26. $4x - 12 = 2x$
27. $7x + 1 = 5x$
28. $2x + 1 = x - 6$
29. $3x - 2 = 2x - 10$
30. $5x - 4 = 2x - 10$

Exercise 6

Solve the equations.

1. $2(x - 1) = 3$
2. $3(x + 1) = 4$
3. $4(x - 2) = 1$
4. $5(x - 3) = 10$
5. $3(2x - 1) = 6$
6. $2(3x + 3) = 12$
7. $5(3x - 2) = 5$
8. $2(3x - 5) = 6$
9. $10(x - 2) = 1$
10. $6(4x + 1) = 18$

11. $3(x - 1) = 2x - 2$
12. $4(x + 2) = 3x + 10$
13. $2(2x - 1) = x + 4$
14. $3(x - 1) = 2(x + 1) - 2$
15. $4(2x - 1) = 3(x + 1) - 2$
16. $5 + 2(x + 1) = 5(x - 1)$
17. $6 + 3(x + 2) = 2(x + 5) + 4$
18. $5(x + 1) = 2x + 3 + x$
19. $4(2x - 2) = 5x - 17$
20. $x + 2(x + 4) = -4$

21. $3x + 2(x + 1) = 3x + 12$
22. $4x - 2(x + 4) = x + 1$
23. $2x - 3(x + 2) = 2x + 1$
24. $5x - 2(x - 2) = 6 - 2x$
25. $3(x + 1) + 2(x + 2) = 10$
26. $4(x + 3) + 2(x - 1) = 4$
27. $3(x - 2) - 2(x + 1) = 5$
28. $5(x - 3) + 3(x + 2) = 7x$
29. $3(2x + 1) - 2(2x + 1) = 10$
30. $4(3x - 1) - 3(3x + 2) = 0$

6.2 SOLVING PROBLEMS WITH EQUATIONS

If I multiply a 'mystery' number by 2 and then add 3 the answer is 14. Find the 'mystery' number.

Let the mystery number be x.
Then $2x + 3 = 14$
$2x = 11$
$x = 5\frac{1}{2}$

The 'mystery' number is $5\frac{1}{2}$

Exercise 7

Find the 'mystery' number in each question by forming an equation and then solving it.

1. If I multiply the number by 3 and then add 4, the answer is 13.

2. If I multiply the number by 4 and then add 5, the answer is 8.

3. If I multiply the number by 2 and then subtract 5, the answer is 4.

4. If I multiply the number by 5 and then subtract 7, the answer is 3.
5. If I double the number and then add 9, the answer is 20.
6. If I treble the number and then subtract 5, the answer is 2.
7. If I multiply the number by 8 and then add 7, the answer is 10.
8. If I treble the number and then subtract 11, the answer is 10.
9. If I multiply the number by 7 and then add 6, the answer is 3.
10. If I multiply the number by 10 and then add 19, the answer is 16.
11. If I add 3 to the number and then multiply the result by 4, the answer is 10.
12. If I add 4 to the number and then multiply the result by 3, the answer is 15.
13. If I subtract 3 from the number and then double the result, the answer is 4.
14. If I add 5 to the number and then multiply the result by 3, the answer is 20.
15. If I treble the number and then subtract 7, the answer is 2.
16. If I multiply the number by 6 and then add 5, the answer is 8.
17. If I subtract 4 from the number and then multiply the result by 5, the answer is 3.
18. If I add 11 to the number and then double the result, the answer is 31.
19. If I multiply the number by 7 and then subtract 6, the answer is 11.
20. If I add 8 to the number and then treble the result, the answer is 16.

If I add 3 to a 'mystery' number and then treble the result, I get the same answer as when I multiply the number by 2 and then subtract 7. Find the 'mystery' number.

Let the mystery number be x

Then $3(x + 3) = 2x - 7$

$$3x + 9 = 2x - 7$$
$$3x - 2x = -7 - 9$$
$$x = -16$$

The mystery number is -16

Exercise 8

Find the 'mystery' number in each question by forming an equation and then solving it.

1. If I double the number and then add 7, I get the same answer as when I add 10 to the number.
2. If I multiply the number by 4 and then add 5, I get the same answer as when I double the number and then add 8.
3. If I treble the number and then add 11, I get the same answer as when I double the number and then add 15.
4. If I multiply the number by 4 and then subtract 1, I get the same answer as when I double the number and then add 9.
5. If I multiply the number by 5 and then subtract 12, I get the same answer as when I treble the number and then subtract 8.
6. If I multiply the number by 7 and then subtract 1, I get the same answer as when I multiply the number by 4 and then add 1.
7. If I multiply the number by 5 and then subtract 12, I get the same answer as when I double the number and then subtract 9.
8. If I treble the number, add 1 and then multiply the result by 2, the answer is 6.
9. If I multiply the number by 4, subtract 1 and then multiply the result by 3, the answer is 9.
10. If I double the number, add 3 and then multiply the result by 5, the answer is 20.
11. If I treble the number, subtract 4 and then multiply the result by 4, the answer is 8.
12. If I multiply the number by 5, subtract 1 and then multiply the result by 6, the answer is 18.
13. If I multiply the number by 4 and then add 1, I get the same answer as when I double the number and then add 7.
14. If I add 2 to the number and then multiply the result by 3, I get the same answer as when I add 4 to the number and then double the result.
15. If I add 5 to the number and then multiply the result by 4, I get the same answer as when I add 1 to the number and then multiply the result by 2.

16. If I subtract 3 from the number and then multiply the result by 6, I get the same answer as when I add 2 to the number and then multiply the result by 4.
17. If I treble the number, subtract 7 and then multiply the result by 5, the answer is 20.
18. If I multiply the number by 4, add 5 and then multiply the result by 7, the answer is 21.
19. If I multiply the number by 6 and then subtract 1, I get the same answer as when I multiply by 3 and then add 8.
20. If I subtract 4 from the number and then multiply the result by 7, I get the same answer as when I add 1 to the number and then multiply the result by 4.

Exercise 9

Answer these questions by forming an equation and then solving it.

1. Find x if the perimeter is 7 cm

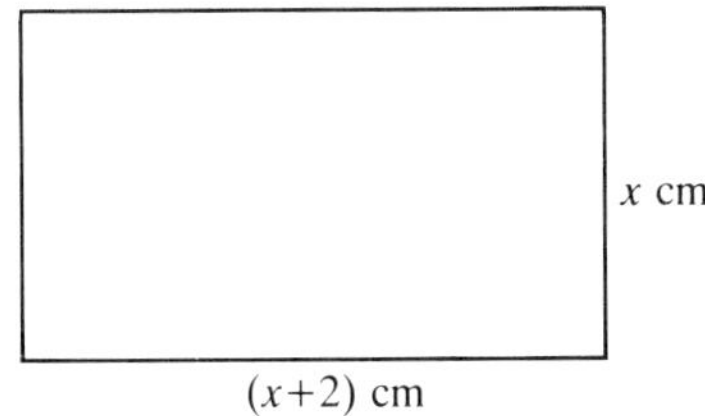

2. Find x if the perimeter is 5 cm.

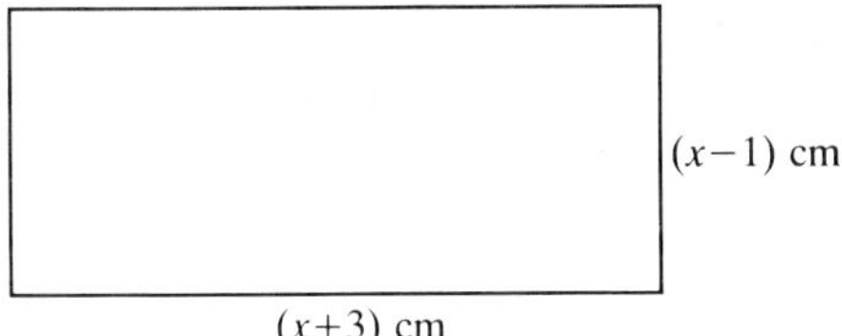

3. Find y if the perimeter is 7 cm.

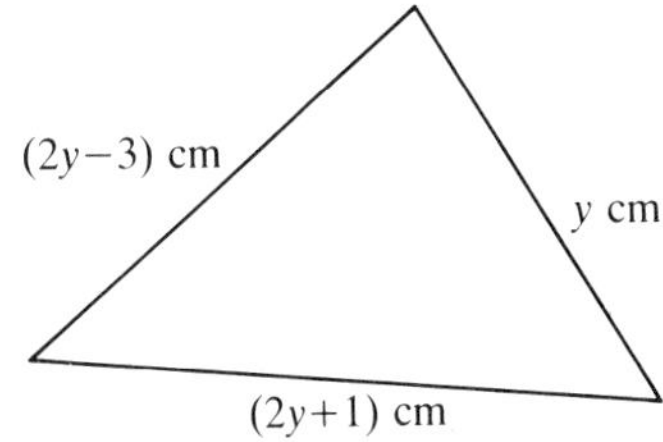

4. Find t if the perimeter is 6 cm.

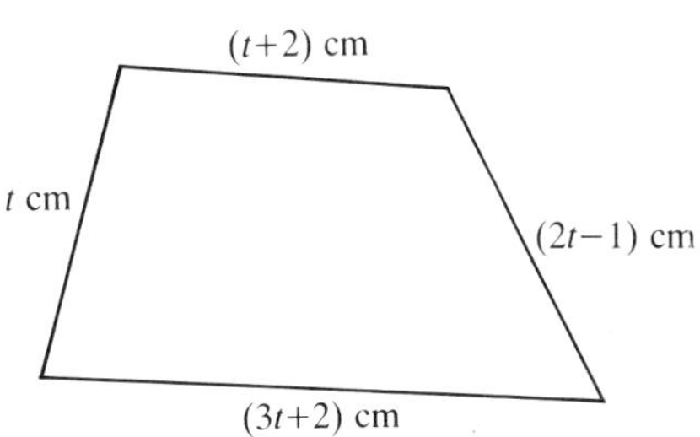

5. The length of a rectangle is 3 times its width. If the perimeter of the rectangle is 11 cm, find its width. Hint: Let the width be x cm.

6. The length of a rectangle is 4 cm more than its width. If its perimeter is 13 cm, find its width.

7. The width of a rectangle is 5 cm less than its length. If the perimeter of the rectangle is 18 cm, find its length.

8. Find x in the following rectangles:

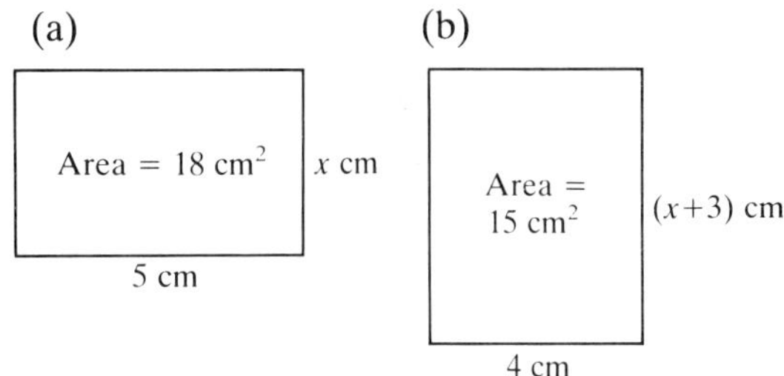

9. Find y in the following triangles:

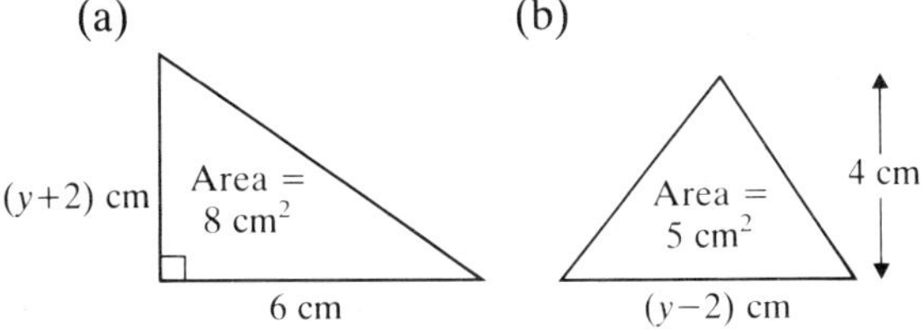

10. The length of a rectangle is 5 cm more than its width. The perimeter of the rectangle is 38 cm. Find the width of the rectangle and hence the area of the rectangle.

11. Find x in the following triangles:

(a)

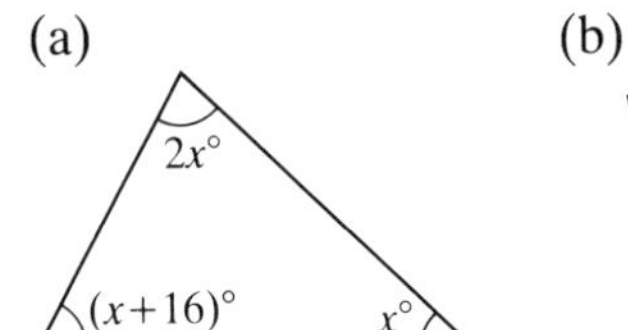

(b)

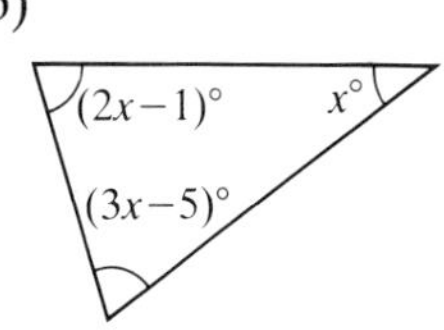

12. The angles of a triangle are 32°, x° and $(4x + 3)$°. Find the value of x.

13. Find a in the diagrams below

(a)

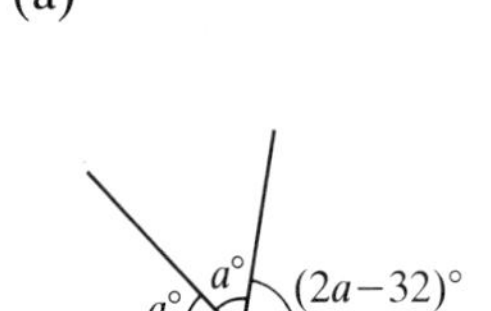

(b)

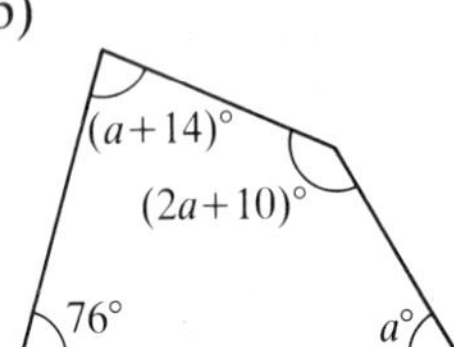

14. Kathryn has some money saved in her piggy bank. On her birthday her father doubles the money she has and then her mother gives her another 75p. She now has 185p. How much did she have to start with?

15. Each diagram in the sequence below consists of a number of dots.

Diagram number	1	2	3
	• • • •	• • • • • • • •	• • • • • • • • • • • •

(a) Draw diagram number 4 and diagram number 5.

(b) Copy and complete the table below:

Diagram number	Number of dots
1	4
2	8
3	
4	
5	
6	

(c) Without drawing the diagrams, state the number of dots in
   (i) diagram number 8
   (ii) diagram number 14
   (iii) diagram number 52

(d) State the number of the diagram which has 64 dots.

(e) If we write x for the diagram number and n for the number of dots, write down a formula involving x and n.

Exercise 10

Multiple choice exercise.

1. What is the value of $-7+(-7)$?
A. 0 **B.** 14 **C.** -14 **D.** 49

2. What is the value of $-8 \div (-2)$?
A. -4 **B.** 4 **C.** 16 **D.** $\frac{1}{4}$

3. What is the value of $-9 + 200$?
A. -209 **B.** -191 **C.** 191
D. -1800

4. If $a = -3$ and $b = 5$, work out $2a - b$.
A. -1 **B.** 1 **C.** 11 **D.** -11

5. If $x = 4$ and $y = -3$, work out $3x - 2y$.
A. 6 **B.** -6 **C.** 18 **D.** -18

6. If $m = -1$ and $n = -2$, work out $m^2 + n^2$
A. -5 **B.** 5 **C.** -3 **D.** 4

7. If $c = -4$, $d = 2$, work out $3(d - c)$.
A. 6 **B.** -18 **C.** 18 **D.** -6

8. If $p = -3$, $q = 2$ and $r = -2$, work out $2q + pr$.
A. -2 **B.** 7 **C.** 9 **D.** 10

9. If $x = -6$ and $y = 3$, work out $2x^2 + y$
A. 75 **B.** 69 **C.** 147 **D.** -141

10. I start with x then add 7, double the result and finally divide by 3. The final result is
A. $\dfrac{2(x+7)}{3}$ **B.** $2x + \dfrac{7}{3}$
C. $\dfrac{2x+7}{3}$ **D.** $3(2x+7)$

11. I start with x, then square it, multiply by 3 and finally subtract 4. The final result is
A. $(3x)^2 - 4$ **B.** $(3x-4)^2$ **C.** $3x^2 - 4$
D. $3(x-4)^2$

12. I start with n, then add 4, then square the result and finally multiply by 3. The final result is
A. $3(n^2+4)$ **B.** $\dfrac{(n+4)^2}{3}$ **C.** $3n^2 + 4$
D. $3(n+4)^2$

13. Solve the equation $3x - 7 = 23$.
A. $x = 5\frac{1}{3}$ **B.** $x = 10$ **C.** $x = 30$
D. $x = 27$

14. Solve the equation $4x + 5 = 3$.
A. $x = \frac{1}{2}$ **B.** $x = 2$ **C.** $x = -\frac{1}{2}$
D. $x = -2$

15. Solve the equation $3x - 1 = 2x + 8$.
A. $x = 9$ **B.** $x = 7$ **C.** $x = 1\frac{4}{5}$
D. $x = 1\frac{2}{5}$

16. Remove the brackets and simplify $2(x + 7) + 3(x - 1)$.
A. $5x - 11$ **B.** $5x + 17$ **C.** $5x + 11$
D. $6x + 14$

17. Remove the brackets and simplify $4(x - 2) - 3(x + 1)$.
A. $x - 5$ **B.** $x - 11$ **C.** $7x - 5$
D. $7x - 11$

18. Solve the equation $4(2x - 1) = 3x + 5$.
A. $x = \frac{5}{9}$ **B.** $x = 1\frac{4}{5}$ **C.** $x = \frac{9}{11}$
D. $x = -\frac{3}{8}$

19. If I add 7 to a certain number and then multiply the result by 5, the answer is 10. What is the number?
A. -20 **B.** 5 **C.** -5 **D.** $1\frac{3}{5}$

20. If I multiply a certain number by 4 and then subtract 11, the answer is 2. What is the number?
A. $11\frac{1}{2}$ **B.** $-2\frac{1}{4}$ **C.** $4\frac{1}{4}$ **D.** $3\frac{1}{4}$

6.3 CHANGING THE SUBJECT

Make x the subject.

(a) $x - e = t$

$x = t + e$

(*b*) $mx = c$

$x = \frac{c}{m}$

(*c*) $B + n = x + a$

$B + n - a = x$

(*d*) $p + q = Ax$

$\frac{p + q}{A} = x$

Exercise 11

Make x the subject

1. $x + a = c$ **2.** $x + d = m$
3. $x + h = m$ **4.** $x + e = t$
5. $x - m = q$ **6.** $x - k = m$
7. $x - n = a + b$ **8.** $x + B = c + b$
9. $x + D = a + d$ **10.** $x - M = m + t$
11. $x - v = u - w$ **12.** $x + T = t - s$
13. $B + x = n$ **14.** $M + x = m$
15. $N + x = a - b$ **16.** $R + x = v - n$
17. $x + K = y^2$ **18.** $x - a^2 = b^2$
19. $x - n^2 = N^2$ **20.** $x + p = -a$

21. $a = x - n$ **22.** $mn = x + r$
23. $c = x + m$ **24.** $B = x - b$
25. $x + b - c = a$ **26.** $x + c - d = e$
27. $x + a^2 - b^2 = c^2$ **28.** $x - v^2 = m^2 - mn$
29. $b = x - a - t$ **30.** $f + g = x - h$
31. $x - B = b + B^2$ **32.** $x + A - a = a$
33. $x - t = T^2 + t$ **34.** $w = x + w^3$
35. $uv = x + w^2$ **36.** $t^3 + x = T^3$
37. $x - abc = a^3$ **38.** $mn^2 = m^3 + x$
39. $a + bc = x - cb$ **40.** $4pq = pq + x$

Exercise 12

Make y the subject.

1. $3y = 12$ **2.** $5y = 30$
3. $ay = c$ **4.** $my = t$
5. $My = m$ **6.** $ty = a$
7. $ym = n$ **8.** $yx = L$
9. $ym^2 = n^2$ **10.** $yq = h$
11. $aby = A$ **12.** $m^2y = M^2$
13. $c = ay$ **14.** $x = ty$
15. $v = dy$ **16.** $u^2 = yv^2$
17. $b = t^2y$ **18.** $B = by$
19. $c = ye$ **20.** $k^2y = a$

21. $xy = a + b$ **22.** $my = e - f$
23. $ny = s + t$ **24.** $Hy = p + q$
25. $zy = ab + c$ **26.** $vy = a^2 - b^2$
27. $pq = My$ **28.** $km - m^2 = ny$
29. $yx^2 = c - k$ **30.** $yp = a - b - A$

31. $zy = \frac{A}{x}$ **32.** $vy = \frac{B}{w}$

33. $ky = \frac{Ba}{d}$ **34.** $m^2y = \frac{1}{n^2}$

35. $xy = \frac{m}{x}$ **36.** $py = \frac{A}{p}$

37. $\frac{N}{n} = yn$

38. $Ly = \frac{A}{B}$

39. $Py = \frac{a+b}{c}$

40. $Qy = \frac{e+t}{k}$

41. $y + t = a$

42. $y - m^2 = v$

43. $b = y + k$

44. $e + y = x$

45. $y + mn = n^2$

46. $ab = y - b^2$

47. $zy = n - a$

48. $py = x - z$

49. $y - t^2 = T^2$

50. $ny = \frac{C}{d}$

Make a the subject.

(a) $am - d = f$
$$am = f + d$$
$$a = \frac{f+d}{m}$$

(b) $c(a - x) = y$
$$ca - cx = y$$
$$ca = y + cx$$
$$a = \frac{y + cx}{c}$$

Exercise 13

Make a the subject.

1. $2a + 1 = 10$
2. $3a - 2 = 19$
3. $na + b = t$
4. $ma + v = q$
5. $pa - A = B$
6. $na - q = A$
7. $ka - w = n^2$
8. $ma + m = n$
9. $at + m = e$
10. $aB - w^2 = v^2$
11. $L + pa = d$
12. $M = ma - n$
13. $x = xa + y$
14. $v^2 = xa - t$
15. $sa - s^2 = z^2$
16. $pq + ra = x^2$
17. $lm + ab = h^2$
18. $t + ae = d + b$
19. $p^2 = m + n + Ba$
20. $km = ma - n^2$
21. $m(a - n) = t$
22. $u(a + x) = x$
23. $p(a + w) = y$
24. $A(a - u) = q$
25. $L(x + a) = m$
26. $n(x^2 + a) = x^3$
27. $r(a - r) = s^2$
28. $x(a - x) = y^2$
29. $3(a - 4) = 1$
30. $5(a + 2) = 8$
31. $T = n(a - t)$
32. $V = w(a - y)$
33. $w + q = m(a - w)$
34. $x^2 - y^2 = z(a - z)$
35. $ut + at = v^2$
36. $MN + ma = L^2$
37. $z(x + a) = x$
38. $y^2 = w(a - w)$
39. $q(a - q) = x^2 + q^2$
40. $k(m + a) = km + n$

Formulae involving fractions

Make k the subject

(a) $\frac{k}{m} = n$
$$k = mn$$

(b) $\frac{k}{a} + b = e$
$$\frac{k}{a} = e - b$$
$$k = a(e - b)$$

Exercise 14

Make k the subject.

1. $\frac{k}{n} = a$
2. $\frac{k}{t} = A$
3. $\frac{k}{x} = x$
4. $z = \frac{k}{p}$
5. $v = \frac{k}{w}$
6. $\frac{k}{n} = n^2$
7. $\frac{k}{m} = -e$
8. $\frac{k}{t} = (a - b)$
9. $\frac{k}{h} = x + y$
10. $\frac{k}{m} = -m$
11. $\frac{k}{(a+b)} = z$
12. $\frac{k}{m-n} = B$
13. $D = \frac{k}{m-p}$
14. $\frac{mk}{n} = a$
15. $\frac{nk}{x} = y$
16. $\frac{ak}{e} = y$
17. $\frac{vk}{a} = z$
18. $\frac{km}{a} = a$
19. $\frac{kz}{x} = y$
20. $\frac{kq}{v} = w$
21. $\frac{x}{a} = \frac{mk}{b}$
22. $\frac{xk}{c} = \frac{A}{m}$
23. $\frac{kz}{v} = \frac{v}{b}$
24. $\frac{ke}{t} = \frac{t}{n}$
25. $\frac{mk}{(x+y)} = a$
26. $\frac{nk}{(p+q)} = d$
27. $\frac{Ak}{q} = (x + t)$
28. $\frac{k}{n} = \frac{1}{a+d^2}$
29. $\frac{w}{B} = \frac{Bk}{w}$
30. $\frac{kz}{v} = \frac{v}{z}$

Think about it 2

Project 1 CROSS NUMBERS

Here we have five cross number puzzles with a difference. There are no clues, only answers, and it is your task to find where the answers go.
(a) Copy out the cross number pattern
(b) Fit all the given numbers into the correct spaces. Tick off the numbers from the lists as you write them in the square.

1.

4	2	1	5	3			6

2 digits	*3 digits*	*4 digits*	*5 digits*	*6 digits*
11	315	2131	14708	137866
13	415	9176	33057	
16	438	5341	42153	
50	578	3726	54780	
79	806	4156		
93	459	3204		
	755	6197		
	619			
	862			
	638			

2.

4	2	1	4					

2 digits	*3 digits*	*4 digits*	*5 digits*	*6 digits*
26	215	5841	21862	134953
41	427	9217	83642	727542
19	106	9131	21362	
71	872	1624	57320	
63	725	1506		
76	385	4214		
	156	5216		
	263	4734		
	234	2007		
	180	2637		

3.

		5					
		6	7	0	5	2	

2 digits	*3 digits*	*4 digits*	*5 digits*	*6 digits*
64	756	8234	31492	There is one but I cannot tell you what it is.
61	725	3938	67052	
29	205	5375	69127	
52	157	7166		
87	852	5781		
78	927	2336		
85	135	1827		
	603	9062		
	846			
	738			

4.

6								
5								
3								

2 digits	*3 digits*	*4 digits*	*5 digits*	*6 digits*
99	571	9603	24715	387566
25	918	8072	72180	338472
52	131	4210	54073	414725
26	328	3824	71436	198264
42	906	8916	82125	
57	249			
30	653			*7 digits*
53	609			8592070
14	111			
61	127			
	276			

5. This one is much more difficult but it *is* possible! Don't give up.

7									
		9							

2 digits	*3 digits*	*4 digits*	*5 digits*	*6 digits*
26	306	3654	38975	582778
28	457	3735	49561	585778
32	504	3751	56073	728468
47	827	3755	56315	
49	917	3819	56435	*7 digits*
52	951	6426	57435	8677056
70		7214	58535	
74		7315	58835	
		7618	66430	
		7643	77435	
		9847	77543	

Exercise A

1. A machine fills 690 oil drums in one hour. How many oil drums will it fill in 20 minutes?

2. Thirty books cost £75 and weigh 6000 g. Find (a) the cost and (b) the weight of 12 of these books.

3. The entire surface area of the solid object shown is covered with paint, the thickness of paint being 1 mm.

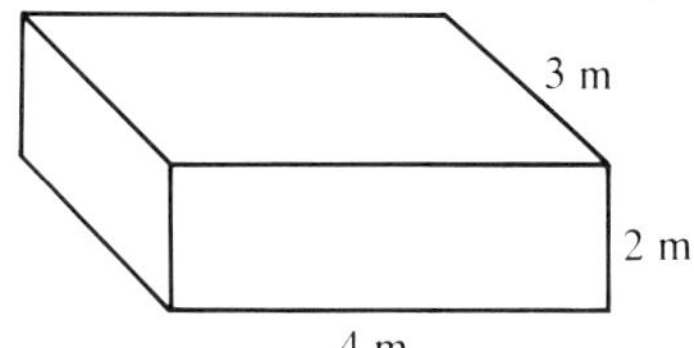

(a) Find the total surface area of the object.
(b) Find the volume of paint used in m^3.

4. The average length of a boy's pace is 70 cm. How many steps would he take in walking a distance of 350 m?

5. Copy and complete

	Fraction	Decimal
(a)	$\frac{1}{4}$	0.25
(b)	$\frac{1}{5}$	
(c)		0.5
(d)	$\frac{3}{4}$	
(e)		0.6
(f)	$\frac{5}{8}$	

6. What change do you receive from £20 after buying 11 tins at 32p, 16 cans at 19p and 14 apples at 6p?

7. Work out, without using a calculator.

(a) 2.42×6 (b) 0.072×9
(c) $17 - 3.6$ (d) $8.1 + 9.95$
(e) $17.92 \div 7$ (f) $210.6 \div 6$

8. A car dealer offers a discount of 5% when a car is paid for with cash. Find the cost of a £800 car after the discount.

9. Which would cost less and by how much: 40 pencils at 8p each or 15 biros at 22p each?

10. 6, 7, 8, 13, 15, 17, 23, 27, 39, 41, 54.
Which of the above numbers are:

(a) even numbers (b) divisible by 3
(c) prime numbers (d) divisible by 9?

Project 2 CALCULATOR WORDS

'LEEOS

If we work out $25 \times 503 \times 4 + 37$ on a calculator we should obtain the number 50337. If we turn the calculator upside down (and use a little imagination) we see the word 'LEEDS'.

Find the words given by the clues below.

1. $83 \times 85 + 50$ (Lots of this in the garden)
2. $211 \times 251 + 790$ (Tropical or Scilly)
3. $19 \times 20 \times 14 - 2.66$ (Not an upstanding man)
4. $(84 + 17) \times 5$ (Dotty message)
5. $0.01443 \times 7 \times 4$ (Three times as funny)
6. $79 \times 9 - 0.9447$ (Greasy letters)
7. $50.19 - (5 \times 0.0039)$ (Not much space inside)
8. $2 \div 0.5 - 3.295$ (Rather lonely)
9. $0.034 \times 11 - 0.00292$; $9^4 - (8 \times 71)$ (two words) (Nice for breakfast)
10. $7420 \times 7422 + 118^2 - 30$ (Big Chief)
11. $(13 \times 3 \times 25 \times 8 \times 5) + 7$ (Dwelling for masons)
12. $71^2 - 11^2 - 5$ (Sad gasp)
13. $904^2 + 89621818$ (Prickly customer)
14. $(559 \times 6) + (21 \times 55)$ (What a surprise!)
15. $566 \times 711 - 23617$ (Bolt it down)
16. $\dfrac{9999 + 319}{8.47 + 2.53}$ (Sit up and plead)
17. $\dfrac{2601 \times 6}{4^2 + 1^2}$; $(401 - 78) \times 5^2$ (two words) (Not a great man)
18. $0.4^2 - 0.1^2$ (Little Sidney)
19. $\dfrac{(27 \times 2000 - 2)}{(0.63 \div 0.09)}$ (Not quite a mountain)
20. $(5^2 - 1^2)^4 - 14239$ (Just a name)
21. $48^4 + 102^2 - 4^2$ (Pursuits)
22. $615^2 + (7 \times 242)$ (Almost a goggle)
23. $14^4 - 627 + 29$ (Good book, by God!)
24. $6.2 \times 0.987 \times 1\,000\,000 - 860^2 + 118$ (Flying ace)
25. $(426 \times 474) + (318 \times 487) + 22018$ (Close to a bubble)
26. $\dfrac{36^3}{4} - 1530$ (Foreign-sounding girl's name)
27. $(594 \times 571) - (154 \times 132) - 38$ (Female Bobby)
28. $(7^2 \times 100) + (7 \times 2)$ (Lofty)
29. $240^2 + 134$; $241^2 - 7^3$ (two words) (Devil of a chime)
30. $1384.5 \times 40 - 1.991$ (Say this after sneezing)
31. $(2 \times 2 \times 2 \times 2 \times 3)^4 + 1929$ (Unhappy ending)
32. $141918 + 83^3$ (Hot stuff in France)

Exercise B

1. Seven books cost £24.15. How many of these books could be bought for £34.50?

2. Write the following correct to the nearest penny:

(a) £6.537 (b) £15.708 (c) £11.6241
(d) £8.029 (e) £0.6267 (f) £1.071

3. A maths teacher bought 40 calculators at £7.20 each and a number of other calculators costing £3.95 each. In all he spent £367. How many of the less expensive calculators did he buy?

4. In the diagram below calculate

(a) the area of rectangle ABCD
(b) the area of the shaded trapezium XBCY
(c) the percentage of the rectangle ABCD which is shaded.

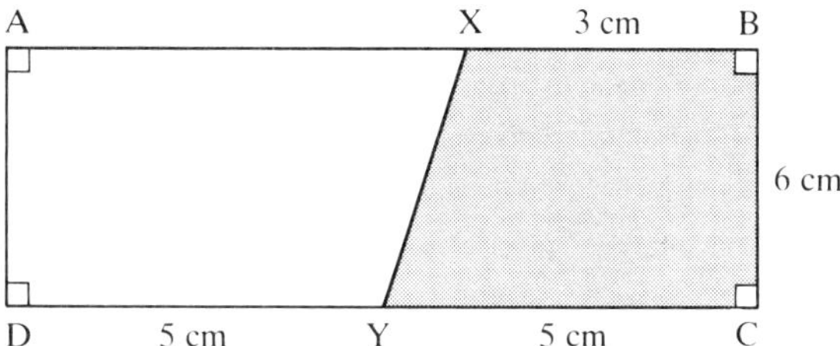

5. Mrs Alexander's salary is £8500 per year. She pays no tax on the first £2100 of her salary but pays 30% on each remaining £.

(a) How much tax does she pay?
(b) How much does she earn after tax?

6. A machine produces 120 articles per hour. How many articles does it produce in $2\frac{1}{4}$ hours?

7. What change do you receive from £10 after buying 6 pens at 25p, 3 rubbers at 18p and 4 pencils at 21p?

8. A slimmer's calorie guide shows how many calories are contained in various foods:

Bread 1.2 calories per g
Cheese 2.5 calories per g
Meat 1.6 calories per g
Butter 6 calories per g

Calculate the number of calories in the following meals:

(a) 50 g bread, 40 g cheese, 100 g meat, 15 g butter.
(b) 150 g bread, 85 g cheese, 120 g meat, 20 g butter.

9. Write as a single number.

(a) 8^2 (b) 1^4 (c) 10^2
(d) 3×10^3 (e) 2^5 (f) 3^4

10. A cylinder has a volume of 200 cm^3 and a height of 10 cm. Calculate the area of its base.

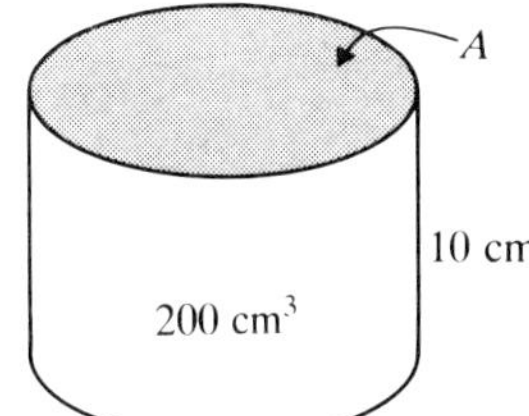

Project 3 MATHEMATICAL WORDSEARCH

These words are hidden in the square shown below.

rectangle, isosceles, multiply, subtract, parallel, infinity, square, number, figure, obtuse, circle, divide, index, power, acute.

They may appear written forwards, backwards or diagonally. Find as many of them as you can.

P	X	Q	E	D	U	B	B	V	K	J	N	O	B	N
B	Q	M	V	N	S	G	A	L	I	Z	G	J	Q	Y
W	I	L	G	R	Y	E	P	K	S	N	J	D	Y	T
O	E	E	V	B	B	L	L	M	V	I	D	W	T	C
E	M	L	E	X	E	F	P	E	R	K	W	W	I	A
S	Q	L	J	V	L	O	E	I	C	G	V	J	N	R
U	G	A	K	T	C	I	T	I	T	S	Y	L	I	T
T	Z	R	T	N	R	Q	U	V	V	L	O	W	F	B
B	O	A	N	R	I	W	C	R	L	R	U	S	N	U
O	F	P	R	E	C	T	A	N	G	L	E	M	I	S
I	K	I	P	O	W	E	R	D	U	O	E	V	N	Q
R	L	B	G	P	A	N	Q	Y	G	M	W	O	D	U
J	A	J	Y	U	D	I	V	I	D	E	B	Y	E	A
N	J	Z	B	D	R	Y	Q	G	R	Z	F	E	X	R
S	E	T	A	L	V	E	Y	N	X	C	J	M	R	E

Exercise C OPERATOR SQUARES

Each empty square contains either a number or a mathematical symbol (+, −, ×, ÷). Copy each square and fill in the missing details.

1.

9		6	→	15
×		÷		
		2	→	6
↓		↓		
36			→	12

2.

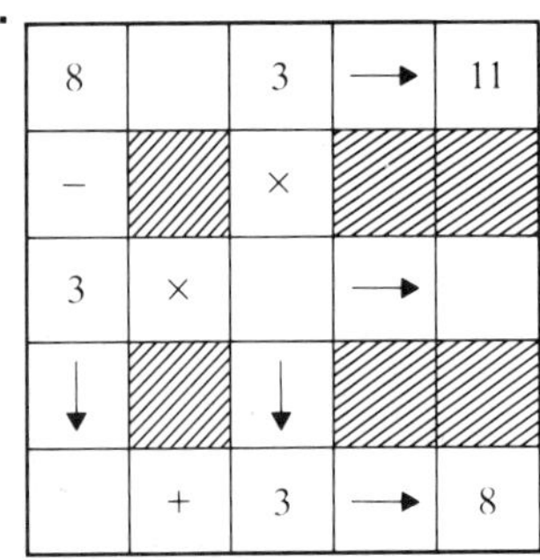

8		3	→	11
−		×		
3	×		→	
↓		↓		
	+	3	→	8

3.

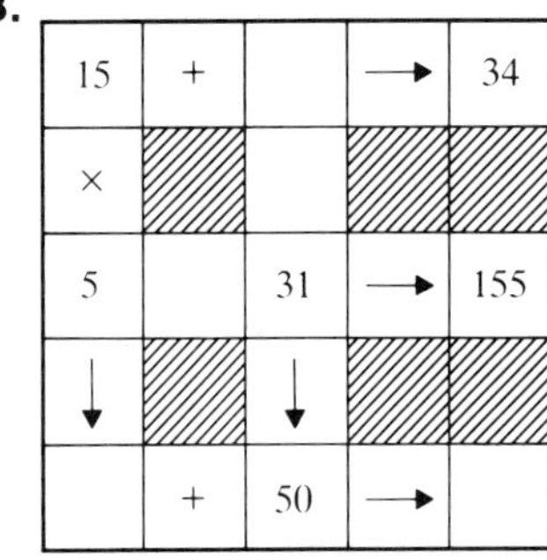

15	+		→	34
×				
5		31	→	155
↓		↓		
	+	50	→	

4.

38			→	52
×		+		
		1	→	3
↓		↓		
	−	15	→	99

5.

	×	10	→	90
+		÷		
			→	$5\frac{1}{2}$
↓		↓		
20	×		→	100

6.

	×		→	42
÷		÷		
	−	3	→	11
↓		↓		
$\frac{1}{2}$		2	→	1

7.

	×	2	→	34
−				
	×		→	36
↓		↓		
8	−		→	$7\frac{1}{2}$

8.

	−		→	83
÷		×		
	÷	8	→	$\frac{1}{4}$
↓		↓		
	+	56	→	101

9.

9			→	45
×		−		
		2	→	2
↓		↓		
9	×		→	27

10.

25	×		→	250
−		÷		
	÷		→	
↓		↓		
9	−	0·1	→	

11.

0·1	×	20	→	
		+		
6	−		→	
↓		↓		
0·6	+		→	20·8

12.

	×	100	→	50
−		×		
		2	→	2·1
↓		↓		
0·4	×		→	

13.

	×	0·1	→	0·7
÷		×		
	÷	0·2	→	10
↓		↓		
	+		→	

14.

	+	6	→	7·2
+				
	÷	5	→	
↓		↓		
8·2		30	→	38·2

15.

	×		→	20
−				
	+	10	→	11·2
↓		↓		
98·8	+	2	→	

16.

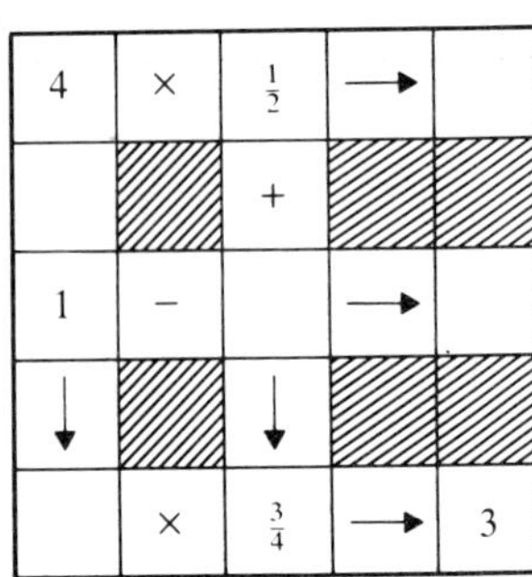

17.

	−	$\frac{1}{8}$	→	$\frac{1}{8}$
×		×		
$\frac{1}{2}$	÷	4	→	
↓		↓		
$\frac{1}{8}$	+		→	

18.

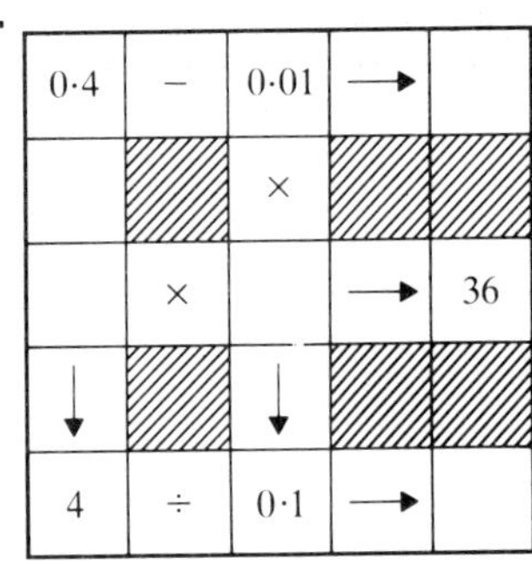

Project 4 DESIGNING SQUARE PATTERNS

The object is to design square patterns of different sizes. The patterns are all to be made from smaller tiles all of which are themselves square.

Designs for a 4 × 4 square:

(a)

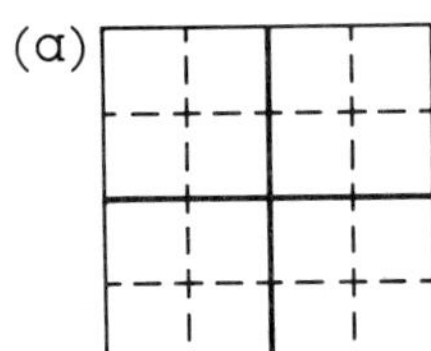

This design consists of four tiles each 2 × 2. The pattern is rather dull.

(b) Suppose we say that the design must contain at least one 1 × 1 square.

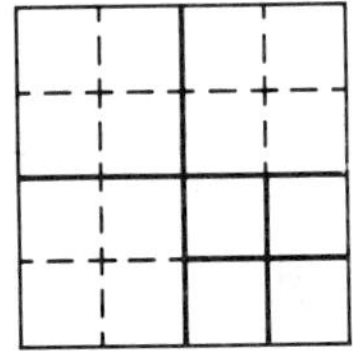

This design is more interesting and consists of seven tiles.

1. Try the 5 × 5 square. Design a pattern which divides the 5 × 5 square into eight smaller squares.
2. Try the 6 × 6 square. Here you must include at least one 1 × 1 square. Design a pattern which divides the 6 × 6 square into nine smaller squares. Colour in the final design to make it look interesting.
3. The 7 × 7 square is more difficult. With no restrictions, design a pattern which divides the 7 × 7 square into nine smaller squares.
4. Design a pattern which divides an 8 × 8 square into ten smaller squares. You must not use a 4 × 4 square.
5. Design a pattern which divides a 9 × 9 square into ten smaller squares. You can use only one 3 × 3 square.
6. Design a pattern which divides a 10 × 10 square into eleven smaller squares. You must include a 3 × 3 square.
7. Design a pattern which divides an 11 × 11 square into eleven smaller squares. You must include a 6 × 6 square.

Exercise D

1. Copy and complete the following bill.

$6\frac{1}{2}$ lb of potatoes at 12p per lb		= £
4 lb of beef at	per lb	= £7.20
jars of coffee at 95p per jar		= £6.65
	Total	= £

2. In a sale, discount at the rate of 10p in the £ is allowed on all articles. What is the sale price of an article for which the normal price is £7?

3. Calculate the area of the shape below. Take $\pi = 3$.

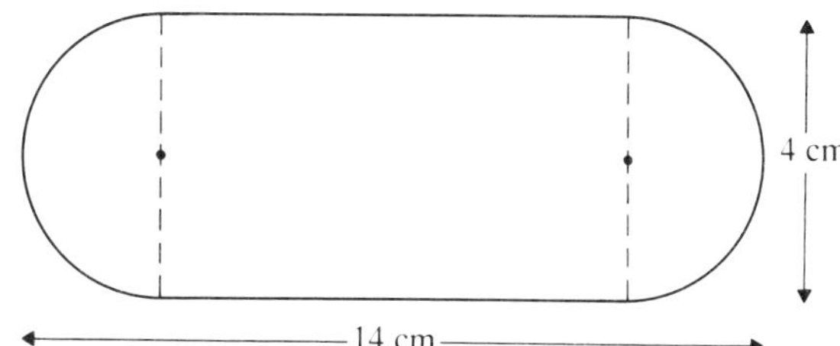

4. 12 pints of milk will feed 5 babies for 2 days. Copy and complete the following:
(a) 6 pints of milk will feed 5 babies for days.
(b) 12 pints of milk will feed 1 baby for days.
(c) 12 pints of milk will feed 2 babies for days.
(d) pints of milk will feed 5 babies for 8 days.

5. (a) A man changed £100 into Italian lire when the exchange rate was 2145 lire = £1. Calculate the number of lire he received.
(b) A woman changed £50 into French francs when the exchange rate was F11.60 = £1. Calculate the number of francs she received.

6. A map uses a scale of 1 cm = 100 m.
(a) Calculate the actual length, in km, of a railway line which is 4 cm long on the map.
(b) A road is 200 m long. Calculate, in cm, the length this would be on the map.

7. Jane is six years old and Sarah is eighteen. In how many years will Sarah be exactly twice as old as Jane?

8. Work out $2\frac{1}{4} \times 3\frac{1}{2}$, giving your answer in its simplest form.

9. Find the missing digits.

(a)

	1		4
+		3	8
	6	8	

(b)

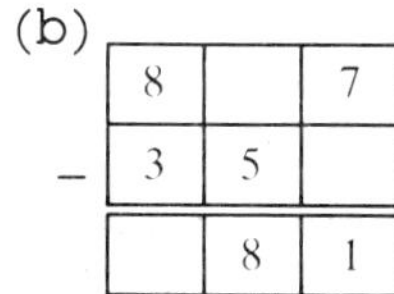

	8		7
−	3	5	
		8	1

10. How many triangles can you see in the diagram below?

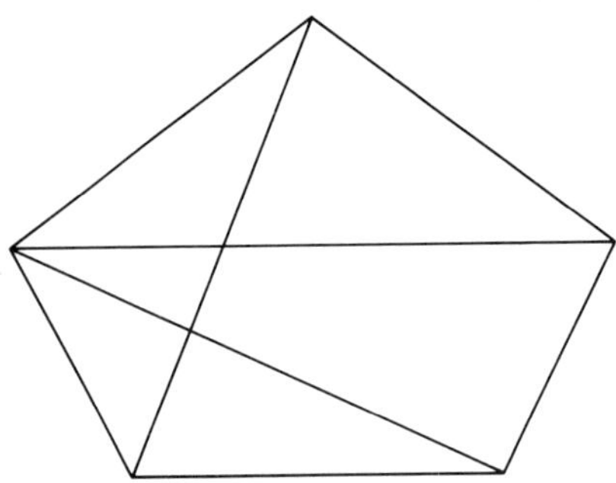

Project 5 CONVERGING SEQUENCES

1. Do the following investigation on a calculator.

1. Take any positive whole number (say 9)
2. Divide by 5
3. Add 1 to the answer
4. Write down the result
5. Repeat steps 2, 3 and 4 a further ten or twenty times.

What is happening?

A flow chart for the operation is shown below.

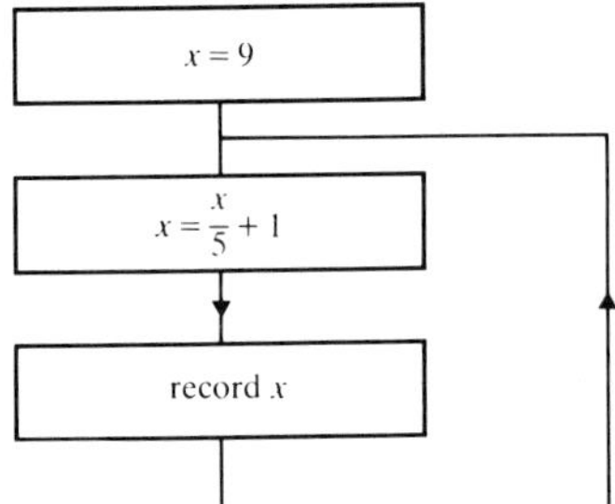

Try the sequence using a different starting number, say 7 or 20.
How about decimal numbers?
How about negative numbers?

2. Now see what happens with a different sequence.

Take any number (say 7) and work through the flow chart below.

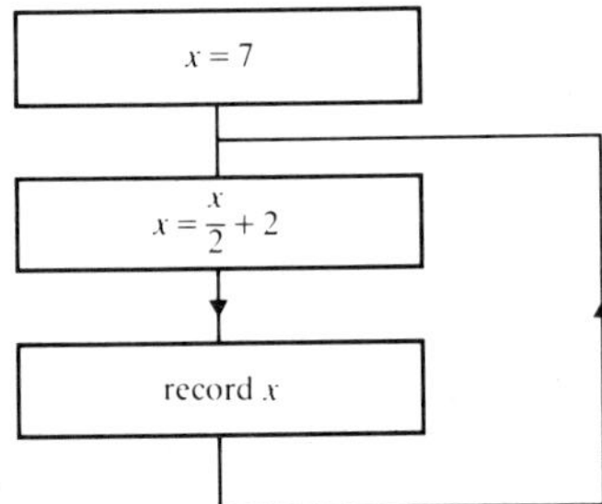

What is happening this time?
Try the sequence using different starting numbers.

3. This one is more difficult.
Take any number (say 7) and work through the flow chart below.

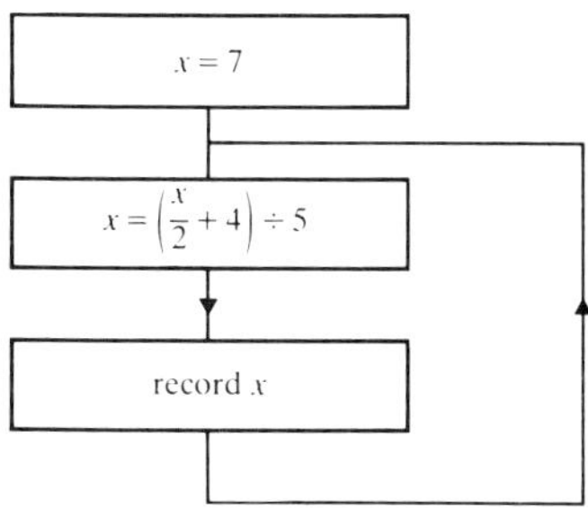

4. Investigate what happens with other flow charts.

Exercise E

Plot the points and join them up in order. You should produce a picture in each case.

1. Draw axes with both x and y from 0 to 10.

A: (3,2), (4,2), (5,3), (3,5), (3,6), (2,7), (1,6), (1,8), (2,9), (3,9), (5,7), (4,6), (4,5), (6,4), (8,4), (8,5), (6,7), (5,7).
B: (7,4), (9,2), (8,1), (7,3), (5,3).
C: (1,6), (2,8), (2,9), (2,7).
D: Draw a dot at (3,8).

2. Draw axes with both x and y from 0 to 10.

A: (6,5), (7,6), (9,5), (10,3), (9,1), (1,1), (3,3), (3,4), (4,5), (5,4), (4,3), (6,4), (8,4), (9,3).
B: (8,3), (8,2), (7,1).
C: (6,3), (6,2), (5,1).
D: (5,2), (4,1).
E: Draw a dot at (3,2).

3. Draw axes with both x and y from 0 to 8.

A: (6,6), (1,6), (2,7), (7,7), (6,6), (6,1), (7,2), (7,7).
B: (1,6), (1,1), (6,1).
C: (3,5), (3,3), (2,2), (2,5), (5,5), (5,2), (2,2), (3,3), (5,3).

4. Draw axes with x from 0 to 8 and y from 0 to 4.

A: (7,1), (8,1), (7,2), (6,2), (5,3), (3,3), (2,2), (6,2), (1,2), (1,1), (2,1).
B: (3,1), (6,1).
C: (3,3), (3,2).
D: (4,3), (4,2).
E: (5,3), (5,2).
F: Draw a circle of radius $\frac{1}{2}$ unit with centre at $(2\frac{1}{2},1)$.
G: Draw a circle of radius $\frac{1}{2}$ unit with centre at $(6\frac{1}{2},1)$.

5. Draw axes with x from -4 to $+4$ and y from 0 to 10.

A: $(3,5)$, $(2,7)$, $(0,8)$, $(-1,8)$, $(-2,7)$, $(-3,7)$, $(-4,8)$, $(-2,9)$, $(0,9)$, $(2,8)$, $(3,7)$, $(3,2)$, $(1,1)$, $(0,3)$, $(-2,2)$, $(-2,4)$, $(-3,4)$, $(-2,6)$, $(-1,6)$, $(-1,5)$, $(-2,6)$, $(-2,7)$.
B: $(-1,3)$, $(-2,3)$.
C: $(1,3)$, $(0,3)$.

6. Draw axes with x from 0 to 17 and y from 0 to 22.

A: $(13,4)$, $(12,4)$, $(14,3)$, $(16,3)$, $(14,4)$, $(13,4)$, $(11,5)$, $(9,4)$, $(10,4)$, $(14,2)$, $(13,1)$, $(14,2)$, $(17,3)$, $(16,3)$. Draw a dot at $(10\frac{1}{2},4\frac{1}{2})$.
B: $(12,6)$, $(12,7)$, $(15,8)$, $(13,8)$, $(14,9)$, $(12,10)$, $(11,9)$, $(9,10)$, $(7,9)$, $(8,9)$, $(12,7)$. Draw a dot at $(8\frac{1}{2},9\frac{1}{2})$.
C: $(11,11)$, $(10,12)$, $(6,14)$, $(5,14)$, $(7,15)$, $(9,14)$, $(10,16)$, $(13,15)$, $(10,14)$, $(12,13)$, $(13,13)$, $(10,12)$. Draw a dot at $(6\frac{1}{2},14\frac{1}{2})$.
D: $(10,17)$, $(9,17)$, $(5,19)$, $(4,19)$, $(6,20)$, $(8,19)$, $(8,21)$, $(10,22)$, $(11,22)$, $(9,19)$, $(11,18)$, $(12,18)$, $(9,17)$. Draw a dot at $(5\frac{1}{2},19\frac{1}{2})$.

7. Draw axes with both x and y from 0 to 14.
A: $(1,3)$, $(9,3)$, $(7,7)$, $(6,5)$, $(8,5)$, $(7,7)$, $(8,9)$, $(12,1)$, $(2,1)$, $(1,3)$, $(6,13)$, $(8,13)$, $(4,5)$, $(6,5)$.
B: $(8,13)$, $(13,3)$, $(12,1)$.

8. Draw axes with x from 0 to 16 and y from 0 to 10.
A: $(2,1)$, $(2,2)$, $(8,10)$, $(16,10)$, $(16,9)$, $(10,1)$, $(2,1)$, $(8,9)$, $(14,9)$, $(10,3)$, $(10,2)$, $(16,10)$.
B: $(8,9)$, $(8,8)$, $(4,2)$, $(10,2)$, $(10,3)$, $(4\frac{2}{3},3)$.
C: $(8,8)$, $(13\frac{1}{3},8)$.

Project 6 KNOCKOUT COMPETITION

1. Eight players entered for a spelling competition organised on a 'knock-out' basis. The results are shown below.

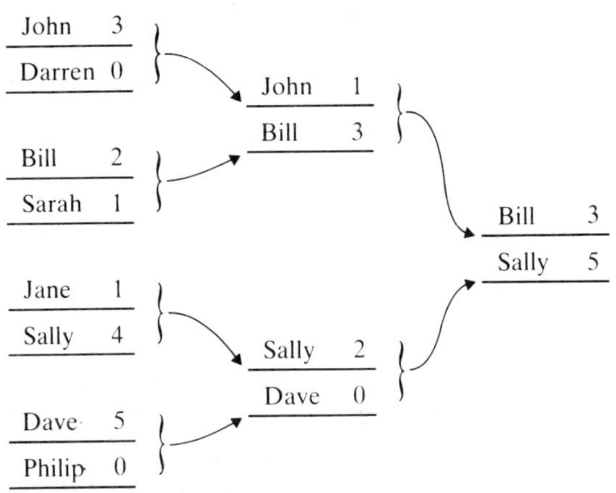

(a) Who was the winner?
(b) Who were the beaten semi-finalists?
(c) Who scored most points in the quarter-finals?
(d) How many matches were played altogether in the whole competition?

2. The diagram below shows a K.O. competition for which 10 players were entered. This time we need a preliminary round involving players W, X, Y and Z.

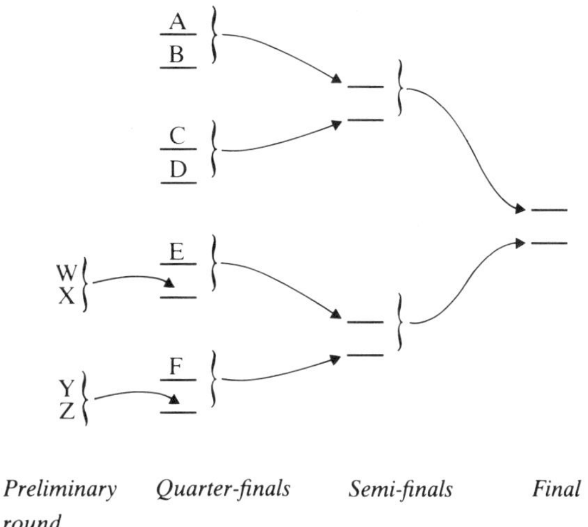

(a) How many players had to play in the preliminary round?
(b) How many matches were played altogether in the whole competition?

3. Draw diagrams similar to those above to show the procedure for organising a knock-out competition for
(a) 20 players
(b) 23 players
(c) 32 players
(d) 43 players
In each case, calculate the total number of matches played up to and including the final.

4. Can you find a rule connecting the number of players p and the number of matches m?

5. In a major tournament like Wimbledon, the better players are seeded from 1 to 16. Can you organise a tournament for 32 players so that, if they win all their games,
(a) seeds 1 and 2 can reach the final,
(b) seeds 1, 2, 3 and 4 can reach the semi-finals,
(c) seeds 1, 2, 3, 4, 5, 6, 7 and 8 can reach the quarter-finals?

Exercise F

1. A group of four adults are planning a holiday in France. The ferry costs, for the return journey, are:

Adult	£25
Car	£62

Travel around France is estimated at 2000 km and petrol costs 5 francs per litre. The car travels 10 km on one litre of petrol.

(a) Calculate the total cost of the return journey on the ferry.
(b) Calculate the number of litres of petrol to be used.
(c) Calculate the total cost, in francs, of the petrol.
(d) Calculate the cost of the petrol in pounds, if £1 is equivalent to 10 francs.

2. A man decorates the room shown in the diagram

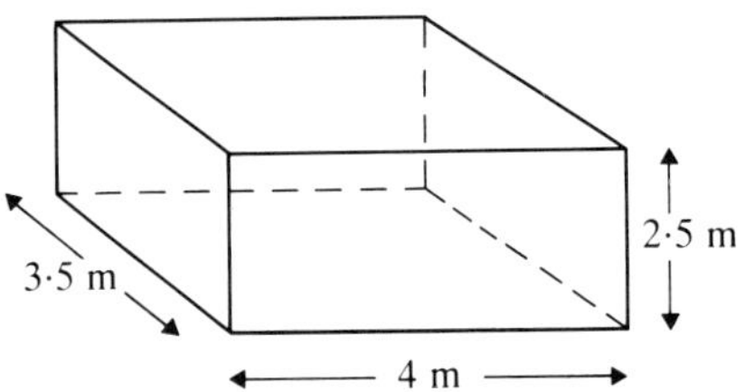

(a) He carpets the floor with carpet costing £8.20 per m^2. How much does the carpet cost?
(b) He paints the four walls with paint which costs 32p per m^2. How much does the paint cost?
(c) He covers the ceiling with tiles, which measure 25 cm by 25 cm. How many tiles does he need?

3. The table below gives details of the repayments on bank loans.

Amount of loan in £'s	12 monthly repayments in £'s	24 monthly repayments in £'s
10	0.93	0.50
30	2.75	1.53
50	4.61	2.52
80	7.40	4.04
400	37.10	20.20
600	55.60	30.50
700	64.70	35.60

(a) What is the monthly repayment on a loan of £80 taken over 24 months?
(b) What is the monthly repayment on a loan of £600 taken over 12 months?
(c) A loan of £400 is taken over 12 months.
  (i) Calculate the total repayment
  (ii) Calculate the interest paid on the loan.
(d) A loan of £730 is taken over 24 months.
  (i) Calculate the total repayment
  (ii) Calculate the interest paid on the loan.

Project 7 AN UNUSUAL SEQUENCE

This work is easier when a calculator is used.

(a) Take a number
  (i) If it is odd, multiply by 3 and then add 1.
  (ii) If it is even, divide by 2.

(b) Take the result and repeat either (i) or (ii) above.

(c) Carry on until you get stuck.
  For example $5 \rightarrow 16 \rightarrow 8 \rightarrow 4 \rightarrow 2 \rightarrow 1$

We will stop when we get to 1 because 1 leads to 4 and back to 1 and so on.

Try the following numbers: 6, 10, 12, 40, 52.

It appears that all the numbers eventually lead to 1. No one has ever found a number which did not produce a final result of 1. If you can find such a number, you will be famous.

Copy and complete the table below.

Number	3	5	13	11	14	17	32	19	23	33	39
Number of steps to reach 1											

Which two-digit number takes the most steps to reach 1?

(More difficult) Which three-digit number takes the most steps to reach 1?

Investigate what happens if you change the rules for the sequence (e.g. If the number is odd, multiply by 3 and subtract 1. If the number is even, divide by 2)

Exercise G

1. In 1986 the costs of running a car for the year were

Petrol	£648
Servicing	£144
Insurance	£ 85.50
Road licence	£105

(a) The cost of petrol was 45p per litre. How many litres were used?

(b) Average petrol consumption was 13 km per litre. What was the total distance travelled?

(c) What was the total cost of running a car in 1986?

(d) In 1987 the petrol costs and the insurance costs remain the same. The cost of servicing goes up by 10% and the cost of the road licence goes up by 20%. What was the total cost of running a car in 1987?

2. A washing machine has a listed price of £320. The machine can be bought in one of two ways:

(i) On hire purchase, in which a deposit of 20% is paid and then a further 24 monthly payments of £13.60.

(ii) A discount price for cash, in which the dealer offers a discount of 8% on the list price. Calculate

(a) the deposit required if the machine is bought on hire purchase

(b) the total amount of the 24 monthly payments

(c) the total hire purchase price

(d) the discount price if the machine is paid for with cash.

3. A shop offers a video recorder at £500 cash or credit terms. The credit terms are 12p in the £ added to the cash price and the whole repayable in 12 equal, monthly instalments. Calculate:

(a) the price of the recorder on credit terms.

(b) the amount of each monthly instalment, to the nearest penny.

4. Nine books cost £22.05. How many of these books could be bought for £36.75?

5. (a) Write down a three-digit number with all digits different — For example: 361

(b) Reverse the order of the digits — 163

(c) Take away the smaller number from the larger number

$$\begin{array}{r} 361 \\ -163 \\ \hline 198 \end{array}$$

(d) Reverse the digits of the answer — 891

(e) Add the last two numbers

$$\begin{array}{r} 198 \\ +891 \\ \hline 1089 \end{array}$$

(f) Try this procedure with four other three-digit numbers. What do you always obtain?

Project 8 MATHEMATICAL SNOOKER

Here we have a rather strange snooker table. There are only four pockets and the base is divided into squares. We are going to play with only one ball. We always play the same shot, starting at the point (1,1)

and each time aiming along the diagonal. When the ball hits the cushion, it bounces off along the next diagonal.

For example the table here is 6 × 4 and there are three rebounds at the cushions before the ball goes into a pocket.

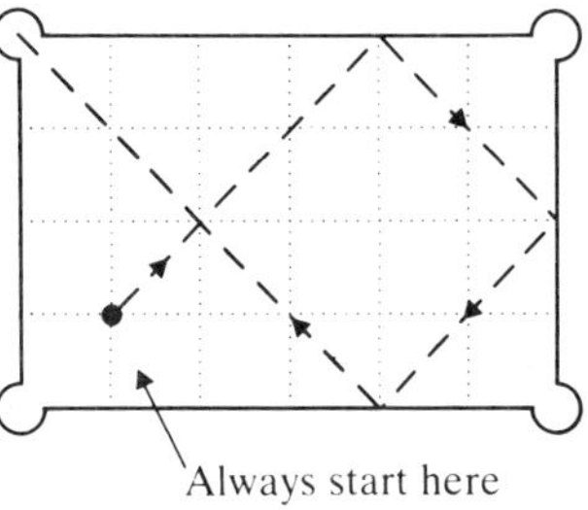

This table is 8 × 6

Into which pocket will the ball go?
How many rebounds were there at the cushions?

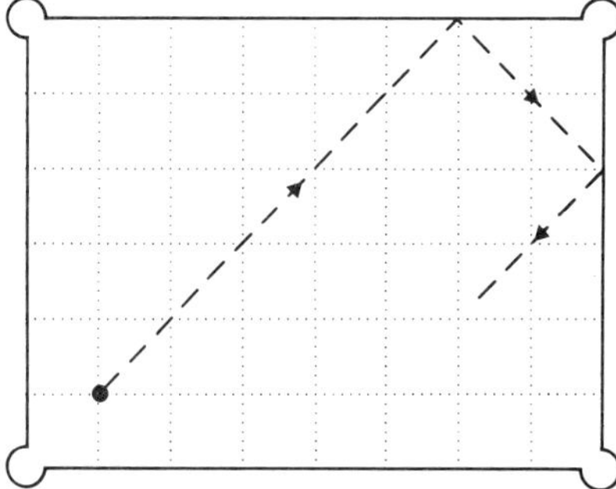

We are going to look at lots of different sizes of table to see if we can discover any rules which might enable us to predict, for any size table, the number of rebounds before the ball goes into a pocket.

Part A
Draw diagrams to show the following size tables and count the number of rebounds. Record the results in a table.
4 × 2, 3 × 2, 8 × 6, 6 × 3, 4 × 3, 6 × 4, 8 × 4, 12 × 9, 9 × 6, 16 × 12.

What do you notice about some of the results?

Part B
(a) Look at tables 8 × 7, 7 × 6, 6 × 5, 5 × 4, 4 × 3, 3 × 2 where the first number is one more than the second number. Is there a rule for the number of rebounds? If you find a rule write it down.
(b) Look at tables 11 × 9, 9 × 7, 7 × 5, 5 × 3 where the first number is two more than the second number.
(Why have we left out 10 × 8, 8 × 6, 6 × 4, 4 × 2? See Part A).
Is there a rule for the number of rebounds?
(c) Look at tables 10 × 7, 8 × 5, 7 × 4, 5 × 2. Is there a rule this time?
(d) Finally look at a mixture: 11 × 5, 12 × 7, 13 × 9, 11 × 2.

Part C
Can you now predict the number of rebounds for *any* size table? See if your predictions are correct.

Part D
So far we have only been looking at the number of rebounds. Is it possible to predict which pocket the ball will go into for any size table? Now you are on your own.

Unit 7

7.1 ANGLES

The angles at a point add up to 360°.
The angles on a straight line add up to 180°.

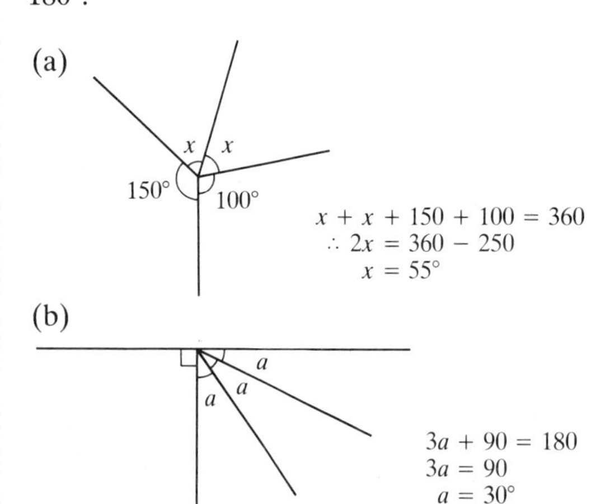

Exercise 1

Find the angles marked with letters. The lines AB and CD are straight.

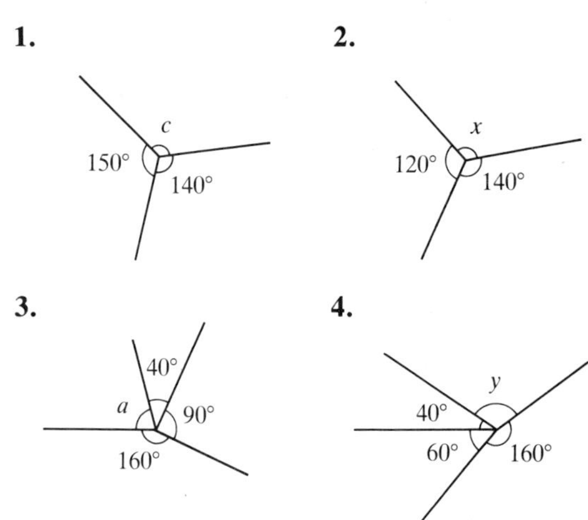

5.

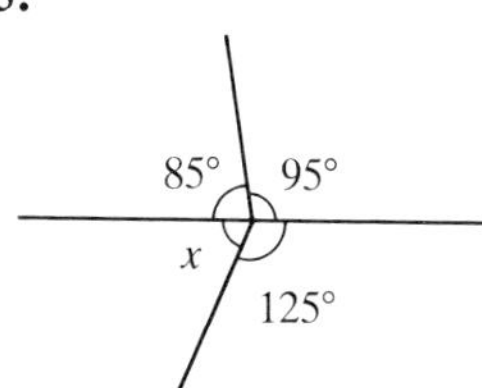

6.

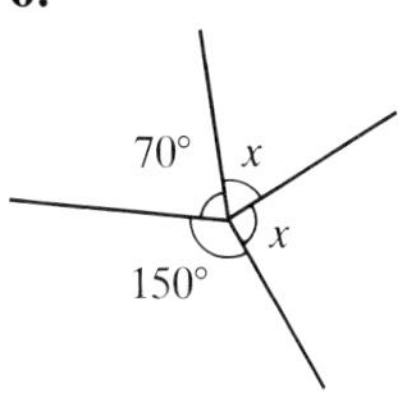

7.

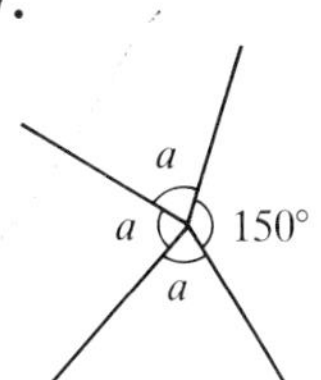

8.

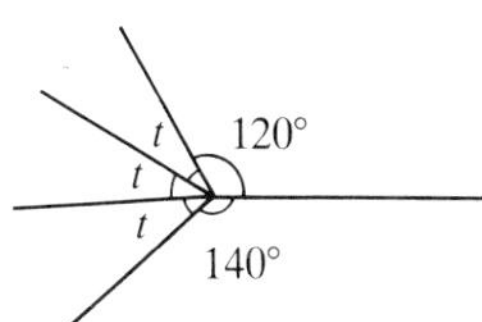

9.

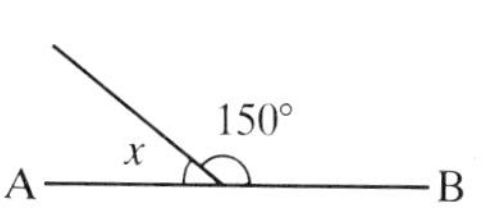

10.

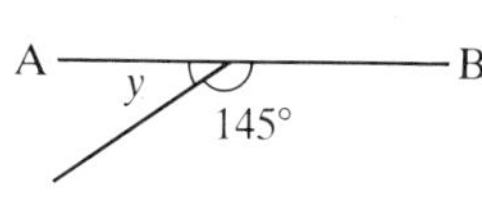

11.

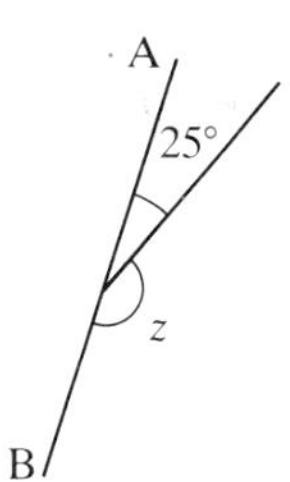

12.

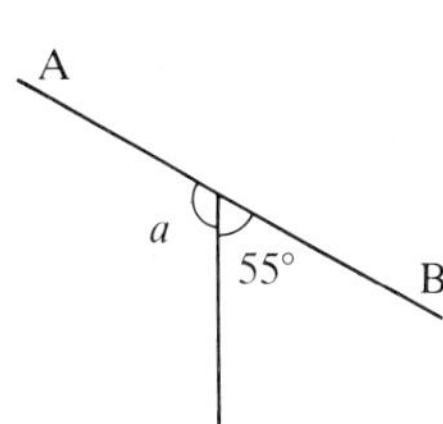

13.

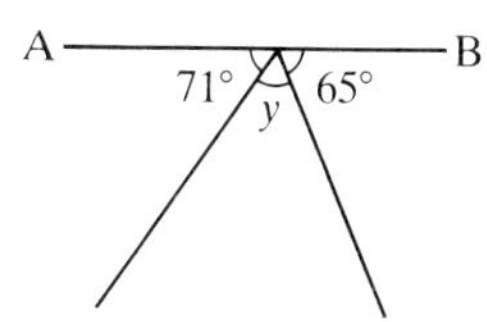

14.

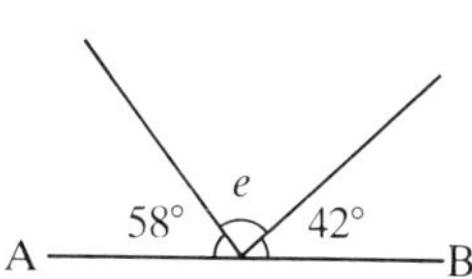

15.

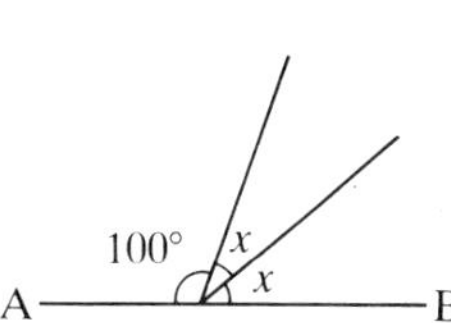

16.

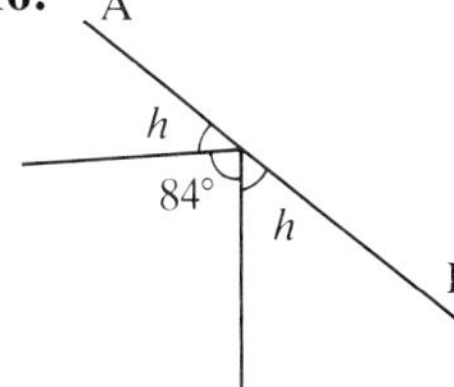

17.

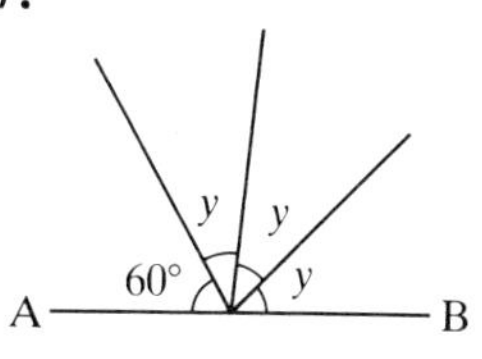

18.

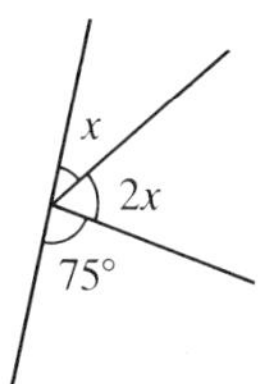

19.

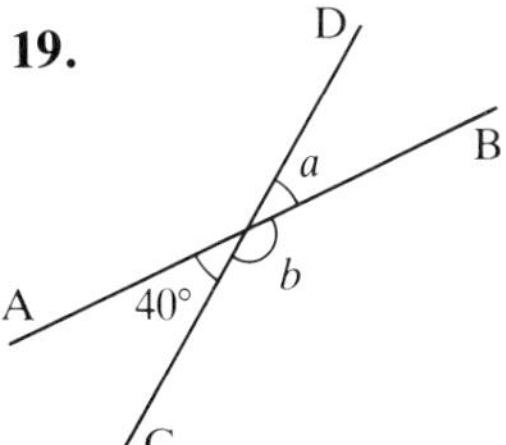

20.

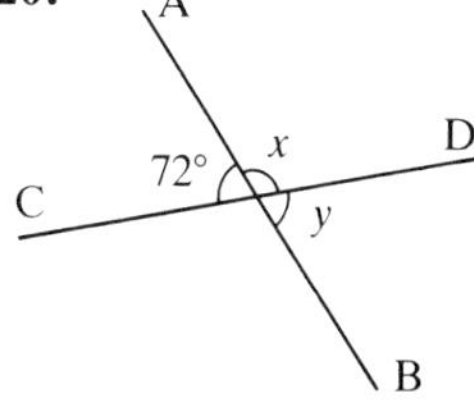

The angles in a triangle add up to 180°.

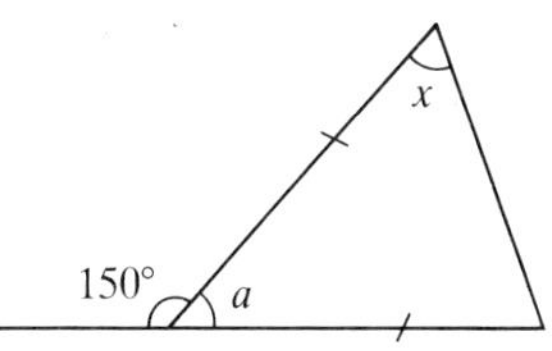

$a = 180 - 150° = 30°$

The triangle is isosceles $\therefore 2x + 30 = 180$

$2x = 150$

$x = 75°$

Exercise 2

Find the angles marked with letters. For the more difficult questions (**9** to **26**) it is helpful to draw a diagram.

1.

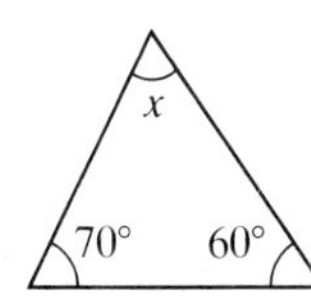

2.

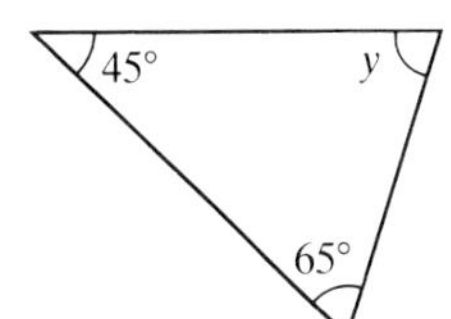

3.

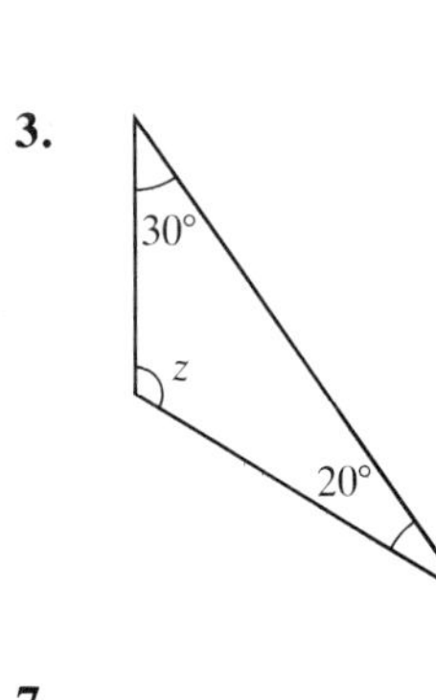

4.

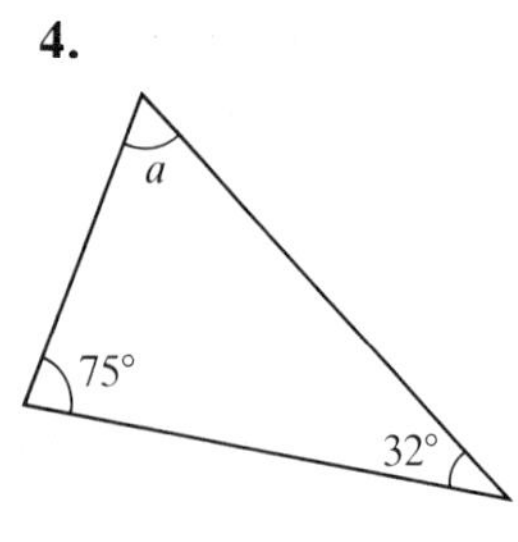

5.

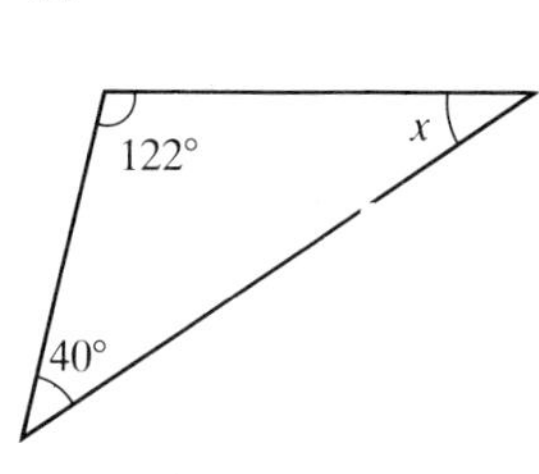

6.

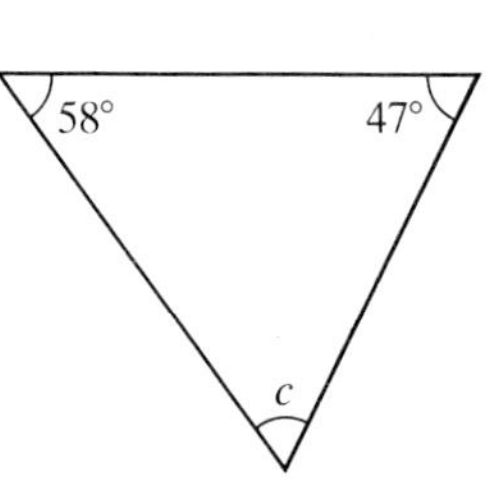

7.

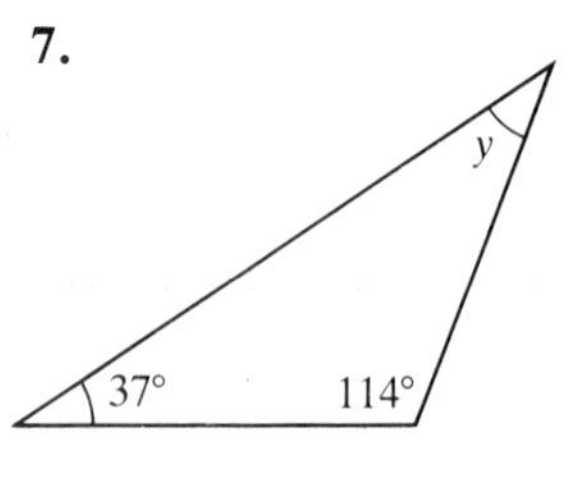

8.

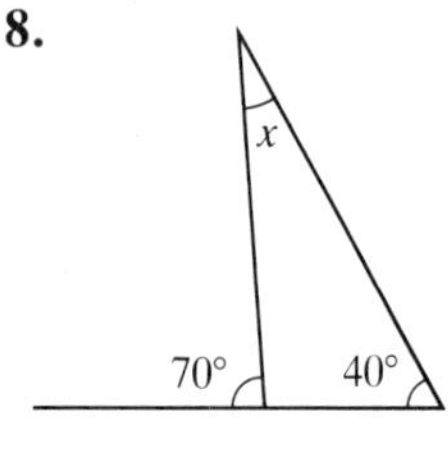

9.

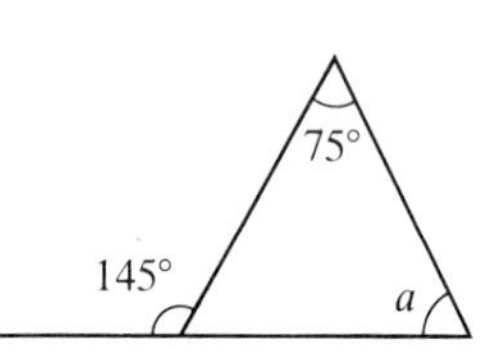

10.

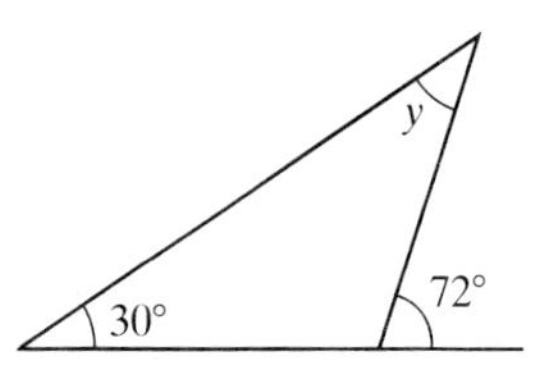

11.

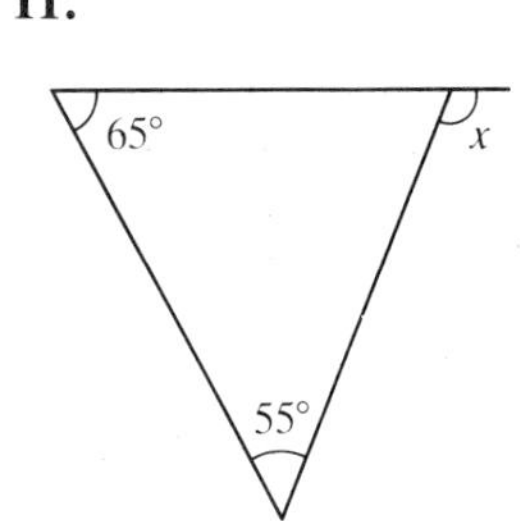

12.

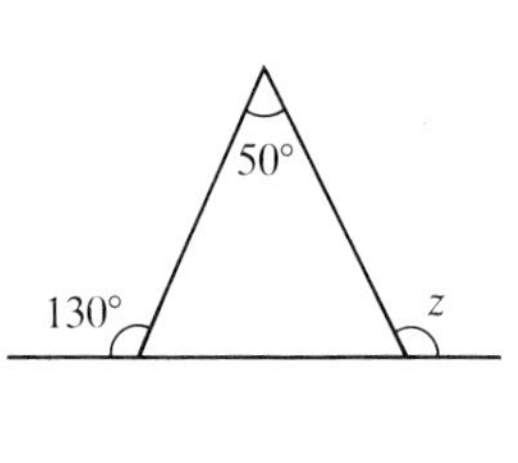

13.

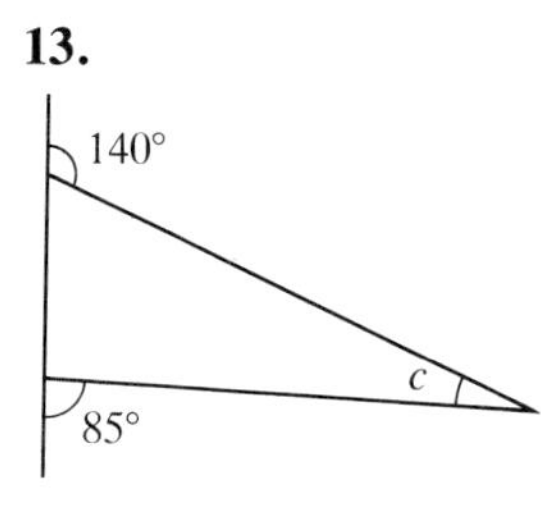

14.

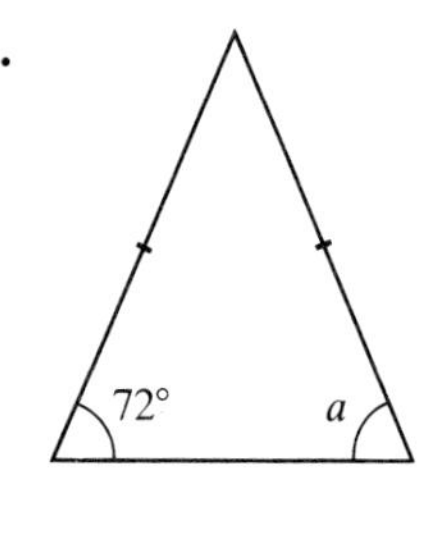

15.

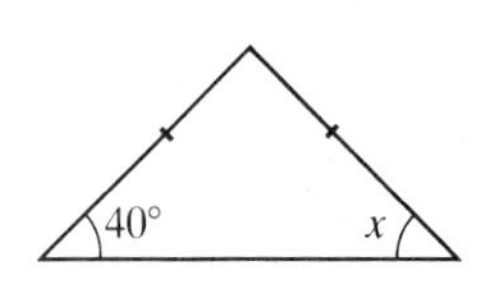

16.

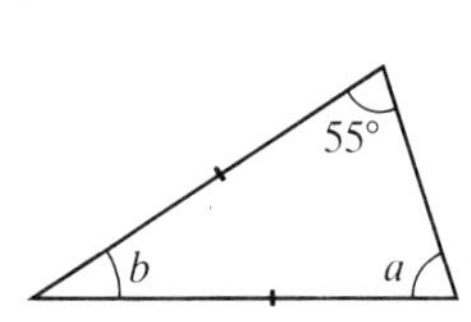

17.

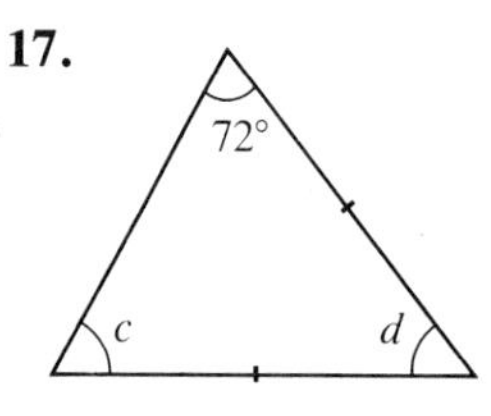

18.

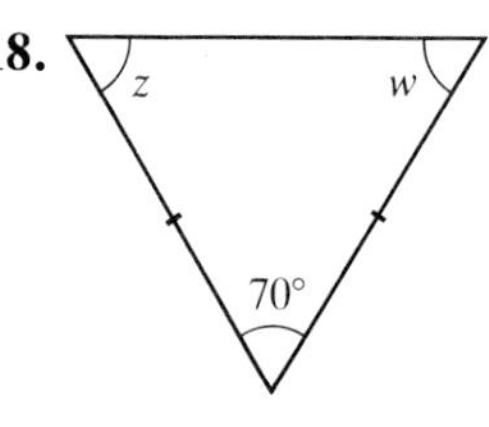

19.

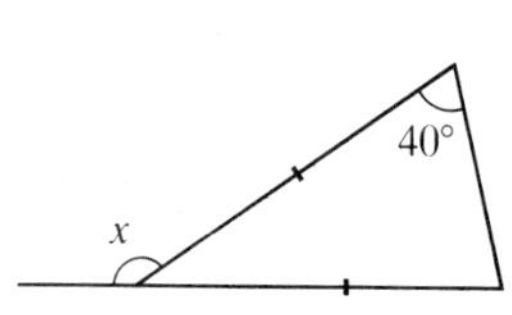

20.

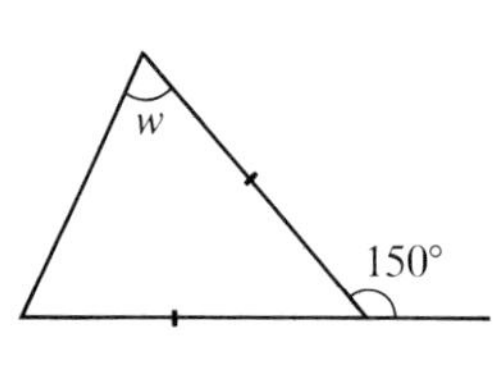

21.

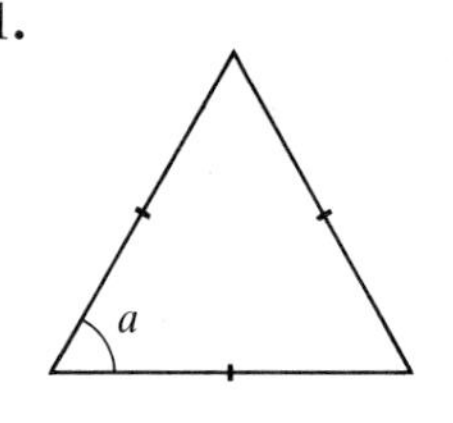

22.

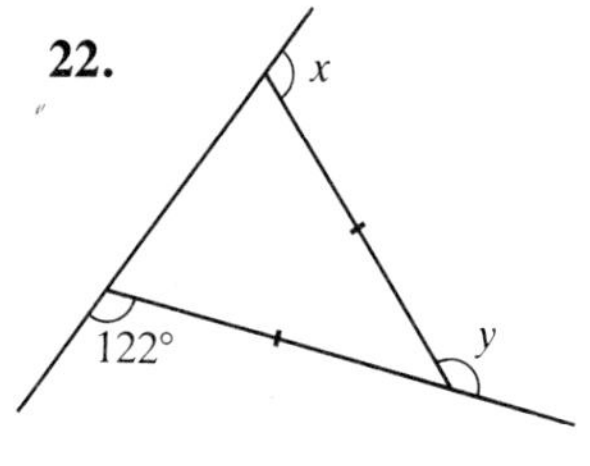

23.

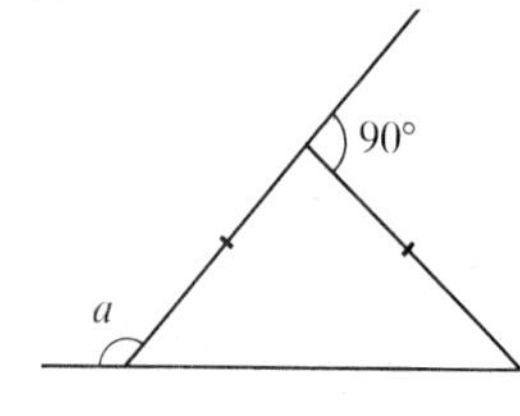

24.

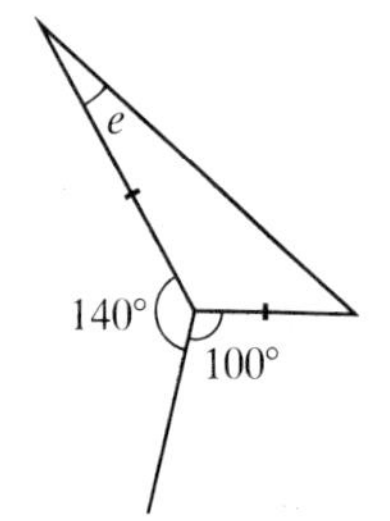

25.

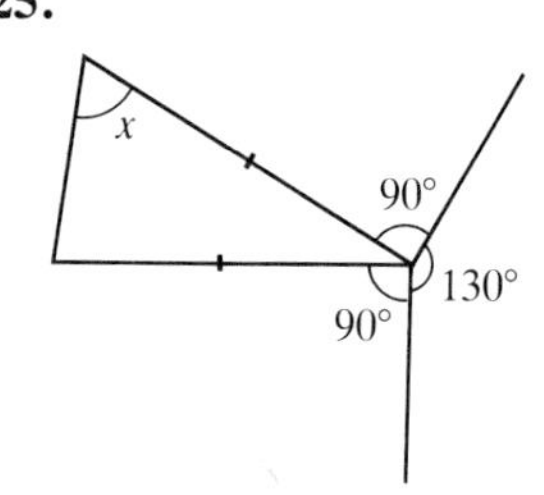

26.

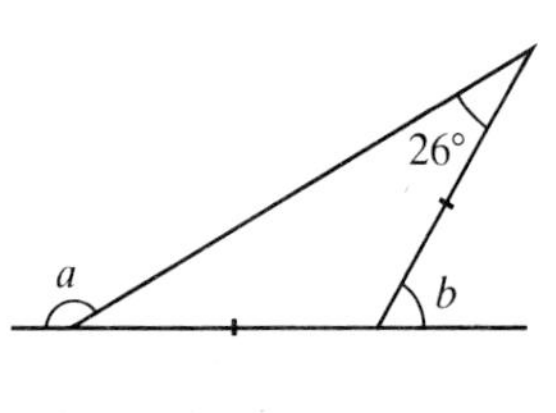

When a line cuts a pair of parallel lines all the acute angles are equal and all the obtuse angles are equal.

(a)

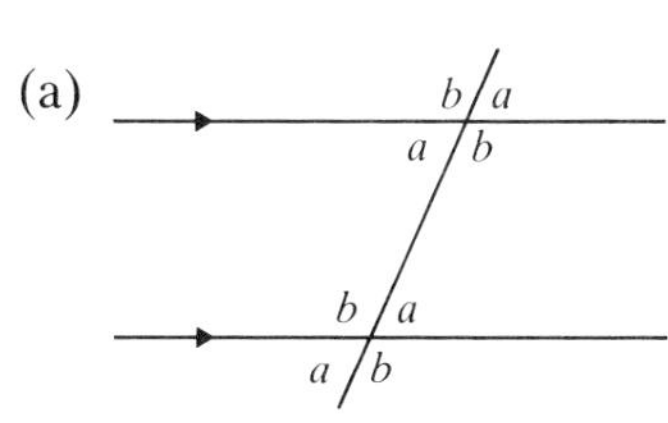

(b)

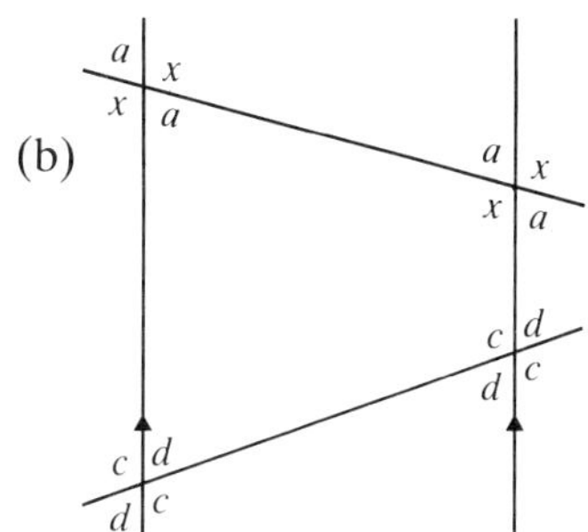

Exercise 3

Find the angles marked with letters.

1.

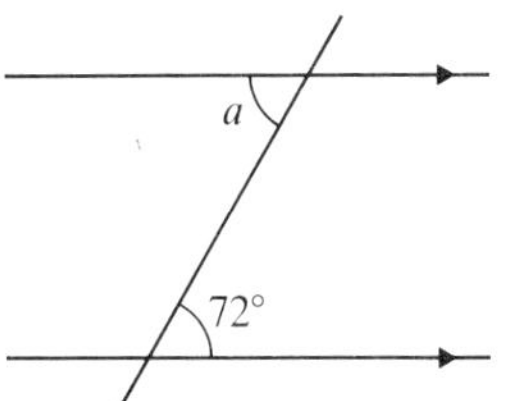

2.

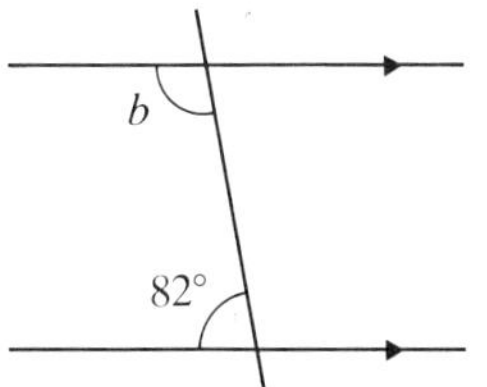

3.

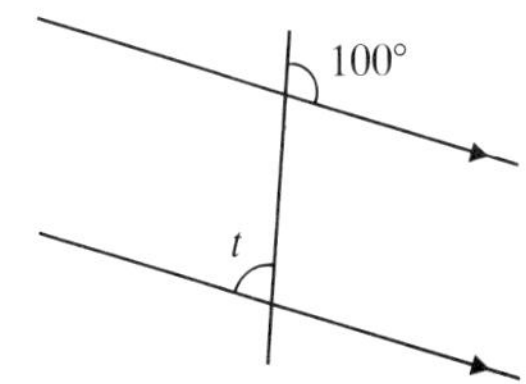

4.

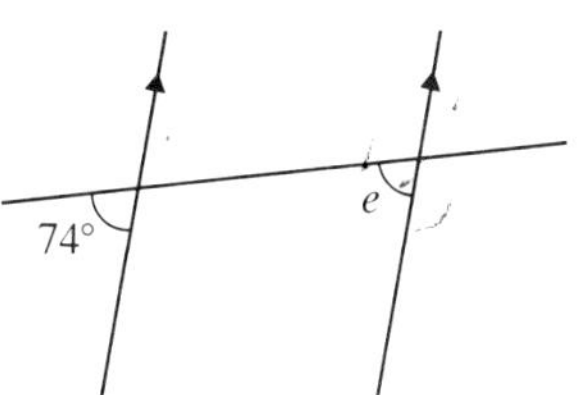

5.

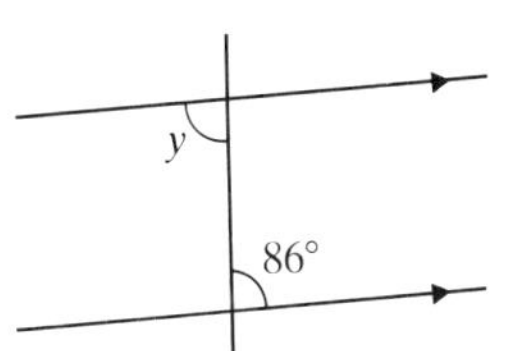

6.

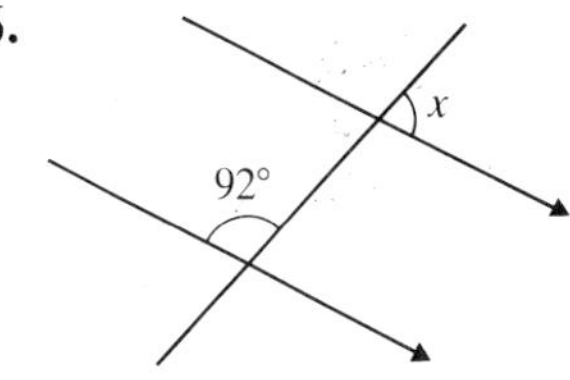

7.

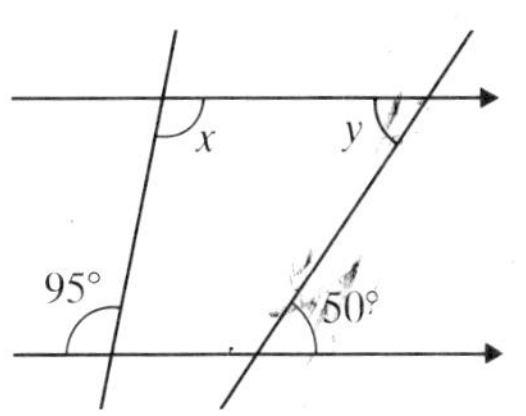

8.

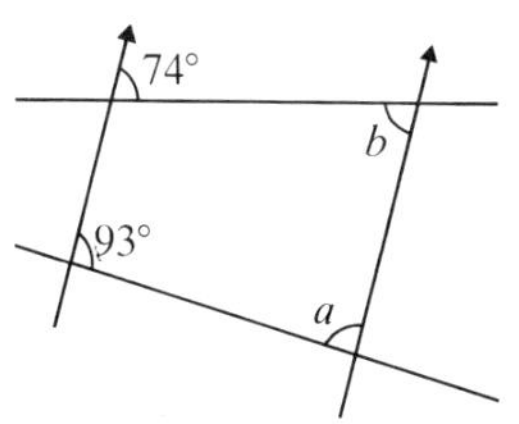

9.

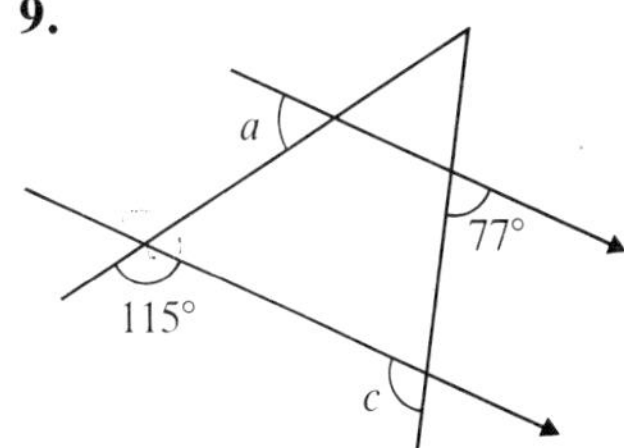

10.

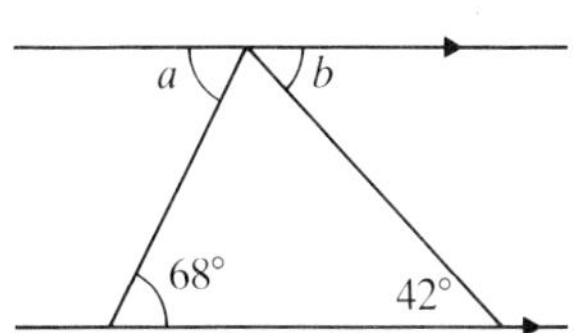

11.

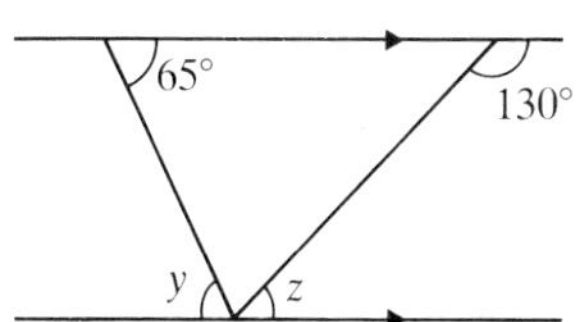

12.

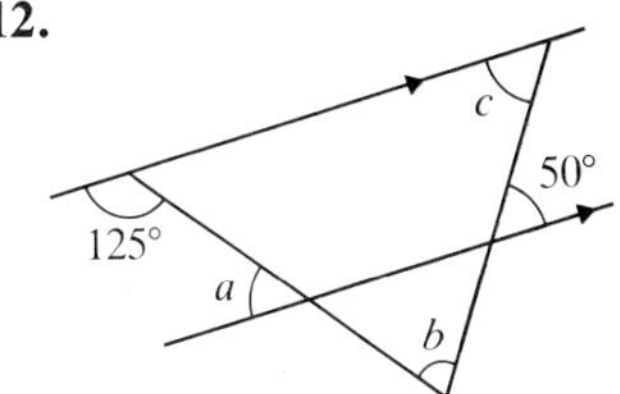

The next exercise contains questions which summarise the work of the last three exercises.

Exercise 4

Find the angles marked with letters.

1.

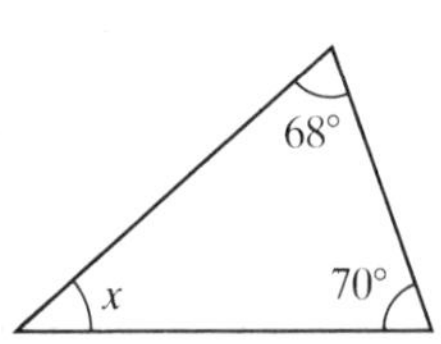

2.

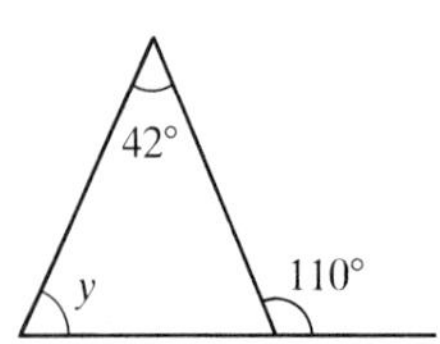

3.

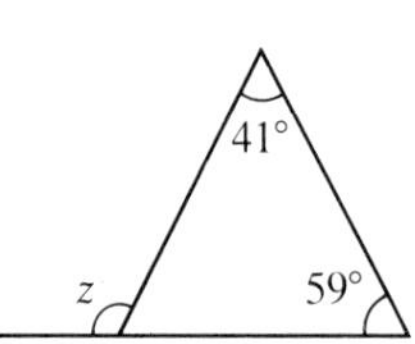

4.

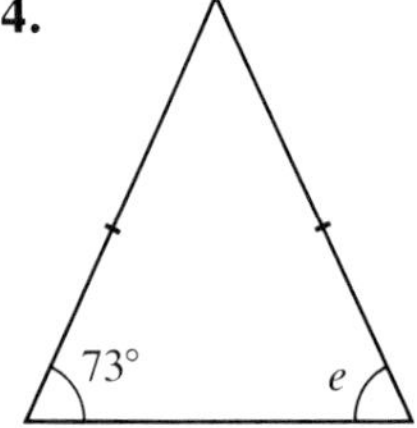

5.

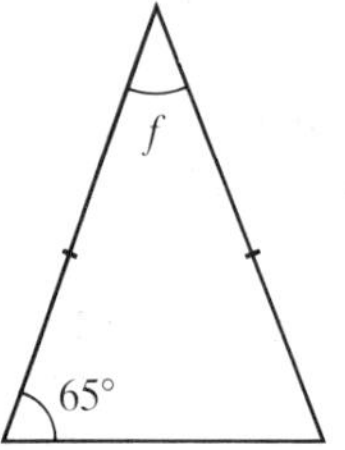

6.

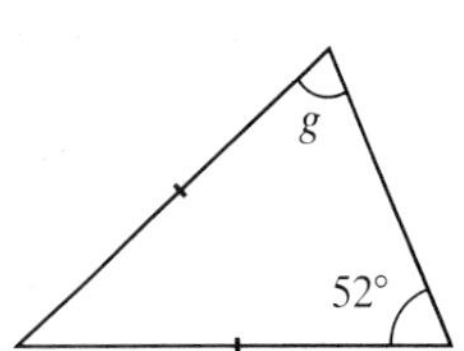

7.

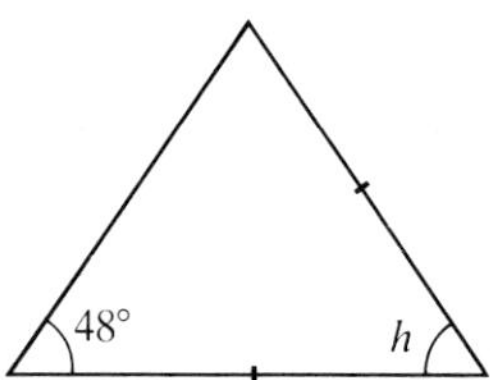

8.

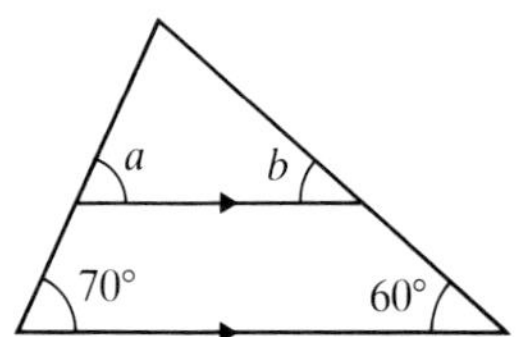

9.

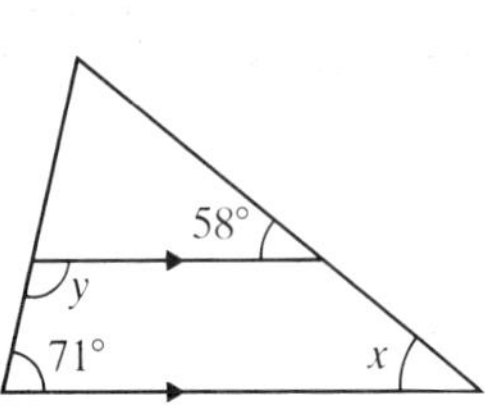

10.

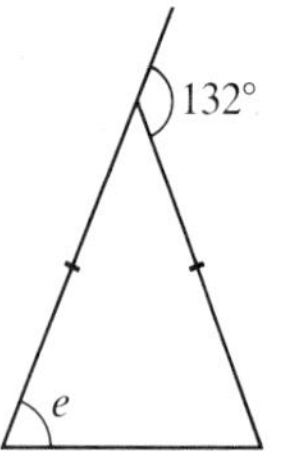

11.

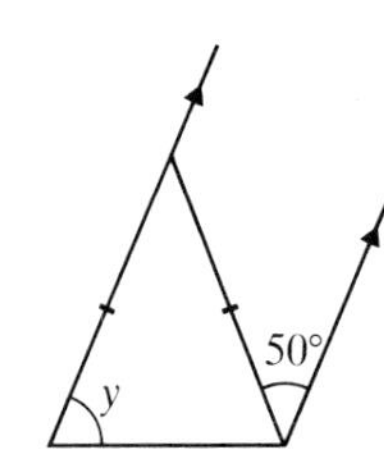

12.

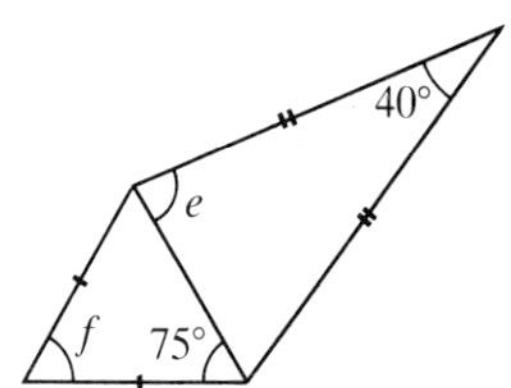

13.

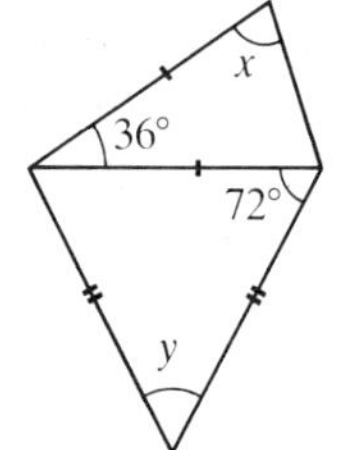

14.

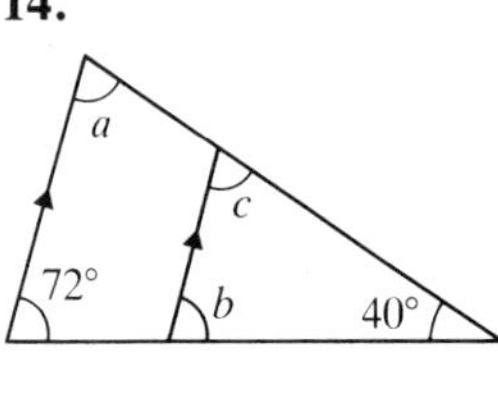

15.

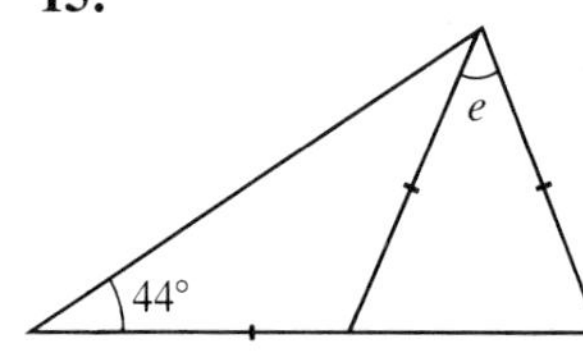

16.

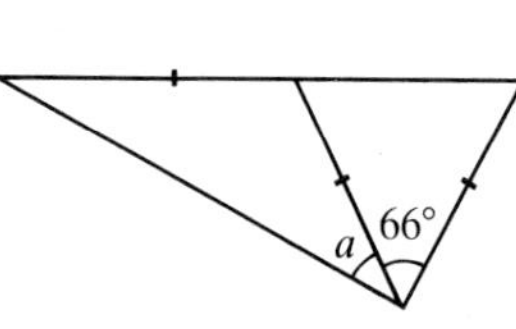

17.

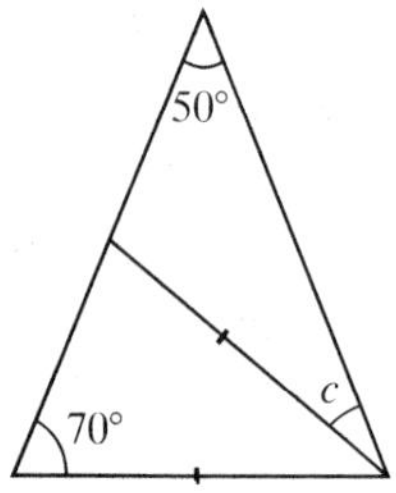

18.

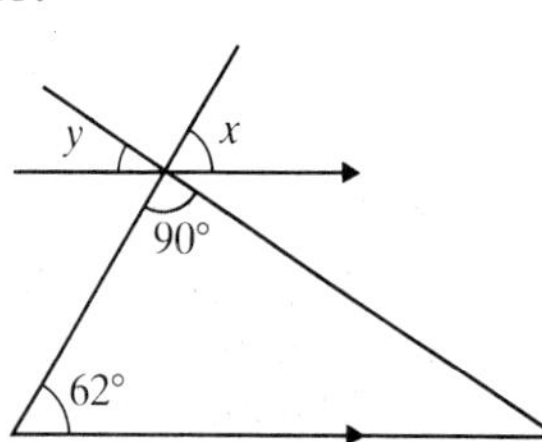

19.

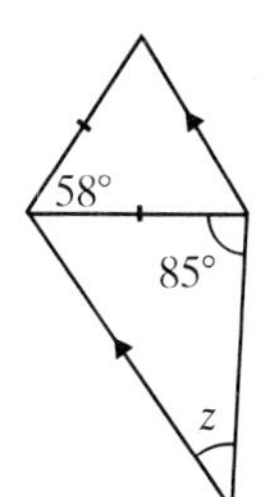

20.

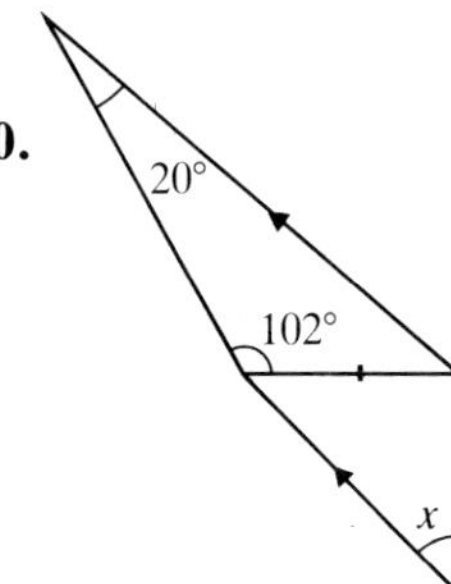

7.2 MENTAL ARITHMETIC

Ideally these questions should be read out by a teacher or friend and you should not be looking at them. Each question should be repeated once and then the answer, and only the answer, should be written down.

Each test, including the recording of results, should take about 30 minutes.

If you do not have anyone to read out the questions for you, try to do the test without writing down any detailed working.

Test 1

1. What number is seventeen more than eighty-two?
2. What is a half of a half of 80?
3. What number is twenty times as big as 30?
4. Write in figures the number two hundred and four thousand and twenty.
5. A television program lasting $2\frac{1}{2}$ hours starts at half-past six. When does it finish?
6. What number is 80 more than 230?
7. How many threes are there in ninety?
8. A record costs £3.20. How much change do I receive from a ten pound note?
9. Find the cost of nine tickets at 20 pence each.
10. What four coins make 44 pence?
11. Work out $\frac{1}{8}$ plus $\frac{3}{8}$ and give the answer as a decimal.
12. A beer crate holds twelve bottles. How many crates are needed for 40 bottles?
13. If the 9th of August is a Saturday, what day of the week is the 19th?
14. By how much is two metres more than 40 cm?
15. Write down 207 pence in pounds and pence.
16. The sides of a square measure 16 cm. Find the total distance around the outside of the square.
17. A television costing £270 is reduced by £58. What is the new price?
18. A lottery prize of £32 000 is shared equally between sixteen people. How much does each person receive?
19. Cold drinks cost twelve pence each. How many can I buy for one pound?
20. What are 19 threes?
21. How many inches are there in three feet?
22. A newsagent stacks 300 magazines into 15 equal piles. How many magazines are in each pile?
23. Add together 37 and 45.
24. What is 10% of £50?
25. Lemons cost eleven pence each. How much do I have to pay for a dozen lemons?
26. A cake costs 36 pence. Find the change from a five pound note.
27. A woman smokes ten cigarettes a day and cigarettes cost £1.30 for 20. How much does she spend in four days?
28. When playing darts you score double ten, double twelve and treble two. What is your total score?
29. What are six fifties?
30. Cheese costs 80 pence a pound. How much do I spend if I buy four ounces of cheese?

Test 2

1. A jacket costing £62 is reduced by £15. What is the new price?
2. Work out a half of a half and give the answer as a decimal.
3. How many sevens are there in sixty-three?
4. What number is ten times as big as 16.6?
5. A sum of £72 is divided equally between six people. How much does each person receive?
6. Find the cost of six bottles of wine at £2.50 each.
7. What four coins make thirty pence?
8. What number is 37 more than 55?
9. By how much is one metre more than 33 cm?
10. Write down 850 pence in pounds and pence.
11. A greengrocer's tray has room for eight melons. How many trays are needed for 30 melons?

12. A film lasting one hour and forty minutes starts at half past seven. When does it finish?
13. If the 14th of June is a Tuesday, what day of the week was the 5th of June?
14. Lemons cost seven pence each. How many can I buy for 60 pence?
15. If you score a treble 18 at darts, how many do you score?
16. What is a half of a half of 56?
17. Write in figures the number five hundred and ten thousand, two hundred and eighty.
18. What are 40 fives?
19. The sides of an equilateral triangle are 17 cm long. Write down the perimeter of the triangle.
20. A librarian stacks 180 books in nine equal piles. How many books are in each pile?
21. How many inches are there in one and a half feet?
22. Add together 9, 13 and 32.
23. A bag of sugar costs 43 pence. Find the change from a five pound note if I buy two bags of sugar.
24. When playing darts you score double five, double ten and treble twenty. What is your total score?
25. A man smokes 60 cigarettes a day and cigarettes cost £1.20 for 20. How much does he spend in two days?
26. Add together 85 and 110.
27. What is 50% of £2000?
28. What are seven 20's?
29. An expensive foreign cheese costs £3.60 a pound. How much does a man pay for eight ounces of cheese?
30. What is the date exactly a fortnight after the 3rd of January?

Test 3

1. Find the cost of seven packets of sweets at nine pence each.
2. What number is 26 more than 25?
3. Write down one thousand pence in pounds.
4. Oranges cost 11 pence each. How many can I buy for 50p?
5. What are eighteen twos?
6. If the 14th of May is a Wednesday, what day of the week is the 19th?
7. A cake weighing 108 ounces is shared equally between nine children. How much does each child receive?
8. A quiz programme on television lasts for an hour and a quarter and starts at ten past six. When does it finish?
9. What four coins make twenty pence?
10. Work out $\frac{1}{10}$ plus $\frac{1}{5}$ and give the answer as a decimal.
11. What is a half of a half of 1000?
12. By how much is 3 metres more than 30 cm?
13. How many fours are there in a hundred?
14. What number is five times as big as forty?
15. An egg box holds six eggs. How many boxes are needed for 15 eggs?
16. Write in figures the number seventeen thousand and nine.
17. How many feet are there in a yard?
18. A car costing £3400 is reduced by £260. What is the new price?
19. If you score a treble fifteen at darts, how many do you score?
20. How many ounces are there in a quarter of a pound?
21. A teacher stacks 1000 books into twenty equal piles. How many books are in each pile?
22. A square has an area of 400 cm^2. How long is each side of the square?
23. Add together 7, 18 and 54.
24. A ball-point pen costs 22 pence. Find the change from a ten pound note.
25. Pencils cost five pence each. How much will two dozen pencils cost?
26. A man drinks three pints of beer a day and beer costs 80 pence a pint. How much does he spend in two days?
27. Add together 38 and 39.
28. What is 15% of £200?
29. A darts player scores double fifteen, double five and treble one. What is his total score?
30. What are fifteen 30's?

Test 4

1. Add together 27 and 32.
2. How many sixes are there in 54?
3. A drink costs 75p. Find the change from a £5 note.
4. What number is twice as big as 59?
5. What four coins make 77 pence?
6. Find the cost of seven ice creams at 12p each.
7. A film lasting $1\frac{1}{2}$ hours starts at ten minutes to nine. When does it finish?
8. If the 6th of January is a Monday, what day of the week is the 12th?
9. Write one fifth as a decimal.
10. Work out $\frac{1}{2}$ plus $\frac{1}{4}$ and give the answer as a decimal.
11. How many inches are there in two feet?
12. How many centimetres are there in 2 m?
13. Apples cost 9 pence each. How many can I buy for 40p?
14. What number is twice as big as 115?
15. A builder stacks 80 blocks into 10 equal piles. How many blocks are in each pile?
16. A coat costing £49 is reduced by £17. What is the new price?
17. What are 17 twos?
18. An egg box holds 6 eggs. How many boxes are needed for 20 eggs?
19. What number is 28 more than 63?
20. Add together 11, 8 and 15.
21. A shopkeeper has 100 footballs. How many are left after he sells two dozen?
22. How many ounces are there in a pound?
23. By how much is 2 metres more than 20 cm?
24. What number is a hundred times as big as 30?
25. Write down 328 pence in pounds and pence.
26. Add together 65 and 165.
27. Work out 20% of £10.
28. A shopkeeper buys a gross of melons. How many is this?
29. A man smokes 40 cigarettes a day and cigarettes cost £1.20 for 20. How much does he spend in three days?
30. A bottle of wine costs £1.95. Find the change from a ten pound note.

Test 5

1. How many ten pence coins are needed to make two pounds?
2. Add three to 9 fours.
3. How many cakes costing 30 pence can be bought for £1.50?
4. Which is the larger: 0.12 or 0.2?
5. How many minutes are there between 9.15 a.m. and 11.15 a.m.?
6. A car does 30 miles per gallon of petrol. How much petrol is used on a journey of 180 miles?
7. I go shopping with three pounds and buy three cakes at twenty pence each. How much money have I left?
8. An escaped prisoner is free for 72 hours. How many days is this?
9. A cake weighing 852 grams is cut in half. How heavy is each piece?
10. What is a half of a half of 30?
11. Find the average of 7 and 23.
12. How many nines are there in one hundred and eighty?
13. What number is twice as big as one hundred and sixty?
14. What four coins make 65 pence?
15. A quarter of a man's wages are taken in deductions. What percentage does he have left?
16. A fishing rod costing £24 is reduced by £5.50. What is the new price?
17. How many minutes are there in three hours?
18. Write in figures the number 'two hundred and two thousand and four'.
19. Write three hundredths as a decimal.
20. A packet of peanuts costs 64 pence. Find the change from a ten pound note.
21. What is 4.30 a.m. on the 24 hour clock?
22. What is 20% of £50?
23. Add together £1.75 and 55 pence.
24. Large eggs cost seven pence each. How many can I buy for sixty pence?

25. Large brown eggs cost nine pence each. How much will a dozen eggs cost?
26. Which is the larger: 0.3 or 0.23?
27. Add together 5, 16 and 22.
28. A pint of milk costs 20 pence and Mrs Green buys two pints a day. What is her bill for seven days?
29. A train took 3 hours to travel 186 miles. What was the average speed of the train?
30. What four coins make 65 pence? Give a different answer to that given in question 14.

Test 6

1. What number divided by 7 gives an answer of 12?
2. Add together four 50 pences and three 20 pences and give the answer in pounds.
3. Which is the larger fraction: $\frac{1}{2}$ or $\frac{1}{3}$?
4. What number multiplied by itself gives an answer of 144?
5. If I change £4 into 20 pence coins, how many will I get?
6. What is the angle between the hands of a clock at 6 o'clock?
7. What is the biggest number that can be made from the figures 5, 9 and 2?
8. Find the difference between $8\frac{1}{2}$ and 20.
9. Rewrite as an ordinary number 2×10^4.
10. Write one centimetre as a fraction of one metre.
11. If meat costs £3.40 per kilo, how much will I pay for 500 g?
12. The profit on a magazine is 10 pence. How many must be sold to make a profit of £35?
13. What number equals ten dozen?
14. What is the smallest number which must be added to 40 to make it exactly divisible by 6?
15. How many 100 ml glasses can be filled from a two-litre bottle?
16. Write in figures the number 'two hundred and seven thousand, eight hundred and twenty'.
17. A ruler costs 5 pence. How many can be bought for £3?
18. The difference between two numbers is 13. One of the numbers is 18. What is the other number?
19. If plastic tube is 20p for 50 cm, how much will 4 m of tube cost?
20. A pile of 12 bricks is 1.2 metres high. What is the thickness of each brick?
21. In a class of 20 children, $\frac{3}{4}$ were girls. What was the number of boys?
22. A car tyre costs £14. How much does a set of five tyres cost?
23. A rectangular pane of glass is 5 feet long and 2 feet wide. Glass costs £1.40 per square foot. How much will the pane cost?
24. The single fare for a journey is £8 and a day return is £13.50. How much is saved by buying a day return rather than two singles?
25. The monthly rental for a television is £6.50. Six months rent must be paid in advance. How much is that?
26. How many 30 pence rulers can be bought for £2?
27. Gas costs 5 pence per unit. How much would you pay for 200 units?
28. How many weeks is 91 days?
29. How long is it between 6.25 p.m. and 8.10 p.m.?
30. A quarter of my wages are taken in deductions. What percentage have I got left?

Test 7

1. Find the average of 8 and 20.
2. If a man earns £4.50 per hour, how much does he earn in 4 hours?
3. How many eights are there in seventy-two?
4. What number is twice as big as thirty-nine?
5. Write in figures the number 'sixty thousand and eleven'.
6. A man stays awake for five days. How many hours is this?
7. What is 8.15 p.m. on the 24-hour clock?
8. How many five pence coins are needed to make one pound?
9. Write four-fifths as a decimal.
10. A video recorder costing £450 is reduced by £55. What is the new price?

11. I go shopping with ten pounds and buy two items at eighty pence each. How much money have I left?
12. A packet of twenty sweets costs 50 pence. How much does each sweet cost?
13. A car consumes one gallon of petrol for every 25 miles travelled. How much petrol is used on a journey of 200 miles?
14. How many seconds are there in $2\frac{1}{2}$ minutes?
15. On a sunny day one-tenth of the water in a pool evaporates. What percentage is left?
16. Add together £4.80 and 50 pence.
17. Add eleven to 8 sixes.
18. What is 50% of £800?
19. How many 25 pence rubbers can be bought for £10?
20. Bananas cost eight pence each. How many can I buy for one pound?
21. A rod of length 188 cm is cut in half. How long is each piece?
22. How many minutes are there between 20.30 and 21.15?
23. Add together 6, 14 and 32.
24. How many half-litre glasses can be filled from a large bowl containing sixteen litres?
25. If a man earns £3.50 per hour, how much does he earn in three hours?
26. A packet of crisps costs 12 pence and a boy eats two packets every day. How much does he spend in five days?
27. An aircraft took four hours to fly a distance of 2000 miles. What was the average speed of the aircraft?
28. The road tax for a car is £100. About how much is this per month?
29. A man died in 1975 aged 68. In what year was he born?
30. By how much is three metres longer than three centimetres?

Test 8

1. Work out 50% of £70.
2. By how much is one kilometre more than one metre?
3. A film lasting an hour and a half starts at a quarter-past seven. When does it finish?
4. There are 20 children in a class and 15 of them are girls. What percentage is this?
5. What number is twice as big as two hundred and sixty?
6. Between midnight and noon the temperature rises by 18°. If the temperature is minus 4 °C at midnight, what is it at noon?
7. From seven times five, take away ten.
8. What four coins make fourteen pence?
9. What is a half of a half of 90?
10. What number is a hundred times fifty-four?
11. A shop assistant is paid £50 a week. About how much is that in a year?
12. Add together £3.75 and 40 pence.
13. How many millimetres are there in one metre?
14. A woman died in 1968 aged 70. In what year was she born?
15. Six pounds of parsnips cost 84 pence. How much do they cost per pound?
16. The maths homework consists of questions 10 to 20. How many questions is that?
17. How many days are there in twenty weeks?
18. Write down ten thousand pence in pounds.
19. If I have £1.40 change from a five pound note, how much have I spent?
20. The time by the school clock is five-past nine. The clock is ten minutes fast. What is the correct time?
21. Spell the word 'isosceles'.
22. The single fare for a journey is £6.50 and a day return is £11. How much is saved by buying a day return rather than two singles?
23. What number is 29 less than 85?
24. There are 50 people on a bus and 30 of them are men. What percentage is this?
25. An egg box holds a dozen eggs. How many boxes are needed for forty eggs?
26. Two angles of a triangle are 60° and 62°. What is the third angle?
27. A car travels at 80 miles per hour for an hour and a quarter. How far does it go?
28. How many two pence coins are needed to make ten pounds?

29. What number is twenty times as big as forty?
30. A ship sails at 25 kilometres per hour for four hours. At what speed is it sailing?

Test 9

1. What number is twice as big as 65?
2. Add together £2.20 and 95 pence.
3. A man died in 1965 aged 70. In what year was he born?
4. Eight pounds of potatoes cost 96 pence. How much do they cost per pound?
5. How many days are there in twelve weeks?
6. By how much is one kilogram more than 50 grams?
7. Write down six pence in pounds and pence.
8. Work out 25% of £800.
9. From four times nine take away seven.
10. How many centimetres are there in 300 millimetres?
11. The time by my watch is a quarter-past eight. My watch is ten minutes slow. What is the correct time?
12. If I have 27 pence change from a one pound note, how much have I spent?
13. A film lasting $2\frac{1}{2}$ hours starts at a quarter to six. When does it finish?
14. Add together 4, 26 and 21.
15. Spell the word 'parallel'.
16. What five coins make 37 pence?
17. What is the date exactly a fortnight after the 8th of June?
18. How many centimetres are there in 30 metres?
19. A teacher sets questions 50 to 100 for homework. How many questions is that?
20. Grapefruit cost twelve pence each. Find the cost of a dozen grapefruit.
21. How many inches are there in a yard?
22. How much less than 140 is 14?
23. Between noon and midnight the temperature falls by 15°. If the temperature is 8 °C at noon, what is the temperature at midnight?
24. There are 24 people in a room. Six are men. What percentage is this?
25. The single fare for a journey is £6 and a day return is £9.50. How much is saved by buying a day return rather than two singles?
26. Two angles of a triangle are 55° and 60°. What is the third angle?
27. A car costing £4000 is reduced by £140. What is the new price?
28. A television programme lasting 45 minutes finished at ten past seven. When did it start?
29. A ship was due to arrive at noon on Wednesday, but arrived at 10 00 on Thursday. How many hours late was it?
30. Write in figures the number 'two hundred million and forty thousand'.

Test 10

1. How many minutes are there in 5 hours?
2. Add together £8.60 and 55 pence.
3. Find the average of 7, 11 and 12.
4. A packet of 20 sweets costs 90 pence. How much is each sweet?
5. The time by my watch is twenty past nine. What is the correct time if my watch is 10 minutes slow?
6. A ship was due at noon on Sunday but arrived at 3.00 p.m. on Monday. How many hours late was the ship?
7. How many days are there in 15 weeks?
8. From nine times eight take away eleven.
9. Thirty-one out of fifty people are men. What percentage is this?
10. Electric cable costs 60 pence per foot. How much do I pay for 3 inches of cable?
11. Spell the word 'equation'.
12. Two angles of a triangle are 55° and 40°. What is the third angle?
13. How many 5 pence coins are needed to make 90 pence?
14. If a man earns £3.20 per hour, how much does he earn in 5 hours?
15. A T.V. programme lasting 35 minutes starts at 12 minutes to 6. When does it finish?
16. How much less than 180 is 34?

17. Nine oranges costing twelve pence each are bought with a £5 note. What is the change?
18. Add 13 to twelve 7's.
19. How many millimetres are there in $3\frac{1}{2}$ cm?
20. A car travels at an average speed of 50 m.p.h. How far does it travel in $2\frac{1}{2}$ hours?
21. What is the perimeter of a square of area 25 cm^2?
22. A rod of length 318 cm is cut in half. How long is each piece?
23. A half is a third of a certain number. What is the number?
24. About how much does a man earn in a week if he is paid £5000 a year?
25. Between midnight and 3.00 a.m. the temperature falls by 7°. If the temperature at midnight was 5 °C, what was the temperature at 3.00 a.m.?
26. An egg box holds 6 eggs. How many boxes are needed for 40 eggs?
27. A car costing £8400 is reduced in price by £270. What is the new price?
28. A man smokes 60 cigarettes a day and cigarettes cost £1.20 for 20. How much does he spend in 3 days?
29. By how much is 1 metre longer than 1 mm? (answer in mm).
30. Write in figures the number 'ten million, forty-two thousand and eleven'.

Test 11

1. A tape cost 95 pence. Find the change from five pounds.
2. The floor of a rectangular room is 8 m by 6 m. What is the distance around the room?
3. Write the number 788 to the nearest ten.
4. By how many does a quarter of 60 exceed 10?
5. Two tapes cost eight pounds. How much will seven tapes cost?
6. What number divided by nine gives five as the answer?
7. What number is ten times as big as 0.3?
8. Write one gram as a fraction of one kilogram.
9. How many 5p coins are there in a bag worth £3?
10. I spend 86 pence and pay with a pound coin. My change consists of three coins. What are they?
11. What fraction must be added to $1\frac{3}{4}$ to make $2\frac{1}{8}$?
12. Twenty per cent of the pupils cycle to school, eight per cent walk, and the rest go by bus. What percentage go by bus?
13. Of the 28 children in a class, a quarter were boys. How many girls were there?
14. Find the cost in pounds of five pens at 25 pence each.
15. I arrive at the docks at 7.25 a.m. and my ferry is due to leave at 8.20 a.m. How long do I have to wait?
16. Find the average of 13 and 27.
17. By how much is 17 greater than $11\frac{1}{2}$?
18. Add together £3.85 and 60 pence.
19. Spell the word 'diagonal'.
20. How many half centimetre lengths can be cut from a piece of string which is 40 centimetres long?
21. A car travelling at 30 m.p.h. takes 20 minutes for a journey. How long will the journey take at 60 m.p.h.?
22. Five light bulbs costing forty pence each are bought with a ten pound note. What is the change?
23. The difference between two numbers is 12. One of the numbers is 20. What is the other?
24. A ruler costs 15 pence. How many can be bought for 90p?
25. How many 20p coins are worth the same as six 50p coins?
26. A certain number multiplied by itself gives 64 as the answer. What is a quarter of that number?
27. If string costs two pounds for one metre, how much will 25 cm cost?
28. After spending £2.35, what change have I from £5?
29. Add together four 50 pence coins and seven 20 pence coins and give the answer in pounds.
30. How many feet are there in ten yards?

7.3 SPEED, DISTANCE, TIME

Finding speed

A lorry takes 5 hours to travel 310 km.
Find the average speed of the lorry.

Use the formula: speed $= \dfrac{\text{distance}}{\text{time}}$

Speed of lorry $= \dfrac{310}{5} = 62$ km/h.

Exercise 5

1. A car travelling at a steady speed takes 4 hours to travel 244 km. What is the speed of the car?
2. A man runs 750 m in a time of 100 s. At what speed does he run?
3. A train takes 6 hours to travel 498 km. What is the speed of the train?
4. After a meal an earthworm moves a distance of 45 cm in 90 s. At what speed does the worm move?
5. During the first month of her life a baby girl grows 4 cm in 28 days. What is the average speed at which she is growing?
6. In the rush-hour a double-decker bus takes 2 hours to travel a distance of 19 km. Find the average speed of the bus.
7. A small plane leaves London at 7.15 p.m. and arrives in Aberdeen, 800 km away, at 9.15 p.m. Find the average speed.
8. A car leaves Norwich at 10.00 a.m. and arrives at York, 290 km away, at 2.00 p.m. Find the average speed.
9. A car leaves Dover at 8.00 a.m. and arrives in London at 10.30 a.m. If the distance is 120 km, find the average speed.
10. A train leaves London at 5.00 a.m. and arrives in Glasgow at 10.15 a.m. If the distance is 630 km, find the average speed.
11. An albatross flies a distance of 470 km in 20 hours. How fast does it fly?
12. A drunken man leaves a public house at 11.15 p.m. and arrives home at midnight. At what average speed does he walk, if he lives $1\frac{1}{2}$ miles from the public house?

Finding distance travelled

How far will a bullet travel in 1.2 s if it is moving at a speed of 1200 m/s?

Use the formula: distance = speed × time.

Distance travelled $= 1200 \times 1.2$
$= 1440$ m.

Exercise 6

1. A car travels at a constant speed of 40 m.p.h. for three hours. How far does it go?
2. An athlete runs at a steady speed of 5 m/s for 100 s. How far does he run?
3. How far will a train travel in 15 s if it is going at a steady speed of 20 m/s?
4. A ball travels for 30 s at a speed of 12 m/s. Find the distance it covers.
5. An aircraft flies at a speed of 800 km/h for $2\frac{1}{2}$ h. How far does it fly?
6. How far will a ship sail in half an hour if it is going at a steady speed of 24 km/h?
7. Calculate the distance from Edinburgh to Glasgow if it takes 12 h to walk between the two towns at a speed of 6 km/h.
8. A killer shark, attacking a fishing boat, swims at a speed of 13 m/s for half a minute. How far does it swim in this time?
9. A well-trained greyhound runs for 25 s at a speed of 22 m/s. How far does it run?
10. A rocket is flying at a speed of 1000 km/h. How far does it go in 15 minutes?
11. A car leaves London at 8.30 a.m. and arrives in Edinburgh at 5.30 p.m. If the car travels at an average speed of 75 km/h, how far is it from London to Edinburgh?
12. A lorry leaves Manchester at 10.00 a.m. and arrives in Dover at 3.30 p.m., having travelled at an average speed of 75 km/h. How far is it from Manchester to Dover?

The three formulae

As an aid to memory use the triangle

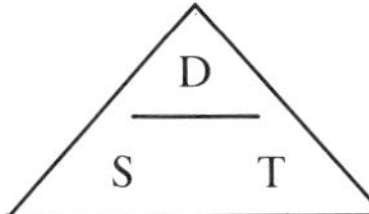

To find speed, cover S so that $S = \frac{D}{T}$

To find distance, cover D so that $D = S \times T$

To find time, cover T so that $T = \frac{D}{S}$

Exercise 7

Copy and complete the table below.

	Speed	Distance	Time
1.	8 m/s	16 m	s
2.	30 km/h	km	3 h
3.	m/s	24 m	2 s
4.	4 m/s	16 m	s
5.	10 km/h	km	5 h
6.	km/h	60 km	3 h
7.	2 m/s	22 m	s
8.	m/s	35 m	5 s
9.	8 km/h	km	4 h
10.	8 m/s	24 m	s
11.	15 km/h	km	3 h
12.	km/h	150 km	3 h
13.	7 m/s	m	8 s
14.	m/s	36 m	4 s
15.	10 m/s	50 m	s
16.	70 km/h	km	4 h
17.	m/s	27 m	9 s
18.	100 km/h	500 km	h
19.	55 km/h	55 km	h
20.	m/s	49 m	7 s
21.	20 m.p.h.	5 miles	h
22.	m.p.h.	8 miles	30 minutes
23.	km/h	4 km	15 minutes
24.	7 km/h	km	30 minutes
25.	22 km/h	km	15 minutes
26.	24 m.p.h.	12 miles	minutes
27.	36 km/h	18 km	minutes
28.	20 m/s	m	0.1 s
29.	300 m/s	m	0.02 s
30.	48 km/h	km	20 minutes

Exercise 8

1. Find the time taken:
(a) 360 km at 20 km/h
(b) 56 miles at 8 m.p.h.
(c) 200 m at 40 m/s
(d) 60 km at 120 km/h.

2. Find the distance travelled:
(a) 55 m.p.h. for 2 hours
(b) 17 m/s for 20 seconds
(c) 63 km/h for 5 hours
(d) 5 cm/day for 12 days.

3. Find the speed:
(a) 98 miles in 7 hours
(b) 364 km in 8 hours
(c) 250 m in 10 seconds
(d) 63 cm in 6 minutes.

The next three questions are more difficult because they involve fractions.
Be careful with the units.

4. Find the time taken:
(a) 6 km at 24 km/h
(b) 12 m at 60 m/s
(c) 8 miles at 80 m.p.h.
(d) 17 km at 51 km/h.

5. Find the distance travelled:
(a) 17 km/h for $\frac{1}{2}$ hour
(b) 26 m.p.h. for 30 minutes
(c) 54 km/h for 15 minutes
(d) 60 m.p.h. for 20 minutes.

6. Find the speed:
(a) 16 miles in $\frac{1}{2}$ hour (in m.p.h.)
(b) 24 km in 30 minutes (in km/h)
(c) 21 miles in 15 minutes (in m.p.h.)
(d) 15 km in 20 minutes (in km/h).

7. A lizard runs 18 m in 5 seconds. Find the speed.

8. A car takes 15 minutes to travel 22 miles. Find the speed in m.p.h.

9. An athlete runs at 9 km/h for 30 minutes. How far does he run?

10. A plane flies 80 miles at a speed of 240 m.p.h. How long does it take in minutes?
11. A killer ant runs at 3 m.p.h. for 30 minutes. How far does she run?
12. An Olympic swimmer takes 20 minutes to swim 2 km. At what speed does he swim in km/h?
13. A cyclist takes 12 minutes to travel 4 miles. At what speed does he cycle in m.p.h.?
14. A train travels at 100 m.p.h. for 6 minutes. How far does it go?
15. A rowing boat covers a distance of 4 miles at a speed of 12 m.p.h. How many minutes does it take?
16. A car goes at 60 m.p.h. for 1 hour 30 minutes. How far does it travel?
17. A horse runs for 2 hours 15 minutes at a speed of 8 m.p.h. How far does it run?
18. An octopus swims 7 km at a speed of 3 km/h. How long does it take in hours and minutes?
19. In a car race the winning car passed the finishing line 8 seconds ahead of the car which came second. If both cars were travelling at 72 m/s, what was the distance between the two cars at the end?
20. The distance from London to Penzance by rail is 420 km. At what average speed must a train travel to cover this distance in 4 hours?
21. In France the T.G.V. does the non-stop Paris to Lyon run, a distance of 448 km in 2 hours 40 minutes. Calculate the average speed in km/h for the journey.
22. The distance from London to Manchester is 295 km. Mr Simpson leaves London for Manchester and drives for 3h 30 min at an average speed of 74 km/h. How far will he be from Manchester after this time?
23. A sprinter runs 100 m in 10 s. Calculate his average speed in km/h.
24. A motorist averaged 50 km/h and 75 km/h over two consecutive 50 km stretches of road.
    (a) Calculate the times taken to cover these two distances.
    (b) Give the total time, in hours, taken to cover the whole distance of 100 km.
    (c) Calculate the motorist's average speed over the whole 100 km.

7.4 TRAVEL GRAPHS

Exercise 9

Make an accurate copy of each graph and then answer the questions which follow.

1. The graph shows a car journey in three stages.
    (a) How far has the car gone after 2 hours?
    (b) How far has the car gone after $2\frac{1}{2}$ hours?
    (c) How long does the car take to go 5 km?
    (d) How long does the car take to go 25 km?
    (e) What is the speed
        (i) from O to A,
        (ii) from A to B,
        (iii) from B to C?

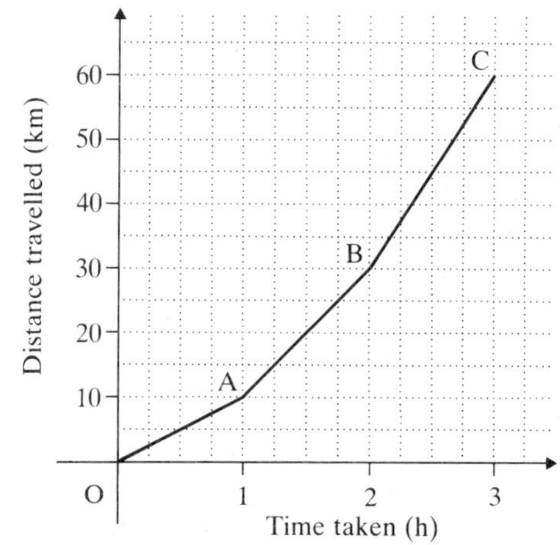

2. The graph shows a train journey in four stages.

(a) How far has the train travelled after
(i) 2 hours, (ii) $1\frac{1}{2}$ hours, (iii) $3\frac{1}{4}$ hours?

(b) How long does the train take to travel
(i) 5 km, (ii) 60 km, (iii) 20 km?

(c) What is the speed
(i) from O to A, (ii) from A to B,
(iii) from B to C, (iv) from C to D?

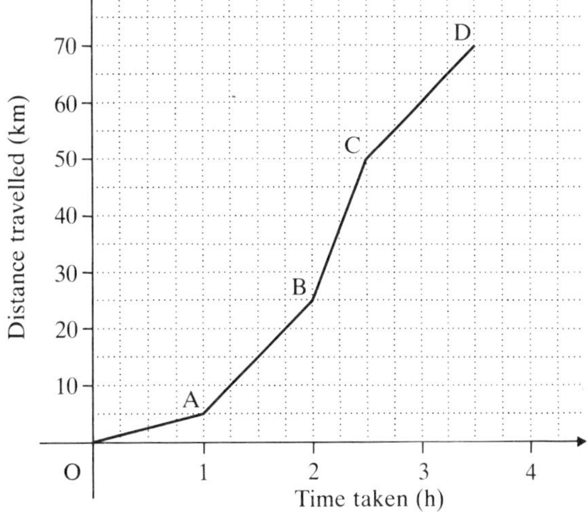

3. The graph shows a bus journey in four stages

(a) How far has the bus travelled after
(i) $1\frac{1}{2}$ hours, (ii) $3\frac{3}{4}$ hours, (iii) 1 hour?

(b) What is the speed
(i) from O to A, (ii) from A to B,
(iii) from B to C, (iv) from C to D?

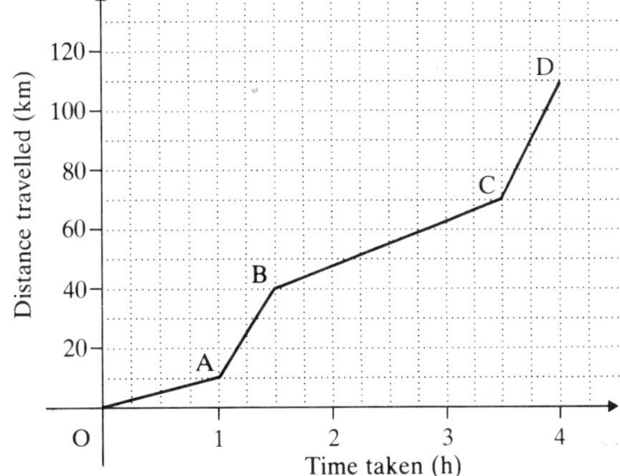

4. The graph shows a return journey by car from Leeds to Scarborough.

(a) How far is it from Leeds to York?

(b) How far is it from York to Scarborough?

(c) At which two places does the car stop?

(d) How long does the car stop at Scarborough?

(e) When does the car
(i) arrive in York,
(ii) leave York,
(iii) arrive in Scarborough,
(iv) arrive back in Leeds?

(f) What is the speed of the car
(i) from Leeds to York,
(ii) from York to Scarborough,
(iii) from Scarborough to Leeds?

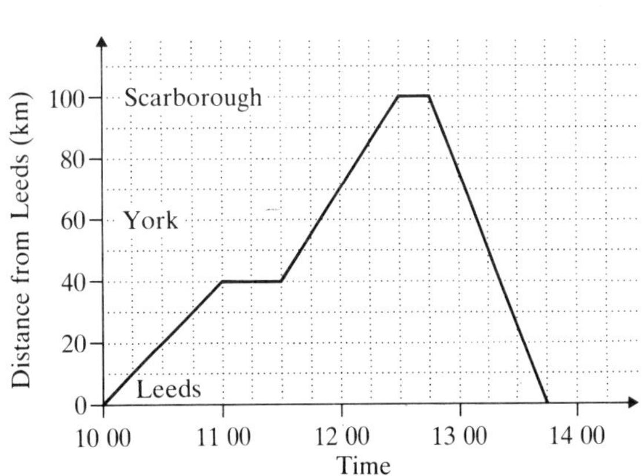

5. The graph shows a return journey by car from Carlisle to Kendal.

(a) How far is it from Carlisle to Kendal?
(b) At which two places does the car stop?
(c) How long does the car stop at Kendal?
(d) When does the car
  (i) arrive in Penrith,
  (ii) arrive in Kendal,
  (iii) leave Kendal,
  (iv) arrive back in Carlisle?
(e) What is the speed of the car
  (i) from Carlisle to Penrith,
  (ii) from Penrith to Kendal,
  (iii) from Kendal back to Carlisle?

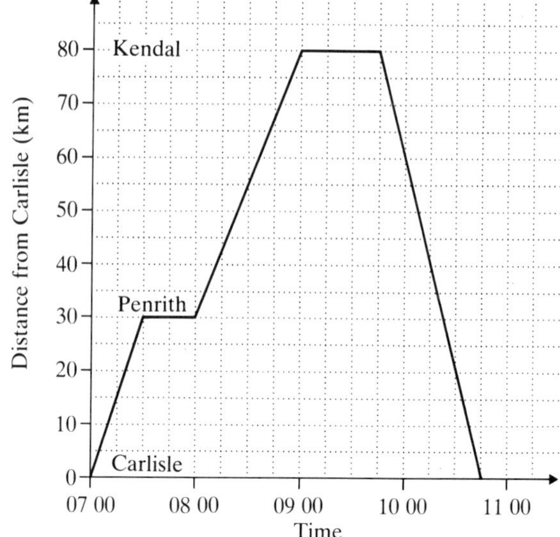

6. The graph shows an athlete on a run from Molash to Thruxted.

(a) At which three places does he stop?
(b) For how long does he stop altogether?
(c) At what time does he
  (i) arrive in Thruxted,
  (ii) leave Chilham,
  (iii) arrive in Bogham on the return journey,
  (iv) arrive back in Molash?
(d) At what speed does he run
  (i) from Molash to Chilham,
  (ii) from Chilham to Thruxted,
  (iii) from Thruxted to Bogham,
(e) At what time on the outward run is he exactly half way between Molash and Chilham?
(f) At what time on the return journey is he exactly half way between Thruxted and Bogham?

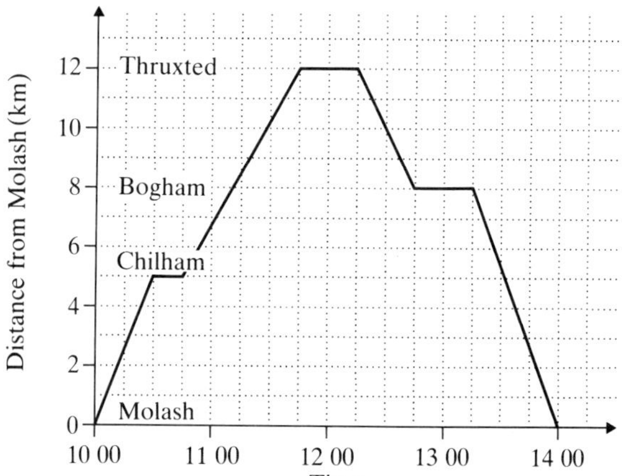

7. The graph shows a man's journey by train, boat and train from London to Paris.

(a) At what time does he
  (i) arrive at Dover,
  (ii) arrive in Paris,
  (iii) leave Calais,
  (iv) leave Dover?
(b) How long does he stop at Dover?
(c) At what speed does he travel
  (i) from Calais to Paris,
  (ii) from London to Dover,
  (iii) from Dover to Calais?
(d) At what time is he exactly half way between Calais and Paris?
(e) Calculate the *average* speed for the whole journey from London to Paris (including stops).

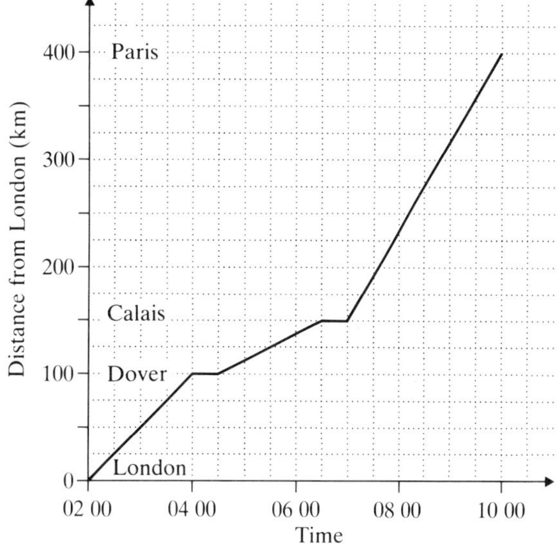

8. The graph shows a woman's journey by plane from London to Aberdeen.

(a) At what time does she
  (i) arrive in Glasgow,
  (ii) leave Birmingham?
(b) How far is she from Aberdeen at 12.15?
(c) At what speed does she fly
  (i) from London to Birmingham,
  (ii) from Birmingham to Glasgow,
  (iii) from Glasgow to Aberdeen?
(d) At what time has she flown one third of the distance from Birmingham to Glasgow?
(e) Calculate the average speed for the whole journey from London to Aberdeen (including stops).

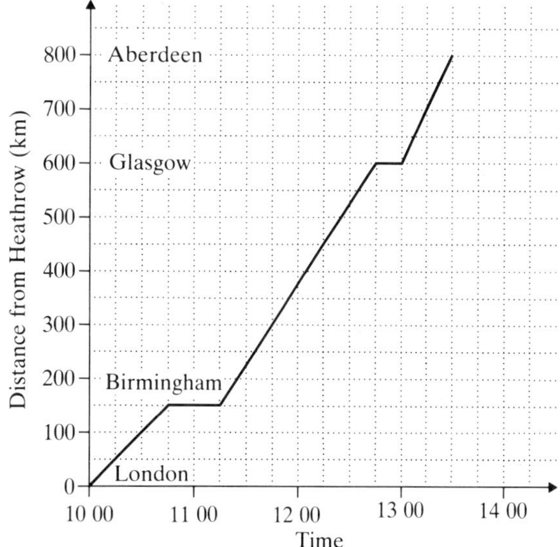

9. Steve cycles to a friend's house but on the way his bike gets a puncture, and he has to walk the remaining distance. At his friend's house, he repairs the puncture, has a game of snooker and then returns home. On the way back, he stops at a shop to buy a book on how to play snooker.

(a) How far is it to his friend's house?
(b) How far is it from his friend's house to the shop?
(c) At what time did his bike get a puncture?
(d) How long did he stay at his friend's house?
(e) At what speed did he travel
  (i) from home until he had the puncture,
  (ii) after the puncture to his friend's house,
  (iii) from his friend's house to the shop,
  (iv) from the shop back to his own home?

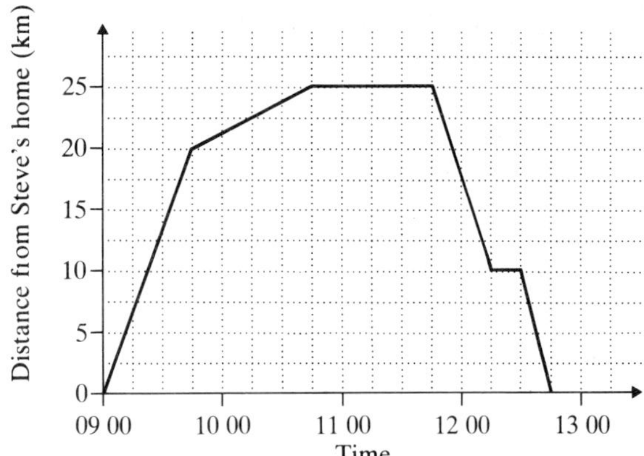

Exercise 10

In questions **1** to **4** make an accurate copy of each graph and then answer the questions which follow.

1. At the same time in the morning Susan leaves home in her car and her brother David leaves home on his bicycle and cycles along the same road as Susan. Susan stops at a garage during the journey but David cycles all the way without stopping. Susan and David arrive in Oxford at the same time.

(a) How far is it from their home to Oxford?
(b) For how long does Susan stop?
(c) How far from Oxford is the garage?
(d) Estimate the time when David passes Susan.
(e) At what speed does
  (i) David cycle,
  (ii) Susan drive to the garage,
  (iii) Susan drive from the garage to Oxford?
(f) How far apart are Susan and David at 11 00 h?

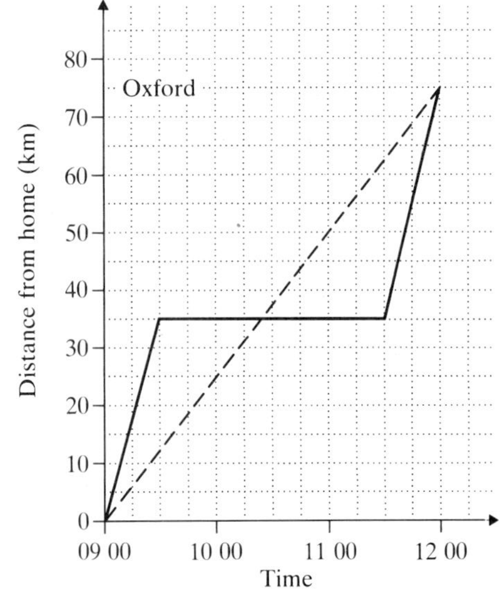

2. The graph shows the journeys made by two trains A and B between London and Brighton.

(a) At what time did
(i) train A leave London,
(ii) train B leave Brighton?

(b) At what speed did train A travel?

(c) At what speed did train B travel?

(d) How far apart were the trains at these times?
(i) 08 30 h (ii) 09 00 h
(iii) 09 30 h (iv) 10 30 h

(e) Estimate how far from London the trains passed each other.

(f) At what time would train A arrive in Brighton if its speed was increased to 60 km/h?

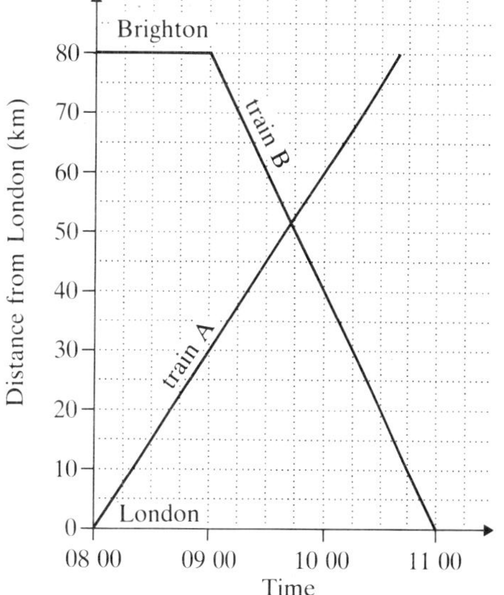

3. The graph shows the journeys of two boys as they travelled along the same road from Hastings.

(a) How long after John did Mark leave?

(b) Calculate the speed of
(i) John for the first two hours
(ii) Mark from Hastings to Tonbridge,
(iii) John for the second part of his journey,
(iv) Mark from Tonbridge to Dartford.

(c) When did Mark overtake John?

(d) When did John overtake Mark?

(e) When did John arrive in Dartford?

(f) How far apart were John and Mark at 15 15 h?

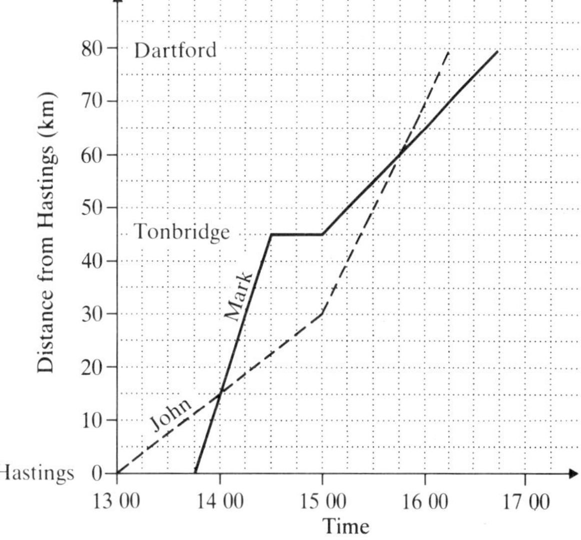

4. Mr Berol and Mr Hale use the same road to travel between Aston and Borton.

   (a) At what time did
       (i) Mr Berol arrive in Borton,
       (ii) Mr Hale leave Aston?

   (b) (i) When did Mr Berol and Mr Hale pass each other?
       (ii) In which direction was Mr Berol travelling?

   (c) Find the following speeds:
       (i) Mr Hale from Aston to Stanley,
       (ii) Mr Berol from Aston to Borton,
       (iii) Mr Hale from Stanley to Borton,
       (iv) Mr Berol from Borton back to Aston.

   (d) (More difficult) When did Mr Hale arrive in Borton?

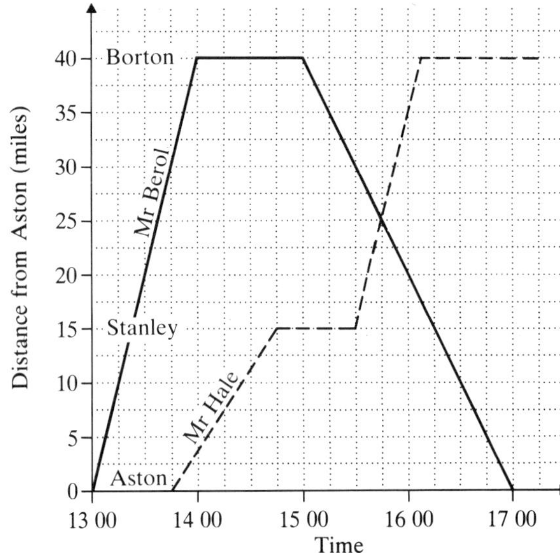

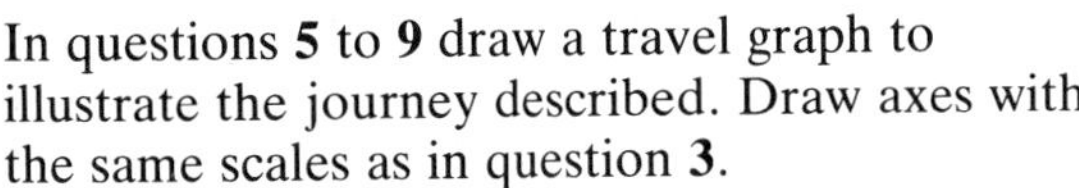

In questions **5** to **9** draw a travel graph to illustrate the journey described. Draw axes with the same scales as in question **3**.

5. (a) A man leaves home at 10 00 and travels to his destination at a speed of 60 km/h for 1 hour. He stops for $1\frac{1}{2}$ hours and then returns home at a speed of 40 km/h.
   (b) Use the graph to find the time at which he arrived home.

6. (a) A man leaves home at midday and travels to his destination at a speed of 40 km/h for $1\frac{1}{2}$ hours. He stops for 1 hour and then returns home at a speed of 60 km/h.
   (b) Use the graph to find the time at which he arrived home.

7. (a) A man leaves home at 08 00 and drives at a speed of 30 km/h. After 1 hour he increases his speed to 50 km/h and continues at this speed for a further 1 hour. He stops for $\frac{3}{4}$ hour and then returns home at a speed of 80 km/h.
   (b) Use the graph to find the time at which he arrived home.

8. (a) Mrs Begg leaves home at 09 00 and drives at a speed of 60 km/h. After $\frac{1}{2}$ hour she reduces her speed to 50 km/h and continues at this speed for a further 1 hour. She stops for 15 minutes and then returns home at a speed of 40 km/h.
   (b) Use the graph to find the time at which she arrives home.

9. (a) It is 40 km from Dundee to Perth and 40 km from Perth to Stirling. Mark Dundee, Perth and Stirling on your graph with Dundee at the bottom.
   (b) A man leaves Dundee at 13 00 and travels at a speed of 40 km/h for 1 hour. He stops for $\frac{1}{2}$ hour at Perth and then continues his journey to Stirling at a speed of 40 km/h. He stops at Stirling for $\frac{1}{2}$ hour and then returns to Dundee at a speed of 80 km/h.
   (c) Use the graph to find the time at which he returns to Dundee.

7.5 STRAIGHT LINE GRAPHS

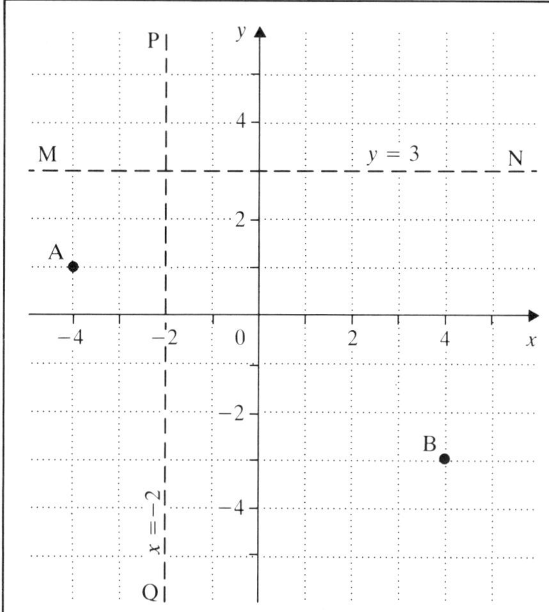

In the diagram above:
A has coordinates (−4,1).
B has coordinates (4,−3).
Line MN has equation $y = 3$.
Line PQ has equation $x = -2$.

Exercise 11

Draw a set of axes with x and y from −8 to +8. Plot and label the following points.

A(3,6), B(2,3), C(−2,4), D(−4,2), E(2,−2), F(−3,−4), G(7,2), H(−6,−3), I(6,−4), J(−6,6), K(7,7), L(3,−5), M(−5,−5), N(1,2), O(7,−2), P(−6,4), Q(4,4), R(−4,4), S(1, 6), T(5,0), U(0,−3), V(−7,−7), W(0,3).

In questions **1** to **10** list the points on the line given.

1. $y = 3$ **2.** $y = -5$
3. $y = 6$ **4.** $x = 7$
5. $x = -4$ **6.** $y = -2$
7. $x = 0$ **8.** $y = 7$
9. $y = x$ **10.** $y = 0$

In questions **11** to **26** write down the equation of the line on which the given points lie.

11. P, R, C, Q **12.** H, U
13. B, E **14.** F, I
15. R, D **16.** M, L
17. W, U **18.** M, Q, K
19. E, O **20.** A, L
21. B, T. O **22.** N, B
23. W, N **24.** H, W, A
25. A, G **26.** N, A

The next two exercises provide revision of negative numbers, which are used extensively in the rest of this section.

Exercise 12

1. $2 \times (-3)$ **2.** -3×3 **3.** $4 \times (-1)$
4. $-1 \times (-2)$ **5.** -3×4 **6.** $-2 \times (-2)$
7. $-3 \times (-4)$ **8.** $5 \times (-2)$ **9.** -1×6
10. $-6 \times (-2)$ **11.** $-3 \times (-5)$ **12.** -3×7
13. -3×1 **14.** $0 \times (-4)$ **15.** $5 \times (-6)$
16. -3×0 **17.** $-7 \times (-1)$ **18.** $-4 \times (-5)$
19. $3 \times (-6)$ **20.** -4×0 **21.** $8 \times (-1)$
22. -1×7 **23.** $0 \times (-3)$ **24.** $4 \times (-4)$

25. $-2 \times (-3)$ **26.** $7 \times (-5)$ **27.** $8 \times (-2)$
28. $(-2)^2$ **29.** $(-3)^2$ **30.** $(-1)^2$
31. $(0)^2$ **32.** -1×9 **33.** $9 \times (-1)$
34. $-9 \times (-1)$ **35.** -8×5 **36.** $(-4)^2$
37. $(2)^2$ **38.** $(-5)^2$ **39.** $0 \times (-7)$
40. $-6 \times (-9)$ **41.** $8 \times (-10)$ **42.** $(-10)^2$
43. $4 \times (-2)$ **44.** $6 \times (-3)$ **45.** $(-8)^2$
46. $0 \times (-10)$ **47.** $-9 \times (-3)$ **48.** $(-7)^2$

Exercise 13

Add together the numbers given.

1. −4, 6 **2.** −2, −2 **3.** −6, −1
4. 8, −5 **5.** 4, −3 **6.** −3, −5
7. 7, −2 **8.** −8, 2 **9.** −9, −4
10. −3, −3 **11.** 9, −12 **12.** 5, −1
13. −6, −2 **14.** 4, −10 **15.** 8, −11
16. −12, −10 **17.** −6, −7 **18.** −2, 5
19. 5, 6 **20.** −7, 2 **21.** 4, 13
22. −8, −5 **23.** −9, 15 **24.** 9, −6

25. −7, −3, 2 **26.** 8, −2, 1
27. −4, −5, 8 **28.** −1, 4, 3
29. −6, 2, 10 **30.** −2, −3, 6
31. −7, −2, 9 **32.** 8, −2, 4

Table of values

Work out a table of values for the graph of $y = 3x - 5$ for values of x from -3 to $+3$.

x	-3	-2	-1	0	1	2	3
$3x$	-9	-6	-3	0	3	6	9
-5	-5	-5	-5	-5	-5	-5	-5
y	-14	-11	-8	-5	-2	1	4

Exercise 14

Copy and complete the tables of values.

1. $y = 2x + 3$

x	-3	-2	-1	0	1	2	3
$2x$	-6	-4		0	2		
$+3$	3	3	3	3			
y				3			

2. $y = 4x - 2$

x	-3	-2	-1	0	1	2	3
$4x$				0	4		12
-2	-2	-2		-2	-2		
y				-2	2		

3. $y = 3x + 4$

x	-4	-3	-2	-1	0	1	2
$3x$							
$+4$							
y							

4. $y = x + 5$

x	-3	-2	-1	0	1	2	3
x	-3	-2					
$+5$	5	5					
y	2						

5. $y = 5x - 9$

x	-4	-3	-2	-1	0	1	2
$5x$							
-9							
y							

Drawing straight line graphs

Draw the graph of $y = 4 - 2x$ for values of x from -2 to $+3$

(a)

x	-2	-1	0	1	2	3
4	4	4	4	4	4	4
$-2x$	4	2	0	-2	-4	-6
y	8	6	4	2	0	-2

(b) Plot the values of x and y from the table

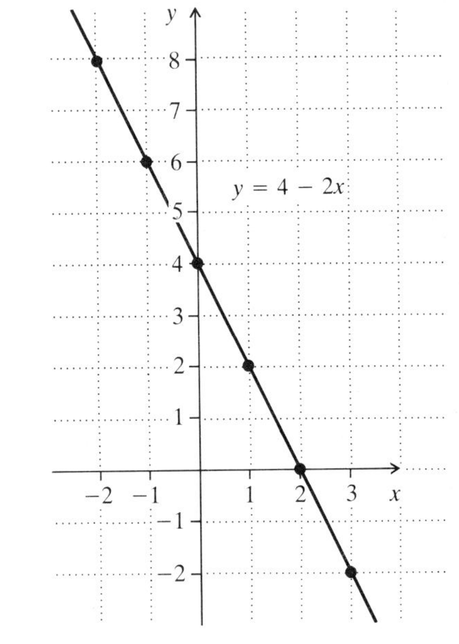

Exercise 15

For each question make a table of values and then draw the graph. Suggested scales: 1 cm to 1 unit on both axes, unless otherwise stated.

1. $y = 2x + 1$; x from -3 to $+3$.

x	-3	-2	-1	0	1	2	3
$2x$	-6	-4					
$+1$	1	1	1				
y	-5	-3					

2. $y = 3x - 5$; x from -2 to $+3$.
3. $y = x + 2$; x from -4 to $+4$.
4. $y = 2x - 7$; x from -2 to $+5$.
5. $y = 4x + 1$; x from -3 to $+3$.
(Use scales of 1 cm to 1 unit on the x-axis and 1 cm to 2 units on the y-axis.)

6. $y = x - 3$; x from -2 to $+5$.
7. $y = 2x + 4$; x from -4 to $+2$.
8. $y = 3x + 2$; x from -3 to $+3$.
9. $y = x + 7$; x from -5 to $+3$.
10. $y = 4x - 3$; x from -3 to $+3$.

    (Use scales of 1 cm to 1 unit on the x-axis and 1 cm to 2 units on the y-axis.)
11. $y = 4 - 2x$; x from -3 to $+3$.

x	-3	-2	-1	0	1	2	3
4	4	4	4	4			4
$-2x$	6	4					-6
y	10	8					-2

12. $y = 8 - 2x$; x from -2 to $+4$.
13. $y = 5 - 3x$; x from -3 to $+3$.
14. $y = 2 - x$; x from -3 to $+3$.

x	-3	-2	-1	0	1	2	3
2	2	2	2	2			
$-x$	3	2					-3
y	5	4					

15. $y = 6 - x$; x from -1 to $+7$.
16. $y = 7 - 4x$; x from -2 to $+4$.

    (Use scales of 1 cm to 1 unit on the x-axis and 1 cm to 2 units on the y-axis.)
17. $y = -2 - 2x$; x from -3 to $+3$.
18. $y = -5 - x$; x from -2 to $+5$.
19. $y = 2x + 3$; x from -3 to $+3$.
20. $y = 10 - 2x$; x from 0 to $+6$.

7.6 CURVED GRAPHS

Table of values

Work out a table of values for the graph of $y = x^2 + 2x$ for values of x from -3 to $+3$

x	-3	-2	-1	0	1	2	3
x^2	9	4	1	0	1	4	9
$2x$	-6	-4	-2	0	2	4	6
y	3	0	-1	0	3	8	15

Exercise 16

Copy and complete the tables of values.

1. $y = x^2 + 3x$.

x	-4	-3	-2	-1	0	1	2
x^2	16	9	4				
$3x$	-12	-9	-6				
y	4	0	-2				

2. $y = x^2 + 5x$.

x	-4	-3	-2	-1	0	1	2
x^2	16						
$5x$	-20						
y	-4						

3. $y = x^2 + 4$.

x	-3	-2	-1	0	1	2	3
x^2							
$+4$	4	4	4	4			
y							

4. $y = x^2 - 7$.

x	-3	-2	-1	0	1	2	3
x^2	9						
-7	-7	-7					
y							

5. $y = x^2 - 2x$.

x	-3	-2	-1	0	1	2	3
x^2							9
$-2x$	6						-6
y							3

6. $y = x^2 - 4x$.

x	-2	-1	0	1	2	3	4
x^2							
$-4x$							
y							

7. $y = x^2 + 2x + 3$.

x	-3	-2	-1	0	1	2	3
x^2	9	4					
$+2x$	-6	-4					
$+3$	3	3	3	3			
y	6	3					

8. $y = x^2 + 3x - 2$.

x	-4	-3	-2	-1	0	1	2
x^2							
$+3x$							
-2	-2	-2					
y							

9. $y = x^2 + 4x - 5$.

x	-3	-2	-1	0	1	2	3
x^2							
$+4x$							
-5							
y							

10. $y = x^2 - 2x + 6$.

x	-3	-2	-1	0	1	2	3
x^2							
$-2x$							
$+6$							
y							

In questions **11** to **20** draw a table of values for the values of x given.

11. $y = x^2 + 4x$; x from -3 to $+3$.
12. $y = x^2 - 6x$; x from -4 to $+2$.
13. $y = x^2 + 8$; x from -3 to $+3$.
14. $y = x^2 + 3x + 1$; x from -4 to $+2$.
15. $y = x^2 - 5x + 3$; x from -3 to $+3$.
16. $y = x^2 - 3x - 5$; x from -2 to $+4$.
17. $y = x^2 - 3$; x from -5 to $+1$.
18. $y = 2x^2 + 1$; x from -3 to $+3$.
19. $y = 2x^2 + 3x$; x from -3 to $+3$.
20. $y = 3x^2 + 2x + 4$; x from -3 to $+3$.

Draw the graph of $y = x^2 + x - 2$ for values of x from -3 to $+3$.

(a)

x	-3	-2	-1	0	1	2	3
x^2	9	4	1	0	1	4	9
$+x$	-3	-2	-1	0	1	2	3
-2	-2	-2	-2	-2	-2	-2	-2
y	4	0	-2	-2	0	4	10

(b) Plot the x and y values from the table.

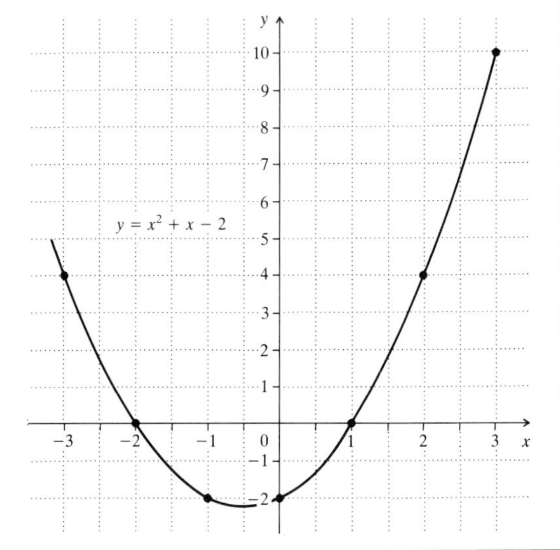

Exercise 17

For each question make a table of values and then draw the graph. Suggested scales: 2 cm to 1 unit on the x-axis and 1 cm to 1 unit on the y-axis.

1. $y = x^2 + 2$; x from -3 to $+3$.

x	-3	-2	-1	0	1	2	3
x^2	9	4	1	0	1		
$+2$	2	2	2				
y	11	6	3				

2. $y = x^2 + 5$; x from -3 to $+3$.
3. $y = x^2 - 4$; x from -3 to $+3$.
4. $y = x^2 - 8$; x from -3 to $+3$.
5. $y = x^2 + 2x$; x from -4 to $+2$.

x	-4	-3	-2	-1	0	1	2
x^2	16	9					4
$+2x$	-8	-6					4
y	8	3					8

6. $y = x^2 + 4x$; x from -5 to $+1$.
7. $y = x^2 + 3x$; x from -4 to $+2$.
8. $y = x^2 - 2x$; x from -3 to $+3$.
9. $y = x^2 - 5x$; x from -1 to $+6$.
10. $y = x^2 + 4x - 1$; x from -2 to $+4$.
11. $y = x^2 + 2x - 5$; x from -4 to $+2$
12. $y = x^2 + 3x + 1$; x from -4 to $+2$.
13. $y = x^2 + 4x - 1$; x from -5 to $+1$.
14. $y = x^2 + x - 2$; x from -3 to $+3$.
15. $y = x^2 - 4x + 1$; x from -1 to $+5$.

Exercise 18

These graphs are more difficult. For each question make a table of values and then draw the graph.

1. $y = x^3 + 1$; x from -3 to $+3$.
   Scales: 2 cm to 1 unit for x;
   1 cm to 5 units for y.

2. $y = \frac{12}{x}$; x from 1 to 12.

3. $y = 2x^2 + 3x - 1$; x from -4 to $+2$.
   Scales: 2 cm to 1 unit for x;
   1 cm to 1 unit for y.
   (Remember $2x^2 = 2(x^2)$. Work out x^2 and then multiply by 2).

4. $y = \frac{16}{x}$; x from 1 to 10.
   Scales: 1 cm to 1 unit for x;
   1 cm to 1 unit for y.

5. $y = x^3 + x^2 - 2$; x from -3 to $+3$.
   Scales: 2 cm to 1 unit for x;
   1 cm to 5 units for y.

6. $y = 3x^2 + 2x - 5$; x from -3 to $+3$.
   Scales: 2 cm to 1 unit for x;
   2 cm to 5 units for y.

7. $y = 2x^2 - 4x - 3$; x from -2 to $+4$.
   Scales: 2 cm to 1 unit for x;
   1 cm to 1 unit for y.

8. $y = x^3 + 1$; x from -3 to $+3$.
   Scales: 2 cm to 1 unit for x;
   1 cm to 5 units for y.

Intersecting line and curve

Draw the graphs of $y = x^2 - 2x$ and $y = x + 2$ and estimate the x-values of the two points where the graphs cut.

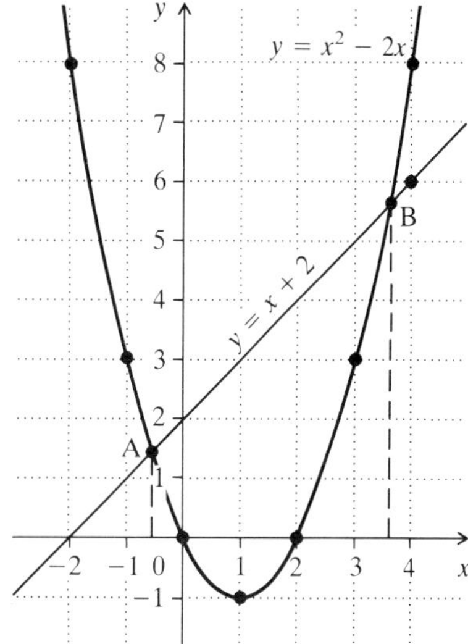

The graphs cut at the points marked A and B.
At A $\quad x \approx -0.6$ (to 1 D.P.)
At B $\quad x \approx 3.6$ (to 1 D.P.)

Exercise 19

In the following questions draw the graphs of the line and the curve and estimate the x-values at the points of intersection. Use scales of 1 cm to 1 unit on both axes.

1. (a) $y = x - 1$,
   (b) $y = x^2 - 3x$. Take values of x from -2 to $+4$.
   The tables of values are started below.

(a)

x	-2	-1	0	1	2	3	4
x	-2	-1	0	1			
-1	-1	-1	-1				
y	-3						

(b)

x	-2	-1	0	1	2	3	4
x^2	4					9	
$-3x$	6				-6		-12
y	10						

2. (a) $y = x - 3$,
(b) $y = x^2 - 7$.
Take values of x from -3 to $+3$.

3. (a) $y = 2x - 1$,
(b) $y = x^2 + 2x - 3$.
Take values of x from -4 to $+2$.

4. From the diagram below estimate the x-values at the two points where the line $y = x + 3$ cuts the curve $y = x^2 + 2x - 1$.

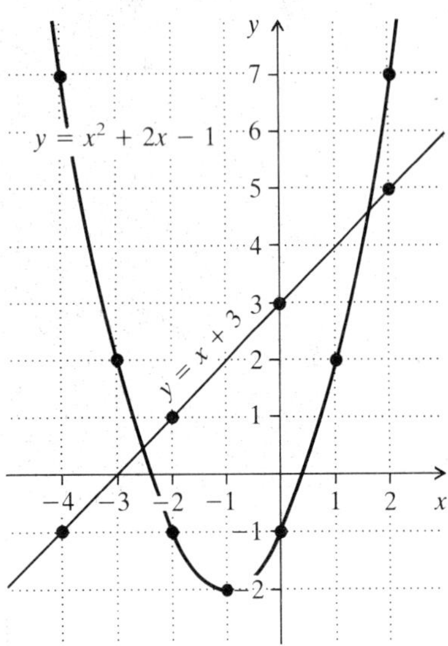

5. (a) $y = x^2 - 2x - 1$,
(b) $y = 4 - x$.
Take values of x from -2 to $+4$.
The table of values for $y = 4 - x$ is started below.

x	-2	-1	0	1	2	3	4
4	4	4	4	4			
$-x$	2	1	0	-1			
y	6						

6. (a) $y = 2x - 8$,
(b) $y = x^2 - 5x$.
Take values of x from 0 to 6.

7. (a) $y = -x$,
(b) $y = 4 - x^2$.
Take values of x from -3 to $+3$.
The line $y = -x$ passes through the points $(-3,3)$, $(-1,1)$, $(2,-2)$ etc.
The table of values for $y = 4 - x^2$ is started below.

x	-3	-2	-1	0	1	2	3
4	4	4	4	4			
$-x^2$	-9	-4				-4	
y							

(Remember: $-x^2 = -(x^2)$.)

8. (a) $y = x$,
(b) $y = x^2 - 2x - 3$.
Take values of x from -2 to $+4$.

9. (a) $y = 7 - x$,
(b) $y = \frac{8}{x}$. Take values of x from 0 to 8.

Plot the points given in the tables below.

(a) $y = 7 - x$:

x	0	2	4	6	7
y	7	5	3	1	0

(b) $y = \frac{8}{x}$:

x	1	2	4	6	8
y	8	4	2	1.3	1

10. (a) $y = x$,
(b) $y = \frac{12}{x}$. Take values of x from 1 to 12.

11. (a) $y = 9 - x$,
(b) $y = \frac{10}{x}$. Take values of x from 1 to 10.

12. (a) $y = x$,
(b) $y = 5 - x^2$.
Take values of x from -3 to $+3$.

Unit 8

8.1 REFLECTIONS

A′B′C′D′ is the image of ABCD after reflection in the broken line.

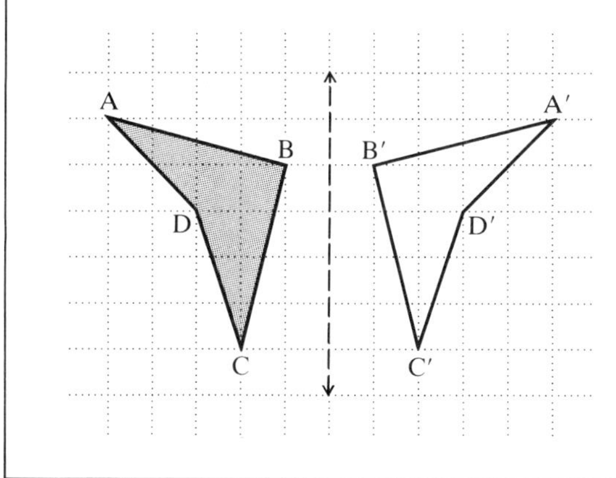

Exercise 1

On squared paper draw the object and its image after reflection in the broken line.

1.

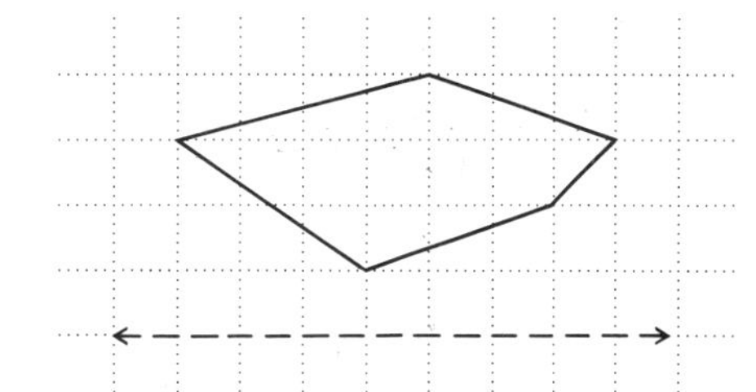

2.

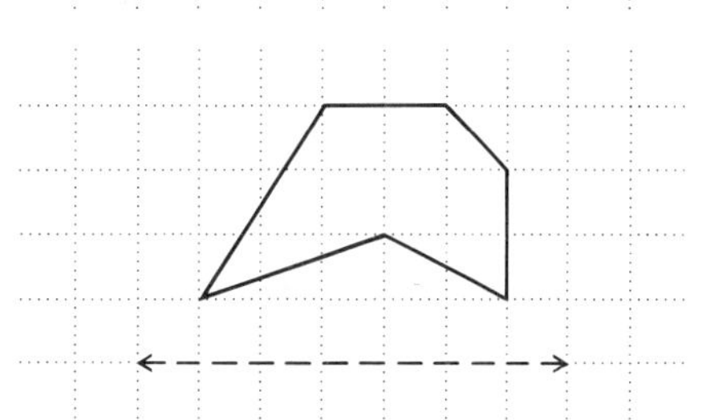

3.

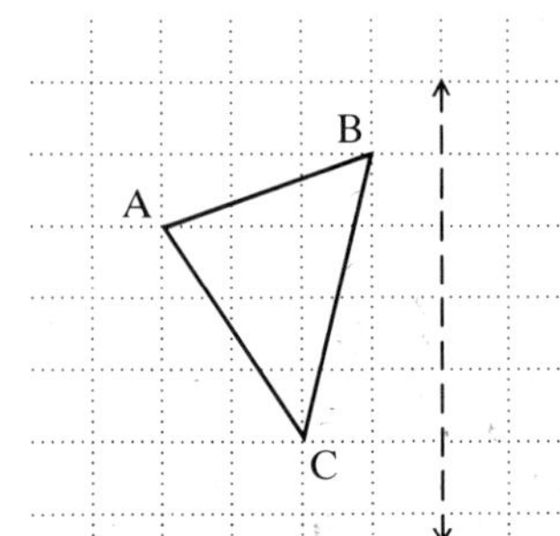

4.

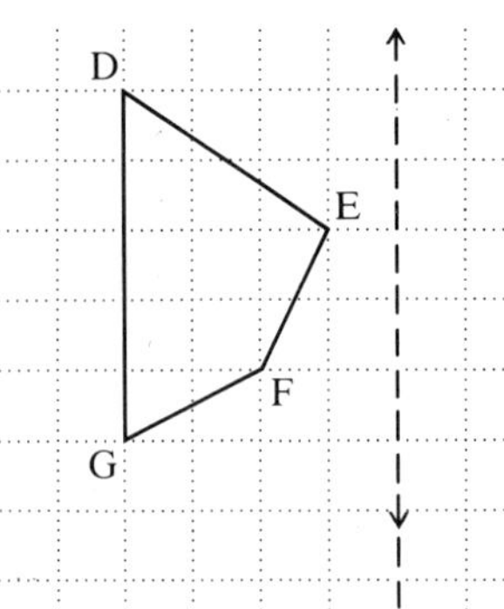

5.

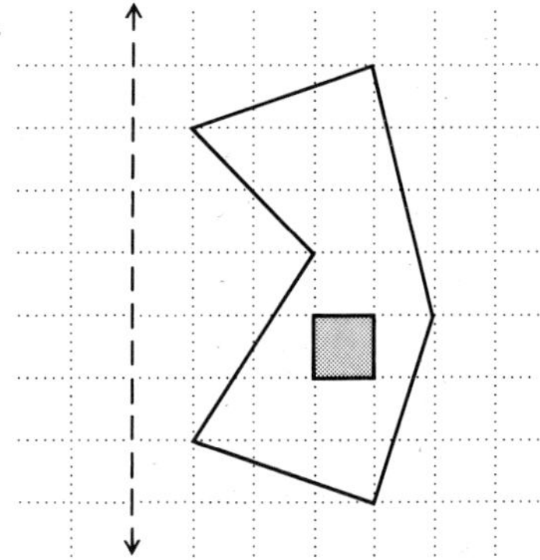

6.

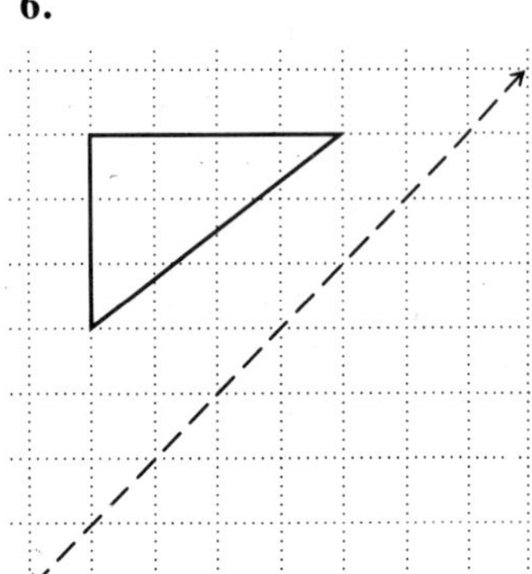

7.

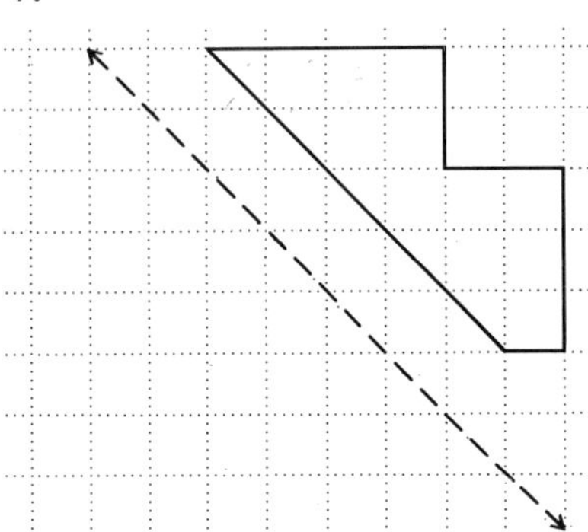

8.

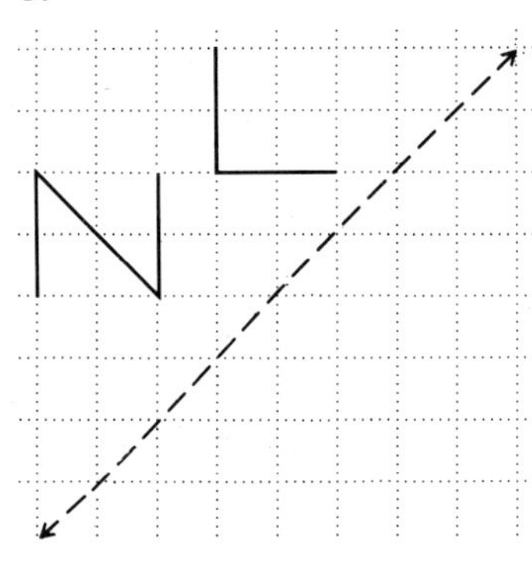

Exercise 2

Draw the image of the given shape after reflection in line AB and then reflect this new shape in line XY.

1.

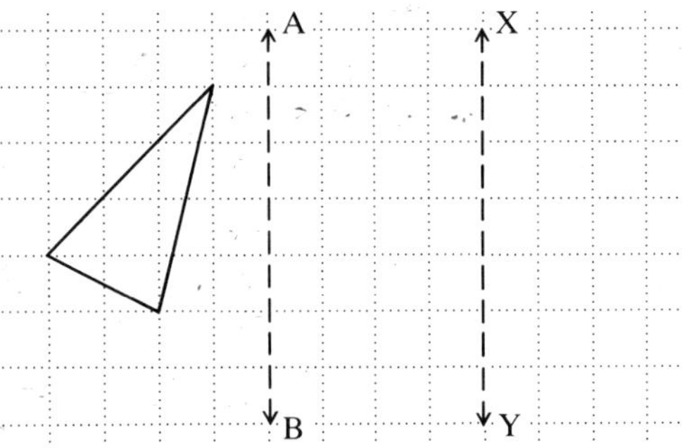

2.

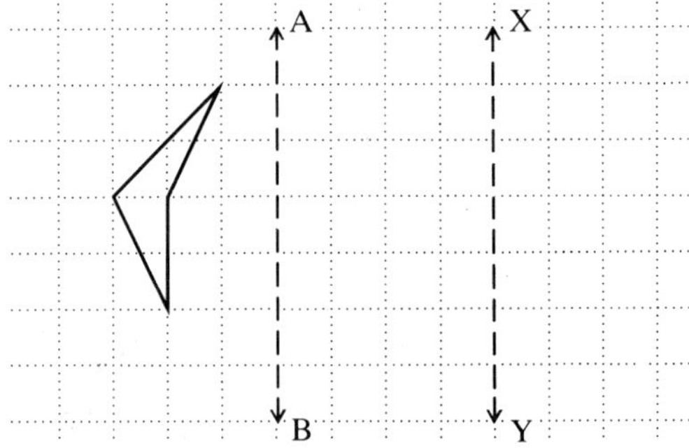

3.

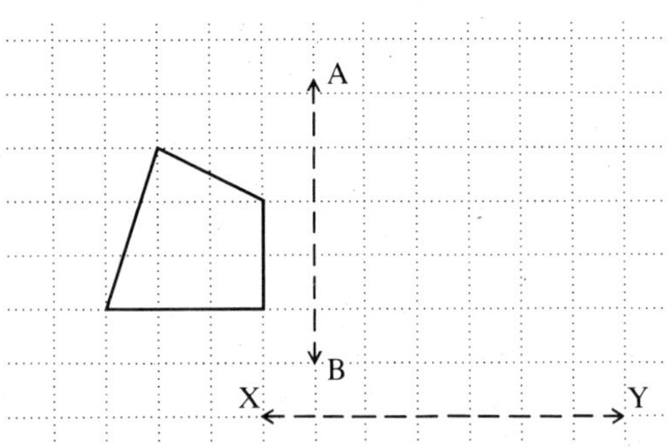

4.

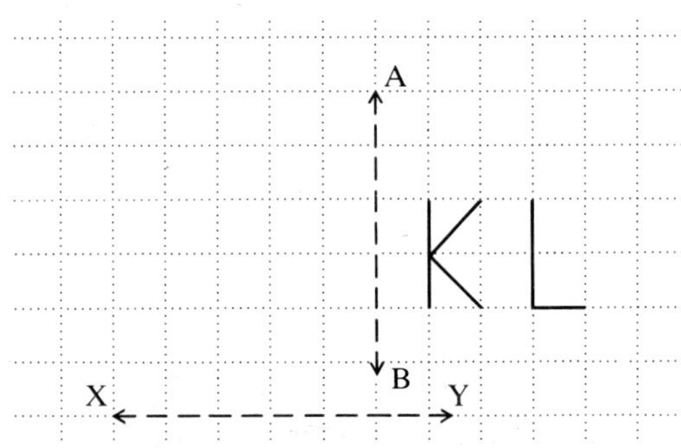

Exercise 3

1. Copy the diagram below.

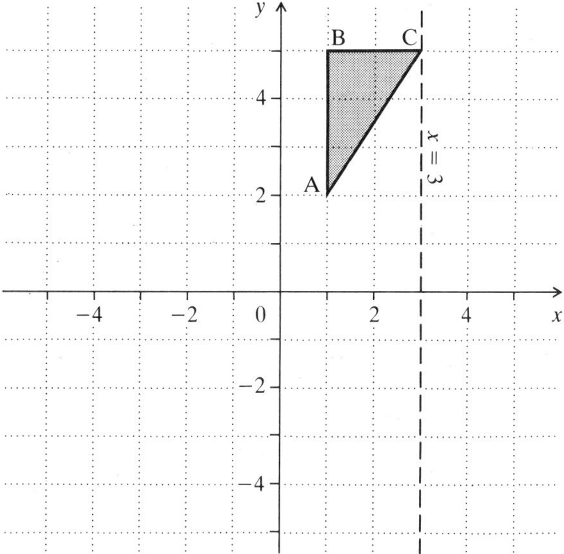

Draw the image of △ ABC after reflection in the lines indicated.
(a) the x-axis. Label it △1.
(b) the y-axis. Label it △2.
(c) the line $x = 3$. Label it △3.

For questions **2** to **5** draw a pair of axes so that both x and y can take values from −7 to +7.

2. (a) Plot and label D(−6,4), E(−6,7), F(−4,7).
(b) Draw the lines $y = 3$ and $x = -2$. [Use dotted lines.]
(c) Draw the image of △ DEF after reflection in:
 (i) the x-axis. Label it △1.
 (ii) the y-axis. Label it △2.
 (iii) the line $y = 3$. Label it △3.
 (iv) the line $x = -2$. Label it △4.
(d) Write down the coordinates of the image of point D in each case.

3. (a) Plot and label P(7,5), Q(7,2), R(5,2).
(b) Draw the lines $y = -1$, $x = 1$ and $y = x$. Use dotted lines.
(c) Draw the image of △PQR after reflection in:
 (i) the line $y = -1$. Label it △1.
 (ii) the line $x = 1$. Label it △2.
 (iii) the line $y = x$. Label it △3.
(d) Write down the coordinates of the image of point P in each case.

4. (a) Plot and label L(7,−5), M(7,−1), N(5,−1).
(b) Draw the lines $y = x$ and $y = -x$. Use dotted lines.
(c) Draw the image of △LMN after reflection in:
 (i) the x-axis. Label it △1.
 (ii) the line $y = x$. Label it △2.
 (iii) the line $y = -x$. Label it △3.
(d) Write down the coordinates of the image of point L in each case.

5. (a) Plot and label A(−7,−6), B(−7,−2), C(−4,−2).
(b) Draw the line $y = x$.
(c) Reflect △ABC in the x-axis. Label the image A′B′C′.
(d) Reflect △A′B′C′ in the y-axis. Label the image A″B″C″.
(e) Reflect △A″B″C″ in the line $y = x$. Label the image A*B*C*.
(f) Write down the coordinates of A′, A″ and A*.

6. (a) Copy the diagram below.

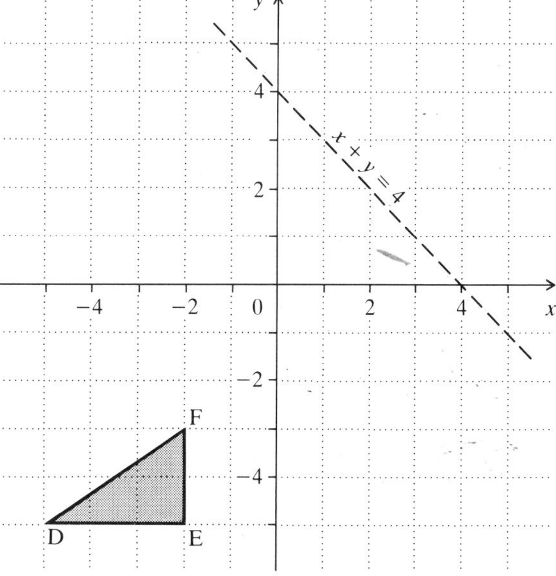

(b) Reflect △DEF in the x-axis. Label the image D′E′F′.
(c) Reflect △D′E′F′ in the y-axis. Label the image D″E″F″.
(d) Reflect △D″E″F″ in the line $x + y = 4$. Label the image D*E*F*.
(e) Write down the coordinates of D′, D″ and D*.

For questions **7** to **10** draw a pair of axes so that both x and y can take values from -7 to $+7$.

7. (a) Draw the line $x + y = 7$. [It passes through (0,7) and (7,0).]
(b) Draw $\triangle 1$ at $(-3,-1)$, $(-1,-1)$, $(-1,-4)$.
(c) Reflect $\triangle 1$ in the y-axis onto $\triangle 2$.
(d) Reflect $\triangle 2$ in the x-axis onto $\triangle 3$.
(e) Reflect $\triangle 3$ in the line $x + y = 7$ onto $\triangle 4$.
(f) Reflect $\triangle 4$ in the y-axis onto $\triangle 5$.
(g) Write down the coordinates of $\triangle 5$.

8. (a) Draw the lines $y = 2$, $x = -1$ and $y = x$.
(b) Draw $\triangle 1$ at $(1,-3)$, $(-3,-3)$, $(-3,-5)$.
(c) Reflect $\triangle 1$ in the line $y = x$ onto $\triangle 2$.
(d) Reflect $\triangle 2$ in the line $y = 2$ onto $\triangle 3$.
(e) Reflect $\triangle 3$ in the line $x = -1$ onto $\triangle 4$.
(f) Reflect $\triangle 4$ in the line $y = x$ onto $\triangle 5$.
(g) Write down the coordinates of $\triangle 5$.

9. (a) Draw the lines $y = x$, $y = -x$ and $y = -1$.
(b) Draw $\triangle 1$ at $(-5,7)$, $(-2,7)$, $(-2,5)$.
(c) Reflect $\triangle 1$ in the line $y = -x$ onto $\triangle 2$.
(d) Reflect $\triangle 2$ in the line $y = x$ onto $\triangle 3$.
(e) Reflect $\triangle 3$ in the line $y = -1$ onto $\triangle 4$.
(f) Reflect $\triangle 4$ in the line $y = x$ onto $\triangle 5$.
(g) Write down the coordinates of $\triangle 5$.

10. (a) Draw the lines $y = -1$, $x = 3$ and $y = x + 4$.
(b) Draw $\triangle 1$ at $(1,7)$, $(-3,7)$, $(-3,5)$.
(c) Reflect $\triangle 1$ in the line $y = x + 4$ onto $\triangle 2$.
(d) Reflect $\triangle 2$ in the line $y = -1$ onto $\triangle 3$.
(e) Reflect $\triangle 3$ in the line $x = 3$ onto $\triangle 4$.
(f) Write down the coordinates of $\triangle 4$.

Describing a given reflection

Exercise 4

1. Copy the diagram below.

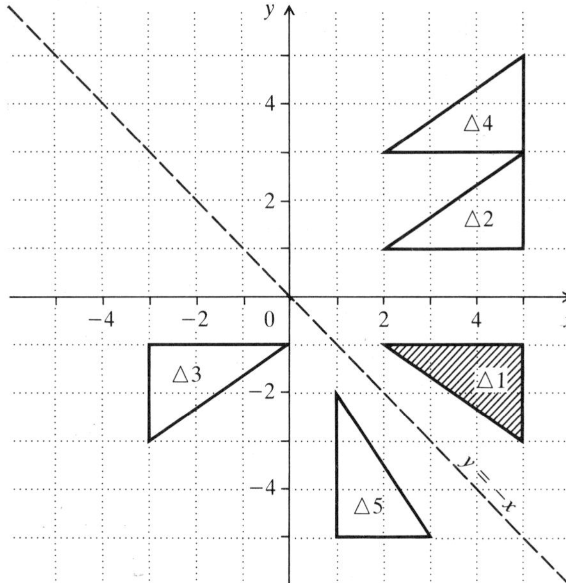

Find the equation of the mirror line for the reflection:
(a) $\triangle 1$ onto $\triangle 2$ (b) $\triangle 1$ onto $\triangle 3$
(c) $\triangle 1$ onto $\triangle 4$ (d) $\triangle 1$ onto $\triangle 5$.

For questions **2** to **5** draw a pair of axes so that both x and y can take values from -7 to $+7$.

2. (a) Draw and label the following triangles:
$\triangle 1$: (3,7), (7,7), (7,5)
$\triangle 2$: (7,−5), (7,−7), (3,−7)
$\triangle 3$: (7,3), (7,1), (3,1)
$\triangle 4$: (−3,7), (−7,7), (−7,5)
$\triangle 5$: (3,7), (−1,7), (−1,5)
(b) Find the equation of the mirror-line for the reflection:
(i) $\triangle 1$ onto $\triangle 2$ (ii) $\triangle 1$ onto $\triangle 3$
(iii) $\triangle 1$ onto $\triangle 4$ (iv) $\triangle 1$ onto $\triangle 5$.

3. (a) Draw and label the following triangles
$\triangle 1$: (2,7), (4,7), (2,4)
$\triangle 2$: (2,−4), (2,−7), (4,−7)
$\triangle 3$: (0,4), (0,7), (−2,7)
$\triangle 4$: (2,4), (2,1), (4,1)
$\triangle 5$: (7,4), (7,2), (4,2)
(b) Find the equation of the mirror-line for the reflection:
(i) $\triangle 1$ onto $\triangle 2$ (ii) $\triangle 1$ onto $\triangle 3$
(iii) $\triangle 1$ onto $\triangle 4$ (iv) $\triangle 1$ onto $\triangle 5$.

4. (a) Draw and label the following triangles:
   $\triangle 1 : (3,5), (-1,5), (-1,3)$
   $\triangle 2 : (5,3), (5,-1), (3,-1)$
   $\triangle 3 : (3,-5), (-1,-3), (-1,-5)$
   $\triangle 4 : (-3, 1), (-5,1), (-5,-3)$
   (b) Find the equation of the mirror-line for the reflection:
   (i) $\triangle 1$ onto $\triangle 2$ (ii) $\triangle 1$ onto $\triangle 3$
   (iii) $\triangle 1$ onto $\triangle 4$.

5. (a) Draw and label the following triangles
   $\triangle 1 : (3,-5), (7,-5), (7,-7)$
   $\triangle 2 : (7,1), (7,-1), (3,-1)$
   $\triangle 3 : (2,-5), (-2,-5), (-2,-7)$
   $\triangle 4 : (7,6), (7,4), (3,4)$
   $\triangle 5 : (-5,3), (-5,7), (-7,7)$
   (b) Find the equation of the mirror-line for the reflection:
   (i) $\triangle 1$ onto $\triangle 2$ (ii) $\triangle 1$ onto $\triangle 3$
   (iii) $\triangle 1$ onto $\triangle 4$ (iv) $\triangle 1$ onto $\triangle 5$.

8.2 ROTATIONS

$\triangle A'B'C'$ is the image of $\triangle ABC$ after a 90° clockwise rotation about centre O.

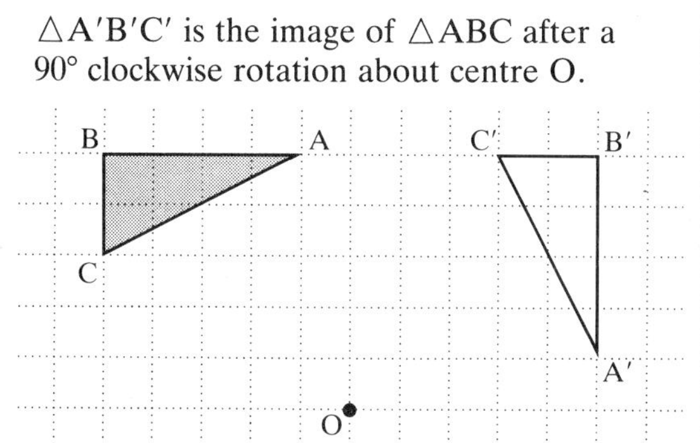

Exercise 5

Draw the object and its image under the rotation given. Take O as the centre of rotation in each case.

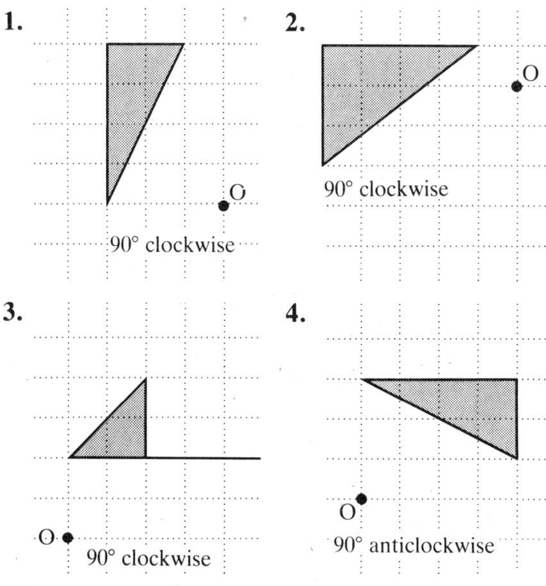

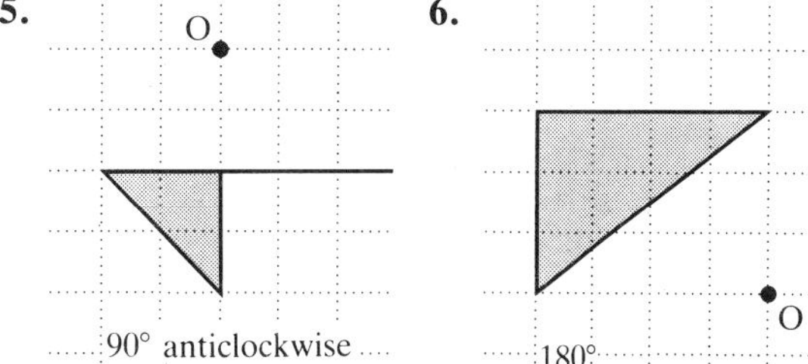

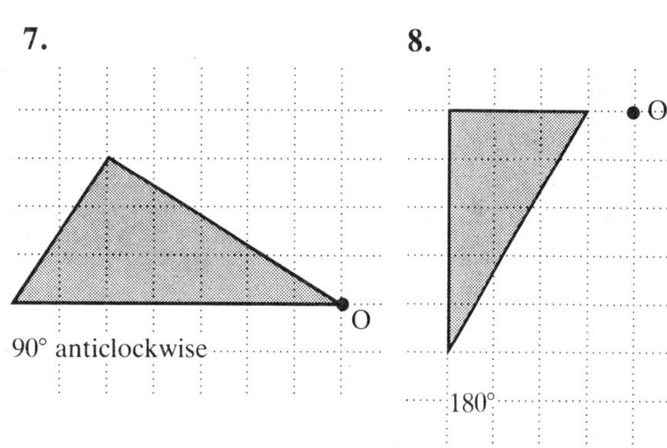

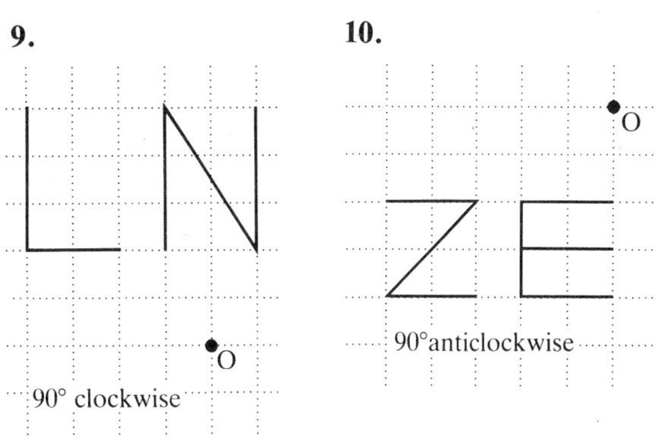

Exercise 6

1. Rotate △ABC 90° clockwise about O and then rotate its image through 90° clockwise about P.

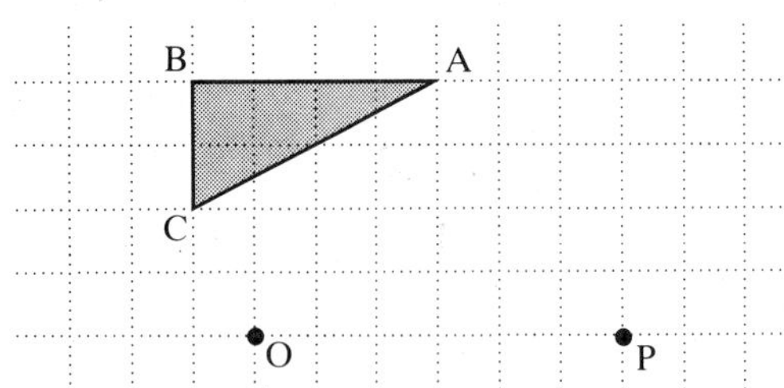

2. Rotate △XYZ through 90° clockwise about O and then rotate its image through 180° about P.

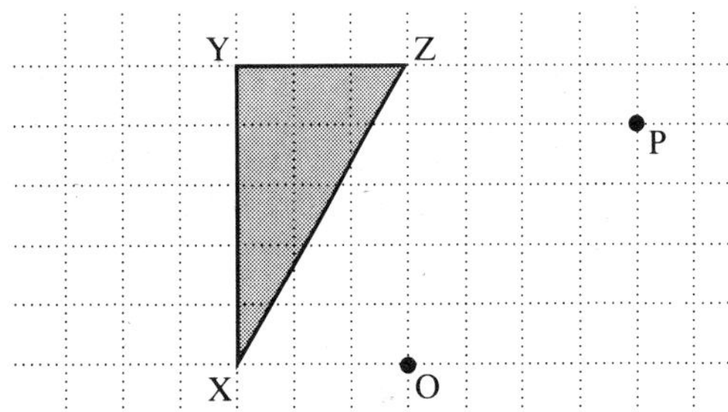

3. Rotate △DEF through 90° anticlockwise about O and then rotate its image through 90° clockwise about P.

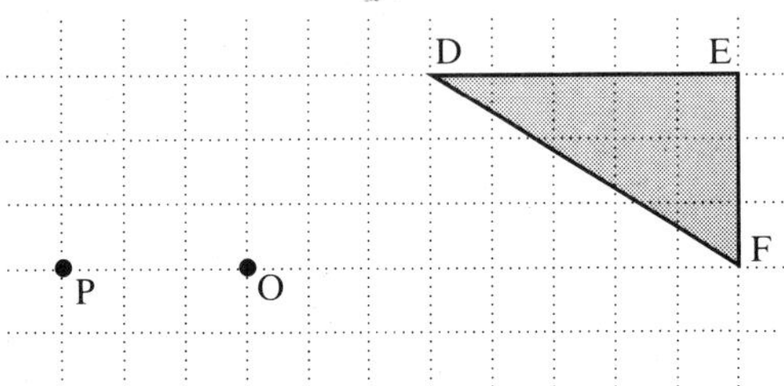

4. Rotate ABCD through 180° about O and then rotate its image through 90° clockwise about P.

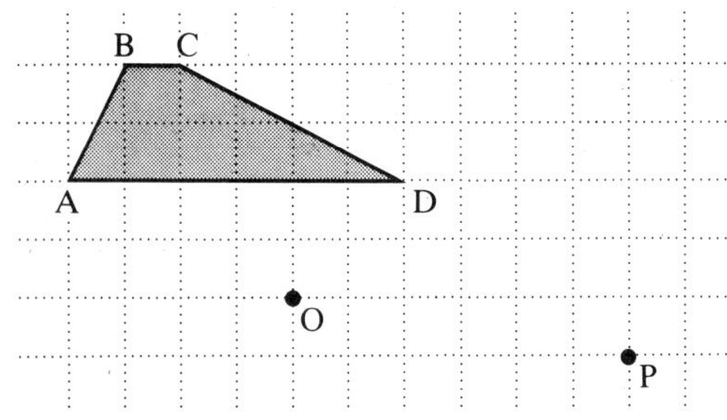

5. Rotate ABCD through 90° anticlockwise about O and then reflect its image in the broken line.

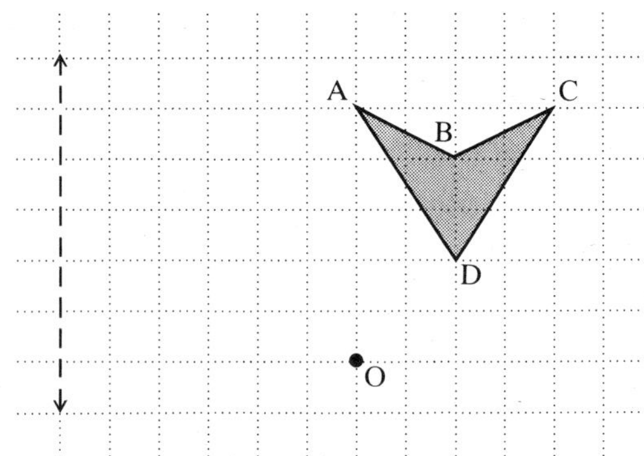

Exercise 7

1. Copy the diagram below.

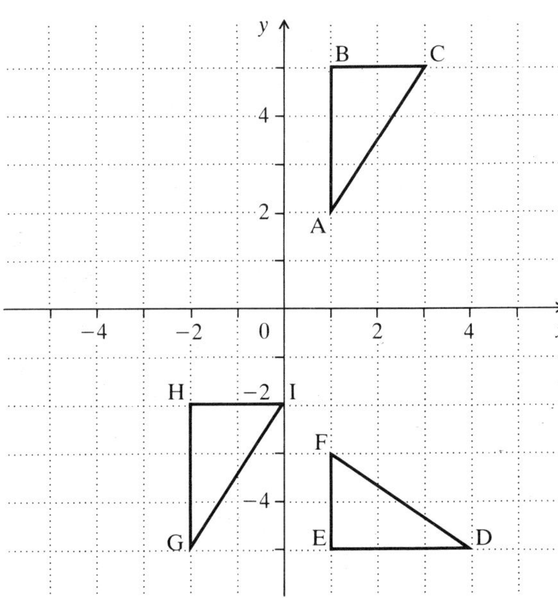

(a) Rotate △ABC 90° clockwise about (0,0) onto △A′B′C′.
(b) Rotate △DEF 180° about (0,0) onto △D′E′F′.
(c) Rotate △GHI 90° clockwise about (0,0) onto △G′H′I′.
(d) Write down the coordinates of A′, D′ and G′.

For questions **2** to **6** draw a pair of axes with values of x and y from -7 to $+7$.

2. (a) Plot and label A(3,3), B(7,3), C(7,1) and D(−1,−3), E(−1,−7), F(−3,−7).
(b) Rotate △ABC 90° anticlockwise about (0,0) onto △A′B′C′.
(c) Rotate △ABC 90° clockwise about (0,0) onto △A″B″C″.
(d) Rotate △DEF 180° about (0,0) onto △D′E′F′.
(e) Write down the coordinates of A′, A″ and D′.

3. (a) Plot and label P(1,6), Q(5,6), R(5,4).
(b) Rotate △PQR 90° clockwise about (2,2) onto △P′Q′R′.
(c) Rotate △PQR 180° about (1,4) onto △P″Q″R″.
(d) Rotate △PQR 90° anticlockwise about (4,−3) onto △P*Q*R*.
(e) Write down the coordinates of P′, P″ and P*.

4. (a) Plot and label K(−6,−6), L(−2,−6), M(−2,−3).
(b) Draw the image of △KLM after the following rotations:
(i) 90° clockwise about (0,0): label it K′L′M′.
(ii) 90° anticlockwise about (−1,−1): label it K″L″M″.
(iii) 180° about (0,−2): label it K*L*M*.
(iv) 90° clockwise about (5,−4): label it K°L°M°.
(c) Write down the coordinates of K′, K″, K* and K°.

5. (a) Plot and label A(1,3), B(3,6), C(1,7).
(b) Draw the image of △ABC after the following rotations:
(i) 90° clockwise about (1,1): label it A′B′C′.
(ii) 180° about (2,1): label it A″B″C″.
(iii) 90° anticlockwise about (1,0): label it A*B*C*.
(iv) 180° about (−2,0): label it A°B°C°.
(c) Write down the coordinates of A′, A″, A* and A°.

6. (a) Plot and label R(−1,6), S(−5,6), T(−5,4).
(b) Draw the image of △RST after the following rotations:
(i) 270° anticlockwise about (0,2): label it R′S′T′.
(ii) 180° about (−2,0): label it R″S″T″.
(iii) 90° anticlockwise about (2,6): label it R*S*T*.
(iv) 270° clockwise about (6,4): label it R°S°T°.
(c) Write down the coordinates of R′, R″, R* and R°.

Finding the centre of a rotation

Exercise 8

In questions **1** to **4** copy the diagram exactly and then use tracing paper to find the centre of the rotation which takes the shaded shape onto the unshaded shape. Mark the centre of rotation with a cross.

1.

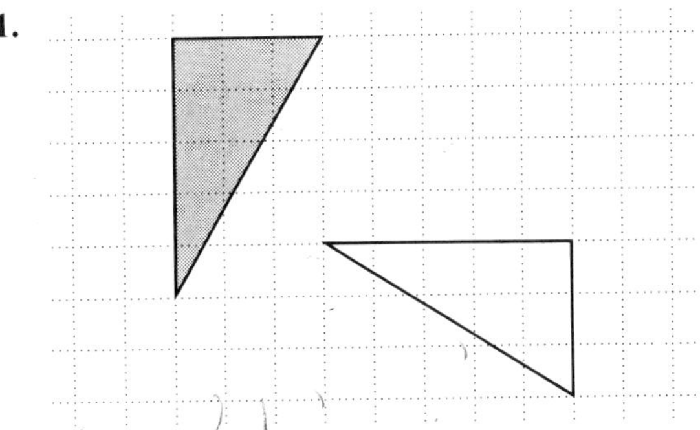

2.

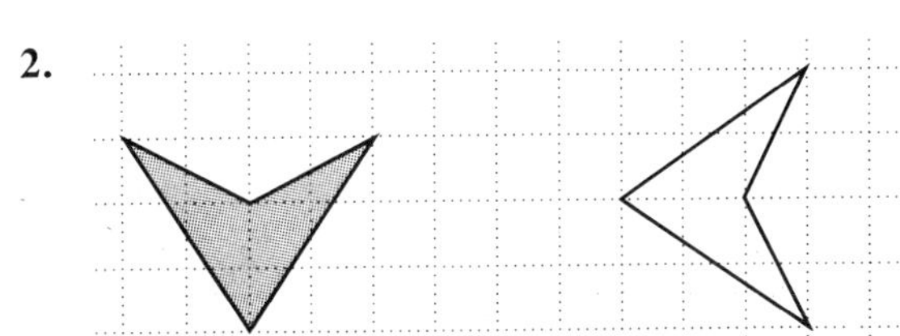

3.

4.

5. Copy the diagram below.

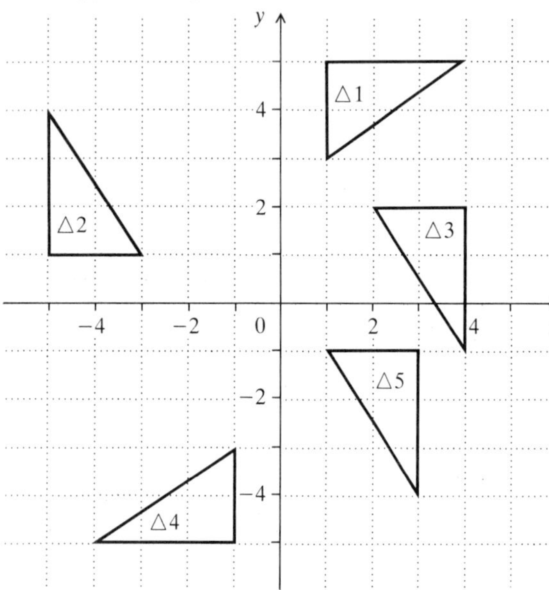

Find the coordinates of the centre of the following rotations:

(a) Δ1 → Δ2 (b) Δ1 → Δ3
(c) Δ1 → Δ4 (d) Δ1 → Δ5

For questions **6** to **9** draw a pair of axes with values of x and y from −7 to +7.

6. (a) Plot and label the following triangles:
Δ1: (3,4), (7,4), (3,7)
Δ2: (3,2), (6,2), (3,−2)
Δ3: (−7,−4), (−3,−4), (−3,−7)
Δ4: (−2,1), (−5,1), (−2,5)
Δ5: (2,−3), (5,−3), (2,−7)
(b) Find the coordinates of the centre of the following rotations:
(i) Δ1 → Δ2
(ii) Δ1 → Δ3
(iii) Δ1 → Δ4
(iv) Δ1 → Δ5.

7. (a) Plot and label the following triangles:
Δ1: (−4,−3), (−4,−7), (−6,−7)
Δ2: (−3,4), (−7,4), (−7,6)
Δ3: (−2,1), (2,1), (2,−1)
Δ4: (0,7), (4,7), (4,5)
Δ5: (2,−3), (4,−3), (2,−7)
(b) Find the coordinates of the centre of the following rotations:
(i) Δ1 → Δ2 (ii) Δ1 → Δ3
(iii) Δ1 → Δ4 (iv) Δ1 → Δ5.

8. (a) Plot and label the following triangles:
Δ1: (1,3), (1,7), (3,7)
Δ2: (3,3), (7,3), (7,1)
Δ3: (−7,3), (−3,3), (−3,1)
Δ4:(−2,−4), (−2,−6),(2,−6)
Δ5: (3,−3), (7,−3), (7,−5)
(b) Find the coordinates of the centre of the following rotations:
(i) Δ1 → Δ2 (ii) Δ1 → Δ3
(iii) Δ1 → Δ4 (iv) Δ1 → Δ5.

9. (a) Plot and label the following triangles:
Δ1: (3,4), (3,7), (7,4)
Δ2: (4,−2), (1,−2), (1,−6)
Δ3: (1,2), (1,6), (−2,2)
Δ4: (−4,1), (−4,−3), (−7,−3)
Δ5: (−3,3), (−3,6), (−7,6)
(b) Find the coordinates of the centre of the following rotations:
(i) Δ1 → Δ2 (ii) Δ1 → Δ3
(iii) Δ1 → Δ4 (iv) Δ1 → Δ5
(v) Δ3 → Δ2 (vi) Δ2 → Δ5
(vii) Δ5 → Δ3 (viii) Δ4 → Δ2

Exercise 9

1. Reflect the letter A in the line PQ and label the image A′. Reflect A′ in the line XY and label the image A″. What is the centre and angle of the rotation which takes A onto A″?

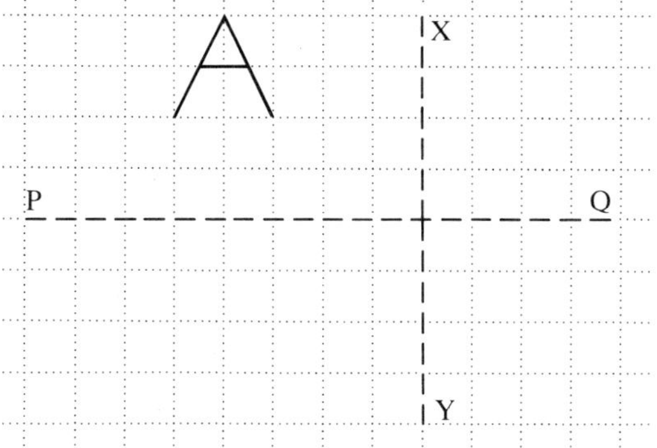

2. Reflect the letter N in the line PQ and label the image N′. Reflect N′ in the line XY and label the image N″. What is the centre and angle of the rotation which takes N onto N″?

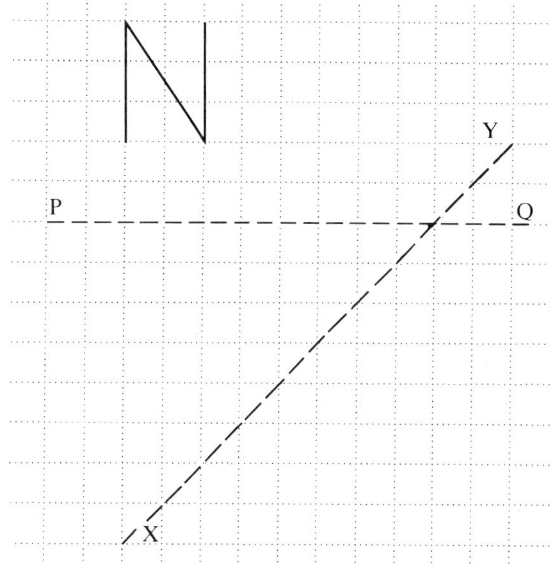

3. Draw a capital L and reflect it successively in any two lines. What is the centre and angle of rotation of the resulting rotation?

8.3 TRANSLATIONS

A translation is simply a 'shift'. There is no turning or reflection and the object stays the same size. In the diagram below:

(a) $\triangle 1$ is mapped onto $\triangle 2$ by the translation with vector $\begin{pmatrix} 4 \\ 2 \end{pmatrix}$

(b) $\triangle 2$ is mapped onto $\triangle 3$ by the translation with vector $\begin{pmatrix} 2 \\ -3 \end{pmatrix}$

(c) $\triangle 3$ is mapped onto $\triangle 2$ by the translation with vector $\begin{pmatrix} -2 \\ 3 \end{pmatrix}$

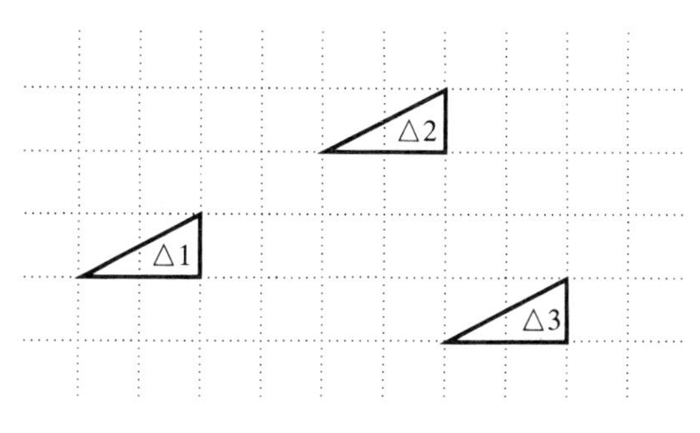

Exercise 10

1. Copy the diagram below.

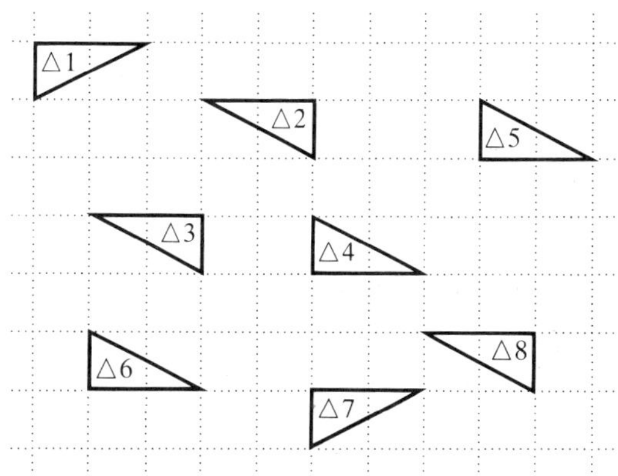

Decide which of these are translations; answer 'yes' or 'no' for each part.

(a)	$\triangle 1 \to \triangle 2$	(b)	$\triangle 1 \to \triangle 3$
(c)	$\triangle 1 \to \triangle 4$	(d)	$\triangle 1 \to \triangle 5$
(e)	$\triangle 1 \to \triangle 6$	(f)	$\triangle 1 \to \triangle 7$
(g)	$\triangle 1 \to \triangle 8$	(h)	$\triangle 2 \to \triangle 3$
(i)	$\triangle 2 \to \triangle 4$	(j)	$\triangle 2 \to \triangle 5$
(k)	$\triangle 2 \to \triangle 6$	(l)	$\triangle 2 \to \triangle 7$
(m)	$\triangle 2 \to \triangle 8$	(n)	$\triangle 3 \to \triangle 6$
(o)	$\triangle 3 \to \triangle 8$	(p)	$\triangle 4 \to \triangle 6$
(q)	$\triangle 4 \to \triangle 5$	(r)	$\triangle 4 \to \triangle 1$
(s)	$\triangle 5 \to \triangle 3$	(t)	$\triangle 6 \to \triangle 4$

2. Copy the diagram below.

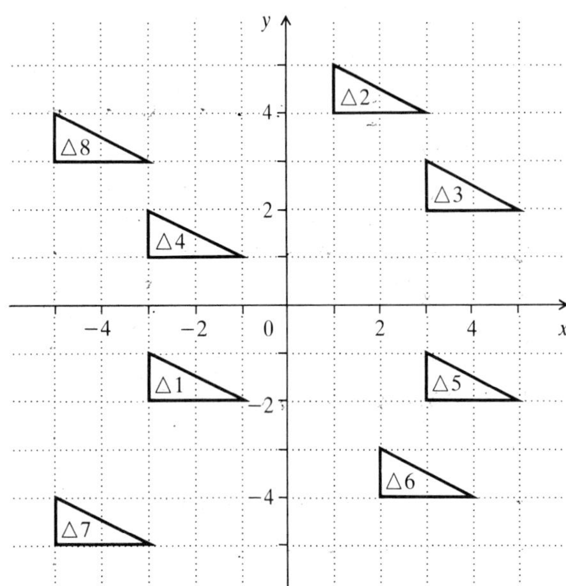

Write down the vector for each of the following translations:

(a) △1 → △2 (b) △1 → △3
(c) △1 → △4 (d) △1 → △5
(e) △1 → △6 (f) △1 → △7
(g) △1 → △8 (h) △2 → △3
(i) △2 → △4 (j) △2 → △5
(k) △2 → △6 (l) △2 → △8
(m) △3 → △5 (n) △8 → △2
(o) △4 → △2 (p) △7 → △5
(q) △6 → △3 (r) △8 → △3
(s) △8 → △7 (t) △4 → △5

3. (a) Draw a pair of axes with values of x and y from -7 to $+7$.

(b) Plot and label △1 at $(-4, 3)$, $(-4, -5)$, $(-3, -3)$.

(c) Draw and label △2, △3, △4, △5, △6, △7 and △8 as follows:

(i) △1 → △2 by translation $\begin{pmatrix} 5 \\ 6 \end{pmatrix}$.

(ii) △1 → △3 by translation $\begin{pmatrix} 6 \\ 1 \end{pmatrix}$.

(iii) △1 → △4 by translation $\begin{pmatrix} 1 \\ 8 \end{pmatrix}$.

(iv) △1 → △5 by translation $\begin{pmatrix} 9 \\ -2 \end{pmatrix}$.

(v) △1 → △6 by translation $\begin{pmatrix} -2 \\ 6 \end{pmatrix}$.

(vi) △1 → △7 by translation $\begin{pmatrix} 1 \\ -2 \end{pmatrix}$.

(vii) △1 → △8 by translation $\begin{pmatrix} 9 \\ 9 \end{pmatrix}$.

(d) Write down the coordinates of the ‘pointed end’ of the triangles △2, △3, △4, △5, △6, △7 and △8.

8.4 ENLARGEMENTS

The picture in fig. 2 below is a three times enlargement of the picture in fig. 1.

Fig. 1

Fig. 2

Notice that the *shape* of the face is exactly the same in both pictures. An enlargement does not change the shape of an object. The enlargement shown above has a *scale factor* of 3.

Exercise 11

1. A photographer makes a four times enlargement of the picture below.

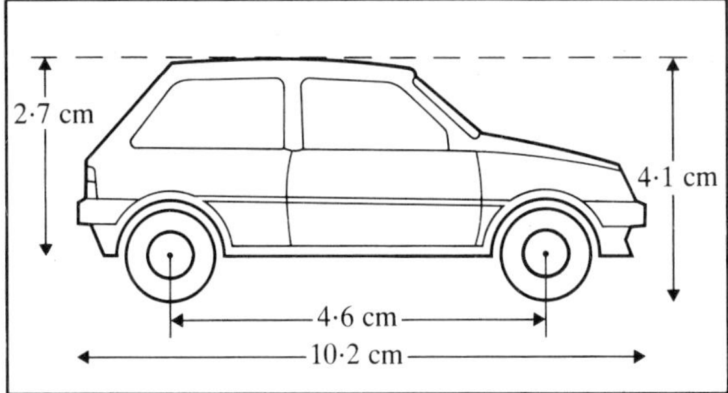

Calculate the corresponding dimensions on the enlarged picture.

2. In a photograph the wing-span of an aircraft is 8.5 cm. Calculate the wing-span of the aircraft as it appears on a ten times enlargement of the photograph.

3. In a photograph the height of a woman is 11.2 cm. Calculate the height of the woman as it appears on a five times enlargement of the photograph.

4. A girl has a model of a house which is an exact copy of the real house but made to a scale of $\frac{1}{10}$. Copy and complete the table.

	On real house	On model
(a) Height of front door	200 cm	
(b) Height of roof	600 cm	
(c) Width of building	850 cm	
(d) Height of windows		18 cm
(e) Length of gutter		70 cm
(f) Number of windows	20	

5. A boy has a model of a train made to a scale of $\frac{1}{5}$. Copy and complete the table.

	On real train	On model
(a) Length of train	20 m	
(b) Height of train		60 cm
(c) Diameter of wheels	1.2 m	
(d) Length of engine		80 cm
(e) Number of wheels	20	
(f) Distance between wheels		30 cm
(g) Number of passengers	100	

6. An architect makes a model of a new town centre to a scale of $\frac{1}{100}$. Copy and complete the table.

	In actual town	In model
(a) Length of main road	120 m	cm
(b) Width of high street	m	5 cm
(c) Height of office block	20 m	
(d) Number of street lights		30
(e) Height of street lights	4.2 m	cm
(f) Length of subway		25 cm
(g) Number of parking meters	300	

Drawing enlargements

For a mathematical description of an enlargement we need two things:
(a) the scale factor
(b) the centre of enlargement.
The triangle ABC is enlarged onto triangle A′B′C′ with a scale factor of 3 and centre O.

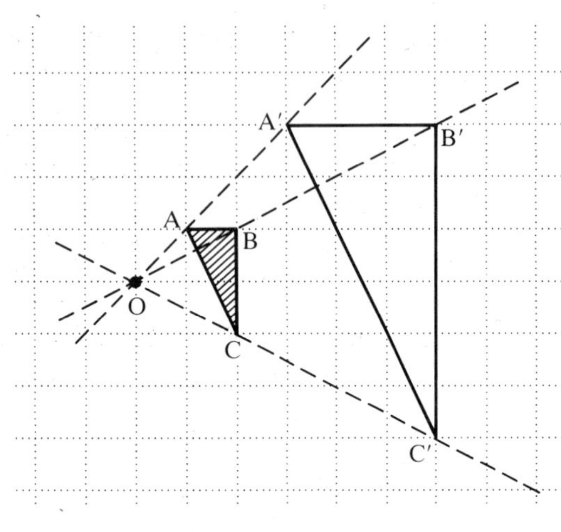

Note: OA′ = 3 × OA; OB′ = 3 × OB; OC′ = 3 × OC. All lengths are measured from the *centre of enlargement*.

Exercise 12

Copy each diagram and draw an enlargement using the centre O and the scale factor given.

1.

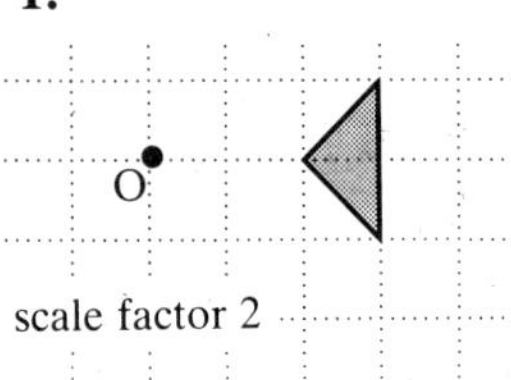

2.

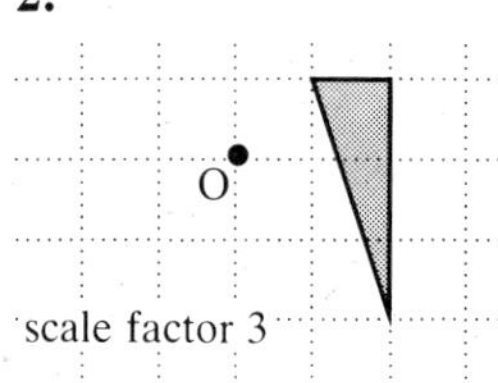

3. **4.**

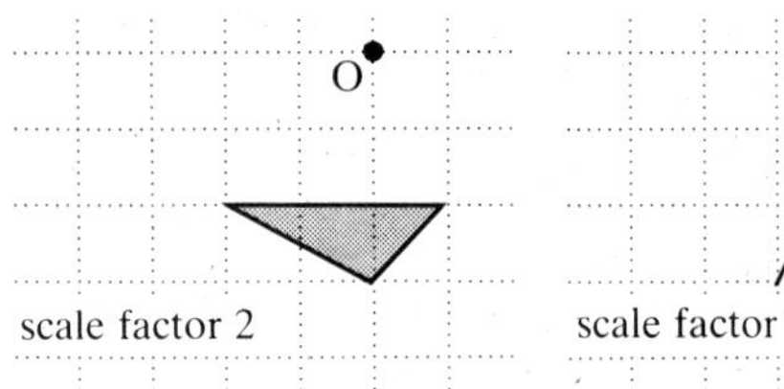

5.

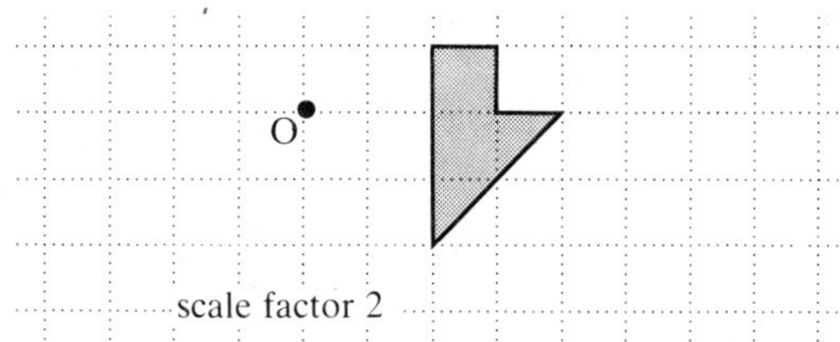

6.

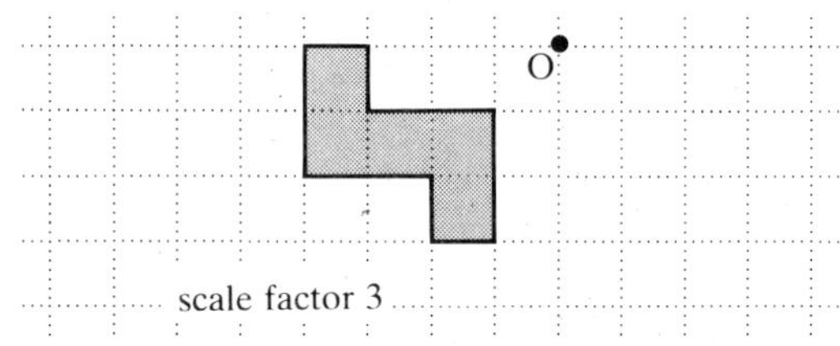

7.

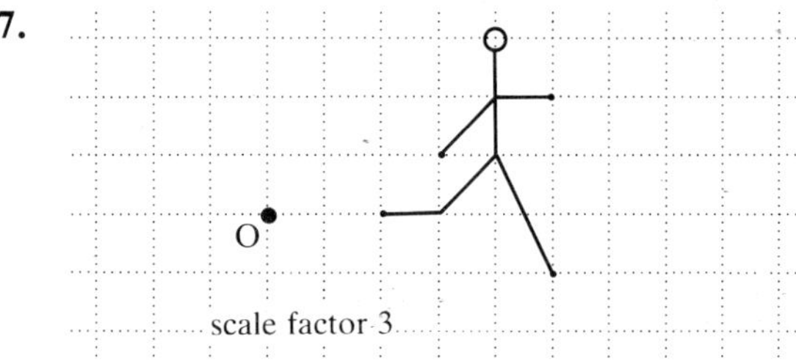

8.

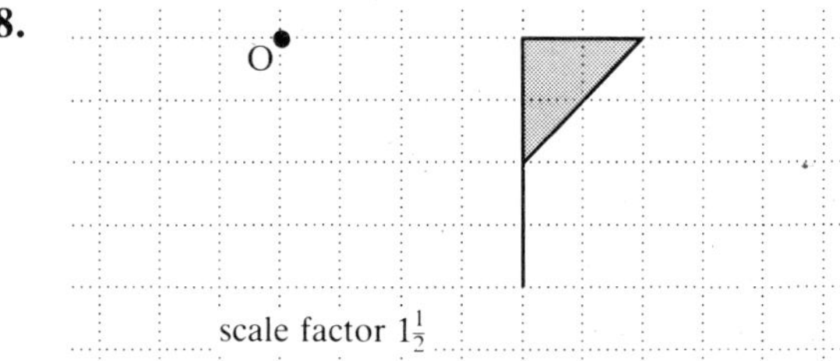

9.

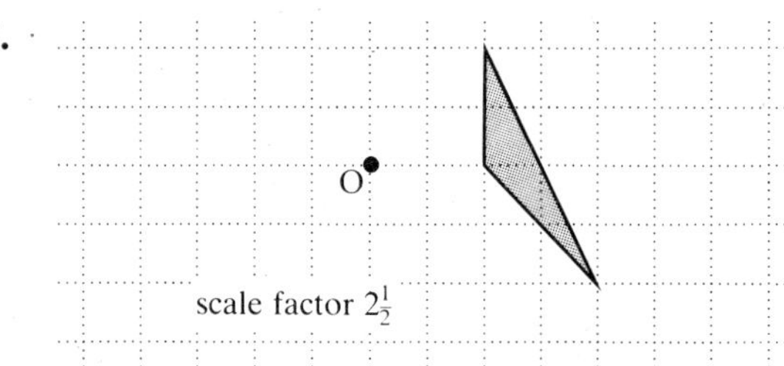

10.

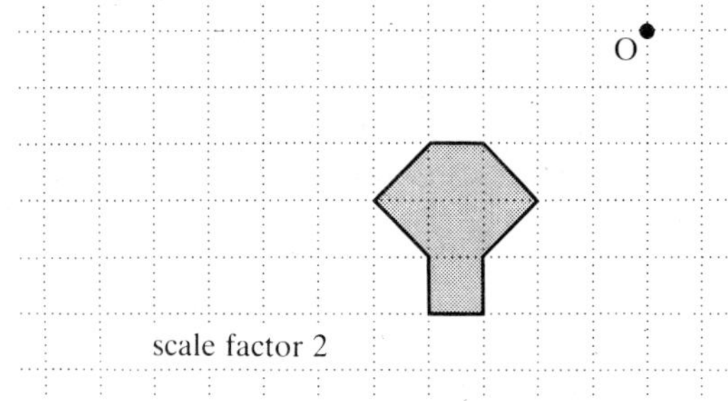

Exercise 13

1. (a) Copy the diagram below.

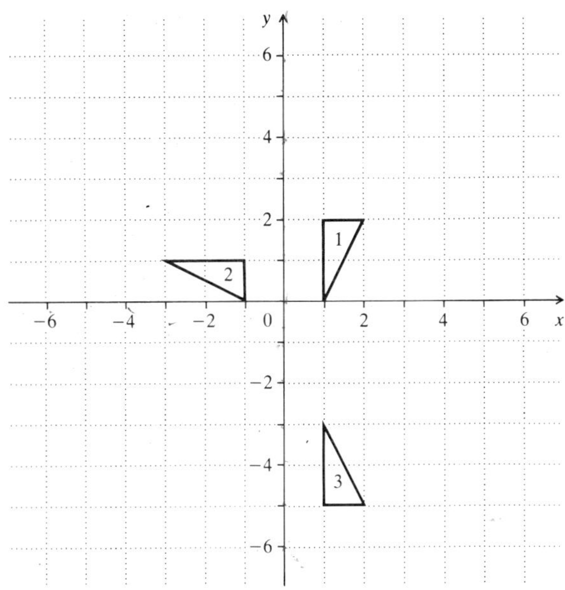

(b) Draw the image of $\triangle 1$ after enlargement with scale factor 3, centre (0,0). Label the image $\triangle 4$.
(c) Draw the image of $\triangle 2$ after enlargement with scale factor 2, centre (−1,3). Label the image $\triangle 5$.
(d) Draw the image of $\triangle 3$ after enlargement with scale factor 2, centre (−1,−5). Label the image $\triangle 6$.
(e) Write down the coordinates of the 'pointed ends' of $\triangle 4$, $\triangle 5$ and $\triangle 6$.
[The 'pointed end' is the vertex of the triangle with the smallest angle.]

For questions **2** to **6** draw a pair of axes with values from −7 to +7.

2. (a) Plot and label the triangles
$\triangle 1$: (5,5), (5,7), (4,7)
$\triangle 2$: (−6,−5), (−3,−5), (−3,−4)
$\triangle 3$: (1,−4), (1,−6), (2,−6).
(b) Draw the image of $\triangle 1$ after enlargement with scale factor 2, centre (7,7). Label the image $\triangle 4$.
(c) Draw the image of $\triangle 2$ after enlargement with scale factor 3, centre (−6,−7). Label the image $\triangle 5$.
(d) Draw the image of $\triangle 3$ after enlargement with scale factor 2, centre (−1,−5). Label the image $\triangle 6$.
(e) Write down the coordinates of the 'pointed ends' of $\triangle 4$, $\triangle 5$ and $\triangle 6$.

3. (a) Plot and label the triangles
$\triangle 1$: (−5,7), (−5,4), (−6,4)
$\triangle 2$: (−6,−2), (−6,−4), (−5,−4)
$\triangle 3$: (2,6), (5,6), (5,5)
(b) Draw the image of $\triangle 1$ after enlargement with scale factor 3, centre (−7,7). Label the image $\triangle 4$.
(c) Draw the image of $\triangle 2$ after enlargement with scale factor 2, centre (−7,−2). Label the image $\triangle 5$.
(d) Draw the image of $\triangle 3$ after enlargement with scale factor 2, centre (4,7). Label the image $\triangle 6$.
(e) Write down the coordinates of the 'pointed ends' of $\triangle 4$, $\triangle 5$ and $\triangle 6$.

4. (a) Plot and label the triangles
$\triangle 1$: (4,3), (7,3), (7,2)
$\triangle 2$: (2,−2), (2,−5), (3,−5)
$\triangle 3$: (−4,−2), (−7,−2), (−7,−3).
(b) Draw the image of $\triangle 1$ after enlargement with scale factor 3, centre (7,4). Label the image $\triangle 4$.
(c) Draw the image of $\triangle 2$ after enlargement with scale factor 2, centre (4,−3). Label the image $\triangle 5$.
(d) Draw the image of $\triangle 3$ after enlargement with scale factor 3, centre (−7,−5). Label the image $\triangle 6$.
(e) Write down the coordinates of the 'pointed ends' of $\triangle 4$, $\triangle 5$ and $\triangle 6$.

5. (a) Plot and label the triangles
$\triangle 1$: (4,−2), (7,−2), (7,−1)
$\triangle 2$: (−6,−1), (−3,−1), (−3,−2)
$\triangle 3$: (−1,−5), (−1,−7), (0,−7).
(b) Draw the image of $\triangle 1$ after enlargement with scale factor 4, centre (7,−3). Label the image $\triangle 4$.
(c) Draw the image of $\triangle 2$ after enlargement with scale factor 2, centre (−5,0). Label the image $\triangle 5$.
(d) Draw the image of $\triangle 3$ after enlargement with scale factor 3, centre (−2,−7). Label the image $\triangle 6$.
(e) Write down the coordinates of the 'pointed ends' of $\triangle 4$, $\triangle 5$ and $\triangle 6$.

6. (a) Plot and label the triangles
△1: (5,3), (5,6), (4,6)
△2: (4,−3), (1,−3), (1,−2)
△3: (−4,−7), (−7,−7), (−7,−6).
(b) Draw the image of △1 after enlargement with scale factor 2, centre (7,7). Label the image △4.
(c) Draw the image of △2 after enlargement with scale factor 3, centre (5,−4). Label the image △5.
(d) Draw the image of △3 after enlargement with scale factor 4, centre (−7,−7). Label the image △6.
(e) Write down the coordinates of the pointed ends of △4, △5 and △6.

Enlargements with fractional scale factors

Exercise 14

Copy each diagram and draw an enlargement using the centre O and the scale factor given.

1.

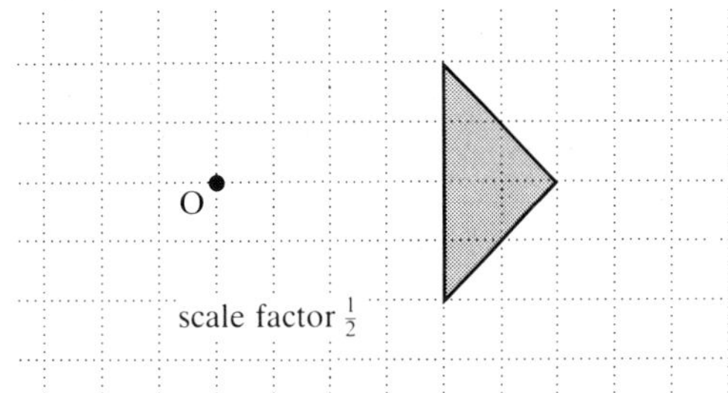

2.

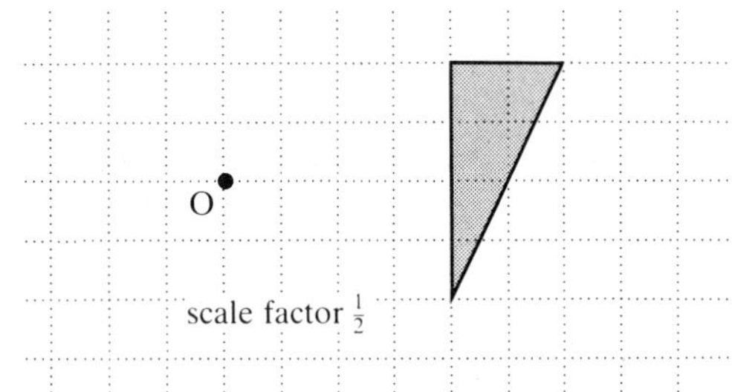

3.

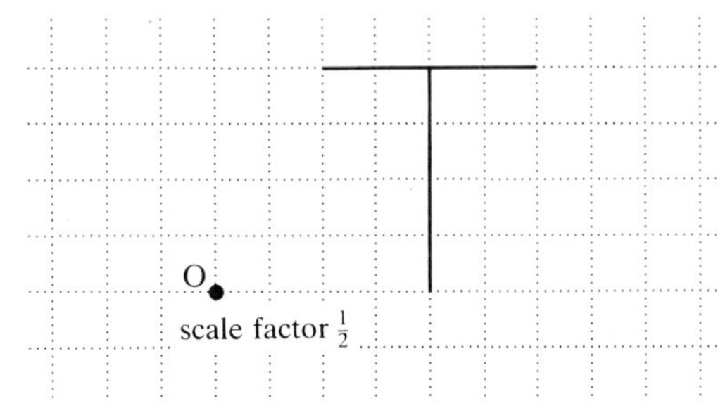

4.

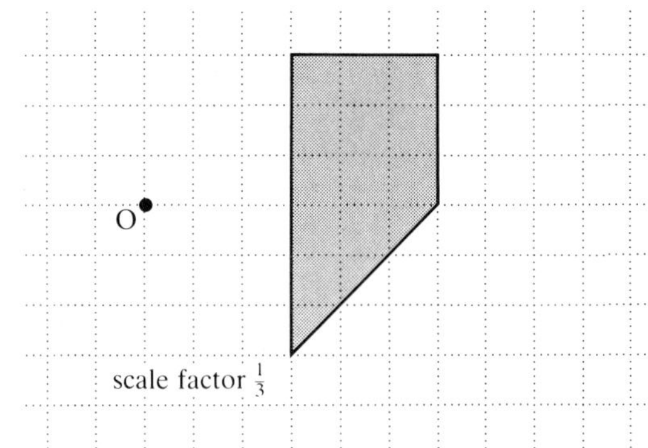

5.

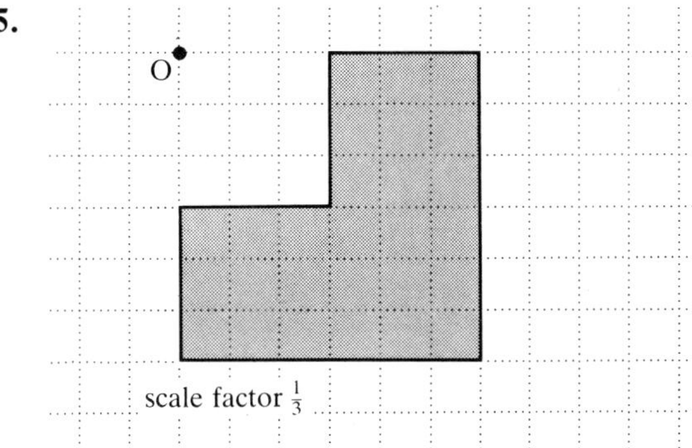

6.

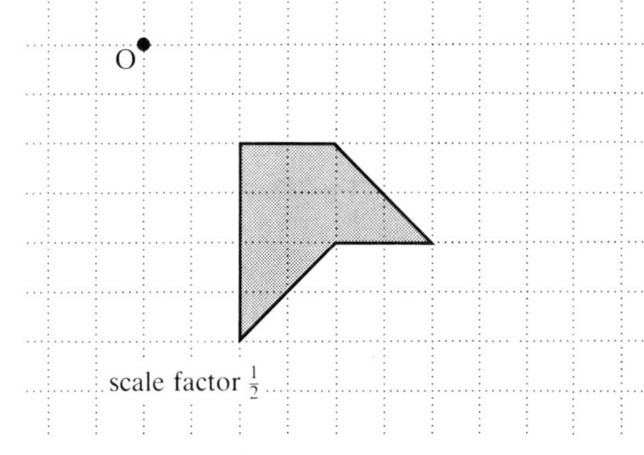

Exercise 15

1. (a) Copy the diagram below.

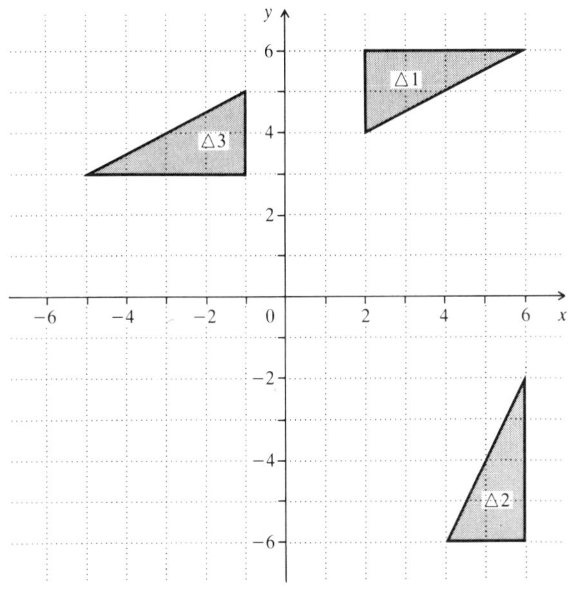

   (b) Draw △4, the image of △1 after an enlargement with scale factor $\frac{1}{2}$, centre (0,0).
   (c) Draw △5, the image of △2 after an enlargement with scale factor $\frac{1}{2}$, centre (0,0).
   (d) Draw △6, the image of △3 after an enlargement with scale factor $\frac{1}{2}$, centre (−3,−1).
   (e) Write down the coordinates of the 'pointed ends' of △4, △5 and △6.

For questions **2** to **5** draw axes with x and y from −7 to +7.

2. (a) Plot and label the triangles
   △1: (7,6), (1,6), (1,3)
   △2: (7,−1), (7,−7), (3,−7)
   △3: (−5,7), (−5,1), (−7,1).
   (b) Draw △4, the image of △1 after an enlargement with scale factor $\frac{1}{3}$, centre (−2,0).
   (c) Draw △5, the image of △2 after an enlargement with scale factor $\frac{1}{2}$, centre (−5,−7).
   (d) Draw △6, the image of △3 after an enlargement with scale factor $\frac{1}{2}$, centre (−7,−5).
   (e) Write down the coordinates of the 'pointed ends' of △4, △5 and △6.

3. (a) Plot and label the triangle △1 at (1,3), (−7,3), (−7,7).
   (b) Draw △2, the image of △1 after an enlargement with scale factor $\frac{1}{4}$, centre (5,3).
   (c) Draw △3, the image of △1 after an enlargement with scale factor $\frac{1}{4}$, centre (−3,−5).
   (d) Draw △4, the image of △1 after an enlargement with scale factor $\frac{1}{2}$, centre (5,−5).
   (e) Write down the coordinates of the 'pointed ends' of △2, △3 and △4.

4. (a) Plot and label the triangle △1 at (1,7), (7,7), (7,4).
   (b) Draw △2, the image of △1 after an enlargement scale factor $\frac{1}{3}$, centre (−5,7).
   (c) Draw △3, the image of △1 after an enlargement scale factor $\frac{1}{3}$, centre (7,−5).
   (d) Draw △4, the image of △1 after an enlargement scale factor $\frac{1}{3}$, centre (−5,−5).
   (e) Write down the coordinates of the 'pointed ends' of △2, △3 and △4.

5. (a) Plot and label the triangle △1 at (5,−7), (−7,−7), (−7,−1).
   (b) Draw △2, the image of △1 after an enlargement with scale factor $\frac{1}{3}$, centre (−7,5).
   (c) Draw △3, the image of △1 after an enlargement with scale factor $\frac{1}{2}$, centre (5,7).
   (d) Draw △4, the image of △2 (not △1) after an enlargement with scale factor $\frac{1}{2}$, centre (−1,7).
   (e) Write down the coordinates of the 'pointed ends' of △2, △3 and △4.

Unit 9

9.1 SCALE DRAWINGS

Measuring angles

Exercise 1

This exercise provides practice in the accurate use of a protractor. Give your answers correct to the nearest half degree.
In questions **1** to **6** measure the angles shown.

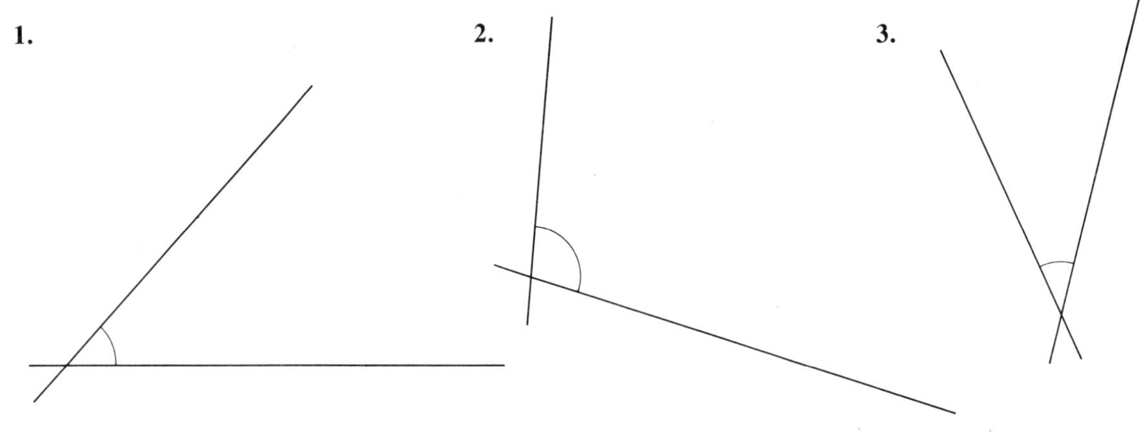

4.

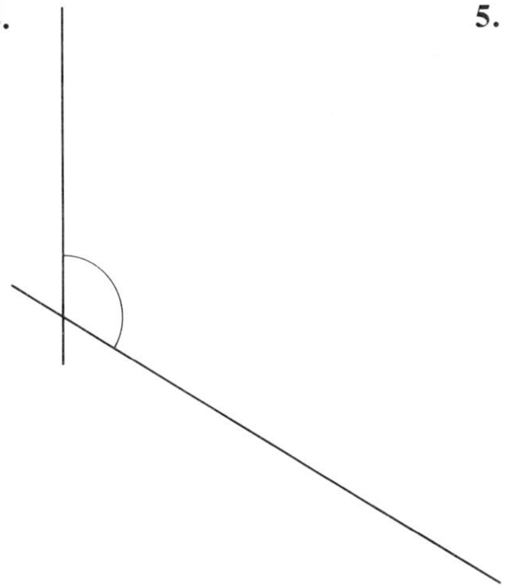

5.

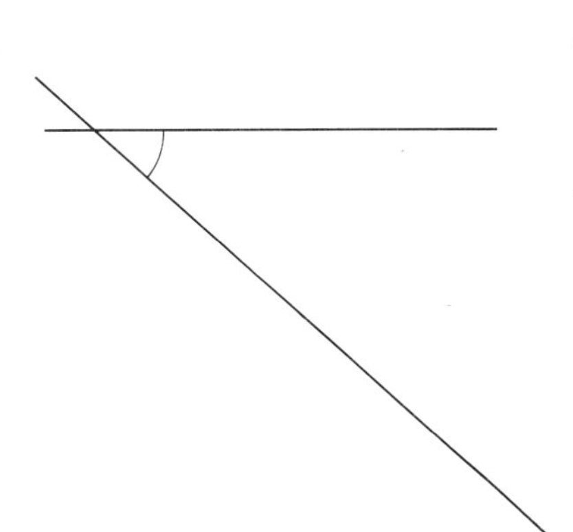

6.

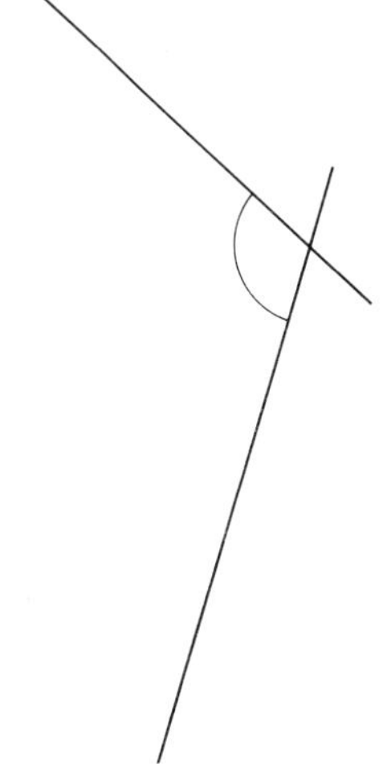

7. Measure the angles given on the diagram below.

(a) $E\hat{G}H$	(b) $A\hat{B}M$	(c) $C\hat{D}N$	(d) $L\hat{K}N$	(e) $I\hat{J}L$
(f) $L\hat{M}F$	(g) $K\hat{F}E$	(h) $B\hat{A}M$	(i) $H\hat{L}J$	(j) $J\hat{C}E$
(k) $L\hat{H}I$	(l) $K\hat{N}D$	(m) $D\hat{H}G$	(n) $N\hat{K}J$	(o) $L\hat{H}D$
(p) $A\hat{B}E$	(q) $H\hat{D}E$	(r) $B\hat{A}I$	(s) $C\hat{E}G$	(t) $C\hat{K}A$

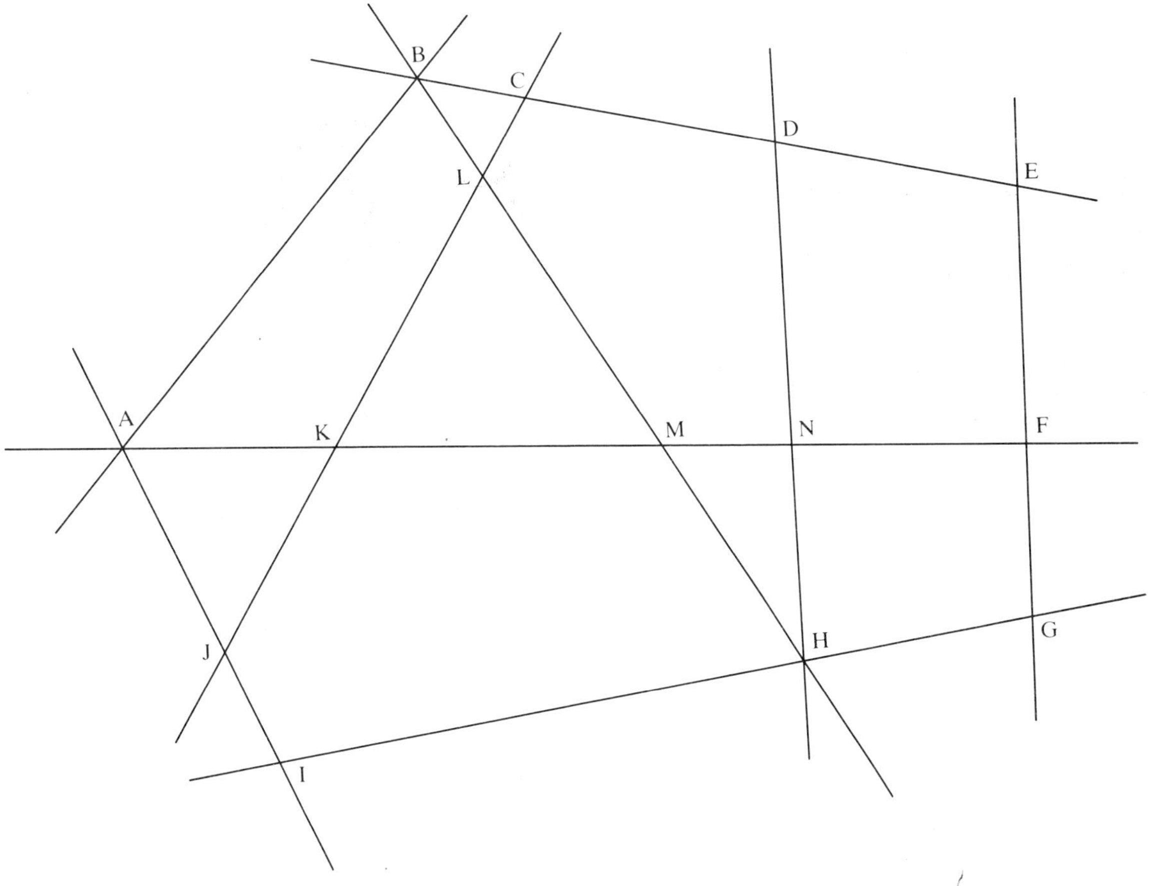

Exercise 2

Use a protractor and ruler to draw full size diagrams and measure the sides marked with letters.

1.

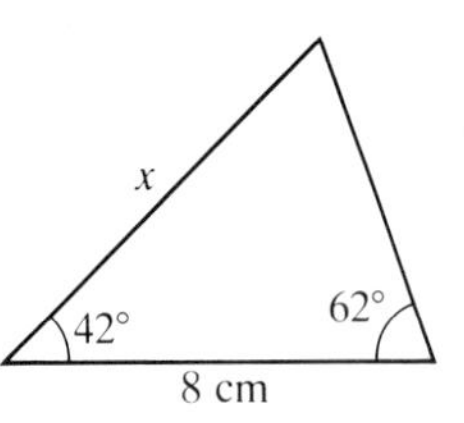

2.

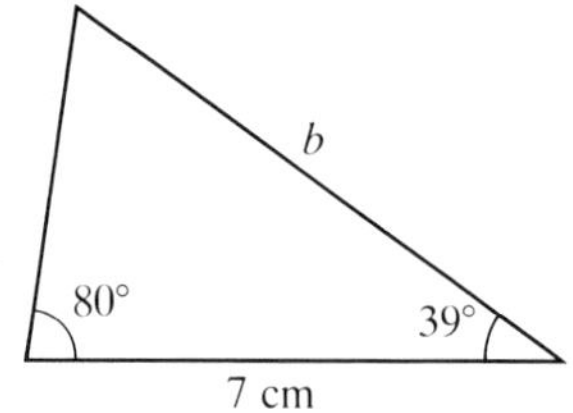

3.

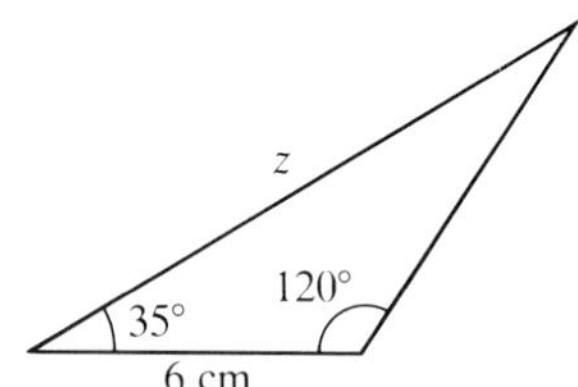

4.

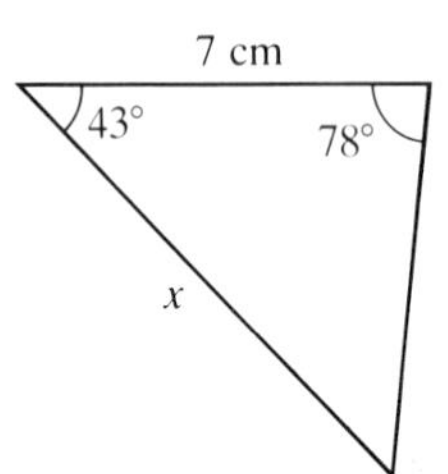

5.

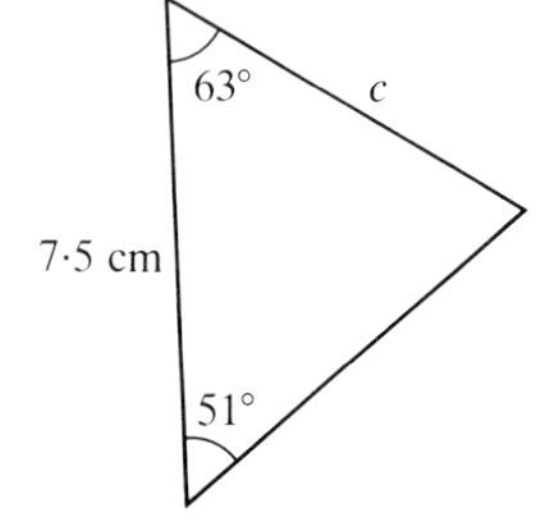

6.

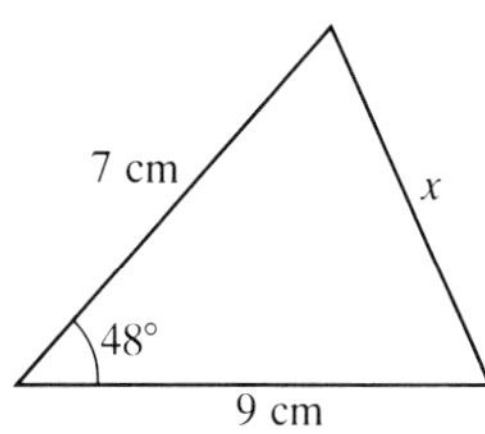

7.

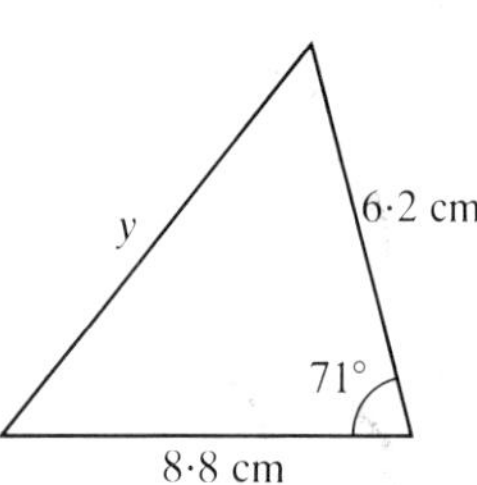

8.

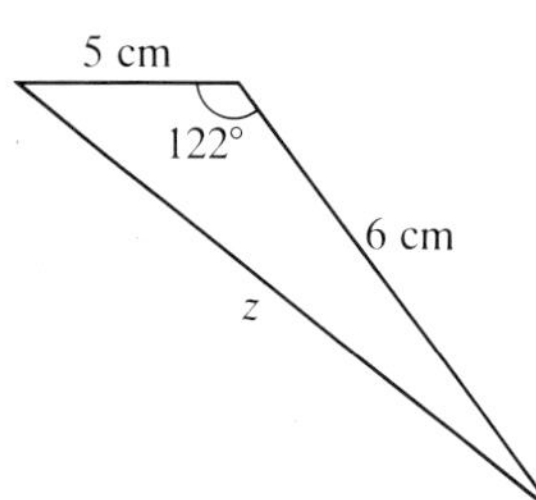

9.

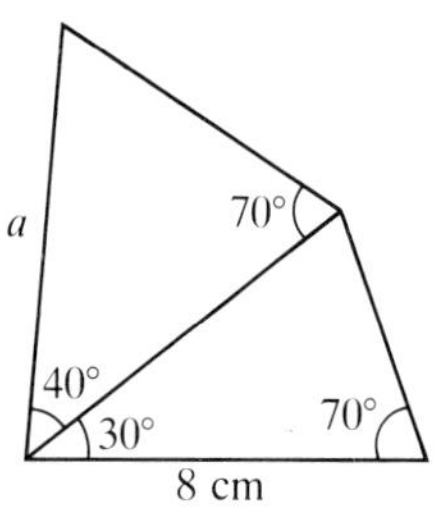

10.

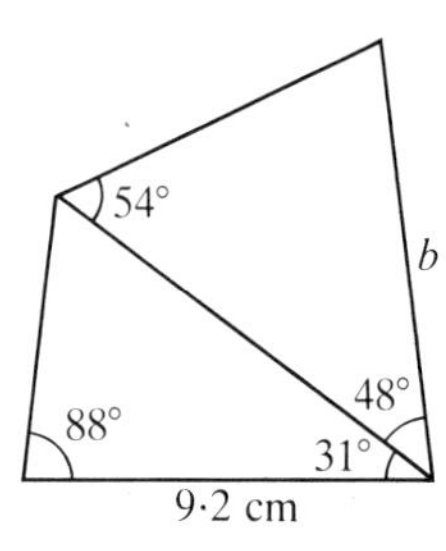

11.

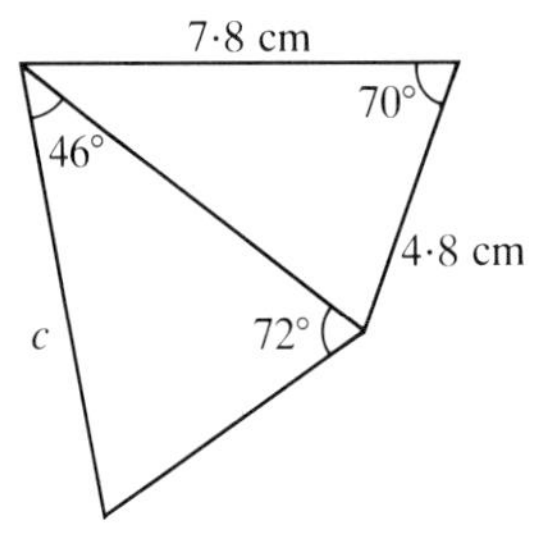

12.

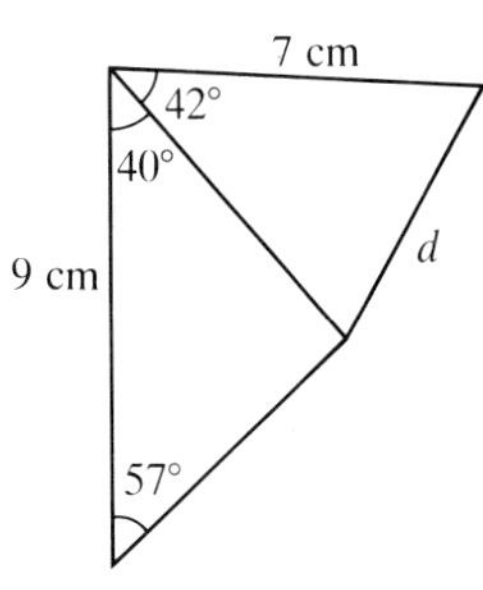

13.

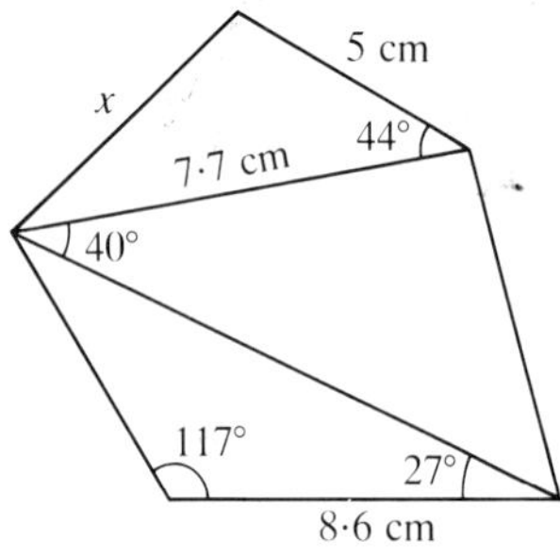

14.

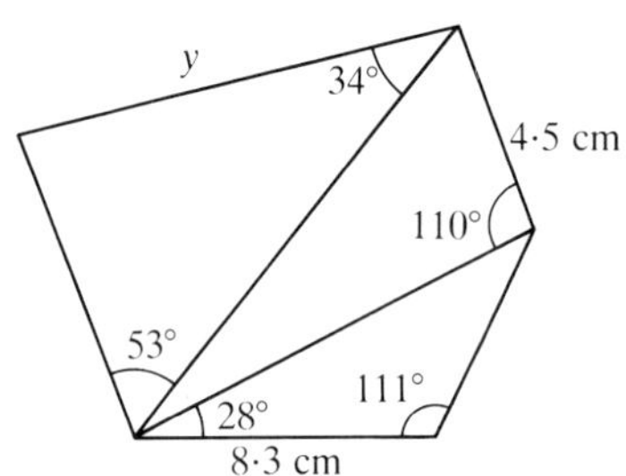

In questions **15** to **20** construct the triangles using a pair of compasses.
Measure the angles marked with letters.

15.

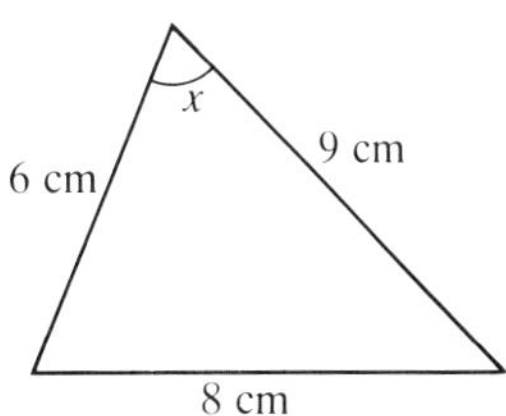

16.

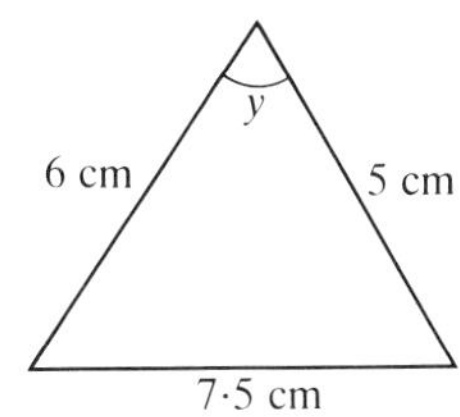

17.

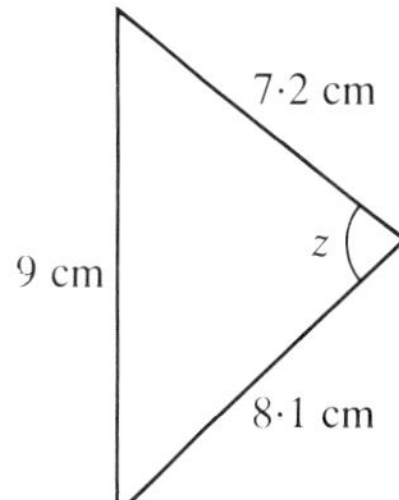

18.

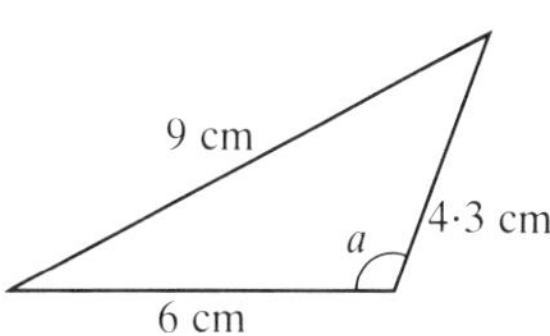

19.

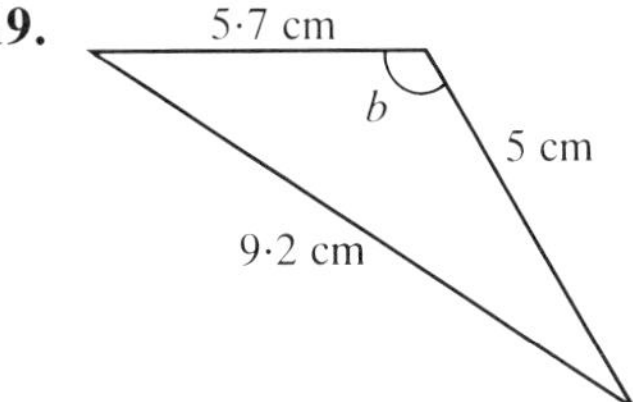

20.

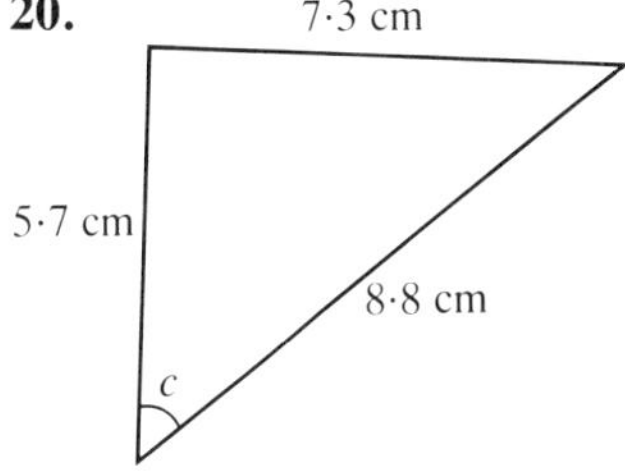

9.2 BEARINGS

Bearings are measured *clockwise from North*.

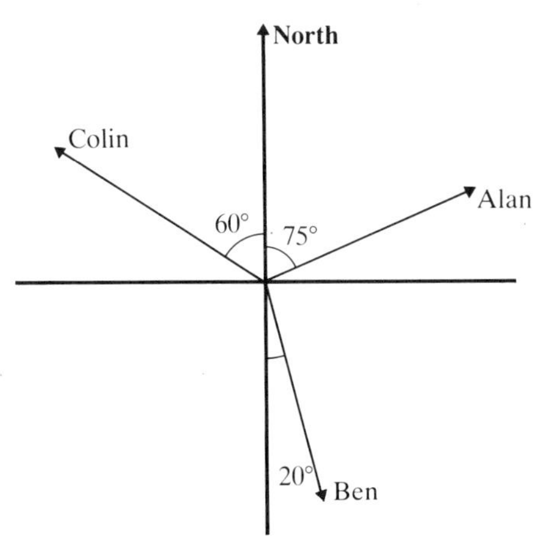

Alan is walking on a bearing of 075°.
Ben is walking on a bearing of 160°.
Colin is walking on a bearing of 300°.

Exercise 3

The diagrams show the directions in which several people are travelling. Copy each diagram and work out the bearing for each person.

1.

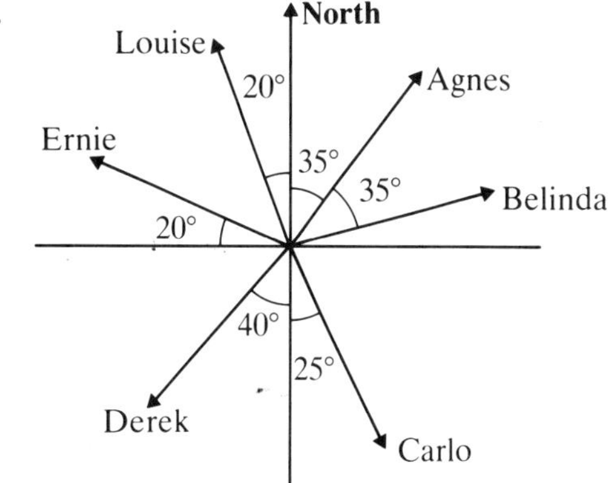

2.

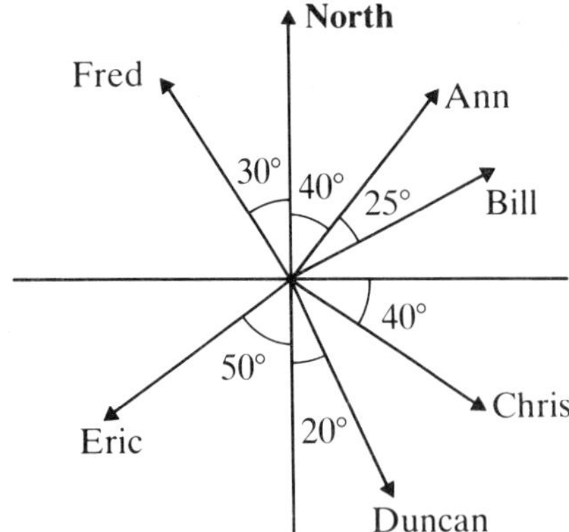

3.

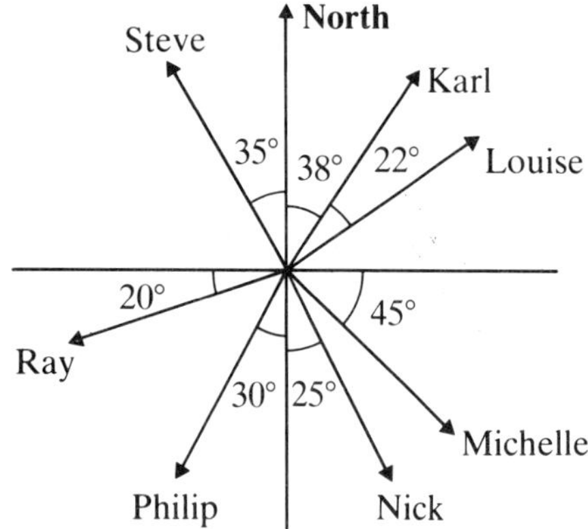

Relative bearings

The bearing of A from B is the direction in which you travel to get to A from B.

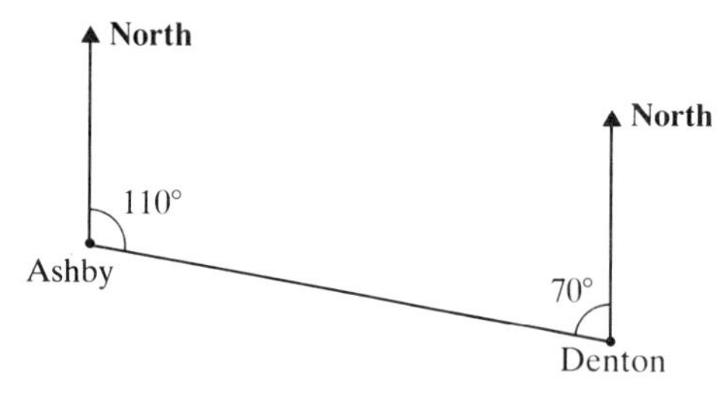

The bearing of Denton from Ashby is 110°.
The bearing of Ashby from Denton is 290°.

Exercise 4

Write down the bearings using the angles given.
Remember: bearings are 'clockwise from North'.

1. (a) The bearing of B from A.
(b) The bearing of A from B.

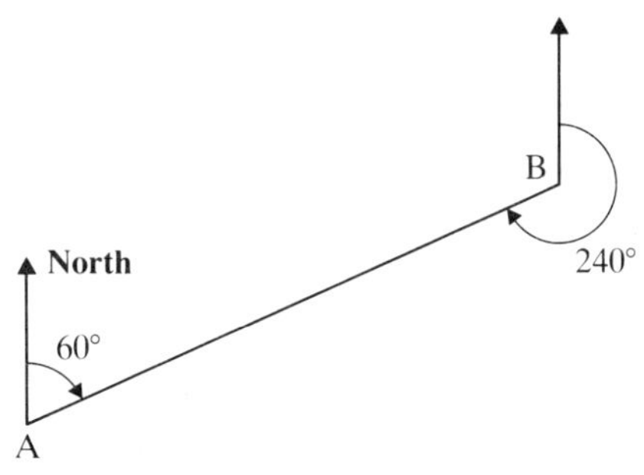

2. (a) The bearing of Q from P.
(b) The bearing of P from Q.

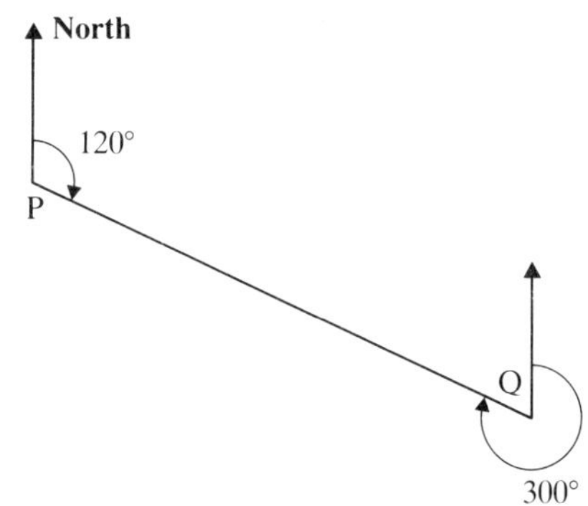

3. (a) The bearing of X from Y.
(b) The bearing of Y from X.

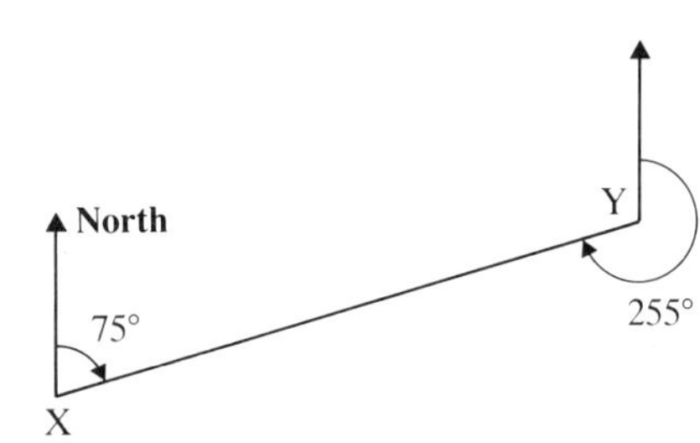

4. (a) The bearing of C from D.
(b) The bearing of D from C.

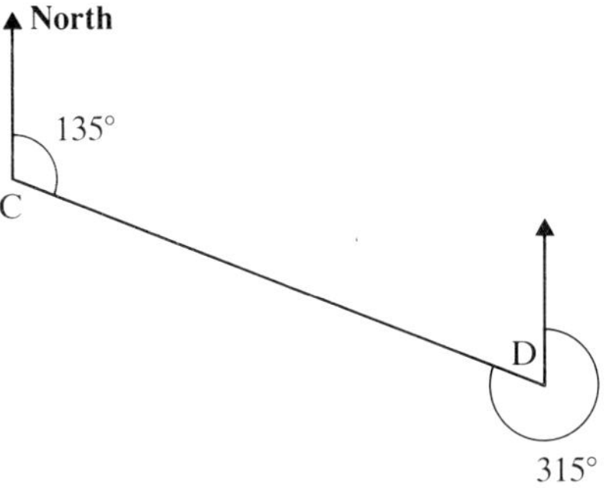

7. (a) The bearing of B from A.
(b) The bearing of B from C.
(c) The bearing of A from B.
(d) The bearing of C from B.

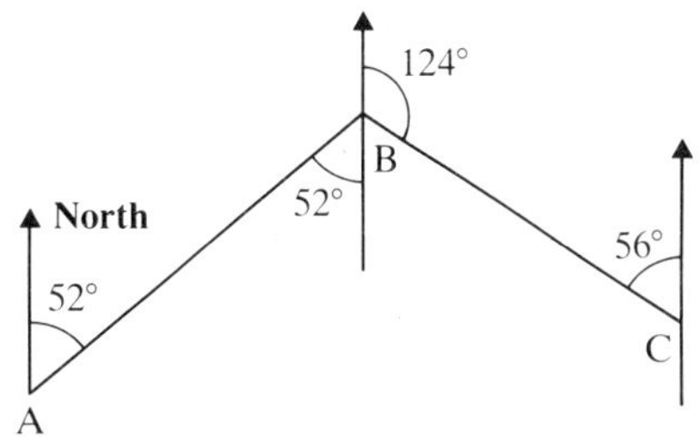

5. (a) The bearing of F from E.
(b) The bearing of E from F.

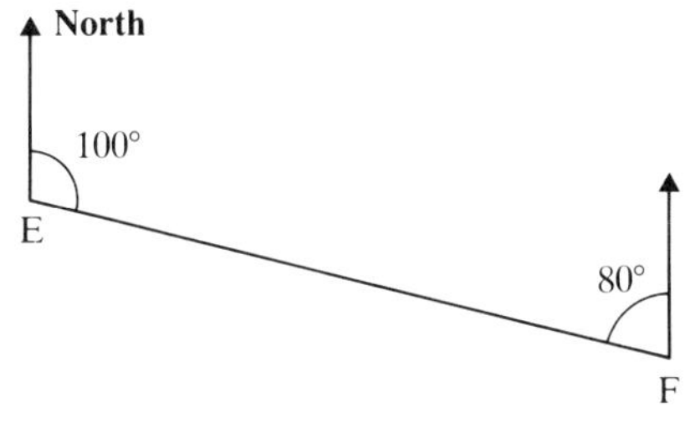

8. (a) The bearing of Q from P.
(b) The bearing of R from Q.
(c) The bearing of P from Q.
(d) The bearing of Q from R.

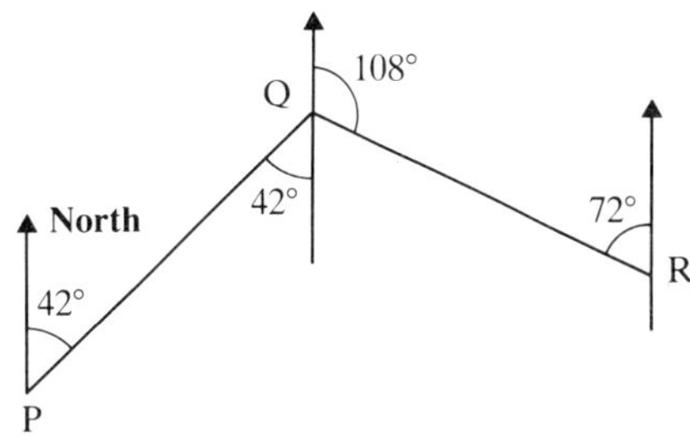

6. (a) The bearing of H from G.
(b) The bearing of G from H.

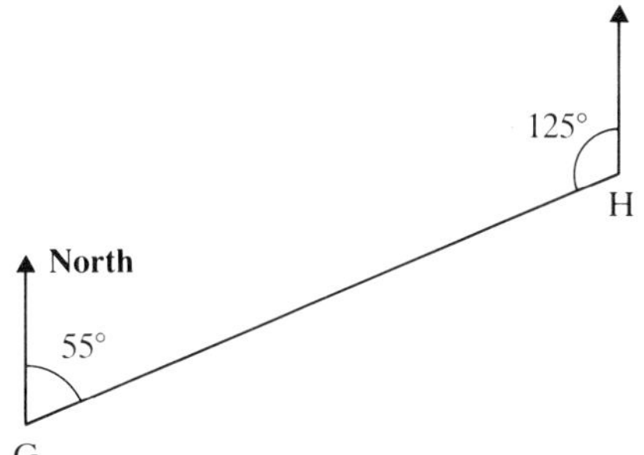

Exercise 5

The map below shows the positions of seven towns: A; B; C; D; E; F; G. Copy the map onto 1 cm graph paper which is at least 20 cm by 15 cm. The axes at the bottom and on the left are shown only to make it easier to draw an accurate copy. You do not use the axes when answering the questions.

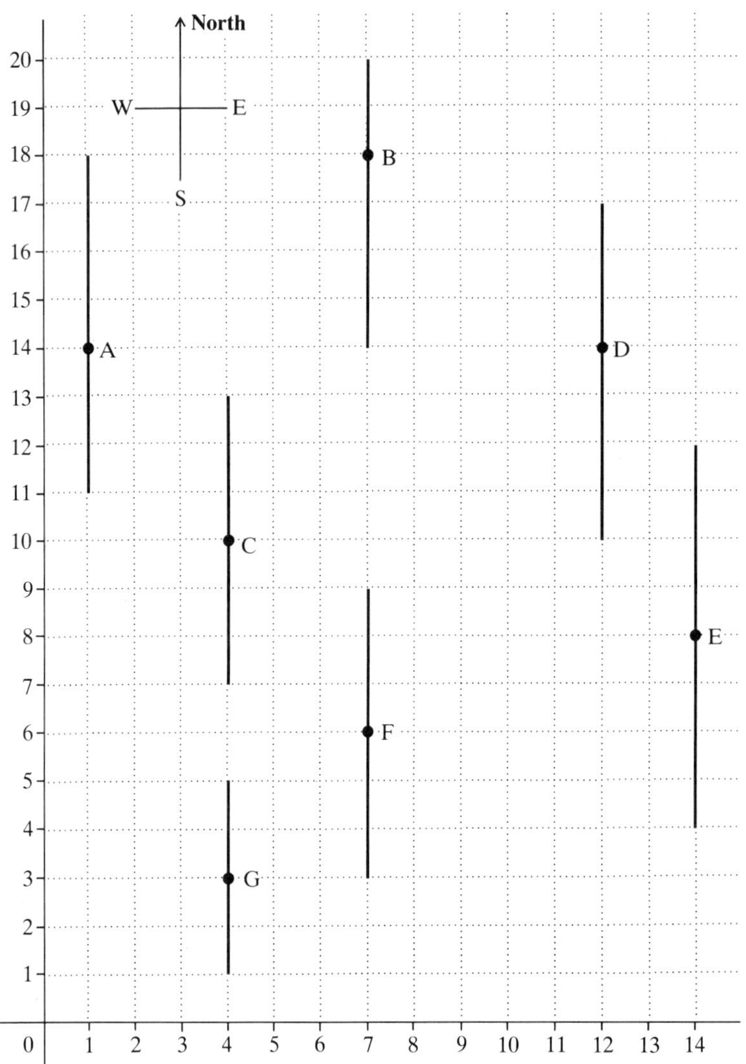

Given that 1 cm represents 1 km, find the distances between the following pairs of places.

1. A and B	**2.** A and C	**3.** A and D
4. A and G	**5.** A and E	**6.** A and F
7. B and C	**8.** B and D	**9.** B and G
10. B and E	**11.** B and F	**12.** C and D
13. C and E	**14.** C and F	**15.** C and G
16. D and E	**17.** D and F	**18.** D and G
19. E and F	**20.** E and G	

Exercise 6

Use the map you made in Exercise 5 to make the following measurements.

1. From A, measure the bearing of (a) B, (b) D, (c) E, (d) C, (e) G.
2. From C, measure the bearing of (a) B, (b) D, (c) E, (d) F, (e) G.
3. From G, measure the bearing of (a) B, (b) D, (c) F, (d) A, (e) E.
4. From B, measure the bearing of (a) D, (b) E, (c) F, (d) C, (e) A.
5. From F, measure the bearing of (a) D, (b) E, (c) G, (d) C, (e) B.
6. From D, measure the bearing of (a) E, (b) F, (c) C, (d) A, (e) B.

Exercise 7

Draw the points P and Q below in the middle of a clean page of squared paper. Mark the points A, B, C, D and E accurately, using the information given.

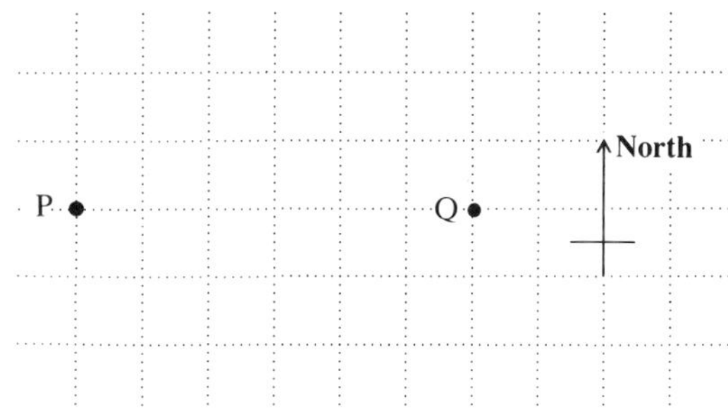

1. A is on a bearing of 040° from P and 015° from Q.
2. B is on a bearing of 076° from P and 067° from Q.
3. C is on a bearing of 114° from P and 127° from Q.
4. D is on a bearing of 325° from P and 308° from Q.
5. E is on a bearing of 180° from P and 208° from Q.

Exercise 8

Draw the points X and Y below in the middle of a clean page of squared paper. Mark the points K, L, M, N and O accurately, using the information given.

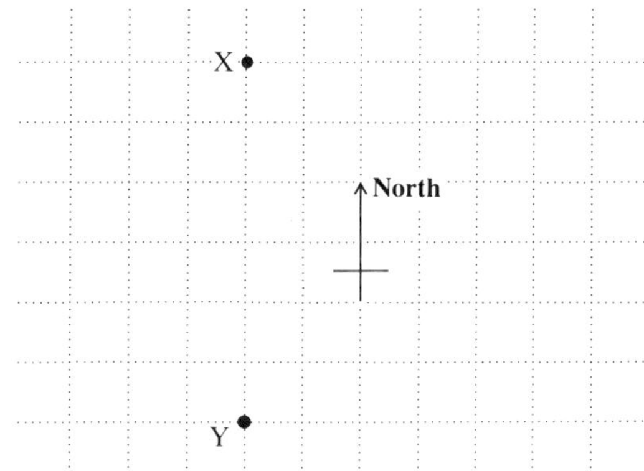

1. K is on a bearing of 041° from X and 025° from Y.
2. L is on a bearing of 090° from X and 058° from Y.
3. M is on a bearing of 123° from X and 090° from Y.
4. N is on a bearing of 203° from X and 215° from Y.
5. O is on a bearing of 288° from X and 319° from Y.

Exercise 9

Make accurate scale drawings with a scale of 1 cm to 1 km. Use squared paper and begin each question by drawing a small sketch of the journey.

1. A ship sails 8 km due North and then a further 7 km on a bearing 080°, as in the diagram (which is not drawn to scale).

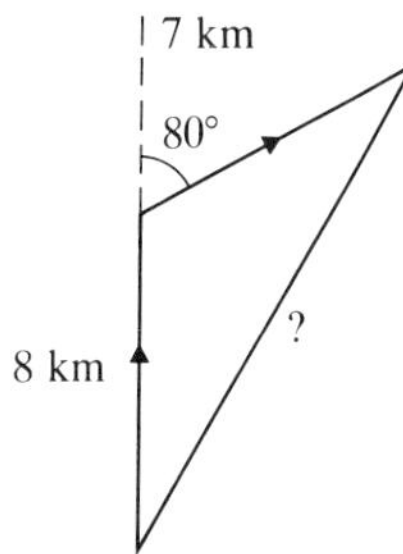

How far is the ship now from its starting point?

2. A ship sails 9 km on a bearing 090° and then a further 6 km on a bearing 050°, as shown in the diagram.

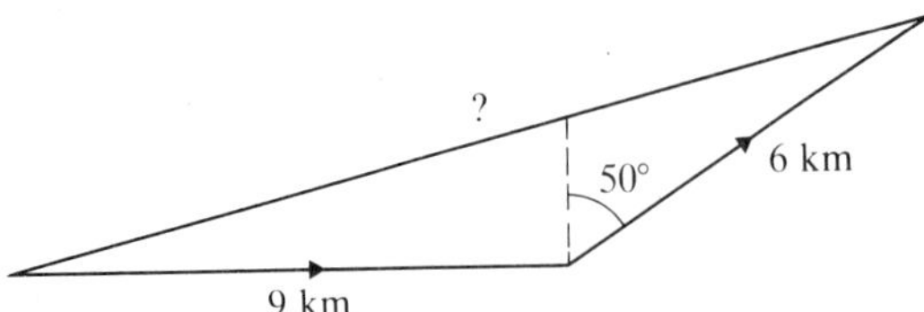

How far is the ship now from its starting point?

3. A submarine sails 7 km on a bearing 180° and then a further 5 km on a bearing 130°. How far is the submarine from its starting point?

4. A ship sails 6 km on a bearing 040° and then a further 6 km on a bearing 100°. How far is the ship from its starting point?

5. A shark swims 7 km on a bearing 055° and then a further 10 km on a bearing 180°. How far is the shark from its starting point?

6. A ship sails 6 km due South and then a further 8 km on a bearing 270°. How far is the ship from its starting point?

7. A ship sails 8 km on a bearing 200° and then a further 9 km on a bearing 100°. How far is the ship from its starting point?

8. A ship sails 6 km on a bearing 160° and then a further 10 km on a bearing 240°, as shown.

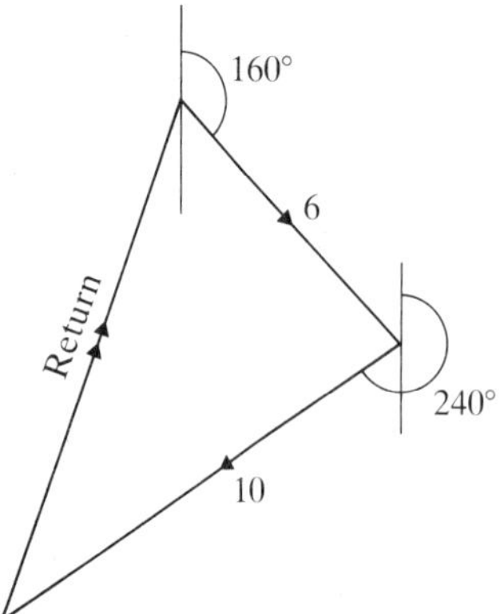

(a) How far is the ship from its starting point?
(b) On what bearing must the ship sail so that it returns to its starting point?

9. A ship sails 5 km on a bearing 030°, then 3 km on a bearing 090° and finally 4 km on a bearing 160°. How far is the ship now from its starting point?

10. A ship sails 6 km on a bearing 070°, then 7 km on a bearing 180° and finally 8 km on a bearing 270°. How far is the ship now from its starting point?

11. Point B is 8 km from A on a bearing 140° from A. Point C is 9 km from A on a bearing 200° from A.
(a) How far is B from C?
(b) What is the bearing of B from C?

12. Point Q is 10 km from P on a bearing 052° from P. Point R is 4 km from P on a bearing 107° from P.
(a) How far is Q from R?
(b) What is the bearing of Q from R?

9.3 TRIGONOMETRY

Labelling the sides of a triangle

The opposite, the hypotenuse and the adjacent are marked with respect to the angle x.

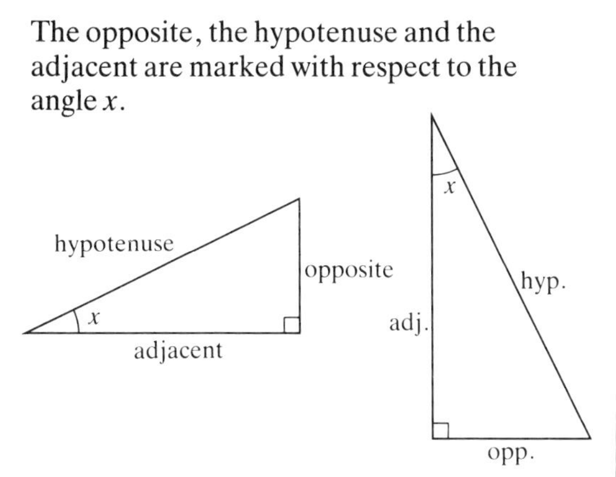

Exercise 10

In each question, use the letters to indicate the opposite, the hypotenuse and the adjacent (in that order) with respect to the angle marked x. The answer to each question will consist of just 3 letters.

1.

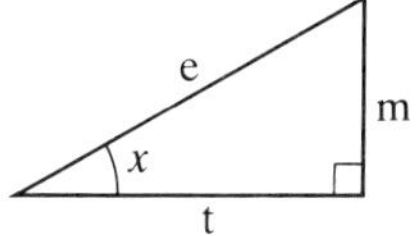

2.

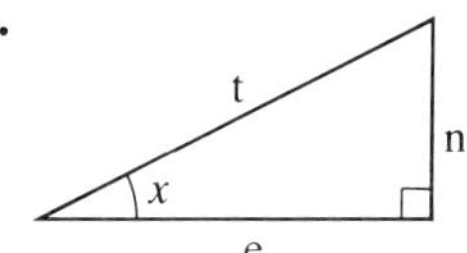

3.

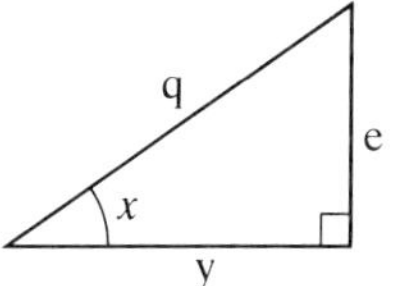

4.

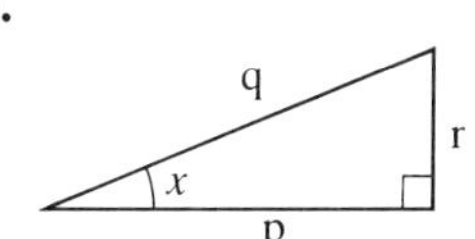

5.

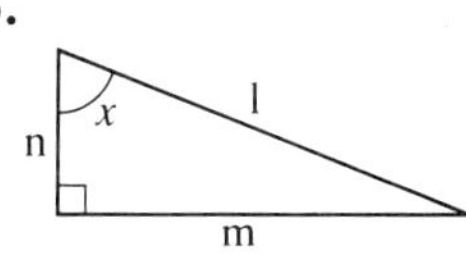

6.

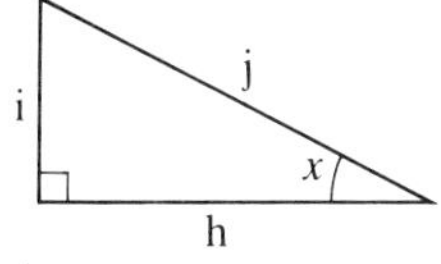

7.

t c x b

8.

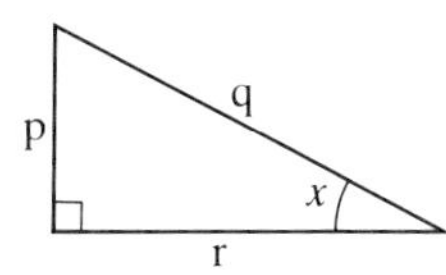

9.

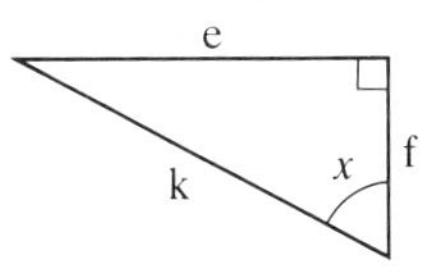

10.

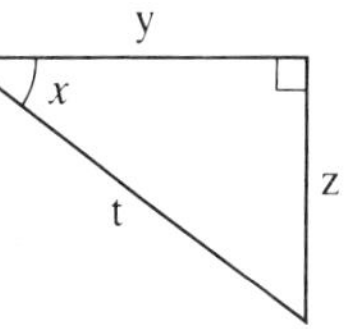

11.

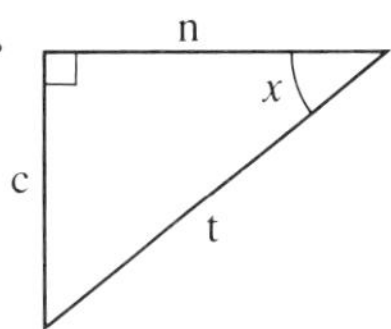

12.

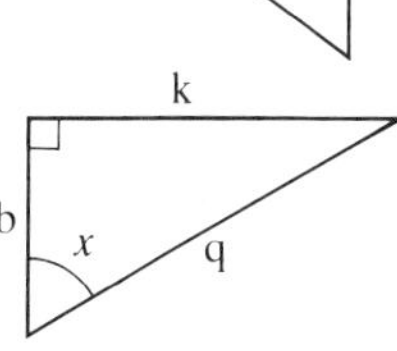

13.

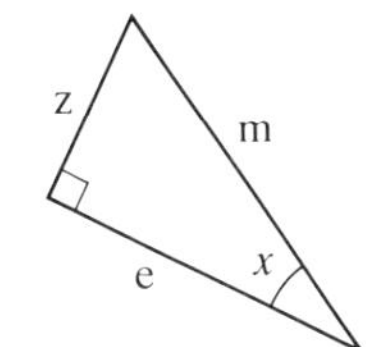

14.

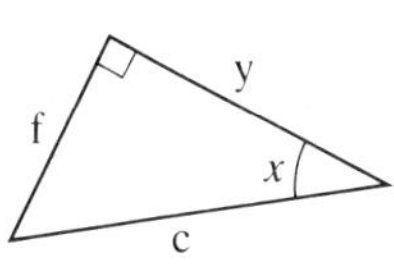

15.

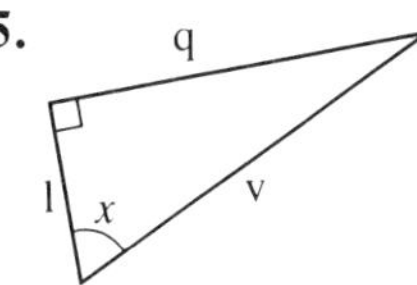

16.

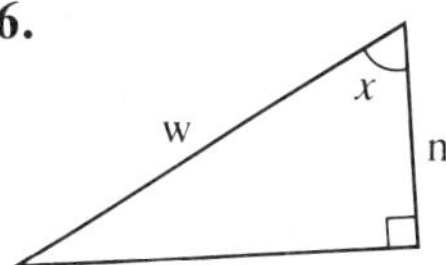

17.

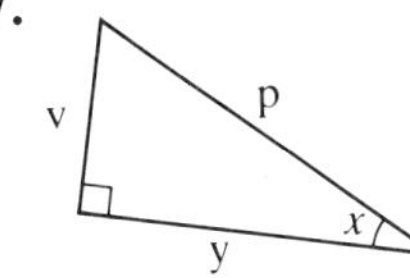

18.

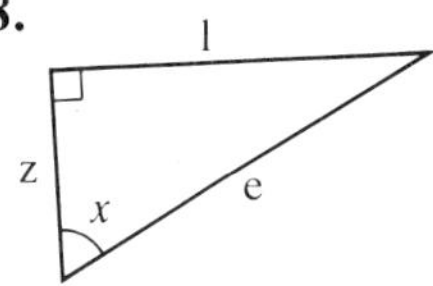

19.

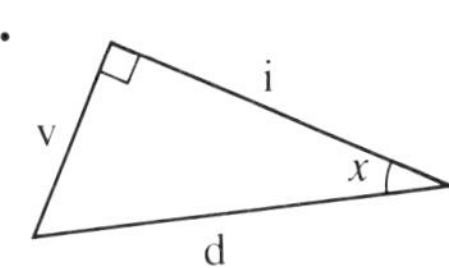

20.

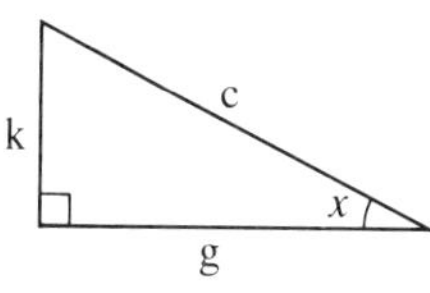

21.

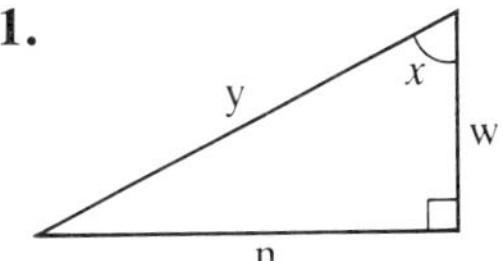

22.

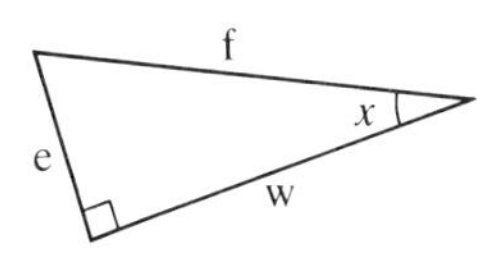

23.

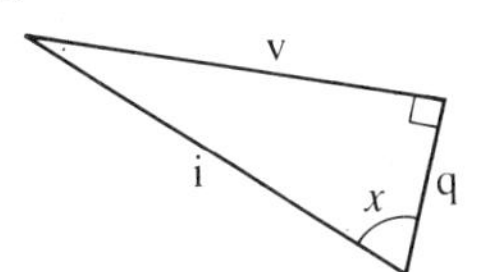

24.

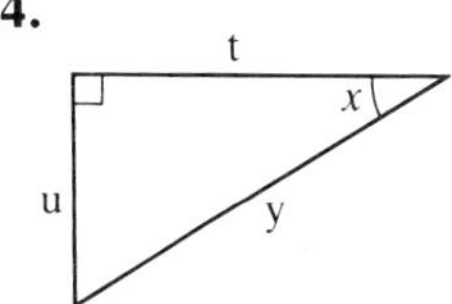

Sine, cosine and tangent

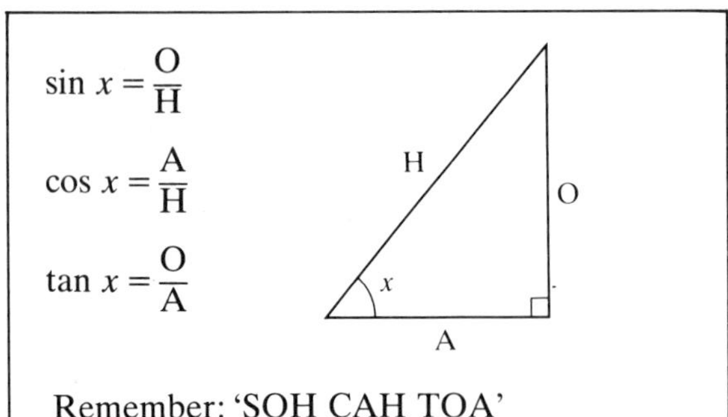

Exercise 11

For questions **1** to **8** in Exercise 10, use the letters given to write down an expression for:

(a) $\sin x$ (b) $\cos x$ (c) $\tan x$

Using tables

Trigonometric tables are given at the end of this book.

Find the following, using 3 figure tables:
(a) sin 28° (b) tan 64° (c) cos 64.3°

(a) sin 28° = 0.469
(b) tan 64° = 2.05
(c) cos 64.3° = 0.434

Exercise 12

Use tables to find the following, correct to 3 S.F.

1. sin 38°	**2.** sin 65°	**3.** sin 82°
4. sin 21°	**5.** sin 8°	**6.** cos 53°
7. cos 82°	**8.** cos 26°	**9.** cos 18°
10. cos 7°	**11.** tan 11°	**12.** tan 53°
13. tan 37°	**14.** tan 66°	**15.** tan 79°
16. sin 31°	**17.** cos 45°	**18.** tan 76°
19. tan 25.4°	**20.** sin 33.1°	**21.** cos 22.4°
22. cos 60.8°	**23.** tan 31.3°	**24.** sin 74.6°
25. sin 18.1°	**26.** cos 9.5°	**27.** tan 69.5°
28. tan 11.4°	**29.** sin 56°	**30.** cos 19°
31. cos 84.7°	**32.** tan 80°	**33.** sin 21.7°
34. sin 6.4°	**35.** cos 0.9°	**36.** tan 28°
37. tan 12.8°	**38.** sin 88°	**39.** cos 17.4°
40. cos 16°	**41.** tan 72.6°	**42.** sin 6.6°
43. sin 29.9°	**44.** cos 57.1°	**45.** tan 88°

Finding the length of a side

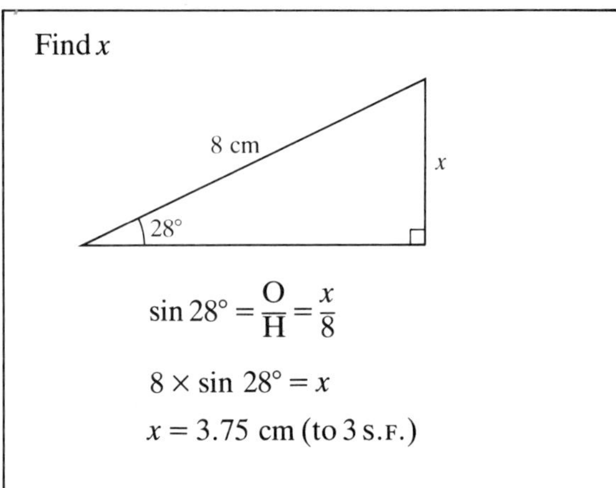

$$\sin 28° = \frac{O}{H} = \frac{x}{8}$$

$$8 \times \sin 28° = x$$

$$x = 3.75 \text{ cm (to 3 S.F.)}$$

Exercise 13

Find the length of the side marked with a letter.

1.

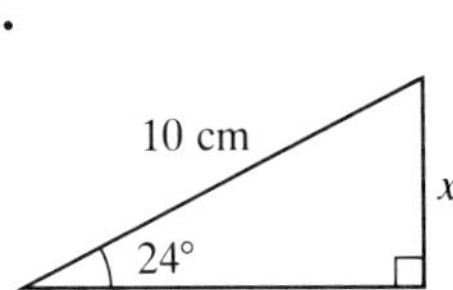

2.

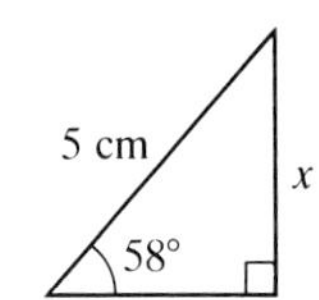

3.

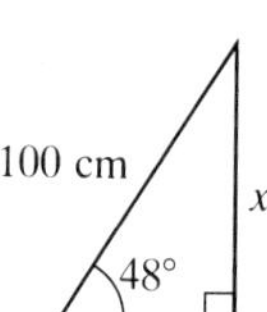

4.

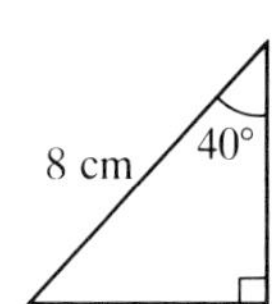

5.

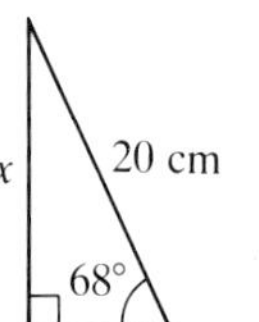

6.

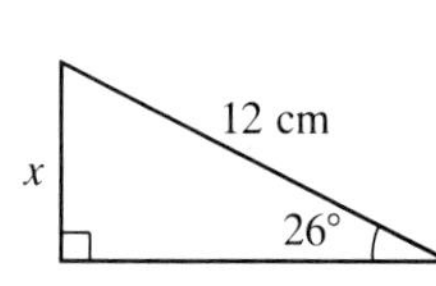

7.

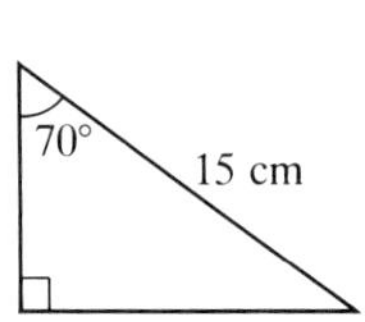

8.

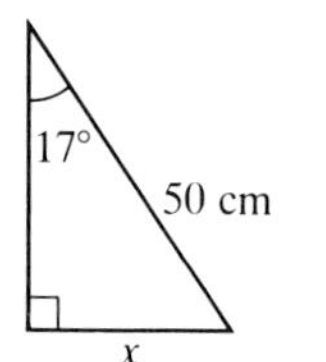

9.

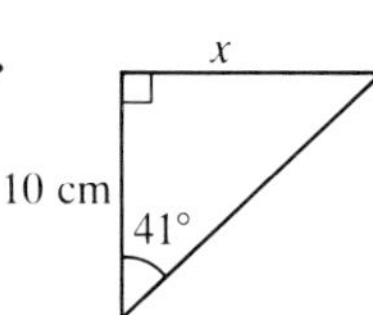

10.

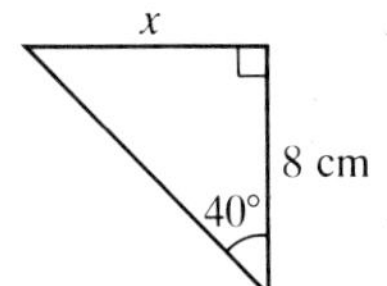

11.

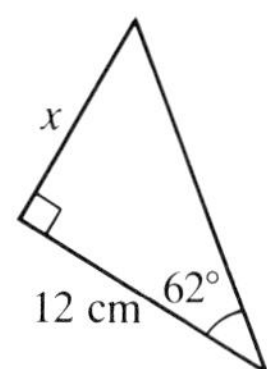

12.

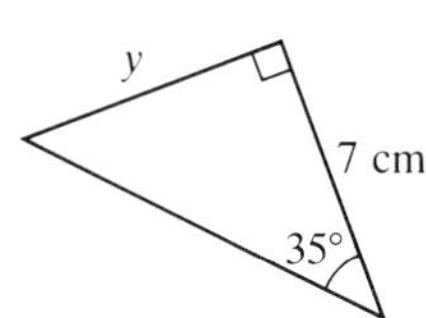

13.

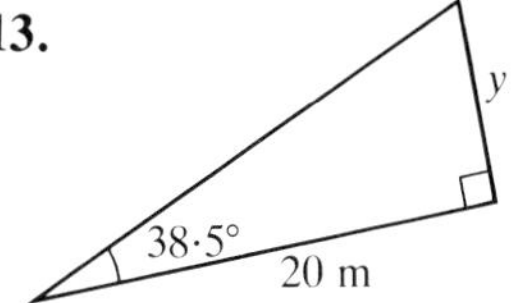

14.

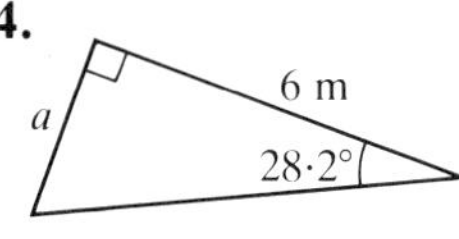

15.

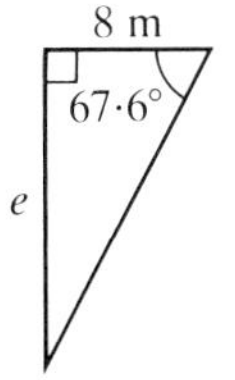

16.

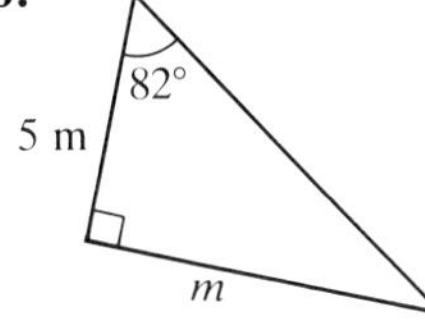

17.

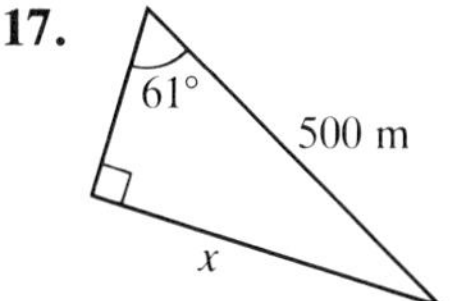

18.

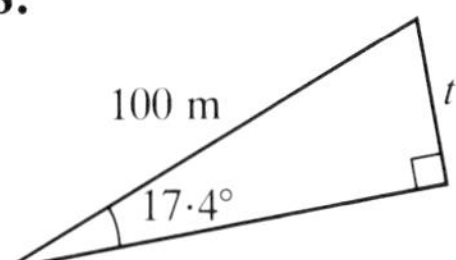

19.

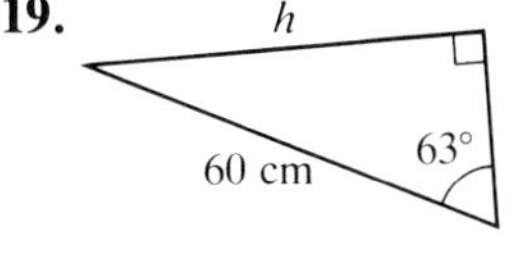

20.

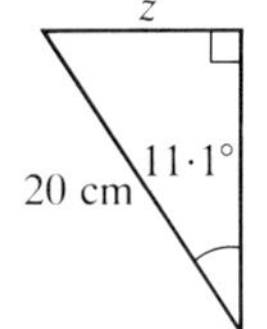

Find y.

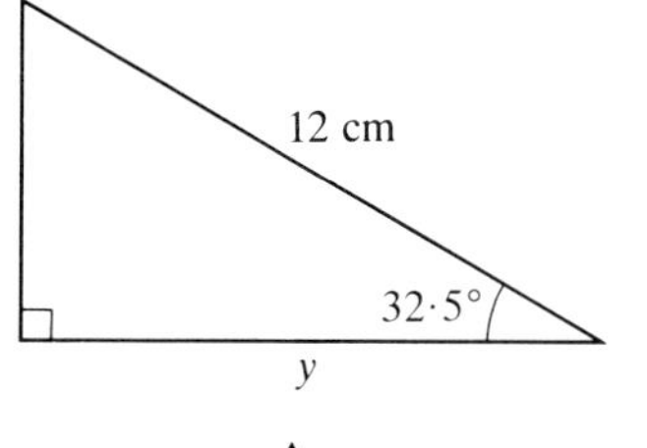

$$\cos 32.5° = \frac{\text{A}}{\text{H}} = \frac{y}{12}$$

$$12 \times \cos 32.5° = y$$

$$y = 10.1 \text{ cm (to 3 s.f.)}$$

Exercise 14

Find the length of the side marked with a letter.

1.

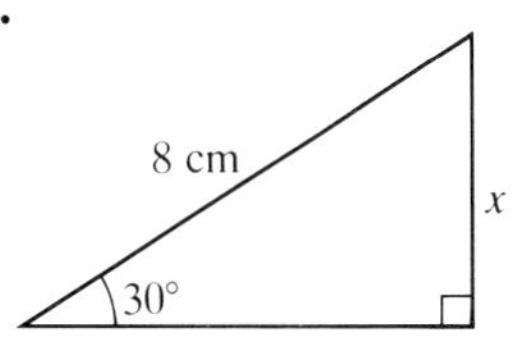

2.

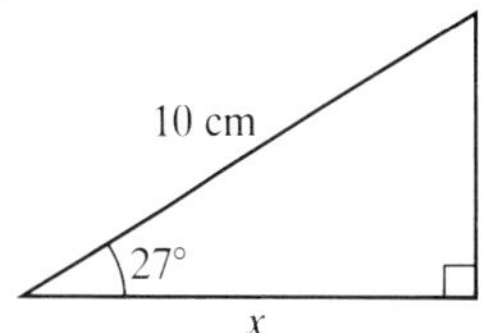

3.

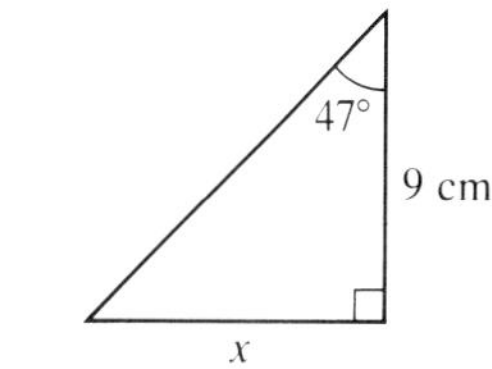

4.

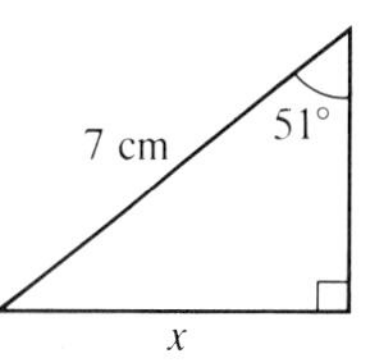

5.

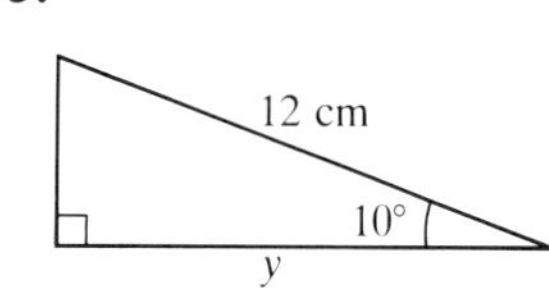

6.

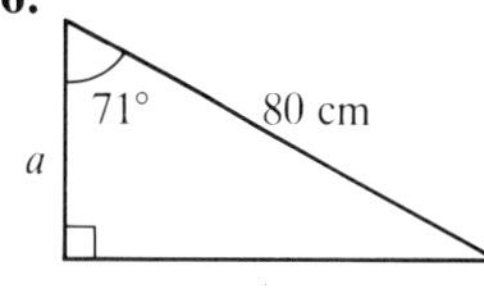

7.

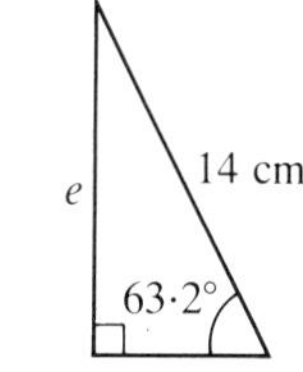

8.

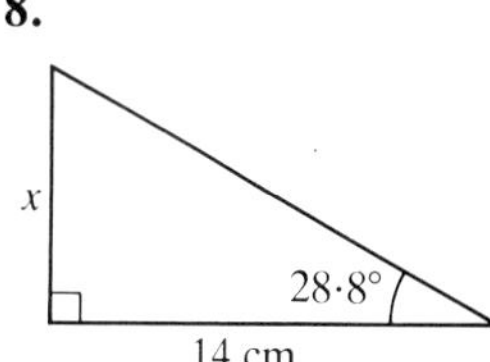

9.

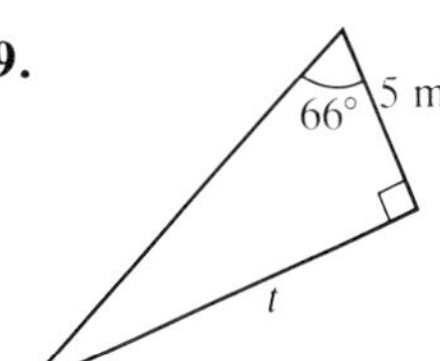

10.

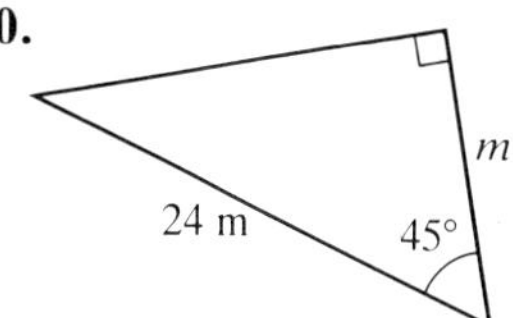

11.

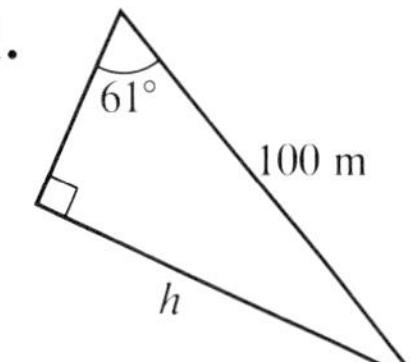

12.

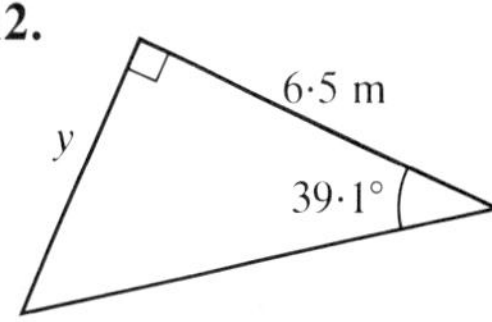

13.

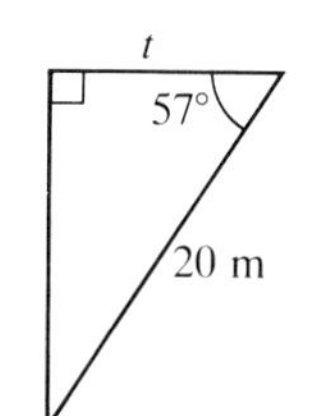

14.

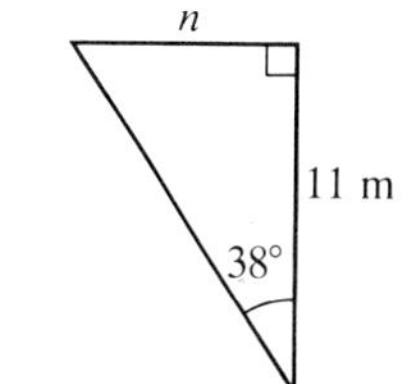

15.

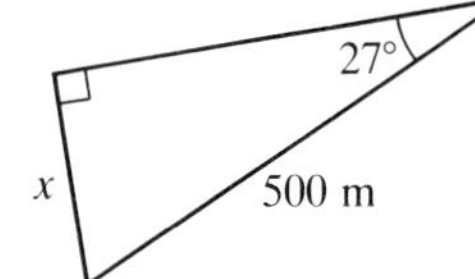

16.

51°
p
6 m

17.

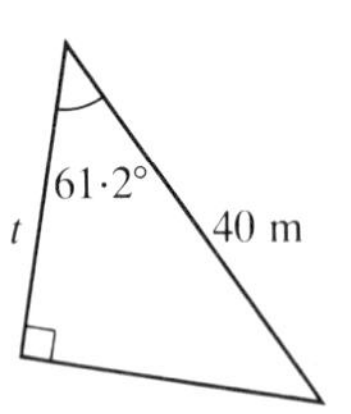

18.

51°
c
25 cm

19.

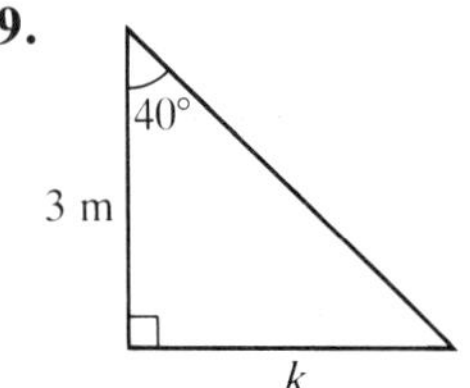

20.

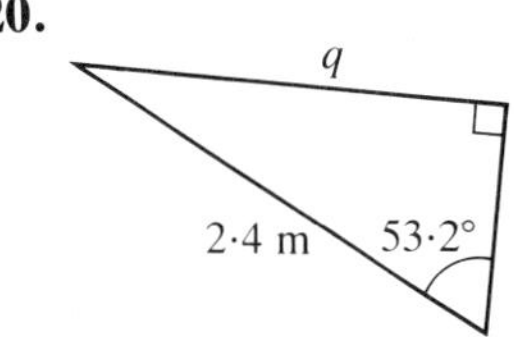

21.

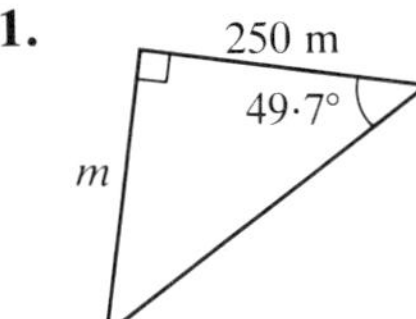

22.

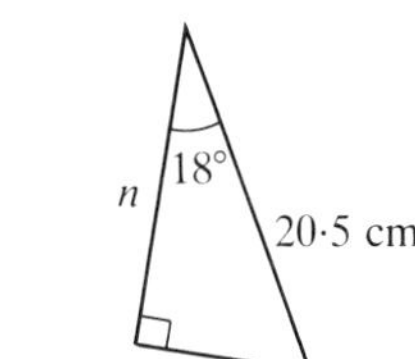

23.

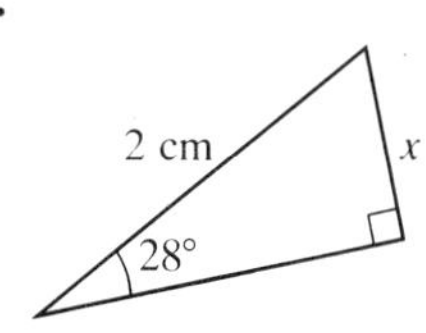

24.

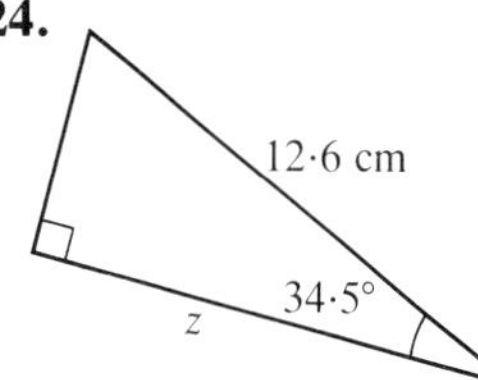

Using tables 'in reverse'

Exercise 15

Find the angle x, correct to one decimal place.

1. $\sin x = 0.857$
2. $\sin x = 0.574$
3. $\sin x = 0.191$
4. $\sin x = 0.620$
5. $\sin x = 0.966$
6. $\sin x = 0.181$
7. $\sin x = 0.915$
8. $\sin x = 0.833$
9. $\sin x = 0.713$
10. $\sin x = 0.774$

11. $\cos x = 0.292$
12. $\cos x = 0.743$
13. $\cos x = 0.866$
14. $\cos x = 0.454$
15. $\cos x = 0.105$
16. $\cos x = 0.765$
17. $\cos x = 0.915$
18. $\cos x = 0.153$
19. $\cos x = 0.049$
20. $\cos x = 0.007$

21. $\tan x = 2.61$
22. $\tan x = 2.39$
23. $\tan x = 0.366$
24. $\tan x = 3.49$
25. $\sin x = 0.54$
26. $\cos x = 0.284$
27. $\cos x = 0.825$
28. $\tan x = 0.735$
29. $\tan x = 0.561$
30. $\sin x = 0.007$

31. $\sin x = 0.8$
32. $\cos x = 0.204$
33. $\cos x = 0.771$
34. $\tan x = 0.264$
35. $\tan x = 3.08$
36. $\sin x = 0.6$
37. $\sin x = 0.605$
38. $\cos x = 0.807$
39. $\cos x = 0.052$
40. $\tan x = 35.8$

41. $\tan x = 1.6$
42. $\sin x = 0.010$
43. $\tan x = 0.620$
44. $\cos x = 0.639$
45. $\sin x = 0.019$
46. $\cos x = 0.815$
47. $\sin x = 0.491$
48. $\tan x = 9.84$
49. $\cos x = 0.187$
50. $\sin x = 0.936$

Finding angles

Find the angle marked with a letter.

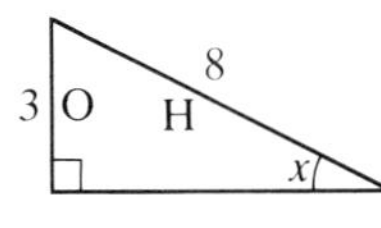

7
O
H
a
11

$$\sin x = \frac{O}{H} = \frac{3}{8}$$

$$\sin x = 0.375$$

$$x = 22.0°$$

$$\sin a = \frac{O}{H} = \frac{7}{11}$$

$$\sin a = 0.6364$$ (4 D.P.)

$$a = 39.5°$$

Exercise 16

Find the angle marked with a letter.

1.

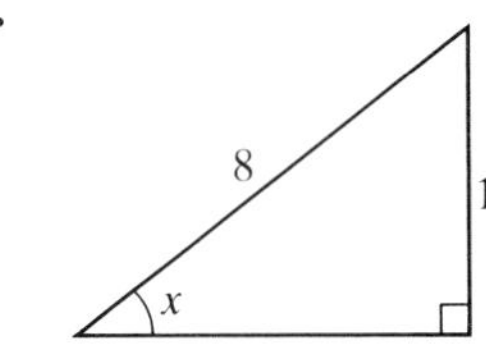

2.

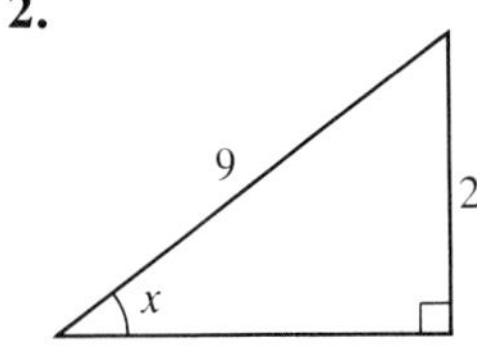

3.

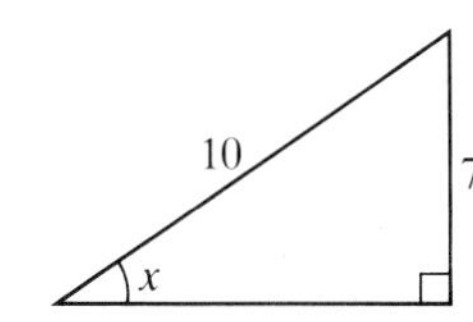

4.

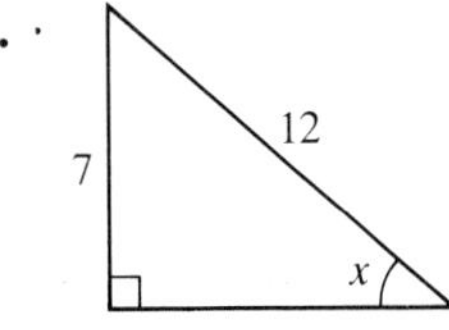

5.

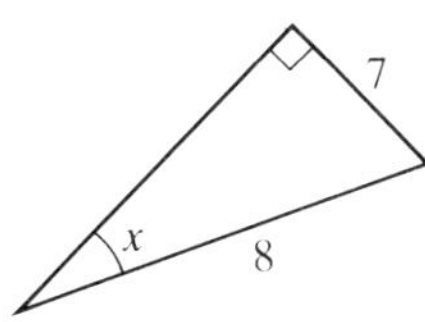

6.

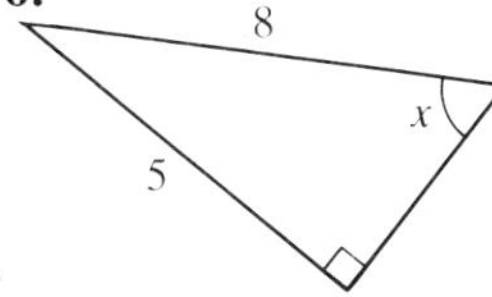

7.

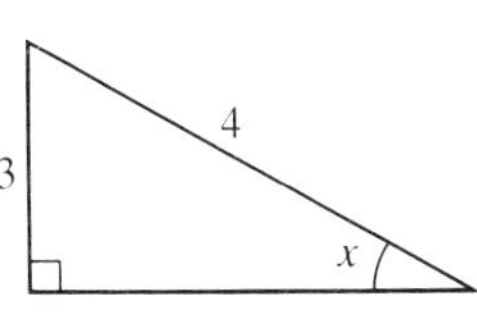

8.

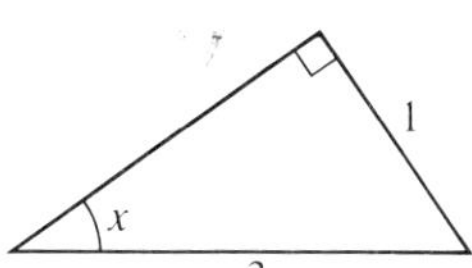

9.

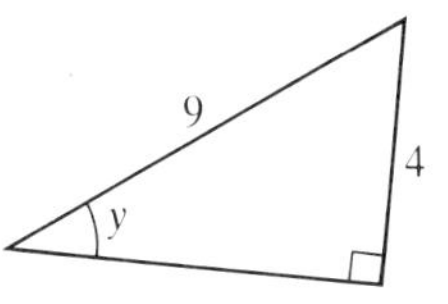

10.

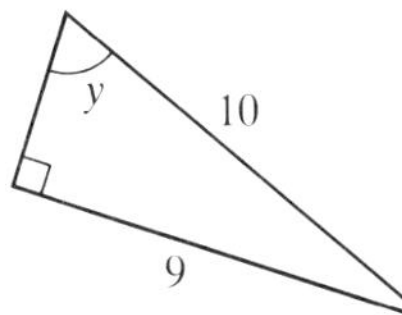

11.

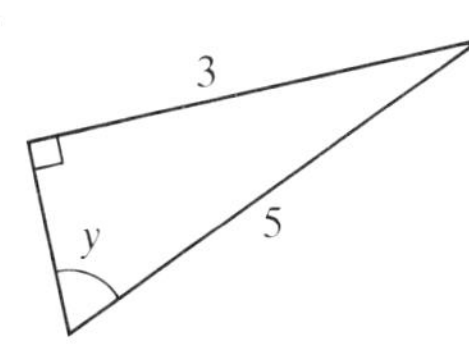

12.

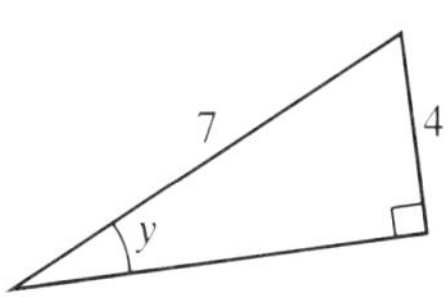

13.

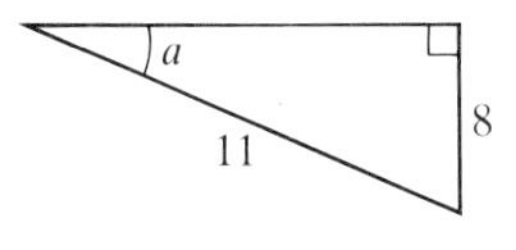

14.

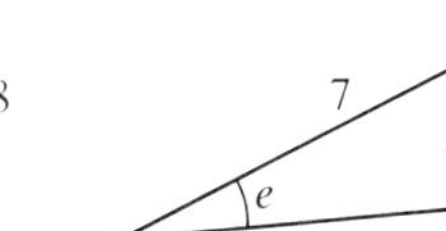

15.

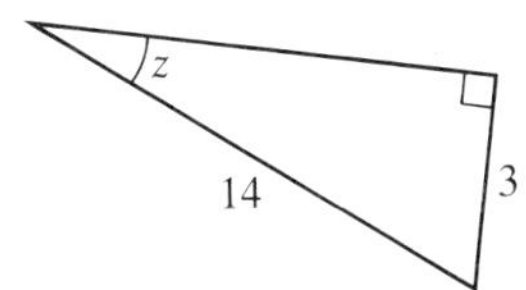

16.

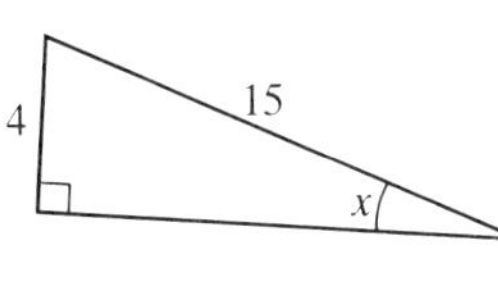

17.

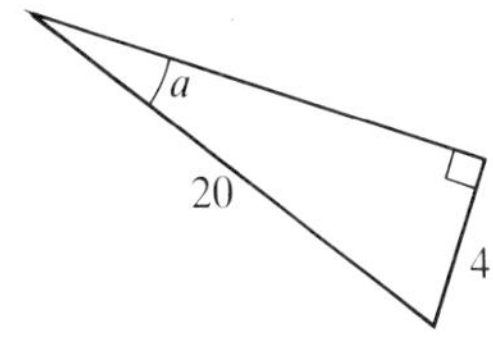

18.

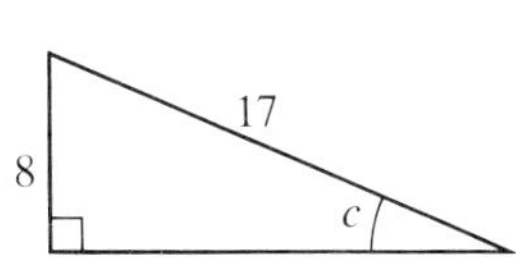

19.

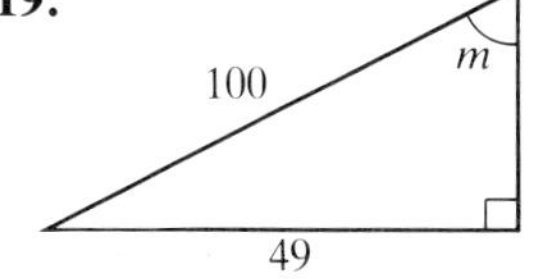

20.

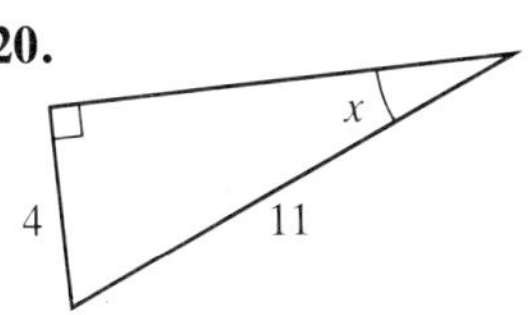

Find the angle y.

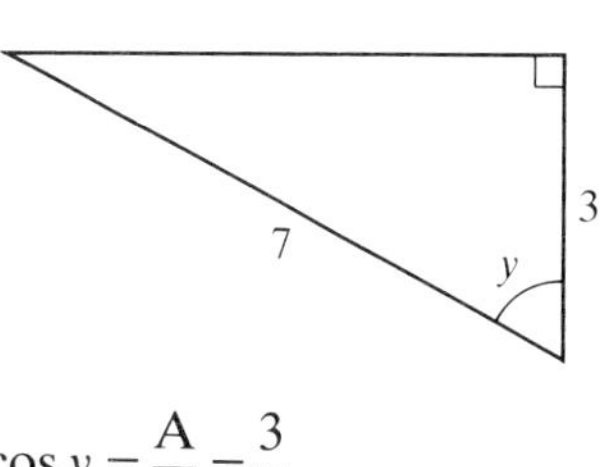

$$\cos y = \frac{\text{A}}{\text{H}} = \frac{3}{7}$$

$$\cos y = 0.4286 \text{ (4 D.P.)}$$

$$y = 64.6°$$

Exercise 17

In each question find the angle marked with a letter.

1.

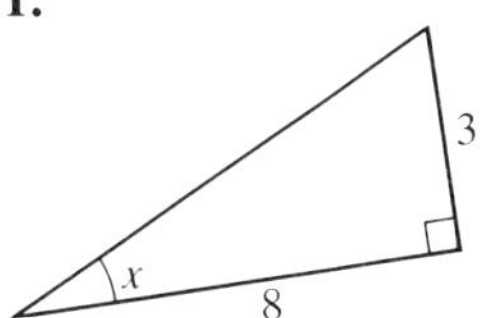

2.

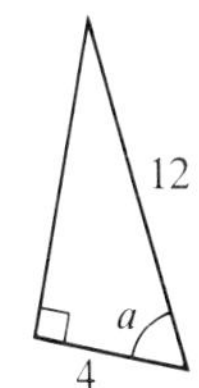

3.

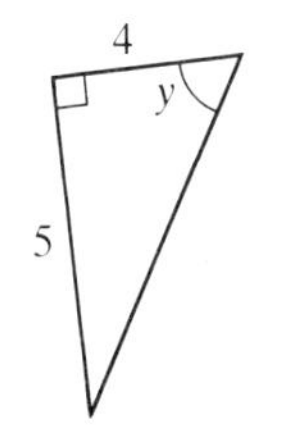

4.

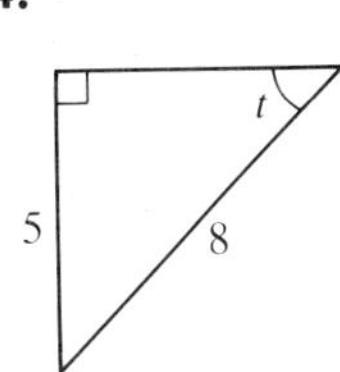

5.

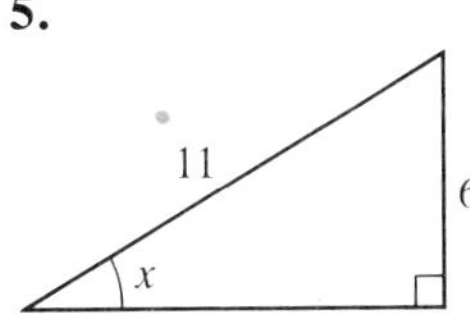

6.

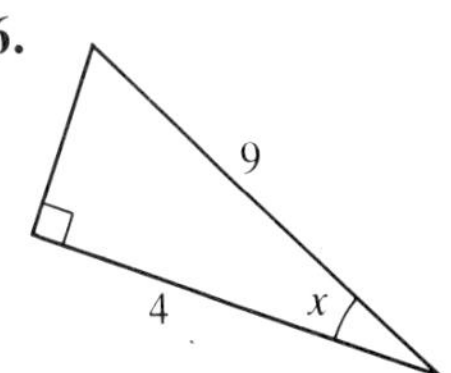

7.

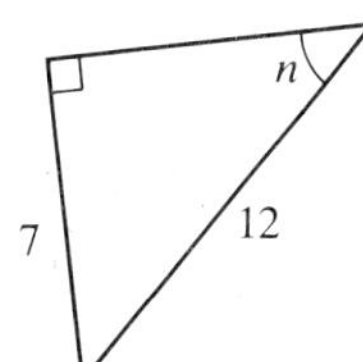

8.

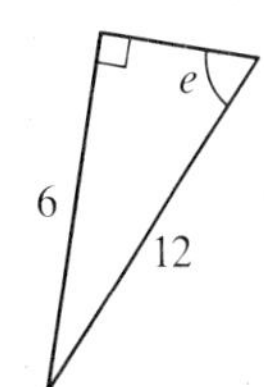

9.

10, 11, a

10.

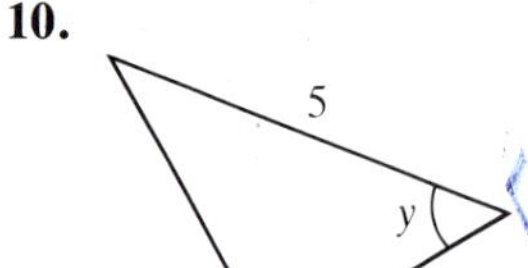

11.

9, 8, z

12.

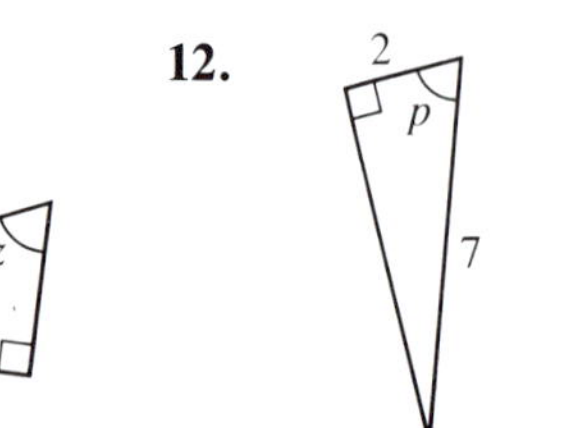

13.

14.

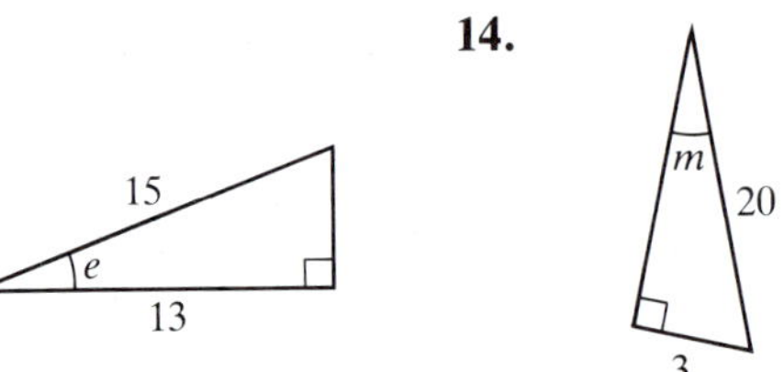

15.

22, 15, n

16.

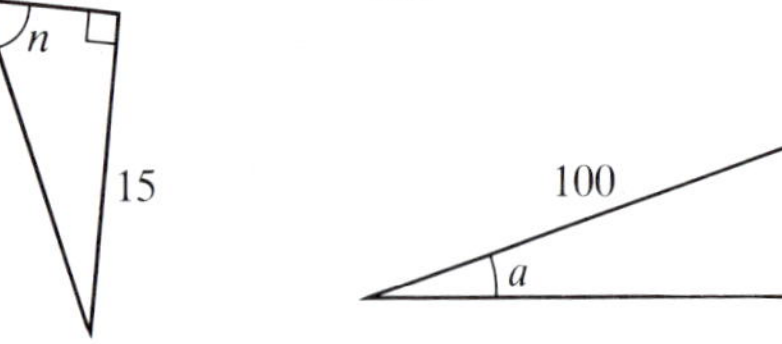

17.

18.

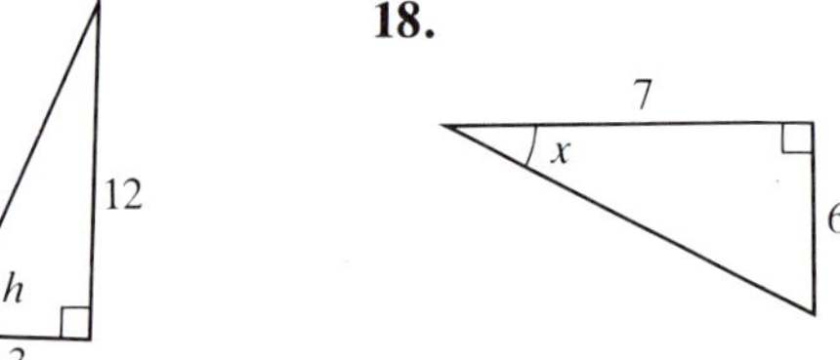

19.

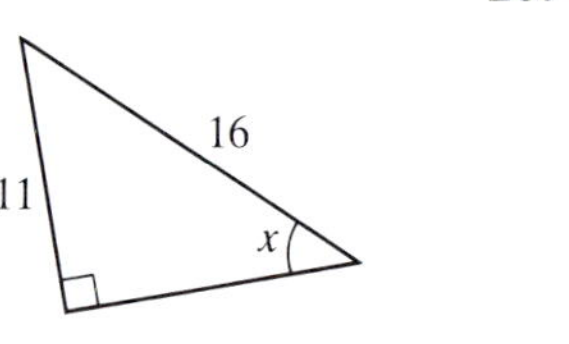

20.

9·9, 8·4, f

21.

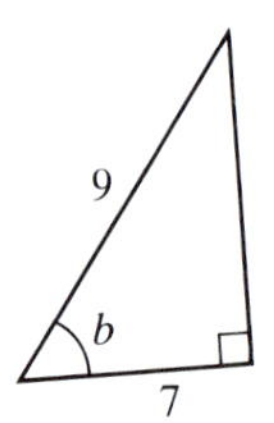

22.

f, 3, 8

23.

24.

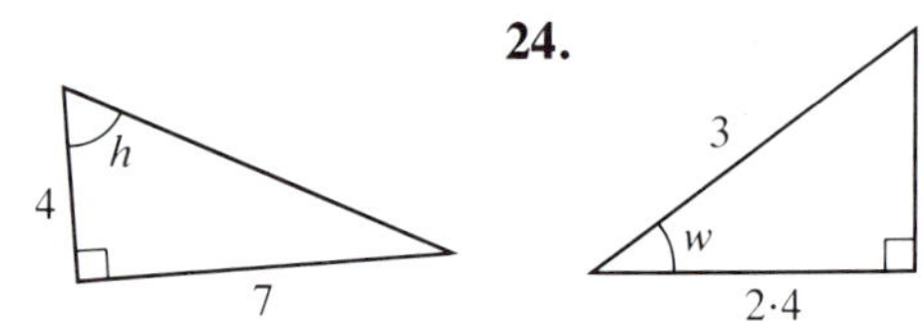

25.

26.

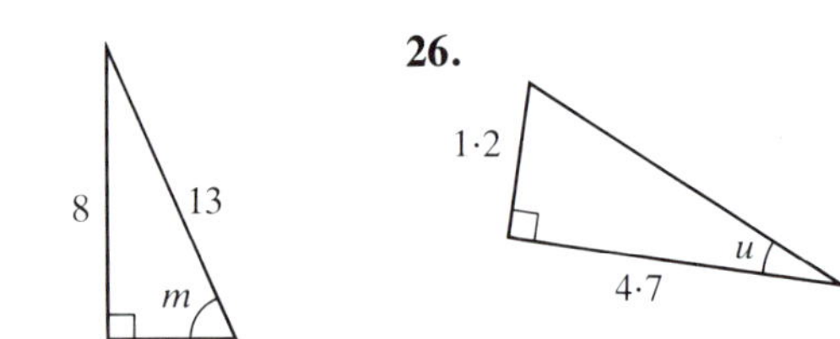

27.

y, 12, 1

28.

9, z, 2

Exercise 18

1. A ladder of length 5 m leans against a vertical wall so that the base of the ladder is 2 m from the wall.

Calculate the angle between the ladder and the wall.

2. A ladder of length 6 m rests against a vertical wall so that the base of the ladder is 2.5 m from the wall. Calculate the angle between the ladder and the wall.
3. A ladder of length 7 m rests against a wall so that the angle between the ladder and the wall is 28°. How far is the base of the ladder from the wall?
4. A ladder of length 5 m rests against a vertical wall so that the angle between the ladder and the ground is 68°. How high does the ladder reach up the wall?

5. An isosceles triangle has sides of length 7 cm, 7 cm and 4 cm.

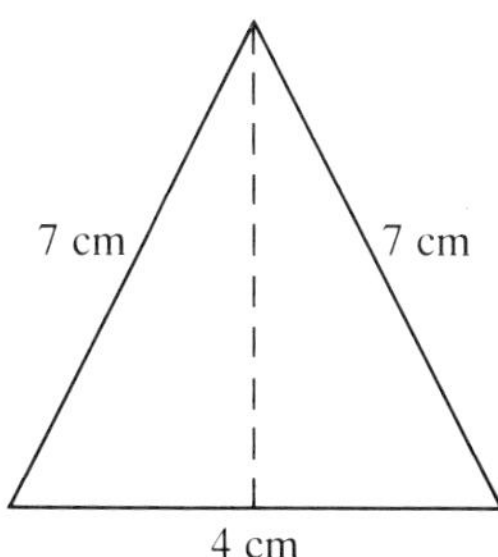

Calculate the angle between the two equal sides.

6. An isosceles triangle has sides of length 8 cm, 8 cm and 4 cm. Calculate the angle between the two equal sides.

7. An isosceles triangle has sides of length 9 cm, 9 cm and 6 cm. Calculate the size of each of the angles in the triangle.

8. A rectangle has sides of length 20 cm and 8 cm.

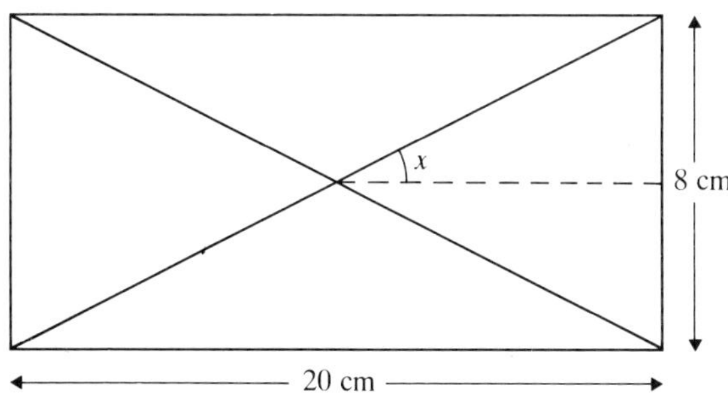

Calculate the size of angle x above and hence find the size of the smaller angle between the diagonals of the rectangle.

9. A rectangle has sides of length 12 cm and 7 cm. Calculate the smaller angle between the diagonals of the rectangle.

10. A rectangle has sides of length 16 cm and 10 cm. Calculate the smaller angle between the diagonals of the rectangle.

11. The points C(2,0) and D(7,4) are plotted on the graph below.

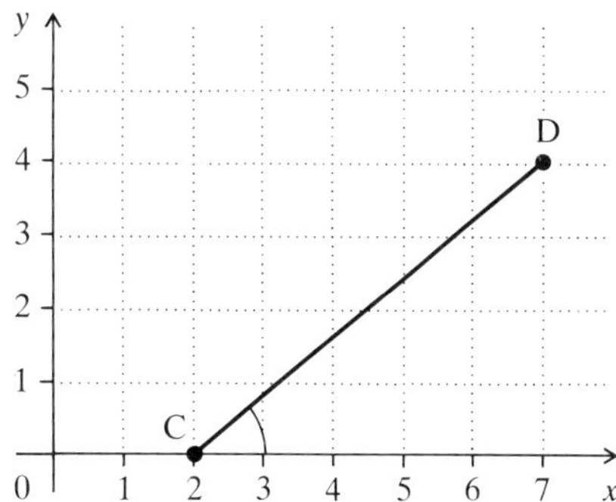

Calculate the angle between the line CD and the x-axis.

For questions **12** to **16** plot the points for each question on a small graph with x- and y-axes drawn to the same scale.
Take x and y from 0 to 8.

12. For the points A(4,0) and B(8,3), calculate the angle between the line AB and the x-axis.

13. For the points M(0,0) and N(7,5), calculate the angle between the line MN and the x-axis.

14. For the points P(7,0) and Q(1,4), calculate the angle between the line PQ and the x-axis.

15. For the points A(3,0), B(6,1) and C(6,5), calculate the angle BAC. (i.e. the angle between BA and CA.)

16. For the points P(6,8), Q(1,3) and R(4,1), calculate the angle PQR. (i.e. the angle between PQ and QR.)

Think about it 3

Project 1 CROSS NUMBERS

Draw a copy of the crossnumber pattern below and work out the answers using the clues. You can check your working by doing *all* the across and *all* the down clues.

1		2		3			4
		5					
6						7	
		8	9				
	10				11		
12			13	14			
		15		16		17	18
19						20	

Part A

Across

1. $327 + 198$
3. $245 \div 7$
5. $3146 - 729$
6. $248 - 76$
7. 2^6
8. $850 \div 5$
10. $10^2 + 1^2$
11. $3843 \div 7$
12. $1000 - 913$
13. $37 \times 5 \times 3$
16. $152\,300 \div 50$
19. 3^6
20. $100 - \left(\frac{17 \times 10}{5}\right)$

Down

1. $3280 + 1938$
2. $65\,720 - 13\,510$
3. 3.1×1000
4. $1284 \div 6$
7. $811 - 127$
9. 65×11
10. $(12^2 - 8) \div 8$
11. $(7^2 + 1^2) \times 11$
12. $7 + 29 + 234 + 607$
14. $800 - 265$
15. $1 + 2 + 3 + 4 + 5 + 6 + 7 + 8 + 13$
17. $(69 \times 6) \div 9$
18. $3^2 + 4^2 + 5^2 + 2^4$

Part B Draw decimal points on the lines between squares where necessary.

Across

1. 4.2 + 1.64
3. 7 × 0.5
5. 20.562 ÷ 6
6. $(2^3 \times 5) \times 10 - 1$
7. 0.034 × 1000
8. 61 × 0.3
10. 8 − 0.36
11. 19 × 50
12. 95.7 ÷ 11
13. 8.1 × 0.7
16. (11 × 5) ÷ 8
19. (44 − 2.8) ÷ 5
20. Number of inches in a yard

Down

1. 62.6 − 4.24
2. 48.73 − 4.814
3. 25 + 7.2 + 0.63
4. 2548 ÷ 7
7. 0.315 × 100
9. 169 × 0.05
10. 770 ÷ 100
11. 14.2 + 0.7 − 5.12
12. 11.4 − 2.64 − 0.18
14. 0.0667×10^3
15. 0.6 + 0.7 + 0.8 + 7.3
17. 0.73 m written in cm
18. 0.028 × 200

Part C

Across

1. Eleven squared take away six
3. Next in the sequence 21, 24, 28, 33,
5. Number of minutes in a day
6. 2 × 13 × 5 × 5
7. Next in the sequence 92, 83, 74,
8. 5% of 11 400
10. $98 + 11^2$
11. (120 − 9) × 6
12. $1\frac{2}{5}$ as a decimal
13. 2387 ÷ 7
16. 9.05 × 1000
19. 8 m − 95 cm (in cm)
20. 3^4

Down

1. Write 18.6 m in cm
2. Fifty-one thousand and fifty-one
3. Write 3.47 km in m
4. $1\frac{1}{4}$ as a decimal
7. 7 m − 54 cm (in cm)
9. 0.0793 × 1000
10. 2% of 1200
11. $\frac{1}{5}$ of 3050
12. 127 ÷ 100
14. Number of minutes between 12 00 and 20 10
15. 4% of 1125
17. $7^2 + 3^2$
18. Last two digits of (67 × 3)

Part D

Across

1. $1\frac{3}{4}$ as a decimal
3. Two dozen
5. Forty less than ten thousand
6. Emergency
7. 5% of 740
8. Nine pounds and five pence
10. 1.6 m written in cm.
11. 5649 ÷ 7
12. One-third of 108
13. 6 − 0.28
16. A quarter to midnight on the 24 h clock
19. 10% of 57.1
20. 'Catch . . .' or 'Yards in a chain' or 3300 ÷ 150

Down

1. Twelve pounds 95 pence
2. Four less than sixty thousand
3. 245 × 11
4. James Bond
7. Number of minutes between 09 10 and 15 30
9. $\frac{1}{20}$ as a decimal
10. Ounces in a pound
11. 8.227 to two decimal places
12. 4 m − 95 cm (in cm)
14. Three to the power six
15. 20.64 to the nearest whole number
17. $(6\frac{1}{2})^2$ to the nearest whole number
18. Number of minutes between 14 22 and 15 14

Exercise A

1. An athlete started a training run at 11 15 and finished at 13 05. How long had he been running in hours and minutes?
2. Calculate the perimeter of a square which has an area of 36 cm^2.
3. The bill for 5 people in a restaurant is £31.80. Find the cost per person correct to the nearest pound.
4. Calculate the area of the shape below.

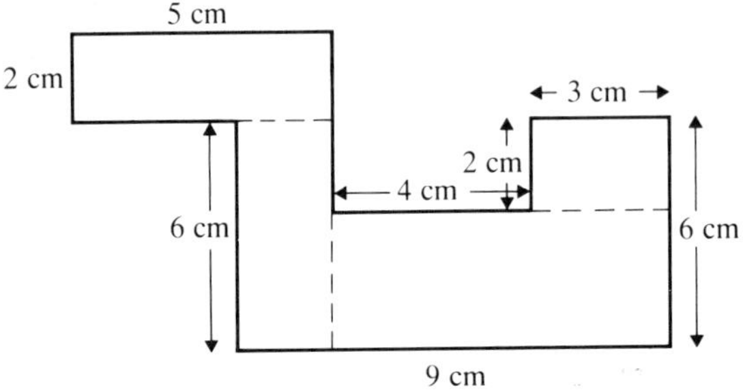

5. A map uses a scale of 1 to 1000.
   (a) Calculate the actual length in metres of a road which is 5 cm long on the map.
   (b) A lake is 800 m long. Calculate in centimetres the length this would be on the map.
6. A shop buys cans of drink at £7.20 for 48 cans and sells them at 17p per can. Calculate the profit on one can.
7. How many seconds are there in 3 days?
8. How many stamps each costing 14p can be bought for £2?
9. Find the angles marked with letters.

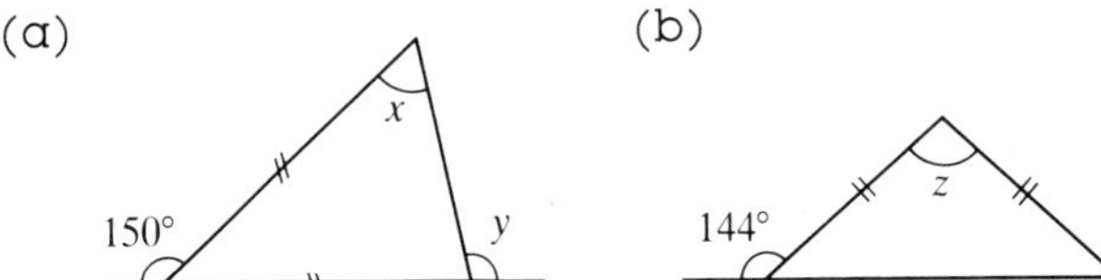

10. There is one road from Ansell to Royton and it passes through Banton, Fixton and Garston. At Ansell a traveller sees the road sign below.

Banton	4 miles
Fixton	$6\frac{1}{2}$ miles
Garston	9 miles
Royton	14 miles

   (a) How far is it from Ansell to Garston?
   (b) How far is it from Banton to Royton?
   (c) How far is it from Fixton to Garston?
   (d) How far is it from Royton to Fixton?

Project 2 TWO UNUSUAL NUMBERS

Here is an interesting exercise with a surprising result. It is easier when a calculator is used but this is not essential.

1. (a) Take a three-digit number (Not a number like 444 or 777 with the same three digits) — 374

(i) Write down the largest number which can be formed using the digits of the number. — 743

(ii) Write down the smallest number which can be formed using the digits of the number. — 347

(iii) Subtract the smaller number from the larger number.

```
  743
- 347
  396
```

(b) Take the answer and repeat (i), (ii) and (iii) above.

```
  963
- 369
  594
```

(c) Repeat (b) until you get stuck with one number.

```
  954
- 459
  459

  954
- 459
  495   stuck!
```

Note: If you obtain a two-digit answer, write a nought at the front.

e.g.

```
  433        990
 -334       -099
  099  →     891  etc.
```

2. Try this sequence of operations with the following starting numbers: 623, 464, 491, 672, 343.
What do you notice each time?

3. Try any starting numbers of your own choice.

4. Now let's try four-digit numbers. The only restriction is that we do not choose numbers like 6666 or 2222 with the same four digits.
Try the following starting numbers: 3591, 5746, 4824, 7345, 9501, 6966.
What do you notice this time?

5. If you are really ambitious, you may like to investigate what happens when you choose five-digit numbers. There are in fact three ways in which you can finish. But now you are on your own!

Exercise B

1. A pile of 56 tiles is 40.32 cm thick. How thick is each tile?

2. Six metres of rope costs £3.30. Find the cost of 11 metres of the same rope.

3. The moving pavement at an airway terminal moves at a speed of 0.8 m/s. If you are standing on the pavement, how far do you travel in (a) 10 s? (b) 1 minute? (c) 45 s?

4. Write correct to the nearest penny:
(a) £5.638 (b) £0.721 (c) £11.655
(d) £2.0725 (e) £8.111 (f) £7.077

5. A businessman is paid travelling expenses at 22.4p per mile. How much does he receive (to the nearest 1p) for (a) a 15 mile journey? (b) an 18 mile journey? (c) a 7.2 mile journey?

6. During a sale the marked price of each article was reduced. Copy and complete.

	Marked price	Percentage reduction	Cash reduction	Sale price
(a)	£20	10%		
(b)	£50	20%		
(c)	£60	75%		

7. Amongst other ingredients 240 g of butter and 2 teaspoons of sugar are needed to make 6 scones.
(a) What weight of butter is needed to make 30 scones?
(b) How many teaspoons of sugar are needed to make 9 scones?

8. A number of tins of soup are packed in a box which weighs 2 kg. The total weight of the box and its contents is 19.5 kg. How many tins are in the box if each tin weighs 350 g?

9. The owner of a garage offers all of his workers a choice of two pay rises. Workers can choose either a 6.2% increase on their salaries or they can accept a rise of £400.
(a) A petrol pump attendant earns £4650 a year. Which pay rise should he choose?
(b) A forecourt manager earns £8600 a year. Which pay rise should he choose?

10. A strand of cotton is 4 m long and is cut into several pieces each of length 30 cm.
(a) How many 30 cm lengths can be cut?
(b) How much cotton is left over?

Project 3 AN EXPANDING DIAGRAM

The first diagram is a single square.

We draw the second diagram by adding squares all around the outside of the first square.

The second diagram has 5 squares in it.

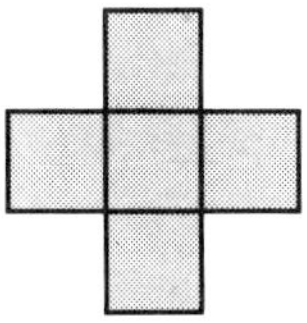

We draw the third diagram by adding squares all around the outside of the second diagram.

The third diagram has 13 squares in it.

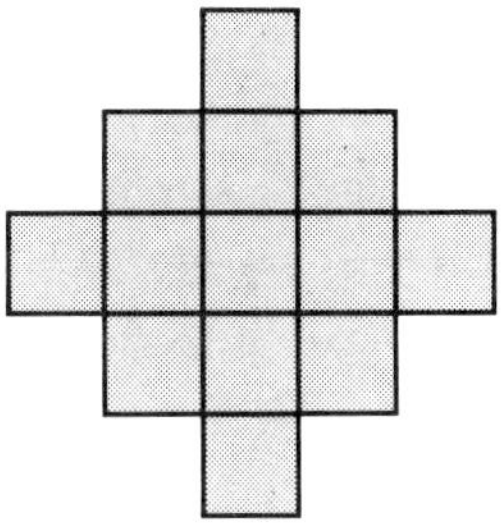

Continue the series by drawing the fourth, fifth and sixth diagrams in the sequence. Each new diagram is obtained by drawing squares all around the outside of the previous diagram. For each diagram count the number of squares it contains.

Using the results of the first six diagrams, can you predict the number of squares in the seventh diagram? See if you were right by drawing the diagram.

Can you predict the number of squares in the eighth diagram? Again draw the diagram to see if you were right.

Can you predict the number of squares in
(a) the 12th diagram,
(b) the 20th diagram?

Try to find a rule which will enable you to predict the number of squares for any member of the sequence of diagrams.

Exercise C

1. How many minutes are there in 2 days?
2. If 208 oranges are divided equally between 9 children, how many will each child get and how many will be left over?
3. During a storm 3 cm of rain falls onto a rectangular field which is 200 m by 100 m. What volume of water in m^3 falls onto the field?
4. Find the angles marked with letters.

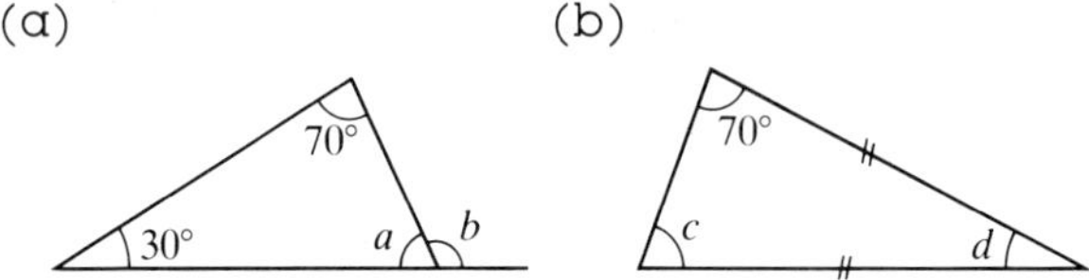

5. A model aeroplane is built to a scale of 1:40. The wing span of the actual aeroplane is 20 m. Find the wing span of the model.
6. Work out $\frac{5}{7} \times \frac{1}{2}$.
7. During the night the temperature falls by 3 °C every hour. Given that the temperature at 8.00 p.m. was 8 °C, find the temperature at:
(a) 9.00 p.m. (b) 11.00 p.m. (c) midnight.
8. A film lasting 1 hour 45 minutes starts at 19 35. At what time does the film finish?
9. We can estimate the value of 19.7×11.2 correct to 1 significant figure by working out $20 \times 10 = 200$. Use this method to estimate, correct to 1 significant figure the value of:

   (a) 198×98.5; (b) 0.102×49.2; (c) $\frac{211 \times 9.85}{10.04}$; (d) $\frac{59.7 \times 98.4}{6.05}$.
10. I am thinking of a number which is less than 100. The number is exactly divisible by 5 but not by 2. The two digits of the number add up to 11. Find the number I am thinking of.

Exercise D

1. The chart shows a patient's temperature in °C.

Time	06 00	08 00	10 00	12 00	14 00
Temperature (°C)	37.5	38.2	39.1	39.6	38.8

The normal temperature is 36.9 °C.
How many degrees above normal was his temperature at (a) 06 00 (b) 10 00 (c) 12 00 (d) 08 00?

2. In 1990 it is forecast that the price of one litre of petrol will be 100p and that the price will rise by 10% each year over the next few years. Calculate the price forecast for (a) 1991 (b) 1992.

3. Paint can be bought in two sizes:
2 litre tin for £5.60
3 litre tin for £7.80.
How much would you save if you bought two 3 litre tins instead of three 2 litre tins?

4. A salesman is paid a basic salary of £5400 per year, plus commission of 5% on all his sales. Calculate his total salary if his sales totalled (a) £40 000 (b) £50 000 (c) £100 000.

5. A glass has a volume of 0.02 litres. How many times can the glass be filled from a can containing 4 litres of water?

6. One hundred small cakes cost £7.50 and weigh 5.5 kg. Find (a) the cost and (b) the weight of 16 of these cakes.

7. In 1984 the population of the Soviet Union was 272 million. Forecasters estimated that the population would increase by 15% by the end of the century. Work out the estimated population at the end of the century, correct to the nearest million.

8. The diagram shows the plan of a room with a carpet shaded.

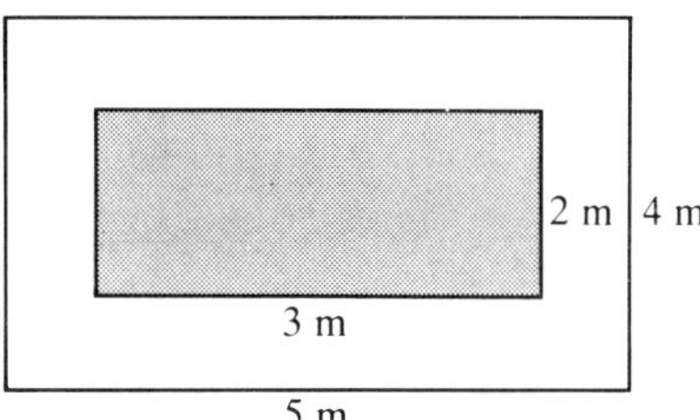

Calculate (a) the length of the carpet as a percentage of the length of the room.
(b) the area of the carpet as a percentage of the area of the room.
(c) the area of the room uncarpeted as a percentage of the area of the room.

9. A car travels for 2 hours at a speed of 65 km/h and for 3 hours at a speed of 70 km/h.
(a) How far does it travel in the 5 hours?
(b) What is the average speed for the whole journey?

10. Train fares are increased by 25%.
Find (a) the new price of a ticket which cost 60p before the increase
(b) the old price of a ticket which costs 50p after the increase.

Project 4 CAR FERRIES

Life can be very complicated! Below there are extracts from the car ferry timetables for three different journeys. In a separate table there is information about the fares for the journeys.

Dover → Calais

August	W	T	F	S	S	M	T	W	T	F	S	S	M	T	W	T	F	S	S	M	T	W	T	F	S	S	M	T	W	T	F
Time	1	2	3	4	5	6	7	8	9	10	11	12	13	14	15	16	17	18	19	20	21	22	23	24	25	26	27	28	29	30	31
0100	D	D	C	C	D	D	D	D	D	C	C	D	D	D	D	D	D	D	D	D	D	D	D	D	D	D	D	D	D	D	D
0500	D	D	D	D	D	D	D	D	D	D	D	D	D	D	D	D	D	D	D	D	D	D	D	D	D	D	D	D	D	D	D
0630	C	C	C	C	C	C	C	C	C	C	C	C	C	C	C	C	C	C	C	C	C	C	C	C	C	C	C	C	C	C	C
0800	C	C	C	C	C	C	C	C	C	C	C	C	C	C	C	C	C	C	C	C	C	C	C	C	C	C	C	C	C	C	C
1000	B	B	B	B	B	B	B	B	B	B	B	B	B	B	B	B	B	B	B	B	B	B	B	B	B	B	B	B	B	B	B
1240	B	B	B	B	B	B	B	B	B	B	B	B	B	B	B	B	B	B	B	B	B	B	B	B	B	B	B	B	B	B	B
1515	B	B	B	B	B	B	B	B	B	B	B	B	B	B	B	B	B	B	B	B	B	B	B	B	B	B	B	B	B	B	B
1730	B	B	B	B	B	B	B	B	B	B	B	B	B	B	B	B	B	B	B	B	B	B	B	B	B	B	B	B	B	B	B
1900	B	B	B	B	B	B	B	B	B	B	B	B	B	B	B	B	B	B	B	B	B	B	B	B	B	B	B	B	B	B	B
2200	C	C	C	C	C	C	C	C	C	C	C	C	C	C	C	C	C	C	C	C	C	C	C	C	C	C	C	C	C	C	C
2330	C	C	C	C	C	C	C	C	C	C	C	C	C	C	C	C	C	C	C	C	C	C	C	C	C	C	C	C	C	C	C

September	S	S	M	T	W	T	F	S	S	M	T	W	T	F	S	S	M	T	W	T	F	S	S	M	T	W	T	F	S	S
Time	1	2	3	4	5	6	7	8	9	10	11	12	13	14	15	16	17	18	19	20	21	22	23	24	25	26	27	28	29	30
0100	D	D	D	D	D	D	D	D	D	D	D	D	D	D	D	D	D	D	D	D	D	D	D	D	D	D	D	D	D	D
0500	D	D	D	D	D	D	D	D	D	D	D	D	D	D	D	D	D	D	D	D	D	D	D	D	D	D	D	D	D	•
0630	C	C	D	D	D	D	D	D	D	D	D	D	D	D	D	D	D	D	D	D	D	D	D	D	D	D	D	D	D	D
0800	C	C	D	D	D	D	D	D	D	D	D	D	D	D	D	D	D	D	D	D	D	D	D	D	D	D	D	D	D	D
1000	B	B	C	C	C	C	C	C	C	C	C	C	C	C	C	C	C	C	C	C	C	C	C	C	C	C	C	C	C	C
1240	B	B	C	C	C	C	C	C	C	C	C	C	C	C	C	C	C	C	C	C	C	C	C	C	C	C	C	C	C	C
1515	B	B	C	C	C	C	C	C	C	C	C	C	C	C	C	C	C	C	C	C	C	C	C	C	C	C	C	C	C	C
1730	B	B	C	C	C	C	C	C	C	C	C	C	C	C	C	C	C	C	C	C	C	C	C	C	C	C	C	C	C	•
1900	B	B	C	C	C	C	C	C	C	C	C	C	C	C	C	C	C	C	C	C	C	C	C	C	C	C	C	C	C	C
2200	C	C	D	D	D	D	D	D	D	D	D	D	D	D	D	D	D	D	D	D	D	D	D	D	D	D	D	D	D	D
2330	C	C	D	D	D	D	D	D	D	D	D	D	D	D	D	D	D	D	D	D	D	D	D	D	D	D	D	D	D	D

Folkestone → Boulogne

June	F	S	S	M	T	W	T	F	S	S	M	T	W	T	F	S	S	M	T	W	T	F	S	S	M	T	W	T	F	S
Time	1	2	3	4	5	6	7	8	9	10	11	12	13	14	15	16	17	18	19	20	21	22	23	24	25	26	27	28	29	30
0745	D	D	D	D	D	D	D	D	D	D	D	D	D	D	D	D	D	D	D	D	D	D	D	D	D	D	D	D	D	D
0945	C	C	C	C	C	C	C	C	C	C	C	C	C	C	C	C	C	C	C	C	C	C	C	C	C	C	C	C	C	C
1145	•	•	C	C	C	C	C	C	C	C	C	C	C	C	C	C	C	C	C	C	C	C	C	C	C	C	C	C	C	C
1345	C	C	C	C	C	C	C	C	C	C	C	C	C	C	C	C	C	C	C	C	C	C	C	C	C	C	C	C	C	C
1545	•	•	C	C	C	C	C	C	C	C	C	C	C	C	C	C	C	C	C	C	C	C	C	C	C	C	C	C	C	C
1745	C	C	C	C	C	C	C	C	C	C	C	C	C	C	C	C	C	C	C	C	C	C	C	C	C	C	C	C	C	C
2200	•	•	D	D	D	D	D	D	D	D	D	D	D	D	D	D	D	D	D	D	D	D	D	D	D	D	D	D	D	D
2345	D	D	•	•	•	•	•	•	•	•	•	•	•	•	•	•	•	•	•	•	•	•	•	•	•	•	•	•	•	•

July	S	M	T	W	T	F	S	S	M	T	W	T	F	S	S	M	T	W	T	F	S	S	M	T	W	T	F	S	S	M	T
Time	1	2	3	4	5	6	7	8	9	10	11	12	13	14	15	16	17	18	19	20	21	22	23	24	25	26	27	28	29	30	31
0345	•	•	•	•	•	•	•	•	•	•	•	•	D	D	D	D	D	D	D	D	D	D	D	D	D	D	D	D	D	D	D
0745	C	C	C	C	C	C	C	C	C	C	C	C	C	C	C	C	C	C	C	C	C	C	C	C	C	C	C	C	C	C	C
0945	B	B	B	B	B	B	B	B	B	B	B	B	B	B	B	B	B	B	B	B	A	B	B	B	B	B	B	A	B	B	B
1145	B	B	B	B	B	B	B	B	B	B	B	B	B	B	B	B	B	B	B	B	A	B	B	B	B	B	B	A	B	B	B
1345	B	B	B	B	B	B	B	B	B	B	B	B	B	B	B	B	B	B	B	A	B	B	B	B	B	B	A	B	B	B	B
1545	B	B	B	B	B	B	B	B	B	B	B	B	B	B	B	B	B	B	B	A	B	B	B	B	B	B	A	B	B	B	B
1745	B	B	B	B	B	B	B	B	B	B	B	B	B	B	B	B	B	B	B	A	B	B	B	B	B	B	A	B	B	B	B
2200	C	C	C	C	C	C	C	C	C	C	C	C	C	C	C	C	C	C	C	C	C	C	C	C	C	C	C	C	C	C	C

Newhaven → Dieppe

July	S	M	T	W	T	F	S	S	M	T	W	T	F	S	S	M	T	W	T	F	S	S	M	T	W	T	F	S	S	M	T
Time	1	2	3	4	5	6	7	8	9	10	11	12	13	14	15	16	17	18	19	20	21	22	23	24	25	26	27	28	29	30	31
0100	•	•	•	•	•	•	•	•	•	•	•	•	•	C	C	C	C	C	C	B	A	B	B	B	B	C	B	A	B	C	C
0700	C	C	C	C	C	B	B	C	C	C	C	C	B	B	B	C	C	C	C	B	A	B	C	B	B	B	B	A	B	B	B
1000	C	C	C	C	C	B	B	B	C	C	C	B	A	A	B	B	B	B	B	A	A	B	B	B	B	B	A	A	B	B	B
1300	C	C	C	C	C	C	C	C	C	C	C	C	B	B	C	C	C	C	C	A	A	B	B	B	B	B	A	A	B	B	B
1830	D	D	D	D	D	C	C	D	D	D	D	D	C	C	C	D	D	D	D	B	B	B	C	C	C	C	B	B	C	C	C
2245	C	C	C	C	C	C	C	C	C	C	C	C	B	B	B	C	C	C	B	A	B	B	C	C	C	B	A	B	C	C	C

August	W	T	F	S	S	M	T	W	T	F	S	S	M	T	W	T	F	S	S	M	T	W	T	F	S	S	M	T	W	T	F
Time	1	2	3	4	5	6	7	8	9	10	11	12	13	14	15	16	17	18	19	20	21	22	23	24	25	26	27	28	29	30	31
0100	C	C	C	B	B	C	C	C	C	C	B	B	C	C	C	C	C	B	B	C	C	C	C	B	B	C	C	C	C	C	C
0700	B	B	B	B	C	B	B	B	B	B	B	C	B	B	B	B	B	B	C	C	C	B	B	B	B	C	C	C	B	B	B
1000	B	B	A	A	B	B	B	B	B	A	A	B	B	B	B	B	A	A	B	B	B	B	B	A	A	B	B	B	B	B	B
1300	C	C	B	B	C	C	C	C	C	B	B	C	C	C	C	C	B	C	C	C	C	C	B	B	C	C	C	C	C	C	C
1830	C	C	C	C	C	C	C	C	C	C	C	C	D	D	D	D	C	C	D	D	D	D	D	C	C	D	D	D	D	D	D
2245	C	B	A	B	B	C	C	C	B	A	B	C	C	C	C	C	B	B	C	C	C	C	C	B	C	C	C	C	C	C	C

Car Ferry Tariffs

Motorist Fares/Vehicle Rates for Single Journeys

	DOVER –CALAIS				FOLKESTONE –BOULOGNE					NEWHAVEN –DIEPPE				
	Tariff	Tariff	Tariff	Tariff	Tariff	Tariff	Tariff	Tariff	Tariff	Tariff	Tariff	Tariff	Tariff	Tariff
MOTORIST FARES (driver and accompanying passengers)	**E** £	**D** £	**C** £	**B** £	**E** £	**D** £	**C** £	**B** £	**A** £	**E** £	**D** £	**C** £	**B** £	**A** £
Adult	10.00	10.00	10.00	10.00	10.00	10.00	10.00	10.00	10.00	15.00	15.00	15.00	15.00	15.00
Child (4 but under 14 years)	5.00	5.00	5.00	5.00	5.00	5.00	5.00	5.00	5.00	7.50	7.50	7.50	7.50	7.50
VEHICLE RATES **Cars, Motorised Caravans, Minibuses and Three-wheeled Vehicles**														
Up to 4.00m in length	16.00	24.00	33.00	43.00	16.00	21.00	33.00	43.00	50.00	19.00	27.00	37.00	47.00	54.00
Up to 4.50m in length	16.00	30.00	42.00	52.00	16.00	27.00	42.00	52.00	60.00	19.00	34.00	47.00	57.00	65.00
Up to 5.50m in length	16.00	34.00	50.00	60.00	16.00	31.00	50.00	60.00	70.00	19.00	39.00	56.00	66.00	75.00
Over 5.50m: each additional metre (or part thereof)	9.00	9.00	9.00	9.00	9.00	9.00	9.00	9.00	9.00	9.00	9.00	9.00	9.00	9.00
CARAVANS/TRAILERS **To Calais, Boulogne, Dieppe**														
Up to 3.00m in length	12.00	16.00	14.00	12.00	12.00	16.00	14.00	12.00	12.00	16.00	16.00	16.00	16.00	16.00
Up to 5.50m in length	12.00	20.00	18.00	16.00	12.00	20.00	18.00	16.00	14.00	38.00	38.00	38.00	38.00	38.00
Over 5.50m: each additional metre (or part thereof)	9.00	9.00	9.00	9.00	9.00	9.00	9.00	9.00	9.00	9.00	9.00	9.00	9.00	9.00

Part A Find the tariff letter for the following journeys.

1. Newhaven → Dieppe; July 28; 10 00.
2. Dover → Calais; August 18; 12 40.
3. Dover → Calais; September 2; 08 00.
4. Newhaven → Dieppe; August 11; 10 00.
5. Folkestone → Boulogne; June 7; 13 45.
6. Dover → Calais; September 25; 08 00.
7. Newhaven → Dieppe; August 28; 10 00.
8. Folkestone → Boulogne; July 18; 09 45.
9. Newhaven → Dieppe; August 5; 07 00.
10. Dover → Calais; September 21; 08 00.
11. Folkestone → Boulogne; June 25; 11 45.
12. Newhaven → Dieppe; August 24; 10 00.
13. Dover → Calais; August 19; 10 00.
14. Newhaven → Dieppe; August 10; 22 45.
15. Folkestone → Boulogne; July 27; 07 45.
16. Dover → Calais; September 2; 19 00.
17. Newhaven → Dieppe; July 25; 13 00.
18. Folkestone → Boulogne; June 29; 22 00.
19. Dover → Calais; August 10; 05 00.
20. Newhaven → Dieppe; July 7; 07 00.

Part B Find the cost for each of the following.

1. Dover–Calais; 1 adult, Tariff B.
2. Dover–Calais; 1 child; Tariff D.
3. Newhaven–Dieppe; 1 adult; Tariff C.
4. Folkestone–Boulogne; car 4.30 m; Tariff E.
5. Dover–Calais; car 5.10 m; Tariff B.
6. Newhaven–Dieppe; car 3.95 m; Tariff A.
7. Newhaven–Dieppe; 2 adults; Tariff C.
8. Folkestone–Boulogne; 4 children; Tariff E.
9. Dover–Calais; car 4.80 m; Tariff B.
10. Newhaven–Dieppe; caravan 4.00 m; Tariff C.
11. Folkestone–Boulogne; caravan 3.60 m; Tariff D.
12. Dover–Calais; 3 adults; Tariff C.
13. Newhaven–Dieppe; car 4.75 m; Tariff E.
14. Folkestone–Boulogne; caravan 5.00 m; Tariff A.
15. Dover–Calais; 3 children; Tariff E.
16. Folkestone–Boulogne; car 4.85 m; Tariff B.
17. Newhaven–Dieppe; 3 children; Tariff D.
18. Dover–Calais; caravan 4.80 m; Tariff B.
19. Folkestone–Boulogne; car 5.25 m; Tariff C.
20. Newhaven–Dieppe; car 5.45 m; Tariff A.

Part C Copy the table below and find the total cost for each of the following journeys.

	Journey	Depart	Adults	Children	Car	Caravan
1.	Newhaven–Dieppe	July 18 07 00	2	2	4.20 m	
2.	Folkestone–Boulogne	June 2 23 45	2	1	4.00 m	
3.	Folkestone–Boulogne	July 3 11 45	2	3	4.80 m	
4.	Dover–Calais	August 13 06 30	2	4	3.80 m	4 m
5.	Newhaven–Dieppe	August 3 10 00	2	1	4.60 m	
6.	Folkstone–Boulogne	June 10 07 45	4	0	5.00 m	5.00 m
7.	Dover–Calais	Sept 12 10 00	3	2	4.80 m	
8.	Newhaven–Dieppe	July 25 13 00	2	4	5.20 m	4.50 m
9.	Folkestone–Boulogne	July 6 11 45	1	6	4.85 m	4.20 m
10.	Dover–Calais	August 27 06 30	2	3	3.75 m	
11.	Newhaven–Dieppe	July 20 13 00	1	4	4.40 m	3.90 m
12.	Folkestone–Boulogne	July 21 09 45	2	2	5.10 m	5.00 m
13.	Dover–Calais	August 20 22 00	4	0	5.20 m	
14.	Newhaven–Dieppe	August 2 10 00	2	5	5.40 m	
15.	Folkestone–Boulogne	July 13 03 45	3	1	4.95 m	
16.	Dover–Calais	August 13 05 00	2	2	4.60 m	
17.	Newhaven–Dieppe	July 14 10 00	3	2	3.95 m	
18.	Folkestone–Boulogne	June 8 09 45	2	4	5.20 m	

Project 5 THE TOWERS OF HANOI

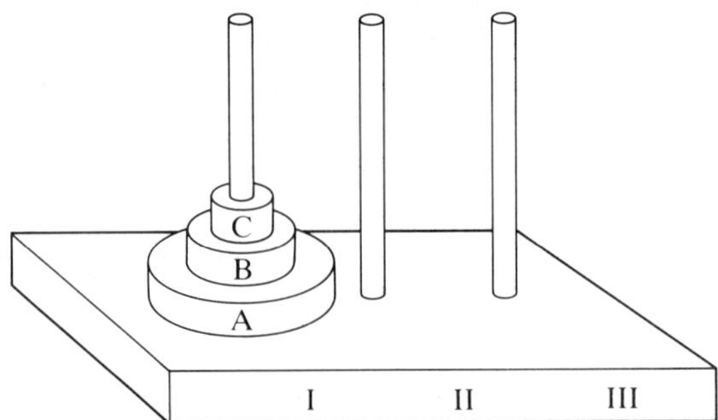

We have a board with three pegs I, II and III.

On one of the pegs we place several discs with the largest at the bottom, the next largest on top of that and so on.

The problem is to transfer all the discs from the first peg to one of the others in such a way that the final arrangement is the same as the original one.

The rules are that only one disc is moved at a time and no disc shall ever be placed on top of a disc smaller than itself.

Start with just two discs and count the minimum number of moves required to transfer the discs to one of the other pegs.

Then try it with 3 discs, 4 discs and so on.

Make a table like the one below.

Number of discs	Minimum number of moves needed
2	3
3	
4	
5	
6	

It is not necessary to use a proper board with pegs. You can perform the investigation with any objects which are different in size (e.g. coins, pieces of cardboard, books).

The final object is to find a rule which connects the number of *moves* with the number of *discs*.

Hint: If the number of discs is even, move the first disc to peg II; if it is odd, move the first disc to peg III.

Exercise E

1. After donations of £825.50, £270 and £585.40 how much is needed to reach a target of £2000?
2. An oil drum contains 39 litres when it is three-quarters full. How many litres will it contain when it is full?
3. The results of a test given to 50 children are shown below.

Mark	0	1	2	3	4	5
Number of pupils	1	4	10	12	15	8

   (a) How many pupils scored less than 3 marks?
   (b) Find the percentage of the pupils who scored
      (i) 2 marks (ii) 5 marks
      (iii) 3 marks or more (iv) No marks.
4. A crate contains 15 dozen tomatoes, of which 11 are squashed. How many good tomatoes are there?
5. A cyclist starts a journey at 3.10 p.m. and travels 70 km at an average speed of 20 km/h. At what time will he finish?
6. Change to top-heavy fractions
   (a) $2\frac{1}{4}$ (b) $1\frac{3}{4}$ (c) $3\frac{1}{2}$ (d) $4\frac{2}{5}$.
7. The thirteenth number in the sequence 1, 3, 9, 27, . . . is 531 441. What is
   (a) the twelfth number
   (b) the fourteenth number?
8. Find the missing digits:

```
(a)    8 2 *   (b)    * 4 1   (c)    3 * 4
       * 1 3          4 5 *          2 1 *
     + 2 * 0        + 2 * 9        + * 0 4
     -------        -------        -------
     1 4 6 4          9 7 3        1 3 7 9
     -------        -------        -------
```

9. An antiques dealer sells a painting at a profit of 70% on the cost price of £250. For how much does he sell the painting?
10. How many triangles can you see in this diagram?

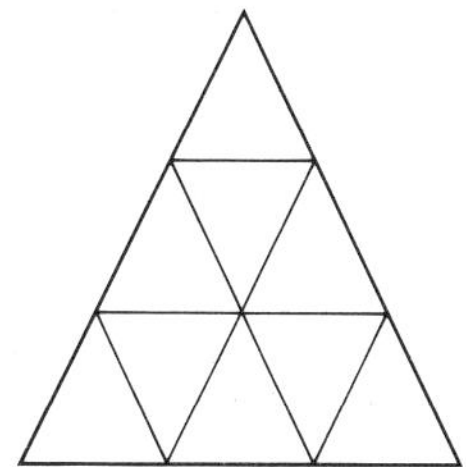

Project 6 FINDING A STRATEGY

Here is an interesting mathematical game where you have two objectives:
(a) to enjoy the game;
(b) to find a strategy so that you always win!

Two players take turns to select one number from the numbers 1, 2, 3, 4, 5, 6. Each number is added to the sum of the others until one player reaches 33. The winner is the player who makes the total up to 33.

Here is a game between David and John

	David	John	David	John	David	John	David	John
	4	5	1	6	6	3	6	2
Total	4	9	10	16	22	25	31	**33**

John is the winner.

(a) Play the game many times and keep the score. After a while you may begin to see how you can win more often. When you think you have discovered a winning strategy try to describe it in words.

(b) Now change the rules so that any number from 1, 2, 3, 4, 5, 6, 7, 8 can be chosen and the target number is **47**. Again try to find the winning strategy and write it down in words.

(c) Change the rules again so that any number from 1, 2, 3, 4, 5, 6, 7, 8, 9 can be chosen and the target number is **63**. What is the winning strategy this time?

Exercise F

1. A girl puts 1p in her piggy-bank on the first day, 2p on the second day, 4p on the third day and carries on like this, doubling the amount each day.
(a) How much does she put in on the 8th day?
(b) How much does she put in on the 12th day?
(c) How much is in the piggy-bank after 5 days?

2. Four boys have weights of 44 kg, 45 kg, 49 kg and 51 kg.
(a) What is their average weight?
When another boy joins them, the average weight becomes 48 kg.
(b) What is the weight of the fifth boy?

3. If 150 bananas are divided equally between 11 girls, how many will each girl receive and how many will be left over?

4. A man drives a car which does 8 km to one litre of petrol and petrol costs 42p per litre. The man drives 144 km every day for a week of 7 days. What is his petrol bill for the week?

5. 6 sacks of corn will feed 80 hens for 12 days.
Copy and complete the following:
(a) 18 sacks of corn will feed 80 hens for . . . days.
(b) 6 sacks of corn will feed 40 hens for . . . days.
(c) 60 sacks of corn will feed 40 hens for . . . days.
(d) 30 sacks of corn will feed 80 hens for . . . days.

6. Calculate the area of the shape below. Take $\pi = 3$.

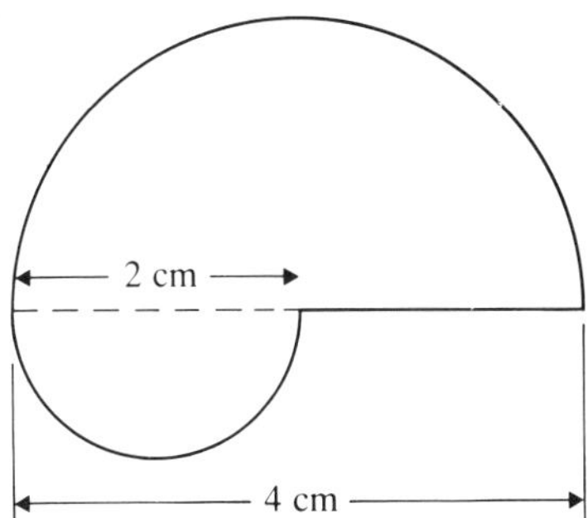

7. Arrange the numbers in order of size, smallest first.
(a) 0.571, 0.5, 0.617, 0.517, 0.5171
(b) 0.03, 0.029, 0.31, 0.1
(c) 0.55, 0.555, 0.505, 0.0555
(d) 0.09, 0.11, 0.011, 0.089

8. Divide £90 in the ratio 2:3:5.

9. An overnight train journey started at 19 40 on Thursday and ended at 06 10 on the Friday. How long was the journey in hours and minutes?

10. Find the missing numbers

(a)
```
  6 * 2
+ * 5 6
-------
  7 9 *
```
(b)
```
  2 5 *
+ * 2 3
-------
1 1 * 7
```
(c)
```
  9 * 2
- * 2 2
-------
  2 4 *
```

Project 7 SQUARE NUMBERS

(a) Write down all the square numbers from 1 to 144.
1, 4, 9, . . . 144.

(b) A famous mathematician named Lagrange stated a theorem that all whole numbers could always be split into square numbers.

e.g. 24 = 16 + 4 + 4
35 = 25 + 9 + 1

Split the following numbers into square numbers.

(i) 29	(ii) 37	(iii) 52	(iv) 72	(v) 47
(vi) 59	(vii) 68	(viii) 91	(ix) 107	(x) 131
(xi) 157	(xii) 137	(xiii) 140	(xiv) 150	(xv) 167

(c) Lagrange also stated that there are no numbers which need more than four square numbers. Try to find a number which *does* need more than four square numbers. If you can think of such a number, a new theorem will be named after you.

Project 8 FIND THE CONNECTION

1. Try this on your calculator.
   (a) Enter any number, e.g. 7.
   (b) Take the square root of the number.
   (c) Take the square root again and this time write down the first 5 digits of the number showing.
   (c) Multiply by the original number.
   (e) Repeat steps (b), (c) and (d) until the number you write down in step (c) is the same as it was last time.

What have you done? What is the connection between the original number and the final number?

Try it out on several other numbers until you can find the connection. (Suggestions: 10; 16; 100; 8; 27).

2. Now try this on your calculator.

Follow the same procedure as given above but this time take the square root *three* times.

Again try to work out the connection between the original number and the final number.
(Suggestions: 7; 128; 2187)

Exercise G

1. How many 18p stamps can be bought for £5 and how much change will there be?
2. A cook uses 250 ml of oil in 4 days. How many days will a 10 litre drum last?
3. Work out the cost per gram of the metal used in various items of jewellery:
   A: gold chain, £33.00, 15 g
   B: silver ring, £6.30, 4.5 g
   C: chrome earrings, £5.85, 7.8 g
   D: steel bracelet, £13.75, 25 g
4. A car left London at 10 00 and arrived in Cardiff at 12 15. Cardiff is 225 km from London. What was the average speed of the car in km/h?
5. The numbers '−2' and '5' multiply to give −10 and add up to 3. Find two numbers which:
   (a) multiply to give −12 and add up to 1.
   (b) multiply to give −12 and add up to 4.
   (c) multiply to give −3 and add up to 2.
6. In a class of 25 children, 11 were girls. What percentage of the class were boys?
7. When a man works 40 hours, he is paid £180. How much is he paid when he works 25 hours?

8. A lady sells a car at a loss of 60% on the original cost price of £5450. How much does she receive for the car?

9. The maps below consist of several roads joining towns. For each map can you plan a route which uses each road only once? Answer 'yes' or 'no'.

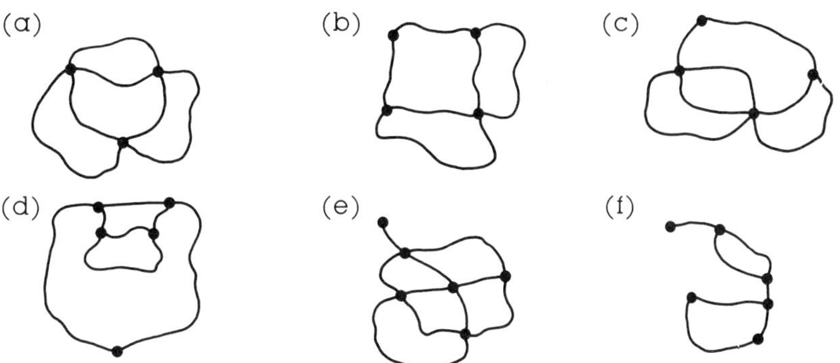

10. The fifteenth number in the sequence 1, 2, 4, 8, 16, . . . is 16 384. What is
(a) the fourteenth number
(b) the sixteenth number?

Project 9 FRACTIONS AND DECIMALS GAME

(a) Draw a large copy of table A.

Table A

0·375	$0{\cdot}\dot{2}$	$2{\cdot}\dot{6}$	0·4	$0{\cdot}\dot{8}$	$1{\cdot}\dot{3}$
1·2	$0{\cdot}\dot{3}$	$0{\cdot}\dot{5}$	0·5	$0{\cdot}\dot{7}$	$0{\cdot}\dot{6}$
0·6	0·625	0·25	0·8	0·875	$1{\cdot}1\dot{6}$
4·5	2·5	$0{\cdot}8\dot{3}$	0·125	1·25	1·6
$0{\cdot}1\dot{6}$	$2{\cdot}\dot{3}$	2·25	3·5	$0{\cdot}\dot{1}$	1·4
$0{\cdot}\dot{4}$	1·8	0·2	1·75	1·125	0·75

Table B

1	2	3
4	5	6
7	8	9

(b) Two players take it in turn to select a pair of numbers from table B and divide them on a calculator. If the answer is in table A and if the number is not yet crossed out the player crosses out that square with a coloured pencil.

(c) The winner is the first player to cross out four squares in a line, either in a column or a row or a diagonal.

Section B

Unit 10

10.1 ARITHMETIC WITHOUT A CALCULATOR

Addition and subtraction

Exercise 1

Work out, without a calculator.

1.	215 + 68	**2.**	322 + 638
3.	39 + 2184	**4.**	62 + 3906
5.	713 + 5607	**6.**	178 + 6058
7.	23 + 615 + 237	**8.**	47 + 205 + 411
9.	27 + 24 078	**10.**	6518 + 6174
11.	274 − 62	**12.**	953 − 22
13.	858 − 74	**14.**	953 − 147
15.	382 − 94	**16.**	410 − 65
17.	715 − 206	**18.**	8926 − 1936
19.	2500 − 2488	**20.**	6163 − 4185

21. Two hundred and six add three hundred and seventeen.

22. Five hundred and eleven add nine hundred and twenty-eight.

23. Fifteen thousand and twenty add four thousand, two hundred and forty-one.

24. Twenty thousand, six hundred and ten add three hundred and ninety-seven.

25. Two hundred and ten thousand, three hundred add twenty-eight thousand eight hundred.

26. Four hundred and eight take away two hundred and eleven.

27. Seven hundred and eighty take away three hundred and thirty-one.

28. Five thousand and nine take away four hundred.

29. Six thousand, two hundred and seven take away three hundred and twelve.

30. Seven thousand and sixteen take away four thousand, two hundred and two.

Exercise 2

Work out, without a calculator.

1. 5.6 + 8.21
2. 3.04 + 5.6
3. 9.5 + 11.4
4. 6.34 + 7.08
5. 6 + 2.4
6. 8 + 2.35
7. 3.09 + 7
8. 7.2 + 11.8
9. 3.1 + 0.6 + 3.7
10. 8.5 + 11.7 + 0.26
11. 8 + 11.7 + 0.34
12. 2.75 + 25
13. 21.65 + 2.45
14. 18 + 2.6 + 11
15. 5.065 + 2.994
16. 3.087 + 2.009
17. 3.64 − 2.12
18. 8.88 − 1.65
19. 9.62 − 1.51
20. 9.85 − 7.17
21. 3.84 − 0.92
22. 11.2 − 0.3
23. 8.9 − 7
24. 13.6 − 7
25. 13.09 − 9
26. 8 − 2.5
27. 11 − 7.4
28. 23 − 15.5
29. 9.9 − 8.16
30. 8.2 − 1.16
31. 9 − 3.6
32. 100 − 99.25
33. 3.07 − 0.09
34. 13 − 7.6
35. 27.8 − 19
36. 258.1 − 17.3
37. 4.825 − 1.666
38. 8.57 − 1.99
39. 8 − 3.63
40. 19 − 12.73

Multiplication and division

Exercise 3

Work out, without a calculator.

1. 27 × 3
2. 82 × 2
3. 33 × 5
4. 49 × 4
5. 82 × 3
6. 232 × 5
7. 216 × 6
8. 323 × 7
9. 305 × 7
10. 411 × 8
11. 201 × 22
12. 314 × 24
13. 62 × 31
14. 84 × 35
15. 712 × 35
16. 818 × 62
17. 714 × 27
18. 923 × 83
19. 607 × 91
20. 425 × 216
21. 316 × 324
22. 718 × 416
23. 509 × 207
24. 306 × 333

Exercise 4

Work out, without a calculator.

1. 693 ÷ 3
2. 1260 ÷ 4
3. 1180 ÷ 5
4. 764 ÷ 2
5. 1668 ÷ 4
6. 3972 ÷ 6
7. 1056 ÷ 3
8. 4795 ÷ 7
9. 12 852 ÷ 6
10. 5376 ÷ 8
11. 22 155 ÷ 7
12. 1254 ÷ 6
13. 4856 ÷ 8
14. 1570 ÷ 5
15. 3069 ÷ 9
16. 10 696 ÷ 4
17. 4830 ÷ 6
18. 28 269 ÷ 9
19. 1660 ÷ 5
20. 24 054 ÷ 6
21. 2948 ÷ 11
22. 28 777 ÷ 7
23. 4424 ÷ 7
24. 96 084 ÷ 12
25. 37 480 ÷ 8
26. 26 609 ÷ 11
27. 34 353 ÷ 9
28. 19 341 ÷ 7
29. 168 945 ÷ 7
30. 34 435 ÷ 5
31. 10.68 ÷ 4
32. 15.3 ÷ 5
33. 20.484 ÷ 6
34. 22.728 ÷ 8
35. 406.3 ÷ 5
36. 10.398 ÷ 3
37. 37.76 ÷ 8
38. 6.732 ÷ 9
39. 57.89 ÷ 7
40. 15.035 ÷ 5

Multiplying and dividing with decimals

Work out (a) 1.7 ×0.6 (b) 3.6 × 0.41
(c) 3.25 ÷ 0.4 (d) 8.6 ÷ 0.02

(a) Ignore the decimal points and work out 17 × 6
17 × 6 = 102
∴ 1.7 × 0.6 = **1.02**

(b) 36 × 41 = 1476
∴ 3.6 × 0.41 = **1.476**

(c) 3.25 ÷ 0.4 = 32.5 ÷ 4
= **8.125**

(d) 8.6 ÷ 0.02 = 860 ÷ 2
= **430**.

Exercise 5

Work out, without a calculator.

1. 3.2 × 0.5
2. 27.4 × 0.4
3. 4.1 × 0.7
4. 3.6 × 0.6
5. 5.5 × 0.8
6. 8.01 × 0.9
7. 3.6 × 1.2
8. 5.6 × 0.06
9. 81.2 × 0.05
10. 74 × 3.1
11. 63.2 × 0.001
12. 120 × 0.11
13. 58 × 0.02
14. 635 × 0.6
15. 63 × 0.04
16. 0.74 × 0.15
17. 0.63 × 0.74
18. 5.62 × 0.07
19. 5.27 × 0.41
20. 99 × 0.007
21. 1.448 ÷ 0.4
22. 0.435 ÷ 0.3
23. 4.12 ÷ 0.5
24. 0.02856 ÷ 0.04
25. 0.2262 ÷ 0.06
26. 0.5782 ÷ 0.07
27. 0.01323 ÷ 0.09
28. 0.000438 ÷ 0.006
29. 5.82 ÷ 0.1
30. 0.1918 ÷ 0.007
31. 64.86 ÷ 0.3
32. 4.114 ÷ 0.11
33. 62.244 ÷ 0.12
34. 1.9584 ÷ 0.008

The next exercise contains a mixture of questions on addition, subtraction, multiplication and division.

Exercise 6

Work out, without a calculator.

1. $0.24 + 3.686$
2. $5.7 - 1.45$
3. 0.62×0.3
4. 36.2×1.1
5. $8.72 \div 0.4$
6. $0.0062 \div 0.02$
7. $18.5 - 9.6$
8. $11 + 3.74$
9. $2.6 \div 0.05$
10. $8 - 1.4$
11. 12.1×0.7
12. 2.6×1000
13. $2.9 + 12$
14. $0.41 \div 100$
15. $0.09 - 0.076$
16. $2184 + 5688$
17. $56.2 \div 0.001$
18. $6324 - 5686$
19. 0.5×0.6
20. $516 \div 10\,000$
21. $45.1 - 8.6$
22. 0.6×100
23. $0.7 + 1.35 + 0.09$
24. $99.9 - 85.95$
25. $5.6 + 2.9 - 1.84$
26. $5.6 \div 0.005$
27. $0.82 + 1.36 - 0.95$
28. 2.45×1.2
29. $0.0043 \times 10\,000$
30. $2583 \div 7$
31. $9.2 - 8.3 - 0.06$
32. $7 - 0.33$
33. $0.21 \div 100$
34. $2856 \div 8$
35. 2.41×3.5
36. $1.8 + 19.6 - 15.55$
37. 0.621×0.31
38. $5346 \div 11$

Making a profit

A shopkeeper buys potatoes at a wholesale price of £180 per tonne and sells them at a retail price of 22p per kg. How much profit does he make on one kilogram of potatoes?

He pays £180 for 1000 kg of potatoes.
$\therefore$ He pays £[180 ÷ 1000] for 1 kg of potatoes.
i.e. He pays 18p for 1 kg
He sells at 22p per kg.
$\therefore$ Profit = 4p per kg.

Exercise 7

Find the profit in each case.

	Commodity	Retail price	Wholesale price	Profit
1.	cans of drink	15p each	£11 per 100	profit per can?
2.	rulers	24p each	£130 per 1000	profit per ruler?
3.	birthday cards	22p each	£13 per 100	profit per card?
4.	soup	27p per can	£8.50 for 50 cans	profit per can?
5.	newspapers	22p each	£36 for 200	profit per paper?
6.	box of matches	37p each	£15.20 for 80	profit per box?
7.	potatoes	22p per kg	£160 per tonne	profit per kg?
8.	carrots	38p per kg	£250 per tonne	profit per kg?
9.	T-shirts	£4.95 each	£38.40 per dozen	profit per T-shirt?
10.	eggs	96p per dozen	£50 per 1000	profit per dozen?
11.	oranges	5 for 30p	£14 for 400	profit per orange?
12.	car tyres	£19.50 each	£2450 for 200	profit per tyre?
13.	wine	55p for 100 ml	£40 for 10 litres	profit per 100 ml?
14.	sand	16p per kg	£110 per tonne	profit per kg?
15.	wire	23p per m	£700 for 10 km	profit per m?
16.	cheese	£2.64 per kg	£87.50 for 50 kg	profit per kg?
17.	copper tube	46p per m	£160 for 500 m	profit per m?
18.	apples	9p each	£10.08 per gross	profit per apple?
19.	carpet	£6.80 per m^2	£1600 for 500 m^2	profit per m^2?
20.	tin of soup	33p per tin	£72 for 400 tins	profit per tin?

10.2 FRACTIONS

Exercise 8

Write the fractions in their simplest form.

1. $\frac{6}{9}$ **2.** $\frac{12}{16}$ **3.** $\frac{18}{20}$ **4.** $\frac{24}{30}$
5. $\frac{12}{18}$ **6.** $\frac{8}{12}$ **7.** $\frac{9}{15}$ **8.** $\frac{6}{24}$
9. $\frac{6}{18}$ **10.** $\frac{4}{18}$ **11.** $\frac{20}{60}$ **12.** $\frac{40}{120}$
13. $\frac{54}{81}$ **14.** $\frac{28}{36}$ **15.** $\frac{18}{30}$ **16.** $\frac{56}{64}$
17. $\frac{72}{162}$ **18.** $\frac{132}{144}$ **19.** $\frac{35}{45}$ **20.** $\frac{55}{60}$
21. $\frac{30}{72}$ **22.** $\frac{42}{60}$ **23.** $\frac{44}{121}$ **24.** $\frac{77}{132}$

25. $\frac{24}{40}$ **26.** $\frac{56}{60}$ **27.** $\frac{64}{120}$ **28.** $\frac{9}{63}$
29. $\frac{45}{100}$ **30.** $\frac{20}{500}$ **31.** $\frac{20}{5000}$ **32.** $\frac{21}{49}$
33. $\frac{70}{560}$ **34.** $\frac{36}{216}$ **35.** $\frac{121}{440}$ **36.** $\frac{25}{400}$
37. $\frac{34}{51}$ **38.** $\frac{6}{15}$ **39.** $\frac{40}{140}$ **40.** $\frac{81}{540}$
41. $\frac{56}{840}$ **42.** $\frac{64}{880}$ **43.** $\frac{7}{630}$ **44.** $\frac{15}{75}$
45. $\frac{52}{65}$ **46.** $\frac{64}{72}$ **47.** $\frac{21}{35}$ **48.** $\frac{96}{108}$
49. $\frac{650}{1040}$ **50.** $\frac{2800}{3600}$ **51.** $\frac{105}{400}$ **52.** $\frac{225}{500}$

Exercise 9

Write as mixed numbers in their simplest form.

1. $\frac{7}{4}$ **2.** $\frac{8}{5}$ **3.** $\frac{9}{4}$ **4.** $\frac{11}{3}$
5. $\frac{8}{3}$ **6.** $\frac{5}{2}$ **7.** $\frac{5}{3}$ **8.** $\frac{6}{5}$
9. $\frac{11}{4}$ **10.** $\frac{7}{3}$ **11.** $\frac{11}{6}$ **12.** $\frac{12}{5}$
13. $\frac{13}{6}$ **14.** $\frac{7}{2}$ **15.** $\frac{9}{7}$ **16.** $\frac{18}{5}$
17. $\frac{21}{5}$ **18.** $\frac{10}{3}$ **19.** $\frac{12}{7}$ **20.** $\frac{60}{11}$
21. $\frac{70}{12}$ **22.** $\frac{24}{7}$ **23.** $\frac{30}{8}$ **24.** $\frac{40}{12}$

25. $\frac{53}{9}$ **26.** $\frac{100}{9}$ **27.** $\frac{41}{5}$ **28.** $\frac{73}{10}$
29. $\frac{38}{9}$ **30.** $\frac{97}{11}$ **31.** $\frac{100}{11}$ **32.** $\frac{20}{7}$
33. $\frac{52}{7}$ **34.** $\frac{84}{10}$ **35.** $\frac{65}{16}$ **36.** $\frac{52}{8}$
37. $\frac{38}{7}$ **38.** $\frac{25}{17}$ **39.** $\frac{30}{13}$ **40.** $\frac{45}{8}$
41. $\frac{33}{9}$ **42.** $\frac{22}{3}$ **43.** $\frac{200}{12}$ **44.** $\frac{75}{50}$
45. $\frac{26}{9}$ **46.** $\frac{200}{55}$ **47.** $\frac{1000}{400}$ **48.** $\frac{250}{40}$
49. $\frac{3}{2}$ **50.** $\frac{58}{12}$ **51.** $\frac{35}{11}$ **52.** $\frac{205}{210}$

Adding and subtracting fractions

(a) $\frac{1}{2} + \frac{5}{8}$
$= \frac{4}{8} + \frac{5}{8}$
$= \frac{9}{8}$
$= 1\frac{1}{8}$

(b) $\frac{3}{5} - \frac{1}{4}$
$= \frac{12}{20} - \frac{5}{20}$
$= \frac{7}{20}$

Exercise 10

Work out.

1. $\frac{1}{4} + \frac{3}{8}$ **2.** $\frac{3}{4} + \frac{1}{2}$ **3.** $\frac{1}{8} + \frac{3}{4}$
4. $\frac{1}{2} + \frac{7}{8}$ **5.** $\frac{3}{4} - \frac{1}{8}$ **6.** $\frac{5}{8} - \frac{1}{4}$
7. $\frac{7}{8} + \frac{1}{16}$ **8.** $\frac{5}{16} + \frac{1}{4}$ **9.** $\frac{3}{8} - \frac{3}{16}$
10. $\frac{7}{8} + \frac{5}{16}$ **11.** $\frac{1}{2} + \frac{7}{16}$ **12.** $\frac{3}{4} - \frac{9}{16}$
13. $\frac{3}{4} - \frac{1}{16}$ **14.** $\frac{11}{16} - \frac{1}{4}$ **15.** $\frac{7}{8} + \frac{13}{16}$

16. $\frac{2}{3} + \frac{1}{4}$ **17.** $\frac{3}{5} + \frac{1}{2}$ **18.** $\frac{4}{5} + \frac{1}{4}$
19. $\frac{3}{5} + \frac{2}{3}$ **20.** $\frac{5}{6} + \frac{1}{2}$ **21.** $\frac{3}{4} + \frac{4}{5}$
22. $\frac{5}{6} + \frac{1}{2}$ **23.** $\frac{5}{7} + \frac{1}{4}$ **24.** $\frac{3}{5} - \frac{1}{3}$
25. $\frac{7}{8} - \frac{2}{3}$ **26.** $\frac{5}{8} - \frac{1}{5}$ **27.** $\frac{6}{7} - \frac{1}{3}$
28. $\frac{3}{8} - \frac{1}{10}$ **29.** $\frac{4}{9} - \frac{1}{4}$ **30.** $\frac{5}{11} - \frac{1}{4}$

Multiplying and dividing fractions

(a) $\frac{5}{6} \times \frac{5}{7} = \frac{25}{42}$ (b) $\frac{2}{3} \times \frac{5}{7} = \frac{10}{21}$
(c) $\frac{4}{5} \div \frac{3}{4} = \frac{4}{5} \times \frac{4}{3} = \frac{16}{15} = 1\frac{1}{15}$

Exercise 11

Work out and simplify where possible.

1. $\frac{2}{3} \times \frac{1}{5}$ **2.** $\frac{3}{4} \times \frac{5}{7}$ **3.** $\frac{4}{5} \times \frac{2}{3}$
4. $\frac{5}{6} \times \frac{5}{7}$ **5.** $\frac{5}{9} \times \frac{2}{3}$ **6.** $\frac{4}{11} \times \frac{5}{6}$
7. $\frac{7}{8} \times \frac{3}{4}$ **8.** $\frac{8}{9} \times \frac{3}{4}$ **9.** $\frac{7}{10} \times \frac{1}{2}$
10. $\frac{4}{7} \times \frac{14}{15}$ **11.** $\frac{3}{5} \times \frac{7}{8}$ **12.** $\frac{5}{8} \times \frac{1}{2}$
13. $\frac{3}{2} \times \frac{1}{4}$ **14.** $\frac{5}{4} \times \frac{1}{3}$ **15.** $\frac{7}{3} \times \frac{1}{4}$
16. $\frac{3}{4} \div \frac{1}{2}$ **17.** $\frac{3}{5} \div \frac{2}{3}$ **18.** $\frac{5}{6} \div \frac{1}{4}$

19. $\frac{2}{3} \div \frac{3}{4}$ **20.** $\frac{5}{6} \div \frac{3}{4}$ **21.** $\frac{5}{7} \div \frac{3}{4}$
22. $\frac{1}{3} \div \frac{1}{10}$ **23.** $\frac{1}{8} \div \frac{3}{4}$ **24.** $\frac{5}{8} \div \frac{1}{2}$
25. $2\frac{1}{2} \times \frac{1}{3}$ **26.** $3\frac{1}{2} \times \frac{1}{4}$ **27.** $1\frac{1}{4} \times \frac{1}{5}$
28. $2\frac{3}{4} \times \frac{1}{2}$ **29.** $3\frac{1}{5} \times \frac{2}{3}$ **30.** $2\frac{1}{5} \times \frac{1}{4}$
31. $1\frac{1}{4} \div 2$ **32.** $3\frac{1}{2} \div 3$ **33.** $2\frac{3}{4} \div 5$
34. $3\frac{1}{10} \div \frac{1}{2}$ **35.** $5\frac{1}{4} \times \frac{1}{7}$ **36.** $3\frac{2}{9} \div \frac{1}{3}$

Exercise 12

Work out and simplify where possible.

1. $\frac{1}{3}+\frac{1}{2}$ 2. $\frac{1}{3}\times\frac{1}{2}$ 3. $\frac{1}{3}\div\frac{1}{2}$
4. $\frac{3}{4}-\frac{1}{3}$ 5. $\frac{3}{4}\times\frac{1}{3}$ 6. $\frac{3}{4}\div\frac{1}{3}$
7. $\frac{2}{5}+\frac{1}{2}$ 8. $\frac{2}{5}\times\frac{1}{2}$ 9. $\frac{2}{5}\div\frac{1}{2}$
10. $\frac{3}{7}+\frac{1}{2}$ 11. $\frac{3}{7}\times\frac{1}{2}$ 12. $\frac{3}{7}\div\frac{1}{2}$
13. $\frac{5}{8}-\frac{1}{4}$ 14. $\frac{5}{8}\times\frac{1}{4}$ 15. $\frac{5}{8}\div\frac{1}{4}$
16. $\frac{1}{6}+\frac{4}{5}$ 17. $\frac{1}{6}\times\frac{4}{5}$ 18. $\frac{1}{6}\div\frac{4}{5}$
19. $\frac{3}{7}+\frac{1}{3}$ 20. $\frac{3}{7}\times\frac{1}{3}$ 21. $\frac{3}{7}\div\frac{1}{3}$
22. $\frac{4}{5}-\frac{1}{4}$ 23. $\frac{4}{5}\times\frac{1}{4}$ 24. $\frac{4}{5}\div\frac{1}{4}$
25. $\frac{2}{3}-\frac{1}{8}$ 26. $\frac{2}{3}\times\frac{1}{8}$ 27. $\frac{2}{3}\div\frac{1}{8}$
28. $\frac{5}{9}+\frac{1}{4}$ 29. $\frac{5}{9}\times\frac{1}{4}$ 30. $\frac{5}{9}\div\frac{1}{4}$
31. $2\frac{1}{2}-\frac{1}{4}$ 32. $2\frac{1}{2}\times\frac{1}{4}$ 33. $2\frac{1}{2}\div\frac{1}{4}$
34. $3\frac{3}{4}-\frac{2}{3}$ 35. $3\frac{3}{4}\times\frac{2}{3}$ 36. $3\frac{3}{4}\div\frac{2}{3}$
37. $\dfrac{\frac{1}{2}+\frac{1}{5}}{\frac{1}{2}-\frac{1}{5}}$ 38. $\dfrac{\frac{3}{4}-\frac{1}{3}}{\frac{3}{4}+\frac{1}{3}}$
39. $\dfrac{2\frac{1}{4}\times\frac{4}{5}}{\frac{3}{5}-\frac{1}{2}}$ 40. $\dfrac{3\frac{1}{2}\times2\frac{2}{3}}{\frac{1}{2}+1\frac{1}{18}}$

Changing fractions to decimals

(a) $\frac{5}{8}$

$$8\overline{)5.000} = 0.625$$

$\frac{5}{8}=0.625$

(b) $\frac{5}{6}$

$$6\overline{)5.0000} = 0.8333\ldots$$

$\frac{5}{6}=0.8\dot{3}$

Exercise 13

Change the fractions to decimals.

1. $\frac{3}{4}$ 2. $\frac{1}{2}$ 3. $\frac{3}{8}$ 4. $\frac{2}{5}$
5. $\frac{7}{8}$ 6. $\frac{1}{4}$ 7. $\frac{4}{5}$ 8. $\frac{3}{10}$
9. $\frac{1}{8}$ 10. $\frac{1}{3}$ 11. $\frac{2}{3}$ 12. $\frac{1}{6}$
13. $\frac{4}{9}$ 14. $\frac{5}{9}$ 15. $\frac{7}{100}$ 16. $\frac{11}{100}$
17. $\frac{7}{50}$ 18. $\frac{1}{20}$ 19. $\frac{9}{1000}$ 20. $\frac{17}{1000}$
21. $\frac{3}{50}$ 22. $\frac{1}{9}$ 23. $\frac{5}{12}$ 24. $\frac{11}{12}$

In questions **25** to **36** write the decimal correct to three decimal places.

25. $\frac{5}{7}$ 26. $\frac{2}{7}$ 27. $\frac{4}{11}$ 28. $\frac{8}{9}$
29. $\frac{1}{7}$ 30. $\frac{7}{11}$ 31. $\frac{5}{13}$ 32. $\frac{8}{13}$
33. $\frac{4}{15}$ 34. $\frac{1}{30}$ 35. $\frac{7}{90}$ 36. $\frac{5}{60}$

Number facts

(a) A *prime* number is divisible only by itself and by one.
e.g. 2, 3, 5, 7, 11, 13 . . .
(b) The *multiples* of 12 are 12, 24, 36, 48 . . .
(c) The *factors* of 12 are 1, 2, 3, 4, 6, 12.
(d) Rational and irrational numbers
The *exact* value of a *rational* number can be written down.
e.g. 3, $2\frac{1}{2}$, 5.72, $-3\frac{3}{4}$.
The exact value of an *irrational* number *cannot* be written down.
e.g. π, $\sqrt{2}$, $\sqrt{3}$, $\sqrt{5}$.

Exercise 14

1. Which of the following are prime numbers?
3, 11, 15, 19, 21, 23, 27, 29, 31, 37, 39, 47, 51, 59, 61, 67, 72, 73, 87, 99.
2. Write down the first five multiples of the following numbers:
(a) 4 (b) 6 (c) 10
(d) 11 (e) 20.
3. Write down the first six multiples of 4 and of 6. What are the first two *common* multiples of 4 and 6? [i.e. multiples of both 4 and 6]
4. Write down the first six multiples of 3 and of 5. What is the lowest common multiple of 3 and 5?
5. Write down all the factors of the following:
(a) 6 (b) 9 (c) 10
(d) 15 (e) 24 (f) 32
6. Decide which of the following are rational numbers and which are irrational:
(a) 3.5 (b) 3.153 (c) $\sqrt{7}$
(d) $\frac{1}{3}$ (e) 0.072 (f) $\sqrt{2}$
(g) $\sqrt{4}$ (h) π (i) $\dfrac{\sqrt{3}}{2}$
(j) $\sqrt{100}$ (k) $-2\frac{3}{7}$ (l) $\sqrt{5}$

10.3 PERCENTAGES

Change into percentages:

(a) $\frac{4}{5}$ (b) $\frac{3}{8}$ (c) 16 out of 40.

(a) $\frac{4}{5} \times \frac{100}{1} = \frac{400}{5} = \mathbf{80\%}$

(b) $\frac{3}{8} \times \frac{100}{1} = \frac{300}{8} = \mathbf{37\frac{1}{2}\%}$

(c) 16 out of 40 $= \frac{16}{40}$

$\frac{16}{40} \times \frac{100}{1} = \frac{1600}{40} = \mathbf{40\%}$

Exercise 15

Change into percentages.

1. $\frac{2}{5}$ **2.** $\frac{3}{4}$ **3.** $\frac{5}{8}$
4. $\frac{7}{100}$ **5.** $\frac{12}{50}$ **6.** $\frac{7}{20}$
7. $\frac{7}{8}$ **8.** $\frac{1}{3}$ **9.** $\frac{1}{8}$
10. $\frac{3}{50}$ **11.** $\frac{19}{100}$ **12.** $\frac{24}{40}$
13. $\frac{64}{80}$ **14.** $\frac{17}{25}$ **15.** $\frac{13}{1000}$

16. 27 out of 50.
17. 72 out of 80.
18. 3 out of 40.
19. 11 out of 20.
20. 220 out of 1000.

Work out: (a) 22% of £400,
(b) $8\frac{1}{2}\%$ of £300.

(a) $\frac{22}{100} \times \frac{400}{1} = £88$

(b) $\frac{8.5}{100} \times 300 = £25.50$

Exercise 16

Work out.

1. 12% of £600 **2.** 6% of £250
3. 8% of £450 **4.** 7% of £440
5. 5% of £22 **6.** 4% of £660
7. 85% of £400 **8.** 6.5% of £200
9. 29% of £2000 **10.** 4.5% of £400
11. 62% of $4000 **12.** 1.4% of $6000
13. 49% of $10 000 **14.** 25% of 64 m
15. $12\frac{1}{2}\%$ of 160 kg **16.** 80% of 600 km
17. 50% of 0.62 kg **18.** $33\frac{1}{3}\%$ of 327 km
19. 1% of £2 **20.** 5% of 200 kg

In questions **21** to **40** give the answer correct to the nearest penny.

21. 13% of £2.13 **22.** 27% of £5.85
23. 11% of £6.27 **24.** 13% of £6.17
25. 37% of £5.20 **26.** 15% of £11.23
27. 6.2% of £8.55 **28.** 31% of £35.04
29. 8.9% of £17.10 **30.** 6.8% of £16.10
31. 81% of £9.32 **32.** 15.1% of £7.87
33. 43% of £185 **34.** 16% of £0.37
35. 1.8% of £2555 **36.** 4% of £0.65
37. 3.7% of £6.12 **38.** 78% of £3.17
39. 17% of £1754 **40.** 23% of £18.05

The next three exercises involve percentages as they are used in everyday life.

Hire purchase

Exercise 17

1. The cash price of an electric cooker is £540.The hire purchase terms are:
Deposit: 20% of cash price
Instalments: 24 monthly payments of £20.75
Calculate (a) the deposit
(b) the total monthly instalments
(c) the total hire purchase price of the cooker.

2. Steve wished to buy a motor cycle priced at £480. He chose to pay by hire purchase. The terms were 30% deposit with 12 monthly payments of £33.80.
Calculate (a) the deposit
(b) the total of the monthly payments
(c) the total hire purchase price of the motor cycle.

3. The cash price of a video recorder is £485. The hire purchase terms are:
Deposit: 30% of cash price
Instalments: 18 monthly payments of £23.
Calculate (a) the deposit
(b) the total monthly instalments
(c) the total hire purchase price.

4. David wishes to buy a computer priced at £360. He choses to pay by hire purchase the terms for which are 30% deposit and 24 monthly payments of £12.50.
Calculate (a) the total hire purchase price
(b) the difference between the cash price and the hire purchase price.

5. A television set is priced at £320 in two different shops A and B, which offer different hire purchase terms.
Shop A requires a 20% deposit and 12 monthly instalments of £26.60.
Shop B requires a 30% deposit and 12 monthly instalments of £23.50.
Calculate (a) the total hire purchase price in Shop A.
(b) the total hire purchase price in Shop B.

6. The cash price of a caravan is £3400. The hire purchase terms are 25% deposit and 12 monthly payments. The total hire purchase price is £4090.
Calculate (a) the deposit
(b) the difference between the deposit and the total hire purchase price
(c) the amount of each monthly instalment.

7. The cash price of a car is £840. The hire purchase terms are $33\frac{1}{3}\%$ deposit and 24 monthly payments. The total hire purchase price is £980.80.
Calculate (a) the deposit
(b) the total of the 24 monthly instalments.
(c) the amount of each monthly instalment.

8. A man may obtain a TV set from a shop in three different ways:
(i) He can buy the set for £285 cash.
(ii) He can pay a deposit of 20% of £285 followed by 24 monthly instalments of £11.60.
(iii) He can rent the set paying £3 a week for the first year and £2.70 a week for the next two years. Calculate
(a) the total hire purchase price.
(b) the cost of renting the set for 3 years.

9. A car costs £1800. Mr Wilson pays by taking out a bank loan for £1800. The bank makes a charge of 22% of the loan. The bank loan plus interest has to be repaid by 18 equal monthly payments. Calculate
(a) the interest charged
(b) the total of the loan plus interest
(c) the amount of each monthly payment.

10.

(a) The cooker can be bought on hire purchase by paying a deposit of 35% and 36 monthly payments of £11.40. How much is
(i) the deposit
(ii) the total of the monthly payments
(iii) the total hire purchase price?

(b) The cooker can also be bought using a bank loan for £460. The bank makes a charge of 20% of the loan and requires the loan plus interest to be repaid by 24 equal monthly payments. Calculate
(i) the interest charged
(ii) the total cost by this method
(iii) the amount of each monthly payment.

Insurance

Exercise 18

The table shows the cost of insuring a motor cycle.

Age of insured in years	Size of engine	Insurance Cover	
		Third Party, Fire and Theft	Comprehensive
16	up to 50 cc	£80	£170
17 to 20	up to 50 cc	£70	£130
	51 to 150 cc	£90	£210
	151 to 300 cc	£130	£260
21 and over	up to 50 cc	£50	£70
	51 to 150 cc	£60	£100
	151 to 300 cc	£80	£170
	301 to 500 cc	£120	£260
'No claim' bonus: one year 10% two years 25% five years or more 60%			

1. David, aged 18, wishes to insure his 175 cc motor cycle.
(a) How much will it cost him for comprehensive cover?
(b) How much will it cost him for 'third party, fire and theft' cover?
(c) How much will it cost him for comprehensive cover if he has a one year no claim bonus?

2. Steve, aged 24, wishes to insure his 250 cc motor cycle.
(a) How much will it cost him for comprehensive cover?
(b) How much will it cost him for comprehensive cover if he has a seven years no claim bonus?

3. Jane, aged 19, wishes to insure her 100 cc motor cycle.
(a) What is her basic premium for 'third party, fire and theft'?
(b) She does not have a no claims bonus but her premium is reduced by 15% because she lives in the countryside. How much does she pay?

Copy and complete the table below

Name	Age	Size of engine	Cover	No claim bonus	Special discount	Cost
4. Peter	18	250 cc	comp.	2 years		
5. Alan	26	500 cc	3rd party	4 years		
6. Patrick	17	300 cc	3rd party		5%	
7. Mark	20	300 cc	comp.	3 years		
8. Roger	28	500 cc	comp.	8 years		
9. Gary	16	50 cc	3rd party			
10. Paul	23	275 cc	comp.	5 years		
11. John	18	250 cc	3rd party		15%	
12. Jim	22	350 cc	3rd party	2 years		

Pay rises

Exercise 19

1. John works for company A and during 1987 he earns £160 per week. From January 1st 1988 company A offer John an extra 5% on his wages and John accepts this offer and is paid this new wage for 52 weeks in 1988.
   (a) How much is John paid each week in 1988?
   (b) How much does John earn in the whole of 1988?

2. Steve works for company B and during 1987 he also earns £160 per week. From January 1st 1988 company B offer Steve an extra 5% but Steve does not accept this and he goes on strike for six weeks, during which time he receives no pay. After six weeks of the strike, company B offer Steve 10% and he immediately accepts this and receives his increased pay for the rest of 1988.
   (a) How much is Steve paid after the strike?
   (b) How much does Steve earn in the whole of 1988?

3. Ann also earns £160 per week during 1987 and she also goes on strike for the first six weeks of 1988. At the end of her strike she accepts a pay offer of 15% and she receives her increased pay for the rest of 1988.
   (a) How much is Ann paid after the strike?
   (b) How much does Ann earn in the whole of 1988?

4. At the beginning of the year the wages of three people working for the same firm are as follows:
   Cleaner £80 per week;
   Secretary £115 per week;
   Personnel manager £15 080 per year.
   (a) The firm awards all of its employees a pay rise of 5%.
      (i) What is the pay increase for a cleaner?
      (ii) What is the pay increase for a secretary?
      (iii) How much does the personnel manager earn in one week before the pay rise?
      (iv) What is the weekly pay increase for the personnel manager?
   (b) The firm's computer makes a mistake with pay increases and awards an increase of 12% for everyone instead of 5%.
      (i) What is the pay increase for a cleaner?
      (ii) What is the pay increase for a secretary?
      (iii) What is the weekly pay increase for the personnel manager?

5. A shop assistant earns £65 per week. She receives a pay rise of 8%. After stoppages for tax and insurance she actually receives 60% of the increase.
   (a) What is the increase in her pay *before* stoppages?
   (b) How much extra money does she receive in her pay packet after stoppages?

6. A car mechanic earns £180 per week. He receives a pay rise of 7%. After stoppages for tax and insurance he actually receives 60% of the increase.
   (a) What is the increase in his pay *before* stoppages?
   (b) How much extra money does he receive in his pay packet after stoppages?

7. An airline pilot earns £17 940 per year. She receives a pay rise of 5.6%. After stoppages for tax and insurance she actually receives only 55% of the increase.
   (a) How much does she earn per week?
   (b) What is the increase in her weekly pay *before* stoppages?
   (c) How much extra money does she actually receive each week after stoppages? Give the answer to the nearest penny.

8. A judge earns £35 040 per year. Parliament awards him a pay rise of 6.2%. After stoppages for tax and insurance he actually receives only 42% of the increase.
   (a) How much does he earn each month?
   (b) What is the increase in his monthly pay before stoppages?
   (c) How much extra money does he actually receive each month after stoppages? Give the answer to the nearest penny.

Income tax

The tax which an employee pays on his income depends on
(a) how much he is paid
(b) his allowances
(c) the rate of taxation.

Tax is paid only on the 'taxable income'.
(i) Taxable income = Total income − allowances.

Allowances depend on whether a person is married or single and on various expenses involved in doing the job.
You can check your allowances by looking at the 'Tax Code Number' on your payslip.

(ii) Allowances = (Tax Code Number) × 10

A man earns £6500 per year. If his Tax Code Number is 238, calculate his taxable income.

Allowances = 238 × 10 = £2380.
Taxable income = £6500 − £2380
= £4120.

Exercise 20

Calculate the taxable income from the details given.

	Earnings	Tax Code Number
1.	£3500 per year	213
2.	£5000 per year	274
3.	£8000 per year	315
4.	£4200 per year	289
5.	£3650 per year	265
6.	£9800 per year	341
7.	£8655 per year	286
8.	£600 per month	412
9.	£450 per month	263
10.	£825 per month	311
11.	£710 per month	278
12.	£985 per month	415
13.	£160 per week	342
14.	£144 per week	214
15.	£180 per week	289

A woman earns £95 per week and her Tax Code Number is 215. Find the total amount of tax paid in a year when the tax rate is 30%.

Amount earned in year = £95 × 52
= £4940

Allowances = 215 × 10 = £2150

∴ Taxable income = £4940 − £2150
= £2790

Tax paid = 30% of £2790
$= \frac{30}{100} \times \frac{2790}{1} = £837$

Exercise 21

In all questions the tax rate is 30%.

1. A man earns £110 per week and his Tax Code Number is 304. Find the total amount of tax paid in a year.

2. A man earns £204 per week and his Tax Code Number is 361. Find the total amount of tax paid in a year.

3. Ann earns £165 per week. How much tax does she pay in a year if her Tax Code Number is 247?

4. John earns £148.50 per week. How much tax does he pay in a year if his Tax Code Number is 302?

5. Louise earns a salary of £620 per month. How much tax does she pay in a year if her Tax Code Number is 342?

6. David earns £950 per month and his Tax Code Number is 357. Find the total amount of tax paid in a year.

7. Mr Tebbit's salary is £9650 per year and his Tax Code Number is 465. Find the total amount of tax paid in a year.

In questions **8** to **15**, find the yearly income tax.

	Earnings	Tax Code Number
8.	£4800 per year	310
9.	£850 per month	267
10.	£85 per week	180
11.	£124 per week	253
12.	£4980 per year	384
13.	£1200 per month	462
14.	£235 per week	318
15.	£760 per month	427

10.4 APPROXIMATIONS

(a) 2.486 = 2.5, correct to 2 significant figures.
(arrow under 4)

(b) 31.924 = 31.9 (to 3 S.F.)

(c) 45671 = 45700 (to 3 S.F.)

(d) 3.2136 = 3.214, correct to 3 decimal places.

(e) 0.455 = 0.46 (to 2 D.P.)

(f) 13.246 = 13.2 (to 1 D.P.)

In each case look at the figure marked with an arrow to see if it is '5 or more'.

Exercise 22

In questions **1** to **10** write the numbers correct to three significant figures.

1. 2.3462 **2.** 0.81438
3. 26.241 **4.** 35.55
5. 112.74 **6.** 210.82
7. 0.8254 **8.** 0.031162
9. 5.6041 **10.** 13.547

In questions **11** to **20** write the numbers correct to two significant figures.

11. 5.894 **12.** 1.232
13. 0.5456 **14.** 0.7163
15. 0.1443 **16.** 1.831
17. 24.83 **18.** 31.37
19. 8.743 **20.** 35.65

In questions **21** to **30** write the numbers correct to four significant figures.

21. 486.72 **22.** 500.36
23. 2.8888 **24.** 3.1125
25. 0.071542 **26.** 3.0405
27. 2463.5 **28.** 488 852
29. 642 628 **30.** 111 224

In questions **31** to **60** write the numbers to the degree of accuracy indicated.

31. 0.5126 (3 S.F.) **32.** 5.821 (2 S.F.)
33. 65.89 (2 S.F.) **34.** 587.55 (4 S.F.)
35. 0.581 (1 S.F.) **36.** 0.0713 (1 S.F.)
37. 5.8354 (3 S.F.) **38.** 87.84 (2 S.F.)
39. 2482 (2 S.F.) **40.** 52 666 (3 S.F.)
41. 6.851 (1 S.F.) **42.** 0.3142 (1 S.F.)
43. 5240 (1 S.F.) **44.** 34.62 (3 S.F.)
45. 63 840 (3 S.F.) **46.** 0.0574 (2 S.F.)
47. 0.0333 (1 S.F.) **48.** 115.62 (3 S.F.)
49. 84 888 (2 S.F.) **50.** 5.0071 (3 S.F.)
51. 5.0063 (3 S.F.) **52.** 18.195 (2 S.F.)
53. 3.4961 (3 S.F.) **54.** 21.982 (3 S.F.)
55. 9.642 (1 S.F.) **56.** 0.7975 (2 S.F.)
57. 3.982 (2 S.F.) **58.** 7.981 (2 S.F.)
59. 3.296 (3 S.F.) **60.** 83.82 (1 S.F.)

Exercise 23

In questions **1** to **10** write the numbers correct to two decimal places (2 D.P.).

1. 5.381 **2.** 11.0482
3. 0.414 **4.** 0.3666
5. 8.015 **6.** 87.044
7. 9.0062 **8.** 0.0724
9. 0.0685 **10.** 5.1555

In questions **11** to **20** write the numbers correct to one decimal place.

11. 8.424 **12.** 0.7413
13. 0.382 **14.** 0.095
15. 6.083 **16.** 19.53
17. 8.111 **18.** 7.071
19. 219.63 **20.** 80.89

In questions **21** to **40** write the numbers to the degree of accuracy indicated.

21. 8.155 (2 D.P.) **22.** 3.042 (1 D.P.)
23. 0.5454 (3 D.P.) **24.** 0.005 55 (4 D.P.)
25. 0.7071 (2 D.P.) **26.** 6.8271 (2 D.P.)
27. 0.8413 (1 D.P.) **28.** 19.646 (2 D.P.)
29. 0.071 35 (4 D.P.) **30.** 60.051 (1 D.P.)
31. 0.551 (2 D.P.) **32.** 0.071 11 (4 D.P.)
33. 8.821 (1 D.P.) **34.** 6.044 (2 D.P.)
35. 3.0129 (3 D.P.) **36.** 18.8201 (3 D.P.)
37. 4.005 (2 D.P.) **38.** 0.0791 (2 D.P.)
39. 8.061 (1 D.P.) **40.** 12.865 (1 D.P.)

10.5 STANDARD FORM

Reminder: 66 000 = 6.6×10^4
125 000 = 1.25×10^5
0.000 76 = 7.6×10^{-4}
0.000 000 4 = 4.0×10^{-7}

Exercise 24

Write the following numbers in standard form.

1. 5500 **2.** 61 400
3. 23 000 000 **4.** 1 700 000
5. 845 000 **6.** 27 100
7. 6 000 000 000 **8.** 8 100 000 000
9. 7 400 000 **10.** 8 960 000
11. 7140 **12.** 66 000
13. 8 400 000 **14.** 746 000
15. 200 **16.** 4400
17. 75 **18.** 826 000 000
19. 2 million **20.** 30 million

21. 0.000 46 **22.** 0.000 023
23. 0.0041 **24.** 0.000 000 075 8
25. 0.0823 **26.** 0.000 095 8
27. 0.000 006 15 **28.** 0.000 001 52
29. 0.0756 **30.** 0.006 164
31. 0.000 008 8 **32.** 0.008 14
33. 0.000 000 009 5 **34.** 0.074
35. 0.08 **36.** 0.95
37. 0.000 714 **38.** 0.999
39. 0.084 15 **40.** 0.000 045

Exercise 25

Write the following numbers in the usual way.

1. 2.3×10^2 **2.** 3.4×10^5
3. 4.1×10^3 **4.** 2.71×10^2
5. 8.2×10^4 **6.** 3×10^8
7. 9×10^2 **8.** 2.2×10^5
9. 6.35×10^1 **10.** 8.95×10^4
11. 4×10^5 **12.** 1.234×10^3
13. 5.14×10^2 **14.** 8×10^1
15. 7×10^3 **16.** 6.05×10^2
17. 8.012×10^4 **18.** 6×10^7
19. 9.6×10^2 **20.** 4.2×10^4

21. 4.2×10^{-2} **22.** 4.7×10^{-3}
23. 1.6×10^{-3} **24.** 8.9×10^{-4}
25. 8.4×10^{-1} **26.** 6×10^{-2}
27. 9.51×10^{-4} **28.** 2×10^{-5}
29. 8×10^{-5} **30.** 4.1×10^{-1}
31. 6.3×10^{-3} **32.** 8.04×10^{-3}
33. 5×10^{-2} **34.** 6.9×10^{-2}
35. 4.8×10^{-4} **36.** 8.95×10^{-1}
37. 6.11×10^{-2} **38.** 8×10^{-7}
39. 9×10^{-6} **40.** 1.11×10^{-3}

41. 5.2×10^3 **42.** 9.4×10^{-3}
43. 8×10^{-2} **44.** 3.8×10^5
45. 6.7×10^{-4} **46.** 6.66×10^{-2}
47. 1.1×10^4 **48.** 8.1×10^{-3}
49. 7×10^{-1} **50.** 5×10^6

Unit 11

11.1 THE METRIC SYSTEM

(a) $3.24 \times 100 = 324$
(Move point two places to the right)

(b) $0.0417 \times 1000 = 41.7$
(Move point three places to the right)

(c) $63.1 \div 100 = 0.631$
(Move point two places to the left)

Exercise 1

This exercise provides revision of multiplying and dividing by 10's, 100's, 1000's etc. Do not use a calculator.

1. 0.36×10 **2.** 0.085×100
3. 0.47×100 **4.** 0.96×10
5. 5.6×10 **6.** 0.74×1000
7. 2.3×1000 **8.** 11.52×100
9. 0.8×100 **10.** $6.54 \times 10\,000$
11. $0.075 \div 10$ **12.** $81.5 \div 1000$
13. $0.047 \div 1000$ **14.** $6.2 \div 10$
15. $0.52 \div 100$ **16.** $310 \div 1000$
17. $1.63 \div 10$ **18.** $7 \div 100$
19. $0.72 \div 100$ **20.** $4500 \div 100\,000$
21. $0.047 \times 10\,000$ **22.** 6.22×100
23. $82.6 \div 10$ **24.** $858 \div 10\,000$
25. 0.007×10 **26.** $0.073 \div 10$
27. $573 \div 1000$ **28.** 1.45×1000
29. $264 \div 10\,000$ **30.** $6 \times 10\,000$
31. 0.06×100 **32.** $0.06 \div 10\,000$
33. 0.0004×1 million **34.** $1.5 \div 100$
35. $85 \div 10$ **36.** 800×10
37. 6.3×1 million **38.** $6000 \div 1$ million
39. $849 \div 1000$
40. $0.000\,06 \times 10$ million

Metric units

Length: 10 mm = 1 cm
100 cm = 1 m
1000 m = 1 km

Mass: 1000 g = 1 kg
1000 kg = 1 t
(t for tonne)

Volume: 1000 ml = 1 l
1000 l = 1 m^3
(l for litre)
Also 1 ml = 1 cm^3

Exercise 2

Copy and complete.

1. 85 cm = m
2. 2.4 km = m
3. 0.63 m = cm
4. 25 cm = m
5. 7 mm = cm
6. 2 cm = mm
7. 1.2 km = m
8. 7 m = cm
9. 0.58 km = m
10. 815 mm = m
11. 650 m = km
12. 25 mm = cm
13. 5 kg = g
14. 4.2 kg = g
15. 6.4 kg = g
16. 3 kg = g
17. 0.8 kg = g
18. 400 g = kg
19. 2 t = kg
20. 250 g = kg

21. 0.5 t = kg
22. 0.62 t = kg
23. 7 kg = t
24. 1500 g = kg
25. 800 ml = l
26. 2 l = ml
27. 1000 ml = l
28. 4.5 l = ml
29. 6 l = ml
30. 3 l = cm^3

31. 2 m^3 = l
32. 5.5 m^3 = l
33. 0.9 l = cm^3
34. 600 cm^3 = l
35. 15 m^3 = l
36. 240 ml = l
37. 28 cm = m
38. 5.5 m = cm
39. 305 g = kg
40. 0.046 km = m

41. 16 ml = l
42. 208 mm = m
43. 28 mm = cm
44. 27 cm = m
45. 788 m = km
46. 14 t = kg
47. 1.3 kg = g
48. 90 l = m^3
49. 2.9 t = kg
50. 19 ml = l

11.2 IMPERIAL UNITS

Exercise 3

(a) 12 inches = 1 foot
3 feet = 1 yard
1760 yards = 1 mile

(b) 16 ounces = 1 pound
14 pounds = 1 stone
2240 pounds = 1 ton

(c) 8 pints = 1 gallon

1. How many inches are there in two feet?
2. How many ounces are there in three pounds?
3. How many feet are there in ten yards?
4. How many pounds are there in two tons?
5. How many pints are there in six gallons?
6. How many yards are there in ten miles?
7. How many inches are there in one yard?
8. How many pounds are there in five stones?
9. How many pints are there in half a gallon?
10. How many yards are there in half a mile?

In questions **11** to **30** copy each statement and fill in the missing numbers.

11. 9 feet = yards
12. 16 pints = gallons
13. 2 miles = yards
14. 5 pounds = ounces
15. 10 stones = pounds
16. 4 yards = feet
17. 4 feet = inches
18. 10 tons = pounds
19. 1 mile = feet
20. 6 feet = yards

21. 2 feet 6 inches = inches.
22. 5 feet 2 inches = inches.
23. 5 stones 6 pounds = pounds.
24. 7 stones 3 pounds = pounds.
25. $1\frac{1}{2}$ feet = inches.
26. $\frac{1}{2}$ pound = ounces.
27. 4 feet 10 inches = inches.
28. 6 stones 8 pounds = pounds.
29. $\frac{1}{4}$ pound = ounces.
30. 10 stones 12 pounds = pounds.

Exercise 4

The following conversions are approximate.

1 inch = 2.54 cm	1 pint = 0.568 litre
1 mile = 1.61 km	1 gallon = 4.55 litres
1 km = 0.621 mile	1 litre = 0.22 gallon
	1 lb = 0.454 kg
	1 kg = 2.2 lb

In questions **1** to **20** copy each statement and fill in the missing numbers.

1. 10 inches = cm
2. 10 miles = km
3. 2 kg = lb
4. 2 km = miles
5. 10 gallons = litres
6. 10 litres = gallons
7. 5 kg = lb
8. 100 km = miles
9. 6 inches = cm
10. 4 miles = km
11. 8 gallons = litres
12. 4 pints = litres
13. 25 kg = lb
14. 1000 miles = km
15. 12 km = miles
16. 10 lb = kg
17. 3 inches = cm
18. 20 litres = gallons
19. 6 litres = gallons
20. 7 km = miles

11.3 PROBLEMS

The next exercises provide practice in using basic arithmetic to solve problems in a wide variety of situations.

Exercise 5

1. 35 000 people saw Spurs play one Saturday. Calculate the takings at the gate if 25 000 stood for £2 each and 10 000 were seated at £3.50 each.

2. A school party caught a train at Victoria station at 0850 and arrived at Dover at 1055. The return train left Dover at 1923 and took exactly the same time on the journey as the morning train. Calculate the time at which the return train arrived at Victoria.

3. A car uses 13 litres of fuel for every 100 km travelled. Calculate the cost, in £, of travelling 300 km if petrol costs 45p per litre.

4. If £1 is equivalent to $1.45,
(a) how many dollars are equivalent to £50,
(b) how many dollars are equivalent to 60p?

5. A worker is paid a basic weekly wage of £20 plus 25p for each item completed. How many items must be completed in a week when he earns a total of £95.50?

6. On the 1st January 1986 Mr Jones has £2754.26 in a bank account. During the year he withdraws £800 and is credited with interest of £65.84 and £43.48. How much is in his account on 1st January 1987?

7. The contents of a house have a total value of £8800. Calculate the insurance premium when the rate is 16p per £100 insured.

8. Write down the next two numbers in each of the following sequences.
(a) 4, 9, 14, 19, . . .
(b) 68, 56, 44, . . .
(c) 5, 6, 4, 7, 3, . . .
(d) 162, 54, 18, 6, . . .

9. A shopkeeper buys tea at £1.15 per kg and sells it at 32p per 100 g. How much profit does he make per kg?

10. A television programme starts at 1755 and ends at 2050. How many hours and minutes does the programme last?

Exercise 6

1. A private hospital charges its patients £150 per day. How much will it cost to stay in this hospital for six days?
2. Mrs Brown earned £76 plus a bonus of £26 in one week. Income tax of £18 was deducted from her wages. Work out her take-home pay.
3. One Saturday last season only 32,163 people watched all the matches in the Scottish League division two. This was 17,584 fewer than the number watching the Manchester United–QPR game. How many people watched the game between Manchester United and QPR?
4. How many shirts costing £15 could you buy for £100?
5. A factory produces 1550 televisions every day. The workers go on strike for nine days. How many televisions are lost because of the strike?
6. A coach journey is going to cost £200. This cost is to be shared by 16 people. How much will each person have to pay?
7. Mr Simpson wants to buy a car costing £4755. The garage offers him a trade-in of £1240 for his old car. How much extra cash does he need to buy the car?
8. An office building has twelve floors and each floor has twenty windows. A window cleaner charges 50p per window. How much will he charge to clean all the windows in the building?

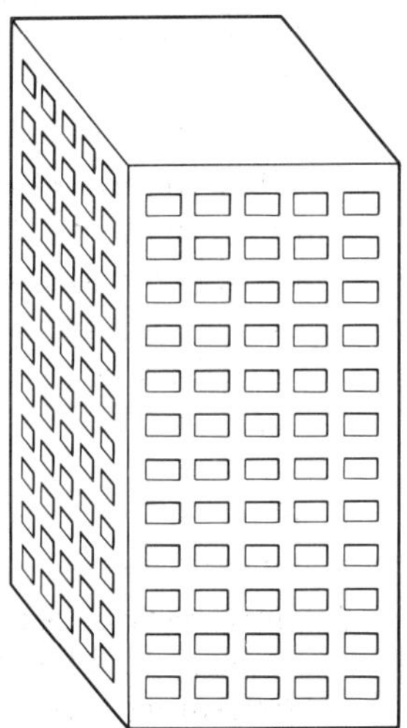

9. An old sailor keeps all of his savings in gold. Altogether the gold weighs ten pounds. One day the price of gold goes up by \$40 an ounce to \$520 an ounce.
   (a) By how much did his gold rise in value?
   (b) How much was it worth after the rise? (1 pound = 16 ounces).
10. This packet of sugar cubes costs 60p

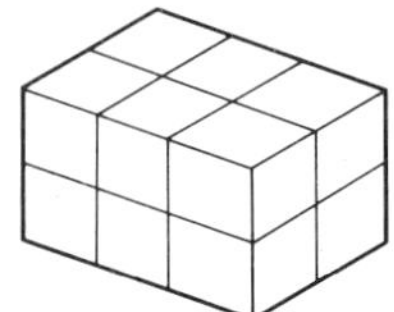

How much would you have to pay for this packet?

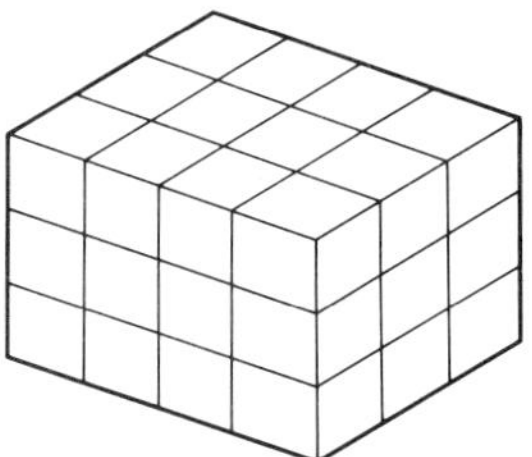

Exercise 7

1. A 7-day holiday in Germany costs £302. Find the average cost per day, correct to the nearest pound.
2. There are 1150 pupils in a school. If 52% of the pupils are girls, how many boys are there?
3. John Lowe made darts history in 1984 with the first ever perfect game played in a tournament, 501 scored in just nine darts. He won a special prize of £100 000 from the sponsors of the tournament. His first eight darts were six treble 20s, treble 17 and treble 18.
   (a) What did he score with the ninth dart?
   (b) How much did he win per dart thrown, to the nearest pound?
4. Eight cans of beer cost £1.28. How many cans of beer could be bought for £8?
5. Reduce the cost of each of the following items by one quarter of its price:
   (a) Video recorder: £480
   (b) Washing machine: £300
   (c) Record: £5.

6. 5, 9, 11, 21, 33, 38, 39
   Which of the above numbers are:
   (a) divisible by 3 (b) prime numbers
   (c) even numbers (d) divisible by 7?
7. Write the following to the degree of accuracy stated:
   (a) 7.243 (to 1 D.P.) (b) 11.275 (to 2 D.P.)
   (c) 0.115 (to 1 D.P.) (d) 0.0255 (to 3 D.P.)
   (e) 28.21 (to 1 D.P.) (f) 0.0072 (to 2 D.P.)
8. Work out, without using a calculator.
   (a) $0.6 + 2.72$ (b) $3.21 - 1.6$
   (c) $2.8 - 1.34$ (d) $8 - 3.6$
   (e) 100×0.062 (f) $27.4 \div 10$
9. A rectangular wheat field is 200 m by 400 m. One hectare is 10 000 m^2 and each hectare produces 3 tonnes of wheat.
   (a) What is the area of the field in hectares?
   (b) How much wheat is produced in this field?
10. A powerful computer is hired out at a rate of 50p per minute. How much will it cost to hire the computer from 06 30 to 18 00?

Exercise 8

1. A bookseller bought 400 copies of a book.
   He sold: 108 in week 1
   145 in week 2
   74 in week 3.
   How many books did he have left after week 3?
2. A market trader sells a coat at a profit of 80% on the cost price of £35. For how much does he sell the coat?
3. A man's heart beats on average 68 times every minute.
   (a) How many times will his heart beat in 10 minutes?
   (b) How many times will his heart beat between 1800 and 2120?
4. How many 50 ml bottles can be filled from a jar containing 7 litres of liquid?

5. What fraction of £1 is
   (a) 10p (b) 5p (c) 50p (d) 75p?
6. Write as a single number:
   (a) 7^2 (b) 1^3 (c) 9^2
   (d) $2^2 + 3^2$ (e) $10^2 + 5^2$ (f) $8^2 - 6^2$
7. Karen is 16 years old and her father is 25 years older than her. Karen's mother is 4 years younger than her father. How old is Karen's mother?
8. A coach holds 60 people. How many people are in the coach when it is
   (a) half full?
   (b) three-quarters full?
   (c) four-fifths full?
9. Find the figures A, B and C if

```
   32A
   6B3
 + C27
 -----
  1764
 -----
```

10. The numbers '5' and '4' multiply to give 20 and add up to 9. Find two numbers which:
    (a) multiply to give 30 and add up to 11.
    (b) multiply to give 36 and add up to 15.
    (c) multiply to give 36 and add up to 13.

Exercise 9

1. Four dozen bags of grain weigh 2016 kg. How much does each bag weigh?
2. A swimming pool 20 m by 12 m contains water to a uniform depth of $1\frac{1}{2}$ m. 1 m^3 of water weighs 1000 kg. What is the weight of the water in the pool?
3. A wall measuring 3 m by 2 m is to be covered with square tiles of side 10 cm.
   (a) How many tiles are needed?
   (b) If the tiles cost £3.40 for ten, how much will it cost?
4. £60 is shared among three people in the ratio 3:4:5. How much is the smallest share?
5. Change the following 12-hour clock times to 24-hour clock times
   (a) 7.30 a.m.
   (b) 7.30 p.m.
   (c) 1.00 p.m.
6. How many apples costing 8p each can be bought with £1?
7. How many cubes, each of edge 1 cm, are required to fill a box with internal dimensions 5 cm by 8 cm by 3 cm?

8. When a car journey starts, the mileometer reads 42 714 miles. After two hours the mileometer reads 42 858 miles. What is the average speed of the car?

9. The map below, which is not drawn to scale, shows the roads joining towns A, B, C, D, E and F. There are signposts at C and F, giving distances in miles.

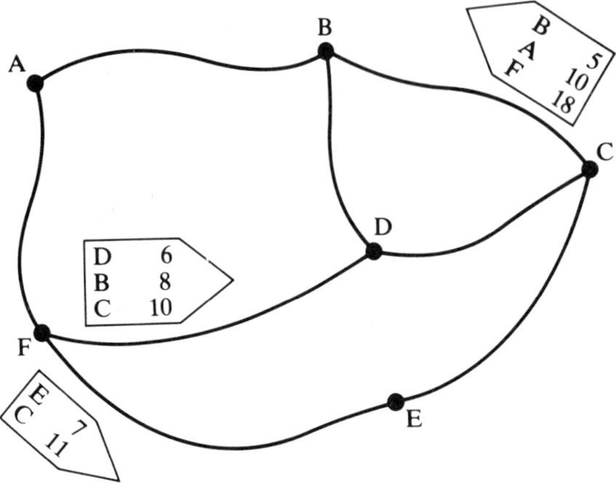

(a) Make a copy of the map and mark on it the lengths of all of the roads.
(b) Work out the *shortest* distance between the following pairs of towns:
(i) F and E
(ii) F and C
(iii) F and B
(iv) D and A
(v) E and A
(vi) B and E

10. I think of a number. If I add 5 and then divide the result by 2 the answer is 8. What number was I thinking of?

Exercise 10

1. A packet of baby food makes 100 feeds. A baby has 5 feeds a day. How many days will the packet last?

2. John is 12 years old and his father is 28 years older than he is. John's mother is 3 years younger than his father. How old is John's mother?

3. Which is greater and by how much: (10% of £600) or (25% of £210)?

4. A rectangular box, without a lid, is to be made from cardboard.

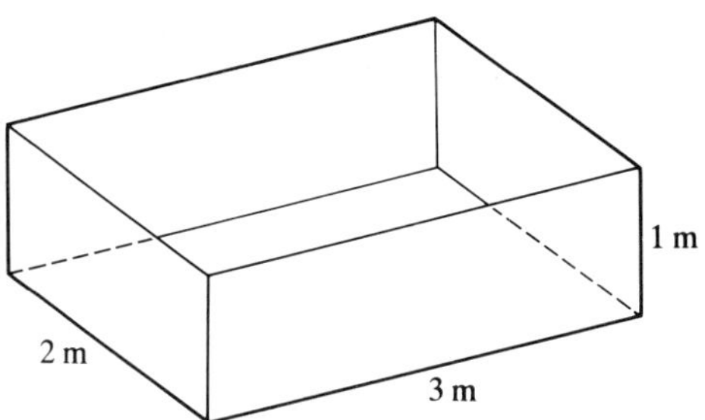

(a) What area of cardboard is required?
(b) What is the volume of the box?

5. (a) Which four coins make a total of 77p?
(b) Which five coins make a total of 86p?
(c) Which five coins make a total of £1.57?

6. Arrange the following numbers in order, smallest first:
8711, 8171, 8117, 817, 8710

7. How much change would I get from £100 after buying two records at £4.95 each, three books at £1.95 each and a turkey for £6.34?

8. A large wheel in a factory turns once every 15 s. How many rotations will it make in 2 hours?

9. Nine bars of chocolate weigh 468 g. They cost £3.15 altogether.
(a) How much does one bar weigh?
(b) How much does one bar cost?
(c) How many bars can I buy for £5.25?

10. The numbers '6' and '2' have a sum of 8 and a product of 12. Find two numbers:
(a) with a sum of 7 and a product of 12,
(b) with a sum of 7 and a product of 10,
(c) with a sum of 11 and a product of 28.

Exercise 11

1. How many stamps each costing 16p can be bought for £1?

2. A typist is paid £4.15 per hour. How much does she earn in a week when she works 40 hours?

3. It needs 100 g of flour to make 20 small cakes. How much flour is needed to make 30 of these cakes?

4. One litre of petrol costs 41.2p and one litre of oil costs 82p.
   (a) Find the cost of 100 litres of petrol
   (b) Find the cost of 10 litres of oil
   (c) Find the total cost of 40 litres of petrol and 20 litres of oil
   (d) Find the total cost of 50 litres of petrol and 8 litres of oil.
5. Calculate the area of the shape below.

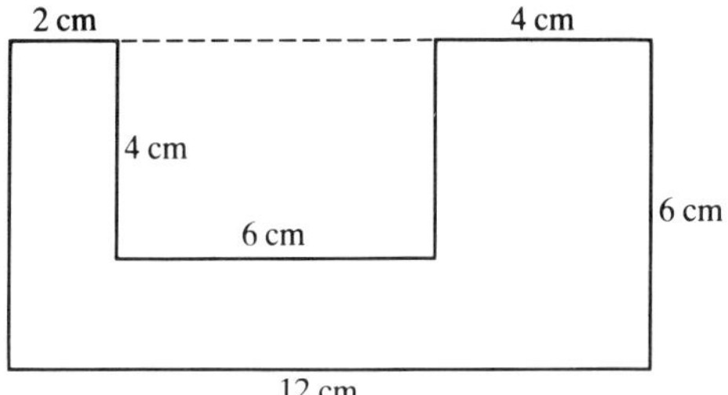

6. A model train is built to a scale of 1:50. The height of the engine of the actual train is 250 cm. Find the height of the engine of the model.
7. Steven has caught ten more fish than Peter and they have caught fifty altogether between them. How many fish has each caught?
8. How many minutes are there between:
   (a) 09 20 and 11 10,
   (b) 07 15 and 10 00,
   (c) 14 45 and 17 15,
   (d) 02 10 and 06 10?
9. Two numbers m and z are such that z is greater than 10 and m is less than 8. Arrange the numbers 9, z and m in order of size, starting with the smallest.
10. Draw the next member of the sequence

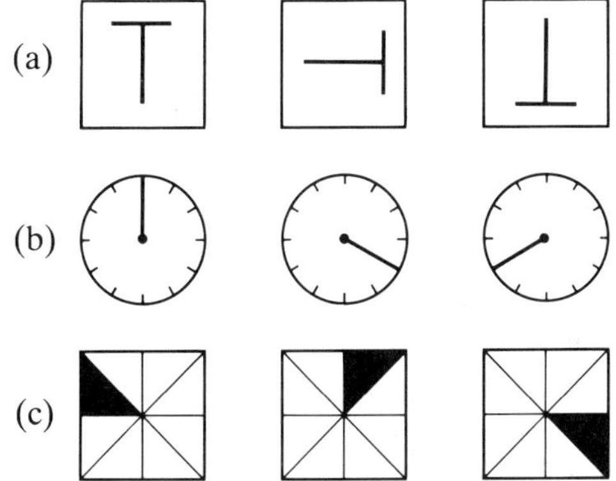

Exercise 12

1. A greengrocer sells 9 kg of potatoes for £2.79.
   Find: (a) the cost of 1 kg,
   (b) how many kg can be bought for £1.86.
2. Arrange the following numbers in order, smallest first:
   2061, 2601, 2106, 2616, 2016.
3. It costs 10p per minute to operate a machine. How much will it cost to operate the machine from 11 50 to 13 15?
4. A garden 9 m by 12 m is to be treated with fertilizer. One cup of fertilizer covers an area of 2 m^2 and one bag of fertilizer is sufficient for 18 cups.
   (a) Find the area of the garden.
   (b) Find the number of bags of fertilizer needed.
5. Copy and complete the pattern below.

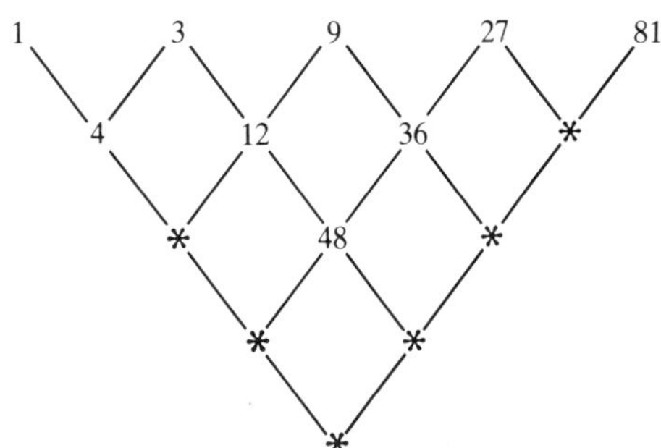

6. A man is 35 cm taller than his daughter, who is 5 cm shorter than her mother. The man was born in 1949 and is 1.80 m tall. How tall is the wife?
7. A car travels from 10 25 to 10 55 at a speed of 84 km/h. How far does it go?
8. During a sale all prices are reduced by 10%. What is the sale price of an article with a marked price of
   (a) £15 (b) £24 (c) £12.50?
9. An examination is marked out of a total of 120 marks. How many marks did Alan get if he scored 65% of the marks?
10. A man gives £3.00 to his two children so that his daughter receives 40p more than his son. How much does the daughter receive?

Exercise 13

1. A man starts work each day at 08 00 and works until 17 30. He stops working for one hour at lunchtime. How many hours does he work in a 5-day week?
2. Place the following numbers in order of size, smallest first:
   0.14, 0.05, 0.062, 0.41, 0.009.
3. The diagram below shows the map of a farm which grows four different crops in the regions shown.

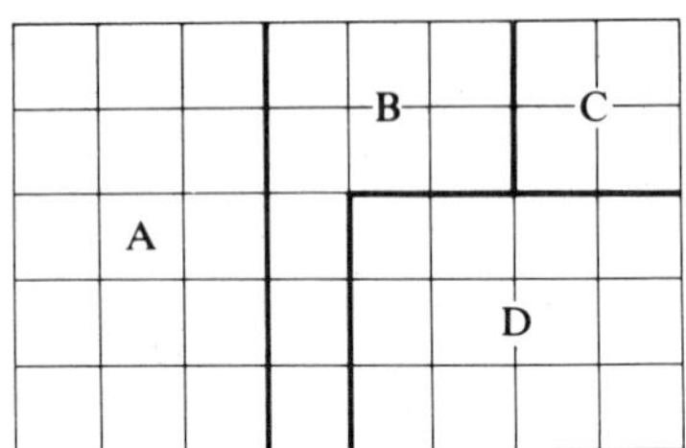

Each square represents one acre.
(a) What is the total area of the farm?
(b) What area is used for crop A?
(c) What percentage of the farm is used for
   (i) crop C (ii) crop D
   (iii) crop A (iv) crop B?
4. One afternoon there are four soccer matches and three rugby matches all being played at the same time. Each soccer team has 11 players and each rugby team has 15 players. How many players are in action altogether?
5. A steel bar of length 2 m is cut into two pieces so that one piece is 8 cm longer than the other. How long is the longer piece?
6. The petrol tank of a car will hold 60 litres, but it contains only 54 litres. To fill it up a bottle full of petrol must be poured in 5 times. Find the capacity of the bottle.
7. A boat journey starts at 08 15. It travels 80.5 km at a speed of 23 km/h. When does the journey finish?
8. An adult and 5 children were charged a total entrance fee of £8. The adult was charged £2 and the children were all charged the same amount. How much was each child charged?
9. A man sells a car at a loss of 30% on the original cost price of £3800. How much does he receive for the car?
10. Write as a single number:
   (a) 4^2 (b) 6^2 (c) 3^3
   (d) 10^4 (e) 3×5^2 (f) 4×10^2

11.4 ORDER OF OPERATIONS

Always perform operations in the following order:
(a) Brackets
(b) Divide and multiply
(c) Add and subtract.

Work out (a) $7 + 6 \div 3$
(b) $8 - 4 \times 2$
(c) $6 \times 4 - 8 \div 2$

(a) $7 + 6 \div 3 = 7 + 2 = 9$
(b) $8 - 4 \times 2 = 8 - 8 = 0$
(c) $6 \times 4 - 8 \div 2 = 24 - 4 = 20$

Exercise 14

Work out

1. $9 + 2 \times 2$
2. $6 + 8 \div 2$
3. $12 - 8 \div 1$
4. $3 \times 5 - 7$
5. $16 \div 4 - 2$
6. $11 - 3 \times 3$
7. $4 + 7 \times 3$
8. $4 \times 5 - 3$
9. $8 + 12 \div 6$
10. $3 + 7 \times 4$
11. $17 - 9 \div 9$
12. $23 + 10 \div 5$
13. $30 + 16 \div 8$
14. $5 \times 6 - 14$
15. $6 \times 3 + 4$
16. $12 \div 2 + 8$
17. $15 - 8 \div 1$
18. $9 - 2 \times 4$
19. $5 + 4 \div 8$
20. $6 \times 7 + 4$
21. $15 \div 3 + 25$
22. $26 - 18 \div 3$
23. $16 \times 2 - 20$
24. $14 + 16 \div 8$
25. $8 - 0 \div 3$
26. $9 \times 8 - 61$
27. $11 - 3 \div 3$
28. $51 - 6 \times 7$
29. $8 \div 1 - 6$
30. $633 \div 3 + 10$
31. $3 \times 2 + 4 \times 1$
32. $4 \times 8 + 2 \times 3$
33. $2 \times 5 + 3 \times 3$
34. $6 \times 6 - 5 \times 5$
35. $7 \times 2 - 4 \times 0$
36. $7 \times 3 - 0 \times 8$
37. $24 \div 6 + 7 \times 2$
38. $6 \div 6 + 7 \times 7$
39. $8 \times 3 - 9 \div 3$
40. $8 \times 3 - 50 \div 5$

41. $16 \div 8 + 8 \times 4$
42. $10 \div 10 + 13 \times 5$
43. $6 \times 2 - 18 \div 9$
44. $0.1 \div 0.1 + 4 \times 5$
45. $27 \div 3 - 14 \div 2$
46. $28 \div 7 - 15 \div 5$
47. $3 \times 5 + 8 \times 3$
48. $9 \times 2 + 36 \div 6$
49. $36 \div 9 - 8 \div 8$
50. $54 \div 9 - 2 \times 2$

51. $9 - 3 \times 2 + 1$
52. $7 - 20 \div 5 + 6$
53. $10 + 4 \times 3 - 8$
54. $8 + 6 \times 6 - 40$
55. $7 - 8 \div 2 - 1$
56. $30 \div 2 - 3 \times 4$
57. $4 + 6 \times 1 - 10$
58. $22 - 3 \times 7 - 1$
59. $3 + 12 \div 2 + 3$
60. $11 + 8 \div 2 - 5$
61. $6 \times 3 + 4 \div 4$
62. $42 \div 7 - 8 \times 0$
63. $8 \times 2 - 2 \times 5$
64. $3 + 5 \times 5 - 20$
65. $10 \div 2 - 3 \div 1$
66. $7 \times 7 + 2 \times 2$
67. $6 + 4 \times 4 - 7$
68. $607 \times 1 - 7 \div 3.5$
69. $7 + 16 \div 8 - 9$
70. $30 - 6 \times 4 + 3$
71. $18 \div 2 + 8 \times 8$
72. $13 - 84 \div 7 + 7$
73. $8 + 200 \div 4 - 41$
74. $600 \div 10 - 8 \times 7$
75. $500 - 7 \times 70 + 3$
76. $8 + 1.7 \times 0 - 7$
77. $55 - 600 \div 12 + 5$
78. $6 + 2 \div 0.5 + 1$
79. $6 \times 5 - 72 \div 8$
80. $8 - 20 \times 0.1 - 2$

Work out (a) $5 + (28 + 5) \div 3$
(b) $7 + (9 - 5) \times 4 - (9 + 5) \div 7$

(a) $5 + (28 + 5) \div 3 = 5 + 33 \div 3$
$= 5 + 11$
$= 16$

(b) $7 + (9 - 5) \times 4 - (9 + 5) \div 7$
$= 7 + 4 \times 4 - 14 \div 7$
$= 7 + 16 - 2$
$= 21$

Exercise 15

Work out

1. $7 + (9 - 5) \times 3$
2. $16 - (6 + 1) \times 2$
3. $8 + (8 + 3) \times 2$
4. $(18 - 7) \times 3 + 10$
5. $(12 + 2) \div 2 - 5$
6. $8 - 12 \div (9 - 6)$
7. $4 + 2 \times (10 - 5)$
8. $(12 \div 3) \times 5 - 19$
9. $20 - (11 - 7) \times 4$
10. $14 - (3 + 4) \times 2$

11. $12 + (17 - 13) \times 5$
12. $5 + (7 + 3) \times 3$
13. $7 \times (26 - 21) - 14$
14. $5 \times (5 + 2) - 15$
15. $20 \div (7 - 3) + 26$
16. $19 - (18 + 6) \div 3$
17. $6 + 7 \times (10 - 3)$
18. $26 + (17 + 7) \div 12$
19. $45 - 9 \times (11 - 6)$
20. $(33 - 29) \times 7 + 5$
21. $(3 + 4) \times 6 - 10$
22. $80 - (8 + 5) \div 13$
23. $14 - (27 - 12) \div 5$
24. $9 + 40 \div (12 - 4)$
25. $(36 + 14) \div 10 + 16$
26. $20 + 7 \times (15 - 6)$
27. $7 + (50 - 43) \times 7$
28. $45 \div (20 - 11) - 2$
29. $48 \div (19 - 7) + 5$
30. $(31 - 21) \times 10 - 65$
31. $60 - (2 \div 2) \times 10$
32. $17 + 4 \times (20 - 20)$
33. $10 + 7 \times (9 - 7)$
34. $8 + (11 - 4) \times 2$
35. $(11 - 8) \times 7 + 11$
36. $34 - 10 \times (9 - 7)$
37. $5 \times (4 + 5) - 15$
38. $18 - 2 \times (24 \div 12)$
39. $3 + 3 \times (8 - 2)$
40. $7 - (13 + 11) \div 4$

41. $(6 - 3) \times 4 - (10 + 4) \div 7$
42. $(12 - 7) \times 2 - (6 + 5) \times 0$
43. $3 \times (8 - 5) + (15 - 9) \div 8$
44. $(8 \div 4) \times 3 + (9 - 8) \times 2$
45. $(38 - 6 \times 6) + (12 + 4 \times 2)$
46. $(17 - 5 \times 3) - (8 - 8 \div 1)$
47. $(5 \times 4 - 15) + (3 + 5 \times 3)$
48. $(7 + 2 \times 2) - (9 - 3 \times 2)$
49. $(9 + 7) \div 4 + 3 \times (11 - 8)$
50. $16 - 2 \times (8 \div 1) + (8 + 4) \div 6$
51. $(20 - 5 \times 3) \times 2 - 4 \div 4$
52. $(8 + 3 \times 1) \div 11 - (3 - 2 \times 1)$
53. $12 - (7 + 9) \div 4 + 3$
54. $28 - [(3 + 7) \div 2] \times 2$
55. $16 + 2 \times [(3 - 2) \times 2 + 1]$
56. $8 + [2 + 3 \times (8 - 5)]$
57. $[(10 - 7) \times 3] \times 3 - 7$
58. $(50 - 9 \times 5) \times 2 + 40 \div 8$
59. $[(2 - 2) \times 11 + 4] \times 3$
60. $[(14 - (8 - 6) \times 2)] \times 4 - 1$

61. $\dfrac{(15 + 24)}{(9 - 6)}$
62. $\dfrac{(36 - 11)}{(14 - 9)}$
63. $\dfrac{(30 - 3 \times 2)}{(4 + 2 \times 1)}$
64. $\dfrac{(12 + 4 \times 2)}{(15 - 7 \times 2)}$
65. $\dfrac{(6 + 9 \times 8)}{(5 - 8 \div 4)}$
66. $\dfrac{(62 - 4 \times 3)}{(4 + 3 \times 2)}$

Exercise 16

This exercise is more difficult. Write down each question and find the missing signs. (+, −, ×, ÷). There are no brackets.

1. 7 5 4 = 27
2. 3 5 10 = 25
3. 4 2 3 = 5
4. 11 3 3 = 20
5. 31 10 2 = 11
6. 10 6 5 = 40
7. 4 8 7 = 25
8. 12 9 2 = 30
9. 18 4 4 = 2
10. 28 10 2 = 8
11. 21 3 5 = 2
12. 7 3 3 = 16
13. 10 2 3 = 8
14. 10 3 12 = 42
15. 18 3 7 = 13
16. 31 40 5 = 39
17. 15 16 4 = 11
18. 15 8 9 = 87
19. 37 35 5 = 44
20. 11 5 9 = 64
21. 8 3 2 4 = 10
22. 12 3 3 1 = 4
23. 11 4 1 6 = 9
24. 15 5 2 4 = 11
25. 7 2 3 3 = 5
26. 12 2 3 4 = 22
27. 8 9 6 11 = 6
28. 20 20 9 0 = 1
29. 20 30 10 8 = 25
30. 30 6 11 11 = 85

11.5 PERCENTAGE INCREASE AND DECREASE

Percentage increase = $\frac{\text{(actual increase)}}{\text{(original value)}} \times \frac{100}{1}$

The price of a car is increased from £6400 to £6800

$$\text{Percentage increase} = \frac{400}{6400} \times \frac{100}{1}$$
$$= 6\tfrac{1}{4}\%$$

Exercise 17

In questions **1** to **15** calculate the percentage increase.

	Original price	Final price
1.	£50	£54
2.	£80	£88
3.	£180	£225
4.	£100	£102
5.	£75	£78
6.	£400	£410
7.	£5000	£6000
8.	£210	£315
9.	£600	£690
10.	$4000	$7200

	Original price	Final price
11.	$2.50	$3.00
12.	$18	$24
13.	$400	$450
14.	£3.20	£3.52
15.	£5.80	£6.09

In questions **16** to **25** calculate the percentage decrease.

	Original price	Final price
16.	£800	£600
17.	£50	£40
18.	£120	£105
19.	£420	£280
20.	£6000	£1200
21.	$880	$836
22.	$15 000	$14 100
23.	$7.50	$6.00
24.	£8.20	£7.79
25.	£16 000	£15 600

Exercise 18

Find the percentage profit/loss using the formula:

$$\text{percentage profit} = \frac{(\text{actual profit})}{(\text{cost price})} \times \frac{100}{1}$$

Give the answers correct to one decimal place.

	Cost price	Selling price
1.	£11	£15
2.	£21	£25
3.	£36	£43
4.	£41	£50
5.	£411	£461
6.	£5.32	£5.82
7.	£6.14	£7.00
8.	£2.13	£2.50
9.	£6.11	£8.11
10.	£18.15	£20
11.	£20	£18.47
12.	£17	£11
13.	£13	£9
14.	£211	£200
15.	£8.15	£7
16.	£2.62	£3
17.	£1.52	£1.81
18.	\$13.50	\$13.98
19.	\$3.05	\$4.00
20.	\$1705	\$1816

Exercise 19

1. The number of people employed by a firm increased from 250 to 280. Calculate the percentage increase in the workforce.

2. During the first four weeks of her life a baby's weight increases from 3000 g to 3870 g. Calculate the percentage increase in the baby's weight.

3. Before cooking, a joint of meat weighs 2.5 kg. After cooking the same joint of meat weighs only 2.1 kg. Calculate the percentage decrease in the weight of the joint.

4. When cold, an iron rod is 200 cm long. After being heated, the length increases to 200.5 cm. Calculate the percentage increase in the length of the rod.

5. A man buys a car for £4000 and sells it for £4600. Calculate the percentage profit.

6. A shopkeeper buys jumpers for £6.20 and sells them for £9.99. Calculate the percentage profit correct to one decimal place.

7. A grocer buys bananas at 20p per pound but after the fruit are spoiled he has to sell them at only 17p per pound. Calculate the percentage loss.

8. Before a service the petrol consumption of a car was 31 miles per gallon. After the service the consumption improved to 35.4 miles per gallon. Calculate the percentage improvement in the petrol consumption, correct to one decimal place.

9. After an outbreak of smallpox, the population of a town went down from 22 315 to 21 987. Calculate the percentage reduction, correct to one decimal place.

10. In 1986 a tennis player earned £2 410 200. In 1987 the same player earned £2 985 010. Calculate the percentage increase in his income, correct to one decimal place.

Exercise 20

This exercise is more difficult.

1. A shopkeeper bought 40 articles for £10 and sold them at 32p each. Calculate
- (a) the cost price of each article.
- (b) the total selling price of the 40 articles.
- (c) the total profit.
- (d) the percentage profit.

2. A grocer bought a crate of 50 tins of peaches at 20p per tin.
- (a) Find the total cost of the crate of peaches.
- (b) He sold all the tins at 27p per tin.
  - (i) How much profit did he make?
  - (ii) Express this profit as a percentage of his total cost price.

3. A shopkeeper bought a crate of 40 tins of pears at 25p per tin.
(a) Find the total cost of the crate of pears.
(b) He sold 10 tins at 37p per tin, and the rest of the crate at 35p per tin.
(i) How much profit did he make?
(ii) Express this profit as a percentage of his total cost price.

4. (a) A shopkeeper buys a number of chairs for £12 each and marks them for sale at £15 each. What percentage profit does he make on the cost price if he sells one chair?
(b) To encourage business he offers 10% off all orders for 6 or more chairs.
(i) How much does he receive for an order of 10 chairs?
(ii) What percentage profit does he make on the cost price when he allows the discount?

5. ABCD is a square of side 100 cm. Side AB is increased by 20% and side AD is reduced by 25% to form rectangle APQR.

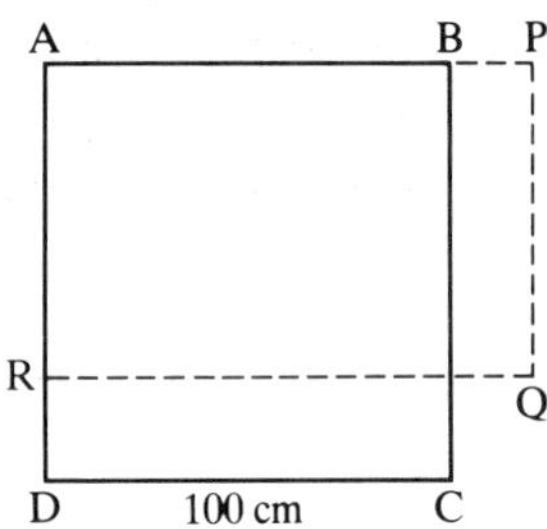

(a) Calculate (i) the length of AP
(ii) the length of AR
(iii) the area of square ABCD
(iv) the area of rectangle APQR.
(b) By what percentage has the area of the square been reduced?

6. ABCD is a square of side 50 cm. Side AB is increased by 16% and side AD is reduced by 40% to form rectangle AKLM.

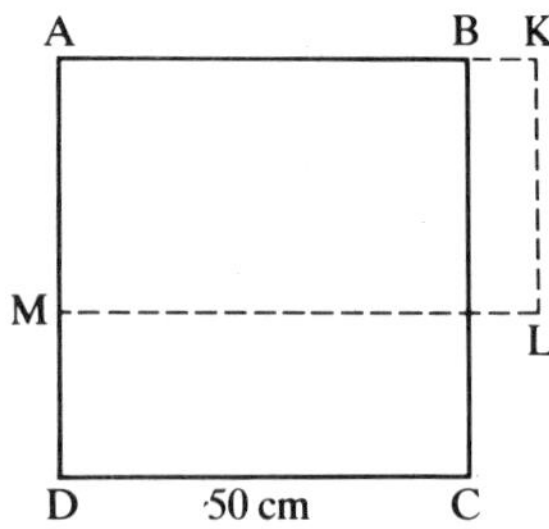

(a) Calculate (i) the length of AK
(ii) the length of AM.
(iii) the area of square ABCD
(iv) the area of rectangle AKLM
(b) By what percentage has the area of the square ABCD been reduced?

7. A jacket costs £60 to make and the shopkeeper adds 25% to give the 'marked price'. During a sale all goods in the shop are labelled 'Sale price 10% off marked price'.
(a) What was the marked price before the sale?
(b) How much did a customer pay for the suit during the sale?
(c) What percentage profit did the shopkeeper make on a suit which was sold in the sale?

8. When a house was built in 1986 the total cost was made up of the following:

wages	£30 000
materials	£16 000
overheads	£4 000

(a) Find the total cost of the house in 1986.
(b) In 1987 the cost of wages increased by 10%, the cost of materials increased by 5% and the overheads remained at their previous cost.
(i) Find the total cost of the house in 1987.
(ii) Calculate the percentage increase in 1986 to 1987.

11.6 TIMETABLES

BBC 2

9.0 **PAGES FROM CEEFAX.**
10.20 **OPEN UNIVERSITY.**
11.25 **PAGES FROM CEEFAX.**
11.50 **CHAMPION THE WONDER HORSE*:** Lost River (rpt.). A drought brings danger.
12.15 **WINDMILL:** Archive film on animals.
1.10 **STATES OF MIND:** Jonathan Miller talks to Professor Richard Gregory (rpt.).
2.0 **RUGBY SPECIAL:** Highlights of a County Championship match and a Welsh Cup match.
2.30 **TENNIS:** Benson and Hedges Final.
4.15 **UNDER SAIL:** New series.
4.35 **RACHMANINOV MASTERCLASS.**
5.20 **THINKING ALOUD:** Denis Healey joins a discussion on espionage.
6.0 **NEWS REVIEW**, with Moira Stewart.
6.30 **THE MONEY PROGRAMME:** Guns for Sale. A look at Britain's defence industry.
7.15 **THE NATURAL WORLD:** City of Coral. A voyage beneath the Caribbean.
8.5 **COMRADES:** Educating Rita. The first of 12 films about life in the Soviet Union profiles a young trainee teacher.
8.50 **100 GREAT SPORTING MOMENTS:** Daley Thompson's Gold in the Moscow Olympics.
9.10 **FAWLTY TOWERS:** Basil and Sybil fall out over alterations to the hotel (rpt.).
9.40 **FILM:** A Dangerous Summer (see Film Guide).
11.5 **TENNIS:** Benson and Hedges Final.
11.55 **MUSIC AT NIGHT. 12.10 CLOSE.**

CHANNEL 4

1.5 **IRISH ANGLE — HANDS:** Basket Maker.
1.30 **FACE THE PRESS:** Graham Kelly, Secretary of the Football League, questioned by Ian Wooldridge of the Daily Mail and Brian Glanville of the Sunday Times.
2.0 **POB'S PROGRAMME**, with Patricia Hodge.
2.30 **FILM*:** Journey Together (see Film Guide).
4.15 **FILM*:** The London Blackout Murders, with John Abbot (see Film Guide).
5.15 **NEWS; WEATHER**, followed by **THE BUSINESS PROGRAMME.**
6.0 **AMERICAN FOOTBALL:** Dallas Cowboys at Washington Redskins.
7.15 **THE HEART OF THE DRAGON:** Understanding (rpt.).
8.15 **THE JEWEL IN THE CROWN (T):** The Towers of Silence (rpt.).
9.15 **THE WRITING ON THE WALL:** Who Governs? The political events of 1974 recalled by Robert Kee.
10.25 **FILM*:** Seven Days to Noon (see Film Guide). **12.10 CLOSE.**

Exercise 21

1. For how many minutes do each of the following programmes last:
   (a) 'The money programme',
   (b) 'Fawlty Towers',
   (c) 'Face the press',
   (d) '100 great sporting moments'?
2. How much of a video tape would be used if 'The Jewel in the Crown' and 'The writing on the wall' were recorded?
3. At what time does 'Comrades' start on the 24-hour clock?
4. There were four films on the two channels. What was the title of the shortest film?
5. A video tape is 3 hours long. How much of the tape is not used after taping the two films in the afternoon on Channel 4?
6. How much time is devoted to sport on BBC 2? [Include 'Under sail'].
7. For how many hours and minutes does Channel 4 broadcast programmes?
8. What is the starting time on the 24-hour clock of the programme in which 'Basil' appears?
9. How many programmes were repeats?
10. For how long are 'Pages from Ceefax' broadcast?
11. What is the starting time on the 24-hour clock of the programme in which the 'Redskins' appear?
12. How much of a two hour video tape is not used after taping 'Windmill' and 'The Natural World'?
13. For how many hours and minutes does BBC 2 broadcast programmes?

Exercise 22

London to Harrow, Watford, Chesham, Amersham and Aylesbury

		⇌						⇌						⇌	
Marylebone	...	1910	...	...	...	...	...	2010	...	...	...	...	...	2110	...
Baker Street	1850	|	1905	1920	1933	1935	1950	|	2005	2020	2033	2035	2050	|	2105
Finchley Road	1856	|	1911	1926	1939	1941	1956	|	2011	2026	2039	2041	2056	|	2111
Wembley Park	1902	|	1917	1932	|	1947	2002	|	2017	2032	|	2047	2102	|	2117
Preston Road	1904	|	1919	1934	|	1949	2004	|	2019	2034	|	2049	2104	|	2119
Northwick Park	1907	↓	1922	1937	↓	1952	2007	↓	2022	2037	↓	2052	2107	↓	2122
Harrow-on-the-Hill	1909	1922	1924	1939	1949	1954	2009	2022	2024	2039	2049	2054	2109	2122	2124
North Harrow	1912	|	1927	1942	|	1957	2012	|	2027	2042	|	2057	2112	|	2127
Pinner	1914	|	1929	1944	|	1959	2014	|	2029	2044	|	2059	2114	|	2129
Northwood Hills	1917	|	1932	1947	|	2002	2017	|	2032	2047	|	2102	2117	|	2132
Northwood	1920	↓	1935	1950	↓	2005	2020	↓	2035	2050	↓	2105	2120	↓	2135
Moor Park	1923	1930	1938	1953	1957	2008	2023	2030	2038	2053	2057	2108	2123	2130	2138
Croxley	1927	|	1942	1957	|	2012	2027	|	2042	2057	|	2112	2127	|	2142
Watford	1933	↓	1947	2003	↓	2017	2033	↓	2047	2103	↓	2117	2133	↓	2147
Rickmansworth	—	1934	—	—	2001	—	—	2034	—	—	2101	—	—	2134	—
Chorleywood	...	1938	...	...	2005	...	...	2038	...	...	2105	...	...	2138	...
Chesham dep	...	*1928c*	...	...	*1958c*	...	...	*2028c*	...	...	*2058c*	...	...	*2128c*	...
Chalfont & Latimer	...	1943	...	...	2009	...	...	2043	...	...	2109	...	...	2143	...
Chesham arr	...	*1954c*	...	...	*2019c*	...	...	*2054c*	...	...	*2119c*	...	...	*2154c*	...
Amersham	...	1948	...	...	2013	...	...	2048	...	...	2113	...	...	2148	...
Great Missenden	...	1955	...	...	—	...	...	2055	...	...	—	...	...	2155	...
Wendover	...	2002	...	...	...	...	...	2102	...	...	...	...	...	2202	...
Stoke Mandeville	...	2006	...	...	...	...	...	2106	...	...	...	...	...	2206	...
Aylesbury	...	2010	...	...	...	...	...	2110	...	...	...	...	...	2210	...

c Change at Chalfont & Latimer (journey time from or to Chesham about 9 minutes)
⇌ British Rail service with First and Second class accommodation

Copy and complete the table below.

	Depart		Arrive	
1.	Baker Street	1920	Harrow-on-the-Hill	*
2.	Baker Street	2033	Moor Park	*
3.	Pinner	1944	Watford	*
4.	Finchley Road	1856	Pinner	*
5.	Wembley Park	2032	Croxley	*
6.	Preston Road	*	Northwood	1920
7.	Baker Street	*	Chalfont & Latimer	2109
8.	Northwick Park	*	Moor Park	2053
9.	Moor Park	*	Amersham	2013
10.	Chorleywood	*	Wendover	2102
11.	Finchley Road	1856	*	1917
12.	Pinner	2014	*	2033
13.	North Harrow	2112	*	2127
14.	Wembley Park	2117	*	2138
15.	Marylebone	2010	*	2110
16.	*	2039	Chorleywood	2105
17.	*	2022	Stoke Mandeville	2106
18.	*	1942	Watford	2003
19.	*	2049	Croxley	2112
20.	*	1910	Wendover	2002

Exercise 23

Refer to the timetable given in the last exercise.

1. How long does it take the 2050 from Baker Street to get to Watford?
2. How long does it take the 1910 from Marylebone to get to Amersham?
3. How long does it take the British Rail train to go from Marylebone to Harrow-on-the-Hill?
4. How long does it take the British Rail train to go from Harrow-on-the-Hill to Moor Park?
5. Jane leaves home at 1920 and it takes her 15 minutes to walk to Harrow-on-the-Hill station. What is the earliest time at which she can arrive at Watford?
6. Mr Ahmed leaves home at 1945 and it takes him 20 minutes to walk to Wembley Park station. What is the earliest time at which he can arrive at Croxley?
7. Mrs Taylor leaves home at 1920 and it takes her 8 minutes to walk to Finchley Road station. What is the earliest time at which she can arrive at Northwood?
8. Mr Jones must arrive in Watford by 2000. What is the departure time of the latest train he can take from Baker Street?
9. Susan must arrive in Aylesbury by 10 p.m. What is the time of the latest train she can take from Marylebone?
10. Mrs Simpson must arrive in Amersham by 8.30 p.m. What is the time of the latest train she can take from Baker Street?
11. It takes David 25 minutes to drive from home to Marylebone station. He must arrive in Aylesbury by 2130. What is the latest time at which he can leave home?
12. Mrs Perrin takes 15 minutes to walk to Baker Street station from home. She must meet her daughter in Amersham at 2030. What is the latest time at which she can leave home?
13. It takes Louise 18 minutes to walk from home to Moor Park station. She must meet her boyfriend in Amersham at 2130. What is the latest time at which she can leave home?
14. Steve can walk from home to Northwick Park station in 21 minutes. He must meet his brother in Watford at 2020. What is the latest time at which he can leave home?

Unit 12

12.1 AREA

Important formulae

Rectangle:
area = $l \times b$

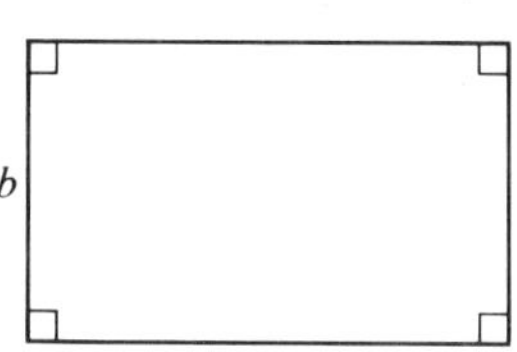

Parallelogram:
area = $b \times h$

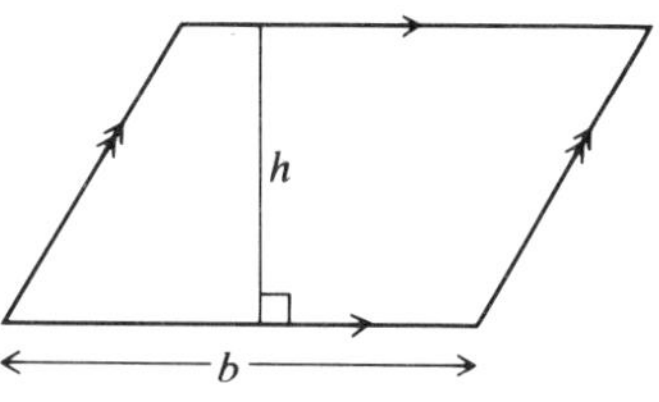

Triangle:

$$\text{area} = \frac{b \times h}{2}$$

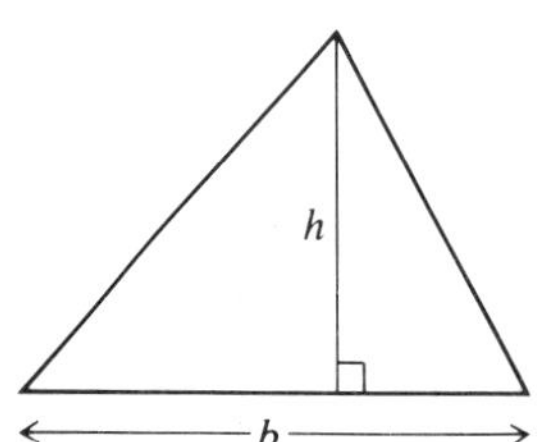

Trapezium:

$$\text{area} = \left(\frac{a + b}{2}\right)h$$

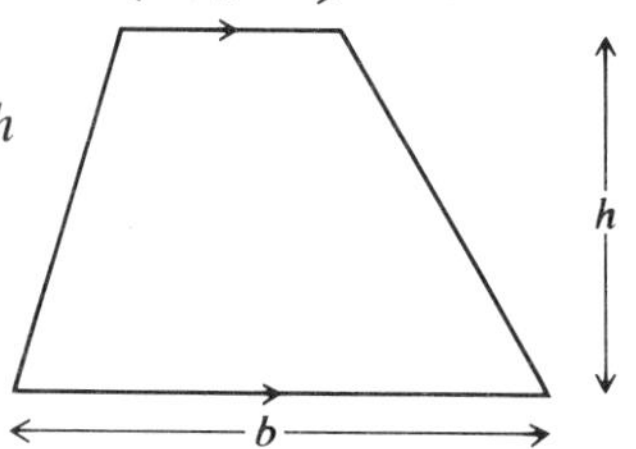

Exercise 1

Draw each shape and find its area.

1.

3·2 cm
10 cm

2.

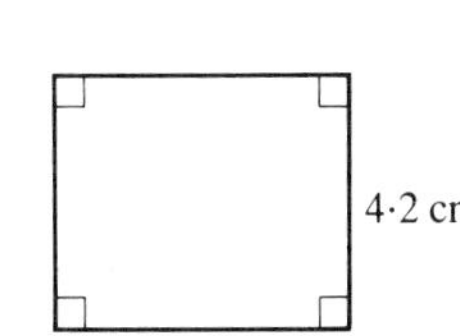

3.

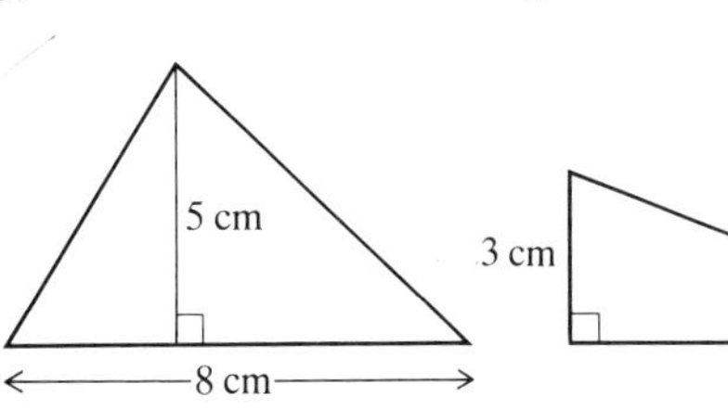

4.

3 cm
9 cm

5.

7 cm
4 cm

6.

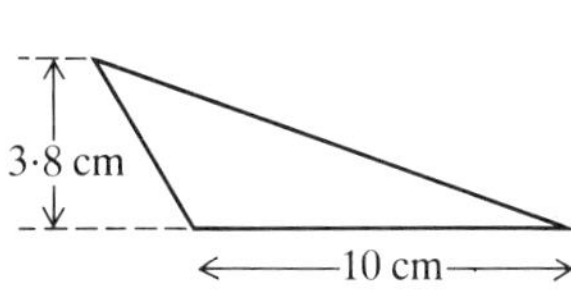

7.

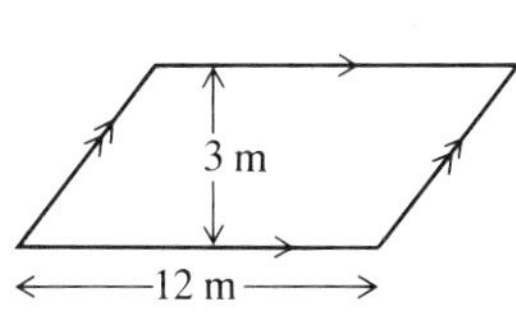

8.

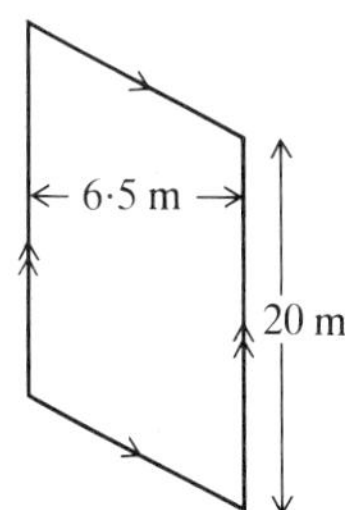

9.

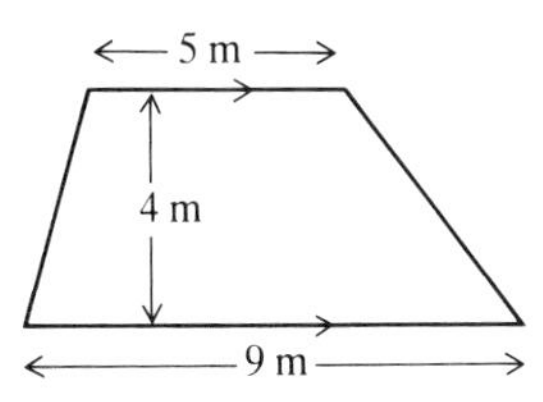

10.

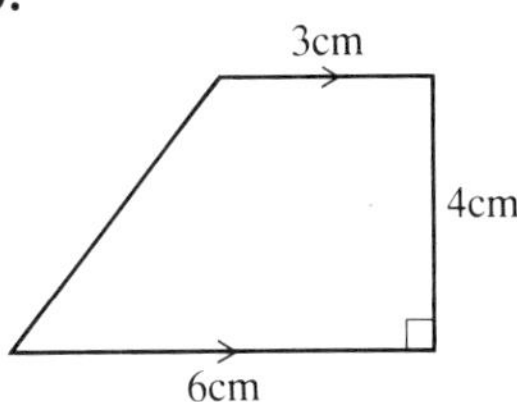

11.

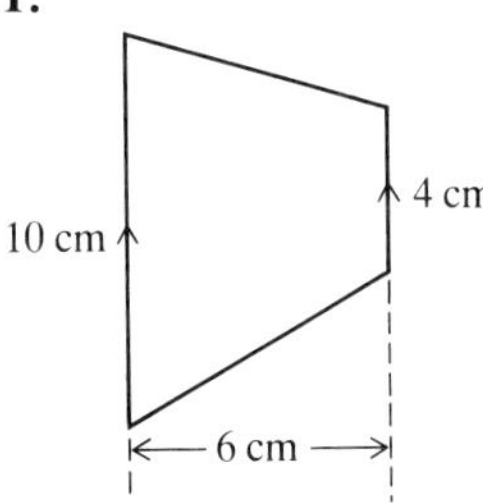

12.

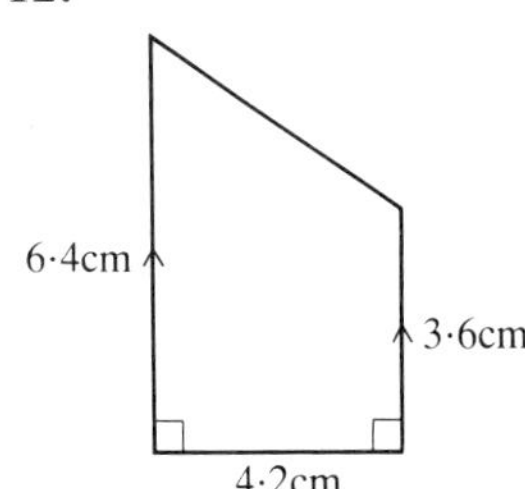

13.

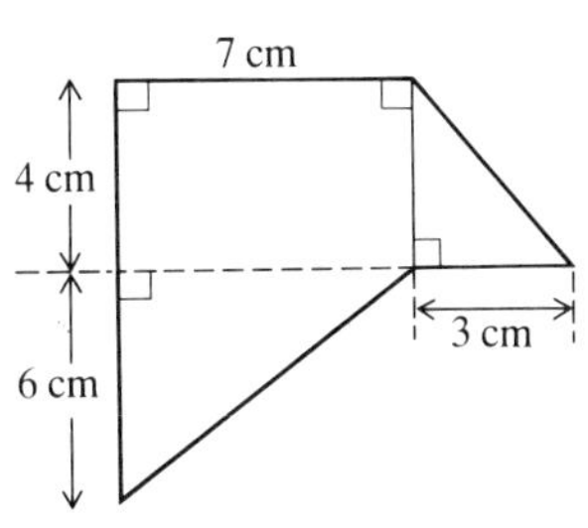

14.

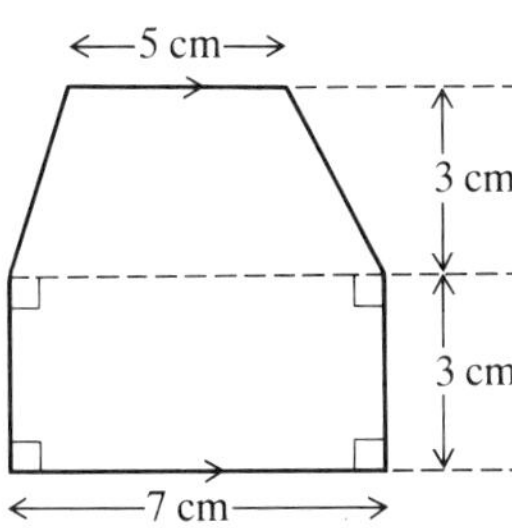

In questions **15** to **18** give the answer in 'square units'.

15.

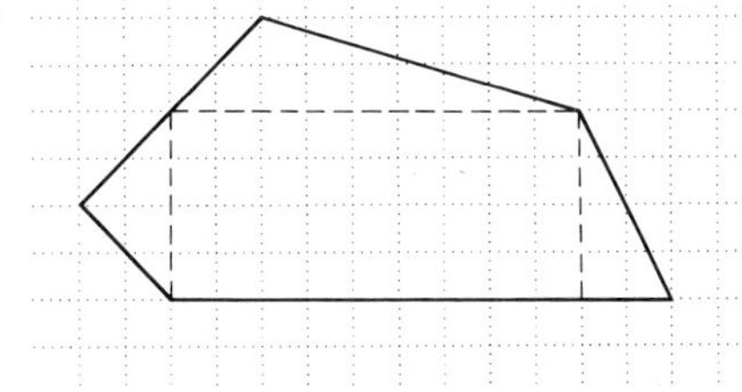

16.

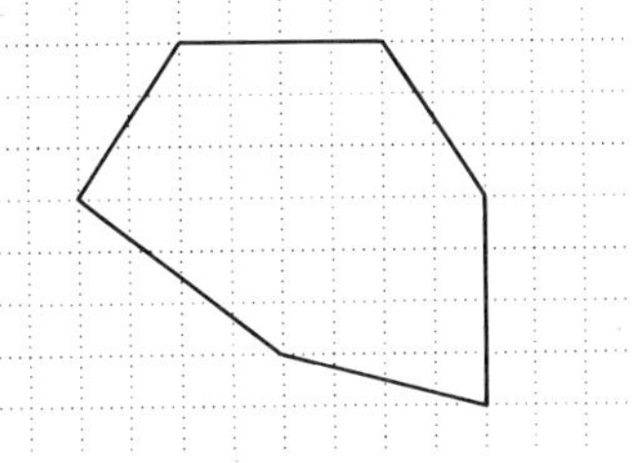

17. Find the shaded area.

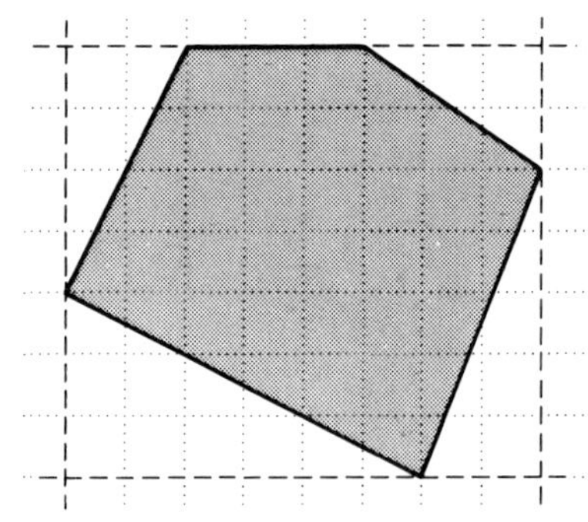

18. Find the shaded area.

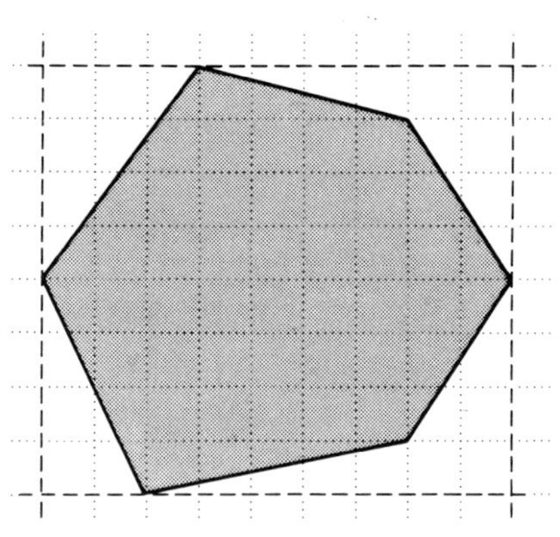

12.2 CIRCLES: CIRCUMFERENCE AND AREA

Find the circumference and area of the circle below.

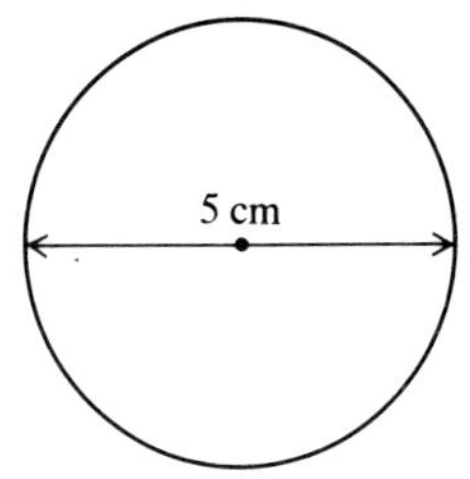

Circumference $= \pi d$
$= \pi \times 5$
$= 15.7$ cm (3 S.F.)

Area $= \pi r^2$
$= \pi \times 2.5^2$
$= 19.6 \text{ cm}^2$ (3 S.F.)

Exercise 2

Use 'π' on a calculator or take $\pi = 3.14$. Give the answers correct to 3 S.F. For each circle find
(a) the circumference
(b) the area.

1.

6 cm

2.

10 cm

3.

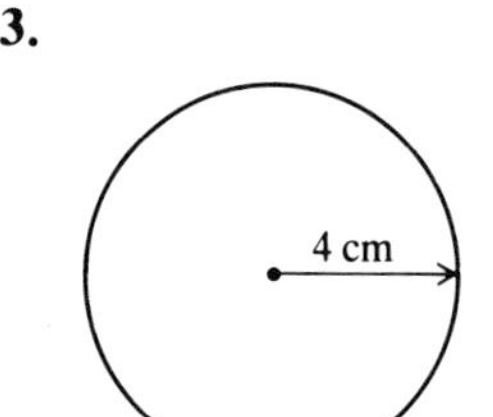

4.

2 cm

5.

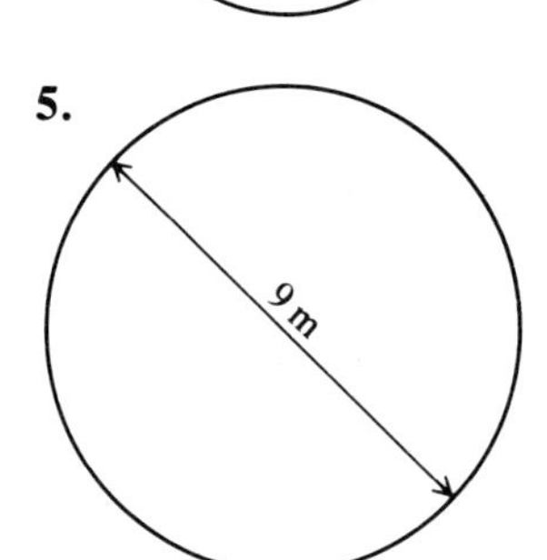

6.

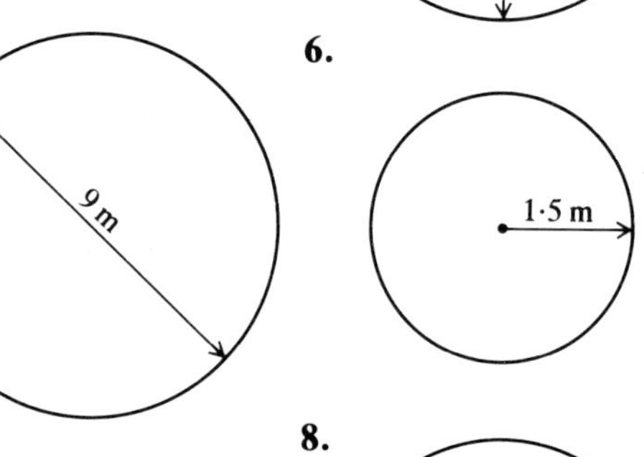

7.

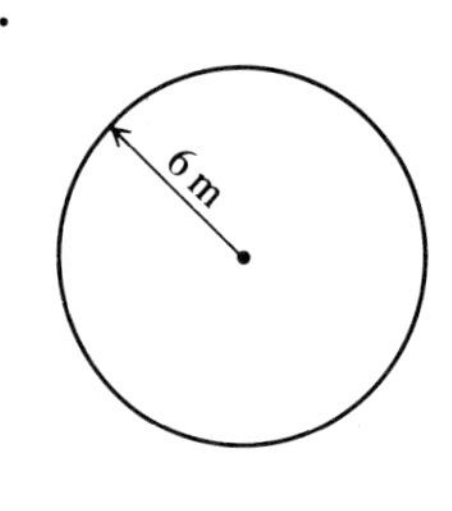

8.

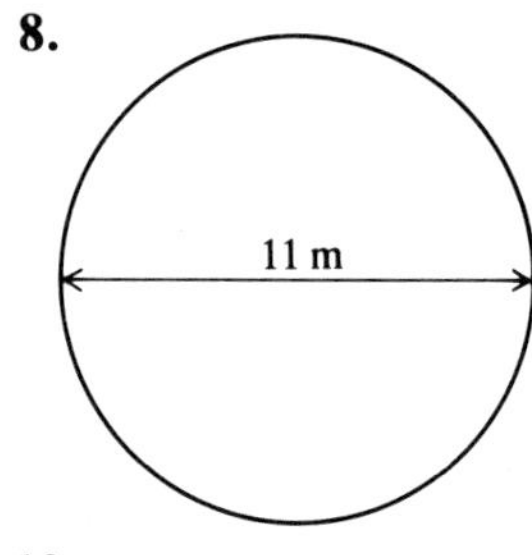

9.

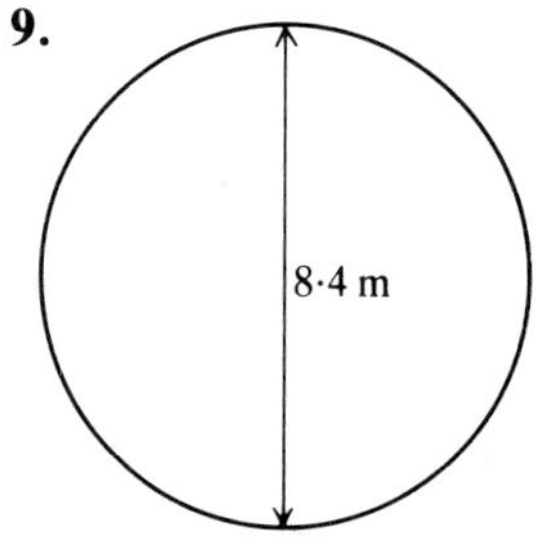

10.

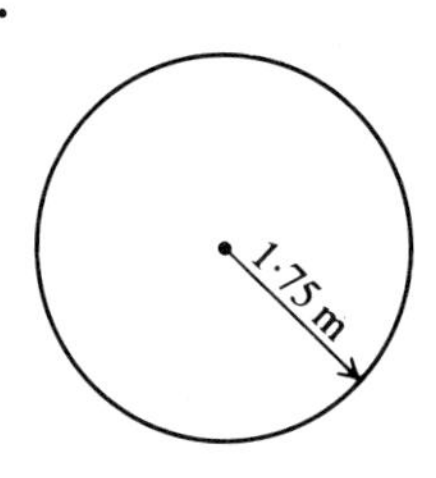

11.

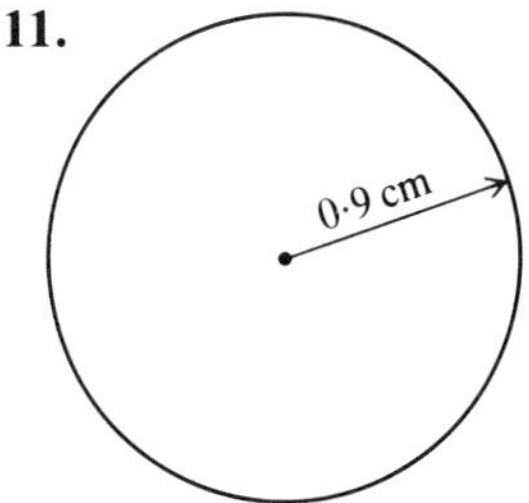

12.

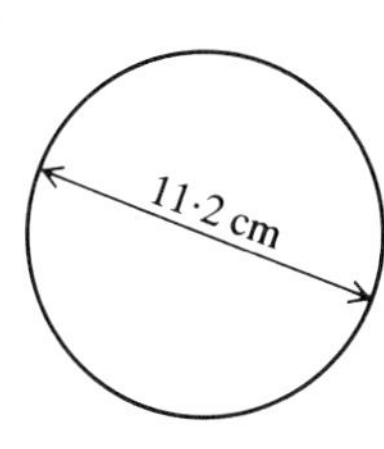

13. Radius = 0.85 cm.
14. Diameter = 7 feet.
15. Diameter = 3.2 km.
16. Radius = 10.1 km.
17. Radius = 0.5 mm.
18. Diameter = $\frac{1}{2}$ mile.
19. Radius = 6.3 km.
20. Diameter = $1\frac{1}{2}$ miles.

More complicated shapes

For the shape below find

(a) the perimeter,
(b) the area.

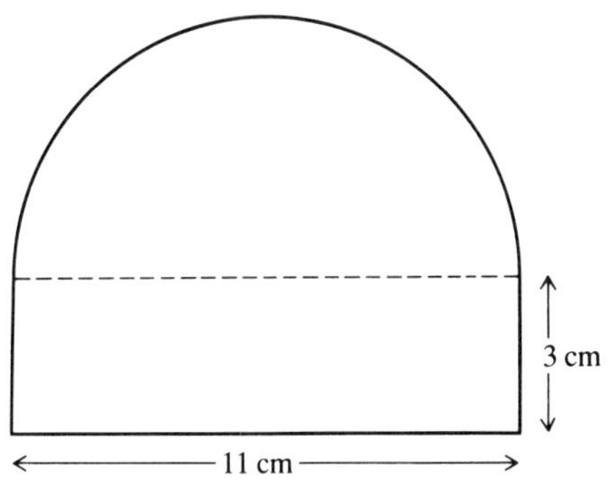

(a) Perimeter $= \left(\frac{\pi \times 11}{2}\right) + 11 + 3 + 3$

$= 34.3$ cm (3 S.F.)

(b) Area $= \left(\frac{\pi \times 5.5^2}{2}\right) + (11 \times 3)$

$= 80.5\ \text{cm}^2$ (3 S.F.)

Exercise 3

Use the 'π' button on a calculator or take $\pi = 3.14$. Give the answers correct to 3 S.F.
For each shape find (a) the perimeter,
(b) the area.

1.

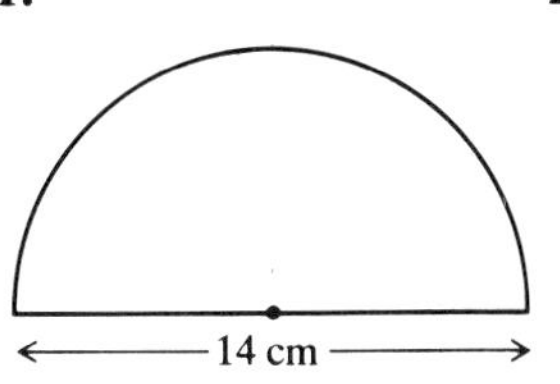

2.

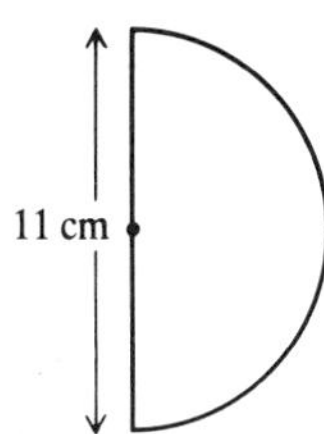

3.

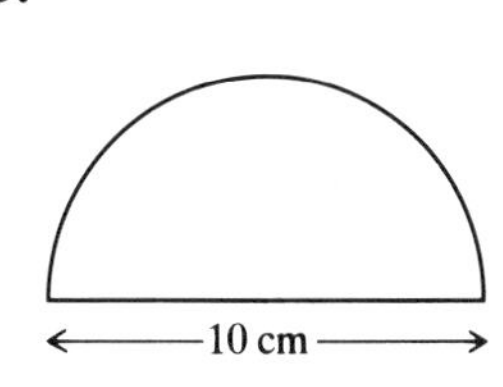

4.

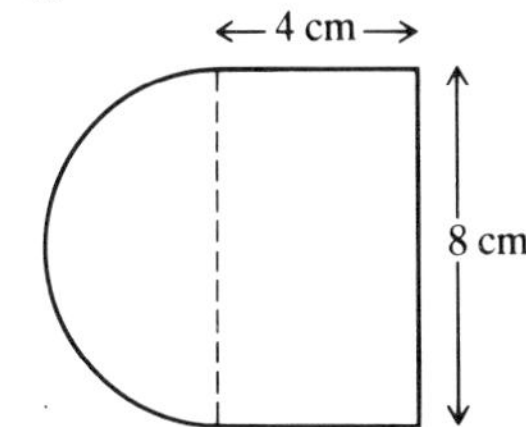

5.

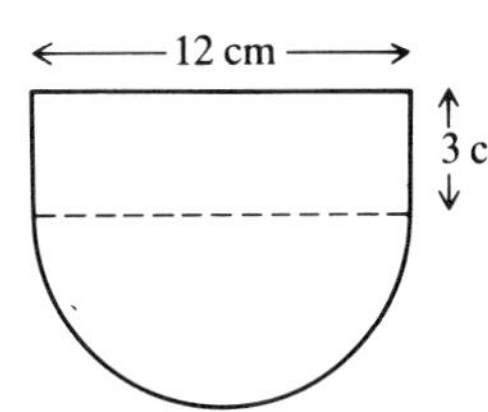

6.

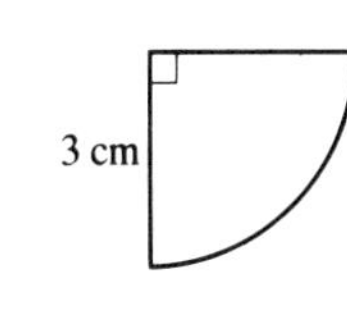

7.

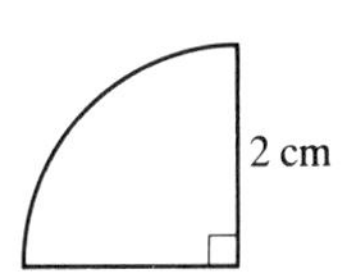

8.

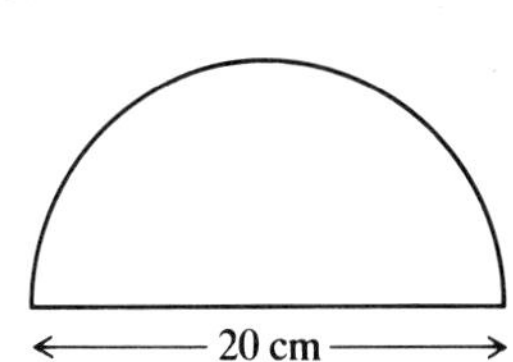

9.

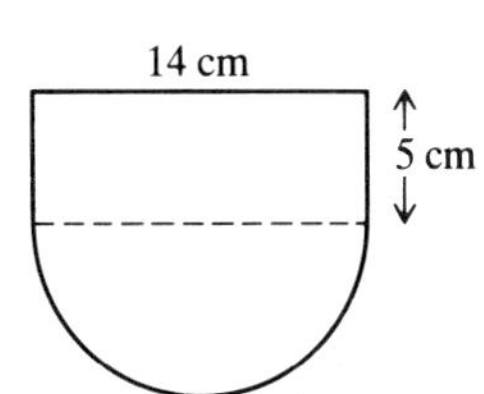

10.

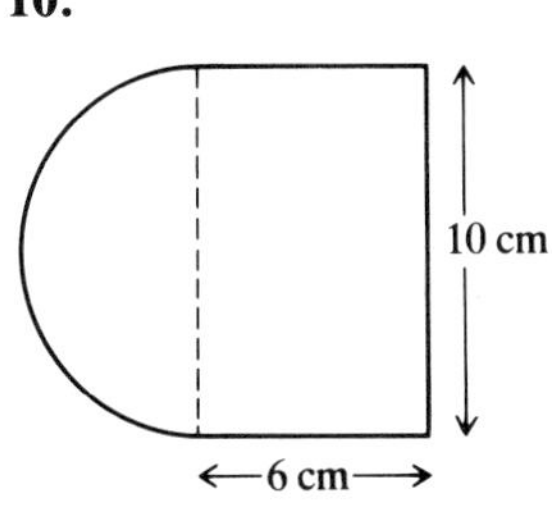

11.

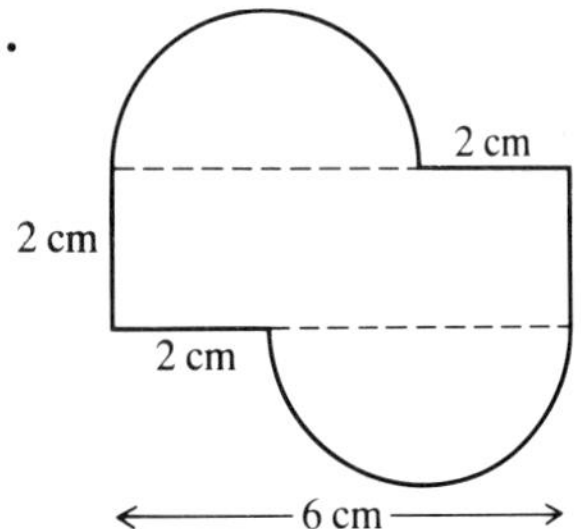

12.

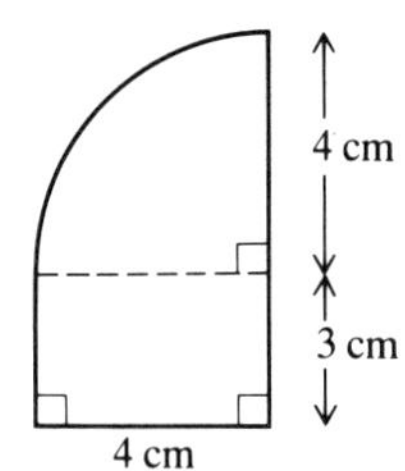

13.

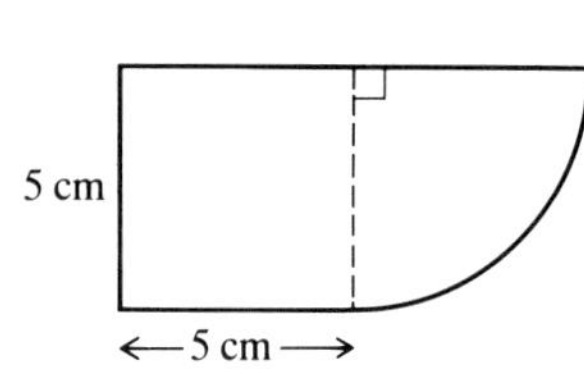

Exercise 4

This exercise is more difficult. Find the area of each shape. If the area is shaded find the shaded area. Give your answers to 3 S.F.

1.

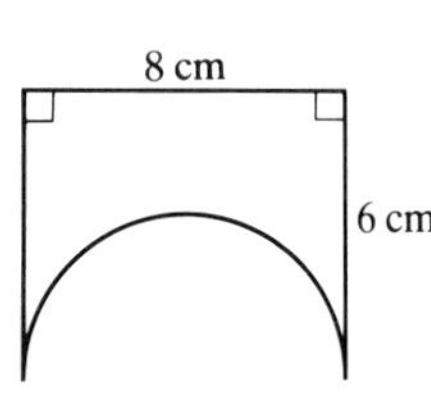

2.

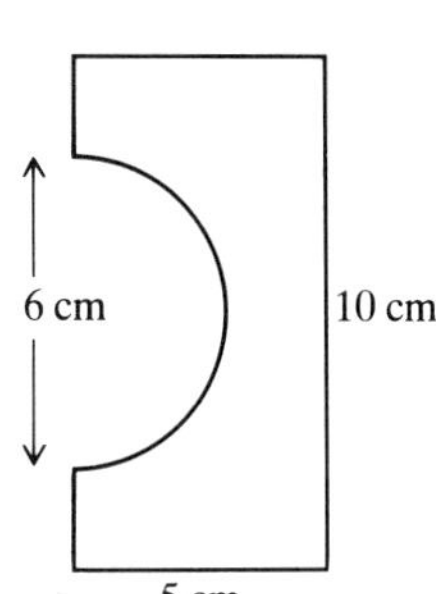

3.

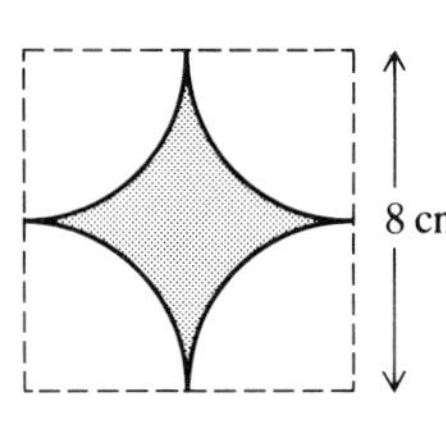

4.

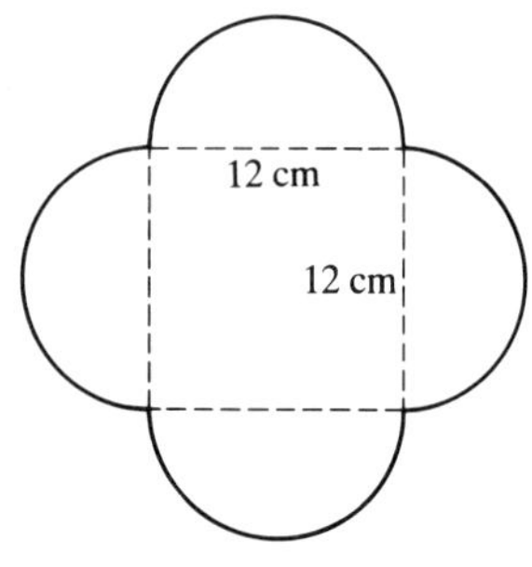

5.

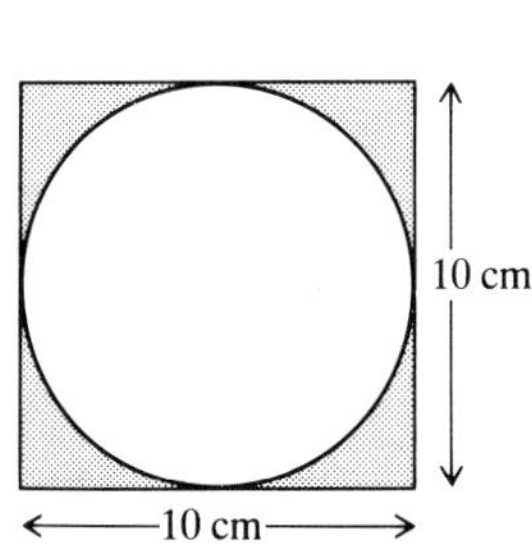

6.

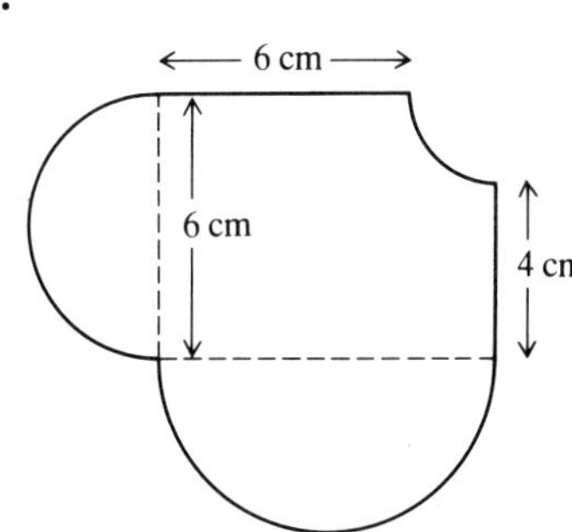

7.

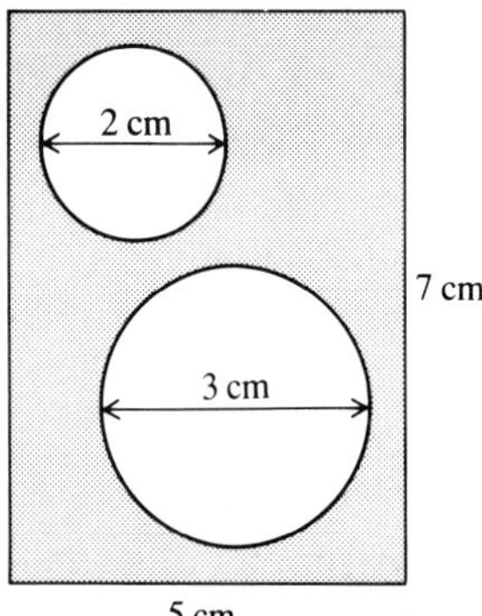

8.

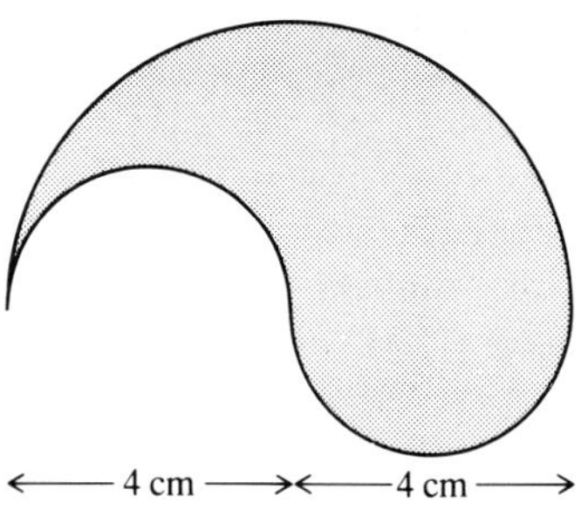

Finding the radius of a circle

(a) The circumference of a circle is 60 cm. Find the radius of the circle.

$$C = \pi d$$

$$\therefore 60 = \pi d$$

$$\therefore \frac{60}{\pi} = d$$

$$\therefore r = \frac{(60/\pi)}{2} = 9.55 \text{ cm (to 3 s.f.)}$$

(b) The area of a circle is 18 m^2. Find the radius of the circle.

$$\pi r^2 = 18$$

$$r^2 = \frac{18}{\pi}$$

$$r = \sqrt{\left(\frac{18}{\pi}\right)} = 2.39 \text{ m (to 3 s.f.)}$$

Exercise 5

In each question, use the information given to calculate the radius of the circle. Use the 'π' button on a calculator or take π = 3.14.

1. The circumference is 15 cm
2. The circumference is 28 m
3. The circumference is 7 m
4. The circumference is 40 cm
5. The area is 54 cm^2
6. The area is 38 cm^2
7. The area is 49 m^2
8. The area is 28 m^2
9. The circumference is 16 m
10. The area is 60 cm^2
11. The circumference is 29 cm
12. The circumference is 35 m
13. The area is 104 cm^2
14. The area is 70 cm^2
15. The circumference is 22 m
16. The circumference is 56 cm
17. The area is 52 m^2
18. The area is 44 cm^2
19. The circumference is 18 m
20. The circumference is 25 cm
21. The area is 30 cm^2
22. The circumference is 30 cm
23. The area is 64 m^2
24. The area is 80 cm^2
25. The circumference is 33 m

Exercise 6

1. The circumference of a circle is 52 m. Find its area.
2. The circumference of a circle is 35 cm. Find its area.
3. The area of a circle is 61 cm^2. Find its circumference.
4. The area of a circle is 29 m^2. Find its circumference.
5. The circumference of a circle is 48 cm. Find its area.
6. The area of a circle is 100 cm^2. Find its circumference.
7. The area of a circle is 86 m^2. Find its circumference.
8. The circumference of a circle is 14 m. Find its area.
9. The area of a circle is 72 m^2. Find its circumference.
10. The circumference of a circle is 25 m. Find its area.
11. The circumference of a circle is 61 cm. Find its area.
12. The area of a circle is 40 cm^2. Find its circumference.
13. The circumference of a circle is 40 cm. Find its area.
14. The area of a circle is 32.5 m^2. Find its circumference.
15. The circumference of a circle is 46.5 cm. Find its area.
16. The circumference of a circle is 12.6 cm. Find its area.

Exercise 7

1. A rectangle has an area of 54 cm^2 and a length of 6 cm. Find its breadth.
2. A rectangle has an area of 60 cm^2 and a length of 8 cm. Find its breadth.
3. Find the area of a rectangle with a perimeter of 26 cm and a side of 8 cm.
4. Find the area of a rectangle with a perimeter of 29 cm and a side of 10 cm.
5. Find the perimeter of a rectangle with an area of 55 cm^2 and a side of 10 cm.
6. Find the perimeter of a square with an area of 144 cm^2.

7. In the diagram below find
   (a) the area of rectangle ABCD,
   (b) the area of triangle DTC.
   [Give answers in square units.]

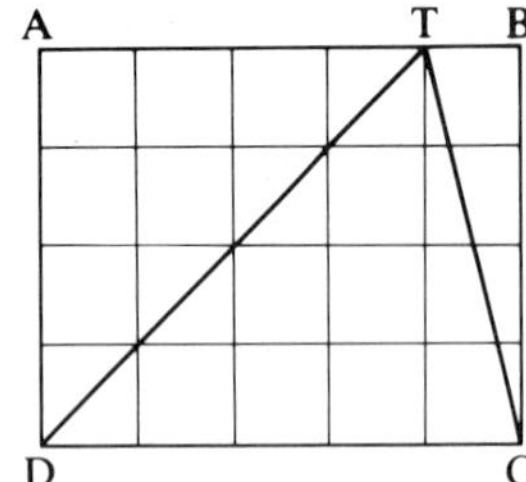

8. Each of the sides of three different rectangles is a whole number of centimetres. Each rectangle has an area of 12 cm^2, but each has a different perimeter. Draw a diagram to show each of the rectangles.

9. The diagram below shows a rectangular wooden door measuring 2 m by 0.9 m in which a rectangular glass window measuring 1.2 m by 0.6 m has been fitted.

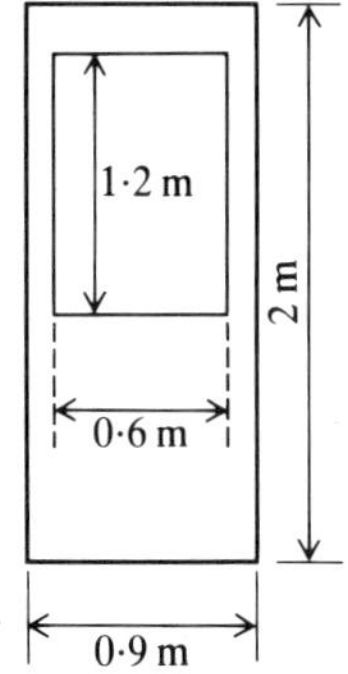

   Find, in square metres,
   (a) the area of glass,
   (b) the area of wood.

10. A running track has two semicircular ends of radius 34 m and two straights of 93.2 m as shown below.

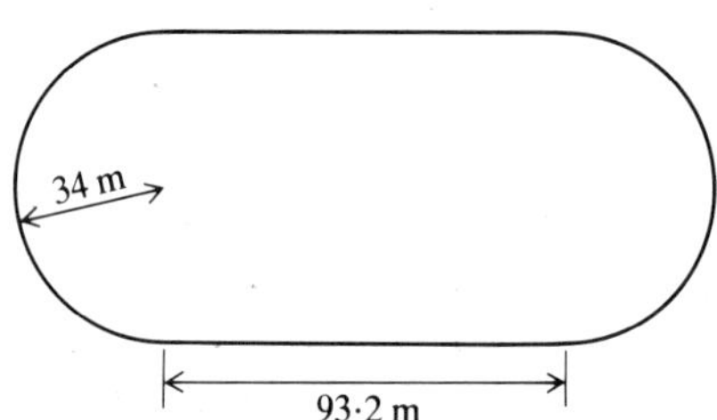

   (a) Calculate the total distance around the track.
   (b) Find the extra distance travelled per lap by a runner who runs 1 m outside the line all the way round.

11. The diagram shows a square ABCD in which DX = XY = YC = AW. The area of the square is 45 cm^2.

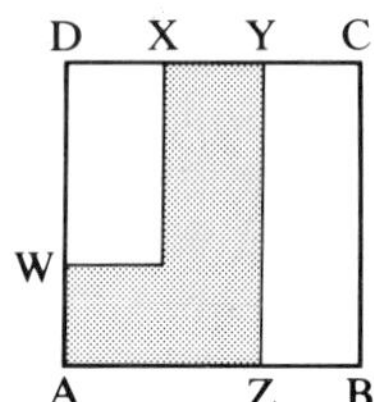

   (a) What is the fraction $\frac{DX}{DC}$?
   (b) What fraction of the square is shaded?
   (c) Find the area of the unshaded part.

12. The diagram below shows a lawn (unshaded) surrounded by a path of uniform width (shaded). The curved end of the lawn is a semi-circle of diameter 10 m.

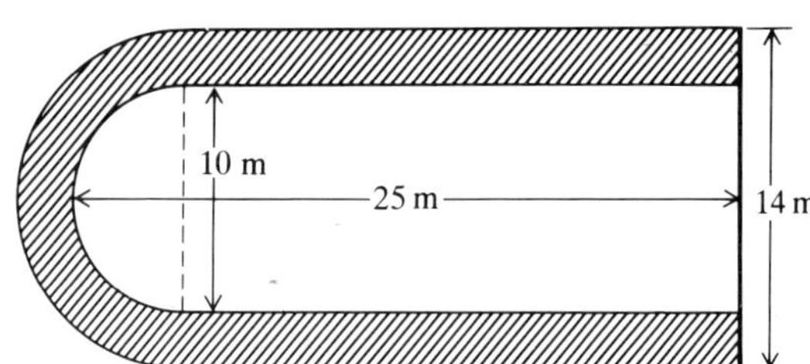

   Calculate:
   (a) the length of the rectangular part of the lawn,
   (b) the area of this rectangular part of the lawn,
   (c) the area of the semi-circular part of the lawn,
   (d) the area of each rectangular part of the path,
   (e) the area of the curved part of the path,
   (f) the total area of the path.

13. Calculate the shaded area below.

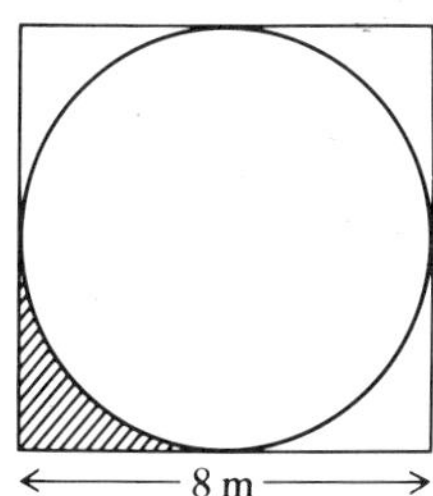

14. How many complete revolutions does a cycle wheel of diameter 60 cm make in travelling 400 m?

15. How many complete revolutions does a car wheel of diameter 70 cm make in travelling 600 m?

16. A sheet of metal measures 60 cm by 20 cm. It is melted down and recast into discs of the same thickness and radius 5 cm. How many complete discs will be cast?

17. A circular duck pond has an area of 65 m^2. Find the radius of the pond.

18. A circular wheel makes 50 complete revolutions in travelling a distance of 100 m. Find the diameter of the wheel.

12.3 VOLUME AND SURFACE AREA

Important formulae

Cuboid : $V = l \times b \times h$
Prism : $V = A \times l$
Cylinder : $V = \pi r^2 h$
Sphere : $V = \frac{4}{3}\pi r^3$
Cone : $V = \frac{1}{3}\pi r^2 h$
Pyramid : $V = \frac{1}{3}$ (base area) $\times$ height.

Exercise 8

1. Find the volume

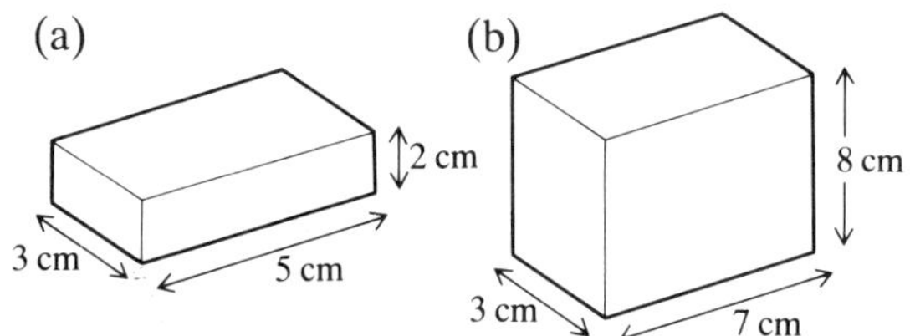

2. Find the length x.

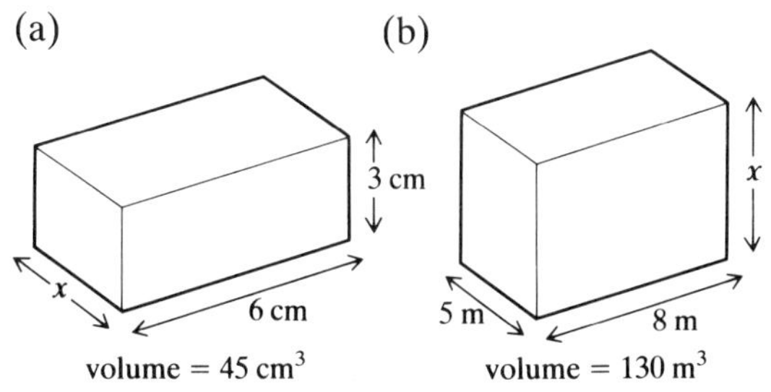

3. Copy and complete the table. All the objects are cuboids.

	length	breadth	height	volume
(a)	3 cm	3 cm	2 cm	
(b)	7 cm	4 cm	$\frac{1}{2}$ cm	
(c)	10 cm	8.5 cm	2 cm	
(d)	6 cm		3 cm	90 cm^3
(e)	8 cm		3 cm	144 cm^3
(f)	5 cm		6 cm	45 cm^3
(g)	7 cm	6 cm		147 cm^3
(h)	9 cm	3 cm		297 cm^3
(i)	8 cm	4 cm		6.4 cm^3
(j)		8 cm	3 cm	54 cm^3
(k)		0.2 cm	0.6 cm	0.012 cm^3
(l)	6 cm	5 cm		72 cm^3
(m)		7 cm	6 cm	357 cm^3
(n)	8 cm		5 cm	284 cm^3

4. A rectangular block of metal has dimensions 20 cm $\times$ 16 cm $\times$ 8 cm. It is melted down and recast into cubes of edge length 4 cm. How many cubes will be cast?

5. A freezer makes ice cubes which are rectangular blocks 5 cm $\times$ 3 cm $\times$ 2 cm. How many ice cubes can be made from 3 litres of water?

6. A wall, 12 m long, 150 cm high and 15 cm thick is constructed using bricks which are 20 cm $\times$ 15 cm $\times$ 10 cm. How many bricks are needed (ignore the cement).

Exercise 9

Find the volume of each of the solid objects below. Give the answers correct to 3 S.F.

1.

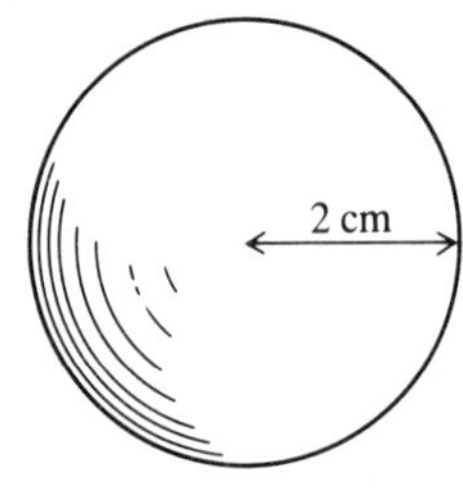

2.

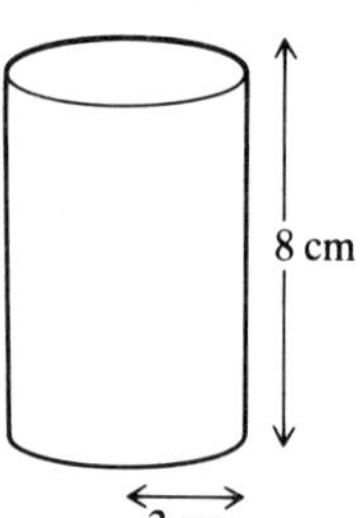

3.

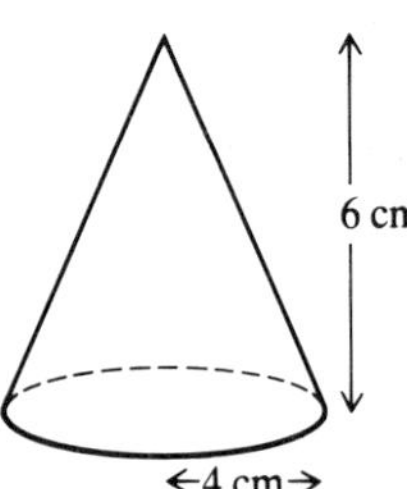

4.

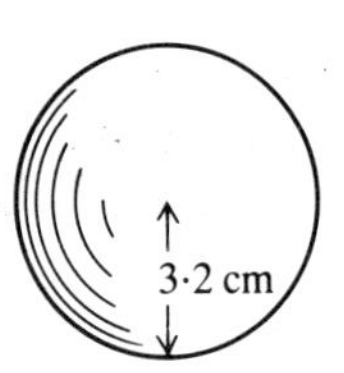

5.

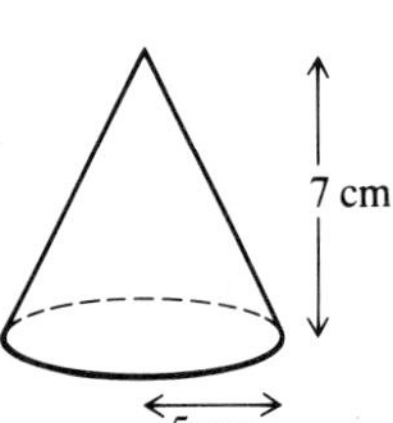

6.

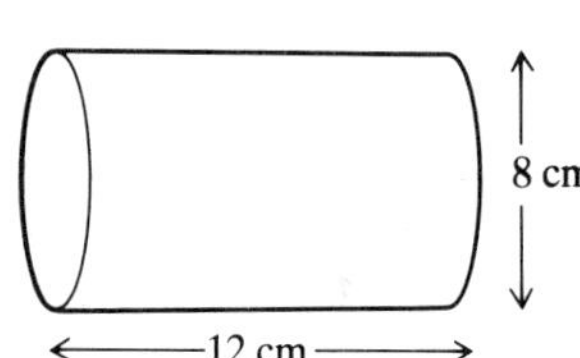

7.

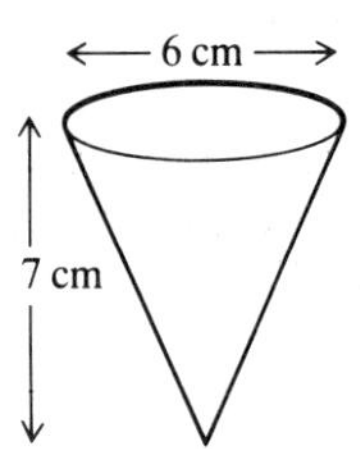

8.

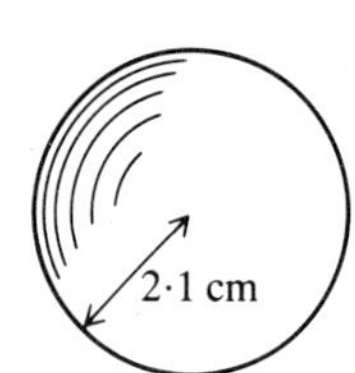

9.

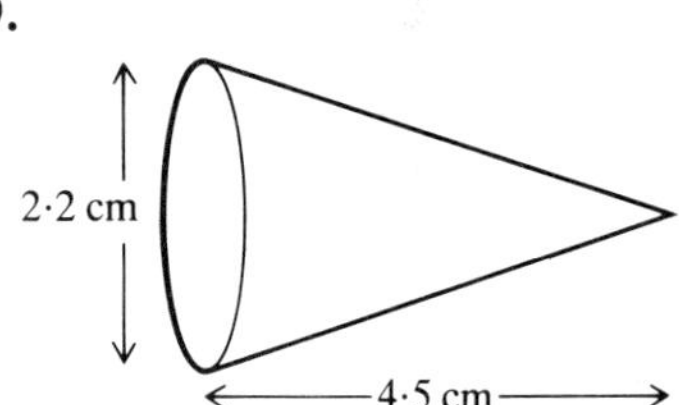

10.

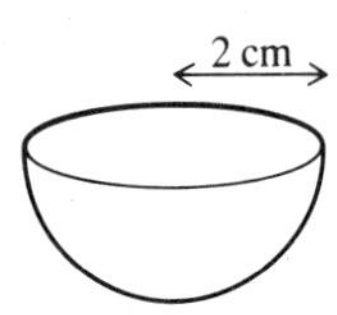

11.

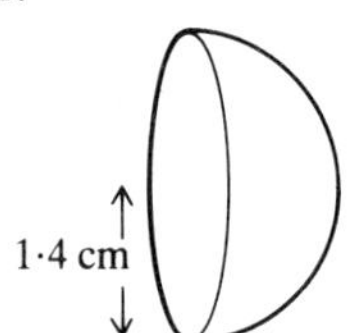

12.

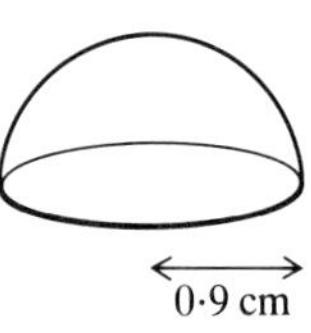

13.

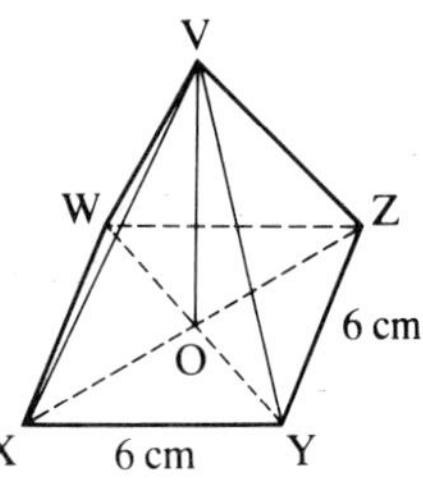

WX = XY = YZ = WZ = 6 cm

VO = 5 cm

14.

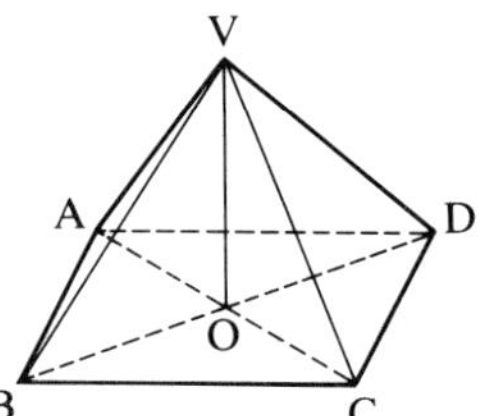

AB = DC = 3 cm

BC = AD = 6 cm

VO = 5 cm

The objects in questions **15** and **16** consist of cones, cylinders and hemispheres joined together.

15.

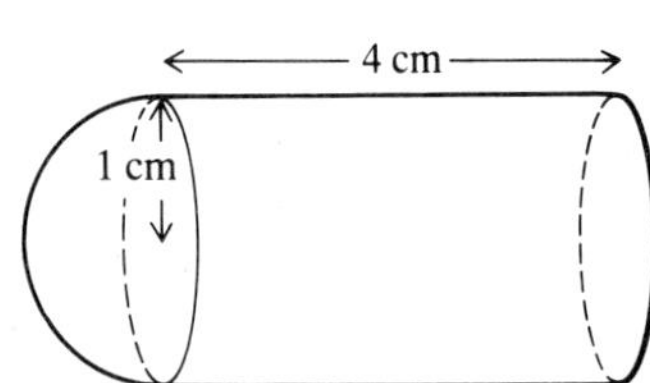

16.

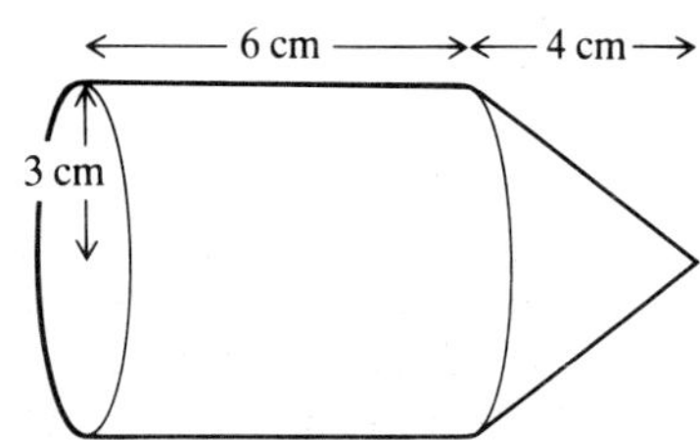

Exercise 10

Use 'π' on a calculator or take $\pi = 3.14$. Give answers correct to 3 S.F.

1. Find the capacity in litres of the oil drum shown below. ($1000 \text{ cm}^3 = 1$ litre).

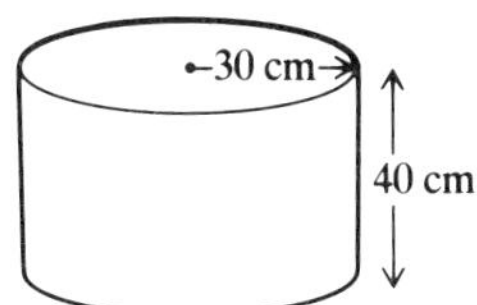

2. Find the volume in litres of a cylinder of height 55 cm and diameter 20 cm.
3. The two objects shown below are made of the same material. Which is the heavier?

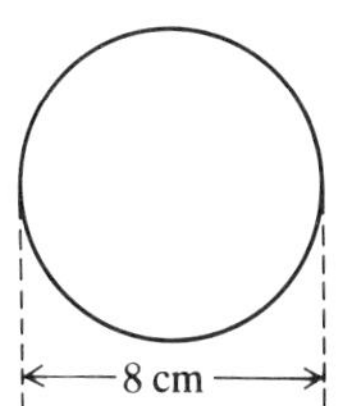

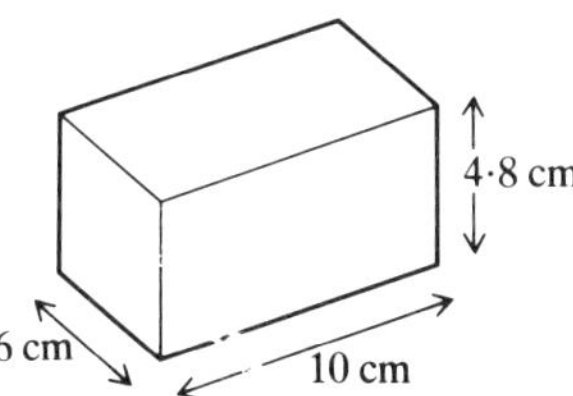

4. A washing powder is sold in two sizes, a giant size for £2.05 and a standard size for 90p

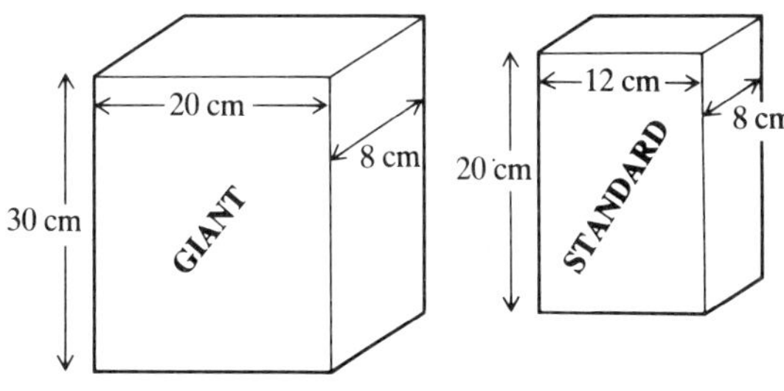

(a) (i) Calculate the volume of the standard size packet.
   (ii) Calculate the volume of the giant size packet.

(b) It takes $2\frac{1}{2}$ packets of standard size to fill the giant size.
   (i) Calculate the cost of 2 standard size packets and half a packet (at half standard-size price).
   (ii) Which is cheaper, a giant packet or $2\frac{1}{2}$ standard packets?
   (iii) How much is saved?

5. Calculate the volume of the object below.

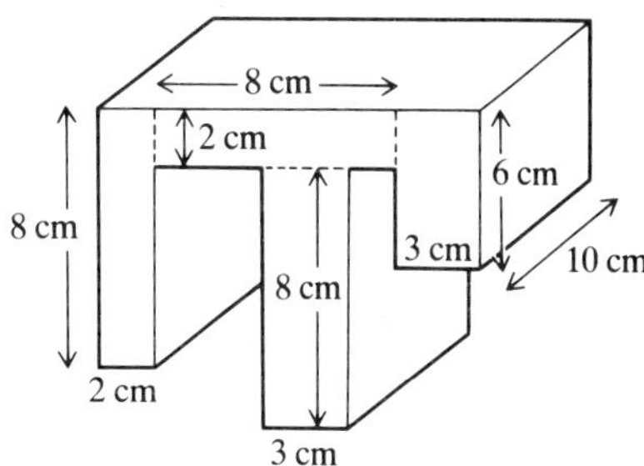

6. A solid sphere of radius 2 cm is melted down and recast into a number of discs of radius 1 cm and thickness 0.2 cm. Calculate
   (a) the volume of the sphere,
   (b) the volume of one disc,
   (c) the number of complete discs which can be made from the sphere.

7. Liquid is poured into an inverted cone of internal radius 10 cm and height 15 cm at a rate of $6 \text{ cm}^3/\text{s}$. How long will it take to fill the cone?

8. Cylinders are cut along the axis of symmetry to form the objects below. Find the volume of each object.

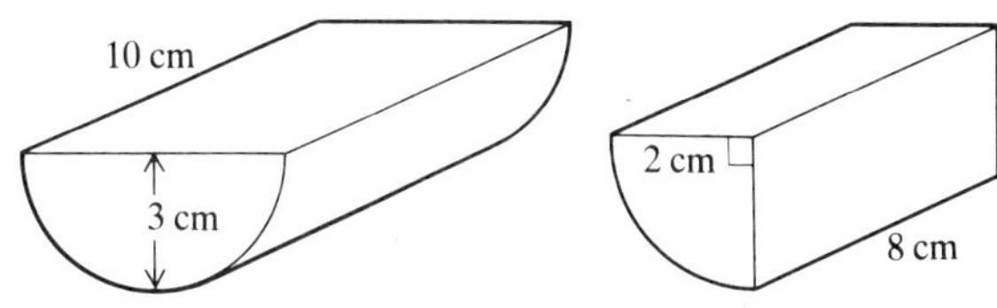

9. The diagram below shows a cross section through the centre of a hollow spherical ball made of steel.

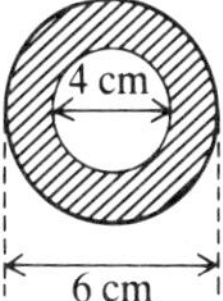

Calculate
   (a) the volume of steel used to make the ball,
   (b) the weight of the ball if the density of steel is 8 g/cm^3.

Exercise 11

1. The solid object shown below is made from 27 small cubes each 1 cm by 1 cm by 1 cm. The small cubes are glued together and then the outside is painted red.

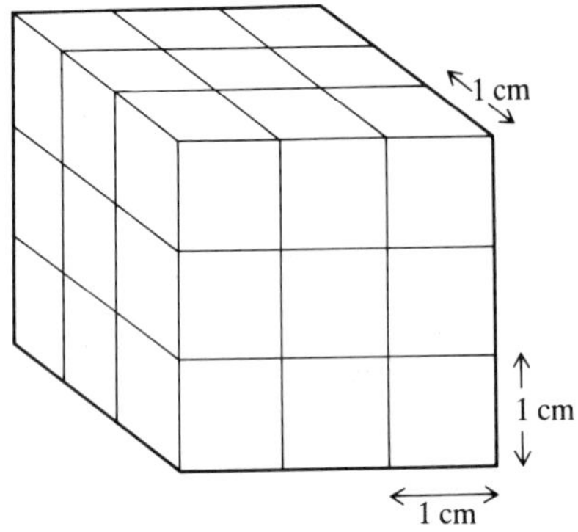

Calculate
(a) the number of cubes with one face painted
(b) the number of cubes with two faces painted
(c) the number of cubes with three faces painted
(d) the number of cubes with no faces painted
(Check that the answers to (a), (b), (c) and (d) add up to the correct number.)

2. Repeat question **1** for the solid objects shown below, each of which is made from 1 cm cubes.

(a)

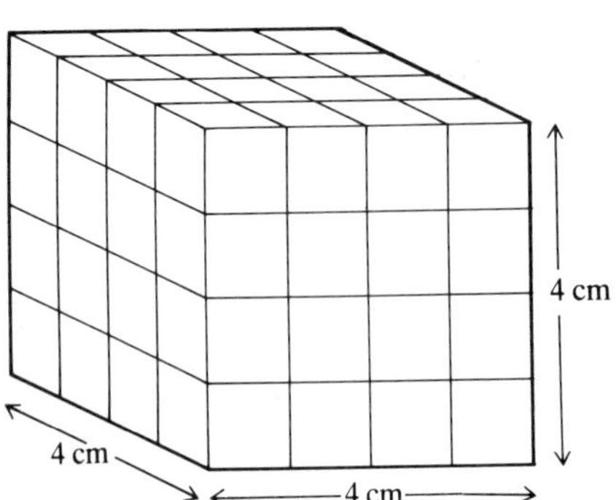

(b)

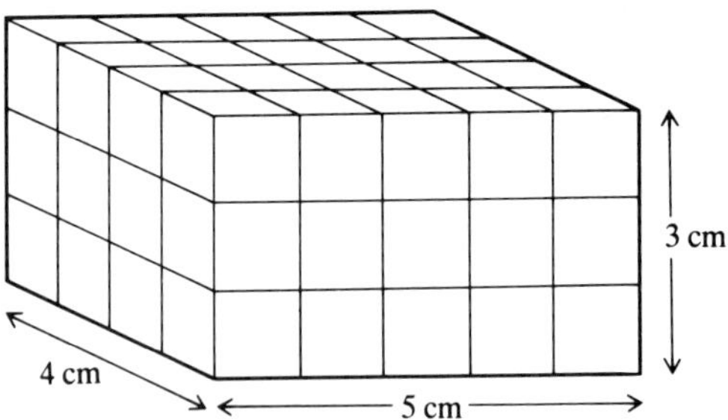

(c)

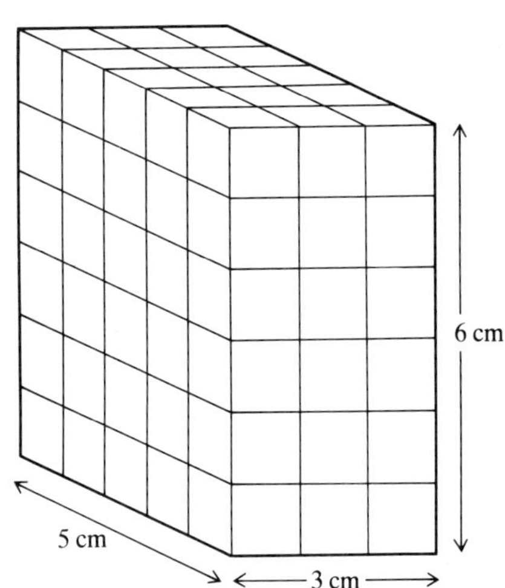

(d)

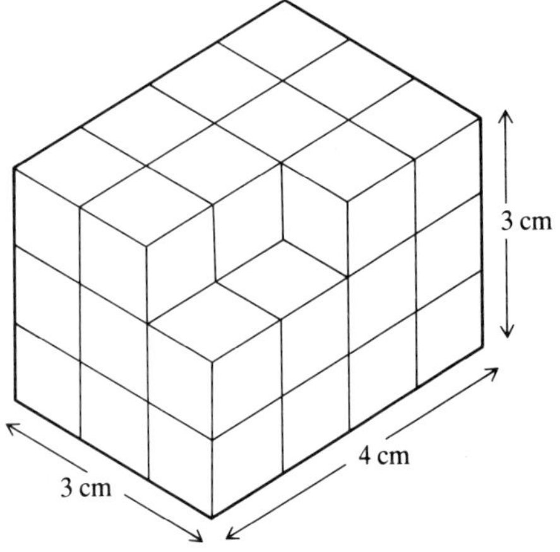

12.4 NETS AND SOLIDS

If the cube below was made of cardboard, and you cut along some of the edges and laid it out flat, you would have the *net* of the cube.

Here is the net for a square-based pyramid.

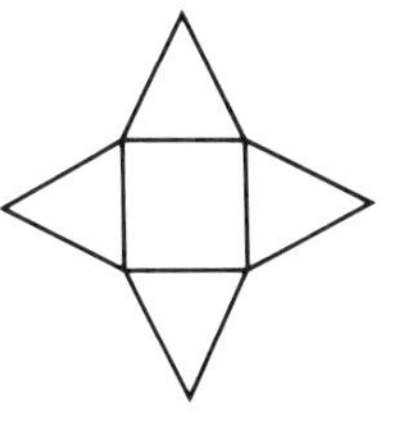

Exercise 12

In question **1** we will construct a series of equilateral triangles using a ruler and a pair of compasses.

1. (a) Draw a straight line AB and draw a pattern of circles of radius 3 cm as shown. The centres of the circles are marked with an O.

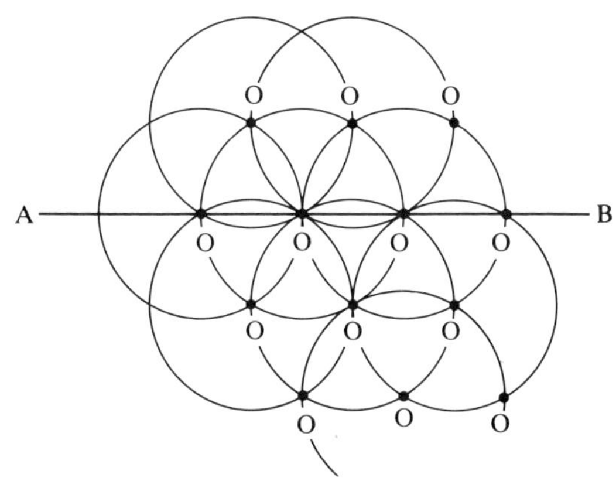

(b) Draw the lines through the O's to produce a series of equilateral triangles.

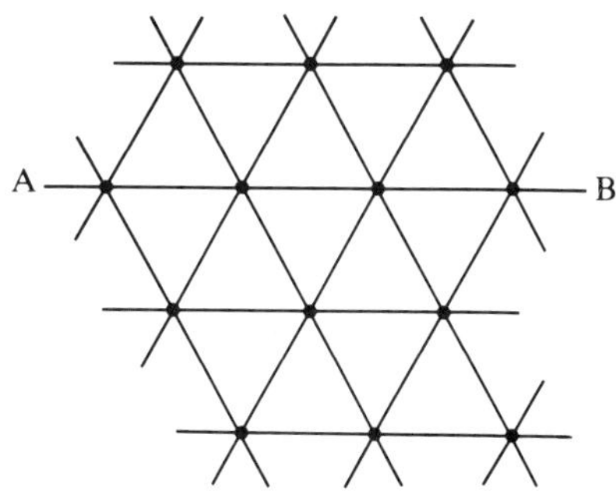

(c) We can also see a series of regular hexagons in the pattern above.

In questions **2** to **5** objects are shown, together with the net which will produce them. Draw the net on a piece of cardboard using the method from question **1**. Cut out the net and fold it to make the object.

2. Tetrahedron

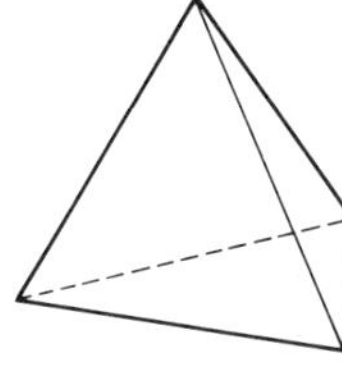

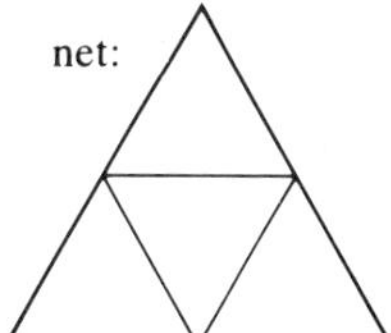

3. Octahedron

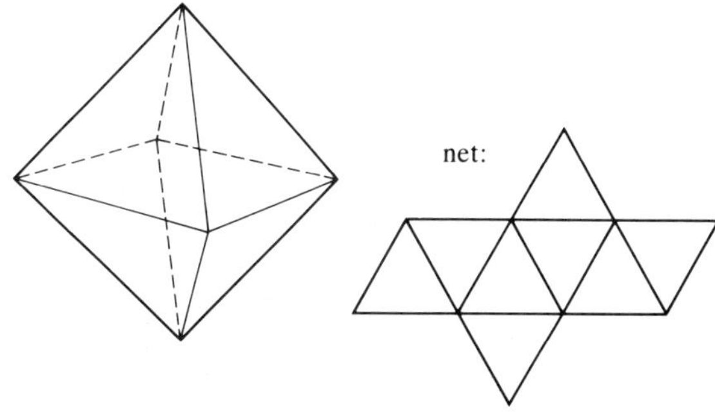

4. Icosahedron (20 faces)

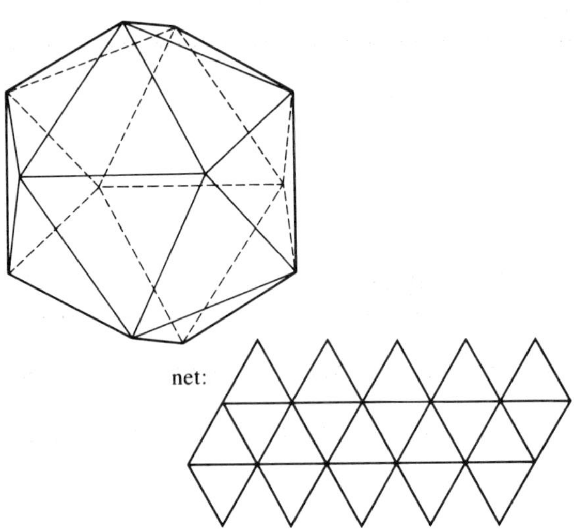

5. Truncated tetrahedron

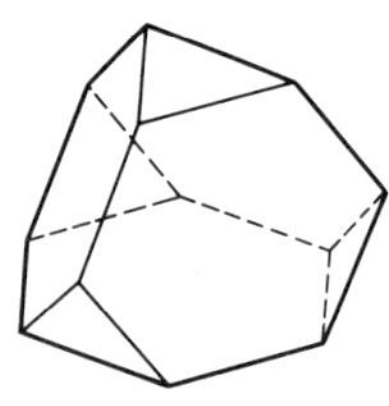

net:

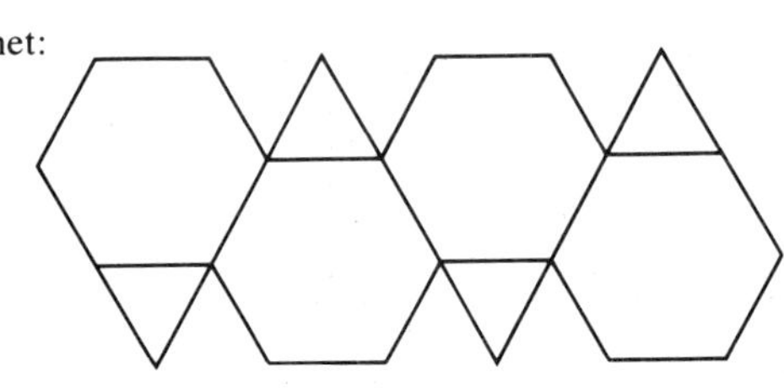

Use the circle pattern method to draw the net of hexagons and equilateral triangles.

6. A cube dissected into three pyramids. Make three solids from the net shown. They can be fitted together to form a cube. This demonstrates the formula for the volume of a pyramid.

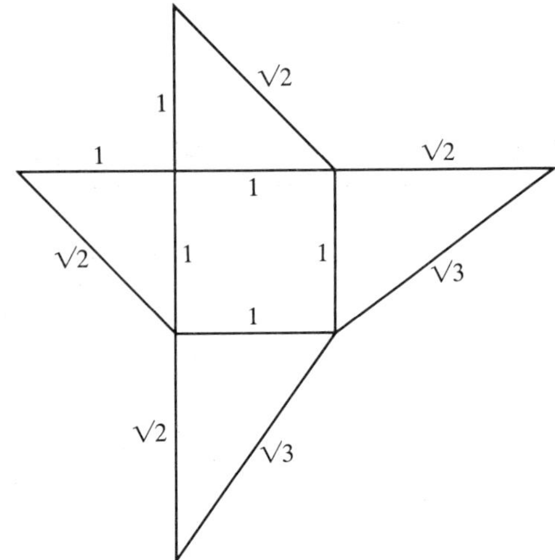

7. Which of the nets below can be used to make a cube?

(a)

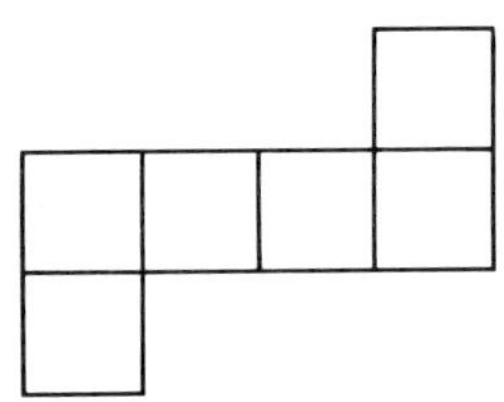

(b)

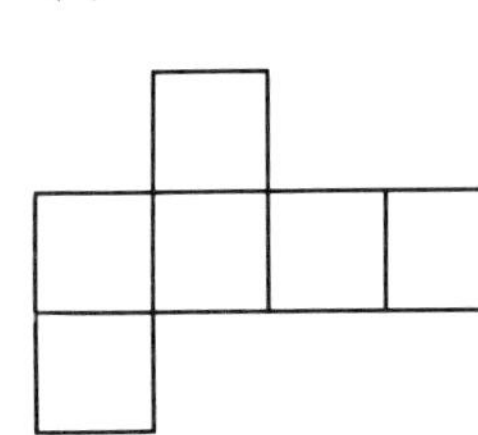

(c)

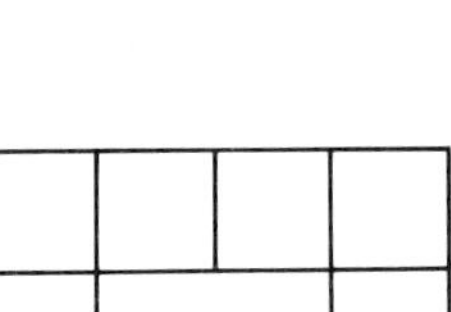

(d)

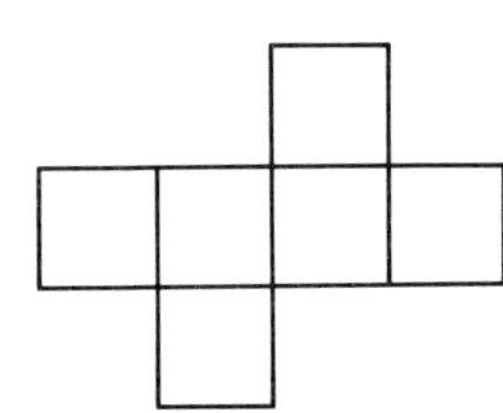

Think about it 4

Project 1 MATHEMATICAL WORDSEARCH

Copy the square below. Find as many mathematical words as possible and make a list.
The words appear written forwards or backwards in any row, column or diagonal.

A	P	M	N	C	I	R	C	L	E	V	Z
E	O	E	D	I	V	I	D	E	B	Q	E
L	R	A	D	I	U	S	R	V	R	T	Q
G	E	T	U	C	A	H	L	M	A	S	U
N	Q	L	N	A	T	M	U	N	C	U	A
A	U	O	L	B	V	L	I	U	K	M	T
P	A	R	N	A	T	D	T	O	E	E	I
Q	L	J	U	I	R	D	F	P	T	R	O
R	M	C	P	O	S	A	X	I	S	T	N
W	K	L	O	G	F	H	P	D	E	N	I
T	Y	C	A	L	C	U	L	A	T	E	Q
L	R	E	T	E	M	A	I	D	R	X	S

Your rating:

10	Average
15	Good
20	Very good
More than 20	Excellent

Exercise A

1. A television programme lasting 2 hours 15 minutes finishes at 21 50. At what time does the film start?

2. How much change from £10 should I receive after spending £2.07?

3. It costs £8 to join a tennis club and 80p for each game. Calculate the total cost of joining the club and then playing 20 games.

4. Work out $\frac{2}{5} \times \frac{3}{4}$, giving your answer in its simplest form.

5. Calculate the area of the shape below.

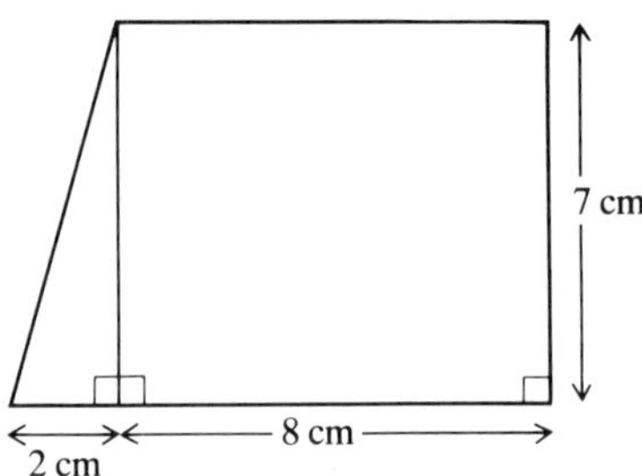

6. The bill for 8 people in a restaurant is £61.60. Find the cost per person correct to the nearest pound.

7. A mechanic is paid £4.80 per hour for normal time and overtime is paid at time and a half. How much does he earn in a week when he works 40 hours normal time and 8 hours overtime?

8. The diagram shows the plan view of a room which is 2.5 m in height.

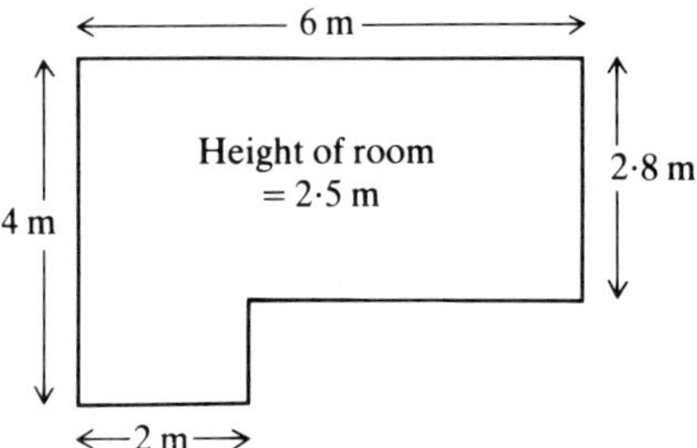

Emulsion paint costs £3.40 per litre.
1 litre of paint covers 7 m^2.
Copy and complete the following table.

Perimeter of room	m
Total area of all walls	m^2
Area of doors and windows	15 m^2
Area which requires painting	m^2
Number of litres of paint needed for 2 coats	
Cost of paint	£

9. A man owed £150. How much does he owe after making payments of £45.50, £27 and £51?

10. The mileometer of a car shows a reading of 14 941 miles. This number is called 'palindromic' because it reads the same backwards or forwards.
(a) What will be the reading when the next palindromic number appears?
(b) How far will the car have travelled by then?

Project 2 CROSSNUMBERS WITHOUT CLUES

Here we have four crossnumbers with no clues, only the answers. Copy the patterns shown and then fill in the answers by working 'backwards'.

1. Copy the pattern below.

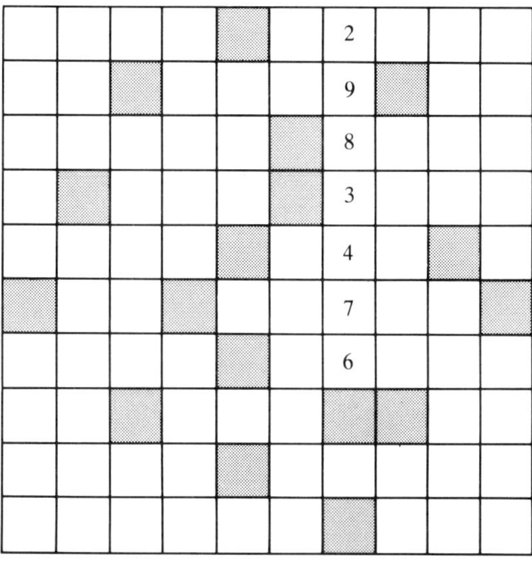

The answers are below. One number has been put in to help you get started. It is a good idea to copy out a list of all the answers so that you can tick them off as you put them onto the pattern.

2 digits: 13, 22, 28, 45, 74, 91, 93, 97.

3 digits: 236, 252, 276, 448, 669, 962.

4 digits: 1219, 2414, 3180, 3436, 3746, 4105, 4254, 5093, 5231, 5636, 8313.

5 digits: 11060, 15283, 16283, 19870, 26105, 35368, 37852, 51273, 60757, 78787, 92523.

6 digits: 191800, 401915, 403645.

7 digits: 2983476.✓

2. Copy the same pattern as for question **1** (without the 2983476). Here are the answers:

2 digits: 15, 22, 23, 23, 24, 26, 31, 81.

3 digits: 126, 127, 356, 357, 414, 651.

4 digits: 1358, 1364, 1527, 2158, 3214, 3216, 3416, 3789, 4177, 5427, 6500.

5 digits: 21011, 24629, 36973, 37189, 45189, 48211, 53636, 64285, 71820, 95890, 97215.

6 digits: 582355, 652748, 653648.

7 digits: 4413516.

3. Copy the same pattern as for question **1** (without the 2983476).
Here are the answers:

2 digits: 28, 56, 66, 67, 68, 88, 92, 93.

3 digits: 171, 372, 387, 415, 485, 675.

4 digits: 1583, 1613, 1683, 2319, 3214, 3217, 3218, 3248, 5218, 8131, 9635.

5 digits: 26561, 26852, 26895, 60911, 60918, 68812, 74164, 82103, 82777, 84266, 91718.

6 digits: 252852, 428151, 448161.

7 digits: 8339822.

4. This question is more difficult. Copy the pattern below.

				■						■
		■	3	7	3	8	■			
					■					
	■				■				■	
3	1	1	8	■				■		
■			■						■	■
6				■				■		
	■	■				■	■			
7				■						■
						■				
		■			■					4

2 digits 13, 16, 19, 49, 60, 63, 65, 68, 74, 84, 85.

3 digits: 168, 316, 516, 610, 616, 617, 735, 785, 801, 815, 833, 885, 928.

4 digits: 3118, 3218, 3738, 5524, 6815, 7516, 7816, 7826, 7856.

5 digits: 21748, 21758, 53674, 53681, 63117, 63546, 63576, 63588, 63781, 63881, 76293, 78151, 92505.

6 digits: 639669, 813849.

7 digits: 3896152.

Exercise B

1. The cash price of a television is £320. It can be bought on hire purchase by paying a deposit of £65 and 24 monthly payments of £12.50. Calculate the total cost of buying the television on hire purchase.

2. A man earns £5980 per annum. How much is this per week?

3. It takes 20 minutes per lb plus an extra 15 minutes to cook a duck. At what time would you put a 9 lb duck into the oven if you wish to have it ready at 1.30 p.m.?

4. What change do you receive from £10 after buying 6 pens at 22p, 4 sharpeners at 32p and 5 pencils at 8p?

5. Two numbers x and t are such that t is greater than 6 and x is less than 4. Arrange the numbers 5, t and x in order of size, starting with the smallest.

6. To the nearest whole number 5.84, 16.23 and 7.781 are 6, 16 and 8 respectively.

(a) Use these approximate values to obtain an approximate result for $\dfrac{5.84 \times 16.23}{7.781}$

(b) Use the same approach to obtain approximate results for

(i) $\dfrac{15.72 \times 9.78}{20.24}$ (ii) $\dfrac{23.85 \times 9.892}{4.867}$

7. King Richard is given three coins which look identical, but in fact one of them is an overweight fake. Describe how he could discover the fake using an ordinary balance and only *one* weighing operation.

8. How many hours are there in February 1987?

9. A cup can be filled fifty times from 18 litres of milk. What is the capacity of the cup in cm^3. ($1000 \text{ cm}^3 = 1$ litre).

10. A pile of 400 sheets of paper is 2.5 cm thick. What is the thickness in cm of one sheet of paper?

Project 3 SPOTTED SHAPES

For this investigation you need dotted paper. If you have not got any you can make your own using a felt tip pen and squared paper.

In Figure 1 there are 10 dots on the perimeter ($p = 10$) and 2 dots inside the shape ($i = 2$). The area of the shape is 6 square units ($A = 6$).

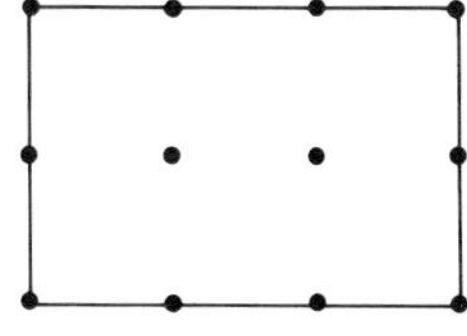

Figure 1

In Figure 2 there are 14 dots on the perimeter ($p = 14$) and 6 dots inside the shape ($i = 6$). The area of the shape is 12 square units ($A = 12$).

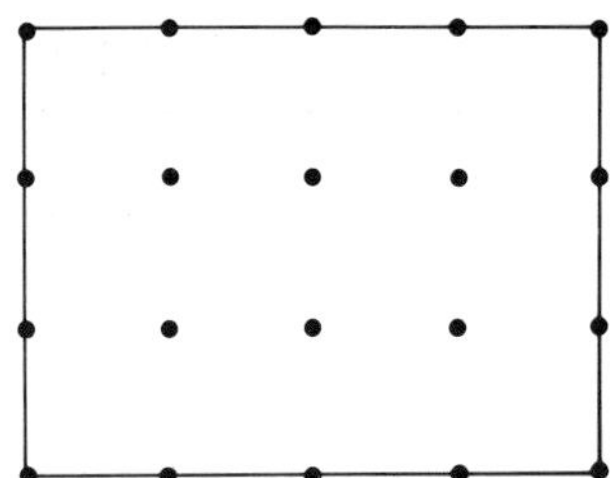

Figure 2

Draw the shapes below and record the values for p, i and A in a table like the one shown.

p	i	A	leave a space
10	2	6	
14	6	12	

Draw more shapes of your own design and record the results in the table. Include some more difficult shapes like those below.

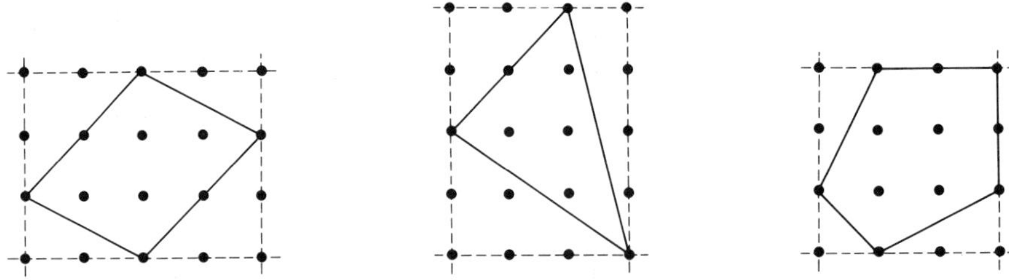

The area of the shape is found by subtracting the areas of the triangles from the area of the surrounding rectangle (shown with a broken line).

In the space you left in the table of results, work out the value of $(\frac{1}{2}p + i)$ for each shape.

Is there a formula connecting p, i and A?

Draw further shapes, even more complicated, to check your formula.

Exercise C OPERATOR SQUARES

Each empty square contains either a number or a mathematical symbol (+, −, ×, ÷). Copy each square and fill in the missing details.

1.

11		4	→	15
×		÷		
		2	→	3
↓		↓		
66			→	132

2.

9		17	→	26
×		−		
5	×		→	
↓		↓		
	÷	9	→	5

3.

14	+		→	31
×				
4		23	→	92
↓		↓		
	−	40	→	

4.

15			→	5
+		×		
		5	→	110
↓		↓		
	−	15	→	22

5.

	×	10	→	90
+		÷		
			→	$5\frac{1}{2}$
↓		↓		
20	×		→	100

6.

	×		→	52
−		×		
	×	4	→	
↓		↓		
8		8	→	1

7.

5			→	60
×		÷		
		24	→	44
↓		↓		
	×	$\frac{1}{2}$	→	50

8.

	×	6	→	42
÷		÷		
14	−		→	
↓		↓		
		2	→	1

9.

	×	2	→	38
−		÷		
			→	48
↓		↓		
7	−		→	$6\frac{1}{2}$

10.

17	×		→	170
−		÷		
	÷		→	
↓		↓		
8	−	0·1	→	

11.

0·3	×	20	→	
		−		
11	÷		→	
↓		↓		
11·3	−		→	2·3

12.

	×	50	→	25
−		÷		
		$\frac{1}{2}$	→	0·6
↓		↓		
0·4	×		→	

13.

7	×		→	0·7
÷		×		
	÷		→	
↓		↓		
1·75	+	0·02	→	

14.

	+	8	→	9·4
−				
	×	0·1	→	
↓		↓		
1·3		0·8	→	2·1

15.

	×		→	30
−				
	÷	10	→	0·25
↓		↓		
97·5	+	3	→	

16.

3	÷	2	→	
÷		÷		
8	÷		→	
↓		↓		
	+	$\frac{1}{8}$	→	

17.

	−	$\frac{1}{16}$	→	$\frac{3}{16}$
×				
	÷	4	→	
↓		↓		
$\frac{1}{8}$		$\frac{1}{4}$	→	$\frac{3}{8}$

18.

0·5	−	0·01	→	
		×		
	×		→	35
↓		↓		
4	÷	0·1	→	

Project 4 NUMBER MESSAGES

(a) Start at the box containing the letter 'Q'.
(b) Work out the answer to the question in the box.
(c) Look for the answer in the corner of another box.
(d) Write down the letter in the box and then work out the answer to the problem in the box.
(e) Look for the answer as before and continue until you arrive back at box 'Q'.
(f) Read the message.

1.

147 **Q** 15 + 19	153 **D** 21 × 7	101 **R** 200 − 47	42 **V** 26 + 98
124 **E** 22 × 3	91 **I** 20 × 6	34 **M** 5 × 15	36 **A** 11 + 90
63 **H** 11 × 11	66 **R** 84 ÷ 4	21 **Y** 110 − 70	81 **T** 36 + 27
75 **A** 100 − 19	40 **H** 216 ÷ 6	121 **S** 95 − 4	120 **S** 61 − 19

2.

27 **Q** 99 − 27	99 **S** 2212 ÷7	125 **W** 211 − 99	444 **N** 110 × 9
766 **I** $(18 - 13)^2$	112 **O** $(21 - 18)^3$	615 **N** 18 × 20	25 **S** 108 + 209
317 **T** 625 ÷ 5	990 **E** 840 ÷ 3	72 **O** 123 + 321	118 **U** $3^2 \times 11$
166 **L** 19 + 99	360 **E** 1000 − 234	316 **O** 5 + 55 + 555	280 **P** 200 − 34

3.

0.42 **Q** 8.1 + 5	3.3 **R** 6.1 ÷ 5	4.1 **B** 19 − 13.7	10.5 **R** 14.5 − 3
5.3 **I** 3.24 ÷ 9	11.5 **S** 0.84 ÷ 4	1.22 **E** 11 − 8.95	0.01 **H** 4.2 × 0.1
2.05 **R** 0.313 × 100	31.3 **U** 8.8 + 9.9	13.1 **S** 8 − 3.7	0.21 **A** 0.33 × 10
4.3 **P** 2.4 + 7	0.36 **S** 10 − 9.99	18.7 **B** 8.2 × 0.5	9.4 **U** 2.1 × 5

4.

6 **Q** 10 + 3 × 2	13 **S** 22 + 20 ÷ 10	33 **R** 19 − 12 ÷ 6	71 **N** 7 × 4 − 15 ÷5
7 **E** 8 + 9 ÷ 3	53 **O** 39 − 17 × 2	25 **D** (25 + 23) ÷ 8	19 **E** 13 − 3 × 2
55 **H** 2 × 3 + 4 × 2	5 **U** 8 × 7 + 3 × 5	16 **T** 12 − 4 × 2	17 **T** (4 + 7) × 5
4 **H** 6 × 3 + 1	24 **R** 3 × 14 + 11	14 **I** 3 × 5 − 1 × 2	11 **A** 5 × 7 − 2

5.

50 **Q** 2.5 × 4 + 3	8.1 **O** 5 × 9 − 2 × 9	2.13 **N** 7 − 0.04 × 10	2 **N** 0.5 × 2 + 17
7.2 **L** 0.3 × 100 − 7	3.5 **O** 8 × 5 + 6 × 7	84 **G** 11 × 9 − 7 × 7	52.2 **G** 10 × (3.4 + 5)
6 **A** 1.7 + 3 ÷ 10	23 **A** 13 ÷ 100 + 2	13 **C** 8 − 0.2 × 10	7.24 **B** 8 + 1 ÷ 10
82 **U** 6.2 ÷ 5 + 6	27 **I** 8 − 0.4 × 2	6.6 **E** 3.2 + 7 × 7	18 **Y** 12.5 − 3 × 3

6.

−13 **Q** − 6 + 2	−7 **C** $(-3)^2 + 4^2$	12 **Y** 12 ÷ (−2)	0 **A** 12 × (−10)	−14 **A** − 8 + 17
−120 **R** 16 ÷ (−16)	−8 **H** − 3 − 15	−18 **E** $(-2)^2$	8 **E** (−8) ÷ (−8)	4 **R** − 3 + 7 − 9
−6 **T** − 8 − 9	13 **E** − 2 + 1 − 1	−4 **M** (−3) × (−4)	25 **L** − 7 + 20	1 **R** − 3 − 2 − 8
9 **C** (−8) ÷ 1	−5 **S** 0 × (−17)	−2 **V** 6 − (−2)	−1 **E** − 2 + 6 − 11	−17 **E** − 2 × 7

7.

3.62 **Q** 12 − 8.99	8 **O** 45 ÷ 9 −5	25 **U** 90 × 2 − 5	300 **S** − 8 − 6	1.3 **L** 6 + 9 ÷ 3
−9 **A** 2.6 × 0.5	6 **Y** 0.7 ÷ 100	0.27 **R** $(-1)^2 + (-2)^2$	21 **N** 200 − 41	159 **G** 25.34 ÷ 7
0 **R** 1.4 + 19	1.24 **A** 9 × 5 − 3 × 7	3.01 **M** 18 − 3 × 4	5 **O** 6 × (11 − 7.5)	175 **L** 6.2 ÷ 5
9 **C** $(-2)^2 + 21$	−14 **W** 2.7 × 0.1	20.4 **I** 0.3 × 1000	24 **T** − 7 + 15	0.007 **C** −36 ÷ 4

Exercise D

1. Eight litres of wine cost £12. Find the cost of 15 litres of the wine.

2. Write correct to the nearest pound:
(a) £57.80 (b) £62.45 (c) £124.85
(d) £6.781 (e) £11.382 (f) £567.60

3. A wooden box when empty weighs 5.2 kg. It contains: 5 tins each weighing 400 g; 7 jars each weighing 675 g; 10 bags each weighing 225 g and 2 bottles each weighing 1050 g. Find the total weight of the box and its contents.

4. A lawnmower has a blade 2 m wide. A groundsman has to cut the grass on a playing surface 100 m by 60 m. He cuts up and down the length of the field.
(a) How many times does he push the mower the length of the field?
(b) What area of grass does he cut each time?

5. Twenty articles cost £50. How many of these articles could be bought for £7.50?

6. How many apples at 16p each would be a fair exchange for 48 oranges costing 11p each?

7. A saleswoman is paid a basic salary of £4200 per year, plus commission of 4% on all her sales. Calculate her total salary if her sales totalled
(a) £10 000 (b) £30 000 (c) £100 000.

8. Peter walks at $4\frac{1}{2}$ km/h and he cycles three times as fast. How long will he take to cycle $33\frac{3}{4}$ km?

9. If we require an estimate of 82 × 43, to the nearest thousand, we may say

$$\begin{aligned} 82 \times 43 &\approx 80 \times 40 \\ &= 3200 \\ &= 3000 \text{ to the nearest thousand.} \end{aligned}$$

Use this method to estimate the value of the following, to the nearest thousand.
(a) 71 × 69 (b) 998 × 41 (c) 11 × 607 (d) 497 × 206

10. Change the fractions $\frac{5}{8}$ and $\frac{7}{11}$ into decimals. Which fraction is larger?

Project 5 THINK OF A NUMBER

Ask someone to follow these instructions:

(a) Think of a number.
(b) Add 11 to the number.
(c) Multiply the answer by 5.
(d) Subtract 7 from the new number.
(e) Double the answer.
(f) Add 4 to the last number.
(g) Read out the final answer.

You can now work out the original number as follows:
'Subtract 100 and divide by 10'.
(e.g. If the final answer is 250, the original number was (250 − 100) ÷ 10. It was 15).

Exercise E

1. Write down the next five lines in this pattern.

$1 \times 999 = 999$
$2 \times 999 = 1998$
$3 \times 999 = 2997$
$4 \times 999 = 3996$

2. Copy the pattern and write down the next four lines.

$1 + 9 \times 0 = 1$
$2 + 9 \times 1 = 11$
$3 + 9 \times 12 = 111$
$4 + 9 \times 123 = 1111$
$5 + 9 \times 1234 =$

3. Copy the pattern and write down the next five lines.

$1 \times 9 - 1 = 8$
$21 \times 9 - 1 = 188$
$321 \times 9 - 1 = 2888$
$4321 \times 9 - 1 = 38888$

4. (a) Write down the next four lines of this pattern.

$1^3 = 1^2 = 1$
$1^3 + 2^3 = (1 + 2)^2 = 9$
$1^3 + 2^3 + 3^3 = (1 + 2 + 3)^2 = 36$

(b) Work out as simply as possible
$1^3 + 2^3 + 3^3 + 4^3 + 5^3 + 6^3 + 7^3 + 8^3 + 9^3 + 10^3$.

5. (a) Write down the next three lines of this pattern.

$(1.5)^2 = (1 \times 2) + 0.25$
$(2.5)^2 = (2 \times 3) + 0.25$
$(3.5)^2 = (3 \times 4) + 0.25$

(b) Copy and complete.

$(9.5)^2 = (\qquad) +$
$(15.5)^2 = (\qquad) +$
$(99.5)^2 = \qquad +$

6. Write down the next five lines of this pattern.

$1 = 1 = 1^3$
$3 + 5 = 8 = 2^3$
$7 + 9 + 11 = 27 = 3^3$
$13 + 15 + 17 + 19 = \quad =$

7. Each diagram in the sequence below consists of a number of dots.

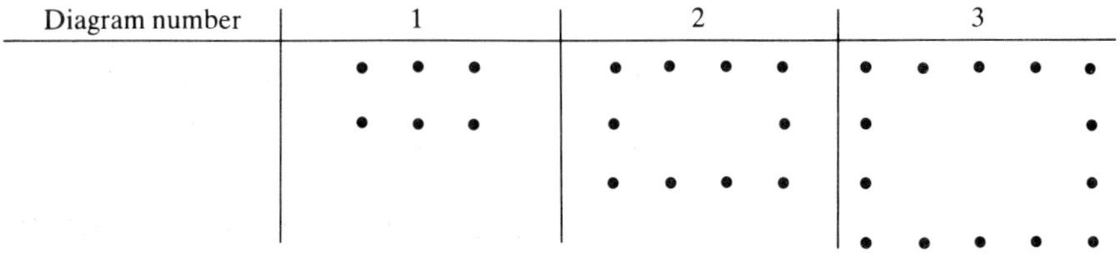

Diagram number	1	2	3
	• • • • • •	• • • • • • • • • •	• • • • • • • • • • • • • •

(a) Draw diagram number 4, diagram number 5 and diagram number 6.

(b) Copy and complete the table below:

Diagram number	Number of dots
1	6
2	10
3	
4	
5	
6	

(c) Without drawing the diagrams, state the number of dots in
  (i) diagram number 10
  (ii) diagram number 15
  (iii) diagram number 50

(d) State the number of the diagram which has
  (i) 50 dots
  (ii) 162 dots

(e) If we write x for the diagram number and n for the number of dots, write down a formula involving x and n.

Project 6 ESTIMATING

(a) Draw a large copy of table A.

Table A

145	441	609	2059	4260	300
1421	969	45	2940	189	459
540	355	399	639	551	261
95	171	1260	1029	105	1071
1740	3060	245	931	2499	255
1140	3621	1479	3479	1349	1491

Table B

5	21	51
9	29	60
19	49	71

(b) Two players take it in turn to select a pair of numbers from table B and multiply them on a calculator. If the answer is in table A and if the number is not yet crossed out the player crosses out that square with a coloured pencil.

(c) The winner is the first player to cross out four squares in a line, either in a column or a row or a diagonal.

Exercise F

Write down the following electricity meter readings. Note the number that the pointer has just passed.

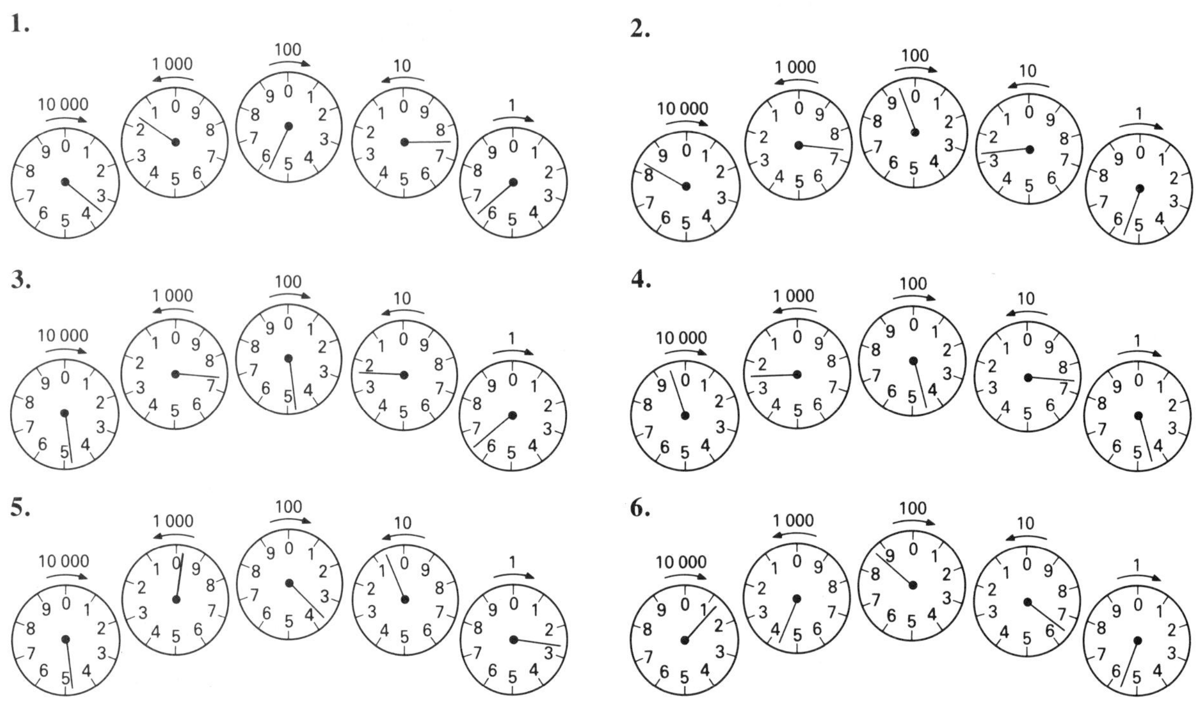

In questions **7**, **8** and **9** find how many units are consumed between each pair of readings.

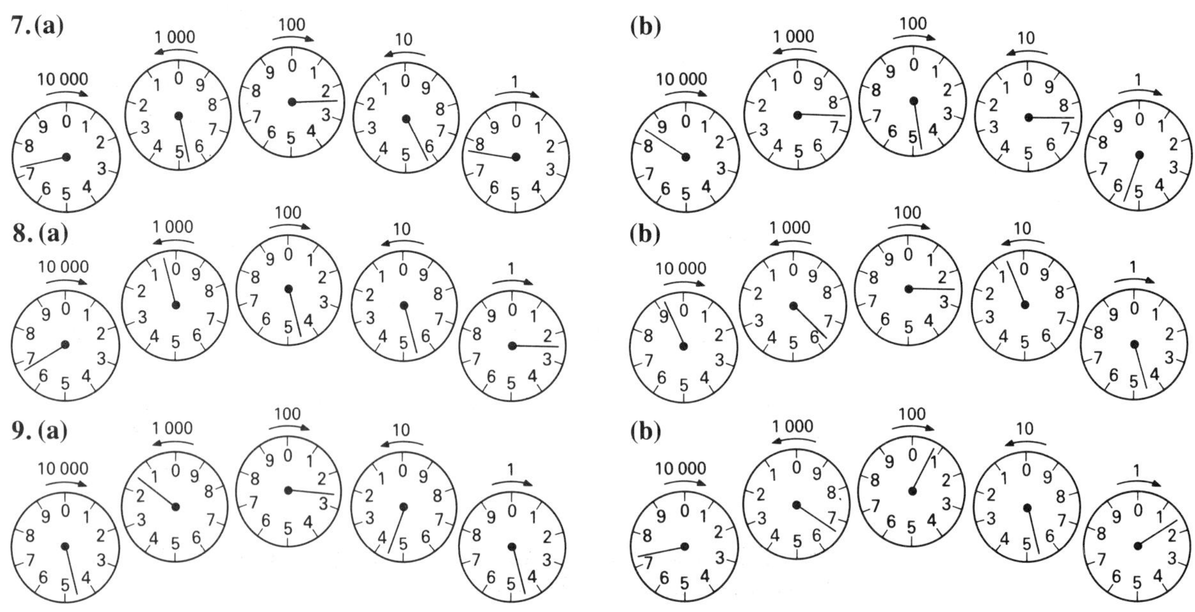

Project 7 BUCKETS

John has two buckets. One holds 5 litres and the other holds 8 litres.

He also has a large tank with a tap.

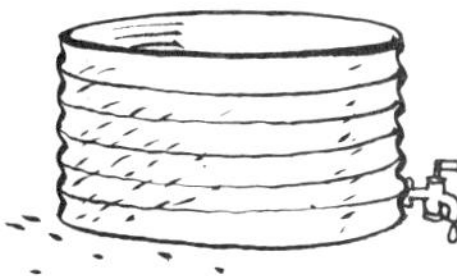

(a) Suppose he needs exactly 18 litres of water. This is easy. He fills the 5 litre bucket twice and the 8 litre bucket once and pours all the water into the tank.

(b) Suppose he needs 7 litres of water.

This is more interesting. He can fill the 5 litre bucket three times and pour all the water into the tank

He can then drain 8 litres from the tank into his 8 litre bucket. In this way he is left with 7 litres of water in the tank.

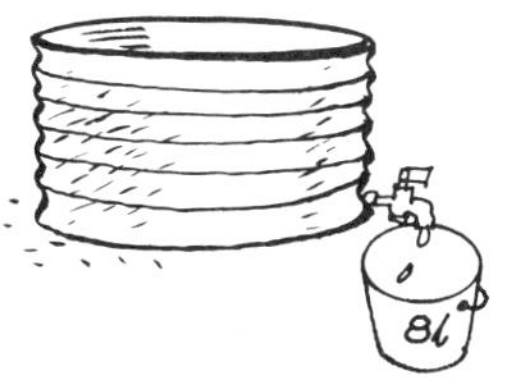

1. Work out ways in which John can obtain the following quantities of water: (remember: no fractions!)
   (a) 3 litres; (b) 13 litres; (c) 2 litres; (d) 11 litres.
2. Work out ways in which he can obtain quantities of water from 1 litre all the way up to 25 litres.
3. Linda also has two buckets. One holds 7 litres and the other holds 9 litres.

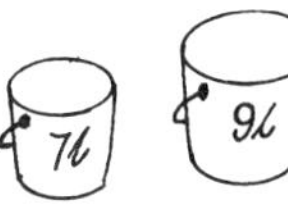

Work out ways in which Linda can obtain quantities of water from 1 litre all the way up to 25 litres.

Unit 13

13.1 NEGATIVE NUMBERS

Addition and subtraction

(a) $-7 + 2 = -5$
(b) $-6 - 5 = -11$
(c) $-3 + (-7) = -3 - 7 = -10$
(d) $-6 - (-10) = -6 + 10 = 4$

Exercise 1

Work out

1. $-6 + 2$
2. $-7 - 5$
3. $-3 - 8$
4. $-5 + 2$
5. $-6 + 1$
6. $8 - 4$
7. $4 - 9$
8. $11 - 19$
9. $4 + 15$
10. $-7 - 10$
11. $16 - 20$
12. $-7 + 2$
13. $-6 - 5$
14. $10 - 4$
15. $-4 + 0$
16. $-6 + 12$
17. $-7 + 7$
18. $2 - 20$
19. $8 - 11$
20. $-6 - 5$
21. $-3 + (-5)$
22. $-5 - (+2)$
23. $4 - (+3)$
24. $-3 - (-4)$
25. $6 - (-3)$
26. $16 + (-5)$
27. $-4 + (-4)$
28. $20 - (-22)$
29. $-6 - (-10)$
30. $95 + (-80)$
31. $-3 - (+4)$
32. $-5 - (+4)$
33. $6 + (-7)$
34. $-4 + (-3)$
35. $-7 - (-7)$
36. $3 - (-8)$
37. $-8 + (-6)$
38. $7 - (+7)$
39. $12 - (-5)$
40. $9 - (+6)$

Multiplication and division

(a) $-7 \times (-3) = 21$
(b) $-8 \times (+2) = -16$
(c) $-8 \div (-4) = 2$
(d) $10 \div (-2) = -5$

Exercise 2

Work out

1. $-3 \times (-2)$
2. $-8 \times (4)$
3. $2 \times (-3)$
4. $-6 \times (2)$
5. $-4 \times (4)$
6. $-3 \times (-3)$
7. $-6 \times (3)$
8. $4 \times (-10)$
9. $5 \times (-5)$
10. $8 \times (-100)$
11. $12 \div (-3)$
12. $16 \div (-1)$
13. $16 \div (-2)$
14. $-15 \div (-3)$
15. $-10 \div (-5)$
16. $-25 \div (5)$
17. $-8 \div (-2)$
18. $20 \div (-4)$
19. $-3 \times (+3)$
20. $-6 \times (0)$
21. $8 \div (-8)$
22. $-7 \div (-7)$
23. $40 \times (-10)$
24. $18 \times (-3)$
25. $100 \div (-1)$
26. $100 \div (-20)$
27. $-6 \times (-6)$
28. $-18 \div (-18)$
29. $0 \div (-7)$
30. $-25 \times (-20)$

Find two numbers

(a) Find two numbers whose *sum* is 12 and whose *product* is 20.
The numbers are 10 and 2.

(b) Find two numbers whose sum is 13 and whose product is 40.
The numbers are 8 and 5.

(c) Find two numbers whose sum is 2 and whose product is -15.
The numbers are -3 and 5.

(d) Find two numbers whose sum is -5 and whose product is 4.
The numbers are -1 and -4.

Exercise 3

1. Find two numbers whose sum is 5 and whose product is 6.

2. Find two numbers whose sum is 6 and whose product is 8.

3. Find two numbers whose sum is 7 and whose product is 12.

4. Find two numbers whose sum is 6 and whose product is 5.

5. Find two numbers whose sum is 8 and whose product is 12.

For questions **6** to **45** copy and complete the table.

	Sum	Product	Two numbers
6.	9	18	
7.	9	14	
8.	9	8	
9.	11	30	
10.	17	30	
11.	13	30	
12.	11	24	
13.	10	24	
14.	14	24	
15.	25	24	
16.	13	36	
17.	-3	2	
18.	-5	6	
19.	-6	8	
20.	-7	12	
21.	-7	10	
22.	-9	20	
23.	-10	24	
24.	-10	21	
25.	-13	42	
26.	-13	30	
27.	2	-3	
28.	-1	-6	
29.	1	-6	
30.	3	-4	
31.	-3	-4	
32.	-3	-10	
33.	-1	-12	
34.	5	-6	
35.	-2	-15	
36.	-2	-8	
37.	9	20	
38.	2	-8	
39.	-5	4	
40.	4	-12	
41.	-6	5	
42.	10	21	
43.	3	-10	
44.	-8	12	
45.	-9	8	

Questions on negative numbers are more difficult when the different sorts are mixed together. The remaining questions are given in the form of six short tests.

Test 1

1. $-8 - 8$ **2.** $-8 \times (-8)$
3. -5×3 **4.** $-5 + 3$
5. $8 - (-7)$ **6.** $20 - 2$
7. $-18 \div (-6)$ **8.** $4 + (-10)$
9. $-2 + 13$ **10.** $+8 \times (-6)$
11. $-9 + (+2)$ **12.** $-2 - (-11)$
13. $-6 \times (-1)$ **14.** $2 - 20$
15. $-14 - (-4)$ **16.** $-40 \div (-5)$
17. $5 - 11$ **18.** -3×10
19. $9 + (-5)$ **20.** $7 \div (-7)$

Test 2

1. $-2 \times (+8)$ **2.** $-2 + 8$
3. $-7 - 6$ **4.** $-7 \times (-6)$
5. $+36 \div (-9)$ **6.** $-8 - (-4)$
7. $-14 + 2$ **8.** $5 \times (-4)$
9. $11 + (-5)$ **10.** $11 - 11$
11. $-9 \times (-4)$ **12.** $-6 + (-4)$
13. $3 - 10$ **14.** $-20 \div (-2)$
15. $16 + (-10)$ **16.** $-4 - (+14)$
17. $-45 \div 5$ **18.** $18 - 3$
19. $-1 \times (-1)$ **20.** $-3 - (-3)$

Test 3

1. $-10 \times (-10)$ **2.** $-10 - 10$
3. $-8 \times (+1)$ **4.** $-8 + 1$
5. $5 + (-9)$ **6.** $15 - 5$
7. $-72 \div (-8)$ **8.** $-12 - (-2)$
9. $-1 + 8$ **10.** $-5 \times (-7)$
11. $-10 + (-10)$ **12.** $-6 \times (+4)$
13. $6 - 16$ **14.** $-42 \div (+6)$
15. $-13 + (-6)$ **16.** $-8 - (-7)$
17. $5 \times (-1)$ **18.** $2 - 15$
19. $21 + (-21)$ **20.** $-16 \div (-2)$

Test 4

1. $-4 + 4$ **2.** $-4 \times (+4)$
3. $-2 - 12$ **4.** $-2 \times (-12)$
5. $3 + (-4)$ **6.** $4 - (-10)$
7. $-22 \div 11$ **8.** $-9 + 7$
9. $-6 - (-13)$ **10.** $-3 \times (-11)$
11. $4 - 5$ **12.** $-20 - (+10)$
13. $4 \times (-7)$ **14.** $7 - (-12)$
15. $9 - 18$ **16.** $56 \div (-7)$
17. $7 - 6$ **18.** $-11 + (+2)$
19. $-2 \times (+8)$ **20.** $-8 \div (-2)$

Test 5

1. $-7 \times (-1)$ **2.** $-7 - 1$
3. $-11 + 2$ **4.** -11×2
5. $7 - (-4)$ **6.** $-3 + 16$
7. $-10 \div 5$ **8.** -6×3
9. $1 - 7$ **10.** $13 - (-2)$
11. $4 + (-7)$ **12.** $-9 - (-9)$
13. $-9 \times (-2)$ **14.** $-64 \div (-8)$
15. $16 - 14$ **16.** $-1 + (+7)$
17. $5 \div (-1)$ **18.** $-4 + (-4)$
19. $-4 \times (+10)$ **20.** $16 - 19$

Test 6

1. $-6 + 2$ **2.** $-6 \times (+2)$
3. $-10 \times (-5)$ **4.** $-10 - 5$
5. $-4 + (-5)$ **6.** $16 - 2$
7. $-14 \div (-2)$ **8.** $7 - (-4)$
9. $-2 + 20$ **10.** $-4 \times (-3)$
11. $17 + (-1)$ **12.** $7 \times (-2)$
13. $2 - 5$ **14.** $-8 - (-7)$
15. $-8 \div 8$ **16.** $-8 \times (-5)$
17. $6 - (-1)$ **18.** $-9 + (+14)$
19. $+81 \div (-9)$ **20.** $11 - 14$

13.2 ALGEBRAIC SUBSTITUTION

(a) A formula connecting velocities with acceleration and time is $v = u + at$.
Find the value of v when $u = 3$
$a = 4$.
$t = 6$.

$v = u + at$
$v = 3 + (4 \times 6)$
$v = 27$

(b) A formula for the tension in a spring is $T = \frac{kx}{a}$.
Find the value of T when $k = 13$,
$x = 5$,
$a = 2$.

$T = \frac{kx}{a}$

$T = \frac{13 \times 5}{2}$

$T = 32\frac{1}{2}$

Exercise 4

1. A formula involving force, mass and acceleration is $F = ma$. Find the value of F when $m = 12$ and $a = 3$.

2. The height of a growing tree is given by the formula $h = 2t + 15$. Find the value of h when $t = 7$.

3. The time required to cook a joint of meat is given by the formula
$T = (\text{mass of joint}) \times 3 + \frac{1}{2}$. Find the value of T when (mass of joint) $= 2\frac{1}{2}$.

4. An important formula in Physics states that $I = mu - mv$.
Find the value of I when $m = 6$, $u = 8$, $v = 5$.

5. The distance travelled by an accelerating car is given by the formula $s = \left(\frac{u+v}{2}\right)t$. Find the value of s when $u = 17$, $v = 25$ and $t = 4$.

6. Einstein's famous formula states that $E = mc^2$. Find the value of E when $m = 5$ and $c = 20$.

7. The height of a stone thrown upwards is given by $h = ut - 5t^2$. Find the value of h when $u = 70$ and $t = 3$.

8. The speed of an accelerating particle is given by the formula $v^2 = u^2 + 2as$. Find the value of v when $u = 11$, $a = 5$ and $s = 6$.

9. If $m = 7x + 15$, find the values of m when
(a) $x = 4$ (b) $x = 7$
(c) $x = -2$ (d) $x = 10$.

10. If $T = 2x^2 - 12$, find the values of T when
(a) $x = 3$ (b) $x = 2$
(c) $x = 1$ (d) $x = 5$

11. If $k = 3x^2 + x$, find the values of k when
(a) $x = 2$ (b) $x = 4$
(c) $x = -1$ (d) $x = 10$

12. If $s = (2y)^2 - 6$, find the values of s when
(a) $y = 2$ (b) $y = 3$
(c) $y = -2$ (d) $y = 5$

13. If $z = t^2 + yt$, find the values of z when
(a) $t = 3, y = 4$ (b) $t = 7, y = 1$

14. If $p = (u - v)t$, find the values of p when
(a) $u = 9$, $v = 2$, $t = 8$
(b) $u = 11$, $v = \frac{1}{2}$, $t = 10$.

15. If $v = ut + \frac{1}{2}at^2$, find the values of v when
(a) $u = 0$, $t = 6$, $a = 10$
(b) $u = -2$, $t = 3$, $a = 10$.

Exercise 5

Work out, using $a = 3$, $b = 4$, $c = 5$, $d = 2$.

1. $a + b$ **2.** $c - b$
3. $3a + d$ **4.** $2b - a$
5. $4d - b$ **6.** $3c - d$
7. $a + 5b$ **8.** $c - 2d$
9. $3a + 2c$ **10.** $5a - 2b$
11. $ab + c$ **12.** $2ac$
13. $3cd$ **14.** $bc + cd$
15. $ad - c$ **16.** $bc - ad$
17. $3ab + c$ **18.** $5d + 2bc$
19. abc **20.** $bcd + 10$

21. $cda - 6$ **22.** $3abd$
23. $acd + 4bd$ **24.** $abcd$
25. $bca - 20$ **26.** $17a - bcd$
27. $13a - cd$ **28.** $10acd + 3$
29. $10abcd$ **30.** $3ac - 5db$
31. $a^2 + 5$ **32.** $b^2 - 3$
33. $c^2 + d^2$ **34.** $a^2 + bc$
35. $d^3 - d$ **36.** $a^3 - b^2$
37. $c^2 - bc$ **38.** $d + d^3$
39. $d^4 - a^2$ **40.** $3a^2$

Exercise 6

Work out the values of the expressions in the exercise above using $a = 2$, $b = 1$, $c = 3$, $d = 4$.

Exercise 7

Work out, using $a = 3$, $b = -2$, $x = -1$, $y = 2$.

1. $a+b$
2. $b+y$
3. $a+x$
4. $y+x$
5. $a-y$
6. $a-b$
7. $y-x$
8. $b-y$
9. $x-a$
10. $y-b$
11. $a+b+x$
12. $b+y+x$
13. $a+b+x+y$
14. $2a+b$
15. $2y+x$
16. $3a-4y$
17. $2b+y$
18. $3x+a$
19. $5a-b$
20. $x+2b$
21. ab
22. by
23. xb
24. abx
25. bxy
26. $2ab$
27. $3bx$
28. $2xy+b$
29. $a+bx$
30. $y(a+b)$
31. $x(a+y)$
32. $b(a-x)$
33. $a(y-b)$
34. $2(ab+x)$
35. $5(xy+a)$
36. $a(bx+y)$
37. a^2+b^2
38. x^2+y^2
39. $2a^2$
40. $(2a)^2$
41. $3b^2$
42. $(3b)^2$
43. $5x^2$
44. $(5x)^2$
45. $(a+b)^2$
46. $(x+b)^2$
47. $(y+b)^3$
48. $(ax+y)^2$
49. $x^2(a-b)$
50. $b^2(a-x)$

Exercise 8

Work out the values of the expressions in the exercise above using $a = 2$, $b = -1$, $x = -3$, $y = 4$.

13.3 SOLVING EQUATIONS

Solve the equations

(a)
$$\begin{aligned} 3x + 14 &= 16 \\ 3x &= 16 - 14 \\ 3x &= 2 \\ x &= \tfrac{2}{3} \end{aligned}$$

(b)
$$\begin{aligned} 4x - 5 &= -2 \\ 4x &= -2 + 5 \\ 4x &= 3 \\ x &= \tfrac{3}{4} \end{aligned}$$

(c)
$$\begin{aligned} 7 &= 2x + 15 \\ -15 + 7 &= 2x \\ -8 &= 2x \\ -4 &= x \end{aligned}$$

Exercise 9

Solve the equations.

1. $x-7=5$
2. $x+11=20$
3. $x+12=30$
4. $x-6=-2$
5. $x-8=9$
6. $x+5=0$
7. $x-13=-7$
8. $x+10=3$
9. $5+x=9$
10. $9+x=17$
11. $y-6=11$
12. $y+8=3$
13. $3x+1=16$
14. $4x+3=27$
15. $2x-3=1$
16. $5x-3=1$
17. $3x-7=0$
18. $2x+5=20$
19. $6x-9=2$
20. $7x+6=6$
21. $9x-4=1$
22. $11x-10=1$
23. $15y+2=5$
24. $7y+8=10$
25. $4y-11=-8$
26. $3z-8=-6$
27. $4p+25=30$
28. $5t-6=0$
29. $9m-13=1$
30. $4+3x=5$
31. $7+2x=8$
32. $5+20x=7$
33. $3+8x=0$
34. $50y-7=2$
35. $200y-51=49$
36. $5u-13=-10$
37. $9x-7=-11$
38. $11t+1=1$
39. $3+8y=40$
40. $12+7x=2$
41. $6=3x-1$
42. $8=4x+5$
43. $9=2x+7$
44. $11=5x-7$
45. $0=3x-1$
46. $40=11+14x$
47. $-4=5x+1$
48. $-8=6x-3$
49. $13=4x-20$
50. $-103=2x+7$

Solve the equations

(a)
$$\begin{aligned} 8x - 3 &= 3x + 1 \\ 8x - 3x &= 1 + 3 \\ 5x &= 4 \\ x &= \tfrac{4}{5} \end{aligned}$$

(b)
$$\begin{aligned} 3x + 9 &= 18 - 7x \\ 3x + 7x &= 18 - 9 \\ 10x &= 9 \\ x &= \tfrac{9}{10} \end{aligned}$$

Exercise 10

Solve the equations

1. $7x - 3 = 3x + 8$	**2.** $5x + 4 = 2x + 9$
3. $6x - 2 = x + 8$	**4.** $8x + 1 = 3x + 2$
5. $7x - 10 = 3x - 8$	**6.** $5x - 12 = 2x - 6$
7. $4x - 23 = x - 7$	**8.** $8x - 8 = 3x - 2$
9. $11x + 7 = 6x + 7$	**10.** $9x + 8 = 10$
11. $5 + 3x = x + 8$	**12.** $4 + 7x = x + 5$
13. $6x - 8 = 4 - 3x$	**14.** $5x + 1 = 7 - 2x$
15. $6x - 3 = 1 - x$	**16.** $3x - 10 = 2x - 3$
17. $5x + 1 = 6 - 3x$	**18.** $11x - 20 = 10x - 15$
19. $6 + 2x = 8 - 3x$	**20.** $7 + x = 9 - 5x$
21. $3y - 7 = y + 1$	**22.** $8y + 9 = 7y + 8$
23. $7y - 5 = 2y$	**24.** $3z - 1 = 5 - 4z$
25. $8 = 13 - 4x$	**26.** $10 = 12 - 2x$
27. $13 = 20 - 9x$	**28.** $8 = 5 - 2x$
29. $5 + x = 7 - 8x$	**30.** $3x + 11 = 2 - 3x$

Solve the equations

(a) $3(x - 1) = 2(x + 7)$

$3x - 3 = 2x + 14$

$3x - 2x = 14 + 3$

$x = 17$

(b) $5(2x + 1) = 3(x - 2) + 20$

$10x + 5 = 3x - 6 + 20$

$10x - 3x = -6 + 20 - 5$

$7x = 9$

$x = 1\frac{2}{7}$

Exercise 11

Solve the equations

1. $2(x + 1) = x + 5$
2. $4(x - 2) = 2(x + 1)$
3. $5(x - 3) = 3(x + 2)$
4. $3(x + 2) = 2(x - 1)$
5. $5(x - 3) = 2(x - 7)$
6. $6(x + 2) = 2(x - 3)$
7. $10(x - 3) = x$
8. $3(2x - 1) = 4(x + 1)$
9. $4(2x + 1) = 5(x + 3)$
10. $3(x - 1) + 7 = 2(x + 1)$
11. $5(x + 1) + 3 = 3(x - 1)$
12. $7(x - 2) - 3 = 2(x + 2)$
13. $5(2x + 1) - 5 = 3(x + 1)$
14. $3(4x - 1) - 3 = x + 1$
15. $2(x - 10) = 4 - 3x$
16. $7(x - 3) = 10 - x$
17. $3(x + 1) = 2(x + 3) - 6$
18. $5(2x - 1) = 9(x + 1) - 8$
19. $3(x + 2) = 4(1 - x)$
20. $7(x + 3) = 2(3 - x)$
21. $3(2x + 1) = 4(5 - x)$
22. $5(x + 1) = 3(x - 2) + 12$
23. $3(x + 7) = 2(x + 1) + 20$
24. $2(2x - 1) = 3(1 - 2x)$
25. $5(3x + 1) = 2 + 3(x - 1)$
26. $3(x - 2) = 5 - 2(x + 2)$
27. $2(x + 1) = 7 - 3(x - 1)$
28. $3x - 1 = 8 - 2(2x + 1)$
29. $5(x - 2) = 6 - 3(x + 2)$
30. $7(2x + 1) = 5 - 4(2x - 3)$

Equations with fractions

Solve the equations (a) $\frac{7}{x} = 8$

(b) $\frac{3x}{4} = 2$

(a) $\frac{7}{x} = 8$

$7 = 8x$

$\frac{7}{8} = x$

(b) $\frac{3x}{4} = 2$

$3x = 8$

$x = \frac{8}{3}$

$x = 2\frac{2}{3}$

Exercise 12

Solve the equations.

1. $\frac{3}{x} = 5$	**2.** $\frac{4}{x} = 7$	**3.** $\frac{11}{x} = 12$
4. $\frac{6}{x} = 11$	**5.** $\frac{2}{x} = 3$	**6.** $\frac{5}{y} = 9$
7. $\frac{7}{y} = 9$	**8.** $\frac{4}{t} = 3$	**9.** $\frac{3}{a} = 6$
10. $\frac{8}{x} = 12$	**11.** $\frac{3}{p} = 1$	**12.** $\frac{15}{q} = 10$
13. $5 = \frac{7}{t}$	**14.** $13 = \frac{4}{y}$	**15.** $3 = \frac{10}{x}$
16. $11 = \frac{4}{a}$	**17.** $-2 = \frac{3}{y}$	**18.** $-1 = \frac{5}{x}$
19. $-16 = \frac{7}{x}$	**20.** $-8 = \frac{4}{e}$	**21.** $\frac{10}{c} = -1$

22. $\dfrac{25}{m}=5$ **23.** $\dfrac{4}{n}=400$ **24.** $13=\dfrac{2}{y}$

25. $\dfrac{5}{t}=1$ **26.** $8=\dfrac{15}{x}$ **27.** $-6=\dfrac{3}{x}$

28. $\dfrac{x}{4}=6$ **29.** $\dfrac{x}{5}=3$ **30.** $\dfrac{y}{5}=-2$

31. $\dfrac{a}{7}=3$ **32.** $\dfrac{t}{3}=7$ **33.** $\dfrac{m}{4}=\dfrac{2}{3}$

34. $\dfrac{x}{7}=\dfrac{5}{8}$ **35.** $\dfrac{2x}{3}=1$ **36.** $\dfrac{4x}{5}=3$

37. $\dfrac{3y}{2}=2$ **38.** $\dfrac{5t}{6}=3$ **39.** $\dfrac{m}{8}=\dfrac{1}{4}$

40. $8=\dfrac{5}{x}$ **41.** $19=\dfrac{7}{y}$ **42.** $-5=\dfrac{3}{a}$

43. $-6=\dfrac{k}{4}$ **44.** $\dfrac{n}{7}=-10$ **45.** $4=\dfrac{33}{q}$

46. $\dfrac{x}{2}=110$ **47.** $\dfrac{500}{y}=-1$ **48.** $-99=\dfrac{98}{f}$

Forming equations

The length of a rectangle is twice the width. If the perimeter is 36 cm, find the width.

(a) Let the width of the rectangle be x cm
Then the length of the rectangle is $2x$ cm

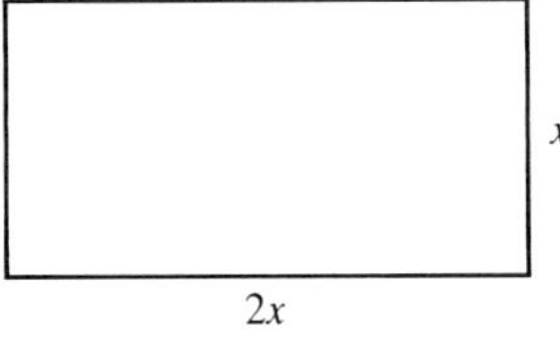

(b) Form an equation.
$x + 2x + x + 2x = 36$

(c) Solve $6x = 36$
$x = 6$
The width of the rectangle is 6 cm

Exercise 13

Solve each problem by forming an equation.

1. The length of a rectangle is three times the width. If the perimeter is 36 cm, find the width. (Let the width be x)

2. The length of a rectangle is five times the width. If the perimeter is 42 cm, find the width.

3. The length of a rectangle is 4 cm greater than its width. If the perimeter is 10 cm, find the width.

4. If the perimeter of the triangle is 29 units, find x.

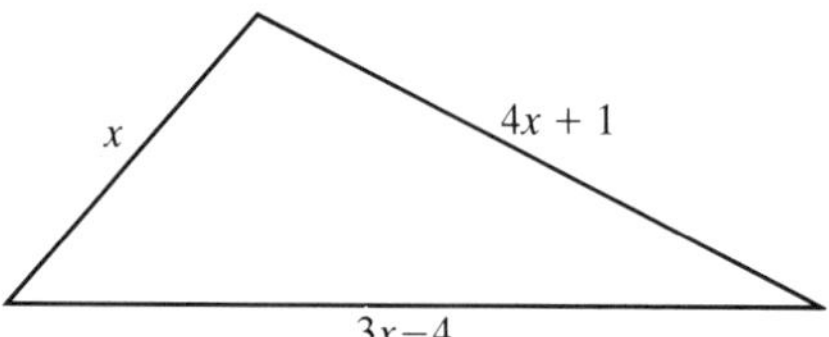

5. When a number is doubled and then added to 15, the result is 38. Find the number.

6. When a number is doubled and then added to 9, the result is 31. Find the number.

7. When a number is trebled and then added to 11, the result is 50. Find the number.

8. Find the area of the rectangle if the perimeter is 30 cm.

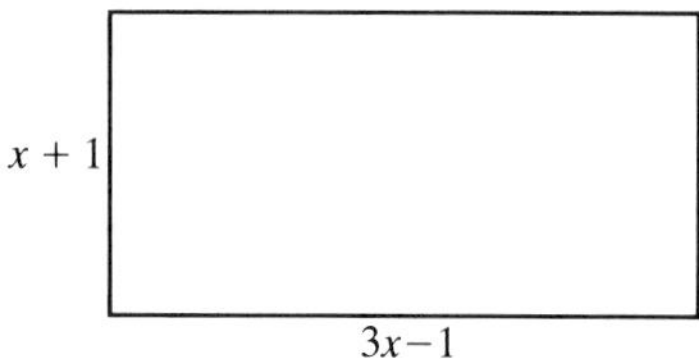

9. The length of a rectangle is 5 cm more than its width. If its perimter is 50 cm, what is its width?

10. If AB is a straight line, find x.

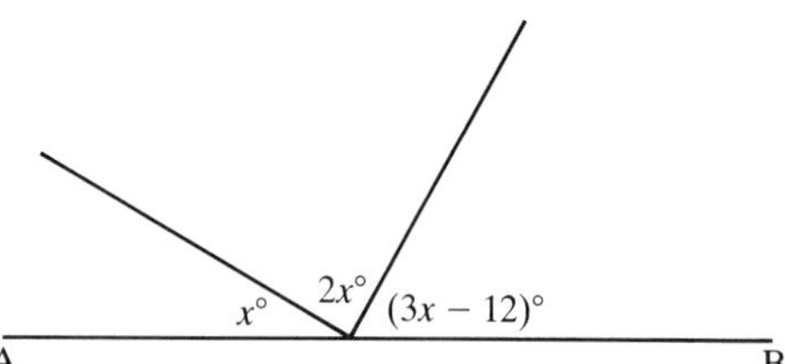

In questions **11** to **18** find the 'mystery' number.

11. If we subtract 3 from the number and then multiply the result by 2, the answer is 3.

12. If we add 9 to the number and then multiply the result by 7, the answer is 147.

13. If we subtract 11 from the number and then treble the result, the answer is 20.

14. If we double the number, add 4 and then multiply the result by 3, the answer is 13.

15. If we treble the number, take away 6 and then multiply the result by 2, the answer is 18.
16. If we double the number and subtract 7 we get the same answer as when we add 5 to the number.
17. If we multiply the number by 5 and subtract 4, we get the same answer as when we add 3 to the number and then double the result.
18. If we multiply the number by 6 and add 1, we get the same answer as when we add 5 to the number and then treble the result.
19. The sum of three consecutive whole numbers is 168. Find the numbers.
20. The sum of four consecutive whole numbers is 170. Find the numbers.

Simple inequalities

(a) Find the largest integer value of x if
$3x < 10$

$3x < 10$
$x < 3\frac{1}{3}$
$\therefore$ Largest integer value of x is 3.
['Integer' means whole number]

(b) Find the smallest integer value of x if
$2x \geqslant 10$

$2x \geqslant 10$
$x \geqslant 5$
$\therefore$ Smallest integer value of x is 5.

Exercise 14

In questions **1** to **16** find the largest integer value of x.

1. $2x<11$ **2.** $3x<8$
3. $4x<21$ **4.** $10x<30$
5. $3x\leqslant 12$ **6.** $2x\leqslant 9$
7. $3x\leqslant 10$ **8.** $5x<7$
9. $3x<50$ **10.** $2x\leqslant 50$
11. $9>2x$ **12.** $11>3x$
13. $16\geqslant 4x$ **14.** $40\geqslant 5x$
15. $1000>2x$ **16.** $100>3x$

In questions **17** to **30** find the smallest integer value of x.

17. $3x>10$ **18.** $4x>9$
19. $2x>13$ **20.** $3x>7$
21. $5x>7$ **22.** $5x>10$
23. $3x\geqslant 12$ **24.** $6x\geqslant 12$
25. $11<3x$ **26.** $801<10x$
27. $10\leqslant 2x$ **28.** $24\leqslant 4x$
29. $50<7x$ **30.** $4x>100$

In questions **31** to **40** list all the integer values of x which satisfy the inequalities.

31. $x < 10\frac{1}{2}$ and $x > 8.1$
32. $2x<12$ and $x>3$
33. $3x<14$ and $x>0$
34. $5x\leqslant 20$ and $x>1$
35. $3x\leqslant 30$ and $2x>15$
36. $4x<19$ and $3x>5$
37. $2x\leqslant 20$ and $5x\geqslant 35$
38. $20<2x\leqslant 30$
39. $10\leqslant 3x\leqslant 18$
40. $975\leqslant 5x\leqslant 1000$

13.4 CHANGING THE SUBJECT OF A FORMULA

Make x the subject in the formulae below.

(a) $ax-p=t$
$ax=t+p$
$$x=\frac{t+p}{a}$$

(b) $y(x+y)=v^2$
$yx+y^2=v^2$
$yx=v^2-y^2$
$$x=\frac{v^2-y^2}{y}$$

Exercise 15

Make x the subject

1. $x+b=e$ **2.** $x-t=m$
3. $x-f=a+b$ **4.** $x+h=A+B$
5. $x+t=y+t$ **6.** $a+x=b$
7. $k+x=m$ **8.** $v+x=w+y$
9. $ax=b$ **10.** $hx=m$
11. $mx=a+b$ **12.** $kx=c-d$
13. $vx=e+n$ **14.** $3x=y+z$
15. $xp=r$ **16.** $xm=h-m$
17. $ax+t=a$ **18.** $mx-e=k$
19. $ux-h=m$ **20.** $ex+q=t$

21. $kx - u^2 = v^2$
22. $gx + t^2 = s^2$
23. $xa + k = m^2$
24. $xm - v = m$
25. $a + bx = c$
26. $t + sx = y$
27. $y + cx = z$
28. $a + hx = 2a$
29. $mx - b = b$
30. $kx + ab = cd$
31. $a(x - b) = c$
32. $c(x - d) = e$
33. $m(x + m) = n^2$
34. $k(x - a) = t$
35. $h(x - h) = k$
36. $m(x + b) = n$
37. $a(x - a) = a^2$
38. $c(a + x) = d$
39. $m(b + x) = e$
40. $n(x - n) = t^2$

Formulae involving fractions

Make x the subject in the formulae below.

(a) $\frac{x}{a} = p$

$x = ap$

(b) $\frac{m}{x} = t$

$m = xt$

$\frac{m}{t} = x$

Exercise 16

Make x the subject.

1. $\frac{x}{t} = m$
2. $\frac{x}{e} = n$
3. $\frac{x}{p} = a$
4. $am = \frac{x}{t}$
5. $bc = \frac{x}{a}$
6. $e = \frac{x}{y^2}$
7. $\frac{x}{a} = (b + c)$
8. $\frac{x}{t} = (c - d)$
9. $\frac{x}{m} = s + t$
10. $\frac{x}{k} = h + i$
11. $\frac{x}{b} = \frac{a}{c}$
12. $\frac{x}{m} = \frac{z}{y}$
13. $\frac{x}{h} = \frac{c}{d}$
14. $\frac{m}{n} = \frac{x}{e}$
15. $\frac{b}{e} = \frac{x}{h}$
16. $\frac{x}{(a + b)} = c$
17. $\frac{x}{(h + k)} = m$
18. $\frac{x}{u} = \frac{m}{y}$
19. $\frac{x}{(h - k)} = t$
20. $\frac{x}{(a + b)} = (z + t)$
21. $t = \frac{e}{x}$
22. $a = \frac{b}{x}$
23. $m = \frac{h}{x}$
24. $\frac{a}{b} = \frac{c}{x}$
25. $\frac{u}{x} = \frac{c}{d}$
26. $\frac{m}{x} = t^2$
27. $\frac{h}{x} = \sin 20°$
28. $\frac{e}{x} = \cos 40°$
29. $\frac{m}{x} = \tan 46°$
30. $\frac{a^2}{b^2} = \frac{c^2}{x}$

Formulae with x^2 and negative x terms

Make x the subject of the formulae.

(a) $ax^2 = e$

$x^2 = \frac{e}{a}$

$x = \pm\sqrt{\left(\frac{e}{a}\right)}$

(b) $h - bx = m$

$h = m + bx$

$h - m = bx$

$\frac{h - m}{b} = x$

Exercise 17

Make x the subject.

1. $cx^2 = h$
2. $bx^2 = f$
3. $x^2t = m$
4. $x^2y = (a + b)$
5. $mx^2 = (t + a)$
6. $x^2 - a = b$
7. $x^2 + c = t$
8. $x^2 + y = z$
9. $x^2 - a^2 = b^2$
10. $x^2 + t^2 = m^2$
11. $x^2 + n^2 = a^2$
12. $ax^2 = c$
13. $hx^2 = n$
14. $cx^2 = z + k$
15. $ax^2 + b = c$
16. $dx^2 - e = h$
17. $gx^2 - n = m$
18. $x^2m + y = z$
19. $a + mx^2 = f$
20. $a^2 + x^2 = b^2$
21. $a - x = y$
22. $h - x = m$
23. $z - x = q$
24. $v = b - x$
25. $m = k - x$
26. $h - cx = d$
27. $y - mx = c$
28. $k - ex = h$
29. $a^2 - bx = d$
30. $m^2 - tx = n^2$
31. $v^2 - ax = w$
32. $y - x = y^2$
33. $k - t^2x = m$
34. $e = b - cx$
35. $z = h - gx$
36. $a + b = c - dx$
37. $y^2 = v^2 - kx$
38. $h = d - fx$
39. $a(b - x) = c$
40. $h(m - x) = n$

The next two exercises are more difficult because they contain a wide variety of different formulae.

Exercise 18

Make the letter in brackets the subject.

1. $ax-d=h$ [x]
2. $zy+k=m$ [y]
3. $d(y+e)=f$ [y]
4. $m(a+k)=d$ [k]
5. $a+bm=c$ [m]
6. $ae^2=b$ [e]
7. $yt^2=z$ [t]
8. $x^2-c=e$ [x]
9. $my-n=b$ [y]
10. $a(z+a)=b$ [z]
11. $\frac{a}{x}=d$ [x]
12. $\frac{k}{m}=t$ [k]
13. $\frac{u}{m}=n$ [u]
14. $\frac{y}{x}=d$ [x]
15. $\frac{a}{m}=t$ [m]
16. $\frac{d}{g}=n$ [g]
17. $\frac{t}{k}=(a+b)$ [t]
18. $y=\frac{v}{e}$ [e]
19. $c=\frac{m}{y}$ [y]
20. $\frac{a^2}{m}=b$ [a]
21. $g(m+a)=b$ [m]
22. $h(h+g)=x^2$ [g]
23. $y-t=z$ [t]
24. $me^2=c$ [e]
25. $a(y+x)=t$ [x]
26. $uv-t^2=y^2$ [v]
27. $k^2+t=c$ [k]
28. $k-w=m$ [w]
29. $b-an=c$ [n]
30. $m(a+y)=c$ [y]
31. $pq-x=ab$ [x]
32. $a^2-bk=t$ [k]
33. $v^2z=w$ [z]
34. $c=t-u$ [u]
35. $xc+t=2t$ [c]
36. $m(n+w)=k$ [w]
37. $v-mx=t$ [m]
38. $c=a(y+b)$ [y]
39. $m(a-c)=e$ [c]
40. $ba^2=c$ [a]
41. $\frac{a}{p}=q$ [p]
42. $\frac{a}{n^2}=e$ [n]
43. $\frac{h}{f^2}=m$ [f]
44. $\frac{v}{x^2}=n$ [x]
45. $v-ac=t^3$ [c]
46. $a(a^2+y)=b^3$ [y]
47. $ah^2-d=b$ [h]
48. $h(h+k)=bc$ [k]
49. $u^2-n^2=v^2$ [n]
50. $m(b-z)=b^3$ [z]

Exercise 19

Make x the subject.

1. $a+x=p$
2. $y+x=m$
3. $z=k+x$
4. $u^2=t^2+x$
5. $a=bc+mx$
6. $z=k+ax$
7. $u^2=e^2+kx$
8. $m(a+x)=b$
9. $h=k(a+x)$
10. $y=p(p+x)$
11. $\frac{x}{k}=y$
12. $\frac{x}{m}=n$
13. $q=\frac{x}{q}$
14. $mn=\frac{x}{n}$
15. $\frac{m}{x}=a$
16. $e=\frac{n}{x}$
17. $w=\frac{u}{x}$
18. $\sin 32°=\frac{e}{x}$
19. $\frac{1}{2}zx=y$
20. $\frac{1}{3}kx=p$
21. $x^2-n=m$
22. $v+x^2=a-b$
23. $bx^2-n=n^2$
24. $a(x-b)=d+e$
25. $k(x^2-k)=mp$
26. $y-x=m$
27. $e(x-d)=u$
28. $a(y+x)=z$
29. $y(ex-f)=w$
30. $t(m+ax)=m$
31. $\frac{x}{(c+d)}=y$
32. $\frac{(a-b)}{x}=p$
33. $\frac{(m+n)}{x}=A$
34. $\frac{k}{x^2}=h$
35. $\frac{(A+B)}{x}=E$
36. $\frac{1}{4}kx=q$
37. $a(x^2-d)=h$
38. $y=k^2-x$
39. $g=m-nx$
40. $k=c(c-x)$

13.5 FACTORS

Factorise the following (a) $12a - 15b$
(b) $3x^2 - 2x$
(c) $2xy + 6y^2$

(a) $12a - 15b = 3(4a - 5b)$
(b) $3x^2 - 2x = x(3x - 2)$
(c) $2xy + 6y^2 = 2y(x + 3y)$

Exercise 20

In questions **1** to **10** copy and complete the statement.

1. $6x + 4y = 2(3x + \quad)$
2. $9x + 12y = 3(\quad + 4y)$
3. $10a + 4b = 2(5a + \quad)$
4. $4x + 12y = 4(\quad + \quad)$
5. $10a + 15b = 5(\quad + \quad)$
6. $18x - 24y = 6(3x - \quad)$
7. $8u - 28v = \quad(\quad - 7v)$
8. $15s + 25t = \quad(3s + \quad)$
9. $24m + 40n = \quad(3m - \quad)$
10. $27c - 72d = \quad(\quad - 8d)$

In questions **11** to **30** factorise the expression.

11. $20a + 8b$ **12.** $30x - 24y$
13. $27c - 33d$ **14.** $35u + 49v$
15. $12s - 32t$ **16.** $40x - 16t$
17. $24x + 84y$ **18.** $12x + 8y + 16z$
19. $12a - 6b + 9c$ **20.** $10x - 20y + 25z$
21. $20a - 12b - 28c$ **22.** $48m + 8n - 24x$
23. $42x + 49y - 21z$ **24.** $6x^2 + 15y^2$
25. $20x^2 - 15y^2$ **26.** $7a^2 + 28b^2$
27. $27a + 63b - 36c$ **28.** $12x^2 + 24xy + 18y^2$
29. $64p - 72q - 40r$ **30.** $36x - 60y + 96z$

Exercise 21

Factorise the following expressions.

1. $3x^2 + 2x$ **2.** $4x^2 - 3x$
3. $5x^2 + x$ **4.** $x^2 - 2x$
5. $2y^2 + 5y$ **6.** $4a^2 - 5a$
7. $6x^2 - 2x$ **8.** $12x^2 + 9x$
9. $10y^2 - 6y$ **10.** $7x^2 - 3x$
11. $10y^2 - 55y$ **12.** $12a^2 + 21a$
13. $x^3 + 2x^2 + 5x$ **14.** $2x^3 - 6x^2 + 2x$
15. $3x^3 + 3x^2 + 6x$ **16.** $2y^3 - 10y$
17. $12t^3 - 28t$ **18.** $u^3 + 2u^2 + 7u$
19. $4x^3 - 8x^2 - 4x$ **20.** $3ax + 2ay$
21. $4ax + 3bx$ **22.** $5cy + 2dy$
23. $4mx - 3my$ **24.** $an + 3bn$
25. $2ax - 10bx$ **26.** $6ax + 3ay$
27. $12ac + 16bc$ **28.** $6mx + 3my + 3mz$
29. $12px - 4py + 12pz$ **30.** $10x^3 - 5x^2 + 10x$
31. $6a^2m + 4am + 2m$ **32.** $6x^2y + 9xy + 12y$
33. $4wx - 5wy - 2wz$ **34.** $8at - 12bt + 14ct$
35. $16xy + 8y^2 + 24y$ **36.** $15ax + 20bx - 25x$
37. $36x^3 - 27x$ **38.** $45ax - 30bx + 60cx$
39. $84x^2y + 24y$ **40.** $18ux^2 + 27uy^2 + 45uz^2$

13.6 ROOTS AND INDICES

Squares and square roots

(a) $11^2 = 11 \times 11 = 121$ (b) $0.3^2 = 0.3 \times 0.3 = 0.09$
(c) $\sqrt{36} = 6$ (d) $\sqrt{0.01} = 0.1$

Exercise 22

Work out, without using a calculator.

1. 7^2 **2.** 3^2
3. 1^2 **4.** 10^2
5. 100^2 **6.** 9^2
7. 20^2 **8.** 0.1^2
9. 0.2^2 **10.** 8^2
11. 5^2 **12.** 4^2
13. 60^2 **14.** 12^2
15. $(\frac{1}{2})^2$ **16.** $\sqrt{4}$

17. $\sqrt{9}$
18. $\sqrt{100}$
19. $\sqrt{900}$
20. $\sqrt{121}$
21. $\sqrt{36}$
22. $\sqrt{10\,000}$
23. $\sqrt{1\,000\,000}$
24. $\sqrt{144}$
25. $\sqrt{1}$
26. $\sqrt{49}$
27. $\sqrt{0.01}$
28. $\sqrt{169}$
29. $\sqrt{\frac{1}{9}}$
30. $\sqrt{0}$
31. $(-1)^2$
32. $(-3)^2$
33. $(-5)^2$
34. $3^2 + (-3)^2$
35. $4^2 + (-4)^2$
36. $100^2 + \sqrt{100}$
37. $8^2 + \sqrt{9}$
38. $(-6)^2 - \sqrt{36}$
39. $1^2 - \sqrt{1}$
40. $5^2 - \sqrt{400}$
41. $(-6)^2 + (-2)^2$
42. $\sqrt{(3^2 + 4^2)}$
43. $\sqrt{(5^2 + 12^2)}$
44. $\sqrt{(6^2 + 8^2)}$
45. $\sqrt{(5^2 - 4^2)}$

Exercise 23

Use a calculator or square root tables to find the square root of the following numbers, correct to three significant figures.

1. 2	**2.** 5	**3.** 17
4. 6	**5.** 10	**6.** 101
7. 5.7	**8.** 8.21	**9.** 200
10. 427	**11.** 18.6	**12.** 0.94
13. 0.21	**14.** 12	**15.** 6072
16. 52 800	**17.** 428.8	**18.** 0.076
19. 0.095	**20.** 0.0074	**21.** 0.008 43
22. 1.1	**23.** 16	**24.** 2.36
25. 8060	**26.** 25 472	**27.** 61 616
28. 2 500 000	**29.** 0.8412	**30.** 72 000
31. 265	**32.** 1.756	**33.** 3.008
34. 19.62	**35.** 11.21	**36.** 0.074
37. 8.652	**38.** 61 111	**39.** 2333
40. 40 000	**41.** 36	**42.** 0.01
43. 7.841	**44.** 0.0085	**45.** 850 000
46. 7777	**47.** 232 323	**48.** 1007
49. 0.1555	**50.** 87.8	**51.** 2000
52. 47 600	**53.** 7	**54.** 1713
55. (a) 0.02	(b) 0.2	(c) 2
(d) 20	(e) 200	(f) 2000
56. (a) 0.05	(b) 0.5	(c) 5
(d) 50	(e) 500	(f) 5000
57. (a) 0.017	(b) 0.17	(c) 1.7
(d) 17	(e) 170	(f) 1700
58. (a) 0.0006	(b) 0.006	(c) 0.06
(d) 0.6	(e) 6	(f) 60

59. Describe the pattern you observe in questions **55** to **58**.

Cube roots by trial and error

Find the cube root of 17, correct to two significant figures, by trial and error.

(a) Try 2. $2^3 = 8$, too small.
(b) Try 3. $3^3 = 27$, too big.
(c) Try 2.5. $2.5^3 = 15.625$, too small.
(d) Try 2.6. $2.6^3 = 17.576$, too big.
(e) Try 2.55. $2.55^3 = 16.58$, too small.
(f) Try 2.58. $2.58^3 = 17.17$, too big.
(g) Try 2.57. $2.57^3 = 16.97$

Finally $\sqrt[3]{17} = 2.57$ correct to three significant figures.

Exercise 24

Find the cube root of the following numbers, using the method above. Give the answers correct to three significant figures.

1. 9	**2.** 11	**3.** 31
4. 60	**5.** 15	**6.** 100
7. 2	**8.** 300	**9.** 0.1
10. 0.01	**11.** 40 000	**12.** 800 000

Indices

Indices are used as a mathematical shorthand.

$2 \times 2 \times 2 \times 2 = 2^4$
$5 \times 5 \times 5 = 5^3$
$7 \times 7 \times 2 \times 2 \times 2 = 7^2 \times 2^3$
$3 \times 3 \times 3 \times 3 \times 10 \times 10 = 3^4 \times 10^2$

Exercise 25

Write in a form using indices.

1. $3 \times 3 \times 3 \times 3$
2. 5×5
3. $6 \times 6 \times 6$
4. $10 \times 10 \times 10 \times 10 \times 10$
5. $1 \times 1 \times 1 \times 1 \times 1 \times 1 \times 1$
6. $8 \times 8 \times 8 \times 8$
7. $7 \times 7 \times 7 \times 7 \times 7 \times 7$
8. $2 \times 2 \times 2 \times 5 \times 5$
9. $3 \times 3 \times 7 \times 7 \times 7 \times 7$
10. $3 \times 3 \times 10 \times 10 \times 10$
11. $5 \times 5 \times 5 \times 5 \times 11 \times 11$
12. $2 \times 3 \times 2 \times 3 \times 3$
13. $5 \times 3 \times 3 \times 5 \times 5$
14. $2 \times 2 \times 3 \times 3 \times 3 \times 11 \times 11$

15. $7 \times 2 \times 3 \times 2 \times 7 \times 2 \times 3$
16. $5 \times 2 \times 2 \times 5 \times 5 \times 7 \times 2$
17. $3 \times 11 \times 3 \times 5 \times 3 \times 11 \times 3$
18. $6 \times 6 \times 5 \times 6 \times 5$
19. $2 \times 7 \times 2 \times 3 \times 2 \times 7 \times 3$
20. $5 \times 9 \times 5 \times 2 \times 7 \times 7 \times 9$
21. $a \times a \times a$
22. $c \times c \times c \times c$
23. $e \times e \times e \times e \times e$
24. $y \times y \times z \times z \times z$
25. $m \times m \times m \times n \times n$
26. $t \times t \times t \times t \times p \times p$
27. $u \times y \times y \times u \times u$
28. $m \times y \times m \times y \times y \times y$
29. $a \times e \times y \times e \times a \times e$
30. $n \times e \times e \times e \times e \times n \times n$

Exercise 26

Work out

1. 2^3 **2.** 3^2 **3.** 1^4
4. 3^3 **5.** 5^2 **6.** 2^2
7. 1^7 **8.** 10^2 **9.** 4^2
10. 4^3 **11.** 10^3 **12.** 2^5
13. 3^4 **14.** 5^3 **15.** 10^6
16. 7^2 **17.** $(-2)^2$ **18.** $(-1)^2$
19. $(-1)^3$ **20.** $(-2)^3$ **21.** $(-3)^3$
22. $(-1)^5$ **23.** $(-5)^2$ **24.** $(-10)^3$
25. $(-4)^3$ **26.** $(-2)^6$ **27.** $(-1)^{10}$
28. $(-100)^2$ **29.** 0.1^2 **30.** $(\frac{1}{2})^2$

Negative indices

$$2^{-3} = \frac{1}{2^3} = \frac{1}{8}$$

$$3^{-2} = \frac{1}{3^2} = \frac{1}{9}$$

$$x^{-5} = \frac{1}{x^5}$$

Exercise 27

In questions **1** to **12**, work out the value of the number given.

1. 2^{-2} **2.** 4^{-2} **3.** 10^{-2}
4. 1^{-4} **5.** 3^{-3} **6.** 4^{-3}
7. 10^{-3} **8.** 5^{-2} **9.** 7^{-2}
10. 5^{-3} **11.** 9^{-2} **12.** 1^{-7}

In questions **13** to **42**, answer 'true' or 'false'.

13. $2^3 = 8$ **14.** $3^2 = 6$ **15.** $5^3 = 125$
16. $2^{-1} = \frac{1}{2}$ **17.** $10^{-2} = \frac{1}{20}$ **18.** $3^{-3} = \frac{1}{9}$
19. $2^2 > 2^3$ **20.** $2^3 < 3^2$ **21.** $2^{-2} > 2^{-3}$
22. $3^{-2} < 3^3$ **23.** $1^9 = 9$ **24.** $(-3)^2 = -9$
25. $5^{-2} = \frac{1}{10}$ **26.** $10^{-3} = \frac{1}{1000}$ **27.** $10^{-2} > 10^{-3}$
28. $5^{-1} = 0.2$ **29.** $10^{-1} = 0.1$ **30.** $2^{-2} = 0.25$
31. $3^{-2} > 3^{-3}$ **32.** $2^5 = 5^2$ **33.** $2^4 = 4^2$
34. $(-2)^2 = 2^2$ **35.** $(-2)^3 = 2^3$ **36.** $10^{-2} = 0.01$
37. $1^{-10} = \frac{1}{10}$ **38.** $3^4 < 4^3$ **39.** $5^2 > 5^{-2}$
40. $2^{-3} > 1$ **41.** $(-2)^3 > 1$ **42.** $7^{-2} > 50^{-1}$

Multiplying and dividing

$3^2 \times 3^4 = (3 \times 3) \times (3 \times 3 \times 3 \times 3) = 3^6$
$2^3 \times 2^2 = (2 \times 2 \times 2) \times (2 \times 2) = 2^5$
$7^3 \times 7^5 = 7^8$ [add the indices].

$$2^4 \div 2^2 = \frac{2 \times 2 \times 2 \times 2}{2 \times 2} = 2^2$$

$\left.\begin{array}{l} 5^6 \div 5^2 = 5^4 \\ 7^8 \div 7^3 = 7^5 \end{array}\right\}$ [subtract the indices].

Exercise 28

Write in a more simple form.

1. $5^2 \times 5^4$ **2.** $6^3 \times 6^2$ **3.** $10^4 \times 10^5$
4. $7^5 \times 7^3$ **5.** $3^6 \times 3^4$ **6.** $8^3 \times 8^3$
7. $2^3 \times 2^{10}$ **8.** $3^6 \times 3^{-2}$ **9.** $5^4 \times 5^{-1}$
10. $7^7 \times 7^{-3}$ **11.** $5^{-3} \times 5^5$ **12.** $3^{-2} \times 3^{-2}$
13. $6^{-3} \times 6^8$ **14.** $5^{-2} \times 5^{-8}$ **15.** $7^{-3} \times 7^9$

16. $7^4 \div 7^2$ **17.** $6^7 \div 6^2$ **18.** $8^5 \div 8^4$
19. $5^{10} \div 5^2$ **20.** $10^7 \div 10^5$ **21.** $9^6 \div 9^8$
22. $3^8 \div 3^{10}$ **23.** $2^6 \div 2^2$ **24.** $3^3 \div 3^5$
25. $7^2 \div 7^8$ **26.** $3^{-2} \div 3^2$ **27.** $5^{-3} \div 5^2$
28. $8^{-1} \div 8^4$ **29.** $5^{-4} \div 5^1$ **30.** $6^2 \div 6^{-2}$

31. $7^5 \times 7^3$ **32.** $6^{-2} \times 6^6$ **33.** $11^3 \times 11^{-5}$
34. $5^{-2} \div 5^3$ **35.** $3^4 \div 3^{-1}$ **36.** $7^5 \div 7^{-2}$
37. $3^{-4} \times 3^{10}$ **38.** $10^{-3} \div 10^{-7}$ **39.** $5^2 \times 5^{20}$
40. $\dfrac{2^3 \times 2^4}{2^2}$ **41.** $\dfrac{3^4 \times 3^5}{3^3}$ **42.** $\dfrac{5^4 \times 5^{-2}}{5^1}$
43. $\dfrac{7^7 \times 7^{-1}}{7^4}$ **44.** $\dfrac{5^{-3} \times 5^{-2}}{5^2}$ **45.** $\dfrac{2^5 \times 2^{-1}}{2^{-2}}$

Unit 14

14.1 SPEED, DISTANCE AND TIME

Distance = Speed × Time.

$$\text{Speed} = \frac{\text{Distance}}{\text{Time}}.$$

$$\text{Time} = \frac{\text{Distance}}{\text{Speed}}.$$

1. A bird takes 20 s to fly a distance of 100 m. Calculate the average speed of the bird.

$\left(S = \frac{D}{T}\right)$ Average speed $= \frac{100}{20} = 5$ m/s.

2. A car travels a distance of 200 m at a speed of 25 m/s. How long does it take?

$\left(T = \frac{D}{S}\right)$

Time taken $= \frac{200}{25} = 8$ seconds

3. A boat sails at a speed of 12 knots for 2 days. How far does it travel?

1 knot = 1 nautical mile/hour
2 days = 48 hours

(D = S × T)

Distance travelled = 12 × 48
= 576 nautical miles

Exercise 1

The map shows several towns with the main roads joining them. The numbers indicate the distances in miles between each pair of towns.

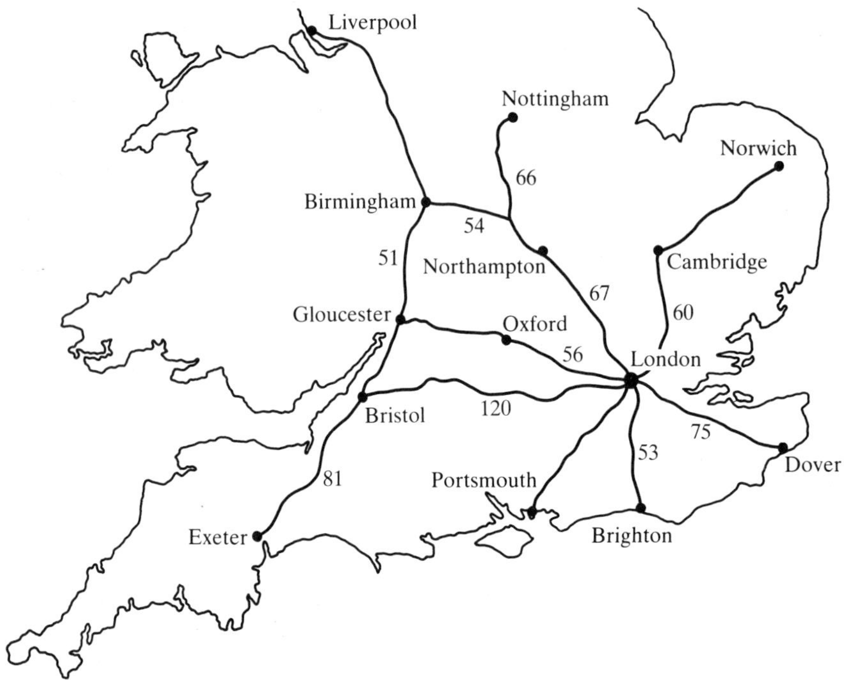

1. How far is it from Liverpool to Birmingham if the journey takes 2 hours at 49 mph?
2. How long does it take to travel from London to Cambridge at a speed of 30 mph?
3. What is the average speed of a car which travels from London to Bristol in three hours?
4. How far is it from Oxford to Gloucester if the journey takes seven hours at 7 mph?
5. An athlete runs from Exeter to Bristol at an average speed of 9 mph. How long does it take?
6. What is the average speed of a lorry which goes from Dover to London in $2\frac{1}{2}$ hours?
7. How far is it from Cambridge to Norwich if a man can walk the distance at a speed of 4 mph in $15\frac{1}{2}$ hours?
8. How long will a dog, running at 6 mph, take to run from Nottingham to Northampton?
9. A vintage car does the London to Brighton run in 20 hours. What is the average speed of the car?
10. A girl on a sponsored walk goes from Bristol to Gloucester in 11 hours at an average speed of 3.2 mph. How far is it from Bristol to Gloucester?
11. How long does it take a cyclist to travel from Birmingham to Northampton at a speed of 12 mph?
12. What is the average speed of a man on a horse who goes from London to Cambridge in 5 hours?
13. How far is it from London to Portsmouth if the journey takes 6 hours 15 minutes at a speed of 10 mph?
14. How long does it take to travel from Bristol to London at a speed of 80 mph?
15. A runaway horse runs from Brighton to London in 4 hours. What is the average speed of the horse?

Exercise 2

Copy and complete the table, giving correct units throughout.

	Speed	Distance	Time
1.	10 m/s	20 m	
2.		12 km	3 h
3.	12 mph	60 miles	
4.	100 cm/s		15 s
5.		15 km	2 h
6.	0.2 m/s		100 s
7.	11.4 km/h		4 h
8.	km/h	18 km	30 minutes
9.	18 feet/minute		10 minutes
10.		0.6 cm	10 s
11.	12 km/h	72 km	
12.	0.2 m/s		20 s
13.	5 cm/day	50 cm	
14.	0.05 m/s		10 s
15.	km/h	200 km	$\frac{1}{2}$ h
16.	0.02 km/year		100 years
17.	km/h	20 km	30 minutes
18.	100 m/s	1 m	
19.	26 cm/s	13 cm	
20.	5 m/day		15 days
21.	2 inches/s	60 inches	
22.	6 inches/s	3 feet	
23.	m/s	0.2 m	10 s
24.	250 mph	miles	15 minutes
25.	mph	18 miles	20 minutes

Exercise 3

1. If a car goes 15 miles in half an hour, how far does it go in one hour at the same speed?
2. If a lorry goes 18 km in 30 minutes, how far does it go in one hour at the same speed?
3. If a train travels 40 km in 20 minutes, how far does it go in one hour at the same speed?
4. A bird flies 8 miles in 15 minutes. How far will it fly in one hour?
5. A man runs at a speed of 9 mph. How far will he run in 20 minutes?
6. An aircraft flies at a speed of 600 mph. How far will it fly in 40 minutes?
7. A car runs at a speed of 40 mph. How far will it go in 1 hour 15 minutes?
8. A large whale swims at a speed of 15 km/h. How far will it swim in 40 minutes?
9. Find the time taken:
   (a) 8 miles at 16 mph
   (b) 20 km at 80 km/h
   (c) 12 miles at 16 mph
   (d) 50 m at 10 m/s.
10. Find the distance travelled:
    (a) 62 mph for 2 hours
    (b) 17 km/h for 4 hours
    (c) 84 mph for 30 minutes
    (d) 120 km/h for 15 minutes
11. Find the speed in km/h:
    (a) 17 km in 30 minutes
    (b) 22 km in 15 minutes
    (c) 15 km in 20 minutes
    (d) 23 km in 20 minutes
12. Find the distance travelled:
    (a) 19 mph for 30 minutes
    (b) 38 mph for 15 minutes
    (c) 36 km/h for 20 minutes
    (d) 80 km/h for 12 minutes
13. The distance from Manchester to Glasgow by road is 357 km. If a driver averages 70 km/h, find the time taken.
14. A car travels at an average speed of 45 mph. How long would a journey of 150 miles take in hours and minutes?
15. A British Rail High Speed Train goes from London to Newport at an average speed of 150 km/h and takes 1 hour 30 minutes over the journey.
    (a) State the time of arrival in Newport if it leaves London at 10 55.
    (b) Calculate the distance in kilometres between London and Newport.

16. In a car race the winning car passed the finishing line 5.5 seconds ahead of the car which came second. If both cars were travelling at 70 m/s, what was the distance between the two cars at the end?

17. Mr Steadman drove his car from Edinburgh to York. The record of his journey in both directions is given below. The distance from Edinburgh to York is 295 km.

Time

07 15	Left Edinburgh
09 15	Stopped for refreshment 160 km from Edinburgh
10 00	The journey to York continued
11 30	Arrived in York
15 00	Left York to travel back to Edinburgh.

(a) Calculate his average speed in km/h before he stopped for refreshment.
(b) Calculate the distance from York when he stopped for refreshment.
(c) Calculate his average speed for the second part of the journey.
(d) On the return journey from York to Edinburgh he averaged 59 km/h. Calculate the time of arrival in York.

14.2 PYTHAGORAS' THEOREM

Find x in the triangle shown.

x 2 cm 6 cm

$x^2 = 2^2 + 6^2$
$x^2 = 40$
$x = \sqrt{40}$
$x = 6.32$ cm (to 3 S.F.)

Exercise 4

Find the side marked with a letter. All lengths are in cm. Give answers correct to 3 S.F.

1.

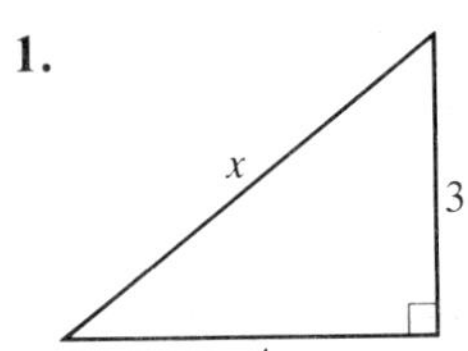

2. x 6 5

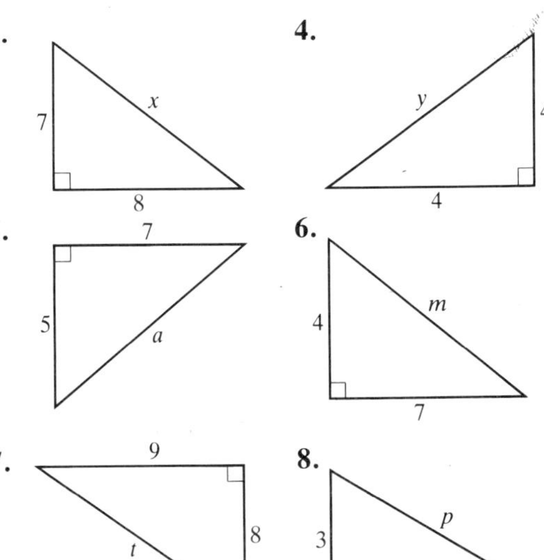

9. x 5 12

10. 6 y 6

11.

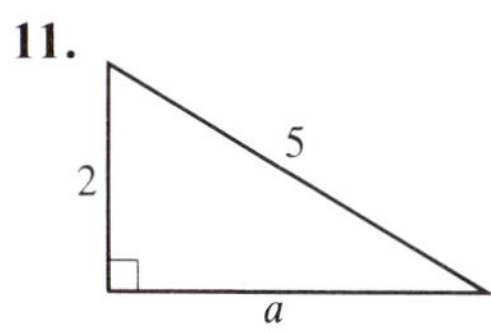

12.

x
3
6

13.

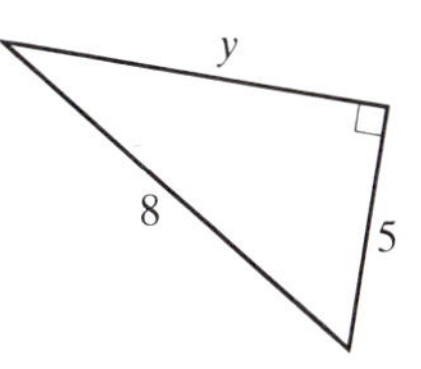

14.

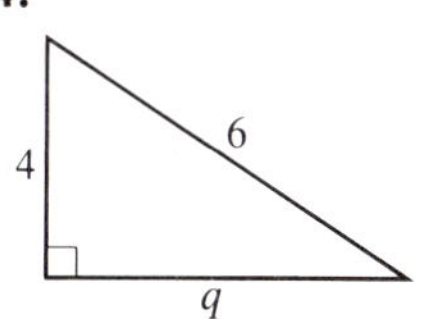

15.

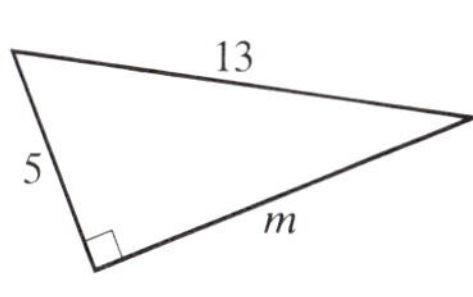

16.

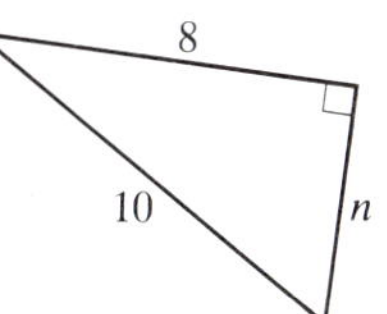

17.

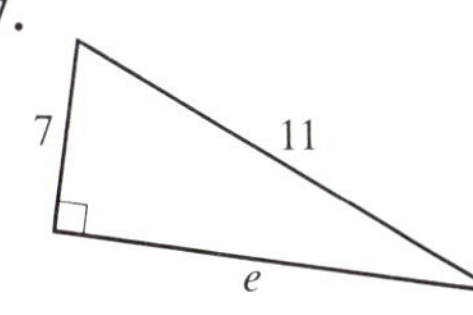

18.

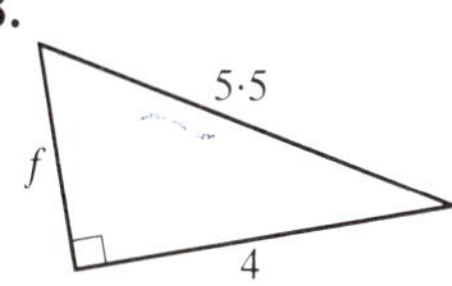

19.

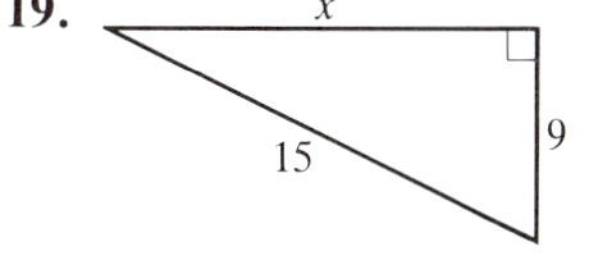

20.

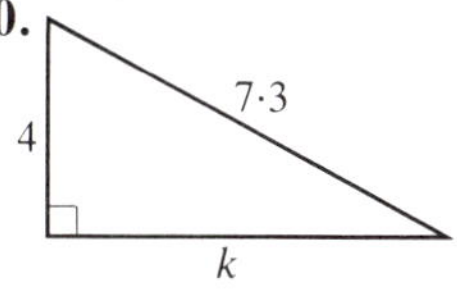

Exercise 5

Find the side marked with a letter. All lengths are in cm. Give answers correct to 3 S.F.

1.

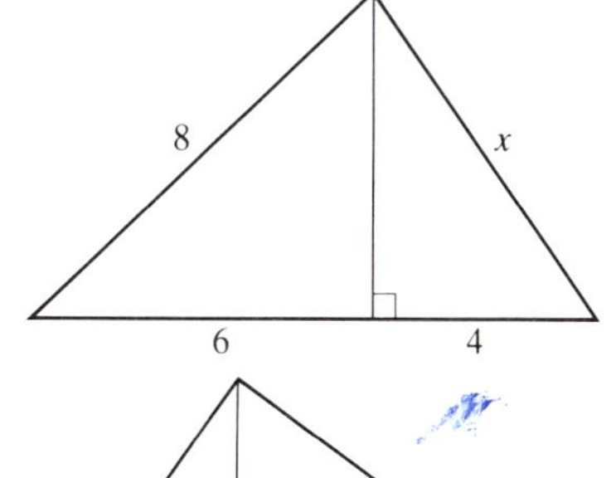

2.

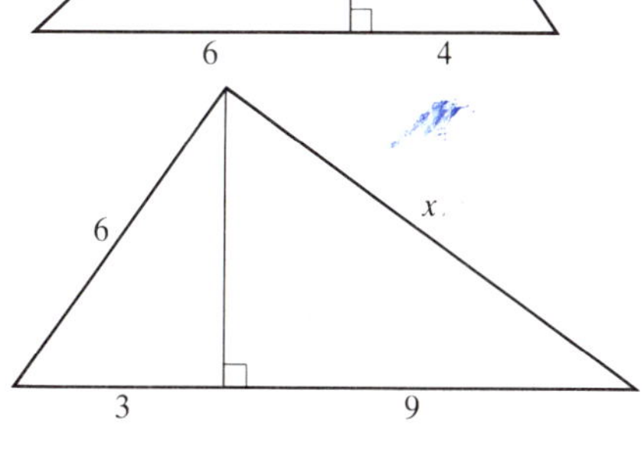

3.

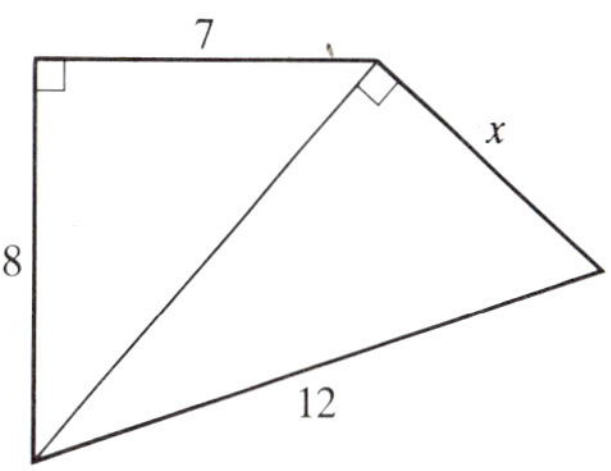

4.

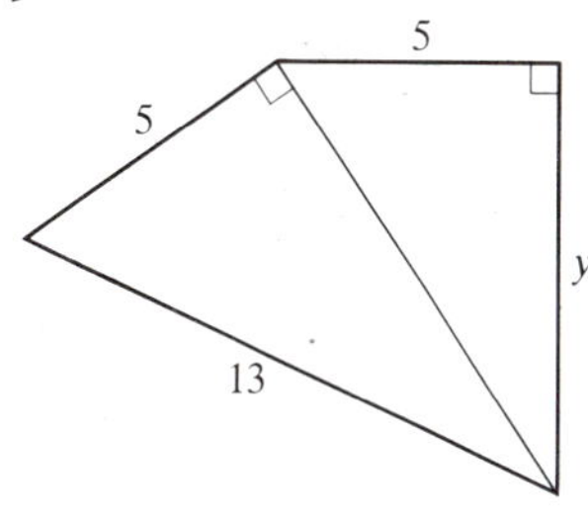

5.

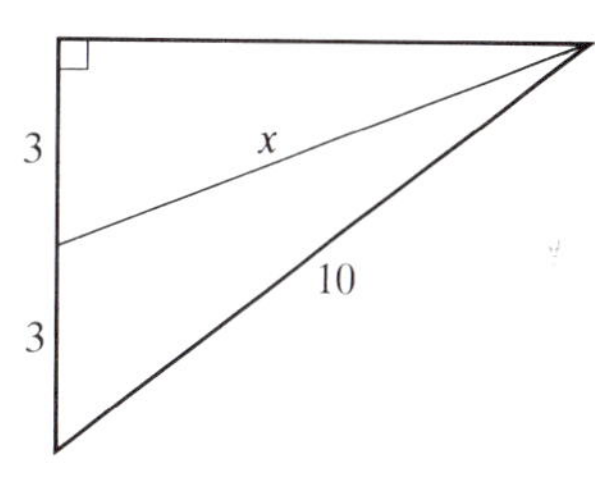

6.

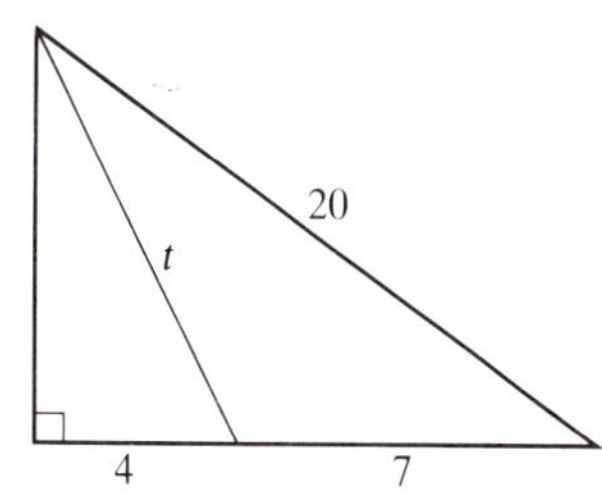

7.

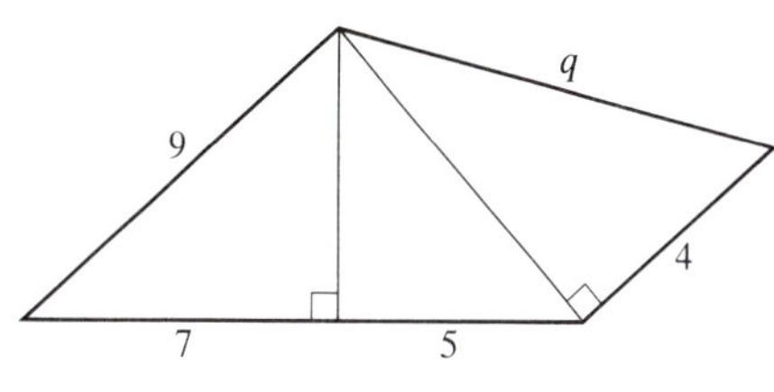

8.

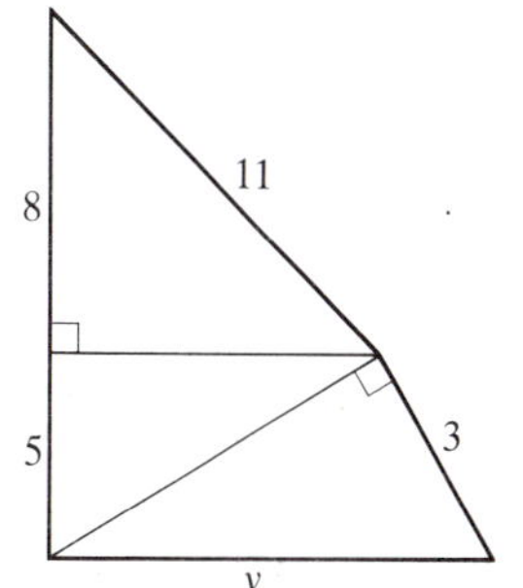

Exercise 6

Begin each question by drawing a clear diagram and let x be the length to be found.

1. A ship sails 9 km due North and then a further 17 km due East. How far is the ship from its starting point?
2. An aircraft flies 400 km due West and then a further 150 km due South. How far is the aircraft from its starting point?
3. A ladder of length 5 m leans against a vertical wall with its feet 2 m from the base of the wall. How high up the wall does the ladder reach?
4. A ship sails 7 km due North and then a further distance x km due West. The ship is then 12 km from its starting point. Calculate x.
5. A ladder of length 6 m leans against a vertical wall with its feet 3 m from the base of the wall. How high up the wall does the ladder reach?
6. A rectangle measures 8 cm by 5 cm. Calculate the length of the diagonals of the rectangle.
7. A rectangle of length 10 cm has diagonals of length 12 cm. Calculate the width of the rectangle.
8. A rectangle of width 6.5 cm has diagonals of length 10 cm. Calculate the length of the rectangle.
9. John is 20 m due North of Steven and Steven is 30 m due West of Peter. How far is John from Peter?
10. The diagram shows a rectangular block.

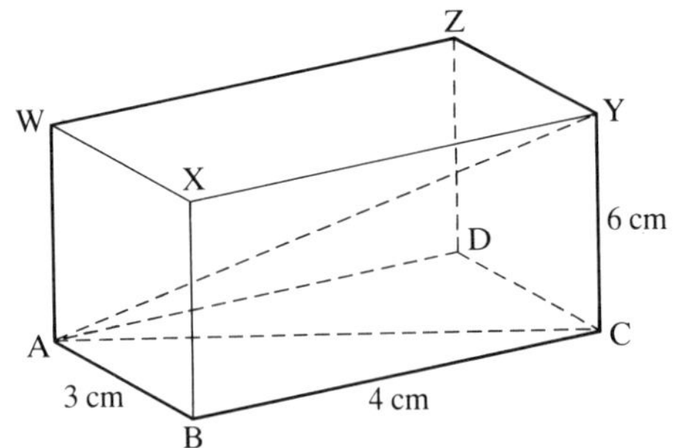

Calculate (a) AC (b) AY

11. The diagram shows a rectangular block.

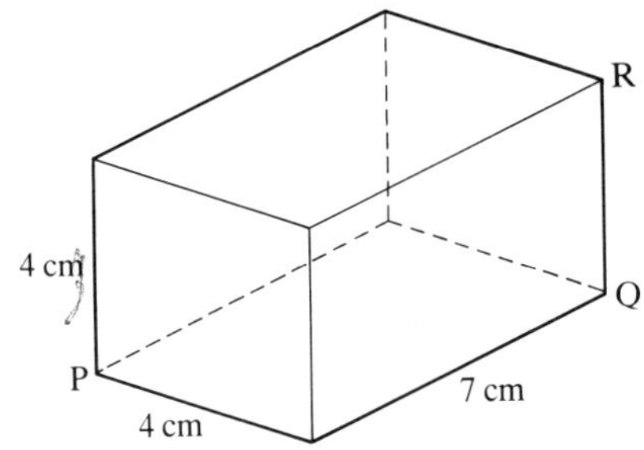

Calculate (a) PQ (b) PR.

12. (a) Draw a diagram of a rectangular block 5 cm by 5 cm by 9 cm.
(b) Calculate the length of the longest diagonal of the block.

14.3 CONVERSION GRAPHS

Exercise 7

Draw the graph and then answer the questions.

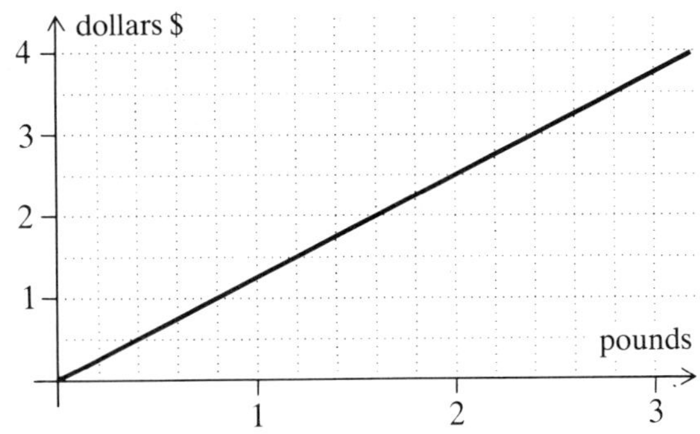

1. (a) Convert into dollars
(i) £2 (ii) £1.60 (iii) £2.40
(b) Convert into pounds
(i) $1 (ii) $3.50 (iii) $2.50

2. (a) Convert into German marks
(i) £1 (ii) £3 (iii) £1.50
(b) Convert into pounds
(i) DM8 (ii) DM10 (iii) DM2
(c) A book costs £2.50 in Britain. What is the equivalent cost in German money?

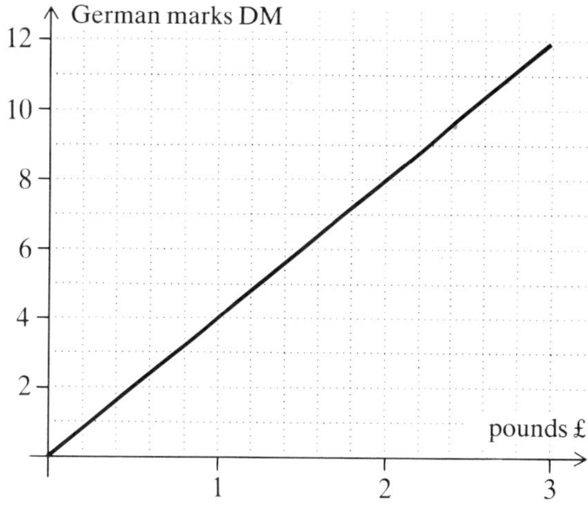

3. Give your answers as accurately as you can. [e.g. 3 lb = 1.4 kg approximately]
(a) Convert into kilograms
(i) 5.5 lb (ii) 8 lb (iii) 2 lb
(b) Convert into pounds
(i) 2 kg (iii) 3 kg (iii) 1.5 kg
(c) A bag of sugar weighs 1 kg. What is its weight in pounds?
(d) A washing machine has a weight limit of 9 lb. What is the weight limit in kilograms?

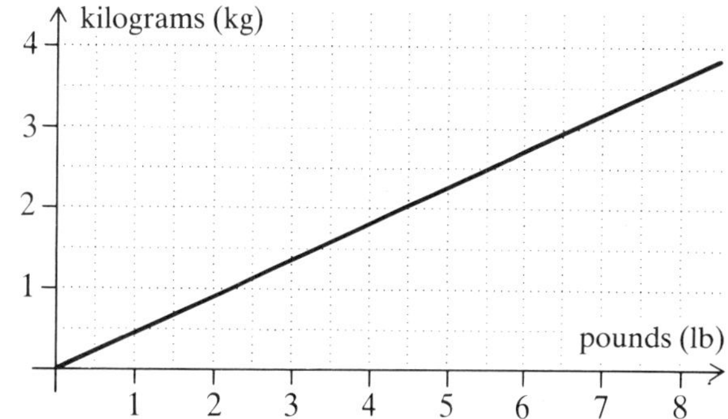

4. (a) Convert into litres
(i) 2 gallons (ii) 1.4 gallons
(iii) 2.8 gallons
(b) Convert into gallons
(i) 10 litres (ii) 7 litres
(iii) 4 litres.
(c) A drum contains 3 gallons of oil. How many litres of oil does it contain?
(d) Car A consumes 2.4 gallons of fuel on a certain journey, while car B consumes 11 litres of fuel. Which car consumes more fuel?

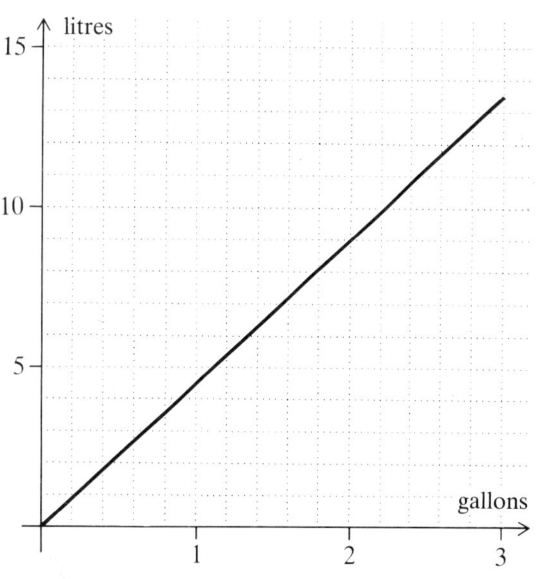

5. (a) Convert into km
 (i) 1 mile (ii) 3 miles
 (iii) 2.2 miles
 (b) Convert into miles
 (i) 2 km (ii) 5 km (iii) 3.5 km
 (c) John can run 2 miles in 12 minutes while Steve can run 3 km in 12 minutes. Who is the faster runner?
 (d) Sarah lives 4.5 km from school and Jane lives 2.7 miles from school. Who lives nearer to school?

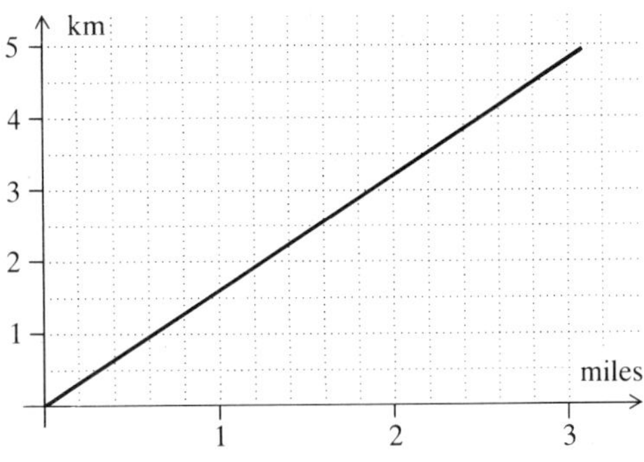

14.4 STRAIGHT LINE GRAPHS

The gradient of a line

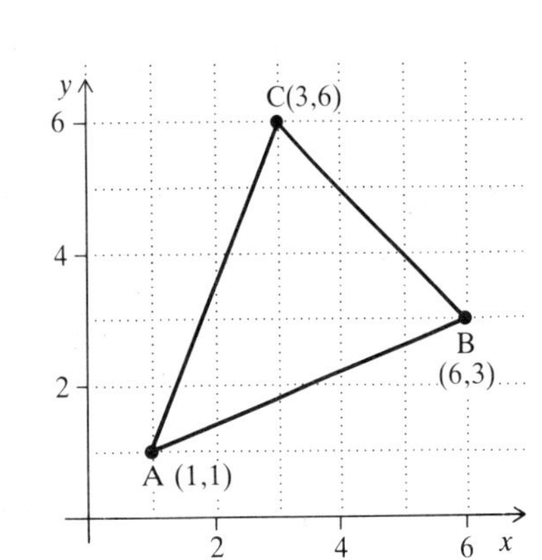

Gradient of line AB $= \frac{3-1}{6-1} = \frac{2}{5}$.

Gradient of line AC $= \frac{6-1}{3-1} = \frac{5}{2}$.

Gradient of line BC $= \frac{6-3}{3-6} = -1$.

A line which slopes upwards to the right has a *positive* gradient.

A line which slopes upwards to the left has a *negative* gradient.

$$\text{Gradient} = \frac{(\text{difference in } y \text{ coordinates})}{(\text{difference in } x \text{ coordinates})}$$

Exercise 8

1. Copy the diagram below.

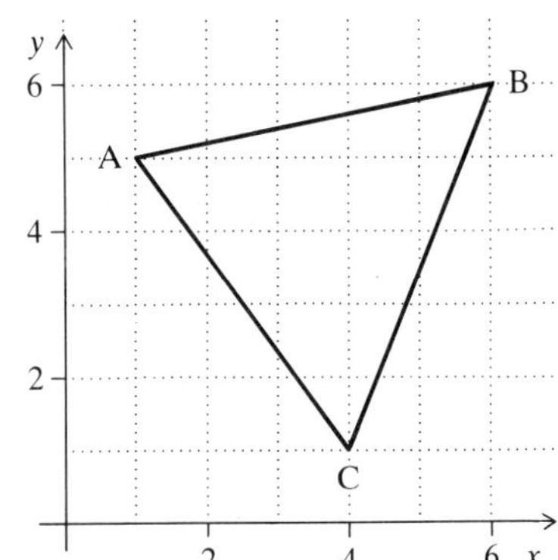

Find the gradients of AB, BC and AC.

2. Copy the diagram below.

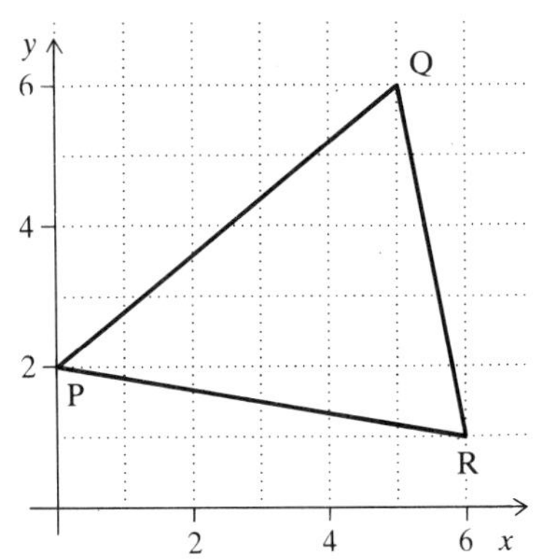

Find the gradients of PQ, PR and QR.

3. Copy the diagram below.

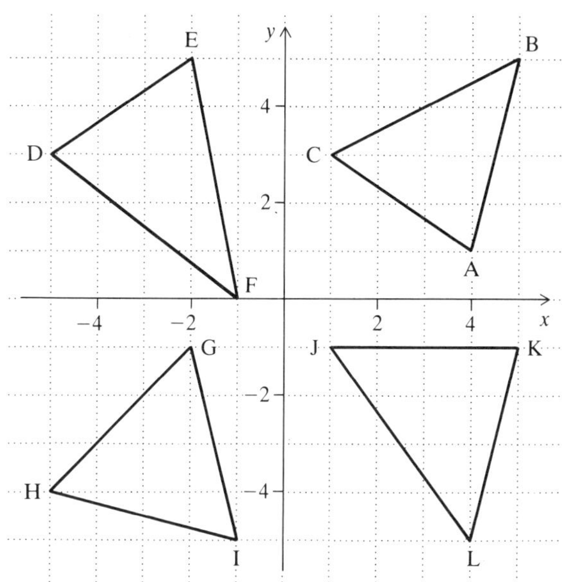

Find the gradients of the lines AB, BC, AC, DE, EF, DF, GH, HI, GI, JK, JL, KL.

4. Find the gradients of the lines joining the following pairs of points:

(a) $(3, 2) \rightarrow (4, 7)$
(b) $(-3, 4) \rightarrow (0, 6)$
(c) $(5, 1) \rightarrow (-2, 4)$
(d) $(-2, 8) \rightarrow (3, 0)$
(e) $(-1, 6) \rightarrow (-2, 7)$
(f) $(-3, -4) \rightarrow (8, -1)$
(g) $(6, 2) \rightarrow (8, 2)$
(h) $(-3, 4) \rightarrow (-2, -6)$
(i) $(0, 7) \rightarrow (-8, 7)$
(j) $(3, 2) \rightarrow (4, -2)$
(k) $(6, 5) \rightarrow (6, 3)$
(l) $(3, -8) \rightarrow (3, 11)$

5. The diagram shows the graph of $y = \dfrac{10}{x}$.

A tangent to the curve has been drawn at the point (2, 5).

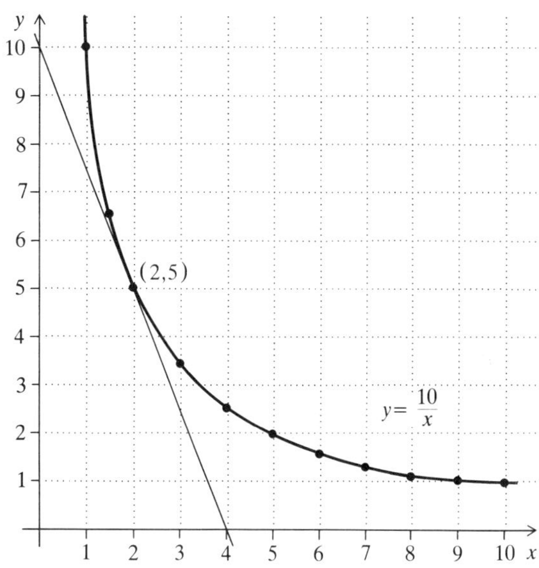

(a) Draw your own graph of $y = \dfrac{10}{x}$ and draw a tangent to the curve at (2, 5)
(b) Find the gradient of the tangent.
(c) Draw a tangent to the curve at (4, 2.5). What is the gradient of the tangent?

6. (a) Draw the graph of $y = x^2$ for values of x from 0 to 5. Use a scale of 2 cm to 1 unit for x and 1 cm to 2 units for y.
(b) Draw a tangent to the curve at (1, 1) and find the gradient of the tangent.
(c) Draw a tangent to the curve at (3, 9) and find the gradient of the tangent.

14.5 PLOTTING GRAPHS

Draw the graph of $y = x^2 - 3x - 2$ for values of x from -2 to 4.

x	-2	-1	0	1	2	3	4
x^2	4	1	0	1	4	9	16
$-3x$	6	3	0	-3	-6	-9	-12
-2	-2	-2	-2	-2	-2	-2	-2
y	8	2	-2	-4	-4	-2	2

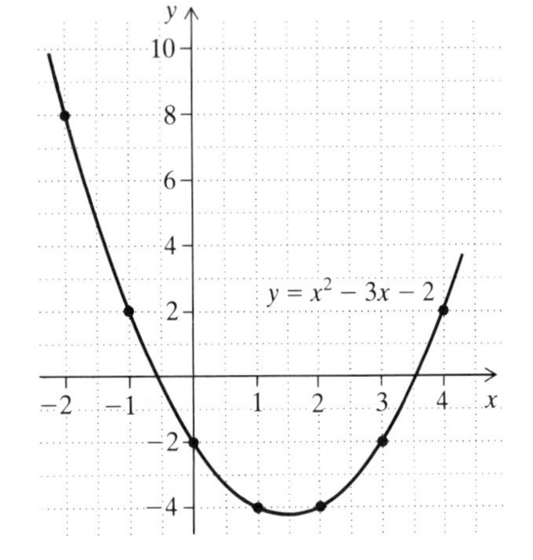

Exercise 9

In each question make a table of values and then draw the graph. Suggested scales: 1 cm to 1 unit on both axes, unless otherwise stated.

1. $y = 2x - 1$; x from -3 to $+3$

x	-3	-2	-1	0	1	2	3
$2x$	-6	-4					
-1	-1	-1	-1				
y	-7	-5					

2. $y = 3x + 1$; x from -2 to $+3$.

3. $y = x - 3$; x from -4 to $+3$.

4. $y = 2x - 7$; x from -2 to $+5$.

5. $y = 4x + 2$; x from -3 to $+3$. [Use scales of 1 cm to 1 unit for x and 1 cm to 2 units for y].

6. $y = 5x - 3$; x from -2 to $+2$. [Scales as in question **5**].

7. $y = 8 - 2x$; x from -2 to $+4$

x	-2	-1	0	1	2	3	4
8	8	8	8				
$-2x$	4	2					
y	12	10					

8. $y = 6 - x$; x from -3 to $+3$.

9. $y = 10 - 3x$; x from -2 to $+3$.

For questions **10** to **16**, use scales of 2 cm to 1 unit for x and 1 cm to 1 unit for y.

10. $y = x^2 + 3x$; x from -4 to $+2$

11. $y = x^2 + 4x$; x from -4 to $+1$.

12. $y = x^2 - 2x$; x from -3 to $+3$.

13. $y = x^2 - 3x + 5$; x from -2 to $+4$.

14. $y = x^2 + 2x - 7$; x from -3 to $+3$.

15. $y = x^2 - 4x + 3$; x from -2 to $+4$.

16. $y = 2x^2 + 3x - 1$; x from -3 to $+2$.

For questions **17** to **20**, use a scale of 1 cm to 1 unit for both axes.

17. $y = \frac{8}{x}$; x from 1 to 8.

18. $y = \frac{12}{x}$; x from 1 to 12.

19. $y = \frac{4}{x}$; x from -4 to 4.

20. $y = \frac{10}{x}$; x from -5 to 5.

Graphical solution of equations

Draw the graphs of $y = x^2 - 2x$ and $y = x + 1$. Hence find approximate solutions to the equation $x^2 - 2x = x + 1$.

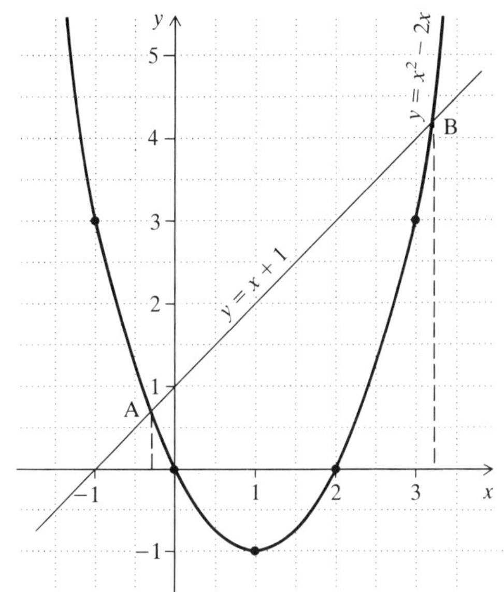

The solutions to the equation are given by the x values at the two points of intersection.

At A $x \approx -0.3$ } These are the
At B $x \approx 3.3$ } approximate solutions

Exercise 10

1. (a) Draw axes with x from -4 to $+6$ and y from -7 to $+7$. Use a scale of 1 cm to 1 unit for both axes.
(b) Draw the graphs of the following: $y = 2x$; $y = x + 3$; $y = x - 2$; $y = 3$; $y = 6 - x$.
(c) Use the graphs to solve the equations
(i) $x - 2 = 6 - x$
(ii) $x + 3 = 2x$,
(iii) $2x = x - 2$,
(iv) $x + 3 = 6 - x$,
(v) $2x = 6 - x$,
(vi) $6 - x = 3$.

2. (a) Draw axes with x from 0 to 8 and y from -4 to 8. Use a scale of 1 cm to 1 unit for both axes.
(b) Draw the graphs of the following: $y = x -=4$; $y = 3$; $y = 0$; $y = 3 - x$; $y = 8 - 2x$.
(c) Hence solve the equations
(i) $x - 4 = 3$,
(ii) $3 - x = 3$,
(iii) $8 - 2x = x - 4$,
(iv) $3 - x = 8 - 2x$,
(v) $x - 4 = 3 - x$,
(vi) $8 - 2x = 3$
(vii) $3 - x = 0$,
(viii) $8 - 2x = 0$.

3. (a) Draw axes with x from -4 to 8 and y from -4 to 8. Use a scale of 1 cm to 1 unit for both axes.
(b) Draw the graphs of the following: $y = 2x - 7$; $y = x$; $y = 5 - x$; $y = 2 - x$; $y = -3$.
(c) Hence solve the equations:
(i) $2x - 7 = x$,
(ii) $2x - 7 = -3$,
(iii) $5 - x = x$
(iv) $5 - x = 2x - 7$,
(v) $2 - x = x$,
(vi) $5 - x = -3$,
(vii) $2 - x = -3$.

4. (a) Draw axes with x from -6 to 4 and y from -20 to 10. Use a scale of 1 cm to 1 unit for x and 2 cm to 5 units for y.
(b) Draw the graphs of the following: $y = x^2 + 2x - 15$; $y = x$; $y = -5$; $y = 0$; $y = -19$.
(c) Hence solve the equations:
(i) $x^2 + 2x - 15 = -5$
(ii) $x^2 + 2x - 15 = 0$
(iii) $x^2 + 2x - 15 = -19$
(iv) $x^2 + 2x - 15 = x$

5. (a) Draw axes with x from -4 to 4 and y from -6 to 8. Use a scale of 1 cm to 1 unit for both axes.
   (b) Draw the graphs of the following: $y = x^2 - 6$; $y = 4 - x$; $y = -3$; $y = 4$; $y = 0$; $y = x$.
   (c) Hence solve the equations:
   (i) $x^2 - 6 = 4$
   (ii) $x^2 - 6 = 0$
   (iii) $x^2 - 6 = -3$
   (iv) $x^2 - 6 = x$
   (v) $x^2 - 6 = 4 - x$

6. (a) Draw axes with x from -8 to 8 and y from -8 to 8. Use a scale of 1 cm to 1 unit for both axes.
   (b) Draw the graphs of the following: $y = 8 - x$; $y = \frac{8}{x}$; $y = x$; $y = 2x$; $y = 6$.
   (c) Hence solve the equations:
   (i) $\frac{8}{x} = 6$ (ii) $\frac{8}{x} = x$
   (iii) $\frac{8}{x} = 2x$ (iv) $\frac{8}{x} = 8 - x$

7. (a) Draw axes with x from -4 to 4 and y from -4 to 4. Use a scale of 2 cm to 1 unit for both axes.
   (b) Draw the graphs of the following: $y = \frac{4}{x}$; $y = \frac{x}{2}$; $y = x - 2$; $y = -3.5$.
   (c) Hence solve the equations:
   (i) $\frac{4}{x} = -3.5$, (ii) $\frac{4}{x} = x - 2$,
   (iii) $\frac{4}{x} = \frac{x}{2}$.

8. (a) Draw axes with x from -4 to 4 and y from 0 to 16. Use a scale of 2 cm to 1 unit for x and 1 cm to 1 unit for y.
   (b) Draw the graphs of the following: $y = x^2$; $y = x + 10$; $y = 2x + 3$; $y = x + 5$; $y = 7 - x$.
   (c) Hence solve the equations:
   (i) $x^2 - x - 5 = 0$
   (ii) $x^2 - x - 10 = 0$
   (iii) $x^2 - 2x - 3 = 0$
   (iv) $x^2 - 7 + x = 0$

Graphical solution of simultaneous equations

Solve the simultaneous equations

$2x + 3y = 12$ . . . [A]

$2x + y = 8$ . . . [B]

Draw lines [A] and [B] and find where they meet.

Quick method:

For line [A] $2x + 3y = 12$
when $x = 0, y = 4$
$y = 0, x = 6$

Draw line [A] through these two points.

For line [B] $2x + y = 8$
when $x = 0, y = 8$
$y = 0, x = 4$

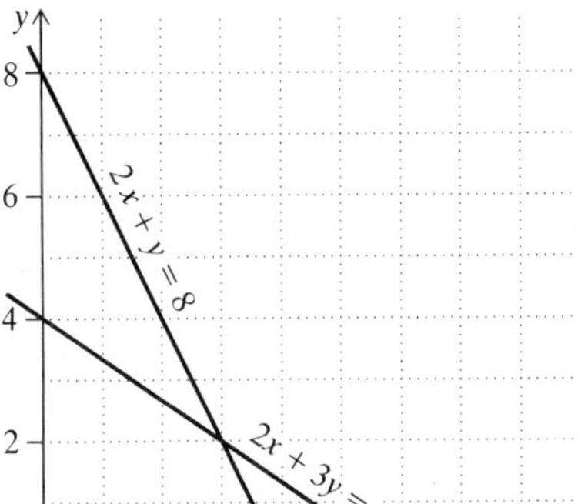

The lines meet at the point (3, 2) so the solutions are $x = 3$, $y = 2$.

Exercise 11

Solve the simultaneous equations by drawing graphs.

1. $x + y = 6$
   $2x + y = 8$
   Draw axes with x and y from 0 to 8.

2. $x + 2y = 8$
   $3x + y = 9$
   Draw axes with x and y from 0 to 9.

3. $x + 2y = 11$
$2x + y = 13$
Draw axes with x and y from 0 to 13.

4. $2x + 3y = 12$
$x + y = 5$
Draw axes with x and y from 0 to 7.

5. $3x + 4y = 24$
$3x + 2y = 18$
Draw axes with x and y from 0 to 9.

6. $x + 3y = 6$
$x - y = 2$
Draw axes with x from 0 to 8 and y from -2 to 4.

7. $5x + y = 10$
$x - y = -4$
Draw axes with x from -4 to 4 and y from 0 to 10.

Exercise 12

The graphs in this exercise are much more difficult and are intended for enthusiasts only! Draw the graphs using the axes indicated.

1. $y = 6 + 2x - x^2$; x from -3 to 4.
Scales: x 2 cm = 1 unit;
y 2 cm = 5 units.

2. $y = 15 - 2x - x^2$; x from -3 to 4.
Scales: x 2 cm = 1 unit;
y 2 cm = 5 units.

3. $y = 3x^2$; x from -3 to 3.
Scales: x 2 cm = 1 unit;
y 2 cm = 5 units.

4. $y = 2x^2 + 4x - 11$; x from -3 to 3.
Scales: x 2 cm = 1 unit;
y 2 cm = 5 units.

5. $y = \frac{8}{x^2}$, $x = \pm 1, \pm 2; \pm 3, \pm 4$.
Scales: x 2 cm = 1 unit;
y 1 cm = 1 unit.

6. $y = 2x + \frac{8}{x}$; $x = \pm\frac{1}{2}, \pm 1, \pm 2, \pm 3, \pm 4, \pm 5, \pm 6$.
Scales: x 1 cm = 1 unit;
y 2 cm = 5 units.

7. $y = x^2 + \frac{10}{x}$; $x = \pm\frac{1}{2}, \pm 1, \pm 2, \pm 3, \pm 4$.
Scales: x 2 cm = 1 unit;
y 2 cm = 5 units.

8. $y = x^3 - 16x$; x from -5 to 5.
Scales: x 1 cm = 1 unit;
y 10 cm = 1 unit.

9. $y = \frac{4}{x^2} + x^2$; $x = \pm\frac{1}{2}, \pm 1, \pm 1\frac{1}{2}, \pm 2, \pm 3, \pm 4$.
Scales: x 2 cm = 1 unit;
y 5 cm = 2 units.

10. $y = \frac{4}{x^2} - x^2$; $x = \pm\frac{1}{2}, \pm 1, \pm 2, \pm 3, \pm 4$.
Scales: x 2 cm = 1 unit;
y 5 cm = 2 units.

11. $y = x^2 + 2x + \frac{4}{x}$;
$x = \pm\frac{1}{4}, \pm\frac{1}{2}, \pm 1, \pm 2, \pm 3, \pm 4$.
Scales: x 2 cm = 1 unit;
y 5 cm = 2 units.

12. $y = 2^x$; $x = -4$ to 4.
Scales: x 2 cm = 1 unit;
y 1 cm = 1 unit.

Unit 15

15.1 TRANSFORMATIONS

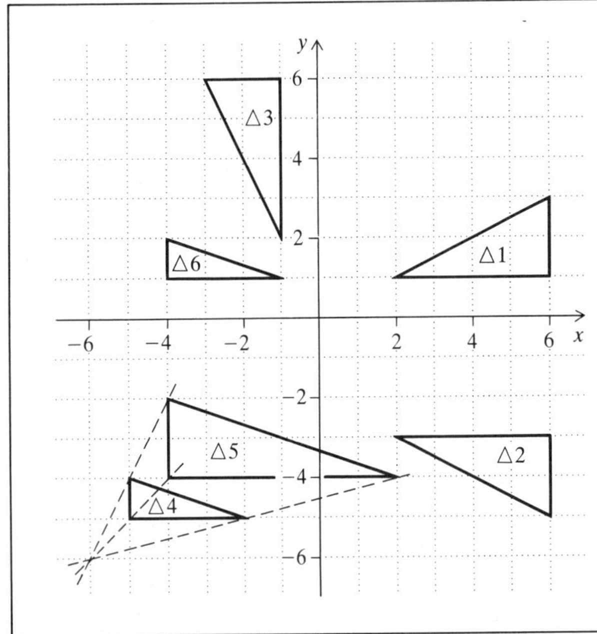

(a) Reminder

△1 → △2: reflection in the line $y = -1$.

△1 → △3: rotation 90° anticlockwise, centre (0, 0).

△4 → △5: enlargement, scale factor 2, centre (−6, −6).

△4 → △6: translation $\begin{pmatrix} 1 \\ 6 \end{pmatrix}$

(b) Congruence

△1, △2 and △3 are congruent.

△4 and △6 are congruent.

△5 is not congruent to any other triangle.

Describing transformations

Exercise 1

In this exercise you are given an object triangle and its image after various unknown transformations. Your task is to describe the transformation which maps the object onto the image. Questions **1** to **6** involve rotations, reflections and translations. Questions **7** and **8** involve enlargements as well.

1. Copy the diagram below.

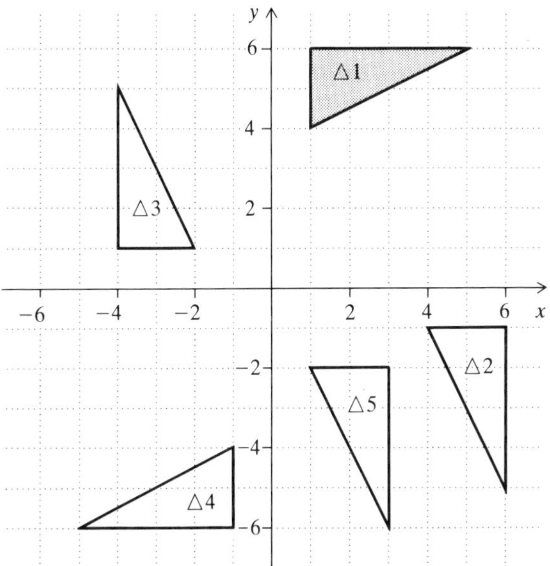

Describe fully the following rotations:
(a) △1 → △2 (b) △1 → △3
(c) △1 → △4 (d) △1 → △5.
[Give the angle, the direction and the centre].

In questions **2** and **3**, draw axes with x and y from −8 to +8.

2. Plot and label the following triangles:
△1: (8, 1), (8, 5), (6, 5)
△2: (1, −8), (5, −8), (5, −6)
△3: (−4, 7), (−4, 3), (−2, 3)
△4: (2, −3), (6, −1), (6, −3)
△5: (−4, −3), (−4, −7), (−2, −7)

Describe fully the following rotations;
(a) △1 → △2 (b) △1 → △3
(c) △1 → △4 (d) △1 → △5
(e) △4 → △5 (f) △3 → △4
(g) △2 → △1

3. Plot and label the following triangles:
△1: (−4, 3), (−4, 5), (0, 5)
△2: (3, 8), (5, 8), (5, 4)
△3: (−4, −7), (0, −5), (0, −7)
△4: (3, −2), (5, −2), (5, −6)
△5: (−5, −4), (−7, −4), (−7, 0)

Describe fully the following rotations:
(a) △1 → △2 (b) △1 → △3
(c) △1 → △4 (d) △1 → △5
(e) △5 → △3 (f) △3 → △4
(g) △5 → △2 (h) △4 → △1

4. Copy the diagram below

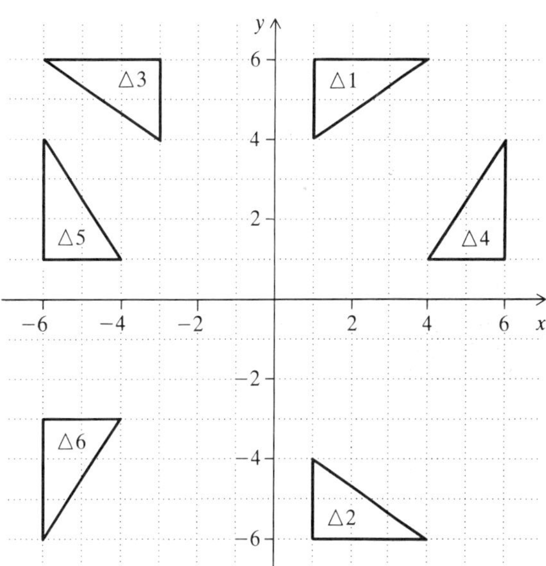

Describe fully the following reflections:
(a) △1 → △2 (b) △1 → △3
(c) △1 → △4 (d) △4 → △5
(e) △5 → △6 (f) △2 → △5

In questions **5** to **8**, draw axes with x and y from −8 to +8.

5. Plot and label the following triangles
△1: (−6, 6), (−2, 6), (−2, 4)
△2: (2, 4), (4, 4), (4, 8)
△3: (4, 3), (8, 3), (8, 1)
△4: (4, −2), (6, −2), (6, −6)
△5: (−2, −4), (−2, −6), (−6, −6)

Describe fully the following transformations
(a) △1 → △2 (b) △1 → △3
(c) △1 → △4 (d) △1 → △5
(e) △2 → △3 (f) △4 → △5

6. Plot and label the following triangles
$\triangle 1$: (2, 6), (2, 8), (6, 8)
$\triangle 2$: (2, −4), (2, −6), (6, −6)
$\triangle 3$: (−6, −2), (−4, −2), (−6, −6)
$\triangle 4$: (4, −2), (6, −2), (6, −6)
$\triangle 5$: (−2, 6), (−2, 4), (2, 4)
$\triangle 6$: (−6, −6), (−2, −4), (−2, −6)
Describe fully the following transformations
(a) $\triangle 1 \rightarrow \triangle 2$ (b) $\triangle 2 \rightarrow \triangle 4$
(c) $\triangle 2 \rightarrow \triangle 3$ (d) $\triangle 2 \rightarrow \triangle 5$
(e) $\triangle 3 \rightarrow \triangle 5$ (f) $\triangle 3 \rightarrow \triangle 6$
(g) $\triangle 1 \rightarrow \triangle 6$ (h) $\triangle 3 \rightarrow \triangle 4$

7. Plot and label the following triangles
$\triangle 1$: (−5, −5), (−1, −5), (−1, −3)
$\triangle 2$: (1, 7), (1, 3), (3, 3)
$\triangle 3$: (3, −3), (7, −3), (7, −1)
$\triangle 4$: (−5, −5), (−5, −1), (−3, −1)
$\triangle 5$: (1, −6) (3, −6), (3, −5)
$\triangle 6$: (−3, 3), (−3, 7), (−5, 7)
Describe fully the following transformations
(a) $\triangle 1 \rightarrow \triangle 2$ (b) $\triangle 1 \rightarrow \triangle 3$
(c) $\triangle 1 \rightarrow \triangle 4$ (d) $\triangle 1 \rightarrow \triangle 5$
(e) $\triangle 1 \rightarrow \triangle 6$ (f) $\triangle 5 \rightarrow \triangle 3$
(g) $\triangle 2 \rightarrow \triangle 3$
Which triangles are congruent to $\triangle 1$?

8. Plot and label the following triangles
$\triangle 1$: (−3, −6), (−3, −2), (−5, −2)
$\triangle 2$: (−5, −1), (−5, −7), (−8, −1)
$\triangle 3$: (−2, −1), (2, −1), (2, 1)
$\triangle 4$: (6, 3), (2, 3), (2, 5)
$\triangle 5$: (8, 4), (8, 8), (6, 8)
$\triangle 6$: (−3, 1), (−3, 3) (−4, 3)
Describe fully the following transformations:
(a) $\triangle 1 \rightarrow \triangle 2$ (b) $\triangle 1 \rightarrow \triangle 3$
(c) $\triangle 1 \rightarrow \triangle 4$ (d) $\triangle 1 \rightarrow \triangle 5$
(e) $\triangle 1 \rightarrow \triangle 6$ (f) $\triangle 3 \rightarrow \triangle 5$
(g) $\triangle 6 \rightarrow \triangle 2$
Which triangles are congruent to $\triangle 1$?

Successive transformations

Exercise 2

This exercise contains questions involving a combination of successive reflections, rotations and translations.

1. (a) Copy the diagram on the right.
(b) Draw the triangles $\triangle 2$, $\triangle 3$, $\triangle 5$ and $\triangle 6$ as follows:
(i) $\triangle 1 \rightarrow \triangle 2$: reflection in y-axis.
(ii) $\triangle 2 \rightarrow \triangle 3$: rotation 90° anticlockwise, centre (0, 0).
(iii) $\triangle 4 \rightarrow \triangle 5$: reflection in y-axis.
(iv) $\triangle 5 \rightarrow \triangle 6$: rotation 90° anticlockwise, centre (2, −2).
(c) Write down the coordinates of the 'pointed ends' of triangles $\triangle 2$, $\triangle 3$, $\triangle 5$ and $\triangle 6$.

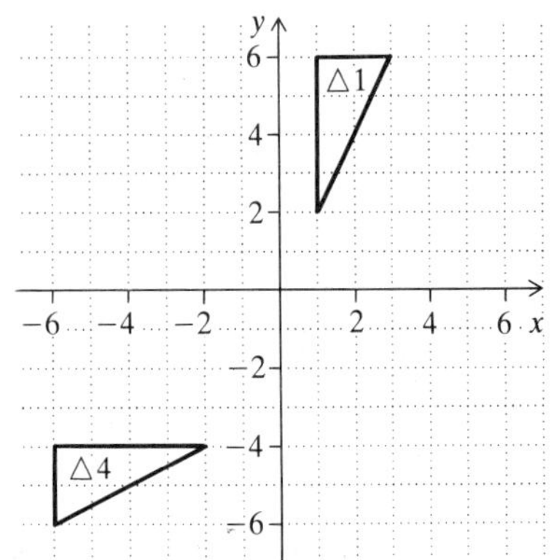

For questions **2** to **5**, draw a pair of axes with values of x and y from -8 to $+8$.

2. (a) Plot and label
$\triangle 1$: (1, 6), (1, 8), (5, 8).
$\triangle 4$: (−2, −8), (−7, −8), (−7, −5).

(b) Draw the triangles $\triangle 2$, $\triangle 3$, $\triangle 5$ and $\triangle 6$ as follows:

(i) $\triangle 1 \to \triangle 2$: reflection in the line $y = x$.

(ii) $\triangle 2 \to \triangle 3$: reflection in the x-axis.

(iii) $\triangle 4 \to \triangle 5$: rotation 90° clockwise, centre (0, 0).

(iv) $\triangle 5 \to \triangle 6$: translation $\begin{pmatrix} 5 \\ -2 \end{pmatrix}$.

(c) Write down the coordinates of the 'pointed ends' of triangles $\triangle 2$, $\triangle 3$, $\triangle 5$ and $\triangle 6$.

3. (a) Plot and label
$\triangle 1$: (−4, 4), (−4, 6), (−8, 6).
$\triangle 4$: (−8, −2), (−8, −6), (−6, −6).

(b) Draw the triangles $\triangle 2$, $\triangle 3$, $\triangle 5$ and $\triangle 6$ as follows:

(i) $\triangle 1 \to \triangle 2$: rotation 90° clockwise, centre (0, 0).

(ii) $\triangle 2 \to \triangle 3$: reflection in the line $y = 3$.

(iii) $\triangle 4 \to \triangle 5$: reflection in the line $y = x$.

(iv) $\triangle 5 \to \triangle 6$: rotation 180°, centre (−2, −5).

(c) Write down the coordinates of the 'pointed ends' of triangles $\triangle 2$, $\triangle 3$, $\triangle 5$ and $\triangle 6$.

4. (a) Plot and label
$\triangle 1$: (−3, 4), (−3, 8), (−1, 8)
$\triangle 5$: (−8, −2), (−8, −6), (−6, −2)

(b) Draw the triangles $\triangle 2$, $\triangle 3$, $\triangle 4$, $\triangle 6$ and $\triangle 7$ as follows:

(i) $\triangle 1 \to \triangle 2$: translation $\begin{pmatrix} 9 \\ -4 \end{pmatrix}$.

(ii) $\triangle 2 \to \triangle 3$: translation $\begin{pmatrix} -4 \\ -8 \end{pmatrix}$.

(iii) $\triangle 3 \to \triangle 4$: reflection in the line $y = x$.

(iv) $\triangle 5 \to \triangle 6$: rotation 90° anticlockwise, centre (−4, −1).

(v) $\triangle 6 \to \triangle 7$: rotation 180°, centre (0, −1).

(c) Write down the coordinates of the 'pointed ends' of triangles $\triangle 2$, $\triangle 3$, $\triangle 4$, $\triangle 6$ and $\triangle 7$.

5. (a) Plot and label
$\triangle 1$: (8, −3), (3, −3), (3, −6).

(b) Draw the triangles $\triangle 2$, $\triangle 3$, $\triangle 4$, $\triangle 5$ and $\triangle 6$ as follows:

(i) $\triangle 1 \to \triangle 2$: rotation 90° anticlockwise, centre (1, 1).

(ii) $\triangle 2 \to \triangle 3$: reflection the line $x = 2$.

(iii) $\triangle 3 \to \triangle 4$: rotation 90° anticlockwise, centre (2, 2).

(iv) $\triangle 4 \to \triangle 5$: translation $\begin{pmatrix} -4 \\ -4 \end{pmatrix}$.

(v) $\triangle 5 \to \triangle 6$: rotation 180°, centre (−2, −6).

(c) Write down the coordinates of the 'pointed ends' of triangles $\triangle 2$, $\triangle 3$, $\triangle 4$, $\triangle 5$ and $\triangle 6$.

15.2 MENTAL ARITHMETIC

Ideally these questions should be read out by a teacher or friend and you should not be looking at them. Each question should be repeated once and then the answer, and only the answer, should be written down.

Each test, including the recording of results, should take about 30 minutes.

If you do not have anyone to read out the questions for you, try to do the test without writing down any detailed working.

Test 1

1. Find the cost in pounds of ten books at 35 pence each.
2. Add together £4.20 and 75 pence.
3. What number divided by six gives an answer of eight?
4. I spend £1.60 and pay with £2. My change consists of three coins. What are they?
5. Find the difference between $13\frac{1}{2}$ and 20.
6. Write one centimetre as a fraction of one metre.
7. How many ten pence coins are there in a pile worth £5.60?
8. Ten per cent of the pupils in a school play hockey, 15% play basketball and the rest play football. What percentage play football?
9. In a room of 20 people, three quarters were women. What was the number of women?
10. Four lemons costing eleven pence each are bought with a one pound coin. What is the change?
11. I arrive at the railway station at 5.20 p.m. and my train is due at 6.10 p.m. How long do I have to wait?
12. What number is ten times as big as 0.65?
13. A hockey pitch measures 25 metres by 40 metres. Find the distance around the pitch.
14. Write the number 768 correct to the nearest ten.
15. By how many does a half of 62 exceed 20?
16. How many 2p coins are worth the same as ten 5p coins?
17. What number must be added to $1\frac{1}{4}$ to make $2\frac{1}{2}$?
18. Three books cost six pounds. How much will five books cost?
19. A rubber costs 20 pence. How many can be bought for £2?
20. What number is a hundred times as big as 0.605?
21. Spell the word 'decimal'.
22. Find the average of 12 and 20.
23. A car travelling at 80 kilometres per hour takes 30 minutes for a journey. How long will the car take at 40 kilometres per hour?
24. A certain number multiplied by itself gives 81 as the answer. What is half of that number?
25. The difference between two numbers is 15. One of the numbers is 90. What is the other?
26. How many half-litre glasses can be filled from a vessel containing ten litres?
27. How much will a dozen oranges cost at 20 pence each?
28. What is the biggest number that can be made from the figures 4, 8 and 1?
29. A prize of £400 000 is shared equally between one hundred people. How much does each person receive?
30. If electric cable is 6 pence for 50 cm, how much will 4 metres cost?

Test 2

1. What are 48 twos?
2. How many fives are there in ninety-five?
3. What is 6.30 a.m. on the 24-hour clock?
4. Add together £2.25 and 50 pence.
5. I go shopping with £2.80 and buy a magazine for ninety pence. How much money have I left?
6. Change $2\frac{1}{2}$ feet into inches.

7. Write in figures the number 'five million, eighteen thousand and one.'
8. How many 20 pence biros can be bought for £3?
9. Work out 1% of £600.
10. A packet of 10 small cakes costs 35 pence. How much does each cake cost?
11. Add eight to 9 fives.
12. A packet of flour weighing 2400 grams is divided into three equal parts. How heavy is each part?
13. Add together 7, 23 and 44.
14. A car does 40 miles per gallon of petrol. How far does the car travel on seven gallons of petrol?
15. How many twenty pence coins are needed to make eight pounds?
16. A certain butterfly lives for just 96 hours. How many days is this?
17. What number is 25 more than 37?
18. Find the average of 2, 5 and 8.
19. Pears cost eleven pence each. How many can I buy for sixty pence?
20. How many minutes are there in eight hours?
21. What number is twice as big as seventy-nine?
22. How many minutes are there between 6.25 p.m. and 8.00 p.m.?
23. Write one-fifth as a decimal.
24. Which is the larger: 0.7, or 0.071?
25. If a woman earns £8.40 per hour, how much does she earn in ten hours?
26. A car costing £2500 is reduced by £45. What is the new price?
27. How many half kilogram packets of sugar can be filled from a large bowl containing 32 kilograms?
28. My daily paper costs 15 pence and I buy the paper six days a week. What is my weekly bill?
29. A car journey of 110 miles took two hours. What was the average speed of the car?
30. How many days will there be in February 1993?

Test 3

1. What number is fifteen more than fifty-five?
2. What is a tenth of 2400?
3. What is twenty times forty-five?
4. Write in figures the number ten thousand, seven hundred and five.
5. A play lasting $2\frac{1}{4}$ hours starts at half-past eight. When does it finish?
6. What number is fifty-five less than 300?
7. How many twelves are there in 240?
8. A book costs £1.95. How much change do I receive from a five pound note?
9. Find the cost of eight biros at 22 pence each.
10. What four coins make 61 pence?
11. Work out $\frac{1}{2}$ plus $\frac{1}{4}$ and give the answer as a decimal.
12. A box holds 16 cans. How many boxes are needed for 80 cans?
13. If the 25th of December is a Tuesday, what day of the week is the first of January?
14. By how much is two kilos more than 500 g?
15. Write down fifteen thousand and fifty pence in pounds and pence.
16. The sides of a square field measure 160 metres. Find the total distance around the field.
17. A three-piece suite costing £970 is reduced by £248. What is the new price?
18. A bingo prize of £150 000 is shared equally between six people. How much does each person receive?
19. Ice creams cost twenty-four pence each. How many can I buy with one pound?
20. A bag contains 22 five pence coins. How much is in the bag?
21. How many pounds are there in two stones?
22. A wine merchant puts 100 bottles in crates of 12. How many crates does he need?
23. Add together 73 and 18.
24. What is 5% of £120?
25. Peaches cost fourteen pence each. How much do I pay for seven peaches?
26. A toy costs 54 pence. Find the change from a five pound note.

27. A boy goes to and from school by bus and a ticket costs 33 pence each way. How much does he spend in a five-day week?
28. In your purse, you have two ten pound notes, three five pound notes and seven one pound coins. How much have you got altogether?
29. What are eighty twelves?
30. Sweets cost 72 pence a pound. How much do I pay if I buy four ounces of sweets?

Test 4

1. What is the change from a £10 note for goods costing £1.95?
2. Add 12 to 7 nines.
3. How many 20 pence coins are needed to make £5?
4. A pile of 100 sheets of paper is 10 cm thick. How thick is each sheet?
5. Lemons cost 7 pence each or 60 pence a dozen. How much is saved by buying a dozen instead of 12 separate lemons?
6. How many weeks are there in two years?
7. What is 1% of £40?
8. How much more than £92 is £180?
9. My watch reads five past 6. It is 15 minutes fast. What is the correct time?
10. If a pint of beer costs 82p, how much does a man pay for a round of 10 pints?
11. A cycle track is 800 metres long. How far do I go in kilometres if I complete 5 laps of the track?
12. A train travels at an average speed of 30 mph for $1\frac{1}{2}$ hours. How far does it travel?
13. I go shopping with £5 and buy 3 items at 25 pence each. How much money have I left?
14. From one thousand and seven take away nine.
15. If I can cycle a mile in 3 minutes, how many miles can I cycle in one hour?
16. How many millimetres are there in 20 cm?
17. A metal rod 90 cm long is cut into four equal parts. How long is one part?
18. Find the cost of fifteen items at 5 pence each.
19. A 2 pence coin is about 2 mm thick. How many coins are in a pile which is 2 cm high?
20. Add up the first four odd numbers.
21. Add up the first four even numbers.
22. My daily paper costs 18 pence. I pay for it with a £10 note. What change do I receive?
23. A film starts at 8.53 p.m. and finishes at 9.15 p.m. How long is the film?
24. We finish school at twenty to four. What is that on the 24-hour clock?
25. Add together £2.34 and £5.60.
26. What is 10% of £7?
27. How many 2 pence coins are needed to make £4?
28. 35% of a class prefer BBC1 and 30% prefer ITV. What percentage prefer the other two channels?
29. How many minutes is it between 6.20 p.m. and 8.00 p.m.?
30. What is the cost of 1000 books at £2.50 each?

Test 5

1. How many minutes are there in 6 hours?
2. Add together £8.65 and 40 pence.
3. Find the average of 6, 14 and 16.
4. A packet of 30 sweets costs 45 pence. How much is each sweet?
5. The time by my watch is twenty past nine. What is the correct time if my watch is 15 minutes slow?
6. A ship was due at noon on Tuesday but arrived at 5.00 p.m. on Wednesday. How many hours late was the ship?
7. How many days are there in 20 weeks?
8. From nine times eight take away fifteen.
9. On a coach forty-one out of fifty people are men. What percentage is this?
10. Electric cable costs 90 pence per foot. How much do I pay for 4 inches of cable?
11. Spell the word 'diagonal'.
12. Two angles of a triangle are 65° and 20°. What is the third angle?
13. How many 5 pence coins are needed to make 120 pence?

14. If a man earns £2.25 per hour, how much does he earn in 4 hours?
15. A T.V. programme lasting 55 minutes starts at 20 minutes to seven. When does it finish?
16. How much less than 260 is 16?
17. Seven apples costing twelve pence each are bought with a £5 note. What is the change?
18. Add 24 to eleven sixes.
19. How many millimetres are there in $5\frac{1}{2}$ cm?
20. A car travels at an average speed of 30 mph. How far does it travel in $1\frac{1}{2}$ hours?
21. What is the perimeter of a square of area 36 cm^2?
22. A rod of length 370 cm is cut in half. How long is each piece?
23. A half is a third of a certain number. What is the number?
24. About how much does a man earn in a week if he is paid £10 000 a year?
25. Between midnight and 3 a.m. the temperature falls by 7°C. If the temperature at midnight was 5°C, what was the temperature at 3 a.m.?
26. An egg box holds 6 eggs. How many boxes are needed for 92 eggs?
27. A car costing £7600 is reduced in price by £750. What is the new price?
28. A man smokes 40 cigarettes a day and cigarettes cost £1.30 for 20. How much does he spend in 3 days?
29. By how much is half a metre longer than 1 millimetre? (answer in mm).
30. Write in figures the number 'eight million, twenty-seven thousand and ten'.

Test 6

1. What is a half of two thousand one hundred?
2. The time by the town hall clock is half-past three but the clock is eight minutes slow. What is the correct time?
3. If I have 65 pence change from a ten pound note, how much have I spent?
4. Find the average of 27 and 31.
5. Work out 10% of £65.
6. For homework a teacher sets questions 30 to 50 inclusive. How many questions is that?
7. How many millimetres are there in 40 centimetres?
8. Between noon and midnight the temperature falls by 20 °C. The temperature at noon is 12 °C. What is the temperature at midnight?
9. How many days are there in thirty weeks?
10. Write down a thousand pence in pounds.
11. What number is three times as big as fifty-one?
12. A man is paid £40 a week. About how much is that in a year?
13. An egg box holds six eggs. How many boxes are needed for seventy eggs?
14. From eight times seven take away eleven.
15. Five pounds of carrots cost one pound. How much do they cost per pound?
16. How many minutes are there in four hours?
17. Spell the word 'equation'.
18. What four coins make 62 pence?
19. Add together £2.90 and 65 pence.
20. A man died in 1981 aged 65. In what year was he born?
21. A tennis match lasting two and a quarter hours starts at a quarter past two. When does it finish?
22. The single fare for a journey is £7 and a day return is £11.25. How much is saved by buying a day return rather than two singles?
23. By how much is one kilogram more than one hundred grams?
24. What is a half of three hundred and ten?
25. Two angles of a triangle are 90° and 41°. What is the third angle?
26. How many weeks are there in two years?
27. A three-piece suite costing £950 is reduced by £280. What is the new price?
28. A train is due to arrive at 6.15 a.m. What is this time on the 24-hour clock?
29. A car travels at 60 miles per hour for $2\frac{1}{2}$ hours. How far does it go?
30. A ship was due to arrive at 7.00 p.m. on Friday, but arrived at 3.00 p.m. on Saturday. How many hours late was it?

Test 7

1. Find the average of 22 and 32.
2. If a man earns £2.50 per hour, how much does he earn in 5 hours?
3. How many fives are there in eighty?
4. What number is twice as big as eighty-five?
5. Write in figures the number three million seventeen thousand and four.
6. A ship sails for five days. How many hours is this?
7. What is 7.22 p.m. on the 24-hour clock?
8. How many two pence coins are needed to make five pounds?
9. Write three hundredths as a decimal.
10. A television costing £340 is reduced by £95. What is the new price?
11. A man goes shopping with £10 and buys three items at seventy pence each. How much money has he left?
12. A packet of twenty chocolates costs 90 pence. How much does each chocolate cost?
13. A car does 30 miles per gallon of petrol. How much petrol is used on a journey of 15 miles?
14. How many minutes are there in $3\frac{1}{2}$ hours?
15. After using slug pellets a gardener kills four-fifths of the slugs in his garden. What percentage is left?
16. Add together £7.85 and 29 pence.
17. Add twelve to 9 nines.
18. What is 10% of £4?
19. How many 40 pence rulers can be bought for £2?
20. Pears cost nine pence each. How many can I buy for one pound?
21. A metal rod of length 350 cm is cut in half. How long is each piece?
22. How many minutes are there between 11.30 a.m. and 2.00 p.m.?
23. Add together 9, 22 and 30.
24. How many half pint glasses can be filled from a barrel containing 19 pints?
25. If a man earns £4.50 per hour, how much does he earn in three hours?
26. A packet of crisps costs 15 pence and a boy eats three packets every day. How much does he spend in ten days?
27. A train took five hours to travel a distance of 400 miles. What was the average speed of the train?
28. A gallon of a precious liquid costs £100. About how much is this per pint?
29. A woman died in 1983 aged 75. In what year was she born?
30. By how much is three kilometres longer than three metres?

Test 8

1. What number multiplied by itself gives an answer of 81?
2. Add together six 50 pences and four 20 pences and give the answer in pounds.
3. If I change £10 into 20 pence coins, how many will I get?
4. The profit on a drink is 20 pence. How many must be sold to make a profit of £10?
5. What number divided by 8 gives an answer of 9?
6. What is the angle between the hands of a clock at 3 o'clock?
7. What is the smallest number that can be made using each of the figures 4, 8 and 1 once only?
8. Find the difference between $11\frac{1}{2}$ and 20.
9. Rewrite as an ordinary number 4×10^3.
10. Write one millimetre as a fraction of one metre.
11. How many 2p coins are worth the same as twenty 5p coins?
12. What number equals nine dozen?
13. Which is the larger fraction: $\frac{7}{10}$ or $\frac{3}{5}$?
14. If fish costs £4.60 per kilo, how much will I pay for 250 g?
15. What is the smallest number which must be added to 41 to make it exactly divisible by 8?
16. How many 50 ml glasses can be filled from a one litre bottle?
17. Write in figures the number 'fifteen thousand and twenty-four'.

18. A pencil costs 5 pence. How many can be bought for £1.20?
19. The difference between two numbers is 15. One of the numbers is 22. What is the other number?
20. A pile of 15 boxes is 3 metres high. What is the depth of each box?
21. In a group of 30 people, $\frac{2}{5}$ were men. What was the number of women?
22. A spark plug for a car costs 75p. How much does a set of six plugs cost?
23. A rectangular pane of glass is 3 feet long and 2 feet wide. Glass costs £1.50 per square foot. How much will the pane cost?
24. The single fare for a journey is £7 and a day return is £9.50. How much is saved by buying a day return rather than two singles?
25. The weekly rent for a flat is £21. Eight weeks rent must be paid in advance. How much is that?
26. How many 15 pence rulers can be bought for £1?
27. Electricity costs 6 pence per unit. How much would you pay for 300 units?
28. How many weeks is 98 days?
29. How long is it between 7.45 p.m. and 9.30 p.m.?
30. One-fifth of my wages is taken in deductions. What percentage have I got left?

Test 9

1. Find the cost of eight stamps at nine pence each.
2. What number is 32 more than 80?
3. Write down six hundred pence in pounds.
4. Apples cost 12 pence each. How many can I buy for 80p?
5. What are nineteen twos?
6. If the 8th of December is a Tuesday, what day of the week is the 18th of December?
7. A sum of £132 is shared equally between twelve people. How much does each person receive?
8. A television programme lasts for two and a quarter hours and starts at half-past six. When does it finish?
9. What four coins make seventy-two pence?
10. Work out $\frac{1}{2}$ take away $\frac{1}{4}$ and give the answer as a decimal.
11. What is a half of a half of 38?
12. What is a quarter of a half of 800?
13. By how much is four metres more than four centimetres? (answer in cm).
14. How many twos are there in a thousand?
15. Spell the word 'parallel'.
16. Write in figures the number thirty thousand and ten.
17. How many inches are there in a foot?
18. A house priced at £60 000 is reduced by £4500. What is the new price?
19. What number is eight times as big as fifty?
20. How many pints are there in a gallon?
21. Spell the word 'circumference'.
22. A square has an area of 144 m^2. How long is each side of the square?
23. Add together 9, 16 and 70.
24. A calculator costs £3.74. Find the change from a ten pound note.
25. Rulers cost ten pence each. How much will two dozen rulers cost?
26. A boy eats three packets of crisps a day and crisps cost 15 pence a packet. How much does he spend on crisps in two days?
27. Add together 74 and 88.
28. Work out 25% of £64.
29. What are fifteen 20's?
30. Which is larger: 0.3 or $\frac{1}{4}$?

Test 10

1. What is the change from a £20 note for goods costing £4.35?
2. Add 12 to 7 nines.
3. How many 20 pence coins are needed to make £20?
4. A pile of 100 sheets of paper is 1 cm thick. How thick is each sheet?

5. Tomatoes cost 6 pence each or 60 pence a dozen. How much is saved by buying a dozen instead of 12 separate tomatoes?
6. How many weeks are there in three years?
7. What is 1% of £60?
8. How much more than £85 is £150?
9. My watch reads five past 7. It is 20 minutes fast. What is the correct time?
10. If a pint of beer costs 85p, how much does a man pay for a round of 10 pints?
11. A cycle track is 600 metres long. How far do I go in km if I complete 5 laps of the track?
12. A train travels at an average speed of 40 mph for $2\frac{1}{2}$ hours. How far does it travel?
13. I go shopping with £5 and buy 3 items at 60 pence each. How much money have I left?
14. From one thousand and two take away three.
15. If I can cycle a mile in four minutes, how many miles can I cycle in one hour?
16. How many millimetres are there in $15\frac{1}{2}$ cm?
17. A metal rod 170 cm long is cut into four equal parts. How long is one part?
18. Find the cost of fifteen items at 4 pence each.
19. A 2 pence coin is about 2 mm thick. How many coins are in a pile which is 1 cm high?
20. Add up the first five odd numbers.
21. Add up the first five even numbers.
22. My daily paper costs 23 pence. I pay for it with a £10 note. What change do I receive?
23. A film starts at 8.47 p.m. and finishes at 9.13 p.m. How long is the film?
24. We finish school at twenty to four. What is that on the 24-hour clock?
25. Add together £2.34 and £5.21.
26. What is 10% of £5.
27. How many 2 pence coins are needed to make £50?
28. 25% of a class prefer BBC1 and 30% prefer ITV. What percentage prefer the other two channels?
29. How many minutes is it between 2.15 p.m. and 4.20 p.m.?
30. What is the cost of 100 books at £4.25 each?

15.3 SYMMETRY

(a) Line symmetry

The letter M has one line of symmetry, shown dotted.

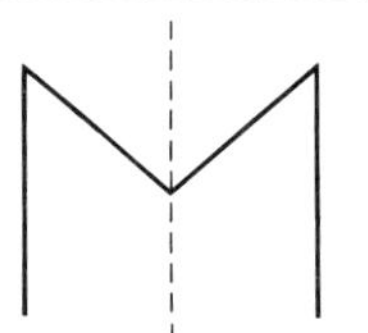

(b) Rotational symmetry

The shape may be turned about O into three identical positions. It has rotational symmetry of order three.

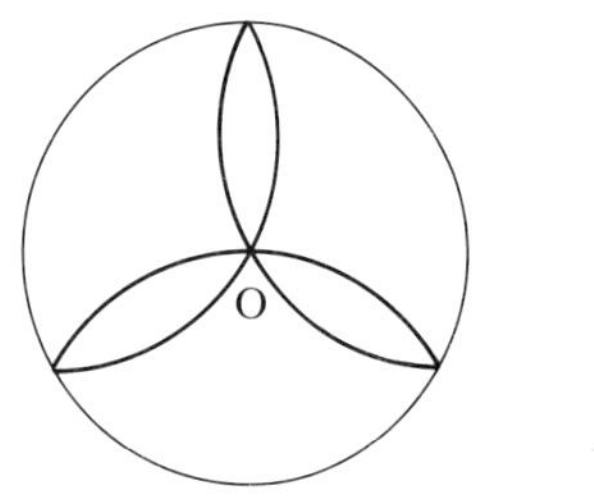

Exercise 3

For each shape state:
(a) the number of lines of symmetry
(b) the order of rotational symmetry.

1.

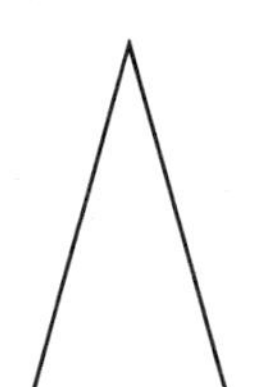

2.

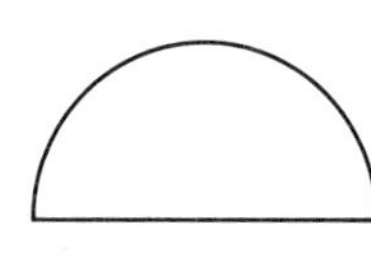

3.

4.

5.

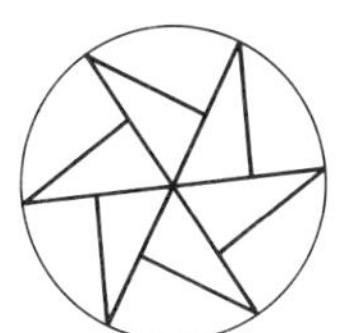

6.

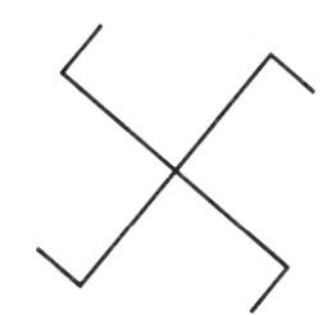

7.

8.

9.

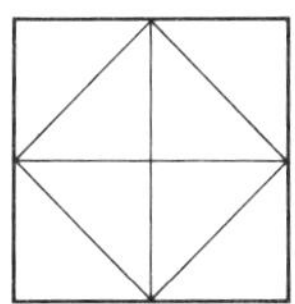

10.

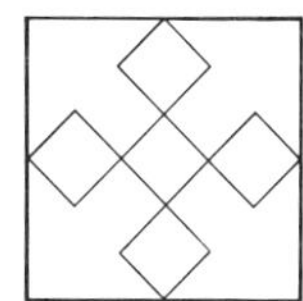

11.

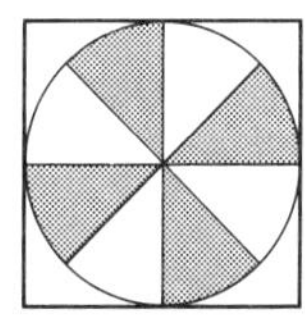

12.

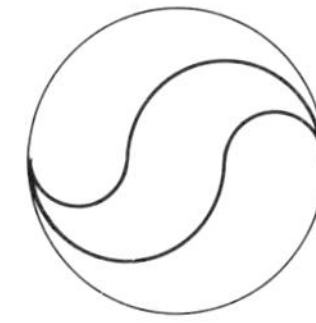

13.

14.

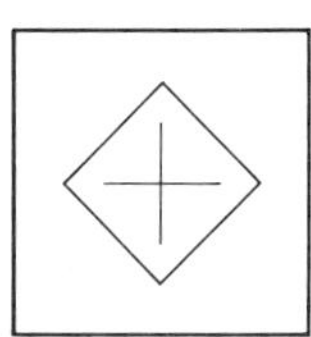

15.

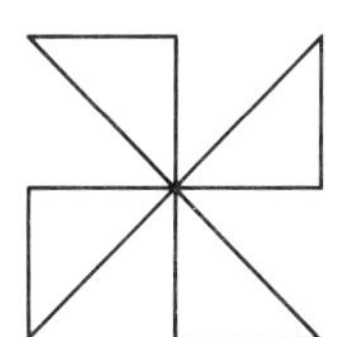

16.

17.

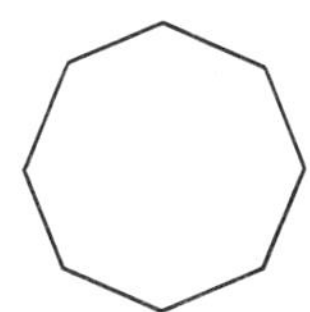

18.

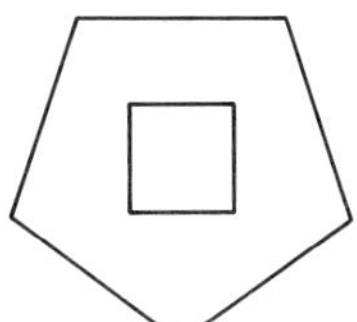

19.

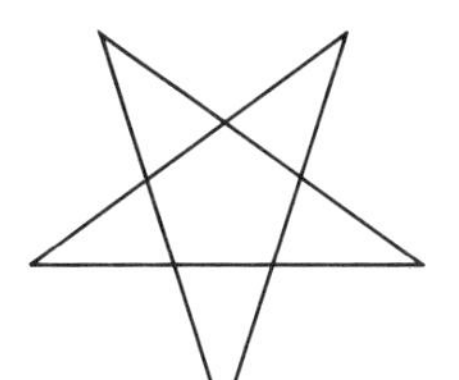

20.

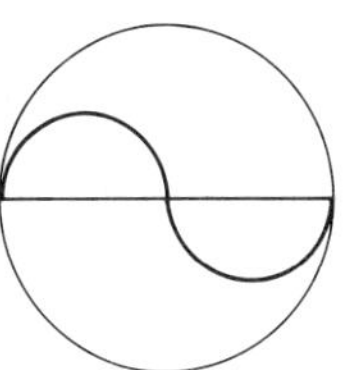

21.

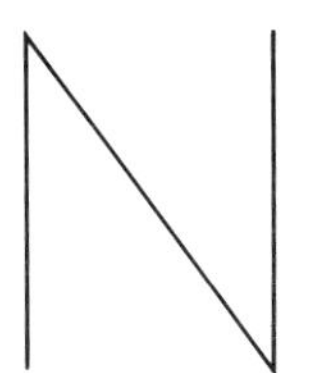

22.

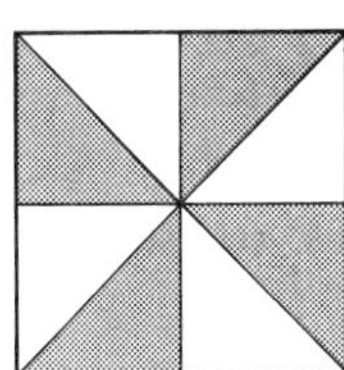

23.

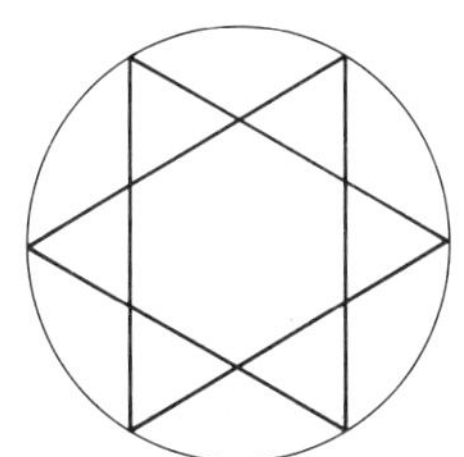

24.

15.4 FLOW DIAGRAMS

Exercise 4

Copy each flow diagram and put each of the numbers 1, 2, 3, 4, 5, 6, 7 in at the box marked N. Work out what number would be printed in each case.

1.

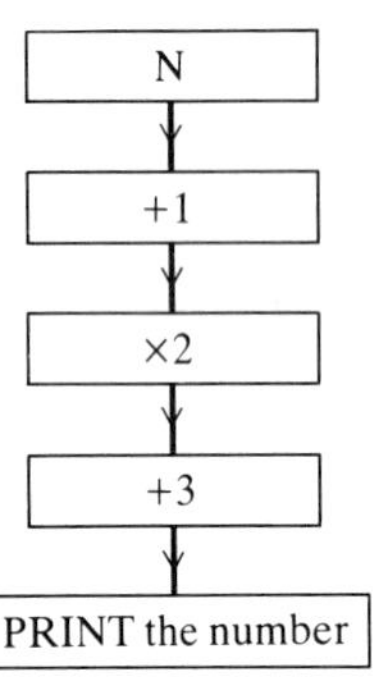

2.

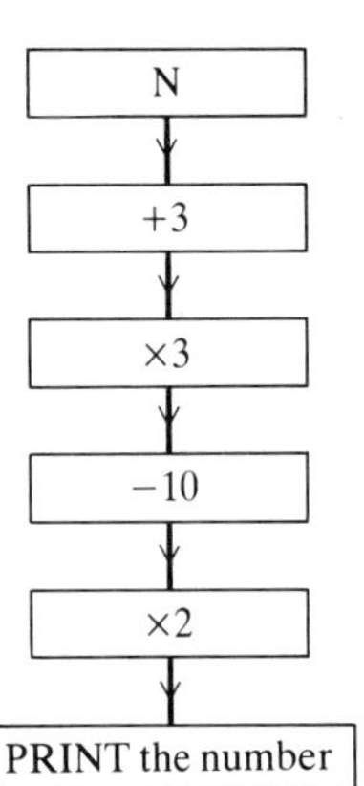

3.

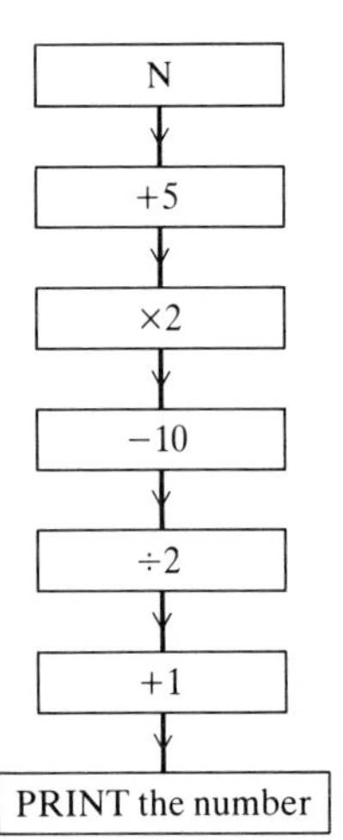

4.

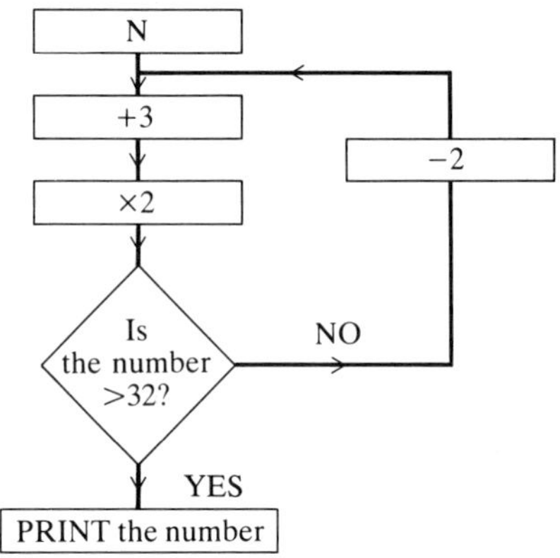

5.

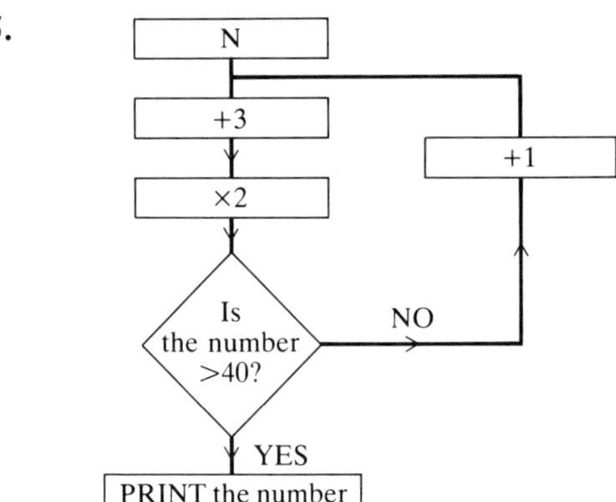

6.

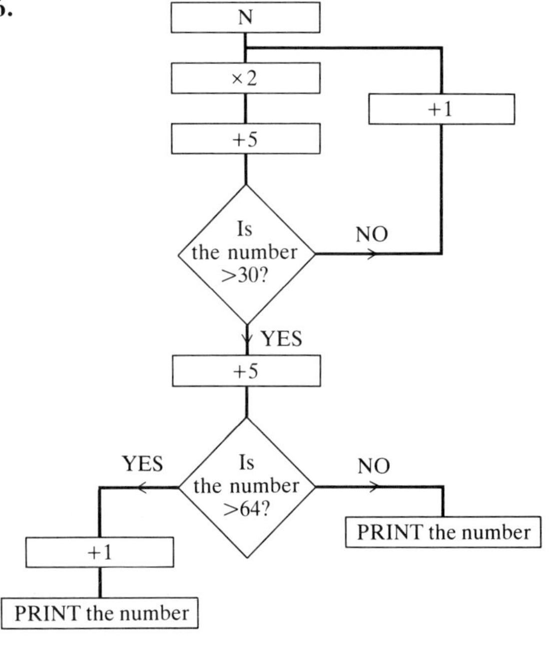

In questions **7** and **8**, use N = 1, 2, 3, . . . 9.

7.

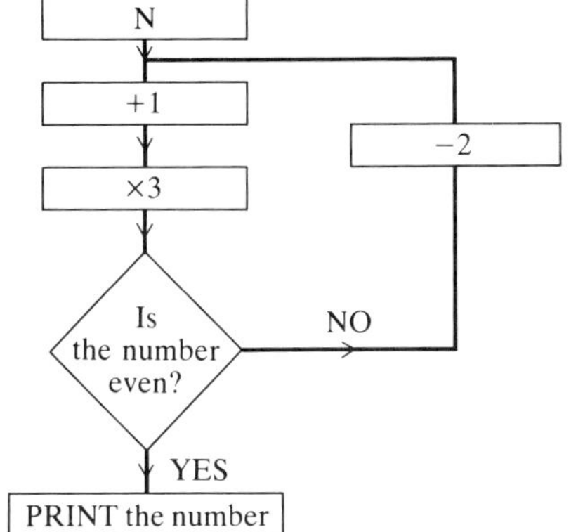

8.

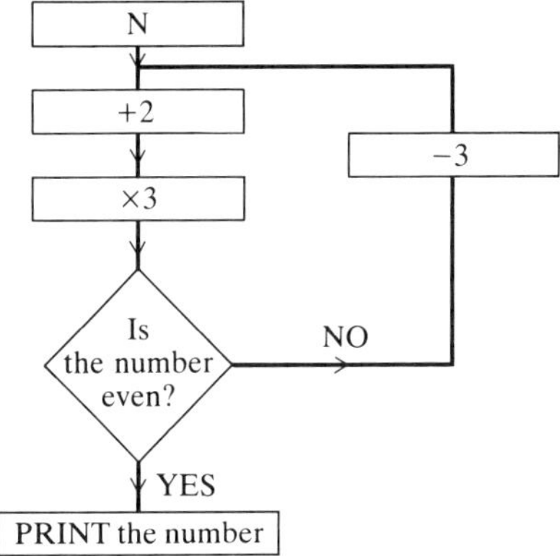

Find the operation

Exercise 5

In the flow charts, the boxes A, B, C and D each contain a single mathematical operation (like +5, ×4, −15, ÷2).

Look at flow charts (i) and (ii) together and work out what is the same operation which will replace A. Complete the flow chart by replacing B, C and D.

Now copy and complete each flow chart on the right, using the same operations.

1. (i)

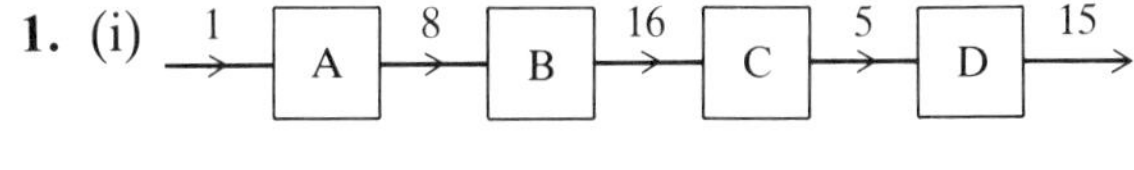

(ii)

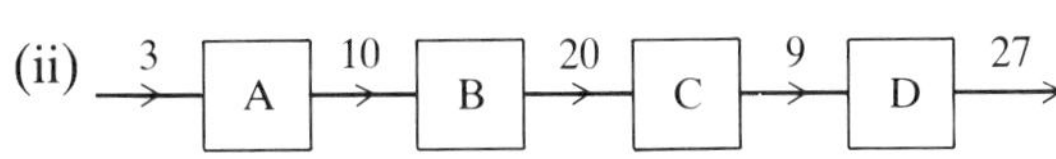

(a)

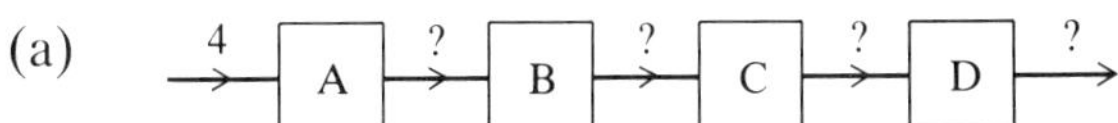

(b)

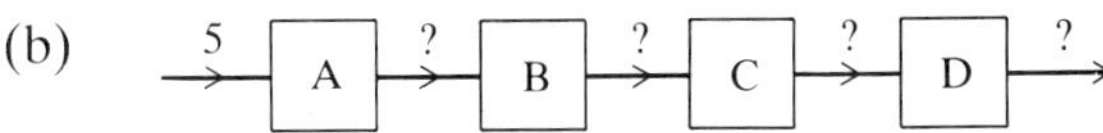

(c)

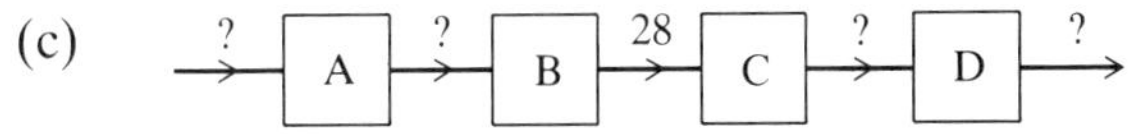

(d) ? → A → 16 → B → ? → C → ? → D → ?

(e) ? → A → ? → B → ? → C → 25 → D → ?

(f) ? → A → ? → B → ? → C → ? → D → 87

2. (i)

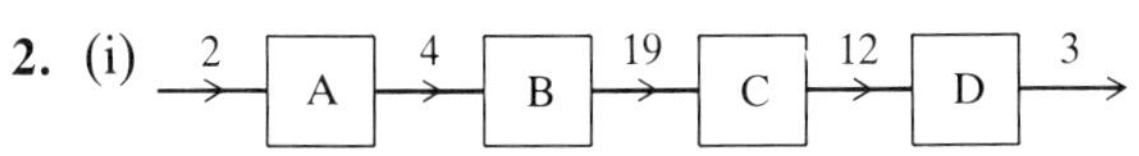

(ii)

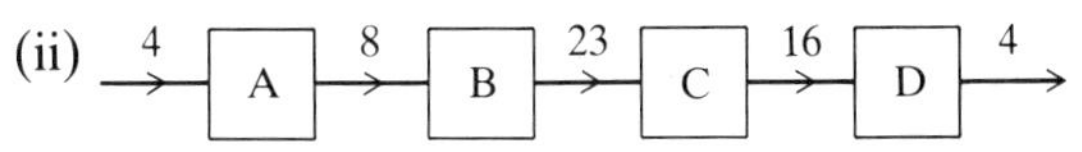

(a)

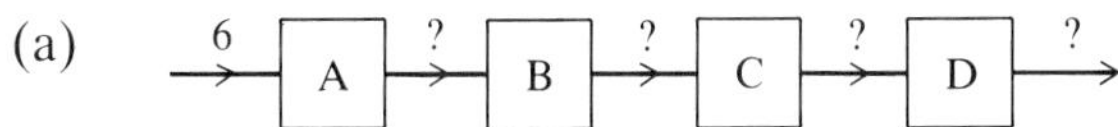

(b)

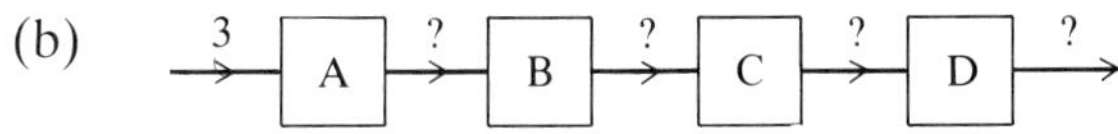

(c) 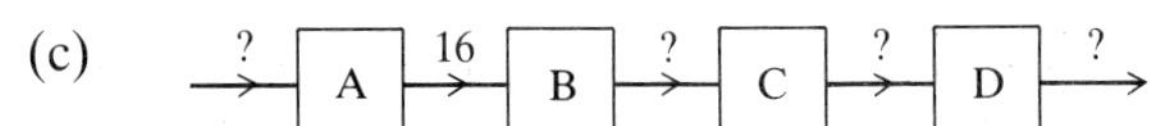
? → A → 16 → B → ? → C → ? → D → ?

(d) ? → A → ? → B → 35 → C → ? → D → ?

(e) ? → A → ? → B → ? → C → ? → D → $2\frac{1}{2}$

(f) ? → A → ? → B → ? → C → ? → D → 8

3. (i) 
2 → ☐ → 17 → ☐ → 34 → ☐ → 12 → ☐ → 3

(ii) 4 → ☐ → 19 → ☐ → 38 → ☐ → 16 → ☐ → 4

(a) 7 → A → ? → B → ? → C → ? → D → ?

(b) 10 → A → ? → B → ? → C → ? → D → ?

(c) ? → A → ? → B → 62 → C → ? → D → ?

(d) ? → A → $15\frac{1}{2}$ → B → ? → C → ? → D → ?

(e) ? → A → ? → B → ? → C → 208 → D → ?

(f) ? → A → ? → B → ? → C → ? → D → 14

4. (i) 2 → ☐ → 4 → ☐ → 12 → ☐ → 2 → ☐ → 1

(ii) 3 → ☐ → 9 → ☐ → 27 → ☐ → 17 → ☐ → $8\frac{1}{2}$

(a) 4 → A → 16 → B → ? → C → ? → D → ?

(b) 5 → A → ? → B → ? → C → ? → D → ?

(c) ? → A → ? → B → 108 → C → ? → D → ?

(d) ? → A → ? → B → ? → C → 182 → D → ?

(e) ? → A → ? → B → 3 → C → ? → D → ?

(f) ? → A → ? → B → ? → C → ? → D → 145

Think about it 5

Project 1 MAXIMUM BOX

(a) You have a square sheet of card 24 cm by 24 cm. You can make a box (without a lid) by cutting squares from the corners and folding up the sides.

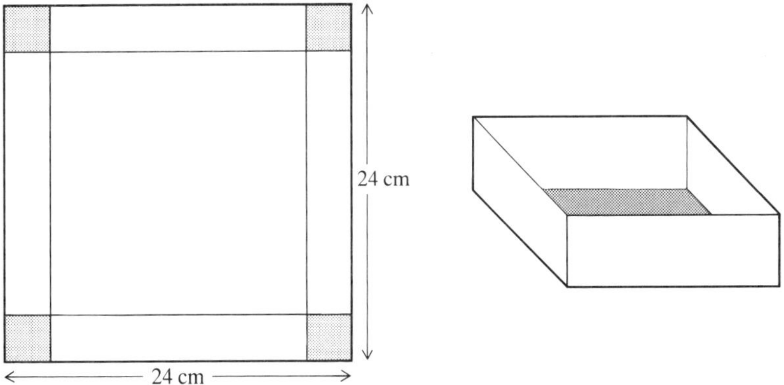

What size corners should you cut out so that the volume of the box is as large as possible? Try different sizes for the corners and record the results in the form of a table:

Length of the side of the corner square (cm)	Dimensions of the open box (cm)	Volume of the open box (cm^3)
1	$22 \times 22 \times 1$	484
2		
⋮		

(b) Now consider boxes made from different sized cards: 15 cm by 15 cm and 20 cm by 20 cm.
What size corners should you cut out this time so that the volume of the box is as large as possible?

(c) Finally investigate the situation when the card is not square. For a rectangular card 20 cm by 12 cm what size corners should you cut out for maximum volume?

Exercise A

1. How many shares of an electronics company, each costing 74p, can be bought for £444?

2. The train fare to York is £5.40 for an adult and £2.20 for a child. How much change will a man get from £20 if he is taking his wife and three children?

3. A jet is flying at 720 km/h.
(a) How many metres will it travel in one hour?
(b) How many metres will it travel in one second?

4. Ten posts are equally spaced in a straight line. It is 450 m from the first to the tenth post. What is the distance between successive posts?

5. A journey by boat takes 2 hours 47 minutes. How long will it take at half the speed?

6. Copy the following tables and write down the next *two* lines

(a)
$2^2 = 1^2 + 3$
$3^2 = 2^2 + 5$
$4^2 = 3^2 + 7$
$5^2 = 4^2 + 9$

(b)
$3^2 = 4 + 1^2 + 2^2$
$5^2 = 12 + 2^2 + 3^2$
$7^2 = 24 + 3^2 + 4^2$
$9^2 = 40 + 4^2 + 5^2$

7. Change the fractions $\frac{3}{5}$ and $\frac{2}{3}$ into decimals. Which fraction is larger?

8. Three girls are 127 cm, 136 cm and 133 cm in height.
(a) What is their average height?
(b) When another girl joins them, the new average height is 134 cm. How tall is the fourth girl?

9. (a) A rectangular floor 5 m by 6 m is to be covered with square tiles, each of side length 50 cm. How many tiles will be required?
(b) If the same floor is covered with smaller tiles of side 25 cm, how many are needed now?

10. A motor cycle averages 75 miles to a gallon of petrol which costs £1.85 per gallon. If the motor cycle goes 24 000 miles in the year, calculate:
(a) The number of gallons of petrol used
(b) The cost of the petrol.

Project 2 REFLECTIONS

Copy each drawing onto squared paper and then draw the reflection of the object in the mirror line shown by the dotted line. When you have done these, make up pictures of your own and draw their reflections.

1.

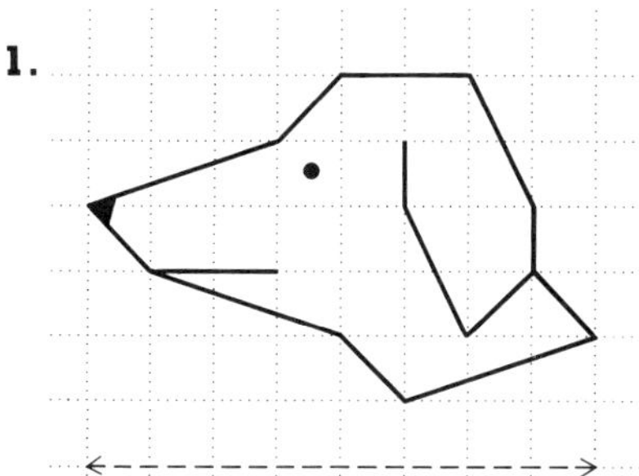

2.

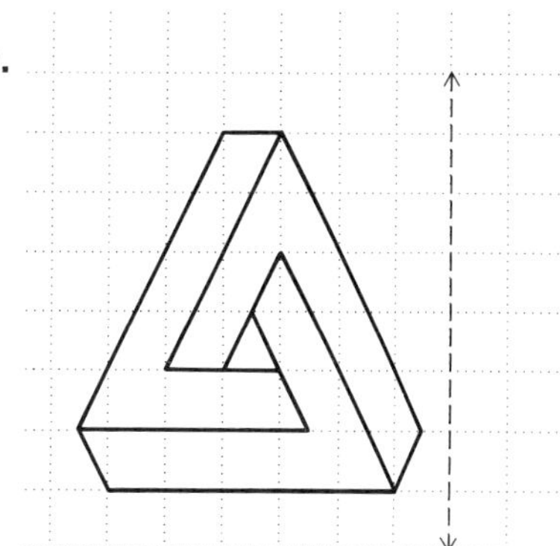

3.

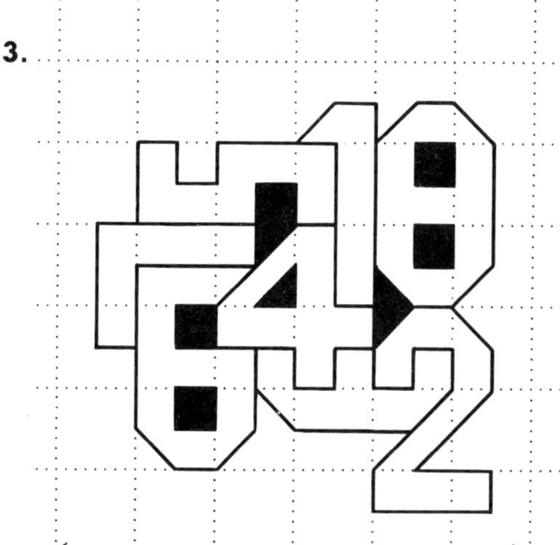

4.

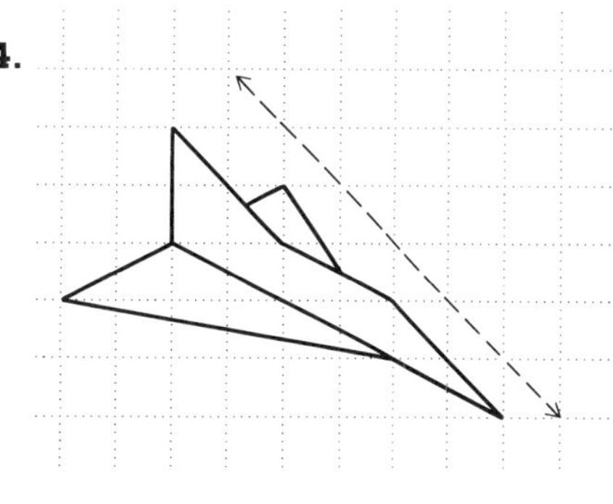

5.

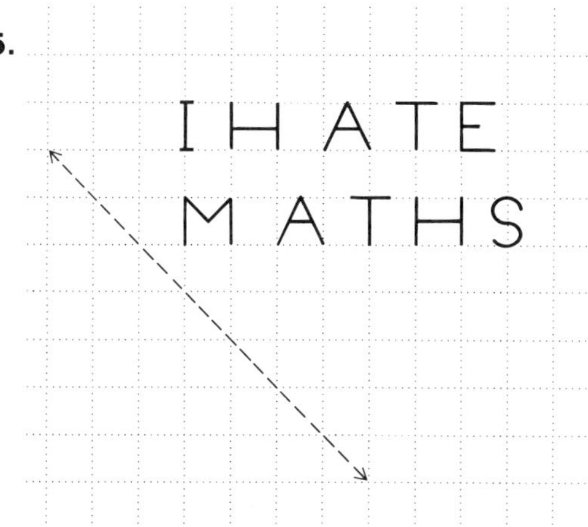

Exercise B

1. Ann weighs 24 kg and her father weighs three times as much.
   (a) How heavy is Ann's father?
   (b) How heavy is Ann's sister, Susan, if their father is four times as heavy as Susan?
2. If 6 kg of flour costs £2.04, how much will it cost for 10 kg?
3. The room shown is to be fitted with carpet tiles. Each tile is 1 m square and costs £8.50.

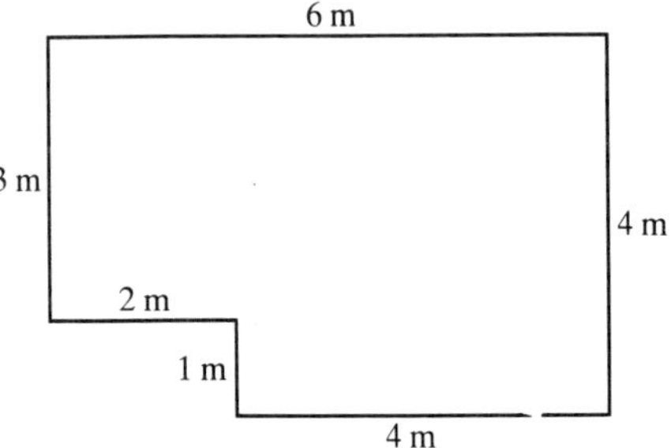

   (a) How many tiles are needed?
   (b) What is the total cost?
   (c) How many tiles were used in another room which cost £425 to cover with tiles?
4. (a) Increase £80 by 25%.
   (b) Decrease 150 kg by 5%.
   (c) Decrease 80 cm by 40%.
5. What fraction of £2 is
   (a) 20p (b) 50p (c) 2p?
6. Of 60 people travelling on a boat, 48 can swim. What percentage of the people is this?
7. V.A.T. of 15% is added to the price of an article costing £12.60.
   (a) How much V.A.T. was paid?
   (b) How much did the article cost, including tax?
8. Seven fig rolls together weigh 560 g. A calorie guide shows that 10 g of fig roll contains 52 calories.
   (a) How much does one fig roll weigh?
   (b) How many calories are there in 1 g of fig roll?
   (c) How many calories are there in one fig roll?
9. An aircraft is flying at an average speed of 750 km/h.
   (a) How far will it fly in 2 hours 30 minutes?
   (b) How long will it take to fly 1650 km?
10. A cinema has 30 rows of seats, with 15 seats in each row. The price of tickets for the first five rows is £3 per seat. All other seats cost £2 each.
   (a) How many seats are there in the cinema?
   (b) Calculate the income from the sale of tickets for 10 performances if all the seats are sold.

Project 3 CROSS NUMBERS

Draw four copies of the pattern below and fill them in using the clues.

1		2		3			4
		5					
6						7	
		8	9				
	10				11		
12			13	14			
		15		16		17	18
19						20	

Part A

Across

1. 111 × 7
3. 145 ÷ 5
5. 15 924 ÷ 4
6. 5 × 121
7. 326 − 248
8. 5148 ÷ 6
10. 152 × 4
11. 37 × 11
12. 603 ÷ 9
13. 7 × 124
16. 8730 ÷ 5
19. 398 + 174
20. $0.7^2 \times 100$

Down

1. 22 683 ÷ 3
2. 73.58 × 1000
3. 312 × 9
4. 829 − 671
7. 7 ÷ 0.01
9. 98 × 6
10. 469 ÷ 7
11. 600 − 113
12. 123 × 5
14. 486 + 129
15. 0.2 × 0.6 × 100
17. 812 − 768
18. 0.069 × 500 × 2

Part B

Across

1. $3368 \div 4$
3. $323 - 249$
5. 814×6
6. $6 \times 7 \times 8$
7. $5 \times 12 - 3$
8. $11^2 - 1^2$
10. $411 + 98$
11. 0.724×10^3
12. $3^2 + 7^2$
13. $8 \times 9 \times 10$
16. 624×11
19. $2056 \div 8$
20. $611 - 564$

Down

1. $24\,411 \div 3$
2. 4922×5
3. $46\,980 \div 6$
4. 3.17×10^2
7. 58×9
9. $15 \times 20 - 3$
10. Half of 116
11. $1000 - 292$
12. 74×8
14. $1325 \div 5$
15. $3^2 + 2^3$
17. $2 \times 2 \times 2 \times 2 \times 2 \times 2$
18. 0.0047×10^4

Part C

Across

1. $(621 + 184) \div 5$
3. Number of inches in a yard
5. $38\,748 \div 6$
6. $6 \times 12 \times 12$
7. Next in the sequence 60, 52, 44, 36, . . .
8. Solve $4x - 11 = 1429$
10. $5096 \div 8$
11. $252 + 187 + 366$
12. 1% of 2500
13. Solve $3x - 5 = 367$
16. $4000 - 889$
19. $10^3 - 1^3$
20. Next in the sequence 41, 45, 50, 56, . . .

Down

1. $2588 - 803$
2. $49\,299 \div 3$
3. 25% of 14 000
4. Double 84 plus treble 60
7. $1820 \div 7$
9. $824 - 153$
10. 10% of 650
11. $30^2 - 59$
12. 0.259×10^3
14. $9 \times (15 + 11)$
15. Next in the sequence 11, 18, 25, 32, . . .
17. Number of ounces in a pound.
18. Solve $2x + 3 = 29$

Part D

Across

1. $427 + 165$
3. Prime number between 32 and 40
5. 742×7
6. $1880 \div 5$
7. $10^2 - 1^2$
8. $882 - 56$
10. 20% of 1200
11. Number of minutes between 1040 and 1305.
12. A quarter of 156
13. $5067 \div 9$
16. $2316 + 1842 + 4317$
19. 42×11
20. Next in the sequence 23, 26, 31, 38, . . .

Down

1. $4658 + 874$
2. $154\,104 \div 6$
3. $4274 - 318$
4. $4719 \div 11$
7. 76 less than a thousand
9. $(9 - 4) \times (50 - 9)$
10. Number of minutes between 1152 and 1221
11. Average of 127, 117 and 158
12. 3% of 10800
14. $(1507 \times 5) \div (50 - 39)$
15. Next in the sequence $1\frac{1}{2}$, 3, 6, . . .
17. 2% of 3700
18. An eighth of 456

Exercise C

Work out the value indicated by the arrow.

1. 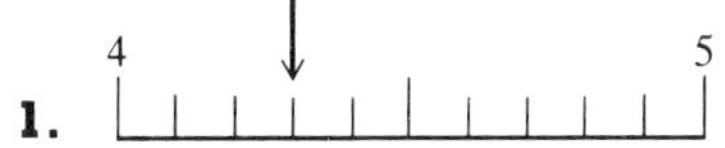

2. 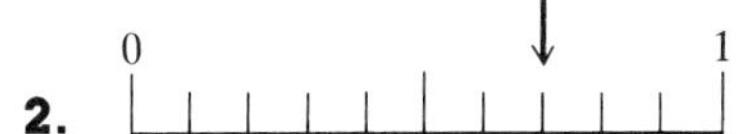

3. 9 10

4. 0 10

5. 40 50

6. 0 2

7. 3 4

8. 0 20

9. 22 24

10. 17 19

11. 120 140

12. 50 55

13. 5 10

14. 2 3

15. 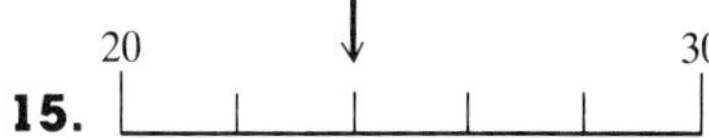

16. 100 200

17. 1 2

18. 

19. 15 15·5

20. 0 1

21. 5 6

22. 0 2

23. 1 1·4

24. 

25. 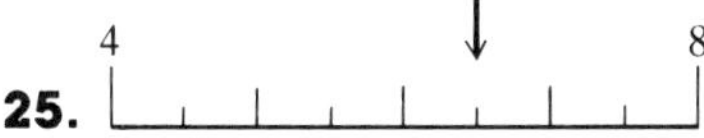

26. 

27. 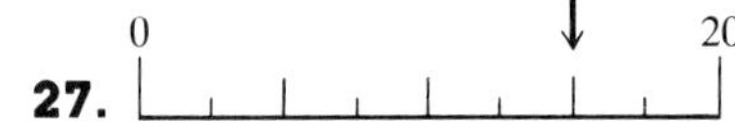

28. 

29. 

30. 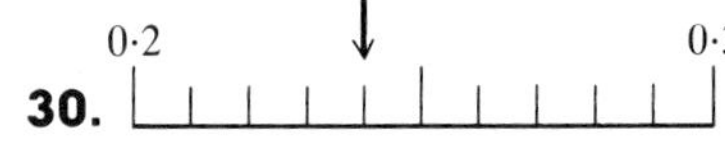

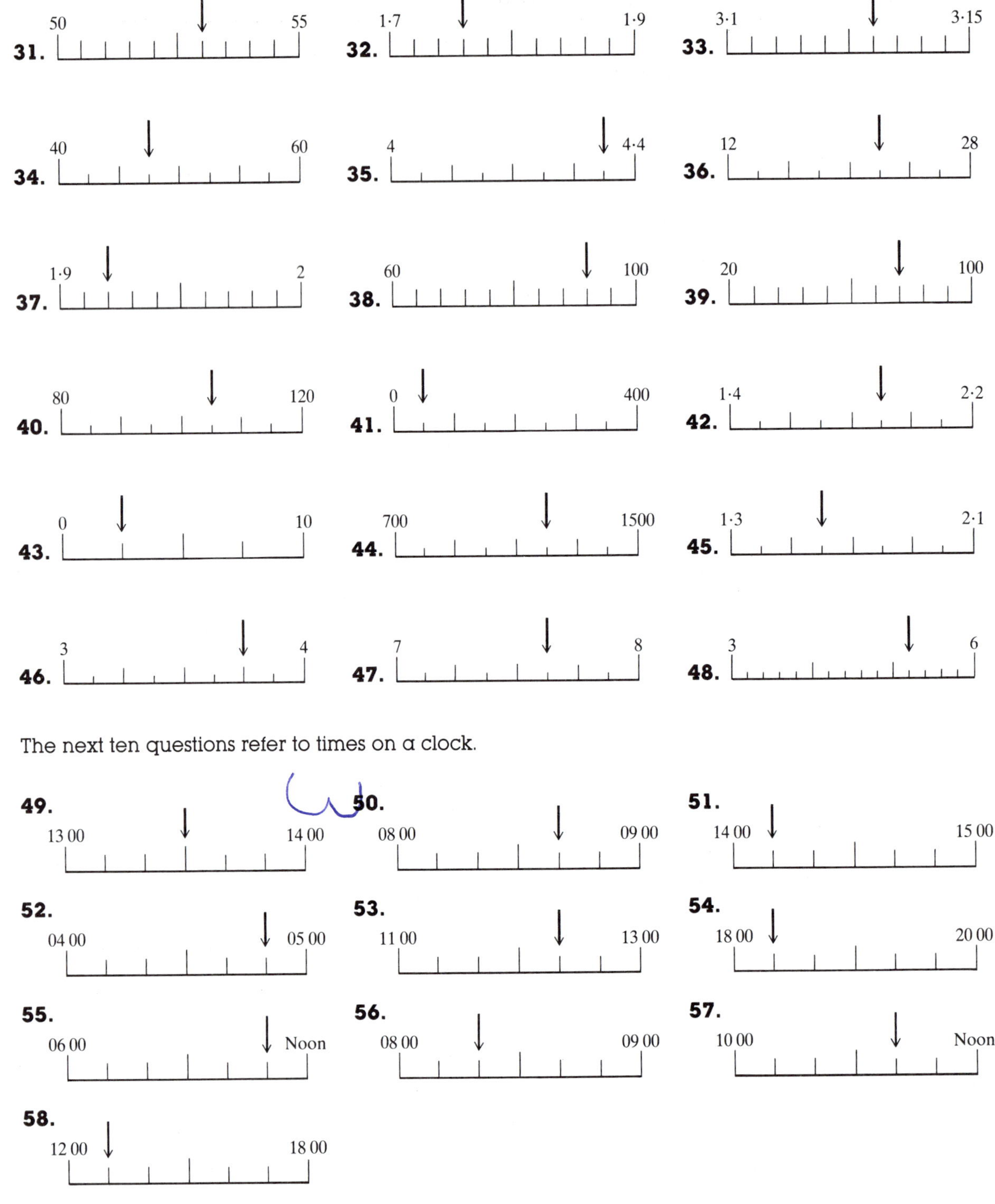
31. 50 55
32. 1·7 1·9
33. 3·1 3·15
34. 40 60
35. 4 4·4
36. 12 28
37. 1·9 2
38. 60 100
39. 20 100
40. 80 120
41. 0 400
42. 1·4 2·2
43. 0 10
44. 700 1500
45. 1·3 2·1
46. 3 4
47. 7 8
48. 3 6
The next ten questions refer to times on a clock.
49. 13 00 14 00
50. 08 00 09 00
51. 14 00 15 00
52. 04 00 05 00
53. 11 00 13 00
54. 18 00 20 00
55. 06 00 Noon
56. 08 00 09 00
57. 10 00 Noon
58. 12 00 18 00

Project 4 CALCULATOR WORDS

On a calculator the number 4915 looks like the word 'SIGH' when the calculator is held upside down.

Find the words given by the clues below.

1. $221 \times 7 \times 5$ (Sounds like 'cell')
2. $5 \times 601 \times 5 \times 3$ (Wet blow)
3. $88^2 - 6$ (Ringer)
4. $0.9 \times 5900 - 1$ (Leaves)
5. $62^2 - (4 \times 7 \times 5)$ (Nothing to it)
6. $0.88^2 - \frac{1}{1000}$ (O Hell)
7. $(5 \times 7 \times 10^3) + (3 \times 113)$ (Gaggle)
8. 44^4 + Half of 67 682 (Readable)
9. $5 \times 3 \times 37 \times 1000 - 1420$ (Stick in mind)
10. $3200 - 1320 \div 11$ (Woodwind)
11. $48^4 + 8929$ (Deceitful dame)
12. $31^2 \times 32^2 - 276^2 + 30$ (Not a twig)
13. $(130 \times 135) + (23 \times 3 \times 11 \times 23)$ (Wobbly)
14. $164 \times 166^2 + 734$ (Almost big)
15. $8794^2 + 25 \times 342.28 + 120 \times 25$ (Thin skin)
16. $0.08 - (3^2 \div 10^4)$ (Ice house)
17. $235^2 - (4 \times 36.5)$ (Shiny surface)
18. $(80^2 + 60^2) \times 3 + 81^2 + 12^2 + 3013$ (ship gunge)
19. $3 \times 17 \times (329^2 + 2 \times 173)$ (Unlimbed)
20. $230 \times 230\frac{1}{2} + 30$ (Fit feet)
21. $33 \times 34 \times 35 + 15 \times 3$ (Beleaguer)
22. $0.32^2 + \frac{1}{1000}$ (Did he or didn't he?)
23. $(23 \times 24 \times 25 \times 26) + (3 \times 11 \times 10^3) - 20$ (Help)
24. $(16^2 + 16)^2 - (13^2 - 2)$ (Slander)
25. $(3 \times 661)^2 - (3^6 + 22)$ (Pester)
26. $(22^2 + 29.4) \times 10$; $(3.03^2 - 0.02^2) \times 100^2$ (Four words) (Goliath)
27. $1.25 \times 0.2^6 + 0.2^2$ (Tissue time)
28. $[710 + (1823 \times 4)] \times 4$ (Liquor)
29. $(3^3)^2 + 2^2$ (Wriggler)
30. $14 + [5 \times (83^2 + 110)]$ (Bigger than a duck)
31. $2 \times 3 \times 53 \times 10^4 + 9$ (Opposite to hello, almost!)
32. $(177 \times 179 \times 182) + (85 \times 86) - 82$ (Good salesman)

Exercise D

1. A wall measuring 3.40 m by 2 m is to be covered with square tiles of side 20 cm.
   (a) How many tiles are needed?
   (b) If the tiles cost £2.60 for ten, how much will it cost?
2. It needs 80 g of flour to make 24 small biscuits. How much flour is needed to make 36 of these biscuits?
3. Work out $\frac{2}{5} + \frac{3}{4}$, giving your answer in its simplest form.
4. Calculate the area of the shape below.

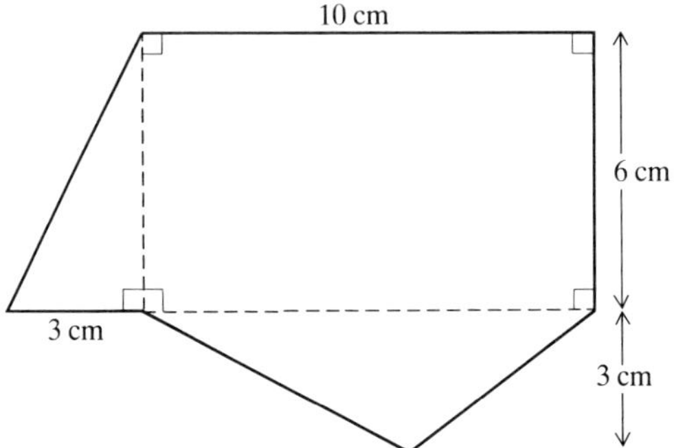

5. Discount at the rate of 12p in the £ is allowed on all articles in a sale. In this sale, what is the sale price of:
   (a) an article with a normal price of £5
   (b) an article with a normal price of £12
6. A shirt and a tie cost £11. If the shirt cost £7 more than the tie, what is the cost of each item?
7. Work out: a) $\frac{2}{3} \times \frac{1}{5}$; b) $\frac{5}{8} + \frac{1}{4}$; c) $\frac{1}{6} - \frac{1}{18}$.
8. It is correct that $8 - 2 \times 3 - 1 = 1$
   (Remember x, ÷ before +, −)
   Also $(8 - 2) \times 3 - 1 = 17$
   (Brackets first)
   By putting either one or two pairs of brackets in the lefthand side, show how the correct answer can be
   (a) 4 (b) 12 (c) 3
9. $9 + 2 \times 4 - 3 = 14$
   Put either one or two pairs of brackets in the lefthand side so that the answer can be
   (a) 41 (b) 11
10. $12 - 5 \times 2 + 4 = 6$
    Put either one or two pairs of brackets in the lefthand side so that the answer can be
    (a) 42 (b) 18 (c) −18 (d) −2

Project 5 BALANCING

In this project □, △, ○ and ∗ represent weights which are always balanced.

1. (a) 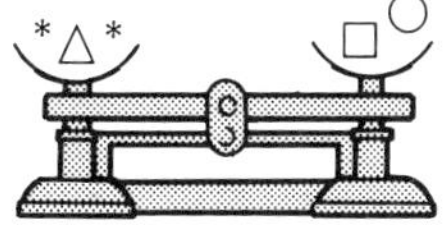 (b) 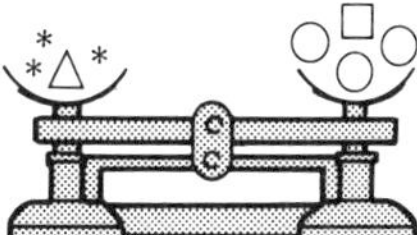

(c) 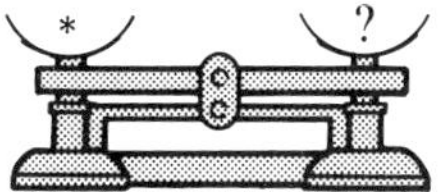 How many ○'s?

2. (a)  (b) 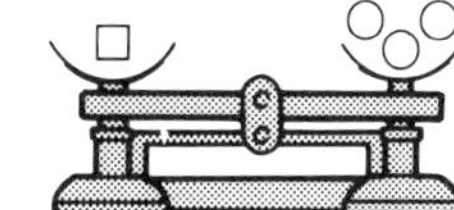

(c) 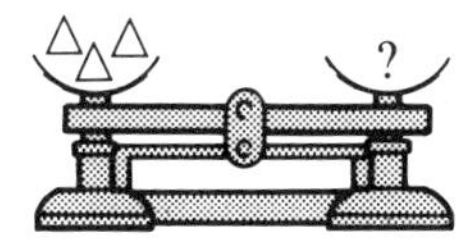 How many ○'s?

3. (a) ○ ○ □ = ∗ ∗
(b) □ □ ○ = ∗ ∗ ○
(c) □ = How many ○'s?

4. (a) □ ○ ○ = △ □ □ □
(b) □ □ □ ○ = △ △ □
(c) □ ○ = △ □
(d) ○ = How many □'s?

5. (a) □ □ = ○ △
(b) ○ ○ ○ □ = □ △
(c) ○ □ □ □ = △ △ ○
(d) □ = How many ○'s?

6. (a) ○ ○ □ = ∗ ○
(b) ∗ ∗ = ○ ○ ○
(c) □ ∗ = ○ ○
(d) ∗ = How many □'s?

7. (a) ○ □ □ = △ ∗
(b) ∗ ∗ ∗ = △ △
(c) ○ □ = △
(d) △ △ △ △ = How many □'s?

8. (a) ○ □ = △
(b) ○ = □ ∗
(c) ○ ○ □ = △ ∗ ∗
(d) □ = How many ∗'s?

Exercise E

1. Change the following fractions to decimals and find the odd one out:

$\frac{3}{5}, \frac{39}{65}, \frac{33}{55}, \frac{36}{54}, \frac{27}{45}.$

2. Find the odd one out: $\frac{98}{112}, \frac{63}{72}, \frac{7}{8}, \frac{119}{138}, \frac{105}{120}$

3. Find the odd one out: $\frac{40}{48}, \frac{5}{6}, \frac{75}{90}, \frac{60}{72}, \frac{95}{115}$

4. Find the odd one out: $\frac{45}{144}, \frac{75}{240}, \frac{135}{435}, \frac{105}{336}, \frac{5}{16}$

5. Find the odd one out: $\frac{56}{96}, \frac{7}{12}, \frac{84}{144}, \frac{147}{252}, \frac{217}{370}$

6. Find the odd one out: $\frac{99}{187}, \frac{135}{255}, \frac{153}{289}, \frac{189}{356}, \frac{9}{17}$

7. Use a calculator to change the fractions to decimals and then arrange the fractions in order of size, smallest first.

(a) $\frac{7}{8}, \frac{17}{20}, \frac{27}{32}.$ (b) $\frac{21}{100}, \frac{9}{40}, \frac{1}{5}$ (c) $\frac{5}{6}, \frac{6}{7}, \frac{3}{4}$

(d) $\frac{2}{3}, \frac{8}{11}, \frac{5}{9}$ (e) $\frac{7}{9}, \frac{11}{12}, \frac{3}{4}, \frac{13}{15}$ (f) $\frac{3}{5}, \frac{15}{19}, \frac{17}{23}$

(g) $\frac{5}{11}, \frac{4}{13}, \frac{7}{19}, \frac{17}{37}$

8. Using a calculator I divided two whole numbers under 10 and found the answer was 0.7777777.
What were the two numbers?

9. Using a calculator I divided two whole numbers under 10 and found the answer was 0.8571428.
What were the two numbers?

10. Using a calculator I divided two whole numbers under 15 and found the answer was 0.5833333.
What were the two numbers?

11. Using a calculator I divided two whole numbers under 20 and found the answer was 0.4705882.
What were the two numbers?

12. I divided two whole numbers under 12 and found the answer was 1.375.
What were the two numbers?

13. I divided two whole numbers under 15 and found the answer was 1.444444.
What were the two numbers?

14. I divided two whole numbers under 15 and found the answer was 1.090909.
What were the two numbers?

15. I divided two whole numbers under 20 and found the answer was 0.1764705.
What were the two numbers?

16. I divided two whole numbers under 20 and found the answer was 0.368421.
What were the two numbers?

Project 6 LARGEST PRODUCT

1. Arrange the digits 1, 2, 3 and 4, one into each box, so that the answer is as large as possible.

$$\begin{array}{r} \square\ \square \\ \times\ \square\ \square \\ \hline \\ \hline \end{array}$$

2. Arrange the digits 1, 2, 3, 4 and 5, one into each box, so that the answer is as large as possible.

$$\begin{array}{r} \square\ \square\ \square \\ \times\ \square\ \square \\ \hline \\ \hline \end{array}$$

3. What is the largest number which can be found with a single multiplication using each of the digits 1, 2, 3, 4, 5 and 6 once only?
4. What is the largest number which can be found with a single multiplication using each of the digits 1, 2, 3, 4, 5, 6 and 7 once only?
5. What is the largest number which can be found with a single multiplication using each of the digits 1, 2, 3, 4, 5, 6, 7 and 8 once only?
6. Can you find a rule which will help you to answer the questions above?

Exercise F

1. A man hires a car and the car hire company charges £8 per day plus 5p per km travelled.
   (a) How much does it cost to hire a car for three days and drive 500 km?
   (b) How much does it cost to hire a car for seven days and drive 750 km?
   (c) A man hired a car for two days and had to pay £21. How far did he drive?
2. The workers in a bank are offered the choice of two pay rises. Workers can choose either a 4.5% increase on their salaries or they can accept a rise of £250.
   (a) A secretary earns £5260 a year. Which pay rise should she accept?
   (b) A cleaner earns £3140 a year. Which pay rise should he accept?

3. The outline of a 50p coin is shown below.

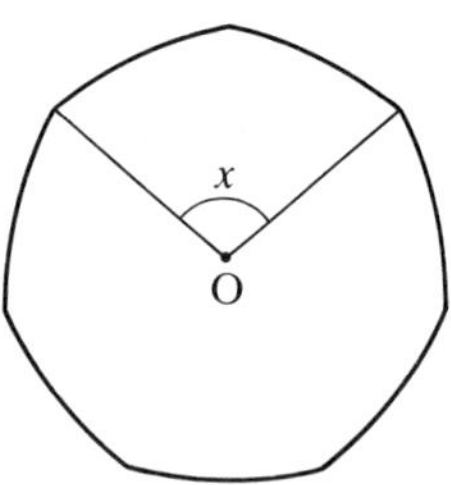

(a) Draw in any lines of symmetry
(b) Calculate the size of the angle marked x (O is the centre of the coin).

4. A shopkeeper bought 30 articles for £4.50 and sold them at 20p each. Find the missing numbers below.
(a) The cost price of each article was *p.
(b) The total selling price was £ *.
(c) The total profit was £ *.

5. Every day on his way to school James walks for $\frac{1}{4}$ hour, rides a horse for $\frac{1}{5}$ hour, takes a boat for $\frac{2}{3}$ hour and finally runs the last part in $\frac{3}{10}$ hour. How long is his journey in minutes?

6. The diagram represents a railway siding. Each ● is a junction where a train can turn left or right. A turn to the left has a code 0 and a turn to the right has a code 1.

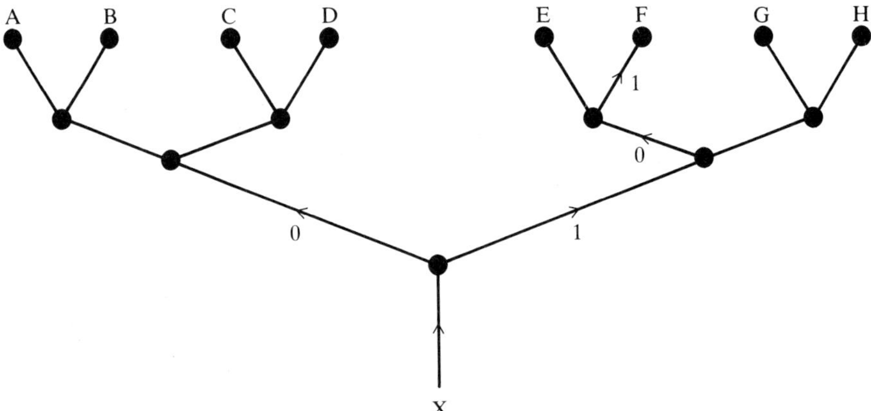

For example, a train starting at X would have code 101 in order to arrive at F.
Copy and complete the table below.

Point	A	B	C	D	E	F	G	H
Code						101		

Project 7 MATHEMATICAL MAGIC

Here is a trick which you can perform to demonstrate that you can add even quicker than a calculator!

(a) Ask someone to give a five-digit number with the figures all jumbled up to make it more 'difficult'.

(b) Ask for two more five-digit numbers. You may now have:

47563 ...A
25608 ...B
87265 ...C

(c) Pretend to add two more five-digit numbers at random. In fact choose the fourth number so that when added to number B it makes 99999. Similarly the fifth number is chosen so that when added to number C it also makes 99999. We now have:

47563
25608
87265
74391
12734

(d) You now add them together 'in your head' and write down the answer. (Check this on a calculator.)

answer = 247561!

How does it work?

The first digit is always a '2'.
The next five digits are simply 2 less than number A.
i.e. 47563 − 2 = 47561.

Here is another example.

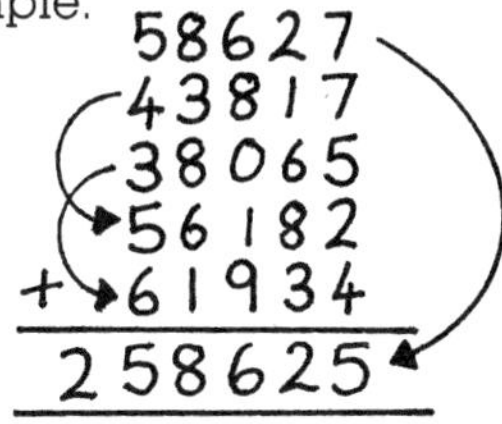

Can you work out why it works?

Now challenge your friends or relatives to an addition race: your brain versus their calculator.

Unit 16

16.1 MEAN, MEDIAN AND MODE

Mean

Five pupils in a class were weighed and their weights were 47 kg, 51 kg, 46 kg, 50 kg and 48 kg.
Find the mean weight of the pupils.

$$\text{Mean weight} = \frac{47 + 51 + 46 + 50 + 48}{5}$$

$$= 48.4 \text{ kg}$$

Exercise 1

In questions **1** to **8** find the mean value of the numbers.

1. 7, 3, 8, 9, 4.
2. 2, 5, 1, 7, 6, 3, 2, 5.
3. 7, 8, 9, 4, 6, 8.
4. 6, 6, 6, 6, 6, 6, 6, 6, 6.
5. 1.2, 0.8, 1.1, 0.8, 3.2.
6. 11; 12, 7, 5, 2, 0, 3, 8, 13, 12.
7. −2, −3, 2, 4, −5, 0, 7, −2.
8. 2350, 3164.

9. In a test the marks were 5, 8, 7, 4, 9, 6, 7, 8, 2, 7. Find the mean mark.

10. The speeds of several cars were measured as they travelled down a road. The speeds were (in m.p.h.) 50, 53, 71, 45, 62, 50, 61, 74. Find the mean speed of the cars.

11. Louise claims that she is better at maths than her brother Peter. Louise's last five marks were 63, 72, 58, 84 and 75 and Peter's last four marks were 69, 73, 81 and 70. Find the mean mark for Louise and for Peter. Is Louise better than Peter?

12. (a) Calculate the mean of the numbers 6, 3, 8, 9, 4, 7, 5.
    (b) Calculate the new mean when the '3' is removed.
13. (a) Calculate the mean of the numbers 8, 11, 5, 2, 9, 1.
    (b) Calculate the new mean when the '8' is removed.
14. (a) Calculate the mean of the numbers 0.8, 1.3, 0.7, 1.4, 2.3, 0.4.
    (b) Calculate the new mean when the '2.3' is removed.
15. (a) Calculate the mean of the numbers 5, 12, 7, 3, 2, 5, 1.
    (b) Calculate the new mean when a '10' is added.
16. (a) Calculate the mean of the numbers 6, 9, 7, 2, 1, 3, 5, 9.
    (b) Calculate the new mean when a '10' and a '4' are added.
17. (a) Calculate the mean of the numbers 13, 6, 8, 5, 3, 8, 6.
    (b) Calculate the new mean when the highest number and the lowest number are removed.
18. Six boys have heights of 1.53 m, 1.49 m, 1.60 m, 1.65 m, 1.90 m and 1.43 m.
    (a) Find the mean height of the six boys.
    (b) Find the mean height of the remaining five boys when the shortest boy leaves.
19. Seven ladies have weights of 44 kg, 51 kg, 57 kg, 63 kg, 48 kg, 49 kg and 45 kg.
    (a) Find the mean weight of the seven ladies.
    (b) Find the mean weight of the remaining five ladies after the lightest and the heaviest ladies leave.
20. In a maths test the marks for the boys were 9, 7, 8, 7, 5 and the marks for the girls were 6, 3, 9, 8, 2, 2.
    (a) Find the mean mark for the boys.
    (b) Find the mean mark for the girls.
    (c) Find the mean mark for the whole class.

Exercise 2

This exercise is more difficult.

1. The mean of four numbers is 4.1.
   The mean of a different six numbers is 3.2.
   Find (a) the total of the first four numbers.
   (b) the total of the second six numbers.
   (c) the mean of the ten numbers altogether.
2. The mean of seven numbers is 3.1.
   The mean of a different three numbers is 4.8.
   Find (a) the total of the first seven numbers.
   (b) the total of the second three numbers.
   (c) the mean of the ten numbers altogether.
3. The mean of two numbers is 11.6.
   The mean of a different eight numbers is 3.3.
   Find (a) the total of the first two numbers.
   (b) the total of the second eight numbers.
   (c) the mean of the ten numbers altogether.
4. The mean of four numbers is 3.4.
   The mean of a different five numbers is 1.4.
   Find (a) the total of the first four numbers.
   (b) the total of the second five numbers.
   (c) the mean of the nine numbers altogether, correct to 3 S.F.
5. The mean of six numbers is 4.7.
   The mean of a different four numbers is 6.5.
   Calculate the mean of the ten numbers altogether.
6. The mean weight of four girls is 48 kg.
   The mean weight of six boys is 53.5 kg.
   Find (a) the total weight of the four girls.
   (b) the total weight of the six boys.
   (c) the mean weight of the group of four girls and six boys.
7. The mean height of three men is 1.78 m.
   The mean height of seven women is 1.59 m.
   Find (a) the total height of the men.
   (b) the total height of the women.
   (c) the mean height of the group of three men and seven women.

Median

Find the median of the numbers
9, 8, 10, 3, 5, 7, 8, 4, 8.

Arrange the numbers in order of size and select the one in the middle.
3, 4, 5, 7, 8, 8, 8, 9, 10
↑

The median is 8.

Exercise 3

In questions **1** to **14** find the median.

1. 3, 4, 8, 2, 1, 5, 6, 2, 9.
2. 8, 6, 7, 13, 3, 9, 4, 8, 14.
3. 6, 5, 10, 15, 5, 8, 16.
4. 4, 1, 7, 8, 1, 9, 3, 3, 10.
5. 7, 6, 11, 30, 12, 6, 9, 13, 21.
6. 4, 5, 1, 4, 9, 1, 7, 3, 3, 10.
7. 7, 3, 11, 8, 4, 9.
8. 4, 3, 4, 3, 4, 3.
9. 0.5, 0.1, 1.2, 1.3, 1.45.
10. 0.7, 0.35, 0.81, 1.2, 1.9.
11. 1, 7, −3, 3, 8, −1, 5.
12. 2, 0.8, 0.1, $\frac{1}{4}$, $\frac{1}{2}$.
13. $\frac{1}{10}$, 3, $\frac{1}{5}$, 0.02, 0.75.
14. 0.05, $\frac{1}{5}$, 0.045, $\frac{11}{12}$, 3, 0.5, $\frac{3}{5}$.
15. The heights in cm of seven children were 151, 160, 148, 143, 127, 159 and 133. What is the median height?
16. A die was thrown ten times and the results are shown below.

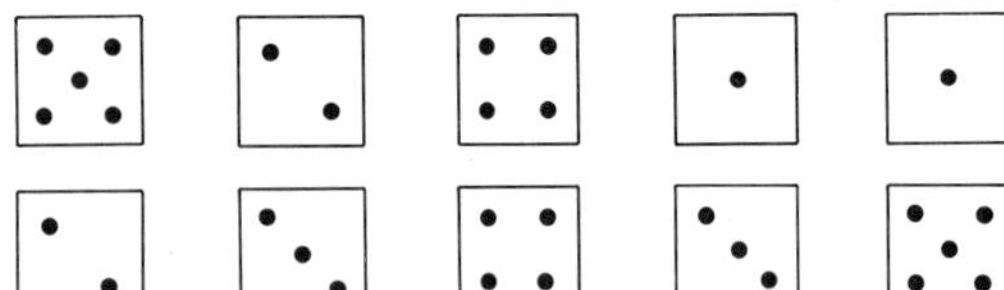

Find the median score

17. Each day a headmaster expels a certain number of pupils for misbehaviour. During one week the number of expulsions was 3, 11, 2, 1, 5. What was the median number of expulsions?
18. In a really hard question a teacher asked a class to find the median of the numbers 7, 1, 7, 1, 12, 8, 13, 3, 12, 4, 4, 11, 14, 25, 20, 19, 20, 18, 15. What was the answer?

Mode

Find the mode of the numbers
3, 2, 4, 3, 2, 3, 4, 3, 4, 4, 4

The mode is the number which occurs most often. There are two '2s', four '3s' and five '4s' so the mode is 4.

Exercise 4

In questions **1** to **6** find the mode.

1. 2, 3, 4, 2, 3, 4, 2, 5, 3, 2, 5.
2. 1, 3, 2, 3, 1, 3, 2, 2, 1, 3, 2, 3.
3. 3, 5, 6, 3, 5, 3, 4, 5, 6, 4, 6, 6.
4. 3, 7, 4, 1, 7, 4, 3, 8, 1, 7, 8.
5. 5, 7, 5, 6, 7, 6, 5, 6, 5, 6, 5, 6, 7, 7, 7, 7.
6. 5, 3, 4, 5, 6, 3, 5, 4, 3, 6, 4, 5, 6.
7. In various shops a tin of beans was priced in pence as follows.
18, 19, 18, 19, 21, 18, 21, 23, 18, 23, 23.
What is the modal price?
8. The temperature in °C on 17 days was:
1, 0, 2, 2, 0, 4, 1, 3, 2, 1, 2, 3, 4, 5, 4, 5, 5.
What was the modal temperature?
9. A die was thrown 14 times as follows:

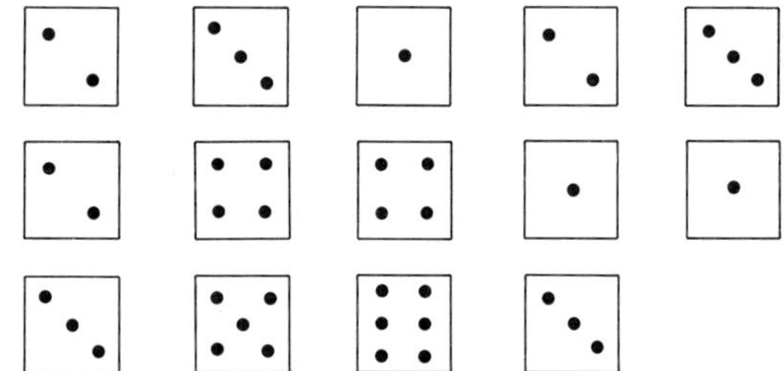

What was the modal score?

10. The bar chart shows the marks scored in a test. What was the modal mark?

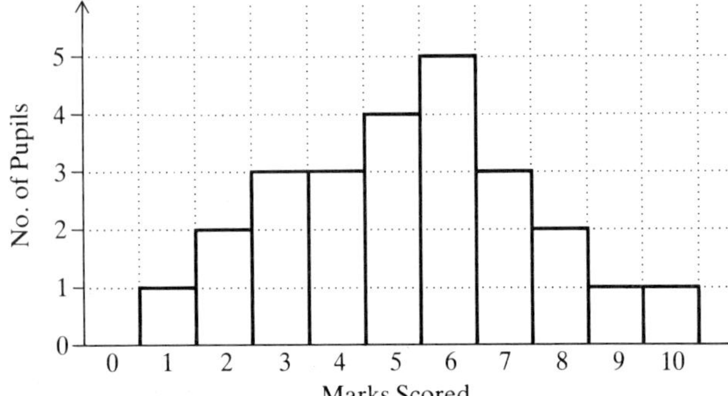

Exercise 5

Find (a) the mean, (b) the median, (c) the mode.
Begin each question by writing out the numbers in order of size.

1. 4, 2, 9, 5, 2.
2. 8, 3, 1, 8, 6, 1, 8.
3. 3, 4, 3, 5, 3, 4, 3, 4.
4. 1.2, 1.8, 0.1, 1.8, 0.6.
5. 17, 18, 18, 17, 18.
6. 4, 7, 8, 3, 4, 11, 8, 4, 4, 8.
7. 0.5, 0.5, 1.05, 0.05, 0.15.
8. 2, 1, 3, 2, 4, 1, 3, 4, 1, 2, 3, 3, 5, 4, 5, 5.
9. $\frac{1}{4}, \frac{3}{4}, \frac{1}{2}, \frac{3}{4}, \frac{1}{4}, \frac{1}{2}, 1\frac{3}{4}, \frac{1}{4}$.
10. −1, −1, 2, −5, 4, −1, 2.
11. 0.8, 0.68, 0.85, 0.85, 0.72.
12. 0, −1, 7, 3, −1, −3, 2.
13. 4, 9, 1, 7, 19, 2, 5, 4, 11, 4, 11.
14. 13, 8, 11, 5, 13, 17, 21, 13, 2, 9, 9.
15. 102, 135, 117, 101, 101.
16. 1, 10, 5, 1, 9, 8, 1, 9, 1, 5, 5.
17. 0.111, 0.1, 0.111, 0.11, 0.01.
18. 0.32, 0.3, 0.302, 0.322, 0.322.
19. −2, 2, −2, −3, 7, 4, −3, 4, −2, 5.
20. 41, 47, 31, 41, 35, 39.

Calculating the mean from a frequency table

The frequency table shows the weights of the eggs bought in a supermarket.

weight	58 g	59 g	60 g	61 g	62 g	63 g
frequency	3	7	11	9	8	2

mean weight of eggs

$$= \frac{(58\times3) + (59\times7) + (60\times11) + (61\times9) + (62\times8) + (63\times2)}{(3 + 7 + 11 + 9 + 8 + 2)}$$

$$= \frac{2418}{40} = 60.45 \text{ g}$$

Exercise 6

1. The frequency table shows the weights of the 40 apples sold in a shop.

weight	70 g	80 g	90 g	100 g	110 g	120 g
frequency	2	7	9	11	8	3

Calculate the mean weight of the apples.

2. The frequency table shows the price of a packet of butter in 30 different shops.

price	49p	50p	51p	52p	53p	54p
frequency	2	3	5	10	6	4

Calculate the mean price of a packet of butter.

3. A box contains 50 nails of different lengths as shown in the frequency table.

length of nail	2 cm	3 cm	4 cm	5 cm	6 cm	7 cm
frequency	4	7	9	12	10	8

Calculate the mean length of the nails.

4. Thirty pupils in a class were asked to estimate the length of a straight line.
Their estimates are given in the frequency table.

estimated length	5 cm	6 cm	7 cm	8 cm	9 cm	10 cm
frequency	4	6	10	5	3	2

Calculate the mean of the estimates.

5. The numbers of eggs in 100 birds' nests are as follows:

number of eggs	1	2	3	4	5	6
frequency	5	15	25	30	15	10

Calculate the mean number of eggs per nest.

6. A group of 50 pupils took a test and their marks were as follows:

marks	5	6	7	8	9	10
frequency	3	8	9	13	9	8

Calculate the mean mark.

7. Twenty-five children were measured and their heights are recorded in the frequency table.

height	1.40 m	1.44 m	1.48 m	1.52 m	1.56 m
frequency	3	5	6	8	3

Calculate the mean height of the 25 children.

8. A class of children were timed when they each ran the length of the playground.

time	6 s	7 s	8 s	9 s	10 s	11 s
frequency	1	4	5	10	7	3

Calculate the mean time for the run.

16.2 CHARTS AND GRAPHS

Pie charts

The pie chart shows the holiday intentions of 600 people.

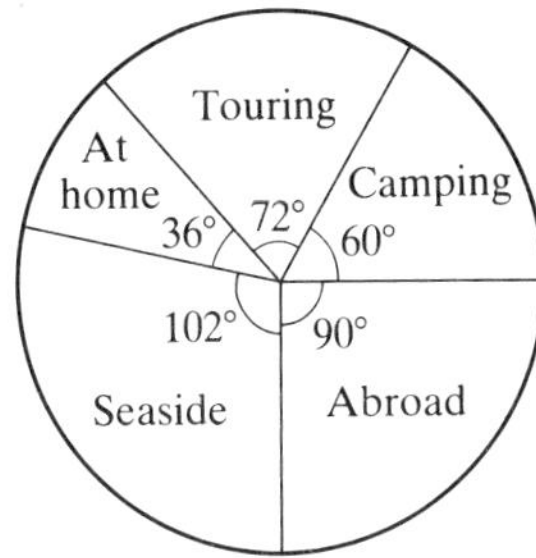

(a) Number of people camping $= \frac{60}{360} \times 600 = 100.$

(b) Number of people touring $= \frac{72}{360} \times 600 = 120.$

(c) Number of people at seaside $= \frac{102}{360} \times 600 = 170.$

Exercise 7

Draw the pie chart and then answer the questions.

1. The total cost of a holiday was £420. The pie chart shows how this cost was made up.

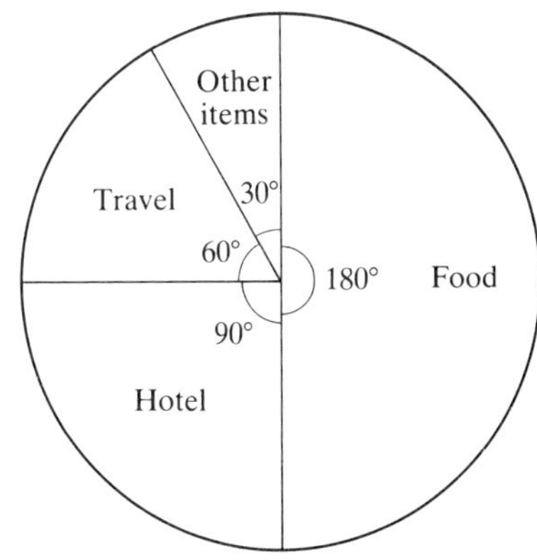

(a) How much was spent on food?
(b) How much was spent on travel?
(c) How much was spent on the hotel?
(d) How much was spent on other items?

2. Mr Billingsgate had an income of £6000. The pie chart shows how he used the money.

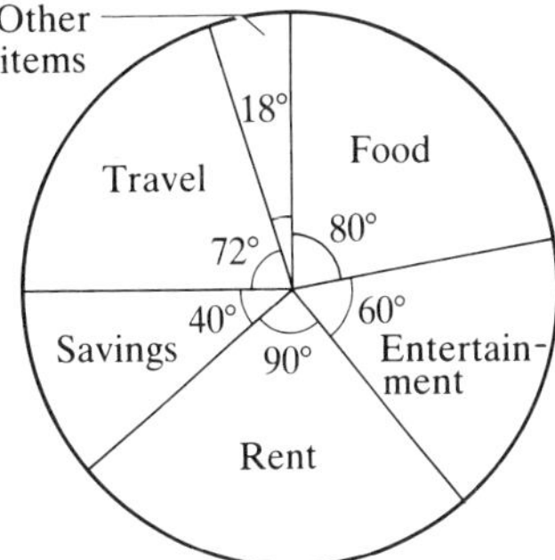

How much did he spend on
(a) Food,
(b) Rent,
(c) Savings,
(d) Entertainment,
(e) Travel?

3. The total expenditure of a County Council is £36 000 000. The pie chart shows how the money was spent.

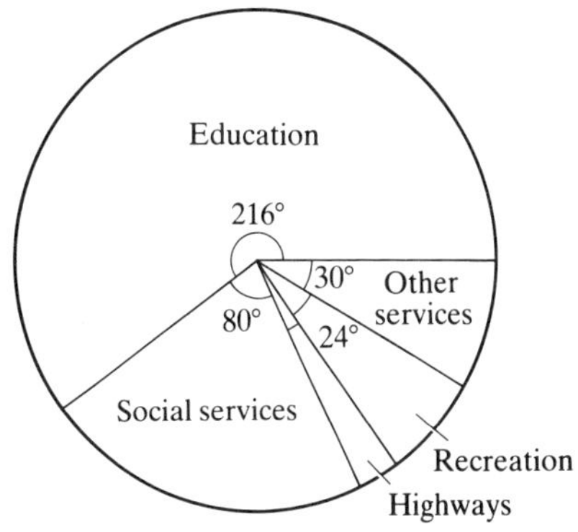

(a) How much was spent on
 (i) Education (ii) Social services?
(b) What is the angle representing expenditure on highways?
(c) How much was spent on highways?

4. A firm employs 720 people in six departments as shown below.

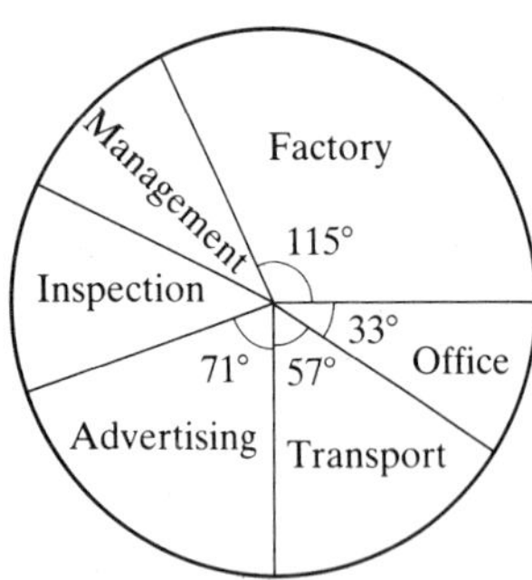

Copy and complete the table below.

Department	Angle on pie chart	Number employed
Factory	115°	
Office	33°	
Transport	57°	
Advertising	71°	
Inspection		140
Management		28

5. The pie chart shows how a pupil spends her time in a maths lesson which lasts 60 minutes.

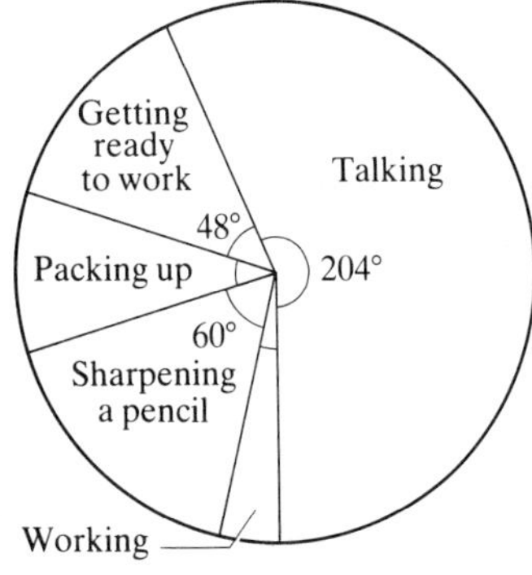

(a) How much time does she spend:
(i) Getting ready to work;
(ii) Talking;
(iii) Sharpening a pencil?
(b) She takes 5 minutes to pack up. What is the corresponding angle on the pie chart?
(c) She spends 3 minutes working. What is the angle on the pie chart for the time spent working?

6. The pie chart below shows the breakdown of cost of an LP having a retail price of £4.99.

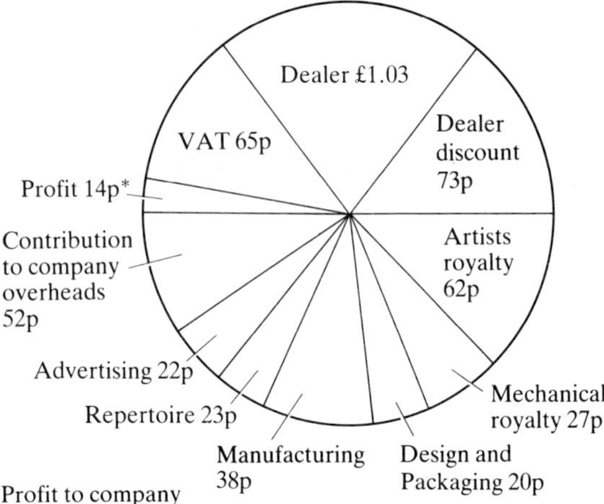

(a) How much does the artist receive if 100 000 records are sold?
(b) How much VAT is paid on a record which sells one million copies?
(c) What are the manufacturing costs for producing 10 000 records?
(d) What is the profit to the company if 500 000 records are sold?

Exercise 8

1. At the semi-final stage of the F.A. Cup 72 neutral referees were asked to predict who they thought would win. Their answers were:

Spurs	9
Manchester United	40
Everton	22
York City	1

(a) Work out
(i) $\frac{9}{72}$ of 360° (ii) $\frac{40}{72}$ of 360°
(iii) $\frac{22}{72}$ of 360° (iv) $\frac{1}{72}$ of 360°
(b) Draw an accurate pie chart to display the predictions of the 72 referees.

2. A survey was carried out to find what 400 pupils did at the end of the fifth year:

120 went into the sixth form
160 went into employment
80 went to F.E. colleges
40 were unemployed.

(a) Simplify the following fractions: $\frac{120}{400}$, $\frac{160}{400}$, $\frac{80}{400}$, $\frac{40}{400}$.
(b) Draw an accurate pie chart to show the information above.

3. In a survey on washing powder 180 people were asked to state which Brand they preferred. 45 chose Brand A.

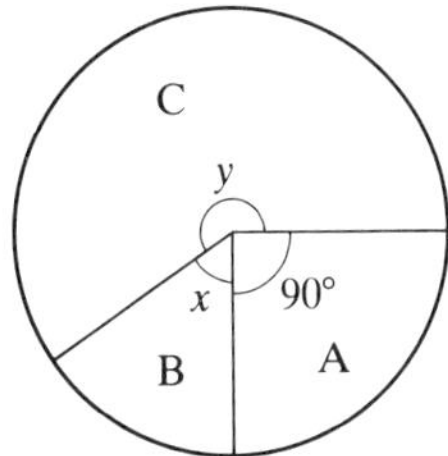

If 30 people chose Brand B and 105 chose Brand C, calculate the angles x and y.

4. A packet of breakfast cereal weighing 600 g contains four ingredients as follows:

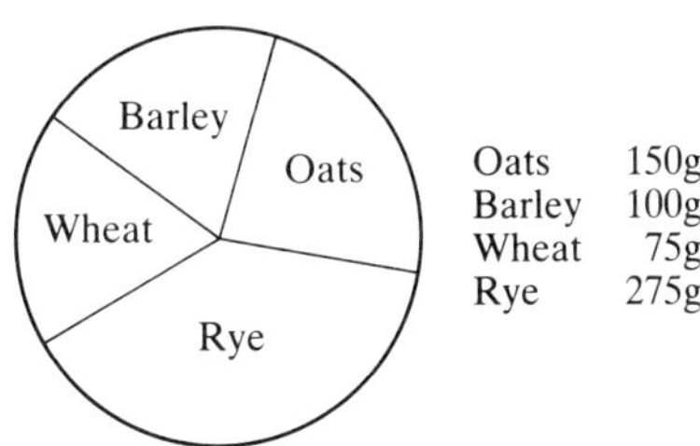

Calculate the angles on the pie chart shown and draw an accurate diagram.

5. The table below shows the share of British car sales achieved by four companies in one year.

Company	A	B	C	D
Share of sales	50%	10%	25%	15%

In a pie chart to show this information, find the angle of the sectors representing
(a) Company A (b) Company B
(c) Company C (d) Company D.

6. The teachers and pupils in a school were asked to state which T.V. channel they preferred. The results were

BBC1	35%
BBC2	5%
ITV	50%
Channel 4	10%

In a pie chart to show this information, find the angle of the sectors representing the four channels in the above order.

7. A pop singer's budget over a three month period was as follows:

Recording latest single	£ 6000
Pressing record and producing sleeve	£ 3000
Poster campaign	£ 5000
Living expenses	£ 2000
Wardrobe	£ 2000
Total	£18000

Draw an accurate pie chart to show the breakdown of his budget.

8. Calculate the angles on a pie chart corresponding to items A, B, C, D and E given in the tables.

(a)

item	A	B	C	D	E
number	5	2	3	6	2

(b)

item	A	B	C	D	E
length (m)	8	3	10	5	10

(c)

item	A	B	C	D	E
mass (g)	15	7	12	16	10

(d)

item	A	B	C	D	E
time (s)	40	7	9	5	11

(e)

item	A	B	C	D	E
number	250	40	100	80	130

Histograms, tally charts and bar charts

A histogram is a diagram which is used to represent a frequency distribution. It consists of a set of rectangles whose *areas* represent the frequency of the various data. If all the rectangles have the same width the frequencies will be represented by the heights of the rectangles.

Example

The tally chart shows the marks obtained by 36 pupils in a test.

Mark	Tally	Frequency
0	IIII	4
1	~~IIII~~ I	6
2	IIII	4
3	~~IIII~~ ~~IIII~~ II	12
4	~~IIII~~ III	8
5	II	2

The same information is shown on a histogram.

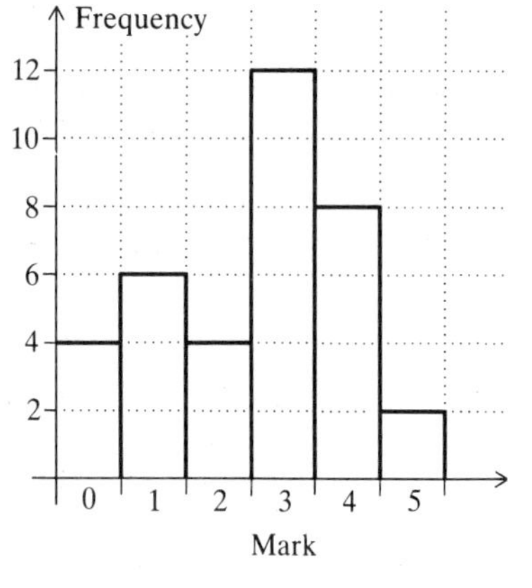

Exercise 9

1. The bar chart shows the sales figures for a firm over a number of years.

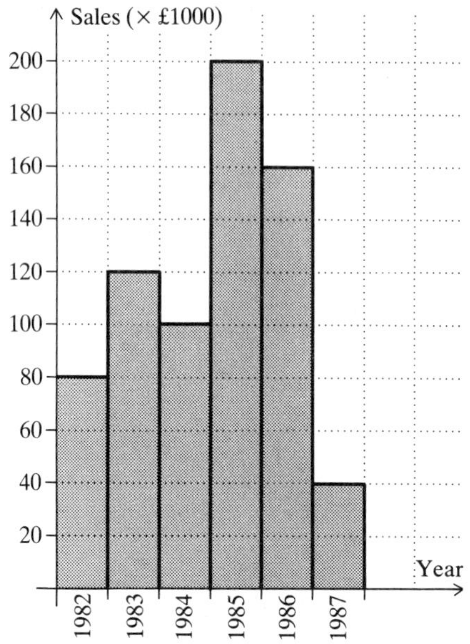

(a) What was the value of sales in 1983?
(b) In what year was the value of sales £160 000?
(c) In what year was the value of sales double the previous year's value?
(d) In 1983 the sales target was £90 000. By how much did the firm exceed its target?
(e) Write the total value of sales over 6 years.

2. The sales of records and cassettes is shown for the years 1980 and 1983.

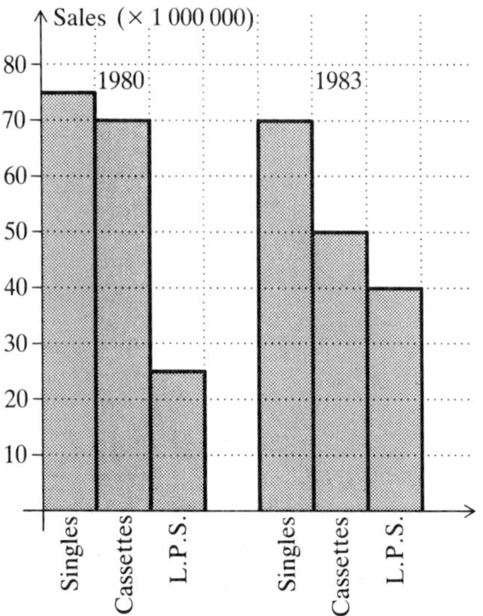

(a) What were the sales of cassettes in 1980?
(b) What were the sales of LP's in 1983?
(c) What was the drop in sales of cassettes between 1980 and 1983?
(d) What was the increase in sales of LP's between 1980 and 1983?
(e) The average price of a single in 1983 was £1.20. How much money was spent on singles in 1983?

3. In a survey the number of occupants in the cars passing a school was recorded.

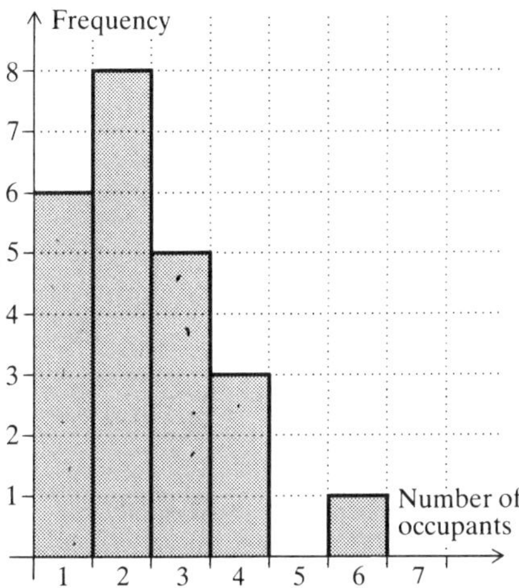

(a) How many cars had 3 occupants?
(b) How many cars had less than 4 occupants?
(c) How many cars were in the survey?
(d) What was the total number of occupants in all the cars in the survey?
(e) What fraction of the cars had only one occupant?

4. The seven best-selling cars in 1984 were:

1. Escort 157 340
2. Cavalier 132 049
3. Fiesta 126 311
4. Metro 117 442
5. Sierra 113 071
6. Maestro 83 072
7. Astra 56 511

(a) Round off the above figures to the nearest 10 000.
(b) Draw a bar chart to illustrate the sales of the cars using the figures obtained in part (a).

5. The bar chart shows the profit/loss figures for a shop.

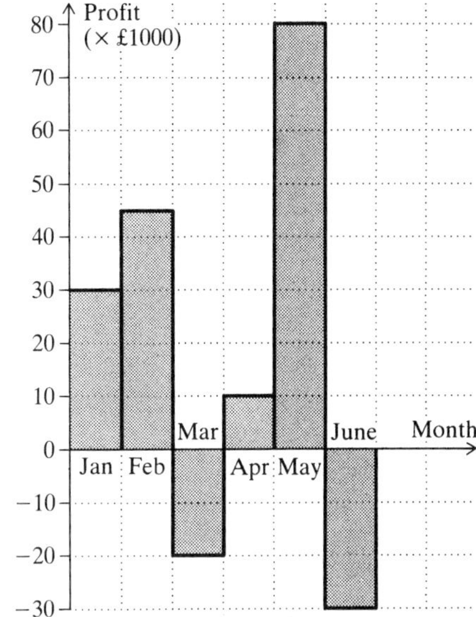

(a) What was the profit in February?
(b) What was the loss in June?
(c) In how many months did the shop make a profit of more than £20 000?
(d) In which two consecutive months did the shop have its best performance?
(e) What was the overall profit for the first six months after the losses were subtracted?

6. In an experiment two dice were thrown sixty times and the total score showing was recorded.

2	3	5	4	8	6	4	7	5	10
7	8	7	6	12	11	8	11	7	6
6	5	7	7	8	6	7	3	6	7
12	3	10	4	3	7	2	11	8	5
7	10	7	5	7	5	10	11	7	10
4	8	6	4	6	11	6	12	11	5

(a) Draw a tally chart to show the results of the experiment. The tally chart is started below.

Score	Tally marks	Frequency
2	II	2
3	IIII	4
4		
:		

(b) Draw a histogram to illustrate the results. Plot the frequency on the vertical axis.

7. In a survey of the cars in a car park the letter at the beginning or the end of the registration number was recorded. Eighty letters were recorded as follows:

D	P	R	B	D	C	D	R	S	A
P	R	T	P	T	B	W	P	T	V
V	B	N	R	W	A	A	N	V	X
T	V	A	C	X	X	T	B	W	W
A	T	C	T	B	A	X	W	X	T
N	D	V	S	S	V	V	C	T	R
V	W	W	V	T	T	R	X	C	S
W	X	X	X	W	S	D	T	D	B

(a) Draw a tally chart so that you can count up the number of cars bearing a particular letter.

(b) Use the tally chart to answer the following questions:
 (i) How many cars had an 'X' registration?
 (ii) What registration letter was most common?

8. In a survey the passengers on an aircraft were asked to state their age in years. The replies are shown below:

29	57	21	41	31	13	43	39	18	5
7	30	28	5	22	38	37	29	47	63
33	25	45	36	35	23	49	5	36	55
10	34	32	15	42	26	32	48	27	68

(a) Draw a tally chart for ages 0–9, 10–19, 20–29 etc.

(b) Draw a histogram to illustrate the results. Plot frequency on the vertical axis.

(c) How many passengers were in the age range 30–39?

Line graphs

Exercise 10

1. Which of the graphs A to D below best fits the following statement:
'Unemployment is still rising but by less each month.'

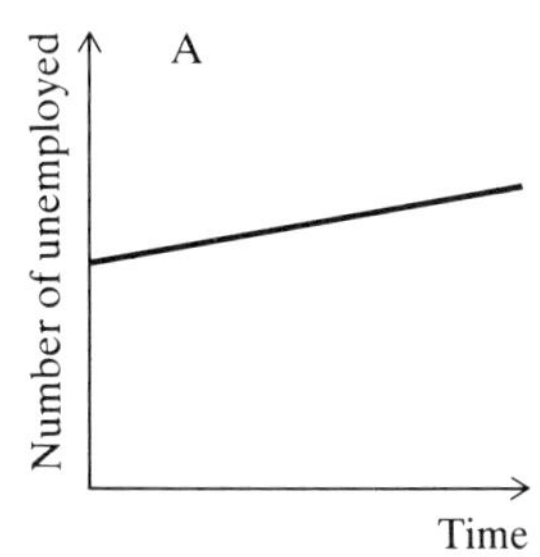

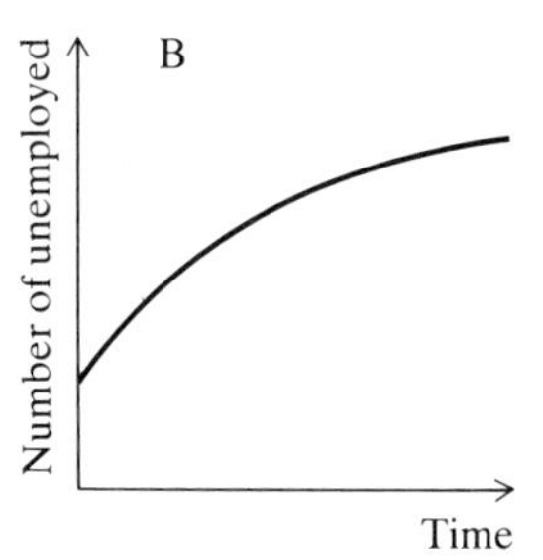

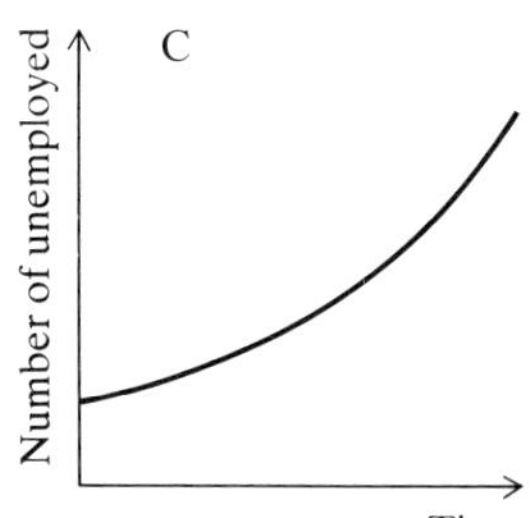

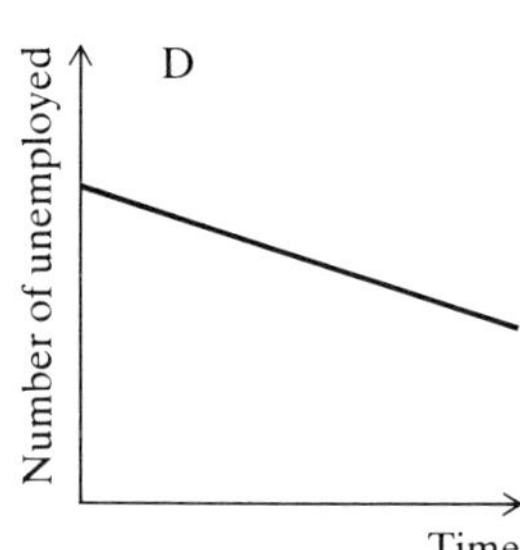

2. Which of the graphs A to D best fits the following statement:
'The price of oil was rising more rapidly in 1983 than at any time in the previous ten years.'

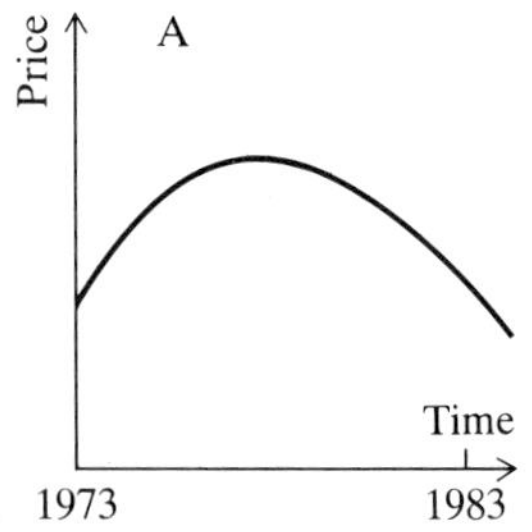

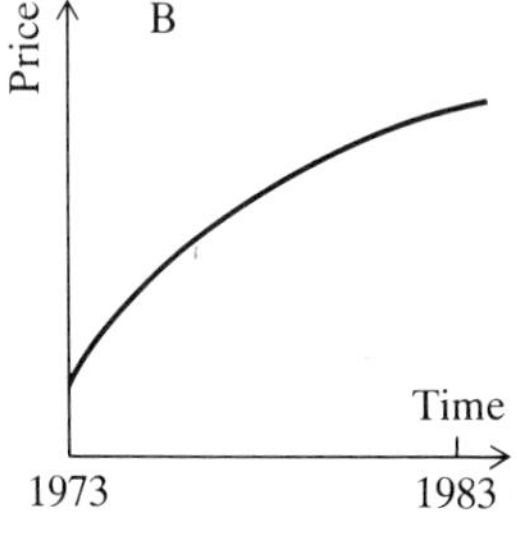

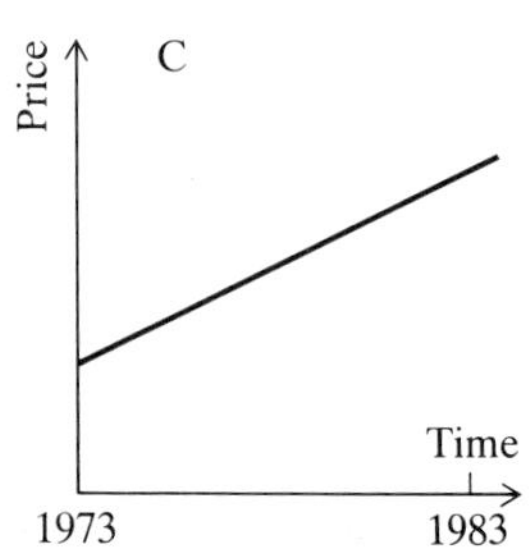

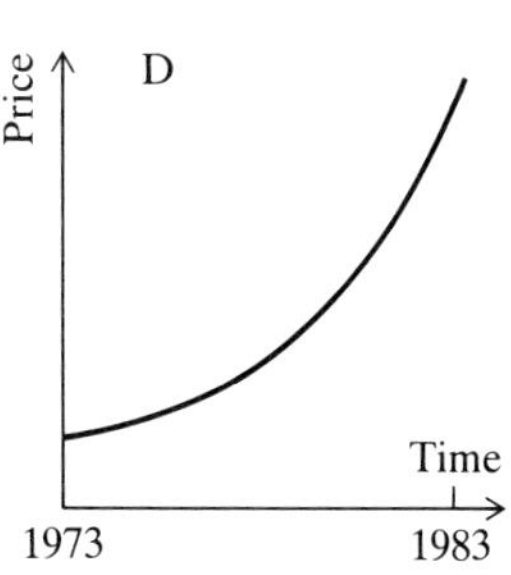

3. Which of the graphs A to D below best fits each of the following statements:
(a) The birthrate was falling but is now steady.
(b) Unemployment, which rose slowly until 1980, is now rising rapidly.
(c) Inflation, which has been rising steadily, is now beginning to fall.
(d) The price of gold has fallen steadily over the last year.

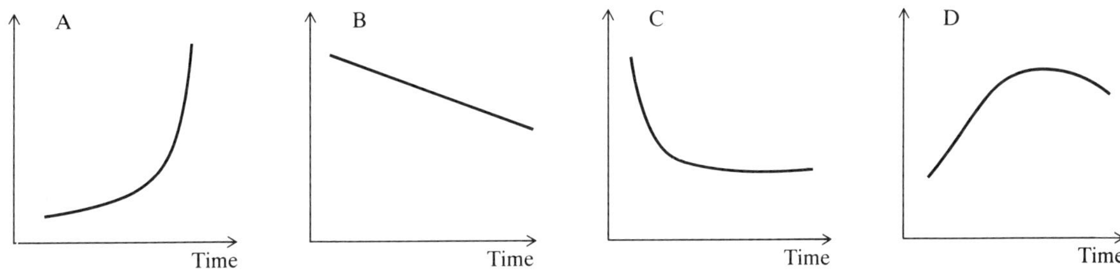

4. The length of a spring is measured with various loads suspended from the spring. The results are shown below.

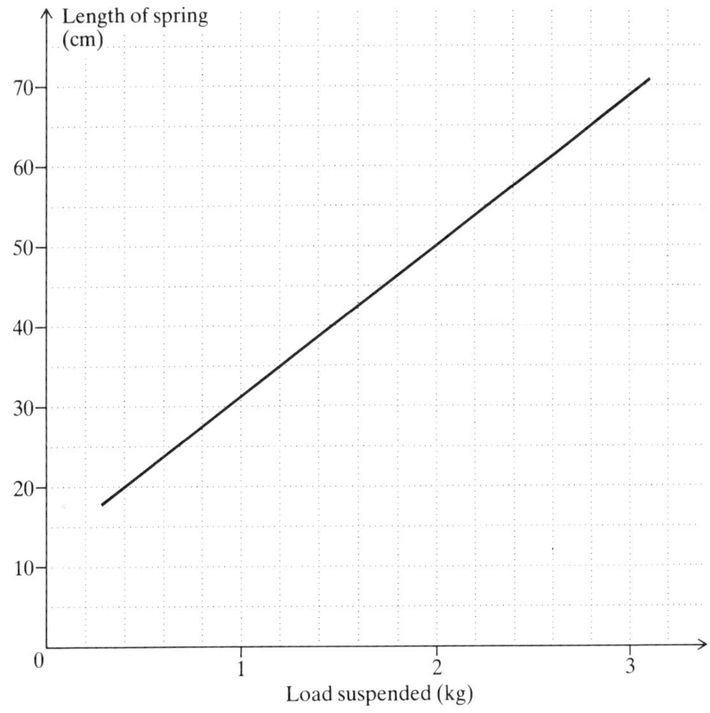

(a) What is the length of the spring with a load of
 (i) 1.2 kg (ii) 2.4 kg (iii) 1.6 kg?
(b) What is the load when the length of the spring is
 (i) 50 cm (ii) 65 cm (iii) 35 cm?
(c) By how much is the length of the spring increased when an extra 1 kg is added to a load of 2 kg?
(d) Estimate the length of the spring with no load.

5. The temperature in a centrally-heated home was recorded every hour for 24 hours. The results are shown below.

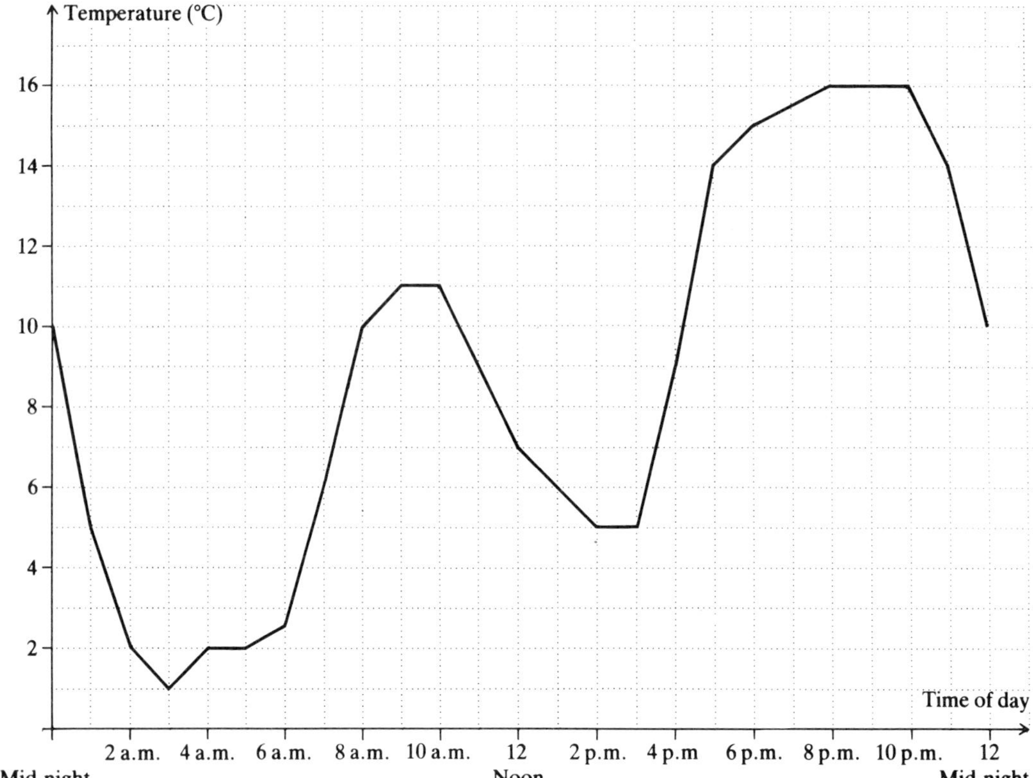

(a) What was the temperature at
  (i) 8 a.m. (ii) 8 p.m. (iii) 7 p.m.?
(b) At what two times was the temperature 14°C?
(c) What was the lowest temperature recorded and when did it occur?
(d) The heating in the house was switched 'on' and then 'off' twice during the day. Estimate
  (i) the two times when it was switched 'on'
  (ii) the two times when it was switched 'off'.
(e) What was the greatest increase in temperature in one hour and when did this occur?

6. The following table gives the cost £C to a householder for the work of a plumber when he works for x hours on a job.

Time x (hours)	1.0	2.0	3.5	4.5	6.5
Cost C (£)	10.50	16.50	25.50	31.50	43.50

(a) Draw a pair of axes with the horizontal scale for x from 0 to 7 and the vertical scale for C from 0 to 50.
(b) Plot the points given in the table and draw a straight line through the points.
(c) Use your graph to find
  (i) the cost to the householder when the plumber is working for 5 hours
  (ii) the length of time he is working when the cost to the householder is £19.50.

7. (a) The graph below gives the charges made by Welwyn Motors for the hire of a van to travel various distances.

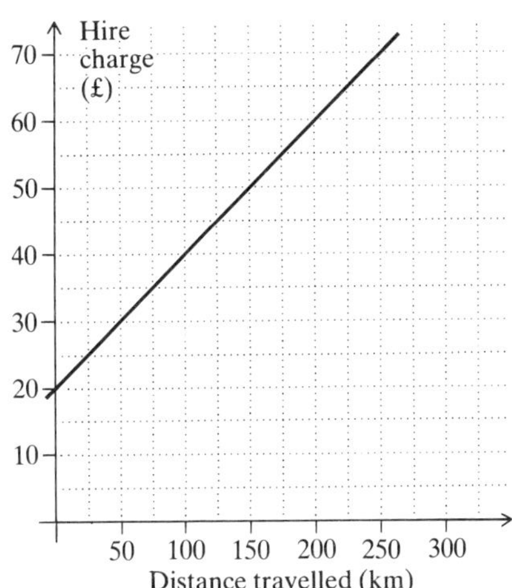

(i) What is the hire charge for a van to travel 100 km?
(ii) What was the distance travelled by a van for which the hire charge was £70?

(b) Cahill Motors also hire out vans. Their charges are shown below.

Distance travelled (km)	50	150	250
Hire charge (£)	45	55	65

(i) Draw a copy of the graph above and on the same graph plot the points representing the hire charges for Cahill Motors. Draw a straight line through the points.
(ii) For what distance do the two firms have the same hire charge?
(iii) For a journey of 50 km, what is the difference in the hire charges made by these two firms?

8. The following table shows the petrol consumption of a car in litres per 100 km at different road speeds.

Road speed km/h	20	30	40	50	60	70	80	90	100
Consumption litres per 100 km	5.5	4.8	4.4	4	4	4.3	4.9	5.8	7.2

(a) Draw a pair of axes with road speed on the horizontal axis and petrol consumption on the vertical axis.
(b) Plot the nine points from the table and draw a smooth curve.
(c) From your graph estimate the most economical road speed for the car.
(d) Estimate the consumption in litres per 100 km at a speed of 95 km/h.
(e) If petrol costs 46p per litre, find the cost of a journey of 200 km if the car travels at a steady speed of 90 km/h.

16.3 PROBABILITY

If a 'trial' can have n equally likely outcomes and a 'success' can occur in s ways (from the n), then the probability of a 'success' $= \frac{s}{n}$.

A single card is drawn from a pack of 52 playing cards. Find the probability of the following results:
(a) the card is a Queen,
(b) the card is a Club,
(c) the card is the Jack of Hearts.

There are 52 equally likely outcomes of the 'trial' (drawing a card).
(a) p (Queen) $= \frac{4}{52} = \frac{1}{13}$
(b) p (Club) $= \frac{13}{52} = \frac{1}{4}$
(c) p (Jack of Hearts) $= \frac{1}{52}$.

Exercise 11

1. If one card is picked at random from a pack of 52 playing cards, what is the probability that it is:
   (a) a King,
   (b) the Ace of Clubs,
   (c) a Heart?
2. Nine counters numbered 1, 2, 3, 4, 5, 6, 7, 8, 9 are placed in a bag. One is taken out at random. What is the probability that it is:
   (a) a '5',
   (b) divisible by 3,
   (c) less than 5,
   (d) divisible by 4?
3. A bag contains 5 green balls, 2 red balls and 4 yellow balls. One ball is taken out at random. What is the probability that it is:
   (a) green,
   (b) red,
   (c) yellow?
4. A cash bag contains two 20p coins, four 10p coins, five 5p coins, three 2p coins and three 1p coins. Find the probability that one coin selected at random is:
   (a) a 10p coin,
   (b) a 2p coin,
   (c) a silver coin.
5. A bag contains 8 orange balls, 5 green balls and 4 silver balls. Find the probability that a ball picked out at random is:
   (a) silver,
   (b) orange,
   (c) green.
6. One card is selected at random from those below.

   Find the probability of selecting:
   (a) a Heart,
   (b) an Ace,
   (c) the 10 of Clubs,
   (d) a Spade,
   (e) a Heart or a Diamond.
7. A pack of playing cards is well shuffled and a card is drawn. Find the probability that the card is:
   (a) a Jack.
   (b) a Queen or a Jack,
   (c) the ten of Hearts,
   (d) a Club higher than the 9 (count the Ace as high).
8. The number of matches in ten boxes is as follows: 48, 46, 45, 49, 44, 46, 47, 48, 45, 46. One box is selected at random. Find the probability of the box containing:
   (a) 49 matches,
   (b) 46 matches,
   (c) more than 47 matches.
9. One ball is selected at random from those below.

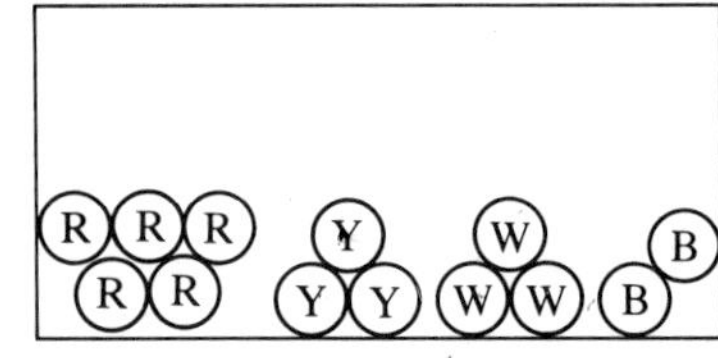

Find the probability of selecting:
(a) a white ball,
(b) a yellow or a black ball,
(c) a ball which is not red.

10. (a) A bag contains 5 red balls, 6 green balls and 2 black balls. Find the probability of selecting:
(i) a red ball (ii) a green ball.
(b) One black ball is removed from the bag. Find the new probability of selecting:
(i) a red ball (ii) a black ball.

11. A small pack of 20 cards consists of the Ace, King, Queen, Jack and ten of all four suits. Find the probability of selecting from this pack:
(a) an Ace,
(b) the Queen of Spades,
(c) a red card,
(d) any King or Queen.

12. A bag contains 12 white balls, 12 green balls and 12 purple balls. After 3 white balls, 4 green balls and 9 purple balls have been removed, what is the probability that the next ball to be selected will be white?

Exercise 12

1. The King of Hearts is drawn from a pack and not replaced. Find the probability that the next card is:
(a) another King,
(b) another Heart,
(c) the Ace of Hearts,
(d) the seven of Diamonds.

2. The Ace, King and Queen of Diamonds are drawn from a pack and not replaced. Find the probability that the next card is:
(a) another Ace,
(b) another Diamond,
(c) the Ace of Spades,
(d) the Queen of Hearts.

3. (a) A bag contains 5 blue discs, 4 orange discs and 2 white discs. What is the probability of picking out:
(i) a blue disc,
(ii) either a white or an orange disc,
(iii) either a blue or a white disc,
(iv) a disc which is not white?
(b) Two of the orange discs are now removed and are replaced by one blue disc and one white disc. What is the new probability of picking out:
(i) a blue disc,
(ii) an orange disc,
(iii) either a white or an orange disc?

4. The 36 possible results, when throwing a red die and a blue die, are shown below. For example the point marked with a cross represents a '6' on the blue die and a '3' on the red die.

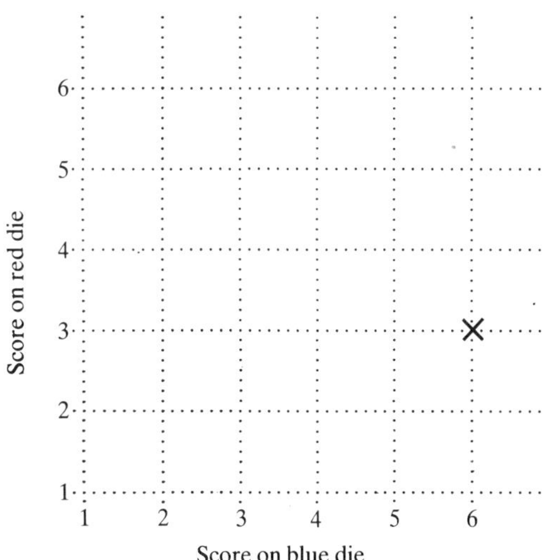

Calculate the probability of scoring in one throw of the two dice:
(a) a total of 12,
(b) a total of 9,
(c) a total of 2,
(d) a double (ie same score on both dice),
(e) a total of more than 9,
(f) a double *and* a total of 10.

5. A boy has 3 coins (5p, 2p and 1p) and he spins all three. Copy and complete the table below to show *all* the possible ways in which they could land. You will need to draw more columns than those shown.

5p	H		
2p	H		
1p	H		

Find the probability of obtaining:
(a) three tails,
(b) two heads and a tail (in any order),
(c) one head and two tails.

6. A girl has 4 coins (50p, 10p, 5p, 2p) and she spins all four. Draw a table to show all the possible ways in which they could land.
Find the probability of obtaining:
(a) four heads,
(b) three heads and a tail (in any order),
(c) two heads and two tails (in any order),
(d) one head and three tails (in any order).

7. Four balls are placed in a bag, 1 red, 1 blue, 1 green and 1 white. Two balls at random are withdrawn in one hand from the bag. List all the different colour combinations which are possible.
Find the probability that:
(a) the red ball and the green ball will be withdrawn,
(b) the blue ball will be withdrawn,
(c) the white ball will be left in the bag.

8. The numbering on a set of 28 dominoes is as follows:

6	6	6	6	6	6	6	5	5	5
6	5	4	3	2	1	0	5	4	3

5	5	5	4	4	4	4	4	3	3
2	1	0	4	3	2	1	0	3	2

3	3	2	2	2	1	1	0
1	0	2	1	0	1	0	0

(a) What is the probability of drawing a domino from a full set with
(i) at least one six on it?
(ii) at least one four on it?
(iii) at least one two on it?
(b) What is the probability of drawing a 'double' from a full set?
(c) If I draw a double five which I do not return to the set, what is the probability of drawing another domino with a five on it?

Tree diagrams

A bag contains 5 yellow balls and 4 green balls. A ball is drawn at random and then replaced. Another ball is drawn. Find the probability of drawing:
(a) two yellow balls,
(b) one ball of each colour.

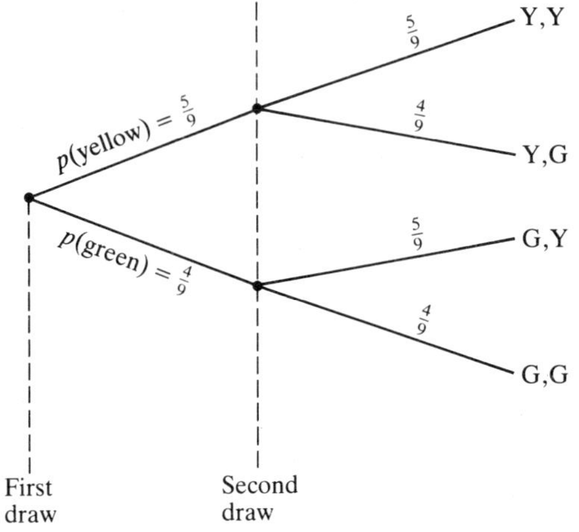

(a) p (two yellow balls) $= \frac{5}{9} \times \frac{5}{9} = \frac{25}{81}$

(b) p (one of each colour)

$$= (\tfrac{5}{9} \times \tfrac{4}{9}) + (\tfrac{4}{9} \times \tfrac{5}{9})$$

$$= \tfrac{20}{81} + \tfrac{20}{81}$$

$$= \tfrac{40}{81}$$

Exercise 13

1. A bag contains 5 green balls and 3 white balls. A ball is drawn at random and then replaced. A second ball is then drawn. Copy and complete the tree diagram below.

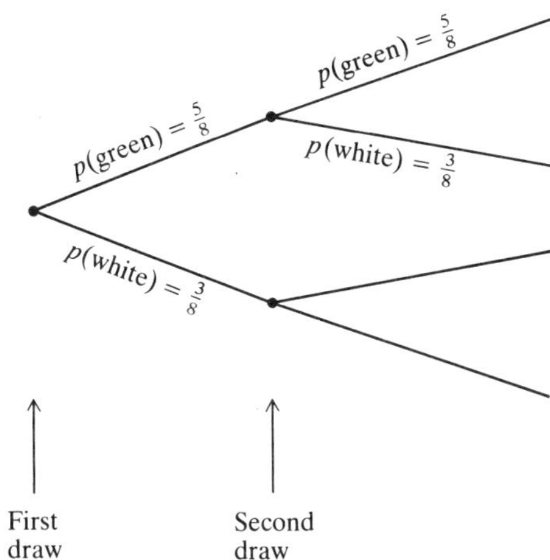

Find the probability of the following:
(a) both balls are green,
(b) both balls are white.

2. A bag contains 3 red balls and 4 yellow balls. A ball is drawn at random and then replaced. A second ball is drawn. Draw a tree diagram to show all the possible outcomes. Find the probability of the following:
(a) both balls are red,
(b) both balls are yellow,
(c) the first ball is red and the second is yellow.

3. A bag contains 4 white balls, 2 black balls and 1 pink ball. A ball is drawn and then replaced. A second ball is drawn. Find the probability of the following:
(a) both balls are pink,
(b) both balls are white,
(c) the first ball is white and the second is black,
(d) the two balls are pink and white in any order.

4. A bag contains 5 red balls and 3 blue balls. A ball is drawn and *not* replaced. A second ball is drawn.
(a) Copy and complete the tree diagram.

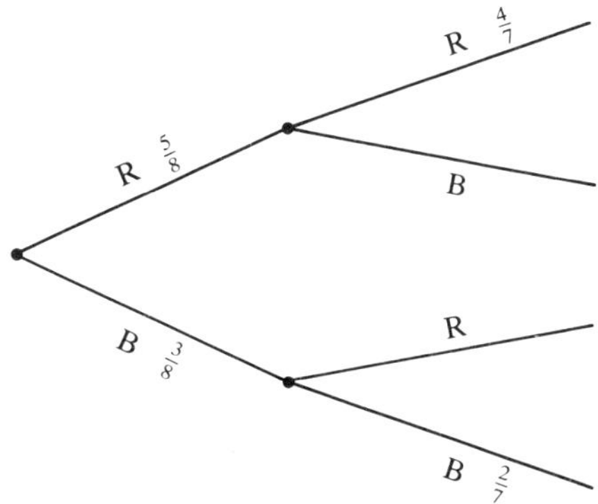

(b) Find the probability of drawing:
(i) two red balls,
(ii) two blue balls.

5. A bag contains 2 orange discs and 5 green discs. A disc is drawn and not replaced. A second disc is drawn. Find the probability of drawing:
(a) two orange discs,
(b) two green discs,
(c) an orange disc and a green disc in that order.

6. A ball is drawn from the box below and not replaced. A second ball is drawn.

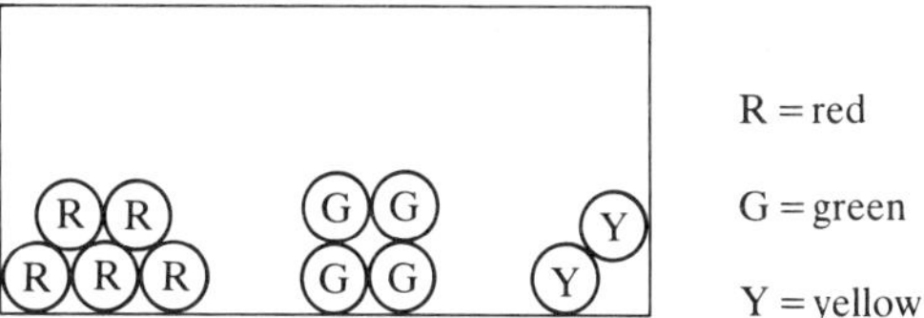

Find the probability of drawing:
(a) two red balls,
(b) two yellow balls,
(c) a red ball and a green ball in that order,
(d) a green ball and a yellow ball in any order.

7. A bag contains 2 white balls and 3 black balls. A ball is drawn and then replaced. A second ball is drawn and then replaced. A third ball is drawn. Find the probability of drawing:
(a) three white balls,
(b) three black balls,
(c) one black ball and two white balls in that order.

8. A card is drawn from a pack of 52 playing cards and is then replaced. Two further draws are made, again with replacement. Draw a tree diagram showing at each branch the two events 'spade' and 'not spade'. What is the probability of drawing:
(a) three spades,
(b) no spades,
(c) one spade and two other suits in any order?

9. An ordinary die is thrown three times. Draw a tree diagram, showing at each branch the two events 'six' and 'not six'. What is the probability of throwing:
(a) three sixes,
(b) no sixes.

10. A fair coin is tossed three times. Draw a tree diagram, showing at each branch the two events 'head' and 'tail'. What is the probability of throwing:
(a) three heads,
(b) no heads,
(c) one head and two tails in any order?

11. The flower seeds in a packet look identical but, in fact, give three differently coloured flowers in the following proportions: 50% red; 30% yellow; 20% white. Assume that all of the seeds will grow into flowers when planted.
(a) What is the probability that a flower will be white?
(b) What is the probability that a flower will not be yellow?
(c) Draw a tree diagram for the colour of the flowers of the first two seeds.
(d) What is the probability that the first two flowers will be:
(i) both red;
(ii) a red and a yellow in any order;
(iii) both white?

12. There are red, white and yellow discs in a bag. The probability of picking a red disc is $\frac{1}{9}$, and the probability of picking a white disc is $\frac{4}{9}$. Find the probability of picking:
(a) a yellow disc,
(b) either a red or a white disc.
(c) If there are 36 discs altogether in the bag, how many are white?
(d) If a disc is picked from the bag, replaced and then a second disc is picked, what is the probability of picking a white disc both times?

13. A fair coin is tossed four times. What is the probability of throwing:
(a) four heads,
(b) two heads and two tails in any order?

14. A coin is biassed so that the probability of a 'head' is $\frac{2}{3}$ and the probability of a 'tail' is $\frac{1}{3}$. The coin is tossed three times. What is the probability of throwing:
(a) three 'tails',
(b) one 'head' and two 'tails' in any order?

15. From a pack of playing cards all the Jacks, Queens and Kings are removed. This leaves the Ace, 2, 3, 4, 5, 6, 7, 8, 9 and 10 of the four suits Spades, Hearts, Diamonds and Clubs; 40 cards in all.
(a) one card is taken from these 40 cards. Find the probability that it is:
(i) a '10', (ii) a Spade,
(iii) the Ace of Clubs,
(iv) the seven of Hearts.
(b) The 40 cards are turned over one by one. The first card turned over is the 8 of Clubs. What is the probability that the next card turned over is the 6 of Spades?
(c) The 40 cards are now shuffled. They are turned over one by one. What is the probability that the first card turned over is the 5 of Diamonds *and* the second card turned over is the 4 of Hearts.

Unit 17

17.1 ANGLES

Basic results

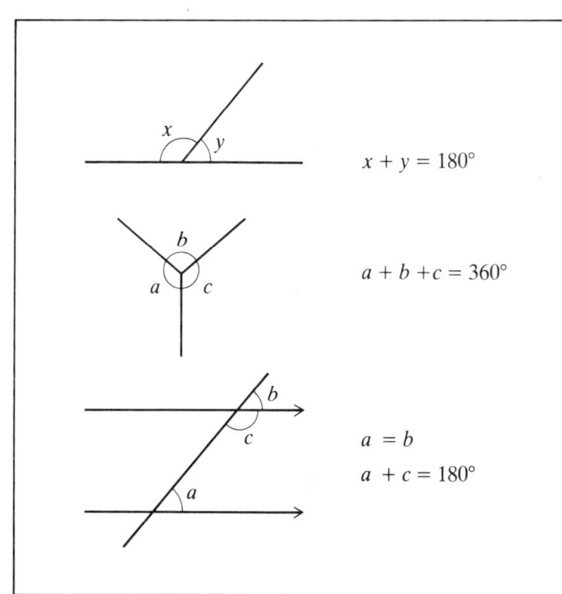

Exercise 1

Find the angles marked with letters. AB and CD are straight lines.

1.

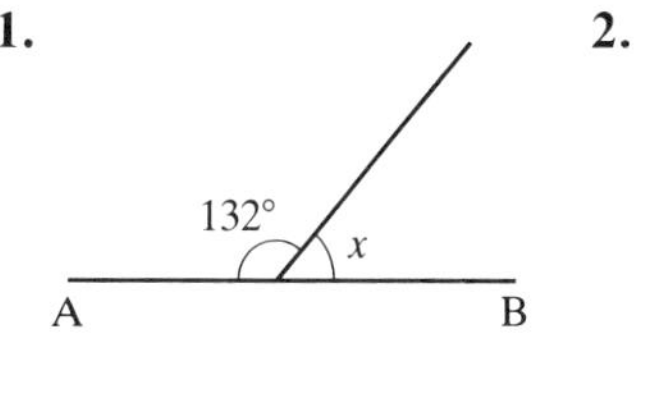

2.

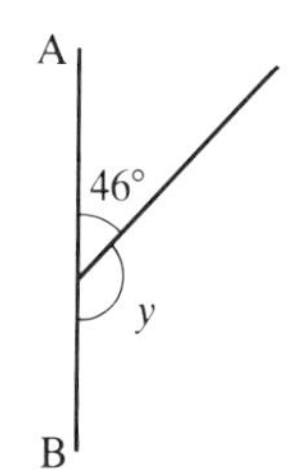

3.

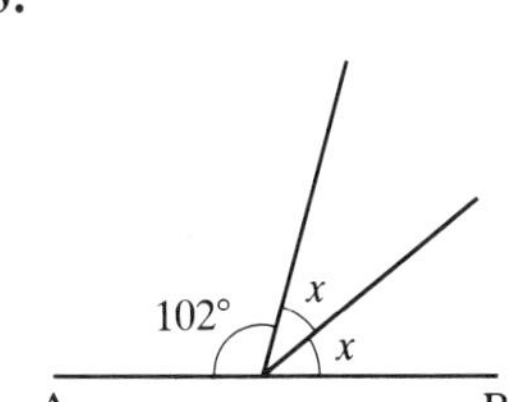

4.

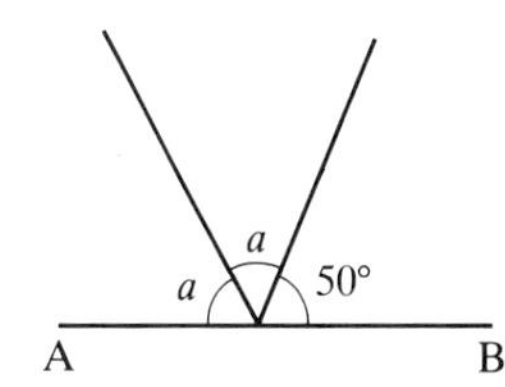

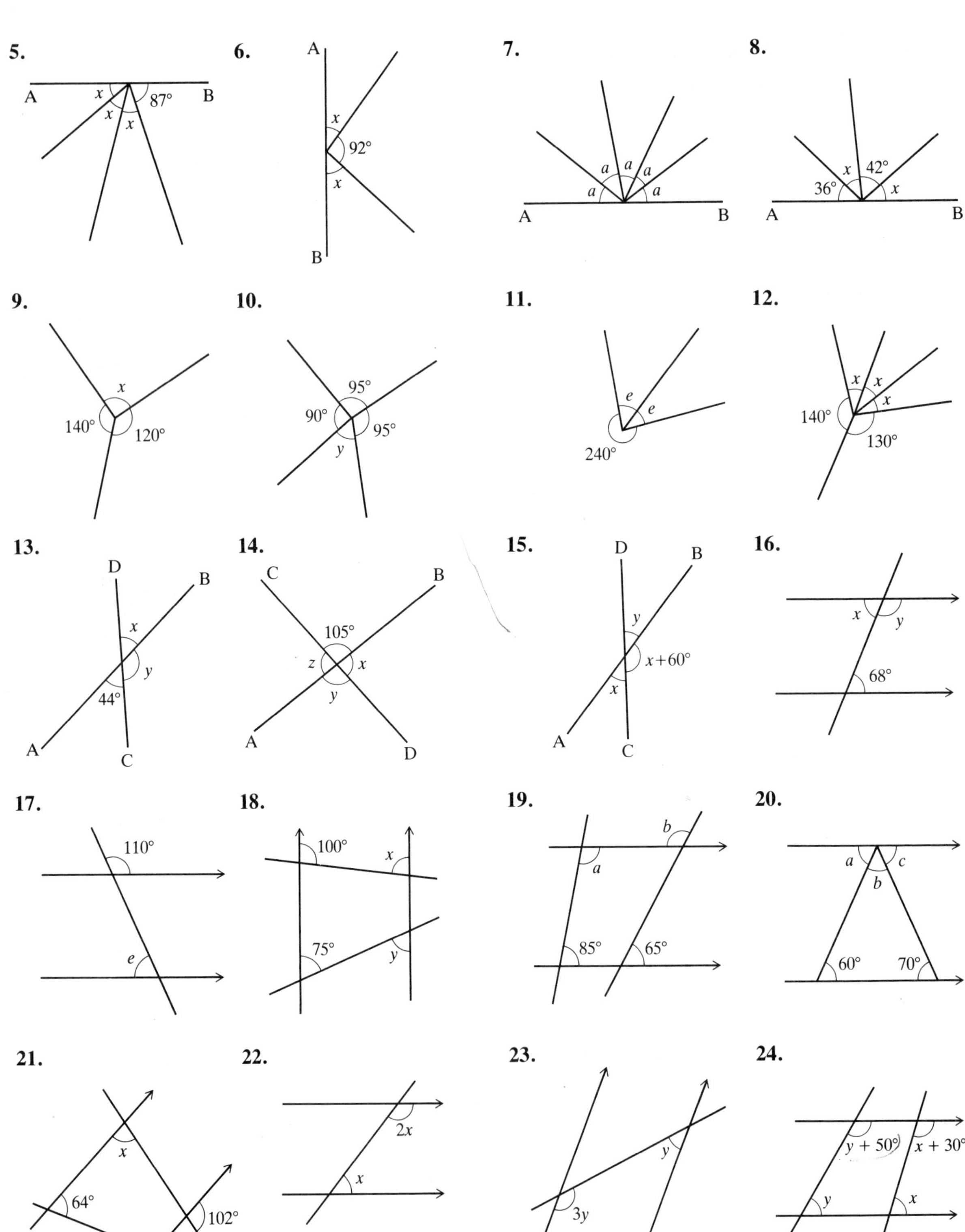
5.
A
B
x
x
x
87°
6.
A
B
x
92°
x
7.
a
a
a
a
a
A
B
8.
x
42°
36°
x
A
B
9.
x
140°
120°
10.
95°
90°
95°
y
11.
e
e
240°
12.
x
x
x
140°
130°
13.
D
B
x
y
44°
A
C
14.
C
B
105°
z
x
y
A
D
15.
D
B
y
x+60°
x
A
C
16.
x
y
68°
17.
110°
e
18.
100°
x
75°
y
19.
b
a
85°
65°
20.
a
c
b
60°
70°
21.
x
64°
102°
y
22.
2x
x
23.
y
3y
24.
y + 50°
x + 30°
y
x

Triangles, quadrilaterals and regular polygons

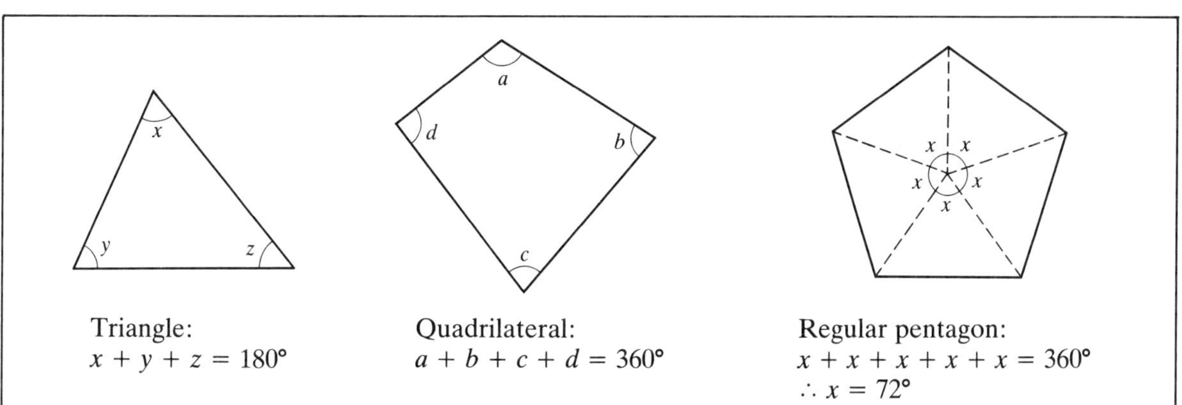

Triangle:
$x + y + z = 180°$

Quadrilateral:
$a + b + c + d = 360°$

Regular pentagon:
$x + x + x + x + x = 360°$
$\therefore x = 72°$

Exercise 2

Find the angles marked with letters.

1.

a
45°
65°

2.

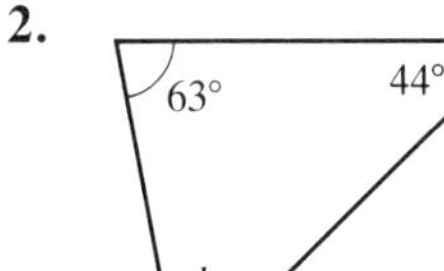

3.

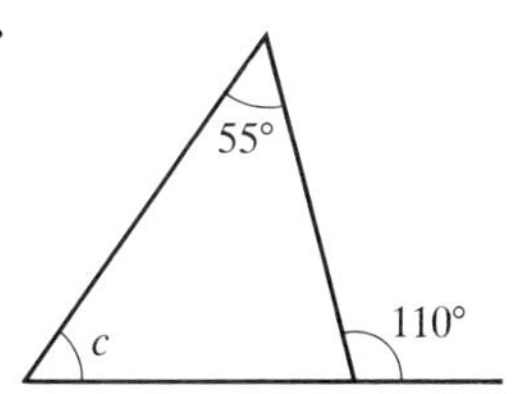

4.

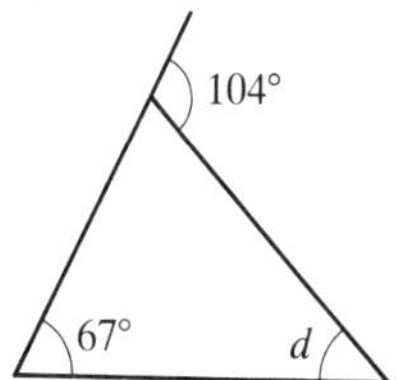

5.

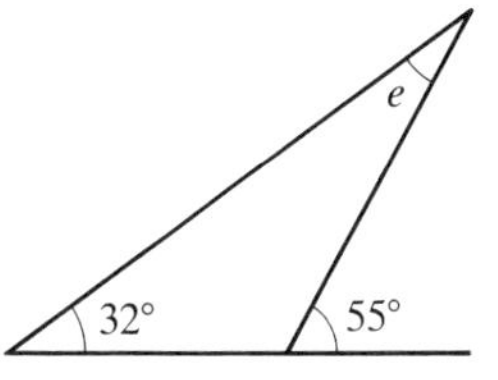

6.

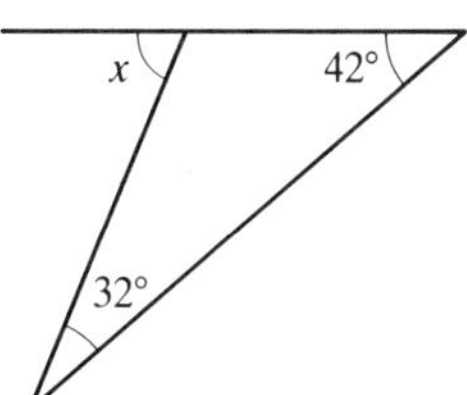

7.

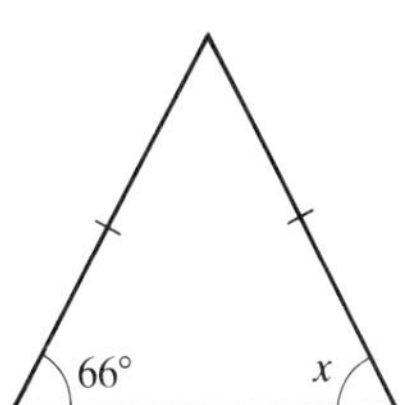

8.

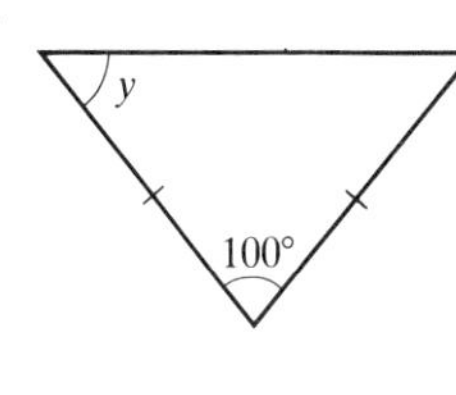

9.

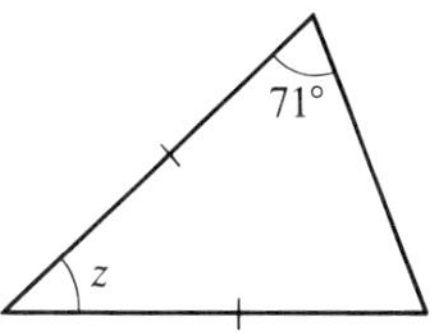

10.

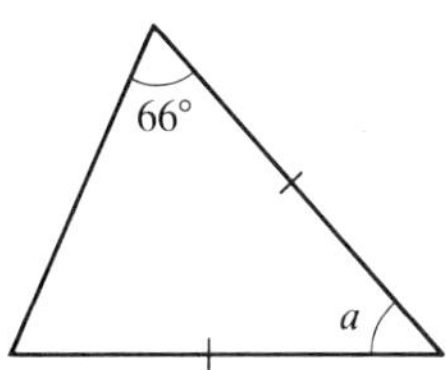

11.

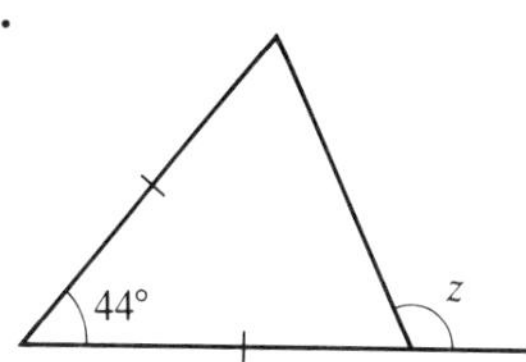

12.

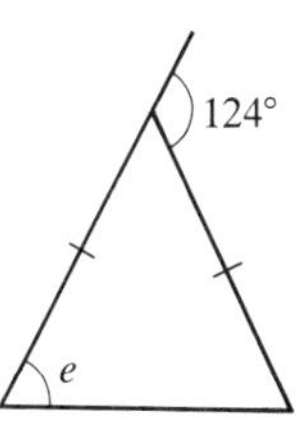

13.

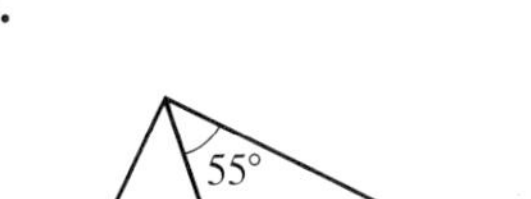

14.

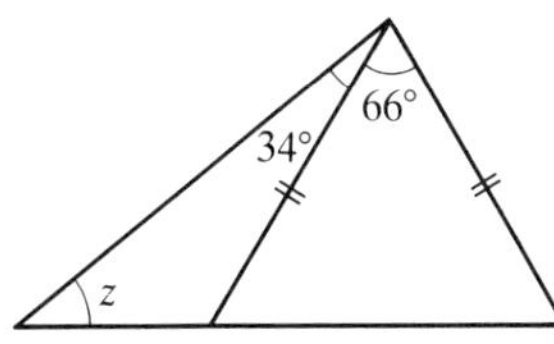

15.

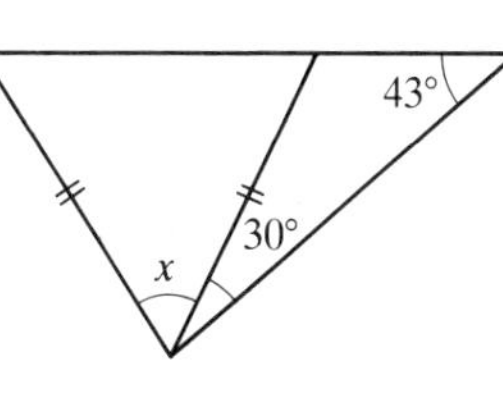

16.

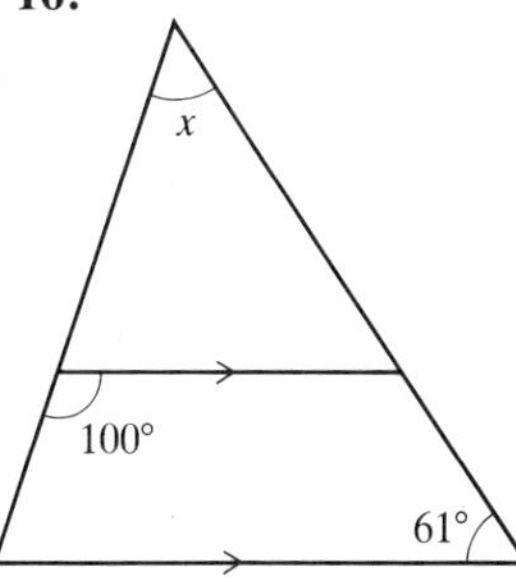

17.

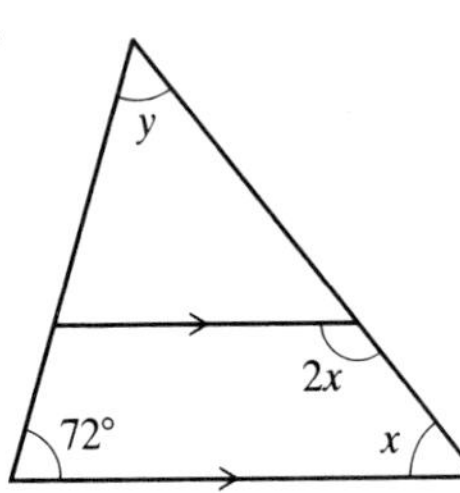

18.

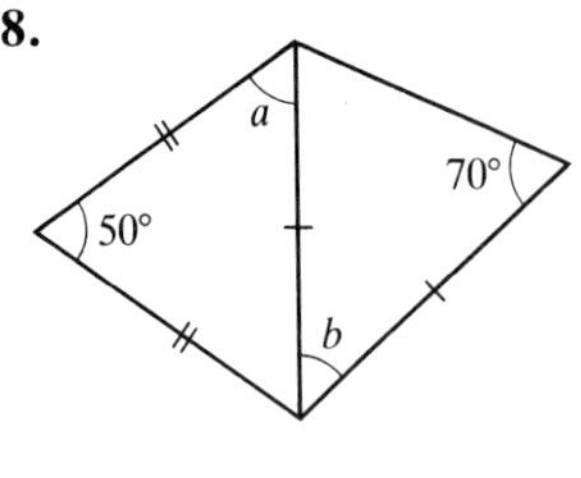

19.

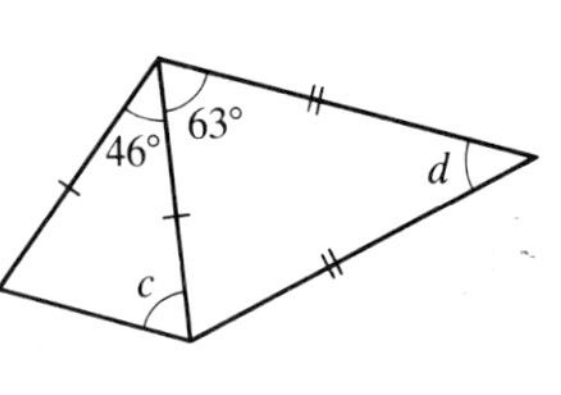

20.

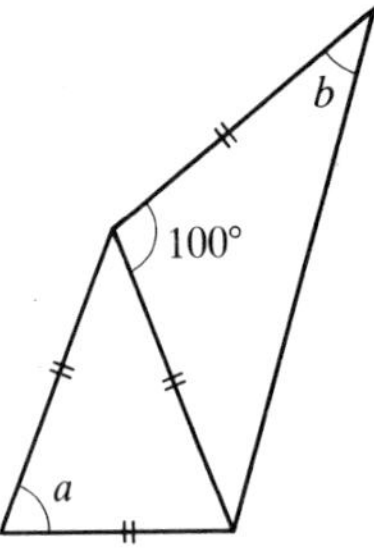

21.

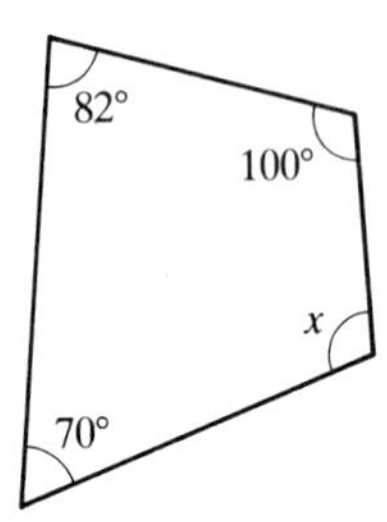

22.

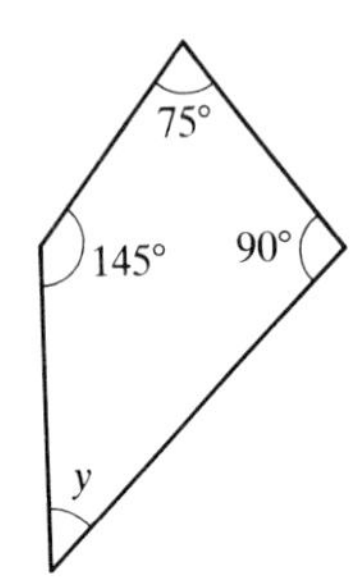

23.

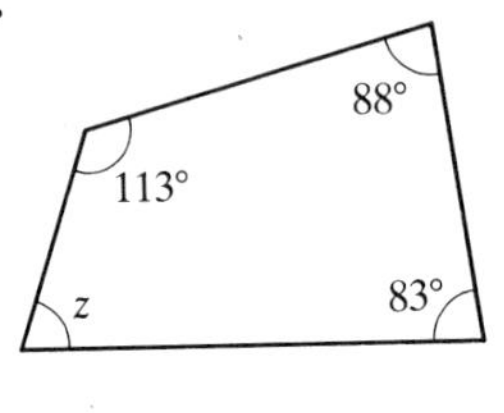

24.

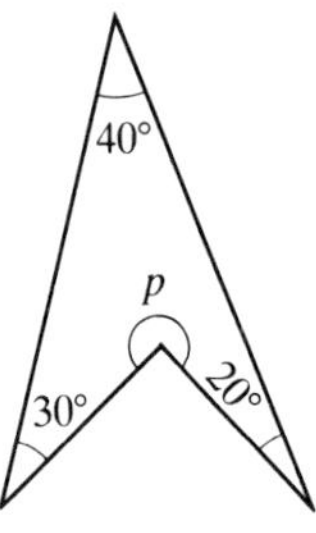

25.

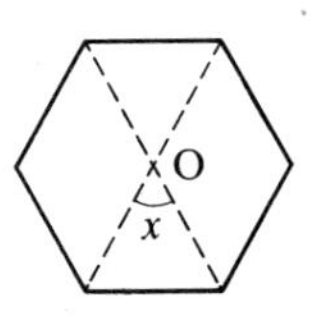

regular hexagon
O is the centre.

26.

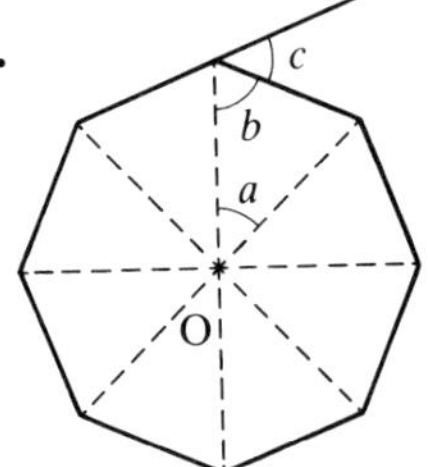

regular octagon
O is the centre.

17.2 CIRCLE THEOREMS

Theorem 1
The angle in a semicircle is a right angle

(a)

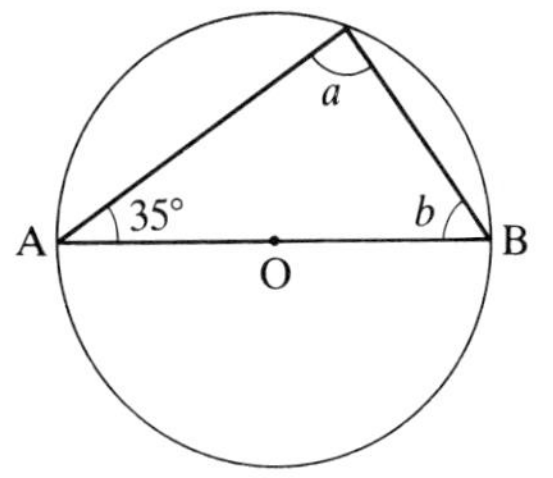

AOB is a diameter.

$a = 90°$
$b = 55°$

(b)

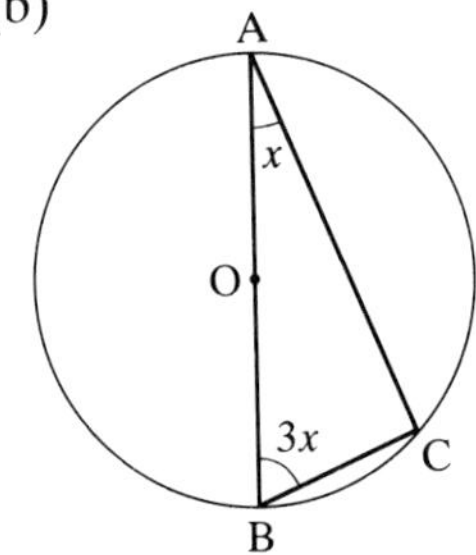

$A\hat{C}B = 90°$

$\therefore\ x + 3x = 90°$

[angle sum of a triangle]

$4x = 90°$

$x = 22\frac{1}{2}°$

Exercise 3

Draw each diagram and find the angles marked with letters. The line AOB is a diameter.

1. **2.** **3.** **4.**

5. **6.** **7.** **8.**

9. **10.** **11.**

Find (a) XÂB
(b) YB̂A
(c) AX̂B

Tangent to a circle

Theorem 2
The angle between a tangent and the radius drawn to the point of contact is 90°

Example.
Find angle x below

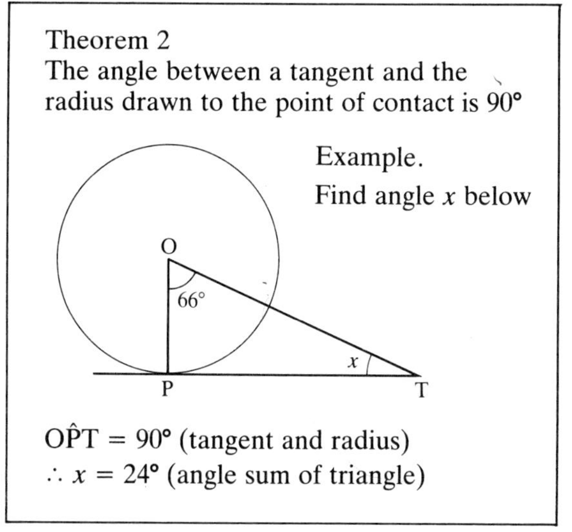

OP̂T = 90° (tangent and radius)
$\therefore x = 24°$ (angle sum of triangle)

Exercise 4

Find the angles marked with letters. The point O is the centre of the circle and TP is a tangent.

1.

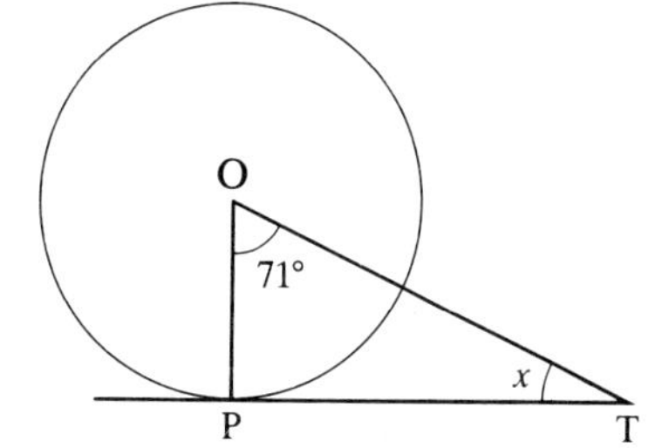

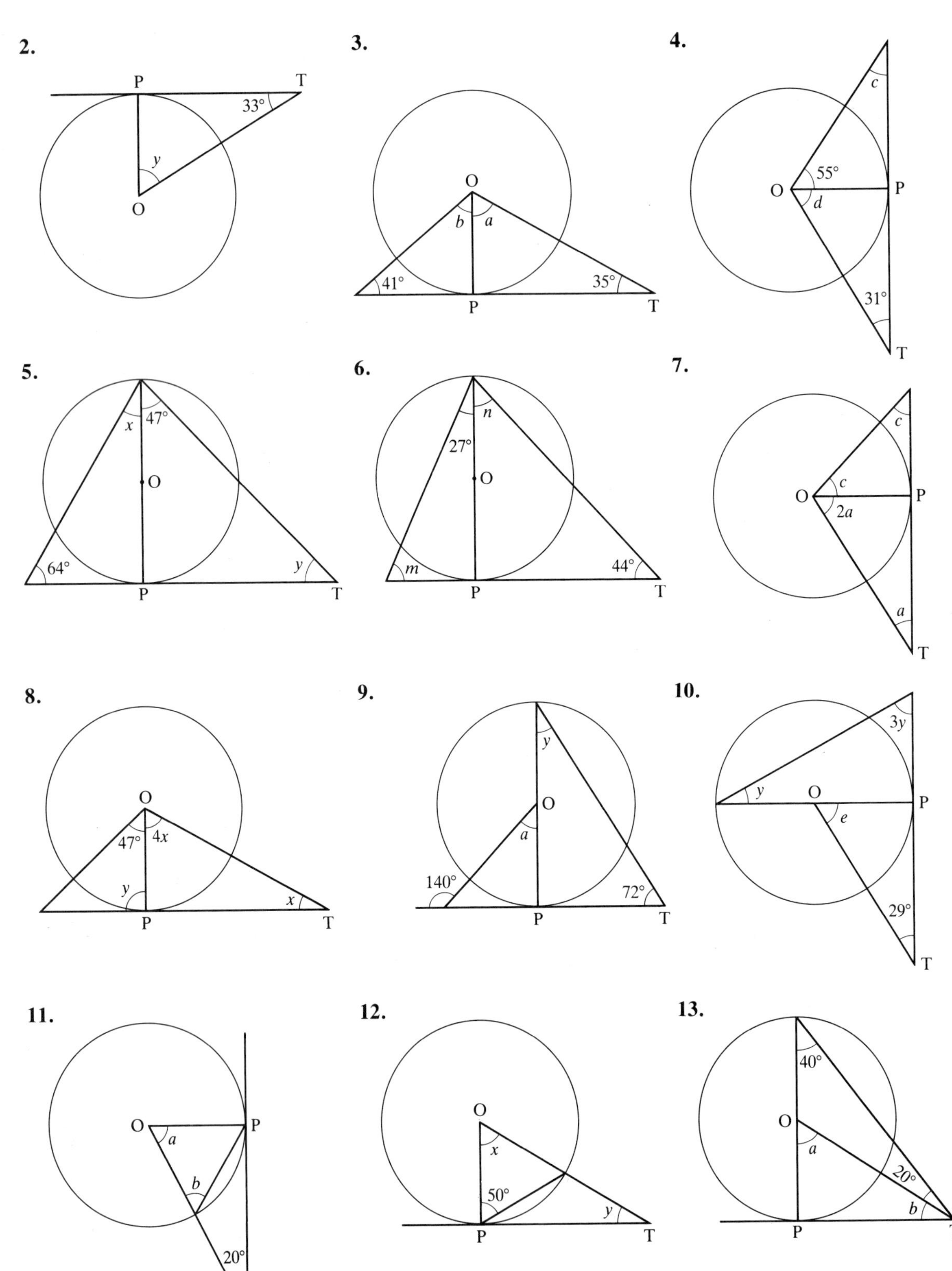

2.
P
T
33°
y
O
3.
O
b
a
41°
35°
P
T
4.
c
55°
O
P
d
31°
T
5.
x
47°
O
64°
y
P
T
6.
n
27°
O
m
44°
P
T
7.
c
O
c
P
2a
a
T
8.
O
47°
4x
y
x
P
T
9.
y
O
a
140°
72°
P
T
10.
3y
y
O
P
e
29°
T
11.
O
a
P
b
20°
T
12.
O
x
50°
y
P
T
13.
40°
O
a
20°
b
P
T

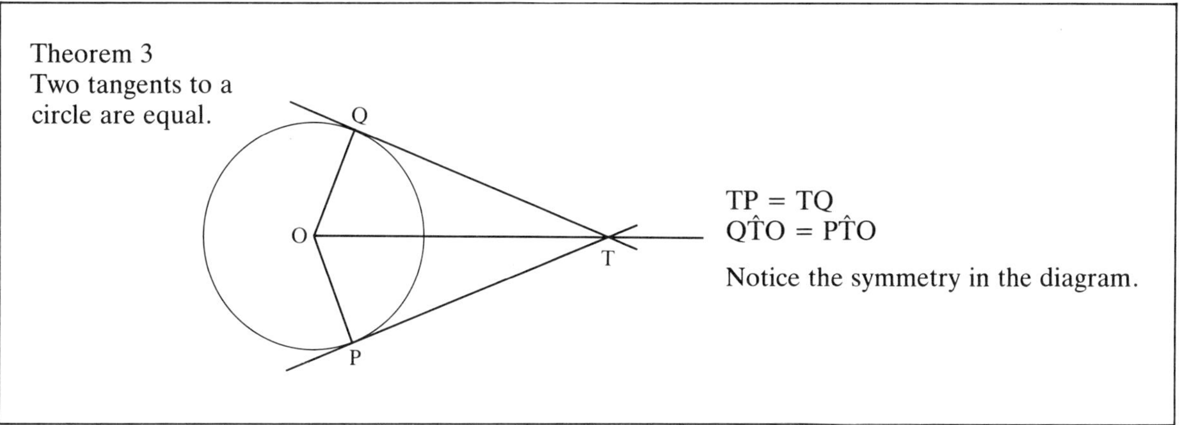

Theorem 3
Two tangents to a circle are equal.

TP = TQ
$\hat{QTO} = \hat{PTO}$

Notice the symmetry in the diagram.

Exercise 5

Find the angles marked with letters.

1.

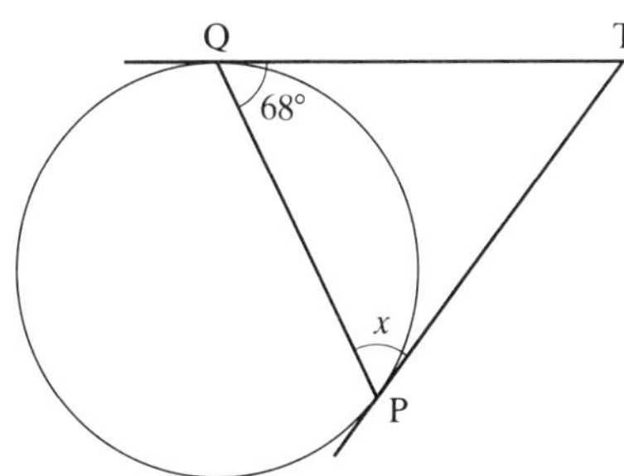

2.

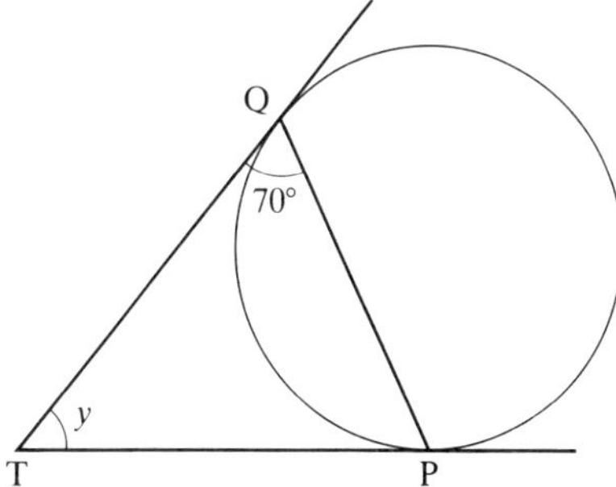

3.

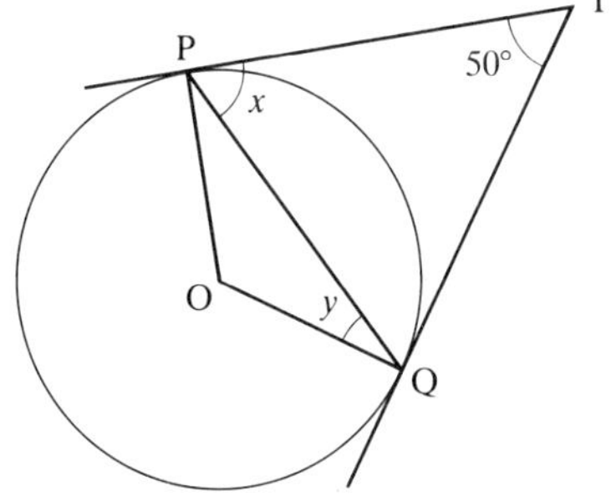

4.

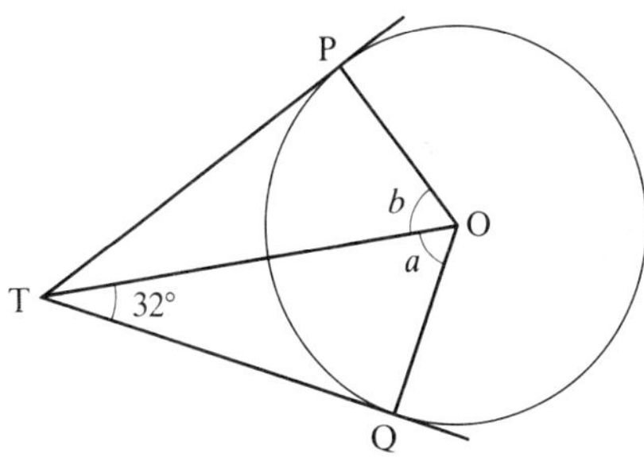

5.

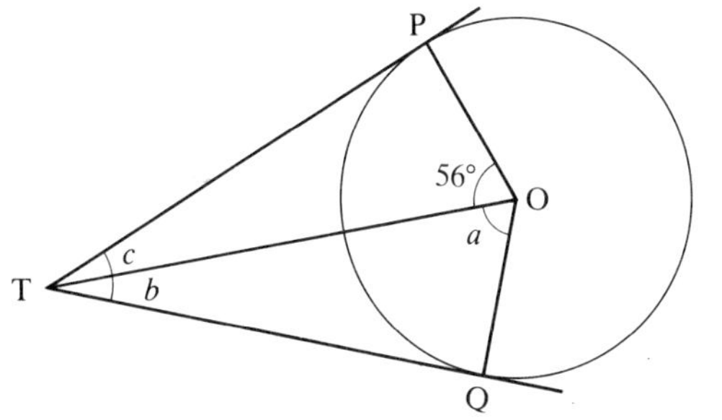

6.

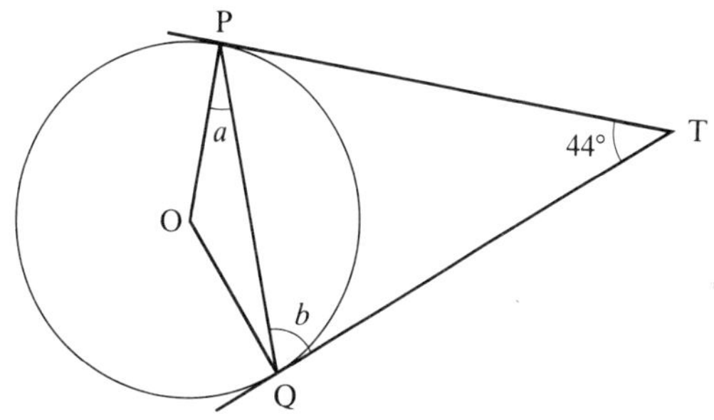

17.3 CONSTRUCTIONS AND LOCUS

(a) Perpendicular bisector of a line

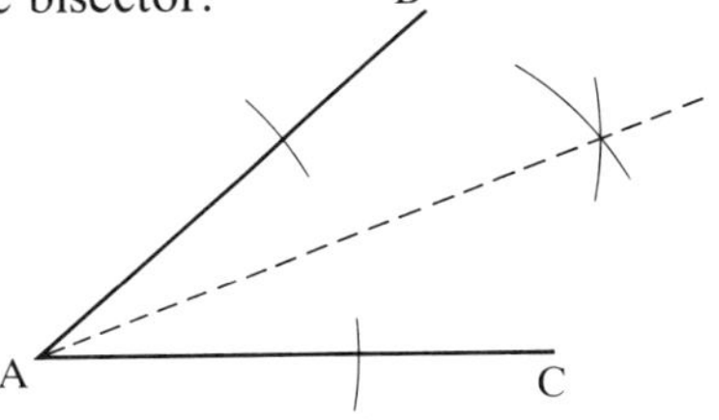

The broken line is the locus of a point which is equidistant from A and from B.

(b) Angle bisector.

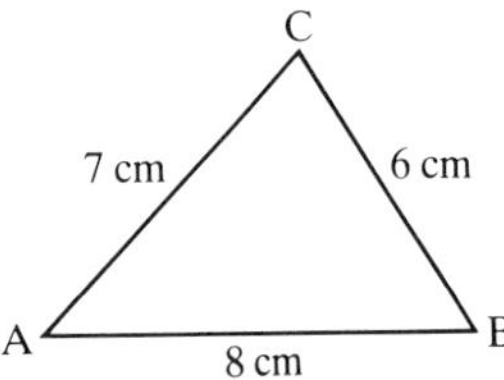

The broken line is the locus of a point which is equidistant from the lines AB and AC.

Exercise 6

You need a pair of compasses, a ruler and a sharp pencil.

1. (a) Construct triangle ABC (full size).

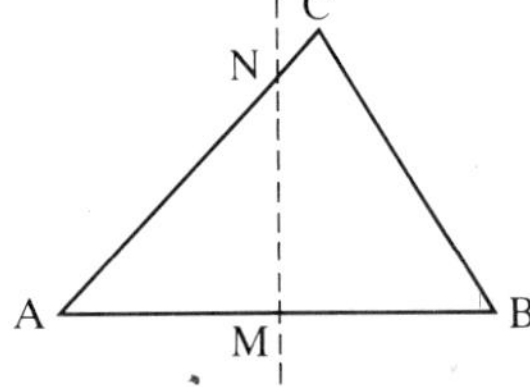

(b) Construct the perpendicular bisector of AB. Measure the length MN.

2. (a) Construct triangle PQR.

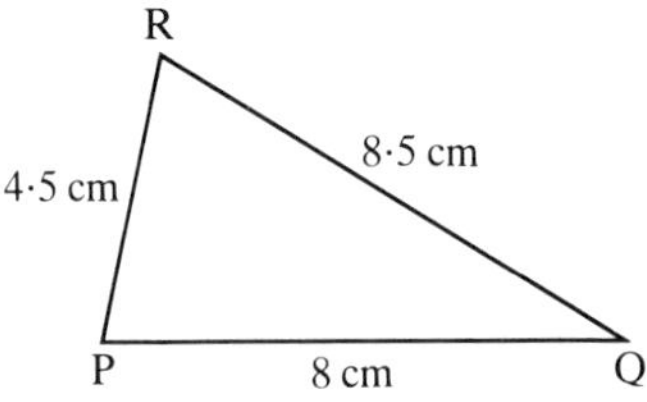

(b) Construct the perpendicular bisector of RQ.
Measure MN.

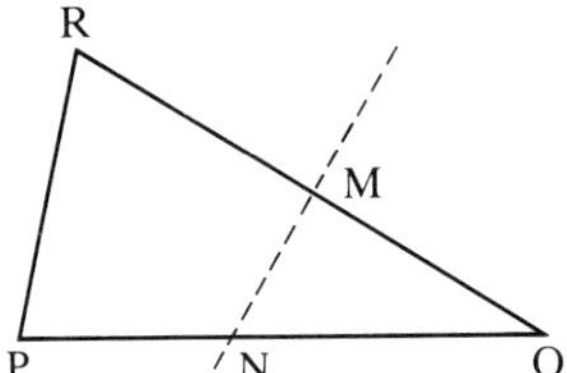

3. (a) Construct triangle ABC.

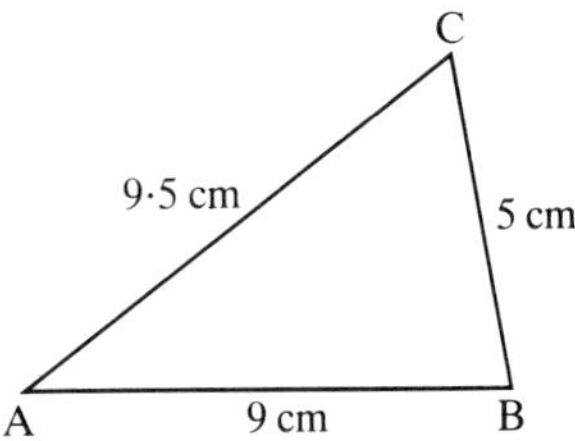

(b) Construct the perpendicular bisectors of AB, AC and BC. They should meet in a single point O.

(c) Draw a circle through A, B and C with centre O and radius OA. This is the *circumcircle* of triangle ABC.

4. (a) Construct triangle PQR.

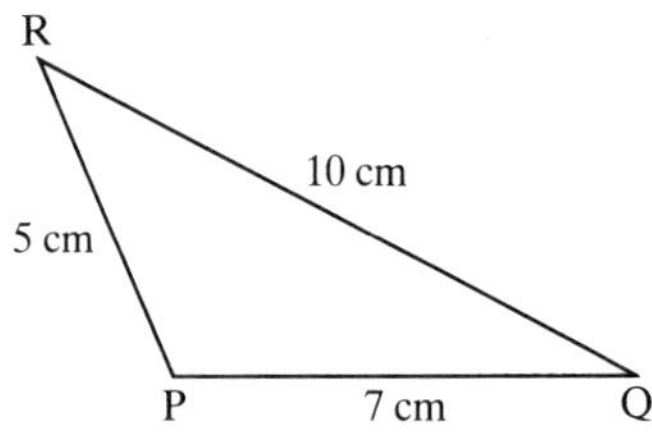

(b) Construct the perpendicular bisectors of PQ, RQ and RP and hence draw the circumcircle of triangle PQR.

5. (a) Construct triangle ABC.

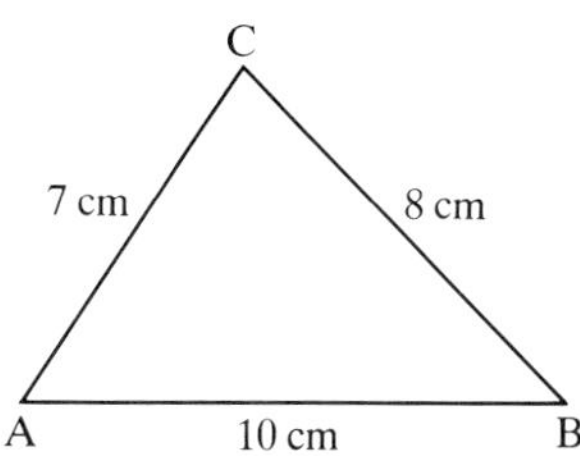

(b) Construct the bisectors of angles A, B and C. They should meet in a single point O.

(c) Draw a circle, with centre O, which just touches the three sides of the triangle. This is the *inscribed* circle of triangle ABC.

6. (a) Construct triangle XYZ.

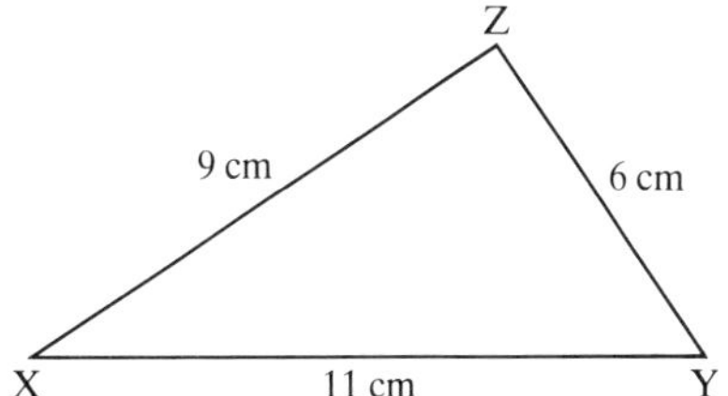

(b) Construct the bisectors of angles X, Y and Z and hence construct the inscribed circle of triangle XYZ.

17.4 TRIGONOMETRY

Finding angles

Find the angle x.

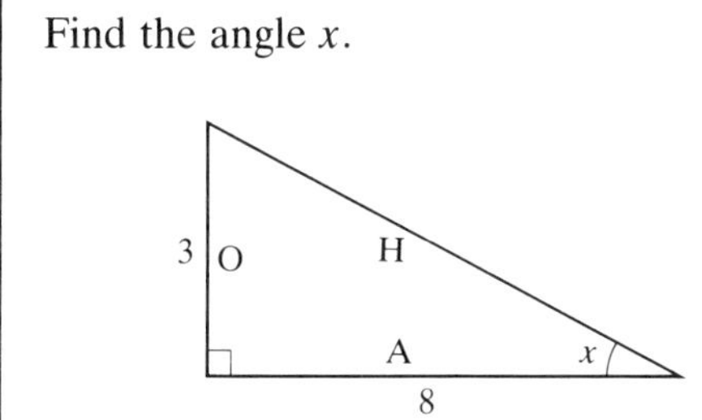

$$\tan x = \frac{O}{A} = \frac{3}{8}$$

$$\tan x = 0.375$$
$$x = 20.6° \text{ (to 1 D.P.)}$$

Remember:

$$\sin x = \frac{O}{H}; \quad \cos x = \frac{A}{H}; \quad \tan x = \frac{O}{A}$$

Exercise 7

Find the angles marked with letters. All the lengths are in cm.

1. 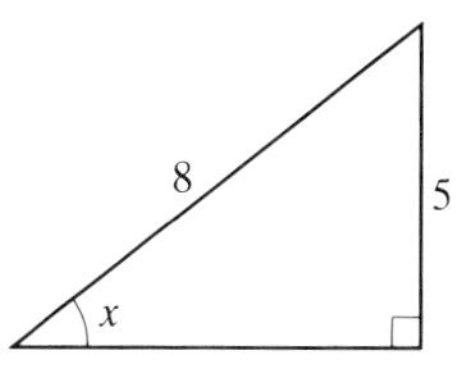

2. 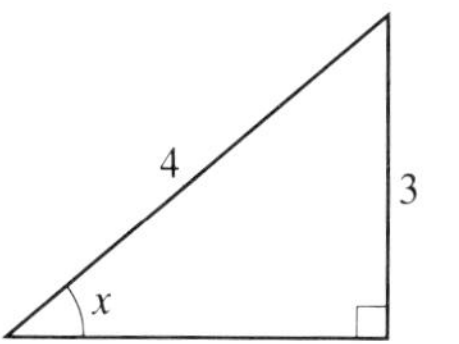

3. 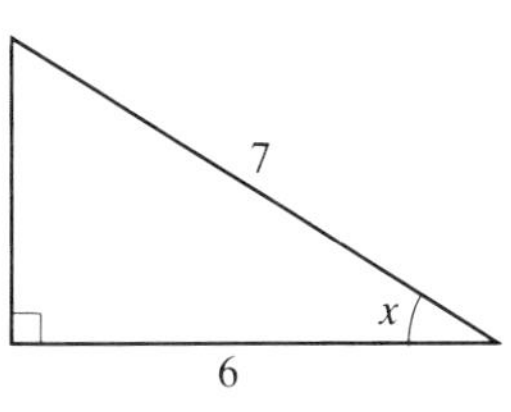

4. 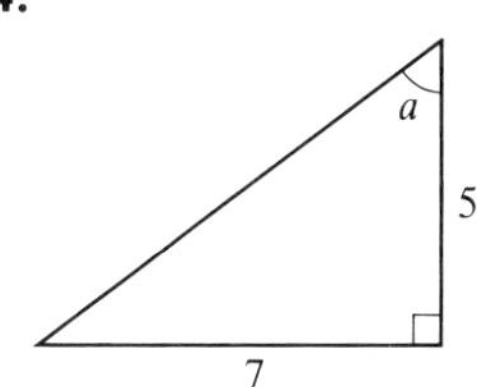

5. 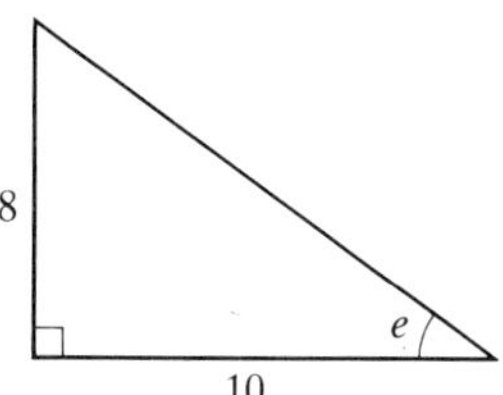

6. 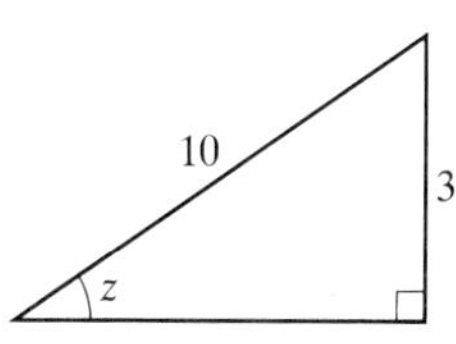

7. 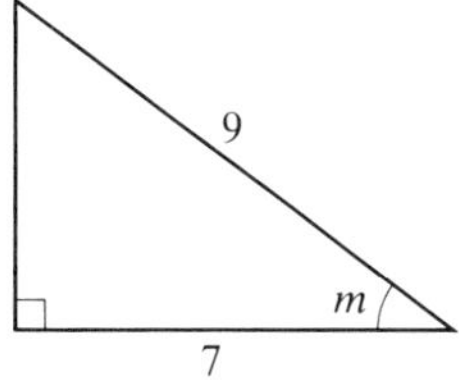

8. 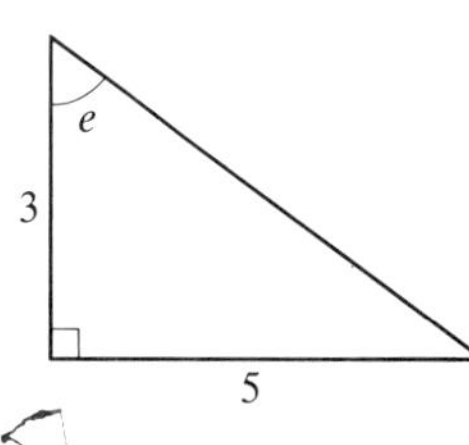

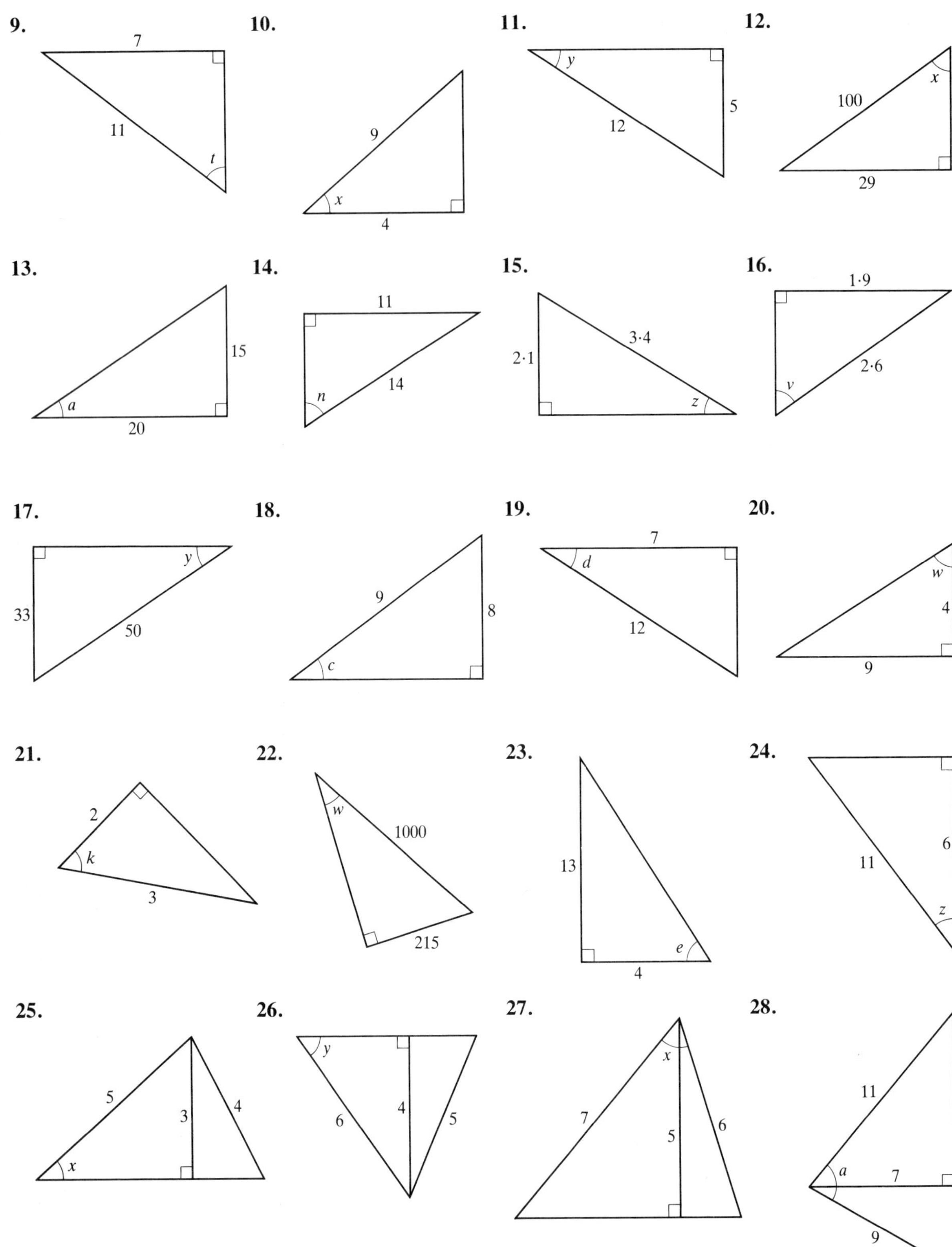
9.
7
11
t
10.
9
x
4
11.
y
5
12
12.
100
x
29
13.
15
a
20
14.
11
n
14
15.
3·4
2·1
z
16.
1·9
2·6
v
17.
y
33
50
18.
9
8
c
19.
7
d
12
20.
w
4
9
21.
2
k
3
22.
w
1000
215
23.
13
e
4
24.
6
11
z
25.
5
4
3
x
26.
y
4
6
5
27.
x
7
6
5
28.
11
a
7
9

Finding the length of a side

Find the length of l.

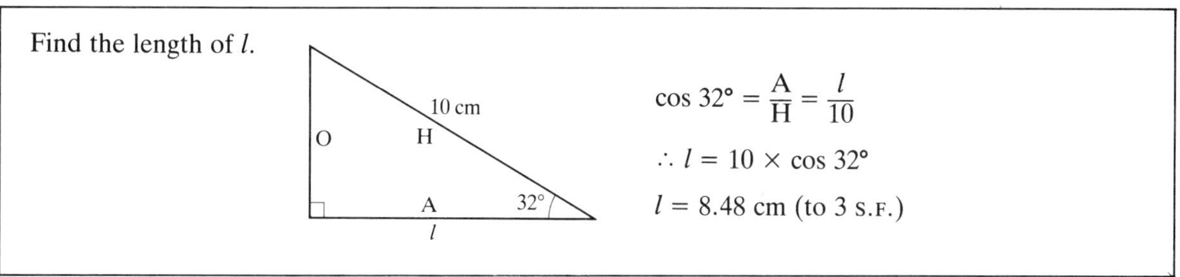

$$\cos 32° = \frac{A}{H} = \frac{l}{10}$$

$$\therefore l = 10 \times \cos 32°$$

$$l = 8.48 \text{ cm (to 3 s.f.)}$$

Exercise 8

Find the lengths marked with letters. All lengths are in cm. Give answers correct to 3 s.f.

1.

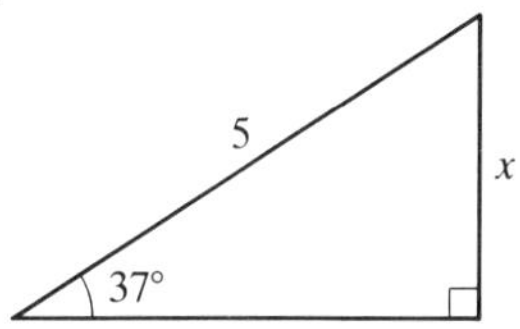

2.

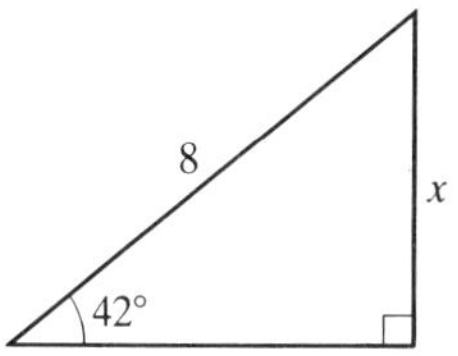

3.

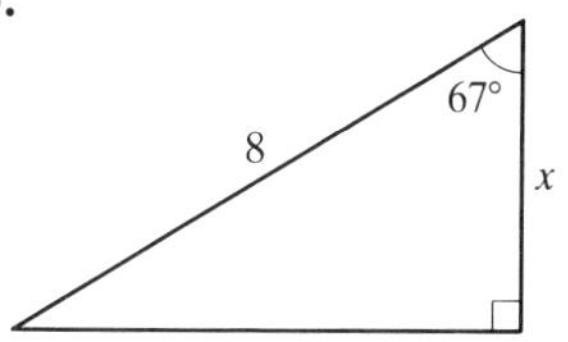

4.

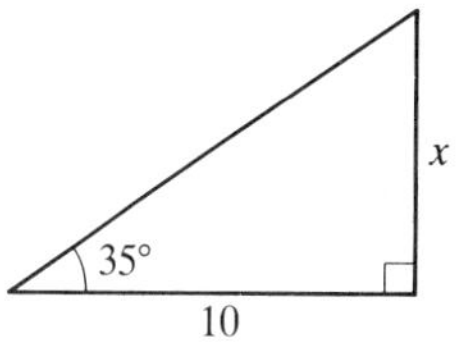

5.

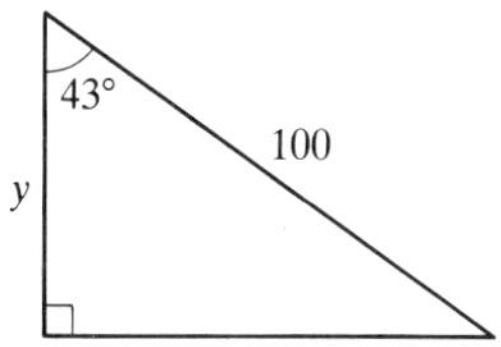

6.

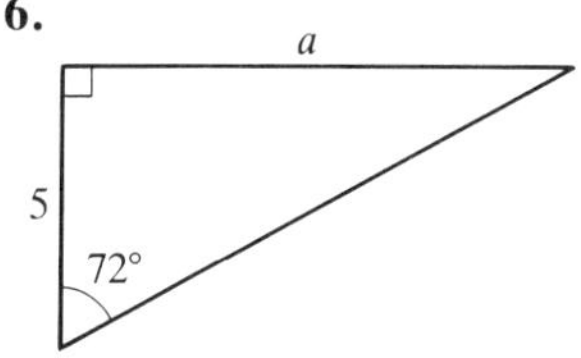

7.

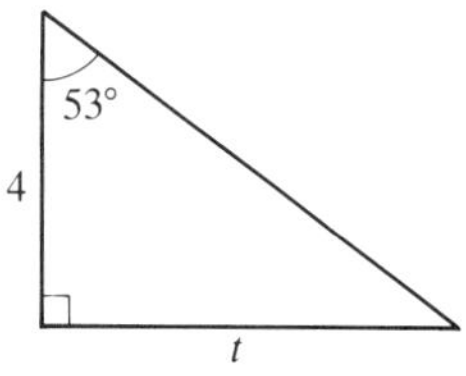

8.

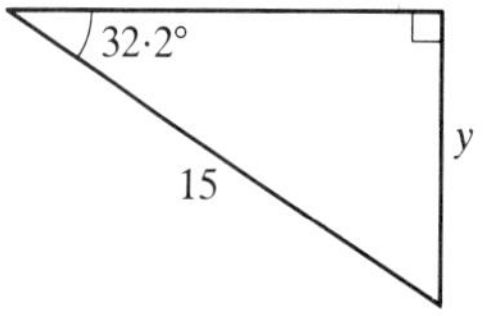

9.

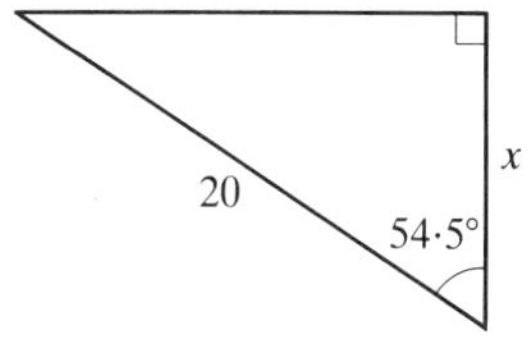

10.

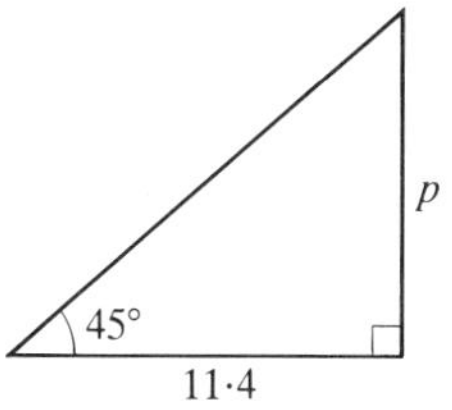

11.

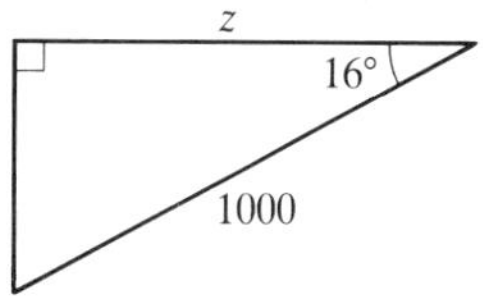

12.

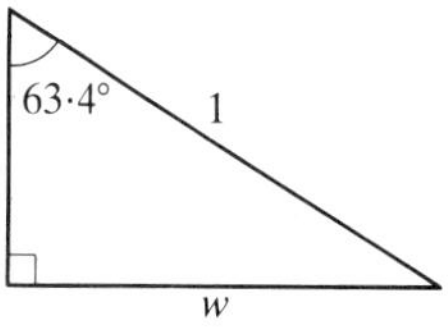

13.

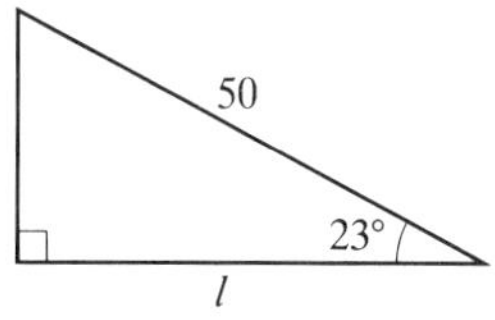

14.

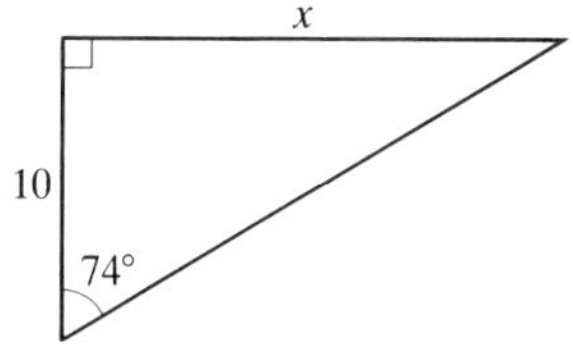

15.

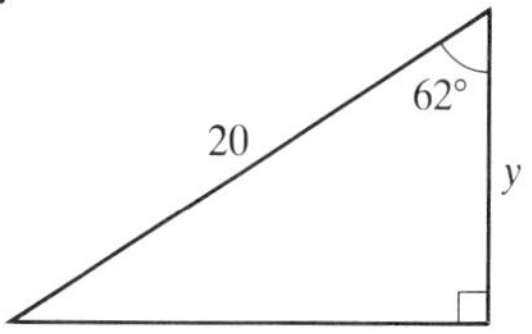

16.

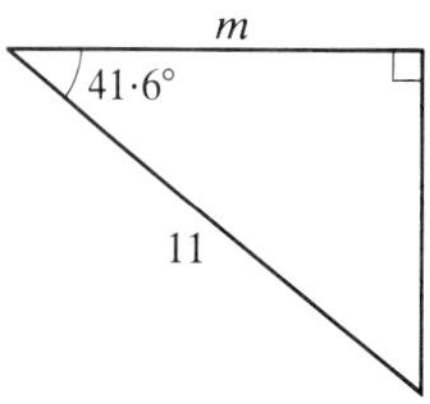

17.

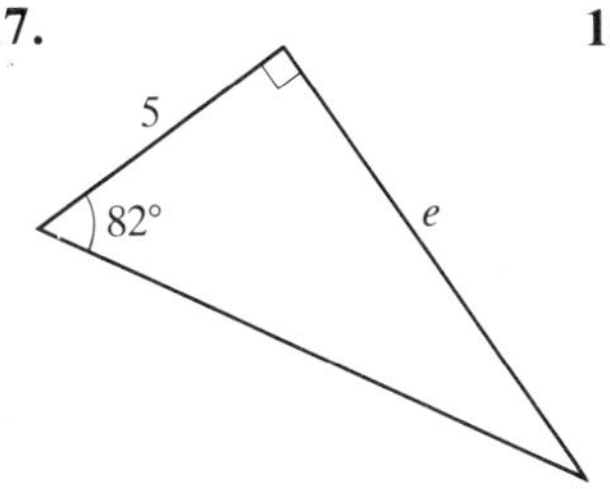

18.

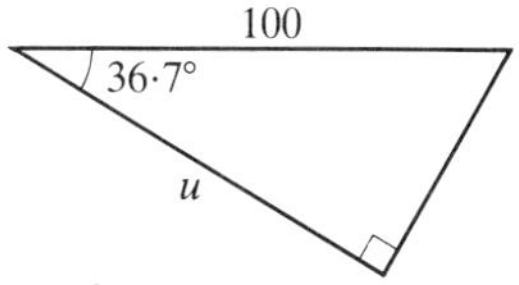

19.

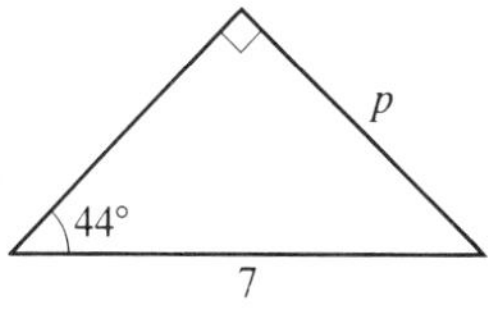

20.

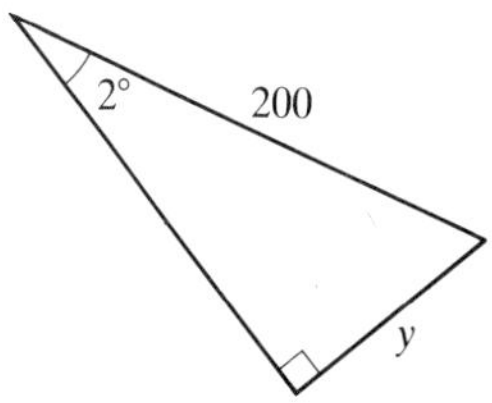

Find the length x.

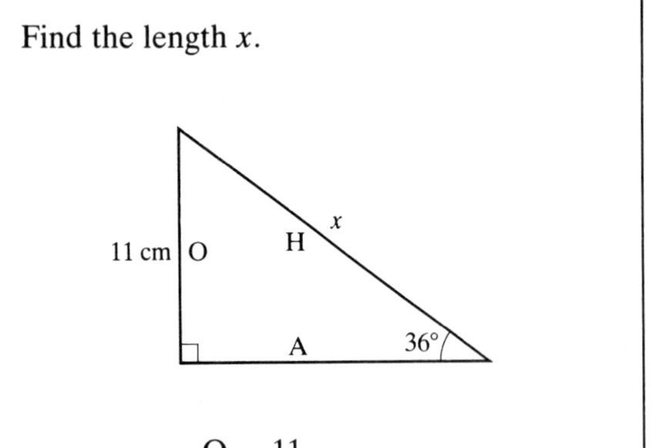

$$\sin 36° = \frac{O}{H} = \frac{11}{x}$$

$$\therefore x \sin 36° = 11$$

$$x = \frac{11}{\sin 36°} = 18.7 \text{ cm (to 3 s.f.)}$$

Exercise 9

This exercise is more difficult. Find the lengths and angles marked with letters.

1.

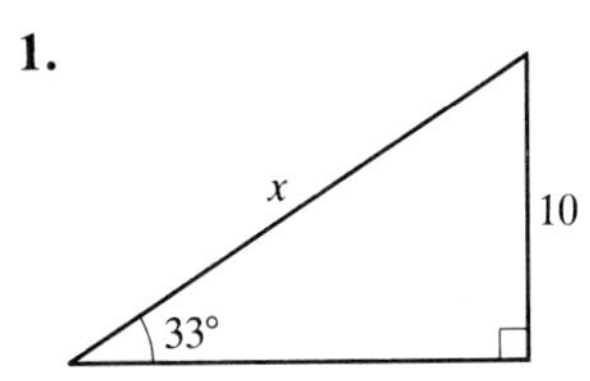

2.

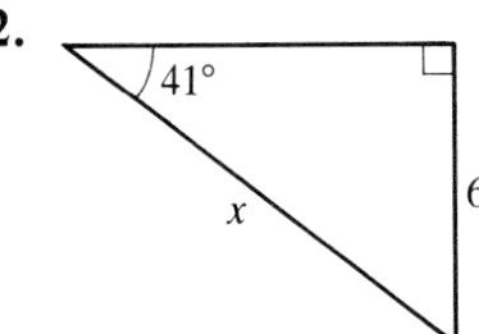

3.

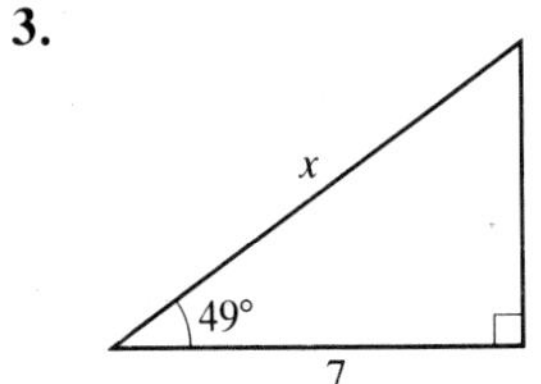

4.

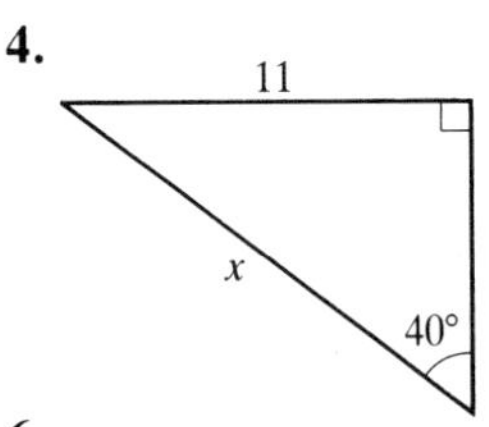

5.

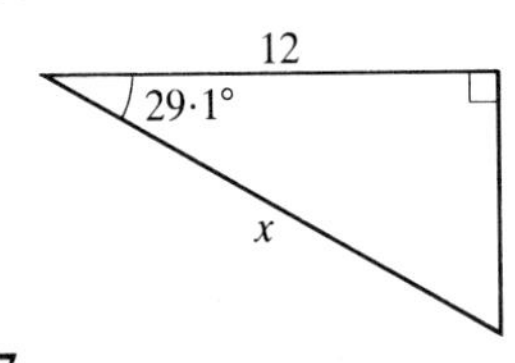

6.

x
37·4°
100

7. **8.**

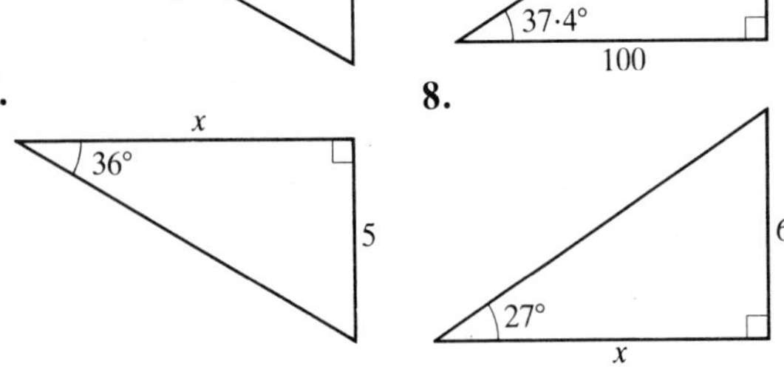

9.

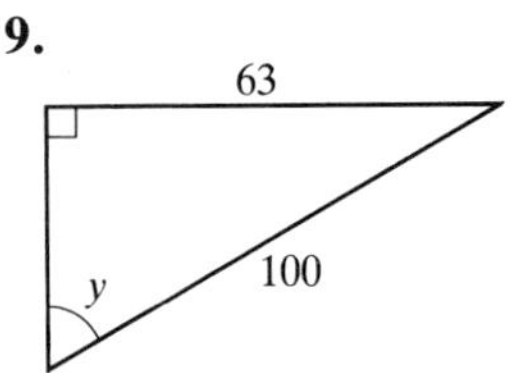

10.

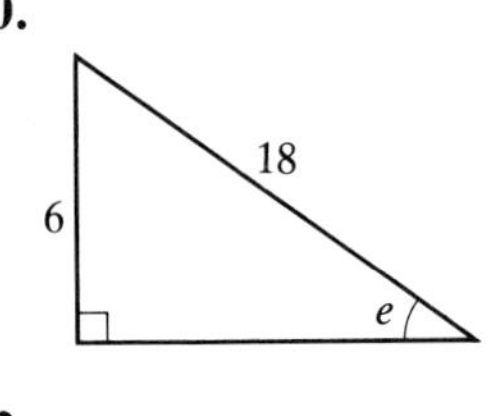

11.

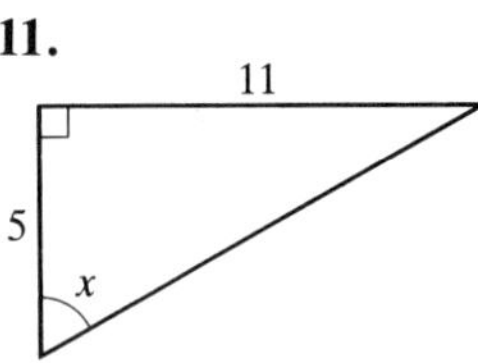

12.

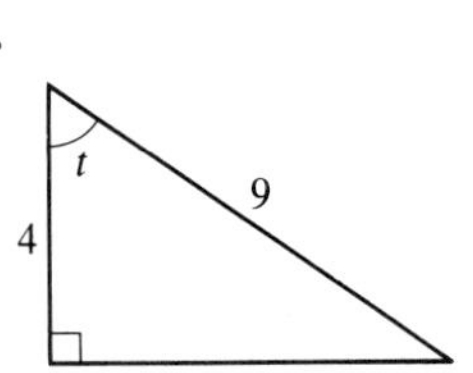

13.

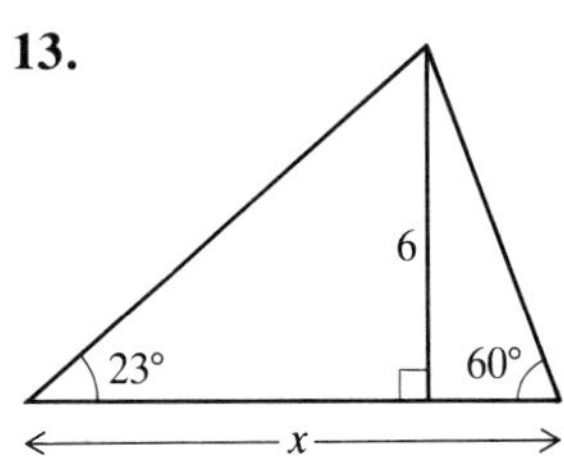

14.

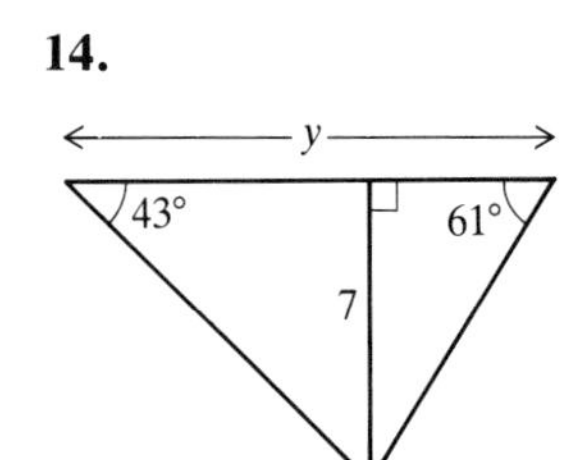

15.

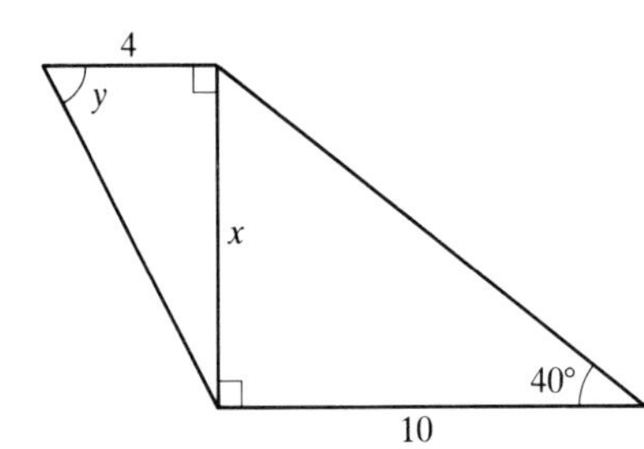

16.

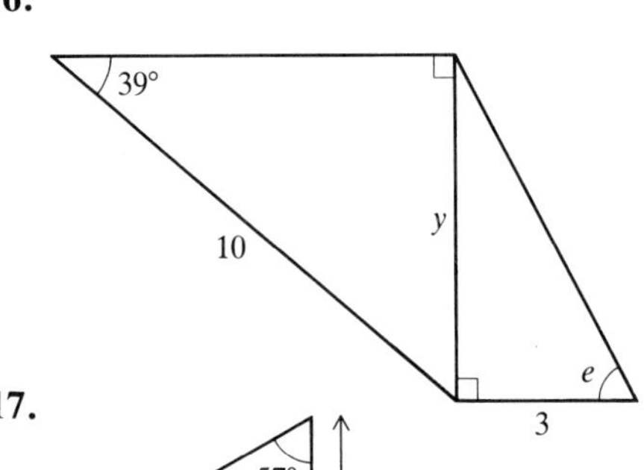

17.

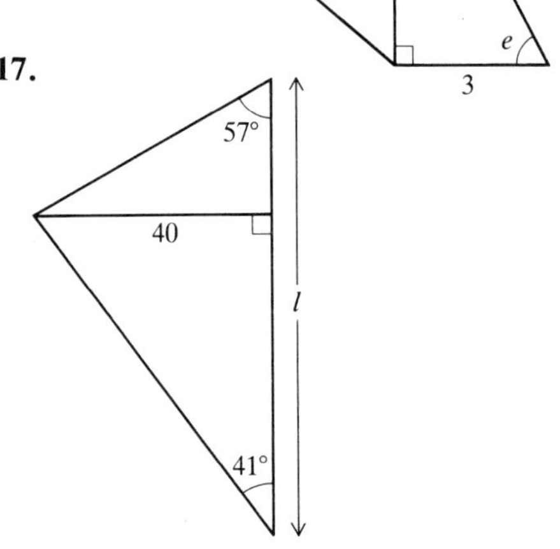

18.

z
40°
y
30°
x
10
72°

19.

63°
20
70°
x
y
31°
z

20.

32°
8
32°
x

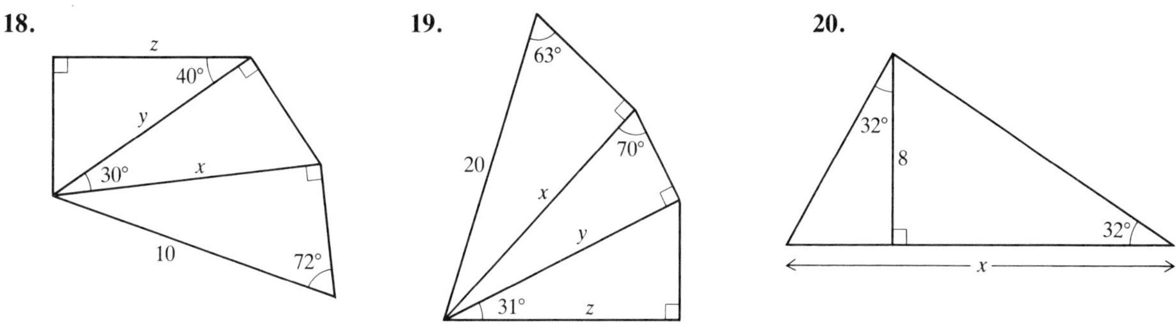

The next exercise is more difficult. It involves finding angles and sides using either trigonometry or Pythagoras' theorem.

Exercise 10

Find the angles and sides marked with letters. All lengths are in cm.

1.

10
34°
x

2.

6
8
y

3.

t
35
28

4.

k
5
7

5.

e
100
64·1°

6.

11
5
m

7.

20
17·4°
h

8.

17
x
20

9.

9
w
7

10.

f
500
62°

11.

7
p
11

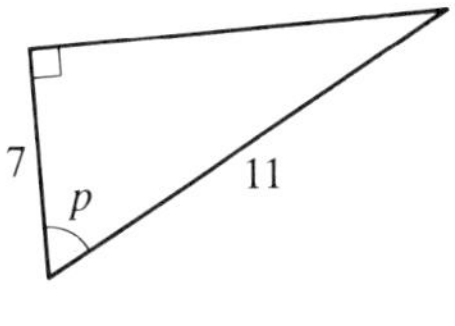

12.

y
5·1
7·4

13.

15
16·1°
a

14.

12
3
x

15.

4
11
h

16.

p
67°
0·5

17.

x
25°
35°
5
y

18.

y
41°
x
62°
10

19.

25°
46°
x
10
30°

20.

10
y
55°
3

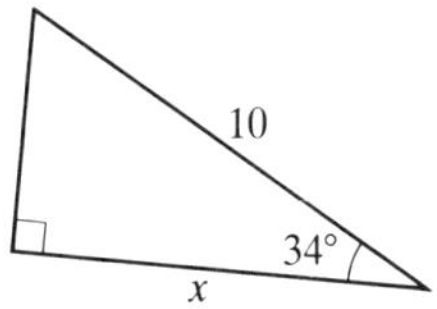

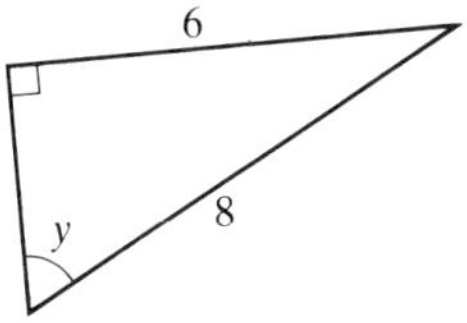

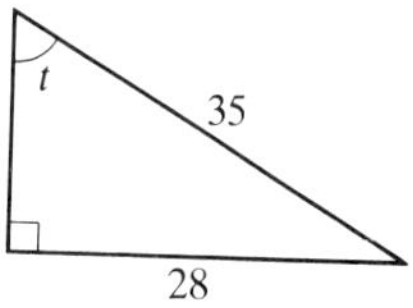

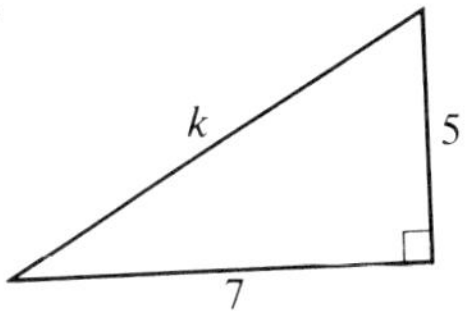

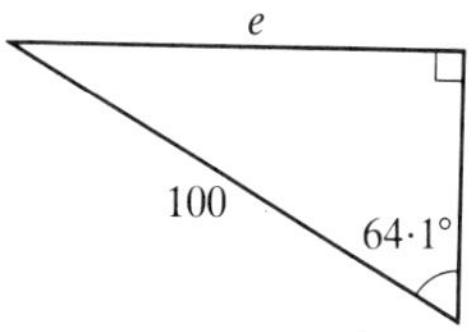

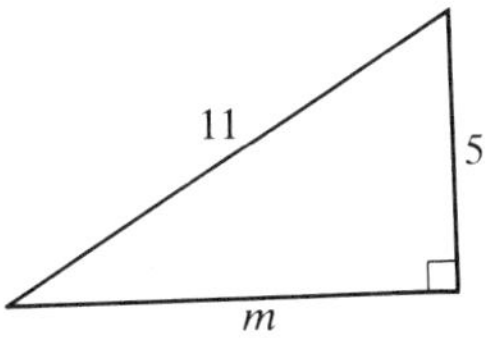

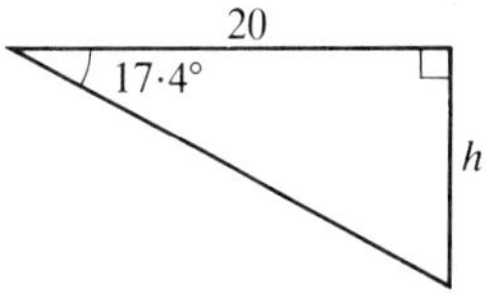

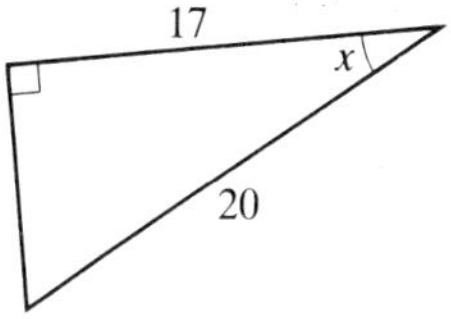

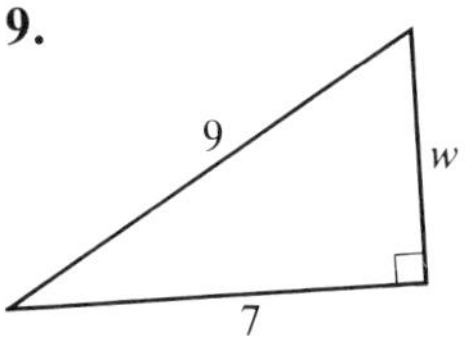

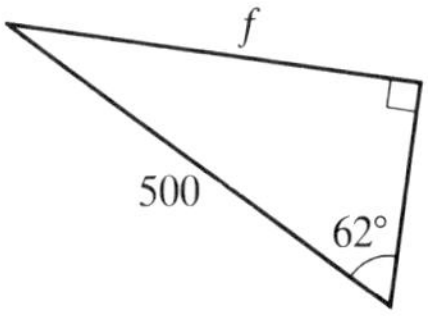

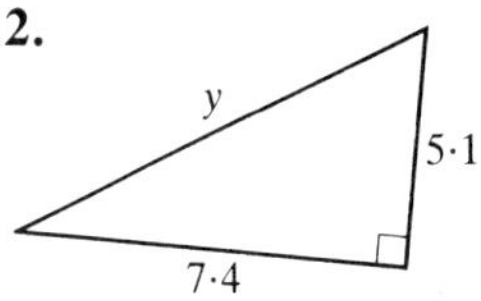

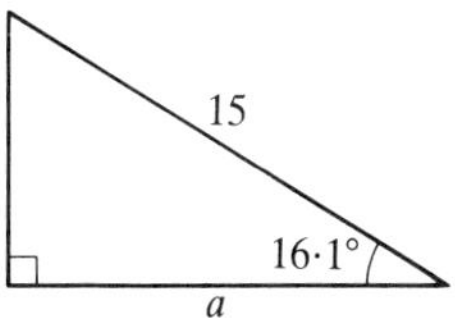

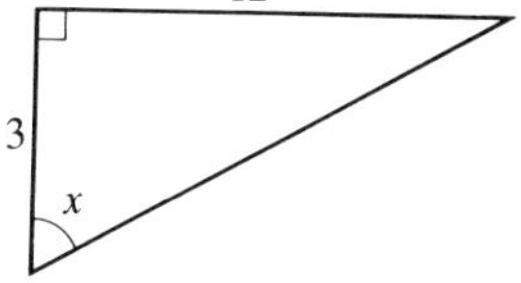

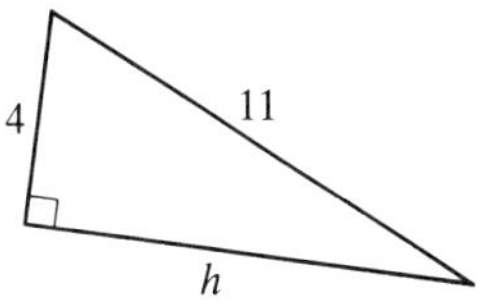

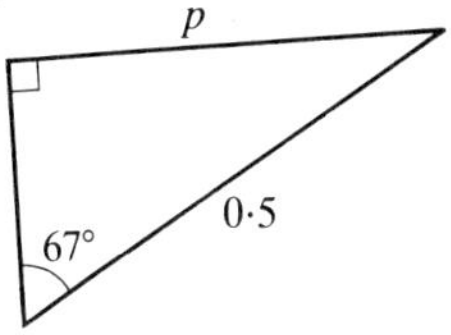

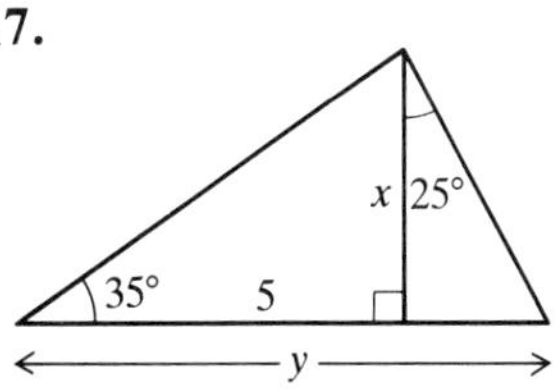

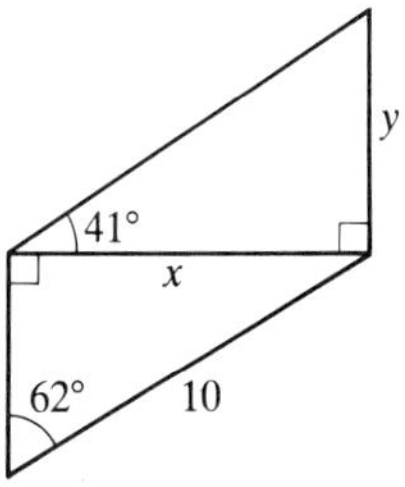

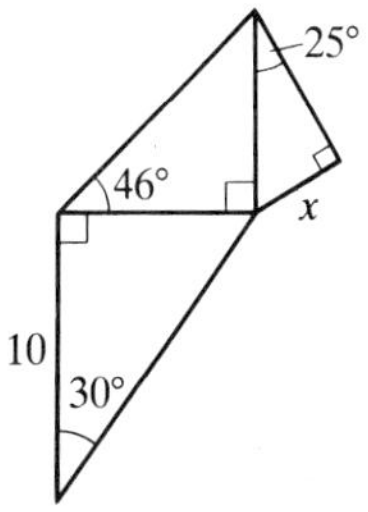

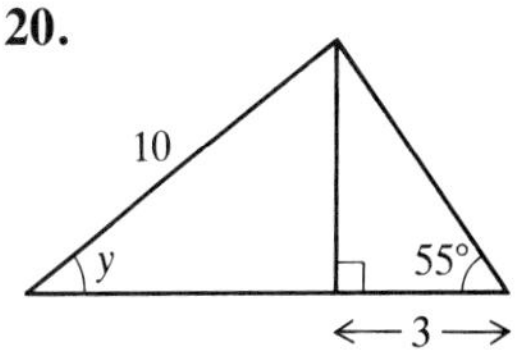

Exercise 11

Begin each question by drawing a large clear diagram.

1. A ladder of length 4 m rests against a vertical wall so that the base of the ladder is 1.5 m from the wall.

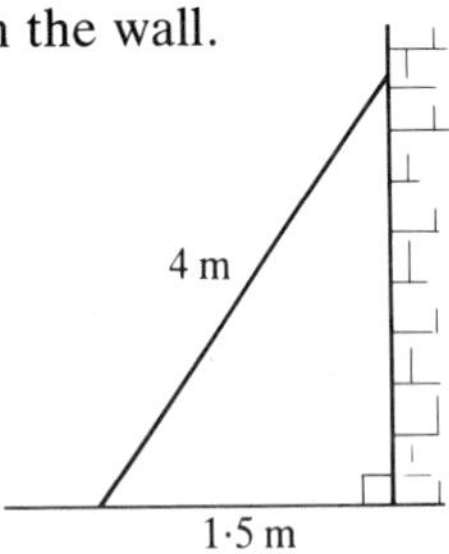

Calculate the angle between the ladder and the ground.

2. A ladder of length 5 m rests against a vertical wall so that the base of the ladder is 3 m from the wall. Calculate the angle between the ladder and the ground.
3. A ladder of length 6 m rests against a vertical wall so that the angle between the ladder and the wall is 25°. How far is the base of the ladder from the wall?
4. A ladder of length 4 m rests against a vertical wall so that the angle between the ladder and the ground is 66°. How far up the wall does the ladder reach?
5. From a distance of 20 m the angle of elevation to the top of a tower is 35°.

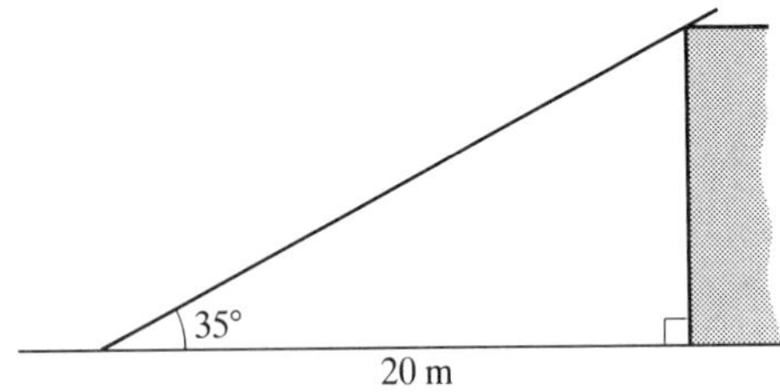

How high is the tower?

6. From a distance of 100 m the angle of elevation to the top of a tall tree is 11.2°. How tall is the tree?
7. From a distance of 30 m, the angle of elevation to the top of a tower is 21.6°. How high is the tower?
8. A point G is 40 m away from a building, which is 15 m high. What is the angle of elevation to the top of the building from G?
9. A point X is 100 m away from a flagpole, which is 27 m high. What is the angle of elevation to the top of the flagpole from X?
10. A boy is flying a kite from a string of length 60 m.

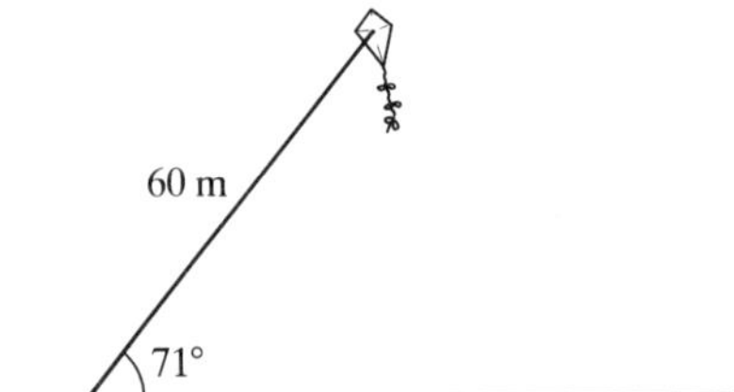

If the string is taut and makes an angle of 71° with the horizontal, what is the height of the kite? Ignore the height of the boy.

11. A girl is flying a kite from a string of length 50 m. If the string is taut and makes an angle of 36° with the horizontal, what is the height of the kite?
12. A man is flying a kite from a taut string of length 40 m. If the kite is 22 m above the ground calculate the angle between the string and the ground.
13. A straight tunnel is 80 m long and slopes downwards at an angle of 11° to the horizontal. Find the vertical drop in travelling from the top to the bottom of the tunnel.
14. The frame of a bicycle is shown in the diagram.

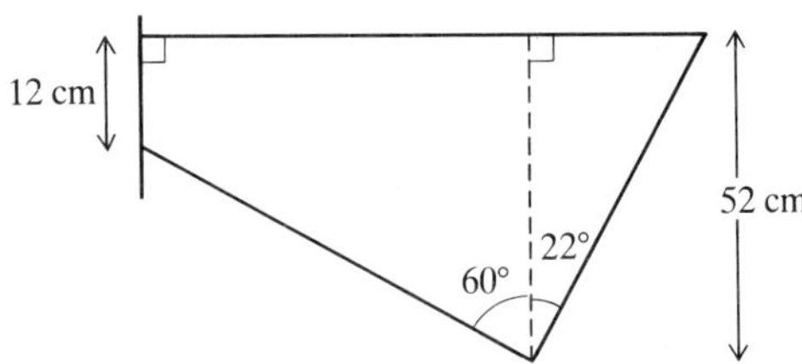

Find the length of the cross bar.

15. Calculate the length x.

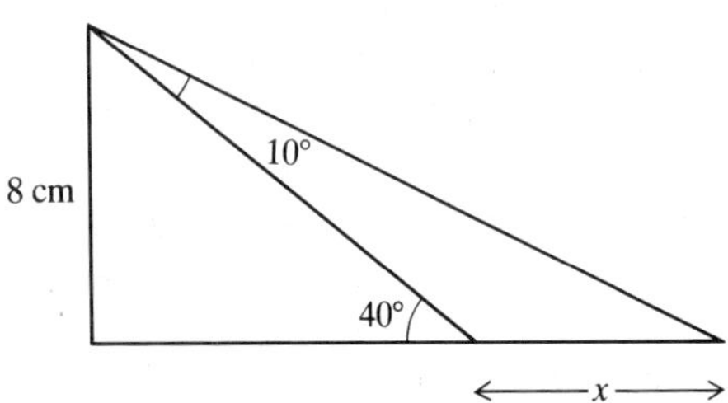

16. AB is a chord of a circle of radius 5 cm and centre O.

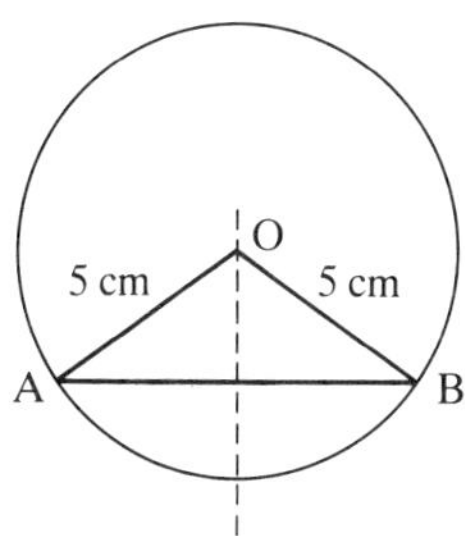

The perpendicular bisector of AB passes through O and also bisects the angle AOB. If $A\hat{O}B = 100°$ calculate the length of the chord AB.

17. A chord XY of length 8 cm is drawn in a circle of radius 6 cm, centre O. Calculate the angle XOY.

18. A chord PQ of length 10 cm is drawn in a circle with centre O. If the angle POQ is 88° calculate the radius of the circle.

Exercise 12

1. A ship is due South of a lighthouse. It sails on a bearing of 055° for a distance of 80 km until it is due East of the lighthouse.

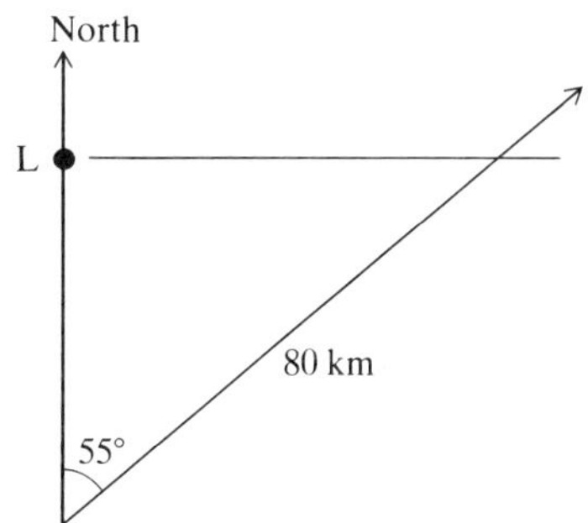

How far is it now from the lighthouse?

2. A ship is due South of a lighthouse. It sails on a bearing of 071° for a distance of 200 km until it is due East of the lighthouse. How far is it now from the lighthouse?

3. An aircraft is due North of a radio tower. It flies for a distance of 100 km on a bearing of 152° until it is due East of the tower. How far is it now from the tower?

4. An aircraft is due West of a control tower. It flies on a bearing of 040° at a speed of 300 km/h for two hours until it is due North of the tower. How far is it now from the tower?

5. A ship is due North of a lighthouse. It sails on a bearing of 200° at a speed of 15 km/h for five hours until it is due West of the lighthouse. How far is it now from the lighthouse?

6. A submarine is due South of an underwater port. It sails on a bearing of 300° for a distance of 160 km until it is due West of the port. How far is it now from the port?

7. Calculate the length y.

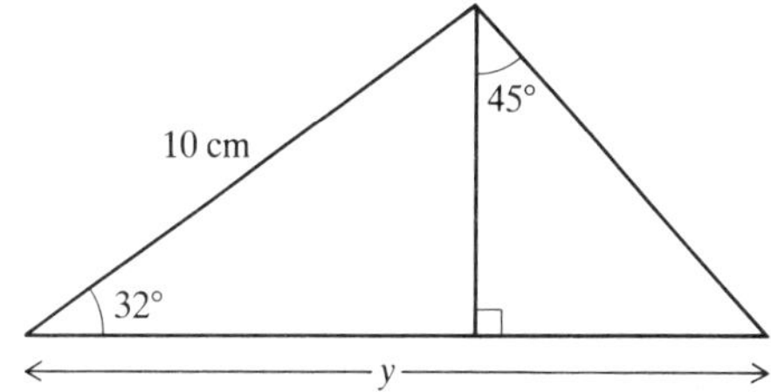

8. From a horizontal distance of 40 m, the angle of elevation to the top of a building is 35.4°. From a point further away from the building the angle of elevation is 20.2°. What is the distance between the two points?

Unit 18

REVISION TESTS

Revision test 1

1. Cheese is on sale at £1.94 per kilogram. Mrs Jones bought half a kilogram and paid with a one pound coin. How much change did she receive?
2. Fifteen books weigh 3 kg altogether. How many grams does one book weigh?
3. A man buys 500 pencils at 2.4 pence each. What change does he receive from £20?
4. Every day at school Stephen buys a roll for 14p, crisps for 11p and a drink for 21p. How much does he spend in pounds in the whole school year of 200 days?
5. An athlete runs 25 laps of a track in 30 minutes 10 seconds.
   (a) How many seconds does he take to run 25 laps?
   (b) How long does he take to run one lap, if he runs the 25 laps at a constant speed?
6. A pile of 250 tiles is 2 m thick. What is the thickness of one tile in cm?
7. Work out
   (a) 20% of £65 (b) 37% of £400 (c) 8.5% of £2000.

8. In a text, the marks of nine pupils were 7, 5, 2, 7, 4, 9, 7, 6, 6. Find
(a) the mean mark (b) the median mark (c) the modal mark.

9. Work out
(a) $-6 - 5$ (b) $-7 + 30$ (c) $-13 + 3$
(d) -4×5 (e) -3×-2 (f) $-4 + -10$

10. Given $a = 3$, $b = -2$ and $c = 5$, work out
(a) $b + c$ (b) $a - b$ (c) ab (d) $a + bc$

11. Solve the equations
(a) $x - 6 = 3$ (b) $x + 9 = 20$ (c) $x - 5 = -2$
(d) $3x + 1 = 22$

12. Find the area of the shapes below.

(a)
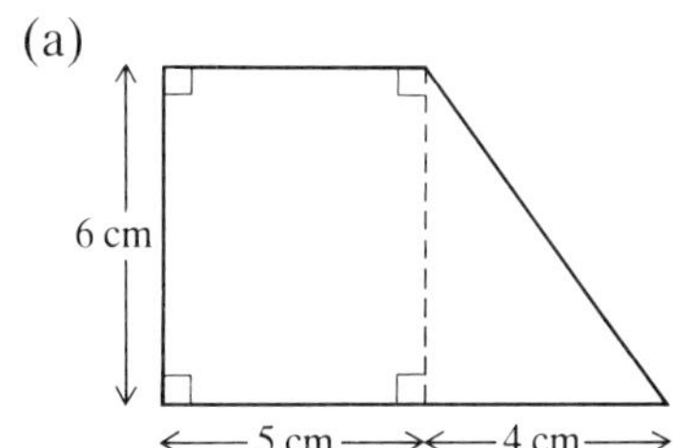

(b)
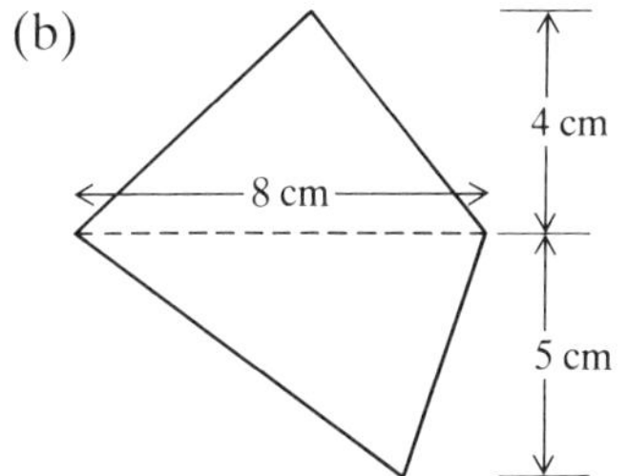

13. (a) Copy and complete the table of values for the graph of $y = 2x - 3$.

x	-2	-1	0	1	2	3	4
$2x$ -3							
y							

(b) Draw the graph of $y = 2x - 3$.

14. (a) Draw a pair of axes for x and y from -7 to $+7$.
(b) Plot and label A(1, 6), B(5, 6), C(5, 4).
(c) Draw the image of $\triangle$ABC after the following rotations:
(i) 90° clockwise about (2, 2). Label it A′B′C′.
(ii) 180° about (1, 4). Label it A″B″C″.
(iii) 90° anticlockwise about (4, −3). Label it A*B*C*.
(d) Write down the coordinates of A′, A″ and A*.

15. (a) Draw a pair of axes for x and y from -7 to $+7$.
(b) Plot and label P(1, 3), Q(1, 7), R(3, 7).
(c) Draw the image of $\triangle$PQR after reflection in
(i) the line $y = 1$. Label it P′Q′R′.
(ii) the line $x = -1$. Label it P″Q″R″.
(iii) the line $y = x$. Label it P*Q*R*.
(d) Write down the coordinates of P′, P″ and P*.

Revision test 2

1. Solve the equations
(a) $3x - 1 = 20$.
(b) $4x + 3 = 4$.
(c) $5x - 7 = -3$.

2. Copy the diagrams and then calculate x, correct to 3 S.F.
(a)

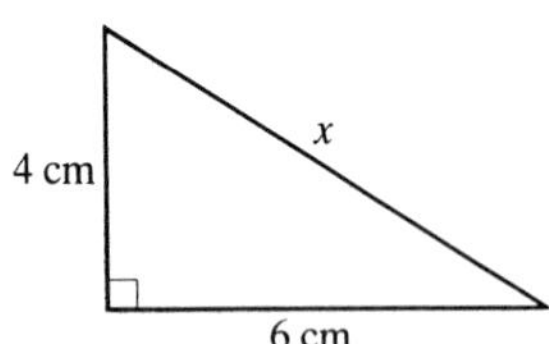

(b)

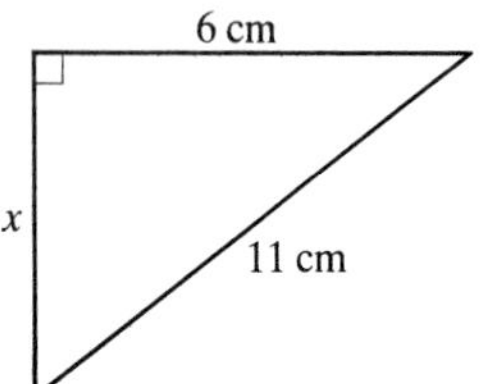

(c)

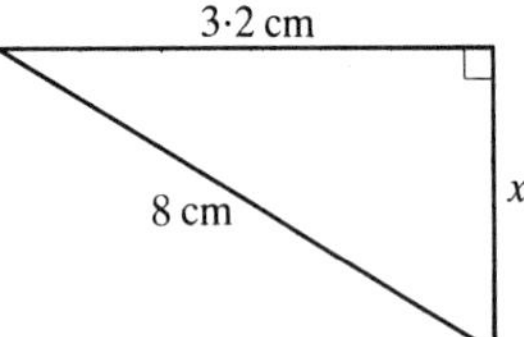

3. A bag contains 3 red balls and 5 white balls. Find the probability of selecting:
(a) a red ball,
(b) a white ball.

4. A box contains 2 yellow discs, 4 blue discs and 5 green discs. Find the probability of selecting:
(a) a yellow disc,
(b) a green disc,
(c) a blue or a green disc.

5. Copy and complete the table, giving correct units.

	Speed	Distance	Time
(a)	10 m/s	200 m	
(b)		120 km	4 h
(c)	24 m.p.h.		30 minutes
(d)	240 km/h	20 km	

6. Work out on a calculator, correct to 4 S.F.
(a) $3.61 - (1.6 \times 0.951)$
(b) $\dfrac{(4.65 + 1.09)}{(3.6 - 1.714)}$.

7. Find the area, correct to 3 S.F.

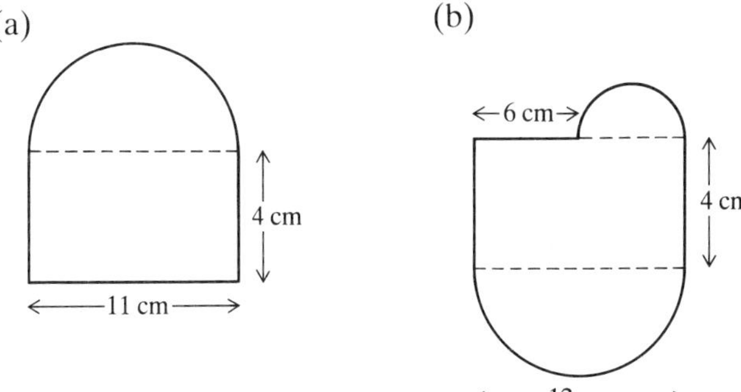

8. Draw the graph of $y = x^2 + 3x - 6$ for values of x from -4 to $+2$.

9. Plot the points given and join them up in order. Find the area of the shape enclosed.
(1, 2), (5, 7), (7,4), (5, 1), (1, 2).

10. Calculate the length x.

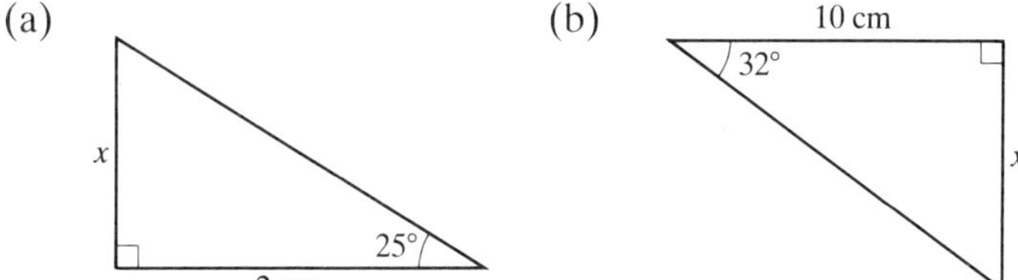

Revision test 3

Formulae: area of a circle $= \pi r^2$
circumference of a circle $= 2\pi r$
volume of cylinder $= \pi r^2 h$
volume of cone $= \frac{1}{3}\pi r^2 h$
volume of sphere $= \frac{4}{3}\pi r^3$

1. A shopkeeper sells 7 kg of potatoes for £1.26. Find
(a) the cost of 1 kg of potatoes
(b) how many kg of potatoes can be bought for £1.98.

2. Arrange the following numbers in order, smallest first.
(a) 3047, 3740, 3407, 3017
(b) 0.31, 0.13, 0.151, 0.301
(c) 0.75, 7.5, 0.075, 0.715
(d) 0.09, 0.089, 0.9, 0.0095

3. An aircraft's flight started at 21 40 on Tuesday and finished at 08 10 on the following Wednesday. How long was the journey in hours and minutes?

4. Copy and complete
(a) 410 cm = m
(b) 63 m = cm
(c) 480 g = kg
(d) 2.2 km = m
(e) 0.07 m = cm

5. Divide £80 in the ratio 1:3:4.

6. Work out, to the nearest penny
(a) 40% of £65 (b) 22% of £16 (c) 7% of £12.40 (d) 11% of £7.63

7. In a sale all prices are reduced by 30%. Find the sale price of an article which normally costs £80.

8. Find the angles marked with letters.

(a)
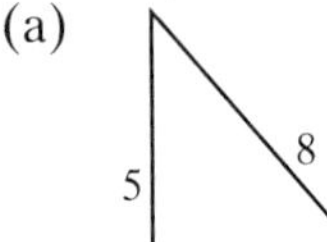
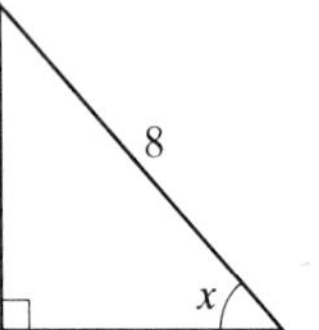

(b)
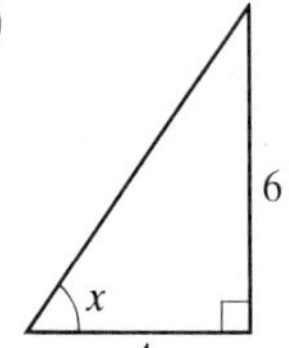

(c)
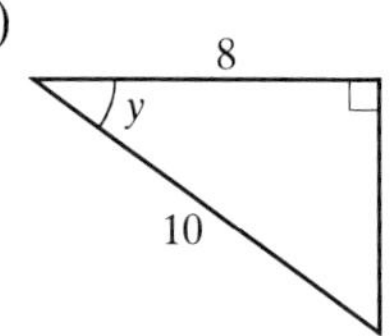

(d)
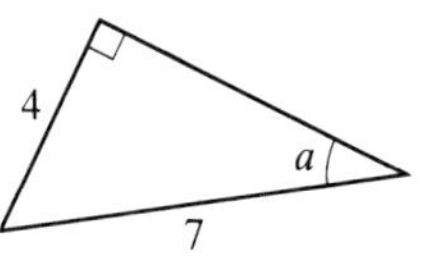

9. Find the volume of the following solid objects. Take $\pi = 3.14$ or use the 'π' button on a calculator. Give the answers to 3 S.F.

(a)
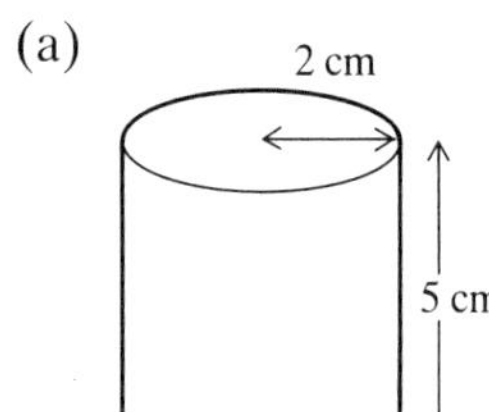

(b)
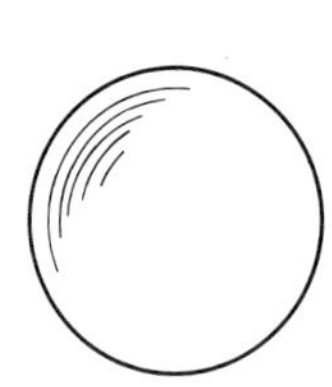
sphere, radius 4 cm

(c)

hemisphere, radius 5 cm

10. Solve the equations:
(a) $5x + 1 = 26$
(b) $3x - 1 = 1$
(c) $4x + 1 = 2x + 9$
(d) $7x - 3 = 2x + 12$

11. Write down each sequence and find the next two numbers.
(a) 2, 9, 16, 23,
(b) 20, 18, 16, 14,
(c) −5, −2, 1, 4,
(d) 128, 64, 32, 16,
(e) 8, 11, 15, 20,

12. (a) Draw a pair of axes for x and y from −7 to +7.
(b) Plot and label A(1, 3), B(1, 6), C(3, 6).
(c) Draw the image of $\triangle$ ABC after reflection in the following lines:
(i) the y-axis. Label it $\triangle 1$.
(ii) the x-axis. Label it $\triangle 2$.
(iii) the line $y = 2$. Label it $\triangle 3$.
(iv) the line $y = x$. Label it $\triangle 4$.
(d) Write down the coordinates of the image of point A in each case.

EXAMINATION EXERCISES

Examination exercise 1

1. Copy the following bill and complete it by filling in the four blank spaces.

8 rolls of wallpaper at £3.20 each	= £ ...
3 tins of paint at £ ... each	= £ 20.10
... brushes at £2.40 each	= £ 9.60
Total	= £ ...

[M]

2. (a) The diagram represents a view of a cubical die. The number of dots on opposite faces adds up to seven. Write down the number of dots on the back face and on the bottom face as indicated in the diagram.

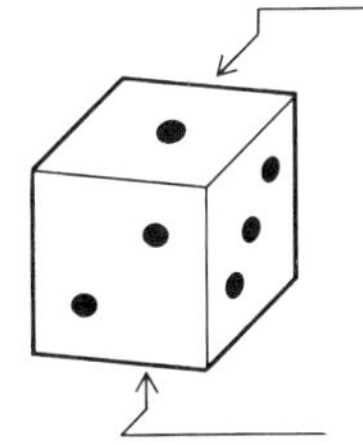

(b) The diagram represents the net of another die. As before, the number of dots on opposite faces adds up to seven. Write down the numbers that would appear on the faces marked A, B and C respectively.

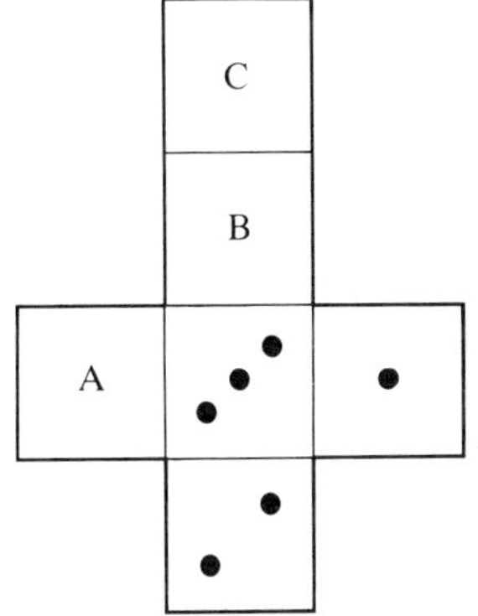

[M]

3. A train travels between Watford and Coventry, a distance of 108 km, in 45 minutes, at a steady speed. It passes through Rugby 40 minutes after leaving Watford. How far, in km, is it from Rugby to Coventry?

[L]

4. Look at the number pattern below.
$(2 \times 1) - 1 = 2 - 1$
$(3 \times 3) - 2 = 8 - 1$
$(4 \times 5) - 3 = 18 - 1$
$(5 \times 7) - 4 = 32 - 1$
$(6 \times a) - 5 = b - 1$
(i) What number does the letter a stand for?
(ii) What number does the letter b stand for?
(iii) Write down the next line in the pattern.

[N]

5. The faces of a round and a square clock are exactly the same area. If the round clock has a radius of 10 cm, how wide is the square clock?

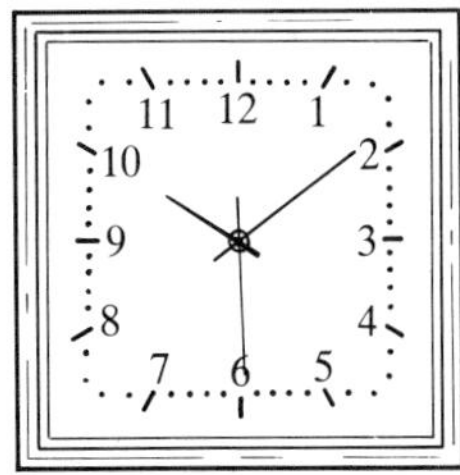

[S]

6. (i) The number of sweets left in a box when 14 have been eaten is given by the equation
$n + 14 = 20$
Solve the equation to find the value of n.
(ii) When calculating the time taken for a car to increase its speed from 20 km/h to 40 km/h, the following equation is produced
$40 = 20 + 4t$
Solve the equation to find the value of t.

[W]

7. A school decides to have a disco from 8 p.m. to midnight. The price of the tickets will be 20p. The costs are as follows:

Disco and D.J., £25
Hire of hall, £5 an hour
200 cans of soft drinks at 15p each
200 packets of crisps at 10p each
Printing of tickets, £5

(i) What is the total cost of putting on the disco?
(ii) How many tickets must be sold to cover the cost?
(iii) If 400 tickets are sold, all the drinks are sold at 20p each and all the packets of crisps at 12p each, calculate the profit or loss the school finally makes.

[N]

8. A ladder of length 10 m rests with its lower end on horizontal ground and its upper end against a vertical wall. Calculate
(a) the horizontal distance from the wall to the lower end of the ladder when it is inclined at an angle of 55° to the horizontal,
(b) the angle that the ladder makes with the horizontal when the upper end is 8 m above the ground.

[S]

9.

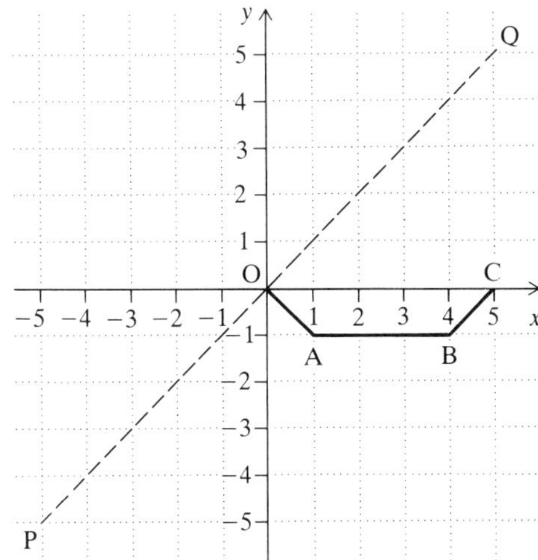

(a) Reflect the figure OABC in the x-axis and draw the image on the given diagram.
(b) The figure and its image are rotated through 90° about the origin in a clockwise direction. Draw the new image on the given diagram.
(c) The complete picture is then reflected in the mirror line PQ. Draw the final image on the same diagram.
(d) How many lines of symmetry has the final figure?
(e) What order of rotational symmetry has the final figure?

[L]

10. A swimming pool is of width 10 m and length 25 m. The depth of water in the pool increases uniformly from the shallow end, where the depth is 1.5 m to the deep end, where the depth is 2.5 m.
(a) Calculate the volume of water in the pool.
(b) This water is emptied into a cylindrical tank of radius 3.5 m. Taking π as $3\frac{1}{7}$, calculate the depth of water in the tank.

[L]

11. The diagram shows a sketch of the net of a pyramid. The base of the pyramid is shaded in the diagram.

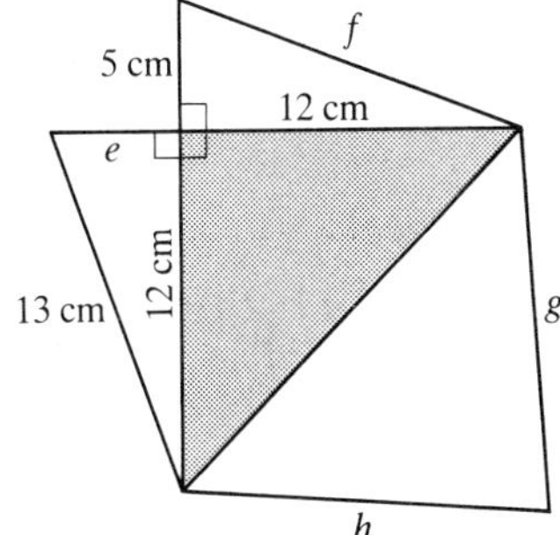

(a) Find the lengths of the lines marked e, f, g, h.
(b) Calculate the volume of the pyramid.
[Volume of a pyramid $= \frac{1}{3}$ (area of base) $\times$ (vertical height).]

[M]

12. A group of children are queueing to select at random either an apple or an orange from a bag. Initially there are 15 apples and 10 oranges in the bag. The first in the queue is Megan and the second is Huw. Find the probability:
    (i) that Megan selects an orange,
    (ii) that Huw selects an apple given that Megan took an apple from the bag,
    (iii) that both Megan and Huw select an apple.

[W]

Examination exercise 2

1. The tables show the rail fares for adults and part of a British Rail timetable for trains between Cambridge and Bury St. Edmunds.

Fares for *one* adult

Cambridge				
£1.00	Dullingham			
£1.20	40p	Newmarket		
£1.30	£1.00	60p	Kennett	
£2.00	£1.30	£1.20	80p	Bury St. Edmunds

Train times

Station	Time
Cambridge	11 20
Dullingham	11 37
Newmarket	11 43
Kennett	11 52
Bury St. Edmunds	12 06

(a) How much would it cost for four adults to travel from Dullingham to Bury St. Edmunds?
(b) How long does this journey take?

[M]

2. The sketch of a clock tower is shown.

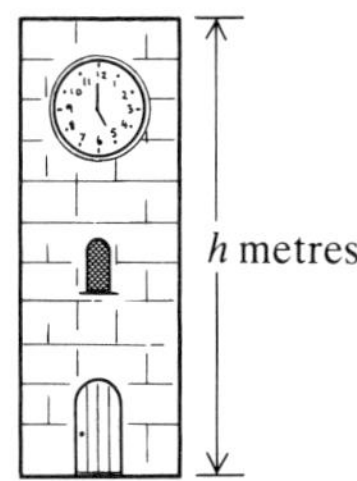

A model of the tower is made using a scale of 1 to 20.
(a) The minute hand on the tower clock is 40 cm long. What is the length of the minute hand on the model?
(b) The height of the model is 40 cm. What is the height h, in metres, of the clock tower?

[S]

3. The Compound Interest Table below shows how much £1 will amount to, in a given number of years, when invested at 10% per year.

No. of Years	1	2	3	4	5	6	7	8	9	10
Amount of £1 (to nearest penny)	£1.10	£1.21	£1.33	£1.46	£1.61	£1.77	£1.95	£2.14	£2.36	£2.59

Use the table to answer the following questions,

(a) How much will £100 amount to in 5 years?
(b) How much will £275 amount to in 7 years?
(c) How much, to the nearest £, must be invested to amount to £500 in 10 years?
(d) What is the least number of complete years for which a sum must be invested to double itself?

[L]

4. $1 + 3 = 2^2$.
$1 + 3 + 5 = 3^2$.

(a) $1 + 3 + 5 + 7 = x^2$.
Calculate x.

(b) $1 + 3 + 5 + \ldots + n = 100$.
Calculate n

[L]

5. The diagram shows a lawn in the shape of a rectangle from which two semi-circles have been removed. The diameter of each semi-circle is 7 metres.

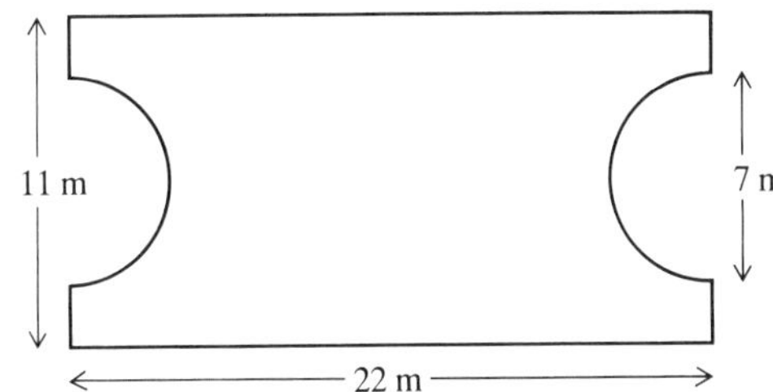

Taking π as $\frac{22}{7}$, calculate, in metres, the perimeter of the lawn.

[L]

6. This electricity bill is not complete.

NEA

Northern Electricity Authority
P.O. Box 6984
Manchester M49 2QQ

Tel: 061 555 2718

Customer:
G. J. Spinner
21 Silk Street
Macclesfield SK27 3BJ

Ref: 0248-6879-5

METER READING on 07-11-84	26819 units	
METER READING on 04-02-85	units	
ELECTRICITY USED	1455 units	
1455 units at 5.44 pence per unit		£
Quarterly charge		£ 6.27
TOTAL (now due)		£

(i) Write down the correct amount to be placed in each box.
(ii) In 1984, in what month was the meter read?

[N]

7. (a) The mean mass of 10 boys in a class is 56 kg.
   (i) Calculate the total mass of these 10 boys.
   (ii) Another boy, whose mass is 67 kg, joins the group. Calculate the mean mass of the 11 boys.

   (b) A group of 10 boys whose mean mass is 56 kg joins a group of 20 girls whose mean mass is 47 kg. Calculate the mean mass of the 30 children.

[M]

8. The shaded pieces are cut from a rectangular card as shown in Figure 1. The remaining piece of card is folded to make the *open* box as shown in Figure 2.

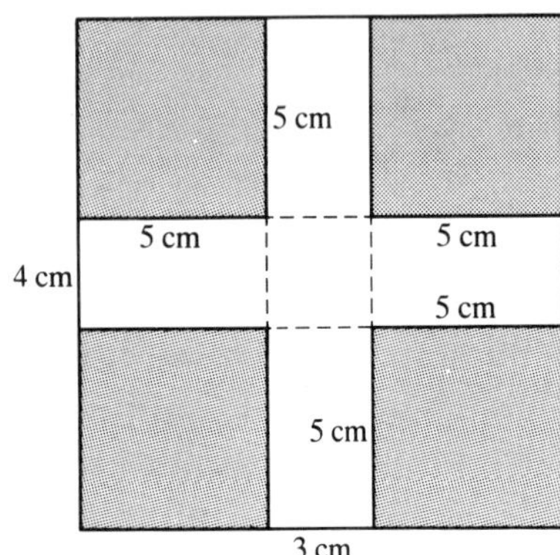

Figure 1

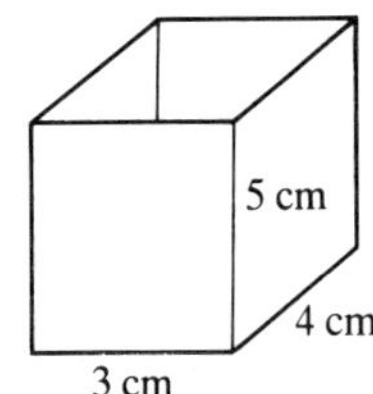

Figure 2

(i) What was the area of the rectangular card?
(ii) What is the area of the card used for the box?
(iii) What is the volume of the box?

[N]

9. On graph paper, using the same scales, draw axes for x to vary from -6 to $+12$, and y to vary from -8 to $+8$.
   (a) Draw triangle ABC, where A is (0, 4), B is (2, 1) and C is (5, 5).

   Transform ABC by the translation $\begin{pmatrix} 6 \\ 2 \end{pmatrix}$ to $A_1B_1C_1$. Reflect $A_1B_1C_1$ in the x-axis to $A_2B_2C_2$.

   (b) On the same graph, draw triangle DEF, where D is $(-1, -3)$, E is $(2, -2)$ and F is $(4, -4)$. Reflect DEF in the y-axis to find $D_1E_1F_1$.

   Translate $D_1E_1F_1$ by the vector $\begin{pmatrix} 0 \\ 5 \end{pmatrix}$ to $D_2E_2F_2$.

[L]

10. A metal ingot is in the form of a solid cylinder of length 7 cm and radius 3 cm.
    (a) Calculate the volume, in cm^3, of the ingot.

    The ingot is to be melted down and used to make cylindrical coins of thickness 3 mm and radius 12 mm.

    (b) Calculate the volume, in mm^3, of each coin.
    (c) Calculate the number of coins which can be made from the ingot, assuming that there is no wastage of metal.

[M]

11. AB is a straight shoreline of length 9 km. On a treasure map, a tall tree T is 6.5 km from point A and angle TAB = 60°.
Using ruler and compasses only, construct a scale drawing of triangle ABT.
The treasure X is equidistant from A and B, and also equidistant from TA and TB. Showing all construction arcs clearly, construct two lines on which X must lie. Hence find and mark the position of X.

[W]

12. The table below gives information about the TT Mountain Course races for motorcycles. It gives the times taken to complete different numbers of laps for average speeds of 100 mph, 104 mph, 106 mph and 108 mph.

Average speed in miles per hour (mph)	Time taken for 1 lap	2 laps	3 laps	4 laps
100	22 min 38 s	45 min 16 s	1 hr 7 min 54 s	1 hr 30 min 32 s
104	21 min 46 s	43 min 32 s	☐	1 hr 27 min 4 s
106	21 min 21 s	42 min 42 s	1 hr 4 min 3 s	1 hr 25 min 24 s
108	20 min 58 s	41 min 56 s	1 hr 2 min 54 s	1 hr 23 min 52 s

(i) How long does it take to do two laps at an average speed of 104 mph?
(ii) Write down the missing entry in the table.
(iii) How long would it take to do six laps at 106 mph?
(iv) Why do the times in each column get less as you go down the table?
(v) A motorcyclist averaging 100 mph started at exactly 9.45 a.m. At what time did he finish the first lap?

[N]

Examination exercise 3

1.

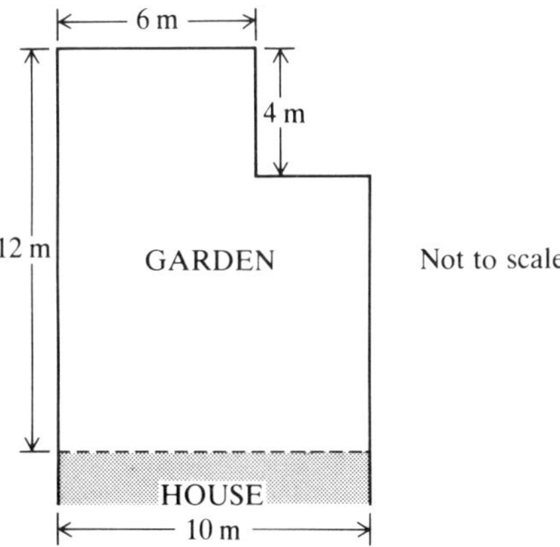

Not to scale

The diagram shows the plan of part of a house and all of its garden.
(a) Find the total length of the sides of the garden shown by solid lines.
(b) How many fence sections, each 2 m long, will be needed to fence the sides of the garden?

[M]

2.

Basic holiday price in £'s per person — Gatwick departures												
Departures between	26 March 27 April		28 April 18 May		19 May 15 June		16 June 13 July		14 July 31 Aug.		1 Sep. 28 Oct.	
Number of nights	7	14	7	14	7	14	7	14	7	14	7	14
Hotel ESPLANADE	218	353	222	360	226	367	231	374	235	380	200	320
Hotel ATLANTIS	152	223	159	236	168	253	174	260	178	291	140	210
Hotel CALYPSO	139	195	150	206	153	219	156	226	162	233	120	181

Addition for Heathrow departure £24 per person.
Addition for balcony and sea view, £1.50 per person per night.
Addition for insurance cover £3.75 per person.

Using the above table, a man reserved a 14 night holiday for himself and family of three (four persons altogether), at the Hotel Atlantis, for the period from 22nd August to 5th September. He wished to fly from Heathrow Airport and to have accommodation with balcony and sea view for himself and his family. Insurance cover was required for each person. Calculate the total cost of the holiday for the man and his family.

[W]

3. The following are the first six numbers, written in order of size, of a pattern.
4, 13, 28, 49, 76, 109.
   (a) Which of these numbers are:
   (i) odd numbers, (ii) square numbers, (iii) prime numbers?
   (b) The difference between the first and second numbers, that is 13–4, is 9; between the second and the third it is 15, between the third and the fourth it is 21. Work out the difference between
   (i) the fourth and the fifth, (ii) the fifth and the sixth.
   (c) By considering your answers in (b), find the seventh and eighth numbers of the pattern.
   Explain how you reached this decision.
   (d) Use the method you have described to write down the next two terms in the following pattern.
   1, 4, 12, 25, 43, 66, —, —.

[S]

4. The diagram below, which is drawn to scale, shows a town B which is due east of town A.

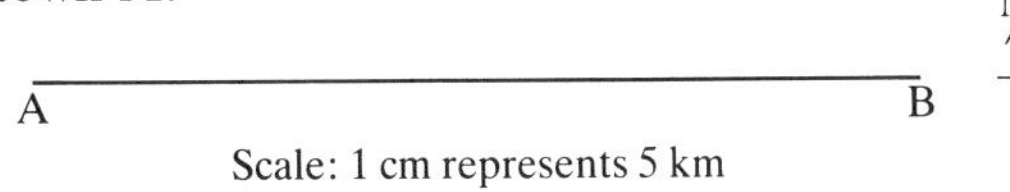

(i) Measure and record the length of AB.
(ii) What is the distance between town A and town B?
(iii) Mark on the diagram the position of town C which is 25 km north of B.
(iv) Using a protractor, measure and record the size of $B\hat{A}C$.
(v) Write down the bearing of C from A.

[W]

5. (a) In 1975, an apprentice electrician's 'take home' pay was £30 per week. His weekly budget was as follows:

Rent, food, heat and light	£9
Clothes	£6
Entertainment	£8
Travel	£4
Savings and other items	£3

Draw a pie chart to represent his weekly budget.

(b) The pie chart represents the 'average family' budget in 1975. The 'average family's' net income in 1975 was £3,240.

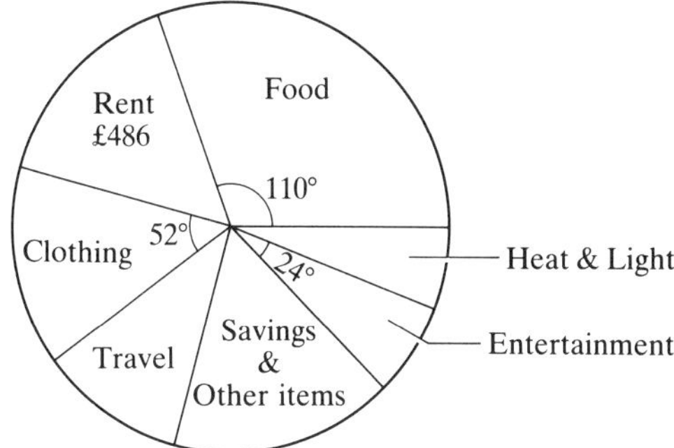

Calculate
(i) how much was spent on food,
(ii) what angle is represented by rent,
(iii) what percentage of the family's net income was spent on entertainment.

(c) By comparing the two pie charts, comment briefly on the major differences between the 'average family' budget and the apprentice's budget.

[S]

6. A cookery book gives the following instructions for cooking a leg of lamb.

'Allow 40 minutes for each kilogram and 20 minutes extra.'

(a) Find the time, in minutes, required to cook a leg of mass 3 kg.
(b) Write a formula for the total cooking time, T minutes, for a leg of mass M kg.

[S]

7. (i) The total weight of a lorry, T tonnes, is related to its load, L tonnes, by the following formula

$$T = 20 + 2L$$

Calculate the value of T when $L = 7$.

(ii) The length, l, of the side of a square is related to the area, a, of the square by the following formula

$$l = \sqrt{a}$$

Calculate the value of l when $a = 81$.

[W]

8. The probability of a train arriving early at a station is $\frac{1}{10}$.
The probability of a train arriving late at a station is $\frac{2}{5}$.
(a) If 400 trains are expected at a station during the day, how many of them are likely to arrive at the correct time?
(b) What is the probability that both the trains arriving at the station from Exeter are late?

[S]

9. A cuboid measures 10 cm by 8 cm by 6 cm.
(a) On your graph sheet, using a scale of 1 cm to represent 2 cm, draw an accurate net which could be folded to make the cuboid.

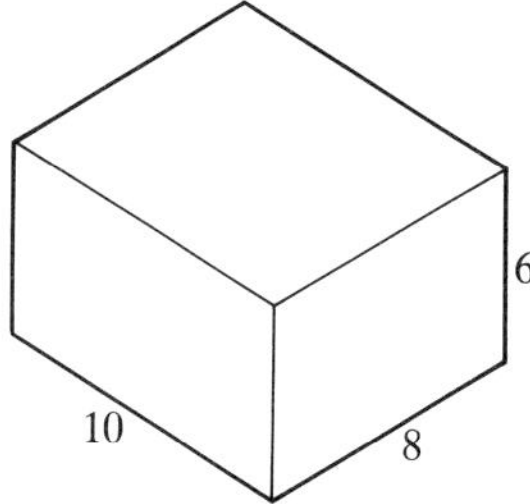

(b) (i) Find the area of the net on your graph paper.
(ii) Find the total surface area of the cuboid.
(c) What is the minimum size rectangle of card you would need if you wanted to make two of the cuboids?

[S]

10. When Diane Wales attends meetings her car expenses worked out as follows.

For journeys of 50 miles or less.

$$\text{Amount} = £\frac{24N}{100}.$$

For journeys of more than 50 miles.

$$\text{Amount} = £12 + £\frac{(N - 50)12}{100}.$$

N is the number of miles travelled.
(i) How much will she be paid for a journey of 26 miles?
(ii) How much will she be paid for a journey of 75 miles?
(iii) How much will she be paid per mile for journeys of less than 50 miles?

[N]

11. Melanie Crisp entered for a sponsored walk in aid of Oxfam. This is her sponsorship form. She walked 13 miles.

AMBRIDGE YOUTH CLUB: SPONSORSHIP WALK for OXFAM: 31/8/85

Signature of sponsor	Amount per mile	Amount given
Mrs Crisp	5p	
Harry Crisp.	1p	
Auntie Jane & Uncle Bill	25p	
B. Kay	3p	
Ben Johnson	15 pence	
J. E. [illegible]	60 pence	

GRAND TOTAL COLLECTED ☐

Name of walker ....Melanie Crisp....

Distance walked ....13.... Signed ....G. Y. Powell....

(i) Complete the column 'Amount given' and fill in the box for the grand total that she collected.

(ii) Melanie wanted to collect at least £20 for Oxfam. How many more miles would she have had to walk in order to do this?

[N]

12. The diagram below shows a straight section of motorway PQ, 900 m long, and a church C which is 700 m from P and 500 m from Q. B is a bridge over the motorway, midway between P and Q.

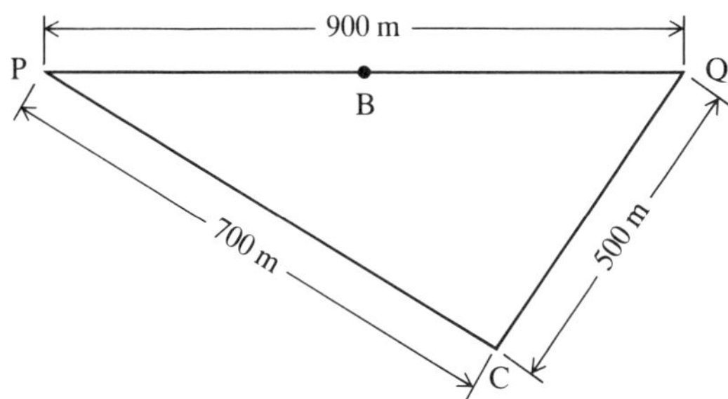

(a) Using a scale of 1 cm representing 100 m, draw an accurate diagram, starting at the point P.

(b) Find the angle PCQ, to the nearest degree.

(c) Find the distance BC to the nearest 10 m.

[S]

Examination exercise 4

1. In December 1984, a factory employed 220 men, each man being paid £130 per week.
(a) Calculate the total weekly wage bill for the factory.
(b) In January 1985, the work force of 220 was reduced by 10 per cent. Find the number of men employed at the factory after the reduction.
(c) Also in January 1985, the weekly wage of £130 was increased by 10 per cent. Find the new weekly wage.
(d) Calculate the total weekly wage bill for the factory in January 1985.
(e) Calculate the difference between the total weekly wage bills in December 1984 and January 1985.

[M]

2. A motorist travelled 800 miles during May, when the cost of petrol was 50 pence per litre. In June the cost of petrol increased by 10% and he reduced his mileage for the month by 5%.
(a) What was the cost, in pence per litre, of petrol in June?
(b) How many miles did he travel in June?

[S]

3. (a) A gardener wishes to sow seeds on a circular lawn of radius 16 metres. He uses 80 grams of seed per square metre of ground. Using $\pi = 3.142$, calculate
(i) the area of the lawn to the nearest square metre,
(ii) the mass of seed used to the nearest kilogram.
(b) The figure ABCDEF is the uniform cross-section of a solid metal bar of length 2 metres. ABEF is a parallelogram and BCDE is a trapezium.

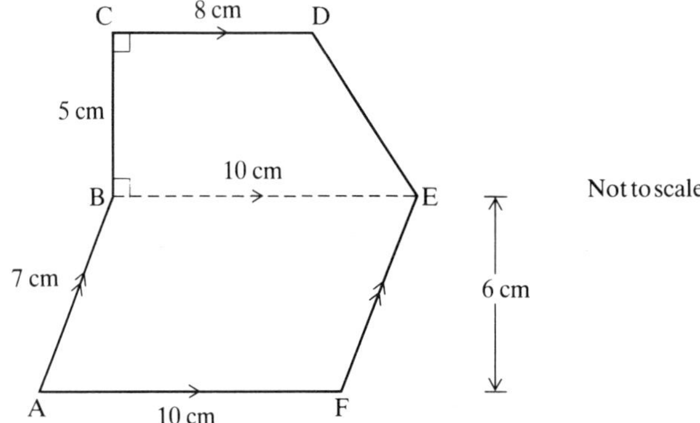

Calculate
(i) the area of the cross-section,
(ii) the volume of the metal bar.

[W]

4. In triangle ABC, angle C = 90° and AC = 10 cm. The foot of the perpendicular from C to AB is N and CN = 6 cm.

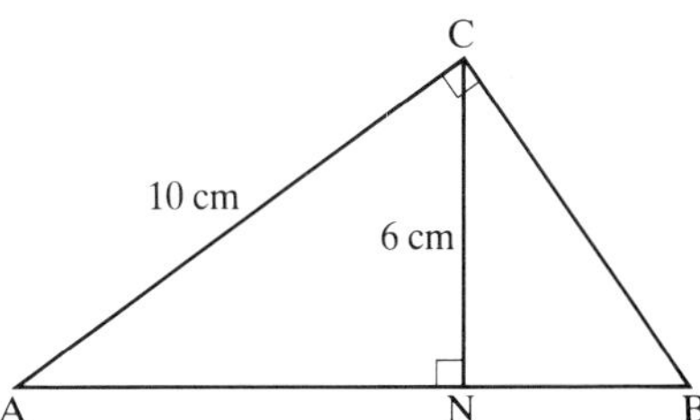

(a) Calculate the length of AN.
(b) Calculate the cosine of angle A.
(c) Calculate the length of AB.

[M]

5. The road and rail distances from Exe to Wye are both 144 km.

(a) The cost of a second class rail return ticket is £13.60 and the cost of a first class rail return ticket is £20.40.
Find how much less a train passenger has to pay to travel, from Exe to Wye and return, by second class rather than first class.

(b) A coach company charges a standard rate of 2p per km for each passenger. A group of four people travel, from Exe to Wye and return, by coach rather than by second class rail. How much less does it cost the group?

(c) The rail fares increase by $12\frac{1}{2}\%$. Find the new price of a first class return rail ticket.

(d)

Rail Timetable

Exe to Wye	Mondays to Fridays				
km 0 64 144	 Exe Dee Wye	 04 38 05 46 06 53	 10 18 11 26 12 33	 13 40 14 48 15 55	 16 18 17 26 18 33

(i) What time does the 13 40 train from Exe arrive at Wye?
(ii) Find the time taken for the journey from Exe to Wye.
(iii) Find the average speed of the 13 40 train from Exe to Wye.

(e) A coach arrived in Wye at 14 20 hours. It had travelled from Exe at an average speed of 60 km/h.
(i) When did the coach leave Exe?
(ii) How much more time did the coach take compared with the train?

[S]

6. Peter carried out a traffic survey of 80 cars passing the school gate, to note the number of persons in each car. The tally column has been filled in for the first 20 cars. The number of persons in the next 60 cars is given in this table.

2	3	4	2	1	1	5	2	2	3	3	4	3	2	1	5	4	4	1	2
5	1	1	2	1	3	1	4	2	1	5	6	5	4	1	2	3	2	2	3
1	4	1	2	5	4	1	2	3	4	1	3	4	2	1	1	3	2	2	1

(i) Complete the tally column for these 60 cars and hence fill in the frequency column for all 80 cars.

Number of persons	Tally	Frequency
1	~~IIII~~ I	
2	~~IIII~~ I	
3	III	
4	III	
5	II	
6		

(ii) Which number of persons per car occurred most frequently?
(iii) Find the mean number of persons per car in these 80 cars.

[N]

7. A factory cafeteria contains a vending machine which sells drinks. On a typical day:

the machine starts half full,
no drinks are sold before 9 a.m. and after 5 p.m.,
drinks are sold at a slow rate throughout the day, except during the morning and lunch breaks (10.30–11 a.m. and 1–2 p.m.) when there is a greater demand.
the machine is filled up just before the lunch break. (It takes about 10 minutes to fill.)

Sketch a graph showing how the number of drinks in the machine may vary from 8 a.m. to 6 p.m.

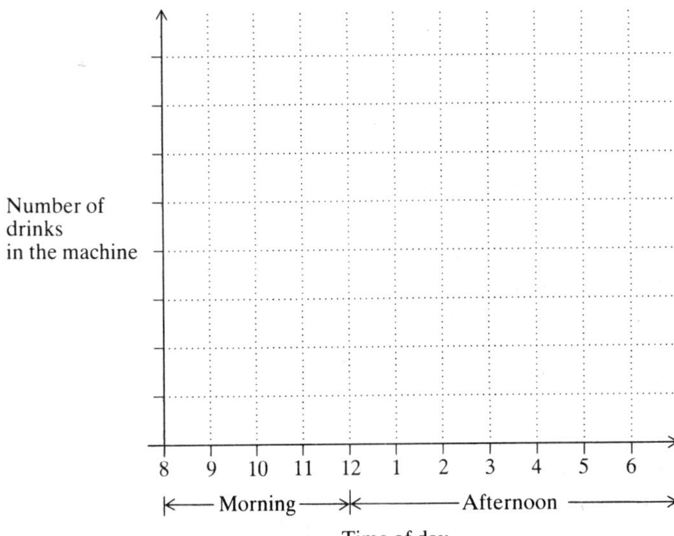

[N]

8.

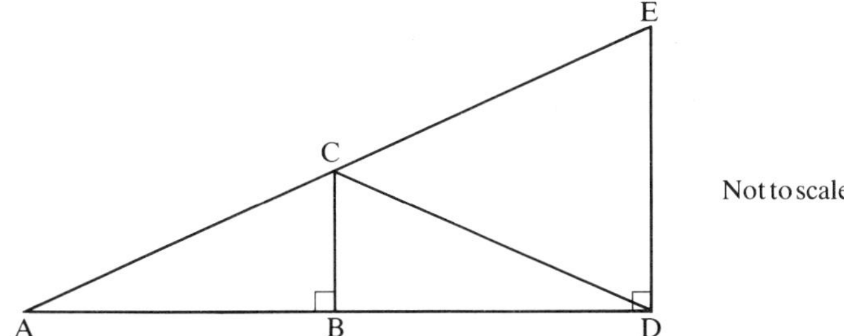

In the diagram above, triangle ADE is the image of triangle ABC after an enlargement, scale factor +2, using A as the centre of enlargement. Angles ABC and ADE are right angles.

(a) Write down the length of AE if AC = 7 cm.
(b) Write down the size of angle CED if angle ACB = 70°.
(c) Name an isosceles triangle in the diagram.
(d) Name two triangles in the diagram which are congruent to each other.

[M]

9. Construct triangle ABC in which AB = 10 cm, BC = 12 cm and $A\hat{B}C = 47°$. Measure and record the length of AC, giving your answer correct to the nearest millimetre.

[W]

10. Having played 26 innings in a season, Emrys Hughes has a batting average of 46. Calculate the number of runs he must score in his 27th innings to increase his average to 48.

[W]

11. Mr Board took his wife and two children to Moscow to see the Olympic Games, and visited his travel agent to obtain the necessary information.

(a) The air timetable was as follows:

	Flight A	Flight B
London departure	11 05	13 50
Moscow arrival	14 35	17 15

(i) How long did Flight A take?
(ii) How long did Flight B take?
(iii) Given that the distance from London to Moscow is 2520 km, calculate the average speed, in km/h, of Flight A.

(b) The cost of a package tour to Moscow was £250 per adult for a holiday, which consisted of travel and hotel only. A discount of 10% off this price was obtained for each child.
(i) Calculate the actual price paid for each child,
(ii) Calculate the total cost for the family of two adults and two children.

(c) Tickets for attending the Games cost 5 roubles per person per day. Mr Board purchased tickets for 12 days for the whole family.
(i) Calculate the total cost, in roubles, of all the tickets.
(ii) Given that there were 1.3 roubles for £1. Calculate, to the nearest pound, the cost of all the tickets.

[L]

12.

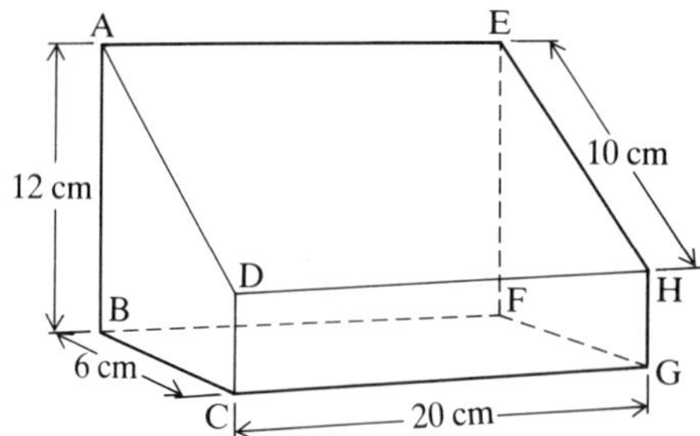

The figure represents a storage box in which
ADHE, ABFE, DCGH and BCGF are rectangles;
EH = 10 cm and CG = 20 cm;
ABCD is a trapezium with AB = 12 cm and BC = 6 cm;
$\angle ABC = \angle BCD = 90°$.

The trapezium EFGH is identical in size and shape to the trapezium ABCD.

(a) Write down the lengths, in cm, of FG and AE.
(b) The rectangle DCGH has an area of 80 cm^2. Calculate
 (i) the length, in cm, of DC,
 (ii) the area, in cm^2, of the trapezium ABCD,
 (iii) the volume, in cm^3, of this box.
 N is a point in AB such that $\angle DNA = 90°$.
(c) Write down the lengths of DN and NA.
 Hence, or otherwise, calculate, to the nearest degree, angle DAN.

[L]

Examination exercise 5

1. The cash price for double glazing the windows of Mr. Sharp's house was £3950. Mr. Sharp decided to pay by hire purchase.
(a) He paid a deposit of 20% of the cash price. Calculate the amount of the deposit.
(b) He also made 36 monthly payments of £118.50 each. Calculate the total of the 36 monthly payments.
(c) Calculate the total amount paid by Mr. Sharp for the double glazing.

[M]

2.

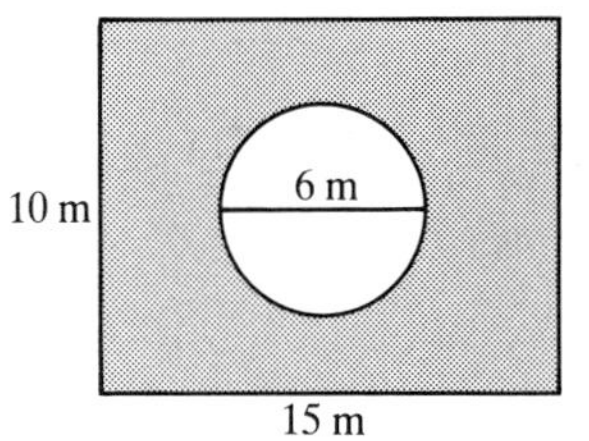

The diagram above represents a rectangular lawn, 15 m by 10 m, with a circular flower bed of diameter 6 m cut from it.
(a) Taking π as 3, calculate the area of the flower bed.
 (Area of circle = πr^2.)
(b) Calculate the area of lawn remaining. (It is shaded in the diagram.)

[M]

3. 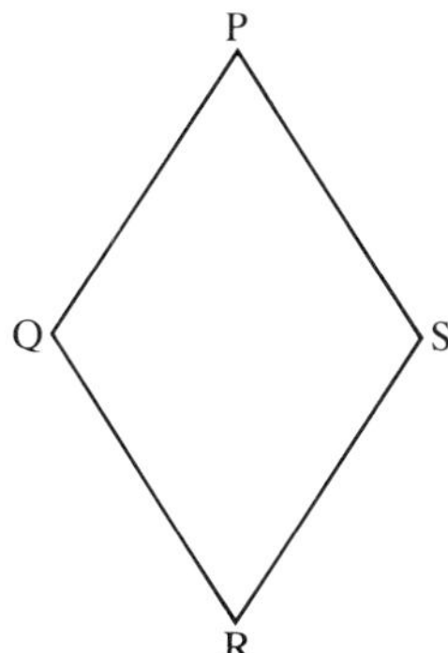

In the diagram, PQRS is a rhombus with each side of length 3 cm. A point X lies inside the rhombus. It is given that X is less than 3 cm from P and that the distance PX is greater than the distance RX. Indicate clearly, by shading in the diagram, the region in which X must lie.

[M]

4. A student asked 30 people arriving at a football ground how long, to the nearest minute, it had taken them to reach the ground. The times they gave (in minutes) are listed below.

35 41 22 15 31 19 12 12 23 30
30 38 36 24 14 20 20 16 15 22
34 28 25 13 19 9 27 17 21 25

(a) (i) Copy and complete the following frequency table using the intervals

Time taken in minutes (to nearest minute)	8–12	13–17	18–22	23–27	28–32	33–37	38–42
Number of people	3	5	7	6	4		

(ii) Draw a histogram to represent the information in the frequency table.

(b) Of the 30 people questioned,
6 paid £2 each to see the football match,
8 paid £3 each,
4 paid £4 each,
10 paid £5 each and
2 paid £6 each.
(i) Calculate the total amount paid by these 30 people.
(ii) Calculate the mean amount paid by these 30 people.

[M]

5. A motorist travelled from Carmarthen to Bristol, calling in at Swansea and Cardiff on the way. The reading on the car's 'distance meter' when starting the journey from Carmarthen was

0	7	9	8	4

The following route diagram shows the motorist's journey.

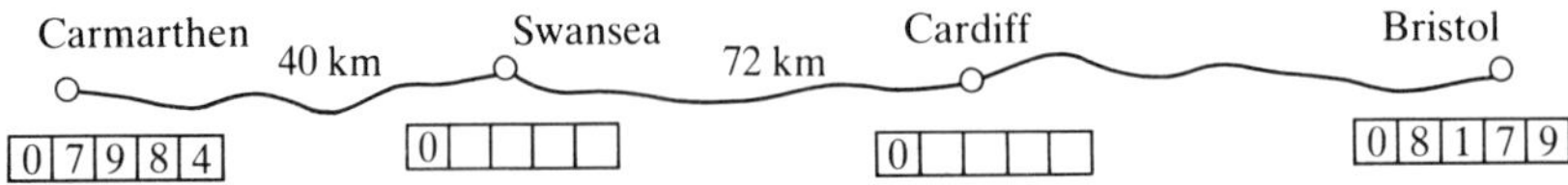

Using the route diagram (*which is not drawn to scale*)

(i) write down the reading on the distance meter when the car arrived in Cardiff,

(ii) find the distance from Cardiff to Bristol.

Given that the total distance from Carmarthen to Bristol is 195 km, and that on average the car used 1 litre of petrol for every 13 km travelled, calculate

(iii) the number of litres of petrol used,

(iv) the total cost of the petrol used for the journey if petrol costs 44p per litre.

[W]

6. A field is in the shape of a quadrilateral ABCD with AB = 80 m, BC = 70 m and CD = 110 m. Angle ABC = 80° and the angle BCD = 120°.
Using a scale of 1 cm to represent 10 m make an accurate scale drawing of the field.

(i) Use your scale drawing to find the length of the side DA.

(ii) A tree is at the point of intersection of the bisector of the angle CDA and the perpendicular bisector of the side BC. Using only ruler and compass construct and indicate the position of the tree.

(iii) Find the distance of the tree from the corner B of the field.

[N]

7. Two bags contain coloured beads.
Bag A contains 3 blue beads and 1 red bead.
Bag B contains 3 blue beads and 3 red beads.
Two draws are made, at random in each case.
Draw 1. A bead is taken from Bag A and put in Bag B.
Draw 2. A bead is taken from Bag B.
Write the appropriate probabilities on the branches of the tree diagram.

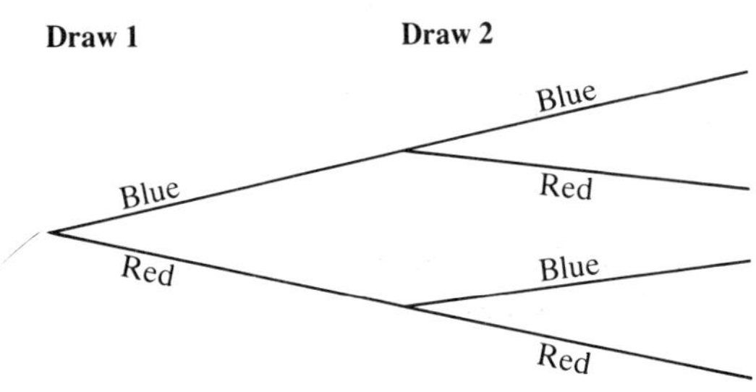

[N]

8. The diagram shows three posts A, B and C on a building site.

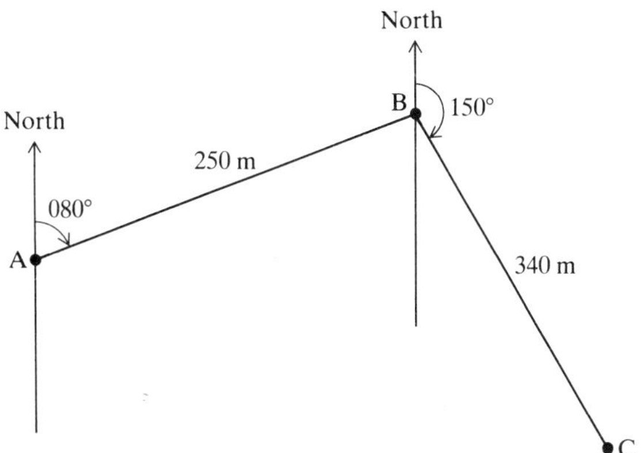

(a) Using the distances and bearings shown on the diagram and with a scale of 1 cm to represent 50 m, make a scale drawing to show the positions of A, B and C.
(b) (i) Join AC and measure its length to the nearest millimetre.
(ii) What is the distance, on the building site, between the two posts A and C?
(c) (i) Measure and write down the size of angle BAC.
(ii) What is the bearing of C from A?
(iii) What is the bearing of A from C?
(d) By drawing further lines on your scale drawing, find how far the post C is East of the post A.

[S]

9. Mrs. Pinks drove her car from Sheffield to Cambridge University. The record of her journey in both directions is given below. The distance between the two cities is 208 kilometres.

Time	
06 30	Left Sheffield.
08 30	Car broke down 140 kilometres from Sheffield.
09 45	Car started again and the journey to Cambridge continued.
10 30	Arrived in Cambridge.
15 55	Left Cambridge for Sheffield.

(a) Calculate her average speed in kilometres per hour *before* the car broke down.
(b) Calculate the distance from Cambridge when the car broke down.
(c) Calculate the average speed between 06 30 and 10 30.
(d) Calculate the length of time in hours and minutes that she spent in Cambridge.
(e) On the return journey from Cambridge to Sheffield she averaged 64 km per hour. Calculate the time of arrival in Sheffield.

[M]

Think about it 6

Project 1 A PATH AROUND THE LAWN

Paving slabs 1 metre square are placed around a square lawn to form a path.
In Figure 1 the side of the lawn is 2 m and there are 12 slabs in the path.

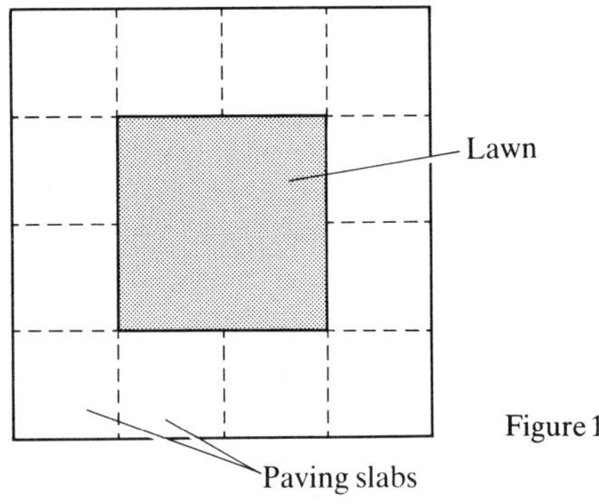

Figure 1

In Figure 2 the side of the lawn is 3 m and there are 16 slabs in the path.

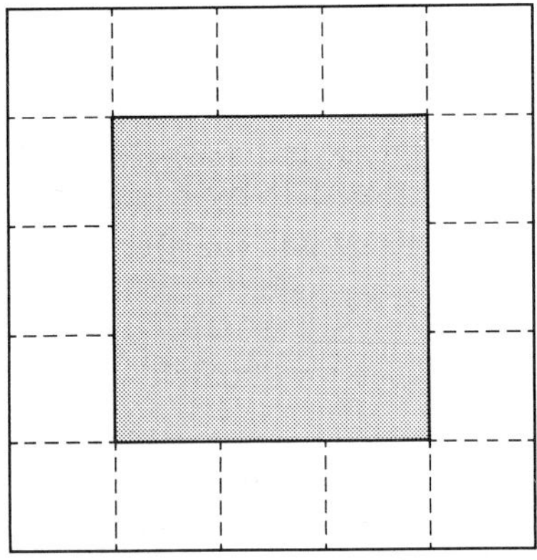
Figure 2

(a) Draw diagrams to show the paths in the following cases:
- (i) lawn 4 m × 4 m
- (ii) lawn 5 m × 5 m
- (iii) lawn 6 m × 6 m
- (iv) lawn 1 m × 1 m

(b) Copy and complete the table

Side of lawn s	number of slabs n
1 m	
2 m	12
3 m	16
4 m	
5 m	
6 m	

(c) How many slabs are needed for a lawn which is
  (i) 12 m square,
  (ii) 22 m square?
(d) What are the dimensions of a lawn where the path has
  (i) 64 slabs,
  (ii) 120 slabs?
(e) Can you find a formula connecting the side of the lawn s and the number of the slabs n?

Oblong lawns

Suppose the lawn is an oblong shape where the length is always 1 m more than the width w. In figure 3 the width is 2 m and there are 14 slabs.

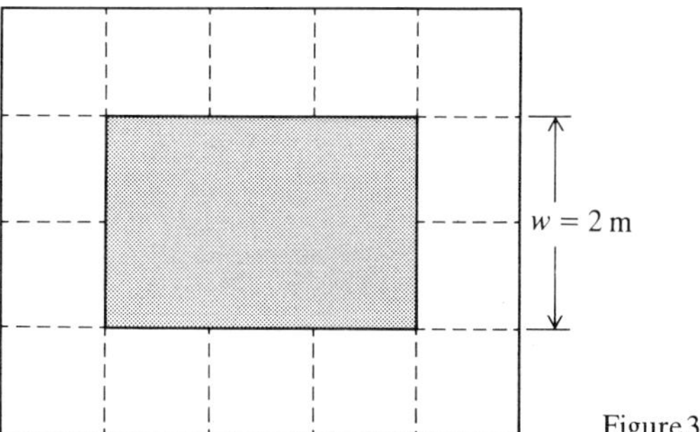

Figure 3

(a) Drawn diagrams to show the paths in the following cases:
  (i) lawn 3 m by 4 m ($w = 3$)
  (ii) lawn 4 m by 5 m ($w = 4$)
  (iii) lawn 5 m by 6 m ($w = 5$)
  (iv) lawn 1 m by 2 m ($w = 1$)
(b) Draw a table of results for the width of the lawn w and the number of slabs n.
(c) Can you find a formula connecting w and n?
(d) Finally consider lawns where the length is always twice the width (1 m by 2 m, 2 m by 4 m, 3 m by 6 m etc).
  Draw diagrams and use the results to find a formula connecting the width of the lawn w and the number of slabs n.

Exercise A

1. When mixing sand and cement a workman puts three times as much sand as cement in the mixture. How much sand does he need for a mixture which weighs 120 kg?

2. Copy and complete the following bill

12 kg of sugar at 42p per kg	=	£
4 kg of potatoes at ...... per kg	=	£1.44
...... boxes of matches at 31p per box	=	£1.86
Total	=	£

3. A car travels at a steady speed of 44 miles per hour for 8 hours. How far does it go in this time?

4. An aircraft flies at a steady speed of 410 nautical miles per hour for 4 hours. How far does it go in this time?

5. A ship sails at a steady speed of 22 nautical miles per hour for $7\frac{1}{2}$ hours. How far does it go in this time?

6. A man bought 30 records at £4.20 each and a number of other records costing £6.80 each. In all he spent £296. How many of the more expensive records did he buy?

7. A train took 8 hours to travel 440 miles. What was the average speed of the train?

8. A lorry took 11 hours to travel 682 km. What was the average speed of the lorry?

9. A man took 3 hours to run a distance of $25\frac{1}{2}$ miles. What was his average speed?

10. Three girls are 144 cm, 147 cm and 153 cm in height.
(a) What is their average height?
When another girl joins them, the average height becomes 149 cm.
(b) What is the height of the fourth girl?

Project 2 DARTS: CAN YOU FINISH?

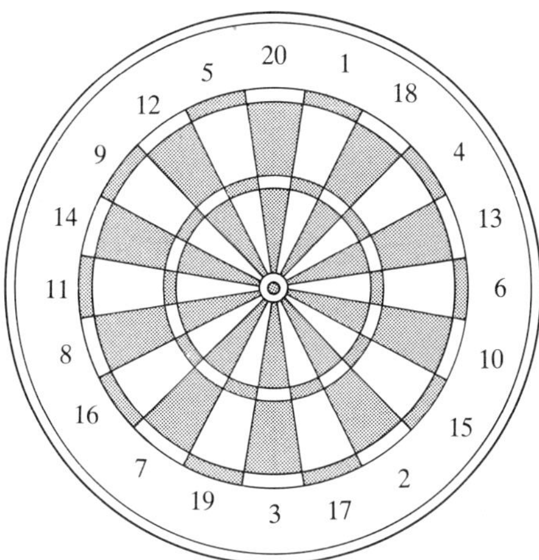

In the game of 501 in darts, players aim to score a total of 501 and they must finish on a double or a bull's eye (50).

For example, if a player has already scored 400 he has 101 left and he could finish 1, treble 20, double 20 (he has just three darts).

If he has 102 left he could finish treble 20, double 20, double 1. There are of course several other ways of finishing from 102.

Find ways of finishing with three darts for scores of 103, 104, 105, and so on up to 140.

What patterns do you notice?

What is the highest possible three-dart finish?

Exercise B

1. A large block of wood measures 10 cm by 10 cm by 20 cm. A small cube of side 4 cm is cut from the block. What volume of wood remains?
2. (a) Find 20% of £20
   (b) Find 5% of 2000 kg
   (c) Find 7% of 1400 m
3. (a) Copy the diagram of the regular hexagon below and draw in any lines of symmetry.
   (b) Calculate the size of the angle marked x.

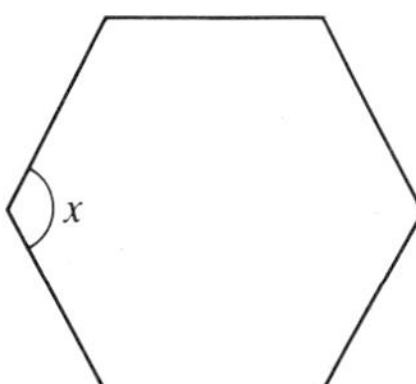

4. A large wheel takes 30 s to turn once. How many rotations will it make in 1 hour?
5. Which is larger: 0.2^2 or ($\frac{1}{2}$ of 0.2)?
6. Sally is 13 years old and Dawn is 10. How many years ago was Sally twice as old as Dawn?
7. A bus travels 32 km on 8 litres of fuel. How many litres of fuel will it need to travel 100 km?
8. A grocer bought a crate of 40 tins of pears at 25p per tin.
   (a) Find the total cost of the crate of pears.
   (b) He wishes to make a profit of 40% on his cost price. For how much must he sell each tin?
   (c) He sold 30 tins at 32p, and the rest of the crate at 40p. How much profit did he make?
9. An aircrafts' flight started at 2150 on Friday and finished at 1020 on the following Saturday. How long was the journey in hours and minutes?
10. A woman drives a car at an average speed of 70 km/h and the car does an average of 25 km per litre of petrol. Petrol costs 43p per litre.
   (a) How far does she drive in 5 hours?
   (b) How much petrol does she use?
   (c) How much does it cost in pounds?
   (d) How much petrol would she need for a journey of 500 km?

Project 3 SLIDING AND HOPPING

Object: To swap the positions of the discs so that they end up the other way round (with a space in the middle).

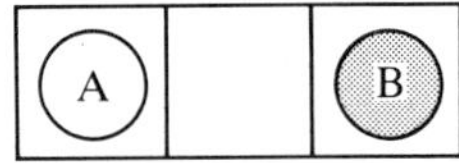

Rules: 1. A disc can be made to slide one square in either direction onto an empty square.
2. A disc can be made to hop over one adjacent disc so that it goes into an empty square.

Example: (a) Slide A one square to the right.

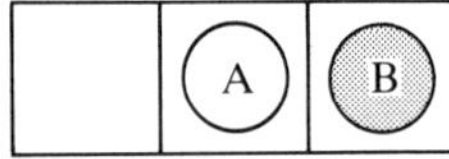

(b) B hops over A to the left.

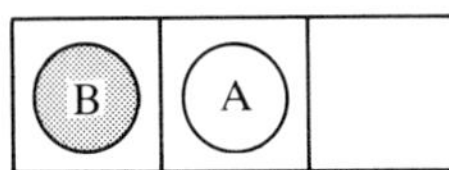

(c) Slide A one square to the right.

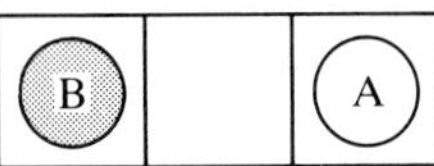

We took 3 moves

1. What is the smallest number of moves needed for two discs of each colour?

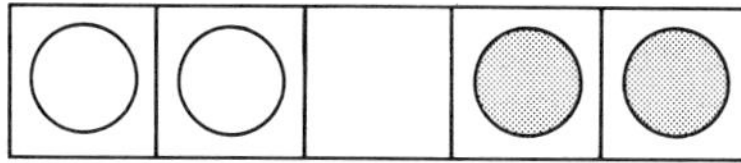

2. Now try three discs of each colour.
Can you complete the task in 15 moves?

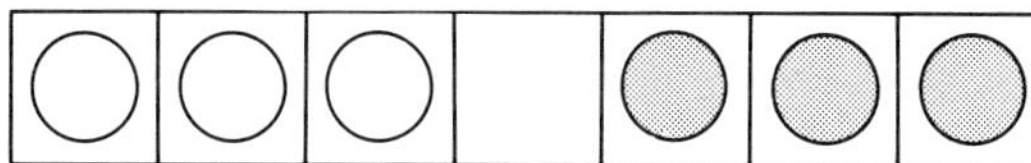

3. Now try four discs of each colour.
Can you complete the task in 24 moves?

4. Results so far (hopefully!)
For 1 disc we took 3 moves.
For 2 discs we took 8 moves.
For 3 discs we took 15 moves.
For 4 discs we took 24 moves.
Use these results to try to *predict* the minimum number of moves needed when five discs of each colour are used.
Now confirm your prediction.

Exercise C

1. The area of a county is 6000 km^2. What volume of rain falls on the county during a day when there is 2 cm of rain? Give the answer in m^3.

2. How many hours and minutes are there between:
(a) 06 40 and 10 00
(b) 11 30 and 14 50
(c) 20 45 and 23 15
(d) 08 55 and 14 00?

3. The basic rate of pay in a factory is £6 per hour for a 37 hour week. Overtime is paid at time and a half.
(a) Calculate the total earnings of Mr Jones who worked the basic week.
(b) Calculate the total earnings of Mr Green who worked 40 hours.
(c) Calculate the number of hours overtime worked by Mr Bradshaw whose total earnings were £267.

4. Calculate the shaded area. Take $\pi = 3$

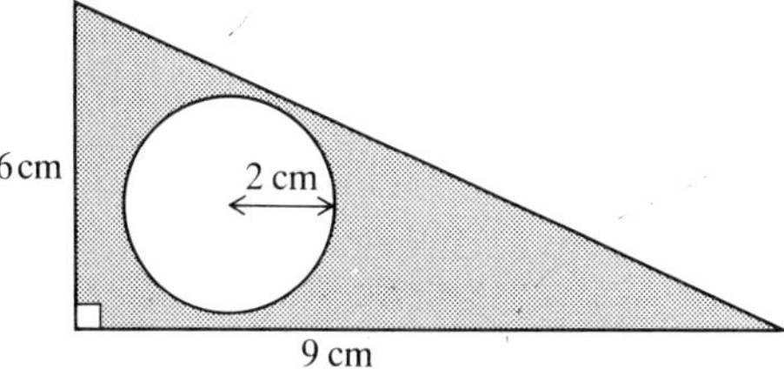

5. At 11 20 the mileometer of a car reads 97 460. At 14 20 the mileometer reads 97 715. What is the average speed of the car?

6. A map uses a scale of 1 to 100 000.
   (a) Calculate the actual length, in km, of a canal which is 5.4 cm long on the map.
   (b) A path is 600 m long. Calculate, in cm, the length this would be on the map.
7. Given the circumference C of a circle it is possible to estimate the area A by the following method:

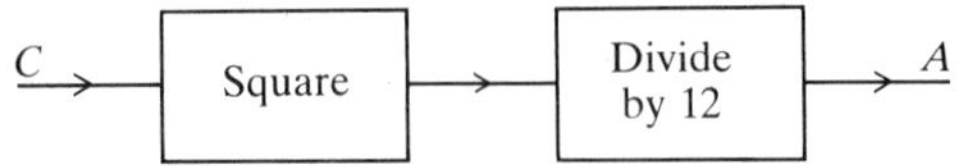

   (a) Find A when $C = 6$ cm.
   (b) Find A when $C = 18$ cm.
   (c) Write down the formula involving A and C.
8. I think of a number. If I subtract 4 and then divide the result by 4 the answer is 3. What number was I thinking of?
9. Try to draw four straight lines which pass through all of the 9 points below, without taking your pen from the paper and without going over any line twice.

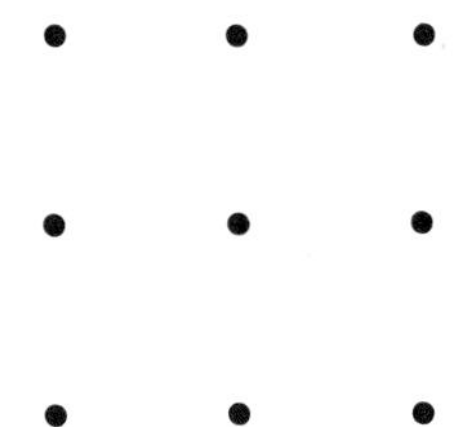

(Hint: The lines may go outside the pattern of dots).

10. Work out (a) $\frac{2}{3} + \frac{2}{5}$ (b) $\frac{2}{3} \times \frac{2}{5}$ (c) $\frac{2}{3} - \frac{2}{5}$

Project 4 EXPERIMENTAL PROBABILITY

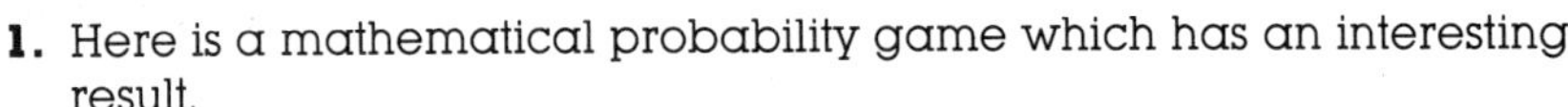

1. Here is a mathematical probability game which has an interesting result.

   Take the ace, two, three, four, . . ., ten of one suit from a pack of playing cards.

   Shuffle the ten cards and then turn them over one by one and as you do so count 'one', 'two', 'three' and so on.
   You 'win' if you turn over at least one card that corresponds to the number you call out as you deal it.

   Before you try the experiment, what do you think is the probability of a 'win' in any one attempt: $\frac{1}{10}$; $\frac{1}{4}$; $\frac{1}{20}$?

   Now work out the experimental probability of a 'win' by playing the game a large number of times.
   Perhaps the whole class can play the game in pairs and then combine the results?

Count the number of trials (every time you start) and the number of 'wins'.

Calculate the experimental probability of a win as

$$p = \frac{\text{number of wins}}{\text{number of trials}}$$

2. Here is another experiment in probability where the result is perhaps even more surprising.

Two people each hold a shuffled pack of cards. Starting at the same time they each turn over the top card from their own pack. They continue to do this, always turning over the cards at the same time, until possibly they both turn over the same card. We will call this a 'success'. Once a 'success' has been achieved they can stop and start again, after shuffling the cards. If several pairs of people can perform this experiment many times we will be able to work out the experimental probability of a 'success' as follows:

$$\text{Experimental probability of a 'success'} = \frac{\text{number of successes}}{\text{number of trials}}$$

Teachers' note: In both experiments the theoretical probability of 'success' is given approximately by the formula

$$p = 1 - \frac{1}{e} \text{ (where e = 2.71828...)}$$

Exercise D

1. Due to overproduction, the EEC destroyed 39 420 000 lb of tomatoes in 1985. Calculate the average weight of tomatoes destroyed
(a) every day
(b) every hour

2. A shopkeeper stocks two different sorts of gloves; he has 80 pairs of leather gloves and 60 pairs of woollen gloves.
(a) He bought each pair of leather gloves for £6.20 and sold them for £8.50.
  (i) Calculate the total cost to the shopkeeper for the 80 pairs of leather gloves.
  (ii) Calculate the total amount of money received from the sale of all 80 pairs of gloves.
(b) He bought the 60 pairs of woollen gloves for a total cost of £150 and sold them for a total of £210.
  (i) Find the total cost to the shopkeeper of the 140 pairs of gloves.
  (ii) Find the total amount of money received from the sale of all 140 pairs of gloves.
(c) Calculate the total profit on the sale of all the gloves.

3. Write the following numbers correct to 2 decimal places:
(a) 1.752 (b) 0.3468 (c) 17.866
(d) 0.0753 (e) 0.0829 (f) 78.094

4. Use Pythagoras' theorem to find x:

(a)
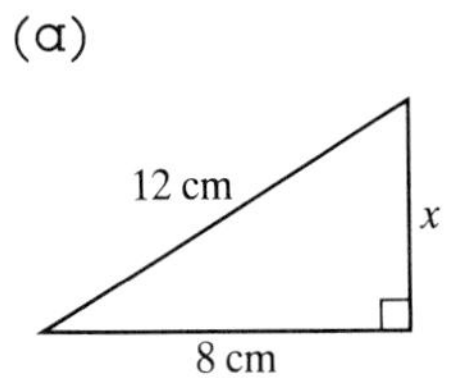

(b)
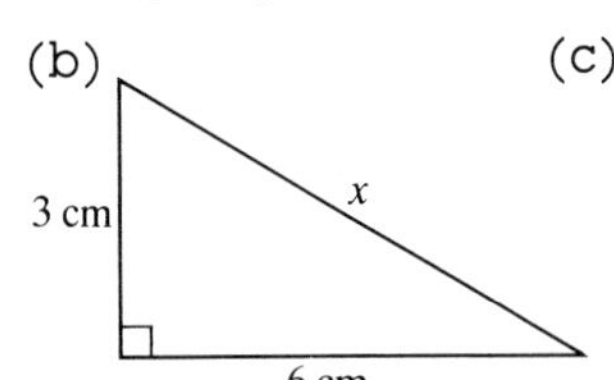

(c)
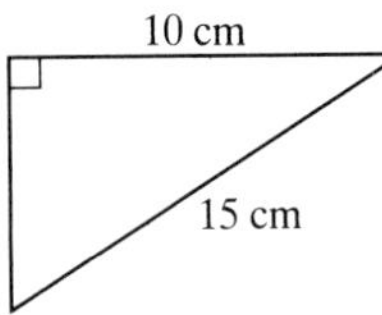

(d)
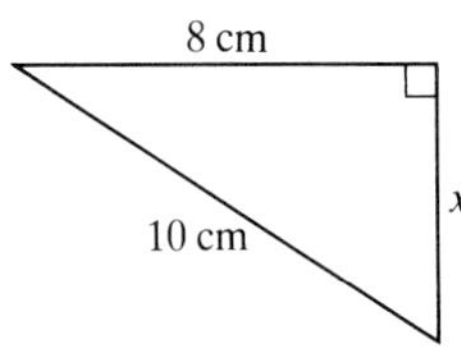

5. A boy spends $\frac{1}{8}$ of his money on sweets, $\frac{1}{4}$ of his money on magazines and the rest of his money on records. If he spends 80p on sweets calculate how much he spends on
(a) magazines, (b) records.

6. (a) Copy the diagram of the regular pentagon below and draw in any lines of symmetry.
(b) Calculate the size of the angle marked x.

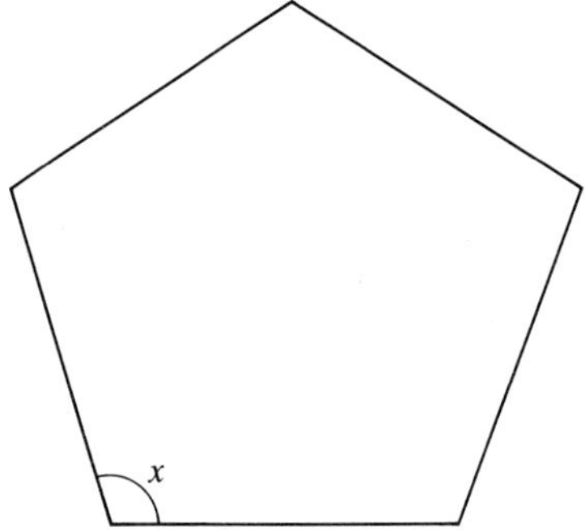

Project 5 COUNT THE BLACK SQUARES

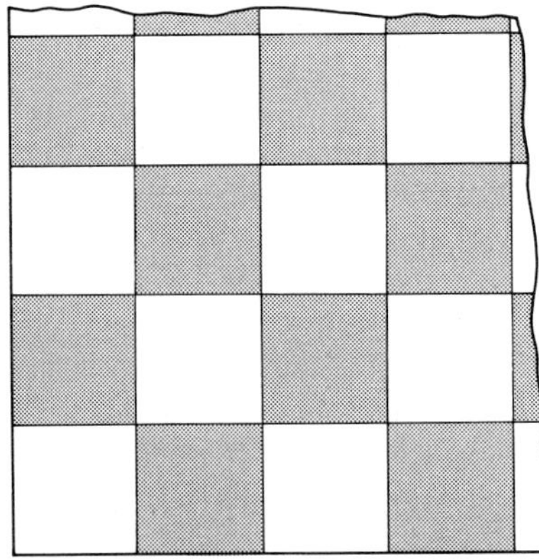

One corner of a variable-sized chess board is shown.
The board consists of black and white squares all 1 cm by 1 cm.

Drawn diagrams to answer the questions below and record the results in a table like this one.

Dimensions	Number of black squares.
6 cm × 8 cm	

Start with a white square in the bottom left-hand corner.

(a) How many black squares are there on a board with the following dimensions:
(i) 6 cm × 8 cm, (ii) 8 cm × 4 cm, (iii) 10 cm × 6 cm?

(b) How many black squares are there on a board with the following dimensions:
(i) 6 cm × 5 cm, (ii) 8 cm × 7 cm, (iii) 10 cm × 9 cm?

(c) How many black squares are there on a board with the following dimensions:
(i) 7 cm × 5 cm, (ii) 5 cm × 3 cm, (iii) 9 cm × 5 cm?

(d) Study the results for (a), (b) and (c) above and use them to predict (without drawing) the number of black squares on a board with the following dimensions:
(i) 13 cm × 12 cm, (ii) 11 cm × 7 cm,
(iii) 12 cm × 8 cm, (iv) 9 cm × 13 cm.

(e) Can you write down a rule (or rules) which enable you to calculate the number of black squares on a board of *any* size?

Project 6 THE MILK CRATE PROBLEM

You have 18 bottles to put into the crate below which has space for 24 bottles.

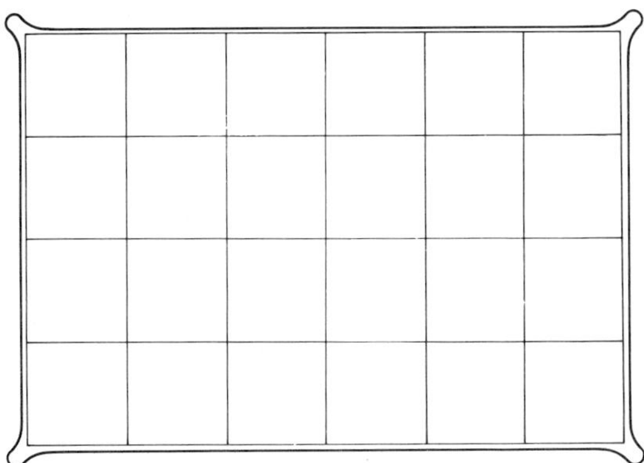

The only condition is that you have to put an *even* number of bottles into every row and every column. Good luck.

Answers

Section A

UNIT 1

Exercise 1 *page 1*

1. 58	**2.** 67	**3.** 251	**4.** 520	**5.** 961
6. 337	**7.** 496	**8.** 511	**9.** 320	**10.** 992
11. 647	**12.** 1071	**13.** 328	**14.** 940	**15.** 197
16. 2384	**17.** 3312	**18.** 5335	**19.** 7008	**20.** 8193
21. 1031	**22.** 3121	**23.** 3541	**24.** 827	**25.** 6890
26. 1021	**27.** 13 011	**28.** 21 844	**29.** 115 387	**30.** 19 885

Exercise 2 *page 1*

1. 34	**2.** 28	**3.** 23	**4.** 82	**5.** 111
6. 204	**7.** 57	**8.** 15	**9.** 56	**10.** 23
11. 137	**12.** 461	**13.** 381	**14.** 542	**15.** 301
16. 113	**17.** 533	**18.** 123	**19.** 522	**20.** 81
21. 265	**22.** 5646	**23.** 4819	**24.** 6388	**25.** 7832
26. 384	**27.** 399	**28.** 5804	**29.** 1361	**30.** 548
31. 355	**32.** 2325	**33.** 7130	**34.** 5071	**35.** 1734
36. 1499	**37.** 1879	**38.** 248	**39.** 3076	**40.** 573
41. 158	**42.** 397	**43.** 1797	**44.** 1416	**45.** 382
46. 9012	**47.** 47	**48.** 9360	**49.** 359	**50.** 16 333

Exercise 3 *page 2*

1.

3	8	1
2	4	6
7	0	5

2.

4	11	6
9	7	5
8	3	10

3.

8	1	6
3	5	7
4	9	2

4.

7	2	9
8	6	4
3	10	5

5.

12	7	14
13	11	9
8	15	10

6.

17	10	15
12	14	16
13	18	11

7.

1	12	7	14
8	13	2	11
10	3	16	5
15	6	9	4

8.

15	6	9	4
10	3	16	5
8	13	2	11
1	12	7	14

9.

3	10	12	17
14	15	5	8
9	4	18	11
16	13	7	6

10.

18	9	12	7
13	6	19	8
11	16	5	14
4	15	10	17

11.

11	24	7	20	3
4	12	25	8	16
17	5	13	21	9
10	18	1	14	22
23	6	19	2	15

12.

16	23	10	17	4
3	15	22	9	21
20	2	14	26	8
7	19	6	13	25
24	11	18	5	12

Exercise 4 *page 3*

1.

	4	7	3	5	9	11	8	6	2	12
4	16	28	12	20	36	44	32	24	8	48
7	28	49	21	35	63	77	56	42	14	84
3	12	21	9	15	27	33	24	18	6	36
5	20	35	15	25	45	55	40	30	10	60
9	36	63	27	45	81	99	72	54	18	108
11	44	77	33	55	99	121	88	66	22	132
8	32	56	24	40	72	88	64	48	16	96
6	24	42	18	30	54	66	48	36	12	72
2	8	14	6	10	18	22	16	12	4	24
12	48	84	36	60	108	132	96	72	24	144

2.

	7	5	9	6	8	11	4	2	12	3
7	49	35	63	42	56	77	28	14	84	21
5	35	25	45	30	40	55	20	10	60	15
9	63	45	81	54	72	99	36	18	108	27
6	42	30	54	36	48	66	24	12	72	18
8	56	40	72	48	64	88	32	16	96	24
11	77	55	99	66	88	121	44	22	132	33
4	28	20	36	24	32	44	16	8	48	12
2	14	10	18	12	16	22	8	4	24	6
12	84	60	108	72	96	132	48	24	144	36
3	21	15	27	18	24	33	12	6	36	9

Exercise 5 *page 3*

1. 63 **2.** 96 **3.** 252 **4.** 140 **5.** 639
6. 230 **7.** 1230 **8.** 168 **9.** 1477 **10.** 2114
11. 1065 **12.** 1923 **13.** 168 **14.** 1884 **15.** 1179
16. 1712 **17.** 4920 **18.** 3684 **19.** 12 846 **20.** 15 125
21. 2592 **22.** 4501 **23.** 2655 **24.** 6410 **25.** 8460
26. 2200 **27.** 4417 **28.** 7965 **29.** 3976 **30.** 12 918

Exercise 6 *page 3*

1. 345 **2.** 459 **3.** 943 **4.** 828 **5.** 1525
6. 1175 **7.** 4453 **8.** 3440 **9.** 464 **10.** 4853
11. 9744 **12.** 9021 **13.** 16 044 **14.** 31 772 **15.** 69 496
16. 65 832 **17.** 67 510 **18.** 143 676 **19.** 256 592 **20.** 734 266

Exercise 7 *page 3*

1. 23	**2.** 143	**3.** 211	**4.** 115	**5.** 178
6. 232	**7.** 527	**8.** 528	**9.** 83	**10.** 497
11. 273	**12.** 6024	**13.** 604	**14.** 271	**15.** 415
16. 383	**17.** 824	**18.** 936	**19.** 321	**20.** 2142
21. 9486	**22.** 2314	**23.** 241	**24.** 7005	**25.** 837
26. 6145	**27.** 2638	**28.** 415	**29.** 2060	**30.** 3104

Exercise 8 *page 3*

1. 325	**2.** 207	**3.** 418	**4.** 416	**5.** 6361
6. 635	**7.** 8089	**8.** 2497	**9.** 5627	**10.** 17 496
11. $535\frac{3}{4}$	**12.** $1283\frac{3}{5}$	**13.** $1506\frac{3}{4}$	**14.** $3440\frac{1}{7}$	**15.** $689\frac{1}{6}$
16. $130\frac{1}{3}$	**17.** $971\frac{1}{7}$	**18.** $2349\frac{1}{3}$	**19.** $254\frac{3}{8}$	**20.** $4420\frac{5}{6}$

Exercise 9 *page 4*

1. 14, 17	**2.** 21, 26	**3.** 12, 10	**4.** 30, 37	**5.** 26, 14
6. 16, 22	**7.** 19, 25	**8.** 40, 35	**9.** 22, 15	**10.** 80, 89
11. 64, 60	**12.** 4, 6	**13.** 7, 10	**14.** −10, −14	**15.** 23, 30
16. −4, −10	**17.** 4, 10	**18.** 51, 43	**19.** 96, 115	**20.** 25, 15

Exercise 10 *page 4*

1. 16, 32	**2.** 81, 243	**3.** 25, $12\frac{1}{2}$	**4.** 58, 67
5. 30 000, 300 000	**6.** 8, 4	**7.** 113, 120	**8.** 26, 20
9. I, K	**10.** N, Q	**11.** P, V	**12.** O, M
13. 155, $77\frac{1}{2}$	**14.** 25, 36	**15.** 120, 720	**16.** 5, 10
17. M, P	**18.** −11, −18	**19.** 26, 33	**20.** 43, 58
21. 3, 14	**22.** 2, $\frac{2}{3}$	**23.** 67, 47	**24.** $\frac{1}{3}$, $\frac{1}{9}$
25. 13, 21	**26.** M, R	**27.** 840, 6720	**28.** 22, 5
29. 32, 47	**30.** 17, 19		

Exercise 11 *page 4*

1. (c)	**2.** (c)	**3.** (b)	**4.** (a)	**5.** (b)	**6.** (c)
7. (c)	**8.** (c)	**9.** (a)	**10.** (c)	**11.** (c)	**12.** (c)
13. F	**14.** T	**15.** T	**16.** T	**17.** T	**18.** F
19. T	**20.** T	**21.** T	**22.** F	**23.** T	**24.** F
25. T	**26.** F	**27.** F	**28.** T	**29.** T	**30.** T
31. T	**32.** F	**33.** F	**34.** T	**35.** F	**36.** F
37. T	**38.** T	**39.** T	**40.** T		

Exercise 12 *page 5*

1. 0.12, 0.21, 0.31	**2.** 0.04, 0.35, 0.4	**3.** 0.67, 0.672, 0.7
4. 0.045, 0.05, 0.07	**5.** 0.089, 0.09, 0.1	**6.** 0.57, 0.705, 0.75
7. 0.041, 0.14, 0.41	**8.** 0.8, 0.809, 0.81	**9.** 0.006, 0.059, 0.6
10. 0.143, 0.15, 0.2	**11.** 0.04, 0.14, 0.2, 0.53	**12.** 0.12, 0.21, 1.12, 1.2
13. 0.08, 0.75, 2.03, 2.3	**14.** 0.26, 0.3, 0.602, 0.62	**15.** 0.5, 1.003, 1.03, 1.3
16. 0.709, 0.79, 0.792, 0.97	**17.** 0.312, 0.321, 1.04, 1.23	**18.** 0.0075, 0.008, 0.09, 0.091
19. 2, 2.046, 2.05, 2.5	**20.** 1.95, 5.1, 5.19, 9.51	**21.** 0.674, 0.706, 0.71, 0.76
22. 0.09, 0.989, 0.99, 1	**23.** 0.204, 0.24, 0.42, 1	**24.** 0.222, 0.3, 0.303, 0.33
25. 0.95, 1.02, 1.2, 1.21	**26.** 0.362, 0.632, 0.662, 3.62	**27.** 0.08, 0.096, 0.4, 1
28. 0.7, 0.72, 0.722, 0.732	**29.** 3.99, 4, 4.025, 4.03	**30.** 0.08, 0.658, 0.66, 0.685

Exercise 13 *page 5*

1. 10.14	**2.** 20.94	**3.** 26.71	**4.** 216.956	**5.** 9.6
6. 23.1	**7.** 12.25	**8.** 17.4	**9.** 0.0623	**10.** 85.47
11. 1.11	**12.** 4.36	**13.** 2.41	**14.** 10.8	**15.** 1.36
16. 6.23	**17.** 2.46	**18.** 12.24	**19.** 8.4	**20.** 15.96
21. 2.8	**22.** 2.2	**23.** 10.3	**24.** 21.8	**25.** 0.137
26. 0.0488	**27.** 6.65	**28.** 4.72	**29.** 0.566	**30.** 3.6

Exercise 14 *page 5*

1. 0.92	**2.** 1.08	**3.** 2.35	**4.** 8.52	**5.** 50
6. 2.982	**7.** 0.126	**8.** 0.302	**9.** 0.0692	**10.** 0.0504
11. 0.459	**12.** 0.002 52	**13.** 127.2	**14.** 10.86	**15.** 284.16
16. 0.0425	**17.** 0.0532	**18.** 3.6036	**19.** 0.000 218	**20.** 0.584
21. 2.99	**22.** 4.76	**23.** 7.815	**24.** 1.3062	**25.** 2.3488
26. 1.2465	**27.** 0.185 24	**28.** 21.164	**29.** 3.2852	**30.** 0.024 072

Exercise 15 *page 6*

1. 2.19	**2.** 9.87	**3.** 2.34	**4.** 2.31	**5.** 1.668
6. 3.45	**7.** 0.159	**8.** 0.313 75	**9.** 5.84	**10.** 2.652
11. 2.15	**12.** 0.35	**13.** 2.36	**14.** 8.59	**15.** 87.5
16. 0.184	**17.** 3.19	**18.** 2.13	**19.** 11.46	**20.** 3.64
21. 5.84	**22.** 36.1	**23.** 6.24	**24.** 0.548	**25.** 6.382
26. 0.259	**27.** 6.547	**28.** 104	**29.** 3575	**30.** 3287.5
31. 5.677	**32.** 6.238	**33.** 0.4963	**34.** 1400	**35.** 69.2
36. 4000	**37.** 0.5846	**38.** 0.002 59	**39.** 62.5	**40.** 2 734 000

Exercise 16 *page 6*

1. 6.34	**2.** 8.38	**3.** 81.5	**4.** 7.4	**5.** 7245
6. 61.05	**7.** 6.4	**8.** 7.5	**9.** 270	**10.** 35 100
11. 0.624	**12.** 0.897	**13.** 0.175	**14.** 0.0236	**15.** 0.048
16. 0.073	**17.** 0.127	**18.** 0.163	**19.** 58	**20.** 6.3
21. 75.1	**22.** 0.0084	**23.** 0.0111	**24.** 8.4	**25.** 16 000
26. 0.07	**27.** 0.008	**28.** 3170	**29.** 0.254	**30.** 99 000

Exercise 17 *page 6*

1. 4.32	**2.** 5.75	**3.** 9.16	**4.** 1.008	**5.** 0.748
6. 20.24	**7.** 10.2	**8.** 2.95	**9.** 4.926	**10.** 34
11. 0.621	**12.** 8.24	**13.** 0.1224	**14.** 12.15	**15.** 2.658
16. 66.462	**17.** 34 100	**18.** 0.0041	**19.** 2.104	**20.** 0.285
21. 0.258 84	**22.** 3.27	**23.** 2.247	**24.** 0.54	**25.** 0.027
26. 6.6077	**27.** 6.56	**28.** 7.84	**29.** 0.005 84	**30.** 742 000

Exercise 18 *page 7*

1. 0.103	**2.** 6.25	**3.** 12.1	**4.** 3.4	**5.** 620
6. 8.26	**7.** 41.42	**8.** 1.605	**9.** 0.009	**10.** 0.34
11. 26 000	**12.** 0.009 624	**13.** 47.8	**14.** 0.3113	**15.** 65.14
16. 5.68	**17.** 3.402	**18.** 9.8	**19.** 8.47	**20.** 177.5
21. 0.8925	**22.** 40 000	**23.** 2.331	**24.** 25.8	**25.** 0.0082
26. 6.548	**27.** 131.8	**28.** 19.98	**29.** 63.49	**30.** 520

Exercise 19 *page 7*

1. 75%	**2.** 40%	**3.** 50%	**4.** 80%	**5.** 25%
6. $62\frac{1}{2}$%	**7.** 90%	**8.** 85%	**9.** 25%	**10.** $87\frac{1}{2}$%
11. 68%	**12.** 35%	**13.** 7%	**14.** $33\frac{1}{3}$%	**15.** $66\frac{2}{3}$%
16. $12\frac{1}{2}$%	**17.** 98%	**18.** 25%	**19.** 61%	**20.** 25%
21. 32%	**22.** $67\frac{1}{2}$%	**23.** $33\frac{1}{3}$%	**24.** $23\frac{1}{2}$%	**25.** 68%
26. 90%	**27.** 65%	**28.** 40%	**29.** $22\frac{1}{2}$%	**30.** 34%
31. 98%	**32.** 25%	**33.** $47\frac{1}{2}$%	**34.** $33\frac{1}{3}$%	**35.** 6.7%

Exercise 20 *page 7*

1. (a) 44% (b) 65% **2.** 21% **3.** (a) 50% (b) 40% (c) 10%
4. (a) 25 (b) 44% (c) 56% **5.** Susan 70%, Jane 54%, Jackie 52%
6. 54% **7.** (a) 48% (b) 76% **8.** 4%
9. (a) $37\frac{1}{2}$% (b) $12\frac{1}{2}$% (c) 0% (d) $37\frac{1}{2}$% **10.** 40%

Exercise 21 *page 8*

1. £12	**2.** £8	**3.** £10	**4.** £3	**5.** £2.40
6. £24	**7.** £45	**8.** £72	**9.** £244	**10.** £9.60
11. $42	**12.** $88	**13.** 8 kg	**14.** 12 kg	**15.** 272 g
16. 45 m	**17.** 40 km	**18.** $710	**19.** 4.94 kg	**20.** 60 g
21. £1340	**22.** 245 kg	**23.** £96.80	**24.** £95.20	**25.** £22.10
26. £70.08	**27.** £66	**28.** £112.50	**29.** £112	**30.** £169.65

Exercise 22 *page 8*

1. £0.28	**2.** £1.16	**3.** £1.22	**4.** £2.90	**5.** £3.57
6. £0.45	**7.** £0.93	**8.** £37.03	**9.** £16.97	**10.** £0.38
11. £0.79	**12.** £1.60	**13.** £13.40	**14.** £50	**15.** £2.94
16. £11.06	**17.** £1.23	**18.** £4.40	**19.** £11.25	**20.** £22.71
21. £0.12	**22.** £0.03	**23.** £1.11	**24.** £93.50	**25.** £95.94
26. £426.87	**27.** £0.04	**28.** £0.13	**29.** £6.80	**30.** £0.88

Exercise 23 *page 9*

1. £13.20	**2.** £42	**3.** £69	**4.** £87.36	**5.** £84
6. £46	**7.** £45	**8.** £60.80	**9.** £7.56	**10.** £8.91
11. £63	**12.** £736	**13.** £77.55	**14.** £104	**15.** £1960
16. £792	**17.** £132	**18.** £45.75	**19.** £110.30	**20.** £42
21. £12.03	**22.** £9.49	**23.** £7.35	**24.** £7.01	**25.** £12.34
26. £16.92	**27.** £31.87	**28.** £9.02	**29.** £8.88	**30.** £14.14

Exercise 24 *page 9*

1. £35.20 **2.** £5724 **3.** £171.50 **4.** £88.35 **5.** 2.828 kg
6. £58.50 **7.** 24 **8.** 59 400 **9.** £9.52 **10.** 3.348 kg
11. 13.054 kg **12.** £2762.50
13. (b) £43.70 (c) £48.30 (d) £243.80 (e) £9.43
14. (a) £25.20 (b) £33.25 (c) £46.75 (d) £156 (e) £7.98

Exercise 25 *page 10*

1. £17.14 **2.** £39.79 **3.** £76.30 **4.** £181.40
5. (a) £28 (b) £21 **6.** (a) £51 (b) £40.80 **7.** £396
8. (a) £480 (b) (i) £16.20 (ii) £1053

Exercise 26 *page 10*

1. (a) £40 (b) £36 (c) £80
2. £28, £15.75, 10%, £37.20, 20%
3. (a) £5000 (b) £1000 (c) £4000, £3200, £2560
4. (a) £45 (b) £495 (c) £41.25
5. 40%, 35%, 10%, 5%
6. (a) 40p (b) £25 (c) £5
7. 4200 kg
8. (a) £5000 (b) 16.7%

Exercise 27 *page 11*

1. £10, £20
2. £45, £15
3. £12, £8
4. £7, £35
5. 330 g, 550 g
6. \$480, \$600
7. 36, 90
8. £10, £20, £30
9. £100, £150, £150
10. £12, £36, £48
11. \$1200, \$1800, \$2400
12. 52, 78, 130
13. 160 g, 320 g, 400 g
14. £70
15. £50
16. £137.50
17. 40 g
18. 3250
19. 45p
20. £24.40

Exercise 28 *page 12*

1. \$9, \$18, \$13.50, \$4.50
2. £66, £44, £110, £110
3. 600 kg, 1500 kg, 300 kg, 1800 kg
4. 224 g
5. £9.10
6. £16
7. £166.50
8. £64, £32
9. £30, £90
10. £48, £24, £12
11. £360, £180, £60
12. £72, £144, £36
13. A £50, B £200, C £100
14. A £96, B £24, C £48
15. A £6, B £36, C £12

Exercise 29 *page 12*

1. 8
2. 5
3. 9
4. £100
5. £42
6. 30 g zinc, 40 g tin
7. 24
8. 36
9. 16 white, 8 green
10. 16 horses, 128 cows

Exercise 30 *page 13*

1. £24
2. £1.08
3. £3.15
4. £5.88
5. £1.26, £4.20
6. £2.20, £22
7. £97.50
8. 2750 g
9. 1400
10. 4.5 litres
11. £3.45
12. £1.61
13. £3.99
14. 125 s
15. 90 min

Exercise 31 *page 13*

1. 10
2. 10
3. 12
4. 20, 35
5. 100
6. 160
7. 450
8. 267, 11
9. £12.75, 20
10. £2.24, £4.20
11. £1.60, £3.60
12. 35 litres
13. 200 litres
14. 70 gallons

Exercise 32 *page 14*

1. 18 h
2. 3 h
3. 6 days
4. 6 h
5. 8 days, $\frac{1}{2}$ day
6. 40 h
7. 24 days
8. 4 days
9. 24
10. 8
11. 12, 3, 4, $1\frac{1}{2}$
12. 80, 24, 1000, $1\frac{1}{2}$
13. 1500, 3000, 1, 120
14. 30
15. 120 min., 40 min.
16. 30 min., 360 min.

UNIT 2

Exercise 1 *page 15*

1. 7.24	**2.** 4.1	**3.** 162.5	**4.** 23.1	**5.** 800
6. 170	**7.** 6000	**8.** 60	**9.** 200	**10.** 1300
11. 110	**12.** 4	**13.** 3200	**14.** 1560	**15.** 7000
16. 700	**17.** 0.7	**18.** 0.2	**19.** 74	**20.** 6230
21. 8.24	**22.** 7.96	**23.** 0.973	**24.** 1.112	**25.** 2.7
26. 3.73	**27.** 0.242	**28.** 0.082	**29.** 0.06	**30.** 0.11
31. 0.004	**32.** 0.002	**33.** 0.0023	**34.** 0.01	**35.** 0.182
36. 0.079	**37.** 0.02	**38.** 0.0071	**39.** 0.013	**40.** 0.084
41. 230	**42.** 0.82	**43.** 410	**44.** 1700	**45.** 1.7
46. 0.06	**47.** 8970	**48.** 1100	**49.** 0.08	**50.** 6
51. 2000	**52.** 18 000			

Exercise 2 *page 16*

1. 127 cm	**2.** 65 cm	**3.** 300 cm	**4.** 7 cm	**5.** 1100 cm
6. 810 cm	**7.** 234 cm	**8.** 0.2 cm	**9.** 0.17 m	**10.** 0.24 m
11. 2.4 m	**12.** 0.11 m	**13.** 0.02 m	**14.** 0.182 m	**15.** 0.031 m
16. 50 m	**17.** 630 cm	**18.** 24 cm	**19.** 0.67 m	**20.** 0.09 m
21. 1.7 cm	**22.** 2.5 cm	**23.** 25 cm	**24.** 1.2 cm	**25.** 20 mm
26. 150 mm	**27.** 28 mm	**28.** 96 mm	**29.** 2000 m	**30.** 1500 m
31. 1240 m	**32.** 324 m	**33.** 76 m	**34.** 18 000 m	**35.** 7100 m
36. 70 m	**37.** 0.4 km	**38.** 0.875 km	**39.** 2.5 cm	**40.** 0.065 km
41. 0.45 kg	**42.** 0.2 kg	**43.** 1.4 kg	**44.** 2.65 kg	**45.** 0.04 kg
46. 0.055 kg	**47.** 0.007 kg	**48.** 7 kg	**49.** 2200 g	**50.** 650 g
51. 2000 kg	**52.** 3200 kg	**53.** 0.5 l	**54.** 4 m^3	**55.** 6 m^3
56. 8 l	**57.** 0.455 l	**58.** 2450 ml	**59.** 2800 kg	**60.** 0.067 kg

Exercise 3 *page 16*

1. 0.32 cm	**2.** 1.5 cm	**3.** 0.234 kg	**4.** 0.072 km	**5.** 750 cm
6. 41 g	**7.** 0.26 l	**8.** 7.1 mm	**9.** 0.09 m	**10.** 100 000 m
11. 0.027 kg	**12.** 0.7 cm	**13.** 18 000 g	**14.** 0.8 l	**15.** 200 m
16. 1110 cm	**17.** 0.4 t	**18.** 1 000 000 g	**19.** 0.085 km	**20.** 0.03 cm
21. 0.08 m	**22.** 0.006 kg	**23.** 10 cm	**24.** 0.95 l	**25.** 7800 kg
26. 70 g	**27.** 0.2 m	**28.** 600 cm	**29.** 0.018 kg	**30.** 0.88 km
31. 0.07 km	**32.** 0.6 m	**33.** 30 mm	**34.** 710 m	**35.** 0.02 t
36. 0.05 m^3	**37.** 0.006 km	**38.** 0.017 kg	**39.** 25 000 cm	**40.** 0.0001 m

Exercise 4 *page 16*

1. 24.3 cm **2.** £2.52 **3.** 73 **4.** 23 **5.** 2576
6. £17.70 **7.** 0.6 kg **8.** (a) 34, 25 (b) 15, 7.5 (c) 12, 17 (d) 44, 32
9. £5 **10.** (a) What time do we finish. (b) Spurs are rubbish. (c) We are under attack.

Exercise 5 *page 17*

1. 582	**2.** £5.12	**3.** 130 years	**4.** £28.50	**5.** 14 55
6. 15 h 5 min	**7.** £10.35	**8.** £21.10	**9.** 3854	**10.** £704

Exercise 6 *page 17*

1. 21	**2.** 50 kg	**3.** 91p	**4.** $1\frac{1}{2}$	**5.** $\frac{2}{3}$
6. 6p	**7.** 16p	**8.** 24	**9.** 24	**10.** Both same (!)

Exercise 7 *page 18*

1. £3.26 **2.** £1.70 **3.** 8 **4.** 215 **5.** 100 m
6. £184.50 **7.** £839.50 **8.** £2
9. (a) $99 + \frac{9}{9}$ (b) $6 + \frac{6}{6}$ (c) $55 + 5$ (d) $55 + 5 + \frac{5}{5}$ (e) $\frac{7+7}{7+7}$ (f) $\frac{88}{8}$
10. From left to right: (a) 7, 3 (b) 4, 3 (c) 7, 8, 6 (d) 3, 7, 0 (e) 3, 6 (f) 6, 8, 0

Exercise 8 *page 18*

1. £62 **2.** £570 **3.** 9 h 15 min **4.** 10. 26 m^2, 1.74 m^2 **5.** 86 400
6. (a) 14, 17 (b) 17, 22 (c) 2, −3 (d) 63, 127 **7.** £37.80 **8.** £1 = F12.1
9. (a) 39, 38, 38, 36, 35, 31, 30, 28 (b) 27, 27, 26, 26, 24, 22, 20, 20 **10.** £5.85

Exercise 9 *page 19*

1. 5p **2.** 0.012, 0.021, 0.03, 0.12, 0.21 **3.** 51.4° 4. Jars by 24p **5.** 4.5 litres
6. 2.05 m, 1.95 m **7.** (a) £66 (b) £720 (c) £2040 **8.** £24
9. 9, 8, 25, 1000, 32, 48 **10.** 6p, 30p, 21p

Exercise 10 *page 19*

1. 9 **2.** 5 m, 50 m, 6 km **3.** £2.50
4. (a) 3, 4 (b) 7, 6 (c) 8, 4 (d) 24, 2
5. (b) 0.25 (c) $\frac{3}{10}$ (d) 0.125 (e) $\frac{1}{20}$ (f) 0.001
6. (a) £800 (b) 8% **7.** 10 h 30 min
8. (a) 0.54 (b) 40 (c) 0.004 (d) 2.2 (e) £9 (f) £40
9. 260 million **10.** (a) 1050 g (b) 3

Exercise 11 *page 20*

1. 22 **2.** 19.35 **3.** 120° **4.** £22.40
5. 2333, 3102, 3120, 3210, 3211, 3301
6. (a) 270 (b) 4100 (c) 0.0084 (d) 5.23
7. 18 000 **8.** 18 **9.** 1296, 322
10. (a) yes (b) no (c) yes (d) yes (e) yes (f) yes (g) yes (h) no

Exercise 12 *page 21*

1. (a) £136 (b) £30.60 (c) £142.05 **2.** 25 cm^2
3. (a) £2.15 (b) £2.45 (c) £2.93 **4.** 44 cm
5. (a) £523 (b) £624 (c) £366.10 **6.** 16 **8.** 64 mph
9. (a) 69 (l) 65 **10.** 4p

Exercise 13 *page 22*

1. (a) £64 (b) £124 (c) 100 km
2. (a) £106, £161, £126, £119 (b) £47 (c) £665 (d) £380
4. (a) £16.50 (b) £20 **5.** (a) 59 040 (b) 21 608 640 (c) £4 321 728

Exercise 14 *page 23*

1. 24 **2.** 9 **3.** 32 **4.** 16 **5.** 42 **6.** 60
7. 17 600 **8.** 80 **9.** 4480 **10.** 36 **11.** 140 **12.** 224
13. 18 **14.** 8 **15.** 440 **16.** 360 **17.** 4 **18.** 2
19. 56 **20.** 16 **21.** 72 **22.** 3520 **23.** 5 **24.** 2
25. 2 **26.** 48 **27.** 108 **28.** 18 **29.** 880 **30.** 4
31. 54 **32.** 54 **33.** 72 **34.** 102 **35.** 152 **36.** 63
37. 73 **38.** 58

Exercise 15 *page 23*

1. 25.4 **2.** 45.5 **3.** 45.4 **4.** 56.8 **5.** 3.22 **6.** 0.908
7. 16.1 **8.** 10.16 **9.** 2.27 **10.** 0.284 **11.** 6.21 **12.** 22
13. 6.6 **14.** 62.1 **15.** 88 **16.** 4.4 **17.** 1.242 **18.** 1.1
19. 44 **20.** 12.42 **21.** 30.48 **22.** 2.84 **23.** 0.66 **24.** 7.62
25. 1.816

Exercise 16 *page 24*

1. F120 **2.** DM80 **3.** DR450 **4.** Ptas20 000 **5.** $1400
6. DR1200 **7.** F84 **8.** $140 **9.** DM64 **10.** DM2000
11. F6 **12.** Ptas100 **13.** $0.70 **14.** DR150 000 **15.** Ptas200 000
16. DM1 **17.** F3 **18.** $70 **19.** DR30 000 **20.** Ptas20
21. $700 **22.** F7200 **23.** DM260 **24.** DR4500 **25.** F18
26. $1.40 **27.** DR225 **28.** Ptas500 **29.** Ptas2200 **30.** $17.50

Exercise 17 *page 24*

1. £3 **2.** £10 **3.** £2 **4.** £5 **5.** £4
6. £10 **7.** £100 **8.** £20 **9.** £25 **10.** £10
11. £8 **12.** £50 **13.** £1.50 **14.** £4.50 **15.** £0.53
16. £5.42 **17.** £42.86 **18.** £20.50 **19.** £8.75 **20.** £32.50
21. £15.50 **22.** £642.86 **23.** £0.47 **24.** £20 **25.** £50
26. £0.63 **27.** £16.07 **28.** £4.83 **29.** £22.10 **30.** £6.05
31. £42.50 **32.** £50.71 **33.** £4.27 **34.** £1.27 **35.** £542.86
36. £79.25 **37.** £4750 **38.** £3000 **39.** £1875 **40.** £182.14

Exercise 18 *page 24*

1. F240 **2.** DM60 **3.** £10 **4.** £3 **5.** Ptas1000
6. £9 **7.** £15 **8.** $428.57 **9.** £2.25 **10.** £21
11. £3.93 **12.** £3333.33 **13.** DR48 000 **14.** £0.93 **15.** Germany £25
16. France £240 **17.** U.S.A. £0.50 **18.** (a) £100 (b) F1200 (c) F1200

Exercise 19 *page 25*

1. 200 m **2.** 500 m **3.** (a) 2 km (b) 3 km (c) 0.8 km
4. (a) 5 km (b) 3 km (c) 6 km
5. (b) 200 m (c) 1 km (d) 0.6 km (e) 1.5 km (f) 2.5 km (g) 2.2 km
(h) 2 km (i) 1.55 km (j) 270 m
6. 1.08 km **7.** 63 m **8.** 24 km **9.** 19.52 km **10.** 5.888 km **11.** 120 m
12. 5.6 m **13.** 5 m **14.** 90 m **15.** 10.5 m

Exercise 20 *page 26*

1. 150 cm **2.** 125 cm **3.** 28 cm **4.** 5.9 cm
5. (a) 60 cm (b) 84 cm (c) 56 cm (d) 140 cm (e) 100 cm (f) 6 cm
(g) 50 cm (h) 220 cm (i) 0.6 cm **6.** 13 cm **7.** 2.5 cm **8.** 1.5 cm

Exercise 21 *page 26*

1. 4.4 km **2.** 250 cm
3. (a) 0.5 km (b) 120 cm (c) 1.68 km (d) 16 cm (e) 6.4 km (f) 0.2 cm
(g) 3 m (h) 1.54 km (i) 1: 10 000 (j) 1: 20 000 (k) 1: 100 000 (l) 1: 20 000
(m) 1: 50 000
4. 1: 10 000 **5.** 1: 20 000 **6.** 1: 50 000 **7.** 7.3 m, 3.5 m, 2.5 m

UNIT 3

Exercise 1 *page 27*

1. 3.18	**2.** 14.8	**3.** 8.05	**4.** 2.63	**5.** 51.3
6. 0.557	**7.** 0.832	**8.** 7.37	**9.** 0.0761	**10.** 18.3
11. 427	**12.** 315	**13.** 6.01	**14.** 11.4	**15.** 2.09
16. 0.007 42	**17.** 318	**18.** 2420	**19.** 3560	**20.** 38 700
21. 5.7	**22.** 18	**23.** 0.77	**24.** 0.52	**25.** 8.3
26. 7.2	**27.** 12	**28.** 25	**29.** 19	**30.** 0.0083
31. 0.071	**32.** 18	**33.** 31	**34.** 61	**35.** 19 000
36. 34 000	**37.** 890	**38.** 72 000	**39.** 40 000	**40.** 160
41. 28.67	**42.** 3.041	**43.** 2.995	**44.** 316.3	**45.** 8.046
46. 0.007 165	**47.** 0.031 11	**48.** 84 210	**49.** 65 530	**50.** 124 900
51. 5.678	**52.** 193.2	**53.** 568.8	**54.** 2002	**55.** 0.038 11
56. 76.06	**57.** 80.05	**58.** 6.067	**59.** 77 780	**60.** 400 300

Exercise 2 *page 28*

1. 8.49	**2.** 6.04	**3.** 1.04	**4.** 12.14	**5.** 11.62
6. 6.05	**7.** 0.56	**8.** 18.08	**9.** 2.05	**10.** 8.95
11. 13.62	**12.** 216.84	**13.** 0.07	**14.** 0.07	**15.** 7.82
16. 3.13	**17.** 4.11	**18.** 24.52	**19.** 206.13	**20.** 8.09
21. 8.6	**22.** 12.6	**23.** 9.0	**24.** 2.6	**25.** 8.6
26. 5.7	**27.** 0.7	**28.** 0.1	**29.** 8.8	**30.** 0.7
31. 207.2	**32.** 10.7	**33.** 0.1	**34.** 8.0	**35.** 4.3
36. 88.7	**37.** 217.1	**38.** 4.0	**39.** 0.9	**40.** 5.0
41. 8.05	**42.** 17.6	**43.** 6.8	**44.** 9.09	**45.** 0.071
46. 0.0333	**47.** 19.6	**48.** 8.076	**49.** 8.09	**50.** 4.08
51. 3.336	**52.** 8.9	**53.** 8.05	**54.** 0.08	**55.** 0.0715
56. 2.3	**57.** 8.072	**58.** 1.350	**59.** 9.9	**60.** 16.0

61. (a) 5.8 cm by 3.6 cm, 5.1 cm by 3.6 cm (b) 20.9 cm^2, 18.4 cm^2

Exercise 3 *page 29*

1. C	**2.** A	**3.** B	**4.** B	**5.** C	**6.** A	**7.** B
8. B	**9.** A	**10.** C	**11.** C	**12.** A	**13.** B	**14.** A
15. C	**16.** B	**17.** C	**18.** A	**19.** B	**20.** B	**21.** C
22. A	**23.** B	**24.** C	**25.** A	**26.** B	**27.** C	**28.** B
29. C	**30.** B					

Exercise 4 *page 30*

1. B	**2.** A	**3.** C	**4.** A	**5.** B	**6.** C	**7.** A
8. B	**9.** A	**10.** C	**11.** B	**12.** A	**13.** C	**14.** A
15. B	**16.** A	**17.** B	**18.** C	**19.** B	**20.** B	**21.** A
22. C	**23.** C	**24.** B	**25.** C	**26.** A	**27.** B	**28.** B
29. C	**30.** B					

Exercise 5 *page 30*

1. 20	**2.** 13	**3.** 16	**4.** 22	**5.** 4	**6.** 13	**7.** 12
8. 10	**9.** 5	**10.** 15	**11.** 20	**12.** 6	**13.** 5	**14.** 47
15. 30	**16.** 22	**17.** 18	**18.** 15	**19.** 1	**20.** 23	**21.** 19
22. 4	**23.** 3	**24.** 0	**25.** 35	**26.** 60	**27.** 16	**28.** 6
29. 13	**30.** 14	**31.** 23	**32.** 71	**33.** 20	**34.** 36	**35.** 9
36. 8	**37.** 32	**38.** 30	**39.** 4	**40.** 0	**41.** 37	**42.** 46

43. 0	**44.** 35	**45.** 74	**46.** 1	**47.** 5	**48.** 7	**49.** 6
50. 20	**51.** 7	**52.** 95	**53.** 14	**54.** 7	**55.** 20	**56.** 89
57. 50	**58.** 8	**59.** 5	**60.** 366			

Exercise 6 *page 31*

1. 13	**2.** 15	**3.** 23	**4.** 27	**5.** 15	**6.** 28	**7.** 97
8. 17	**9.** 7	**10.** 5	**11.** 22	**12.** 16	**13.** 20	**14.** 5
15. 13	**16.** 58	**17.** 29	**18.** 80	**19.** 9	**20.** 10	**21.** 20
22. 34	**23.** 18	**24.** 5	**25.** 44	**26.** 28	**27.** 13	**28.** 32
29. 5	**30.** 21	**31.** 17	**32.** 36	**33.** 39	**34.** 80	**35.** 51
36. 1	**37.** 5	**38.** 54	**39.** 14	**40.** 78	**41.** 51	**42.** 14
43. 97	**44.** 4	**45.** 24	**46.** 41	**47.** 23	**48.** 17	**49.** 23
50. 11	**51.** 5	**52.** 6	**53.** 4	**54.** 4	**55.** 6	**56.** 5
57. 1	**58.** 47	**59.** 6	**60.** 3	**61.** 16	**62.** 12	**63.** 52
64. 15	**65.** 87	**66.** 17	**67.** 23	**68.** 8	**69.** 2	**70.** 26

Exercise 7 *page 32*

1. 1851	**2.** 6.889	**3.** 1.214	**4.** 0.4189	**5.** 7.889
6. 19.35	**7.** 0.049 47	**8.** 221.5	**9.** 24.37	**10.** 6.619
11. 3.306	**12.** 2.303	**13.** 41.73	**14.** 8.163	**15.** 0.1090
16. 0.5001	**17.** 20.63	**18.** 10.09	**19.** 6.191	**20.** 10.27
21. 8.627	**22.** 22.02	**23.** 1.093	**24.** 44.72	**25.** 45.66
26. 52.86	**27.** 22.51	**28.** 5.479	**29.** 5.272	**30.** 0.2116
31. 4.605	**32.** 1.153			

Exercise 8 *page 32*

1. 14.52	**2.** 1.666	**3.** 1.858	**4.** 0.8264	**5.** 2.717
6. 4.840	**7.** 10.87	**8.** 7.425	**9.** 13.49	**10.** 0.7392
11. 1135	**12.** 13.33	**13.** 5.836	**14.** 86.39	**15.** 10.23
16. 5540	**17.** 14.76	**18.** 8.502	**19.** 57.19	**20.** 19.90
21. 6.578	**22.** 9.907	**23.** 0.082 80	**24.** 1855	**25.** 2.367
26. 1.416	**27.** 7.261	**28.** 3.151	**29.** 149.9	**30.** 74 020
31. 8.482	**32.** 75.21	**33.** 1.226	**34.** 6767	**35.** 5.964
36. 15.45	**37.** 25.42	**38.** 2.724	**39.** 4.366	**40.** 0.2194

Exercise 9 *page 33*

1. 5.6×10^5	**2.** 2.44×10^8	**3.** 7.2×10^4	**4.** 1.31×10^5
5. 8.5×10^7	**6.** 9×10^8	**7.** 7.34×10^{10}	**8.** 8.42×10^9
9. 6.6×10^4	**10.** 2×10^{12}	**11.** 1×10^8	**12.** 2×10^9
13. 4.4×10^2	**14.** 6×10^4	**15.** 1.6×10^5	**16.** 4.85×10^9
17. 1.8472×10^4	**18.** $6.358\ 11 \times 10^5$	**19.** $3.333\ 333 \times 10^6$	**20.** $8.211\ 111 \times 10^6$
21. 4×10^{-6}	**22.** 5.2×10^{-6}	**23.** 7.411×10^{-6}	**24.** 4.32×10^{-3}
25. 7.5×10^{-3}	**26.** 8.239×10^{-3}	**27.** 7×10^{-9}	**28.** 1.5×10^{-8}
29. 2×10^{-10}	**30.** 4.6×10^{-3}	**31.** 7.4×10^{-3}	**32.** 6.31×10^{-3}
33. 8.4×10^4	**34.** 1.2×10^7	**35.** 2×10^{-6}	**36.** 4.53×10^{-8}
37. 1.6×10^{10}	**38.** 7.24×10^{-1}	**39.** $2.844\ 44 \times 10^5$	**40.** 2.22×10^{-6}
41. 3.2×10^6	**42.** 6×10^9	**43.** 1.82×10^6	**44.** 4×10^{-7}
45. 7×10^{-7}	**46.** 7×10^{-8}	**47.** 6.66×10^{10}	**48.** 7.1×10^{11}
49. 3.2×10^{-8}	**50.** 1.62×10^{-6}		

Exercise 10 *page 33*

1. 360 000	**2.** 72 200 000	**3.** 82 000	**4.** 6 000 000
5. 1 100 000 000	**6.** 324 000	**7.** 100 000 000 000	**8.** 6 360 000

9. 8 020 000 000 10. 32 000 11. 670 12. 30 300
13. 89 900 000 14. 10 200 000 000 15. 6 200 000 16. 0.000 26
17. 0.081 18. 0.000 01 19. 0.000 003 20. 0.000 000 44
21. 0.008 22. 0.000 000 12 23. 0.000 000 095 24. 0.000 000 000 046
25. 88 000 26. 2750 27. 0.001 01 28. 0.000 009 6
29. 0.000 07 30. 320

Exercise 11 *page 33*

1. 10^7 2. 10^9 3. 10^{10} 4. 10^5 5. 10^6 6. 10^2 7. 10^{-7}
8. 10^{-2} 9. 10^{-8} 10. 10^{-5} 11. 10^{-8} 12. 10^2 13. 10^4 14. 10^5
15. 10^8 16. 10^{-4} 17. 10^{-13} 18. 10^6 19. 10^8 20. 10^{11} 21. 10^{-8}
22. 10^7 23. 10^{-3} 24. 10^8

Exercise 12 *page 33*

1. 6×10^9 2. 3×10^{13} 3. 6.6×10^{17} 4. 8.8×10^{13} 5. 8×10^4
6. 8.5×10^9 7. 6.9×10^{-6} 8. 7×10^5 9. 6.28×10^{16} 10. 7.2×10^{-4}
11. 4.4×10^6 12. 4.5×10^3 13. 1.5×10^6 14. 8×10^3 15. 3×10^{-5}
16. 2×10^{-6} 17. 3.6×10^{-6} 18. 1.7×10^6 19. 3×10^9 20. 3.1×10^7

THINK ABOUT IT 1

Exercise A *page 35*

1. 23 and 2 over 2. 42 3. 2675 4. £9.20 5. 6
6. 6, 4 7. 6 km 8. 740 9. $5\frac{1}{2}$ h 10. 3

Exercise B *page 36*

1. 273 377 2. 120°, 30° 3. 845 4. £58.05 5. 61 6. 1000, 96
7. £274 8. 4400, £2.50 9. $x = 203.13$, $y = 777.21$, $z = 585.71$ 10. £26.25

Exercise C *page 38*

3. Man. Utd 19 points
Liverpool 19 points
Everton 18 points
Arsenal 10 points
Notts Forest 9 points
West Ham 7 points

4. £115 625 5. £113 808 6. £479 770 7. £11 034

Exercise D *page 41*

1. 2.3 kg 2. (a) 2 m (b) 230 cm (c) 7200 m (d) 80 cm (e) 0.028 km (f) 2.5 cm
3. £1320 5. 50, $\frac{3}{4}$ 6. £19 7. £53 250 8. £1860 9. 12
10. (a) 100 cm^2 (b) 3 cm (c) 30 cm^2

Project 5 *page 42*

triangle, fraction, decimal, degree, ruler, seven, total, area, volume, two, add, one, ten, centimetre, pencil, dozen, foot, inch, gram, even.

Exercise E *page 43*

1. 480 g **2.** (c) 5 cm^2 **3.** (a) 70 m (b) 700 m (c) 42 km
4. £17, 8.4 kg **5.** 50p **6.** 5% of £80 = £4
7. (a) 5 (b) 30 (c) 12 (d) 100 (e) 9 (f) 0.1
8. (a) $\frac{1}{5}$ (b) $\frac{3}{4}$ (c) 50% (d) $\frac{9}{10}$ (e) 25% (f) $\frac{1}{10}$
9. 30, $\frac{1}{3}$ **10.** £8.75

Exercise F *page 45*

1. 0.03, 0.058, 0.07, 0.085, 0.11 **2.** (a) £270 (b) £4050 (c) £4.05 **3.** 13
4. (a) 17, 21 (b) 37, 46 (c) 3, $1\frac{1}{2}$ (d) 25, 36 **5.** 69 **6.** $7\frac{1}{2}$
7. (a) $\frac{3}{4}$ (b) $\frac{2}{3}$ (c) $\frac{5}{8}$ (d) $\frac{2}{5}$
8. 0.5, 50%; $\frac{1}{5}$, 20%; $\frac{1}{10}$, 0.1; 0.375, $37\frac{1}{2}$%; $\frac{9}{10}$, 0.9
9. £3750, £33 750 **10.** (a) 260 km (b) 26 litres (c) £11.05

Exercise G *page 46*

1. 15, 17 **2.** 10, 7 **3.** 36, 43 **4.** 17, 23 **5.** 41, 36
6. 16, 32 **7.** 29, 20 **8.** 6, 3 **9.** 120, 720 **10.** 10, 13
11. 13, 12 **12.** 39, 65 **13.** 25, 36 **14.** 18, $4\frac{1}{2}$ **15.** $\frac{1}{4}$, $\frac{1}{16}$
16. 7, 9 **17.** 240, 1440 **18.** 30, 15 **19.** 8, 216 **20.** 82, 100

21. (a) $6 \times 7 = 6 + 6^2$
$7 \times 8 = 7 + 7^2$
(b) $10 \times 11 = 10 + 10^2$
$30 \times 31 = 30 + 30^2$

22. (a) $7^2 = 5^2 + 4 \times 5 + 4$
$8^2 = 6^2 + 4 \times 6 + 4$
(b) $12^2 = 10^2 + 4 \times 10 + 4$
$22^2 = 20^2 + 4 \times 20 + 4$

23. (a) $5^2 = 1 + 3 + 5 + 7 + 9$
$6^2 = 1 + 3 + 5 + 7 + 9 + 11$
(b) $10^2 = 1 + 3 + 5 + \ldots + 19$
$15^2 = 1 + 3 + 5 + \ldots + 29$

UNIT 4

Exercise 1 *page 50*

1. 24 cm^2 **2.** 14 cm^2 **3.** 144 cm^2 **4.** 15 cm^2 **5.** 33 cm^2 **6.** 75 mm^2 **7.** 25 m^2
8. 12 cm^2 **9.** 153 cm^2 **10.** 20 m^2 **11.** 42 cm^2 **12.** $7\frac{1}{2}$ cm^2 **13.** 20 km^2 **14.** 24 mm^2

Exercise 2 *page 51*

1. 36 cm^2 **2.** 77 m^2 **3.** 96 cm^2 **4.** 36 m^2 **5.** 54 m^2 **6.** 25 m^2 **7.** 28 m^2
8. 39 cm^2 **9.** 20 cm^2 **10.** 75 cm^2 **11.** 36 mm^2 **12.** 48 cm^2

Exercise 3 *page 51*

1. 36 cm^2 **2.** 29 cm^2 **3.** 51 cm^2 **4.** 36 cm^2 **5.** 24 cm^2 **6.** 24 cm^2 **7.** 57 cm^2
8. 48 cm^2 **9.** 36 cm^2 **10.** 41 cm^2

Exercise 4 *page 52*

1. (a) 14.6 m (b) 6 (c) £19.20 (d) 11.22 m^2
2. A. (a) 13.2 m (b) 6 (c) £19.20 (d) 9.32 m^2
B. (a) 15.6 m (b) 8 (c) £25.60 (d) 11.17 m^2
C. (a) 9.4 m (b) 4 (c) £12.80 (d) 3.76 m^2
D. (a) 19.4 m (b) 9 (c) £28.80 (d) 13 m^2

Exercise 5 *page 53*

1. All in square units (b) 10, 6, 3 (c) 36 (d) 17 **2.** (b) 5, 14, 6 (c) 42 (d) 17
3. $13\frac{1}{2}$ **4.** $14\frac{1}{2}$ **5.** $21\frac{1}{2}$ **6.** 15 **7.** $17\frac{1}{2}$ **8.** 24 **9.** 22
10. 21 **11.** 12 **12.** 14 **13.** 28 **14.** 29

Exercise 6 *page 54*

1. 34.6 cm **2.** 25.1 cm **3.** 37.7 cm **4.** 15.7 cm **5.** 28.3 cm **6.** 53.4 m
7. 44.6 m **8.** 72.3 m **9.** 52.2 m **10.** 78.5 m **11.** 56.5 km **12.** 47.1 cm
13. 3.27 m **14.** 2.98 m **15.** 19.5 m **16.** 25.8 km **17.** 5.28 mm **18.** 11.7 cm
19. 57.2 m **20.** 19.5 mm **21.** 15.1 miles **22.** 26.1 feet **23.** 24.5 km **24.** 0.289 m
25. 8.98 cm

Exercise 7 *page 55*

1. 23.1 cm **2.** 38.6 cm **3.** 20.6 m **4.** 8.23 cm **5.** 129 m **6.** 56.6 cm
7. 28.6 cm **8.** 39.4 m **9.** 53.7 m **10.** 28.1 m **11.** 24.8 cm **12.** 46.3 m
13. 28.8 cm **14.** 51.7 m

Exercise 8 *page 57*

1. 95.0 cm^2 **2.** 78.5 cm^2 **3.** 28.3 m^2 **4.** 38.5 m^2 **5.** 113 cm^2 **6.** 201 cm^2
7. 19.6 m^2 **8.** 380 cm^2 **9.** 346 m^2 **10.** 314 cm^2 **11.** 18.1 km^2 **12.** 5.31 m^2
13. 296 cm^2 **14.** 284 km^2 **15.** 52.8 cm^2 **16.** 0.126 m^2 **17.** 106 m^2 **18.** 10.2 cm^2
19. 2.27 m^2 **20.** 11.9 km^2

Exercise 9 *page 58*

1. 25.1 cm^2 **2.** 14.1 cm^2 **3.** 56.5 m^2 **4.** 0.393 m^2 **5.** 127 m^2 **6.** 6.28 cm^2
7. 19.6 cm^2 **8.** 95.0 m^2 **9.** 0.385 m^2 **10.** 157 m^2 **11.** 88.4 cm^2

Exercise 10 *page 59*

1. 18.3 cm^2 **2.** 19.9 cm^2 **3.** 43.4 cm^2 **4.** 37.7 cm^2 **5.** 28.3 cm^2
6. 74.6 cm^2 **7.** 3.43 cm^2 **8.** 17.4 cm^2
9. (a) 12.5 cm^2 (b) 50 cm^2 (c) 78.5 cm^2 (d) 28.5 cm^2
10. (a) 4.5 (b) 18 (c) 28.3 (d) 10.3

Exercise 11 *page 60*

1. 36 cm^3 **2.** 40 cm^3 **3.** 50 cm^3 **4.** 84 m^3 **5.** 5000 cm^3
6. 0.1 cm^3 **7.** 93 cm^3 **8.** 0.84 m^3 **9.** $\frac{1}{2}$ cm **10.** $3\frac{1}{2}$ cm
11. $5\frac{1}{4}$ cm **12.** 0.2 cm **13.** 10 cm^3 **14.** 12 cm^3 **15.** 18 cm^3
16. 22 cm^3 **17.** 21 cm^3 **18.** 12 cm^3 **19.** 18 cm^3

Exercise 12 *page 62*

1. 150 cm^3 **2.** 60 m^3 **3.** 480 cm^3 **4.** 60 m^3 **5.** 300 cm^3
6. 56 m^3 **7.** 340 cm^3 **8.** 145 cm^3 **9.** 448 cm^3 **10.** 108 cm^3

Exercise 13 *page 63*

1. 62.8 cm^3 **2.** 113 cm^3 **3.** 198 cm^3 **4.** 763 cm^3 **5.** 157 cm^3
6. 385 cm^3 **7.** 770 cm^3 **8.** 176 m^3 **9.** 228 m^3 **10.** 486 cm^3
11. 0.665 m^3 **12.** 17.6 cm^3 **13.** 5.99 m^3 **14.** 29.8 m^3 **15.** 118 ft^3
16. 99.5 ft^3 **17.** 876 in^3 **18.** 32.6 cm^3

Exercise 14 *page 64*

1. (a) 2400 cm^3 (b) 0.0024 m^3 2. (a) 200 m^2 (b) 2400 m^3
3. 770 cm^3 4. (a) 2.25 cm^2 (b) 0.451 cm^3 (c) 4510 cm^3
5. 25 6. (a) 76 cm^2 (b) 30 400 cm^3 (c) 237 kg (d) 33
7. 8 cm^3 8. (a) 7 (b) 35, 6 (c) 1200 cm^3, 14 000 cm^3 (d) 48p, £5.60, £50.40 (e) 140

UNIT 5

Exercise 1 *page 66*

1. −4°C 2. −6°C 3. 5°C
4. (a) 4°C (b) −3°C (c) 5°C (d) −8°C (e) 2°C (f) −3°C (g) −4°C
(h) 1°C (i) 2°C (j) −5°C (k) 12°C (l) −3°C (m) +4°C (n) +5°C
(o) −6°C (p) +6°C (q) +3°C (r) +8°C (s) 10°C (t) 3°C (u) 3°C
(v) 11°C (w) 3°C (x) −5°C (y) −6°C (z) −10°C

Exercise 2 *page 67*

1. T 2. T 3. T 4. F 5. F 6. T 7. F
8. T 9. F 10. T 11. F 12. F 13. T 14. T
15. T 16. T 17. F 18. F 19. T 20. F 21. <
22. > 23. > 24. > 25. < 26. < 27. > 28. >
29. < 30. > 31. > 32. > 33. < 34. > 35. <
36. < 37. > 38. > 39. > 40. >

41. −4, −3, −2 42. −5, −3, 7 43. −5, 0, 5 44. −8, −3, 1
45. −4, −2, −1 46. −4, −3, 2, 6 47. −2, −1, 1, 3 48. −3, −2, 0, 4
49. −5, −3, 1, 4 50. −7, −3, 2, 7 51. −4, −1, 0, 4 52. −6, −2, −1, 2
53. −4, −1, 5, 6 54. −8, −4, −1, 10 55. −8, −3, 0, 1, 7 56. −9, −6, −5, 0, 1
57. −3, −2, −1, 4, 5 58. −9, −2, −1, 6, 8 59. −4, −3, 1, 4, 5 60. −60, −20, −6, 2, 17
61. 2, 0 62. 3, 0 63. −2, −3 64. −4, −6
65. −6, −12 66. 0, 1 67. −2, 0 68. −2, −6
69. −15, −25 70. 2, 6 71. 2, 5 72. −6, −10
73. 12, 17 74. 2, −3 75. 10, 15 76. −6, −11
77. 0, 5 78. −7, −10 79. −18, −32 80. 1, 5

Exercise 3 *page 67*

1. 4 2. −3 3. 6 4. −4 5. 7 6. 5 7. −6
8. −6 9. −2 10. 1 11. 0 12. −13 13. −16 14. 1
15. 0 16. 3 17. −10 18. −5 19. −1 20. −2 21. −10
22. −4 23. −13 24. −20 25. −10 26. −9 27. −7 28. −5
29. 2 30. 1 31. −11 32. −14 33. −13 34. −5 35. −2
36. −12 37. −23 38. −23 39. −22 40. 3 41. −18 42. −11
43. −93 44. −90 45. 24 46. −46 47. −20 48. −18 49. −10
50. 0 51. −11 52. −11 53. −53 54. −99 55. 30 56. −20
57. −41 58. −1 59. −21 60. 2

Exercise 4 *page 68*

1. 1 2. 4 3. 4 4. 14 5. 10 6. 2 7. 1
8. −14 9. −8 10. −5 11. −4 12. −1 13. 7 14. 5
15. 2 16. −5 17. −20 18. −15 19. −2 20. 16 21. −11
22. 6 23. −8 24. −6 25. −2 26. −17 27. 0 28. −16
29. 6 30. 15 31. 16 32. −3 33. −8 34. −7 35. −10
36. 17 37. −12 38. 0 39. 2 40. 95

Exercise 5 *page 68*

1. −6 **2.** −4 **3.** −15 **4.** 9 **5.** −8 **6.** −15 **7.** −24
8. 6 **9.** 12 **10.** −18 **11.** −21 **12.** 25 **13.** −60 **14.** 21
15. 48 **16.** −16 **17.** −42 **18.** 20 **19.** −42 **20.** −66 **21.** −4
22. −3 **23.** 3 **24.** −5 **25.** 4 **26.** −4 **27.** −4 **28.** −1
29. −2 **30.** 4 **31.** −16 **32.** −2 **33.** −4 **34.** 5 **35.** −10
36. 11 **37.** 16 **38.** −2 **39.** −4 **40.** −5 **41.** 64 **42.** −27
43. −600 **44.** 40 **45.** 2 **46.** 36 **47.** −2 **48.** −8 **49.** 160
50. −2

Exercise 6 *page 68*

1. −4 **2.** −12 **3.** 1 **4.** −4 **5.** 16 **6.** −13 **7.** 2
8. −3 **9.** −6 **10.** 0 **11.** −12 **12.** 8 **13.** −4 **14.** −100
15. −12 **16.** −5 **17.** −2 **18.** −11 **19.** −20 **20.** 5 **21.** −6
22. −9 **23.** −1 **24.** 9 **25.** 6 **26.** 0 **27.** −5 **28.** −15
29. 12 **30.** −4

Exercise 7 *page 68*

1. −27 **2.** −13 **3.** −10 **4.** 1 **5.** −2 **6.** 0 **7.** 0
8. −400 **9.** 16 **10.** 42 **11.** −1 **12.** 33 **13.** 15 **14.** −60
15. −13 **16.** −11 **17.** 200 **18.** 52 **19.** −44 **20.** 0 **21.** −9
22. −49 **23.** −10 **24.** −38 **25.** −20 **26.** 501

Exercise 8 *page 69*

1.

add	−2	1	4	0	−3	6	−1	5
−3	−5	−2	1	−3	−6	3	−4	2
2	0	3	6	2	−1	8	1	7
4	2	5	8	4	1	10	3	9
−2	−4	−1	2	−2	−5	4	−3	3
−1	−3	0	3	−1	−4	5	−2	4
5	3	6	9	5	2	11	4	10
−4	−6	−3	0	−4	−7	2	−5	1
1	−1	2	5	1	−2	7	0	6

2.

multiply	−2	5	2	6	−4	0	−3	3
3	−6	15	6	18	−12	0	−9	9
−1	2	−5	−2	−6	4	0	3	−3
−2	4	−10	−4	−12	8	0	6	−6
4	−8	20	8	24	−16	0	−12	12
5	−10	25	10	30	−20	0	−15	15
−4	8	−20	−8	−24	16	0	12	−12
1	−2	5	2	6	−4	0	−3	3
−3	6	−15	−6	−18	12	0	9	−9

Exercise 9 *page 69*

1. $3x + 6$ **2.** $5x + 7$ **3.** $2x - 4$ **4.** $3x + 10$ **5.** $6y + 3$
6. $2y - 7$ **7.** $5m - 8$ **8.** $6x - y$ **9.** $3y + t$ **10.** $6p - a$
11. $3(x + 4)$ **12.** $5(x + 3)$ **13.** $6(y + 11)$ **14.** $9(m - 5)$ **15.** $5t - 7$
16. $4(x - 6)$ **17.** $\frac{x + 3}{4}$ **18.** $\frac{x - 7}{3}$ **19.** $\frac{y - 8}{5}$ **20.** $\frac{x + m}{7}$
21. $3(2x + 7)$ **22.** $\frac{3x - y}{5}$ **23.** $\frac{2(4a + 3)}{5}$ **24.** $\frac{3(m - 6)}{4}$ **25.** $\frac{4(t + x)}{5}$
26. $x^2 + 4$ **27.** $x^2 - 6$ **28.** $\frac{x^2 + 3}{4}$ **29.** $(n + 2)^2$ **30.** $(w - x)^2$

31. $(y + t)^2$ 32. $\frac{x^2 - 7}{3}$ 33. $3x^2 + 4$ 34. $2(y^2 + 4)$ 35. $\frac{a^3 - 3}{7}$
36. $\frac{z^3 + 6}{8}$ 37. $4(p^2 - x)$ 38. $(x - 9)^2 + 10$ 39. $\frac{(y + 7)^2}{x}$ 40. $\frac{(a - x)^3}{y}$

Exercise 10 *page 70*

1. $(x + y - 7)$ cm 2. $(l + t - 10)$ cm 3. $(l - 3)$ cm
4. $(15 - x)$ cm 5. £$(c + 195)$ 6. $(x + 25 - y)$ pence
7. $3n + 55$ 8. $(c + w + 2000)$ m 9. $(y + d + x)$ cm
10. $(2t + 3)$ km, $(3t + 3)$ km 11. £ $2x + 100$ 12. $(l + 200 - m)$ kg
13. $4(n + 2)$ 14. $6w$ kg 15. xl kg
16. $\frac{n}{6}$ pence 17. £$\frac{p}{5}$ 18. $\frac{12}{n}$ kg
19. $\frac{m}{4}$ kg 20. $3x - 11$

Exercise 11 *page 71*

1.

1	2	0	5	−5
4	1	5	7	11
3	0	1	−2	−1
−4	4	2	9	10
−4	5	−3	6	3

2.

5	1	0	1	−1
−5	0	0	0	8
−4	1	2	1	2
7	−5	6	5	7
4	−1	6	6	−6

3.

−6	−8	−4	−6	6
0	−2	6	10	30
−10	−9	−12	0	0
3	−12	−15	18	24
4	0	2	8	0

Exercise 12 *page 72*

1. 4 2. −4 3. 4 4. 12 5. 8 6. −5 7. 7
8. 3 9. 6 10. 12 11. −2 12. 14 13. 4 14. 15
15. −2 16. −3 17. 7 18. −4 19. 2 20. 10 21. 5
22. 2 23. −4 24. 10 25. 9 26. −2 27. −8 28. 2
29. 0 30. 15 31. 2 32. −8 33. 4 34. 11 35. −14
36. −15 37. 4 38. 0 39. 5 40. −4

Exercise 13 *page 72*

1. 2 2. −3 3. −3 4. 2 5. 5 6. −6 7. −1
8. 1 9. 5 10. 10 11. 5 12. 13 13. 3 14. 13
15. −3 16. −5 17. 6 18. 3 19. 10 20. 7 21. 1
22. −5 23. 4 24. 4 25. −3 26. −1 27. −7 28. 5
29. 6 30. 9 31. −3 32. −1 33. −3 34. 0 35. −6
36. −14 37. 11 38. −12 39. 4 40. 1

Exercise 14 *page 72*

1. −9 2. −8 3. 8 4. 8 5. 24 6. 6 7. −9
8. −27 9. −4 10. −18 11. −16 12. −4 13. −6 14. 6
15. −15 16. 20 17. −6 18. 28 19. 8 20. 6 21. −12
22. 36 23. −20 24. −8 25. 12 26. −6 27. −6 28. 12
29. −10 30. 6 31. −3 32. −22 33. −12 34. 20 35. −18
36. −21 37. −4 38. 40 39. 15 40. 27 41. 16 42. −4
43. 16 44. −6 45. −11 46. −8 47. 4 48. 2 49. 9
50. 33 51. 3 52. −30 53. 30 54. 21 55. −10 56. 44
57. −3 58. −2 59. 12 60. −2

Exercise 15 *page 72*

1. 15	**2.** −8	**3.** 4	**4.** −12	**5.** 12	**6.** −9	**7.** −35
8. 45	**9.** −12	**10.** 30	**11.** −32	**12.** −24	**13.** −36	**14.** −20
15. 25	**16.** −30	**17.** −15	**18.** 14	**19.** −6	**20.** −14	**21.** 20
22. 18	**23.** −40	**24.** −16	**25.** 6	**26.** 10	**27:** 28	**28.** −14
29. −20	**30.** 21	**31.** −18	**32.** −44	**33.** 10	**34.** 10	**35.** −36
36. 35	**37.** −8	**38.** 20	**39.** −35	**40.** −63	**41.** −24	**42.** 12
43. 8	**44.** −12	**45.** −66	**46.** −48	**47.** −6	**48.** 24	**49.** −21
50. −77	**51.** −30	**52.** 50	**53.** −70	**54.** −49	**55.** −60	**56.** 22
57. 42	**58.** −12	**59.** −28	**60.** 18			

Exercise 16 *page 72*

1. −5	**2.** 8	**3.** −17	**4.** 8	**5.** −2	**6.** −27	**7.** 1
8. −22	**9.** −22	**10.** −22	**11.** −10	**12.** −2	**13.** 23	**14.** −44
15. 26	**16.** 25	**17.** −4	**18.** 0	**19.** −16	**20.** 22	**21.** −5
22. 30	**23.** 13	**24.** 25	**25.** 40	**26.** 3	**27.** −5	**28.** −12
29. −34	**30.** 2	**31.** 12	**32.** 39	**33.** 40	**34.** 7	**35.** 3
36. 10	**37.** 51	**38.** −2	**39.** 1	**40.** 11	**41.** 10	**42.** 1
43. −20	**44.** −21	**45.** 16	**46.** −14	**47.** −5	**48.** −25	**49.** −45
50. −23						

Exercise 17 *page 73*

1. 9	**2.** −13	**3.** 11	**4.** 0	**5.** 14	**6.** 15	**7.** 6
8. 13	**9.** 28	**10.** 24	**11.** 8	**12.** −6	**13.** −5	**14.** 48
15. −16	**16.** −3	**17.** 17	**18.** 5	**19.** 7	**20.** 1	**21.** 1
22. −15	**23.** −11	**24.** −6	**25.** −9	**26.** 0	**27.** 25	**28.** 13
29. 13	**30.** −12	**31.** −22	**32.** −24	**33.** −2	**34.** −2	**35.** 0
36. −25	**37.** −6	**38.** 10	**39.** 16	**40.** −13	**41.** 13	**42.** −26
43. −20	**44.** 16	**45.** 18	**46.** −21	**47.** −31	**48.** 42	**49.** −38
50. 19						

Exercise 18 *page 73*

1. 4	**2.** 4	**3.** 9	**4.** 16	**5.** 8	**6.** −8	**7.** −27
8. 64	**9.** 8	**10.** 16	**11.** 8	**12.** 16	**13.** 18	**14.** 36
15. 48	**16.** 16	**17.** 20	**18.** 54	**19.** 144	**20.** 24	**21.** 13
22. 10	**23.** 1	**24.** 18	**25.** 13	**26.** 19	**27.** 10	**28.** 32
29. 16	**30.** 144	**31.** 36	**32.** 36	**33.** 4	**34.** 1	**35.** 2
36. −14	**37.** −5	**38.** −5	**39.** −10	**40.** 10	**41.** 0	**42.** 4
43. 50	**44.** 4	**45.** −10	**46.** −4	**47.** −6	**48.** −16	**49.** 28
50. 44	**51.** 2	**52.** −1	**53.** −1	**54.** 3	**55.** $\frac{1}{2}$	**56.** 1

Exercise 19 *page 73*

1. 1	**2.** 16	**3.** 9	**4.** 25	**5.** −1	**6.** −64	**7.** 27
8. −125	**9.** 2	**10.** 4	**11.** 32	**12.** 64	**13.** 18	**14.** 36
15. 75	**16.** 4	**17.** 80	**18.** 54	**19.** 225	**20.** −3	**21.** 13
22. 19	**23.** 13	**24.** 9	**25.** 25	**26.** 19	**27.** −11	**28.** −25
29. 16	**30.** 225	**31.** 144	**32.** −45	**33.** 3	**34.** −7	**35.** −4
36. −26	**37.** −1	**38.** 7	**39.** −7	**40.** −17	**41.** −15	**42.** −8
43. −55	**44.** −8	**45.** 1	**46.** −10	**47.** −12	**48.** 28	**49.** −8
50. 128	**51.** $-4\frac{2}{3}$	**52.** $-4\frac{1}{2}$	**53.** $-\frac{1}{5}$	**54.** 1	**55.** $-\frac{1}{4}$	**56.** $\frac{8}{11}$

Exercise 20 *page 74*

1. $5x + 8$
2. $9x + 5$
3. $7x + 4$
4. $7x + 4$
5. $7x + 7$
6. $8x + 12$
7. $12x - 6$
8. $2x + 5$
9. $2x - 5$
10. $2x - 5$
11. $9x - 9$
12. $3x - 5$
13. $9x + 6$
14. $13x$
15. 6
16. $7y - 2$
17. $10y - 2$
18. $4y$
19. -8
20. $4y + 8$
21. $13a + 3b - 1$
22. $10m + 3n + 8$
23. $3p - 2q - 8$
24. $2s - 7t + 14$
25. $2a + 1$
26. $x + y + 7z$
27. $5x - 4y + 4z$
28. $5k - 4m$
29. $4a + 5b - 9$
30. $a - 4x - 5e$

Exercise 21 *page 74*

1. $x^2 + 7x + 3$
2. $x^2 + 7x + 8$
3. $x^2 + 3x + 3$
4. $3x^2 + 6x + 5$
5. $2x^2 + 6x - 7$
6. $3x^2 + x + 12$
7. $2x^2 + x + 3$
8. $2x^2 - x$
9. $x^2 - 4x - 2$
10. $3x^2 - 2x - 2$
11. $8a + 9$
12. $2m^2 + 8m - 10$
13. $10 + x - 3x^2$
14. $2 - 4x - 3x^2$
15. $22 + 4t + 2t^2$
16. 23
17. 4
18. $4x^2 - 7x + 29$
19. $4 - x - 2x^2$
20. $11x$
21. $x^2 + 5xy + 5x$
22. $4x^2 + 6xy - 2x$
23. $7x^2 + 8xy + x$
24. $5x^2 + 2xy + x$
25. $4x^2 + 3xy + x$
26. $4m^2 + 3mn + 2m$
27. $8a^2 - 5a + 4ab$
28. $6cd$
29. $3z^2 + 10xz + 5z$
30. $4p^2 - 10p$
31. $5x^2 + 4y^2 + x$
32. $x + 12$
33. $5y^2 - 6y + 2$
34. $3ab - 3b$
35. $2cd - 2d^2$
36. $4ab - 2a^2 + 2a$
37. $2x^3 + 5x^2$
38. $x^3 + x^2 + 11$
39. $3xy$
40. $p^2 - q^2$

Exercise 22 *page 75*

1. $2x + 8$
2. $5 + x + y$
3. $16 + x + y$
4. $3l + 13$
5. $3x + d + 11$
6. $4t + m + 3$
7. $3a + b + 3$
8. $6x + 2y + 12$
9. $10x + 8$

Exercise 23 *page 75*

1. $6x$
2. $8x$
3. $6x$
4. $15x$
5. $6y$
6. $20y$
7. $21x$
8. $-6x$
9. $-20x$
10. $-10x$
11. $28a$
12. $15a$
13. $6x$
14. $12y$
15. $25y$
16. $2x^2$
17. $4x^2$
18. $6x^2$
19. $3y^2$
20. $10y^2$
21. $7x^2$
22. $5a^2$
23. $6x^2$
24. $12x^2$
25. $10x^2$
26. $8x^2$
27. $14x^2$
28. $18x^2$
29. $10y^2$
30. $24t^2$
31. $2x^3$
32. $6x^3$
33. $4y^3$
34. $6a^3$
35. $9y^3$
36. $5x^3$
37. $21p^2$
38. $12x^2$
39. $60x^2$
40. $30x^2$
41. $30x^3$
42. $12x^3$
43. $4x^3$
44. $12y^2$
45. $12a^3$
46. $3x^4$
47. $2xy$
48. $6a^3$
49. $6ab$
50. $10pq$
51. $15xy$
52. $18x^3$
53. $24a^4$
54. $36x^3$
55. $2a^2b$
56. $3xy^2$
57. $5c^2d$
58. a^2b^2
59. $2x^2y^2$
60. $6cd$

Exercise 24 *page 76*

1. $6x^2$ cm^2
2. $10x^2$ cm^2
3. $4x^2$ cm^2
4. $9y^2$ cm^2
5. $9x^2$ cm^2
6. $12d^2$ cm^2
7. $10x^2$ cm^2
8. $26x^2$ cm^2
9. $18z^2$ cm^2

Exercise 25 *page 76*

1. $6x^2$ cm^2
2. $3x + 15$
3. $4x + 24$
4. $4x + 2$
5. $10x + 15$
6. $12x - 4$
7. $12x - 12$
8. $15x - 6$
9. $15x - 20$
10. $14x - 21$
11. $4x + 6$
12. $6x + 3$
13. $5x + 20$
14. $12x + 12$
15. $4x + 12$
16. $12x + 84$
17. $6x - 9$
18. $10x + 40$
19. $18x + 45$
20. $24x - 48$
21. $-4x - 6$
22. $-8x - 4$
23. $-3x - 6$
24. $-6x - 8$
25. $-8x + 2$
26. $-10x + 10$
27. $-6x - 3$
28. $-2x - 1$
29. $-3x - 2$
30. $-4x + 5$
31. $x^2 + 3x$
32. $x^2 + 5x$
33. $x^2 - 2x$
34. $x^2 - 3x$
35. $2x^2 + x$
36. $3x^2 - 2x$
37. $3x^2 + 5x$
38. $2x^2 - 2x$
39. $2x^2 + 4x$
40. $6x^2 + 9x$

Exercise 26 *page 77*

1. (a) $2x - 2$ (b) $3x - 1$ (c) $x - 1$ (d) $x + 2$ (e) $x - 3$ (f) $x + 3$
(g) $x + 3$
2. (a) $3x + 3$ (b) $4x + 6$ (c) $x + 5$ (d) $2x + 1$ (e) $2x - 2$ (f) 7
(g) $x + 6$ (h) $x + 7$ (i) $x + 5$

UNIT 6

Exercise 1 *page 79*

1. 8 **2.** 10 **3.** 13 **4.** 3 **5.** 5 **6.** 6 **7.** 4
8. 1 **9.** 8 **10.** −2 **11.** −3 **12.** −5 **13.** 2 **14.** −2
15. 10 **16.** −5 **17.** 1 **18.** −10 **19.** 5 **20.** 2 **21.** 16
22. −8 **23.** 4 **24.** −6 **25.** 5 **26.** 12 **27.** 11 **28.** 19
29. −6 **30.** 23 **31.** 9 **32.** 12 **33.** −16 **34.** 1 **35.** 5
36. −12

Exercise 2 *page 79*

1. 3 **2.** 6 **3.** 7 **4.** 6 **5.** 8 **6.** 9
7. 9 **8.** 10 **9.** 30 **10.** 5 **11.** 100 **12.** 12
13. $\frac{2}{5}$ **14.** $\frac{5}{7}$ **15.** $\frac{3}{8}$ **16.** $\frac{1}{4}$ **17.** $\frac{1}{2}$ **18.** $\frac{5}{9}$
19. $1\frac{2}{3}$ **20.** $1\frac{3}{4}$ **21.** $2\frac{1}{3}$ **22.** $4\frac{1}{2}$ **23.** $3\frac{1}{3}$ **24.** $2\frac{1}{5}$
25. $-\frac{4}{5}$ **26.** −4 **27.** −2 **28.** −9 **29.** $-\frac{2}{3}$ **30.** $-\frac{1}{12}$
31. $-1\frac{3}{7}$ **32.** $\frac{1}{5}$ **33.** $-2\frac{1}{4}$ **34.** −1 **35.** −1 **36.** −4
37. 2 **38.** 5 **39.** 4 **40.** 8 **41.** $1\frac{1}{5}$ **42.** $7\frac{1}{2}$
43. −4 **44.** $-3\frac{1}{2}$ **45.** −3 **46.** −3 **47.** 10 **48.** 10

Exercise 3 *page 80*

1. 12 **2.** 20 **3.** 20 **4.** 28 **5.** 72 **6.** −12
7. −4 **8.** 0 **9.** 1 **10.** 360 **11.** 1 **12.** 2
13. $3\frac{1}{2}$ **14.** 2 **15.** 70 **16.** 35 **17.** 36 **18.** 77
19. −9 **20.** −8 **21.** −5 **22.** −80 **23.** −160 **24.** $\frac{1}{2}$
25. 20 **26.** 7 **27.** 16 **28.** 45

Exercise 4 *page 80*

1. 3 **2.** 2 **3.** 2 **4.** 6 **5.** 2 **6.** 4
7. $2\frac{1}{2}$ **8.** 4 **9.** $\frac{3}{4}$ **10.** $1\frac{1}{5}$ **11.** $2\frac{3}{5}$ **12.** $\frac{1}{3}$
13. $\frac{1}{2}$ **14.** 1 **15.** $-\frac{1}{2}$ **16.** −1 **17.** 0 **18.** $\frac{2}{3}$
19. $\frac{4}{5}$ **20.** $-\frac{4}{7}$ **21.** $\frac{7}{9}$ **22.** $\frac{3}{10}$ **23.** $2\frac{4}{5}$ **24.** $-\frac{5}{6}$
25. $-2\frac{1}{3}$ **26.** $1\frac{1}{2}$ **27.** $-2\frac{1}{2}$ **28.** 2 **29.** 4 **30.** $3\frac{1}{4}$
31. $\frac{5}{8}$ **32.** $-1\frac{1}{5}$ **33.** $-\frac{1}{7}$ **34.** $-1\frac{3}{5}$ **35.** −3 **36.** −2
37. $3\frac{1}{2}$ **38.** 2 **39.** 3 **40.** 1 **41.** $\frac{1}{3}$ **42.** −2
43. $3\frac{1}{3}$ **44.** $-1\frac{1}{2}$ **45.** $\frac{1}{10}$ **46.** $-\frac{2}{11}$ **47.** 4 **48.** 0

Exercise 5 *page 81*

1. 2 **2.** 3 **3.** 1 **4.** 2 **5.** 4 **6.** 3
7. $\frac{1}{2}$ **8.** 1 **9.** 2 **10.** 5 **11.** 3 **12.** 2
13. 4 **14.** 1 **15.** 1 **16.** $\frac{1}{2}$ **17.** $\frac{9}{10}$ **18.** 8
19. 7 **20.** $2\frac{2}{3}$ **21.** 8 **22.** $\frac{5}{12}$ **23.** $\frac{3}{4}$ **24.** $\frac{8}{9}$
25. 5 **26.** 6 **27.** $-\frac{1}{2}$ **28.** −7 **29.** −8 **30.** −2

Exercise 6 *page 81*

1. $2\frac{1}{2}$ **2.** $\frac{1}{3}$ **3.** $2\frac{1}{4}$ **4.** 5 **5.** $1\frac{1}{2}$ **6.** 1
7. 1 **8.** $2\frac{2}{3}$ **9.** $2\frac{1}{10}$ **10.** $\frac{1}{2}$ **11.** 1 **12.** 2
13. 2 **14.** 2 **15.** 1 **16.** 4 **17.** 2 **18.** -1
19. -3 **20.** -4 **21.** 5 **22.** 9 **23.** $-2\frac{1}{3}$ **24.** $\frac{2}{5}$
25. $\frac{3}{5}$ **26.** -1 **27.** 13 **28.** 9 **29.** $4\frac{1}{2}$ **30.** $3\frac{1}{3}$

Exercise 7 *page 81*

1. 3 **2.** $\frac{3}{4}$ **3.** $4\frac{1}{2}$ **4.** 2 **5.** $5\frac{1}{2}$ **6.** $2\frac{1}{3}$
7. $\frac{3}{8}$ **8.** 7 **9.** $-\frac{3}{7}$ **10.** $-\frac{3}{10}$ **11.** $-\frac{1}{2}$ **12.** 1
13. 5 **14.** $1\frac{2}{3}$ **15.** 3 **16.** $\frac{1}{2}$ **17.** $4\frac{3}{5}$ **18.** $4\frac{1}{2}$
19. $2\frac{3}{7}$ **20.** $-2\frac{2}{3}$

Exercise 8 *page 82*

1. 3 **2.** $1\frac{1}{2}$ **3.** 4 **4.** 5 **5.** 2 **6.** $\frac{2}{3}$
7. 1 **8.** $\frac{2}{3}$ **9.** 1 **10.** $\frac{1}{2}$ **11.** 2 **12.** $\frac{4}{5}$
13. 3 **14.** 2 **15.** -9 **16.** 13 **17.** $3\frac{2}{3}$ **18.** $-\frac{1}{2}$
19. 3 **20.** $10\frac{2}{3}$

Exercise 9 *page 83*

1. $\frac{3}{4}$ **2.** $\frac{1}{4}$ **3.** $1\frac{4}{5}$ **4.** $\frac{3}{7}$ **5.** $1\frac{3}{8}$ **6.** $1\frac{1}{4}$ **7.** 7
8. (a) $3\frac{3}{5}$ (b) $\frac{3}{4}$ **9.** (a) $\frac{2}{3}$ (b) $4\frac{1}{2}$ **10.** width = 7 cm, area = 84cm^2
11. (a) 41 (b) 31 **12.** 29 **13.** (a) 53 (b) 65 **14.** 55p
15. (c) 32, 56, 208 (d) 16 (e) $n = 4x$

Exercise 10 *page 84*

1. C **2.** B **3.** C **4.** D **5.** C **6.** B **7.** C
8. D **9.** A **10.** A **11.** C **12.** D **13.** B **14.** C
15. A **16.** C **17.** B **18.** B **19.** C **20.** D

Exercise 11 *page 85*

1. $c - a$ **2.** $m - d$ **3.** $m - h$ **4.** $t - e$
5. $q + m$ **6.** $m + k$ **7.** $a + b + n$ **8.** $c + b - B$
9. $a + d - D$ **10.** $m + t + M$ **11.** $u - w + v$ **12.** $t - s - T$
13. $n - B$ **14.** $m - M$ **15.** $a - b - N$ **16.** $v - n - R$
17. $y^2 - K$ **18.** $b^2 + a^2$ **19.** $N^2 + n^2$ **20.** $-a - p$
21. $a + n$ **22.** $mn - r$ **23.** $c - m$ **24.** $B + b$
25. $a - b + c$ **26.** $e - c + d$ **27.** $c^2 - a^2 + b^2$ **28.** $m^2 - mn + v^2$
29. $b + a + t$ **30.** $f + g + h$ **31.** $b + B^2 + B$ **32.** $2a - A$
33. $T^2 + 2t$ **34.** $w - w^3$ **35.** $uv - w^2$ **36.** $T^3 - t^3$
37. $a^3 + abc$ **38.** $mn^2 - m^3$ **39.** $a + 2bc$ **40.** $3pq$

Exercise 12 *page 85*

1. 4 **2.** 6 **3.** $\frac{c}{a}$ **4.** $\frac{t}{m}$ **5.** $\frac{m}{M}$
6. $\frac{a}{t}$ **7.** $\frac{n}{m}$ **8.** $\frac{L}{x}$ **9.** $\frac{n^2}{m^2}$ **10.** $\frac{h}{q}$
11. $\frac{A}{ab}$ **12.** $\frac{M^2}{m^2}$ **13.** $\frac{c}{a}$ **14.** $\frac{x}{t}$ **15.** $\frac{v}{d}$

16. $\frac{u^2}{v^2}$ 17. $\frac{b}{t^2}$ 18. $\frac{B}{b}$ 19. $\frac{c}{e}$ 20. $\frac{a}{k^2}$

21. $\frac{a+b}{x}$ 22. $\frac{e-f}{m}$ 23. $\frac{s+t}{n}$ 24. $\frac{p+q}{H}$ 25. $\frac{ab+c}{z}$

26. $\frac{a^2-b^2}{v}$ 27. $\frac{pq}{M}$ 28. $\frac{km-m^2}{n}$ 29. $\frac{c-k}{x^2}$ 30. $\frac{a-b-A}{p}$

31. $\frac{A}{xz}$ 32. $\frac{B}{wv}$ 33. $\frac{Ba}{dk}$ 34. $\frac{1}{n^2m^2}$ 35. $\frac{m}{x^2}$

36. $\frac{A}{p^2}$ 37. $\frac{N}{n^2}$ 38. $\frac{A}{BL}$ 39. $\frac{a+b}{cP}$ 40. $\frac{e+t}{kQ}$

41. $a-t$ 42. $v+m^2$ 43. $b-k$ 44. $x-e$ 45. n^2-mn

46. $ab+b^2$ 47. $\frac{n-a}{z}$ 48. $\frac{x-z}{p}$ 49. T^2+t^2 50. $\frac{C}{dn}$

Exercise 13 *page 86*

1. $\frac{9}{2}$ 2. 7 3. $\frac{t-b}{n}$ 4. $\frac{q-v}{m}$ 5. $\frac{B+A}{p}$

6. $\frac{A+q}{n}$ 7. $\frac{n^2+w}{k}$ 8. $\frac{n-m}{m}$ 9. $\frac{e-m}{t}$ 10. $\frac{v^2+w^2}{B}$

11. $\frac{d-L}{p}$ 12. $\frac{M+n}{m}$ 13. $\frac{x-y}{x}$ 14. $\frac{v^2+t}{x}$ 15. $\frac{z^2+s^2}{s}$

16. $\frac{x^2-pq}{r}$ 17. $\frac{h^2-lm}{b}$ 18. $\frac{d+b-t}{e}$ 19. $\frac{p^2-m-n}{B}$ 20. $\frac{km+n^2}{m}$

21. $\frac{t+mn}{m}$ 22. $\frac{x-ux}{u}$ 23. $\frac{y-pw}{p}$ 24. $\frac{q+Au}{A}$ 25. $\frac{m-Lx}{L}$

26. $\frac{x^3-nx^2}{n}$ 27. $\frac{s^2+r^2}{r}$ 28. $\frac{y^2+x^2}{x}$ 29. $\frac{13}{3}$ 30. $-\frac{2}{5}$

31. $\frac{T+nt}{n}$ 32. $\frac{V+wy}{w}$ 33. $\frac{w+q+mw}{m}$ 34. $\frac{x^2-y^2+z^2}{z}$ 35. $\frac{v^2-ut}{t}$

36. $\frac{L^2-MN}{m}$ 37. $\frac{x-zx}{z}$ 38. $\frac{y^2+w^2}{w}$ 39. $\frac{x^2+2q^2}{q}$ 40. $\frac{n}{k}$

Exercise 14 *page 86*

1. an 2. At 3. x^2 4. zp 5. vw
6. n^3 7. $-em$ 8. $t(a-b)$ 9. $h(x+y)$ 10. $-m^2$

11. $z(a+b)$ 12. $B(m-n)$ 13. $D(m-p)$ 14. $\frac{an}{m}$ 15. $\frac{yx}{n}$

16. $\frac{ey}{a}$ 17. $\frac{az}{v}$ 18. $\frac{a^2}{m}$ 19. $\frac{xy}{z}$ 20. $\frac{vw}{q}$

21. $\frac{bx}{am}$ 22. $\frac{Ac}{mx}$ 23. $\frac{v^2}{bz}$ 24. $\frac{t^2}{en}$ 25. $\frac{a(x+y)}{m}$

26. $\frac{d(p+q)}{n}$ 27. $\frac{q(x+t)}{A}$ 28. $\frac{n}{a+d^2}$ 29. $\frac{w^2}{B^2}$ 30. $\frac{v^2}{z^2}$

THINK ABOUT IT 2

Exercise A *page 89*

1. 230 **2.** (a) £30 (b) 2400 g **3.** (a) 52 m^2 (b) 0.052 m^3 **4.** 500
5. (b) 0.2 (c) $\frac{1}{2}$ (d) 0.75 (e) $\frac{3}{5}$ (f) 0.625 **6.** £12.60
7. (a) 14.52 (b) 0.648 (c) 13.4 (d) 18.05 (e) 2.56 (f) 35.1 **8.** £760
9. pencils by 10p **10.** (a) 6, 8, 54 (b) 6, 15, 27, 39, 54 (c) 7, 13, 17, 23, 41 (d) 27, 54

Project 2 *page 90*

1. SOIL **2.** ISLES **3.** HE LIES **4.** SOS
5. HO HO HO **6.** ESSO OIL **7.** SOLID **8.** SOLO
9. BOILED EGGS **10.** HE IS BOSS **11.** LODGE **12.** SIGH
13. HEDGEHOG **14.** GOSH **15.** GOBBLE **16.** BEG
17. BIG SLOB **18.** SID **19.** HILL **20.** LESLIE
21. HOBBIES **22.** GIGGLE **23.** BIBLE **24.** BIGGLES
25. BOBBLE **26.** HEIDI **27.** BOBBIE **28.** HIGH
29. HELLS BELLS **30.** GOD BLESS **31.** SHE DIES **32.** SOLEIL

Exercise B *page 91*

1. 10 **2.** (a) £6.54 (b) £15.71 (c) £11.62 (d) £8.03 (e) £0.63 (f) £1.07
3. 20 **4.** (a) 60 cm^2 (b) 24 cm^2 (c) 40% **5.** (a) £1920 (b) £6580
6. 270 **7.** £7.12 **8.** (a) 410 (b) 704.5
9. (a) 64 (b) 1 (c) 100 (d) 3000 (e) 32 (f) 81 **10.** 20 cm^2

Exercise C *page 92*

1.

9	+	6	→	15
×		÷		
4	+	2	→	6
↓		↓		
36	÷	3	→	12

2.

8	+	3	→	11
−		×		
3	×	1	→	3
↓		↓		
5	+	3	→	8

3.

15	+	19	→	34
×		+		
5	×	31	→	155
↓		↓		
75	+	50	→	125

4.

38	+	14	→	52
×		+		
3	÷	1	→	3
↓		↓		
114	−	15	→	99

5.

9	×	10	→	90
+		÷		
11	÷	2	→	$5\frac{1}{2}$
↓		↓		
20	×	5	→	100

6.

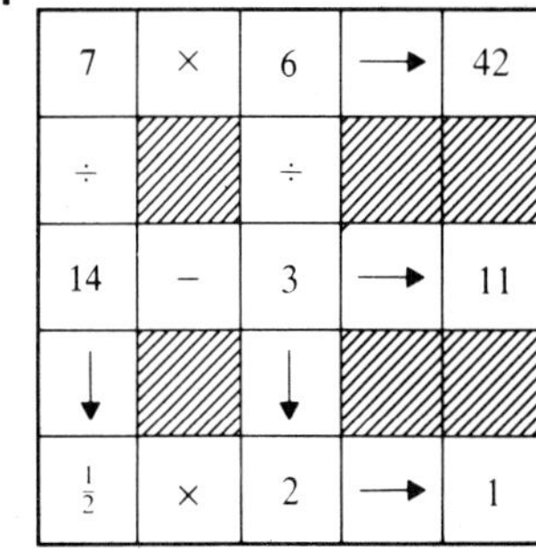

7	×	6	→	42
÷		÷		
14	−	3	→	11
↓		↓		
$\frac{1}{2}$	×	2	→	1

7.

17	×	2	→	34
−		÷		
9	×	4	→	36
↓		↓		
8	−	$\frac{1}{2}$	→	$7\frac{1}{2}$

8.

90	−	7	→	83
÷		×		
2	÷	8	→	$\frac{1}{4}$
↓		↓		
45	+	56	→	101

9.

9	×	5	→	45
×		−		
1	×	2	→	2
↓		↓		
9	×	3	→	27

10.

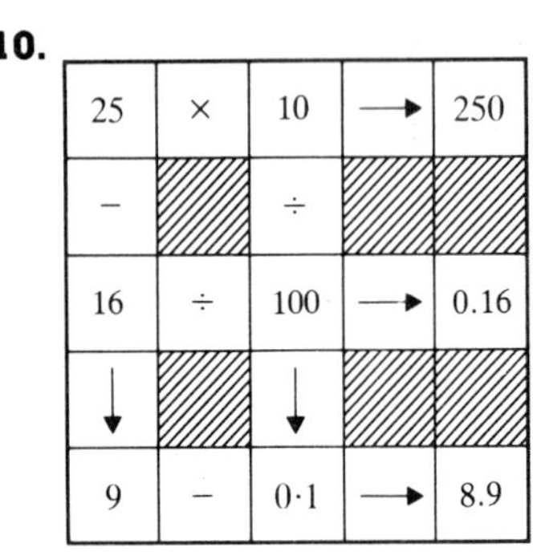

25	×	10	→	250
−		÷		
16	÷	100	→	0.16
↓		↓		
9	−	0·1	→	8.9

11.

0·1	×	20	→	2
×		+		
6	−	0.2	→	5.8
↓		↓		
0·6	+	20.2	→	20·8

12.

$\frac{1}{2}$	×	100	→	50
−		×		
0.1	+	2	→	2·1
↓		↓		
0·4	×	200	→	80

13.

7	×	0·1	→	0·7
÷		×		
5	÷	0·2	→	10
↓		↓		
1.4	+	0.02	→	1.42

14.

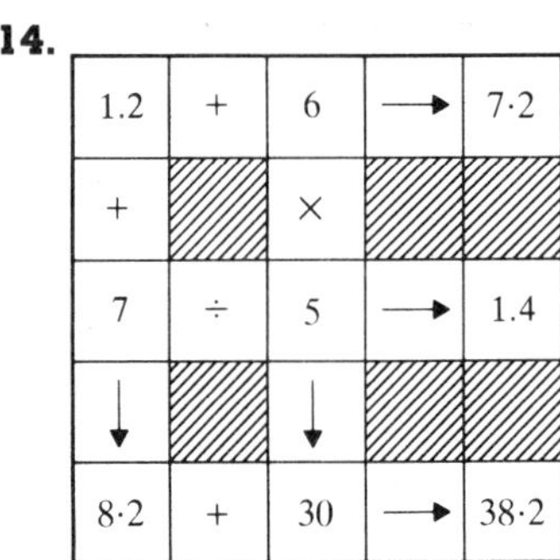

1.2	+	6	→	7·2
+		×		
7	÷	5	→	1.4
↓		↓		
8·2	+	30	→	38·2

15.

100	×	0.2	→	20
−		×		
1.2	+	10	→	11·2
↓		↓		
98·8	+	2	→	100.8

16.

4	×	$\frac{1}{2}$	→	2
÷ ×		+		
1	−	$\frac{1}{4}$	→	$\frac{3}{4}$
↓		↓		
4	×	$\frac{3}{4}$	→	3

17.

$\frac{1}{4}$	−	$\frac{1}{8}$	→	$\frac{1}{8}$
×		×		
$\frac{1}{2}$	÷	4	→	$\frac{1}{8}$
↓		↓		
$\frac{1}{8}$	+	$\frac{1}{2}$	→	$\frac{5}{8}$

18.

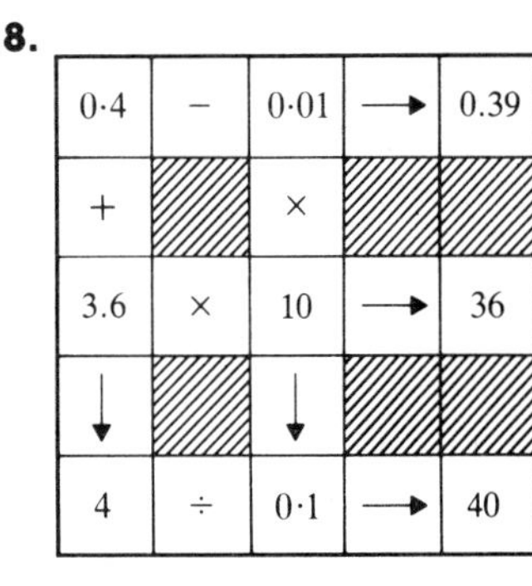

0·4	−	0·01	→	0.39
+		×		
3.6	×	10	→	36
↓		↓		
4	÷	0·1	→	40

Exercise D *page 95*

1. £0.78; £1.80; 7; £14.63 **2.** £6.30 **3.** 52 cm^2
4. 1, 10, 5, 48 **5.** (a) 214 500 (b) 580 **6.** (a) 0.4 km (b) 2 cm **7.** 6 years
8. $7\frac{7}{8}$ **9.** (a) 144 + 538 = 682 (b) 837 − 356 = 481 **10.** 9

Project 6 *page 98*

1. (a) Sally (b) John, Dave (c) Dave (d) 7 **2.** (a) 4 (b) 9
3. (a) 19 (b) 22 (c) 31 (d) 42 **4.** $m = p - 1$

Exercise F *page 100*

1. (a) £162 (b) 200 (c) F1000 (d) £100
2. (a) £114.80 (b) £12 (c) 224 tiles
3. (a) £4.04 (b) £55.60 (c) (i) £445.20 (ii) £45.20 (d) (i) £891.12 (ii) £161.12

Project 7 *page 101*

Number	3	5	13	11	14	17	32	19	23	33	39
Number of steps to reach 1	7	5	9	14	17	12	5	20	15	26	34

Exercise G *page 101*

1. (a) 1440 (b) 18 720 km (c) £982.50 (d) £1017.90
2. (a) £64 (b) £326.40 (c) £390.40 (d) £294.40
3. (a) £560 (b) £46.67 **4.** 15 **5.** (f) 1089

UNIT 7

Exercise 1 *page 104*

1. 70° **2.** 100° **3.** 70° **4.** 100°
5. 55° **6.** 70° **7.** 70° **8.** $33\frac{1}{3}°$
9. 30° **10.** 35° **11.** 155° **12.** 125°
13. 44° **14.** 80° **15.** 40° **16.** 48°
17. 40° **18.** 35° **19.** $a = 40°$, $b = 140°$ **20.** $x = 108°$, $y = 72°$

Exercise 2 *page 105*

1. 50° **2.** 70° **3.** 130° **4.** 73°
5. 18° **6.** 75° **7.** 29° **8.** 30°
9. 70° **10.** 42° **11.** 120° **12.** 100°
13. 45° **14.** 72° **15.** 40° **16.** $a = 55°$, $b = 70°$
17. $c = 72°$, $d = 36°$ **18.** $w = 55°$, $z = 55°$ **19.** 80° **20.** 75°
21. 60° **22.** $x = 122°$, $y = 116°$ **23.** 135° **24.** 30°
25. 65° **26.** $a = 154°$, $b = 52°$

Exercise 3 *page 107*

1. 72° **2.** 98° **3.** 80° **4.** 74°
5. 86° **6.** 88° **7.** $x = 95°$, $y = 50°$ **8.** $a = 87°$, $b = 74°$
9. $a = 65°$, $c = 103°$ **10.** $a = 68°$, $b = 42°$ **11.** $y = 65°$, $z = 50°$ **12.** $a = 55°$, $b = 75°$, $c = 50°$

Exercise 4 *page 108*

1. 42° **2.** 68° **3.** 100° **4.** 73°
5. 50° **6.** 52° **7.** 84° **8.** $a = 70°$, $b = 60°$
9. $x = 58°$, $y = 109°$ **10.** 66° **11.** 65° **12.** $e = 70°$, $f = 30°$
13. $x = 72°$, $y = 36°$ **14.** $a = 68°$, $b = 72°$, $c = 68°$ **15.** 4° **16.** $28\frac{1}{2}°$
17. 20° **18.** $x = 62°$, $y = 28°$ **19.** 34° **20.** 58°

Test 1 *page 109*

1. 99	**2.** 20	**3.** 600	**4.** 204 020	**5.** 9 o'clock
6. 310	**7.** 30	**8.** £6.80	**9.** £1.80	**10.** 20p, 20p, 2p, 2p
11. 0.5	**12.** 4	**13.** Tuesday	**14.** 160 cm	**15.** £2.07
16. 64 cm	**17.** £212	**18.** £2000	**19.** 8	**20.** 57
21. 36	**22.** 20	**23.** 82	**24.** £5	**25.** £1.32
26. £4.64	**27.** £2.60	**28.** 50	**29.** 300	**30.** 20p

Test 2 *page 109*

1. £47	**2.** 0.25	**3.** 9	**4.** 166	**5.** £12
6. £15	**7.** 10, 10, 5, 5	**8.** 92	**9.** 67 cm	**10.** £8.50
11. 4	**12.** 9.10	**13.** Sunday	**14.** 8	**15.** 54
16. 14	**17.** 510 280	**18.** 200	**19.** 51 cm	**20.** 20
21. 18	**22.** 54	**23.** £4.14	**24.** 90	**25.** £7.20
26. 195	**27.** £1000	**28.** 140	**29.** £1.80	**30.** 17th January

Test 3 *page 110*

1. 63p	**2.** 51	**3.** £10	**4.** 4	**5.** 36
6. Monday	**7.** 12 ounces	**8.** 7.25	**9.** 5, 5, 5, 5	**10.** 0.3
11. 250	**12.** 270 cm	**13.** 25	**14.** 200	**15.** 3
16. 17 009	**17.** 3	**18.** £3140	**19.** 45	**20.** 4
21. 50	**22.** 20 cm	**23.** 79	**24.** £9.78	**25.** £1.20
26. £4.80	**27.** 77	**28.** £30	**29.** 43	**30.** 450

Test 4 *page 111*

1. 59	**2.** 9	**3.** £4.25	**4.** 118
5. 50, 20, 5, 2	**6.** 84p	**7.** 20 past 10 (10.20)	**8.** Sunday
9. 0.2	**10.** 0.75	**11.** 24	**12.** 200
13. 4	**14.** 230	**15.** 8	**16.** £32
17. 34	**18.** 4	**19.** 91	**20.** 34
21. 76	**22.** 16	**23.** 180 cm	**24.** 3000
25. £3.28	**26.** 230	**27.** £2	**28.** 144
29. £7.20	**30.** £8.05		

Test 5 *page 111*

1. 20	**2.** 39	**3.** 5	**4.** 0.2	**5.** 120
6. 6 gallons	**7.** £2.40	**8.** 3	**9.** 426 g	**10.** $7\frac{1}{2}$
11. 15	**12.** 20	**13.** 320	**14.** 50, 5, 5, 5 or 20, 20, 20, 5	
15. 75%	**16.** £18.50	**17.** 180	**18.** 202 004	**19.** 0.03
20. £9.36	**21.** 04 30	**22.** £10	**23.** £2.30	**24.** 8
25. £1.08	**26.** 0.3	**27.** 43	**28.** £2.80	**29.** 62 m.p.h.
30. see Qu. **14**				

Test 6 *page 112*

1. 84	**2.** £2.60	**3.** $\frac{1}{2}$	**4.** 12	**5.** 20
6. 180°	**7.** 952	**8.** $11\frac{1}{2}$	**9.** 20 000	**10.** $\frac{1}{100}$
11. £1.70	**12.** 350	**13.** 120	**14.** 2	**15.** 20
16. 207 820	**17.** 60	**18.** 5 or 31	**19.** £1.60	**20.** 10 cm
21. 5	**22.** £70	**23.** £14	**24.** £2.50	**25.** £39
26. 6	**27.** £10	**28.** 13	**29.** 1 hr 45 min	**30.** 75%

Test 7 *page 112*

1. 14 **2.** £18 **3.** 9 **4.** 78 **5.** 60 011
6. 120 **7.** 2015 **8.** 20 **9.** 0.8 **10.** £395
11. £8.40 **12.** $2\frac{1}{2}$p **13.** 8 gallons **14.** 150 **15.** 90%
16. £5.30 **17.** 59 **18.** £400 **19.** 40 **20.** 12
21. 94 cm **22.** 45 **23.** 52 **24.** 32 **25.** £10.50
26. £1.20 **27.** 500 m.p.h. **28.** £8 → £9 **29.** 1907 **30.** 297 cm

Test 8 *page 113*

1. £35 **2.** 999 m **3.** quarter to nine **4.** 75%
5. 520 **6.** 14°C **7.** 25 **8.** 2, 2, 5, 5, or 1, 1, 2, 10
9. $22\frac{1}{2}$ **10.** 5400 **11.** £2500 → £2600 **12.** £4.15
13. 1000 **14.** 1898 **15.** 14p **16.** 11
17. 140 **18.** £100 **19.** £3.60 **20.** five to nine
21. isosceles **22.** £2 **23.** 56 **24.** 60%
25. 4 **26.** 58° **27.** 100 miles **28.** 500
29. 800 **30.** 25 km/h

Test 9 *page 114*

1. 130 **2.** £3.15 **3.** 1895 **4.** 12p
5. 84 **6.** 950 g **7.** £0.06 **8.** £200
9. 29 **10.** 30 **11.** 8.25 **12.** 73p
13. 8.15 **14.** 51 **15.** parallel **16.** 2, 5, 10, 10, 10 or 1, 1, 5, 10, 20
17. 22nd June **18.** 3000 **19.** 51 **20.** £1.44
21. 36 **22.** 126 **23.** −7°C **24.** 25%
25. £2.50 **26.** 65° **27.** £3860 **28.** 6.25
29. 22 **30.** 15

Test 10 *page 114*

1. 300 **2.** £9.15 **3.** 10 **4.** $4\frac{1}{2}$p
5. half past nine **6.** 27 **7.** 105 **8.** 61
9. 62% **10.** 15p **11.** equation **12.** 85°
13. 18 **14.** £16 **15.** 6.23 **16.** 146
17. £3.92 **18.** 97 **19.** 35 **20.** 125 miles
21. 20 cm **22.** 159 cm **23.** $1\frac{1}{2}$ **24.** £90 → £100
25. −2°C **26.** 7 **27.** £8130 **28.** £10.80
29. 999 mm **30.** 10 042 011

Test 11 *page 115*

1. £4.05 **2.** 28 m **3.** 790 **4.** 5 **5.** £28
6. 45 **7.** 3 **8.** $\frac{1}{1000}$ **9.** 60 **10.** 10p, 2p, 2p
11. $\frac{3}{8}$ **12.** 72% **13.** 21 **14.** £1.25 **15.** 55 min
16. 20 **17.** $5\frac{1}{2}$ **18.** £4.45 **19.** diagonal **20.** 80
21. 10 min **22.** £8 **23.** 8 or 32 **24.** 6 **25.** 15
26. 2 **27.** 50p **28.** £2.65 **29.** £3.40 **30.** 30

Exercise 5 *page 116*

1. 61 km/h **2.** 7.5 m/s **3.** 83 km/h **4.** $\frac{1}{2}$ cm/s **5.** $\frac{1}{7}$ cm/day
6. $9\frac{1}{2}$ km/h **7.** 400 km/h **8.** $72\frac{1}{2}$ km/h **9.** 48 km/h **10.** 120 km/h
11. $23\frac{1}{2}$ km/h **12.** 2 m.p.h.

Exercise 6 *page 116*

1. 120 miles **2.** 500 m **3.** 300 m **4.** 360 m **5.** 2000 km **6.** 12 km
7. 72 km **8.** 390 m **9.** 550 m **10.** 250 km **11.** 675 km **12.** $412\frac{1}{2}$ km

Exercise 7 *page 117*

1. 2 s **2.** 90 km **3.** 12 m/s **4.** 4 s **5.** 50 km **6.** 20 km/h
7. 11 s **8.** 7 m/s **9.** 32 km **10.** 3 s **11.** 45 km **12.** 50 km/h
13. 56 m **14.** 9 m/s **15.** 5 s **16.** 280 km **17.** 3 m/s **18.** 5 h
19. 1 h **20.** 7 m/s **21.** $\frac{1}{4}$ h **22.** 16 mph **23.** 16 km/h **24.** $3\frac{1}{2}$ km
25. $5\frac{1}{2}$ km **26.** 30 min **27.** 30 min **28.** 2 m **29.** 6 m **30.** 16 km

Exercise 8 *page 117*

1. (a) 18 h (b) 7 h (c) 5 s (d) $\frac{1}{2}$ h
2. (a) 110 miles (b) 340 m (c) 315 km (d) 60 cm
3. (a) 14 m.p.h. (b) 45.5 km/h (c) 25 m/s (d) 10.5 cm/min
4. (a) $\frac{1}{4}$ h (b) 0.2 s (c) $\frac{1}{10}$ h (d) 20 min ($\frac{1}{3}$ h)
5. (a) 8.5 km (b) 13 miles (c) 13.5 km (d) 20 miles
6. (a) 32 m.p.h. (b) 48 km/h (c) 84 m.p.h. (d) 45 km/h
7. 3.6 m/s **8.** 88 m.p.h. **9.** 4.5 km **10.** 20 min **11.** $1\frac{1}{2}$ miles
12. 6 km/h **13.** 20 m.p.h. **14.** 10 miles **15.** 20 min **16.** 90 miles
17. 18 miles **18.** 2 h 20 min **19.** 576 m **20.** 105 km/h **21.** 168 km/h
22. 36 km **23.** 36 km/h **24.** (a) 1 h, 40 min (b) $1\frac{2}{3}$ h (c) 60 km/h

Exercise 9 *page 118*

1. (a) 30 km (b) 45 km (c) $\frac{1}{2}$ h (d) $1\frac{3}{4}$ h
(e) (i) 10 km/h (ii) 20 km/h (iii) 30 km/h
2. (a) (i) 25 km (ii) 15 km (iii) 65 km
(b) (i) 1 h (ii) 3 h (iii) $1\frac{3}{4}$ h
(c) (i) 5 km/h (ii) 20 km/h (iii) 50 km/h (iv) 20 km/h
3. (a) (i) 40 km (ii) 90 km (iii) 10 km
(b) (i) 10 km/h (ii) 60 km/h (iii) 15 km/h (iv) 80 km/h
4. (a) 40 km (b) 60 km (c) York, Scarborough (d) 15 min
(e) (i) 11 00 (ii) 11 30 (iii) 12 30 (iv) 13 45
(f) (i) 40 km/h (ii) 60 km/h (iii) 100 km/h
5. (a) 80 km (b) Penrith, Kendal (c) $\frac{3}{4}$ h
(d) (i) 07 30 (ii) 09 00 (iii) 09 45 (iv) 10 45
(e) (i) 60 km/h (ii) 50 km/h (iii) 80 km/h
6. (a) Chilham, Thruxsted, Bogham (b) $1\frac{1}{4}$ h
(c) (i) 11 45 (ii) 10 45 (iii) 12 45 (iv) 14 00
(d) (i) 10 km/h (ii) 7 km/h (iii) 8 km/h
(e) 10 15 (f) 12 30
7. (a) (i) 04 00 (ii) 10 00 (iii) 07 00 (iv) 04 30
(b) $\frac{1}{2}$ h
(c) (i) $83\frac{1}{3}$ km/h (ii) 50 km/h (iii) 25 km/h (d) 08 30
(e) 50 km/h
8. (a) (i) 12 45 (ii) 11 15 (b) 350 km
(c) (i) 200 km/h (ii) 300 km/h (iii) 400 km/h
(d) 11 45 (e) 229 km/h (to 3 S.F.)
9. (a) 25 km (b) 15 km (c) 09 30 (d) $1\frac{1}{4}$ h
(e) (i) 40 km/h (ii) 5 km/h (iii) 30 km/h (iv) 40 km/h

Exercise 10 *page 122*

1. (a) 75 km (b) 2 h (c) 40 km (d) 10 24
(e) (i) 25 km/h (ii) 70 km/h (iii) 80 km/h (f) 15 km
2. (a) (i) 08 00 (ii) 09 00 (b) 30 km/h (c) 40 km/h
(d) (i) 65 km (ii) 50 km (iii) 15 km (iv) 55 km
(e) 51 km (f) 09 20
3. (a) $\frac{3}{4}$ h
(b) (i) 15 km/h (ii) 60 km/h (iii) 40 km/h (iv) 20 km/h
(c) 14 00 (d) 15 45 (e) 16 15 (f) 10 km
4. (a) (i) 14 00 (ii) 13 45 (b) (i) 15 45 (ii) towards Aston
(c) (i) 15 m.p.h. (ii) 40 m.p.h. (iii) 40 m.p.h. (iv) 20 m.p.h.
(d) $1607\frac{1}{2}$
5. (b) 14 00 6. (b) 15 30 7. (b) 11 45 8. (b) 12 45
9. (c) 17 00

Exercise 11 *page 125*

1. B, W 2. L, M 3. A, J, S 4. G, K, O 5. D, R
6. E, O 7. U, W 8. K 9. K, M Q, V 10. T
11. $y = 4$ 12. $y = -3$ 13. $x = 2$ 14. $y = -4$ 15. $x = -4$
16. $y = -5$ 17. $x = 0$ 18. $y = x$ 19. $y = -2$ 20. $x = 3$
21. $x + y = 5$ 22. $y = x + 1$ 23. $x + y = 3$ 24. $y = x + 3$ 25. $x + y = 9$
26. $y = 2x$

Exercise 12 *page 125*

1. −6 2. −9 3. −4 4. 2 5. −12 6. 4 7. 12
8. −10 9. −6 10. 12 11. 15 12. −21 13. −3 14. 0
15. −30 16. 0 17. 7 18. 20 19. −18 20. 0 21. −8
22. −7 23. 0 24. −16 25. 6 26. −35 27. −16 28. 4
29. 9 30. 1 31. 0 32. −9 33. −9 34. 9 35. −40
36. 16 37. 4 38. 25 39. 0 40. 54 41. −80 42. 100
43. −8 44. −18 45. 64 46. 0 47. 27 48. 49

Exercise 13 *page 125*

1. 2 2. −4 3. −7 4. 3 5. 1 6. −8 7. 5
8. −6 9. −13 10. −6 11. −3 12. 4 13. −8 14. −6
15. −3 16. −22 17. −13 18. 3 19. 11 20. −5 21. 17
22. −13 23. 6 24. 3 25. −8 26. 7 27. −1 28. 6
29. 6 30. 1 31. 0 32. 10

Exercise 14 *page 126*

[y values are given]

1. −3, −1, 1, 3, 5, 7, 9
2. −14, −10, −6, −2, 2, 6, 10
3. −8, −5, −2, 1, 4, 7, 10
4. 2, 3, 4, 5, 6, 7, 8
5. −29, −24, −19, −14, −9, −4, 1

Exercise 15 *page 126*

[y values are given]

1. −5, −3, −1, 1, 3, 5, 7
2. −11, −8, −5, −2, 1, 4
3. −2, −1, 0, 1, 2, 3, 4, 5, 6
4. −11, −9, −7, −5, −3, −1, 1, 3
5. −11, −7, −3, 1, 5, 9, 13
6. −5, −4, −3, −2, −1, 0, 1, 2
7. −4, −2, 0, 2, 4, 6, 8
8. −7, −4, −1, 2, 5, 8, 11

9. 2, 3, 4, 5, 6, 7, 8, 9, 10
11. 10, 8, 6, 4, 2, 0, −2
13. 12, 10, 8, 6, 4, 2, 0
15. 7, 6, 5, 4, 3, 2, 1, 0, −1
17. 4, 2, 0, −2, −4, −6, −8
19. −3, −1, 1, 3, 5, 7, 9

10. −15, −11, −7, −3, 1, 5, 9
12. 5, 4, 3, 2, 1, 0, −1
14. 14, 11, 8, 5, 2, −1, −4
16. 15, 11, 7, 3, −1, −5, −9
18. −3, −4, −5, −6, −7, −8, −9, −10
20. 10, 8, 6, 4, 2, 0, −2

Exercise 16 *page 127*

[*y* values are given]

1. 4, 0, −2, 2, 0, 4, 10
3. 13, 8, 5, 4, 5, 8, 13
5. 15, 8, 3, 0, −1, 0, 3
7. 6, 3, 2, 3, 6, 11, 18
9. −8, −9, −8, −5, 0, 7, 16
11. −3, −4, −3, 0, 5, 12, 21
13. 17, 12, 9, 8, 9, 12, 17
15. 27, 17, 9, 3, −1, −3, −3
17. 22, 13, 6, 1, −2, −3, −2
19. 9, 2, −1, 0, 5, 14, 27

2. −4, −6, −6, −4, 0, 6, 14
4. 2, −3, −6, −7, −6, −3, 2
6. 12, 5, 0, −3, −4, −3, 0
8. 2, −2, −4, −4, −2, 2, 8
10. 21, 14, 9, 6, 5, 6, 9
12. 40, 27, 16, 7, 0, −5, −8
14. 5, 1, −1, −1, 1, 5, 11
16. 5, −1, −5, −7, −7, −5, −1
18. 19, 9, 3, 1, 3, 9, 19
20. 25, 12, 5, 4, 9, 20, 37

Exercise 17 *page 128*

[*y* values are given]

1. 11, 6, 3, 2, 3, 6, 11
3. 5, 0, −3, −4, −3, 0, 5
5. 8, 3, 0, −1, 0, 3, 8
7. 4, 0, −2, −2, 0, 4, 10
9. 6, 0, −4, −6, −6, −4, 0, 6
11. 3, −2, −5, −6, −5, −2, 3
13. 4, −1, −4, −5, −4, −1, 4
15. 6, 1, −2, −3, −2, 1, 6

2. 14, 9, 6, 5, 6, 9, 14
4. 1, −4, −7, −8, −7, −4, 1
6. 5, 0, −3, −4, −3, 0, 5
8. 15, 8, 3, 0, −1, 0, 3
10. 10, 4, 0, −2, −2, 0, 4
12. 5, 1, −1, −1, 1, 5, 11
14. 4, 0, −2, −2, 0, 4, 10

Exercise 18 *page 129*

1. −26, −7, 0, 1, 2, 9, 28
3. 19, 8, 1, −2, −1, 4, 13
5. −20, −6, −2, −2, 0, 10, 34
7. 13, 3, −3, −5, −3, 3, 13

2. 12, 6, 4, 3, 2.4, 2, 1.7, 1.5, 1.3, 1.2, 1.1, 1
4. 16, 8, 5.3, 4, 3.2, 2.7, 2.3, 2, 1.8, 1.6
6. 16, 3, −4, −5, 0, 11, 28
8. −35, −13, −3, 1, 5, 15, 37

Exercise 19 *page 129*

1. 0.3, 3.7
5. −1.8, 2.8
9. 1.4, 5.6

2. −1.6, 2.6
6. 1.4, 5.6
10. 3.5

3. −1.4, 1.4
7. −1.6, 2.6
11. 1.3, 7.7

4. −2.6, 1.6
8. −0.8, 3.8
12. −2.8, 1.8

UNIT 8

Exercise 3 *page 133*

2. (d) (−6, −4), (6, 4), (−6, 2), (2, 4)
4. (d) (7, 5), (−5, 7), (5, −7)
6. (e) (−5, 5), (5, 5), (−1, −1)
8. (g) (3, 1), (7, 1), (7, 3)
10. (f) (3, −3), (3, −7), (5, −3)

3. (d) (7, −7), (−5, 5), (5, 7)
5. (f) (−7, 6), (7, 6), (6, 7)
7. (g) (−3, 6), (−6, 6), (−6, 4)
9. (g) (5, 5), (5, 2), (3, 2)

Exercise 4 page 134

1. (a) x axis ($y = 0$) (b) $x = 1$ (c) $y = 1$ (d) $y = -x$
2. (b) (i) x axis ($y = 0$) (ii) $y = 4$ (iii) y axis ($x = 0$) (iv) $x = 3$
3. (b) (i) x axis (ii) $x = 1$ (iii) $y = 4$ (iv) $y = x$
4. (b) (i) $y = x$ (ii) x axis (iii) $y = -x$
5. (b) (i) $y = -3$ (ii) $x = 2\frac{1}{2}$ (iii) $y = -\frac{1}{2}$ (iv) $y = x$

Exercise 7 page 136

1. (d) (2, −1), (−4, 5), (−5, 2)
2. (e) (−3, 3), (3, −3), (1, 3)
3. (e) (6, 3), (1, 2), (−5, −6)
4. (c) (−6, 6), (4, −6), (6, 2), (3, 7)
5. (c) (3, 1), (3, −1), (−2, 0), (−5, −3)
6. (c) (4, 3), (−3, −6), (2, 3), (4, −3)

Exercise 8 page 137

5. (a) (0, 0) (b) (1, 2) (c) (0, 0) (d) (−1, 1)
6. (b) (i) (2, 3) (ii) (0, 0) (iii) (2, 0) (iv) (−1, 1)
7. (b) (i) (0, 0) (ii) (−5, 0) (iii) (−7, 4) (iv) (−1, −5)
8. (b) (i) (2, 2) (ii) (−3, 7) (iii) (6, −1) (iv) (−1, −1)
9. (b) (i) (−1, 2) (ii) (3, 2) (iii) (3, −3) (iv) (0, 5)
   (v) (1, 0) (vi) (3, 4) (vii) (−3, 2) (viii) $(-1\frac{1}{2}, -2\frac{1}{2})$

Exercise 9 page 138

1. Centre is intersection of PQ and XY, angle is 180°
2. Centre is intersection of PQ and XY, angle is 90°

Exercise 10 page 139

1. (a) no (b) no (c) no (d) no (e) no
   (f) yes (g) no (h) yes (i) no (j) no
   (k) no (l) no (m) yes (n) no (o) yes
   (p) yes (q) yes (r) no (s) no (t) yes
2. (a) $\begin{pmatrix}4\\6\end{pmatrix}$ (b) $\begin{pmatrix}6\\4\end{pmatrix}$ (c) $\begin{pmatrix}0\\3\end{pmatrix}$ (d) $\begin{pmatrix}6\\0\end{pmatrix}$ (e) $\begin{pmatrix}5\\-2\end{pmatrix}$
   (f) $\begin{pmatrix}-2\\-3\end{pmatrix}$ (g) $\begin{pmatrix}-2\\5\end{pmatrix}$ (h) $\begin{pmatrix}2\\-2\end{pmatrix}$ (i) $\begin{pmatrix}-4\\-3\end{pmatrix}$ (j) $\begin{pmatrix}2\\-6\end{pmatrix}$
   (k) $\begin{pmatrix}1\\-8\end{pmatrix}$ (l) $\begin{pmatrix}-6\\-1\end{pmatrix}$ (m) $\begin{pmatrix}0\\-4\end{pmatrix}$ (n) $\begin{pmatrix}6\\1\end{pmatrix}$ (o) $\begin{pmatrix}4\\3\end{pmatrix}$
   (p) $\begin{pmatrix}8\\3\end{pmatrix}$ (q) $\begin{pmatrix}1\\6\end{pmatrix}$ (r) $\begin{pmatrix}8\\-1\end{pmatrix}$ (s) $\begin{pmatrix}0\\-8\end{pmatrix}$ (t) $\begin{pmatrix}6\\-3\end{pmatrix}$
3. (d) (i) (1, 1) (ii) (2, −4) (iii) (−3, 3) (iv) (5, −7) (v) (−6, 1)
   (vi) (−3, −7) (vii) (5, 4)

Exercise 11 page 141

1. 2.7 → 10.8 cm, 4.6 → 18.4 cm, 10.2 → 40.8 cm, 4.1 → 16.4 cm
2. 85 cm
3. 56 cm
4. (a) 20 cm (b) 60 cm (c) 85 cm (d) 180 cm (e) 700 cm (f) 20
5. (a) 4 m (b) 3 m (c) 24 cm (d) 4 m (e) 20 (f) 1.5 m
   (g) 100
6. (a) 120 cm (b) 5 m (c) 20 cm (d) 30 (e) 4.2 cm (f) 25 m
   (g) 300

Exercise 13 *page 143*

1. (e) (3, 0), (−5, −1), (3, −1) **2.** (e) (3, 3), (−6, −1), (3, −3)
3. (e) (−1, 7), (−5, −2), (0, 5) **4.** (e) (−2, 1), (0, −1), (2, 4)
5. (e) (−5, 1), (−7, −2), (1, −1) **6.** (e) (3, −1), (2, −1), (5, −7)

Exercise 15 *page 145*

1. (e) (3, 3), (3, −1), (−4, 1) **2.** (e) (1, 2), (1, −4), (−6, 1)
3. (e) (4, 3), (−2, −3), (3, −1) **4.** (e) (−3, 7), (5, −1), (−3, −1)
5. (e) (−3, 1), (5, 0), (−2, 4)

UNIT 9

Exercise 1 *page 146*

1. $47\frac{1}{2}°$ **2.** 102° **3.** 39° **4.** $120\frac{1}{2}°$ **5.** 41° **6.** 116°
7. (a) 98° (b) 73° (c) 104° (d) 61° (e) 124°
(f) 124° (g) 88° (h) 51° (i) 62° (j) 108°
(k) 66° (l) 86° (m) 83° (n) 120° (o) 31°
(p) 120° (q) 76° (r) $114\frac{1}{2}°$ (s) $102\frac{1}{2}°$ (t) 119°

Exercise 2 *page 148*

1. 7.3 cm **2.** 7.9 cm **3.** 12.3 cm **4.** 8.0 cm **5.** 6.4 cm **6.** 6.8 cm
7. 9.0 cm **8.** 9.6 cm **9.** 7.6 cm **10.** 8.7 cm **11.** 8.2 cm **12.** 5.3 cm
13. 5.4 cm **14.** 11.2 cm **15.** $60\frac{1}{2}°$ **16.** $85\frac{1}{2}°$ **17.** 72° **18.** 121°
19. $118\frac{1}{2}°$ **20.** $55\frac{1}{2}°$

Exercise 3 *page 149*

1. A 035°, B 070°, C 155°, D 220°, E 290°, L 340°
2. A 040°, B 065°, C 130°, D 160°, E 230°, F 330°
3. Karl 038°, Louise 060°, Michelle 135°, Nick 155°, Philip 210°, Ray 250°, Steve 325°

Exercise 4 *page 150*

1. (a) 060° (b) 240° **2.** (a) 120° (b) 300° **3.** (a) 255° (b) 075°
4. (a) 315° (b) 135° **5.** (a) 100° (b) 280° **6.** (a) 055° (b) 235°
7. (a) 052° (b) 304° (c) 232° (d) 124°
8. (a) 042° (b) 108° (c) 222° (d) 288°

Exercise 5 *page 152*

1. 7.2 km **2.** 5.0 km **3.** 11.0 km **4.** 11.4 km **5.** 14.3 km **6.** 10.0 km
7. 8.5 km **8.** 6.4 km **9.** 15.3 km **10.** 12.2 km **11.** 12.0 km **12.** 8.9 km
13. 10.2 km **14.** 5.0 km **15.** 7.0 km **16.** 6.3 km **17.** 9.4 km **18.** 13.6 km
19. 7.3 km **20.** 11.2 km

Exercise 6 *page 153*

1. (a) 056° (b) 090° (c) 115° (d) 143° (e) 165°
2. (a) $020\frac{1}{2}°$ (b) $063\frac{1}{2}°$ (c) 101° (d) 143° (e) 180°
3. (a) 011° (b) 036° (c) 045° (d) 345° (e) 063°
4. (a) $128\frac{1}{2}°$ (b) 145° (c) 180° (d) $200\frac{1}{2}°$ (e) 236°
5. (a) 032° (b) 074° (c) 225° (d) 323° (e) 000°
6. (a) $161\frac{1}{2}°$ (b) 212° (c) $243\frac{1}{2}°$ (d) 270° (e) $308\frac{1}{2}°$

Exercise 9 *page 153*

1. 11.5 km **2.** 14.1 km **3.** 10.9 km **4.** 10.4 km **5.** 8.3 km
6. 10.0 km **7.** 10.95 km **8.** 12.5 km, 032° **9.** 6.9 km **10.** 5.5 km
11. 8.5 km, 074° **12.** 8.4 km, 029°

Exercise 10 *page 155*

1. m, e, t **2.** n, t, e **3.** e, q, y **4.** r, q, p **5.** m, l, n **6.** i, j, h
7. t, c, b **8.** p, q, r **9.** e, k, f **10.** z, t, y **11.** c, t, n **12.** k, q, b
13. z, m, e **14.** f, c, y **15.** q, v, l **16.** e, w, n **17.** v, p, y **18.** l, e, z
19. v, d, i **20.** k, c, g **21.** n, y, w **22.** e, f, w **23.** v, i, q **24.** u, y, t

Exercise 12 *page 156*

1. 0.545 **2.** 0.906 **3.** 0.990 **4.** 0.358 **5.** 0.139 **6.** 0.602
7. 0.139 **8.** 0.899 **9.** 0.951 **10.** 0.993 **11.** 0.194 **12.** 1.33
13. 0.754 **14.** 2.25 **15.** 5.14 **16.** 0.515 **17.** 0.707 **18.** 4.01
19. 0.475 **20.** 0.546 **21.** 0.925 **22.** 0.488 **23.** 0.608 **24.** 0.964
25. 0.311 **26.** 0.986 **27.** 2.67 **28.** 0.202 **29.** 0.829 **30.** 0.946
31. 0.092 **32.** 5.67 **33.** 0.370 **34.** 0.111 **35.** 1.00 **36.** 0.532
37. 0.227 **38.** 0.999 **39.** 0.954 **40.** 0.961 **41.** 3.19 **42.** 0.115
43. 0.498 **44.** 0.543 **45.** 28.6

Exercise 13 *page 157*

1. 4.07 cm **2.** 4.24 cm **3.** 74.3 cm **4.** 5.14 cm **5.** 18.5 cm **6.** 5.26 cm
7. 14.1 cm **8.** 14.6 cm **9.** 8.69 cm **10.** 6.71 cm **11.** 22.6 cm **12.** 4.90 cm
13. 15.9 m **14.** 3.22 m **15.** 19.4 m **16.** 35.6 m **17.** 437 m **18.** 29.9 m
19. 53.5 cm **20.** 3.85 cm

Exercise 14 *page 157*

1. 4.00 cm **2.** 8.91 cm **3.** 9.65 cm **4.** 5.44 cm **5.** 11.8 cm **6.** 26.0 cm
7. 12.5 cm **8.** 7.70 cm **9.** 11.2 m **10.** 17.0 m **11.** 87.5 m **12.** 5.28 m
13. 10.9 m **14.** 8.59 m **15.** 227 m **16.** 7.41 m **17.** 19.3 m **18.** 19.4 cm
19. 2.52 m **20.** 1.92 m **21.** 295 m **22.** 19.5 cm **23.** 0.939 cm **24.** 10.4 cm

Exercise 15 *page 158*

1. 59.0° **2.** 35.0° **3.** 11.0° **4.** 38.3° **5.** 75.0° **6.** 10.4° **7.** 66.2°
8. 56.4° **9.** 45.5° **10.** 50.7° **11.** 73.0° **12.** 42.0° **13.** 30.0° **14.** 63.0°
15. 84.0° **16.** 40.1° **17.** 23.8° **18.** 81.2° **19.** 87.2° **20.** 89.6° **21.** 69.0°
22. 67.3° **23.** 20.1° **24.** 74.0° **25.** 32.7° **26.** 73.5° **27.** 34.4° **28.** 36.3°
29. 29.3° **30.** 0.4° **31.** 53.1° **32.** 78.2° **33.** 39.6° **34.** 14.8° **35.** 72.0°
36. 36.9° **37.** 37.2° **38.** 36.2° **39.** 87.0° **40.** 88.4° **41.** 58.0° **42.** 0.6°
43. 31.8° **44.** 50.3° **45.** 1.1° **46.** 35.4° **47.** 29.4° **48.** 84.2° **49.** 79.2°
50. 69.4°

Exercise 16 *page 158*

1. 7.2° **2.** 12.8° **3.** 44.4° **4.** 35.7° **5.** 61.0° **6.** 38.7° **7.** 48.6°
8. 19.5° **9.** 26.4° **10.** 64.2° **11.** 36.9° **12.** 34.8° **13.** 46.7° **14.** 16.6°
15. 12.4° **16.** 15.5° **17.** 11.5° **18.** 28.1° **19.** 29.3° **20.** 21.3°

Exercise 17 *page 159*

1. 20.6° **2.** 70.5° **3.** 51.3° **4.** 38.7° **5.** 33.1° **6.** 63.6° **7.** 35.7°
8. 30.0° **9.** 24.6° **10.** 53.1° **11.** 62.7° **12.** 73.4° **13.** 29.9° **14.** 8.6°

15. 34.3° **16.** 4.0° **17.** 76.0° **18.** 40.6° **19.** 43.4° **20.** 32.0° **21.** 38.9°
22. 69.4° **23.** 60.3° **24.** 36.9° **25.** 38.0° **26.** 14.3° **27.** 4.8° **28.** 77.5°

Exercise 18 *page 160*

1. 23.6° **2.** 24.6° **3.** 3.29 m **4.** 4.64 m
5. 33.2° **6.** 29.0° **7.** 38.9°, 70.5°, 70.5° **8.** 21.8°, 43.6°
9. 60.5° **10.** 64.0° **11.** 38.7° **12.** 36.9°
13. 35.5° **14.** 33.7° **15.** 40.6° **16.** 78.7°

THINK ABOUT IT 3

Project 1 *page 162*

Part A

5	2	5		3	5		2
2		2	4	1	7		1
1	7	2		0		6	4
8		1	7	0		8	
	1	0	1		5	4	9
8	7		5	5	5		
7		4		3	0	4	6
7	2	9				6	6

Part B

5	8	4		3	5		3
8		3	4	2	7		6
3	9	9		8		3	4
6		1	8	3		1	
	7	6	4		9	5	0
8	7		5	6	7		
5		9		6	8	7	5
8	2	4		7		3	6

Part C

1	1	5		3	9		1
8		1	4	4	0		2
6	5	0		7		6	5
0		5	7	0		4	
	2	1	9		6	6	6
1	4		3	4	1		
2		4		9	0	5	0
7	0	5		0		8	1

Part D

1	7	5		2	4		0
2		9	9	6	0		0
9	9	9		9		3	7
5		9	0	5		8	
	1	6	0		8	0	7
3	6		5	7	2		
0		2		2	3	4	5
5	7	1		9		2	2

Exercise A *page 164*

1. 1 hr 50 min **2.** 24 cm **3.** £6 **4.** 56 cm^2 **5.** 50 m, 80 cm
6. 2p **7.** 259 200 **8.** 14 **9.** (a) 75°, 105° (b) 108°
10. (a) 9 miles (b) 10 miles (c) $2\frac{1}{2}$ miles (d) $7\frac{1}{2}$ miles

Exercise B *page 166*

1. 0.72 cm **2.** £6.05 **3.** (a) 8 m (b) 48 m (c) 36 m
4. (a) £5.64 (b) £0.72 (c) £11.66 (d) £2.07 (e) £8.11 (f) £7.08
5. (a) £3.36 (b) £4.03 (c) £1.61
6. (a) £2, £18 (b) £10, £40 (c) £45, £15 **7.** (a) 1200 g (b) 3
8. 50 **9.** (a) £400 (6.2% = £288.30) (b) 6.2% = £533.20 **10.** (a) 13 (b) 10 cm

Exercise C *page 168*

1. 2880 **2.** 23, 1 over **3.** 600 m^3 **4.** (a) $a = 80°$, $b = 100°$ (b) $c = 70°$, $d = 40°$
5. 0.5 m **6.** $\frac{5}{14}$ **7.** (a) 5°C (b) −1°C (c) −4°C
8. 2120 **9.** (a) 20 000 (b) 5 (c) 200 (d) 1000 **10.** 65

Exercise D *page 168*

1. (a) 0.6°C (b) 2.2°C (c) 2.7°C (d) 1.3°C **2.** (a) 110p (b) 121p
3. £1.20 **4.** (a) £7400 (b) £7900 (c) £10 400 **5.** 200
6. (a) £1.20 (b) 880 g **7.** 313 million **8.** (a) 60% (b) 30% (c) 70%
9. (a) 340 km (b) 68 km/h **10.** (a) 75p (b) 40p

Project 4 *page 170*

Part A

1. A **2.** B **3.** C **4.** A **5.** C **6.** D **7.** B
8. B **9.** C **10.** D **11.** C **12.** A **13.** B **14.** A
15. C **16.** B **17.** B **18.** D **19.** D **20.** B

Part B

1. £10 **2.** £5 **3.** £15 **4.** £16 **5.** £60 **6.** £54
7. £30 **8.** £20 **9.** £60 **10.** £38 **11.** £20 **12.** £30
13. £19 **14.** £14 **15.** £15 **16.** £60 **17.** £22.50 **18.** £16
19. £50 **20.** £75

Part C

1. £92 **2.** £46 **3.** £95 **4.** £91 **5.** £112.50 **6.** £91
7. £90 **8.** £164 **9.** £116 **10.** £68 **11.** £148 **12.** £114
13. £90 **14.** £133.50 **15.** £66 **16.** £64 **17.** £114 **18.** £90

Exercise E *page 175*

1. £319.10 **2.** 52
3. (a) 15 (b) (i) 20% (ii) 16% (iii) 70% (iv) 2% **4.** 169
5. 6.40 p.m. **6.** (a) $\frac{9}{4}$ (b) $\frac{7}{4}$ (c) $\frac{7}{2}$ (d) $\frac{22}{5}$
7. (a) 177 147 (b) 1 594 323 **8.** (a) 821 + 413 + 230 = 1464 (b) 241 + 453 + 279 = 973
(c) 364 + 211 + 804 = 1379 **9.** £425 **10.** 13

Exercise F *page 176*

1. (a) £1.28 (b) £20.48 (c) 31p **2.** (a) 47.25 kg (b) 51 kg **3.** 13 each, 7 left over
4. £52.92 **5.** (a) 36 (b) 24 (c) 240 (d) 60 **6.** $7\frac{1}{2}$ cm^2

7. (a) 0.5, 0.517, 0.5171, 0.617 (b) 0.029, 0.03, 0.1, 0.31
(c) 0.0555, 0.505, 0.55, 0.555 (d) 0.011, 0.089, 0.09, 0.11
8. £18, £27, £45 **9.** 10 h 30 min **10.** (a) 642 + 156 = 798 (b) 254 + 923 = 1177
(c) 962 − 722 = 240

Exercise G *page 178*

1. 27, 14p change **2.** 160 **3.** £2.20, £1.40, £0.75, £0.55 **4.** 100 km/h
5. (a) −3, 4 (b) −2, 6 (c) −1, 3 **6.** 56% **7.** £112.50 **8.** £2180
9. (a) yes (b) yes (c) yes (d) no (e) yes (f) no
10. (a) 8192 (b) 32 768

Section B

UNIT 10

Exercise 1 *page 183*

1. 283 **2.** 960 **3.** 2223 **4.** 3968 **5.** 6320 **6.** 6236
7. 875 **8.** 663 **9.** 24 105 **10.** 12 692 **11.** 212 **12.** 931
13. 784 **14.** 806 **15.** 288 **16.** 345 **17.** 509 **18.** 6990
19. 12 **20.** 1978 **21.** 523 **22.** 1439 **23.** 19 261 **24.** 21 007
25. 239 100 **26.** 197 **27.** 449 **28.** 4609 **29.** 5895 **30.** 2814

Exercise 2 *page 184*

1. 13.81 **2.** 8.64 **3.** 20.9 **4.** 13.42 **5.** 8.4 **6.** 10.35 **7.** 10.09
8. 19 **9.** 7.4 **10.** 20.46 **11.** 20.04 **12.** 27.75 **13.** 24.1 **14.** 31.6
15. 8.059 **16.** 5.096 **17.** 1.52 **18.** 7.23 **19.** 8.11 **20.** 2.68 **21.** 2.92
22. 10.9 **23.** 1.9 **24.** 6.6 **25.** 4.09 **26.** 5.5 **27.** 3.6 **28.** 7.5
29. 1.74 **30.** 7.04 **31.** 5.4 **32.** 0.75 **33.** 2.98 **34.** 5.4 **35.** 8.8
36. 240.8 **37.** 3.159 **38.** 6.58 **39.** 4.37 **40.** 6.27

Exercise 3 *page 184*

1. 81 **2.** 164 **3.** 165 **4.** 196 **5.** 246 **6.** 1160
7. 1296 **8.** 2261 **9.** 2135 **10.** 3288 **11.** 4422 **12.** 7536
13. 1922 **14.** 2940 **15.** 24 920 **16.** 50 716 **17.** 19 278 **18.** 76 609
19. 55 237 **20.** 91 800 **21.** 102 384 **22.** 298 688 **23.** 105 363 **24.** 101 898

Exercise 4 *page 184*

1. 231 **2.** 315 **3.** 236 **4.** 382 **5.** 417 **6.** 662
7. 352 **8.** 685 **9.** 2142 **10.** 672 **11.** 3165 **12.** 209
13. 607 **14.** 314 **15.** 341 **16.** 2674 **17.** 805 **18.** 3141
19. 332 **20.** 4009 **21.** 268 **22.** 4111 **23.** 632 **24.** 8007
25. 4685 **26.** 2419 **27.** 3817 **28.** 2763 **29.** 24 135 **30.** 6887
31. 2.67 **32.** 3.06 **33.** 3.414 **34.** 2.841 **35.** 81.26 **36.** 3.466
37. 4.72 **38.** 0.748 **39.** 8.27 **40.** 3.007

Exercise 5 *page 184*

1. 1.6 **2.** 10.96 **3.** 2.87 **4.** 2.16 **5.** 4.4 **6.** 7.209
7. 4.32 **8.** 0.336 **9.** 4.06 **10.** 229.4 **11.** 0.0632 **12.** 13.2

13. 1.16 **14.** 381 **15.** 2.52 **16.** 0.111 **17.** 0.4662 **18.** 0.3934
19. 2.1607 **20.** 0.693 **21.** 3.62 **22.** 1.45 **23.** 8.24 **24.** 0.714
25. 3.77 **26.** 8.26 **27.** 0.147 **28.** 0.073 **29.** 58.2 **30.** 27.4
31. 216.2 **32.** 37.4 **33.** 518.7 **34.** 244.8

Exercise 6 *page 185*

1. 3.926 **2.** 4.25 **3.** 0.186 **4.** 39.82 **5.** 21.8 **6.** 0.31
7. 8.9 **8.** 14.74 **9.** 52 **10.** 6.6 **11.** 8.47 **12.** 2600
13. 14.9 **14.** 0.0041 **15.** 0.014 **16.** 7872 **17.** 56 200 **18.** 638
19. 0.3 **20.** 0.0516 **21.** 36.5 **22.** 60 **23.** 2.14 **24.** 13.95
25. 6.66 **26.** 1120 **27.** 1.23 **28.** 2.94 **29.** 43 **30.** 369
31. 0.84 **32.** 6.67 **33.** 0.0021 **34.** 357 **35.** 8.435 **36.** 5.85
37. 0.192 51 **38.** 486

Exercise 7 *page 185*

1. 4p **2.** 11p **3.** 9p **4.** 10p **5.** 4p **6.** 18p **7.** 6p
8. 13p **9.** £1.75 **10.** 36p **11.** 2.5p **12.** £7.25 **13.** 15p **14.** 5p
15. 16p **16.** £0.89 **17.** 14p **18.** 2p **19.** £3.60 **20.** 15p

Exercise 8 *page 186*

1. $\frac{2}{3}$ **2.** $\frac{3}{4}$ **3.** $\frac{9}{10}$ **4.** $\frac{4}{5}$ **5.** $\frac{2}{3}$ **6.** $\frac{2}{3}$ **7.** $\frac{3}{5}$
8. $\frac{1}{4}$ **9.** $\frac{1}{3}$ **10.** $\frac{2}{9}$ **11.** $\frac{1}{3}$ **12.** $\frac{1}{3}$ **13.** $\frac{2}{3}$ **14.** $\frac{7}{9}$
15. $\frac{3}{5}$ **16.** $\frac{7}{8}$ **17.** $\frac{4}{9}$ **18.** $\frac{11}{12}$ **19.** $\frac{7}{9}$ **20.** $\frac{11}{12}$ **21.** $\frac{5}{12}$
22. $\frac{7}{10}$ **23.** $\frac{4}{11}$ **24.** $\frac{7}{12}$ **25.** $\frac{3}{5}$ **26.** $\frac{14}{15}$ **27.** $\frac{8}{15}$ **28.** $\frac{1}{7}$
29. $\frac{9}{20}$ **30.** $\frac{1}{25}$ **31.** $\frac{1}{250}$ **32.** $\frac{3}{7}$ **33.** $\frac{1}{8}$ **34.** $\frac{1}{6}$ **35.** $\frac{11}{40}$
36. $\frac{1}{16}$ **37.** $\frac{2}{3}$ **38.** $\frac{2}{5}$ **39.** $\frac{2}{7}$ **40.** $\frac{3}{20}$ **41.** $\frac{1}{15}$ **42.** $\frac{4}{55}$
43. $\frac{1}{90}$ **44.** $\frac{1}{5}$ **45.** $\frac{4}{5}$ **46.** $\frac{8}{9}$ **47.** $\frac{3}{5}$ **48.** $\frac{8}{9}$ **49.** $\frac{5}{8}$
50. $\frac{7}{9}$ **51.** $\frac{21}{80}$ **52.** $\frac{9}{20}$

Exercise 9 *page 186*

1. $1\frac{3}{4}$ **2.** $1\frac{3}{5}$ **3.** $2\frac{1}{4}$ **4.** $3\frac{2}{3}$ **5.** $2\frac{2}{3}$ **6.** $2\frac{1}{2}$ **7.** $1\frac{2}{3}$
8. $1\frac{1}{5}$ **9.** $2\frac{3}{4}$ **10.** $2\frac{1}{3}$ **11.** $1\frac{5}{6}$ **12.** $2\frac{2}{5}$ **13.** $2\frac{1}{6}$ **14.** $3\frac{1}{2}$
15. $1\frac{2}{7}$ **16.** $3\frac{3}{5}$ **17.** $4\frac{1}{5}$ **18.** $3\frac{1}{3}$ **19.** $1\frac{5}{7}$ **20.** $5\frac{5}{11}$ **21.** $5\frac{5}{6}$
22. $3\frac{3}{7}$ **23.** $3\frac{3}{4}$ **24.** $3\frac{1}{3}$ **25.** $5\frac{8}{9}$ **26.** $11\frac{1}{9}$ **27.** $8\frac{1}{5}$ **28.** $7\frac{3}{10}$
29. $4\frac{2}{9}$ **30.** $8\frac{9}{11}$ **31.** $9\frac{1}{11}$ **32.** $2\frac{6}{7}$ **33.** $7\frac{3}{7}$ **34.** $8\frac{2}{5}$ **35.** $4\frac{1}{16}$
36. $6\frac{1}{2}$ **37.** $5\frac{3}{7}$ **38.** $1\frac{8}{17}$ **39.** $2\frac{4}{13}$ **40.** $5\frac{5}{8}$ **41.** $3\frac{2}{3}$ **42.** $7\frac{1}{3}$
43. $16\frac{2}{3}$ **44.** $1\frac{1}{2}$ **45.** $2\frac{8}{9}$ **46.** $3\frac{7}{11}$ **47.** $2\frac{1}{2}$ **48.** $6\frac{1}{4}$ **49.** $1\frac{1}{2}$
50. $4\frac{5}{6}$ **51.** $3\frac{2}{11}$ **52.** $\frac{41}{42}$

Exercise 10 *page 186*

1. $\frac{5}{8}$ **2.** $1\frac{1}{4}$ **3.** $\frac{7}{8}$ **4.** $1\frac{3}{8}$ **5.** $\frac{5}{8}$ **6.** $\frac{3}{8}$ **7.** $\frac{15}{16}$
8. $\frac{9}{16}$ **9.** $\frac{3}{16}$ **10.** $1\frac{3}{16}$ **11.** $\frac{15}{16}$ **12.** $\frac{3}{16}$ **13.** $\frac{11}{16}$ **14.** $\frac{7}{16}$
15. $1\frac{11}{16}$ **16.** $\frac{11}{12}$ **17.** $1\frac{1}{10}$ **18.** $1\frac{1}{20}$ **19.** $1\frac{4}{15}$ **20.** $1\frac{1}{3}$ **21.** $1\frac{11}{20}$
22. $1\frac{1}{3}$ **23.** $\frac{27}{28}$ **24.** $\frac{4}{15}$ **25.** $\frac{5}{24}$ **26.** $\frac{17}{40}$ **27.** $\frac{11}{21}$ **28.** $\frac{11}{40}$
29. $\frac{7}{36}$ **30.** $\frac{9}{44}$

Exercise 11 *page 186*

1. $\frac{2}{15}$ **2.** $\frac{15}{28}$ **3.** $\frac{8}{15}$ **4.** $\frac{25}{42}$ **5.** $\frac{10}{27}$ **6.** $\frac{10}{33}$ **7.** $\frac{21}{32}$
8. $\frac{2}{3}$ **9.** $\frac{7}{20}$ **10.** $\frac{8}{15}$ **11.** $\frac{21}{40}$ **12.** $\frac{5}{16}$ **13.** $\frac{3}{8}$ **14.** $\frac{5}{12}$
15. $\frac{7}{12}$ **16.** $1\frac{1}{2}$ **17.** $\frac{9}{10}$ **18.** $3\frac{1}{3}$ **19.** $\frac{8}{9}$ **20.** $1\frac{1}{9}$ **21.** $\frac{20}{21}$
22. $3\frac{1}{3}$ **23.** $\frac{1}{6}$ **24.** $1\frac{1}{4}$ **25.** $\frac{5}{6}$ **26.** $\frac{7}{8}$ **27.** $\frac{1}{4}$ **28.** $1\frac{3}{8}$
29. $2\frac{2}{15}$ **30.** $\frac{11}{20}$ **31.** $\frac{5}{8}$ **32.** $1\frac{1}{6}$ **33.** $\frac{11}{20}$ **34.** $6\frac{1}{5}$ **35.** $\frac{3}{4}$
36. $9\frac{2}{3}$

Exercise 12 *page 187*

1. $\frac{5}{6}$ **2.** $\frac{1}{6}$ **3.** $\frac{2}{3}$ **4.** $\frac{5}{12}$ **5.** $\frac{1}{4}$ **6.** $2\frac{1}{4}$ **7.** $\frac{9}{10}$
8. $\frac{1}{5}$ **9.** $\frac{4}{5}$ **10.** $\frac{13}{14}$ **11.** $\frac{3}{14}$ **12.** $\frac{6}{7}$ **13.** $\frac{3}{8}$ **14.** $\frac{5}{32}$
15. $2\frac{1}{2}$ **16.** $\frac{29}{30}$ **17.** $\frac{2}{15}$ **18.** $\frac{5}{24}$ **19.** $\frac{16}{21}$ **20.** $\frac{1}{7}$ **21.** $1\frac{2}{7}$
22. $\frac{11}{20}$ **23.** $\frac{1}{5}$ **24.** $3\frac{1}{5}$ **25.** $\frac{13}{24}$ **26.** $\frac{1}{12}$ **27.** $5\frac{1}{3}$ **28.** $\frac{29}{36}$
29. $\frac{5}{36}$ **30.** $2\frac{2}{9}$ **31.** $2\frac{1}{4}$ **32.** $\frac{5}{8}$ **33.** 10 **34.** $3\frac{1}{12}$ **35.** $2\frac{1}{2}$
36. $5\frac{5}{8}$ **37.** $2\frac{1}{3}$ **38.** $\frac{5}{13}$ **39.** 18 **40.** 6

Exercise 13 *page 187*

1. 0.75 **2.** 0.5 **3.** 0.375 **4.** 0.4 **5.** 0.875 **6.** 0.25 **7.** 0.8
8. 0.3 **9.** 0.125 **10.** $0.\dot{3}$ **11.** $0.\dot{6}$ **12.** $0.1\dot{6}$ **13.** $0.\dot{4}$ **14.** $0.\dot{5}$
15. 0.07 **16.** 0.11 **17.** 0.14 **18.** 0.05 **19.** 0.009 **20.** 0.017 **21.** 0.06
22. $0.\dot{1}$ **23.** $0.41\dot{6}$ **24.** $0.91\dot{6}$ **25.** 0.714 **26.** 0.286 **27.** 0.364 **28.** 0.889
29. 0.143 **30.** 0.636 **31.** 0.385 **32.** 0.615 **33.** 0.267 **34.** 0.033 **35.** 0.078
36. 0.083

Exercise 14 *page 187*

1. 3, 11, 19, 23, 29, 31, 37, 47, 59, 61, 67, 73
2. (a) 4, 8, 12, 16, 20 (b) 6, 12, 18, 24, 30 (c) 10, 20, 30, 40, 50
(d) 11, 22, 33, 44, 55 (e) 20, 40, 60, 80, 100
3. 4, 8, 12, 16, 20, 24; 6, 12, 18, 24, 30, 36; common multiples 12, 24
4. 3, 6, 9, 12, 15, 18; 5, 10, 15, 20, 25, 30; L.C.M. = 15
5. (a) 1, 2, 3, 6 (b) 1, 3, 9 (c) 1, 2, 5, 10
(d) 1, 3, 5, 15 (e) 1, 2, 3, 4, 6, 8, 12, 24 (f) 1, 2, 4, 8, 16, 32
6. (a) rational (b) rational (c) irrational (d) rational
(e) rational (f) irrational (g) rational (h) irrational
(i) irrational (j) rational (k) rational (l) irrational

Exercise 15 *page 188*

1. 40% **2.** 75% **3.** 62.5% **4.** 7% **5.** 24% **6.** 35% **7.** 87.5%
8. $33\frac{1}{3}$% **9.** 12.5% **10.** 6% **11.** 9.5% **12.** 60% **13.** 80% **14.** 68%
15. 1.3% **16.** 54% **17.** 90% **18.** 7.5% **19.** 55% **20.** 22%

Exercise 16 *page 188*

1. £72 **2.** £15 **3.** £36 **4.** £30.80 **5.** £1.10 **6.** £26.40
7. £340 **8.** £13 **9.** £580 **10.** £18 **11.** $2480 **12.** $84
13. $4900 **14.** 16 m **15.** 20 kg **16.** 480 km **17.** 0.31 kg **18.** 109 km
19. £0.02 **20.** 10 kg **21.** £0.28 **22.** £1.58 **23.** £0.69 **24.** £0.80
25. £1.92 **26.** £1.68 **27.** £0.53 **28.** £10.86 **29.** £1.52 **30.** £1.09
31. £7.55 **32.** £1.19 **33.** £79.55 **34.** £0.06 **35.** £45.99 **36.** £0.03
37. £0.23 **38.** £2.47 **39.** £298.18 **40.** £4.15

Exercise 17 *page 188*

1. (a) £108 (b) £498 (c) £606
2. (a) £144 (b) £405.60 (c) £549.60
3. (a) £145.50 (b) £414 (c) £559.50
4. (a) £408 (b) £48
5. (a) £383.20 (b) £378
6. (a) £850 (b) £3240 (c) £270
7. (a) £280 (b) £700.80 (c) £29.20
8. (a) £335.40 (b) £436.80
9. (a) £396 (b) £2196 (c) £122
10. (a) (i) £161 (ii) £410.40 (iii) £571.40
 (b) (i) £92 (ii) £552 (iii) £23

Exercise 18 *page 190*

1. (a) £260 (b) £130 (c) £234
2. (a) £170 (b) £68
3. (a) £90 (b) £76.50
4. £195
5. £90
6. £123.50
7. £195
8. £104
9. £80
10. £68
11. £110.50
12. £90

Exercise 19 *page 191*

1. (a) £168 (b) £8736
2. (a) £176 (b) £8096
3. (a) £184 (b) £8464
4. (a) (i) £4 (ii) £5.75 (iii) £290 (iv) £14.50 (b) (i) £9.60 (ii) £13.80 (iii) £34.80
5. (a) £5.20 (b) £3.12
6. (a) £12.60 (b) £7.56
7. (a) £345 (b) £19.32 (c) £10.63
8. (a) £2920 (b) £181.04 (c) £76.04

Exercise 20 *page 192*

1. £1370
2. £2260
3. £4850
4. £1310
5. £1000
6. £6390
7. £5795
8. £3080
9. £2770
10. £6790
11. £5740
12. £7670
13. £4900
14. £5348
15. £6470

Exercise 21 *page 192*

1. £804
2. £2099.40
3. £1833
4. £1410.60
5. £1206
6. £2349
7. £1500
8. £510
9. £2259
10. £786
11. £1175.40
12. £342
13. £2934
14. £2712
15. £1455

Exercise 22 *page 193*

1. 2.35
2. 0.814
3. 26.2
4. 35.6
5. 113
6. 211
7. 0.825
8. 0.0312
9. 5.60
10. 13.5
11. 5.9
12. 1.2
13. 0.55
14. 0.72
15. 0.14
16. 1.8
17. 25
18. 31
19. 8.7
20. 36
21. 486.7
22. 500.4
23. 2.889
24. 3.113
25. 0.071 54
26. 3.041
27. 2464
28. 488 900
29. 642 600
30. 111 200
31. 0.513
32. 5.8
33. 66
34. 587.6
35. 0.6
36. 0.07
37. 5.84
38. 88
39. 2500
40. 52 700
41. 7
42. 0.3
43. 5000
44. 34.6
45. 63 800
46. 0.057
47. 0.03
48. 116
49. 85 000
50. 5.01
51. 5.01
52. 18
53. 3.50
54. 22.0
55. 10
56. 0.80
57. 4.0
58. 8.0
59. 3.30
60. 80

Exercise 23 *page 193*

1. 5.38
2. 11.05
3. 0.41
4. 0.37
5. 8.02
6. 87.04
7. 9.01
8. 0.07
9. 0.07
10. 5.16
11. 8.4
12. 0.7
13. 0.4
14. 0.1
15. 6.1
16. 19.5
17. 8.1
18. 7.1
19. 219.6
20. 80.9
21. 8.16
22. 3.0
23. 0.545
24. 0.0056
25. 0.71
26. 6.83
27. 0.8
28. 19.65
29. 0.0714
30. 60.1
31. 0.55
32. 0.0711
33. 8.8
34. 6.04
35. 3.013
36. 18.820
37. 4.01
38. 0.08
39. 8.1
40. 12.9

Exercise 24 page 194

1. 5.5×10^3	**2.** 6.14×10^4	**3.** 2.3×10^7	**4.** 1.7×10^6
5. 8.45×10^5	**6.** 2.71×10^4	**7.** 6×10^9	**8.** 8.1×10^9
9. 7.4×10^6	**10.** 8.96×10^6	**11.** 7.14×10^3	**12.** 6.6×10^4
13. 8.4×10^6	**14.** 7.46×10^5	**15.** 2×10^2	**16.** 4.4×10^3
17. 7.5×10^1	**18.** 8.26×10^8	**19.** 2×10^6	**20.** 3×10^7
21. 4.6×10^{-4}	**22.** 2.3×10^{-5}	**23.** 4.1×10^{-3}	**24.** 7.58×10^{-8}
25. 8.23×10^{-2}	**26.** 9.58×10^{-5}	**27.** 6.15×10^{-6}	**28.** 1.52×10^{-6}
29. 7.56×10^{-2}	**30.** 6.164×10^{-3}	**31.** 8.8×10^{-6}	**32.** 8.14×10^{-3}
33. 9.5×10^{-9}	**34.** 7.4×10^{-2}	**35.** 8×10^{-2}	**36.** 9.5×10^{-1}
37. 7.14×10^{-4}	**38.** 9.99×10^{-1}	**39.** 8.415×10^{-2}	**40.** 4.5×10^{-5}

Exercise 25 page 194

1. 230	**2.** 340 000	**3.** 4100	**4.** 271	**5.** 82 000
6. 300 000 000	**7.** 900	**8.** 220 000	**9.** 63.5	**10.** 89 500
11. 400 000	**12.** 1234	**13.** 514	**14.** 80	**15.** 7000
16. 605	**17.** 80 120	**18.** 60 000 000	**19.** 960	**20.** 42 000
21. 0.042	**22.** 0.004 7	**23.** 0.001 6	**24.** 0.000 89	**25.** 0.84
26. 0.06	**27.** 0.000 951	**28.** 0.000 02	**29.** 0.000 08	**30.** 0.41
31. 0.006 3	**32.** 0.008 04	**33.** 0.05	**34.** 0.069	**35.** 0.000 48
36. 0.895	**37.** 0.061 1	**38.** 0.000 000 8	**39.** 0.000 009	**40.** 0.001 11
41. 5200	**42.** 0.009 4	**43.** 0.08	**44.** 380 000	**45.** 0.000 67
46. 0.066 6	**47.** 11 000	**48.** 0.008 1	**49.** 0.7	**50.** 5 000 000

UNIT 11

Exercise 1 page 195

1. 3.6	**2.** 8.5	**3.** 47	**4.** 9.6	**5.** 56
6. 740	**7.** 2300	**8.** 1152	**9.** 80	**10.** 65 400
11. 0.0075	**12.** 0.0815	**13.** 0.000 047	**14.** 0.62	**15.** 0.005 2
16. 0.31	**17.** 0.163	**18.** 0.07	**19.** 0.007 2	**20.** 0.045
21. 470	**22.** 622	**23.** 8.26	**24.** 0.0858	**25.** 0.07
26. 0.007 3	**27.** 0.573	**28.** 1450	**29.** 0.0264	**30.** 60 000
31. 6	**32.** 0.000 006	**33.** 400	**34.** 0.015	**35.** 8.5
36. 8000	**37.** 6 300 000	**38.** 0.006	**39.** 0.849	**40.** 600

Exercise 2 page 196

1. 0.85 m	**2.** 2400 m	**3.** 63 cm	**4.** 0.25 m	**5.** 0.7 cm
6. 20 mm	**7.** 1200 m	**8.** 700 cm	**9.** 580 m	**10.** 0.815 m
11. 0.65 km	**12.** 2.5 cm	**13.** 5000 g	**14.** 4200 g	**15.** 6400 g
16. 3000 g	**17.** 800 g	**18.** 0.4 kg	**19.** 2000 kg	**20.** 0.25 kg
21. 500 kg	**22.** 620 kg	**23.** 0.007 t	**24.** 1.5 kg	**25.** 0.8 l
26. 2000 ml	**27.** 1 l	**28.** 4500 ml	**29.** 6000 ml	**30.** 3000 cm^3
31. 2000 l	**32.** 5500 l	**33.** 900 cm^3	**34.** 0.6 l	**35.** 15 000 l
36. 0.24 l	**37.** 0.28 m	**38.** 550 cm	**39.** 0.305 kg	**40.** 46 m
41. 0.016 l	**42.** 0.208 m	**43.** 2.8 cm	**44.** 0.27 m	**45.** 0.788 km
46. 14 000 kg	**47.** 1300 g	**48.** 0.09 m^3	**49.** 2900 kg	**50.** 0.019 l

Exercise 3 page 196

1. 24	**2.** 48	**3.** 30	**4.** 4480	**5.** 48	**6.** 17 600
7. 36	**8.** 70	**9.** 4	**10.** 880	**11.** 3	**12.** 2

13. 3520 14. 80 15. 140 16. 12 17. 48 18. 22 400
19. 5280 20. 2 21. 30 22. 62 23. 76 24. 101
25. 18 26. 8 27. 58 28. 92 29. 4 30. 152

Exercise 4 page 197

1. 25.4 cm 2. 16.1 km 3. 4.4 lb 4. 1.242 miles 5. 45.5 litres
6. 2.2 gallons 7. 11 lb 8. 62.1 miles 9. 15.24 cm 10. 6.44 km
11. 36.4 litres 12. 2.272 litres 13. 55 lb 14. 1610 km 15. 7.452 miles
16. 4.54 kg 17. 7.62 cm 18. 4.4 gallons 19. 1.32 gallons 20. 4.347 miles

Exercise 5 page 197

1. £85 000 2. 2128 3. £17.55 4. (a) $72.50 (b) $0.87 5. 302
6. £2063.58 7. £14.08
8. (a) 24, 29 (b) 30, 20 (c) 8, 2 (d) 2, $\frac{2}{3}$ 9. £2.05 10. 2h 55 min

Exercise 6 page 198

1. £900 2. £84 3. 49 747 4. 6 5. 13 950 6. £12.50
7. £3515 8. £120 9. (a) $6400 (b) $83 200 10. £1.80

Exercise 7 page 198

1. £43 2. 552 3. (a) double 18 (b) £11,111 4. 50
5. (a) £360 (b) £225 (c) £3.75
6. (a) 9, 21, 33, 39 (b) 5, 11 (c) 38 (d) 21
7. (a) 7.2 (b) 11.28 (c) 0.1 (d) 0.026 (e) 28.2 (f) 0.01
8. (a) 3.32 (b) 1.61 (c) 1.46 (d) 4.4 (e) 6.2 (f) 2.74
9. (a) 8 (b) 24 10. £345

Exercise 8 page 199

1. 73 2. £63 3. (a) 680 (b) 13 600 4. 140
5. (a) $\frac{1}{10}$ (b) $\frac{1}{20}$ (c) $\frac{1}{2}$ (d) $\frac{3}{4}$ 6. (a) 49 (b) 1 (c) 81 (d) 13 (e) 125
(f) 28 7. 37 8. (a) 30 (b) 45 (c) 48 9. A = 4, B = 1, C = 8
10. (a) 6, 5 (b) 12, 3 (c) 9, 4

Exercise 9 page 199

1. 42 kg 2. 360 000 kg 3. (a) 600 (b) £204 4. £15
5. (a) 07 30 (b) 19 30 (c) 13 00 6. 12 7. 120 8. 72 m.p.h.
9. (b) (i) 7 miles (ii) 10 miles (iii) 8 miles (iv) 7 miles (v) 14 miles (vi) 9 miles
10. 11

Exercise 10 page 200

1. 20 2. 37 3. 10% of £600 is greater by £7.50 4. (a) 16 m^2 (b) 6 m^3
5. (a) 50, 20, 5, 2 (b) 50, 20, 10, 5, 1 (c) £1, 50, 5, 1, 1 6. 817, 8117, 8171, 8710, 8711
7. £77.91 8. 480
9. (a) 52 g (b) 35p (c) 15 10. (a) 3, 4 (b) 5, 2 (c) 7, 4

Exercise 11 page 200

1. 6 2. £166 3. 150 g
4. (a) £41.20 (b) £8.20 (c) £32.88 (d) £27.16
5. 48 cm^2 6. 5 cm 7. Steven 30, Peter 20
8. (a) 110 (b) 165 (c) 150 (d) 240
9. m, 9, z

10. 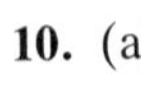 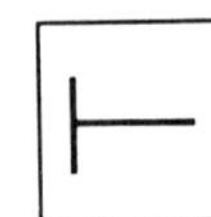 (b)   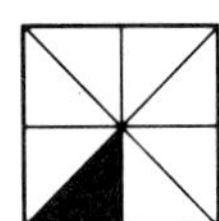

Exercise 12 *page 201*

1. (a) 31p (b) 6 **2.** 2016, 2061, 2106, 2601, 2616 **3.** £8.50
4. (a) 108 m^2 (b) 3 **6.** 1.50 m **7.** 42 km
8. (a) £13.50 (b) £21.60 (c) £11.25 **9.** 78 **10.** £1.70

Exercise 13 *page 201*

1. $42\frac{1}{2}$ h **2.** 0.009, 0.05, 0.062, 0.14, 0.41
3. (a) 40 acres (b) 15 acres (c) 10%, 30%, 37.5%, 22.5% **4.** 178
5. 104 cm **6.** 1.2 l **7.** 1145 **8.** £1.20 **9.** £2660
10. (a) 16 (b) 36 (c) 27 (d) 10 000 (e) 75 (f) 400

Exercise 14 *page 201*

1. 13 **2.** 10 **3.** 4 **4.** 8 **5.** 2 **6.** 2 **7.** 25 **8.** 17
9. 10 **10.** 31 **11.** 16 **12.** 25 **13.** 32 **14.** 16 **15.** 22 **16.** 14
17. 7 **18.** 1 **19.** $5\frac{1}{2}$ **20.** 46 **21.** 30 **22.** 20 **23.** 12 **24.** 16
25. 8 **26.** 11 **27.** 10 **28.** 9 **29.** 2 **30.** 221 **31.** 10 **32.** 38
33. 19 **34.** 11 **35.** 14 **36.** 21 **37.** 18 **38.** 50 **39.** 21 **40.** 14
41. 34 **42.** 66 **43.** 10 **44.** 21 **45.** 2 **46.** 1 **47.** 39 **48.** 24
49. 3 **50.** 2 **51.** 4 **52.** 9 **53.** 14 **54.** 4 **55.** 2 **56.** 3
57. 0 **58.** 0 **59.** 12 **60.** 10 **61.** 19 **62.** 6 **63.** 6 **64.** 8
65. 2 **66.** 53 **67.** 15 **68.** 605 **69.** 0 **70.** 9 **71.** 73 **72.** 8
73. 17 **74.** 4 **75.** 13 **76.** 1 **77.** 10 **78.** 11 **79.** 21 **80.** 4

Exercise 15 *page 202*

1. 19 **2.** 2 **3.** 30 **4.** 43 **5.** 2 **6.** 4 **7.** 14 **8.** 1
9. 4 **10.** 0 **11.** 32 **12.** 35 **13.** 21 **14.** 20 **15.** 31 **16.** 11
17. 55 **18.** 28 **19.** 0 **20.** 33 **21.** 32 **22.** 79 **23.** 11 **24.** 14
25. 21 **26.** 83 **27.** 56 **28.** 3 **29.** 9 **30.** 35 **31.** 50 **32.** 17
33. 24 **34.** 22 **35.** 32 **36.** 14 **37.** 30 **38.** 14 **39.** 21 **40.** 1
41. 10 **42.** 10 **43.** $9\frac{3}{4}$ **44.** 8 **45.** 22 **46.** 2 **47.** 23 **48.** 8
49. 13 **50.** 2 **51.** 9 **52.** 0 **53.** 11 **54.** 18 **55.** 22 **56.** 19
57. 20 **58.** 15 **59.** 12 **60.** 39 **61.** 13 **62.** 5 **63.** 4 **64.** 20
65. 26 **66.** 5

Exercise 16 *page 203*

1. $7 + 5 \times 4$ **2.** $3 \times 5 + 10$ **3.** $4 \div 2 + 3$ **4.** $11 + 3 \times 3$
5. $31 - 10 \times 2$ **6.** $10 + 6 \times 5$ **7.** $4 \times 8 - 7$ **8.** $12 + 9 \times 2$
9. $18 - 4 \times 4$ **10.** $28 - 10 \times 2$ **11.** $21 \div 3 - 5$ **12.** $7 + 3 \times 3$
13. $10 \div 2 + 3$ **14.** $10 \times 3 + 12$ **15.** $18 \div 3 + 7$ **16.** $31 + 40 \div 5$
17. $15 - 16 \div 4$ **18.** $15 + 8 \times 9$ **19.** $37 + 35 \div 5$ **20.** $11 \times 5 + 9$
21. $8 + 3 \times 2 - 4$ **22.** $12 - 3 \times 3 + 1$ **23.** $11 + 4 - 1 \times 6$ **24.** $15 \div 5 + 2 \times 4$
25. $7 \times 2 - 3 \times 3$ **26.** $12 - 2 + 3 \times 4$ **27.** $8 \times 9 - 6 \times 11$ **28.** $20 \div 20 + 9 \times 0$
29. $20 - 30 \div 10 + 8$ **30.** $30 + 6 \times 11 - 11$

Exercise 17 page 204

1. 8% **2.** 10% **3.** 25% **4.** 2% **5.** 4% **6.** $2\frac{1}{2}$%
7. 20% **8.** 50% **9.** 15% **10.** 80% **11.** 20% **12.** $33\frac{1}{3}$%
13. $12\frac{1}{2}$% **14.** 10% **15.** 5% **16.** 25% **17.** 20% **18.** $12\frac{1}{2}$%
19. $33\frac{1}{3}$% **20.** 80% **21.** 5% **22.** 6% **23.** 20% **24.** 5%
25. $2\frac{1}{2}$%

Exercise 18 page 205

1. 36.4% **2.** 19.1% **3.** 19.4% **4.** 22.0% **5.** 12.2% **6.** 9.4%
7. 14.0% **8.** 17.4% **9.** 32.7% **10.** 10.2% **11.** 7.7% **12.** 35.3%
13. 30.8% **14.** 5.2% **15.** 14.1% **16.** 14.5% **17.** 19.1% **18.** 3.6%
19. 31.1% **20.** 6.5%

Exercise 19 page 205

1. 12% **2.** 29% **3.** 16% **4.** 0.25% **5.** 15% **6.** 61.1%
7. 15% **8.** 14.2% **9.** 1.5% **10.** 23.8%

Exercise 20 page 205

1. (a) 25p (b) £12.80 (c) £2.80 (d) 28%
2. (a) £10 (b) (i) £3.50 (ii) 35% **3.** (a) £10 (b) (i) £4.20 (ii) 42%
4. (a) 25% (b) (i) £135 (ii) 12.5%
5. (a) (i) 120 cm (ii) 75 cm (iii) 10 000 cm^2 (iv) 9000 cm^2 (b) 10%
6. (a) (i) 58 cm (ii) 30 cm (iii) 2500 cm^2 (iv) 1740 cm^2 (b) 30.4%
7. (a) £75 (b) (i) £67.50 (ii) 12.5% **8.** (a) £50 000 (b) (i) £53 800 (ii) 7.6%

Exercise 21 page 207

1. (a) 45 (b) 30 (c) 30 (d) 20 **2.** 2 h 10 min **3.** 2005
4. 'The London Blackout Murders' **5.** 15 min **6.** 225 min (=$3\frac{3}{4}$ h) **7.** 11 h 5 min
8. 21 10 **9.** 5 **10.** 1h 45 min **11.** 18 00
12. 15 min **13.** 15 h 10 min

Exercise 22 page 208

1. 1939 **2.** 2057 **3.** 2003 **4.** 1914
5. 2057 **6.** 1904 **7.** 2033 **8.** 2037
9. 1957 **10.** 2038 **11.** Northwood Hills **12.** Watford
13. Croxley **14.** Moor Park **15.** Aylesbury **16.** Finchley Road
17. Harrow-on-the-Hill **18.** North Harrow **19.** Preston Road **20.** Marylebone

Exercise 23 page 209

1. 43 min **2.** 38 min **3.** 12 min **4.** 8 min **5.** 2003 **6.** 2042
7. 2005 **8.** 1905 **9.** 2010 **10.** 1933 **11.** 1945 **12.** 1918
13. 2039 **14.** 1931

UNIT 12

Exercise 1 page 211

1. 32 cm^2 **2.** 21 cm^2 **3.** 20 cm^2 **4.** 13.5 cm^2 **5.** 14 cm^2
6. 19 cm^2 **7.** 36 m^2 **8.** 130 m^2 **9.** 28 m^2 **10.** 18 cm^2
11. 42 cm^2 **12.** 21 cm^2 **13.** 55 cm^2 **14.** 39 cm^2 **15.** 52 sq. units
16. $35\frac{1}{2}$ sq. units **17.** 35 sq. units **18.** $48\frac{1}{2}$ sq. units

Exercise 2 page 212

1. 18.8 cm, 28.3 cm^2
2. 31.4 cm, 78.5 cm^2
3. 25.1 cm, 50.3 cm^2
4. 12.6 cm, 12.6 cm^2
5. 28.3 m, 63.6 m^2
6. 9.42 cm, 7.07 cm^2
7. 37.7 m, 113 m^2
8. 34.6 m, 95.0 m^2
9. 26.4 cm, 55.4 cm^2
10. 11.0 m, 9.62 m^2
11. 5.65 cm, 2.54 cm^2
12. 35.2 cm, 98.5 cm^2
13. 5.34 cm, 2.27 cm^2
14. 22.0 feet, 38.5 sq feet
15. 10.1 km, 8.04 km^2
16. 63.5 km, 320 km^2
17. 3.14 mm, 0.785 mm^2
18. 1.57 miles, 0.196 sq. miles
19. 39.6 km, 125 km^2
20. 4.71 miles, 1.77 sq. miles

Exercise 3 page 213

1. 36.0 cm, 77.0 cm^2
2. 28.3 cm, 47.5 cm^2
3. 25.7 cm, 39.3 cm^2
4. 28.6 cm, 57.1 cm^2
5. 36.8 cm, 92.5 cm^2
6. 10.7 cm, 7.07 cm^2
7. 7.14 cm, 3.14 cm^2
8. 51.4 cm, 157 cm^2
9. 46.0 cm, 147 cm^2
10. 37.7 cm, 99.3 cm^2
11. 20.6 cm, 24.6 cm^2
12. 20.3 cm, 24.6 cm^2
13. 27.9 cm, 44.6 cm^2

Exercise 4 page 214

1. 22.9 cm^2
2. 35.9 cm^2
3. 13.7 cm^2
4. 370 cm^2
5. 21.5 cm^2
6. 84.1 cm^2
7. 24.8 cm^2
8. 25.1 cm^2

Exercise 5 page 215

1. 2.39 cm
2. 4.46 m
3. 1.11 m
4. 6.37 cm
5. 4.15 cm
6. 3.48 cm
7. 3.95 m
8. 2.99 m
9. 2.55 m
10. 4.37 cm
11. 4.62 cm
12. 5.57 m
13. 5.75 cm
14. 4.72 cm
15. 3.50 m
16. 8.91 cm
17. 4.07 m
18. 3.74 cm
19. 2.86 m
20. 3.98 cm
21. 3.09 cm
22. 4.77 cm
23. 4.51 m
24. 5.05 cm
25. 5.25 m

Exercise 6 page 215

1. 215 m^2
2. 97.5 cm^2
3. 27.7 cm
4. 19.1 m
5. 183 cm^2
6. 35.4 cm
7. 32.9 m
8. 15.6 m^2
9. 30.1 m
10. 49.7 m^2
11. 296 cm^2
12. 22.4 cm
13. 127 cm^2
14. 20.2 m
15. 172 cm^2
16. 12.6 cm^2

Exercise 7 page 215

1. 9 cm
2. 7.5 cm
3. 40 cm^2
4. 45 cm^2
5. 31 cm
6. 48 cm
7. (a) 20 sq. units (b) 10 sq. units
8. 3×4, 6×2, 1×12
9. (a) 0.72 m^2 (b) 1.08 m^2 (c) 25 cm^2
10. (a) 400 m (b) 6.3 m
11. (a) $\frac{1}{3}$ (b) $\frac{4}{9}$
12. (a) 20 m (b) 200 m^2 (c) 39.3 m^2 (d) 40 m^2 (e) 37.7 m^2 (f) 117.7 m^2
13. 3.43 m^2
14. 212
15. 272
16. 15
17. 4.55 m
18. 0.637 m

Exercise 8 page 217

1. (a) 30 cm^3 (b) 168 cm^3
2. (a) 2.5 cm (b) 3.25 cm
3. (a) 18 cm^3 (b) 14 cm^3 (c) 170 cm^3 (d) 5 cm (e) 6 cm (f) 1.5 cm (g) 3.5 cm (h) 11 cm (i) 0.2 cm (j) 2.25 cm (k) 0.1 cm (l) 2.4 cm (m) 8.5 cm (n) 7.1 cm
4. 40
5. 100
6. 900

Exercise 9 page 218

1. 33.5 cm^3
2. 226 cm^3
3. 101 cm^3
4. 137 cm^3
5. 183 cm^3
6. 603 cm^3
7. 66.0 cm^3
8. 38.8 cm^3
9. 5.70 cm^3
10. 16.8 cm^3
11. 5.75 cm^3
12. 1.53 cm^3
13. 60 cm^3
14. 30 cm^3
15. 14.7 cm^3
16. 207 cm^3

Exercise 10 *page 219*

1. 113 l **2.** 69.1 l **3.** B
4. (a) (i) 1920 cm^3 (ii) 4800 cm^3 (b) (i) £2.25 (ii) giant (iii) 20p **5.** 740 cm^3
6. (a) 33.5 cm^3 (b) 0.628 cm^3 (c) 53 **7.** 262 sec (4 min 22 s)
8. (a) 141 cm^3 (b) 9.42 cm^3 **9.** (a) 79.6 cm^3 (b) 637 g

Exercise 11 *page 220*

1. (a) 6 (b) 12 (c) 8 (d) 1
2. (a) 24, 24, 8, 8 (b) 22, 24, 8, 6 (c) 38, 32, 8, 12 (d) 8, 14, 10, 2

THINK ABOUT IT 4

Project 1 *page 223*

circle, divide, radius, axis, log, calculate, angle, equal, add, bracket, test, equation, sum, sin, tan, three, multiply, coordinate, parallel, six, pi, four, diameter.

Exercise A *page 223*

1. 19 35 **2.** £7.93 **3.** £24 **4.** $\frac{3}{10}$ **5.** 63 cm^2 **6.** £8
7. £249.60 **8.** 20 m, 50 m^2, 35 m^2, 10, £34 **9.** £26.50 **10.** (a) 15051 (b) 110 miles

Exercise B *page 227*

1. £365 **2.** £115 **3.** 10.15 a.m. **4.** £7 **5.** x, 5, t **6.** (a) 12 (b) 8, 48
8. 672 **9.** 360 cm^3 **10.** 0.006 25 cm

Project 3 *page 227*

Formula is $A = \frac{1}{2}p + i - 1$ [Pick's theorem]

Exercise C *page 229*

1.

11	+	4	→	15
×		÷		
6	÷	2	→	3
↓		↓		
66	×	2	→	132

2.

9	+	17	→	26
×		−		
5	×	8	→	40
↓		↓		
45	÷	9	→	5

3.

14	+	17	→	31
×		+		
4	×	23	→	92
↓		↓		
56	−	40	→	16

4.

15	÷	3	→	5
+		×		
22	×	5	→	110
↓		↓		
37	−	15	→	22

5.

9	×	10	→	90
+		÷		
11	÷	2	→	$5\frac{1}{2}$
↓		↓		
20	×	5	→	100

6.

26	×	2	→	52
−		×		
18	×	4	→	72
↓		↓		
8	÷	8	→	1

7.

5	×	12	→	60
×		÷		
20	+	24	→	44
↓		↓		
100	×	$\frac{1}{2}$	→	50

8.

7	×	6	→	42
÷		÷		
14	−	3	→	11
↓		↓		
$\frac{1}{2}$	×	2	→	1

9.

19	×	2	→	38
−		÷		
12	×	4	→	48
↓		↓		
7	−	$\frac{1}{2}$	→	$6\frac{1}{2}$

10.

17	×	10	→	170
−		÷		
9	÷	100	→	0.09
↓		↓		
8	−	0·1	→	7.9

11.

0·3	×	20	→	6
+		−		
11	÷	11	→	1
↓		↓		
11·3	−	9	→	2·3

12.

$\frac{1}{2}$	×	50	→	25
−		÷		
0.1	+	$\frac{1}{2}$	→	0·6
↓		↓		
0·4	×	100	→	40

13.

7	×	0.1	→	0·7
÷		×		
4	÷	0.2	→	20
↓		↓		
1·75	+	0·02	→	1.77

14.

1.4	+	8	→	9·4
−		×		
0.1	×	0·1	→	0.01
↓		↓		
1·3	+	0·8	→	2·1

15.

100	×	0.3	→	30
−		×		
2.5	÷	10	→	0·25
↓		↓		
97·5	+	3	→	100.5

16.

3	÷	2	→	1.5
÷		÷		
8	÷	16	→	$\frac{1}{2}$
↓		↓		
$\frac{3}{8}$	+	$\frac{1}{8}$	→	$\frac{1}{2}$

17.

$\frac{1}{4}$	−	$\frac{1}{16}$	→	$\frac{3}{16}$
×		×		
$\frac{1}{2}$	÷	4	→	$\frac{1}{8}$
↓		↓		
$\frac{1}{8}$	+	$\frac{1}{4}$	→	$\frac{3}{8}$

18.

0·5	−	0·01	→	0.49
+		×		
3.5	×	10	→	35
↓		↓		
4	÷	0·1	→	40

Project 4 *page 230*

1. Maths is very hard.
2. One plus one is two.
3. Spurs are rubbish.
4. The earth is round.
5. Can you boil an egg.
6. My teachers are clever.
7. My calculator is wrong.

Exercise D *page 233*

1. £22.50
2. (a) £58 (b) £62 (c) £125 (d) £7 (e) £11 (f) £568
3. 16.275 kg
4. (a) 30 (b) 200 m^2
5. 3
6. 33
7. (a) £4600 (b) £5400 (c) £8200
8. 2 h 30 min
9. (a) 5000 (b) 40 000 (c) 6000 (d) 100 000
10. $\frac{5}{8} = 0.625$, $\frac{7}{11} = 0.\dot{6}\dot{3}$

Project 5 *page 233*

$2[5(x + 11) - 7] + 4 = 10x + 100.$

Exercise E page 234

1. $5 \times 999 = 4995$
   $6 \times 999 = 5994$
   $7 \times 999 = 6993$
   $8 \times 999 = 7992$
   $9 \times 999 = 8991$

2. $5 + 9 \times 1234 = 11111$
   $6 + 9 \times 12345 = 111111$
   $7 + 9 \times 123456 = 1111111$
   $8 + 9 \times 1234567 = 11111111$
   $9 + 9 \times 12345678 = 111111111$

3. $54321 \times 9 - 1 = 488888$
   $654321 \times 9 - 1 = 5888888$
   $7654321 \times 9 - 1 = 68888888$
   $87654321 \times 9 - 1 = 788888888$
   $987654321 \times 9 - 1 = 8888888888$

4. (a) $1^3 + 2^3 + 3^3 + 4^3 = (1 + 2 + 3 + 4)^2 = 100$
   $1^3 + 2^3 + \ldots + 5^3 = (1 + 2 + \ldots + 5)^2 = 225$
   $1^3 + 2^3 + \ldots + 6^3 = (1 + 2 + \ldots + 6)^2 = 441$
   $1^3 + 2^3 + \ldots + 7^3 = (1 + 2 + \ldots + 7)^2 = 784$
   (b) $1^3 + 2^3 + \ldots + 10^3 = (1 + 2 + \ldots + 10)^2 = 3025$

5. (a) $(4.5)^2 = (4 \times 5) + 0.25$
   $(5.5)^2 = (5 \times 6) + 0.25$
   $(6.5)^2 = (6 \times 7) + 0.25$
   (b) $(9.5)^2 = (9 \times 10) + 0.25$
   $(15.5)^2 = (15 \times 16) + 0.25$
   $(99.5)^2 = (99 \times 100) + 0.25$

6. $13 + 15 + 17 + 19 = 64 = 4^3$
   $21 + 23 + 25 + 27 + 29 = 125 = 5^3$
   $31 + 33 + 35 + 37 + 39 + 41 = 216 = 6^3$
   $43 + 45 + 47 + 49 + 51 + 53 + 55 = 343 = 7^3$
   $57 + 59 + 61 + 63 + 65 + 67 + 69 + 71 = 512 = 8^3$

7. (b) $3 \to 14$, $4 \to 18$, $5 \to 22$, $6 \to 26$ (c) (i) 42 (ii) 62 (iii) 202
   (d) (i) 12 (ii) 40 (e) $n = 4x + 2$

Exercise F page 235

1. 31576 **2.** 87925 **3.** 47426 **4.** 92474 **5.** 49302 **6.** 14865 **7.** 12218
8. 35752 **9.** 34807

UNIT 13

Exercise 1 page 238

1. −4 **2.** −12 **3.** −11 **4.** −3 **5.** −5 **6.** 4 **7.** −5 **8.** −8
9. 19 **10.** −17 **11.** −4 **12.** −5 **13.** −11 **14.** 6 **15.** −4 **16.** 6
17. 0 **18.** −18 **19.** −3 **20.** −11 **21.** −8 **22.** −7 **23.** 1 **24.** 1
25. 9 **26.** 11 **27.** −8 **28.** 42 **29.** 4 **30.** 15 **31.** −7 **32.** −9
33. −1 **34.** −7 **35.** 0 **36.** 11 **37.** −14 **38.** 0 **39.** 17 **40.** 3

Exercise 2 page 239

1. 6 **2.** −32 **3.** −6 **4.** −12 **5.** −16 **6.** 9 **7.** −18
8. −40 **9.** −25 **10.** −800 **11.** −4 **12.** −16 **13.** −8 **14.** 5
15. 2 **16.** −5 **17.** 4 **18.** −5 **19.** −9 **20.** 0 **21.** −1
22. 1 **23.** −400 **24.** −54 **25.** −100 **26.** −5 **27.** 36 **28.** 1
29. 0 **30.** 500

Exercise 3 page 239

1. 3, 2 **2.** 2, 4 **3.** 3, 4 **4.** 1, 5 **5.** 2, 6 **6.** 3, 6
7. 2, 7 **8.** 1, 8 **9.** 5, 6 **10.** 2, 15 **11.** 3, 10 **12.** 3, 8
13. 4, 6 **14.** 2, 12 **15.** 1, 24 **16.** 4, 9 **17.** −1, −2 **18.** −3, −2
19. −2, −4 **20.** −3, −4 **21.** −2, −5 **22.** −5, −4 **23.** −4, −6 **24.** −3, −7
25. −7, −6 **26.** −3, −10 **27.** 3, −1 **28.** 2, −3 **29.** 3, −2 **30.** 4, −1

31. 1, −4 **32.** 2, −5 **33.** 3, −4 **34.** 6, −1 **35.** 3, −5 **36.** 2, −4

37. 4, 5 **38.** 4, −2 **39.** −4, −1 **40.** 6, −2 **41.** −5, −1 **42.** 7, 3

43. 5, −2 **44.** −6, −2 **45.** −8, −1

Test 1 page 240

1. −16 **2.** 64 **3.** −15 **4.** −2 **5.** 15 **6.** 18 **7.** 3 **8.** −6

9. 11 **10.** −48 **11.** −7 **12.** 9 **13.** 6 **14.** −18 **15.** −10 **16.** 8

17. −6 **18.** −30 **19.** 4 **20.** −1

Test 2 page 240

1. −16 **2.** 6 **3.** −13 **4.** 42 **5.** −4 **6.** −4 **7.** −12 **8.** −20

9. 6 **10.** 0 **11.** 36 **12.** −10 **13.** −7 **14.** 10 **15.** 6 **16.** −18

17. −9 **18.** 15 **19.** 1 **20.** 0

Test 3 page 240

1. 100 **2.** −20 **3.** −8 **4.** −7 **5.** −4 **6.** 10 **7.** 9 **8.** −10

9. 7 **10.** 35 **11.** −20 **12.** −24 **13.** −10 **14.** −7 **15.** −19 **16.** −1

17. −5 **18.** −13 **19.** 0 **20.** 8

Test 4 page 240

1. 0 **2.** −16 **3.** −14 **4.** 24 **5.** −1 **6.** 14 **7.** −2 **8.** −2

9. 7 **10.** 33 **11.** −1 **12.** −30 **13.** −28 **14.** 19 **15.** −9 **16.** −8

17. 1 **18.** −9 **19.** −16 **20.** 4

Test 5 page 240

1. 7 **2.** −8 **3.** −9 **4.** −22 **5.** 11 **6.** 13 **7.** −2 **8.** −18

9. −6 **10.** 15 **11.** −3 **12.** 0 **13.** 18 **14.** 8 **15.** 2 **16.** 6

17. −5 **18.** −8 **19.** −40 **20.** −3

Test 6 page 240

1. −4 **2.** −12 **3.** 50 **4.** −15 **5.** −9 **6.** 14 **7.** 7 **8.** 11

9. 18 **10.** 12 **11.** 16 **12.** −14 **13.** −3 **14.** −1 **15.** −1 **16.** 40

17. 7 **18.** 5 **19.** −9 **20.** −3

Exercise 4 page 241

1. 36 **2.** 29 **3.** 8 **4.** 18 **5.** 84 **6.** 2000

7. 165 **8.** $\sqrt{181}$

9. (a) 43 (b) 64 (c) 1 (d) 85

10. (a) 6 (b) −4 (c) −10 (d) 38

11. (a) 14 (b) 52 (c) 2 (d) 310

12. (a) 10 (b) 30 (c) 10 (d) 94

13. (a) 21 (b) 56 **14.** (a) 56 (b) 105 **15.** (a) 180 (b) 39

Exercise 5 page 241

1. 7 **2.** 1 **3.** 11 **4.** 5 **5.** 4 **6.** 13 **7.** 23

8. 1 **9.** 19 **10.** 7 **11.** 17 **12.** 30 **13.** 30 **14.** 30

15. 1 **16.** 14 **17.** 41 **18.** 50 **19.** 60 **20.** 50 **21.** 24

22. 72 **23.** 62 **24.** 120 **25.** 40 **26.** 11 **27.** 29 **28.** 303

29. 1200 **30.** 5 **31.** 14 **32.** 3 **33.** 29 **34.** 29 **35.** 6

36. 11 **37.** 5 **38.** 10 **39.** 7 **40.** 27

Exercise 6 page 242

1. 3 **2.** 2 **3.** 10 **4.** 0 **5.** 15 **6.** 5 **7.** 7
8. −5 **9.** 12 **10.** 8 **11.** 5 **12.** 12 **13.** 36 **14.** 15
15. 5 **16.** −5 **17.** 9 **18.** 26 **19.** 6 **20.** 22 **21.** 18
22. 24 **23.** 40 **24.** 24 **25.** −14 **26.** 22 **27.** 14 **28.** 243
29. 240 **30.** −2 **31.** 9 **32.** −2 **33.** 25 **34.** 7 **35.** 60
36. 7 **37.** 6 **38.** 68 **39.** 252 **40.** 12

Exercise 7 page 242

1. 1 **2.** 0 **3.** 2 **4.** 1 **5.** 1 **6.** 5 **7.** 3
8. −4 **9.** −4 **10.** 4 **11.** 0 **12.** −1 **13.** 2 **14.** 4
15. 3 **16.** 1 **17.** −2 **18.** 0 **19.** 17 **20.** −5 **21.** −6
22. −4 **23.** 2 **24.** 6 **25.** 4 **26.** −12 **27.** 6 **28.** −6
29. 5 **30.** 2 **31.** −5 **32.** −8 **33.** 12 **34.** −14 **35.** 5
36. 12 **37.** 13 **38.** 5 **39.** 18 **40.** 36 **41.** 12 **42.** 36
43. 5 **44.** 25 **45.** 1 **46.** 9 **47.** 0 **48.** 1 **49.** 5
50. 16

Exercise 8 page 242

1. 1 **2.** 3 **3.** −1 **4.** 1 **5.** −2 **6.** 3 **7.** 7
8. −5 **9.** −5 **10.** 5 **11.** −2 **12.** 0 **13.** 2 **14.** 3
15. 5 **16.** −10 **17.** 2 **18.** −7 **19.** 11 **20.** −5 **21.** −2
22. −4 **23.** 3 **24.** 6 **25.** 12 **26.** −4 **27.** 9 **28.** −25
29. 5 **30.** 4 **31.** −18 **32.** −5 **33.** 10 **34.** −10 **35.** −50
36. 14 **37.** 5 **38.** 25 **39.** 8 **40.** 16 **41.** 3 **42.** 9
43. 45 **44.** 225 **45.** 1 **46.** 16 **47.** 27 **48.** 4 **49.** 27
50. 5

Exercise 9 page 242

1. 12 **2.** 9 **3.** 18 **4.** 4 **5.** 17 **6.** −5 **7.** 6
8. −7 **9.** 4 **10.** 8 **11.** 17 **12.** −5 **13.** 5 **14.** 6
15. 2 **16.** $\frac{4}{5}$ **17.** $2\frac{1}{3}$ **18.** $7\frac{1}{2}$ **19.** $1\frac{5}{6}$ **20.** 0 **21.** $\frac{5}{9}$
22. 1 **23.** $\frac{1}{5}$ **24.** $\frac{2}{7}$ **25.** $\frac{3}{4}$ **26.** $\frac{2}{3}$ **27.** $1\frac{1}{4}$ **28.** $1\frac{1}{5}$
29. $1\frac{5}{9}$ **30.** $\frac{1}{3}$ **31.** $\frac{1}{2}$ **32.** $\frac{1}{10}$ **33.** $-\frac{3}{8}$ **34.** $\frac{9}{50}$ **35.** $\frac{1}{2}$
36. $\frac{3}{5}$ **37.** $-\frac{4}{9}$ **38.** 0 **39.** $4\frac{5}{8}$ **40.** $-1\frac{3}{7}$ **41.** $2\frac{1}{3}$ **42.** $\frac{3}{4}$
43. 1 **44.** $3\frac{3}{5}$ **45.** $\frac{1}{3}$ **46.** $2\frac{1}{14}$ **47.** −1 **48.** $-\frac{5}{6}$ **49.** $8\frac{1}{4}$
50. −55

Exercise 10 page 243

1. $2\frac{3}{4}$ **2.** $1\frac{2}{3}$ **3.** 2 **4.** $\frac{3}{5}$ **5.** $\frac{1}{2}$ **6.** 2 **7.** $5\frac{1}{3}$
8. $1\frac{1}{5}$ **9.** 0 **10.** $\frac{2}{9}$ **11.** $1\frac{1}{2}$ **12.** $\frac{1}{6}$ **13.** $1\frac{1}{3}$ **14.** $\frac{6}{7}$
15. $\frac{4}{7}$ **16.** 7 **17.** $\frac{5}{8}$ **18.** 5 **19.** $\frac{2}{5}$ **20.** $\frac{1}{3}$ **21.** 4
22. −1 **23.** 1 **24.** $\frac{6}{7}$ **25.** $1\frac{1}{4}$ **26.** 1 **27.** $\frac{7}{9}$ **28.** $-1\frac{1}{2}$
29. $\frac{2}{9}$ **30.** $-1\frac{1}{2}$

Exercise 11 page 243

1. 3 **2.** 5 **3.** $10\frac{1}{2}$ **4.** 4 **5.** $\frac{1}{3}$ **6.** $-4\frac{1}{2}$ **7.** $3\frac{1}{3}$
8. $3\frac{1}{2}$ **9.** $3\frac{2}{3}$ **10.** −2 **11.** $-5\frac{1}{2}$ **12.** $4\frac{1}{5}$ **13.** $\frac{3}{7}$ **14.** $\frac{7}{11}$
15. $4\frac{4}{5}$ **16.** $3\frac{7}{8}$ **17.** −3 **18.** 6 **19.** $-\frac{2}{7}$ **20.** $-1\frac{2}{3}$ **21.** $1\frac{7}{10}$

22. $\frac{1}{2}$ **23.** 1 **24.** $\frac{1}{2}$ **25.** $-\frac{1}{2}$ **26.** $1\frac{2}{5}$ **27.** $1\frac{3}{5}$ **28.** 1
29. $1\frac{1}{4}$ **30.** $\frac{5}{11}$

Exercise 12 *page 243*

1. $\frac{3}{5}$ **2.** $\frac{4}{7}$ **3.** $\frac{11}{12}$ **4.** $\frac{6}{11}$ **5.** $\frac{2}{3}$ **6.** $\frac{5}{9}$ **7.** $\frac{7}{9}$
8. $1\frac{1}{3}$ **9.** $\frac{1}{2}$ **10.** $\frac{2}{3}$ **11.** 3 **12.** $1\frac{1}{2}$ **13.** $1\frac{2}{5}$ **14.** $\frac{4}{13}$
15. $3\frac{1}{3}$ **16.** $\frac{4}{11}$ **17.** $-1\frac{1}{2}$ **18.** -5 **19.** $-\frac{7}{16}$ **20.** $-\frac{1}{2}$ **21.** -10
22. 5 **23.** $\frac{1}{100}$ **24.** $\frac{2}{13}$ **25.** 5 **26.** $1\frac{7}{8}$ **27.** $-\frac{1}{2}$ **28.** 24
29. 15 **30.** -10 **31.** 21 **32.** 21 **33.** $2\frac{2}{3}$ **34.** $4\frac{3}{8}$ **35.** $1\frac{1}{2}$
36. $3\frac{3}{4}$ **37.** $1\frac{1}{3}$ **38.** $3\frac{3}{5}$ **39.** 2 **40.** $\frac{5}{8}$ **41.** $\frac{7}{19}$ **42.** $-\frac{3}{5}$
43. -24 **44.** -70 **45.** $8\frac{1}{4}$ **46.** 220 **47.** -500 **48.** $-\frac{98}{99}$

Exercise 13 *page 244*

1. $4\frac{1}{2}$ cm **2.** $3\frac{1}{2}$ cm **3.** $\frac{1}{2}$ cm **4.** 4 **5.** $11\frac{1}{2}$ **6.** 11 **7.** 13
8. 15 cm^2 **9.** 10 cm **10.** 32 **11.** $4\frac{1}{2}$ **12.** 12 **13.** $17\frac{2}{3}$ **14.** $\frac{1}{3}$
15. 5 **16.** 12 **17.** $3\frac{1}{3}$ **18.** $4\frac{2}{3}$ **19.** 55, 56, 57 **20.** 41, 42, 43, 44

Exercise 14 *page 245*

1. 5 **2.** 2 **3.** 5 **4.** 2 **5.** 4 **6.** 4
7. 3 **8.** 1 **9.** 16 **10.** 25 **11.** 4 **12.** 3
13. 4 **14.** 8 **15.** 499 **16.** 33 **17.** 4 **18.** 3
19. 7 **20.** 3 **21.** 2 **22.** 3 **23.** 4 **24.** 2
25. 4 **26.** 81 **27.** 5 **28.** 6 **29.** 8 **30.** 26
31. 9, 10 **32.** 4, 5 **33.** 1, 2, 3, 4 **34.** 2, 3, 4 **35.** 8, 9, 10 **36.** 2, 3, 4
37. 7, 8, 9, 10 **38.** 11, 12, 13, 14, 15 **39.** 4, 5, 6 **40.** 195, 196, 197, 198, 199, 200

Exercise 15 *page 245*

1. $e - b$ **2.** $m + t$ **3.** $a + b + f$ **4.** $A + B - h$ **5.** y
6. $b - a$ **7.** $m - k$ **8.** $w + y - v$ **9.** $\frac{b}{a}$ **10.** $\frac{m}{h}$
11. $\frac{a+b}{m}$ **12.** $\frac{c-d}{k}$ **13.** $\frac{e+n}{v}$ **14.** $\frac{y+z}{3}$ **15.** $\frac{r}{p}$
16. $\frac{h-m}{m}$ **17.** $\frac{a-t}{a}$ **18.** $\frac{k+e}{m}$ **19.** $\frac{m+h}{u}$ **20.** $\frac{t-q}{e}$
21. $\frac{v^2+u^2}{k}$ **22.** $\frac{s^2-t^2}{g}$ **23.** $\frac{m^2-k}{a}$ **24.** $\frac{m+v}{m}$ **25.** $\frac{c-a}{b}$
26. $\frac{y-t}{s}$ **27.** $\frac{z-y}{c}$ **28.** $\frac{a}{h}$ **29.** $\frac{2b}{m}$ **30.** $\frac{cd-ab}{k}$
31. $\frac{c+ab}{a}$ **32.** $\frac{e+cd}{c}$ **33.** $\frac{n^2-m^2}{m}$ **34.** $\frac{t+ka}{k}$ **35.** $\frac{k+h^2}{h}$
36. $\frac{n-mb}{m}$ **37.** $2a$ **38.** $\frac{d-ac}{c}$ **39.** $\frac{e-mb}{m}$ **40.** $\frac{t^2+n^2}{n}$

Exercise 16 *page 246*

1. mt
2. en
3. ap
4. amt
5. abc
6. ey^2
7. $a(b+c)$
8. $t(c-d)$
9. $m(s+t)$
10. $k(h+i)$
11. $\frac{ab}{c}$
12. $\frac{mz}{y}$
13. $\frac{ch}{d}$
14. $\frac{em}{k}$
15. $\frac{hb}{e}$
16. $c(a+b)$
17. $m(h+k)$
18. $\frac{mu}{y}$
19. $t(h-k)$
20. $(z+t)(a+b)$
21. $\frac{e}{t}$
22. $\frac{b}{a}$
23. $\frac{h}{m}$
24. $\frac{bc}{a}$
25. $\frac{ud}{c}$
26. $\frac{m}{t^2}$
27. $\frac{h}{\sin 20°}$
28. $\frac{e}{\cos 40°}$
29. $\frac{m}{\tan 46°}$
30. $\frac{b^2c^2}{a^2}$

Exercise 17 *page 246*

1. $\pm\sqrt{\frac{h}{c}}$
2. $\pm\sqrt{\frac{f}{b}}$
3. $\pm\sqrt{\frac{m}{t}}$
4. $\pm\sqrt{\frac{a+b}{y}}$
5. $\pm\sqrt{\frac{t+a}{m}}$
6. $\pm\sqrt{(a+b)}$
7. $\pm\sqrt{(t-c)}$
8. $\pm\sqrt{(z-y)}$
9. $\pm\sqrt{(a^2+b^2)}$
10. $\pm\sqrt{(m^2-t^2)}$
11. $\pm\sqrt{(a^2-n^2)}$
12. $\pm\sqrt{\frac{c}{a}}$
13. $\pm\sqrt{\frac{n}{h}}$
14. $\pm\sqrt{\frac{z+k}{c}}$
15. $\pm\sqrt{\frac{c-b}{a}}$
16. $\pm\sqrt{\frac{h+e}{d}}$
17. $\pm\sqrt{\frac{m+n}{g}}$
18. $\pm\sqrt{\frac{z-y}{m}}$
19. $\pm\sqrt{\frac{f-a}{m}}$
20. $\pm\sqrt{(b^2-a^2)}$
21. $a-y$
22. $h-m$
23. $z-q$
24. $b-v$
25. $k-m$
26. $\frac{h-d}{c}$
27. $\frac{y-c}{m}$
28. $\frac{k-h}{e}$
29. $\frac{a^2-d}{b}$
30. $\frac{m^2-n^2}{t}$
31. $\frac{v^2-w}{a}$
32. $y-y^2$
33. $\frac{k-m}{t^2}$
34. $\frac{b-e}{c}$
35. $\frac{h-z}{g}$
36. $\frac{c-a-b}{d}$
37. $\frac{v^2-y^2}{k}$
38. $\frac{d-h}{f}$
39. $\frac{ab-c}{a}$
40. $\frac{hm-n}{h}$

Exercise 18 *page 247*

1. $\frac{h+d}{a}$
2. $\frac{m-k}{z}$
3. $\frac{f-ed}{d}$
4. $\frac{d-ma}{m}$
5. $\frac{c-a}{b}$
6. $\pm\sqrt{\left(\frac{b}{a}\right)}$
7. $\pm\sqrt{\left(\frac{z}{y}\right)}$
8. $\pm\sqrt{(e+c)}$
9. $\frac{b+n}{m}$
10. $\frac{b-a^2}{a}$
11. $\frac{a}{d}$
12. mt
13. mn
14. $\frac{y}{d}$
15. $\frac{a}{t}$
16. $\frac{d}{n}$
17. $k(a+b)$
18. $\frac{v}{y}$
19. $\frac{m}{c}$
20. $\pm\sqrt{mb}$
21. $\frac{b-ag}{g}$
22. $\frac{x^2-h^2}{h}$
23. $y-z$
24. $\pm\sqrt{\left(\frac{c}{m}\right)}$

25. $\frac{t - ay}{a}$ 26. $\frac{y^2 + t^2}{u}$ 27. $\pm\sqrt{(c - t)}$ 28. $k - m$ 29. $\frac{b - c}{a}$

30. $\frac{c - am}{m}$ 31. $pq - ab$ 32. $\frac{a^2 - t}{b}$ 33. $\frac{w}{v^2}$ 34. $t - c$

35. $\frac{t}{x}$ 36. $\frac{k - mn}{m}$ 37. $\frac{v - t}{x}$ 38. $\frac{c - ab}{a}$ 39. $\frac{ma - e}{m}$

40. $\pm\sqrt{\frac{c}{b}}$ 41. $\frac{a}{q}$ 42. $\pm\sqrt{\left(\frac{a}{e}\right)}$ 43. $\pm\sqrt{\left(\frac{h}{m}\right)}$ 44. $\pm\sqrt{\left(\frac{v}{n}\right)}$

45. $\frac{v - t^3}{a}$ 46. $\frac{b^3 - a^3}{a}$ 47. $\pm\sqrt{\left(\frac{b + d}{a}\right)}$ 48. $\frac{bc - h^2}{h}$ 49. $\pm\sqrt{(u^2 - v^2)}$

50. $\frac{mb - b^3}{m}$

Exercise 19 *page 247*

1. $p - a$ 2. $m - y$ 3. $z - k$ 4. $u^2 - t^2$

5. $\frac{a - bc}{m}$ 6. $\frac{z - k}{a}$ 7. $\frac{u^2 - e^2}{k}$ 8. $\frac{b - ma}{m}$

9. $\frac{h - ka}{k}$ 10. $\frac{y - p^2}{p}$ 11. ky 12. mn

13. q^2 14. mn^2 15. $\frac{m}{a}$ 16. $\frac{n}{e}$

17. $\frac{u}{w}$ 18. $\frac{e}{\sin 32°}$ 19. $\frac{2y}{z}$ 20. $\frac{3p}{k}$

21. $\pm\sqrt{(m + n)}$ 22. $\pm\sqrt{(a - b - v)}$ 23. $\pm\sqrt{\left(\frac{n^2 + n}{b}\right)}$ 24. $\frac{d + e + ab}{a}$

25. $\pm\sqrt{\left(\frac{mp + k^2}{k}\right)}$ 26. $y - m$ 27. $\frac{u + ed}{e}$ 28. $\frac{z - ay}{a}$

29. $\frac{w + yf}{ye}$ 30. $\frac{m - tm}{at}$ 31. $y(c + d)$ 32. $\frac{a - b}{p}$

33. $\frac{m + n}{A}$ 34. $\pm\sqrt{\frac{k}{h}}$ 35. $\frac{A + B}{E}$ 36. $\frac{4q}{k}$

37. $\pm\sqrt{\left(\frac{h + ad}{a}\right)}$ 38. $k^2 - y$ 39. $\frac{m - g}{n}$ 40. $\frac{c^2 - k}{c}$

Exercise 20 *page 248*

1. $2(3x + 2y)$ 2. $3(3x + 4y)$ 3. $2(5a + 2b)$ 4. $4(x + 3y)$
5. $5(2a + 3b)$ 6. $6(3x - 4y)$ 7. $4(2u - 7v)$ 8. $5(3s + 5t)$
9. $8(3m - 5n)$ 10. $9(3c - 8d)$ 11. $4(5a + 2b)$ 12. $6(5x - 4y)$
13. $3(9c - 11d)$ 14. $7(5u + 7v)$ 15. $4(3s - 8t)$ 16. $8(5x - 2t)$
17. $12(2x + 7y)$ 18. $4(3x + 2y + 4z)$ 19. $3(4a - 2b + 3c)$ 20. $5(2x - 4y + 5z)$
21. $4(5a - 3b - 7c)$ 22. $8(6m + n - 3x)$ 23. $7(6x + 7y - 3z)$ 24. $3(2x^2 + 5y^2)$
25. $5(4x^2 - 3y^2)$ 26. $7(a^2 + 4b^2)$ 27. $9(3a + 7b - 4c)$
28. $6(2x^2 + 4xy + 3y^2)$ 29. $8(8p - 9q - 5r)$ 30. $12(3x - 5y + 8z)$

Exercise 21 *page 248*

1. $x(3x + 2)$ 2. $x(4x - 3)$ 3. $x(5x + 1)$ 4. $x(x - 2)$
5. $y(2y + 5)$ 6. $a(4a - 5)$ 7. $2x(3x - 1)$ 8. $3x(4x + 3)$
9. $2y(5y - 3)$ 10. $x(7x - 3)$ 11. $5y(2y - 11)$ 12. $3a(4a + 7)$
13. $x(x^2 + 2x + 5)$ 14. $2x(x^2 - 3x + 1)$ 15. $3x(x^2 + x + 2)$ 16. $2y(y^2 - 5)$
17. $4t(3t^2 - 7)$ 18. $u(u^2 + 2u + 7)$ 19. $4x(x^2 - 2x - 1)$ 20. $a(3x + 2y)$
21. $x(4a + 3b)$ 22. $y(5c + 2d)$ 23. $m(4x - 3y)$ 24. $n(a + 3b)$
25. $2x(a - 5b)$ 26. $3a(2x + y)$ 27. $4c(3a + 4b)$ 28. $3m(2x + y + z)$
29. $4p(3x - y + 3z)$ 30. $5x(2x^2 - x + 2)$ 31. $2m(3a^2 + 2a + 1)$ 32. $3y(2x^2 + 3x + 4)$
33. $w(4x - 5y - 2z)$ 34. $2t(4a - 6b + 7c)$ 35. $8y(2x + y + 3)$ 36. $5x(3a + 4b - 5)$
37. $9x(4x^2 - 3)$ 38. $15x(3a - 2b + 4c)$ 39. $12y(7x^2 + 2)$ 40. $9u(2x^2 + 3y^2 + 5z^2)$

Exercise 22 *page 248*

1. 49 2. 9 3. 1 4. 100 5. 10 000 6. 81
7. 400 8. 0.01 9. 0.04 10. 64 11. 25 12. 16
13. 3600 14. 144 15. $\frac{1}{4}$ 16. 2 17. 3 18. 10
19. 30 20. 11 21. 6 22. 100 23. 1000 24. 12
25. 1 26. 7 27. 0.1 28. 13 29. $\frac{1}{3}$ 30. 0
31. 1 32. 9 33. 25 34. 18 35. 32 36. 10 010
37. 67 38. 30 39. 0 40. 5 41. 40 42. 5
43. 13 44. 10 45. 3

Exercise 23 *page 249*

1. 1.41 2. 2.24 3. 4.12 4. 2.45 5. 3.16 6. 10.0
7. 2.39 8. 2.87 9. 14.1 10. 20.7 11. 4.31 12. 0.970
13. 0.458 14. 3.46 15. 77.9 16. 230 17. 20.7 18. 0.276
19. 0.308 20. 0.0860 21. 0.0918 22. 1.05 23. 4 24. 1.54
25. 89.8 26. 160 27. 248 28. 1580 29. 0.917 30. 268
31. 16.3 32. 1.33 33. 1.73 34. 4.43 35. 3.35 36. 0.272
37. 2.94 38. 247 39. 48.3 40. 200 41. 6 42. 0.1
43. 2.80 44. 0.0922 45. 922 46. 88.2 47. 482 48. 31.7
49. 0.394 50. 9.37 51. 44.7 52. 218 53. 2.65 54. 41.4
55. (a) 0.141 (b) 0.447 (c) 1.41 (d) 4.47 (e) 14.1 (f) 44.7
56. (a) 0.224 (b) 0.707 (c) 2.24 (d) 7.07 (e) 22.4 (f) 70.7
57. (a) 0.130 (b) 0.412 (c) 1.30 (d) 4.12 (e) 13.0 (f) 41.2
58. (a) 0.0245 (b) 0.0775 (c) 0.245 (d) 0.775 (e) 2.45 (f) 7.75

Exercise 24 *page 249*

1. 2.08 2. 2.22 3. 3.14 4. 3.91 5. 2.47 6. 4.64 7. 1.26
8. 6.69 9. 0.464 10. 0.215 11. 34.2 12. 92.8

Exercise 25 *page 249*

1. 3^4 2. 5^2 3. 6^3 4. 10^5
5. 1^7 6. 8^4 7. 7^6 8. $2^3 \times 5^2$
9. $3^2 \times 7^4$ 10. $3^2 \times 10^3$ 11. $5^4 \times 11^2$ 12. $2^2 \times 3^3$
13. $3^2 \times 5^3$ 14. $2^2 \times 3^3 \times 11^2$ 15. $2^3 \times 3^2 \times 7^2$ 16. $2^3 \times 5^3 \times 7$
17. $3^4 \times 5 \times 11^2$ 18. $5^2 \times 6^3$ 19. $2^3 \times 3^2 \times 7^2$ 20. $2 \times 5^2 \times 7^2 \times 9^2$
21. a^3 22. c^4 23. e^5 24. $y^2 \times z^3$
25. $m^3 \times n^2$ 26. $t^4 \times p^2$ 27. $u^3 \times y^2$ 28. $m^2 \times y^4$
29. $a^2 \times e^3 \times y$ 30. $e^4 \times n^3$

Exercise 26 *page 250*

1. 8 **2.** 9 **3.** 1 **4.** 27 **5.** 25
6. 4 **7.** 1 **8.** 100 **9.** 16 **10.** 64
11. 1000 **12.** 32 **13.** 81 **14.** 125 **15.** 1 000 000
16. 49 **17.** 4 **18.** 1 **19.** −1 **20.** −8
21. −27 **22.** −1 **23.** 25 **24.** −1000 **25.** −64
26. 64 **27.** 1 **28.** 10 000 **29.** 0.01 **30.** $\frac{1}{4}$

Exercise 27 *page 250*

1. $\frac{1}{4}$ **2.** $\frac{1}{16}$ **3.** $\frac{1}{100}$ **4.** 1 **5.** $\frac{1}{27}$ **6.** $\frac{1}{64}$ **7.** $\frac{1}{1000}$ **8.** $\frac{1}{25}$
9. $\frac{1}{49}$ **10.** $\frac{1}{125}$ **11.** $\frac{1}{81}$ **12.** 1 **13.** T **14.** F **15.** T **16.** T
17. F **18.** F **19.** F **20.** T **21.** T **22.** T **23.** F **24.** F
25. F **26.** T **27.** T **28.** T **29.** T **30.** T **31.** T **32.** F
33. T **34.** T **35.** F **36.** T **37.** F **38.** F **39.** T **40.** F
41. F **42.** T

Exercise 28 *page 250*

1. 5^6 **2.** 6^5 **3.** 10^9 **4.** 7^8 **5.** 3^{10} **6.** 8^6 **7.** 2^{13}
8. 3^4 **9.** 5^3 **10.** 7^4 **11.** 5^2 **12.** 3^{-4} **13.** 6^5 **14.** 5^{-10}
15. 7^6 **16.** 7^2 **17.** 6^5 **18.** 8^1 **19.** 5^8 **20.** 10^2 **21.** 9^{-2}
22. 3^{-2} **23.** 2^4 **24.** 3^{-2} **25.** 7^{-6} **26.** 3^{-4} **27.** 5^{-5} **28.** 8^{-5}
29. 5^{-5} **30.** 6^4 **31.** 7^8 **32.** 6^4 **33.** 11^{-2} **34.** 5^{-5} **35.** 3^5
36. 7^7 **37.** 3^6 **38.** 10^4 **39.** 5^{22} **40.** 2^5 **41.** 3^6 **42.** 5
43. 7^2 **44.** 5^{-7} **45.** 2^6

UNIT 14

Exercise 1 *page 252*

1. 98 miles **2.** 2 h **3.** 40 m.p.h. **4.** 49 miles **5.** 9 h
6. 30 m.p.h. **7.** 62 miles **8.** 11 h **9.** 2.65 m.p.h. **10.** 35.2 miles
11. $4\frac{1}{2}$ h **12.** 12 m.p.h. **13.** $62\frac{1}{2}$ miles **14.** $1\frac{1}{2}$ h **15.** $13\frac{1}{4}$ m.p.h.

Exercise 2 *page 253*

1. 2 s **2.** 4 km/h **3.** 5 h **4.** 1500 cm **5.** 7.5 km/h
6. 20 m **7.** 45.6 km **8.** 36 km/h **9.** 180 feet **10.** 0.06 cm/s
11. 6 h **12.** 4 m **13.** 10 days **14.** 0.5 m **15.** 400 km/h
16. 2 km **17.** 40 km/h **18.** 0.01 s **19.** 0.5 s **20.** 75 m
21. 30 s **22.** 6 s **23.** 0.02 m/s **24.** 62.5 miles **25.** 54 m.p.h.

Exercise 3 *page 253*

1. 30 miles **2.** 36 km **3.** 120 km **4.** 32 miles
5. 3 miles **6.** 400 miles **7.** 50 miles **8.** 10 km
9. (a) $\frac{1}{2}$ h (b) $\frac{1}{4}$ h (c) $\frac{3}{4}$ h (d) 5 s
10. (a) 124 miles (b) 68 km (c) 42 miles (d) 30 km
11. (a) 34 km/h (b) 88 km/h (c) 45 km/h (d) 69 km/h
12. (a) $9\frac{1}{2}$ miles (b) $9\frac{1}{2}$ miles (c) 12 km (d) 16 km
13. 5.1 h **14.** 3 h 20 mins **15.** (a) 12 25 (b) 225 km **16.** 385 m
17. (a) 80 km/h (b) 135 km (c) 90 km/h (d) 2000

Exercise 4 page 254

1. 5 cm **2.** 7.81 cm **3.** 10.6 cm **4.** 5.66 cm **5.** 8.60 cm **6.** 8.06 cm
7. 12.0 cm **8.** 7.62 cm **9.** 13 cm **10.** 8.49 cm **11.** 4.58 cm **12.** 5.20 cm
13. 6.24 cm **14.** 4.47 cm **15.** 12 cm **16.** 6 cm **17.** 8.49 cm **18.** 3.77 cm
19. 12 cm **20.** 6.11 cm

Exercise 5 page 255

1. 6.63 cm **2.** 10.4 cm **3.** 5.57 cm **4.** 10.9 cm **5.** 8.54 cm **6.** 17.2 cm
7. 8.54 cm **8.** 9.54 cm

Exercise 6 page 256

1. 19.2 km **2.** 427 km **3.** 4.58 m **4.** 9.75 km **5.** 5.20 m **6.** 9.43 cm
7. 6.63 cm **8.** 7.60 cm **9.** 36.1 m **10.** (a) 5 cm (b) 7.81 cm
11. (a) 8.06 cm (b) 9 cm **12.** (b) 11.4 cm

Exercise 7 page 256

1. (a) (i) \$2.50 (ii) \$2 (iii) \$3
(b) (i) £0.80 (ii) £2.80 (iii) £2
2. (a) (i) DM4 (ii) DM12 (iii) DM6
(b) (i) £2 (ii) £2.50 (iii) £0.50 (c) DM10
3. (a) (i) 2.5 kg (ii) 3.6 kg (iii) 0.9 kg
(b) (i) 4.4 lb (ii) 6.6 lb (iii) 3.3 lb (c) 2.2 lb
(d) 4.1 kg
4. (a) (i) 9.1 l (ii) 6.3 l (iii) 12.7 l
(b) (i) 2.2 gallons (ii) 1.5 gallons (iii) 0.9 gallons (c) 13.6
(d) car B (11 l to 10.9 l)
5. (a) (i) 1.6 km (ii) 4.8 km (iii) 3.5 km
(b) (i) 1.25 miles (ii) 3.1 miles (iii) 2.2 miles
(c) John (2 miles = 3.2 km) (d) Jane (2.7 miles = 4.3 km)

Exercise 8 page 258

1. $\frac{1}{5}, \frac{5}{2}, -\frac{4}{3}$ **2.** $\frac{4}{5}, -\frac{1}{6}, -5$
3. AB : 4; BC : $\frac{1}{2}$; AC : $-\frac{2}{3}$; DE : $\frac{2}{3}$; EF : -5; DF : $-\frac{3}{4}$; GH : 1; HI : $-\frac{1}{4}$; GI : -4; JK : 0; JL : $-\frac{4}{3}$; KL : 4.
4. (a) 5 (b) $\frac{2}{3}$ (c) $-\frac{3}{7}$ (d) $-\frac{8}{5}$ (e) -1
(f) $\frac{3}{11}$ (g) 0 (h) -10 (i) 0 (j) -4
(k) infinite (l) infinite **5.** (b) -2.5 (c) -0.625 **6.** (b) 2 (c) 6

Exercise 10 page 261

1. (c) (i) $x = 4$ (ii) $x = 3$ (iii) $x = -2$ (iv) $x = 1.5$ (v) $x = 2$ (vi) $x = 3$
2. (c) (i) 7 (ii) 0 (iii) 4 (iv) 5 (v) 3.5 (vi) 2.5
(vii) 3 (viii) 4
3. (c) (i) 7 (ii) 2 (iii) 2.5 (iv) 4 (v) 1 (vi) 8
(vii) 5
4. (c) (i) 2.3, −4.3 (ii) −5, 3 (iii) no solutions (iv) −4.4, 3.4
5. (c) (i) ±3.16 (ii) ±2.45 (iii) ±1.73 (iv) −2, 3 (v) −3.7, 2.7
6. (c) (i) 1.3 (ii) ±2.8 (iii) ±2 (iv) 1.2, 6.8
7. (c) (i) −1.14 (ii) −1.24, 3.24 (iii) ±2.83
8. (c) (i) −1.8, 2.8 (ii) −2.7, 3.7 (iii) −1, 3 (iv) −3.2, 2.2

Exercise 11 page 262

1. $x = 2, y = 4$ **2.** $x = 2, y = 3$ **3.** $x = 5, y = 3$ **4.** $x = 3, y = 2$
5. $x = 4, y = 3$ **6.** $x = 3, y = 1$ **7.** $x = 1, y = 5$

UNIT 15

Exercise 1 page 265

1. (a) 90° clockwise, (0, 0) (b) 90° anticlockwise, (1, 1)
   (c) 180°, (0, 0) (d) 90° clockwise, (−2, 1)
2. (a) 90° clockwise, (0, 0) (b) 180° (2, 4)
   (c) 90° clockwise, (3, 2) (d) 180°, (2, −1)
   (e) 90° clockwise, (−1, 0) (f) 90° anticlockwise, (4, 5)
   (g) 90° anticlockwise, (0, 0)
3. (a) 90° clockwise, (2, 2) (b) 180°, (−2, −1)
   (c) 90° clockwise, (−3, −3) (d) 90° anticlockwise, (−1, −1)
   (e) 90° anticlockwise, (−2, −2) (f) 90° anticlockwise, (0, −2)
   (g) 180°, (−1, 2) (h) 90° anticlockwise, (−3, −3)
4. (a) x-axis (b) $x = -1$ (c) $y = x$ (d) y-axis (e) $y = -1$ (f) $y = x$
5. (a) rotation 90° clockwise, (0, 2) (b) translation $\begin{pmatrix} 10 \\ -3 \end{pmatrix}$
   (c) reflection in $y = x$ (d) reflection in x axis
   (e) rotation 90° anticlockwise, ($6\frac{1}{2}$, $5\frac{1}{2}$) (f) rotation 90° clockwise, (0, 0)
6. (a) reflection in $y = 1$ (b) reflection in $y = -x$
   (c) rotation 90° clockwise, (0, 0) (d) translation $\begin{pmatrix} -4 \\ 10 \end{pmatrix}$
   (e) rotation 90° anticlockwise, (−7, 3) (f) reflection in $y = x$
   (g) rotation 180°, (0, 1) (h) reflection in y axis
7. (a) rotation 90° clockwise, (4, −2) (b) translation $\begin{pmatrix} 8 \\ 2 \end{pmatrix}$
   (c) reflection in $y = x$ (d) enlargement; scale factor $\frac{1}{2}$, (7, −7)
   (e) rotation 90° anticlockwise, (−8, 0) (f) enlargement; scale factor 2, (−1, −9)
   (g) rotation 90° anticlockwise, (7, 3)

   Congruent to △1 : △2, △3, △4, △6
8. (a) enlargement; scale factor $1\frac{1}{2}$, (1, −4) (b) rotation 90° clockwise, (0, −4)
   (c) reflection in $y = -x$ (d) translation $\begin{pmatrix} 11 \\ 10 \end{pmatrix}$
   (e) enlargement; scale factor $\frac{1}{2}$, (−3, 8) (f) rotation 90° anticlockwise, ($\frac{1}{2}$, $6\frac{1}{2}$)
   (g) enlargement; scale factor 3, (−2, 5)

   Congruent to △1 : △3, △4, △5.

Exercise 2 page 266

1. (c) (i) (−1, 2) (ii) (−2, −1) (iii) (2, −4) (iv) (4, −2)
2. (c) (ii) (8, 5) (ii) (8, −5) (iii) (−8, 2) (iv) (−3, 0)
3. (c) (i) (6, 8) (ii) (6, −2) (iii) (−2, −8) (iv) (−2, −2)
4. (c) (ii) (6, 0) (ii) (2, −8) (iii) (−8, 2) (iv) (1, −5) (v) (−1, 3)
5. (c) (ii) (5, 8) (ii) (−1, 8) (iii) (−4, 1) (iv) (−8, −5) (v) (4, −7)

Test 1 page 268

1. £3.50	2. £4.95	3. 48	4. 10p, 10p, 20p	5. $6\frac{1}{2}$
6. $\frac{1}{100}$	7. 56	8. 75%	9. 15	10. 56p
11. 50 min	12. 6.5	13. 130 m	14. 770	15. 11
16. 25	17. $1\frac{1}{4}$	18. £10	19. 10	20. 60.5

21. Decimal **22.** 16 **23.** 1 h **24.** $4\frac{1}{2}$ **25.** 75 or 105
26. 20 **27.** £2.40 **28.** 841 **29.** £4000 **30.** 48p

Test 2 page 268

1. 96 **2.** 19 **3.** 06 30 **4.** £2.75 **5.** £1.90
6. 30 **7.** 5 018 001 **8.** 15 **9.** £6 **10.** 3.5p
11. 53 **12.** 800 g **13.** 74 **14.** 280 miles **15.** 40
16. 4 **17.** 62 **18.** 5 **19.** 5 **20.** 480
21. 158 **22.** 95 **23.** 0.2 **24.** 0.7 **25.** £84
26. £2455 **27.** 64 **28.** 90p **29.** 55 m.p.h. **30.** 28

Test 3 page 269

1. 70 **2.** 240 **3.** 900 **4.** 10 705 **5.** 10 45 **6.** 245
7. 20 **8.** £3.05 **9.** £1.76 **10.** 20, 20, 20, 1 or 50, 5, 5, 1
11. 0.75 **12.** 5 **13.** Tuesday **14.** 1.5 kg **15.** £150.50 **16.** 640 m
17. £722 **18.** £25 000 **19.** 4 **20.** £1.10 **21.** 28 **22.** 9
23. 91 **24.** £6 **25.** 98p **26.** £4.46 **27.** £3.30 **28.** £42
29. 960 **30.** 18p

Test 4 page 270

1. £8.05 **2.** 75 **3.** 25 **4.** 0.1 cm **5.** 24p **6.** 104
7. 40p **8.** £88 **9.** 5:50 **10.** £8.20 **11.** 4 km **12.** 45 miles
13. £4.25 **14.** 998 **15.** 20 **16.** 200 **17.** 22.5 cm **18.** 75p
19. 10 **20.** 16 **21.** 20 **22.** £9.82 **23.** 22 min **24.** 1540
25. £7.94 **26.** 70p **27.** 200 **28.** 35% **29.** 100 **30.** £2500

Test 5 page 270

1. 360 **2.** £9.05 **3.** 12 **4.** 1.5p **5.** 9:35 **6.** 29
7. 140 **8.** 57 **9.** 82 **10.** 30p **11.** Diagonal **12.** 95°
13. 24 **14.** £9 **15.** 7:35 **16.** 244 **17.** £4.16 **18.** 90
19. 55 **20.** 45 miles **21.** 24 cm **22.** 185 cm **23.** $1\frac{1}{2}$ **24.** £200
25. −2°C **26.** 16 **27.** £6850 **28.** £7.80 **29.** 499 mm **30.** 8 027 010

Test 6 page 271

1. 1050 **2.** 3:38 **3.** £9.35 **4.** 29 **5.** £6.50 **6.** 21
7. 400 **8.** −8°C **9.** 210 **10.** £10 **11.** 153 **12.** £2000
13. 12 **14.** 45 **15.** 20p **16.** 240 **17.** Equation
18. 50, 10, 1, 1 or 20, 20, 20, 2 or 50, 5, 5, 2 **19.** £3.55 **20.** 1916 **21.** 4:30
22. £2.75 **23.** 900 g **24.** 155 **25.** 49° **26.** 104 **27.** £670
28. 06 15 **29.** 150 miles **30.** 20

Test 7 page 272

1. 27 **2.** £12.50 **3.** 16 **4.** 170 **5.** 3 017 004
6. 120 **7.** 19 22 **8.** 250 **9.** 0.03 **10.** £245
11. £7.90 **12.** 4.5p **13.** $\frac{1}{2}$ gallon **14.** 210 **15.** 20%
16. £8.14 **17.** 93 **18.** 40p **19.** 5 **20.** 11
21. 175 cm **22.** 150 **23.** 61 **24.** 38 **25.** £13.50
26. £4.50 **27.** 80 m.p.h. **28.** £12 → £13 **29.** 1908 **30.** 2997 m

Test 8 page 272

1. 9 **2.** £3.80 **3.** 50 **4.** 50 **5.** 72 **6.** 90°
7. 148 **8.** $8\frac{1}{2}$ **9.** 4000 **10.** $\frac{1}{1000}$ **11.** 50 **12.** 108

13. $\frac{7}{10}$	**14.** £1.15	**15.** 7	**16.** 20	**17.** 15 024	**18.** 24
19. 7 or 37	**20.** 20 cm	**21.** 18	**22.** £4.50	**23.** £9.00	**24.** £4.50
25. £168	**26.** 6	**27.** £18	**28.** 14	**29.** $1\frac{3}{4}$ h	**30.** 80%

Test 9 *page 273*

1. 72p	**2.** 112	**3.** £6	**4.** 6	**5.** 38	**6.** Friday
7. £11	**8.** 8:45	**9.** 50, 10; 10, 2 or 50, 20, 1, 1		**10.** 0.25	**11.** 9.5
12. 100	**13.** 396 cm	**14.** 500	**15.** Parallel	**16.** 30 010	**17.** 12
18. £55 500	**19.** 400	**20.** 8	**21.** Circumference	**22.** 12 m	**23.** 95
24. £6.26	**25.** £2.40	**26.** 90p	**27.** 162	**28.** £16	**29.** 300
30. 0.3					

Test 10 *page 273*

1. £15.65	**2.** 75	**3.** 100	**4.** 0.01 cm	**5.** 12p	**6.** 156
7. 60p	**8.** £65	**9.** 6:45	**10.** £8.50	**11.** 3 km	**12.** 100 miles
13. £3.20	**14.** 999	**15.** 15 miles	**16.** 155	**17.** $42\frac{1}{2}$ cm	**18.** 60p
19. 5	**20.** 25	**21.** 30	**22.** £9.77	**23.** 26 mins	**24.** 15 40
25. £7.55	**26.** 50p	**27.** 2500	**28.** 45%	**29.** 125 mins	**30.** £425

Exercise 3 *page 274*

1. (a) 1	(b) 1	**2.** (a) 1	(b) 1	**3.** (a) 4	(b) 4	**4.** (a) 2	(b) 2
5. (a) 0	(b) 6	**6.** (a) 0	(b) 4	**7.** (a) 0	(b) 2	**8.** (a) 1	(b) 1
9. (a) 4	(b) 4	**10.** (a) 4	(b) 4	**11.** (a) 0	(b) 4	**12.** (a) 0	(b) 2
13. (a) 4	(b) 4	**14.** (a) 4	(b) 4	**15.** (a) 0	(b) 4	**16.** (a) 4	(b) 4
17. (a) 8	(b) 8	**18.** (a) 1	(b) 1	**19.** (a) 5	(b) 5	**20.** (a) 0	(b) 2
21. (a) 0	(b) 2	**22.** (a) 0	(b) 4	**23.** (a) 12	(b) 6	**24.** (a) infinite	(b) infinite

Exercise 4 *page 276*

1. 7, 9, 11, 13, 15, 17, 19
2. 4, 10, 16, 22, 28, 34, 40
3. 2, 3, 4, 5, 6, 7, 8
4. 38, 46, 54, 62, 34, 38, 42
5. 56, 64, 72, 80, 88, 44, 48
6. 54, 62, 71, 38, 42, 46, 50
7. 6, 24, 12, 42, 18, 60, 24, 78, 30
8. 24, 12, 42, 18, 60, 24, 78, 30, 96

Exercise 5 *page 277*

1. (a) 11, 22, 11, 33 (b) 12, 24, 13, 39 (c) 7, 14, 28, 17, 51
(d) 9, 16, 32, 21, 63 (e) 11, 18, 36, 25, 75 (f) 13, 20, 40, 29, 87
2. (a) 6, 12, 27, 20, 5 (b) 3, 6, 21, 14, $3\frac{1}{2}$ (c) 8, 16, 31, 24, 6
(d) 10, 20, 35, 28, 7 (e) 1, 2, 17, 10, $2\frac{1}{2}$ (f) 12, 24, 39, 32, 8
3. (a) 7, 22, 44, 22, $5\frac{1}{2}$ (b) 10, 25, 50, 28, 7 (c) 16, 31, 62, 40, 10
(d) $\frac{1}{2}$, $15\frac{1}{2}$, 31, 9, $2\frac{1}{4}$ (e) 100, 115, 230, 208, 52 (f) 24, 39, 78, 56, 14
4. (a) 4, 16, 48, 38, 19 (b) 5, 25, 75, 65, $32\frac{1}{2}$ (c) 6, 36, 108, 98, 49
(d) 8, 64, 192, 182, 91 (e) 1, 1, 3, −7, $-3\frac{1}{2}$ (f) 10, 100, 300, 290, 145

THINK ABOUT IT 5

Project 1 *page 279*

(a) cut out 4 cm squares (b) 3.5 cm, $3\frac{1}{3}$ cm. Always $\frac{1}{6}$ × side of square card. (c) 2.43 cm (3 s.f.)

Exercise A *page 280*

1. 600 **2.** £2.60 **3.** (a) 720 000 (b) 200 **4.** 50 m

5. 5 h 34 min **6.** (a) $6^2 = 5^2 + 11$, $7^2 = 6^2 + 13$ (b) $11^2 = 60 + 5^2 + 6^2$, $13^2 = 84 + 6^2 + 7^2$
7. $\frac{2}{3}$ is larger **8.** (a) 132 cm (b) 140 cm **9.** (a) 120 (b) 480
10. (a) 320 (b) £592

Exercise B *page 282*

1. (a) 72 kg (b) 18 kg **2.** £3.40 **3.** (a) 22 (b) £187 (c) 50
4. (a) £100 (b) 142.5 kg (c) 48 cm **5.** (a) $\frac{1}{10}$ (b) $\frac{1}{4}$ (c) $\frac{1}{100}$ **6.** 80°
7. (a) £1.89 (b) £14.49 **8.** (a) 80 g (b) 5.2 (c) 416
9. (a) 1875 km (b) 2 h 12 min **10.** (a) 450 (b) £9750

Project 3 *page 283*

Part A

[1] 7	7	[2] 7	■	[3] 2	9	■	[4] 1
5	■	[5] 3	9	8	1	■	5
[6] 6	0	5	■	0	■	[7] 7	8
1	■	[8] 8	[9] 5	8	■	0	■
■	[10] 6	0	8	■	[11] 4	0	7
[12] 6	7	■	[13] 8	[14] 6	8	■	■
1	■	[15] 1	■	[16] 1	7	[17] 4	[18] 6
[19] 5	7	2	■	5	■	[20] 4	9

Part B

[1] 8	4	[2] 2	■	[3] 7	4	■	[4] 3
1	■	[5] 4	8	8	4	■	1
[6] 3	3	6	■	3	■	[7] 5	7
7	■	[8] 1	[9] 2	0	■	2	■
■	[10] 5	0	9	■	[11] 7	2	4
[12] 5	8	■	[13] 7	[14] 2	0	■	■
9	■	[15] 1	■	[16] 6	8	[17] 6	[18] 4
[19] 2	5	7	■	5	■	[20] 4	7

Part C

[1] 1	6	[2] 1	■	[3] 3	6	■	[4] 3
7	■	[5] 6	4	5	8	■	4
[6] 8	6	4	■	0	■	[7] 2	8
5	■	[8] 3	[9] 6	0	■	6	■
■	[10] 6	3	7	■	[11] 8	0	5
[12] 2	5	■	[13] 1	[14] 2	4	■	■
5	■	[15] 3	■	[16] 3	1	[17] 1	[18] 1
[19] 9	9	9	■	4	■	[20] 6	3

Part D

[1] 5	9	[2] 2	■	[3] 3	7	■	[4] 4
5	■	[5] 5	1	9	4	■	2
[6] 3	7	6	■	5	■	[7] 9	9
2	■	[8] 8	[9] 2	6	■	2	■
■	[10] 2	4	0	■	[11] 1	4	5
[12] 3	9	■	[13] 5	[14] 6	3	■	■
2	■	[15] 1	■	[16] 8	4	[17] 7	[18] 5
[19] 4	6	2	■	5	■	[20] 4	7

Exercise C *page 285*

1. 4.3 **2.** 0.7 **3.** 9.4 **4.** 7 **5.** 42 **6.** 1.2 **7.** 3.3
8. 16 **9.** 23.4 **10.** 17.4 **11.** 128 **12.** 54 **13.** 8 **14.** 2.6
15. 24 **16.** 120 **17.** 1.8 **18.** 190 **19.** 15.2 **20.** 0.2 **21.** 5.5
22. 0.5 **23.** 1.2 **24.** 1.75 **25.** 6.5 **26.** 10.75 **27.** 15 **28.** 11
29. 8.6 **30.** 0.24 **31.** 53 **32.** 1.76 **33.** 3.13 **34.** 47.5 **35.** 4.35
36. 22 **37.** 1.92 **38.** 92 **39.** 76 **40.** 105 **41.** 50 **42.** 1.9
43. 2.5 **44.** 1200 **45.** 1.6 **46.** 3.75 **47.** 7.625 **48.** 5.2 **49.** 1330
50. 08 40 **51.** 14 10 **52.** 04 50 **53.** 12 20 **54.** 18 20 **55.** 11 00 **56.** 08 20
57. 11 20 **58.** 13 00

Project 4 page 287

1. Sell **2.** Slosh **3.** Bell **4.** Goes **5.** Hole
6. Hello **7.** Geese **8.** Legible **9.** Obsess **10.** Oboe
11. She lies **12.** Big log **13.** Loose **14.** Biggish **15.** Eggshell
16. Igloo **17.** Gloss **18.** Bilge **19.** Legless **20.** Shoes
21. Siege **22.** He did **23.** Oblige **24.** Libel **25.** Besiege
26. He is so big **27.** Boo Hoo **28.** Booze **29.** Eel **30.** Goose
31. Goodbie **32.** He sells

Exercise D page 288

1. (a) 170 (b) £44.20 **2.** 120 g **3.** $1\frac{3}{20}$ **4.** 84 cm^2
5. (a) £4.40 (b) £10.56 **6.** shirt £9, tie £2 **7.** (a) $\frac{2}{15}$ (b) $\frac{7}{8}$ (c) $\frac{1}{9}$
8. (a) $8 - 2 \times (3 - 1)$ (b) $(8 - 2) \times (3 - 1)$ (c) $8 - (2 \times 3 - 1)$
9. (a) $(9 + 2) \times 4 - 3$ (b) $9 + 2 \times (4 - 3)$ or $(9 + 2) \times (4 - 3)$
10. (a) $(12 - 5) \times (2 + 4)$ (b) $(12 - 5) \times 2 + 4$ (c) $12 - 5 \times (2 + 4)$
(d) $12 - (5 \times 2 + 4)$

Project 5 page 289

1. 2 **2.** 3 **3.** 2 **4.** 2 **5.** 2 **6.** 3 **7.** 6 **8.** 1

Exercise E page 290

1. $\frac{36}{54}$ **2.** $\frac{119}{138}$ **3.** $\frac{95}{115}$ **4.** $\frac{135}{435}$ **5.** $\frac{217}{370}$ **6.** $\frac{189}{356}$
7. (a) $\frac{27}{32}, \frac{17}{20}, \frac{7}{8}$ (b) $\frac{1}{5}, \frac{21}{100}, \frac{9}{40}$ (c) $\frac{3}{4}, \frac{5}{6}, \frac{6}{7}$ (d) $\frac{5}{9}, \frac{2}{3}, \frac{8}{11}$ (e) $\frac{3}{4}, \frac{7}{9}, \frac{13}{15}, \frac{11}{12}$
(f) $\frac{3}{5}, \frac{17}{23}, \frac{15}{19}$ (g) $\frac{4}{13}, \frac{7}{19}, \frac{5}{11}, \frac{17}{37}$
8. $\frac{7}{9}$ **9.** $\frac{6}{7}$ **10.** $\frac{7}{12}$ **11.** $\frac{8}{17}$ **12.** $\frac{11}{8}$ **13.** $\frac{13}{9}$ **14.** $\frac{12}{11}$ **15.** $\frac{3}{17}$
16. $\frac{7}{19}$

Project 6 page 291

1. 41×32 **2.** 431×52 **3.** $631 \times 542 = 342\ 002$ **4.** $742 \times 6531 = 4\ 846\ 002$
5. $8531 \times 7642 = 65\ 193\ 902$

Exercise F page 291

1. (a) £49 (b) £93.50 (c) 100 km **2.** (a) £250 (b) £250
3. (b) 102.86° **4.** (a) 15 (b) 6 (c) £1.50 **5.** 85
6. 000, 001, 010, 011, 100, 101, 110, 111

Project 7 page 293

Second number + fourth number = 99 999
Third number + fifth number = 99 999
∴ Sum of five numbers = first number + 199 998
= first number + 200 000 − 2

UNIT 16

Exercise 1 page 294

1. 6.2 **2.** 3.875 **3.** 7 **4.** 6 **5.** 1.42 **6.** 7.3 **7.** $\frac{1}{8}$
8. 2757 **9.** 6.3 **10.** 58.25 **11.** 70.4, 73.25, no
12. (a) 6 (b) 6.5 **13.** (a) 6 (b) 5.6
14. (a) 1.15 (b) 0.92 **15.** (a) 5 (b) 5.625
16. (a) 5.25 (b) 5.6 **17.** (a) 7 (b) 6.6

18. (a) 1.6 m (b) 1.634 m 19. (a) 51 kg (b)
20. (a) 7.2 (b) 5 (c) 6

Exercise 2 page 295

1. (a) 16.4 (b) 19.2 (c) 3.56 2. (a) 21.7
3. (a) 23.2 (b) 26.4 (c) 4.96 4. (a) 13.6
5. 5.42 6. (a) 192 kg
7. (a) 5.34 m (b) 11.13 m (c) 1.647 m

Exercise 3 page 296

1. 4 2. 8 3. 8 4. 4 5. 11 6. 4
7. 7.5 8. 3.5 9. 1.2 10. 0.81 11. 3 12. $\frac{1}{2}$
13. $\frac{1}{5}$ 14. 0.5 15. 148 cm 16. 3 17. 3 18. 12

Exercise 4 page 296

1. 2 2. 3 3. 6 4. 7 5. 7 6. 5 7. 18p
8. 2°C 9. 3 10. 6

Exercise 5 page 297

1. 4.4, 4, 2 2. 5, 6, 8 3. 3.625, 3.5, 3 4. 1.1, 1.2, 1.8
5. 17.6, 18, 18 6. 6.1, 5.5, 4 7. 0.45, 0.5, 0.5 8. 3, 3, 3
9. 0.625, $\frac{1}{2}$, $\frac{1}{4}$ 10. 0, −1, −1 11. 0.78, 0.8, 0.85 12. 1, 0, −1
13. 7, 5, 4 14. 11, 11, 13 15. 111.2, 102, 101 16. 5, 5, 1
17. 0.0884, 0.11, 0.111 18. 0.3132, 0.32, 0.322 19. 1, 0, −2 20. 39, 40, 41

Exercise 6 page 297

1. 96.25 g 2. 51.9p 3. 4.82 cm 4. 7.1 cm 5. 3.65 6. 7.82
7. 1.48 m 8. 8.9 s

Exercise 7 page 299

1. (a) £210 (b) £70 (c) £105 (d) £35
2. (a) £1333.33 (b) £1500 (c) £666.67 (d) £1000 (e) £1200
3. (a) £21 600 000 (b) £8 000 000 (c) £1 000 000 4. 230, 66, 114, 142, 70°, 14°
5. (a) 8 min, 34 min, 10 min (b) 30° (c) 18°
6. (a) £62 000 (b) £650 000 (c) £3800 (d) £70 000

Exercise 8 page 300

1. (a) (i) 45° (ii) 200° (iii) 110° (iv) 5° 2. (a) $\frac{3}{10}$, $\frac{4}{10}$, $\frac{1}{5}$, $\frac{1}{10}$
3. $x = 60°$, $y = 210°$ 4. Barley 60°, Oats 90°, Rye 165°, Wheat 45°
5. (a) 180° (b) 36° (c) 90° (d) 54° 6. BBC1 126°, BBC2 18°, ITV 180°, Channel 4 36°
7. (From top to bottom) 120°, 60°, 100°, 40°, 40°
8. (a) 100°, 40°, 60°, 120°, 40° (b) 80°, 30°, 100°, 50°, 100° (c) 90°, 42°, 72°, 96°, 60°
(d) 200°, 35°, 45°, 25°, 55° (e) 150°, 24°, 60°, 48°, 78°

Exercise 9 page 301

1. (a) £120 000 (b) 1986 (c) 1985 (d) £30 000 (e) £700 000
2. (a) £70 000 000 (b) £40 000 000 (c) £20 000 000 (d) £15 000 000 (e) £84 000 000
3. (a) 5 (b) 19 (c) 23 (d) 55 (e) $\frac{6}{23}$
5. (a) £45 000 (b) £30 000 (c) 3 months (d) April and May (e) £115 000
6. Frequency: 2, 4, 5, 7, 9, 13, 6, 0, 5, 6, 3

6, C 5, D 6, N 3, P 4, R 6, S 5, T 12, V 9, W 9, X 9. All others 0. (b) (i) 9 (ii) T

…cise 10 page 304

1. B 2. D 3. (a) C (b) A (c) D (d) B
4. (a) (i) 35 cm (ii) 57.5 cm (iii) 42.5 cm (b) (i) 2 kg (ii) 2.8 kg (iii) 1.2 kg
(c) 18 cm approximately (d) 12.5 cm 5. (a) (i) 10°C (ii) 16°C (iii) 15.5°C
(b) 5 p.m. and 11 p.m. (c) 1°C at 3 a.m. (d) (i) 6 a.m. and 3 p.m. (ii) 10 a.m. and 10 p.m.
(e) 5°C between 4 p.m. and 5 p.m. 6. (c) (i) £34.50 (ii) $2\frac{1}{2}$ h
7. (a) (i) £40 (ii) 250 km (b) (ii) 200 km (iii) £15
8. (c) 55 km/h (d) 6.5 (e) £5.34

Exercise 11 page 308

1. (a) $\frac{1}{13}$ (b) $\frac{1}{52}$ (c) $\frac{1}{4}$ 2. (a) $\frac{1}{9}$ (b) $\frac{1}{3}$ (c) $\frac{4}{9}$ (d) $\frac{2}{9}$
3. (a) $\frac{5}{11}$ (b) $\frac{2}{11}$ (c) $\frac{4}{11}$ 4. (a) $\frac{4}{17}$ (b) $\frac{3}{17}$ (c) $\frac{11}{17}$
5. (a) $\frac{4}{17}$ (b) $\frac{8}{17}$ (c) $\frac{5}{17}$
6. (a) $\frac{2}{9}$ (b) $\frac{2}{9}$ (c) $\frac{1}{9}$ (d) 0 (e) $\frac{5}{9}$
7. (a) $\frac{1}{13}$ (b) $\frac{2}{13}$ (c) $\frac{1}{52}$ (d) $\frac{5}{52}$ 8. (a) $\frac{1}{10}$ (b) $\frac{3}{10}$ (c) $\frac{3}{10}$
9. (a) $\frac{3}{13}$ (b) $\frac{5}{13}$ (c) $\frac{8}{13}$ 10. (a) (i) $\frac{5}{13}$ (ii) $\frac{6}{13}$ (b) (i) $\frac{5}{12}$ (ii) $\frac{1}{12}$
11. (a) $\frac{1}{5}$ (b) $\frac{1}{20}$ (c) $\frac{1}{2}$ (d) $\frac{2}{5}$ 12. $\frac{9}{20}$

Exercise 12 page 309

1. (a) $\frac{1}{17}$ (b) $\frac{4}{17}$ (c) $\frac{1}{51}$ (d) $\frac{1}{51}$
2. (a) $\frac{3}{49}$ (b) $\frac{10}{49}$ (c) $\frac{1}{49}$ (d) $\frac{1}{49}$
3. (a) (i) $\frac{5}{11}$ (ii) $\frac{6}{11}$ (iii) $\frac{7}{11}$ (iv) $\frac{9}{11}$ (b) (i) $\frac{6}{11}$ (ii) $\frac{2}{11}$ (iii) $\frac{5}{11}$
4. (a) $\frac{1}{36}$ (b) $\frac{1}{9}$ (c) $\frac{1}{36}$ (d) $\frac{1}{6}$ (e) $\frac{1}{6}$ (f) $\frac{1}{36}$
5. (a) $\frac{1}{8}$ (b) $\frac{3}{8}$ (c) $\frac{3}{8}$ 6. (a) $\frac{1}{16}$ (b) $\frac{1}{4}$ (c) $\frac{3}{8}$ (d) $\frac{1}{4}$
7. (a) $\frac{1}{6}$ (b) $\frac{1}{2}$ (c) $\frac{1}{2}$ 8. (a) (i) $\frac{1}{4}$ (ii) $\frac{1}{4}$ (iii) $\frac{1}{4}$ (b) $\frac{1}{4}$ (c) $\frac{6}{27} = \frac{2}{9}$

Exercise 13 page 311

1. (a) $\frac{25}{64}$ (b) $\frac{9}{64}$ 2. (a) $\frac{9}{49}$ (b) $\frac{16}{49}$ (c) $\frac{12}{49}$
3. (a) $\frac{1}{49}$ (b) $\frac{16}{49}$ (c) $\frac{8}{49}$ (d) $\frac{8}{49}$ 4. (b) (i) $\frac{20}{56} = \frac{5}{14}$ (ii) $\frac{6}{56} = \frac{3}{28}$
5. (a) $\frac{1}{21}$ (b) $\frac{10}{21}$ (c) $\frac{5}{21}$
6. (a) $\frac{2}{11}$ (b) $\frac{1}{55}$ (c) $\frac{2}{11}$ (d) $\frac{8}{55}$
7. (a) $\frac{8}{125}$ (b) $\frac{27}{125}$ (c) $\frac{12}{125}$ 8. (a) $\frac{1}{64}$ (b) $\frac{27}{64}$ (c) $\frac{27}{64}$
9. (a) $\frac{1}{216}$ (b) $\frac{125}{216}$ 10. (a) $\frac{1}{8}$ (b) $\frac{1}{8}$ (c) $\frac{3}{8}$
11. (a) $\frac{1}{5}$ (b) $\frac{7}{10}$ (d) (i) $\frac{1}{4}$ (ii) $\frac{3}{10}$ (iii) $\frac{1}{25}$
12. (a) $\frac{4}{9}$ (b) $\frac{5}{9}$ (c) 16 (d) $\frac{16}{81}$ 13. (a) $\frac{1}{16}$ (b) $\frac{3}{8}$
14. (a) $\frac{1}{27}$ (b) $\frac{2}{9}$ 15. (a) (i) $\frac{1}{10}$ (ii) $\frac{1}{4}$ (iii) $\frac{1}{40}$ (iv) $\frac{1}{40}$
(b) $\frac{1}{39}$ (c) $\frac{1}{40} \times \frac{1}{39} = \frac{1}{1560}$

UNIT 17

Exercise 1 page 313

1. 48° 2. 134° 3. 39° 4. 65° 5. 31° 6. 44° 7. 36°
8. 51° 9. 100° 10. 80° 11. 60° 12. 30°

13. $x = 44°$, $y = 136°$ **14.** $x = 75°$, $y = 105°$, $z = 75°$ **15.** $x = 60°$, $y = 60°$
16. $x = 68°$, $y = 112°$ **17.** 70° **18.** $x = 80°$, $y = 75°$
19. $a = 95°$, $b = 115°$ **20.** $a = 60°$, $b = 50°$, $c = 70°$
21. 78° **22.** $x = 60°$ **23.** $y = 45°$ **24.** $x = 75°$, $y = 65°$

Exercise 2 *page 315*

1. 70° **2.** 73° **3.** 55° **4.** 37°
5. 23° **6.** 74° **7.** 66° **8.** 40°
9. 38° **10.** 48° **11.** 112° **12.** 62°
13. $a = 110°$, $b = 55°$ **14.** 23° **15.** 34° **16.** 39°
17. $x = 60°$, $y = 48°$ **18.** $a = 65°$, $b = 40°$ **19.** $c = 67°$, $d = 54°$ **20.** $a = 60°$, $b = 40°$
21. 108° **22.** 50° **23.** 76° **24.** 270°
25. 60° **26.** $a = 45°$, $b = 67\frac{1}{2}°$, $c = 45°$

Exercise 3 *page 317*

1. 57° **2.** 49° **3.** $c = 37°$, $d = 50°$ **4.** $x = 90°$, $y = 33°$
5. $e = 44°$, $f = 52°$ **6.** $g = 90°$, $h = 34°$ **7.** 30° **8.** 18°
9. $m = 45°$, $n = 90°$ **10.** $x = 48°$, $y = 42°$ **11.** (a) 54° (b) 51° (c) 90°

Exercise 4 *page 317*

1. 19° **2.** 57° **3.** $a = 55°$, $b = 49°$ **4.** $c = 35°$, $d = 59°$ **5.** $x = 26°$, $y = 43°$
6. $m = 63°$, $n = 46°$ **7.** $a = 30°$, $c = 45°$ **8.** $x = 18°$, $y = 90°$ **9.** $a = 50°$, $y = 18°$
10. $e = 61°$, $y = 22\frac{1}{2}°$ **11.** $a = 70°$, $b = 55°$ **12.** $x = 80°$, $y = 10°$ **13.** $a = 60°$, $b = 30°$

Exercise 5 *page 319*

1. 68° **2.** 40° **3.** $x = 65°$, $y = 25°$ **4.** $a = 58°$, $b = 58°$
5. $a = 56°$, $b = 34°$, $c = 34°$ **6.** $a = 22°$, $b = 68°$

Exercise 6 *page 320*

1. (b) 4.2 cm **2.** (b) 2.6 cm

Exercise 7 *page 321*

1. 38.7° **2.** 48.6° **3.** 31.0° **4.** 54.5° **5.** 38.7° **6.** 17.5° **7.** 38.9°
8. 59.0° **9.** 39.5° **10.** 63.6° **11.** 24.6° **12.** 16.9° **13.** 36.9° **14.** 51.8°
15. 38.1° **16.** 47.0° **17.** 41.3° **18.** 62.7° **19.** 54.3° **20.** 66.0° **21.** 48.2°
22. 12.4° **23.** 72.9° **24.** 56.9° **25.** 36.9° **26.** 41.8° **27.** 78.0° **28.** 89.4°

Exercise 8 *page 323*

1. 3.01 cm **2.** 5.35 cm **3.** 3.13 cm **4.** 7.00 cm **5.** 73.1 cm **6.** 15.4 cm
7. 5.31 cm **8.** 7.99 cm **9.** 11.6 cm **10.** 11.4 cm **11.** 961 cm **12.** 0.894 cm
13. 46.0 cm **14.** 34.9 cm **15.** 9.39 cm **16.** 8.23 cm **17.** 35.6 cm **18.** 80.2 cm
19. 4.86 cm **20.** 6.98 cm

Exercise 9 *page 324*

1. 18.4 **2.** 9.15 **3.** 10.7 **4.** 17.1 **5.** 13.7 **6.** 126 **7.** 6.88
8. 11.8 **9.** 39.1° **10.** 19.5° **11.** 65.6° **12.** 63.6° **13.** 17.6 **14.** 11.4
15. $x = 8.39$, $y = 64.5°$ **16.** $y = 6.29$, $e = 64.5°$ **17.** 72.0 **18.** $x = 9.51$, $y = 8.24$, $z = 6.31$
19. $x = 17.8$, $y = 16.7$, $z = 14.4$ **20.** 17.8

Exercise 10 *page 325*

1. 8.29 **2.** 48.6° **3.** 53.1° **4.** 8.60 **5.** 90.0 **6.** 9.80 **7.** 6.27

8. 31.8° **9.** 5.66 **10.** 441 **11.** 50.5° **12.** 8.99 **13.** 14.4 **14.** 76.0°
15. 10.2 **16.** 0.460 **17.** $x = 3.50$, $y = 6.63$ **18.** $x = 8.83$, $y = 7.68$
19. 2.53 **20.** 25.4°

Exercise 11 *page 326*

1. 68.0° **2.** 53.1° **3.** 2.54 m **4.** 3.65 m **5.** 14.0 m **6.** 19.8 m
7. 11.9 m **8.** 20.6° **9.** 15.1° **10.** 56.7 m **11.** 29.4 m **12.** 33.4°
13. 15.3 m **14.** 90.3 cm **15.** 4.32 cm **16.** 7.66 cm **17.** 83.6° **18.** 7.20 cm

Exercise 12 *page 327*

1. 65.5 km **2.** 189 km **3.** 46.9 km **4.** 460 km **5.** 25.7 km **6.** 139 km
7. 13.8 cm **8.** 37.3 m

UNIT 18

Revision test 1 *page 328*

1. 3p **2.** 200 g **3.** £8 **4.** £92 **5.** (a) 1810 s (b) 72.4 s **6.** 0.8 cm
7. (a) £13 (b) £148 (c) £170 **8.** (a) $5\frac{8}{9}$ (b) 6 (c) 7
9. (a) −11 (b) 23 (c) −10 (d) −20 (e) 6 (f) −14
10. (a) 3 (b) 5 (c) −6 (d) −7
11. (a) 9 (b) 11 (c) 3 (d) 7 **12.** (a) 42 cm^2 (b) 36 cm^2
13. (a) y-values −7, −5, −3, −1, 1, 3, 5 **14.** (d) A′(6, 3), A″(1, 2), A*(−5, −6)
15. (d) P′(1, −1), P″(−3, 3), P*(3, 1)

Revision test 2 *page 330*

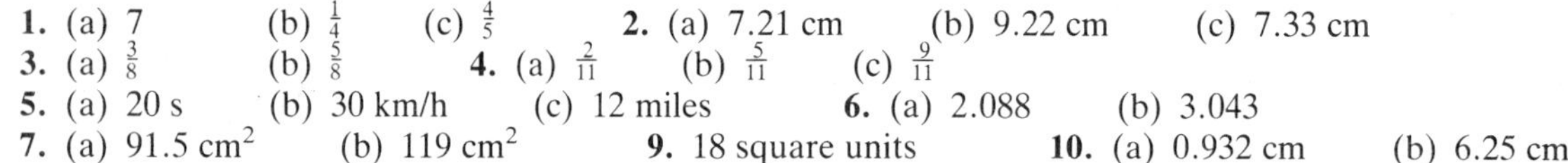

1. (a) 7 (b) $\frac{1}{4}$ (c) $\frac{4}{5}$ **2.** (a) 7.21 cm (b) 9.22 cm (c) 7.33 cm
3. (a) $\frac{3}{8}$ (b) $\frac{5}{8}$ **4.** (a) $\frac{2}{11}$ (b) $\frac{5}{11}$ (c) $\frac{9}{11}$
5. (a) 20 s (b) 30 km/h (c) 12 miles **6.** (a) 2.088 (b) 3.043
7. (a) 91.5 cm^2 (b) 119 cm^2 **9.** 18 square units **10.** (a) 0.932 cm (b) 6.25 cm

Revision test 3 *page 331*

1. (a) £0.18 (b) 11 kg (c) 0.075, 0.715, 0.75, 7.5 **2.** (a) 3017, 3047, 3407, 3740 (b) 0.13, 0.151, 0.301, 0.31 (d) 0.0095, 0.089, 0.09, 0.9 **3.** 10 h 30 min
4. (a) 4.1 m (b) 6300 cm (c) 0.48 kg (d) 2200 m (e) 7 cm **5.** £10; £30; £40
6. (a) £26 (b) £3.52 (c) £0.87 (d) £0.84 **7.** £56
8. (a) 38.7° (b) 56.3° (c) 36.9° (d) 34.8°
9. (a) 62.8 cm^3 (b) 268 cm^3 (c) 262 cm^3 **10.** (a) 5 (b) $\frac{2}{3}$ (c) 4 (d) 3
11. (a) 30, 37 (b) 12, 10 (c) 7, 10 (d) 8, 4 (e) 26, 33
12. (d) (−1, 3), (1, −3), (1, 1), (3, 1)

Examination exercise 1 *page 333*

1. £25.60, £6.70, 4, £55.30 **2.** (a) back 5, bottom 6 (b) A 6, B 5, C 4 **3.** 12 km
4. (i) 9 (ii) 50 (iii) (7 × 11) − 6 = 72 − 1 **5.** 17.7 cm **6.** (i) 6 (ii) 5
7. (i) £100 (ii) 500 (iii) £44 profit **8.** (a) 5.74 m (b) 53.1° **9.** (d) 4 (e) 4
10. (a) 500 m^3 (b) 13 m **11.** (a) 5 cm, 13 cm, 13 cm, 13 cm (b) 120 cm^3
12. (i) $\frac{2}{5}$ (ii) $\frac{7}{12}$ (iii) $\frac{7}{20}$

Examination exercise 2 *page 336*

1. (a) £5.20 (b) 29 min **2.** (a) 2 cm (b) 8 m
3. (a) £161 (b) £536.25 (c) £193 (d) 8

4. (a) 4 (b) 19 **5.** 74 m **6.** 28274, £79.15, £85.42, November
7. (a) 560 kg, 57 kg (b) 50 kg **8.** (i) 182 cm^2 (ii) 82 cm^2 (iii) 60 cm^3
10. (a) 198 cm^3 (b) 1357 mm^3 (c) 145 **12.** (i) 43 min 32 s (ii) 1 hr 5 min 18 s
(iii) 2 hr 8 min 6 s (v) 10:07:38

Examination exercise 3 page 339

1. (a) 34 m (b) 17 **2.** £1359
3. (a) (i) 13, 49, 109 (ii) 4, 49 (iii) 13, 109 (b) (i) 27 (ii) 33 (c) 148, 193
(d) 94, 127
4. (ii) 30 km (iv) 40° (v) 050° **5.** (b) (i) £990 (ii) 54° (iii) 6.67%
6. (a) 140 min (b) $T = 40M + 20$ **7.** (i) 34 (ii) 9 **8.** (a) 200 (b) $\frac{4}{25}$
9. (b) (i) 94 cm^2 (ii) 376 cm^2 **10.** (i) £6.24 (ii) £15 (iii) 24p **11.** (i) £14.17 (ii) 6
12. (b) 96° (±1°) (c) 410 m (±10 m)

Examination exercise 4 page 344

1. (a) £28 600 (b) 198 (c) £143 (d) £28 314 (e) £286
2. (a) 55p (b) 760
3. (a) (i) 804 m^2 (ii) 64 (b) (i) 105 cm^2 (ii) 21 000 cm^3
4. (a) 8 cm (b) 0.8 (c) 12.5 cm **5.** (a) £6.80 (b) £31.36 (c) £22.95
(d) (i) 1555 (ii) 2 h 15 min (iii) 64 km/h (e) (i) 1156 (ii) 9 min
6. (i) 23, 22, 13, 13, 8, 1 (ii) 1 (iii) 2.55
8. (a) 14 cm (b) 70° (c) ADC, CDE (d) ABC, BCD **9.** 9.0 cm
10. 100
11. (a) (i) 3 h 30 min (ii) 3 h 25 min (iii) 720 km/h (b) (i) £225 (ii) £950
(c) (i) 240 (ii) £185
12. (a) 6 cm, 20 cm (b) (i) 4 cm (ii) 48 cm^2 (iii) 960 cm^3 (c) 6 cm, 8 cm, 37°

Examination exercise 5 page 348

1. (a) £790 (b) £4266 (c) £5056 **2.** (a) 27 m^2 (b) 123 m^2
4. (b) (i) £114 (ii) £3.80 **5.** (i) 08096 (ii) 83 km (iii) 15
(iv) £6.60 **6.** (i) 111 m (iii) 48 m
8. (b) (i) 9.7 cm (±0.1) (ii) 485 m (±5 m) (c) (i) 42° (±1°) (ii) 122° (iii) 302°
(d) 410 m **9.** (a) 70 km/h (b) 68 km (c) 52 km/h (d) 5 h 25 min (e) 1910

THINK ABOUT IT 6

Project 1 page 352

(e) $n = 4s + 4$ Oblong lawns (c) $n = 4w + 6$ (d) $n = 6w + 4$

Exercise A page 354

1. 90 kg **2.** £5.04; 36p; 6; £8.34 **3.** 352 miles **4.** 1640 nautical miles **5.** 165 nautical miles
6. 25 **7.** 55 m.p.h. **8.** 62 km/h **9.** $8\frac{1}{2}$ m.p.h. **10.** (a) 148 cm (b) 152 cm

Project 2 page 355

Highest finish = 170 (60 + 60 + 50)

Exercise B page 355

1. 1936 cm^3 **2.** (a) £4 (b) 100 kg (c) 98 m **3.** 120° **4.** 120
5. $\frac{1}{2}$ of 0.2 **6.** 7 years **7.** 25 litres **8.** (a) £10 (b) 35p (c) £3.60
9. 12 h 30 min **10.** (a) 350 km (b) 14 litres (c) £6.02 (d) 20 litres

Project 3 *page 356*

For five discs 35 moves are needed.

Exercise C *page 357*

1. 120 000 000 m^3 **2.** (a) 3 h 20 min (b) 3 h 20 min (c) 2 h 30 min (d) 5 h 5 min
3. (a) £222 (b) £249 (c) 5 h **4.** 15 cm^2 **5.** 85 km/h
6. (a) 5.4 km (b) 0.6 cm **7.** (a) 3 cm^2 (b) 27 cm^2 (c) $A = \frac{C^2}{12}$
8. 16 **10.** (a) $1\frac{1}{15}$ (b) $\frac{4}{15}$ (c) $\frac{4}{15}$

Exercise D *page 359*

1. (a) 108 000 lb (b) 4500 lb
2. (a) (i) £496 (ii) £680 (b) (i) £646 (ii) £890 (c) £244
3. (a) 1.75 (b) 0.35 (c) 17.87 (d) 0.08 (e) 0.08 (f) 78.09
4. (a) 8.94 cm (b) 6.71 cm (c) 11.2 cm (d) 6.00 cm **5.** (a) £1.60 (b) £4.00
6. (b) 108°

Project 5 *page 360*

(a) (i) 24 (ii) 16 (iii) 30 (b) (i) 15 (ii) 28 (iii) 45
(c) (i) 17 (ii) 7 (iii) 22 (d) (i) 78 (ii) 38 (iii) 48 (iv) 58
(e) If one or both numbers are even: multiply numbers and divide by 2.
If both numbers are odd: multiply numbers, take away one and divide by 2.

Project 6 *page 361*

One solution is:

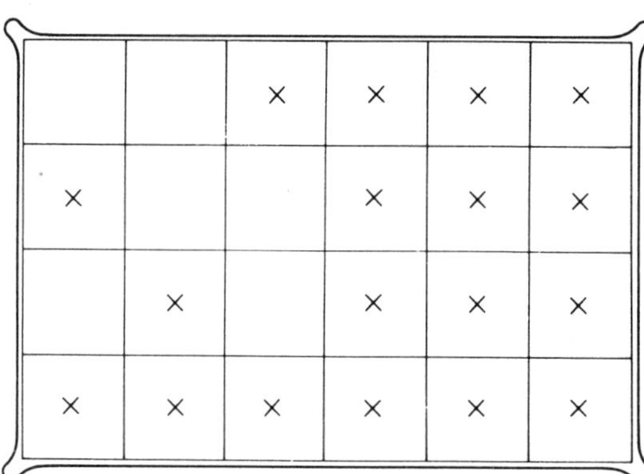

TRIGONOMETRIC TABLES

TABLE OF SINES

Angle in degrees	.0	.1	.2	.3	.4	.5	.6	.7	.8	.9
0	0.000	.002	.003	.005	.007	.009	.010	.012	.014	.016
1	0.017	.019	.021	.023	.024	.026	.028	.030	.031	.033
2	0.035	.037	.038	.040	.042	.044	.045	.047	.049	.051
3	0.052	.054	.056	.058	.059	.061	.063	.065	.066	.068
4	0.070	.071	.073	.075	.077	.078	.080	.082	.084	.085
5	0.087	.089	.091	.092	.094	.096	.098	.099	.101	.103
6	0.105	.106	.108	.110	.111	.113	.115	.117	.118	.120
7	0.122	.124	.125	.127	.129	.131	.132	.134	.136	.137
8	0.139	.141	.143	.144	.146	.148	.150	.151	.153	.155
9	0.156	.158	.160	.162	.163	.165	.167	.168	.170	.172
10	0.174	.175	.177	.179	.181	.182	.184	.186	.187	.189
11	0.191	.193	.194	.196	.198	.199	.201	.203	.204	.206
12	0.208	.210	.211	.213	.215	.216	.218	.220	.222	.223
13	0.225	.227	.228	.230	.232	.233	.235	.237	.239	.240
14	0.242	.244	.245	.247	.249	.250	.252	.254	.255	.257
15	0.259	.261	.262	.264	.266	.267	.269	.271	.272	.274
16	0.276	.277	.279	.281	.282	.284	.286	.287	.289	.291
17	0.292	.294	.296	.297	.299	.301	.302	.304	.306	.307
18	0.309	.311	.312	.314	.316	.317	.319	.321	.322	.324
19	0.326	.327	.329	.331	.332	.334	.335	.337	.339	.340
20	0.342	.344	.345	.347	.349	.350	.352	.353	.355	.357
21	0.358	.360	.362	.363	.365	.367	.368	.370	.371	.373
22	0.375	.376	.378	.379	.381	.383	.384	.386	.388	.389
23	0.391	.392	.394	.396	.397	.399	.400	.402	.404	.405
24	0.407	.408	.410	.412	.413	.415	.416	.418	.419	.421
25	0.423	.424	.426	.427	.429	.431	.432	.434	.435	.437
26	0.438	.440	.442	.443	.445	.446	.448	.449	.451	.452
27	0.454	.456	.457	.459	.460	.462	.463	.465	.466	.468
28	0.469	.471	.473	.474	.476	.477	.479	.480	.482	.483
29	0.485	.486	.488	.489	.491	.492	.494	.495	.497	.498
30	0.500	.502	.503	.505	.506	.508	.509	.511	.512	.514
31	0.515	.517	.518	.520	.521	.522	.524	.525	.527	.528
32	0.530	.531	.533	.534	.536	.537	.539	.540	.542	.543
33	0.545	.546	.548	.549	.550	.552	.553	.555	.556	.558
34	0.559	.561	.562	.564	.565	.566	.568	.569	.571	.572
35	0.574	.575	.576	.578	.579	.581	.582	.584	.585	.586
36	0.588	.589	.591	.592	.593	.595	.596	.598	.599	.600
37	0.602	.603	.605	.606	.607	.609	.610	.612	.613	.614
38	0.616	.617	.618	.620	.621	.623	.624	.625	.627	.628
39	0.629	.631	.632	.633	.635	.636	.637	.639	.640	.641
40	0.643	.644	.645	.647	.648	.649	.651	.652	.653	.655
41	0.656	.657	.659	.660	.661	.663	.664	.665	.667	.668
42	0.669	.670	.672	.673	.674	.676	.677	.678	.679	.681
43	0.682	.683	.685	.686	.687	.688	.690	.691	.692	.693
44	0.695	.696	.697	.698	.700	.701	.702	.703	.705	.706
45	0.707	.708	.710	.711	.712	.713	.714	.716	.717	.718

TABLE OF SINES – *continued*

Angle in degrees	.0	.1	.2	.3	.4	.5	.6	.7	.8	.9
45	0.707	.708	.710	.711	.712	.713	.714	.716	.717	.718
46	0.719	.721	.722	.723	.724	.725	.727	.728	.729	.730
47	0.731	.733	.734	.735	.736	.737	.738	.740	.741	.742
48	0.743	.744	.745	.747	.748	.749	.750	.751	.752	.754
49	0.755	.756	.757	.758	.759	.760	.762	.763	.764	.765
50	0.766	.767	.768	.769	.771	.772	.773	.774	.775	.776
51	0.777	.778	.779	.780	.782	.783	.784	.785	.786	.787
52	0.788	.789	.790	.791	.792	.793	.794	.795	.797	.798
53	0.799	.800	.801	.802	.803	.804	.805	.806	.807	.808
54	0.809	.810	.811	.812	.813	.814	.815	.816	.817	.818
55	0.819	.820	.821	.822	.823	.824	.825	.826	.827	.828
56	0.829	.830	.831	.832	.833	.834	.835	.836	.837	.838
57	0.839	.840	.841	.842	.842	.843	.844	.845	.846	.847
58	0.848	.849	.850	.851	.852	.853	.854	.854	.855	.856
59	0.857	.858	.859	.860	.861	.862	.863	.863	.864	.865
60	0.866	.867	.868	.869	.869	.870	.871	.872	.873	.874
61	0.875	.875	.876	.877	.878	.879	.880	.880	.881	.882
62	0.883	.884	.885	.885	.886	.887	.888	.889	.889	.890
63	0.891	.892	.893	.893	.894	.895	.896	.896	.897	.898
64	0.899	.900	.900	.901	.902	.903	.903	.904	.905	.906
65	0.906	.907	.908	.909	.909	.910	.911	.911	.912	.913
66	0.914	.914	.915	.916	.916	.917	.918	.918	.919	.920
67	0.921	.921	.922	.923	.923	.924	.925	.925	.926	.927
68	0.927	.928	.928	.929	.930	.930	.931	.932	.932	.933
69	0.934	.934	.935	.935	.936	.937	.937	.938	.938	.939
70	0.940	.940	.941	.941	.942	.943	.943	.944	.944	.945
71	0.946	.946	.947	.947	.948	.948	.949	.949	.950	.951
72	0.951	.952	.952	.953	.953	.954	.954	.955	.955	.956
73	0.956	.957	.957	.958	.958	.959	.959	.960	.960	.961
74	0.961	.962	.962	.963	.963	.964	.964	.965	.965	.965
75	0.966	.966	.967	.967	.968	.968	.969	.969	.969	.970
76	0.970	.971	.971	.972	.972	.972	.973	.973	.974	.974
77	0.974	.975	.975	.976	.976	.976	.977	.977	.977	.978
78	0.978	.979	.979	.979	.980	.980	.980	.981	.981	.981
79	0.982	.982	.982	.983	.983	.983	.984	.984	.984	.985
80	0.985	.985	.985	.986	.986	.986	.987	.987	.987	.987
81	0.988	.988	.988	.988	.989	.989	.989	.990	.990	.990
82	0.990	.991	.991	.991	.991	.991	.992	.992	.992	.992
83	0.993	.993	.993	.993	.993	.994	.994	.994	.994	.994
84	0.995	.995	.995	.995	.995	.995	.996	.996	.996	.996
85	0.996	.996	.996	.997	.997	.997	.997	.997	.997	.997
86	0.998	.998	.998	.998	.998	.998	.998	.998	.998	.999
87	0.999	.999	.999	.999	.999	.999	.999	.999	.999	.999
88	0.999	.999	1.000	1.000	1.000	1.000	1.000	1.000	1.000	1.000
89	1.000	1.000	1.000	1.000	1.000	1.000	1.000	1.000	1.000	1.000
90	1.000									

TABLE OF COSINES

Angle in degrees	.0	.1	.2	.3	.4	.5	.6	.7	.8	.9
0	1.000	1.000	1.000	1.000	1.000	1.000	1.000	1.000	1.000	1.000
1	1.000	1.000	1.000	1.000	1.000	1.000	1.000	1.000	1.000	0.999
2	0.999	.999	.999	.999	.999	.999	.999	.999	.999	.999
3	0.999	.999	.998	.998	.998	.998	.998	.998	.998	.998
4	0.998	.997	.997	.997	.997	.997	.997	.997	.996	.996
5	0.996	.996	.996	.996	.996	.995	.995	.995	.995	.995
6	0.995	.994	.994	.994	.994	.994	.993	.993	.993	.993
7	0.993	.992	.992	.992	.992	.991	.991	.991	.991	.991
8	0.990	.990	.990	.990	.989	.989	.989	.988	.988	.988
9	0.988	.987	.987	.987	.987	.986	.986	.986	.985	.985
10	0.985	.985	.984	.984	.984	.983	.983	.983	.982	.982
11	0.982	.981	.981	.981	.980	.980	.980	.979	.979	.979
12	0.978	.978	.977	.977	.977	.976	.976	.976	.975	.975
13	0.974	.974	.974	.973	.973	.972	.972	.972	.971	.971
14	0.970	.970	.969	.969	.969	.968	.968	.967	.967	.966
15	0.966	.965	.965	.965	.964	.964	.963	.963	.962	.962
16	0.961	.961	.960	.960	.959	.959	.958	.958	.957	.957
17	0.956	.956	.955	.955	.954	.954	.953	.953	.952	.952
18	0.951	.951	.950	.949	.949	.948	.948	.947	.947	.946
19	0.946	.945	.944	.944	.943	.943	.942	.941	.941	.940
20	0.940	.939	.938	.938	.937	.937	.936	.935	.935	.934
21	0.934	.933	.932	.932	.931	.930	.930	.929	.928	.928
22	0.927	.927	.926	.925	.925	.924	.923	.923	.922	.921
23	0.921	.920	.919	.918	.918	.917	.916	.916	.915	.914
24	0.914	.913	.912	.911	.911	.910	.909	.909	.908	.907
25	0.906	.906	.905	.904	.903	.903	.902	.901	.900	.900
26	0.899	.898	.897	.896	.896	.895	.894	.893	.893	.892
27	0.891	.890	.889	.889	.888	.887	.886	.885	.885	.884
28	0.883	.882	.881	.880	.880	.879	.878	.877	.876	.875
29	0.875	.874	.873	.872	.871	.870	.869	.869	.868	.867
30	0.866	.865	.864	.863	.863	.862	.861	.860	.859	.858
31	0.857	.856	.855	.854	.854	.853	.852	.851	.850	.849
32	0.848	.847	.846	.845	.844	.843	.842	.842	.841	.840
33	0.839	.838	.837	.836	.835	.834	.833	.832	.831	.830
34	0.829	.828	.827	.826	.825	.824	.823	.822	.821	.820
35	0.819	.818	.817	.816	.815	.814	.813	.812	.811	.810
36	0.809	.808	.807	.806	.805	.804	.803	.802	.801	.800
37	0.799	.798	.797	.795	.794	.793	.792	.791	.790	.789
38	0.788	.787	.786	.785	.784	.783	.782	.780	.779	.778
39	0.777	.776	.775	.774	.773	.772	.771	.769	.768	.767
40	0.766	.765	.764	.763	.762	.760	.759	.758	.757	.756
41	0.755	.754	.752	.751	.750	.749	.748	.747	.745	.744
42	0.743	.742	.741	.740	.738	.737	.736	.735	.734	.733
43	0.731	.730	.729	.728	.727	.725	.724	.723	.722	.721
44	0.719	.718	.717	.716	.714	.713	.712	.711	.710	.708
45	0.707	.706	.705	.703	.702	.701	.700	.698	.697	.696

TABLE OF COSINES – *continued*

Angle in degrees	.0	.1	.2	.3	.4	.5	.6	.7	.8	.9
45	0.707	.706	.705	.703	.702	.701	.700	.698	.697	.696
46	0.695	.693	.692	.691	.690	.688	.687	.686	.685	.683
47	0.682	.681	.679	.678	.677	.676	.674	.673	.672	.670
48	0.669	.668	.667	.665	.664	.663	.661	.660	.659	.657
49	0.656	.655	.653	.652	.651	.649	.648	.647	.645	.644
50	0.643	.641	.640	.639	.637	.636	.635	.633	.632	.631
51	0.629	.628	.627	.625	.624	.623	.621	.620	.618	.617
52	0.616	.614	.613	.612	.610	.609	.607	.606	.605	.603
53	0.602	.600	.599	.598	.596	.595	.593	.592	.591	.589
54	0.588	.586	.585	.584	.582	.581	.579	.578	.576	.575
55	0.574	.572	.571	.569	.568	.566	.565	.564	.562	.561
56	0.559	.558	.556	.555	.553	.552	.550	.549	.548	.546
57	0.545	.543	.542	.540	.539	.537	.536	.534	.533	.531
58	0.530	.528	.527	.525	.524	.522	.521	.520	.518	.517
59	0.515	.514	.512	.511	.509	.508	.506	.505	.503	.502
60	0.500	.498	.497	.495	.494	.492	.491	.489	.488	.486
61	0.485	.483	.482	.480	.479	.477	.476	.474	.473	.471
62	0.469	.468	.466	.465	.463	.462	.460	.459	.457	.456
63	0.454	.452	.451	.449	.448	.446	.445	.443	.442	.440
64	0.438	.437	.435	.434	.432	.431	.429	.427	.426	.424
65	0.423	.421	.419	.418	.416	.415	.413	.412	.410	.408
66	0.407	.405	.404	.402	.400	.399	.397	.396	.394	.392
67	0.391	.389	.388	.386	.384	.383	.381	.379	.378	.376
68	0.375	.373	.371	.370	.368	.367	.365	.363	.362	.360
69	0.358	.357	.355	.353	.352	.350	.349	.347	.345	.344
70	0.342	.340	.339	.337	.335	.334	.332	.331	.329	.327
71	0.326	.324	.322	.321	.319	.317	.316	.314	.312	.311
72	0.309	.307	.306	.304	.302	.301	.299	.297	.296	.294
73	0.292	.291	.289	.287	.286	.284	.282	.281	.279	.277
74	0.276	.274	.272	.271	.269	.267	.266	.264	.262	.261
75	0.259	.257	.255	.254	.252	.250	.249	.247	.245	.244
76	0.242	.240	.239	.237	.235	.233	.232	.230	.228	.227
77	0.225	.223	.222	.220	.218	.216	.215	.213	.211	.210
78	0.208	.206	.204	.203	.201	.199	.198	.196	.194	.193
79	0.191	.189	.187	.186	.184	.182	.181	.179	.177	.175
80	0.174	.172	.170	.168	.167	.165	.163	.162	.160	.158
81	0.156	.155	.153	.151	.150	.148	.146	.144	.143	.141
82	0.139	.137	.136	.134	.132	.131	.129	.127	.125	.124
83	0.122	.120	.118	.117	.115	.113	.111	.110	.108	.106
84	0.105	.103	.101	.099	.098	.096	.094	.092	.091	.089
85	0.087	.085	.084	.082	.080	.078	.077	.075	.073	.071
86	0.070	.068	.066	.065	.063	.061	.059	.058	.056	.054
87	0.052	.051	.049	.047	.045	.044	.042	.040	.038	.037
88	0.035	.033	.031	.030	.028	.026	.024	.023	.021	.019
89	0.017	.016	.014	.012	.010	.009	.007	.005	.003	.002
90	0.000									

TABLE OF TANGENTS

Angle in degrees	.0	.1	.2	.3	.4	.5	.6	.7	.8	.9
0	0.000	.002	.003	.005	.007	.000	.010	.012	.014	.016
1	0.017	.019	.021	.023	.024	.026	.028	.030	.031	.033
2	0.035	.037	.038	.040	.042	.044	.045	.047	.049	.051
3	0.052	.054	.056	.058	.059	.061	.063	.065	.066	.068
4	0.070	.072	.073	.075	.077	.079	.080	.082	.084	.086
5	0.087	.089	.091	.093	.095	.096	.098	.100	.102	.103
6	0.105	.107	.109	.110	.112	.114	.116	.117	.119	.121
7	0.123	.125	.126	.128	.130	.132	.133	.135	.137	.139
8	0.141	.142	.144	.146	.148	.149	.151	.153	.155	.157
9	0.158	.160	.162	.164	.166	.167	.169	.171	.173	.175
10	0.176	.178	.180	.182	.184	.185	.187	.189	.191	.193
11	0.194	.196	.198	.200	.202	.203	.205	.207	.209	.211
12	0.213	.214	.216	.218	.220	.222	.224	.225	.227	.229
13	0.231	.233	.235	.236	.238	.240	.242	.244	.246	.247
14	0.249	.251	.253	.255	.257	.259	.260	.262	.264	.266
15	0.268	.270	.272	.274	.275	.277	.279	.281	.283	.285
16	0.287	.289	.291	.292	.294	.296	.298	.300	.302	.304
17	0.306	.308	.310	.311	.313	.315	.317	.319	.321	.323
18	0.325	.327	.329	.331	.333	.335	.337	.338	.340	.342
19	0.344	.346	.348	.350	.352	.354	.356	.358	.360	.362
20	0.364	.366	.368	.370	.372	.374	.376	.378	.380	.382
21	0.384	.386	.388	.390	.392	.394	.396	.398	.400	.402
22	0.404	.406	.408	.410	.412	.414	.416	.418	.420	.422
23	0.424	.427	.429	.431	.433	.435	.437	.439	.441	.443
24	0.445	.447	.449	.452	.454	.456	.458	.460	.462	.464
25	0.466	.468	.471	.473	.475	.477	.479	.481	.483	.486
26	0.488	.490	.492	.494	.496	.499	.501	.503	.505	.507
27	0.510	.512	.514	.516	.518	.521	.523	.525	.527	.529
28	0.532	.534	.536	.538	.541	.543	.545	.547	.550	.552
29	0.554	.557	.559	.561	.563	.566	.568	.570	.573	.575
30	0.577	.580	.582	.584	.587	.589	.591	.594	.596	.598
31	0.601	.603	.606	.608	.610	.613	.615	.618	.620	.622
32	0.625	.627	.630	.632	.635	.637	.640	.642	.644	.647
33	0.649	.652	.654	.657	.659	.662	.664	.667	.669	.672
34	0.675	.677	.680	.682	.685	.687	.690	.692	.695	.698
35	0.700	.703	.705	.708	.711	.713	.716	.719	.721	.724
36	0.727	.729	.732	.735	.737	.740	.743	.745	.748	.751
37	0.754	.756	.759	.762	.765	.767	.770	.773	.776	.778
38	0.781	.784	.787	.790	.793	.795	.798	.801	.804	.807
39	0.810	.813	.816	.818	.821	.824	.827	.830	.833	.836
40	0.839	.842	.845	.848	.851	.854	.857	.860	.863	.866
41	0.869	.872	.875	.879	.882	.885	.888	.891	.894	.897
42	0.900	.904	.907	.910	.913	.916	.920	.923	.926	.929
43	0.933	.936	.939	.942	.946	.949	.952	.956	.959	.962
44	0.966	.969	.972	.976	.979	.983	.986	.990	.993	.997
45	1.00	1.00	1.01	1.01	1.01	1.02	1.02	1.02	1.03	1.03

TABLE OF TANGENTS – *continued*

Angle in degrees	.0	.1	.2	.3	.4	.5	.6	.7	.8	.9
45	1.00	1.00	1.01	1.01	1.01	1.02	1.02	1.02	1.03	1.03
46	1.04	1.04	1.04	1.05	1.05	1.05	1.06	1.06	1.06	1.07
47	1.07	1.08	1.08	1.08	1.09	1.09	1.10	1.10	1.10	1.11
48	1.11	1.11	1.12	1.12	1.13	1.13	1.13	1.14	1.14	1.15
49	1.15	1.15	1.16	1.16	1.17	1.17	1.17	1.18	1.18	1.19
50	1.19	1.20	1.20	1.20	1.21	1.21	1.22	1.22	1.23	1.23
51	1.23	1.24	1.24	1.25	1.25	1.26	1.26	1.27	1.27	1.28
52	1.28	1.28	1.29	1.29	1.30	1.30	1.31	1.31	1.32	1.32
53	1.33	1.33	1.34	1.34	1.35	1.35	1.36	1.36	1.37	1.37
54	1.38	1.38	1.39	1.39	1.40	1.40	1.41	1.41	1.42	1.42
55	1.43	1.43	1.44	1.44	1.45	1.46	1.46	1.47	1.47	1.48
56	1.48	1.49	1.49	1.50	1.51	1.51	1.52	1.52	1.53	1.53
57	1.54	1.55	1.55	1.56	1.56	1.57	1.58	1.58	1.59	1.59
58	1.60	1.61	1.61	1.62	1.63	1.63	1.64	1.64	1.65	1.66
59	1.66	1.67	1.68	1.68	1.69	1.70	1.70	1.71	1.72	1.73
60	1.73	1.74	1.75	1.75	1.76	1.77	1.77	1.78	1.79	1.80
61	1.80	1.81	1.82	1.83	1.83	1.84	1.85	1.86	1.86	1.87
62	1.88	1.89	1.90	1.90	1.91	1.92	1.93	1.94	1.95	1.95
63	1.96	1.97	1.98	1.99	2.00	2.01	2.01	2.02	2.03	2.04
64	2.05	2.06	2.07	2.08	2.09	2.10	2.11	2.12	2.13	2.13
65	2.14	2.15	2.16	2.17	2.18	2.19	2.20	2.21	2.23	2.24
66	2.25	2.26	2.27	2.28	2.29	2.30	2.31	2.32	2.33	2.34
67	2.36	2.37	2.38	2.39	2.40	2.41	2.43	2.44	2.45	2.46
68	2.48	2.49	2.50	2.51	2.53	2.54	2.55	2.56	2.58	2.59
69	2.61	2.62	2.63	2.65	2.66	2.67	2.69	2.70	2.72	2.73
70	2.75	2.76	2.78	2.79	2.81	2.82	2.84	2.86	2.87	2.89
71	2.90	2.92	2.94	2.95	2.97	2.99	3.01	3.02	3.04	3.06
72	3.08	3.10	3.11	3.13	3.15	3.17	3.19	3.21	3.23	3.25
73	3.27	3.29	3.31	3.33	3.35	3.38	3.40	3.42	3.44	3.46
74	3.49	3.51	3.53	3.56	3.58	3.61	3.63	3.66	3.68	3.71
75	3.73	3.76	3.78	3.81	3.84	3.87	3.89	3.92	3.95	3.98
76	4.01	4.04	4.07	4.10	4.13	4.17	4.20	4.23	4.26	4.30
77	4.33	4.37	4.40	4.44	4.47	4.51	4.55	4.59	4.63	4.66
78	4.70	4.75	4.79	4.83	4.87	4.92	4.96	5.00	5.05	5.10
79	5.14	5.19	5.24	5.29	5.34	5.40	5.45	5.50	5.56	5.61
80	5.67	5.73	5.79	5.85	5.91	5.98	6.04	6.11	6.17	6.24
81	6.31	6.39	6.46	6.54	6.61	6.69	6.77	6.85	6.94	7.03
82	7.12	7.21	7.30	7.40	7.49	7.60	7.70	7.81	7.92	8.03
83	8.14	8.26	8.39	8.51	8.64	8.78	8.92	9.06	9.21	9.36
84	9.51	9.68	9.84	10.0	10.2	10.4	10.6	10.8	11.0	11.2
85	11.4	11.7	11.9	12.2	12.4	12.7	13.0	13.3	13.6	14.0
86	14.3	14.7	15.1	15.5	15.9	16.3	16.8	17.3	17.9	18.5
87	19.1	19.7	20.4	21.2	22.0	22.9	23.9	24.9	26.0	27.3
88	28.6	30.1	31.8	33.7	35.8	38.2	40.9	44.1	47.7	52.1
89	57.3	63.7	71.6	81.8	95.5	115	143	191	286	573

INDEX